Managing Organizational Behavior

The Irwin Series in Management and The Behavioral Sciences

L. L. Cummings and E. Kirby Warren *Consulting Editors*

Managing Organizational Behavior

W. Alan Randolph
University of Baltimore

Richard S. Blackburn
University of North Carolina
at Chapel Hill

1989

IRWIN

Homewood, IL 60430
Boston, MA 02116

Sponsoring editor: William R. Bayer
Developmental editor: Eleanore Snow
Project editor: Margaret Haywood
Production manager: Carma W. Fazio
Designer: Paula Lang
Compositor: Weimer Typesetting Co., Inc.
Typeface: 10/12 Palatino
Printer: R. R. Donnelley & Sons Company

LIBRARY OF CONGRESS
Library of Congress Cataloging-in-Publication Data

Randolph, W. Alan.
    Managing organizational behavior / W. Alan Randolph, Richard S.
Blackburn
        p.   cm.
    Includes index.
    ISBN 0-256-06520-9
    1. Organizational behavior.   I. Blackburn, Richard S.   II. Title.
HD58.7.R356 1989
302.3'5—dc19   88–18574
                                                                                       CIP

Printed in the United States of America
1 2 3 4 5 6 7 8 9 0 DO 6 5 4 3 2 1 0 9

*Dedicated with respect and admiration to
those professors who labor to teach organizational behavior
and to those students who labor to learn it*

Preface

Why would anyone in their right mind write a textbook on organizational behavior? There are many other books on this topic already available. And whenever you put your ideas into print, professors and students alike are going to criticize them. We may be masochists, but we also felt we had a point of view worth sharing and decided to give that viewpoint a life of its own. Hence, the book you hold in your hands.

For the past decade, there has been a growing interest in examining behavior in organizations from a developmental perspective. This means that to better understand the impact of events on companies, hospitals, schools, and so on, researchers and managers must appreciate that such events occur over time. For example, the nature of the relationship between a manager and an employee is not a one-day occurrence. It developed over time—past to present—and will continue to develop in the future. What happens today is partially determined by what happened in the past and by what may happen in the future. We use a developmental perspective in this book to explore the behavior of individuals, groups, and organizations.

Our primary goal has been to write a book that provides useful information based on rigorous research, and to provide this information in a way that is easy to comprehend and easy to apply. To this end, the developmental perspective allows us to tie together the major concepts and theories of organizational behavior, demonstrate how these concepts and theories relate to effective management, and make it easier to use these ideas in management situations.

Most organizational behavior texts are designed to teach *about* management. This book, too, is designed to teach *about* management, but it is also designed to teach *how* to manage. To do this, we have gone beyond a simple discussion of organizational behavior theories. For example, we explore many theories of motivation, as do most organizational behavior texts. But, we also develop a model of motivation that ties these theories together—making them more useful in management settings. We provide the same integrative approach in our summary of leadership theories.

We have designed three features to help you apply the information presented in each chapter. First, you can follow the Home Computers Company case throughout the book. In nearly every chapter, you will learn about the Home Computers Company. You will meet many of its employees and share their personal and organizational problems. This integration of the case into each chapter should make the usefulness of the theories in real-world situations become much clearer. The case also integrates material from chapter to chapter; discussions in one chapter frequently refer back to discussions in earlier chapters. Students have responded favorably to this case; some tell us they read the case before reading the text material. They want to see what is new at Home Computers Company. It may not be "Dallas" or "Knots Landing" or "Falconcrest," but the case does make many of our theoretical discussions come alive.

The second feature designed to aid in the application and integration of the text material are excerpts from *The Wall Street Journal* and other business publications. We call these excerpts Insights, for they provide added insights into the way real organizations apply the ideas we have presented. As with the Home Computers Company case, students and professors alike have enjoyed the vivid examples that the Insights provide.

The final application and integration design feature appears at the end of most chapters. Short cases, exercises, and questionnaires are provided to make the text material more personal and applied. Each major part of the book is followed by a longer, more sophisticated case that integrates the information learned over several chapters. We are confident you will enjoy each of these features as well as the learning that comes from their use.

As they say in the business world, "What's the bottom line?" This book is written for both student and professor. While rigorous in its adherence to research-based ideas, it is also flexible—meeting the needs of many professors. For the student, it is written to explain complicated ideas in as straightforward a manner as possible. To ensure this happens, **key points throughout the chapters are highlighted in boldface type;** real-world examples are woven into the text; and Chapter Highlights (more extensive than in most organizational behavior texts) make recall and review of key issues much easier.

The field of organizational behavior, though young compared to physics or mathematics, has matured to the point where we know a great deal about behavior in organizations. Our purpose is to share that information with you as though we were sitting together in someone's living room. We want to share that information in a way that will help you become a more effective manager. Much as the employees of Home Computers Company want to make their computers user-friendly, we have tried to do the same with your text—to make it student- and professor-friendly. Work with us. By carefully reading each chapter, thinking about the relationships between the Home Computers Company case, the Insights, and the text material, and completing the end of chapter materials, you will be well on your way to being a better manager. Good luck!

Acknowledgments

No book can be written in a vacuum. All authors need help and support to complete a project of this magnitude. We would like to thank a number of individuals who aided us in this venture. First of all, we want to thank those colleagues who carefully reviewed portions of our work and gave us helpful feedback—though it was sometimes hard to take:

Jerry Anderson, Xavier University
Brendan Bannister, Northeastern University
Mary Elizabeth Beres, Mercer University
John Bunch, Lehigh University
Paul Collins, Purdue University
Ed Conlon, University of Iowa
David Cowan, University of Notre Dame
Alan Hamlin, Southern Utah State College
Lynn Johnson, North Texas State University
Patrick Liverpool, University of Toledo
Herb Tilley, Johnson State University
Ken Whelan, Baldwin-Wallace College
Kent Zimmerman, James Madison University

We would also like to thank Randy Sleeth at Virginia Commonwealth University for suggesting the cases and exercises for each chapter and for preparing the Manual of Tests that accompanies this book. In addition, our heartfelt appreciation is offered to Peter Frost, University of British Columbia, who reviewed the entire manuscript.

Each of these individuals has made substantial contributions to improving the quality of the text. Nevertheless, we accept full responsibility for any errors that may have found their way into print—errors of both omission and commission.

A number of people at the Richard D. Irwin Company also deserve our thanks. First, we appreciate the support and guidance from consulting editors Larry Cummings and Kirby Warren. We especially appreciate the masterful red pen of Eleanore Snow, who worked with us to ensure that the material was presented as clearly as possible. Paula Lang and Margaret Haywood deserve our thanks for their work on the design and production of the book, as does Nancy Lanum for her work on the Instructor's Manual. We also appreciate the support and encouragement provided by Jerry Saykes and Frank Burrows. And last, but certainly not least, this project could not have been completed were it not for the supervision and interest of our editor, Bill Bayer.

We must also add a note of thanks for the secretarial support provided by Alan's institutions. Sandy Murrah and Susie Gorsage at the University of South Carolina performed legion work in making revisions with short timelines. Alan also appreciates the support and encouragement of both his former dean, Jim Kane at the University of South Carolina, and his current dean, Syd Stern at the University of Baltimore.

Dick would like to thank Dean Paul Rizzo of the Graduate School of Business at the University of North Carolina at Chapel Hill for his support. Additional support during the writing of this text was provided by the Business Foundation, Graduate School of Business, University of North Carolina and The Frank Hawkins Kenan Institute of Private Enterprise, University of North Carolina. Dick also would like to thank his colleagues Tom Bateman, Benson Rosen, and Richard Woodman for their assistance. If not for the golf, this effort would have been completed much earlier.

Finally, we recognize the part played by friends and family in the process of writing a textbook. Without the support and love of such people, we would never have completed this project. Alan would like to especially thank his wife, Ruth Anne, and his children, Ashley, Shannon, and Elizabeth for their continued love and support. Dick would like to thank his parents Andy and Lois, Michelle (without whom this manuscript was written), and Felix and Weber (the cats).

W. Alan Randolph
Richard S. Blackburn

Contents

A Developmental Framework for Studying Organizations

DYNAMIC ENVIRONMENTAL INFLUENCES

Past	Present	Future
Change	**Organizations** Environments Goals/Effectiveness Structure Design Development	Change
Develop	**Work Groups** Structure Processes Cohesion Groupthink Intergroup Behavior	Develop
Evolve	**Interpersonal Relationships** Leadership Power Politics Communications	Evolve
Grow	**Individuals** Perception Learning Attitudes Values Personality Motivation Outcomes	Grow

Managing Organizational Behavior

PART ONE

Organizational Behavior: A Developmental Perspective

Chapter 1

Organizations and People as Dynamic Beings

Chapter 2

Managing as a Changing Role

C H A P T E R 1

Organizations and People as Dynamic Beings

*A*n early researcher of organizations once said that we can neither live with nor without organizations.[1] Indeed, we depend upon organizations for most of the goods and services necessary for our survival and also for the leisure aspects of our lives. We have been influenced by and involved in organizations since our birth (for example, the hospital where we were born, our family, schools, clubs, and current jobs). Organizations have made our high standard of living possible, but they have also heightened the stresses and tribulations of modern life. For those hoping to have a successful career working and managing in one or more organizations, a question of paramount interest is how to be effective in an organization.

Chapter 1 begins to answer this question by introducing both the levels of organizational behavior and the developmental perspective. In it we develop an analytical framework consisting of four levels of organizational behavior—individuals, interpersonal relationships, work groups, and organizations. These levels then form the major sections of this book and are key aspects for an effective manager to understand and manage. Once we have the levels defined, we will overlay the developmental perspective to make the framework more useful to us as managers.

Chapter 2 then brings this developmental perspective down to a personal level. We will discuss the career aspects of a manager's job by focusing on how different skills are needed at different career phases. We also will explore the key stages of a working career and the key factors in the changing role of a manager during a career. As we get into the book, it will be helpful to reflect on personal experiences. By doing so, we will achieve a major goal of the book—that is, making the material really useful to managers. ▪▶

[1] G. C. Homans, *The Human Group* (New York: Harcourt, Brace and World, 1950).

As we begin our quest to understand and manage organizational behavior, it is important to appreciate the two most critical components of concern—people and organizations. Let us begin by exploring the nature of organizations, since it is the behavior of people *in organizations* that is our concern.

THE NATURE OF ORGANIZATIONS

Most simply defined, **an organization is a pattern of rational and political interactions and activities invented by people to fulfill the goals of individuals and groups.** Managing in an organization is defined as **working with and through other people and groups of people to accomplish the goals set for the organization.** The process of managing is difficult because of the interactive nature of the elements comprising any organization, whether it is a business, a hospital, a school, a union, or a club. There are at least five main elements of an organization system that constantly interact in determining both **individual and organizational effectiveness:**

1. The **task, or goal,** chosen by the organization (that is, the product or service to be provided, the markets to be served, and some desired level of performance).
2. The **technology and design** chosen to accomplish the task.
3. The **structure** chosen to define jobs and interrelationships of people.
4. The **people** who comprise the organization.
5. The **external and internal environments** in which the organization exists.[1]

And it is important to remember that all five of these elements must coexist within a world of constant **organizational change and development.**

One of a manager's critical challenges is working with and through other people in the dynamic context that results from the interaction of task/goal, technology/design, structure, and environment to achieve desired individual and organizational effectiveness. Each of the five main elements of organizations represents a complex system that is brought to life through such processes as communications, influence, decision making, goal implementation, and action plans. And in action, these elements are all interdependent upon one another, and their interactions ultimately determine individual and organizational effectiveness.

In this text, the primary focus is on the people element of organizations, within the context of the other four elements. This people aspect of organizations is what is meant by the term *organizational behavior*. More specifically, **organizational behavior is the study of actions, feelings, and effectiveness of people in organizational settings.** The focus is on what happens within individuals, between individuals (that is, interpersonal relations), within groups of people and between groups of people (that is, intergroup relations), and within organizations. Effective managers must learn both to understand and to manage organizational behavior.

But in this endeavor to understand organizational behavior, we managers must also understand organizations and their environments. And we must recognize that organizations are dynamic, developmental entities. That is, organizations change over time. They change goals, structures, and designs; and they may improve or decline in effectiveness. In other words, organizations are not static. And this dynamic nature applies both to the main organizational elements (task, technology, structure, people, and environment) and to the subdivisions under the people element (that is, individuals, interpersonal relations, groups, and intergroup relations).

As we proceed through the text and the four subdivisions of organizational behavior, we will use a developmental, dynamic, and change-oriented set of glasses for viewing and analyzing situations. By taking this time-based perspective, we will be better able to understand why people and organizations operate as they do. Put another way, in order to understand why people and organizations behave the way they do **now,** we need to know something about their past history and development from past to present. We must also recognize that things will change as the future unfolds. Thus, our analysis must be continual if we are to effectively manage people in the present and the future. **This historical, evolving, and changing nature of people and organizations is what we mean when we use the term "developmental perspective."**

When we consider the dynamic nature of organizations and people, as well as the interactive nature of the elements of organizations, it is easy to appreciate the complexity of understanding the behavior of people and organizations. Learning how to be effective in an organizational context and how to manage the behavior of others in an organization is even more difficult. To illustrate this point, take a look at Insight 1–1 for a sense of how automakers have found it difficult to effectively blend people, technology, and organizations as advances are made.

To show why a developmental perspective will be helpful, consider the case that follows.

I N S I G H T 1–1

The Human Factor

When mixing autos with automation, Detroit is finding that success isn't automatic.

The U.S. auto industry has spent billions of dollars in the past four years on sophisticated robots for welding and installing parts, laser systems for inspecting fit and finish, and computer systems to integrate entire assembly operations. These "factories of the future" are supposed to produce better quality autos at a lower cost—and thus compete better with Japanese rivals.

But the new manufacturing methods are running into giant snafus with workers who don't have the skills to handle them. And restrictive union rules that limit job assignments and even training programs only compound the people problem.

What's happening to auto makers is a common difficulty in U.S. industry. After identifying automation as their salvation, the Big Three auto makers rushed to acquire all kinds of new systems that couldn't be easily integrated because they were built by a myriad of manufacturers. Operators were an afterthought—brought in not at the design and development stages when the workers could begin to master new procedures, but only later when training was more difficult.

"The domestic auto companies' faith in technology was unbounded, and so the hidden cost was very high complexity that would fail in actual performance," says Harley Shaiken, an expert on factory automation at the University of California in San Diego. "No amount of training could prepare the work force to handle that kind of overreliance on technology."

Auto makers acknowledge that they underestimated the importance of pairing technology with people. General Motors Corp., for example, has experienced delayed startups and constant production interruptions at its newest plants. Such problems threaten to plague auto makers for years. In the future, says GM chairman Roger Smith, "solid human partnerships will form the ground floor on which high-technology systems will be built."

For now, however, auto makers must contend with an ill-equipped work force. At GM, roughly 15% of hourly employees—and as much as 30% at some plants—can't read or write; a GM employee publication says some workers can't read such simple safety signs as "do not enter." Only 8% of GM's 425,000 hourly workers have college degrees.

Yet today's technologies call for more sophisticated skills than assembly-line workers needed in the past. Although a major goal of automation is to reduce the number of production workers, those who survive cutbacks need some understanding of computers and electronics.

Home Computers Case

The Home Computers Company Case

Harvey Brown and his cousin Bill Adams decided, after several years of working for a large computer firm, to start their own computer manufacturing business. Following the entrepreneurial spirit, they felt they could offer a computer that could be used in the homes of all Americans. Imagining huge sales of the computer, they set up business in Harvey's garage and basement in the fall of 1974. Today, Home Computers Company enjoys sales of over $800 million, has offices from coast to coast, has 1,000 employees, and has three main divisions in the organization. But how did this happen? And what has happened to Harvey and Bill?

Back in the garage in the mid-1970s, Harvey and Bill, then in their mid-30s, were quite energetic and highly motivated to put in long days. They worked through many failures for over a year before they developed a prototype of their computer. There were many problems, not the least of which was a messy divorce for Bill. At the computer show where they first demonstrated EZ1, the printer failed to work, and many people criticized the speed of the processor. Harvey and Bill did, however, manage to sell one computer to an older man who later became a source of financing for a revised and improved model. In fact, without Mr. Hearn's backing, Home Computers Company would have folded.

By early 1977, EZ2 was in the market, and at $1,195 for the basic microcomputer unit, it received acceptance almost immediately. Sales demand was so great that Harvey and Bill leased a building to use for production and hired 16 employees. Now they had to be concerned not only with their own work habits and productivity, but also with the work habits and productivity of 16 other people. Questions of pay scales, fringe benefits, organizational structure, and a host of other business questions had to be addressed. Harvey and Bill quickly discovered that Bill's leadership style and motivational drives made him too overbearing for the employees, whereas Harvey was able to work well with them. To deal with this difference, Harvey became the production manager and Bill the sales manager.

This division of responsibility worked well for everyone concerned, and business prospered. Sales grew from 250 units in 1977 to 3,000 in 1980. Sales offices were opened in 14 locations around the country, and the number of employees grew to 500. Naturally, the organization also changed during this time period. An extensive sales division and full accounting department were added. Production expanded to include two plants to reduce distribution costs. Several layers of management hierarchy were added as Harvey became president and Bill became national sales vice president. Under Bill were three regional managers and a sales force of 45 people. A production vice president supervised the two plant managers, and each plant had approximately 200 employees.

But now Bill was not happy. The entrepreneurial flavor was gone from the company for him, and in 1981, he left to go into resort property development. Harvey decided to reorganize the sales division along product lines rather than geographic lines, since there were three distinct models of the Home Computers product, each with numerous options and special features. One model was designed for home use; one model was better suited to schools and libraries; and the third model appealed to small business owners.

Business continued to grow, and in 1983, HCC began to export to Canada and Europe. Also, in 1983, an attempt to unionize the plant in Ohio failed by a narrow margin. But the closeness of the vote suggested that his work force of 750 was not altogether happy with the Home Computers Company.

In 1986, the largest manufacturer of computers in the world entered the personal computer business, not to mention all of the clones that followed the big fellow. Growth rates in HCC have been severely cut since 1986, and profit margins have been hit especially hard. Harvey is unsure of what goals to set for his business—whether, for example, to focus on the business or the educational markets. He is unsure of how to better organize the business to be more efficient in its operation. And the prospect of changing the organization scares Harvey to death. With the help of a consultant, Harvey has begun to explore the current situation and is finding numerous problems. Many employees feel the company has become too bureaucratic, with all decisions being made at the top. The spirit of a new organization has waned. A number of managers report personnel problems and problems of coordination between the various divisions. The friction between sales and production is especially noticeable. Production cannot keep pace with sales, and sales makes promises it knows cannot be kept.

These signs of decay are present despite the fact that sales have begun to rebound a little. Harvey is unsure of what to do next; he does not want to make a fatal error at this critical time. And he is certain of one thing: Time will not stand still for him to conduct his analysis and make the best decisions.

THE DEVELOPMENTAL NATURE OF ORGANIZATIONS

Imagine yourself in Harvey's position, or as one of the employees who has been around since the early years, or even as a new employee at HCC. Could you make sense of the many events that are simultaneously unfolding? What would you do now if you were Harvey? How would you begin to analyze this situation? To come close to understanding these events and learning what to do, we must draw on a number of organizational behavior theories and view them in a developmental perspective. In the remainder of this chapter, we will focus on what a developmental perspective is and why it is so important to a manager. We will then look at an analytical framework that is helpful in structuring the remaining chapters of the book. The framework deals with the four levels of analysis mentioned earlier—namely, people, interpersonal relationships, work groups, and organizations. Each of these will be explored briefly in this chapter and in more detail in the chapters that follow. And we will also encounter the Home Computers Company case in the other chapters, as a vehicle for exploring the application of the theories presented.

Organizations and change

As the Home Computers case illustrates, the name of the game in organizations is change. Like people, organizations are always evolving and developing, though their progression is less orderly. While we can view organizations such as Home Computers as passing through phases of birth, growth, maturity, and possibly decline, organizations—unlike people—can backtrack in their development. For example, an organization that is beginning to decline may introduce a new product line, begin a new marketing campaign, or implement other strategic decisions that can take it back to the growth stage. But an organization can also move directly from birth to decline and failure, to which the many small business failures each year attest.

It is important in understanding people and organizations to appreciate their dynamic, changing, and developmental nature. Neither people nor organizations suddenly appear on the spot in their present form. They develop over time to their present state and then evolve into different states as the future unfolds. **Organizations and people exist within a time context, where their histories affect current perceptions of the world, and where past decisions affect their current structure, processes, and effectiveness.**

Some writers have likened this developmental perspective for studying organizations to using motion pictures, as compared to still pictures.[2] In still photos, one can get a clear picture of how things are at present and how they fit together to form the whole. Many theories in organizational behavior have been constructed in this fashion via cross-sectional research. That is, research data has been collected on a number of variables at only one point in time. Thus, we understand a great deal about critical relationships among organizationally relevant variables, but we do not always understand how to apply these relationships in dynamic settings. By viewing organizations as if through a motion picture lens, we can gain an understanding of how the still picture came to be and how to apply organizational behavior concepts in a dynamic setting.

Imagine freezing a frame of a movie so that a group of people are sitting on the steps in front of a house. Looking at the still frame, we can determine who is on the top step, who is on the right or the left, and who is on the bottom step. But did they all come out of the house, or did some come from the yard? Was there some jockeying for the seated positions? By backing up the film and then running it forward, we can find answers to these and other questions. If we think about organizations as motion pictures, we can employ existing behavior science theories in an analytical process that better portrays reality and that allows for an integrated view of events.

Analyzing organizations developmentally

Thus, it might be wise to use an analytical approach that is longitudinal in nature. If we look at the position of Harvey and Home Computers now in terms of the development of the organization since those days in the garage in the mid-1970s, we can better understand and see how to manage the present situation. Certainly, Harvey has changed since then. He has aged from his mid-30s to late 40s. And as we shall discuss later in the book, important changes occur in people from their 30s to their 40s. For one thing, Harvey is probably much more conscious of security issues. He may have children approaching college age. In short, he is a different person than he was in 1974, and he will continue to change.

Likewise, Home Computers Company is a very different company now than it was in the 1970s. It has evolved from a struggling, small company to a successful and growing organization to a firm facing new challenges. During this time, it has also evolved into an organization with a more complicated structure and design. Coordination and communication now involve the activities of many groups of people rather than just the activities of a few individuals. All is not rosy, as personnel and morale problems are becoming visible. Home Computers is thus showing signs of decline (or at least of inefficiency). Harvey is finding it difficult to manage HCC in its more competitive environment. To understand and manage this business, we need to look into: (1) the history of the company, (2) the previous decisions that affect the current state, and (3) the current developmental state of the people and the organization. By taking this approach, we can more effectively analyze Home Computers and decide what needs to be done. Things just do not occur in a time vacuum. In this book, we will use an analytical framework that explicitly employs a time-based perspective in order to gain a better understanding of organizational life.

THE ANALYTICAL FRAMEWORK FOR THIS TEXT

The analytical framework for this book involves a diagnostic and predictive process that views issues in both an organizational and a historical context. All topics are studied as they exist within an organization. For example, individuals are analyzed in the context of interpersonal and group relationships and within the structure of an entire organization and its environment. This organizational context is also embedded within a time dimension. All events are viewed in terms of their past, present, and future. This approach forces us to continually integrate topics and to review them at several points throughout the book. A more static application of theories would not encourage this integration. Nor would it be representative of the ever-changing way in which things occur in organizations. And since managers must operate in a dynamic, organizational world, this book offers a dynamic and developmental analytical framework that can help in applying the many organizational behavior theories.

The four levels of the framework

The framework used in the text involves the four levels of organizational behavior, which are shown in Exhibit 1–1. The first level focuses on understanding individuals in organizations. It deals with perception, learning, attitudes, values, personality, motivation, and outcomes of individual organizational members. The second level builds upon the first and focuses on the interpersonal aspects of people working together in organizations. It deals with leadership, influence and power relationships, as well as politics and communications among organizational members. The third level builds on the first two and focuses on the interplay between individuals and the organizational structure. It deals with work teams in organizations and explores group structure and processes, and group cohesion and groupthink. It also focuses on the interface between work teams in organizations, that is, the interplay between groups of people and the organization structure. This level also deals with intergroup conflict and coordination. The fourth level deals with the organization and its environment. It focuses on organizational goals and effectiveness, and on structure and design issues. This level also focuses on just how organizations change and develop over time. And all of these organizational behavior levels are embedded in the dynamic environmental forces of change and evolution.

Exhibit 1–1 is also designed to show the interrelationships among individuals, interpersonal relationships, work groups, organizations, and the environment. All five of these elements interact to determine an organization's effectiveness. For example, who we are as individuals affects our interpersonal relationships, effectiveness in a work group, and success in an organization. In return, we are affected by our work group, interpersonal relationships, and organization. Likewise, the interpersonal relationships of people influence work group effectiveness and organizational performance, as well as the individuals involved. And in return, the group, the organization, and the individuals affect

EXHIBIT 1–1
A Framework for Studying Organizations

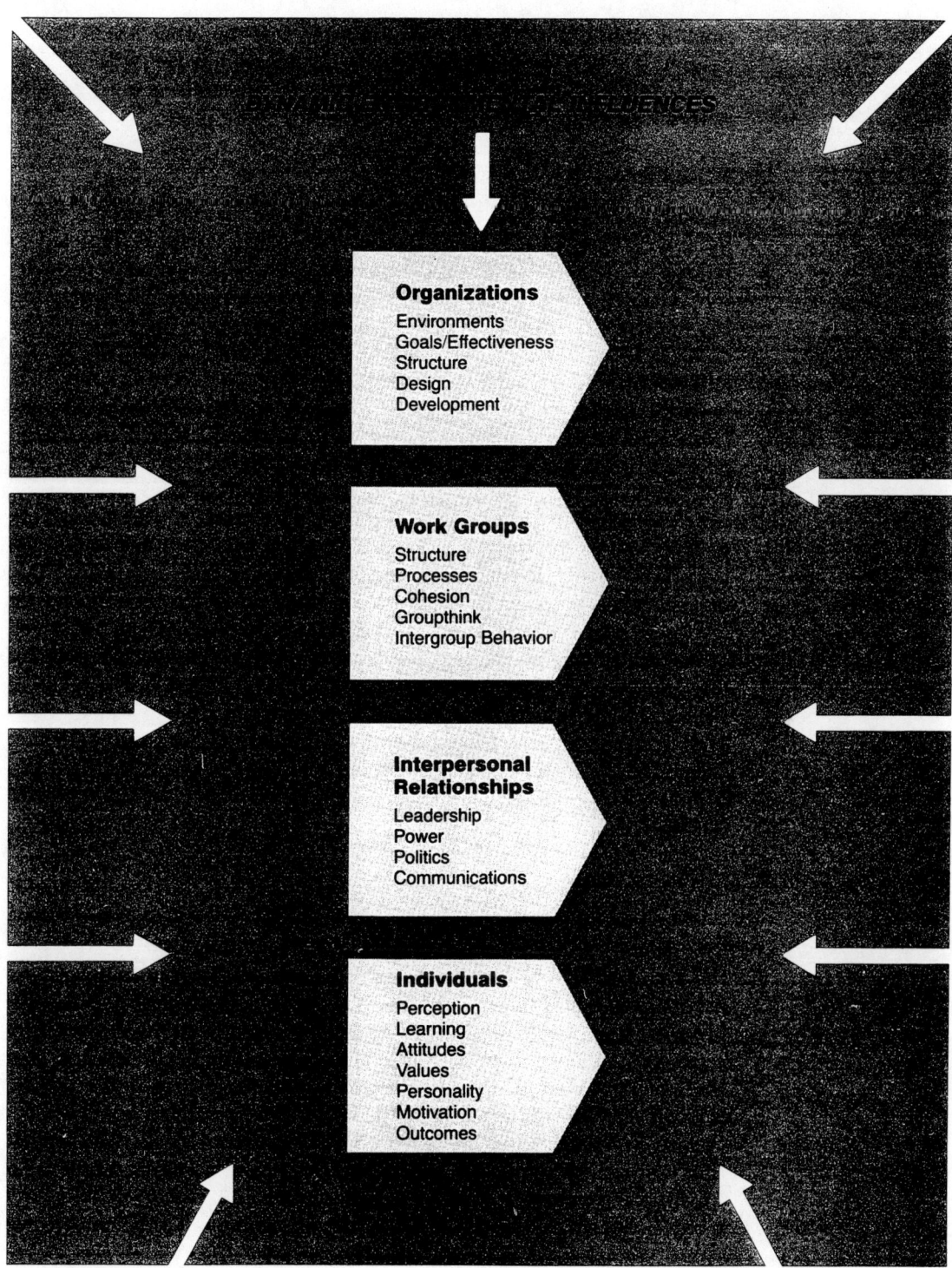

ENVIRONMENTAL/CULTURAL INFLUENCES

Organizations
Environments
Goals/Effectiveness
Structure
Design
Development

Work Groups
Structure
Processes
Cohesion
Groupthink
Intergroup Behavior

Interpersonal Relationships
Leadership
Power
Politics
Communications

Individuals
Perception
Learning
Attitudes
Values
Personality
Motivation
Outcomes

interpersonal relationships. As we work through the book one level at a time, it will be important to keep in mind that the other levels have a bearing on each topic we discuss. An organization exists with all four organizational behavior levels simultaneously interacting together and with the environment.

The dynamic dimension of the framework

In addition to the four organizational behavior levels, there is also a dynamic dimension to our analytical framework, which is depicted in Exhibit 1–2. The labels *Past* and *Future* show the developmental perspective. The key point here is that the four levels are always changing, and the interrelationships among the four levels are subject to influence by changes in any one of the four levels. In addition, all four levels are subject to changes in the environment, as well.

Think about the environmental changes that have occurred in the United States in the 1980s. We have had a recession, then a revitalized economy, then concern over budget deficits, a stock market crash—and who knows what will be next? Likewise, organizations change over time. They either grow and prosper, or they decline and fail. Work groups also go through developmental stages, as do interpersonal relationships. Finally, individuals grow and change as the years pass. Thus, our analytical framework must acknowledge the dynamism of all four levels of organizational behavior. Let us now look briefly at the developmental aspects of the four levels as an introduction to the plan for this text. First, we explore the individual level, which is the focus of Part 2 of the book. Then we look at interpersonal relationships, which are the focus of Part 3. Next, we look at groups and intergroup behavior, which are the focus of Part 4. And in Part 5, we focus on the organization as a whole, as well as the environments in which the organization operates.

Growth and change in people

People who study organizations and managers in organizations agree that people are the basic building blocks in any organization—and also the source of many organizational problems. Managers often lament how nice it would be if the business could be run without people, still knowing that people are vital to the organization. Even the designers of sophisticated new machines and office equipment have learned that their designs must incorporate the concerns of the people who must use the equipment, as illustrated by the NASA example in Insight 1–2. People are complex beings, and each person represents a unique character that will change over time. **To understand the employees in any organization and to understand ourselves, we must appreciate the developmental aspects of people.** Even if we can understand the people we

EXHIBIT 1–2
A Developmental Framework for Studying Organizations

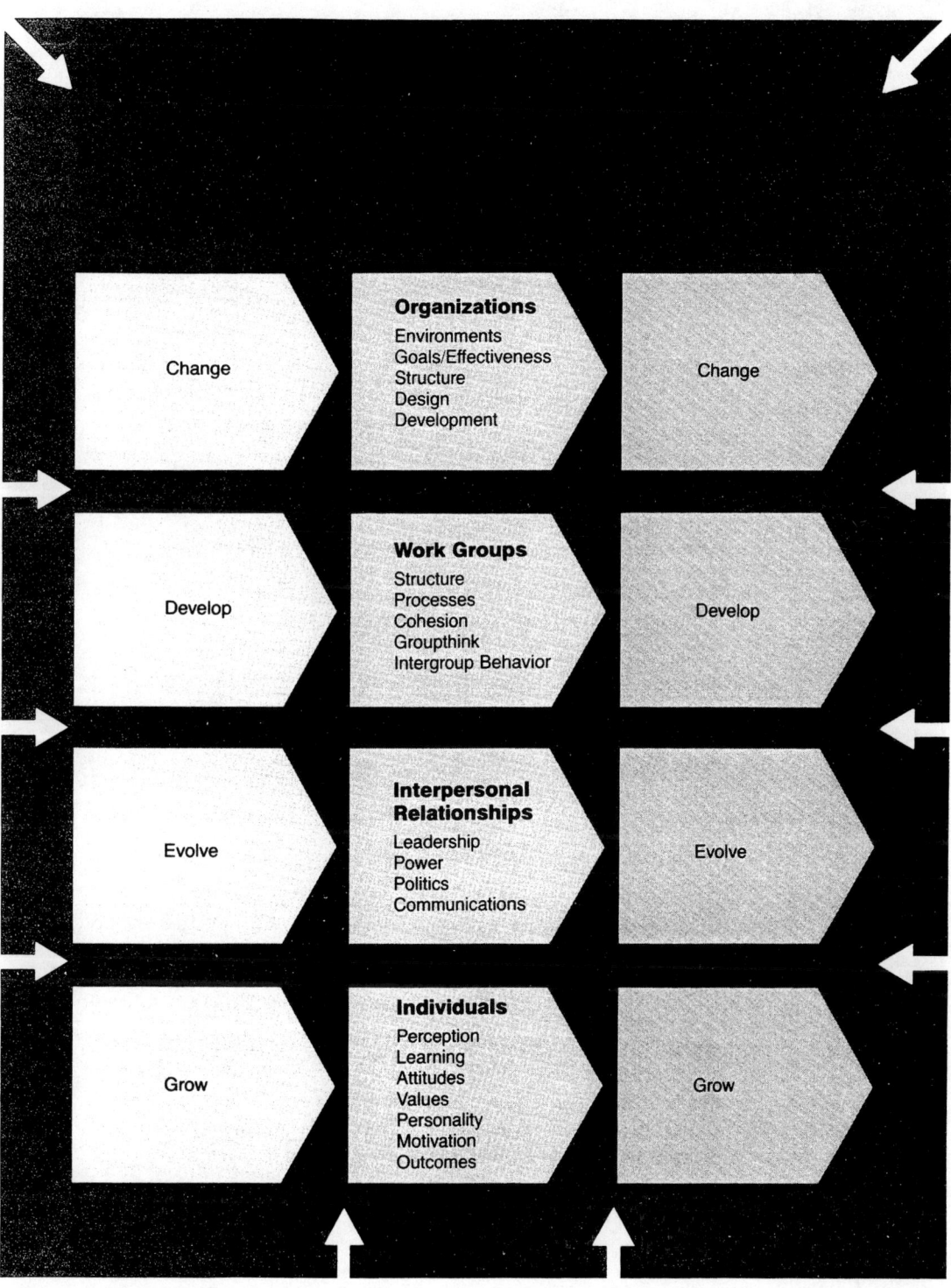

Future Schlock

Space station plans have critics wondering whether all that high technology is necessary

Astronauts are questioning the practicality of some of the space station's robotics technology. In an internal report circulated in August, Air Force Col. Gordon Fullerton, a veteran of two shuttle missions, sharply criticized the station design and NASA's plan to assemble it with a sophisticated robot arm.

Machines like the arm typify NASA's reliance on "too much Buck Rogers" technology that is prone to mechanical breakdown or error, Col. Fullerton says in an interview. "If it doesn't work, the whole station grinds to a halt," he adds. The space station is "a gadget with moving arms that never comes back to the hangar for maintenance. That really worries me."

The respected astronaut's 20-page report caused such a stir in the ranks of NASA management that the agency agreed to redesign certain aspects of the station. The high-tech arm, however, will stay.

Astronauts also have bridled at other state-of-the-art space station technology. NASA contractors designing the astronaut's helmets are enthusiastic about a high-tech visor equipped with a tiny screen that displays images directing an astronaut through a maintenance or repair task. NASA hopes the system, which would be triggered by the astronaut's voice, will some day be a training tool for a wide range of complex tasks.

But the astronauts contend that the technicians hadn't taken into account some natural human tendencies, such as boredom. A position paper prepared by the astronauts asserted that the device "would lead to crew indifference and ignorance due to concentration on manipulative nuts-and-bolts tasks at the expense of intellectual involvement and comprehension." NASA hasn't acted on the astronauts' complaints.

manage right now, will we understand them tomorrow after they change? And if we are to really understand people in the present, we must know something about their past and the process of human development.

A number of recent books based on documented studies indicate that understanding a person's past helps us understand present behavior. In turn, this can help us direct work behavior in ways that are useful to the organization. People who come to work for any organization bring a history of experiences with them. We simply do not get a "new" person as we can buy a new car, a new computer, or a new piece of machinery. Each person who is of employment age has had many years of experiences, contacts with many groups, and training in a number of locations and topics. Burton White's book *The First Three Years of Life* suggests that a great deal of education has already transpired before a child reaches three years of age.[3] Social skills, attitudes, and intellectual abilities are well along in their development by the age of three. People, of course, do continue to develop beyond the age of three, but White argues that their degree of flexibility in lifestyle, intellectual capacity, attitudes, and so forth are significantly influenced by events that occur during those first three years. We will encounter these issues in detail in Chapter 3, as we discuss the process of perception.

Eric Erikson, a well-known personality theorist, argues that human beings develop in important ways from birth to death.[4] To be born is to begin the simultaneous process of growth and death; each day we live, we grow a little, and we die a little. We constantly learn and constantly forget as we progress through life. We learn at different rates, learn different things from similar experiences, and are motivated by various stimuli to perform actions that differ from person to person. The same is true of forgetting. It is likely that many of these differences in learning and forgetting could be traced to differences in early childhood experiences.

But changes also continue into adulthood. As Gail Sheehy indicates in *Passages,* there are "predictable crises of adult life."[5] She provides insight into the developmental stages people pass through during their teenage years and beyond. Sheehy describes the teenage years as a time of pulling up roots. The "trying 20s" are a time of trying out different life scenarios and different partners with whom to make our lives. The "catch 30s" are a time to make, break, or deepen life commitments. The "forlorn 40s" are the years of reassessment, sexual panic, and opportunity for self-discovery. The "refreshed or resigned 50s" are the time to let go of old roles and find a renewal of purpose. Certainly Harvey of Home Computers Company is affected as he approaches his refreshed or resigned 50s—which shall it be? How is he different than he was when the company started and he was in the catch 30s? We explore these stages in greater detail in Chapters 5 and 6, as we work to understand the factors that motivate people.

The purpose of mentioning the stages of life and the importance of one's early years is twofold. First, they help us gain an understanding of ourselves and how we might fit into an organization. Second, they provide the basis for understanding the behavior of other people and should prove useful to us as managers. We will return to these issues in Chapter 4 as we discuss personality and in Chapters 5 and 6 on motivation. For now, let us recognize that **by understanding what people are like in the present, how they got there, and something about where they are headed, we are in a much better position to effectively work with and manage them.** Furthermore, the same analytical process can help us to understand ourselves and our potential in various situations.

Of course, we must not forget that people will continue to change throughout their careers. While the organization gets a "used product" in any new employee, the product is not a finished one in terms of organizational influence. Our analysis of people must continue into the future as they develop. For example, a new employee must learn about the basic goals of the organization, the preferred means for attaining those goals, job responsibilities, and the accepted ways of behaving in the organization. As the employee moves from one position to another, and up the hierarchy, the organization will exert its influence, causing the employee to change. How will the employee be different 10 years down the road? And we must not forget that evolutionary processes can create dramatic differences in people from different generations. For example, Insight 1–3 shows how a father and son can have quite different perspectives on the world. These issues will be explored in more detail in Chapters 2 and 4.

Interpersonal relationships over time

The second level of analysis in our model is interpersonal relations. As in the case of friendships, working relationships in organizations develop over time, may change for better or worse, and may end. Imagine yourself as a new employee going to work in one of the offices of a large business. You are introduced to your supervisor and to the people with whom you will work. To perform effectively, you will usually have to develop good working relations with these people.

But people manage (or lead) in different ways. By learning from other employees about their past experiences with this supervisor, you begin to learn what to expect from the manager. The combination of both of your personal histories and your own experience with the supervisor results in a relationship that may range from good to poor. From the supervisor's perspective, you will be analyzed and may be found to need a great deal of supervision in this new work situation. In time, however, the supervisor may decide that you are quite capable and then shift to a more general supervision. Various leadership theories allow us to analyze and understand the dynamics underlying the changes that will take place from day one to six months or several years later. But we must not forget that the past experiences of both you and the supervisor will interact in the present situation to determine the outcome of this relationship. We explore these interrelationships in detail in Chapters 8 and 9. For now it is important to understand that **the developmental aspects of leader-follower relationships interact with the dynamic properties of individuals.**

In addition to your relationship with the supervisor, you must develop working relationships and possibly social relationships with the other employees in your work unit. The work itself may dictate interac-

I N S I G H T 1–3

Quiet Mills

As Steel Jobs Dwindle, Blue-Collar Families Face Vexing Changes

Pittsburgh—Bill Gorol, a laid-off USX Corp. steelworker, walked the picket line during the 116-day steel strike of 1959, and now he fervently backs the current strike against the nation's largest steelmaker. "We fought for everything for 80 years," he says, "and now they want it back."

But the son born to Mr. Gorol and his wife as the 1959 strike loomed disagrees with him. "I'm a businessman," says Bill Gorol Jr., a 27-year-old former steelworker who has embarked on a new life as a car salesman. "If you're not making a profit and your costs are too high, I say shut the plants down. Why operate in the red?"

Such are the sharply clashing views dividing blue-collar fathers and white-collar sons these days. Just as America's industrial landscape is changing radically, so are the families that helped build it. The traditional working-class family, once the backbone of the U.S. economy, is disappearing as rapidly as did the smoke from this region's smokestacks.

Nowhere is that more evident than in USX-dominated mill-towns such as Clairton and Homestead, Pa., Gary, Ind., and Lorain, Ohio—places where men long carried union cards and passed on their workday traditions like keepsakes. Sons followed fathers into the mills as surely as the 4 p.m. whistle signaled an end to the first shift. But the closing of many mills has shattered all that.

Emerging from the crumbling world of steel is a class of young workers whose jobs, attitudes and values are often confusing to their working-class parents. These sons and daughters found little but bitter memories in the forbidding, abandoned mills that dominate places such as the Monongahela Valley south of here. While their fathers collect unemployment benefits, they have entered the white-collar world, taking jobs programming computers, preparing electric bills, managing restaurants, tending bars and selling cars, water beds and shoes.

But these "new-collar" workers, as they have been tagged, often pay a heavy price in the transition. While their new fields hold potential for salaries and promotions that their fathers never dreamed of, they often also engender bewildering pressures and uncertain futures. Forsaking coveralls for ties and jackets may guarantee that they never will have a leg severed on the job. But it probably also requires working longer hours—and for lower pay—than their fathers. The changes that these younger workers undergo often trigger tensions between the generations, tensions that can be especially painful in tightly knit working-class families. Many say they feel trapped between the blue- and white-collar life styles.

tions between you and certain other people in the office. Interpersonal relations theories indicate that initial impressions also determine who you will come to know best, at least initially. People to whom you are attracted will become the focus of your interactions, and the more you interact with someone, the more likely you are to become friends. Sometimes, though, interactions can lead to the discovery that your initial attraction cannot be sustained, and the relationship wanes. **Exchange theory** suggests that people continue a relationship for as long as the benefits equal or outweigh the costs of the relationship.[6] The now famous case of how John Sculley was hired by Steven Jobs to run Apple Computers and then forced Jobs, the cofounder, out of the company is one such example of how business relationships can end.

Our experience tells us that change is the nature of interpersonal relationships. For example, people meet and become friends, one moves away, and the friendship declines. Or, employees meet, learn to work together, and become good coworkers; then something happens (for example, one gets transferred or promoted), and the relationship deteriorates. And we could think of countless other examples. Just look at what happened between Bill and Harvey at HCC. Their relationship changed because of changes in the company and probably because of changes in both Bill and Harvey, and Bill has moved on to other endeavors. Likewise, think about what happened to Bill's marriage. And as Insight 1-4 suggests, maintaining these relationships can be a real source of stress in business. Managers must become adept at understanding and managing changing relationships. The key point is that **relationships take time to develop; they continue to change indefinitely; and they may end.** The interpersonal processes of leadership (discussed in Chapters 8 and 9), power and political relationships (discussed in Chapter 10), and communications (discussed in Chapter 11) must be viewed in this fashion if we are to understand how to effectively manage in organizations.

Work teams and their development

The third level in our model is the work team or group of people who work together in organizational settings. What organization can operate without committees, task forces, work teams, and other groups of people? Yet some people suggest that a camel is a horse made by committee—that groups cannot make decisions as efficiently as one person. The fact is that while **organizations depend very heavily upon groups of people, it is difficult to make a group operate effectively.** Fortunately, it is possible to have some very effective groups. And one key to understanding the operation of a work team is to appreciate and analyze the individuals who make up the team. As we have discussed, each person is unique and will bring unique elements to a group. The task of the

---

I N S I G H T 1–4

Business Stress, If Neglected, Can Be a Company's Undoing

*B*usiness is off sharply. The owner and founder of a small Massachusetts company is convinced he must cut back to survive. But that means firing members of "the family," employees who have been with the company from the beginning. He can't do it, so he calls in someone else to do the firing.

The stress problem for middle-aged owners is especially difficult because they are likely to be at the stage where they are reassessing their goals in life. "Often the problems of the organization have to do with the problems of the middle-aged manager or owner," says Dr. Rosenthal, consultant to businesses.

The death of a parent or parents often occurs during this period. Children leave home. Today, while the man may be considering tapering off at work, his wife may be preparing to go back to work or start a career. Small-business owners must be aware that such changes occur during middle age and be prepared to deal with them, Dr. Rosenthal says. "He must keep his relationships with family well oiled and greased."

By Johnnie L. Roberts, *The Wall Street Journal*, December 14, 1982. Reprinted by permission of *The Wall Street Journal*, © Dow Jones & Company, Inc., 1982. All rights reserved.

---

group and its manager is to put the pieces of the puzzle together to form a complete picture. But there are exceptions to this puzzle analogy: (1) There is no guarantee that all the pieces will be present; (2) There is no guarantee that the pieces will fit together; and (3) The pieces continue to change through growth and development.

Another key, then, to understanding a group is to recognize that it—like individuals—will change over time. It is easy to see that groups add and lose people and must deal with people who have changed, and these changes make adjustments in the group necessary. But aside from these obvious changes, even an intact team evolves through different stages over time. Schutz has defined three stages through which groups evolve: inclusion, control, and affection.[7]

Inclusion is the initial process of determining who is really going to commit to the group; what skills, abilities, and other resources they bring to the group; and what their standards and motivation levels are. It is basically a time to get acquainted and to lay groundwork for later stages. The inclusion stage varies in length of time, and groups may later come back to it if they add or lose people. However, once these inclusion issues are basically settled, the **control** stage (which has already begun during inclusion) comes into focus.

The **control** stage involves the issue of who is going to lead the group—who is going to influence the direction of the team and with what style. Sometimes one person emerges as the leader; sometimes two or three people are in control; and sometimes influence is more or less equally shared by all team members. It can also happen that a group becomes stuck in the control stage when two or more people compete for primary influence and cannot resolve the issue.

Once the control issues are basically settled, however, the group can enter the final stage of **affection.** This stage is basically a time of cohesion for the group. Members are clear on the commitment levels of other members; they know who has influence in the group; they have developed norms of operation; and they know what to expect from the group as a whole and from its individual members. Still, it takes continuing effort to maintain this cohesion. As we have discussed, changes in group membership can force the team back to earlier stages. And changes in the tasks assigned the group, in its relationship with other groups, or in its physical workspace can also take the group back to previous stages of evolution. In addition, unsuccessful groups may dissolve at any point in the three-stage process.

The key idea is that work teams that are successful over the long run are dynamic entities. They evolve over time, and their evolution is influenced by many factors. In Chapters 12 and 13, we explore groups in detail and discuss research and theory development concerning these vital components in organizations. In Chapter 14, we deal with the important issues of intergroup conflict and coordination.

The dynamic aspects of organizations

The development of people, interpersonal relationships, and work teams occurs in the context of the developmental nature of organizations as a whole. Thus, the organizational context is the fourth level of analysis. At this level, we have to be concerned with organizational environments, goals, and effectiveness (as discussed in Chapters 15 and 16).[8] We must focus on the structures and designs that can be used to achieve desired levels of organizational effectiveness. And all of these factors occur within a dynamic process of change and development.

In the case of Home Computers Company, we saw that organizations are created; they grow and develop; their goals change. They may also decline in effectiveness and eventually fail. A number of writers have attempted to explain the development of organizations using a life-cycle metaphor. Lippitt and Schmidt defined three basic stages of organizational evolution: birth, growth, and maturity.[9] Greiner explained organizational development in terms of five stages, each involving a particular crisis:

1. Creativity, with the crisis of leadership.
2. Direction, with the crisis of autonomy.

3. Delegation, with the crisis of control.
4. Coordination, with the crisis of red tape.
5. Collaboration, with the crisis unspecified.[10]

More recently, Tansik, Chase, and Aquilano identified eight life-cycle phases of organizational evolution:

1. Birth of the organization.
2. Design of the organization.
3. Staffing the organization.
4. Startup of the organization.
5. Organization in steady state.
6. Improving the organization.
7. Revision of the organization.
8. Termination of the organization.[11]

However, this life-cycle analogy is not completely satisfactory in understanding organizational evolution. Perhaps the most obvious shortcoming is, as stated before, that organizations are born, grow, and decline. But, instead of dying, they can be reborn (via a new product line, for example) and thus go back to an earlier stage of the process. Insight 1–5 provides a good example of this type of revitalization, describing how Mr. Taylor brought Rockford Headed Products, Inc. back from near death. Another problem is that the timing of the evolutionary steps is not at all predictable. Two organizations in the same industry may vary substantially in the length of time they remain in each stage of growth and development. Furthermore, some subdivisions of an organization may be growing and prospering, while others in the same organization are declining and experiencing significant problems. The four levels of analysis allow the possibility for different developmental rates at each level.

The point to learn from the life-cycle metaphor is that the past history of an organization has a major influence on its present state. **Past decisions of management and past events in the organization's history have a direct influence on present and future events and decisions in the organization's life.** For example, the past decision of Home Computers Company to manufacture small computers may limit the organization's ability to produce other products. The commitment of human, financial, equipment, and time resources to the computer business may not leave the resources to go into, say, portable typewriters. Or a previous decision to locate on the East Coast may impede HCC's development of markets on the West Coast, at least until a certain size operation is achieved.

A developmental perspective to understanding organizations includes their historical context, plus their natural evolution and planned

**How an Entrepreneur Revived
Faltering Firm Despite Slump**

*I*n 1978, Mr. [Frank] Taylor bought Rockford Headed Products Inc., Rockford, Ill., a small, privately owned maker of screws, bolts and other fasteners that was losing sales to cheap imports. After Mr. Taylor took over, the economy soured, industrial production fell and fastener demand shrank. Yet the company has done well under his direction. First quarter sales set a record, and the 56-year-old entrepreneur predicts sales for the year will be $4.4 million, 10% ahead of last year.

Mr. Taylor has transformed the entire business from the bookkeeping office to the manufacturing floor. Accounts receivable that chronically ran 50 days late are current. Shipments go out on time where half used to be late. There is a cost accounting system that the previous managers didn't have. "They had no idea what their costs were,"

Mr. Taylor says. He has slashed overhead and improved quality. Most important, he moved the company away from a cutthroat part of the market.

For many years the company sold standard screws and bolts to distributors who resell to end users.

Mr. Taylor's research showed that special-purpose fasteners were a way out of the price-cutting competition that sapped many small bolt and screw companies. Today, 47 production employees tend 65 machines in the company's new plant, producing millions of screws and bolts. A homely bolt, with a nick cut out of its flat head, is one that makes Mr. Taylor especially proud. Six months to develop, it replaces three pieces in an electrical terminal, saving a manufacturer assembly time and parts costs.

change efforts (which we explore in Chapter 19). Certain aspects of organizations tend to evolve in predictable patterns. Technologies of organizations (that is, the methods of completing the organization's tasks) tend to evolve from a nonroutine and relatively unpredictable state to a routine and predictable state, as the bugs are worked out and systems are refined. The designs of organizations (the subject of Chapter 18) may change from functional organization to product organization to matrix in order to respond to changes both internal and external to the organization. The structure and procedures of organizations (discussed in Chapter 17) tend to evolve from loose and organic to rigid and bureaucratic. And people in organizations tend to evolve from unskilled to highly skilled in their jobs. **Overall, organizations that survive over time generally evolve from uncertainty to a relative degree of certainty in accomplishing their objectives and tasks, but they also must evolve to fit the world around them.** Numerous examples have been reported in the literature of the 1980s. Bank of America changed its culture to fit current trends; AT&T reorganized dramatically after its 1984 divestiture of the Bell companies; and Honeywell had to refocus its Information Systems operation to stay competitive.[12] And a popular book by Tom Peters, *Thriving on Chaos,* is built on the theme of managing change.[13]

While such developments may be generally predictable, effective managers pay attention to the details of the evolution. Some organizations may not evolve toward certainty and control of their situations, or their direction of evolution may reverse toward uncertainty. Thus, these organizations may become additions to the statistics on business failures. Then, too, changes in the environment may dictate that the organization remain less structured in order to meet the demands of a rapidly changing environment and still remain viable. Chrysler is a good example of a company that did not adapt well to a changing environment. Among other problems, it continued to make large cars when the public wanted high-quality small cars. Chrysler's successful shift in direction to be more competitive, under Lee Iacocca, is now legend.[14] The developmental perspective allows us to understand the forces operating in and around an organization and to determine what needs to be done either to rectify problems or to take advantage of opportunities. Knowing where an organization has been and having an appreciation for past decisions will help a manager understand why the organization is where it is now, and where it may be going. Indeed, as Insights 1–6 and 1–7 show, picture phones, teleconferencing, and robots are creating alternatives only dreamed about a few years ago.

The changing environment

We saw earlier that the developmental perspective allows us to incorporate the organization's history into our analysis. It also allows us to consider the organization's environment. As Exhibits 1–1 and 1–2 show, the environment of the organization is the final element in our model of organizations. Environment is both external and internal to the organization, as we discuss in Chapter 15. We must recognize that environments play a role in the application of individual, interpersonal, group, and organization theories and research that we explore in this text.

To appreciate the influence of an organization's environment, consider what has transpired in the U.S. industrial community since 1900. In 1900, the United States was basically an agrarian society only beginning to enter the age of industry. As the United States began to industrialize, people had to learn new skills as well as how to live and work in cities. Industrial technology dictated that jobs be engineered for efficiency and designed to accommodate the lack of skills of the average worker. Scientific management (a method for breaking down jobs into simple tasks) led the way to an efficient and effective economy that saw the United States become a world leader.[15] As this environmental evo-

INSIGHT 1-6

In This Futuristic Office, Intimacy Exists Between Workers Separated by 500 Miles

*F*or a year, in rooms filled with computers, cameras, microphones and xylophones, Xerox Corp. scientists in cities 500 miles apart have been collaborating as if they were in the same building.

The scientists hope to achieve an electronic "office of the future" that goes well beyond such temporary and awkward methods as picture phones and teleconferences. To study the daunting sociological and technological challenges of such an office, the company has put labs in Palo Alto, Calif., and Portland, Ore., in constant communication, using an assortment of commercially available devices.

The workers watch and talk to each other via video and speaker-phone connections that are always open. They exchange documents over a network that links the computers on their desks.

By examining life in this environment, Xerox hopes to learn how to combine the disparate links into one super work station that functions as both a computer and a TV monitor, running programs, projecting images from other offices and storing paper work and video images.

Some strange things may appear in such files. Last National Secretaries Day, for example, researchers in the two cities gathered in a "circle" to belt out a pastiche of "Seventy-Six Trombones." The circle's halves were joined by cameras, speaker phones and a computer network.

Yet far more is at stake than a better way for widely dispersed colleagues to make dubious music together. Corporate executives have long complained that poor coordination between far-flung operations hurts productivity. Moreover, as the rise of two-career marriages makes many professionals more reluctant to relocate, companies are trying harder to link offices electronically rather than uproot employees.

lution continued, the standard of living increased and resulted in more highly educated and skilled workers. A series of studies conducted at the Hawthorne plant of the Western Electric Company in the late 1920s highlighted the need to seriously consider the impact of people on the job, as their skills began to catch up with the skill demands of the technologies employed in industry.[16]

In the 1950s, the advent of computers and other sophisticated technologies that grew out of World War II moved the United States into an era of tremendous growth and expanded influence. For a while, it seemed that the sky really was the limit. But the 1960s brought serious unrest among people who were being left behind in this country and in other countries. The sky began to fall. Leaders were assassinated, and the United States could not seem to win the conflict in Southeast Asia.

I N S I G H T   1–7

Robots: Next Step for Garment Makers

*I*n Cambridge, Mass., scientists are putting the final touches on a machine that does what no machine has been able to do before: automatically construct the sleeves for a man's coat and sew them onto the body of the jacket.

In Japan, government planners foresee bolts of fabric entering one end of a robot assembly line and emerging at the other end as finished men's business suits—all done with a minimum of human assistance.

An in Europe, companies are developing space-age contraptions for handling and assembling garments, including lasers and ultra-high-pressure water jets to cut fabric to computer-controlled patterns.

Automating the Rag Trade

Automation is a tall order for an industry that remains among the most labor-intensive world-wide. Indeed, garment-making robots are years off, and clothing makers and unions in the U.S. and elsewhere continue to press for more immediate relief through tariff protection. (Just yesterday, the House up-

held a presidential veto of a bill that would have cut textile imports by an average of 30%.) But automation must happen, the industry believes, if Japan and the West are to provent further loss of jobs to China, Hong Kong, South Korea and other low-cost places.

The loss of garment-industry jobs explains why the rush to robotize has been joined by the labor unions, even though the machines are designed to cut labor. "We felt that we couldn't compete on the basis of wage levels," says Jack Sheinkman, secretary-treasurer of the Amalgamated Clothing and Textile Workers Union, which has seen its membership in the U.S. slip 20%, to 360,000 from 450,000 in 1980.

"If we don't go this route, the jobs will be wiped out. It'll save what is left of a much smaller industry." Adds Tyuyoshi Takagi, a Japanese union leader, "We may have mixed feelings (about automation), but this technology is essential to our survival."

By the time the 1970s rolled around, Americans were fighting among themselves, being threatened by oil magnates in the Middle East, and dealing with numerous rules and regulations imposed by the Washington bureaucracy.[17]

Currently, we find ourselves searching for solutions to these economic, political, and social ills. The White House and Congress search for ways to stabilize our economic ship. Business and government search for methods of dealing with an economy that consists of international competitors, suppliers, and inflationary influences. At the same time, individuals try to cope with a world where they have difficulty affording a house and where each year they lose ground economically.[18] Managers try to lead people whose skills do not match the needs of a computerized, high-tech society. The complexity and dynamism of the world has been multiplied many times since 1900, and many historical and current factors interact to create the management problems faced by organizations and individuals. By gaining an appreciation for the environmental history of our organizations, we will be better able to find solutions for today's problems.

This point is made vividly by a sign at the entrance to the Dachau, West Germany, concentration camp, which has been made a memorial to World War II by the West Germans. It reads: "Those who forget the past are condemned to repeat it." Managers who ignore the past may attempt solutions that have already been tried and have failed. Furthermore, a knowledge of past trends, though not a perfect predictor of the future, may help managers anticipate problems before they occur. In times of rapid change, things may occur that upset the trend of events; but often several trends all predict the same future events and should not be ignored. For example, long before the oil shortages of the 1970s, people in oil companies were reporting a declining level of reserves in domestic oil, while the trend of oil consumption was clearly moving upward. No one seemed to take this seriously until the "surprising" oil shortage of 1973–74. What lies ahead for managers in the 1990s and beyond? What skills will they need? What signals must be read if they are to be successful? This text should provide some of the answers.

CHAPTER HIGHLIGHTS

The purpose of this book is to help the reader gain an understanding of the dynamics of behavior in organizations and learn how to effectively manage people in organizations. In the following chapters, we explore the basic levels of organizational behavior (individuals, interpersonal relations, groups, and organizations) from a developmental perspective. Everything we discuss is viewed as in a state of flux. Nothing is static; even the theories we discuss are viewed as dynamic rather than as the final answer. As a philosopher once said, "The only good answer to a question is one that leads to the asking of another good question." **We must dig deeper and deeper in our understanding of concepts and theories; that is, we must search for greater understanding by constantly asking questions.**

As students of organizational behavior and as managers, we must **learn to learn.** If we only retain the theories as we presently know them, we will quickly become obsolete. For example, managers today who have not kept up with the explosive use of computers are truly behind in their organizations. **One key ingredient common to successful people in organizations is the ability to continue learning and adapting.**

Analytical skills need to be developed in school, and we need to learn to use the theories and research that do exist. However, we also need to keep questioning things over and over again in order to use a developmental perspective to understand and manage organizational behavior.

In this book, we rely on the four levels of analysis of organizational behavior, overlaid with the developmental perspective. This system of analysis gives us a set of building blocks for understanding organizational behavior. First, we gain an understanding of individuals in organizations, including their motivations, attitudes, and other key aspects, as well as their developmental properties. We then use this information to develop an understanding of interpersonal relationships. In other words, if we are to understand leadership, power, and communications, we need an understanding of what makes individuals operate as they do. We build on this understanding of individuals and interpersonal relations as we explore group and intergroup effectiveness issues. Finally, we build on the first three levels to explore organizations as whole entities. We try to integrate these four levels as we proceed through the book, since things in real organizations occur in a simultaneous, integrated, and developmental fashion.

By overlaying the developmental perspective on the four dimensions, we become aware of another integrating factor: namely, all four levels of analysis occur within a historical, developmental context. Awareness of the past, present, and future of organizational events forces us to integrate the four levels in our search for a realistic perspective on organizational behavior. For example, while we can discuss theories and research related to individuals, we cannot forget that their behavior takes place in an organizational and historical context. Organizations and people simply are not static entities, as the Home Computers Company case illustrates. To solve Harvey's problems, we must ask questions about how the organization, its people, and its subdivisions arrived at their present state. To ignore (1) the rapid growth of the company, (2) its evolution toward bureaucracy, (3) the past history of conflict between sales and production, (4) the history of interpersonal relationships such as between Harvey and Bill, and (5) the growth and change in Harvey and his stage in life, means that we will not be able to adequately assess the present situation and determine what needs to be done to rectify the problems surfacing in Home Computers. For example, to determine that Harvey needs to devote more time to personnel issues may ignore a possible desire on his part to become less involved in the daily detail of HCC. In his late 40s and after more than 15 years of making this company go, Harvey may really need a reorganization that frees him rather than a solution that ties him down. Likewise, the conflict between sales and production is quite likely more than a simple case of interdepartmental strife created by goal and priority differences. The rapid growth of the company suggests that some key people may have been moved up the ladder more quickly than was consistent with their ability and development. Thus, the solution to this conflict may rest in better selection of qualified people or training for present managers, especially given the current, more competitive environment. Whatever the real solution for Harvey and Home Computers, a developmental and historical perspective will be more useful in the analysis process than a static look at things would be.

The remaining chapters of this book provide much detailed information for enhancing developmental analytical skills. By the time you finish, you should have a well-integrated, developmental understanding of behavior in organizations. You will also have become familiar with the language of a developmental perspective. Primarily, this means that words take the *-ing* form, such as act*ing*, manag*ing*, lead*ing*, behav*ing*, mov*ing*, think*ing*. Everything you study will be in a state of be*ing* and becom*ing*, and your knowledge will be increas*ing* and form*ing* a solid beginn*ing* for manag*ing* organizational behavior.

REVIEW QUESTIONS

1. How would you define *organizations, managing,* and *organizational behavior?*

2. What are the five main elements of organizations, and how are they interrelated?

3. What does it mean to take a *developmental perspective* to understanding and managing organizational behavior? Why is this a useful perspective?

4. How does the analytical framework for the book integrate the levels of organizational analysis with the developmental perspective?

5. What are the developmental aspects of people in organizations?

6. "Relationships with others in an organization are dynamic and evolutionary in nature." What does this mean, and why is it important to appreciate this process?

7. Explain the developmental process as it applies to work groups.

8. Why are past decisions made by organizations important for a manager to understand and consider?

9. Explain the dynamic aspects of organizational goals and effectiveness, as well as organization environments.

10. What are the key developmental issues that relate to organizational structures and designs?

RESOURCE READINGS

Bradford, D. L., and A. R. Cohen. *Managing for Excellence.* New York: John Wiley & Sons, 1984.

Greiner, L. E. "Evolution and Revolution as Organizations Grow." *Harvard Business Review,* July-August 1972, pp. 37–46.

Kimberly, J. R.; R. H. Miles; and Associates. *The Organizational Life Cycle: Issues in the Creation, Transformation, and Decline of Organizations.* San Francisco: Jossey-Bass, 1980.

Kimberly, J. R., and R. E. Quinn. *Managing Organizational Transitions.* Homewood, IL: R. D. Irwin, 1984.

Peters, T. *Thriving on Chaos.* New York: A. A. Knopf, 1987.

NOTES

1. H. J. Leavitt, *Managerial Psychology* (Chicago: The University of Chicago Press, 1958); D. A. Nadler and M. L. Tushman, "A Model for Diagnosing Organizational Behavior: Applying a Congruence Perspective," *Organizational Dynamics,* Autumn 1980, pp. 35–51.

2. J. R. Kimberly and M. J. Evanisko, "Organizational Technology, Structure, and Size." In *Organizational Behavior,* ed. S. Kerr (Columbus, Ohio: Grid, 1979), pp. 263–87.

3. B. L. White, *The First Three Years of Life* (New York: Avon Books, 1975).

4. E. Erikson, *Childhood and Society* (New York: W. W. Norton, 1950).

5. G. Sheehy, *Passages* (New York: E. P. Dutton, 1974).

6. J. W. Thibaut and H. H. Kelly, *The Social Psychology of Groups* (New York: John Wiley & Sons, 1959), pp. 9–30.

7. W. C. Schutz, "Interpersonal Underworld," *Harvard Business Review,* July-August 1958, pp. 38–56.

8. W. A. Randolph and G. G. Dess, "The Congruence Perspective of Organizational Design: A Conceptual Model and Multivariate Research Approach," *Academy of Management Review* 9 (1984), pp. 114–27; K. S. Cameron, "A Study of Organizational Effectiveness and Its Predictors," *Management Science* 32 (1986), pp. 87–112.

9. G. L. Lippitt and W. H. Schmidt, "Crisis in a Developing Organization," *Harvard Business Review,* November-December 1967, pp. 102–11.

10. L. E. Greiner, "Evolution and Revolution as Organizations Grow," *Harvard Business Review,* July-August 1972, pp. 37–46.

11. D. A. Tansik, R. B. Chase, and N. J. Aquilano, *Management: A Life Cycle Approach* (Homewood, Ill.: Richard D. Irwin, 1980).

12. Z. E. Barnes, "Change in the Bell System," *Academy of Management Executive* 1 (1987), pp. 43–46; R. N. Beck, "Visions, Values and Strategies:

Changing Attitudes and Culture," *Academy of Management Executive* 1 (1987), pp. 33–42; J. J. Renier, "Turnaround of Information Systems at Honeywell," *Academy of Management Executive* 1 (1987), pp. 47–50.

13. T. Peters, *Thriving on Chaos* (New York: Alfred A. Knopf, 1987).

14. L. Iacocca with W. Novak, *Iacocca: An Autobiography* (New York: Bantam Books, 1984).

15. F. Taylor, *Scientific Management* (New York: Harper & Row, 1947).

16. E. Mayo, *The Social Problems of an Industrial Civilization* (Boston, Mass.: Harvard University, Graduate School of Business, 1945).

17. C. A. Reich, *The Greening of America* (New York: Random House, 1970).

18. N. Jonas, A. Bernstein, J. Berger, O. Port, J. W. Wilson, and K. Penner, "Can America Compete?," *Business Week*, April 20 (1987), pp. 45–66.

CASE: Elizabeth Sternberg*

Elizabeth had always admired her parents. Of course, she argued with them from time to time, but she loved to be home, to cook and sew, and to help with her younger brothers and sisters. To her parents, Liz was a model child. She never did especially well in school, but never received an F either. School social life was more important than studies to Elizabeth. Yet she was a little shy, more a group follower than a leader. Although she dated frequently, most of the boys seemed too immature for her.

Liz never planned to go to college. Her real dream was to get married and have children. At 17, however, this seemed a way off, and after high school graduation she expected to look for a job—but not for about six months. The summer and autumn went very slowly. Many of her friends left the neighborhood; some of the boys joined the military, some traveled, others went off to college. Liz missed the excitement of the crowded halls and active conversation of high school. Finally, in November she took a clerical job in the regional office of a large insurance company.

From the beginning, Liz fit right in. She did what she was told, was polite and willing. She thought the work was fine, but she really enjoyed the beautiful new office, so clean and neat, and even more she liked the friends she made.

It was her social sensitivity that prompted Liz to drop a note into the suggestion box. The office had been arranged in long straight rows and columns, all rather forbidding looking. Liz suggested that the setup be modified to several semicircles. This would facilitate communicating with the group leader located in the middle and between cooperating desks. It would also create a sense of belonging (and perhaps promote gossip). Management subsequently introduced the arrangement, and everyone was pleased.

As time passed, Liz perfected her typing, shorthand, and telephone style so much that she received several merit raises. She was even assigned a

*Source: Adapted from R. A. Webber, *Management* (Homewood, IL: Richard D. Irwin, 1975), pp. 139–40.

position as office claims agent and became the first female to handle routine policyholder claims over the telephone. She was flattered by the promotion, but the job did make it more difficult to keep up with her friends in the office. Nonetheless, she enjoyed talking with policyholders, who also liked to deal with her. Everyone thought she did an outstanding job.

Shortly after Liz's 25th birthday last year her mother passed away. At first, Liz wanted to quit her job to take care of the family, but her father said it wasn't necessary and she had her own life to live. It has been a rough twelve months for Liz.

Last week, the regional vice president called Liz into his office, praised her, and offered her a promotion to assistant office manager in charge of hiring and training all clerical employees. The position included a private office and salary that exceeded her father's. Liz was in a terrible quandary. She just couldn't see herself as a manager giving orders to friends she had worked with before. And she did not want to be thought of as a career woman.

This morning Elizabeth Sternberg quit her job and went home.

Questions

1. What did Liz want from work?
2. Why was she successful at the insurance office?
3. What was her problem with regard to the promotion? Why do you think she felt as she did?
4. What developmental aspects did you observe in Liz?
5. Why do you think she quit her job?

CASE: Managers for All Seasons?*

Most business people believe that to be an effective manager and enjoy a fulfilling career, an individual need only be competent and have an in-depth knowledge of the industry. Lee Iacocca, for example, is a competent and skilled manager who is an expert on the automobile industry. Other observers believe that a manager's unique skills must be related to the life-cycle of the product line. Those who hold this opinion cite the different demands on entrepreneurs and managers of established firms. An individual seeking a career in management must consider the pros and cons of these two conflicting theories.

Consider the experience of Robert C. Hazard, Jr., and Gerald W. Petitt. From 1977 to 1980, Hazard was chief executive and Petitt was second in command of Best Western International, Inc. Under their leadership, Best Western expanded from 800 to 2,597 hotels, began operations in 19 countries, and set up the industry's premier computerized reservation system. The out-

*Source: Adapted from "Matching Managers to a Company's Life Cycle," *Business Week*, February 23, 1981, pp. 62, 67, 70, 74, as presented in J. H. Donnelly, Jr., J. L. Gibson, J. M. Ivancevich, *Fundamentals of Management* (Plano, TX: Business Publications, 1984), pp. 778–79.

position as office claims agent and became the first female to handle routine policyholder claims over the telephone. She was flattered by the promotion, but the job did make it more difficult to keep up with her friends in the office. Nonetheless, she enjoyed talking with policyholders, who also liked to deal with her. Everyone thought she did an outstanding job.

Shortly after Liz's 25th birthday last year her mother passed away. At first, Liz wanted to quit her job to take care of the family, but her father said it wasn't necessary and she had her own life to live. It has been a rough twelve months for Liz.

Last week, the regional vice president called Liz into his office, praised her, and offered her a promotion to assistant office manager in charge of hiring and training all clerical employees. The position included a private office and salary that exceeded her father's. Liz was in a terrible quandary. She just couldn't see herself as a manager giving orders to friends she had worked with before. And she did not want to be thought of as a career woman.

This morning Elizabeth Sternberg quit her job and went home.

Questions

1. What did Liz want from work?
2. Why was she successful at the insurance office?
3. What was her problem with regard to the promotion? Why do you think she felt as she did?
4. What developmental aspects did you observe in Liz?
5. Why do you think she quit her job?

CASE: Managers for All Seasons?*

Most business people believe that to be an effective manager and enjoy a fulfilling career, an individual need only be competent and have an in-depth knowledge of the industry. Lee Iacocca, for example, is a competent and skilled manager who is an expert on the automobile industry. Other observers believe that a manager's unique skills must be related to the life-cycle of the product line. Those who hold this opinion cite the different demands on entrepreneurs and managers of established firms. An individual seeking a career in management must consider the pros and cons of these two conflicting theories.

Consider the experience of Robert C. Hazard, Jr., and Gerald W. Petitt. From 1977 to 1980, Hazard was chief executive and Petitt was second in command of Best Western International, Inc. Under their leadership, Best Western expanded from 800 to 2,597 hotels, began operations in 19 countries, and set up the industry's premier computerized reservation system. The out-

*Source: Adapted from "Matching Managers to a Company's Life Cycle," *Business Week*, February 23, 1981, pp. 62, 67, 70, 74, as presented in J. H. Donnelly, Jr., J. L. Gibson, J. M. Ivancevich, *Fundamentals of Management* (Plano, TX: Business Publications, 1984), pp. 778–79.

ward signs of success included an increase in room occupancy from 5 percent in 1974 to 11 percent in 1980, and an increase in pretax profits from 3 percent in 1974 to 15 percent in 1980. Best Western was transformed from a regional chain to an international giant.

The management style that Hazard and Petitt used was "go-go growth." They made and implemented decisions without consultation with the company's board members—a group representing the views of owners and managers of affiliate Best Western motels. Their individual styles were complementary, and they were able to get their ideas accepted on the basis of past successes. They were neither interested nor skilled in persuasion or politics. They had achieved their greatest accomplishments by working toward bottom-line results and avoiding the in-fighting that often accompanies high-risk decisions.

Eventually, Hazard and Petitt were no longer able to perform at Best Western. The apparent unbridled growth began to cause the affiliates some uneasiness. The 1979 gasoline shortage reduced travel and caused depressed profits. Programs to increase growth no longer seemed appealing in the face of declining business. Board members increasingly rejected Hazard and Petitt's proposals, and neither man was adept at obtaining support from the stubborn groups. So, in 1980, Hazard and Petitt left Best Western.

Both were hired by Quality Inns because that company's board wanted the Hazard/Petitt entrepreneurial flair. Quality Inns had abundant cash and was ready to take off, but it needed direction and a push. The Hazard/Petitt team announced its growth strategy only two months after it took over: By 1983, the number of Quality Inns will increase from 345 to 750, and reservations will be handled by a sophisticated computer system. Sound familiar? After three years of bare survival, 1975–77, when growth was the last item on the corporate agenda, Quality Inns is now primed for growth. Enter Hazard and Petitt.

Questions

1. Can an individual be an effective top manager and enjoy career success throughout the product life cycle? What are the implications of your opinion for your own career planning?
2. How can a growth-oriented company provide for top management succession from within its own ranks of managers?
3. Where would you rather be in top management in the years to come: In Best Western? Or in Quality Inns? Explain.

Managing as a Changing Role

I n Chapter 1, we defined **managing** as working with and through other people and groups of people to accomplish the goals set for an organization. In this chapter, we explore what is involved in successfully managing *your* career. The reason for dealing with the aspects of your career at this point is to make the developmental perspective we defined in Chapter 1 more personal. The developmental perspective is a cornerstone of this book, and you should become aware of its impact on everything you do as a manager, coworker, and subordinate. And since your career occurs over time, it makes a natural bridge between developmental ideas and your work as a manager.

Stop for a moment now, and think about the developmental perspective as it applies to your managerial career. Certainly, you can reflect on changes you have encountered and can imagine many changes that you will encounter. The people and groups you manage change; so does the organization or organizations in which you work. And of course, you change too, as you progress in your working career. Let us begin our look at managing as a changing role by exploring what managers actually do.

BASIC MANAGERIAL SKILLS

To be effective in performing a managerial role, managers need three basic types of skills: technical, human relations, and conceptual.[1] And as we shall see, the importance of these skills changes as managers progress through the management hierarchy.

Technical skill is the ability to perform the specific kinds of activities required in a job. Included are the specific methods, procedures, and techniques that are a part of performing a job. For example, if the job is programming computers, the technical skills include knowledge of particular computer languages, the ability to use computer terminology, and an understanding of how computers operate. Katz suggests that technical skill is important at all levels of management; but it is most important to first-line managers, since they are so intimately involved with producing a product or providing a service. In the Home Computers Company case, first-line supervisors in the two plants must rely heavily on their technical skill to get the work out. In the past, Harvey also needed a great deal of technical skill; but at his level in the organization now, he is much less dependent on his own technical skill, and more dependent on the technical skill of others.

Human relations skill is the ability to motivate, lead, and communicate with other people. A manager must be able to relate to people to get work done through them. Managers cannot perform all the work for which they are responsible, but must depend on others to complete the work. Thus, human relations skill is vital to their performance. Katz suggests that this skill is important for managers at all levels. Consider Harvey, for example. In the early stages of HCC, he had to manage production of the 16 employees through communicating, motivating, and leading. While this work demanded technical skill, it also required human relations skill. At present, Harvey still manages the upper-level management people and must get work done through them. Thus, his human relations skill is still important even though his technical skill is less important.

Finally, **conceptual skill is the ability to see the organization as a system of interacting parts and as a system interacting with its environment.** It is also the ability to diagnose and resolve a host of organizational problems. As Katz suggests, this is a top-management skill. It is not as essential at lower levels of management, though its importance is increasing as businesses become more professional and service oriented. But, conceptual skill is even more important for top management. For example, Harvey, as president of Home Computers Company, must conceptualize the business, set priorities for the company, and analyze trends in the market. He must understand the interactions between sales and production if he is to eliminate any friction that exists. He must know what the competition is doing so that plans can be developed to maintain the company's growth pattern. In short, he must deal more with the external environment. In a recent book, *Running American Business,* author Robert Lamb reports that 90 percent of the CEOs he interviewed were unprepared to deal with community groups, the media, government agencies, and other parts of the external environment.[2]

To recap, managers need three very important skills. **All three skills are important at all levels of management. But at lower levels, technical skill is the most important, while at top levels, conceptual skill is the most important. Human relations skill is important at all levels.** This pattern of skill emphasis (shown in Exhibit 2–1) suggests that a successful manager develops all three kinds of skills. Because of its importance throughout a manager's career, human relations skill is the primary focus of both this book and the field of organizational behavior itself.

WHAT MANAGERS DO

In thinking about the career of a manager, it is useful to consider in more specific terms what managers do. Research has suggested that first-level supervisors, who directly manage the work force, engage in literally hundreds of incidents each day, few of which last more than two minutes.[3] These incidents consist primarily of giving orders, answering questions, dealing with problems, seeking information, listening to

EXHIBIT 2–1

Managerial Skill Emphasis at Different Management Levels

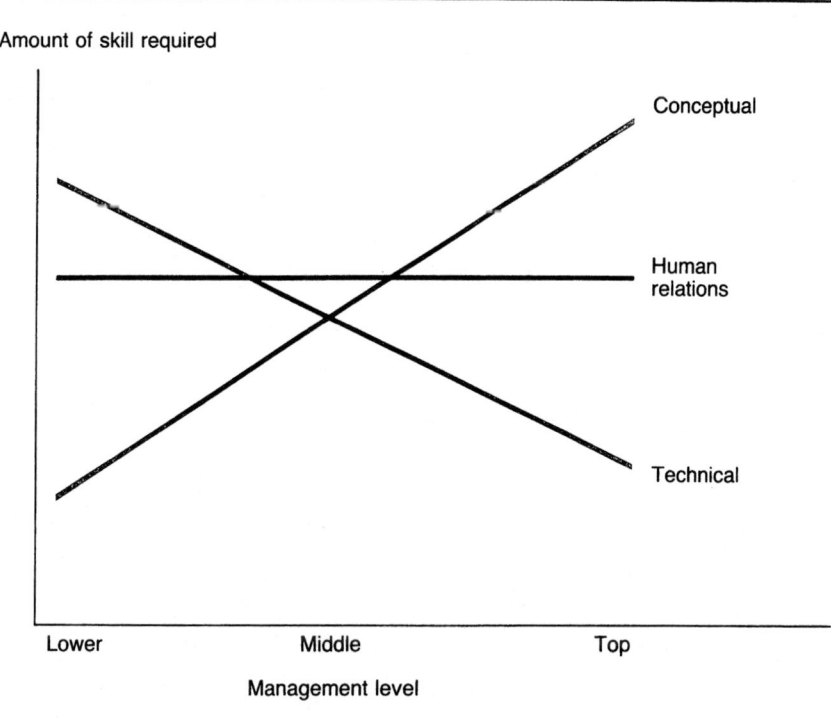

Amount of skill required

Conceptual

Human relations

Technical

Lower   Middle   Top

Management level

complaints, evaluating work, receiving instructions, granting and denying permission, and so forth, almost without stop during the day. Because of this rapid pace, supervisors must be very current in the technical aspects of their subordinates' jobs. They must also be capable of handling a wide range of situations that involve human interactions. Supervisors often feel overwhelmed by paperwork and by meetings with other supervisors and with their bosses. The communication and information demands on them are enormous.[4]

As a person's career shifts to the middle levels of the hierarchy, the pace is no less swift. A typical middle manager may spend up to 80 percent of the day in verbal exchanges with subordinates, peers, and superiors—on the telephone, in face-to-face meetings, and in one-to-one exchanges.[5] Whereas the supervisor must carry out relatively specific activities within the unit of responsibility, the middle manager is responsible for developing specific action plans from the broad objectives laid out by top management. However, with advances in computer technology and alternative work designs, the lines between supervisor and middle manager can become blurred. Another major activity category of middle managers, then, is the preparation of written reports—activity plans to be distributed to supervisors, or reports to top management about the execution of those plans.

At top-management levels, the pattern of fragmented, interrupted, and brief activity persists. A study of chief executive officers determined that on average these managers engaged in over 50 activities each day, with approximately half lasting less than nine minutes.[6] Top managers spent 59 percent of the day in scheduled meetings, another 10 percent in unscheduled meetings, and 6 percent on the telephone. Desk work (reading reports and processing mail) accounted for 22 percent of the day; the remaining 3 percent was spent on tours of the workplace. In fact, this study suggests that top-level managers spend very little time in reflective thinking. The conceptual issues of policy setting, goal setting, and strategic planning are certainly dealt with by these managers, but it does not appear that they do this work when they are alone. Rather, the conceptual issues are dealt with in interpersonal settings—which explains why human relations skill is still important at the top levels of management.

Now that we have seen a cross-section of managers' activities at various levels in an organization, we need to view the pieces from a developmental and longitudinal perspective. We need to look at a managerial career as a changing role. How does one evolve through these various levels of management? How do the managerial skills evolve over a career? To do this, let us look at the career of an employee of Home Computers Company.

Home Computers Case

The Case of Louise of Home Computers Company

Louise is 45 years old and has had a very successful career working in the computer industry since her graduation from college 23 years ago. When Louise graduated from her computer science undergraduate program, she was immediately hired by one of the largest multinational computer manufacturing companies in the world. Having been raised in the South, she was excited to have the opportunity to move to New York as she began her career. She rented an apartment on the Upper East Side and began the process of adjusting to the New York culture. She took the subway to work her first day in September 1966.

Louise was fortunate to be given a challenging job in her initial assignment. She knew that many companies feel they should bring new employees along slowly, starting them on an easy project and then gradually adding more challenge and responsibility as the employees prove their ability. But Louise's first job was to work on the development of an accounts receivable package for one of the company's largest customers. Of course, she did not work on the project alone, and her supervisor was quite willing to help whenever Louise encountered problems. Louise worked on this project for six months in the corporate offices. Then she was asked to go to the customer's headquarters along with George Davis, an experienced programmer, to help install and debug the accounts receivable system.

Upon completing this initial assignment, Louise was given a series of challenging projects over the next few years. Louise's short-term goal was to become a project leader, so she could use her technical expertise in supervising others. In 1973, she achieved her goal. At this time, she was also asked to move to the Phoenix, Arizona, office where the demand for services was growing rapidly. Although she hated to leave New York, Louise saw this as a strategic move in her career. Her next goal was to become a systems manager, overseeing the accounts and projects of several customers. In Phoenix, there was currently one systems manager, and the rapid growth suggested that the addition of another one was quite likely. While Louise was not sure what the company's plans were for her, she hoped to make the best of this opportunity.

In Phoenix, Louise found that her technical and human relations skills were constantly utilized. She had to assist new programmers, explain the clients' desires to the programmers, decide which programmer would work on which piece of the project, and deal with programmer complaints and conflicts. It was a challenging assignment, but Louise enjoyed it very much. She was also very good at it.

While in Phoenix, Louise met a programmer named Steve, and they began dating. After several months of casual dates, it became apparent that there was something special about their relationship. They were married in April, 1976. In late 1977, they had a child. Because Louise valued her career so much, she took a maternity leave of only eight weeks.

In that same year, Steve was transferred back East to Washington, D.C., to become a systems manager. Louise had been a systems manager for a year already and found that she liked the shift in emphasis from the technical to the conceptual aspects of the work. The separation was difficult for Steve and Louise, as well as for their child, but they decided it was the best for their respective careers. Nine months later, Louise also had an opportunity to transfer back East to Baltimore. With Steve working in Washington, they were able to live together again. Now both their careers were taking off, with both operating at the company's middle-management level.

In 1978, Louise learned of the success that a former colleague, Harvey Brown, and his cousin, Bill Adams, had had in starting their own business, called Home Computers Company. She was very interested in their venture and discussed it with Harvey at a party a few months later. Things were going well for HCC at that time. Louise told Steve of her interest in the company, but Steve suggested she forget it—she had a good career already. But she could not forget Home Computers.

Louise and Steve were both committed to having successful careers and a successful family life. And both of their lives were becoming extremely busy with work and the demands of a baby. In 1979, Steve turned down a promotion that would have moved him to corporate headquarters in New York, because he did not want to disrupt the family. Later that same year, Louise had an opportunity to go to work for HCC when Harvey and Bill saw the need for technically experienced sales managers.

Louise jumped at the chance, especially since she would not have to move, but could handle her work via travel. She became a regional sales manager for Home Computers in 1980, reporting to National Sales Vice President Bill Adams. She found Bill a little difficult to work with, but the job was the most challenging of her career. Home Computers Company was so new and was growing so fast that Louise had many opportunities to draw upon all of her skills and abilities. Plans and decisions had to be developed for marketing and sales goals. She had to be aware of what the competition was doing. And because the company was so small, she knew the 15 people working for her very well. She liked interacting with them.

Because of her success as regional sales manager, Harvey promoted Louise to national sales vice president in 1981 when Bill Adams left the company. In fact, it was Louise's idea to reorganize the sales division along product lines, rather than on geographic lines. Now Louise was really using her conceptual skill and no longer had much contact with the salespeople.

Since 1986, the problems the company has encountered in the computer industry consolidation have made Louise's job very difficult. Louise has had to spend longer hours at work, at a time when she wanted to be at home more with her child. Steve's career has also been very demanding over the last few years. These career demands have contributed to some personal problems for their family.

Louise is happy with the career decisions she has made and with the opportunities that have come her way. She has some concerns about the future of HCC but her real regrets revolve around her family life. Steve seems jealous of her success, though he has tried hard not to be. Louise also feels that she has not spent enough time with her child. She wonders what will happen in her family and in her career over the next few years.

Imagine yourself beginning a career now, or making a career change. What will it be like? What important decisions will you have to make? What can you learn by looking at Louise's career? Does the career viewpoint help you appreciate the importance of a developmental perspective to organizational behavior? In the remainder of this chapter, we explore what we mean by a career and the stages of a career. We also look at the key factors that influence the changing role of a manager.

CAREER STAGES

We have now used the term **career** several times without defining it. Before we discuss the stages of a career, let us arrive at a definition. First of all, career does not imply either success or failure. Even if Louise had not moved up the corporate ladder so rapidly, we would still define her series of jobs as a career. In addition, her rapid movement might not be thought of as completely successful, as the end of the case suggests. A career consists not only of behaviors, but also of attitudes: How does Louise feel about her work life? **A career is a sequence of work-related experiences and activities over a person's lifespan, and it includes the person's sequence of attitudes and behaviors in these work-related experiences.**[7] Let us turn to a model of the various stages of a career. As we do, we see how the developmental perspective applies to a managerial career.

A career-stage model

Drawing from the early work of Super and his associates, **we can define a career-stage model with five stages: exploration, establishment, advancement, maturity, and withdrawal**[8] (see Exhibit 2–2). But it is important to note that these stages and ages are not fixed in stone, especially in today's world. And they vary from person to person. For example, some people backtrack from the advancement stage to the exploration stage, as they change careers in mid-life. Some women raise their children first and then begin the exploration stage in their 40s or 50s, as shown in Insight 2–1. Some people alter their career path because of takeovers of their companies or forced early retirement. We will explore these variables after first considering the basic career-stage model in Exhibit 2–2. This exhibit provides a general framework that can aid in managing people and careers in organizations.

The first stage, **exploration** (ages 15 to 25), is where initial job choices are made and sampled in discussion, courses, and part-time work. The realities of abilities and motivation are tested as the person enters the job market or professional training.

The second stage, **establishment** (ages 26 to 35), is where a person has found an appropriate field of work and is trying to make a place in that field. The person may make several changes before finding a suitable field or realizing that a career will consist of a series of unrelated jobs.

INSIGHT 2-1

One Who Took the Big Step

*T*he mother of five children, Mrs. Daley had worked at various secretarial and clerical jobs, so that both at home and at work, she had held "nurturing and mothering positions."

When she decided to change careers, "I made some basic changes in myself," she says.

Building on her college degree and aptitude in music and her facility for math, she took accounting and data processing courses. She went from jobs in which she catered to the needs of others to a position in which, as a programmer analyst, she is in charge.

Mrs. Daley has her own checklist of what it takes to change careers:

√ Be dissatisfied.
√ Decide you're going to change.
√ Find out how to go about it, the technique.
√ Find out what's selling.
√ Add up your pluses and minuses.
√ Get whatever training you need.
√ See what compromises you have to make. (Find out what's totally unacceptable, what's tolerable, what's desirable.)

EXHIBIT 2–2

Career Stages

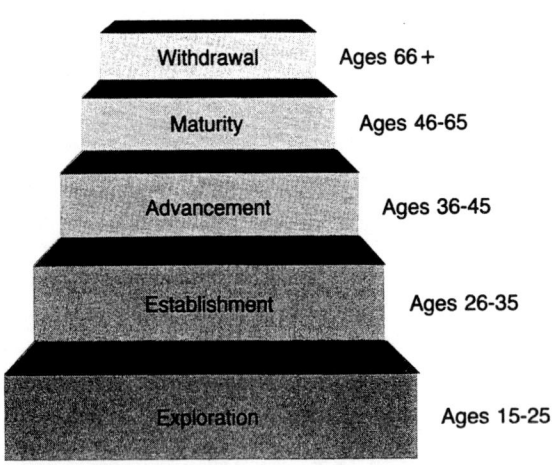

Withdrawal	Ages 66 +
Maturity	Ages 46-65
Advancement	Ages 36-45
Establishment	Ages 26-35
Exploration	Ages 15-25

Mid-Life Entrepreneurs

What nobody ever taught Richard Alexander about starting a business could fill a textbook.

Alexander gave up an executive marketing position seven years ago to start a telecommunications manufacturing business with two partners. Within three years, the company was floundering.

"You have to be a little nuts to start your own business," Alexander said. "There are so many things you have to learn on the job."

After bailing out of the telecommunications company, he set up a marketing consulting firm that is thriving.

But Alexander's success hardly is universal. Many corporate executives who decide to become entrepreneurs in mid career find the going unexpectedly tough.

Despite their maturity and experience in the business world, mid-life entrepreneurs still face the same pitfalls and problems as their younger counterparts—and perhaps several additional roadblocks.

"Guys who have been working for a big corporation all their lives do things differently. They have different mind sets," said Richard Buskirk, director of the entrepreneur program at the University of Southern California's School of Business Administration. "The average business employee isn't a businessman. He's a specialist or a bureaucrat."

Another source of stress for the mid-life entrepreneur is a family's financial needs. By middle age, workers commonly have accumulated mortgages and life style expectations that exceed those of their younger counterparts. For example, middle-age workers are likely to have child support and education expenses at the same time that they want to provide for their retirement.

Although no one knows for sure how many of the nearly 700,000 new U.S. businesses created last year belong to middle-aged workers, experts say persistent corporate layoffs, expanding use of forced early retirement and a renewed attraction to small business are giving rise to increasing numbers of mid-life entrepreneurs.

Adapted from Carla Lazzareschi, "Mid-Life Entrepreneurs," *Los Angeles Times*, May 24, 1987. Copyright 1987 *Los Angeles Times*. Reprinted by permission.

The third stage, **advancement** (ages 36–45), is where a person works hard to develop a secure place in the chosen field of work. As we have already noted in Insight 2–1, there can be some major shifts or backtracking during these ages.

The fourth stage, **maturity** (ages 46–65), is defined as the time to hold on to one's place in the chosen field of work. It can be a time of little change, a continuation in already-established directions, or it can be a volatile time of starting a new career. Many people now experience significant changes in their chosen field during midcareer and preretirement periods. Insight 2–2 describes a man who decided to go into business for himself. You can probably think of other examples, as well.

Finally, the last stage, **withdrawal** (age 66 and up), is the period in a career when abilities sometimes begin to decline and people reach retirement age. Work activities shift to coincide with these changes. People may shift to part-time jobs or to less active roles in their organizations. Some people completely retire from work; others continue to gear down gradually. Still others find new challenges and continue working as hard as ever, either in new jobs or in hobbies and volunteer work. For example, see Insight 2–3 about the salesman at Texas Refinery Corporation.

The AT&T studies

A number of studies have attempted to analyze career stages in field settings. One study of particular interest was conducted in the late 1960s at American Telephone and Telegraph (AT&T). A group of young managers was studied over a five-year period.[9] During the first year of employment, these managers expressed a great deal of concern about gaining recognition and establishing themselves in the organization. As we discuss later, these are **safety needs;** they relate to the question of motivation. By the fifth year of employment, though, this need for safety had significantly declined for these managers. In fact, it was the least important of the needs measured. It makes sense that gaining a feeling of establishment with the organization would be a high priority in the early years of employment. These initial years are clearly related to the establishment stage.

During the same five-year period, the need for achievement and esteem in the job increased dramatically for these AT&T managers. By the fifth year, they were concerned with moving upward and mastering the organization. This new stage was labeled the advancement stage, just as we call it in Exhibit 2–2. During this time in a person's career, promotion and achievement are the predominant goals. It is the time to be creative and to strive for advancement in the organization.

The Schein career model

One other career model is worthy of our attention, because it explicitly recognizes the connection between the career as it relates to the individual and the career as it relates to the organization's needs. In 1971, Edgar Schein of MIT proposed a model that defines career growth opportunities in terms of moving in three directions within an organization: vertically, radially, and laterally (see Exhibit 2–3).[10] **Vertical movement** is defined as moving up or down the hierarchy of the organization. **Radial movement** is defined as moving toward a greater or lesser amount of influence in the organization: How central will the person be to the

```
I  N  S  I  G  H  T   2–3
```

**Firm Recruits Older People
as Salesmen**

Robert Stacey is one of Texas Refinery
Corp.'s top salesmen. After joining the company last year, he earned $3,000 on his first
sale, and ultimately was named "rookie of
the year," with total commissions of $45,000.

The Elberta, Ala., salesman is so keen on
peddling Texas Refinery's roof-protective
coatings that he carries a pair of roofing
shoes in his car, just in case he spots an
opportunity to clamber onto a roof.

Mr. Stacey is 74 years old. He was a
pharmacist in his first working life. "This is
better than a lot of years I put behind the
prescription counter," he says.

At Fort Worth-based Texas Refinery, Mr.
Stacey is one of 20 salesmen over 70 who
joined last year. A fifth of the firm's 3,000 or
so salesmen are over 65, and one is 84. The
company is one of the growing number of
firms recruiting elderly workers.

By Maria T. Padilla, *The Wall Street Journal,* April 19,
1982. Reprinted by permission of *The Wall Street Journal,*
© Dow Jones & Company, Inc., 1982. All rights reserved.

decision making of the organization? How much influence will he or
she have in the organization? Finally, **lateral movement** is defined as
transferring horizontally to different functions, programs, or projects in
the organization.

Schein argues that as people move in these three directions, they will
change through a process called **socialization.** (We explore this process
in more detail in Chapter 4.) They develop new attitudes, values, competencies, self-images, and new ways of conducting themselves in social
settings. This socialization process occurs with peaks and valleys
throughout a career. It even transcends movement from one organization to another. Schein suggests that the pressure for change will be
strongest just before or just after a move—whether that move is vertical,
radial, or lateral. Thus, **the organization exerts forces that will change
a person throughout his or her career.** These pressures do, however,
tend to decrease over one's career.

Schein also points out a reverse set of influences; namely, the influence a person has on an organization. This process he calls **innovation.**
Once a person has learned their role in a particular part of an organization, but before they look ahead to their next career position, they can
exert the greatest influence to change the organization. This innovation
process tends to increase over the course of a career, though it probably
drops off toward the very end. Schein's model points out the directions
a person can move in an organization as he or she travels through the
stages of a career.

EXHIBIT 2–3
Directions of Career Movement

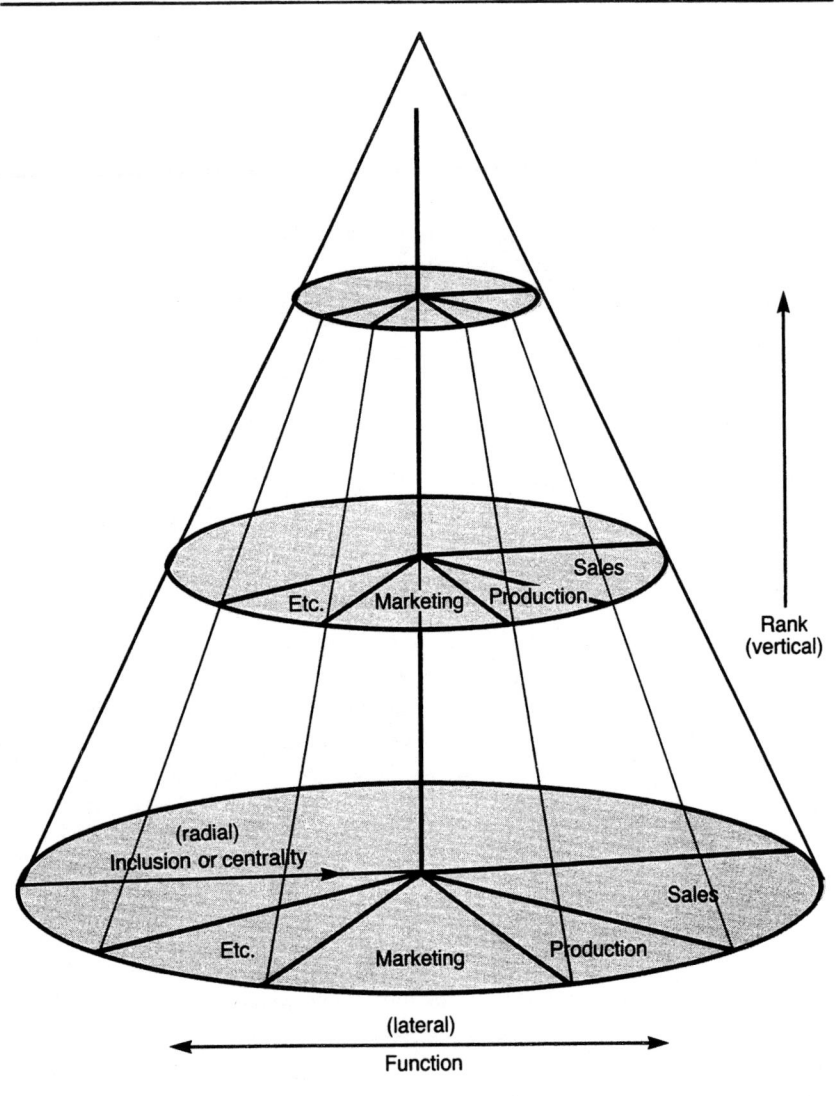

Applying the career stages model

Let us briefly apply these career stages to the case of Louise. In Louise's case, we do not have much information about the exploration stage, except that she studied computer science in college. We can speculate that her discussions, courses, and perhaps part-time work involved computer-related situations that influenced her decision to enter this field. The case does reveal that Louise was given a challenging first assignment at the age of 22. She was also fortunate to have an effective supervisor, as she explored her first job. With regard to the establishment stage, some researchers have argued that upward mobility is greatly influenced by promotions that occur early in one's career. But fortunately, others have found that other factors such as number of jobs held, functional area, and economic factors can allow for a slow career start but a fast rise later.[11] The case revealed that Louise worked hard on a series of challenging projects during her first few years on the job. By the time she reached age 29 and was transferred to Phoenix, she was beginning to feel established in her field.

As Louise entered the advancement stage, the case shows that she made the move to HCC and took on the role of regional sales manager. Home Computers Company was a small and growing company compared to her old company, and its expectations were quite different. Also, Louise was making a lateral move into sales. She had to learn to be more of a generalist in the small company and to sell hardware and software. But she had considerable experience, which placed her in a position of influence. Up to this point, she had shown very little concern for leveling out her career aspirations, and she continued to desire advancement and influence. With her vertical move to national sales vice president (a position previously held by the cofounder of the company), she moved radially toward Harvey and the control of the company. We must also point out something that we will discuss in detail later: The advancement stage often coincides with the family stage of raising children, as it did for Louise. This interaction of career and family stages is not always easy to manage, especially in a two-career family.

As Louise approaches the career stage of maturity, several things are occurring simultaneously. Home Computers is undergoing some hard times; Louise and Steve's child is 12 years old going on 20 as she enters middle school; and Steve and Louise are approaching middle age. What will happen next to Louise we cannot say; but we do know that her career can go any of several ways. If you were Louise, understanding how you got where you are would help you anticipate your next move. Should she stay at HCC, especially given the shakeout that is occurring in the industry? Does she have a real chance to become president of the company? What will happen in her personal life?

We now want to consider some specific factors of managing as a changing role. Also, we will examine some factors that may cause us to reconsider the career-stage model in Exhibit 2–2. Our purpose here is to focus on the developmental aspects of a managerial career and to set the stage for our analysis of individuals in organizations.

KEY FACTORS IN THE CHANGING ROLE OF A MANAGER

Three factors primarily influence people as they move through careers as managers: their movement within organizations, new people they encounter, and changes in the organizations themselves. We discuss each of these factors below and how they create the developmental forces that act upon a management career.

Movement within organizations

As Schein's career model and our earlier discussion of technical, human relations, and conceptual skills suggest, movement within an organization can significantly change a managerial role.

Lateral moves

First of all, there are the lateral moves from one functional area to another. Louise experienced that in her move from programming at her old company to sales at Home Computers Company. It was also another type of lateral move; namely, from one organization to another. In the functional change from programming to sales, Louise moved from one culture to another. The two functions are different in norms, goals, time frames, types of people, and so forth. To be successful, Louise had to become socialized to the new situation quickly. Her move was also a change of cultures of a different order. Her old company was much larger than Home Computers. It was more formally organized, and her work was more specialized. At HCC, her technical, human relations, and conceptual skills were called upon.

Vertical moves

As Louise moved upward in responsibility during her career at the two companies, she encountered new demands and was called on to develop different skills. She had to learn to rely less on technical skill and more on conceptual skill. She had to learn to see the bigger picture. But other aspects of vertical moves are also apparent in this case. Louise's husband Steve turned down a promotion—something that was seldom done in the past for fear that one such refusal would mean the end of upward vertical movement. But with dual-income families and an increased concern for quality-of-life issues, that fear has subsided to some extent, as shown in Insight 2–4.

The flip side of this is that some people who desire to get to the top of their organization do not make it. There are always fewer positions in top management than there are people who want them. Thus, some people do not achieve this career goal. This realization often occurs during the life stage where one expects to be climbing to the top. The

---

More Workers Are Refusing Promotions

A chemical company official rejected a transfer from his beloved South. A canny electronics executive refused a promotion on the theory—correct as it turned out—that it would detour him from the surest road to the executive suite.

These managers did what was once unthinkable—refused a promotion. And while employees aren't rejecting advancement in droves, they are doing it more than they used to. "There was a time when no one would consider saying no," says Betty Nelson, manager of employee relations for InterNorth Inc., a diversified energy company based in Omaha. That just isn't so anymore, she says, though she adds that "I won't say it never hurts them."

Resisting a promotion can brand an employee as disloyal or lacking in ambition, and reputations like that can scuttle promising careers. But personnel officers, consultants and career counselors say there can be good reasons to pass up a new job. Sometimes, refusing a position can save a worker from a dead-end job, protect him from a difficult boss or simply give him more time to enjoy life.

Concerns About Travel, Life Style

Take the chemical company executive. He passed up a $30,000 raise because it meant relocating at the company's Northeastern headquarters. "I love to play golf," he says. "I have a house on the golf course of the club that I belong to. It would be next to impossible to do that" at the home office.

Adapted from Heywood Klein, *The Wall Street Journal*, May 18, 1982. Reprinted by permission of *The Wall Street Journal*, © Dow Jones & Company, Inc. 1982. All rights reserved.

---

difficult task then is to adjust career goals, to make a job or field change, or to substitute external goals for those in the organization. Another option that is gaining more and more acceptability is downward movement (that is, demotion) in an organization.[12] And, of course, downward movement must be managed quite differently to maintain an employee's motivation (a topic we shall discuss in Chapters 5 and 6). Such transitions are trying for both employee and company. It is essential to the continued motivation of all employees that it be managed well.

Radial moves

Radial movement in a career is the most subtle and difficult to detect. It relates most directly to the attitudinal aspects of a career. As we shall see in the motivation chapters, everyone has, to varying degrees, a need for power and influence. Radial movement gets a person closer to the seat of power and decision making in the organization. As this change occurs, there goes with it a shift in responsibility, both legal and moral.

The coalition of people who make key decisions in an organization have the legitimate or legal right to obligate the organization by setting goals and policy and by making plans. They also are accountable for those decisions; that is, they are morally and socially responsible to the organization's employees, stockholders, and customers, as well as to the society and community in which the organization exists. These responsibilities demand that a manager have real wisdom—and they probably relate directly to the increase in gray hair in higher-level managers!

But there is also the other direction of radial movement—that is, away from power and influence in an organization. Indeed, the ultimate such movement could be to be fired. Because of changes both internal and external to organizations, people sometimes must leave an organization. But companies in the 1980s have begun to increase their responsibility in this arena by smoothing the exit transitions and helping employees find new jobs that result in career growth.[13] Depending on the individual, the environmental conditions at the time, and the way an organization handles outplacement, being fired can actually enhance one's career.

Managers must be prepared for all of these career moves. In addition, other forces will cause these managers to change over the life of their career.

New people you encounter

As we have discussed, managers meet many different people as they move vertically, radially, and laterally in the firm. If their careers are to continue on successfully, they must be able to draw on their human relations skills to work with and through these people. Let us look at the sources of some of the different types of people managers encounter.

Functional and level differences

As a manager's career takes her into different functions within organizations, she encounters people with varying backgrounds, training, and expertise. For example, in programming, Louise encountered highly technical people who were very precise in their thinking and who probably had little tolerance for others who could not understand their jargon. When she moved to sales at HCC, she met people with less technical training. They could be ambiguous at times, and liked to talk in general terminology. These stereotypes of programmers and salespeople may not be totally accurate; the point is that Louise had to recognize and deal with such differences to be successful. Likewise, as Louise moved up the corporate ladder, she first encountered people with a need to achieve and to have a challenging job. Further up the ladder, she met people who wanted to influence the company. Could Louise operate in exactly the same way with these different types of people? Of course not.

From a different perspective, the people Louise encountered also offered possibilities to aid her in her career advancement. It has long been known that it is helpful to a person's career to have a mentor—that is, someone who is older and at a higher organizational level.[14] Mentors offer tremendous learning opportunities, as well as connections that can help get a career off to a good start. But recent evidence suggests that peers in an organization can also offer many unique mentoring possibilities.[15] They offer the chance to achieve a feeling of expertise, equality, and empathy that is often missing from the traditional mentor relationship. While Louise may have had more senior mentors, she would be wise to have developed helping relationships with peers, as well.

New people from the environment

As we discussed in Chapter 1, there has been a trend for several decades toward a more highly educated and skilled work force. Today, people receive more education in their earliest years through formal education than they did in the 1940s or even in the 1960s. They also learn to expect more from a job and from life in general. For this reason, some employees feel the company owes them a job and good pay; they do not have to earn it. But this trend has also created employees who want a challenge and will not be satisfied with a boring job. In fact, a 1985 *Business Week* article noted that the new generation of employees and managers is more eager to take risks, more optimistic, more female, more ethnically diverse, more independent, and more desirous of instant gratification than managers who grew up in the 1950s and 1960s.[16] This evolution may stimulate management to find new ways to motivate employees who want to have more control over their careers.[17] And managers must learn to manage and work with this new type of employee. Indeed, the manager may be one, too.

Furthermore, this *Business Week* article implies that managers must be able to work with women, minorities, people of different nationalities, and dual-career family members, if they are to be effective. Since the early 1970s, there has been a concerted effort to bring women and minorities into the workplace. Affirmative action and equal employment opportunity efforts have been especially successful in blue-collar and clerical jobs. Recent years have seen advances for women and minorities in the ranks of middle management and, to a lesser extent, in the executive suite. The changes brought on by these developments continue to occur, and the increase in multinational operations plus the hiring of people from a variety of countries have created changes that have far-reaching effects and that will influence managers. Just imagine having

I N S I G H T 2–5

Many Hurdles, Old and New, Keep Black Managers Out of Top Jobs

*T*wenty years after blacks began moving into corporations in significant numbers, many black managers say their companies have clamped a lid on their climb up management ranks.

Despite their MBAs and their initial attractiveness to corporate recruiters, many black managers say they are blocked by an array of obstacles. Some are longstanding, such as white executives' discomfort with non-whites, the predilection to pick managers of similar backgrounds and outright prejudice. Others arose more recently, including the kind of jobs that blacks found themselves funneled into as well as the management

layoffs that have accompanied mergers and acquisitions.

Moreover, many companies have downgraded, if not abandoned, affirmative-action programs in response to the Reagan administration's opposition to many such endeavors.

John L. Jones, director of corporate resources for Xerox Corp., is a black who believes there is an "invisible ceiling that blacks, and women as well, hit as they move up the corporate ladder, regardless of their achievements, motivation, preparation and training."

to manage people from Mexico and Japan working with Americans. Or imagine dealing with child-care problems or granting paternity leave as part of managerial responsibilities. Or imagine having to deal with the growing frustration of black and female managers who see a lid (or what some people call a glass ceiling) on their career aspirations just as they enter the career stage of advancement. (See Insight 2–5.) These are very recent considerations for managers and their companies. They reflect the developmental aspects of dealing with people over a career.

We can also carry this issue one step further by considering the impact of dual-career families, where both husband and wife work full time. In such cases, child care and paternity leave issues are very important. And there are more than 26.7 million dual-career families in the United States, with the number increasing rapidly.[18] In addition, a whole new group of dual-income couples are emerging called *DINKs*— dual income, no kids. These couples have chosen career over family. With both wife and husband working—and working with a long-term outlook on jobs, kids or no kids—a number of problems are encountered by managers. When job transfers or hirings are considered by the dual-career couple, both careers must be considered. Transferring one spouse means that the other spouse must likely relocate, too. And if a company wants to hire a person in a dual-career family, both people may have to be hired, or the company may have to help the spouse locate a suitable job. Managers must become familiar with such issues and learn to deal effectively with members of dual-career couples.

You, too, may be part of a dual-career couple. If so, you will no doubt face the relocation problem—which ultimately means the establishing of priorities. Just how important will your career be? What about for your spouse? The dual-career family must also face the issues of child-care and household responsibilities. How are the children cared for while both parents work? Who stays home when a child is sick? Do you even have children, and if yes, then when? Who does the laundry, the dishes, the vacuuming? Do you hire someone to do these things? A survey by the Catalyst Career and Family Center in 1980 revealed that wives and husbands agreed that allocation of time, finances, poor family communications, and conflicts over housework were the most troublesome problems for two-career couples.[19] The problems of the dual-career family will affect you in one way or another as you progress through your career. If you are to be successful both in work and personal life, you will have to manage all of these issues. As we will discuss later, **the interacting aspects of career, family, and life stages are difficult for anyone to manage.**

Changing needs of people

Another source of "new" people is the change that occurs in individuals over their lifetime. As we saw in Chapter 1, the evolution of life stages brings on changes in people as they progress from the trying 20s to the catch 30s to the forlorn 40s and beyond. People change their goals; they change the perceptions of their capabilities; and they change their needs. For example, a 60-year-old person given a new and challenging job may not respond the same way a 30-year-old would. In the early years of a career (the establishment and advancement stages), people usually look for challenges and chances for advancement. They often overestimate their abilities and only later, through experience, become aware of this overestimation. By mid-career and middle age (the maturity career stage), they have learned what they can accomplish. They may also be ready to move into the more conceptual and administrative aspects of their work. By the time they reach the withdrawal career stage, they start to anticipate retirement (which is really a new career itself). Or as shown earlier in Insight 2–3, they may actually explore and get into a totally new line of work after retiring from one job.

As a manager, how will you motivate these different people toward the goals of your organization? How will you provide effective leadership for all of them? How will you manage your own evolution through the career, life, and family stages? These questions need to be answered if you are to be a successful manager, in both your work and your personal life.

Changes in the organization

The final key factor in the changing role of a manager is the change that occurs in the organizations for which a person works during a career. Is the company a high-growth company? Is it a company that is about to make a significant change in goals? Is it on the decline?

High-growth companies

In the Home Computers Company case, it is apparent that up until 1985, the company grew very rapidly. Certainly this growth was welcomed by managers in the establishment and advancement stages of their careers. The growth of a company opens up many challenging opportunities, and it allows rapid vertical movement in the organization. At first glance, this growth and expansion would seem to be all positive: Who would not want the chance for rapid advancement? The only real catch is that people may be promoted before they have gained the experience and knowledge necessary to succeed at the next higher level. The result can be disastrous for the manager, the employees, and the organization.

For a person to grow professionally as fast as some high-growth organizations require, it takes real dedication to the company. It means long hours of work and sacrifice by the person and by the person's family. The career stages may come much faster than is compatible with the life and family stages. A successful manager must anticipate this development by determining if the company is a rapid-growth company. If it is, the manager must ask, "Am I prepared to grow rapidly with it?"

Companies changing direction

If top management makes a significant change in a company's direction, it can have a far-reaching effect on the careers of company managers. Imagine, for example, that you work for Home Computers, which decides to acquire a small company that manufactures portable telephones. You are asked to be a manager in this new division. Immediately, your technical expertise in computers loses some value; and you will have to develop expertise in telephones. Are the employees that make telephones motivated by the same things as those who make computers? The change could become either a real plus or a real problem for your career, depending on how you handle this change in direction.

Now imagine the reverse situation: Home Computers is purchased by another company. How will things be different under the new top

---

INSIGHT 2-6

After a Takeover: More Managers Run or Are Pushed, Out the Door

After Masonite Corp. was acquired by U.S. Gypsum Co., Donald Slocum, Masonite's vice president of advanced technology, tried to adapt to his new employer's corporate practices.

But in seeking support for his projects and staff, Mr. Slocum found that he had to fight through several tiers of management and thought that the parent company was wary of spending in uncharted technical areas.

After nine months, he resigned. "I gave it a shot, but I felt there was a climate change," says Mr. Slocum, who now works with companies to develop new products.

Although mergers and takeovers have traditionally prompted some senior executives to quit, managers these days are bailing out—or getting pushed—faster and more often. One recent survey of senior executives whose companies were acquired found that almost half sought other positions within one year; a similar study in 1981 found that only 20% left in the first year.

Management consultants and recruiters attribute the greater number of departures to: the increasing number of hostile takeovers, which often create a sour climate and a clash in management styles; the increasingly steep stock price premiums in buyouts that give managers holding the stock greater freedom and mobility; a lessening of corporate loyalty, and the proliferation of so-called golden parachutes.

---

management? What changes will be made in the operation of the company? Will you and your department have the same influence in decision making as before? If not, will it be more or less? Increasingly since the early 1980s, managers in many companies have had to deal with these very issues. Sometimes the results have significant impacts on the careers of managers in the acquired company. As the story in Insight 2–6 shows, the changes brought on by a takeover can be devastating for managers in the acquired company.

Declining organizations

The Masonite story in Insight 2–6 also suggests another possibility: Suppose the company a manager works for suffers a decline in business. The decline may be only temporary, due to a normal business cycle or to circumstances in the economy. But it could also be a sustained decline, resulting in the eventual death of the organization. Every year, thousands and thousands of companies go out of business. What effect does this have on the careers of the managers in those companies? Certainly, it may necessitate a relocation to find a new job. Problems could arise here because of a dual-career family or because of age or other factors. It may be a real setback in the advancement of a career—or it could be the break that allows someone to find a job that offers even better opportunities. While managers may not be able to plan for this event, it is important to recognize that it can happen to anyone.

If the decline is temporary, it may only mean a slight delay in a manager's desired career path. But for some managers, even a slight decline is unacceptable. In such a case, it will be important to analyze the situation carefully. How long might the decline last? Are there other opportunities the manager should explore at this time? What must the manager do to retain his or her position if layoffs are a possibility? What is the manager's responsibility toward others that work with him in the organization? In short, **many forces at the organizational level that are not controllable by the manager may have a big impact on his or her career.**

And on top of these organizational issues are environmental issues—mainly economic and technological—that can cause considerable downsizing of organizations. For example, nearly a half million U.S. management positions were eliminated between 1982 and 1987, at a time when the number of MBAs granted was increasing.[20] Clearly, such pressures suggest that our early career-stage model may need to be more complex to reflect the realities a manager faces.

REFINING THE FIVE CAREER STAGES

As we discussed earlier, there are five basic career stages. (Refer back to Exhibit 2–2.) However, when we laid out those five stages, it was as though a person could expect to move through the stages in a fairly predictable way, and at predictable ages. What we have just explored about key factors in the changing role of a manager suggests, however, that career stages may be far more complicated. Consider just a few of the variations that may be relevant during a career.

First of all, the **exploration** stage can occur at any age. Many people, especially women, may decide to delay a work career until after raising children. Hence, they may be exploring career options at age 35 to 45. And, many people begin to have second thoughts about their chosen career in their early 40s, after 15 to 20 years of growing in one direction. Often referred to as the mid-life crisis, this revisiting of the exploration stage can create serious upheaval for the individuals, their families, and the organizations for which they have been working. As we saw in Insight 2–2, more and more people decide to become entrepreneurs at this stage of life. Tired of working for others, they decide to go it on their own. And many of these entrepreneurs are women.[21]

Naturally, such changes upset any sort of natural flow into the **establishment** and **advancement** stages. In fact, these changes may come right in the middle of the advancement stage of the first career. Furthermore, from a life-stage and family-stage perspective, these changes may come in the midst of children in school with their own friends, interests, and desires. And they may come when people are in their 40s, when energy levels often begin to decline. In other words, many forces converge during a person's 40s. There can be a real tug to leave a job, while at the same time there are many forces that tend to keep the person there. Because of age and responsibilities, such dramatic change and the associated risks may not be feasible. But for people caught in such a trap, what happens to their motivation on their current job? How would you effectively manage such a person?

Earlier we referred to DINKs—dual income, no kids—who try to keep their options open by not committing themselves to the responsibility of children. However, because of their concern for two successful careers, they may find themselves locked into careers they might otherwise change if it were not for the careers of their spouses. Transfers and relocations are the most difficult issues for dual-income couples—and for their organizations.[22] In addition, the two incomes for these couples make them far less dependent on their employer, and may make them harder for a manager to motivate.

The **maturity** stage has certainly become a much more volatile career stage than earlier models would suggest. Not all careers settle into a comfortable stage where the individual begins to exert greater degrees of influence on the organization. For a considerable number of people, the maturation that takes place is the realization that all the dreams of how high they could climb are not going to be achieved. Their career curve is flat from here on out. Perhaps this is why a growing number of people decide to change careers at this juncture in their lives. For some employees, though, the career change is brought on by being fired. With mergers, market restructuring, technological change, and downsizing, many organizations find they need fewer people than before. Hence, some people have to go. For example, consider the case of AT&T during the mid-1980s. Divestiture, downsizing, massive reorganization, and early retirement options resulted in many long-term, loyal AT&Ters out looking for a new career. In addition, technological changes at AT&T have eliminated thousands of jobs, while creating thousands of new jobs—but jobs requiring different skills.[23] However, as we noted earlier, AT&T is one of the companies that has taken on the task of managing outplacement, retraining, and other creative options for employees.

For some people at AT&T, as well as at other companies, the choice that is being offered is a downward movement in the company. As we might expect, this option often does not meet with overwhelming excitement by the employee.[24] But when family and life-stage issues leave the person with no options, it becomes much more attractive, compared to leaving the company. Still, it must be presented positively and with as much ceremony as a promotion if a manager hopes to maintain the self-esteem and motivation of the demoted employee.

Finally, with regard to the **withdrawal** stage, advances in life expectancy and the health of people in general have made this the stage of second careers, starting exciting projects, and working at what a person has always wanted to do. Early retirement options have sometimes even moved the withdrawal stage down into the 50s and early 60s. But other employees want to continue working for the company, and there has been increasing upward pressure on the age of mandatory retirement. Indeed, there appears to be no end to the opportunities for the healthier-than-ever senior citizen (see Insight 2–7). For those who stay with the company, managers must determine how to use their talents effectively. And for those who leave, managers must figure out how to replace their experience.

Overall, our goal here has been to clarify that the stages of a career are probably much more complex than indicated by the simple model shown in Exhibit 2–2. **The five stages of exploration, establishment, advancement, maturity, and withdrawal may reflect the various stages that occur, but it is clear that the ordering and duration of those stages can take on an almost limitless number of possibilities.**

WHAT CAN YOU DO ABOUT YOUR CAREER?

Now that we have discussed the factors that affect the changing role of a manager, let us conclude this chapter with a brief discussion of what you can do about your career. Simply **having an appreciation of the developmental aspects of career, life, and family stages can prepare you to better manage your career.** We have said that people are goal oriented and that they develop a perception of their abilities. Both of these are subject to change, as are the goals and operations of the companies for which we work. However, **when your goals/abilities and the goals/development plans of the organization are in agreement, a successful career is more likely.** Such a convergence will encourage you to develop the skills and abilities needed for new jobs within the organization. It will also encourage the organization to invest in your career development. If, however, there is a lack of agreement between you and the organization, you will be dissatisfied—and so will the organization. In such an event, the best career move may be to look for work elsewhere.

I N S I G H T   2–7

Early Retirement

More People Quit Jobs before 65, but Ways of Using Time Vary

*B*efore he took early retirement seven years ago, Howard Shank made a list of the things he wanted to do when he was no longer the president and chief creative officer at Leo Burnett Co., a Chicago advertising agency. High on his agenda were painting, writing, golf and traveling.

But Mr. Shank, who was then 57 years old, wasn't ready for his own advice. Instead, he let others tell him how a man of his talent, experience and vigor should spend his retirement years. So he taught, consulted and was miserable for 18 months.

He didn't snap out of his melancholy until he realized that his professional achievements no longer mattered. "Retirement forced me to reinvent myself," he says. And what the new Howard Shank really wanted to do was write, which had been on his list from the start. "I've written one book (about retirement) and I'm struggling cheerfully to write another," he says from his home-office in Lake Forest, Ill.

Robert Swinarton, who retired six years ago at 54 as vice chairman of Dean Witter Reynolds, a major brokerage house, also planned to retire early. But serving as a director or trustee wasn't part of his plan. "I cold-turkeyed," he says from his mountain home in Dorset, Vt. "I made my deal on Thursday, packed my office and left on Friday, and I've been back only once, a year ago." In the past six years, he adds, "I haven't done a lick of work for pay."

With the developmental perspective, it is important to recognize the sources of your career orientations. It is also important to recognize that they may change over time. First of all, your goals and abilities are influenced by your childhood experiences. Social class is probably one of the primary factors that enters in here.[25] Children raised in a home where achievement is stressed will develop a different career orientation than those brought up in a home where other values are stressed.[26] **It is important to get a sense of what your goals and aspirations are, where they come from, and how they may change over time.**

Another factor important in determining your career orientation is your previous organizational and job experiences. As we pointed out in Chapter 1, you are already a used product. Your past experiences have given you feedback about your goals and abilities; and future experiences will continue to shape your perceptions. If you experience success, you will probably adjust your goals and perceptions of abilities upward. This can result in a reassessment of career aspirations and can begin a cycle of success: Higher goals, when achieved, lead to setting even higher goals. But it is also possible for another scenario to develop: Continued success can breed a complacency that inhibits continued growth.[27]

Of course, if you experience failure, the result can be quite different. Such negative feedback can lead to a downward adjustment in career aspirations; and continued failure can begin to push you into a downward cycle. However, research has shown that initial failures can also lead to the exertion of greater effort to avoid repeated failure.[28] Thus, the scenario again has two main possibilities. And it is quite possible that your childhood experiences will determine your reaction to success and failure.

Other factors can also influence your career orientation both today and in the future. We have noted the impact that family stages can have on your career, and we have also discussed the impact of life stages. Both factors interact with your career in significant ways. We will explore them more in Chapters 3 and 4. For now, focus specifically on your career by completing the career-planning exercise at the end of this chapter. The steps outlined can be completed alone, but you should discuss the results with friends and/or relatives. And as you go through the exercise, think about the factors we have discussed that affect your career and its various stages. Then take a look at the chapter highlights and review questions that follow.

CHAPTER HIGHLIGHTS

The purpose of this chapter has been to think more personally about the developmental aspects of organizations. We need to gain a true appreciation for this perspective before we proceed through the four levels of organizational behavior. To do this, we have focused on managing as a changing role. More specifically, we have focused on the elements of a career—your career. Different skills are required as you progress through your managerial career. In particular, we discussed three types of skills. **Technical skill is important at lower levels of management but less important at upper levels. Conceptual skill is important at upper levels of management and less important at lower levels. Human relations skill is necessary at all levels.**

We also talked about how a career can be broken down into various stages. Several breakdowns were explored and resulted in the definition of five career stages. The **exploration** stage is the period in our lives (ages 15–25) when we begin to choose our life's work. The **establishment** stage (ages 26–35) is the period of exploring various career paths and becoming comfortable in one field of endeavor (at least for the time being). The third stage, **advancement** (ages 36–45), is the time during which we determine how far we will go in our field of endeavor. At the end of this period, people sometimes change fields when they realize they will not be able to climb as high as they would like. The fourth stage is the **maturity** stage (ages 46–65). It is during this time that the real change from technical to conceptual skill utilization usually takes place. We will either reach a plateau at the beginning of this period or become a mentor for others. We can also exercise influence in the organization. The final career stage is **withdrawal** (ages 66 and on). During this period, people begin to withdraw from their field of endeavor and may pick up another career in retirement. In fact, retirement may be a career all its own as people live longer.

Another important way to view your career is from the point of view of the organization. Schein's model explicitly recognizes three directions of career movement in an organization: **vertically** up or down the organization ladder, **laterally** from one functional area to another, and **radially** toward the center of influence in the organization. **And as your career takes you vertically, laterally, and radially through one or more organizations, you will be changed as a result of the experiences you have. You will also have to manage and work in a context and with people who are different at each step of the way.** People in the different functions have unique orientations, goals, and norms of operation.

In addition, you will encounter changes in the work force. We discussed the effects of increased numbers of women and minorities in the work force, as well as the multicultural influences of working with people from different countries. We discussed the rapid growth of dual-career couples. Such couples create special challenges for managers and organizations—and for the husband and wife, too. As you move into different family and career stages, you, too, may have to manage the stresses associated with a dual-career couple. You will certainly encounter the situation in one way or another.

The last two factors creating changes in your managerial career are changes in you and in the organizations where you work. Indeed, these are the fundamental developmental focuses in this book. As we discussed, **you will experience changes in your needs, goals, and abilities as you traverse your career.** The organization (or organizations) for which you work will also change and create forces for change in your career. **The organization may grow rapidly, change directions, or decline, but regardless of the direction of movement, your career will be affected.**

Next, we discussed how all of these factors suggest the need for refining the five career stages. We explored how the **five stages can occur at different ages,** as shown in Exhibit 2–2. We also looked at how dual-career couples, expanded retirement options, downsizing, and technological change **may also reorder and change the duration of the**

five career stages. Indeed, the notion of a career can take on many possible variations.

Throughout the chapter, we referred to Louise and Home Computers Company. By understanding Louise's career stages, her movement through the two organizations, the different people she has encountered, her dual-career situation, plus the changes in Louise's needs and the changes in her organizations, we can better understand what is happening to Louise. By asking questions such as these of yourself, you will be better prepared to manage the career that unfolds before you.

We have now fully introduced the developmental perspective as it applies to the levels of organizational behavior and to your personal career as a manager. By this point, you should have gained an appreciation for why the developmental perspective is so important in understanding and managing organizational behavior. As we begin to explore the individual level of organizational behavior in the next chapter, understanding this perspective will be most helpful.

REVIEW QUESTIONS

1. Define the three basic skills of management: technical, human relations, and conceptual. How do these skills relate to levels of management?

2. What is the work of a manager like on a day-to-day basis? How does this work vary across different levels of management?

3. What is the definition of *career?* How does this definition relate to a developmental view of work life?

4. What are the five stages of a career presented in this text? What typically happens during each career stage?

5. Schein defines three directions of career movement within organizations. What are they, and how are they defined?

6. How do Schein's directions of movement relate to various changes in the role of a manager?

7. As you move through your career, one factor creating changes for you will be the people you encounter. What are the three sources of "new" people who will change your role as a manager? How might each source affect you?

8. How might the impact of belonging to a dual-career couple interact with the changing needs of a manager? What challenges will be encountered as the manager passes through various career stages?

9. What types of changes could occur in the organizations for which you work during your career and have an impact on your career? How would these changes affect your career?

10. What current factors might alter the smooth progression of career stages in Exhibit 2–2? In what ways might these factors change the progression?

11. How do the elements of career stages and the key factors in the changing role of a manager interact in the life of Louise at Home Computers? How does the developmental perspective help in understanding her situation?

RESOURCE READINGS

Derr, C. B. *Managing the New Careerists*. San Francisco: Jossey-Bass, 1986.

Hall, D. T., ed. *Organizational Career Development*. San Francisco: Jossey-Bass, 1986.

Jelinek, M. *Career Management for the Individual and the Organization*. New York: John Wiley & Sons, 1979.

Kotter, J. *The General Managers*. New York: Free Press, 1982.

Schein, E. H. *Career Dynamics: Matching Individual and Organizational Needs*. Reading, Mass: Addison-Wesley Publishing, 1978.

NOTES

1. R. Katz, "Skills of the Effective Administrator," *Harvard Business Review,* January–February 1955, pp. 33–42.

2. R. B. Lamb, *Running American Business* (New York: Basic Books, 1987).

3. L. R. Bittel and J. E. Ramsey, "The Limited Traditional World of Supervisors," *Harvard Business Review* 60 (July–August 1982), pp. 26–36.

4. Bittel and Ramsey, "The Limited Traditional World of Supervisors."

5. L. Sayles, *Leadership: What Effective Managers Really Do . . . and How They Do It* (New York: McGraw-Hill, 1979); E. E. Lawler, L. W. Porter, and A. S. Tannenbaum, "Managers' Attitudes toward Interaction Episodes," *Journal of Applied Psychology* 52 (1968), pp. 432–9; and R. Stewart, *Managers and Their Jobs* (New York: Macmillan, Ltd., 1967).

6. H. Mintzberg, *The Nature of Managerial Work* (New York: Harper & Row, 1973).

7. D. T. Hall, *Careers in Organizations* (Glenview, Ill.: Scott, Foresman, 1976), p. 4.

8. D. Super, J. Crites, R. Hummel, H. Moser, P. Overstreet, and C. Warnath, *Vocational Development: A Framework for Research* (New York: Teachers College Press, 1957), pp. 40–1.

9. D. T. Hall and K. Nougaim, "An Examination of Maslow's Need Hierarchy in an Organizational Setting," *Organizational Behavior and Human Performance* (1968), pp. 12–35.

10. E. H. Schein, "The Individual, the Organization, and the Career: A Conceptual Scheme," *Journal of Applied Behavioral Science* 7 (1971), pp. 401–26.

11. J. E. Rosenbaum, *Career Mobility in a Corporate Hierarchy* (Orlando, Fla: Academic Press, 1984); and J. B. Forbes, "Early Intraorganizational Mobility: Patterns and Influences," *Academy of Management Journal* 30 (1987), pp. 110–25.

12. D. T. Hall and L. A. Isabella, "Downward Movement and Career Development," *Organizational Dynamics,* Summer 1985, pp. 5–23.

13. J. C. Latack and J. B. Dozier, "After the Ax Falls: Job Loss as a Career Transition," *Academy of Management Review* 11 (1986), pp. 375–92.

14. G. R. Roche, "Much Ado about Mentors," *Harvard Business Review* 57 (1979), pp. 14–28.

15. K. E. Kram and L. A. Isabella, "Mentoring Alternatives: The Role of Peer Relationships in Career Development," *Academy of Management Journal* 28 (1985), pp. 110–32.

16. T. Carson, "Fast-Track Kids," *Business Week,* November 10, 1985, pp. 90–2.

17. W. A. Randolph, B. Z. Posner, and M. S. Wortman, "A New Ethic for Work? The Worth Ethic," *Human Resource Management* 14 (Fall 1975), pp. 15–20.

18. *American Demographics,* August 1987, p. 24.

19. *Corporations and Two-Career Families: Directions for the Future* (New York: Catalyst Career and Family Center, 1981).

20. T. Jackson and A. Vitberg, "Career Development, Part 1: Careers and Entrepreneurship," *Personnel,* February 1987, pp. 12–7.

21. D. D. Bowen and R. D. Hisrich, "The Female Entrepreneur: A Career Development Perspective," *Academy of Management Review* 11 (1986), p. 393.

22. F. S. Hall and D. T. Hall, *The Two-Career Couple* (Reading, Mass: Addison-Wesley, 1979).

23. Jackson and Vitberg, "Career Development."

24. Hall and Isabella, "Downward Movement and Career Development."

25. M. Carter, *Into Work* (New York: Penguin Books, 1966).

26. J. G. Goodale, "Effects of Personal Background and Training on Work Values of the Hard-Core Unemployed," *Journal of Applied Psychology* 57 (1973), pp. 1–9.

27. A. S. DeNisi, W. A. Randolph, and A. Blencoe, "Reactions to Peer Ratings," *Academy of Management Journal* 26 (1983), pp. 457–64.

28. DeNisi, Randolph, and Blencoe, "Reactions to Peer Ratings."

CASE: Down and out Jane*

At the age of twenty-eight, Jane returned to college after going through a divorce. The divorce left Jane solely responsible for the support of herself and her two small children. With no home, no car, no furniture, and no professional job training, Jane remembered the words of her father: "The only way to get ahead in this world is to get yourself a college degree. Without that piece of paper, they don't care how much you know or how much experience you have; you won't get a chance to get ahead." Although neither of Jane's parents ever graduated from high school, they stressed achievement and education to their children. Having been raised in a small mill town in the South, Jane was fortunate that she had a strong academic background from high school. Her high academic performance enabled her to enter college.

Within six months, Jane secured a low-skilled job, received a Basic Equal Opportunity Grant, and gained acceptance into the nursing program at a local university. Jane vowed to never allow herself to be so desolate again. Jane chose nursing because of her interest in science and human behavior, and because there was a guaranteed job market at a time when the unemployment rate for even professional college graduates was high. In 1981, Jane graduated at the top of her nursing class, and passed the state nursing boards with high national scores. During that same year, Jane remarried. Her new husband Don was a health care administrator and a small-business investor who also had been divorced and had custody of his two small children.

After graduation, Jane began working as a staff nurse in a local private hospital. Jane worked at the private hospital for a year, during which time she improved her clinical skills and observed various management styles. In 1982, Jane decided to move from the small private hospital to a larger VA medical center. The decision resulted from a conflict of principles between Jane and management. Jane felt that management expected nurses to tolerate rude, unprofessional behavior from physicians because physicians brought in patients and thus financial support to the hospital. Nurses were discouraged from addressing rude behavior from physicians, and management tolerated their unprofessional behavior without reprimand. Jane could not accept this position from management, so she quit.

Jane began her new job as a staff nurse within a medical intensive care unit. This highly technical nursing position was a challenging new learning experience for Jane. Although the VA high-level nursing administrators were authoritarian in their management style, Jane's head nurse was an excellent manager with good technical, human relations, and conceptual skills. Jane felt fortunate to work with her on a close basis. For two years, Jane worked long hours, gained an excellent clinical background, and developed an appreciation for the VA system. In 1984, the hospital created assistant head nurse positions. Jane applied and was selected over several other more experienced nurses. Being selected fed Jane's needs for self-esteem, power, and achievement. Jane began to finely tune her human relations skills, as she maintained a sense of unity within the group. The position also provided Jane with

*Source: © Alan Randolph, 1988; adapted from a course assignment by June Jones.

opportunities to make out time schedules, to attend committee meetings, and to work with middle-level management. Shortly after Jane took the position, the head nurse had to go away on leave for several months. Over the few months prior to this, the area of supervision for the head nurse had expanded to three intensive care units and over thirty nurses. During the absence of the head nurse, Jane was asked to assume the head nurse position. Again, Jane's self-esteem was lifted by her achievements and the power she had gained. She felt compelled to maintain her career. She vowed to always remain financially independent and to never have her basic needs threatened as they were at the time of her divorce.

Jane received an excellent evaluation for her supervision of the units during the absence of the head nurse. However, the experience allowed Jane to realize that clinical nursing management was not what she wanted to do. Even as a head nurse, she had to work long irregular hours and come in to cover staff quite frequently on days off. At the age of 36 and after five years of bedside nursing, Jane realized the pace would be a physical challenge in later years. Jane wanted to have more control over her schedule and workload. Upper-level hospital management now intrigued Jane. In the summer of 1986, the position opened for an infection control nurse to work directly under the chief of staff (COS). Jane competed against four other nurses, all of whom had more nursing experience and two of which had a master's degree. The chief of staff interviewed and selected Jane. Jane was sent to the Communicable Disease Center in Atlanta for training and was given sole responsibility for coordinating the hospital program.

During the next year, Jane did an outstanding job and received excellent performance ratings. Over the same year, the hospital was directed by the VA central office to develop a utilization review program, to revise the quality assurance program, and to intensify their infection control program in an effort to prepare for the next accreditation review. The budgets for the hospital were chopped to the bone, and hiring was frozen.

The chief of staff created a new section called the Appropriateness Review Section (ARS). He chose three nurses, a secretary, and a medical records technician to compose the group. Jane was selected to be one of those three nurses. The ARS was created to accomplish the task of developing a program to meet the requirements for Infection Control, Quality Assurance, and Utilization Review. The members of the group would work with chiefs of services, committees, and other staff to develop these programs. After the ARS had been in existence five months, the COS interviewed the three nurses and chose an inner group supervisor. Jane competed against two other nurses, both of whom had a master's degree and greater than 10 years' experience in nursing. Jane was told by the COS that she was one-half point short of the chosen nurse. This represented the first time Jane had failed to obtain a position for which she applied.

Jane intends to continue striving for a position in upper-level management, but right now she continues to work within a dynamic group where subtle inner-group conflicts exist. This situation is challenging, but at times it threatens the group's effectiveness. An ongoing subtle conflict between the other two nurses is of increasing concern to Jane. Jane enjoys her involvement with top-level management, and encounters new learning experiences daily.

Her job is a valuable resource, with which she can meet her needs and provide a valuable service. The job allows Jane to maintain her financial independence, and to meet her needs for power, self-esteem, and achievement. Her family has been very supportive, and her husband has been understanding toward her career aspirations. Jane, now 37, has taken the opportunity offered her by her administrative schedule to return to school for her MBA degree.

Questions

1. What career stages has Jane experienced thus far in her life?
2. How do you think her personal life has affected her career?
3. What do you anticipate the remainder of Jane's career will be like? What advice would you offer to Jane?
4. How would you feel about your career if you were Jane?

EXERCISE: Career planning

Purpose

To develop or reassess your career and life plans.

Introduction

This exercise will give you an opportunity to examine your own values and priorities for your life and to set career goals for yourself. It is helpful in an exercise like this to share the ideas you generate with other people in a small group setting because the feedback, support, and questions of others are helpful in clarifying your own values and goals. However, you should always feel free to withhold any personal data from others if you would be uncomfortable in sharing it.

Procedure

Step 1. On a piece of notebook paper, write *WHO AM I* at the top. Then make 3 columns on the sheet. Label the first column *CAREER*, the second *AFFILIATIONS*, and the third *PERSONAL FULFILLMENT*. Write the numerals 1 to 5 in the left margin.

In the first column, list 5 adjectives that describe you most accurately in regard to your *career*.

In the second column, list 5 adjectives that describe you most accurately in regard to your *personal affiliations*.

In the third column, list 5 adjectives that describe you most accurately in regard to you *personal fulfillment*.

Step 2.   Take three more sheets of paper. Head them up as follows:

WHERE DO I WANT TO BE?—CAREER
WHERE DO I WANT TO BE?—AFFILIATIONS
WHERE DO I WANT TO BE—PERSONAL FULFILLMENT

On each sheet, write the numbers 1 to 3, leaving a blank in front of the numbers like this:

_____ 1.
_____ 2.
_____ 3.
etc.

Fill in the first sheet as follows:

List 3 goals that describe your conception of ideal attainments in your *career.* Be as free as possible in selecting these goals. Summarize your career fantasies on this page. Example: I want to become president of my company.

Then fill in the second sheet:

What would be your conception of 3 ideal attainments in your *personal affiliations?* Be as free as possible in selecting these goals. Summarize your affiliation fantasies on this page. Example: I want to behave in such a way that my mother-in-law will be more accepting of me.

And then the third sheet:

What would be your conception of 3 ideal attainments with regard to your *personal fulfillment?* Be as free as possible in selecting these goals. Summarize your personal fulfillment fantasies on this page. Example: I want to learn to fly an airplane.

Go back to the first sheet and, in the blank in front of the numbers, assign a priority value to each of your *career* goals.

a. Using the following four-point scale, write the appropriate value in the space provided in front of each goal.
    1—of little importance
    2—of moderate importance
    3—of great importance
    4—of very great importance
b. Assign a priority value to each of your *personal affiliation* goals (the second sheet). Using the four-point scale above, write the appropriate value in the space provided in front of each goal.
c. Assign a priority value to each of your *personal fulfillment* goals (the third sheet). Using the four-point scale above, write the appropriate value in the space provided in front of each goal.
d. Which of the three sheets (career, affiliations, personal fulfillment) has the most 4s? The most 1s? What does this tell you about the relative importance of these aspects of your life?

Step 3.   Take 1 more sheet of paper; head it up with *MY THREE GOALS*. From your three lists of goals in Step 2, select three that you want most to attain. Discuss these three in terms of the following questions:

a.   What are *my strengths and weaknesses* affecting my ability to achieve these goals?

b.   What *obstacles* are to prevent me from achieving these goals?

c.   Are these *goals realistic?* What will happen if I do not achieve these goals?

Reprinted from: J. William Pfeiffer and John E. Jones (Eds.), *A Handbook of Structured Experiences for Human Relations Training,* Vol. II. San Diego, Calif.: University Associates, Inc., 1984, pp. 101–12. Used with permission.

A Developmental Framework for Studying Organizations

DYNAMIC ENVIRONMENTAL INFLUENCES

Past	Present	Future

Change

Organizations
Environments
Goals/Effectiveness
Structure
Design
Development

Change

Develop

Work Groups
Structure
Processes
Cohesion
Groupthink
Intergroup Behavior

Develop

Evolve

Interpersonal Relationships
Leadership
Power
Politics
Communications

Evolve

Grow

Individuals
Perception
Learning
Attitudes
Values
Personality
Motivation
Outcomes

Grow

PART TWO

Individuals in Organizations

*T*his section of the book takes an in-depth look at the behavior of individuals in organizations. The next five chapters deal with several important processes and outcomes of individual behavior.

Chapter 3 deals with the process of perception—how it is error-prone and how it affects behavior and interactions—and with the related process of learning. We explore how learning takes place over time, how forgetting occurs, and how learning and perception are interrelated. These discussions progress in Chapter 4 to attitudes and values, and then to personality which is the integration of learning, perception, and attitudes. With this information in hand, we look at the interaction of people and organizations by focusing on the process of socialization. This process, in particular, highlights the developmental perspective of this book.

Chapters 5 and 6 focus on how managers can motivate people. We discuss such questions as: What motivates different people? How does motivation change over a person's life? What can managers do to increase the motivation of subordinates and peers? And we also discuss an integrative model of the process of motivation. The final chapter in this section (Chapter 7) focuses on several positive and negative individual outcomes that managers need to understand and manage, in themselves and in others.

Throughout these five chapters, it will be important to do three things to maximize learning about individual behavior. First, keep in mind that people are the basic building blocks of any organization. The remainder of this book builds upon these five chapters which deal with the individual. Second, remember that each person is unique and develops in significant ways from birth to death. And third, think about how this material relates to ourselves. What new things can we learn about ourselves in organizational settings? ▪▶

C H A P T E R 3

Perception and Learning as Dynamic Processes

I ndividuals are the basic building blocks of organizations. They create organizations, and they perform the work of organizations. Managers need to know a great deal about individuals to be effective.

WHY MANAGERS NEED TO UNDERSTAND INDIVIDUAL BEHAVIOR

It is important for managers to understand the elements that make up individual behavior—such things as perception, learning, attitudes, values, personality, socialization, and motivation. These internal elements determine the behavior a person will exhibit as a result of external stimuli. For example, imagine a supervisor who tries to get a worker to do a certain task by yelling and pushing him or her around. Based upon perception, previous learning, personality, and so forth, the worker may perform the desired action, or the worker may turn around and punch the supervisor. Of course, different people respond differently to the same situation because of their unique personalities. Also, the *same* person may respond differently at different times due to stress or other dynamic factors. And people may respond differently at different points in their lives because of the evolution of personality. This developmental process is summarized in Exhibit 3–1.

In the exhibit, persons A and B are both exposed to the same external stimuli at Time 1. But because of their uniqueness (as represented by their individual and current—A1 and B1—perception, learning, attitudes, values, personality, socialization, stress, and motivation), their behaviors at Time 1 may differ. Furthermore, person A (or B) may respond to the same external stimuli with different behavior at another time (Time 2). This is because the person has changed (as represented by the changed—A2—perception, learning, attitudes, and so forth). People are unique and dynamic beings, and **to be most effective, managers must be very familiar with the elements that make up the individuals they supervise: perception, learning, attitudes, values, personality, socialization, stress, and motivation.** This means being familiar with the theory that relates to each of these behavioral elements, as well as their interactions and developmental aspects, all of which we will be exploring in this and the next four chapters. And familiarity with these elements means that managers should be able to apply the theoretical concepts to the people they manage. To make this discussion more concrete, let us return to the case of Louise of Home Computers Company and her husband Steve.

EXHIBIT 3–1

The Elements of Individual Behavior from a Developmental Perspective

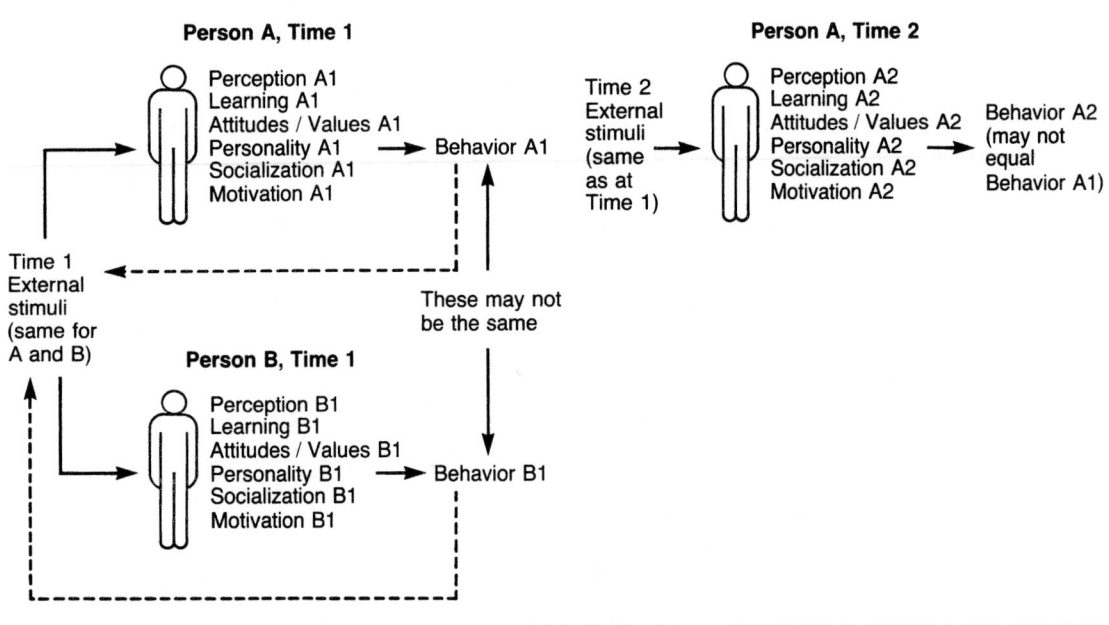

Louise of Home Computers Company (continued)

Louise's first job in 1966, long before joining HCC, was to work on the development of an accounts receivable system for one of her company's largest customers. She had just received her degree in computer science. Louise was fortunate to have attended an excellent school with some first-rate professors of computer science. She had developed a logical, analytical approach to learning and problem solving. Furthermore, she was fortunate to have had several women professors as role models in developing a self-concept of strength and confidence. Her attitude toward managerial problems and challenges was both optimistic and realistic. Louise was well prepared intellectually and psychologically to accept the challenges of her first job.

On Louise's first day, she met her boss Sam Stewart, who had retired from the Navy with nearly 20 years' experience in computers and programming. Sam explained to Louise that she would be working on an important project for one of the company's largest customers. In fact, she and George Davis, an experienced programmer, would be coleaders on the project. Their job was to work with the customer's representatives to determine exactly what they needed and then deliver it on time. They could call upon other programmers and resources within the company, as long as they kept Sam informed of their progress. Sam told Louise that he wanted progress reports every two weeks and that he wanted the job done right.

In addition to receiving these instructions from Sam on her first day, Louise met George Davis and began to get to know him. She also started to familiarize herself with the written description of the project. Soon she met the representatives from the customer company and learned more details about the project and the time schedule. In addition, she learned about the rest of her organization: how to get supplies, who she could trust and count on, where things and people were located, and so forth. And on top of this, she had to adjust to a new city and a new home.

Louise handled these varied and numerous stimuli very well. Her past training and life experiences had prepared her to deal selectively with her environment. She could distinguish the important facts and relationships from the unimportant ones. Also, she learned well from her first assignment and was asked to implement the system for the customer. She was then given a series of challenging projects.

In 1979, Louise's husband turned down a promotion because he would have had to move to New York and disrupt his family life. Instead, Steve chose to put his family before his career. Louise wondered what she would have done had the situation been reversed. Would she have chosen her career and the related stress on her family, or would she have made the same decision Steve did? Would the differences between Louise and Steve have resulted in a different decision for Louise? Well, one year later, Louise jumped at the chance to go to work for Home Computers Company as a sales manager, even though Steve advised against it. The job change did not mean having to move, but it did mean more travel.

Currently, Louise is national sales vice president of HCC and is very happy in her career. However, she is now 45 years old and feels left out of her child's life. She also feels that Steve is envious of her success. She wonders what would happen now if Harvey stepped aside as president of HCC and offered her the job. If she accepted, her family might have to move, or she might have to commute to the headquarters outside New York City and stay over several nights each week. It would certainly be a step up the career ladder, and it might not involve moving to another location. But Louise is wondering whether she should accept if the possibility arises. She is older now than when she came to Home Computers Company. She wonders about her career and how such a change would be received by her family. And what would Harvey think if she turned it down?

A number of aspects of this case are important to note. First, as Louise began her career, she encountered a large number of stimuli from her environment. She received instructions from Sam; met people;

learned a new city; and so forth. Could she pay equal attention to all of these stimuli? No.

Second, if Louise had been a different person, she might have felt threatened by Sam and the tough first assignment he gave her. She might also have perceived negative things about having to work with many men. For example, she could have felt inferior, or patronized, or sexually harassed. Someone with a high need to be liked, as opposed to Louise's high need to accomplish things, might have succumbed to such perceptions and been less effective on the job. And a person with less self-confidence than Louise might have felt overwhelmed by the challenging job.

Third, it is clear that Louise learned her jobs well and was very successful. However, as the case closes, Louise ponders her next career move. She may have to move to a new location and take on additional responsibility. She questions whether her current family and life stages will cause her to perceive these options differently than similar ones she encountered when first joining HCC. Will the present state of her learning, socialization, and motivation compel Louise to accept or reject the offer to become president of HCC, should it arise? And how will her family and Harvey react to her next career decision?

Let us now explore the process of perception in more detail. An understanding of this process will help you better understand Louise and the situations in her life. And it will also help you understand the situations you will face in your own career.

THE PROCESS OF PERCEPTION

In the preceding Home Computers excerpt, several aspects of the **perception** process are apparent. But just what is the perception process? Why is it so important? And why is it so error-prone? **Perception is defined as the process by which people select, organize, interpret, and assign meaning to external phenomena.**[1] In other words, it is the process people use to make sense of the world around them.

Before discussing a model of the perception process in detail, let us consider several reasons why the process is so important for managers to understand. First, it is unlikely that any person's definition of reality will be identical to an objective assessment of reality. In fact, reality may only be perception. For example, Louise's and Steve's perceptions of reality are influenced by their individual past experiences as well as by their sensory processes. Second, it is unlikely that two people's definition of reality will be exactly the same. The uniqueness of Louise's and Steve's pasts plus individual selection mechanisms determine that they will assign different meanings to the same situation. As another example, Insight 3–1 makes this point by illustrating how different peo-

**More People Face Career Plateaus:
A Relief for Some, Shock for Others**

*F*or some, it is a career crisis of major proportions, often resulting in agonizing soul-searching, marital troubles, and drinking problems.

For others, it is a comfortable and relaxing time, when family and personal interests come before the job.

It is the plateau, that point in a career when further advancement looks unlikely or impossible. Popular conception holds that the career plateau is the menace of only middle-aged managers. But with the baby-boom generation reaching its 30s and 40s during a time of widespread unemployment and record numbers of business-school graduates, a career plateau can come to anybody in any profession at nearly any age.

"It's like aging," says the 50-year-old vice president of a pharmaceutical concern. "You hardly notice it until you wake up one morning and you've had the same job for five years and it isn't anywhere near where you planned to be by this time."

But some recent corporate studies show that a sizable number of executives and managers welcome a plateau as relief from the competition and pressure to keep moving ahead. An American Telephone & Telegraph Co. survey shows that after 20 years at the company, one-third of the managers deem advancement as "not important." And only 36% say they would give up more personal time for career success.

ple respond to career plateaus. Third, individual perception directly influences the behavior exhibited in a given situation. **The bottom line is that people who work together often see things differently, and this difference can create problems in their ability to work together effectively.** Furthermore, who is to say what the *objective reality* is? All people in a situation may be wrong in the different meanings they assign to the same phenomena.

To understand perception, let us look at the model of the perception process in Exhibit 3–2. A glance at the model suggests its complexity as well as the potential for error and differences among people. But there is no way to avoid the perception process. It is physiologically impossible to jump from external phenomena to assignment of meaning. A person must go through the senses, observation, and frame of reference filters before assigning meaning. Everything a person sees in the world is seen through this process. As we walk through the model step by step, think about the potential points where errors may creep into the process. Also, think about the developmental nature of the process.

EXHIBIT 3–2

Model of the Perception Process

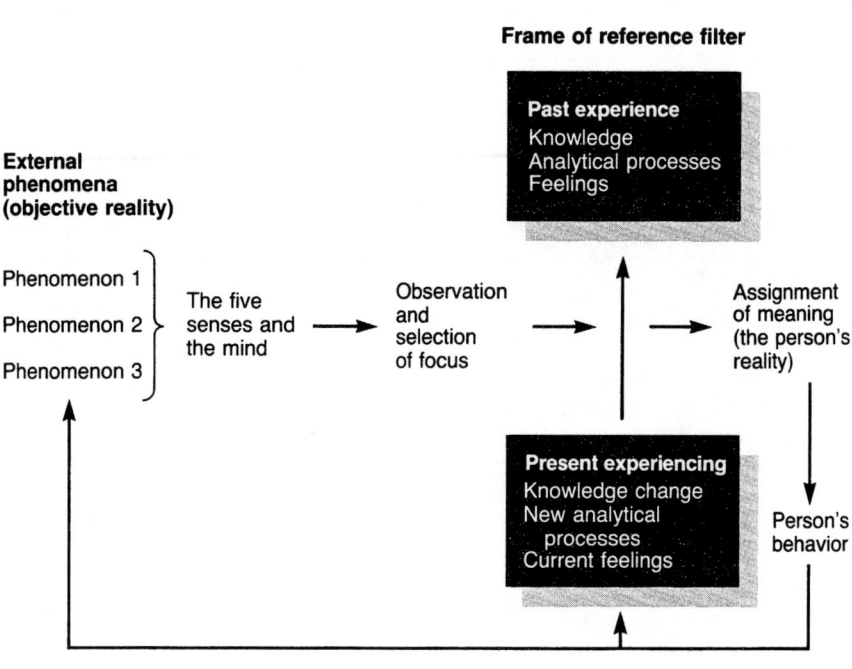

The senses and external phenomena

The first step in the model in Exhibit 3–2 (starting on the left side) is that multiple phenomena occur around us at all times. We begin to notice these phenomena via our five senses: taste, smell, sight, hearing, and touch.[2] For example, at this very moment, while you are reading this text, you are obviously seeing the words on the page; but what else is happening around you? You may hear a radio in the background, or someone talking to you, or a truck passing by your window. You may also smell coffee brewing, or taste the cup of coffee you are drinking as you try to stay awake to finish the chapter. You may also feel your chair getting very hard, or feel someone touching you on the shoulder to get your attention. Your mind may be on other things as well as on what you are reading. Perhaps you are thinking about your plans for the evening or about something that happened earlier in the day. The main point here is: Which of these external phenomena will you pay attention to? Which ones will you ignore?

Herein lies the first potential for variation from the objective reality and variation in the realities of two people. Perhaps you are highly motivated to absorb what is in this chapter. You therefore focus on the written page and ignore the external phenomena. Another person may be very concerned about an upcoming date and thus find that the words on these pages are not registering. What we are really talking about is the **selection mechanism** that is part of the perceptual process.

Observation and selection of focus

What is it that makes two people observe the same phenomena but "see" different things? The most obvious reason is that people must select their focus in the process of perception. There simply are more phenomena bombarding our senses than we can absorb, which means we must select which ones to notice.[3] The characteristics of the perceived object, person, or problem, the characteristics of the situation, and the characteristics of the perceiver all affect the selection mechanism.

Characteristics of the perceived

Physical properties of perceived objects, persons, or problems include size, intensity, contrast, and novelty. Dynamic properties include motion, repetition, and ordering.[4]

Size is an important physical property. Larger objects, people, and problems tend to receive more attention than smaller ones. For example, the size of an office will influence people's perception of someone's importance in an organization. Or a request from a large customer may be perceived as more important than a request from a smaller one.

Intensity has to do with the brightness and loudness of a person or object. If a manager speaks loudly to an employee, she is more likely to get the person's attention than if she speaks in a whisper. Or suppose a father is talking on the telephone at home, and his baby starts to cry. If the crying is loud he will probably put the phone down to go to the baby.

Contrast refers to the principle that objects that stand out against their background are more likely to be noticed. For example, material in this text that is printed in bold face or color contrasts with the regular print and receives greater attention.

Novelty (compared to familiarity) means that something is not as it is expected to be. Such novel items or people tend to stand out and demand attention. How often does a person notice the shoes of a business associate? Probably not very often. Yet, one time on "The Tonight Show," Johnny Carson's guest was a rock singer who was dressed in a conservative blue suit. But as the camera pulled back to give a full view, viewers could see that the guest was wearing white tennis shoes. Now, that got attention!

Dynamic Properties

Motion is probably the most obvious dynamic property. Objects or people that are moving are more likely to get attention than those standing still. A public speaker who stands like a statue behind the podium will not keep a listener's attention as well as one who is animated. And a problem in the workplace that is becoming progressively worse is more likely to receive attention than one that may be severe but is static.

Repetition is another dynamic factor in the selection mechanism. The more often a stimulus is repeated, the more likely it is to receive attention. For example, suppose a person is reading a mystery, and the telephone rings. If it rings only once, the person might ignore it; but persistent ringing will invariably make him answer it. Likewise, work instructions that are repeated several times are more often heard than those given once. Of course, too much repetition can lead to boredom.

The final property of a perceived person or object that affects the selection mechanism is **ordering.** Information that is entered early into the perception process will receive more weight than information entered later.[5] Furthermore, early information tends to distort later data to make it more consistent with this early information. For example, in hiring interviews, recruiters often make their decisions in the first five minutes, even though they may not realize it; and the interview may go on for another half hour. However, information that is the last to be received can also have a great impact on perception because there is no further information to weaken the impact of this last bit of data.

Overall, these physical and dynamic properties of the perceived object, person, or problem are important determinants of which stimuli we will attend to in forming our perceptions. If the focus is on people as the perceived, some of these properties can expand to include other aspects. For example, size can be broadened to include age, sex, race, and dress—in other words, physical appearance. Could the fact that Louise of Home Computers is a woman make a difference in the way she is perceived on the job? With regard to intensity, we immediately think about verbal communications. Certainly, volume is one element; but so are tone of voice, accent, and choice of words. If someone heard two people speaking, and one had a foreign accent, which person would more quickly attract the listener's attention? As for tone, there are at least two ways for a boss to say, "Come into my office for a minute." One is loud and gruff, letting a person know he or she is in trouble. Another is of moderate volume and said in a pleasant tone of voice. Finally, in combination with the verbal expression of people is nonverbal expression. If the verbal and nonverbal cues suggest different things, to which does a person pay attention? These communications issues will surface again in Chapter 11.

Characteristics of the situation

Three elements of any situation make a difference in the phenomena that a person selects to notice: the social context, the place of people within the organization (that is, their organizational roles), and the location of the perceptual incident.[6]

— If the **social context** is, for example, one of stress and time pressure, a person's selection mechanism may focus on different things than it would in a more relaxed atmosphere. Under stress, people often miss cues in the environment or imagine cues that are not present. The presence or absence of stress and time pressure is a dynamic variable; and over time, people may learn to function well under stress. Of course, social context can consist of other factors, as well—for example, nature of the work, relationship with others in the situation, and so forth.

— One's **organizational role** can also influence the phenomena that a person notices. For example, the superior in a two-person interaction will pay attention to different things than will the subordinate. The superior might focus on when a project will be completed and how the employee must work with little supervision. The subordinate might focus on what is expected of her on the project and where she will obtain support to complete it on time.

A classic study of functional units in an organization makes this point quite well.[7] Executives from different functional units were asked to analyze facts about their company and determine the first problem a new president should address. Sales executives saw sales problems as the priority. Production executives saw production problems as the priority. And industrial relations people saw human relations problems as the priority. These executives all had the same facts to study; their organizational roles made the difference.

— Finally, the **location of an incident** can influence which phenomena receive notice. Wrapping an arm around someone on the golf course may be interpreted differently than wrapping an arm around a coworker in the office. Being on time is valued in the United States; it is rude in South America. People will notice different things about a coworker at a formal luncheon than they will at the company picnic.

Characteristics of the perceiver

The last element in the selection mechanism is the individual perceiver. Basically, three aspects of the perceiver influence selection: learning, motivation, and personality.

— From past experiences, we **learn** to expect certain things to go together. For example, when we ask someone "How are you doing?" we expect an answer of "Fine." But what if that is not the answer? Do we still hear "Fine?" Sometime for fun, try responding to the question

"How are you doing?" with "Terrible." See if the other person notices. Usually learning to expect certain things serves us well—without it, we would have to start from scratch each time we met someone new or encountered a new situation. It is the basis of attitudes which we formulate to help guide our behavior.

Motivation also plays a role in the phenomena we select to notice. In a given situation involving a superior and a subordinate trying to solve a problem, a superior with a high need for power may attend to different cues from the subordinate than the superior with a high need for affiliation. If a person wants to solve a problem, not just get credit for the

"Now, I'm a reasonable fellow, but it seems to me that in case after case and time after time in these labor disputes the fairer, more enlightened position has always been held by management."

Drawing by Stan Hunt; © 1982 The New Yorker Magazine, Inc.

selected solution, the person is more likely to attend to all of the facts than just those that support the solution.

— Finally, the **personality** of the perceiver will influence the selection mechanism.[8] An individual's personality is the total person, involving emotional and cognitive elements. As we discuss in detail in Chapter 4, some people collect information about their world based on feeling; others depend on thinking. *Feeling* people pay attention to their own and others' emotions; *thinking* people are analytical and focus on facts. An individual's personality type will influence his or her selection mechanism.

Obviously, the selection mechanism is an area where many differences among people can occur. For example, Steve and Louise of the Home Computers case may have perceived their promotion opportunities differently because of their differences in personality and motivation or because of differences in their work situations and in what the promotions meant. Furthermore, the selection mechanism is also an area that is very dynamic. People may select a different set of phenomena to focus on today than they did at a previous time or they will in the future. People may even form different perceptions of the same phenomena on two different days. Perhaps this dynamism will yield a different perception for Louise on her second promotion than on her first. Furthermore, this is only the beginning of the perception process. The next step in the model in Exhibit 3–2 is the frame of reference filter.

The frame of reference filter

Once the senses have selected particular phenomena, the phenomena are processed through a frame of reference (see Exhibit 3–2). This begins the assignment of meaning to the phenomena. Two aspects of a human mind come into play at this point: the rational, analytical aspect, and the feeling, emotional aspect. In essence, the characteristics of the perceiver become predominant in the perception process. A look at the model reveals that this personal filter is comprised of two parts: past experiences and present experiencing.

Past experiences

The knowledge stored in people's minds from previous experiences is a sounding board for the phenomena that have entered their system.[9] If people have been in similar situations before, their experiences will affect them in the present. As we said in Chapter 1, we all have a history that we carry around with us, based on our individual set of past experiences. The comments in Insight 3–2 suggest that past experiences may cause black managers to perceive their options in organizations differently from white managers. And it is not hard to appreciate the impact of culture on this filtering process.

I N S I G H T 3–2

How the Corporate World Looks to Black Managers

While many conclusions about the status of black managers are based on anecdotal evidence, a 1985 survey of the nation's 1,000 largest companies by Korn/Ferry International found only four black senior executives, one more than the search firm found in 1979.

"We're no further today than we were 20 years ago," says Renee DuJean, director of the National Urban League's black executive exchange program.

Companies acknowledge that black executives are rare, but attribute the fact to the relatively limited time blacks have been managers and the intense competition all managers face for the ever-narrowing number of top jobs.

These companies believe that many blacks, particularly MBAs in such high-profile areas as finance and marketing, are now poised to break into upper management ranks. "It's just a function of time," says Robert Belden, a Southwestern Bell Corp. manager for affirmative action. "We see continuing growth at the middle-management level and within a very few years we'll see dramatic change."

But black managers say that for many of them it is more than a question of time. For one thing, the first wave of blacks who entered corporations in the 1960s and 1970s often were placed in such staff positions as public relations and affirmative action and thus aren't in line for top executive jobs.

"It was the easy route in," says Mr. Jones of Xerox, whose first corporate job was with General Foods Corp.'s personnel depart-

ment in 1965. "We had no role models, so we joined the corporate family in personnel (or) public relations, because those were available to us." Mr. Jones says that his own opportunities were limited by being placed in a staff position, but he says he is doing what he wants to do.

Dama Stephenson, a black marketing officer at Philadelphia National Bank, says she thinks her company is one of the best in the country. Still, she feels she has been passed over for several promotions, partly because of her color and sex. "People who started when I did are now assistant vice presidents. I think it's a function of their manager. They were pushed," she says.

'Golden Boys'

Ms. Stephenson, who holds an MBA from George Washington University, chalks it up to "human behavior," adding, "I can work harder than anybody in this institution but I think because I'm black and female the chances are remote of being president. It's not so much racism or sexism, but there are so many other white guys out there who have the same credentials as me and (who are) identified early on as golden boys."

The general cultural and social separation of blacks and whites spills over to corporate settings, Ms. Stephenson adds. "People in the senior ranks might have gone to the same prep school, college, fraternity, church," she says. "Put yourself in corporate America's shoes. You hire who you feel most comfortable with."

For example, suppose a person has an appointment with a supervisor at 10:00 A.M., and the supervisor arrives at 10:25 A.M. Is the supervisor late? Well, that depends. If this takes place in Switzerland, the answer is a resounding YES! In Switzerland, a person can set his watch by the train departures—promptness is highly valued. But if these people live in Brazil, the answer is NO! A study by Levine and Wolff found that people are not considered late in Brazil until they are tardy 30 minutes or more.[10] Our culture plays a vital role in how we interpret phenomena around us. Furthermore, research has shown that experiences that occur in our lives during the first three years have a profound effect on our knowledge base.[11] By the age of four, we have developed intellectual abilities that will be used the rest of our lives. By this time, we have also developed a base level of trust that underlies our feelings about other people.

Our past experiences have also brought us into contact with various groups of people. Often it appears that all people who belong to a particular group exhibit similar properties. For example, all Southerners are slow-moving and laid-back; all Northerners are fast-moving and curt. This stereotyping is useful in the filtering process because it helps us draw conclusions more quickly; but it can also lead to perception errors.

On the more emotional side, past experiences have been associated with particular feelings. When similar experiences are encountered, people tend to rely upon past feelings to help interpret the phenomena. If, for example, a motorist was once stopped for speeding and felt very anxious about the police officer giving her a ticket, being stopped again may bring on the same anxiety. But this time, the officer may be stopping the motorist just to say that her rear tire is almost flat.

In short, these past experiences illustrate the developmental aspects of the perception process. The past makes a difference in how people interpret the present and think about the future. But the process is also developmental in that the present experiencing part of the filter allows new things to influence people's perception. The present experiencing also modifies the past experiences part of the filter by providing new information.

Present experiencing

As present phenomena enter the perception process, they bring in new knowledge, new analytical processes, and current feelings. This present experiencing also plays a part in the assignment of meaning to the phenomena entering people's systems. Perhaps new knowledge tells people that this slow-moving, laid-back Southerner is also very bright and very wealthy, and this alters the pure stereotypical image from their past experiences. If people meet someone from a different background, they may also encounter new ways of analyzing things or new ways of organizing ideas. Of course, encountering situations at different points in their lives may encourage them to use different approaches for their analysis. For example, Louise's analysis of the promotion to HCC president would probably be different than her previous analysis of the promotion to national sales vice president. Her present experiencing will be different because of her different stage in life.

In fact, Louise's current feelings are probably different than they were when she joined Home Computers Company. Her expressed feelings about family have changed since the earlier job decision, and these current feelings will influence her assignment of meaning. As another example, why is it that a man sometimes meets a beautiful woman, feels very little emotional attraction, and simply becomes a friend. The man then meets another woman, feels a strong emotional tug, falls in love, and marries her. Needless to say, the same can happen to a woman. The different reactions to similar situations are heavily influenced by the man or woman's current feelings.

The assignment of meaning and behavior

The final step in perception formation (see Exhibit 3–2) is the assignment of meaning to the external phenomena that have been selected and processed through the frame of reference filter. This final step is an interaction of characteristics of the perceived person or object, of the situation, and of the perceiver within a dynamic selection mechanism. It is also an interaction involving past experiences and present experiencing in the actual assignment of meaning. And the assignment of meaning brings into play a process of attribution.

Attribution theory

Attribution relates to the way people try to understand the behavior of others.[12] When through the process of perception people try to assign meaning to the phenomena coming through the system, they invariably ask "Why?" In other words, if people can understand why a person behaves the way he or she does, they can better understand what to make of this person's behavior. Suppose a traveler observes someone at an airport ticket counter berating the agent about a flight that has been delayed for an hour. Why is this person doing this? Is he upset because this delay means he may not get home before his very ill father dies, or is he just an obnoxious customer? The traveler's assessment of the cause of the behavior will affect the meaning he or she assigns to it, and may, in turn, affect his or her own behavior.

Let's look at how the attribution process works. The central issue revolves around whether we attribute the cause of a behavior to internal or external causes. As in the example above, if the man behaves outrageously due to stress resulting from his father's illness (an external factor), the traveler would be much more understanding than if the man's behavior is just his typical nature. Research by Kelley has suggested that people focus on three major factors in making their attributions: (1) consensus, (2) consistency, and (3) distinctiveness.[13] **Consensus** relates to the extent to which others—when faced with the same situation—would behave in a manner similar to the perceived person. **Consistency** is the extent to which the perceived person behaves in the same manner on other occasions when faced with the same situation. **Distinctiveness** is the extent to which the perceived person acts in the same manner in different situations.

As Exhibit 3–3 shows, when there is high consensus, high consistency, and high distinctiveness, people tend to attribute behavior to external causes. On the other hand, when there is low consensus, high consistency, and low distinctiveness, people tend to attribute behavior to internal causes. An example will help make this point clear. Suppose someone observes a supervisor in the plant chewing out one of the employees. Suddenly, the employee starts yelling back and then slugs the supervisor. What conclusion does the observer draw? She has never seen the employee get so angry with anyone else (distinctiveness is high), but she has seen the employee argue with this supervisor (consistency is high), and has seen others argue with this supervisor, too (consensus is high). Hence, the observer would probably attribute the employee's behavior to external factors: the employee must be under a great deal of stress. However, if she has seen this employee get angry with many other people (distinctiveness is low), and has often seen this employee almost come to blows with this supervisor (consistency is high), while she has never seen other employees argue with this supervisor (consensus is low), the observer would probably attribute the employee's behavior to internal factors: that's just the way this employee is.

The process of perception is quite complex, and it is very dynamic and developmental. It should be clear that past events in people's lives will influence their perceptions and that present and anticipated future events will also have an impact. Take a look at the newspaper excerpt in Insight 3–3 (on page 95) about dual-income, no-kids (DINK) couples. How do your perceptions compare with those expressed in the excerpt? What past experiences help you draw your conclusions?

With a perception of reality in hand, a person's behavior follows directly. Behavior is consistent with a person's perceptions of the situation and the people involved. Of course, behavior now becomes an objective phenomenon in the situation as the cycle in Exhibit 3–2 begins over again. In turn then, a person's behavior can influence the perceptions he or she forms at a later date. Perhaps a worker perceives himself as quite capable of completing a job, but his experience in the job is not

EXHIBIT 3–3

The Attribution Process

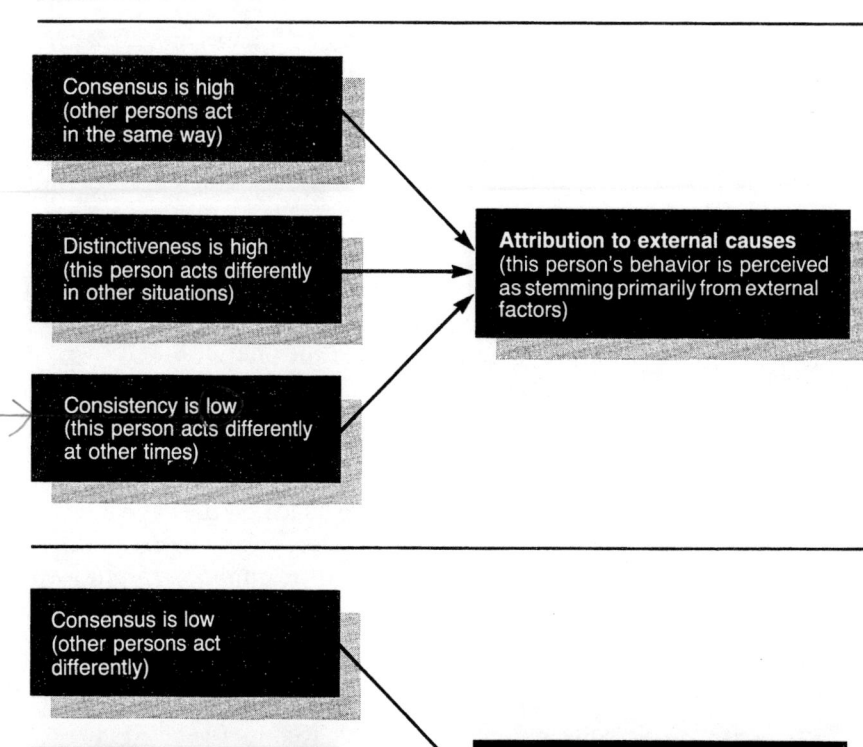

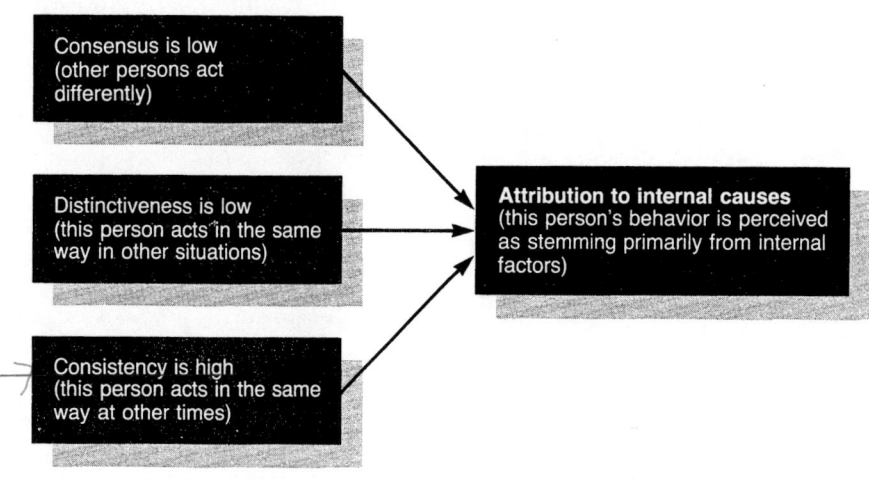

Adapted from R. A. Baron, *Behavior in Organizations*, 2nd ed. Boston: Allyn & Bacon, 1986, p. 115.

good. This may convince the worker that he really is not capable of doing the job, thus altering his original perception. This scenario clearly demonstrates the developmental aspect of the perceptual process. People constantly process new stimuli as they enter the perceptual system; and the new stimuli alter past experiences, as well as behavior. Also, people may become more sophisticated in using their senses, selecting phenomena to attend to, and filtering things through their frame of reference. But, by falling into a number of perceptual errors, they may also decline in their ability to form accurate perceptions.

ERRORS IN PERCEPTION

The perception process we just described is filled with possibilities for error. Certainly, we have seen some of these possibilities as we have discussed the model in Exhibit 3–2. This section explores some of these perceptual errors, including stereotyping, implicit personality theories, halo or horn effect, selective perception, perceptual defense, projection, and the self-fulfilling prophecy. As the text does so, it will relate them to the various steps in the perception process.

Stereotyping

One of the most common perceptual errors is **stereotyping.** Stereotyping is the process of assigning attributes to people on the basis of a category to which they belong. In other words, a person is looked upon as a type instead of as a person. Think about the perceptions that come to mind when we hear the following categories of people: police officer, business school dean, priest, real estate salesperson, top-level female manager, top-level male manager. Do the attributes we have imagined accurately describe any one person in these categories? No, but we often use stereotypes, especially when meeting new people. And they are useful if we do not depend on them too much. Take a look at the stereotypes presented in Insight 3–4. What is your reaction? The use of stereotypes grows primarily out of the knowledge part of our past experiences. Stereotypes are often based on facts gathered in the past, but are applied to new and different people who may not fit the mold.

A study of business students found that the sex of a manager influenced the perceptions of the effectiveness of the manager's style.[14] Using the same behavior descriptions but varying the sex of the manager, the study found that female managers were perceived as more effective when using an interpersonal style of leadership. Male managers were perceived as more effective when they emphasized task accomplishment.

Implicit personality theories

Closely connected to stereotyping is the creation of **implicit personality theories.** Based upon experience, people develop over time their own theory about people and their traits.[15] For example, a person may come to believe that a neat desk relates to efficient behavior, while a cluttered desk means disorganization. Perhaps this person relates a cluttered desk to being creative. What does this person then conclude about her professor whose office looks like a tornado just struck? That the professor must be creative, but she'll never get her test back? In fact, though, this professor may be on top of the tests but without a creative idea since graduate school. And people can even carry such associations beyond observed traits, as they make the halo or horn perceptual error.

Halo or horn effects

The process by which we allow our perception of observed traits to influence our perception of other unobserved traits is called the **halo (or horn) effect.** If we view observed traits as positive, we tend to apply a

**He Works, She Works·
But What Different Impressions
They Make**

Have you ever found yourself up against the old double-standard at work? Then you know how annoying it can be and how alone you can feel. Supervisors and co-workers still judge us by old stereotypes that say women are emotional, disorganized, and inefficient. Here are some of the most glaring examples of the typical office double-standard.

The family picture is on HIS desk:
Ah, a solid, responsible family man.

The family picture is on HER desk:
Hmm, her family will come before her career.

HIS desk is cluttered:
He's obviously a hard worker and a busy man.

HER desk is cluttered:
She's obviously a disorganized scatterbrain.

HE'S talking with co-workers:
He must be discussing the latest deal.

SHE'S talking with co-workers:
She must be gossiping.

HE'S not at his desk:
He must be at a meeting.

SHE'S not at her desk:
She must be in the ladies' room.

HE's not in the office:
He's meeting customers.

SHE'S not in the office:
She must be out shopping.

HE'S having lunch with the boss.
He's on his way up.

SHE'S having lunch with the boss.
They must be having an affair.

The boss criticized HIM:
He'll improve his performance.

The boss criticized HER:
She'll be very upset.

HE got an unfair deal:
Did he get angry?

SHE got an unfair deal:
Did she cry?

HE'S getting married:
He'll get more settled.

She's getting married:
She'll get pregnant and leave.

HE'S having a baby:
He'll need a raise.

SHE'S having a baby:
She'll cost the company money in maternity benefits.

HE'S going on a business trip:
It's good for his career.

SHE'S going on a business trip:
What does her husband say?

HE'S leaving for a better job:
He recognizes a good opportunity.

SHE'S leaving for a better job:
Women are undependable.

By Natasha Josephowitz, *Paths to Power*, © 1980, Addison-Wesley Publishing Co., Inc., Reading, Massachusetts. Chart on p. 60. Reprinted with permission.

halo (positive) effect to other traits. If we think observed traits are negative, we apply a horn (negative) effect. This application of the knowledge part of present experiencing is an efficient way to form an impression of someone, but generalizing from limited information can also lead to errors. The process of **closure** is really what brings about the halo or horn error. People take a limited outline of a person and flesh it out into a total person. For example, if a student makes a good grade on his first test in a course, the professor may assume the student is tops in all his classes, a leader in many situations, and a good tennis player. Thus, the professor may be making a halo-effect error. (But then again, maybe the student's professor is correct!)

Selective perception

While **selective perception** is a necessary process, as we have discussed, it can also be a perceptual error. Selective perception also demonstrates the time dimension of the process. Once we have formed a perception of a person or a situation, we tend to select into our system only external phenomena that support our perception. Insight 3–5 on former Interior Secretary James Watt is a good example of selective perception. Even when Watt tried to be conciliatory by reversing his position on off-shore drilling, California's Governor Jerry Brown chose to focus on the things that the secretary had not changed. By doing so, Governor Brown could retain his negative perception of Secretary Watt.

Perceptual defense

Another closely associated perceptual error is **perceptual defense.** Basically, perceptual defense takes the selected phenomena and alters them to be consistent with our existing perceptions. We do this to protect our egos when we get caught up in the belief that our perceptions of the world are always right. Through our analytical processes (part of our present experiencing), stimuli that mean one thing are distorted to mean something else. For example, a man who was competing with Louise for the job of national sales vice president might know that the best-qualified people are promoted at HCC; but this might be hard to swallow since Louise is a woman. Hence, the man might distort the facts and believe that Louise was promoted because Harvey wanted to look good from an affirmative action point of view or because Louise and Harvey had a special relationship.

Projection

Another perceptual error is called **projection.** Past or current knowledge and feelings sometimes cause us to project onto other people traits or feelings that are really our own. In other words, we often see others as

I N S I G H T 3–5

Watt Softens His Line but Image as Extremist Cuts His Effectiveness

His Bid to Seem Conciliatory Only Inflames Foes, Who Include Some Republicans

*D*uring his first few months on the job, Interior Secretary James Watt was too busy discarding policies and staff left by the Carter administration to worry about his public image.

"I pledged to lock myself in my office," Mr. Watt recalls, "until I had brought about the policy changes" promised by President Reagan. Through tough management, intimate knowledge of the issues and rigid adherence to ideological principles, the Wyoming conservative hoped to defy critics and single-handedly open more federal lands for energy and mineral development.

Now that self-imposed exile is over. But the strategy has backfired, and Mr. Watt appears stymied in completing many of the changes close to his heart. "When I finally looked up from my work," the Interior chief confided in frustration to a group of newspaper editors last fall, "the hounds were in full cry (and) I was the prey."

Secretary Watt went out of his way to announce that federal offshore oil-and-gas leasing won't be permitted in four controversial Northern California basins. Apparently prompted by stiff opposition from state officials, environmental groups and local GOP leaders, Mr. Watt did an abrupt aboutface and acknowledged that the environmental risks are too great to allow drilling there. "We considered it quite a big step to appease critics," one department official recalls.

But it had just the opposite effect. Environmentalists and Gov. Jerry Brown immediately blasted the decision as a "hoax" and a "hollow concession" because Mr. Watt refused to rule out leasing of nine million additional acres along the central and Northern California coastline. Democratic Rep. Leon Panetta of California charged that the administration was "playing a shell game with the environment and economy" of unspoiled areas. Several Republican politicians fumed that the move reopened the entire issue during an election year.

By Andy Pasztor, *The Wall Street Journal,* June 2, 1982. Reprinted by permission of *The Wall Street Journal,* © Dow Jones & Company, Inc. 1982. All rights reserved.

reflections of ourselves without realizing it. In fact, projection often means that we believe something is true about another person but not true about ourselves. For example, we may not carry our share of the load in a group project, but we project that another group member is doing even less.

Attribution errors

There is a tendency for people to underestimate the impact of external or situational causes of behavior and to overestimate the impact of internal or personal causes. This perception error is called the **fundamental**

attribution error.[16] In other words, we may hold someone responsible for his or her actions without taking into account the circumstances surrounding the behavior. Perhaps a mother robs a store because her children are hungry, but she is still guilty of robbery. On top of this fundamental attribution error, we tend to attribute our own success to our effort and ability (that is, to internal causes) and our failure to bad luck or other external factors. In other words, we tend to view the world with a **self-serving bias.**

Self-fulfilling prophecy

The final perceptual error we will discuss is closely tied to projection and attribution errors. The **self-fulfilling prophecy** is the process by which our projections or perceptions of a person actually alter the external phenomena to become consistent with our perceptions. For example, suppose a manager is lazy on Friday afternoons. The manager then projects this trait onto his subordinates, expecting them also to be lazy; and the manager treats them as if they do not want to work. As a result, the employees do not work and therefore do appear lazy. As another example, a student goes to see her professor after taking an exam to discuss a question she did not understand. What the student really wants is to learn something; she is not concerned with getting a few extra points. The professor, however, has just had a heated discussion with another student about the test and assumes this student, too, will attack it. The professor thus responds to the student in a defensive and counterattacking manner and proceeds to make her angry. She begins to fight back, and the professor's perception is confirmed. Here, the past experience has influenced the present—and perhaps the future.

The entire perceptual process is one of continuous action and development. The past influences the present; the present influences the future. And behavior that is influenced by perception also influences subsequent perception. Furthermore, as we discussed earlier, there is no way to avoid the perceptual process and the errors associated with it. But a person may ask, "Is there any way to improve the perceptual process?"

Overcoming perceptual errors

Can anyone say what the objective reality is? No, all we really have is perception. But there are several ways to increase the probability that our perceptions approximate reality and are equal to the perceptions of others. First and foremost is to keep in mind the way the perceptual process works. By doing this, we will be aware of the tendency to make perceptual errors. And if we are aware of where errors can enter the process, we can do a better job of minimizing their effect. We will be

"What did you expect a financial wizard to look like?"

From *The Wall Street Journal*, with permission of Cartoon Features Syndicate.

more open to information that can correct our errors, as the perceptual process develops into the future. Second, one of the best ways to determine if we have made a perceptual error is to compare our perception with those of several other people, especially if they represent different backgrounds, cultures, or training. Even though there is no way to know for sure if anyone has the correct perception, we can learn from this comparative process. If everyone agrees, there is a good chance we are correct. But if there is disagreement, communications can help us sort out the differences.

Third, we must focus on understanding other people's points of view; it may help us know when we are wrong. The key here is to listen to and understand the other person rather than try to convince him or her that we are right. Fourth, we must be willing to change our perceptions when we encounter new information; this can help us overcome stereotypes, halo/horn effects, and perceptual defenses. Finally, we should view the world in dynamic terms and recognize that while a current perception may be correct, phenomena may change to make it incorrect over time. Also, our own behavior can alter the phenomena that are the basis of our perceptions; therefore, we must notice the impact of our own behavior.

Perception is a vital process in our organizational lives. It plays a key role in forming the basis of our behavior, since it is the vehicle for formulating our view of the world. Perception is also closely associated with the learning process—which is very important for managers to understand. Let us now take a look at learning.

LEARNING—A DEVELOPMENTAL PROCESS

Next to perception, **learning is one of the most important individual processes that occurs in organizations.** Just as perception influences behavior, so does learning. Furthermore, learning and perception are highly interrelated. The model of perception (Exhibit 3–2) shows how learning through past experiences influences current perceptions; but it also suggests how perception of external phenomena influences new learning. As defined here, **learning is a relatively permanent change in an attitude or behavior that occurs as a result of repeated experience.**[17] The following pages explore two basic approaches to learning: operant conditioning and cognitive learning.

Operant conditioning

Operant conditioning is really an extension of classical conditioning, where a connection is made between a stimulus and a response.[18] For example, someone learning to type might be told by the instructor to hit the return key every time the bell rings, indicating the end of a line. Eventually, the typist learns to associate the ringing of the bell with the hitting of the return key. Operant conditioning adds the dimension of **reinforcement,** associated with the stimulus-response connection. For this reason, it is often referred to as reinforcement theory. In the typing example, the typing instructor might say "Good!" when the typist hits the return key after hearing the bell ring, thus reinforcing the appropriate stimulus-response connection.

According to reinforcement theory, learning results from the consequences of previous behavior. When behavior is rewarded, we would expect it to be repeated and eventually learned. If no reward is forthcoming—of if punishment is administered after a behavior—we would expect the behavior not to be repeated. In a work setting, the use of reinforcements can cause the extinguishing of undesirable behavior and the learning of desirable behavior. From a managerial point of view, this type of learning is extremely important. There are several alternative methods of reinforcement. Suppose a manager has an employee who is absent too much. What can the manager do? Exhibit 3–4 illustrates four possible supervisory actions and labels the type of reinforcement applied. While any of the four could be applied, they will not be equally effective, as we shall see.

EXHIBIT 3–4

An Example of Reinforcement Theory on the Job

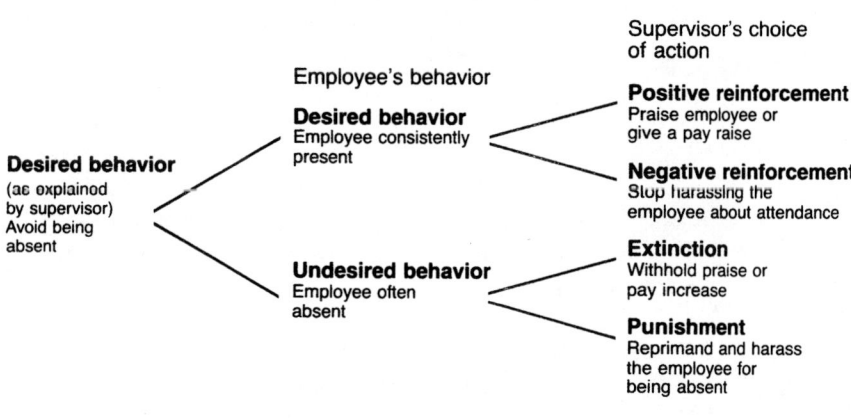

Positive reinforcement

As the figure shows, **positive reinforcement** is the giving of a valued reward when the employee, for example, consistently shows up for work. It is important to recognize several important factors about positive reinforcement. First, the employee must value the reward; thus, perception plays an important role. If the employee in our example wants more responsibility and a bigger title, praise and a pay increase may not result in learning the desired behavior. Second, the reward must be clearly tied to the desired behavior. There must be little lapse of time between performing the desired behavior and receiving the reward. And the reward will have to be given numerous times for the desired behavior to become the employee's habit. Any manager who thinks that one word of praise for attendance on several consecutive days will correct a long-standing problem of absenteeism is in for a real shock. Time is a critical element in this process—both its length and the proximity of behavior and reward.

Negative reinforcement

Another form of reinforcement, which is often hard for people to understand, is **negative reinforcement.** In the preceding example, the employee is spared harassment when the desired behavior is performed. In other words, when the employee has been absent, he or she is harassed constantly by the supervisor; when the employee is present, the supervisor stops the harassment. Something negative is taken away, thus reinforcing the desired behavior. The employee learns to avoid unpleasant penalties by doing what the supervisor desires. And the supervisor hopes that the desire to avoid these negative consequences will maintain this employee's behavior—being present for work every day.

Extinction

Extinction is really the reverse of positive reinforcement. Here, the employee is told to be present for work and what reward to expect if he or she is consistently present. If the employee is absent, the desired reward is withheld until the appropriate behavior is performed. Thus, the undesired behavior of being absent is extinguished. Extinction and positive reinforcement can work together in eliminating undesired behavior and learning desired behavior.

Punishment

Finally, Exhibit 3–4 shows **punishment** as a way of molding behavior. If the employee is consistently absent, the supervisor reprimands and harasses the employee. The idea is that the employee will be present in order to avoid the supervisor's punishment. However, if the desired behavior is not just the opposite of the undesired behavior (as being present is of being absent), punishment may only extinguish the undesired behavior without replacing it with the desired behavior.

Application of reinforcement theory suggests that the most efficient combination of reinforcers involves extinction and positive reinforcement. Negative reinforcement does not appear to be as powerful as positive reinforcement. And punishment may only deal with half of the problem, as explained above. If a manager clearly tells employees what is desired and what reward will be given for performing the desired behavior, the manager can withhold the reward until the desired behavior is performed. This results in extinguishing the undesired behavior (extinction) while simultaneously helping the employee learn the desired behavior with rewards (positive reinforcement). Insight 3–6 describes one of the early applications of these ideas in altering behavior at Emery Air Freight. In this case, the feedback was self-administered, and the praise was a simple pat on the back. And if good progress was not reported, there was no punishment—just no praise.

The Emery case also suggests that it is important to apply reinforcers very soon after the behavior. That way, there is less chance of the employee linking the reinforcer to the wrong behavior. Furthermore, a particular reinforcer applied indefinitely may start to lose its effectiveness. This suggests that the topic of learning is more complex than a simple stimulus-response connection. Indeed, researchers have again discovered that learning must go beyond mastery of things and responses to a point of meaning or cognition if we are to effectively oper-

---

INSIGHT 3–6

The Case of Emery Air Freight

The program. Perhaps the most widely known example of the application of behavior modification in industry is that of Emery Air Freight. Under the direction of Edward J. Feeney, Emery selected behavior modification as a simple answer to the persistent problems of inefficiency and low productivity. In an air freight firm, rapid processing of parcels is important to corporate profitability.

Emery Air Freight began with a performance audit, which attempted to identify the kind of job behaviors which had the greatest impact on profit and the extent to which these behaviors were shown in the company. One area of special concern was the use of containers. Emery loses money if shipping containers are not fully loaded when shipped. Hence, one goal was to ensure that empty container space was minimized. Before the program was implemented, workers reported that they believed they were filling the containers about 90% of the time. However, the performance audit revealed that this was really so only about 45% of the time. In other words, over half of the containers were shipped unfilled.

The results. Through the use of feedback (in the form of self-report checklists provided to each worker) and positive reinforcement

(praise), the percentage of full containers rose swiftly from 45% to 95%. Cost reductions for the first year alone exceeded $500,000, and rose to $2 million during the first three years. In other words, when workers were given consistent feedback and kept informed of their performance, subsequent output increased rapidly. As a result of this initial success, similar programs were initiated at Emery, including the setting of performance standards for handling customer problems on the telephone and for accurately estimating the container sizes needed for shipment of lightweight packages. Again, positive results were claimed.

The aftermath. While the use of praise as a reinforcer proved initially to be a successful and inexpensive reinforcer, its effects diminished over time as it became repetitious. As a result, Emery had to seek other reinforcers. These included invitations to business luncheons, formal recognition such as a public letter or a letter home, being given a more enjoyable task after completing a less desirable one, delegating responsibility and decision making, and allowing special time off from the job.

By R. M. Steers, *Introduction to Organizational Behavior* (Santa Monica, CA: Goodyear 1981), p. 142 as adapted from W. C. Hamner and E. P. Hamner, "Behavior Modification on the Bottom Line." *Organizational Dynamics* 4 (1976), pp. 8–21.

---

ate in the world around us.[19] People need to know why to do something, not just what to do when. Let us explore this cognitive aspect of learning.

Cognitive learning

Learning involves the total personality, including both reinforcement-type learning and thought processes. The cognitive model suggests that learning occurs by thinking about a situation and by synthesizing facts about it.[20] Such learning is very close to problem solving.

The Kolb model

There are numerous cognitive learning models, but this chapter focuses on a simple model that summarizes the important elements of learning as a problem-solving approach. David Kolb provides this model, which shows learning as a four-stage, cyclical process (see Exhibit 3–5).[21] Learning can begin with any of the four stages shown in the figure.

One stage in the Kolb model is the **concrete experience.** As we encounter new experiences, we begin the process of learning from those events (much like the process of perception). The experience may then be followed by **observation and reflection.** During this time, we try to

EXHIBIT 3–5
Kolb's Model of Learning

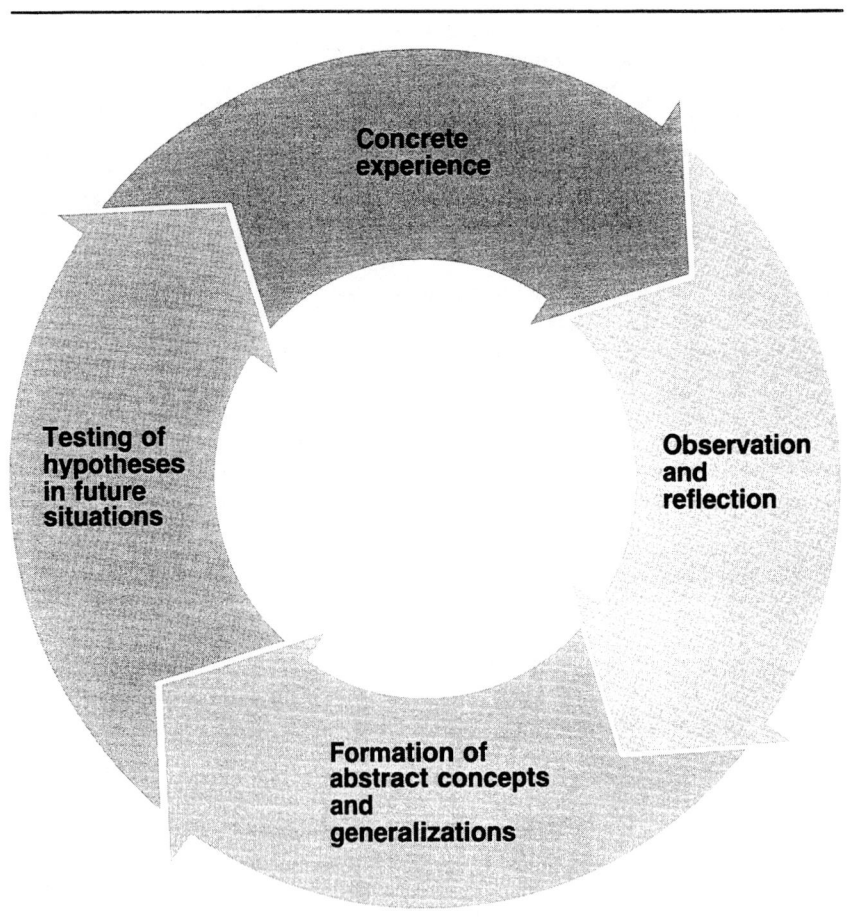

make sense of what has happened. Of course, we can also observe and reflect on experiences of other people. This stage then leads into the **formation of abstract concepts and generalizations.** Here, we try to compare our current experience to previous experiences, just like the process that occurs in perception. But the focus here is on the modification of those past experiences to take into account the new concrete experience. This stage can also involve the use of written material (for example, books) as a basis of comparison between theory and our experience. The next stage is the **testing of hypotheses in future situations,** which leads us back to new concrete experiences. Perhaps an example would make this model clearer.

Suppose a person goes for a job interview and gets turned down for the job (concrete experience). In thinking back over the interview, the person feels that she came on too strong and made too many demands (observation and reflection). So she concludes that to be successful in job interviews, she should try to be less aggressive (generalization). On the next job interview, she tries out this idea (testing hypothesis) as the cycle continues with this new concrete experience.

Several aspects of this model are important to note. First, the model shows learning to be more than a stimulus-response process. Thinking and analysis occur during reflection and generalization, as well as in the testing of hypotheses. Second, the learning cycle is continuous. Previous learning influences current learning; and current learning influences future learning in a developmental process. While a great deal of base learning occurs before the age of four, important learning does continue throughout life. Certain motor-skill abilities are primarily developed in the earlier years of life; complex cognitive abilities develop during the teenage years. A sense of responsibility for others occurs later, as the individual matures.

In fact, forgetting can also be explained by this model of learning. Forgetting is caused not merely by the passage of time, but rather by the events that occur after the initial learning experience.[22] After the learning cycle is completed, an individual begins a new learning cycle. Perhaps the new learning invalidates the old learning or just consumes the person, not allowing practice of the previously learned behavior. If managers expect a person to remember something he or she has just learned, they must allow the person to continue to repeat it, so that forgetting does not occur. It also does not hurt to continue to reward desired behavior. As discussed earlier, withholding a reward can cause extinction of behavior, which is much like forgetting.

The third point about Kolb's model is that since the learning process is cyclical, it is possible to begin new learning at any stage of the process. For example, a person may read about a theory of golf before going out to experiment with a new grip. Here, the person enters at the abstract conceptualization stage and then progresses to the testing hypothesis stage. Where a person starts and the direction his or her learning takes depend on the individual's goals and needs as well as on previous learning and the stage that has been rewarded in the past.

The three preceding points suggest the final point: Learning is a highly individualized process. It is also difficult for others to observe, since it is an internal process. People have different styles of learning. Think about which of the four styles in Exhibit 3–6 best describes the way you learn.[23] When you have a feel for your learning style, you will find it interesting to compare it with the styles of others. Also, think about how managers might use this information in understanding and managing subordinates, peers, and superiors. For example, should a work team have people of similar learning styles, or would it be better to have a variety of styles? With a very complicated problem to solve,

EXHIBIT 3–6

Kolb's Four Basic Learning Styles

An **orientation toward concrete experience** focuses on being involved in experiences and dealing with immediate human situations in a personal way. It emphasizes feeling as opposed to thinking, a concern with the uniqueness and complexity of present reality as opposed to theories and generalizations, an intuitive, "artistic" approach as opposed to the systematic, scientific approach to problems. People with a concrete experience orientation enjoy and are good at relating to others. They are often good intuitive decision makers and function well in unstructured situations. People with this orientation value relating to people, being involved in real situations, and having an open-minded approach to life.

An **orientation toward reflective observation** focuses on understanding the meaning of ideas and situations by carefully observing and impartially describing them. It emphasizes understanding as opposed to practical application; a concern with what is true or how things happen as opposed to what is practical; an emphasis on reflection as opposed to action. People with a reflective orientation enjoy thinking about the meaning of situations and ideas and are good at seeing their implications. They are good at looking at things from different perspectives and at appreciating different points of view. They like to rely on their own thoughts and feelings to form opinions. People with this orientation value patience, impartiality, and considered, thoughtful judgment.

An **orientation toward abstract conceptualization** focuses on using logic, ideas, and concepts. It emphasizes thinking as opposed to feeling; a concern with building general theories as opposed to intuitively understanding unique, specific areas; a scientific as opposed to an artistic approach to problems. A person with an abstract conceptual orientation enjoys and is good at systematic planning, manipulation of abstract symbols, and quantitative analysis. People with this orientation value precision, the rigor and discipline of analyzing ideas, and the aesthetic quality of a neat, conceptual system.

An **orientation toward active experimentation** focuses on actively influencing people and changing situations. It emphasizes practical applications as opposed to reflective understanding; a pragmatic concern with what works as opposed to what is absolute truth; an emphasis on doing as opposed to observing. People with an active experimentation orientation enjoy and are good at getting things accomplished. They are willing to take some risk to achieve their objectives. They also value having an impact and influence on the environment around them and like to see results.

By D. A. Kolb, Irwin M. Rubin, James M. McIntyre, *Organizational Psychology: An Experiential Approach to Organizational Behavior*, 4th ed. Englewood Cliffs, N.J.: Prentice-Hall, 1984.

what combination of styles would be most useful? How can managers give different training to people with different learning styles?

In closing this chapter, remember that learning and perception are very important elements of individual behavior for managers to understand. Both processes occur continually, and both directly influence behavior. They also influence our ability to deal with new situations, the formation of attitudes and values, and ultimately, the development of personalities. These important individual elements are discussed in the next chapter.

CHAPTER HIGHLIGHTS

This chapter has begun an analysis of individual behavior in organizations by noting the extreme importance of managers' understanding of individual behavior. **Primarily, an individual interprets external stimuli before behavior follows; therefore, the reaction managers get from a subordinate may not be what they expect unless they have some idea of how their behavior toward the subordinate may be interpreted.**

Next, the text explored the process of perception—the vehicle for assigning meaning to external phenomena. **There is no way to avoid the perception process even if it is an error-prone process.** People's senses are the initial means by which stimuli enter their individual systems. People also select phenomena to focus on, since there are more phenomena out there than they can pay attention to at any one time. This selection mechanism is influenced by characteristics of the perceived object, person, or problem; the situation; and the perceiver. The selection mechanism is developmental in nature. **It is heavily influenced by time, past experiences, and the behavior that follows perception and then becomes part of the external phenomena.**

The developmental aspects of perception become very clear in the next step in the process—the frame of reference filter. People use past experiences to try to make sense of current experiences. **Knowledge from past experiences, along with analytical processes and feelings formulated in the past, are used to allow the past to help people interpret the present.** However, the present experiencing part of this filter allows new phenomena to alter the knowledge, analytical processes, and feelings that have been developed in the past. Hence, the frame of reference is constantly developing and providing new data to be used in assigning meaning to external phenomena.

The final step in the perception process is the assignment of meaning to external phenomena. And the attribution of causes also ties into people's interpretation of behavior they observe. This assignment of meaning then relates directly to the individual's behavior. And the behavior is then part of the objective reality that will be processed through the perception mechanism for interpretation and influence on subsequent behavior. Thus, even in the short run, perception is a dynamic and developmental process.

The chapter then discussed a number of common perceptual errors: stereotyping, halo/horn effect, selective perception, perceptual defense, projection, attribution, and self-fulfiling prophecy. The final points on perception dealt with ways of overcoming such errors. **The basic thrust of these ideas was to be open to new information and to modification of perceptions, and to actively communicate with others while keeping in mind the perceptual process.**

Finally, the chapter discussed the related process of learning. **Learning was defined as a relatively permanent change in an attitude or behavior that occurs as a result of repeated experience.** Discussion focused first on operant conditioning, especially the reinforcement aspects of this learning model. There are four forms of reinforcement: positive reinforcement, negative reinforcement, extinction, and punishment. The definition of learning suggests that change over time is a vital aspect of the learning process. And these reinforcers aid in this developmental process.

But there is more to learning than the simple stimulus-response connection of reinforcement theory with people. A person's mind plays a vital role in learning as the cognitive theories of learning point out. The text explored the Kolb model of cognitive learning which involves four steps: concrete experience, observation and reflection, abstract conceptualization and generalization, and testing of hypotheses in new situations.

Throughout this discussion of perception and learning, this text has tried to make it clear that these are developmental processes. **Learning and perception are both continuing cycles of activity, with each new cycle altering people to varying degrees.** Especially as people encounter new experiences, their perceptual processes are put to the test, and their frames of reference are altered for the future. As we continue through this book, we will engage in exploration of ourselves, allowing our perceptions to be altered and new learning to take place. To be effective, managers need to understand themselves both now and as they will be in the future. Without understanding and managing themselves, people cannot hope to successfully understand and manage others.

REVIEW QUESTIONS

1. Why do managers need to understand individual behavior in organizations?
2. What are the basic elements of individual behavior?

3. Why is the perception process so important for managers to understand?

4. Describe the process of perception. What are the key elements of the process, and how are they ordered in time?

5. How do the characteristics of the perceived influence the selection mechanism? Which are physical properties, and which are dynamic properties?

6. How do the characteristics of the situation and the perceiver influence the selection mechanism?

7. Focusing on the frame of reference part of the perception process, explain why perception is a developmental process. How is the frame of reference developmental?

8. How is attribution theory tied into the process of perception of behavior?

9. How do errors creep into the perception process? How can a person overcome these perception errors?

10. What is *learning?* Why is the process of learning so important for managers to understand?

11. Explain *reinforcement theory* and the four types of reinforcers. Which ones work best in which kinds of situations?

12. Explain Kolb's model of learning. How does it differ from the operant conditioning model of learning?

RESOURCE READINGS

Adams, J. S. *Learning and Memory.* Homewood, Ill.: Dorsey Press, 1976.

Heil, J. *Perception and Cognition.* Berkeley, Cal.: University of California Press, 1983.

Jaspars, J.; F. D. Fincham; and M. Hewstone. *Attribution Theory and Research: Conceptual, Developmental and Social Dimensions.* London: Academic Press, 1983.

Matlin, M. W. *Perception.* Boston: Allyn & Bacon, 1983.

NOTES

1. S. Asch, "Forming Impressions of Persons," *Journal of Abnormal and Social Psychology* 40 (1946), pp. 258–90; M. W. Matlin, *Perception* (Boston: Allyn & Bacon, 1983).

2. J. Heil, *Perception and Cognition* (Berkeley, Calif.: University of California Press, 1983), pp. 3–29.

3. S. T. Fiske and S. E. Taylor, *Social Cognition* (Reading, Mass.: Addison-Wesley, 1984).

4. D. Krech, R. Crutchfield, and E. Balachey, *Individual and Society* (New York: McGraw-Hill, 1962), pp. 20–34.

5. S. Penrod, *Social Psychology* (Englewood Cliffs, N.J.: Prentice-Hall, 1983) pp. 176–7.

6. S. Zalkind and T. W. Costello, "Perception: Some Recent Research and Implications for Administration," *Administrative Science Quarterly* 9 (1962), pp. 218–35.

7. D. C. Dearborn and H. A. Simon, "Selective Perception: A Note on Departmental Identification of Executives," *Sociometry* 21 (1958), pp. 140–4.

8. S. E. Hampson, "Personality Traits: In the Eye of the Beholder or the Personality of the Perceived," in *Issues in Person Perception* ed. M. Cook (London: Methuen, 1984), pp. 28–47.

9. H. Helson, *Adaptation Level Theory* (New York: Harper & Row, 1964).

10. R. Levine and E. Wolff, "The Heartbeat of Culture," *Psychology Today,* March 1985, p. 35.

11. B. L. White, *The First Three Years of Life* (New York: Avon Books, 1975).

12. J. Jaspars, F. D. Fincham, and M. Hewstone, *Attribution Theory and Research: Conceptual, Developmental, and Social Dimensions* (London: Academic Press, 1983).

13. H. H. Kelley and J. L. Michela, "Attribution Theory and Research," *Annual Review of Psychology* 31 (1980), pp. 400–5.

14. K. M. Bartol and D. A. Butterfield, "Sex Effects in Evaluating Leaders," *Journal of Applied Psychology* 61 (1976), pp. 446–54.

15. M. Cook, *Perceiving Others: The Psychology of Interpersonal Perception* (London: Methuen, 1979).

16. J. H. Harvey and G. Weary, "Current Issues in Attribution Theory and Research," *Annual Review of Psychology* 35 (1984), p. 428.

17. G. A. Kimble and N. Garmezy, *Principles of General Psychology* (New York: Ronald Press, 1963).

18. B. F. Skinner, "Operant Behavior," *American Psychologist* 18 (1963), pp. 503–15.

19. G. Schuck, "Intelligent Technology, Intelligent Workers: A New Pedagogy for the High-Tech Work Place," *Organizational Dynamics* (Autumn, 1985), pp. 66–79.

20. P. G. Zimbardo and F. L. Ruch, *Psychology and Life* (Glenview, Ill.: Scott, Foresman, 1975), pp. 109–11.

21. D. A. Kolb, I. M. Rubin, and J. M. McIntyre, *Organizational Psychology: An Experiential Approach,* 3rd ed. (Englewood Cliffs, N.J.: Prentice-Hall, 1979), p. 37–42.

22. M. Manis, *Cognitive Processes* (Monterey, Calif.: Brooks/Cole Publishing, 1966), pp. 18–24.

23. A questionnaire to measure your learning style is available for purchase from McBer and Company in Boston, Massachusetts.

CASE: Volunteers can't be punished

Ann-Marie Jackson is the head of a volunteer agency in a large city. She is in charge of a volunteer staff of over twenty-five people. Weekly she holds a meeting with this group in order to keep them informed and teach them the specifics of any new laws or changes in state and federal policies and procedures that might affect their work, and she discusses priorities and assignments for the group. This meeting is also a time when members can share some of the problems and concerns for what they are personally doing and what the agency as a whole is doing. The meeting is scheduled to begin at 9 A.M. sharp every Monday. Lately, the volunteers have been filtering in every five minutes or so until almost 10 A.M. Ann-Marie has felt she has to delay the start of the meetings until all the people arrive. The last few weeks the meetings haven't started until 10 A.M.; in fact, at 9 A.M. nobody has shown up. Ann-Marie cannot understand what has happened. She feels it is important to start the meetings at 9 A.M. so that they can be over before the whole morning is gone. On the other hand, she feels that her hands are tied because, after all, the people are volunteers and she can't punish them or make them get to the meetings on time.

1. What advice would you give Ann-Marie? In terms of reinforcement theory, explain what is happening here and what Ann-Marie needs to do to get the meetings started on time.

2. What learning theories could be applied to Ann-Marie's efforts to teach her volunteers the impact of new laws and changes in state and federal policies and procedures?

3. How could someone like Ann-Marie use reinforcement to train her staff to do a more effective job?

Source: F. Luthans, *Organizational Behavior*, 4th ed. New York: McGraw-Hill, 1985, p. 300.

EXERCISE: The Mary Manager role play

Objectives

1. To experience a superior-subordinate situation in which the superior is female and the subordinates are male.

2. To expose people to the kinds of perceptual errors we all can make.

3. To provide an opportunity to learn how to overcome one's perceptual errors and how to deal with a job-related problem in spite of perceptual difficulties.

Procedure

1. The instructor introduces the situation by putting the names of the three role players on the board (or newsprint) in a hierarchical configuration and indicating that observers will be utilized.

2. The instructor describes the existing organizational situation by indicating that there is a productivity and training problem in the Accounting Unit and indicating that Ron Rushworth and Mary Manager were recently in competition for the promotion which Mary received.

3. The instructor divides the group according to roles (women as Mary Manager and men as Rushworth and O'Malley, as much as possible) and instructs people to meet together with others of like role in the place specified by the instructor. The observers also meet together. If possible, the Rushworth's and O'Malley's meet in another room or in the hall.

4. The students read the general role descriptions and the appropriate specific role descriptions or instructions for observers. The instructor allows 10 minutes for discussion of how to play the roles. Discussion is only with others of like role.

5. When the role players are ready, the Mary Managers set up their offices, and the observers find a spot from which to work. The Rushworths and O'Malleys wait in the hall. Mary Managers are instructed that the meeting can last no longer than 20 minutes.

6. To help the subordinates find a superior, the Mary Managers raise their hands as the Rushworths and O'Malleys enter the room. The meeting begins as soon as both subordinates locate their superior.

7. At the end of 20 minutes the instructor calls time and leads a discussion about what happened. Such questions as the following can be asked:

    a. What was Mary's style of leading the meeting?
    b. Was Mary effective?
    c. Was a solution reached? If yes, what was it?
    d. Who first offered the solution agreed upon?
    e. What was the problem at issue?
    f. What perceptual errors might have hindered the meeting's effectiveness?
    g. How were the facts on the Facts Sheet used? Ask observers.
    h. Does it matter that the Manager was female? How might it have been different if Ron were the manager?

Role Descriptions

Role for Mary Manager. You are Ms. Mary Manager, newly promoted to your position from that of supervisor of an accounting unit. At this time you are the supervisor of four unit supervisors, each of whom has charge of approximately 30 persons in their respective units.

Since assuming your new responsibilities, you have noticed that Ronald Rushworth (who was the person competing against you for this job) has been giving less time and effort to the supervision of the women in his department than he has given the men. Since many of them have been hired recently through the affirmative action programs, they are in need of more direct training until they have learned the ways of the office and their particular jobs.

You think it is possible, in this case, that Ron is overlooking this part of his work because of his feeling that he was passed over by a woman, and you know that Ron is not particularly in favor of women in management, certainly not over him.

Also, Ron's friend, Jim O'Malley, another unit supervisor, seems to be getting involved in some unknown way, probably due to Ron's influence. Jim would be more willing to accept you and continue doing his usually fine job, but Ron is exerting a fair amount of pressure on him and his allegiance is split.

You call both Jim and Ron in to try to sort out the real problem, concentrating on the situation of training and supervision of new employees; hopefully, you can promote some cooperation and understanding.

Here are some things you know about the behavior of men when compared to women in the Accounting Unit:

Absenteeism is 10% lower.	More willing to work overtime.
More time in restrooms.	Take fewer leaves of absence.
Less willing to do detailed jobs.	Make 10% more errors.
Don't get as emotional on the job.	Have 5% greater production rate.
Adapt more slowly to changes on the job.	Complain more about co-workers.

Role for Ronald Rushworth.   You are Ronald Rushworth, Unit Supervisor in Accounting, and have been called in to see your manager. She has been in the position only a short time, before which you were in competition with her for the position she now holds. Both you and another supervisor, Jim O'Malley, have been called in to her office.

The past few weeks have been rather trying for you. First, you did not get the promotion you had hoped for and had been trying rather hard to get. While you know Mary's work from having seen her as supervisor of her accounting unit, you feel that you really deserved the job. She just got the job because of Affirmative Action. And, to be honest, you think it is a man's job and don't like the idea of working for a woman.

Nevertheless, you are being called in to speak with Mary and Jim about the employee training and supervision in your and Jim's departments. You can't see any reason for this, but of course you will go. They have dumped a flock of women into your unit due to the affirmative action programs, and women are just not as easy to train and never stay very long. You feel they have been given a fair shake, anyway, and can't see what the problem is.

You are annoyed at the prospect of wasting time in another meeting and especially don't intend to be called down by Mary Manager.

Here are some things you know about the behavior of men when compared to women in the Accounting Unit:

Absenteeism is 10% lower.

More time in restrooms.

Less willing to do detailed jobs.

Don't get as emotional on the job.

Adapt more slowly to changes on the job.

More willing to work overtime.

Take fewer leaves of absence.

Make 10% more errors.

Have 5% greater production rate.

Complain more about co-workers.

Role for Jim O'Malley.   You are Jim O'Malley, Unit Supervisor in Accounting. You like your job, do well at it, and are quite satisfied with your position in the company hierarchy. You have just gotten a new manager, a woman who had been one of the Unit Supervisors until recently. Almost simultaneously, the company has hired several new women employees, the first women you have had working in the unit except one long-time employee.

Your friend Ron Rushworth, also a Unit Supervisor in Accounting, and who competed with Mary Manager to be your new manager has been called in along with you to see Ms. Manager, supposedly regarding problems with the training of new employees. You have been trying to give all your employees, particularly the new ones, a good chance and your work has continued to be of a high caliber. You realize that it is likely that the problem is with Ron's treatment of the new women employees in his unit, probably stemming from the fact that Ron does not feel that women belong in management and has made it clear that he does not like working for a woman manager.

Nevertheless, Ron is your friend, and you have seen him work very well with his employees in the past; he also had a good working relationship with his old manager. You have begun to wonder if maybe he is right and women shouldn't be in that position, especially if they are over men and, perhaps as Ron suggested, taking a man's job from him.

You are split between your allegiance to Ron, a good friend, and your desire to do your best and let the best "man" win.

Here are some things you know about the behavior of men when compared to women in the Accounting Unit:

Absenteeism is 10% lower.

More time in restrooms.

Less willing to do detailed jobs.

Don't get as emotional on the job.

Adapt more slowly to changes on the job.

More willing to work overtime.

Take fewer leaves of absence.

Make 10% more errors.

Have 5% greater production rate.

Complain more about co-workers.

Instructions for Observers

In their roles, Manager, Rushworth and O'Malley are given the same facts concerning men and women in the department. However, they will likely disagree with each other as they begin their discussion because they have been given different attitudes toward "women." Rushworth's role is designed to induce an unfavorable attitude, while O'Malley is neutral. You should observe the extent to which the participants use primarily the facts concerning men and women that are consistent with their own attitudes. One purpose of this case is to illustrate how persons with different attitudes may disagree even when they both have the same facts.

The facts supplied the role players are given below. For your convenience they are divided into two groups: (1) those favorable to "men"; and (b) those unfavorable to "men." While observing the role playing, place the initial M, R or O before a fact to indicate whether Manager, Rushworth or O'Malley were the first to bring it into the conversation.

Facts about "men" as compared to women in the Department:

Favorable

_____ Absenteeism is 10% lower
_____ Do not get as emotional on the job
_____ More willing to work overtime
_____ Take fewer leaves of absence
_____ Have a 5% greater production rate

Unfavorable

_____ More time in restrooms
_____ Less willing to do detailed jobs
_____ Adapt more slowly to changes on the job
_____ Make 10% more errors
_____ Complain more about co-workers

In addition, you should pay attention to:

I. Observations concerning *process* of the meeting
   A. How did Manager open the meeting?
   B. What was Rushworth's emotional state at the beginning of the meeting? At the end? O'Malley's?
   C. Who talked the most during the meeting? Who talked the least?
   D. Has the relationship between Manager and Rushworth improved as a result of the meeting? Between Manager and O'Malley?
   E. What specific things did Manager do that seemed especially effective . . . ineffective?
   F. Does it seem to matter that Manager is female?

II. Observations concerning *content* of the meeting
   A. Did any conflicts arise? If yes, about what?
   B. What was the most important issue in the meeting?
   C. What action will result from the meeting?

Source: © Alan Randolph, 1988. The author wishes to thank former student, Judy Spangenberg, for suggesting this role play and providing some initial ideas regarding its design.

CHAPTER 4

Attitudes, Values, and Personality

I n Chapter 3, we looked at the processes of perception and learning as fundamental to the understanding of people as dynamic beings. In this chapter, we will explore attitudes and values that people formulate as guides to behavior. We will also take a brief look at the importance of ethics in determining behavior. Finally, we will discuss personality as a means of gaining an appreciation of the person as a whole. Personality will be the vehicle to integrate learning, perception, attitudes, and values. As such, personality is important to managers in understanding and managing people in organizations. In closing the chapter, we will look carefully at the interaction between the person and the organization by examining the socialization process. In so doing, we will gain a better appreciation of how to manage these factors that influence ourselves and our employees. This chapter will also prepare us for the study of motivation in Chapters 5 and 6.

WHO WE ARE

This chapter begins an exploration of who we are. One of the most thoughtful books on leadership published in the 1980s was titled simply *Leaders.*[1] In that book, the authors explain that a person's understanding of himself or herself is a key to being an effective leader who can take charge. As this text explores concepts like attitudes, values, ethics, and personality, we should use this material as a mirror for looking at ourselves.

THE JOHARI WINDOW

A simple vehicle for making sense of who we are is the **Johari Window.**[2] It categorizes what we know about ourselves and what others know about us. As Exhibit 4–1 shows, there are two dimensions to the window: the horizontal dimension is a person as perceived by himself or herself ("things known to self" and "things not known to self"). The vertical dimension is a person as perceived by others ("things known to others" and "things not known to others").

Quadrant I is the **open area** of a person's life where things are known both to the person and to others. This is the area in which we should generally operate to be effective in interpersonal relationships. The more we operate in the open area, the more we understand each other. Hence, perceptions will be more consistent; communications will be better; and it will be easier to work together. Furthermore, we will know ourselves better if we operate in the open area. As discussed, one key

EXHIBIT 4–1

The Johari Window

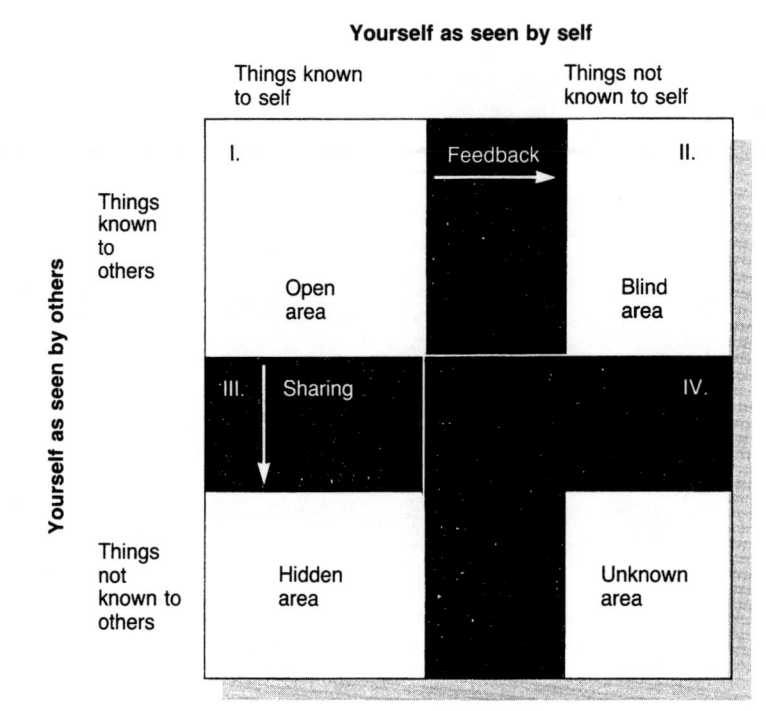

to effective management is for managers to know themselves and their people; and operating in the open area means just that.

Quadrant II contains things unknown to individuals about themselves, but known to those around them. This is the **blind area** of a person's life. As the figure shows, feedback from others is the way to decrease this blind area and enlarge the open area. By being open to feedback and by asking for it, we can learn a great deal about ourselves. If we operate in the blind area, we are more likely to unknowingly hurt other people and do things they do not like. We may be poor managers and not even know it.

Quadrant III is the **hidden area** of a person's life where things are known to the person, but not to others. As the figure shows, sharing is the way to decrease this hidden area and enlarge the open area. Of course, there will always be certain things we will want to keep to ourselves but minimizing these hidden things will make for better interpersonal relationships at work and in our personal lives. It will also increase our likelihood of feedback, since others see that we desire to be open about who we are.

Finally, Quadrant IV is the **unknown area** of a person's life where things are not known to that person or to others. By sharing and receiving feedback, we can reduce the unknown area; but the best way to reduce it is to encounter new and different situations. If we are then open to feedback and to the sharing of ourselves in these new situations, we can reduce the unknown area and enlarge the open area.

These steps of sharing and feedback will help ensure that our self-perception is a reasonably accurate measure of our personality, at least as it exists at this point in time. As this chapter proceeds, we should share things about ourselves with others and be open to feedback. We should take this opportunity to learn who we are.

ATTITUDES

As we begin to explore who we are and to provide concepts to help us understand others, it is important to recall from Chapter 1 that each person has a past history to carry around. Over that past, we have formulated our attitudes, values, and ultimately our personality as it exists now. Of course, the future will also bring change. As a way to begin understanding who we and others are, let us look at the formation of attitudes. First of all, attitudes, beliefs, and values are closely associated concepts. **Attitudes are opinions about things or people; that is, they represent our likes and dislikes. Beliefs are perceptions that a relationship exists between two things. And values are basic and pervasive standards by which we evaluate end-states of existence and modes of conduct.**[3] An example will help illustrate these points. We may have a **value** that says we should work hard at our job—the work ethic. We may have a **belief** that doing a good job at work will result in a promotion. And we may have an **attitude** that says we like what we do.

The attitude formation process

In perception and learning, stereotypes are very important. Stereotypes are an example of attitudes and beliefs. And as discussed in Chapter 3, stereotypes grow out of the past experiences part of our frame of reference. We develop stereotypes and other attitudes about a person or situation in three ways: (1) direct experience with the person or situation, (2) association with other similar persons or situations, and (3) learning from others about their association with the person or situation. These ways of formulating attitudes are styles of learning, according to the Kolb model of learning, discussed in Chapter 3. **Direct experience** is the concrete experience stage of learning. **Association** is similar to abstract conceptualization and generalization. And **learning from others** is like reflection and observation. Hence, attitudes and the underlying values are an extension of the learning and perception processes. Through the perception process, we learn about the world around us. We also formulate attitudes and values to help us interpret the world. Thus, attitudes both derive from and affect learning and perception.

Most behavioral scientists agree that we are not born with attitudes, beliefs, and values—we acquire them through life experiences. In particular, many of our basic attitudes are formed during our early years of life. Research by Erik Erikson suggests that a basic life attitude of trust or mistrust occurs during infancy.[4] If a child's basic needs are met in a loving manner, the child will develop a sense of trust toward the world. In the reverse situation, a sense of mistrust develops. In early childhood (one to two years), the child also develops either a sense of autonomy or one of shame and doubt. Of course, personal development continues throughout life, but basic attitudes are strongly grounded in the early years.[5] Later, this chapter explores Erikson's work in more detail. For now, it is important to note only that these individual aspects (values, beliefs, attitudes, learning, and perception) all affect a person's behavior, and are influenced by that behavior. These points are summarized in Exhibit 4–2.

EXHIBIT 4–2

The Interrelationships of Perception, Learning, and Attitudes and Their Impact on Behavior

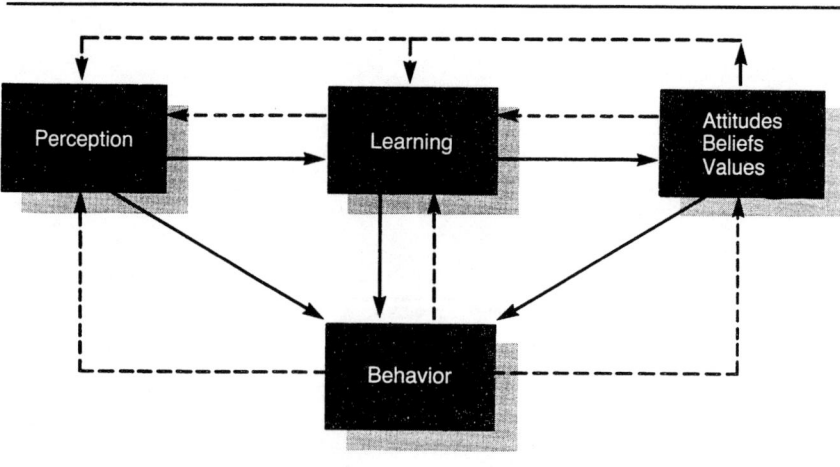

And this linkage to behavior is what managers are concerned with; it is the behavior of people that determines paychecks, promotions, and so forth. To be effective, managers need to know how perception, learning, and attitudes affect behavior. They also need to understand the ways in which behavior affects attitudes.

Attitudes and behavior

There can be little doubt that attitudes do affect behavior.[6] People's opinions, likes, and dislikes about things and people influence how they behave. For example, if a person dislikes a coworker, he will not be able to work with her as well as if he liked her. However, the person may be forced to work with that coworker, putting him in a situation where his attitude and behavior are not consistent.

This mismatch is referred to as **cognitive dissonance.**[7] And usually something has to give. Either the attitude will change, or the behavior will change. Or, the individual will experience stress and perhaps try to rationalize or deny the inconsistency. As Insight 4–1 (on page 124) shows, people in controversial industries—like the weapons industry—often have to deal with this issue.

What is also suggested, though, is the reality that attitudes are not perfect predictors of behavior. Still, managers must understand people's attitudes in order to understand their behavior. Consider, for example, one of the most studied of all worker attitudes—job satisfaction—which is discussed at length in Chapter 7. When employees are dissatisfied with their jobs, the results will often be high absenteeism, tardiness, low productivity, high turnover, and high job stress (sometimes resulting in physical or mental problems).[8]

Hence, managers may be interested not only in understanding the attitudes of people, but also in changing them. Clearly, since attitudes are learned, they can be changed. Managers often try to use techniques of persuasive communications to change attitudes. In so doing, their credibility is probably the single most important characteristic affecting their success.[9] Expertise and apparent motive indicate to people whether managers should be believed or not. Furthermore, a manager's chance of success will depend on how different the new attitude is from the old one. Moderate changes in attitude are usually easier to pull off than large changes.

But it is also important to recognize that attitudes may be slow to change. Some of the basic attitudes in the United States regarding women in the workplace have been especially slow to change. One longitudinal study from 1975 to 1983 found the attitudes of male MBA students toward women executives did not change that much over the eight year period, in spite of the fact that this period was marked by intensive efforts to enhance opportunities for women and the status of women.[10]

I N S I G H T   4–1

Conscience Crisis

In the Star Wars Era, Scientists Grow Warier About Jobs in Defense

Polling its 10,000 members last year, the Institute of Electrical and Electronics Engineers, a mainstream professional group, found that a third of them considered assignment to nonmilitary work an important factor when changing jobs. And a survey of 85 nuclear scientists at Sandia and Los Alamos National Laboratories found that a majority of them were deeply ambivalent about their work.

No Consensus

For most scientists, the struggle with conscience is a private one, unrevealed until a decision point is reached. Alfred Beebe, who worked four years at Hughes Aircraft Co. developing software for small tactical missiles, says that at first he could ignore the "human implications" of his work. But they intruded more and more often, and gradually the joy went out of his job.

When colleagues celebrated new Hughes contracts, "I just couldn't identify with the euphoria," the 41-year-old mathematician

and computer scientist recalls. "I often found I had a lot of trouble just getting through each day." He quit in 1983 for a university communications-research post.

Lockheed, along with other employers, has had to adjust to changing attitudes. When systems engineer William Cutler grew disenchanted with weapons work, Lockheed reluctantly transferred him from a defense project to a space-station job he wanted. He was lucky, however. Often, nonmilitary work isn't immediately available in the same company.

For some people, intracompany transfers or new jobs at new companies aren't enough. They get out of science and engineering altogether, as Joseph Roehrig did.

He was an engineer and a director of a small Louisville company working on nuclear-weapons contracts. Disturbed by what he was doing, he shifted to nondefense work but was still ambivalent. Now he runs the spousal-abuse center at the Louisville YWCA. On his wall is a plaque quoting Albert Einstein: "Try not to become a man of success, but rather a man of value."

Perhaps one of the reasons for this slow change is that attitudes are based on deep-seated beliefs and values. Let us explore values and beliefs to see how they form the foundation for attitudes.

VALUES AND BELIEFS: THE FOUNDATION FOR ATTITUDES

Values and beliefs are the fundamental concepts of individuals. More deeply ingrained than attitudes, they are the basis for attitude formation—and they are difficult to change. In addition, values are hard to see. A report on values by the American Management Association indicated that values are at the core of a personality, and that they are a powerful, *though silent,* force affecting behavior.[11]

Values, it seems, are so deep-seated that we can only infer them from people's behavior and their expressed attitudes. But values are a strong force in people. What may *appear* to be strange behavior in an employee can make sense if managers understand the values underlying that behavior. For example, company managers in various functional groups may have different values and hence react differently to a particular situation.[12] A better understanding of each other's values can help the departments work together.

Two basic frameworks can help us better understand values. First, Rokeach has divided values into two broad categories.[13] **Terminal values** relate to *ends* to be achieved. Examples of terminal values are: comfortable life, family security, self-respect, and sense of accomplishment. **Instrumental values** relate to *means* for achieving desired ends. Examples of instrumental values include: ambition, courage, honesty, and imagination. Terminal values reflect what a person is ultimately striving to achieve, whereas instrumental values reflect how the person gets there. For example, a person may want family security (a terminal value), and pursues it only through honest means (an instrumental value).

The second values perspective helps us to understand the fact that **values are learned.** It reflects how values that are related to organizational life vary across different cultures. Hofstede studied the work-related values of over 116,000 personnel in a large multinational firm operating in 40 countries.[14] Hofstede's research defined four basic value dimensions that can distinguish individuals in different countries.

First **power distance** is the degree to which a person feels there should be an unequal distribution of power in organizations. Managers in Sweden and Denmark, for example, feel the power distance should be smaller than what U.S. managers feel. But U.S. managers do not expect nearly as large a power distance as managers in Venezuela or Mexico.

Second, **uncertainty avoidance** is the degree to which a person feels that ambiguity and uncertainty should be avoided. Managers in the United States are not nearly so willing to deal with uncertainty as are managers in Ireland or Great Britain. But U.S. managers are more comfortable with uncertainty than managers in Japan.

Third, **individualism** is the degree to which a person feels the key resource for work and problem solving is the individual versus the group. Managers in the United States and Australia feel the focus should be on the individual. Managers in Venezuela and Colombia feel the focus should be on the group. Japan, interestingly enough, rates near the middle on Hofstede's individualism/collectivism scale.

Fourth, **masculinity** is the degree to which a person feels managers should be assertive, independent, and insensitive to feelings. It is unfortunate that Hofstede chose the term masculine (versus feminine) to describe this value dimension. Perhaps this reflects his Dutch heritage; but clearly, a term like **assertiveness** could just as easily have been chosen. Hofstede found that Japanese managers feel they should be assertive and strong, whereas managers from Sweden and Norway do not believe this is necessary. U.S. managers, along with those from Germany and Switzerland, scored near the middle of this scale but still fairly high on being assertive and independent.

This study by Hofstede clearly supports the idea that values are learned. The culture in which we grow up influences many of the values we develop. Other factors that have an influence but are more micro in nature are groups we belong to (such as labor versus management), past work experiences, and our families.

Ethics: A special case of values

In recent years, a focus on ethics in business has gained increasing attention, partly due to media coverage of a number of unethical actions. As shown in Insight 4–2, a 1987 cover story in *Time* magazine documented the apparent demise of ethics in both the public and private sector of the United States.

Ethics are standards of conduct that assess whether actions are right or wrong in a moral sense. They reflect a common moral code in a society. As such, ethical standards can vary, depending on the society. And ethical standards can change over time.

The article in *Time* suggests that the cult of personhood that originated in the "me generation" of the 1970s has created a more selfish view of ethics.[15] What this may reflect is a change in the priorities of instrumental values. More than ever, the end seems to justify the means, so long as it is legal or deemed all right by management. Indeed, when there are no laws (or vague laws) to cover a situation, it seems that anything goes. And employees often follow the dictates of managers even if they feel it is wrong. Naturally, such a view of ethics creates problems for many people.

Debates have often transpired over who is at fault for this state of frayed ethics. The point here is not to assess blame, but rather to understand the fact that values and ethics change. As Insight 4–3 (on page 128) suggests, ethics, like values, are influenced from many angles. And ethics are clearly more than laws.

Indeed, a recent book by Hosmer suggests that ethical dilemmas are going to occur more and more frequently in the future.[16] He asks such questions as: What do companies owe employees who are let go after 30 years of service? Is it right for management to cancel out a loyal distrib-

I N S I G H T 4-2

What's Wrong

Hypocrisy, Betrayal and Greed Unsettle the Nation's Soul

"*J*ust about every place you look, things are looking up. Life is better—America's back—and people have a sense of pride they never thought they'd feel again."
—Voice-over from 1984 Ronald Reagan TV commercial

*O*nce again it is morning in America. But this morning Wall Street financiers are nervously scanning the papers to see if their names have been linked to the insider-trading scandals. Presidential candidates are peeking through drawn curtains to make sure that reporters are not staking out their private lives. A congressional witness, deeply involved in the Reagan Administration's secret foreign policy, is huddling with his lawyers before facing inquisitors. A Washington lobbyist who once breakfasted regularly in the White House mess is brooding over his investigation by an independent counsel. In Quantico, Va., the Marines are preparing to court-martial one of their own. In Palm Springs, Calif., a husband-and-wife televangelist team, once the adored cyno-

sures of 500,000 faithful, are beginning another day of seclusion.

Such are the scenes of morning in the scandal-scarred spring of 1987. Lamentation is in the air, and clay feet litter the ground. A relentless procession of forlorn faces assaults the nation's moral equanimity, characters linked in the public mind not by any connection between their diverse dubious deeds but by the fact that each in his or her own way has somehow seemed to betray the public trust: Oliver North, Robert McFarlane, Michael Deaver, Ivan Boesky, Gary Hart, Clayton Lonetree, Jim and Tammy Bakker, maybe Edwin Meese, perhaps even the President. Their transgressions—some grievous and some petty—run the gamut of human failings, from weakness of will to moral laxity to hypocrisy to uncontrolled avarice. But taken collectively, the heedless lack of restraint in their behavior reveals something disturbing about the national character. America, which took such back-thumping pride in its spiritual renewal, finds itself wallowing in a moral morass. Ethics, often dismissed as a prissy Sunday School word, is now at the center of a new national debate. Put bluntly, has the mindless materialism of the '80s left in its wake a values vacuum?

utor just because it is cheaper to use other means? Is it proper to develop condominiums on land that has been a bird sanctuary? These are tough questions, the answers to which go beyond economic and legal analyses. They bring into play our ethics about what is right, proper, and fair.

Another recent book on ethics by noted authors Ken Blanchard and Norman Vincent Peale clarifies this issue and provides an ethics check to guide behavior.[17] The first question in their ethics check is: "Is it legal?" If the answer is no, an action is usually also unethical. However, there have been cases of civil disobedience where an action was illegal,

---

I N S I G H T 4–3

Business Schools Say Lack of Ethics Not Their Fault

"**Y**ou learn ethics at home," says Donald Jacobs, dean of the graduate business school at the University of Chicago.

Russell E. Palmer, dean of the Wharton Business School added, "If people think we can take a person 23 to 26 years old and within two years totally retool them, they're wrong. Putting the entire focus on business schools is ridiculous."

"Ethics and morality is a continuum of experience from the time you're born," he said. "Graduate school is part of the continuum, but it's only one piece. Whatever has happened to that person in their 30 to 40 years are the factors that have caused them to be what they are. We're a two-year piece of that."

Academics also consider the current focus on Levine, Boesky and other Wall Street figures who have pleaded guilty to crimes to be a red herring.

"Ethics—that's not Boesky," Jacobs says. "Boesky and Levine broke the law. We don't have to tell people not to break the law."

"People don't necessarily go to jail for poor ethics," said Robert K. Jaedicke, dean of the graduate school of business at Stanford University. "They go to jail for breaking laws. You shouldn't have to go to business school to learn you ought to do business within the law."

By Sallie Gaines, adapted from *Chicago Tribune*. Reprinted in *State Paper*, Columbia, S.C., May 29, 1987.

---

but deemed ethical. And, of course, something may certainly be legal but unethical. The second and third questions help sort things out: second, "Is it balanced and fair to all parties involved?" and third, "How will it make you feel about yourself?" To be truly ethical, an action must pass the test on all three questions. What Blanchard and Peale suggest is that effective managers implicitly follow this ethics check in determining their action in a given situation. This leads back to the fact that values, beliefs, and now ethics influence our attitudes and ultimately our behavior. Before turning to a discussion of personality, let us drop in on Louise of Home Computers and her husband Steve.

Home Computers Case

Steve worked for the same large computer company that Louise did originally. Steve had received a degree in computer science at his state's major university. He came from a very strict family. His parents always pressed him to do better work in school. And his professors in college figured Steve to be a bright student, but without much drive and ambition.

His personal attitude and self-concept was one of self-doubt when it came to the big challenges in life. In fact, Louise proposed marriage to Steve rather than the reverse.

Steve's first job was as a programmer with very little responsibility. As a new employee, he completed for the personnel office a self-assessment questionnaire. This was a standard practice of the company as a means of identifying talent and determining the proper channel of training and experience. On the basis of this questionnaire, Steve was identified as an introvert, a thinking type, a sensing type, and a judging type. Louise, on the other hand, was identified as an extrovert, a thinking type, an intuitive type, and a perceptive type.

The personnel department knew that Steve and Louise represented different personality types. But since the test results were not adequately explained to Louise and Steve, they did not think about them very long. Still, their personalities were different as a result of their unique past experiences.

Louise was the first child in her family, and she received a great deal of support and love in her early years. She was encouraged to experiment within clearly defined limits, and her many successes were rewarded. In school, she also encountered a great deal of success and gained a strong sense of identity. When she went to college, it was a first-rate school several hundred miles from home.

In contrast, Steve was the second child. His older brother had a learning disability that required a great deal of his parents' attention. Steve received varying degrees of guidance, and he was sometimes made to feel guilty for his brother's disability. Steve learned to doubt himself and to lack self-confidence. In school, he encountered numerous social and scholastic problems, though none were serious. Steve went to college at the state university in his hometown. Fortunately, the school had an excellent computer science program. Because Steve did well in his courses and seemed to gain in self-confidence, one of his professors recommended him for a job with a large computer company in nearby Phoenix.

Steve did a good job for the company, but he had trouble making friends at work. He had been working there for five years when Louise moved out from New York. The relationship between Steve and Louise was good for Steve. It began to change his attitude from one of distrust of people to one of trust. Steve gradually developed a capability both for achievement and for intimacy. After he and Louise were married and had a child, Steve was offered the chance for a better job in Washington, D.C. It was not without a great deal of thought and discussion that he accepted the transfer. His attitude toward himself had grown to be one of respect, and he had developed a desire to succeed in his career. During this same period, in his 20s and 30s, Steve also developed a sense of family and an attitude of wanting more than just a career.

On the other hand, Louise seemed to put her career before everything. She was very capable and jumped at chances to advance her career. Steve seemed to reflect more on his total life with his career only a part of it. But Louise is now having some doubts about where her life is headed. Is her personality gradually changing? Is Steve's? The work, family, and life stage forces operating now might result in a different score on the personality tests Steve and Louise took back in the early 1970s.

PERSONALITY: THE TOTAL PERSON

We can use the concept of personality to better understand Louise and Steve as total people. As discussed, personality is a vehicle to integrate perception, learning, values, and attitudes and thus to understand the total person. **Personality is an individual's total sense of self; it is an organizing force for the person's particular pattern of exhibited traits and behaviors.**[18] In essence, personality is the culmination to date of experiences and genetic influences. As such, it is a dynamic construct which can be influenced by things in an individual's personal life and by the organization through things like socialization. That is not to say, however, that personality is constantly flip-flopping from one type to another. The process of personality change is more evolutionary in nature. As with attitudes, a certain level of inertia is present.[19]

Aspects of personality

At this point, it is important to explore several aspects of personality. **First, personalities are based on the past and the present, since personality is largely determined through the processes of perception and learning. Second, personality is a result of growth and development.** Each of us is goal-oriented and is striving to live up to our capabilities. **Third, although personality is dynamic, it is characterized by internal consistency in our behaviors.** That is, we attempt to engage in actions which are compatible with our personality, and this consistency makes sense, given that personality is the total construct of a person.

In addition, there are several factors that influence the evolution of personality: group experiences, group roles, situations, physical properties, and mental abilities.[20] These factors are shown in Exhibit 4–3 and discussed below.

Physical properties and mental abilities are important factors because they reflect our capabilities. For example, if a person is very intelligent, he or she may develop a different self-concept of his or her achievement potential than someone who is less intelligent. But mental abilities vary

EXHIBIT 4–3

Determinants of Personality

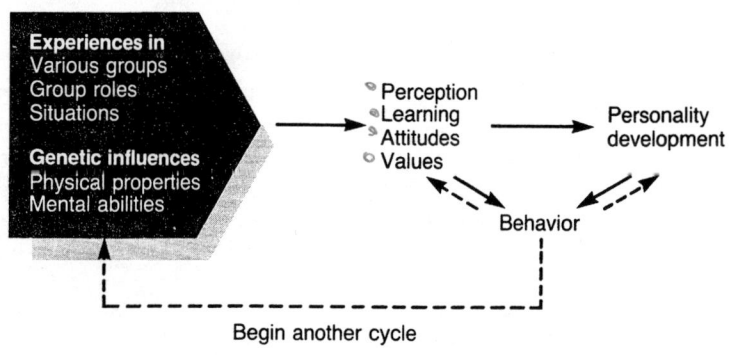

with age. They increase rapidly until about age 20; and they tend to continue increasing, though more gradually, as one's age increases.[21] Such things as accidents and illness can cause rather dramatic changes in mental abilities (and thus in personality).

A second factor affecting the formation and evolution of personality is membership in various groups. As we are exposed to a new group situation, we go through a socialization process that helps us fit into the group. And since we are members of different groups over time, our personalities are altered over time. Closely connected with group membership is the role we fill in each group. For example, Louise and Steve of the Home Computers case fill different roles at work than they do at home. Indeed, the family is another group which influences a person's personality. Birth order, family size, family education level, family economics, and other such factors influence who people are. Both family roles and work group roles, and the interaction between the two sets, help determine Louise's and Steve's personalities.

Finally, the situations to which we are exposed influence our personalities. We have already noted, in discussing values, the important role culture plays in our values. Likewise, culture heavily influences personality development. We have also discussed how the love and affection we receive during the first year of life heavily influence our basic trust of people. Such situational influences continue at work and throughout our personal lives. Probably one of the most dramatic examples of situational influences on personality occurs when we are placed in stressful situations. For example, the death of a loved one, getting married or divorced, the birth of a child, losing a job, and so forth are all stressful situations that may result in changes in our personalities.

Development of personality: Erikson's eight life stages

As a way of further understanding how personalities develop over a lifetime, let us explore Erikson's life stages.[22] Erikson identified eight stages of life that characterize the unending development of a person. He characterized each stage by a particular conflict that needs to be resolved successfully before a person can move to the next stage. However, these eight stages are not totally separate; and the crises are never fully resolved. Thus, movement between stages is developmental. Movement can even involve regression to earlier stages when traumatic events occur. Let us briefly consider each of the eight stages.

Stage one: infancy.   During the first year of life a person resolves the basic crisis of **trust versus mistrust.** An infant who is cared for in a loving and affectionate way learns to trust other people. Lack of love and affection results in mistrust. While neither result is carved in stone, this first year makes a serious imprint on a child that influences events for the remainder of life.

Stage two: early childhood.   In the second and third years of life, a child begins to assert independence. If the child is allowed to control those aspects of life that the child is capable of controlling, a sense of **autonomy** will develop. If the child encounters constant disapproval or inconsistent rule setting, a sense of **self-doubt and shame** is likely to develop.

Stage three: play age.   The four- and five-year-old seek to discover just how much they can do. If a child is encouraged to experiment and to achieve reasonable goals, he or she will develop a sense of **initiative.** If the child is blocked and made to feel incapable, he or she will develop a sense of **guilt and lack of self-confidence.** As Erikson points out, these first three stages are the most important crises a child must successfully resolve. Without such resolution, the child will not be prepared to face the future problems of development. And adults who have never re-solved these issues must be managed differently than those who have resolved them. Imagine managing someone who lacks trust, autonomy, an initiative compared to someone who has these qualities. It would be quite different.

Stage four: school age.   From ages 6 to 12, a child learns many new skills and develops social abilities. If a child experiences real progress at a rate compatible with his or her abilities, the child will develop a sense of **industry.** The reverse situation results in a sense of **inferiority.**

Stage five: adolescence.   The crisis of the teenage years is to gain a sense of **identity** rather than to become **confused** about who you are.

While undergoing rapid biological changes, the teenager is also trying to establish himself or herself as socially separate from the parents. The teenager, as discussed in Chapter 2, is also usually beginning the exploration stage of a career. Many events unfold simultaneously during these years. The autonomy, initiative, and industry developed in earlier stages are very important in helping the teenager successfully resolve this crisis and prepare for adulthood. Judging from the facts presented in the case of Steve and Louise, probably Steve's sense of identity was not as clear and positive as Louise's as they entered adulthood.

Stage six: young adulthood. The young adult (20s and 30s) faces the crisis of **intimacy versus isolation.** The sense of identity developed during the teenage years allows the young adult to begin developing deep and lasting relationships. Simultaneously, though, the young adult is usually establishing himself or herself in a career and beginning advancement (as discussed in Chapter 2). Thus, it is easy for a person's achievement orientation to overshadow the need for people and intimate relationships, resulting in isolation. In the Home Computers case, we saw how Steve learned intimacy from Louise and how Louise's ability for intimacy may be influenced by her career drives. Certainly, she faces a choice between the two.

Stage seven: adulthood. During their 40s and 50s, adults face the crisis of **generativity versus self-absorption.** Self-absorbed persons never develop an ability to look beyond themselves. They may become absorbed in career advancement and maintenance; and they may never learn to have concern for future generations, the welfare of organizations to which they belong, or the welfare of society as a whole. Generative people see the world as much bigger than themselves. Productivity in work or child rearing or societal advancement become important to them. Through innovation and creativity, they begin to exert influence that benefits their organization. In the Home Computers case, it appears that Steve is developing this sense of generativity. The issue is still open for Louise.

Stage eight: later life. In their 60s and beyond, people who have followed a healthy development of personality in previous stages reach a level of **integrity,** while the alternative is **disgust with one's life.** The adult of integrity has gained a sense of wisdom and perspective that can truly help guide future generations. The career stage of influence and the innovative and creative influence on organizations to which a person belongs go along with the adult of integrity.

The stages of life and the corresponding development of personality are intertwined with the stages of one's career and the stages of family life. All of these influences help determine and alter people's personalities. Insight 4–4 describes the changes in one woman's life that may have a bearing on her personality. Is Mrs. Kurtzig's personality different now than before she started ASK Computer Systems, Inc.?

To gain a perspective on personality, let us explore several different facets of personality. First, we will look at locus of control; then Machiavellianism; then Type A or Type B; and finally, Jung's Personality Theory.

Locus of control

Whether people feel in control of the events that affect their lives or whether they feel that other factors like fate are in control depends on their **locus of control**.[23] *Internals* are people who believe they are in control of their own destiny. *Externals* believe that much of what happens to them is controlled by outside forces, such as their boss, their luck, and their circumstances. Rotter has developed an inventory designed to assess whether a person has an internal or external locus of control. Take a moment now to complete this inventory, as reproduced at the end of this chapter. Is your locus of control internal or external? From the information provided in the Home Computers case, probably Steve is more of an internal than Louise, but then maybe they should take the inventory, too.

p. 157

Research has shown that internals differ from externals with regard to several important organizational issues.[24] For example, with regard to job satisfaction, internals tend to be more satisfied. Internals make more attempts to influence and persuade others. Internals exhibit greater self-control. Externals respond more easily to leadership attempts by others. Externals are more comfortable with directive leadership. Of course, locus of control is not the only element of an individual's personality.

Machiavellianism

In the 16th century, Niccoló Machiavelli, an Italian philosopher, wrote *The Prince*.[25] He wrote about some rather ruthless ways to acquire and use power. For example, he noted, "It is far better to be feared than loved if you cannot be both." In essence, Machiavelli wrote about ways to manipulate other people. And some more recent books, such as Michael Korda's *Power! How to Get It, How to Use It,* suggest that many people are still drawn to a philosophy of how to manipulate others.[26]

p. 160

To help people understand their tendency to want to manipulate others, psychologists have created Machiavellianism scales. Take a few moments to honestly complete the scale at the end of this chapter. Remember, if you want to know yourself, you need to be honest with yourself.

Some of the characteristics which distinguish high Machs are as follows.[27] High Machs tend to take control, especially in loosely structured situations; indeed, they prefer such situations. Low Machs, on the other hand, like and respond well to structure. High Machs tend to be more logical, rational, and pragmatic than low Machs. High Machs are often skilled at influence and coalition building. Indeed, there is probably at least a little Machiavellianisim in all good leaders. It would be easy to imagine some Machiavellian tendencies for Louise of the Home Computers Company case as well as more celebrated leaders like Lee Iaccoca of Chrysler Corporation.

Type A or Type B

Are you the kind of person who is hard-driving, impatient, aggressive, and super-competitive? Or are you more easygoing, sociable, laid-back, and noncompetitive? Researchers call the former a Type A personality, and the latter Type B.[28] These differences were first noted in distinguishing people who had premature heart disease from those who did not. Exhibit 4–4 (on page 136) summarizes the characteristics of the Type A personality. About 40 percent of the population are Type A, while 60 percent are Type B.[29] Do these Type A characteristics describe you? Or are you just the opposite—hence a Type B? What about Steve and Louise in the Home Computers case?

Type A people tend to be very productive and work very hard. Some might say these people are workaholics. Type As are always juggling several balls in the air and pushing themselves to get things done. But

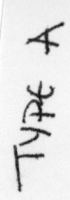

EXHIBIT 4–4

Characteristics of the Type A Behavior Pattern

1. Eagerness to undertake all activities in a spirit of competition
2. Compulsion to win
3. Inclination to dominate in social as well as in business situations
4. Easily aroused irritability
5. Fixed and staunchly defended positions on various political, economic, and sociological issues
6. Failure to be elated at the success of others
7. Self-awareness of impatience
8. Keeps hectic pace of activities
9. Difficulty in sitting and doing nothing
10. Intense dislike of waiting in line
11. Fast walking, fast eating and unwillingness to dawdle at the table after meals
12. Habitual substitution of numbers as metaphors and nouns
13. Polyphasic thought and actions; i.e., doing two or more things at once (such as "doubling-up" a conversation—thinking about or doing something else while "listening" to someone on the phone, eating or drinking while driving, reading or watching TV while eating)

Adapted from M. Friedman and D. Ulmer, *Treating Type A Behavior and Your Heart* (New York: Alfred A. Knopf, 1984); used with permission; all rights reserved.

there is also a more negative side to Type A people at work. They tend to be impatient with others; they often are not good team players; they are more irritable; and they may exercise poor judgment. It appears that Type A people may be better at tasks that can be done alone and where there is great time pressure. Type B people do better on complex tasks involving judgment, accuracy rather than speed, and teamwork.

These three aspects of personality (locus of control, Machiavellianism, Type A/B) can begin to give people a picture of themselves and others. But a more complete theory of personality has been provided by Carl Jung.[30] There are four dimensions to his theory.

JUNG'S PERSONALITY THEORY

In considering Jung's theory, it is important to note that it has become very popular in business circles in recent years. The Myers–Briggs Type Indicator, developed to assess personality using Jung's theory, is commercially available.[31] It was given to some 1.5 million people in 1986 and was used by such companies as AT&T, GE, 3M, and Exxon.[32] The inventory results are used in a variety of ways, most notably to improve communications and to build communications and to build teams. As we explore the four dimensions of the theory, take time to seriously consider yourself in relation to each dimension. You will learn some interesting things about yourself. And by discussing and sharing your results with others, you will begin learning how to use these ideas to make you a better team member and a better manager.

Jung made three basic assumptions in his theory. First, **Jung asserted that our personalities are developmental in that they are influenced by our past and by our hopes for the future.** Second, he viewed people optimistically in assuming that **all people have the potential for growth and change.** And third, Jung suggested that **personality is the totality of a person's interacting subsystems.** In particular, he discussed the conscious mind, the subconscious mind, emotional orientations, problem-solving styles, and general attitudes. The last three subsystems can help people determine their personality along four dimensions.

Emotional orientations

The two basic orientations of people are extroversion and introversion. While few people are purely one or the other, one orientation will tend to dominate. Exhibit 4–5 (on page 138) indicates that **introverts are quiet people who like to work alone and stay to themselves. They tend to be comfortable with themselves. On the other hand, extroverts like action and interaction with people. They do not mind interruptions, and they communicate freely.** Based on these definitions, are you an introvert or an extrovert? It is important to point out that neither orientation is better. Each has its strengths and weaknesses. The point is that managers should gain an understanding of themselves and learn how understanding others can make them better managers. For example, managers often have to draw out an introverted person while quieting down an extroverted employee.

Problem-solving styles

Jung identified two basic steps in problem solving: collecting information and making a decision. Collecting data for problem solving occurs along a continuum from **sensing** to **intuition**. Exhibit 4–6 (on page 139) gives details of these two extremes. As the figure indicates, **sensing types like to approach a problem in a step-by-step organized way. They work steadily and patiently with details. Intuitive types work in bursts and are impatient with details; however, they can be very patient with complicated situations.** Are you mainly a sensing or an intuitive type?

Which type is better—sensing or intuitive? Neither; the world needs both. Intuitives need sensing types to bring up facts, attend to details, and maintain a sense of realism. Sensing types need intuitives to bring

EXHIBIT 4–5

Extroverts versus Introverts: Characteristics of Each

Extroverts	Introverts
Like variety and action.	Like quiet for concentration.
Tend to work faster, dislike complicated procedures.	Tend to be careful with details, dislike sweeping statements.
Are often good at greeting people.	Have trouble remembering names and faces.
Are often impatient with long slow jobs.	Tend not to mind working on one project for a long time uninterruptedly.
Are interested in the results of their job, in getting it done and in how other people do it.	Are interested in the idea behind their job.
Often do not mind interruption of answering the telephone.	Dislike telephone intrusions and interruptions.
Often act quickly, sometimes without thinking.	Like to think a lot before they act, sometimes without acting.
Like to have people around.	Work contentedly alone.
Usually communicate freely.	Have some problems communicating.

up new possibilities, generate enthusiasm, and tackle difficulties with zest. Which type would a person want to prepare his or her income tax statement? What about to do a painting for a person's home?

In terms of making a decision, the continuum ranges from **thinking** to **feeling** types. Exhibit 4–7 (on page 140) describes **the thinking type as one who does not show a lot of emotion, who can put things into a logical order, and who can be firm and fair. The feeling type is very aware of other people, dislikes telling people unpleasant things, and prefers harmony among people.** Which type are you?

As with the sensing and intuitive types, the thinking and feeling types each have strengths and weaknesses. Feeling types need thinkers to analyze, organize, and help make the tough decisions. On the other hand, thinkers need feeling types to conciliate, sell, and be aware of how others might accept the decision. As an example of how these types can complement each other, consider the man who was having an operation by a very well-respected and competent surgeon. He had to do a very thorough analysis and make tough decisions about the surgery (thinking type). But the surgeon was not very personable. To compensate, he had an assistant who met with the patient's family to deal with their concerns and emotions (feeling type). They made a very good team.

The interaction of these two aspects of problem solving results in four problem-solving types. (1) The **sensing-feeling person** likes to collect data in an orderly way and make decisions that take into account the

EXHIBIT 4–6

Sensing Types versus Intuitive Types: Characteristics of Each

Sensing Types	Intuitive Types
Dislike new problems unless there are standard ways to solve them.	Like solving new problems.
Like an established way of doing things.	Dislike doing the same thing repeatedly.
Enjoy using skills already learned more than learning new ones.	Enjoy learning a new skill more than using it.
Work more steadily, with realistic idea of how long it will take.	Work in bursts of energy powered by enthusiasm, with slack periods in between.
Usually reach a conclusion step by step.	Reach a conclusion quickly.
Are patient with routine details.	Are impatient with routine details.
Are impatient when the details get complicated.	Are patient with complicated situations.
Are not often inspired, and rarely trust the inspiration when they are.	Follow their inspirations, good or bad.
Seldom make errors of fact.	Frequently make errors of fact.
Tend to be good at precise work.	Dislike taking time for precision.

needs of people. This person is very concerned with high-quality decisions that people will accept and implement. (2) The **intuitive-feeling person** is equally concerned with the people side of decisions, but the focus is on new ideas which are often broad in scope and lacking in details. (3) **Sensing-thinkers** emphasize details and the quality of a decision. They are not as concerned with the people aspect of an organization as with a technically sound decision. And (4) **intuitive-thinking types** like to tackle new and innovative problems, but make decisions primarily on technical terms. They tend to be good planners, but not so good at implementing.

While few people are any of these pure types, we all have dominant styles. We need to recognize the strengths and weaknesses of our dominant style and what we can do to compensate for our weaknesses (as in the example of the surgeon). What is your dominant problem-solving style? What are the dominant styles of people with whom you work?

General attitudes

The last personality subsystem Jung identified was the general attitude toward work, namely **judging** or **perceptive**. As Exhibit 4–8 (on page 141) shows, **judging types like to follow a plan, like to make decisions, and want only the essentials for their work. On the other hand, perceptive types adapt well to change, want to know all about a job, and may get overcommitted.** Which type are you?

EXHIBIT 4–7

Thinking Types versus Feeling Types: Characteristics of Each

Thinking Types	Feeling Types
Do not show emotion readily and are often uncomfortable dealing with people's feelings.	Tend to be very aware of other people and their feelings.
May hurt people's feelings without knowing it.	Enjoy pleasing people, even in unimportant things.
Like analysis and putting things into logical order; can get along without harmony.	Like harmony. Efficiency may be badly disturbed by office feuds.
Tend to decide impersonally, sometimes paying insufficient attention to people's wishes.	Often let decisions be influenced by their own or other people's personal likes and wishes.
Need to be treated fairly.	Need occasional praise.
Are able to reprimand people or fire them when necessary.	Dislike telling people unpleasant things.
Are more analytically oriented; respond more easily to people's thoughts.	Are more people-oriented; respond more easily to people's values.
Tend to be firm-minded.	Tend to be sympathetic.

The interaction of these four dimensions yields a dominant personality type—1 of 16. Based on your assessments of each of the four dimensions shown in Exhibits 4–5 to 4–8, you can locate your personality type in Exhibit 4–9 (on page 142).

I = introvert	S = sensing
E = extrovert	N = intuitive
(from Exhibit 4–5)	(from Exhibit 4–6)
T = thinking	J = judging
F = feeling	P = perceptive
(from Exhibit 4–7)	(from Exhibit 4–8)

You should be able to select four of the eight letters to describe yourself; for example, ISTP or ENFJ. Then, in Exhibit 4–9, locate your four-letter combination to find your personality type and its description.

It is important to recognize that each dimension of personality is a continuum, and the figures help identify only a dominant personality style. It is also important to recognize that there is no ideal personality type for managers. While some business schools have focused heavily on developing sensing and thinking skills, it is clear that managers must also be intuitive and feeling if they are to be effective in more ambiguous situations.[33] And it is important to realize that this is a snapshot of an

EXHIBIT 4–8

Judging Types versus Perceptive Types: Characteristics of Each

Judging Types	Perceptive Types
Work best when they can plan their work and follow the plan.	Adapt well to changing situations.
Like to get things settled and finished.	Do not mind leaving things open for alterations.
May decide things too quickly.	May have trouble making decisions.
May dislike to interrupt the project they are on for a more urgent one.	May start too many projects and have difficulty finishing them.
May not notice new things that need to be done.	May postpone unpleasant jobs.
Want only the essentials needed to begin their work.	Want to know all about a new job.
Tend to be satisfied once they reach a judgment on a thing, situation, or person.	Tend to be curious and welcome new information on a thing, situation, or person.

individual's personality. Various factors in our lives cause the evolution of our personalities. We have already discussed some of these in exploring how a personality develops (genetics, family situation, groups, life experiences). In closing the chapter we will discuss one other factor—namely socialization. But first, let us look at the personality types of Steve and Louise.

Home Computers Case

Steve and Louise (continued)

Steve's scores on the personality questionnaire indicated that he was an introvert, a sensing type, a thinking type, and a judging type. Overall, then, Steve was an ISTJ personality type. Steve was told he was serious, quiet, and earned success through concentration and thoroughness. He was the type to see that everything was well organized and to take responsibility (see further description in Exhibit 4–9).

Louise, on the other hand, was an extrovert, an intuitive type, a thinking type, and a perceptive type. Overall, then, Louise was an ENTP personality type. She was told she was quick, ingenious, and good at many things. She was resourceful in solving new problems, but might neglect routine assignments (see further description in Exhibit 4–9).

FIGURE 4–9

Sixteen Personality Types Based on Jung's Four Dimensions

	Sensing Types	
	With Thinking	**With Feeling**
Introverts / Judging	**ISTJ** Serious, quiet, earn success by concentration and thoroughness. Practical, orderly, matter-of-fact, logical, realistic and dependable. See to it that everything is well organized. Take responsibility. Make up their own minds as to what should be accomplished and work toward it steadily, regardless of protests or distractions. Live their outer life more with thinking, inner more with sensing.	**ISFJ** Quiet, friendly, responsible and conscientious. Work devotedly to meet their obligations and serve their friends and school. Thorough, painstaking, accurate. May need time to master technical subjects, as their interests are not often technical. Patient with detail and routine. Loyal, considerate, concerned with how other people feel. Live their outer life more with feeling, inner more with sensing.
Introverts / Perceptive	**ISTP** Cool onlookers, quiet, reserved, observing and analyzing life with detached curiosity and unexpected flashes of original humor. Usually interested in impersonal principles, cause and effect, or how and why mechanical things work. Exert themselves no more than they think necessary, because any waste of energy would be inefficient. Live their outer life more with sensing, inner more with thinking.	**ISFP** Retiring, quietly friendly, sensitive, modest about their abilities. Shun disagreements, do not force their opinions or values on others. Usually do not care to lead but are often loyal followers. May be rather relaxed about assignments or getting things done, because they enjoy the present moment and do not want to spoil it by undue haste or exertion. Live their outer life more with sensing, inner more with feeling.
Extroverts / Perceptive	**ESTP** Matter-of-fact, do not worry or hurry, enjoy whatever comes along. Tend to like mechanical things and sports, with friends on the side. May be a bit blunt or insensitive. Can do math or science when they see the need. Dislike long explanations. Are best with real things that can be worked, handled, taken apart or put back together. Live their outer life more with sensing, inner more with thinking.	**ESFP** Outgoing, easygoing, accepting, friendly, fond of a good time. Like sports and making things. Know what's going on and join in eagerly. Find remembering facts easier than mastering theories. Are best in situations that need sound common sense and practical ability with people as well as with things. Live their outer life more with sensing, inner more with feeling.
Extroverts / Judging	**ESTJ** Practical realists, matter-of-fact, with a natural head for business or mechanics. Not interested in subjects they see no use for, but can apply themselves when necessary. Like to organize and run activities. Tend to run things well, especially if they remember to consider other people's feelings and points of view when making their decisions. Live their outer life more with thinking, inner more with sensing.	**ESFJ** Warm-hearted, talkative, popular, conscientious, born cooperators, active committee members. Always doing something nice for someone. Work best with plenty of encouragement and praise. Little interest in abstract thinking or technical subjects. Main interest is in things that directly and visibly affect people's lives. Live their outer life more with feeling, inner more with sensing.

	Intuitives	
	With Feeling	**With Thinking**
Introverts — Judging	**INFJ** Succeed by perseverance, originality and desire to do whatever is needed or wanted. Put their best efforts into their work. Quietly forceful, conscientious, concerned for others. Respected for their firm principles. Likely to be honored and followed for their clear convictions as to how best to serve the common good. Live their outer life more with feeling, inner more with intuition.	**INTJ** Have original minds and great drive which they use only for their own purposes. In fields that appeal to them they have a fine power to organize a job and carry it through with or without help. Skeptical, critical, independent, determined, often stubborn. Must learn to yield less important points in order to win the most important. Live their outer life more with thinking, inner more with intuition.
Introverts — Perceptive	**INFP** Full of enthusiasms and loyalties, but seldom talk of these until they know you well. Care about learning, ideas, language, and independent projects of their own. Apt to be on yearbook staff, perhaps as editor. Tend to undertake too much, then somehow get it done. Friendly, but often too absorbed in what they are doing to be sociable or notice much. Live their outer life more with intuition, inner more with feeling.	**INTP** Quiet, reserved, brilliant in exams, especially in theoretical or scientific subjects. Logical to the point of hair-splitting. Interested mainly in ideas, with little liking for parties or small talk. Tend to have very sharply defined interests. Need to choose careers where some strong interest of theirs can be used and useful. Live their outer live more with intuition, inner more with thinking.
Extroverts — Perceptive	**ENFP** Warmly enthusiastic, high-spirited, ingenious, imaginative. Able to do almost anything that interests them. Quick with a solution for any difficulty and ready to help anyone with a problem. Often rely on their ability to improvise instead of preparing in advance. Can always find compelling reasons for whatever they want. Live their outer life more with intuition, inner more with feeling.	**ENTP** Quick, ingenious, good at many things. Stimulating company, alert and outspoken, argue for fun on either side of a question. Resourceful in solving new and challenging problems, but may neglect routine assignments. Turn to one new interest after another. Can always find logical reasons for whatever they want. Live their outer life more with intuition, inner more with thinking.
Extroverts — Judging	**ENFJ** Responsive and responsible. Feel real concern for what others think and want, and try to handle things with due regard for other people's feelings. Can present a proposal or lead a group discussion with ease and tact. Sociable, popular, active in school affairs, but put time enough on their studies to do good work. Live their outer life more with feeling, inner more with intuition.	**ENTJ** Hearty, frank, able in studies, leaders in activities. Usually good in anything that requires reasoning and intelligent talk, such as public speaking. Are well-informed and keep adding to their fund of knowledge. May sometimes be more positive and confident than their experience in an area warrants. Live their outer life more with thinking, inner more with intuition.

Source: Reproduced by special permission of the Publisher, Consulting Psychologists Press, Inc., Palo Alto, CA 94306, from *Introduction to Type* by Isabel Briggs Myers. Copyright 1980. Further reproduction is prohibited without the Publisher's consent.

Note: A questionnaire to assess these 16 types, called the Myers-Briggs Type Indicator, is available for purchase from Consulting Psychologists Press, Inc.

If you have not already done so, you should now make a general assessment of your personality type using Exhibit 4–9. Again, it is important to recognize that each personality type has its strengths and weaknesses. Managers are more effective when they know the pluses and minuses of their personality and learn to utilize their strengths and to compensate for their weaknesses. And when managers know the personality types of their subordinates, peers, and superiors, they will be in a better position to motivate and lead them, as we will discuss in later chapters.

Before moving on to discuss one of the organizational factors that can change a personality, we need to make one point about the personality types we have just interpreted. Steve and Louise (and we, too) were subject to perceptual bias in their assessments. As mentioned in Chapter 3, the perception process is error-prone; and this problem applies to self-perception as well as to perception of others. We must understand that the way we see ourselves may not be the way others see us. And others will respond to us in terms of how they see us—not how we see ourselves. To gain some insight into your own bias, you might ask someone else to assess you on the four personality dimensions in Exhibits 4–5 to 4–8 and then compare the assessments. Such feedback and sharing is an excellent vehicle for gaining a better understanding of ourselves, as we explored in discussing the Johari Window.

SOCIALIZATION'S INFLUENCE ON PERSONALITY, VALUES, AND ATTITUDES

In closing this chapter, think about the interplay between people and an organization. As a major factor in people's lives, organizations to which they belong and where they work can have significant impact on people's personality, values, and attitudes. One primary mechanism for this is the socialization process briefly discussed in Chapters 1 and 2. **Socialization is the process by which an individual is assimilated into and gains loyalty and commitment to an organization.** Through this process, a person learns the goals of the organization, the preferred means to achieve those goals, an employee's responsibilities, and accepted ways of behaving in the organization. In addition, the person learns the organization's attitudes and values. Thus, it should be clear that socialization is a learning process, as described in Chapter 3. And as the person becomes socialized in the organization, there is also a tendency to adopt the attitudes and values of the organization. Herein lies the potential impact of the organization on the personality, values, and attitudes of an individual.

Socialization from an organizational perspective

As a way of exploring the impact of socialization on personality, values, and attitudes, let us delve more deeply into this process of change. From the organization's point of view, there is a need to develop the commitment of its employees. Of course, there are many ways this socialization can occur. Some organizations have very formal and even severe socialization mechanisms. For example, the Marine Corps' approach is to tear down the person who enters basic training and build back the kind of person they want. Other organizations, such as Digital Equipment Corporation, use a more informal and drawn-out process. That is, gradual experience on the job reveals the company expectations to each new employee. Insight 4–5 (on page 16) illustrates how IBM goes about the socialization process. Could this change you if you worked for IBM? Indeed, your personality, values, and attitudes could be affected as you attempted to achieve consistency between your attitudes and values and those of IBM.

Imagine a new employee in a large American business, for example— like Louise in her first job—at a large computer company. As a new employee, the individual will be exposed to various direct methods of socialization, such as orientation programs, employee handbooks, training programs, and assignments to particular work experiences. In addition, a number of informal mechanisms will be working simultaneously, such as the influence of coworkers, supervisors, and subordinates. Socialization, then, is not a completely planned and controlled process. **Many factors dictate the amount of influence the socialization process has—not the least of which is the individual's background and existing personality.** There are also stages associated with the process.

Stages of socialization

Steers identifies three basic stages of socialization.[34] First is the **prearrival stage.** Individuals develop preconceived notions about an organization based on previous education, work experiences, and contacts with organization members. For example, a person may already know that a company expects hard work and efficiency from its employees. That person is thus already on his or her way to being socialized, assuming the perceptions are correct.

The second stage is the **encounter with the organization.** A person's initial orientation, training, and experiences with other employees who exhibit the accepted attitudes in the organization all influence and change the person.

The final stage is the **change of the person and acquisition of the new attitudes and values.** As a person works in a company, he or she gradually learns what is expected and begins to develop a new personality that is consistent with the organization—assuming the person

I N S I G H T 4–5

Life at IBM: Rules and Discipline, Goals and Praise Shape IBMers' Taut World

When Thomas J. Watson Sr. died in 1956, some might have thought the IBM spirit of the stiff white collar was destined to die with him. But indications are that the founder's legacy of decorum to International Business Machines Corp. still burns bright. Consider the way an IBM man on a witness stand in San Francisco the other day replied when questioned about an after-hours encounter with a competitor:

Q: "All of you were in the hot tub with the Qyx district manager?"

A: "The party adjourned to a hot tub, yes. Fully clothed, I might add."

That an IBMer invited to a California hot tub should fear that propriety demanded a swimsuit wouldn't surprise many people who have ever worked for the giant company. For, besides its great success with computers, IBM has a reputation in the corporate world for another standout trait: an almost proprietary concern with its employee's behavior, appearance and attitudes.

What this means to employees is a lot of rules. And these rules, from broad, unwritten ones calling for "tasteful" dress to specific ones setting salesmen's quotas, draw their force at IBM from another legacy of the founder: the value placed on loyalty. Mr. Watson believed that joining IBM was an act calling for absolute fidelity to the company in matters big and small.

Esprit de Corps

And just in case an IBM employee isn't a self-starter in the loyalty department, the company has a training regimen geared to instilling it. In brief, this consists of supervising new trainees closely, grading them, repeatedly setting new goals for them, and rewarding them amply for achievement. Suffused in work and pressure to perform, employees often develop a camaraderie, an esprit de corps.

What it all amounts to is a kind of IBM culture, a set of attitudes and approaches shared to a greater or lesser degree by IBMers everywhere. This culture, as gleaned from talks with former as well as current employees, is so pervasive that, as one nine-year (former) employee puts it, leaving the company "was like emigrating."

By Susan Chace, *The Wall Street Journal*, April 8, 1982. Reprinted by permission of *The Wall Street Journal*, © Dow Jones & Company, Inc., 1982. All rights reserved.

stays a member for a sustained period of time. To truly become a member of an organization, a person must be transformed, if only slightly and, usually, subtly. Otherwise, the employee or the organization may decide that it is better for the employee to move along.

It is also important to note that **the socialization process is not limited to the entry point in an organization. Rather, it is a continuous process throughout a career path.** Two reasons are primary for this continuation.

First, as discussed in Chapter 2, socialization occurs every time employees make a move in an organization. As people move vertically up the organization's hierarchy, they encounter different norms, values, and attitudes. As at the entry stage, employees must assimilate these new factors if they are to be successful, and the potential is there for an alteration in their personality. For example, at lower levels of the organization, the norm may be to make decisions based on thinking, rational processes, and use of technical skill. At higher levels, feeling, intuition, and conceptual skill may be more valued. People must make the same shift if they are to succeed. The same process will occur as employees move laterally from one function to another and as they move radially toward greater or lesser influence in the organization.

The second reason that socialization continues throughout a career is that the organization itself may change. Economic conditions, competition, and technological advances, to name only a few, can cause an organization to change its basic orientation. The resulting adaptation will bring new forces to bear on each organization member—forces which may alter personalities.

Socialization from the individual perspective

There is, of course, another side to the issue of socialization. Each individual exerts influence on his or her own socialization. Obviously, people respond to situational and organizational forces for socialization based on their own perceptions of the forces and on unique past experiences. As discussed in Chapter 1, people enter organizations as used products. They are a product of their past—and there have been many years of past before a person enters a full-time job. The works by Erikson and White emphasize the importance of the past in establishing one's personality.[35]

The influence that a person exerts on his or her own socialization is really an influence on the organization itself. Steers refers to **this process of a person trying to shape an organization to fit his or her own needs as individualization.**[36] Schein calls it innovation.[37] The point is that an individual's current personality exerts an influence on what his or her personality will be in the future. Also, people are proactive creatures, exerting influence on their surroundings, as well as being influenced by the surroundings.

The Schein socialization model

Schein identified three ways in which individuals respond to the socialization forces of the organization and thus exert influence on their own personalities.[38] How would a person exert influence on an organization he or she had just joined? Schein suggests that one approach is **rebellion.** The new employee could attempt to fight the organization. The result might be dismissal, or change in the organization, or change in the person (regardless of whether the individual wins or loses). If the employee loses, he or she moves closer to what the organization desires; if the employee wins, his or her existing personality will probably be strengthened. A second alternative is **creative individualism,** where an employee accepts the organization's values and attitudes that are pivotal, but rejects the others. The employee uses a combination of personal and organizational values in relating to the organization. For example, he or she may accept the value of responding to the customer as if the customer is always right, while rejecting the idea that he or she must come to the Christmas party every year. Usually this compromise works well unless the person or the organization is too rigid. Finally, a person could simply **conform** to the organizational forces and exert very little influence on the organization.

Thus, socialization is a process that exerts influence toward changing a personality. But previous socialization, learning, and attitude formation create forces that operate to maintain personality as a consistent type. Finally, a perceptual process filters socialization forces in an attempt to maintain consistency between people's surroundings and their self-concept. The result depends on the strength of these forces, but one thing is clear: people can be sure that their personality, values, and attitudes will continue to develop and evolve over time.

CHAPTER HIGHLIGHTS

The purpose of this chapter has been to integrate the concepts of perception, learning, attitudes, values, and beliefs through the concept of personality.

First, the text explored the Johari Window as a way of seeing who we are. People may see themselves as others see them (the open area); people may have blind spots; they may have hidden areas; and they may have things that are unknown both to them and to others. **It is desirable to have a large open area, and feedback and sharing are two ways to expand this area. In addition, we mentioned people should be open to new experiences as a third way to expand the open area.**

The text then looked at the process of attitude formation as an extension of the processes of perception and learning. Attitudes are opinions about things. Beliefs are closely related and represent our perceptions about relationships between things. And values represent deep-seated standards by which people evaluate their world.

We learned about **terminal** and **instrumental** values and something about the cultural impact on values. We explored Hofstede's value dimensions of: (1) **power distance,** (2) **uncertainty avoidance,** (3) **individualism,** and (4) **masculinity** (which we preferred to call assertiveness).

To help us better understand values, the text also took a look at the emerging issues of **ethics—those moral standards of conduct.** We discussed some of the ethical issues of today and an ethics check from a book by Blanchard and Peale.

In further exploring attitudes, we discussed how attitudes evolve. **The past plays an important role in the development of attitudes, beliefs, and values.** And people's attitudes and values tend to be in line with their behavior. Otherwise, people experience **cognitive dissonance,** which they will move to reduce either by attitude or behavior change.

Through the Home Computers case example of Steve and Louise, we began to explore the integrating concept of personality. **Personality is the culmination to date of a person's experiences and genetic influences.** Personality is determined by past experiences, growth, and development. Personality is dynamic, but it is characterized by internal consistency in people's behaviors. We looked at several **factors that determine personality: physical properties, membership in various groups, roles played in the groups, and exposure to various situations.**

The chapter moved on to discuss Erikson's eight stages of personality development. In so doing, the text reemphasized the importance of the first few years (stages 1 and 2) of life in establishing a base and direction for an individual's personality. Successful resolution of the crises of previous stages is essential to normal development at later stages.

During stages 3 to 5, people gain a sense of initiative, industry, and overall sense of identity. A positive identity is very important as a person enters adulthood, because he or she must deal simultaneously with important career and perhaps family stages. At this time, the issue of intimacy becomes paramount, but the development of personality does not stop here. Erikson suggests that we still have the crises of generativity versus self-absorption and integrity versus disgust with life, while we simultaneously engage in the development of a career and movement through family stages.

To provide some concreteness to the concept of personality, the text explored several aspects of personality. **Locus of control** refers to our tendency to be internally or externally oriented. **Machiavellianism** refers to our tendency to want to manipulate others. **Type A or B** refers to our tendency to be workaholics. Since these three concepts are only pieces of personality, the text then turned to Jung's Personality Theory, which has become increasingly popular in the 1980s.

Jung's theory was discussed via its four dimensions. **Emotional orientations were defined as extroversion or introversion. Problem-solving styles were defined along two dimensions: sensing or intuitive, and thinking or feeling. Finally, general attitudes were defined as judging or perceptive.** Your assessment of these four dimensions then identified you as 1 of 16 personality types, at least at present and as you see yourself.

Finally, we turned to one aspect of organizational life that directly alters our personalities, values, and attitudes: **socialization.** As we anticipate and encounter a new organization or a new part of an organization (due to transfer or promotion), we encounter forces that try to shape us to better fit the new situation. **Through direct and indirect means, the organization acts to socialize us. At the same time, we exert forces that influence our own socialization,** not the least of which is our previously developed personality. We try to make the situation fit us the way we are. Depending on the strength of these forces, our personalities are altered in various directions; but it is certain that they are altered in some direction to some extent.

This chapter has reemphasized the fact that personality is the integration of values and attitudes that occurs through the perception and learning processes. As such, **personality is developed from previous experiences, and a person's existing personality influences the next cycle through perception, learning, attitude, and value formation.** Socialization is not the only force that alters personality, but it is an extremely important factor for managers to understand in order to be effective, since it relates directly to a work organization.

REVIEW QUESTIONS

1. What is the Johari Window, and why is it a useful way to look at our own personalities?
2. How are beliefs and attitudes related to each other and to the process of learning?
3. What are *terminal* and *instrumental values?* How does culture relate to values?
4. What are *ethics,* and why are they important for managers to understand?
5. How are attitudes related to behavior? What is *cognitive dissonance?*
6. What is *personality,* and what are the important aspects to understand?
7. Explain why personality is developmental in nature. What are the primary factors that influence the evolution of personality?
8. Why are the first three stages of Erikson's model of personality development so crucial to long-term personality development? How do the crises of these three stages relate to the crises of the remaining stages?
9. Describe *locus of control, Machiavellianism,* and *Type A or B* as aspects of personality.

10.   Describe the subsystems of Jung's Personality Theory. Also explain the four dimensions of the theory.

11.   Describe *socialization* from an organizational perspective, and explain how it might influence someone's personality.

12.   How does a person's existing personality impact the socialization process and influence the individual's future personality?

RESOURCE READINGS

Erikson, E. H. "Youth and the Life Cycle." *Children* 7 (1960), pp. 43–9.

Hosmer, L. T. *The Ethics of Management.* Homewood, Ill.: Richard D. Irwin, 1987.

Jung, C. G. *Collected Works.* Edited by H. Read, M. Fordham, and G. Adler. Princeton, N.J.: Princeton University Press, 1953.

Pervin, L. A. *Current Controversies and Issues in Personality.* 2d ed. New York: John Wiley & Sons, 1984.

Rokeach, M. *The Nature of Human Values.* New York: The Free Press, 1973.

Schein, E. H. "Organizational Socialization and the Profession of Management." *Industrial Management Review* 9 (1968), pp. 1–16.

NOTES

1.   W. Bennis and B. Nanus, *Leaders: The Strategies for Taking Charge* (New York: Harper & Row, 1985).

2.   J. Luft, *Group Processes* (Palo Alto, Calif.: National Press Books, 1970).

3.   D. J. Bem, *Beliefs, Attitudes, and Human Affairs* (Monterey, Calif.: Brooks/Cole Publishing, 1970), pp. 4–15.

4.   E. H. Erikson, "Youth and the Life Cycle," *Children* 7 (1960), pp. 43–49.

5.   B. L. White, *The First Three Years of Life* (New York: Avon Books, 1975).

6.   J. Cooper and R. T. Groyle, "Attitudes and Attitude Change," *Annual Review of Psychology* 35 (1984), pp. 395–426.

7.   L. Festinger, *A Theory of Cognitive Dissonance* (Palo Alto, Calif.: Stanford University Press, 1957).

8.   R. Mowday, S. Parker, and R. M. Steers, *Employee-Organization Linkages* (New York: Academic Press, 1982).

9.   R. A. Baron and D. Byrne, *Social Psychology: Understanding Human Interaction,* 4th ed. (Boston: Allyn & Bacon, 1984).

10. P. Dubno, "Attitude Toward Women Executives: A Longitudinal Approach," *Academy of Management Journal* 28 (1985), pp. 235–39.

11. W. H. Schmidt and B. Z. Posner, *Managerial Values and Expectations: The Silent Power in Personal and Organizational Life* (New York: American Management Association, 1982).

12. B. Z. Posner, W. A. Randolph, and W. H. Schmidt, "Managerial Values Across Functions: A Source of Organizational Problems," *Group & Organization Studies* 12 (1987), pp. 373-385.

13. M. Rokeach, *The Nature of Human Values* (New York: Free Press, 1973).

14. G. Hofstede, "Motivation, Leadership, and Organization: Do American Theories Apply Abroad?," *Organizational Dynamics* (Summer, 1980), pp. 42–63.

15. E. Bowen, "Looking to Its Roots: At a Time of Moral Disarray, America Seeks to Rebuild a Structure of Values," *Time*, May 25, 1987, pp. 26–28.

16. L. T. Hosmer, *The Ethics of Management* (Homewood, Ill.: Richard D. Irwin, 1987).

17. K. H. Blanchard and N. V. Peale, *The Power of Ethical Management* (New York: William Morrow and Company, Inc., 1987).

18. L. A. Pervin, *Personality: Theory and Research*, 4th ed. (New York: John Wiley & Sons, 1984).

19. Ibid.

20. L. A. Pervin, *Current Controversies and Issues in Personality*, 2d ed. (New York: John Wiley & Sons, 1984).

21. J. B. Miner and M. G. Miner, *Personnel and Industrial Relations*, 3d ed. (New York: Macmillan, 1977), p. 72.

22. Erikson, "Youth and the Life Cycle."

23. J. B. Rotter, "Generalized Expectancies for Internal Versus External Control of Reinforcement," *Psychological Monographs* 80 (1966), pp. 1–28.

24. Research summarized in J. R. Schermerhorn, Jr., J. G. Hunt, and R. N. Osborn, *Managing Organizational Behavior*, 2d ed. (New York: John Wiley & Sons, 1985).

25. N. Machiavelli, *The Prince*, trans. G. Bull (Middlesex: Penguin Books, 1961).

26. M. Korda, *Power!: How to Get It, How to Use It* (New York: Random House, 1975).

27. R. Christie and F. L. Geis, *Studies in Machiavellianism* (New York: Academic Press, 1970).

28. M. Friedman and R. Rosenman, *Type A Behavior and Your Heart* (New York: Alfred A. Knopf, 1974).

29. D. C. Glass, *Behavior Patterns, Stress, and Coronary Disease* (Hillsdale, N.J.: Erlbaum, 1977).

30. C. G. Jung, *Collected Works*, ed. H. Read, M. Fordham, and G. Adler (Princeton, N.J.: Princeton University Press, 1953).

31. The Myers-Briggs Type Indicator could not be reproduced in this book due to its copyright. It is, however, available commercially from Consulting Psychologists Press, Palo Alto, Calif.

32. W. Woods, "Personality Tests Are Back," *Fortune*, March 30, 1987, pp. 74–82.

33. H. A. Simon, "Making Management Decisions: The Role of Intuition and Emotion," *Academy of Management Executive* 1 (1987), pp. 57–64.

34. R. Steers, *Introduction to Organizational Behavior,* 3d ed. (Glenview, Ill.: Scott, Foresman, 1987).

35. Erikson, "Youth and the Life Cycle," pp. 43–9; White, *The First Three Years of Life.*

36. Steers, *Introduction to Organizational Behavior.*

37. E. H. Schein, "The Individual, the Organization and the Career: A Conceptual Scheme," *Journal of Applied Behavioral Science* 7 (1971), pp. 401–26.

38. E. H. Schein, "Organizational Socialization and the Profession of Management," *Industrial Management Review* 9 (1968), pp. 1–16.

CASE: People don't change, or do they?*

Paul Smith is a recruiter in the personnel department of a large organization. One day he was chatting with Dick Witte, a top manager. Paul was lamenting the fact that when he visited college campuses he had only fifteen minutes to talk with, and make a judgment about, a potential job candidate. "How can you decide in that short a period of time?" he asked. "I just hope the persons I choose to come back here for follow-up interviews will meet with your approval." Dick assured him that they would, and the conversation went as follows:

"Don't let it worry you, Paul. You've got a knack for picking out good people. Besides, I know you can't allow anyone more than fifteen minutes with your busy schedule, and that doesn't give you a lot of time for making judgments. You know, though, I've often thought that it would be easier on interviewers if they talked to the neighbors of the interviewees who knew these people when they were kids."

"I don't think I follow you."

"Well, I'll bet you that if you knew a person as a kid and then met the person as an adult, you would find basically the same individual. I mean, the person wouldn't have changed very much at all."

"Do you really think so?"

"I'm positive of it. People just don't change."

"I'm not so sure that I agree with you, Dick. As people get older, they tend to do things differently from the way they did as children."

"Not quite. They might do things somewhat differently, but they would be predictable. I'm sure of it. For example, you take a kid who's a bookworm when he's seven or eight years old. The guy is going to be either a teacher or a librarian."

"Well, if that's true, why doesn't every kid become a doctor? At some stage they all seem to want to be one."

"Sure, but you have to distinguish between fleeting fancy and deep interest. I think this is possible to determine."

*Source: F. Luthans, *Organizational Behavior* (4th ed.), New York: McGraw-Hill, 1985, pp. 343–45.

"Do you really think you can prove that?"

"You bet. I'll tell you what; get that yearbook from the shelf over there." Paul did so and handed it to Dick.

"This is my high school yearbook. Now it's been almost twenty-five years since I graduated from high school, but I'll bet you that I can tell you what anyone in here is doing today if you just call out the name."

"Well, you might know just on the basis of the alumni get-togethers."

"If you'll take my word for it, I have never attended one of them. Furthermore, if you look at the address inside the cover, you'll see that the school is located on the other coast. Right after high school my folks moved here, and I haven't been back since. In fact, I never did see any of those people again."

"All right, Dick. What do you think Mary Aaron is doing today? It says here that she liked chemistry and wanted to major in it at college."

"Don't take her because we have no way of checking. Choose someone with a rare name, and we'll call the city and try to locate him."

"All right, here's one. Theodore X. Culpepahr."

"Good choice. Old Teddy's father was a very successful mortician, but Teddy never seemed to express an interest in joining that business. As I remember him, he was always in school plays and loved to recite poetry."

"It says here that he wanted to major in English in college."

"I believe it. Now let's see. From what I remember of him he would be either an English teacher or the director of a local theater guild. I'll tell you what; I'll bet you that today he's teaching drama at a college somewhere on the coast."

"How can we find out?"

"With a name like that? Let's call information and see if he's still living in the same city. In any event, it shouldn't be too difficult to locate him."

The operator informed Dick that there was no one by the name of Theodore X. Culpepahr living in the city. Dick then asked her to give him the number of the Culpepahr mortuary. He placed a call there and asked for Teddy's father.

"Mr. Culpepahr? This is Dick Whitson. I was a high school classmate of Teddy's. I have a business trip scheduled for your area, and I was just calling ahead to find out where Teddy was. I thought I might drop by and look him up."

"Well, he doesn't live here any more. He and his wife have a house about 100 miles up the shore."

"I see. Well tell me, what's he doing these days?"

"Oh, he's teaching English composition and literature at a junior college."

"Well, isn't that great! Listen, tell him I called, won't you, and I'll try to get in touch with him sometime."

After hanging up, Dick turned back to Paul.

"What did I tell you? He's teaching English at a junior college. Now I'll concede that I was a little off, but not very much, right?"

"No, you were pretty accurate. However, I'm still not so certain that I hold with your theory concerning the fact that people don't change."

"Oh, heck, Paul. By the time people are five years old, their futures are already spelled out. From there on they're just going through the motions of a prewritten script. If you want to find out about people, learn something of their early personality and environment. From there you can merely extrapolate."

Questions:

1. What personality theory is Dick supporting in his argument? If you were Paul, what personality theories would you suggest as alternatives to counter Dick's argument?

2. What kinds of perceptions does a recruiter like Paul form of a job applicant in a fifteen-minute interview? What are some perceptual principles that will affect his impressions of candidates? Is there some way that recruiters could improve the accuracy of their perceptions?

3. How do you account for the fact that Paul seems to be doing a good job of recruiting good people? How do you account for the fact that Dick was fairly accurate in his prediction of what an old classmate was doing twenty-five years later?

4. Are there any implications for motivation and learning in this case? How are needs derived? What learning principles are found in this case?

EXERCISE: Attitude measure of women as managers

Purpose

The purpose of this exercise is to assess attitudes people have about women in business.

The Exercise in Class

1. Have each student complete the following Women as Managers Scale (WAMS). The best answer to each statement is your *personal opinion*. The statements cover many different and opposing points of view; you may find yourself agreeing strongly with some of the statements, disagreeing just as strongly with others, and perhaps uncertain about others. Whether you agree or disagree with any statement, you can be sure that many people feel the same way you do.

Rating Scale

1 = Strongly Disagree   5 = Slightly Agree
2 = Disagree   6 = Agree
3 = Slightly Disagree   7 = Strongly Agree
4 = Neither Disagree nor Agree

Using the numbers from 1 to 7 on the rating scale above, mark your personal opinion about each statement in the blank that immediately precedes it. Remember, give your *personal opinion* according to how much you agree or disagree with each item. Please respond to all 21 items.

_____ 1. It is less desirable for women than men to have a job that requires responsibility.

_____ 2. Women have the objectivity required to evaluate business situations properly.

_____ 3. Challenging work is more important to men than it is to women.

_____ 4. Men and women should be given equal opportunity for participation in management training programs.

_____ 5. Women have the capability to acquire the necessary skills to be successful managers.

_____ 6. On the average, women managers are less capable of contributing to an organization's overall goals than are men.

_____ 7. It is not acceptable for women to assume leadership roles as often as men.

_____ 8. The business community should someday accept women in key managerial positions.

_____ 9. Society should regard work by female managers as valuable as work by male managers.

_____ 10. It is acceptable for women to compete with men for top executive positions.

_____ 11. The possibility of pregnancy does not make women less desirable employees than men.

_____ 12. Women would no more allow their emotions to influence their managerial behavior than would men.

_____ 13. Problems associated with menstruation should not make women less desirable than men as employees.

_____ 14. To be a successful executive, a woman does not have to sacrifice some of her femininity.

_____ 15. On the average, a woman who stays at home all the time with her children is a better mother than a woman who works outside the home at least half time.

_____ 16. Women are less capable of learning mathematical and mechanical skills than are men.

_____ 17. Women are not ambitious enough to be successful in the business world.

_____ 18. Women cannot be assertive in business situations that demand it.

_____ 19. Women possess the self-confidence required of a good leader.

_____ 20. Women are not competitive enough to be successful in the business world.

_____ 21. Women cannot be aggressive in business situations that demand it.

Source: James R. Terborg, Lawrence H. Peters, Daniel R. Ilgen, and Frank Smith, "Organizational and Personal Correlates of Attitudes toward Women as Managers," *Academy of Management Journal*, March 1977, p. 93. With permission.

2. Receive the scoring instructions from your instructor.
3. After students have scored their individual forms set up groups of 5 to 6 students. (Try to have men and women in each group.) The group discussion should focus on the individual scores.

The Learning Message

The scores on the WAMS will provide some indication of how comfortable a person is with women in managerial positions. Since women are entering management in greater numbers, attitudes about them as managers are important and should be understood.

Source: J. H. Donnelley, Jr., J. L. Gibson, and J. M. Ivancevich, *Fundamentals of Management*, 5th ed. (Plano, Tx: Business Publications, 1984, pp. 753-754).

QUESTIONNAIRE: Locus of control scale

For each pair of statements below, select the one which you believe to be the most true. Check the statement (either *a* or *b*) which you believe to be most true. Please answer all items.

1. [ ]*a.* Children get into trouble because their parents punish them too much.
   [ ]*b.* The trouble with most children nowadays is that their parents are too easy with them.

2. [ ]*a.* Many of the unhappy things in people's lives are partly due to bad luck.
   [ ]*b.* People's misfortunes result from the mistakes they make.

3. [ ]*a.* One of the major reasons why we have wars is because people don't take enough interest in politics.
   [ ]*b.* There will always be wars, no matter how hard people try to prevent them.

4. [ ]*a.* In the long run, people get the respect they deserve in this world.
   [ ]*b.* Unfortunately, an individual's worth often passes unrecognized no matter how hard he or she tries.

5. [ ]a. The idea that teachers are unfair to students is nonsense.
   [ ]b. Most students don't realize the extent to which their grades are influenced by accidental happenings.

6. [ ]a. Without the right breaks, one cannot be an effective leader.
   [ ]b. Capable people who fail to become leaders have not taken advantage of their opportunities.

7. [ ]a. No matter how hard you try, some people just don't like you.
   [ ]b. People who can't get others to like them don't understand how to get along with others.

8. [ ]a. Heredity plays the major role in determining one's personality.
   [ ]b. It is one's experiences in life which determine what one is like.

9. [ ]a. I have often found that what is going to happen will happen.
   [ ]b. Trusting to fate has never turned out as well for me as making a decision to take a definite course of action.

10. [ ]a. In the case of the well-prepared student, there is rarely, if ever, such a thing as an unfair test.
    [ ]b. Many times, exam questions tend to be so unrelated to course work that studying is really useless.

11. [ ]a. Becoming a success is a matter of hard work; luck has little or nothing to do with it.
    [ ]b. Getting a good job depends mainly on being in the right place at the right time.

12. [ ]a. The average citizen can have an influence in government decisions.
    [ ]b. This world is run by the few people in power, and there is not much the little guy can do about it.

13. [ ]a. When I make plans, I am almost certain that I can make them work.
    [ ]b. It is not always wise to plan too far ahead because many things turn out to be a matter of good or bad fortune anyhow.

14. [ ]a. There are certain people who are just no good.
    [ ]b. There is some good in everybody.

15. [ ]a. In my case, getting what I want has little or nothing to do with luck.
    [ ]b. Many times, we might just as well decide what to do by flipping a coin.

16. [ ]a. Who gets to be the boss often depends on who was lucky enough to be in the right place first.
    [ ]b. Getting people to do the right thing depends upon ability; luck has little or nothing to do with it.

17. [ ]a. As far as world affairs are concerned, most of us are the victims of forces which we can neither understand, nor control.
    [ ]b. By taking an active part in political and social affairs, the people can control world events.

18. [ ]a. Most people don't realize the extent to which their lives are controlled by accidental happenings.
    [ ]b. There is really no such thing as "luck."

19. [ ]a. One should always be willing to admit mistakes.
    [ ]b. It is usually best to cover up one's mistakes.

20. [ ]a. It is hard to know whether or not a person really likes you.
    [ ]b. How many friends you have depends on how nice a person you are.

21. [ ]a. In the long run, the bad things that happen to us are balanced by the good things.
    [ ]b. Most misfortunes are the result of lack of ability, ignorance, laziness, or all three.

22. [ ]a. With enough effort, we can wipe out political corruption.
    [ ]b. It is difficult for people to have much control over the things politicians do in office.

23. [ ]a. Sometimes I can't understand how teachers arrive at the grades they give.
    [ ]b. There is a direct connection between how hard I study and the grades I get.

24. [ ]a. A good leader expects people to decide for themselves what they should do.
    [ ]b. A good leader makes it clear to everybody what their jobs are.

25. [ ]a. Many times I feel that I have little influence over the things that happen to me.
    [ ]b. It is impossible for me to believe that chance or luck plays an important role in my life.

26. [ ]a. People are lonely because they don't try to be friendly.
    [ ]b. There's not much use in trying too hard to please people; if they like you, they like you.

27. [ ]a. There is too much emphasis on athletics in high school.
    [ ]b. Team sports are an excellent way to build character.

28. [ ]a. What happens to me is my own doing.
    [ ]b. Sometimes I feel that I don't have enough control over the direction my life is taking.

29. [ ]a. Most of the time I can't understand why politicians behave the way they do.
    [ ]b. In the long run, the people are responsible for bad government on a national as well as on a local level.

Scoring Key

1. Circle *a* on the
   following questions
2
6
7
9
16
17
18
20
21
23
25
29

2. Circle *b* on the
   following questions
3
4
5
10
11
12
13
15
22
26
28

3. Count the number of times your checks appear in any of the circles.
   Total _____
   Note: Questions 1, 8, 14, 19, 24, and 27 are filler items and are not scored.

4. If your score is above 14, you are "externally" oriented; below 7, you are "internally" oriented. For scores 7 to 14, the higher the score the more "externally" oriented you are.

Source: J. B. Rotter, "Generalized Expectancies for Internal Versus External Control of Reinforcement," *Psychological Monographs* 80 (1966), pp. 1-28.

QUESTIONNAIRE: Mach V attitude inventory

Instructions: You will find twenty groups of statements listed below. Each group is composed of three statements. Each statement refers to a way of thinking about people or things in general. The statements reflect opinions and not matters of fact—there are no "right" or "wrong" answers, and different people have been found to agree with different statements.

Read each of the three statements in each group. First decide which of the statements is *most true* or *the closest* to your own beliefs. Put a plus sign (+) in the space provided before that statement. Then decide which of the remaining two statements is *most false* or *the farthest* from your own beliefs. Put a minus sign (−) in the space provided before that statement. Leave the last of the three statements unmarked.

Most True = +
Most False = −
Here is an example:

_____ A. It is easy to persuade people but hard to keep them persuaded.

__+__ B. Theories that run counter to common sense are a waste of time.

__−__ C. It is only common sense to go along with what other people are doing and not be too difficult.

In this example, statement B would be the one you believe in *most strongly* and statements A and C would be ones that are *not* as characteristic of your opinions. Of these two, statement C would be the one you believe in *least strongly* and the one that is *least* characteristic of your beliefs.

You will find some of the choices easy to make; others will be quite difficult. Do not fail to make a choice no matter how hard it may be. Remember: mark *two* statements in each group of three—the one that is the closest to your own beliefs with a + and the one that is the farthest from your beliefs with a −. Do not mark the remaining statement. *Do not omit any group of statements.*

1. _____ A. It takes more imagination to be a successful criminal than a successful business person.

   _____ B. The phrase "the road to hell is paved with good intentions" contains a lot of truth.

   _____ C. Most people forget more easily the death of their parents than the loss of their property.

2. _____ A. People are more concerned with the car they drive than with the clothes their spouses wear.

   _____ B. It is very important that imagination and creativity in children be cultivated.

   _____ C. People suffering from incurable diseases should have the choice of being put painlessly to death.

3. _____ A. Never tell anyone the real reason you did something unless it is useful to do so.

   _____ B. The well-being of the individual is the goal that should be worked for before anything else.

   _____ C. Once a truly intelligent person makes up his mind about the answer to a problem he rarely continues to think about it.

4. _____ A. People are getting so lazy and self-indulgent that it is bad for our country.

   _____ B. The best way to handle people is to tell them what they want to hear.

   _____ C. It would be a good thing if people were kinder to others less fortunate than themselves.

5. _____ A. Most people are basically good and kind.

   _____ B. The best criterion for a wife or husband is compatibility—other characteristics are nice but not essential.

_____ C. Only after you have gotten what you want from life should you concern yourself with the injustices in the world.

6. _____ A. Most people who get ahead in the world lead clean, moral lives.

_____ B. Any person worth his salt should not be blamed for putting career above family.

_____ C. People would be better off if they were concerned less with how to do things and more with what to do.

7. _____ A. A good teacher is one who points out unanswered questions rather than gives explicit answers.

_____ B. When you ask someone to do something for you, it is best to give the real reasons for wanting to rather than giving reasons that might carry more weight.

_____ C. A person's job is the best single guide to the sort of person he or she is.

8. _____ A. The construction of such monumental works as the Egyptian pyramids was worth the enslavement of the workers who built them.

_____ B. Once a way of handling problems has been worked out it is best to stick to it.

_____ C. You should take action only when you are sure that it is morally right.

9. _____ A. The world would be a much better place to live in if people would let the future take care of itself and concern themselves only with enjoying the present.

_____ B. It is wise to flatter important people.

_____ C. Once a decision has been made, it is best to keep changing it as new circumstances arise.

10. _____ A. It is a good policy to act as if you are doing the things you do because you have no other choice.

_____ B. The biggest difference between most criminals and other people is that criminals are stupid enough to get caught.

_____ C. Even the most hardened and vicious criminal has a spark of decency somewhere inside.

11. _____ A. All in all, it is better to be humble and honest than to be important and dishonest.

_____ B. People who are able and willing to work hard have a good chance of succeeding in whatever they want to do.

_____ C. If a thing does not help us in our daily lives, it is not very important.

12. _____ A. People should not be punished for breaking a law that they think is unreasonable.

_____ B. Too many criminals are not punished for their crimes.

_____ C. There is no excuse for lying to someone else.

13. _____ A. Generally speaking, people will not work hard unless they are forced to do so.
    _____ B. Every person is entitled to a second chance, even after committing a serious mistake.
    _____ C. People who cannot make up their minds are not worth bothering about.

14. _____ A. A person's first responsibility is to spouse, not to parents.
    _____ B. Most people are brave.
    _____ C. It is best to pick friends who are intellectually stimulating rather than ones who are comfortable to be around.

15. _____ A. There are very few people in the world worth concerning oneself about.
    _____ B. It is hard to get ahead without cutting corners here and there.
    _____ C. A capable person motivated for his or her own gain is more useful to society than a well-meaning but ineffective person.

16. _____ A. It is best to give others the impression that you can change your mind easily.
    _____ B. It is a good working policy to keep on good terms with everyone.
    _____ C. Honesty is the best policy in all cases.

17. _____ A. It is possible to be good in all respects.
    _____ B. To help oneself is good; to help others is even better.
    _____ C. War and threats of war are unchangeable facts of human life.

18. _____ A. Barnum was probably right when he said that there is at least one sucker born every minute.
    _____ B. Life is pretty dull unless one deliberately stirs up some excitement.
    _____ C. Most people would be better off if they controlled their emotions.

19. _____ A. Sensitivity to the feelings of others is worth more than poise in social situations.
    _____ B. The ideal society is one in which all people know their place and accept it.
    _____ C. It is safest to assume that all people have a vicious streak and that it will come out when the chance arises.

20. _____ A. People who talk about abstract problems usually do not know what they are talking about.
    _____ B. Anyone who completely trusts anyone else is asking for trouble.
    _____ C. It is essential for the functioning of a democracy that everyone vote.

Mach V Attitude Inventory Score Key

Instructions: To find your score on the Mach V Attitude Inventory, locate the combination of letters and plus or minus signs that you chose for each item (group of statements) in the inventory. For example, if for the first group of statements you marked statement B with a plus (+) and statement C with a minus (−), your score for that item would be 3.

Item	1	3	3	5	5	7	Score
1	A+ C−	B+ C−	A+ B−	B+ A−	C+ B−	C+ A−	3

Mark your score for each item in the appropriate place in the score column. Do this for each of the twenty items. Then sum the scores.

Points per Item by Response Patterns

Item	1	3	3	5	5	7	Score
1	A+ C−	B+ C−	A+ B−	B+ A−	C+ B−	C+ A−	
2	A+ C−	B+ C−	A+ B−	B+ A−	C+ B−	C+ A−	
3	C+ A−	B+ A−	C+ B−	B+ C−	A+ B−	A+ C−	
4	A+ B−	C+ B−	A+ C−	C+ A−	B+ C−	B+ A−	
5	A+ B−	C+ B−	A+ C−	C+ A−	B+ C−	B+ A−	
6	A+ C−	B+ C−	A+ B−	B+ A−	C+ B−	C+ A−	
7	B+ A−	C+ A−	B+ C−	C+ B−	A+ C−	A+ B−	
8	C+ B−	A+ B−	C+ A−	A+ C−	B+ A−	B+ C−	
9	C+ B−	A+ B−	C+ A−	A+ C−	B+ A−	B+ C−	
10	A+ B−	C+ B−	A+ C−	C+ A−	B+ C−	B+ A−	
11	A+ B−	C+ B−	A+ C−	C+ A−	B+ C−	B+ A−	
12	C+ B−	A+ B−	C+ A−	A+ C−	B+ A−	B+ C−	
13	C+ A−	B+ A−	C+ B−	B+ C−	A+ B−	A+ C−	
14	B+ C−	A+ C−	B+ A−	A+ B−	C+ A−	C+ B−	
15	C+ B−	A+ B−	C+ A−	A+ C−	B+ A−	B+ C−	
16	C+ B−	A+ B−	C+ A−	A+ C−	B+ A−	B+ C−	

Item	1	3	3	5	5	7	Score
17	A+ C−	B+ C−	A+ B−	B+ A−	C+ B−	C+ A−	
18	C+ A−	B+ A−	C+ B−	B+ C−	A+ B−	A+ C−	
19	B+ C−	A+ C−	B+ A−	A+ B−	C+ A−	C+ B−	
20	A+ B−	C+ B−	A+ C−	C+ A−	B+ C−	B+ A−	
						Total score	
						Now add 20	+20
						Mach score	

Your Mach score can range from 40 to 160. The higher your score, the higher your Machiavellian tendencies. Scores above 100 are considered high Mach; below 100 are low Mach.

Source: Richard Christie and Florence L. Geis, *Studies in Machiavellianism* (Orlando, Fla: Academic Press, 1970).

Foundations of Motivation

$\mathbf{T}$he last two chapters looked at several important aspects of individual behavior. By gaining an understanding of the **perception** and **learning** processes, we were able to better understand the formation of **attitudes and values** and ultimately of one's **personality.** By considering **socialization,** we could begin to appreciate the interaction between individuals and the organizations in which they work. This chapter delves further into this interaction as we begin to explore the dynamic process of **motivation.** We will explore a number of theories of motivation that will lay the foundation for developing in Chapter 6 an integrated model of the motivation process. By learning about these motivation theories and the integrated model, managers are better able to create a situation where employees are motivated to work to accomplish organizational goals. In the process, managers also learn a great deal about their own motivation.

MOTIVATION AND ITS IMPORTANCE TO A MANAGER

Motivation can be defined as a force that energizes, directs, and sustains an individual to perform goal-directed actions. People are generally motivated to do something that will satisfy their needs. A manager's job is to see that employees' actions are directed not only toward personal goals but also toward goals of the unit and the organization. Thus, there are several reasons why managers must understand motivation.

Why study motivation?

First of all, employees are the vehicle for accomplishing the goals of a unit and an organization. And although their ability plays a crucial role in determining their work performance, so does their motivation. Managers must be sure that employees are motivated to perform their tasks to the best of their abilities. Managers need creative and innovative workers who are motivated to complete their tasks in spite of unexpected interruptions.[1] Recall the old saying that performance on a job is 20 percent ability and 80 percent effort. **Motivation is the critical factor in mobilizing the efforts of employees.**

The second reason to study motivation is that organizations in the future will need to more effectively use all of their resources, including their human resources. With continuously tightening constraints from the economy, world competition, government controls, and consumer groups, organizations must draw heavily on their employees to increase productivity. A manager's knowledge of motivation can be extremely useful in achieving gains in the short- and long-run productivity of an organization. In the short run, managers must use selection, placement, and rewards to ensure that there is a fit between employee needs and the demands of a job. In the long run, managers must prepare employees (through training and on-the-job experience) to be future resources in new, different, or altered capacities. For example, can one of a manager's employees replace her when she is promoted?

Third, motivation is important because it is a complex process that ultimately influences employees in a variety of ways. And often it is not easy to motivate people to do what someone else wants them to do. Indeed, people ultimately determine their own motivation. Recall our discussions from Chapters 3 and 4 that explained how each person is unique. **Each employee brings to the workplace a unique set of needs that has been determined by past experiences. Therefore, two employees may be motivated very differently by the same situation, by the same job, or by the same reward.** It has often been said in union negotiations that managers must treat all employees equally. But if managers treat every employee the same—and if every employee is unique—are managers not then treating people unequally? Some employees will be pleased with a nice pay raise; others might have preferred a promotion or more responsibility. Motivation occurs in a complicated process that influences the actions of each employee. It pays managers to understand this.

Fourth, motivation is important to understand because managers must also be concerned with their own motivation. By knowing what motivates themselves to perform productively, managers will be in a better position to maximize their work efforts and find jobs that are best for them. **For a manager's work to be meaningful and to contribute to overall personal satisfaction and health in life, the manager will need to understand how motivation works for him or her.**

Problems associated with motivation

Another major reason for studying motivation is that motivation is linked to a number of organizational problems. For example, managers often lament that workers do not put forth the kind of effort managers want. Managers are constantly concerned with **productivity** of their employees, and this concern seems to be growing in the face of foreign competition and increased constraints on profits. Many managers are searching for quick, simple solutions, but the problem is more long-term and complex than that. Our exploration of the motivation process will help in the analysis of the productivity problem.

Managers also frequently mention the problem of employee **dependability.** Often managers must deal with high levels of employee tardiness or absenteeism. These problems in dependability are costly; they disrupt work schedules, lead to overstaffing, and reduce the organization's productivity. Steers has suggested that the costs associated with absenteeism in the United States—including salary, fringe benefits, temporary replacement, and profit loss—total over $26 billion annually, using 1977 costs.[2] Taking inflation into account, the costs today probably exceed $60 billion annually. As our study of motivation will reveal, an employee makes a choice each day either to go to work or to do something else; to work hard or to take it easy. Two factors that influence this decision—and that can be influenced by managers—are the employee's satisfaction with the work and the various rewards associated with attendance. Both of these relate to motivation.

A third problem area associated with employee motivation is **turnover,** that is employees quitting their jobs. As with absenteeism, turnover is rooted in employees' dissatisfaction with their jobs. But quitting involves a longer decision process. The decision to quit involves the exploration of alternative jobs, the development of an intention to quit, and finally, the act of quitting.[3] Absenteeism merely involves a choice between going to work or doing something else for the day, with the intention of going to work the next day. As with absenteeism and tardiness, the problem of turnover can be analyzed from a motivation perspective using the motivation theories and model explored in this and the following chapters.

Besides the three problem areas mentioned above, low motivation can lead to a number of other problems: poor quality of work, presence on the job physically but not mentally, lack of innovation and of suggestions for improvement, low employee morale, and many other undesirable outcomes. Studies have reported that less than 25 percent of employees say they work at full potential; 50 percent say they do only what is required to hold on to their jobs; and 75 percent say they could be significantly more productive than they are now.[4] Managers have to be concerned with increasing and maintaining the motivation of employees. If motivation is relatively low, managers have to try to raise it, and if motivation is relatively high, managers have to work to maintain it. At the same time, managers also have to be concerned with their own motivation on the job now and as it may change over time.

Motivation as a dynamic process

Throughout the first four chapters we have noted changes that people undergo in the various stages of developing a career, life, and family. We have seen that **people are likely to be motivated by different things at different points in their lives.** For example, a 22-year-old may be looking for more money and greater challenge in a job; a 58-year-old may be more concerned about retirement pension and maintaining a level of importance in a company. In fact, people vary from day to day in their motivation. Each of us has good and bad days—days when we are highly motivated to work and days when we have little desire to work.

Employee motivation can also be altered by changes in a job or in an organization itself. Technological advances in a job can take away or add interesting components to a job. Automation both eliminates and adds jobs. In both cases, jobs are changed. The question is: How is the motivation aspect of a job altered? As we will see, **a job itself is a very important factor in the motivation process of employees.** For example, if a job is changed to include greater decision-making responsibility for the employee, the motivation potential of the job has been altered.

Organizational changes can also affect motivation—for example, growth, decline, or change in direction, as discussed in Chapter 2. In a growing organization, there are many opportunities for advancement and increased responsibility that can influence the motivation of employees. As Insight 5–1 illustrates, the reverse may be true in a declining organization. People often operate with the fear that they may lose their job; their motivation to work or to search for alternative employment can be altered by the forces in this situation. By the same token, a change in company direction can influence the motivation of employees. Remember, **people are usually motivated to do something; the question is, What?** Later we will explore these dynamic aspects of motivation in more detail. But now, let us discuss a number of theories of motivation that have been developed over the years. As we do so, keep in mind that an employee's motivation depends on the person, job, supervisor, peers, organization, and general environment.

AN INTRODUCTION TO MOTIVATION THEORIES

As discussed earlier, motivation operates through a complex process that ultimately influences the behavior of people in organizations. And because motivation is so complex, many theories have been advanced in an effort to explain it. We will explore a number of them in this chapter to form the foundation for the integrative model explained in Chapter 6.

The existing theories of motivation can be classified as either **content theories** or **process theories.** Content theories deal with *what* motivates people, while process theories deal with *how* they are motivated. In general, content theories historically predate process theories. There has been a progression from simple theories of motivation to more complex models as researchers have learned more about the motivation process; and there is still a great deal more to learn. Many managers are familiar with at least one of the content theories—Maslow's **need hierarchy theory.** Other content theories include Herzberg's **two-factor theory** and McClelland's **need for achievement, affiliation, and power theory.** More recently, we have witnessed the development of Alderfer's **ERG (existence, relatedness, and growth) needs theory** as an extension of Mas-

---

Fear of Unemployment Takes Emotional Toll at White-Collar Levels

*T*he human-resources manager at an ailing manufacturing company in Pittsburgh sits alone in an office at the end of a long corridor dotted by empty offices. "I still get here at 8 A.M. every day and put in nine, sometimes 10 hours, but more and more I'm asking myself why," he says.

Since February, nearly 20% of his co-workers have been laid off "and now all anyone can talk about is who's going to be next. It's depressing. You end up feeling that what you do doesn't matter, that it won't make a difference."

Similar feelings echo in corporate offices around the nation. In conference rooms and cubicles, managers ranging from first-line supervisors to vice presidents talk incessantly about the loss of job security and the stresses of keeping going in companies that are suffering production and people losses.

For those still employed, many who thought themselves immune to layoffs suddenly are facing uncertainty and must make do with less. Many are frightened—even ashamed—to discuss their situation, insisting on anonymity.

Manifestations of grief

In fact, the retrenchment going on in corporations is affecting those who survive layoffs almost as much as those who are let go. The survivors go through the same traumas of thinking they may be fired and then, once they've been spared, often find themselves "overworked and overpressured," says James Lotz, a consultant at International Management Advisors Inc. in New York. "The leaves left on the tree are shaking," he says.

The search for new jobs goes on undercover. "People are terribly frightened that if they're seen looking, they'll be judged disloyal and fired," says Mr. Young, the executive recruiter. "One guy I had lunch with last week didn't want to be seen walking down the street with me."

---

low's theory. Also, we have seen the emergence of **social-facilitation theory,** which suggests that people are influenced by the expectations of others around them. **Content theories highlight the differences among people. Different people are motivated by different things.**[5]

The process theories that have been developed since about the mid-1960s include Vroom's **expectancy theory,** Adams's **equity theory,** and an application of Skinner's **operant conditioning** to motivation. Closely following the development of these models of motivation came Locke's **goal-setting theory.** While the models differ in terms of the motivational mechanism that causes behavior, all four of **these process models define motivation as an individual choice process.**[6] The models suggest that individuals rely on past and current information about their goals, expectations, and sense of fairness to choose their behaviors. People also rely on their expectations of the rewards or punishments associated with certain behaviors to make their choices.

Both content and process theories focus on the individual and certain characteristics about the individual (for example, needs and expectations) in explaining motivation. To some extent, the theories also include other people who interact with the employee (such as the supervisor and peers). In addition, these theories focus on the reward and information systems of the organization. But one aspect of the motivational puzzle that seems to be slighted is the job that the person is performing. In the 1970s, a job-design theory of motivation was developed by Hackman and his associates at Yale University. Hackman's theory directly considers the motivating potential of a job. Thus we are provided with yet another aspect of the complex motivational process. No doubt other motivation theories will follow. Indeed, the authors of a recent article in *Organizational Dynamics* focus on perceptual/motor and biological factors of jobs—factors brought back into the forefront by issues of the 1980s.[7] Let us now look into each of these 10 theories in more detail.

CONTENT THEORIES OF MOTIVATION

Content theories of motivation help us to understand the basic needs that people satisfy by their actions. **An unsatisfied need results in a driving force toward satisfaction of the need.** A look at these theories as shown in Exhibit 5–1 reveals the types of needs that can motivate people. The exhibit also shows how the four major content theories can be related to one another.

Maslow's need hierarchy theory

The first—and still the most popular—content theory was developed by Abraham Maslow in 1943.[8] Since this is a familiar theory, we will not spend much time discussing it. As Exhibit 5–1 shows, Maslow proposed that there is a hierarchy of needs ranging from physiological to self-actualization. **As long as lower-level needs are unsatisfied, an individual will choose actions designed to move toward satisfaction of those needs.** But once physiological needs are basically satisfied (and there is an expectation that they will remain satisfied), a person will turn to safety needs, and continue up the hierarchy.

Research on Maslow's hierarchy has resulted in some criticisms of the model, but none of the criticisms have been fatal. First, as suggested throughout this text, a person's needs change over time. Certainly the needs of a young college graduate will differ from the veteran employee.

EXHIBIT 5–1

Major Content Theories of Motivation

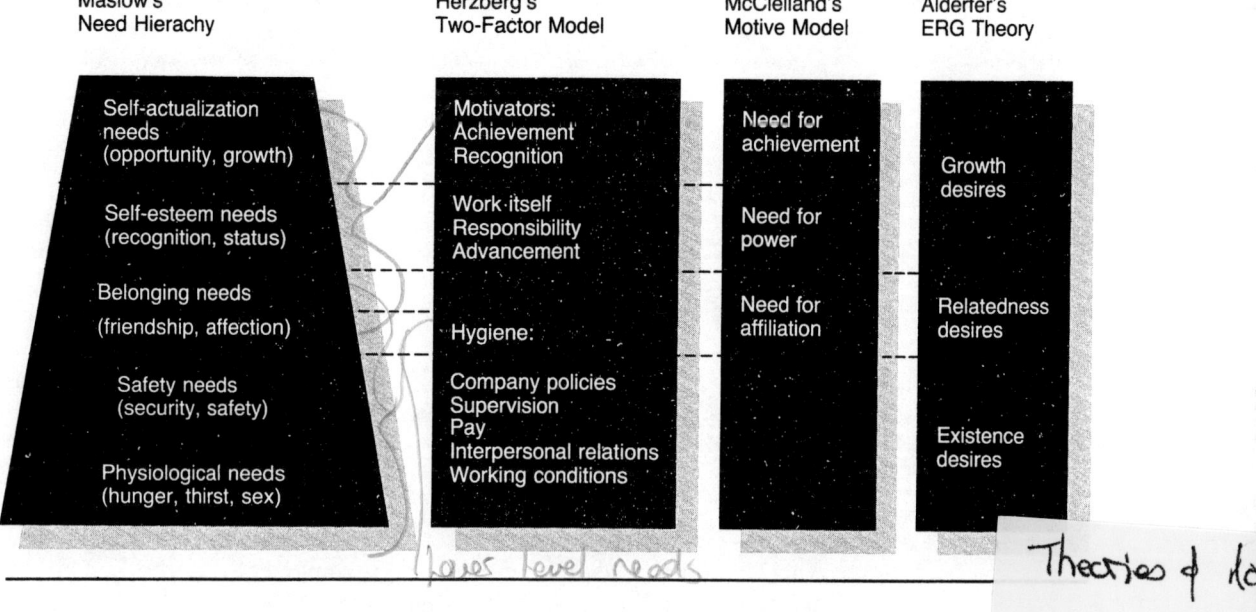

And changes in a situation may result in changes in the priority of needs. For example, a recessionary economy with high unemployment may cause a person to refocus from self-actualization needs to safety and physiological needs. Indeed, the 500-point Dow Jones Industrials crash of 1987 caused many people to reconsider their priorities and lifestyles. Second, research suggests that more than one need level may be operational at a time. People may, for example, work to satisfy their safety needs and self-esteem needs at the same time. But despite these criticisms, Maslow's theory has remained popular because it is simple to understand and because individual needs appear to be critical to understanding individual behavior.[9] Take a few minutes now to complete and score the Motivation Feedback Opinionnaire at the end of the chapter. Be honest with yourself, and see which of Maslow's needs are most important to you at this point in your life.

Alderfer's ERG theory

A more recently developed theory, Alderfer's ERG theory (shown on the far right in Exhibit 5–1), seems to address many of the criticisms of the Maslow hierarchy.[10] First of all, Alderfer reduces Maslow's five needs to three more general needs: existence, relatedness, and growth. Included under **existence needs** are hunger, thirst, shelter, pay and working conditions—that is, the physiological and safety needs from Maslow. **Relatedness needs** include basically the same desires as Maslow's belongingness needs—namely friendship and affection from others. Finally, **growth needs** are the desires to be creative, to develop additional skills and abilities, and to feel a sense of status in an organization—that is, the self-esteem and self-actualization needs from Maslow.

Second, ERG theory suggests that the more lower-level needs (for example, existence desires) have been satisfied, the greater the drive to satisfy higher-level needs (like relatedness or growth). This implies that **people are not dependent upon full satisfaction of a lower-level need before moving on to a higher-level need.** ERG theory clearly allows for the simultaneous pursuit of both existence needs and relatedness needs. Third, ERG theory builds in a frustration response. An individual who has difficulty satisfying a higher-level need (say growth) may focus more importance and effort on lower-level needs where there is a greater chance of satisfaction. Thus, this theory allows for movement both up and down the hierarchy. But **the primary proposition of need theory holds here as well; namely, the less a need is satisfied, the more it will be desired.**

McClelland's need theory

Another content theory expresses needs somewhat differently. The theory by David McClelland and his associates at Harvard defines the needs for achievement, power, and affiliation.[11] **Need for achievement** is the desire to perform to high standards or to excel at a job. If people are high-need achievers, they like to set their own goals; they set goals that are neither too easy nor too difficult to achieve; and they like to receive immediate feedback on their work. Insight 5–2 provides an interesting illustration of this need. The chirigami kokan is clearly working on his achievement need, as well as self-actualization, in a society that does not encourage individualism. The **need for power** is the desire to influence and control others. If people have a high need for power, they seek positions of leadership in groups; they freely give their opinion on matters; and they try to convince others to change their opinions. However, a high need for power is, by itself, neither good nor bad. What a person does with power determines whether this need is good or bad. Indeed, managers who are effective tend to have a high need for power. Looking ahead to future chapters, we can note now that leadership is defined as influencing the behavior of others; hence, leadership and power are intertwined. A leader must have some base of power to utilize his or her need for power. Finally, **need for affiliation** is defined as the desire to develop close interpersonal relationships with others. If people are high in need for affiliation, they exhibit a real interest in the feelings

---

**It Isn't Easy to Work Alone in Japan—
Ask a Chirigami Kokan**

'Toilet-Paper Exchanger'
Has Zero Prestige but Is
Free of Bosses and
Their Edicts

*T*okyo—A small, weather-beaten truck inches along a street in a residential neighborhood, a public-address system on its roof. The voice of the driver, Tsuguo Suzuki, summons the populace.

"This is your familiar chirigami kokan," comes the voice from the loudspeaker. "If you have old newspapers, magazines, used cardboard or telephone directories you don't need, please let me know. I will come to your doorway to get them, and in return give you rolls of high-quality toilet paper."

Chirigami kokan—literally, "toilet-paper exchangers"—have become familiar sights and sounds on the streets of big Japanese cities. Toyko alone has more than 6,000 of them. Working alone, often driving old trucks rented by day, they scour the neighborhoods for wastepaper and sell it to junkyards that compress if for recycling. From the junkyards they pick up a supply of recycled tissue paper—to attract more wastepaper the next day.

Chirigami kokan exist because this island nation needs to conserve resources. There is a government-sponsored institution in Japan called the Paper Recycling Promotion Center, and it says the toilet-paper exchangers play a vital role in reducing woodpulp imports.

But the job of chirigami kokan also serves another function in Japan: It offers a role for the individualist, for the lone wolf.

This is a nation where young people compete strenuously, from junior high to high school to college, for a chance to go to work for a large corporation. Big companies offer higher pay, better benefits and, above all, the promise of lifetime employment. From these flows a fourth advantage—prestige. "It is for social status and respect as well as for the money" that Japanese strive to be part of a large corporate organization, says Hitoshi Hashimoto, a professor of social psychology at Tokyo's Waseda University.

Thus, in a nation of teamwork and team players, the chirigami kokan constitutes one answer to a question foreigners often ask about Japan: What happens to small entrepreneurs who go bankrupt and to those individualistic types who don't like working in big groups?

---

of others; they like a great deal of interpersonal contact; and they look for support and/or approval from others.

As Exhibit 5–1 suggests, these three needs are not unlike the needs in Alderfer's and Maslow's models. Need for achievement is similar to self-actualization and growth needs. Need for power is similar to self-esteem needs and growth needs. And need for affiliation is similar to relatedness and belonging needs. In a manner similar to Alderfer,

McClelland suggests that all three needs are operative at all times, but one or two of them will tend to dominate the individual at a point in time. Thus, a person might have high achievement and power needs and a low affiliation need. And if so, this individual would have to be motivated differently than someone high in affiliation and power needs and low in achievement need. McClelland adds one other key point for understanding the needs aspect of motivation. He argues that **all needs are learned, which means that they reflect our pasts and can be altered via a continued learning process.** Hence, McClelland's theory is clearly consistent with a developmental focus on motivation. Take a few moments to complete the Motivation Needs Survey at the end of this chapter to see how you score on these three needs.

Herzberg's two-factor theory

One last content theory that has received a great deal of attention from managers must be explained. Herzberg defines a number of motivators and hygiene factors, as shown in Exhibit 5–1.[12] They relate to the basic needs defined by Maslow, McClelland, and Alderfer. **Motivators** relate to satisfaction of higher-level needs (self-actualization, self-esteem, and belonging), while **hygiene** factors relate to lower-level needs (physiological, safety, and belonging).

Herzberg argues that motivators are what lead to satisfaction on the job, while a lack of sufficient hygiene factors can lead to job dissatisfaction. The lack of motivators does not lead to dissatisfaction, and the presence of hygiene factors does not lead to satisfaction. Further, a recent study by Herzberg found these same results in a variety of countries, including Europe, Israel, Japan, Zambia, South Africa, and India.[13] Still, Herzberg's ideas have been severely criticized in research literature, primarily because of the way in which Herzberg has collected his data.[14] He basically asked people to describe what made them feel good about their jobs and what made them feel bad about their jobs. The problem is that people have a tendency to attribute positive things to their own efforts and negative things to others' efforts. Hence, the hygiene factors all relate to the company and the supervisor, while the motivators relate more to personal events.

In spite of this criticism, the two-factor theory continues to have broad appeal to managers. One reason is that managers see immediate applicability to real situations. Recognition, responsibility, and the other motivators give managers more concrete direction than saying that workers have unsatisfied self-esteem needs. This same practicality exists for the hygiene factors. Thus, for example, if assembly-line workers are unhappy because of a lack of recognition (a motivator), putting more money into hygiene factors (pay, working conditions) will not alleviate the problem. If managers want these workers to be more

don't accept responsibility for their contribution to that negativity

motivated, they must determine how to introduce more recognition into the job.

Herzberg's theory can be even more useful if we talk in terms of employee potential that can be tapped via hygiene and motivating factors. Exhibit 5–2 depicts a possible explanation. Below an average level of employee motivational potential (say, 30 percent of potential), the hygiene factors can produce improvement in the level of employee motivation. This would be true because supervision, working conditions, and so forth may be inhibiting the employee's motivation to do the job. **However, to tap the motivational potential of outstanding employees and break through the 30 percent barrier, managers must rely more heavily on the motivating factors.** The area between 30 percent and 85 percent (a reasonable guess at the maximum achievable) is the challenge for managers. Not all employees will want the motivators in their jobs; some workers are happy with a lack of responsibility and the predicta-

EXHIBIT 5–2

An Adaptation of Herzberg's Motivational Model

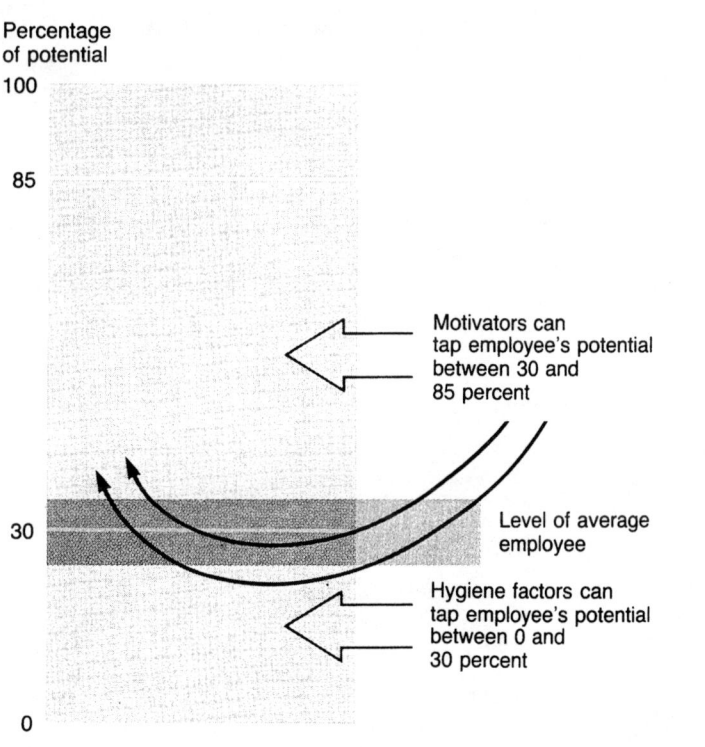

Source: Adapted from F. Herzberg, B. Mausner, and B. Snyderman, *The Motivation to Work*, copyright © 1959 John Wiley & Sons, Inc.

bility of their job. But for those who want motivators, the hygiene factors are no substitute. Later, we will discuss Hackman's job design theory that draws heavily on Herzberg's model and on the differences in individuals.

Social-facilitation theory

While it is not strictly a content theory, **social-facilitation** theory qualifies because it is connected to the belongingness needs. The theory suggests that our needs and goals are influenced by the expectations that our peers, superiors, and subordinates have for us.[15] As we go about our jobs, we come into contact with others in the organization upon whom we depend and who depend upon us. We develop expectations about the behaviors of these people, and they develop expectations about us. But what is most crucial is that these coworkers influence our sense of what is important.[16] What goals do we value? What needs are important? For example, in one department in Home Computers Company there may be a great deal of discussion about salary and other money matters. As a result, a person working in that department might place greater importance on salary increments than a person working in a department where there is a great deal of discussion about advancement, recognition, and responsibility.

Another way to look at this theory is to think of interactions with coworkers as a source of motivation for a person's actions. If someone's peers, for example, have set an informal norm of producing 10 computers per day, then that person will be motivated to work up to, but not above that level. People learn some of their needs from those with whom they work. **The needs in content theories are basically learned and are therefore subject to change over time. Coworkers are one source of influence on needs.**

As stated earlier, content theories help managers understand the basic needs that motivate people. In turning now to the process theories, we focus more on how motivation works.

PROCESS THEORIES OF MOTIVATION

There are several important process theories of motivation, each of which defines motivation as a choice process for individuals. We will discuss expectancy theory, operant conditioning, equity theory, and goal-setting theory.

Expectancy theory

The first truly comprehensive explanation of expectancy theory was provided by Victor Vroom in the 1960s.[17] The basic premise of the theory is that people make choices about what to do at a given point in time. Which behavior they choose depends on which one they believe will lead to desired rewards. For example, a person with a report due at 5 P.M. today might choose between the following two behaviors: (1) work on the report over lunch to try to finish it on time, or (2) go to lunch and then rush to finish the report later. The question is, Which behavior will lead to a good, timely report? And a good report is important because it could lead to one of several possible rewards: (1) a bonus, (2) a promotion, or (3) an excellent performance review.

Expectancy theory suggests people look at a choice in three steps, as shown in Exhibit 5–3. The first step involves **expectancy.** Essentially, **expectancy is an assessment of the probability that a particular level of effort will lead to a desired level of performance.** The questions are: Can I do it? What is the probability that I can? Referring to the example above, what is the probability that working over lunch will lead to a good and timely report? What is the probability that rushing the work won't?

The second step involves **instrumentality, which is an assessment of the probability that the desired level of performance will lead to a desired reward.** The questions are: Does performance lead to what I

EXHIBIT 5–3

An Expectancy Theory Model

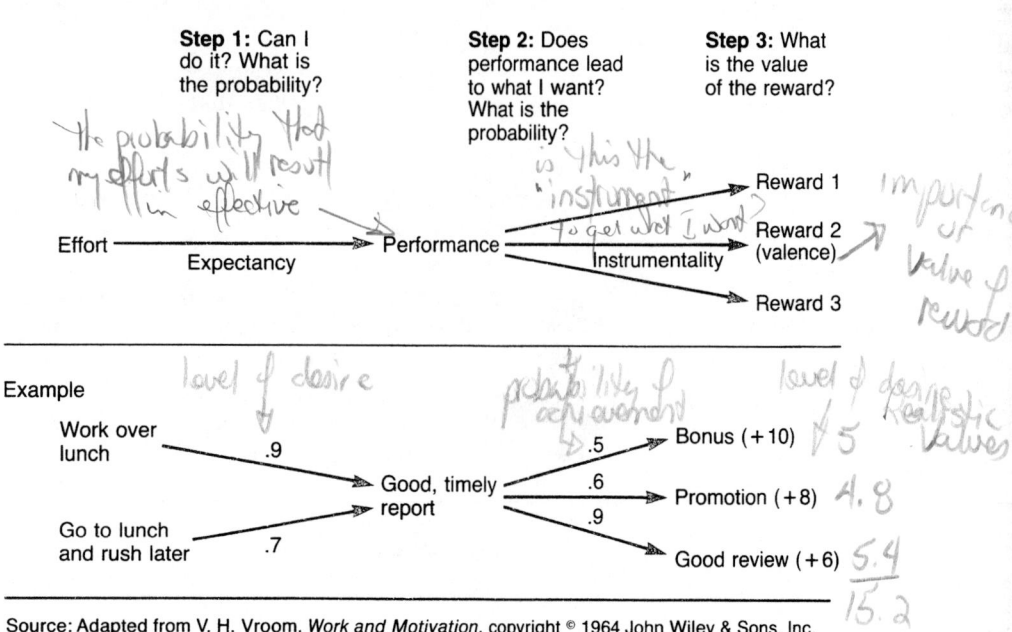

Source: Adapted from V. H. Vroom, *Work and Motivation,* copyright © 1964 John Wiley & Sons, Inc.

want? What is the probability that it does? In the above example, what is the probability that a good, timely report will lead to a bonus, a promotion, and/or a good review?

The third step then assigns to each reward a **valence, which is the importance or value placed on each possible reward.** In the example, how important is a bonus, a promotion, a good review? But the expected value of the reward is really a function of the instrumentality between performance and reward. A person might desire a bonus the most (valence of +10), a promotion next (valence of +8), and a good review least (valence of +6). But the probability of each, as associated with a good, timely report, may be .5, .6, and .9, respectively (as shown in Exhibit 5–3). Thus, the realistic values of the bonus, promotion, and good review are +5, +4.8, and +5.4, respectively. These values are obtained by multiplying the valence by the instrumentality. Overall, the value of a good, timely report is the sum of these three realistic values— +15.2. The value could be much higher if the instrumentalities for a bonus and a promotion were higher.

To determine the motivational strength for the two behaviors suggested in the example, multiply the expectancy that each behavior will lead to the desired performance by the value of the report. Thus, work over lunch is rated $.9 \times 15.2 = +13.7$, and go to lunch/rush later is rated $.7 \times 15.2 = +10.6$. Clearly, the motivational strength related to working over lunch is stronger than going to lunch. Of course, this relates only to getting the report done. It may be that the lunch has a higher motivational value because it is a romantic lunch that may result in engagement, which has a high value for the person. The key point of the theory is not the numbers; it is the process of choice.

A great deal of research has been conducted on the basic expectancy theory model, and it suggests that the model is probably more complete than the content theories.[18] One of the problems with the expectancy theory, though, is that it is a complex theory to test fully. Still, the logic of the model is clear, and the steps are useful for clarifying how managers can motivate people. For example, managers should first find out which rewards under their control have the highest valences for their employees. Managers should then link these to the performance they desire. And if any expectancies are low, managers might provide coaching, leadership, and training to raise them.

It is clear that expectancy theory is consistent with the developmental theme of this book. The valences, expectancies, and instrumentalities come from people's past experience, and the step-by-step fashion of the model also introduces a time aspect. Indeed, the model will form the framework for integrating in Chapter 6 all of the various motivation theories discussed in this chapter.

Operant conditioning

Chapter 3 looked at operant conditioning as a model of learning. The discussion of it here as a process theory of motivation suggests the close link between learning and motivation. **Operant conditioning (or reinforcement theory) is a model for rewarding the kind of behavior managers desire from employees and for not rewarding undesired behavior.** Thus, motivation is viewed specifically in terms of getting the employee to do what the organization wants. If the employee does what the organization wants and receives a valued reward, the employee's behavior should continue to fit the desires of the organization. An employee who does not do what the organization wants will not receive the reward—and may instead receive punishment for the undesired behavior. Hence, the employee's behavior will probably change.

Application of this theory involves choices of the particular reward or punishment to be used and the frequency with which the reward or punishment is given. To be most effective in producing desired results, the reward must be tied closely to the accomplishment of organizational goals. And more and more companies are tying pay to performance. As Insight 5–3 on page 182 points out, companies like General Motors are changing their pay systems to tie pay directly to performance.

Of course, it is important to understand that if managers want significant improvements in performance, they must apply the reinforcers repeatedly over time.[19] Praising a child once for playing nicely with her brother does little to ensure the continuation of this behavior. As any parent knows, it takes at least "487" such instances to get the good behavior to sink in. The same principle applies with employees. Repeated recognition of success is needed to get good behavior to stick.

But managers must be careful to reward the behavior they desire. If an employee who wants a promotion and works hard with good results sees the promotion go to someone who is connected with the boss's family, the desired result of continued hard work may not be forthcoming. And the same result may come about if the wrong reward is given— for example, a pay raise instead of a promotion. The bottom line is that for reinforcement theory to be most useful, **managers must recognize that rewards only accomplish the desires of the organization when their receipt is tied to accomplishment of organizational goals and when the rewards are valued by the individuals receiving them.** Research has tended to favor the use of rewards over punishment in achieving desired results. And as the Dagwood cartoon below suggests, managers must not forget nonfinancial rewards. There are times, though, where punishment can be very effective.[20] For example, when college graduates fail to repay their student loans, some U.S. attorneys have taken away their cars. Usually this ends the delinquency and payments resume. The

GM's New Compensation Plan Reflects General Trend Tying Pay to Performance

*D*etroit—Throughout the 1980s, General Motors Corp. has struggled to overhaul its technology and bureaucracy.

Now, it's intensifying efforts to reform its people.

For decades the auto maker appeared to be running a white-collar welfare system: salaried employees, regardless of individual performance or market conditions, were practically assured of high pay and lifetime employment. But this month, GM is setting up a new compensation system that it hopes will push its salaried employees to work harder—or will help push those who don't out the door.

"We enjoyed so much success that we didn't have to be as sensitive about the business as we have to be today," says Roy S. Roberts, vice president for corporate personnel. "This business is so competitive we need everybody pulling their weight."

The move, which will affect 112,000 low-level managers, clerical workers and other white-collar staffers, is part of a trend across corporate America to tie compensation more closely to performance and to make pay more variable from year to year. "We are moving away from the entitlement era," says Steven E. Gross, a compensation consultant for Hay Management Group in Phila-delphia. "There's a lot of experimentation going on."

'The Time Has Arrived'

GM made major changes two years ago when it dropped annual cost-of-living raises for salaried employees and established a "pay-for-performance" system. The company also began eliminating 40,000 white-collar positions—in part by "voluntary" buy-outs that many employees say were involuntary. Last year, GM temporarily suspended all salary increases.

This year raises have been reinstated, but the differences among employees will be greater than ever. "A merit increase . . . is something you have to earn," says Mr. Roberts. "To treat people fairly you have to treat people differently."

Previously, most GM managers gave employees a performance grade, like "superior" or "outstanding." The vast majority got the top rankings, and "merit" raises were "quasi-automatic," Mr. Roberts says.

Now, GM ranks employees against each other, essentially grading on a curve. Bosses have to pick the top 10%, the next 25%, the next 55%, and the bottom 10% of their group, and enforce pay differences between the tiers. The specifics are up to individual offices.

cars are then returned. Thus, punishment as a final approach can be useful when undesired behavior must be stopped quickly. But it is safe to say that too many managers overutilize punishment, and underutilize rewards, which are more powerful in terms of shaping behavior.

Equity theory

Equity theory is a model of motivation which involves the comparison of an employee's efforts and output with either some internal standard of performance or the performance of other employees.[21] Motivation is tied to a judgment of fairness in a given work situation. For example, if an employee perceives that the rewards from her job (pay, promotion, etc.) relative to what she puts into the job (effort, skills, etc.) are equal to what other employees receive, she will be satisfied and motivated to continue working she has been. In other words, the employee perceives equitable treatment of herself and her coworkers. Of course, it is also possible to perceive inequitable treatment. An employee may feel that the ratio of his rewards to his input is greater than the ratio for other employees; thus, he is being overrewarded. Or he may feel the ratio of his rewards to his input is less than the ratio for others; thus, he is being underrewarded. In these situations, a worker's motivation could be altered by this information, depending upon his or her equity sensitivity.[22] As discussed in Chapters 3 and 4, different people respond differently to the same situation. The reactions to inequity are no different. Some people are more willing to accept being underrewarded than are others. And some people may expect to be overrewarded. But if the perceived inequity results in a change in motivation, the inequity may also alter effort and performance. You can probably think of instances in school where you worked harder than others on a paper, yet received a lower grade. Your sense of equity was violated—you felt underre-

Source: © King Features Syndicate Inc. 1976.

warded. As Insight 5–4 shows, the same issues have been occurring among various medical specialties.

The inequity of being **underrewarded** can result in several behaviors. A person could reduce his or her efforts so that the ratio of rewards to input would be reduced and become more comparable to the ratio for other people. Another way to increase the equity ratio would be to ask for an increase in rewards. And since the key factor in this model is the perception of the individual, a person could also distort the perception of personal rewards and input, and the rewards and input of others. This would either increase the individual's personal ratio or reduce the perceived ratio of others.

In the case of being **overrewarded,** the same perceptual distortion processes can result in lowering a personal ratio or raising the ratio of others. An individual can also lower a personal ratio by reducing some of the subjective rewards received or by increasing the effort put into a job. It would seem that there are greater motivational problems in the case of underreward than overreward. One research study found that in organizations where the top rate of pay for new employees is substantially lower than that for old employees (two-tier wage structures), the motivation and work effort for new employees tends to be lower.[23] In order to balance their input/output ratio, new employees reduce their effort to be in line with their pay.

Research, in general, appears to lend stronger support to such underreward aspects of the theory than to overreward situations.[24] However, one recent study of equity theory found that when people are overrewarded based on what is perceived to be merit conditions (e.g., they did the job better and hence were not laid off), they perceive their input to be greater.[25] By perceiving their input to be greater, the fact that they were not laid off seems more equitable.

These points also reinforce the fact that perception is an important aspect of equity theory. **And since perception is influenced so heavily by developmental properties (as discussed in Chapter 3), equity theory is also influenced by one's past and present experiencing of a situation.** Hence, equity theory is quite consistent with the developmental theme of this book.

Locke's goal-setting theory

As the final process theory, let us explore Locke's goal-setting theory.[26] Basically, **the goal-setting model of motivation asserts that we all have values and desires that determine the goals we set for ourselves. In turn, these goals directly influence our behavior.** An individual's actions are directly influenced by both the individual and the organizational goals desired. In particular, goal-setting theory has revealed several findings that directly affect its use in organizational settings.

I N S I G H T   5–4

Physicians' Not-So-Civil War

*L*ate last year, the American Medical Association announced that physician incomes, before income tax, averaged about $120,000 in 1986. Some papers that don't like rich doctors played the item up. Others, inured to high incomes by knowledge about what people get in TV, professional sports and Wall Street, buried the story or ignored it.

What was astonishing was the way in which the press missed the really interesting story. The story concerns the huge differences in the incomes of various medical specialties and the political civil war those differences have touched off among doctors' organizations.

We can refer to that same AMA survey for the basic facts to set the stage. In 1986 when the overall average income was $119,500, radiologists averaged about $168,800 and general surgeons about $162,400. But general practitioners and their modern successors, the family physicians, averaged only about $80,300, while pediatricians were only slightly better off at an average income of $81,800. Internists—at $109,000—were better off than GPs and

pediatricians, but nowhere near the radiologists and surgeons.

As Karl Marx might have predicted, a bitter medical class struggle has been raging about these differences. The internists, the best organized of the relatively low-income specialties, have been complaining for years about these "unfair" disparities. Surgeons and the like are being paid far too richly for "procedures," they maintain, while internists are being grossly underpaid for "cognitive services"—that is, for talking to patients, taking a medical history, and the like.

The surgeons' response has been predictably frosty. Anyone who suggests that a surgeon does no cognition—i.e., thinking—before, during and after an operation, just doesn't know what goes into successful surgery, they sniff. In effect the surgeons have argued they too give all the cognitive services of their less prosperous colleagues plus perform operations that frequently save lives. And doing a complex operation is far more difficult than merely listening to a patient and writing a prescription, they assert.

By Harry Schwartz, *The Wall Street Journal*, February 9, 1988. Reprinted by permission of *The Wall Street Journal*, © Dow Jones & Company, Inc. 1988. All rights reserved.

First, specific, clearly defined goals are more likely to result in better performance than are vague goals. Some consultants argue that simply setting clear goals for people can often increase performance by 15 percent to 20 percent. Tying rewards to goals can increase performance by as much as 40 percent. Second, the more difficult a goal is, the more effort a person will put forth. However, if goals are set unreasonably high, the individual may become discouraged, though this possibility can be reduced if the person participates in the goal setting. Third, participation in setting goals leads to greater acceptance of the goal and tends to lead to increased performance.[27] It seems that participation in the goal-setting process helps people better understand the goal and helps lead to higher levels of commitment.[28] And if people understand a goal and are committed to it, performance tends to go up. Insight 5–5 shows how one turnaround expert uses many of these principles to save companies.

However, one rather interesting study has suggested the importance of cultural context on the usefulness of participation in goal setting. Comparing Israeli employees working in the private sector, the public sector, and on kibbutzim, researchers found that participative goal setting yielded the best results in the kibbutzim where collectivistic values are strong.[29] As suggested in Chapter 4 when discussing culturally based values, it appears that whether a particular management approach works depends on where it is applied—the culture at least partially dictates how the technique will be received.

One final point to recognize is that managers must compete for an employee's effort. Employees pursue both individual and organizational goals. The extent to which employees accept the organizational goals has a direct influence on the effort they will expend. **If organizational goals and individual goals are compatible, the employee's actions will be directed toward organizational goals. If there is a lack of congruence between these two types of goals, the individual will try to accomplish individual goals unless there is external pressure to accomplish organizational goals.**

JOB DESIGN AND MOTIVATION

With an understanding of content theories that focus on individual needs and of process theories that focus on individual choices, managers have a great deal of information to aid them in motivating people. To some extent, these theories even take peers and supervisors into account. However, these theories tend to ignore the job as a potential source of motivation, except for Herzberg's mention that the work itself is a motivator. This omission is understandable because, historically, the design of a job has been viewed as a technical question. But over the years, managers have learned that the job a person performs directly affects motivation. This type of motivation is often referred to as **intrinsic** motivation.

History of job-design concerns

In the days of Frederick Taylor, scientific management encouraged the simplification and standardization of jobs in order to achieve the greatest efficiency.[30] This approach made a great deal of sense, given the abilities of the unskilled, uneducated work force of the early 1900s. Without simplified jobs, the demands of industrialized work would have

Dr. Fix-It

Q.T. Wiles Revives Sick High-Tech Firms with Strong Medicine

*I*ndian Wells, Calif.—A strange ritual is taking place around a long conference table here, where 60 young men and women are sitting in a circle. A rumpled man in a baseball cap and golf shirt has summoned them to this desert resort, and one by one each addresses him in the same chantlike format:

"Q.T., this is my charter," they begin. "Q.T., these are my five most important tasks. . . . Q.T., these are my operating principles. . . . Q.T., these are my shortfalls. . . ." The session looks a little like a scene from a movie about zombies. Actually, the people around the table are the top managers of MiniScribe Corp., a small personal-computer disk-drive company that was nearly destroyed last year when the electronics business fell apart.

Amid the 1985 chaos, Q.T. Wiles, the man in the baseball cap, took over MiniScribe. He fired a fifth of its employees and split up its managers into a dozen little groups, each responsible for a product, a customer, a research project or some other narrowly defined task. In every case, he authorized the units to plan their own budgets and sales targets.

This restructuring is the heart of Wiles turnarounds. In his view, it combats a common threat to young high-tech companies: overoptimistic planning by executives lacking a feel for what their staff can accomplish. Mr. Wiles prefers to let managers set their own business targets. Then, top executives can add up all those numbers to plan for the overall company.

"I'm one for forecasting from the bottom up rather than deciding at the top what the hell it's going to be and then making everyone else fit it," he explains.

To keep track of his groups, Mr. Wiles demands a torrent of paper work. Every manager has to commit to writing his official "charter," his "operating principles" and his five most important tasks. The managers also have to file monthly payroll reports, weekly profit-and-loss statements and trip summaries, and they must keep lists of their major customers, top 10 orders and top 10 receivables.

So far, the treatment has been paying off. MiniScribe forecasts 1986 pre-tax earnings of at least $21 million on revenue of about $185 million. Its stock, which was trading at about $3 a share when Mr. Wiles came in (and which the Hambrecht & Quist group bought for $1.45 a share), has leaped to the $7-to-$8 range.

exceeded the skills of immigrant and poorly educated workers. The success of this approach resulted in a prosperous economy and an infatuation with technological efficiency that lingers today. The standardization of jobs also resulted in a rapid improvement of workers' job skills.

The Hawthorne studies of the 1930s were the first real indication that there was more to a job than technical factors.[31] But it was not until the late 1940s that efforts were directed at the apparent convergence of job demands and the job skills of the workers. The 1950s saw job rotation (moving people from one job to another during the day) and job enlargement (combining jobs of equal difficulty into one bigger job), but neither approach really changed the nature of jobs that much. All the while, worker skills continued to improve and to surpass the demands of the job. By the 1960s, a real mismatch was developing between job demands and worker skills and desires. Worker skills had increased beyond what was needed for many jobs, and workers' desires for job growth and opportunity had increased even more. The result of this mismatch was lower motivation—a widespread problem in the United States. But with the advent of increased use of computers, process control work, robotics, and the like, the late 1980s suggest that this mismatch is now reversed. Jobs have become significantly more complex in the last few years, and worker skills have not kept up. But worker desires for the good life continue to grow. A *Business Week* article in 1987 hinted at what is happening.[32] For example, banks want secretaries to have computer skills, not dictation skills. Insurance companies want claim processors to verify that doctors and dentists have used the appropriate procedure. Manufacturing plants need workers with better math skills to run process-control equipment. The result is that job demands often outstrip worker skills, but employees still desire interesting work. Hackman's job characteristics model gives managers a framework to help them analyze the situation.

Hackman's job characteristics model

In the late 1960s, Herzberg's model of motivation formed the basis of job enrichment as managers tried to build motivators into jobs. Their intent was to expand jobs vertically by adding more managerial aspects, thus increasing job responsibilities and opportunities for growth and development in the job. And in the 1970s, Hackman and his associates at Yale added depth to job enrichment by identifying five core dimensions of jobs.[33] The five were skill variety, task identity, task significance, autonomy, and feedback. **Skill variety** is the extent to which a job involves doing different things and using different skills. **Task identity** is the extent to which a job involves performing a task from beginning to end (that is, a complete job). **Task significance** is the importance of a job in the overall work of the plant or company. As shown in Exhibit 5–4, these three core dimensions result in the level of meaningfulness experienced by the employee performing the job. And these factors have virtually nothing to do with the employee's supervisor. Rather, they are dependent upon how the job is designed technologically. The next core dimension, **autonomy,** is the degree to which a job provides freedom and independence for the employee to make important decisions related to the performance of the job—for example, setting work schedules. As shown in Exhibit 5–4, autonomy affects the degree of responsibility experienced by the employee in doing the job. Finally, **feedback** is the degree to which carrying out work activities results in employees receiving direct information about how well they are doing. Such feedback directly affects the knowledge of actual results that the employee receives on a very timely basis.

This model thus **suggests that the higher a job is in skill variety, task identity, and task significance, the higher it will be in meaningfulness.** The greater the autonomy, the greater the experienced responsibility. And the greater the direct feedback from the job, the greater the knowledge of actual results—and without possible distortion as it passes through other people. In turn, Exhibit 5–4 shows that **the greater the meaningfulness, experienced responsibility, and knowledge of actual results, the greater will be internal work motivation, quality of work, and satisfaction with work, and the lower will be absenteeism and**

EXHIBIT 5–4

The Job Characteristics Model of Work Motivation

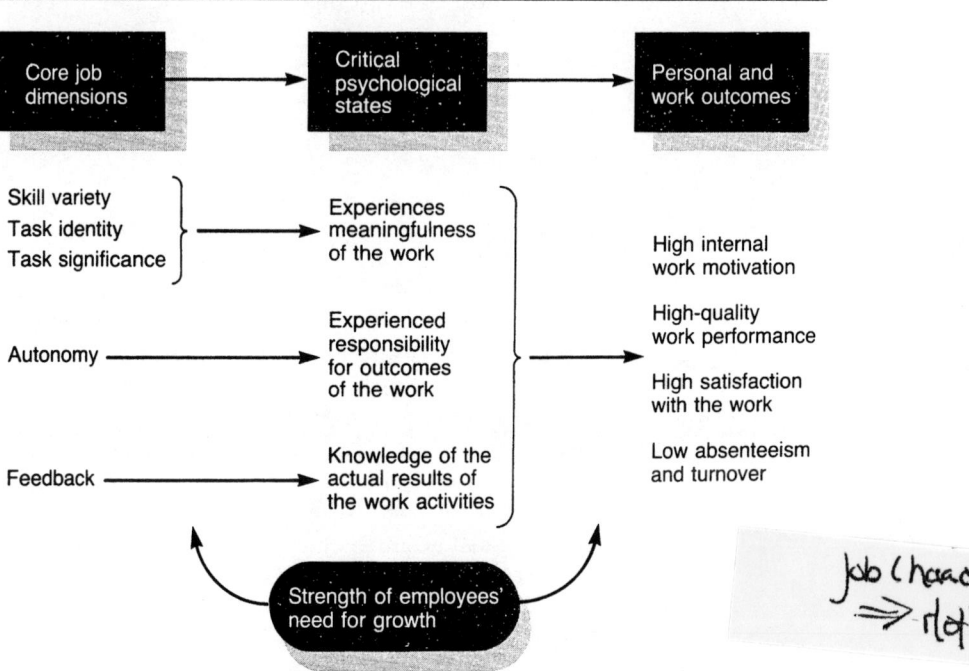

Source: Copyright 1975 by the Regents of the University of California. Adapted from J. R. Hackman, G. Oldham, R. Janson, and K. Purdy, "A New Strategy for Job Enrichment," *California Management Review*, vol. 17, no. 4, p. 62. By permission of the Regents.

turnover. However, there is one major qualifier to this statement: **this relationship holds only for people who are high in what Hackman calls** *growth need strength.* This concept refers to the desire an employee has for development of skills and abilities and for performing interesting and challenging work. If an employee does not have a high need for growth, increases in the core job dimensions will overwhelm the person and result in erratic performance, adjustment problems, and possible turnover and absenteeism.[34] The person with low growth need is best suited for a job which is low in the five core dimensions, whereas the high-growth-need person will be bored and unchallenged by a job low in the core dimensions. Recent research has added credibility to this prediction.[35] The message here is clear, and it is one we have discussed before. **There must be a fit between the person and the job if desired outcomes are to result.** And this applies both to cases where people are over- and underqualified.

An interesting issue which has often been raised is the impact of external rewards (for example, pay) on the intrinsic motivation created by the five core job dimensions. The questions to consider combine operant conditioning with job-design theory. Is pay more important to people than the job itself in determining motivation? Can pay wash out the effects of job design? A study conducted in 1985 seems to suggest an answer of no for both questions.[36] In this research, the intrinsic motivation in a job high on the five core dimensions was not different regardless of whether people received no pay, a fixed pay regardless of performance, or pay based on performance. Thus, it would appear that managers can gain real motivational payoffs by learning how to alter the core dimensions to create motivating jobs for people with a high need for growth.

But how does a manager go about altering the core job dimensions? Exhibit 5–5 shows several ways to modify them.[37] By **combining tasks** into larger modules (basically job enlargement), both skill variety and task identity can be increased. **Forming natural work units**—that is, making the worker responsible for a more complete and identifiable body of work (for example, sales of all products to a certain set of customers rather than sales of only one product)—leads to greater task identity and task significance. **Establishing client relationships**—that is, relationships with the users of the employee's work—increases skill variety, autonomy, and feedback. **Vertical loading**—that is, giving the employee greater discretion and decision-making authority—leads to greater task identity, task significance, and autonomy. Finally, by **opening feedback channels** from the job itself, the employee can measure his or her own performance and thus receive better feedback. An early analysis of a keypunch operator's job, as reported by Hackman, will help illustrate these ideas. (See Insight 5–6 on page 192.)

EXHIBIT 5–5

Principles for Changing Jobs

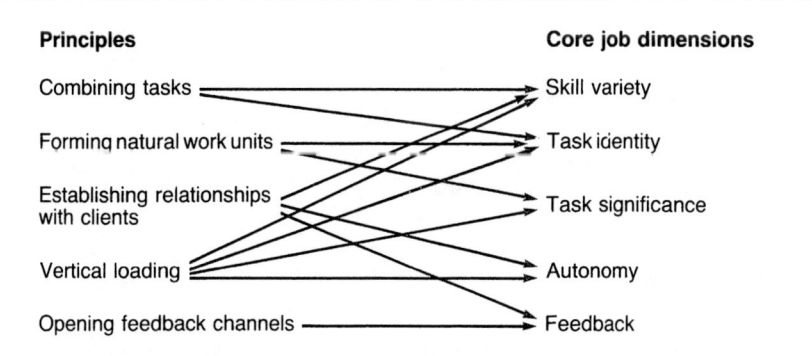

Source: Copyright 1975 by the Regents of the University of California. Adapted from J. R. Hackman, G. Oldham, R. Janson, and K. Purdy, "A New Strategy for Job Enrichment," *California Management Review*, vol. 17, no. 4, p. 62. By permission of the Regents.

The Hackman model essentially focuses on enlarging a job in order to create greater job involvement and greater challenge. One negative aspect is that this approach increases training time, as well as the chances of stress and overload, not to mention that job enlargement is just not right for some people. In many ways, Hackman's approach is the exact opposite of the scientific management approach, which attempts to simplify a job, thus decreasing the training time and reducing the chances of stress and overload. Again, this approach is not for everyone.

Recent developments in the workplace such as computerization and an influx of women have caused some additional job design aspects to surface.[38] **Perceptual/motor** job-design aspects relate to issues like lighting, ease of reading displays, user friendliness, and memory requirements. In the industrial organizations of the past, these issues were not that relevant. But current jobs like air traffic controller, computer operator, and process control machinist require consideration of these elements if employees are to be able and motivated to perform a desired job.

A second set of new issues revolves around **biological** job-design aspects. As more women join the workforce, especially in heavy-industry jobs, managers have to consider such issues as the physical strength and endurance requirements for a job, size differences of people, and seating requirements. For example, hand tools are now made with small handles, as well as large ones. Chairs are orthopedically designed for people who must sit at a computer terminal all day. Without such con-

I N S I G H T 5–6

Redesigning a Keypunch Operator's Job

*T*he problem. Perhaps one of the clearest examples of the application of the Job Characteristics Model can be seen in one effort, to redesign the job of keypunch operators at Traveler's Insurance Company. Using the core job dimensions described in the model, the job of keypunch operator prior to enrichment can be described as follows:

Skill variety. None. Only a single skill was needed: the ability to accurately punch data on cards.

Task identity. Little. Batches were assembled to provide an even work load, but not whole identifiable jobs.

Task significance. Not apparent. While keypunching is a necessary step in providing service to company customers, the individual operators were isolated by an assignment clerk and a supervisor from any knowledge of what the operation meant to the receiving department, let alone to the ultimate consumer.

Autonomy. Little. The operators had no freedom to arrange their daily tasks to meet schedules, to resolve problems with receiving departments, or even to correct information that was obviously wrong.

Feedback. None. Once a batch was completed, the operators received no feedback on performance quality.

Work redesign. The investigators, using the Job Characteristics Model, made the following simple changes:

Natural work units. Instead of randomly assigning batches of work, each operator was assigned continuing responsibility for certain accounts (particular departments or recurring jobs). All work for an account was given to the same operator.

Task combination. Some planning and controlling functions were integrated with the main task of keypunching.

Client relationships. Each operator was given several channels of direct contact with clients. Operators, not assignment clerks, could now examine documents for legibility and autonomy. When a problem arises, the operator, not the supervisor, contacts the client.

Feedback. In addition to client feedback, the operators also receive feedback from the job itself. For example, all incorrect cards are returned to the operator for correction. Weekly computer printouts are provided listing error rates and productivity. These are sent directly to the operator, not the supervisor.

Vertical loading. Operators were given authority to correct obvious errors on their own. They could also set their own schedules and plan their daily work.

Results. As a result of the work redesign experiment, several desired outcomes emerged: (1) While the control group (where no changes were made) showed an increase in productivity of 8.1 percent during the trial period, the work redesign group showed an increase of 39.6 percent. (2) Prior to the study the experimental group had an error rate of 1.53 percent; following the intervention, the average error rate fell to 0.99 percent. (3) During the study period, absenteeism in the experimental group declined 24.1 percent, while it increased 29 percent in the control group. (4) While no attitude changes occurred in the control group, overall job satisfaction increased 16.5 percent in the experimental group after intervention. (5) Because of the improved operator proficiency, fewer controls were necessary, reducing supervisory needs. (6) Since the operators took over many of

193

the mundane supervisory responsibilities, supervisors were now able to devote more time to developing feedback systems, setting up work modules, overseeing the enrichment effort, and planning. In short, supervisors were now able to manage instead of dealing with day-to-day problems.

Source: Copyright 1975 by the Regents of the University of California. Adapted from J. R. Hackman, G. Oldham, R. Janson, and K. Purdy, "A New Strategy for Job Enrichment," *California Management Review*, vol. 17, no. 4, p. 62. By permission of the Regents.

siderations, employees tend to have a hard time doing their job, and they may also grow tired. Both factors can result in lower productivity and lower motivation to do the job. Hence, managers must not underestimate the importance of biological and perceptual/motor factors in the design of a job.

We now have 10 motivation theories to draw on. Let us look into some motivational problems at Home Computers Company to see if we can pose some solutions based on these theories.

Home Computers Case

Motivation at Home Computers Company

In the HCC plant in Dayton, Ohio, 330 employees work on the assembly of the EZ3 computer, which is designed for home use. The EZ3 was introduced in 1983, six years after the EZ2. In addition to the 330 assembly line employees, there are 75 clerical people in the plant, and 85 management employees in five hierarchical levels above the assembly line and clerical workers. Beside the plant manager, there are four department heads, a number of section heads, an even larger number of shift supervisors, and a large number of first-line supervisors. But while 490 employees form a relatively large plant with a number of jobs and employee categories, it has not always been that way.

The Dayton plant was the first plant leased by Harvey and Bill back in 1977. At that time, there were 16 employees in addition to Harvey and Bill. Everyone was on a first-name basis, and people generally worked on a computer from start to finish. There was a real feeling of involvement, challenge, and responsibility. In fact, the workers tested each computer after assembling it to ensure that it worked—a self-administered quality-control system. Each employee worked on an hourly pay system with bonuses based on company profits at the end of each year. Hence, there was a great deal of incentive to do the best job possible in the shortest time possible.

From 1977 to 1980, sales increased dramatically (from 250 units to 3,000). Approximately 60 percent of these units were still produced in Dayton after the opening of a second plant in Denver, Colorado. With the number of computers produced in Dayton going from 250 to 1,800 in three years, a number of changes occurred in the plant. First, the number of employees working on production increased from 16 to 150. Second, the plant established a more structured hierarchy with line supervisors, shift supervisors, and several middle managers. The structure also involved the addition of approximately 30 clerical workers. Third, the plant operation went to two and then to three shifts to maximize use of plant faciities and equipment. The fourth major change was the shift from a craft operation where each employee built an entire computer to an assembly line operation where each employee worked with only one part of the final product. For a while, HCC did maintain the hourly pay plus bonuses. But it was so difficult for employees to feel any personal impact on profits that the fifth change was to go to a simple hourly pay scale. Fortunately, most of the original 16 employees (plus others who had joined HCC under the old pay plan) had either moved up into supervisory and managerial positions or had quit the company. Otherwise, there could have been some problems.

These changes toward a more structured organization, a more sophisticated technology for computer assembly, and a conservative pay plan have continued at the Dayton plant from 1980 through the present. Life on the HCC assembly line in Dayton is not exciting or challenging. As one employee recently said, "It takes more brains to change my kid's diaper than it does to do my job here." However, some of the employees seem to like the lack of responsibility in their job and the predictability of the work. They get a steady paycheck and can go home at night and forget about HCC. However, some employees take advantage of the situation by being late or absent a great deal. In fact, productivity at HCC has dropped off steadily since 1987, and part of this problem involves turnover and absenteeism of the work force. Of course, it has not helped to have strong competition the last three years from the largest computer manufacturer in the world.

Harvey has begun to explore the problems with his work force, with the help of a consultant. An attitude survey was administered to the employees in Dayton, and many of the managers were interviewed in order to delve into the problems. The attitude survey was designed to assess the need satisfaction of the employees. In general, the consultant reported that employees' existence desires and lower-level needs were basically satisfied. The assembly line employees seemed happy with their working conditions, their pay, and most company policies. There was some concern expressed about the constant changes in supervision due to growth and turnover and about the wide variety of people on the assembly line.

As for the higher-level needs, the assembly line workers expressed very little satisfaction. In fact, the consultant pointed out that the concerns expressed about supervision and coworkers were probably unsatisfied belongingness needs. The workers felt very little sense of achievement in their work. They also felt little sense of responsibility and thought the work was boring and unchallenging. However, some of the workers reported liking their job; they liked having very little responsibility and still receiving a good paycheck. As for the managers, some felt they had too much responsibility given their background; others felt they were not advancing fast enough. Some managers felt their work was too constraining and gave them no opportunity to exercise real control and decision making. Harvey interrupted the consultant during his report to say, "Things really seem to be messed up and very complicated. Some people seem to like what the others dislike. What am I going to do?" The consultant responded, "Yes, things are complicated, but let's not talk yet about what you are going to do. There's more data here to tell you about."

While the data suggested that employees were satisfied with their pay, they reported that they were not happy with the reward system of HCC. Very little recognition was given for a job well done. And employees were often reprimanded only when a situation had really become severe; they were given no previous warning. But workers were more upset about their jobs. On the job-design part of the survey, employees rated their jobs low on meaningfulness, responsibility, and feedback. Many of the employees have associate degrees in computer science or computer experience from the military. But their jobs only allowed them to do set, specific things. They felt quality would be better if they had more control over the production.

As for the managers, they, too, felt their jobs to be constraining, though some were overwhelmed by the managerial task. They felt that feedback was inadequate. But what really seemed to upset the managers was a lack of clear company goals. They felt that Home Computers Company was just being swept along by the tide with little direction. This meant constantly changing guidelines and responsibilities for the managers. Sometimes they were the last to know about a change; but if clear goals were established, managers felt there would not be as much change anyway.

Harvey is sitting with the consultant, mulling over these results and wondering what to do. Indeed, what needs to be done to correct a growing motivation problem at Home Computers Company?

APPLYING MOTIVATION THEORIES TO HOME COMPUTERS COMPANY

With the data supplied by the consultant's survey, we can now use the motivational theories to dig into the Home Computers Company situation. Let us see what the content theories suggest for our analysis.

Content theories

The HCC survey has revealed that most employees satisfy their lower-level needs. There is, however, a problem with their belonging needs and with the higher-level, growth-oriented needs. The employees seem to want more responsibility, more recognition for their work, and a greater sense of achievement. So, what can be done? More information would seem to deal directly with the issues of concern to the employees. And a more orderly plan for employee development and career movement would also signal that the company is responding to the desires of the employees, while still focusing on company goals.

But the survey data also suggested that some of the employees liked the lack of responsibility in their jobs. How can managers satisfy employees with such divergent needs? Ah, such is the life of a manager. Two options seem possible. First, managers can try to group employees together by the kinds of needs they are trying to satisfy. Or second, managers can try to match employees with their jobs and see that employees with high growth needs get the more motivating jobs and those with low growth needs get the less motivating ones. Managers can probably eliminate the first option because they do not want to create pockets of unmotivated employees in the company. The second option addresses the critical need for a match between worker and job. Essentially, higher-need-level employees can be allowed to participate in weekly meetings and can be expected to make better use of the information and goals that will be available to everyone. Of course, some people's needs may change, depending on events that transpire; but the plans discussed above allow room for such change.

Process theories

It seems that goals for HCC employees are not always clearly defined, and goal-setting theory suggests that this is a problem source. But goals do not appear to be the only problem. Employees also do not know which rewards are associated with good or poor performance, and reinforcement theory suggests that this is a problem. The old bonus system appears to have failed because control was taken away from the employees on the job. With clearer goals, a performance-linked reward system should be possible, hence clarifying the instrumentalities suggested by expectancy theory.

It is clear that HCC employees are making personal choices (for example, some are quitting), but the choices are not compatible with organizational goals. Equity theory suggests that there are perceived inequities. Some of the managers welcome responsibility, while others feel overwhelmed. Perhaps more training could help alleviate the problem. Likewise, some employees welcome the lack of responsibility in their jobs, while others want more responsibility. As suggested, this inequity could be handled by matching people and jobs. Indeed, the interaction of different personalities on the job can easily create feelings of inequity. As the employees at HCC who are unhappy interact with other employees, their unhappiness can spread, and a morale problem can develop. A key factor for avoiding these problems brought on by different people is the job/person fit, so let us see what job design theory offers our analysis.

Job-design theory

The survey results suggest that the assembly-line workers feel their jobs lack meaningfulness, responsibility, and feedback. Job-design theory suggests that employees with a high need for growth will not be motivated in these jobs. High absenteeism, high turnover, and low satisfaction with the work—all problems presently experienced at Home Computers Company—are likely to result. The case does point out that the employees value higher-level needs. Thus, all the pieces seem to be in place to cause the problems experienced at Home Computers. Exhibit 5–6 suggests several principles which could be applied to improve the motivation of the work itself: (1) combining tasks, (2) forming natural work units, (3) establishing relationships with clients, (4) vertical loading, and (5) opening feedback channels. Not all of these may apply here, but Harvey and the consultant can consider several possibilities.

One option would be to have employees move along the assembly line with a computer so they can work on several steps in the assembly process. This combining of tasks should increase skill variety and task identity and result in more meaningful jobs. This approach should not create any severe training or staffing problems, since most of the tasks are simple. A second option would be to have all the workers for a particular section of the line (that is, those who do the same job) meet each week for an hour to discuss problems and suggestions for improvement on the line. In addition, two team representatives from each shift could meet to discuss any problems that cut across shift boundaries. Recommendations from these meetings could be forwarded to management for consideration and written response. This establishment of relationships and vertical loading (that is, allowing decision making and problem solving) should increase the autonomy of a job. Finally, employees on the line could conduct quality-control procedures, keep a tally, and pass information along the assembly line. This change should increase feedback. We have thus identified several promising changes that could make the employees' jobs more motivating and move them into the upper levels of their motivational potential (see Exhibit 5–2).

In summary, we can see how these 10 motivation theories are helpful in analyzing the Home Computers case. But the analysis still seems to fall short. First, we have no way to integrate the use of the theories to assist our analysis. It is as though we are using a shotgun approach. Second, our analysis up to this point tends to be rather static—yet we know that these motivational problems are grounded in a dynamic process. The problems did not come about overnight. The next chapter will try to address these two deficiencies through an integrative model of motivation.

CHAPTER HIGHLIGHTS

This chapter has begun our examination of motivation in work settings. First, we explored why motivation is important for managers to understand. **Motivation was defined as that which energizes, directs, and sustains an individual to perform goal-directed actions.** People are usually motivated to do something; a manager's job is to see that employees' actions help the organization achieve its goals. We also pointed out the complexity of the motivation process by recalling the uniqueness of each individual. This point then led to consideration of some organizational problems which can be directly tied to motivation. These problems include low productivity, tardiness, absenteeism, turnover, poor-quality work, lack of mental presence on the job, lack of innovativeness, and low employee morale.

We briefly discussed how motivation is a dynamic process and that **people are likely to be motivated by different things at different times in their lives.** And just as people change over time, so do their jobs and organizations. Organizations grow or decline and thus provide new or reduced opportunities for individuals to meet their needs and be motivated. And jobs can become more or less challenging and exciting due to technological and structural changes in the organization.

We then discussed a number of content and process theories of motivation. **Content theories highlight the differences among people's needs;** they include theories by Maslow, Herzberg, McClelland, and Alderfer. **Process theories focus on the choice process of individuals regarding their actions;** they include theories by Vroom, Adams, Skinner, and Locke. We also mentioned Hackman's theory of job design and the social-facilitation theory as two other important theories of motivation.

Maslow's hierarchy of needs was the starting point for tying together the four content theories of motivation. Because of the developmental implications of Maslow's theory, we used it to relate Alderfer's ERG theory, Herzberg's two-factor theory, and McClelland's motive model.

These theories all suggest the importance of employees' needs; **the less a need is satisfied, the more it will be desired, and the more individual action will be directed toward satisfying that need.**

McClelland's motive (need) theory added another important element to our analysis: **Individual needs are learned.** This developmental aspect means that needs change over time. It also means that different individuals have unique needs (or at least strengths of needs), since each has a unique background. Herzberg's theory added the important idea that **needs can, in a sense, become oversatisfied and thus fail to motivate behavior.** More of the same reward will not always motivate employees; sometimes managers have to discover new rewards that will address new needs.

After a brief discussion of social-facilitation theory—which helps managers appreciate the impact of peers and superiors on motivation— we discussed several process theories of motivation. First, we discussed Vroom's expectancy theory and stated that it will form the basis for the integrative motivational model in Chapter 6. We discussed three steps in the expectancy model (expectancy, instrumentality, and valence). This step-by-step aspect of the model highlights its developmental nature.

We then discussed operant conditioning (reinforcement theory) as a motivation theory. This model helps managers understand the interface between the organization and the individual. **One critical point managers must remember in applying this theory is that the reward must be perceived as important by the employee receiving it if it is to be an effective motivator. And rewards are not always money.**

Equity theory helps managers appreciate the way employees compare their perceived inputs and outputs to those of other employees. **Managers must be aware that employees are influenced by what they perceive happens both to themselves and to others.**

The last process theory we discussed was Locke's goal-setting theory. Goals are an important element in motivation, and participation in goal setting, tying rewards to the goal accomplishment, and feedback on progress appear to be critical to the effective use of goals. **One of the challenges managers face is the encouragement of employee actions which help accomplish both organizational and individual goals.**

Next, we turned to a discussion of job design as it relates to motivation. Job design has been an important concern to managers since the early 1900s, but the primary focus has been on technical aspects of jobs rather than on full utilization of employee job skills. Since the 1970s, managers have had a theory of job design which focuses on creating a job that is matched to the employee. **Giving an enriched job to a person who wants no challenge is as bad as giving an unenriched job to a**

person who seeks challenge. Current changes in jobs suggest that managers must also focus attention on perceptual/motor and biological aspects of jobs.

To better understand how to apply these various theories, we then looked into the motivational problems at Home Computers Company. Drawing upon all 10 motivational theories, we developed a number of suggested solutions. In closing, we discussed the need for a vehicle to integrate our use of these theories and to place them in a developmental framework. This will be the focus of Chapter 6.

REVIEW QUESTIONS

1. How should *motivation* be defined to be useful to managers?
2. Why is it important for managers to understand motivation? How does a manager's job relate to motivation?
3. What are some key organizational problems that are related to motivation of employees?
4. Explain why motivation is a dynamic process. What work-setting factors create changes in employee motivation?
5. What is the primary distinction between content and process theories of motivation? What other motivation theories are important background for an understanding of motivation?
6. How can the theories of Maslow, Alderfer, Herzberg, and McClelland be tied together?
7. What unique contributions do the theories of Maslow, Alderfer, Herzberg, and McClelland provide for understanding motivation?
8. What is the importance of social facilitation theory for understanding motivation?
9. How do operant conditioning and equity theory tie together to provide useful information for understanding motivation?
10. Goal-setting theory, developed by Locke, is helpful in understanding which aspects of motivation? What challenge for management grows out of this theory?
11. Detail the development of job-design theory and how it has led to both a current dilemma and a new theory of job design (Hackman's model).
12. Describe the important elements and relationships in Hackman's model of job design. Where do individual differences enter into the model?
13. How do perceptual/motor and biological job design aspects relate to Hackman's model?

RESOURCE READINGS

Adams, J. S. "Injustice in Social Exchange." In *Advances in Experimental Social Psychology* 2, ed. L. Berkowitz. New York: Academic Press, 1965.

Alderfer, C. P. *Existence, Relatedness, and Growth.* New York: Free Press, 1972.

Blanchard, K. H., and S. Johnson. *The One Minute Manager.* New York: William Morrow, 1982.

Hackman, R., Jr., and G. R. Oldham. *Work Redesign.* Reading, Mass.: Addison-Wesley, 1980.

Hamner, W. C. "Reinforcement Theory." In *Organizational Behavior and Management: A Contingency Approach*, ed. H. T. Tosi and W. C. Hamner. New York: John Wiley & Sons, 1977, pp. 93–112.

Herzberg, F.; B. Mausner; and B. Snyderman. *The Motivation to Work.* New York: John Wiley & Sons, 1959.

Locke, E. A. "The Nature and Causes of Job Satisfaction." In *Handbook of Industrial and Organizational Psychology*, ed. M. D. Dunnette. Skokie, Ill.: Rand McNally, 1976.

Maslow, A. H. *Motivation and Personality.* New York: Harper & Row, 1954.

McClelland, D. C. *Human Motivation.* Glenview, Ill.: Scott, Foresman, 1985.

Vroom, V. H. *Work and Motivation.* New York: John Wiley & Sons, 1964.

NOTES

1. D. Katz and R. Kahn, *The Social Psychology of Organizations*, 2nd ed. (New York: John Wiley & Sons, 1978).

2. R. M. Steers, *Introduction to Organizational Behavior* (Glenview, Ill.: Scott, Foresman, 1981), p. 328.

3. W. H. Mobley, "Intermediate Linkages in the Relationship between Job Satisfaction and Employee Turnover," *Journal of Applied Psychology* 62 (1977), pp. 237–40.

4. D. Yankelovich & Associates, *Work and Human Values* (New York: Public Agenda Foundation, 1983), pp. 6–7.

5. T. R. Mitchell, "Motivation: New Directions for Theory, Research, and Practice," *Academy of Management Review* 7 (1982), pp. 80–88.

6. Ibid.

7. M. A. Campion and P. W. Thayer, "Job Design: Approaches, Outcomes, and Trade-offs," *Organizational Dynamics* (Winter, 1987), pp. 66–79.

8. A. Maslow, "A Theory of Human Motivation," *Psychological Review* 80 (1943), pp. 370–96.

9. G. R. Salancick and J. Pfeffer, "An Examination of Need-Satisfaction Models of Job Attitudes," *Administrative Science Quarterly* 22 (1977), pp. 427–56.

10. C. P. Alderfer, *Existence, Relatedness, and Growth* (New York: Free Press, 1972).

11. D. C. McClelland, "Power Is the Great Motivator," *Harvard Business Review* 54 (1976), pp. 100–10.

12. F. Herzberg, B. Mausner, and B. Snyderman, *The Motivation to Work* (New York: John Wiley & Sons, 1959).

13. F. Herzberg, "Worker's Needs: The Same Around the World," *Industry Week*, September 21, 1987, pp. 29–32.

14. S. Kerr, A. Harlan, and R. Stogdill, "Preference for Motivator and Hygiene Factors in a Hypothetical Interview Situation," *Personnel Psychology* 25 (1974), pp. 109–24.

15. G. R. Ferris, T. A. Beehr, and D. C. Gilmore, "Social Facilitation: A Review and Alternative Conceptual Model," *Academy of Management Review* (1987), pp. 338–47.

16. G. Schuck, "Intelligent Technology, Intelligent Workers: A New Pedagogy for the High-Tech Work Place," *Organizational Dynamics* (Autumn, 1985), pp. 66–79.

17. V. H. Vroom, *Work and Motivation* (New York: John Wiley & Sons, 1964).

18. T. R. Mitchell, "Expectancy Models of Job Satisfaction, Occupational Preference, and Effort: A Theoretical, Methodological, and Empirical Appraisal," *Psychological Bulletin* 81 (1974), pp. 1096–112.

19. T. C. Mawhinney, "Learning What's Inside the Teaching Machine from the Outside: Operant Technology Applied to Cognitive Phenomena," *Journal of Management* (1985), pp. 134–39.

20. D. J. Cherrington, H. J. Reitz, and W. E. Scott, "Effects of Contingent and Non-Contingent Rewards on the Relationship between Satisfaction and Performance," *Journal of Applied Psychology* 56 (1971), pp. 531–36; W. C. Hamner, "Reinforcement Theory and Contingency Management in Organizational Settings." In H. L. Tosi and W. C. Hamner, *Organizational Behavior and Management: A Contingency Approach* (New York: John Wiley & Sons, 1974), pp. 86–112.

21. J. S. Adams, "Injustice in Social Exchange." In *Advances in Experimental Social Psychology* 2, ed. L. Berkowitz (New York: Academic Press, 1965); L. A. Meese and B. L. Watts, "Complex Nature of the Sense of Fairness: Internal Standards and Social Comparison as Bases for Reward Evaluations," *Journal of Personality and Social Psychology* 45 (1983), pp. 84–93.

22. R. C. Huseman, J. D. Hatfield, and E. W. Miles, "A New Perspective on Equity Theory: The Equity Sensitivity Construct," *Academy of Management Review* (1987), pp. 222–34.

23. J. E. Martin and M. M. Peterson, "Two-Tier Wage Structures: Implications for Equity Theory," *Academy of Management Journal* (1987), pp. 297–315.

24. R. T. Mowday, "Equity Theory Predictions of Behavior in Organizations." In *Motivation and Work Behavior*, 2nd ed., ed. R. M. Steers and L. W. Porter (New York: McGraw-Hill, 1979).

25. J. Brockner, J. Greenberg, A. Brockner, J. Bartz, J. Deavy, and C. Carter, "Layoffs, Equity Theory, and Work Performance: Further Evidence of

the Impact of Survivor Guilt," *Academy of Management Journal* (1986), pp. 373–84.

26. E. A. Locke, "Toward a Theory of Task Performance and Incentive," *Organizational Behavior and Human Performance* 3 (1986), pp. 157–89.

27. M. Erez, R. C. Earley, and C. L. Hulin, "The Impact of Participation on Goal Acceptance and Participation: A Two-Step Model," *Academy of Management Journal* (1985), pp. 50–66.

28. E. A. Locke and D. M. Schweiger, "Participation in Decision-Making: One More Look." In *Research in Organizational Behavior,* ed. B. M. Staw (Greenwich, Conn.: JAI Press, 1979), pp. 265–339.

29. M. Enez, "The Congruence of Goal-Setting Strategies with Socio-Cultural Values and Its Effect on Performance," *Journal of Management* (1986), pp. 585–92.

30. F. W. Taylor, *The Principles of Scientific Management* (New York: Harper & Row, 1911).

31. F. Roethlisberger and W. J. Dickson, *Management and the Worker* (Cambridge, Mass.: Harvard University Press, 1939).

32. A. Bernstein, R. W. Anderson, and W. Zellner, "Help Wanted: America Faces an Era of Worker Scarcity that May Last to the Year 2000," *Business Week,* August 10, 1987, pp. 48–53.

33. J. R. Hackman, G. Oldham, R. Janson, and K. Purdy, "A New Strategy for Job Enrichment," *California Management Review* 27 (1975), pp. 57–71.

34. Ibid.

35. Y. Fried and G. R. Ferris, "The Validity of the Job Characteristics Model: A Review and Meta-Analysis," *Personnel Psychology* (1987), pp. 287–322.

36. H. J. Arnold, "Task Performance, Perceived Competence, and Attributed Causes of Performance as Determinants of Intrinsic Motivation," *Academy of Management Journal* (1985), pp. 876–88.

37. Ibid.

38. This section is drawn from Campion and Thayer, "Job Design: Approaches, Outcomes, and Trade offs."

CASE: Back to piecework: More companies want to base pay increases on the output of their employees

A recent survey of 600 companies by Hay Management Consultants found that one-third intend to push pay-for-performance down the corporate ladder; about 11% currently do so. Another survey, by Hewitt Associates, finds a surprising surge in the use of incentive bonuses for all sorts of workers.

Source: *The Wall Street Journal,* November 15, 1985. Reprinted by permission of *The Wall Street Journal,* © Dow Jones & Company, Inc. 1985. All rights reserved.

Earlier this month, General Motors Corp. became the largest company to change, saying it will place all 110,000 of its North American salaried staff on pay-for-performance, abandoning automatic cost-of-living adjustments. GM joins such other U.S. corporations as TRW Inc., Honeywell Inc. and Hewlett-Packard Co. in using an entirely merit-based pay plan.

The concept of basing pay on output is old indeed, but it hasn't been prevalent in the U.S. since piecework began to fade after the rise of unionization. Economic forces are moving corporations to bring it back.

What's in it

Many companies, because of competition and diminished inflation, find it hard to justify raising wages and passing along higher labor costs to customers. At the same time, they want to increase labor productivity by motivating employees to do their best work, and by dumping laggards. Many companies have found that group-based merit pay, including profit sharing, works best only when they are highly profitable, and even then group-based pay rewards workers similarly. Pay-for-performance is seen as a way to stretch wage dollars, to motivate top performers and to provide a defensible reason for punishing or discharging the least productive.

The companies that tend to jump at basing pay increases on merit are in the most competitive businesses. BankAmerica, for instance, didn't get serious about pay-for-performance until its earnings and market share sharply declined over the past five years; its work force is bloated compared with lean-and-mean competitors such as Citicorp and Wells Fargo & Co. General Motors is in a constant struggle to pare the labor-cost advantage enjoyed by Japanese companies in making popular small cars.

But many of the managers who must implement pay-for-performance and the employees who work under it are skeptical, even critical. According to management consultants, most workers dislike being judged, and most managers who work closely with their employees dislike sitting in judgment.

Spread evenly

"An awful lot of it (pay-for-performance) is rhetoric, "observes Jerrold Bratkovich, a Hay consultant. "Middle managers would rather use the 'peanut-butter approach' of handing out raises, just spreading a little to everybody."

Mr. Bratkovich cites one company that sought advice last year when it had only a small pool of money allocated for raises. The consultants suggested giving the best employees bonuses of up to $10,000. "Not one manager opted to give a bonus," he says. "They were so afraid of making a judgment and getting the other employees mad at them."

Workers have their own concerns. They and their unions say that performance on many jobs can't be measured objectively, that pay-for-performance may be an excuse for favoritism and for firing people. Some companies agree that the system can destroy rather than lift morale, and even those employees who prosper under it complain bitterly if other groups of fellow workers, such as unionized blue-collar workers, are kept on the old system of automatic cost-of-living adjustments.

But where pay-for-performance has been universally and rigorously applied, it has often had dramatic results. Frank Schultz, a BankAmerica senior vice president, runs the company's credit-card division. He has put all of his 3,500 employees under a pay-for-performance system, which ranks them against their peers, using 200 specific criteria. "I measure everything that moves," Mr. Schultz says.

The rankings lump workers into five groups, or quintiles. Under ostensibly companywide policy, the top performers are supposed to receive raises at least 40% higher than the worst get, and the bottom 20% have a limited time in which to get out of their quintile or get out of the company. In Mr. Schultz's division, the best workers have received raises 64% higher than those on the bottom. He has sacked 6% of the workforce in the past year.

"Some people had retired while they were still on the payroll," he says.

Employees are rated on how many payments they process, how many new accounts they generate, how many phone calls they handle. Computers and surveillance are essential to pay-for-performance systems. Supervisors now listen in on customer-service representatives 10 times a week; the employees don't know which 10 calls are monitored. An outside agency has been hired to make calls posing as customers. It rates representatives on such qualities as helpfulness and cheerfulness, and on how long they keep customers on hold. The monitoring becomes another cost of doing business. It takes 20 people, a lot of computer software and about $1 million a year to keep tabs on the employees in Mr. Schultz's division.

Mr. Schultz says that his measures "are required for a turnaround in the corporate culture, and for us to compete in a deregulated environment." He says that morale is high, because good workers are receiving hefty raises and think that justice is being done by firing the deadwood. Mr. Schultz also says that credit-card division profit has doubled in the past three years, but he won't disclose numbers. He adds that quality of service has increased.

The difficulty of implementing pay-for-performance can be seen even at BankAmerica. Some division managers aren't convinced that the system works for everybody, and others don't want to rank their employees. William Carstens, a vice president of business services, doesn't think all jobs can be measured objectively. And some workers, he says, might become so nervous working under a quota system that it hurts their work. "You don't want them so worried about being able to pay their rent that they can't do their job," Mr. Carstens says.

Another BankAmerica executive, who manages a group of branches, says he hasn't confronted any employees over poor ranking, nor has he fired anyone. "It is my biggest weakness," he says. "I find [such confrontation] very unpleasant."

Other companies, and other managers, are willing to endure some unpleasantness because they see no other choice. When annual, across-the-board raises are eliminated, "someone is always going to be unhappy," says John Hillins, the director of executive compensation for Honeywell Inc. "The question is: who do you want to be unhappy? When everyone gets the same raise, the top performers are unhappy. Under a merit system, the poor performers are unhappy."

What would you recommend to managers? Why?

EXERCISE: Expectancy theory: A case exercise approach

Purpose: To clarify and operationalize Expectancy Theory.

Advance Preparation: The students should have a basic understanding of Expectancy Theory.

Group Size: This may be done as an individual assignment and/or as a group task. The group size should range from 4 to 6.

Time Required: The exercise requires from 35 to 50 minutes. This excludes the advance preparation stage, i.e., an understanding of Expectancy Theory. This may be covered immediately before conducting this exercise.

Procedure

Step 1.   This step requires approximately 5 minutes and consists of reading the following case.

You have been asked to interview Harry and find out how he feels about his job and a few aspects relating to it. The following is the dialogue that resulted.

Interviewer: Hi, Harry. I have been asked to talk to you about your job. Do you mind if I ask you a few questions?

Harry: No, not at all.

Interviewer: Thanks, Harry. What are the things that you would anticipate getting satisfaction from as a result of your job?

Harry: What do you mean?

Interviewer: Well, what is important to you with regard to your job here?

Harry: I guess most important is job security. As a matter of fact, I can't think of anything that is more important to me. I think getting a raise would be nice, and a promotion would be even better.

Interviewer: Anything else that you think would be nice to get, or for that matter, that you would want to avoid?

Harry: I certainly would not want my buddies to make fun of me. We're pretty friendly, and this is really important to me.

Interviewer: Anything else?

Harry: No, not really. That seems to be it.

How satisfied do you think you would be with each of these?

Harry: What do you mean?

Interviewer: Well, assume that something that you would really like has a value of $+1.0$ and something you would really not like, that is you would want to avoid, has a value of -1.0, and something you are indifferent about has a value of 0.

Harry: Ok. Getting a raise would have a value of .5; a promotion is more important, so I'd say .7; and having my buddies make fun of me, .9.

Interviewer: But, I thought you didn't want your buddies to make fun of you.

Harry: I don't.

Interviewer: But, you gave it a value of .9.

Harry: Oh, I guess it should be $-.9$.

Interviewer: Ok, I just want to be sure I understand what you're saying. Harry, what do you think the chances are of these things happening?

Harry: That depends.

Interviewer: On what?

Harry: On whether my performance is high or just acceptable.

Interviewer: What if it is high?

Harry: I figure I stand about a 50–50 chance of getting a raise and/or a promotion, but I also think that there is a 90% chance that my buddies will make fun of me.

Interviewer: What about job security?

Harry: I am certain my job is secure here, whether my performance is high or just acceptable. I can't remember the last guy, who was doing his job, and got fired. But if my performance is just acceptable, my chances of a raise or promotion are about 10%. However, then the guys will not make fun of me. That I am certain about.

Interviewer: What is the likelihood of your performance level being high?

Harry: That depends. If I work very hard and put out a high degree of effort, I'd say that my chances of my performance being high is about 90%. But if I put out a low level of effort, you know—if I just take it easy, then I figure that the chances of my doing an acceptable job is about 80%.

Interviewer: Well, which would you do: put out a low level, or a high level, of effort?

Harry: With all the questions you asked me, you should be able to tell me.

Interviewer: You may be right!

Harry: Yeah? That's nice. Hey, if you don't have any other questions, I'd like to join the guys for coffee.

Interviewer: Ok, thanks for your time.

Harry: You're welcome.

Step 2. This step requires approximately 15 minutes when being done individually, and 20 minutes when being done in a group, or 25 minutes when being done individually and then in a group. If the latter approach is taken, allocate 10 minutes for the individual activity, and 15 minutes for the group activity.

Answer the following question based upon the information in the above case. Calculate, according to Expectancy Theory model, whether Harry will choose to exert a high level of effort, or a low level of effort. Your calculations should clearly demonstrate the values of expectancies, instrumentalities, and valences. (Use the chart below.)

Step 3. This step requires approximately 15 to 20 minutes. Member(s) of the class are to answer the following questions. According to Expectancy Theory, would Harry choose to exert a low or a high level of effort and why? This may entail the explanation of the calculations performed, the basis for the figures used, and the rationale for using those particular figures. (Use the chart below.)

Step 4. The following discussion question may be asked: What are the different things you might do to motivate Harry if you were Harry's boss?

Source: Robert J. Oppenheimer, *Proceedings of Eastern Academy of Management Meeting*, 1981, pp.15–16.

Please fill in the blanks and calculate the effort motivation for each choice.

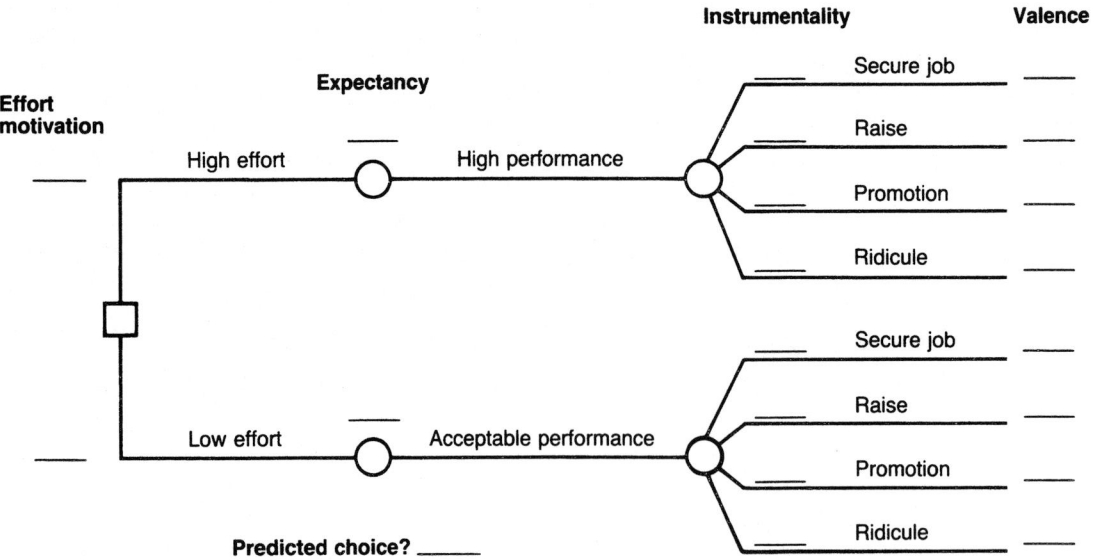

Predicted choice? _____

QUESTIONNAIRE: Motivation Feedback Opinionnaire

Part 1

Directions:
The following statements have seven possible responses.

Strongly Agree	Agree	Slightly Agree	Don't Know	Slightly Disagree	Disagree	Strongly Disagree
+3	+2	+1	0	−1	−2	−3

Please mark one of the seven responses by circling the number that corresponds to the response that fits your opinion. For example: if you "Strongly Agree," circle the number "+3."

Complete every item.

1. Special wage increases should be given to employees who do their jobs very well.   +3+2+1   0−1−2−3

2. Better job descriptions would be helpful so that employees will know exactly what is expected of them.   +3+2+1   0−1−2−3

3. Employees need to be reminded that their jobs are dependent on the company's ability to compete effectively.   +3+2+1   0−1−2−3

4. A supervisor should give a good deal of attention to the physical working conditions of his or her employees.   +3+2+1   0−1−2−3

5. The supervisor ought to work hard to develop a friendly working atmosphere among his or her people.   +3+2+1   0−1−2−3

6. Individual recognition for above-standard performance means a lot to employees.   +3+2+1   0−1−2−3

7. Indifferent supervision can often bruise feelings.   +3+2+1   0−1−2−3

8. Employees want to feel that their real skills and capacities are put to use on their jobs.   +3+2+1   0−1−2−3

9. The company retirement benefits and stock programs are important factors in keeping employees on their jobs.   +3+2+1   0−1−2−3

10. Almost every job can be made more stimulating and challenging.   +3+2+1   0−1−2−3

11. Many employees want to give their best in everything they do.   +3+2+1   0−1−2−3

12. Management could show more interest in the employees by sponsoring social events after-hours. $+3+2+1$ $0-1-2-3$

13. Pride in one's work is actually an important reward. $+3+2+1$ $0-1-2-3$

14. Employees want to be able to think of themselves as "the best" at their own jobs. $+3+2+1$ $0-1-2-3$

15. The quality of the relationships in the informal work group is quite important. $+3+2+1$ $0-1-2-3$

16. Individual incentive bonuses would improve the performance of employees. $+3+2+1$ $0-1-2-3$

17. Visibility with upper management is important to employees. $+3+2+1$ $0-1-2-3$

18. Employees generally like to schedule their own work and to make job-related decisions with a minimum of supervision. $+3+2+1$ $0-1-2-3$

19. Job security is important to employees. $+3+2+1$ $0-1-2-3$

20. Having good equipment to work with is important to employees. $+3+2+1$ $0-1-2-3$

Part 2

Scoring:

1. Transfer the numbers you circled in Part 1 to the appropriate places in the chart below:

Statement Number	Score	Statement Number	Score
10	_____	2	_____
11	_____	3	_____
13	_____	9	_____
18	_____	19	_____
· · · · · · ·		· · · · · · ·	
Total	_____	Total	_____
(Self-Actualization Needs)		(Safety Needs)	

Statement Number	Score	Statement Number	Score
6	_____	1	_____
8	_____	4	_____
14	_____	16	_____
17	_____	20	_____
· · · · · · ·		· · · · · · ·	
Total	_____	Total	_____
(Esteem Needs)		(Physiological Needs)	

	Statement Number	Score
	5	_____
	7	_____
	12	_____
	15	_____
		. . . .
	Total	_____

(Belonging Needs)

2. Record your total scores in the chart below by marking an "X" in each row next to the number of your total score for that area of needs motivation.

	−12	−10	−8	−6	−4	−2	0	+2	+4	+6	+8	+10	+12
Self-Actualization									X				
Esteem												X	
Belonging										X			
Safety						X							
Physiological										X			

Low use   High use

Once you have completed this chart, you can see the relative strength of your use of each of these areas of needs motivation. There is, of course, no "right" answer. What is right for you is what matches the actual needs of your employees and that, of course, is specific to each situation and each individual. In general, however, the "experts" tell us that today's employees are best motivated by efforts in the areas of Belonging and Esteem.

Source: Reprinted from J. William Pfeiffer and John E. Jones, eds., *The 1973 Annual Handbook for Group Facilitators* (San Diego, Calif.: University Associates, Inc., 1973). Used with permission.

QUESTIONNAIRE: Motivation Needs Survey

Please respond to each statement below in terms of how often the statement describes you. Use the scale below for responses:

Never	Almost never	Seldom	Sometimes	Usually	Almost always	Always
1	2	3	4	5	6	7

_____ 1. I do my best work when my job assignments are fairly difficult.

_____ 2. When I have a choice, I try to work in a group instead of by myself.

_____ 3. I seek an active role in the leadership of a group.

_____ 4. I try to influence those around me to see things my way.

_____ 5. I try very hard to improve on my past performance at work.

_____ 6. I pay a good deal of attention to the feelings of others at work.

_____ 7. I find myself organizing and directing the activities of others.

_____ 8. I strive to gain more control over the events around me at work.

_____ 9. I take moderate risks and stick my neck out to get ahead at work.

_____ 10. I prefer to do my work with others.

_____ 11. I strive to be "in command" when I am working in a group.

_____ 12. I try to seek out added responsibilities on my job.

_____ 13. I do not openly express my disagreements with others.

_____ 14. I try to perform better than my co-workers.

_____ 15. I find myself talking to those around me about non-business related matters.

Scoring for Motivation Needs Survey

Record your responses from the survey and total the three columns to get your scores for Need for Achievement, Need for Affiliation and Need for Power.

Need for Achievement	Need for Affiliation	Need for Power
1 _____	2 _____	3 _____
5 _____	6 _____	4 _____
9 _____	10 _____	7 _____
12 _____	13 _____	8 _____
14 _____	15 _____	11 _____
Total _____	Total _____	Total _____
÷ 5	÷ 5	÷ 5
Score = _____	Score = _____	Score = _____

Averages for samples of 712 employees:

| 4.3 | 4.1 | 4.1 |

Sources: R. M. Steers and D. N. Braunstein, "A Behaviorally-Based Measure of Manifest Needs in Work Settings," *Journal of Vocational Behavior* 9 (1976), pp.251–61; and R. M. Steers, "Antecedents and Outcomes of Organizational Commitment," *Administrative Science Quarterly* 22 (1977), pp. 46–56. Samples consisted of scientists, engineers, hospital employees, white collar employees, and management students.

An Integrative Approach to Motivation

C hapter 5 discussed 10 different theories of motivation. In exploring both content and process theories, as well as social facilitation and job-design theories, we gained a great deal of information for analyzing motivational problems. And we applied these theories to the Home Computers Company case. This chapter will go one step further in making these theories useful by providing an integrative model of motivation. With the 10 theories as background, an integrative model should make it easier to fully analyze motivational problems in organizations.

AN INTEGRATIVE MODEL OF MOTIVATION

The integrative model of motivation is based on the expectancy theory discussed in Chapter 5.[1] This theory provides a strong basis for the model because it is both process oriented and developmental, as discussed in the last chapter. By modifying the model somewhat and expanding it in certain areas, managers can develop a very useful integrative framework for understanding motivation in organizations. The model is shown in Exhibit 6–1 on page 216. It describes the motivational process that unfolds in determining an individual's motivational level. Arrows 1a, 2, 3a, 4, and 5 represent the five basic steps in the process. The model also shows the interaction between the internal motivational process of an individual and the managerial practices of an organization (arrows 1b, 3b, and 3c). This model helps managers tie together the content, process, and job-design theories discussed in Chapter 5. It integrates individual needs, feedback of information, desired rewards, the impact of supervisors and peers, organizational goals, and the job itself. Let us use an example to go through the model and see how it works. As we explore the example, constant reference to Exhibit 6–1 will help you understand the integrative model.

Imagine that an employee has an unsatisfied need for greater recognition in her work (arrow 1a). The organization, via her supervisor, has given Betty a goal of handling five more customer complaints each week than she presently handles (arrow 1b). In arrow 2, Betty considers alternative actions which she thinks will lead to satisfaction of that need (arrow 5). She might consider: (1) increasing her contacts with her boss so he knows her better, (2) working harder on the job to increase her productivity, or (3) attending training courses to demonstrate her interest in advancement. At this point, Betty's choice will be influenced by the reward she believes will lead to satisfaction of her need for esteem (arrows 4 and 5), as well as the desired outcome of the organization (arrow 3b). Let us say that Betty feels it will take a promotion to satisfy her esteem need. Furthermore, she believes that in her organization, a promotion will follow high productivity in her present job; that is, high productivity in handling customer complaints has the highest instrumentality value. Betty's opinion is developed from her experiences in the organization. Thus, high productivity becomes her desired outcome (arrow 3a), which is consistent with the organization's goal (arrow 1b). And of her three action options, working harder is the choice (arrow 2) she believes will lead to higher productivity (arrow 3a); that is, it has the highest expectancy value.

The amount of motivation

The actual amount of a person's motivation (according to expectancy theory) depends on several factors shown in the model. First is the **expectancy** that hard work (arrow 2) will lead to a desired outcome (arrow 3a). Using our example, if Betty feels that she is a capable worker

EXHIBIT 6–1

An Integrative Model of an Individual's Motivational Process

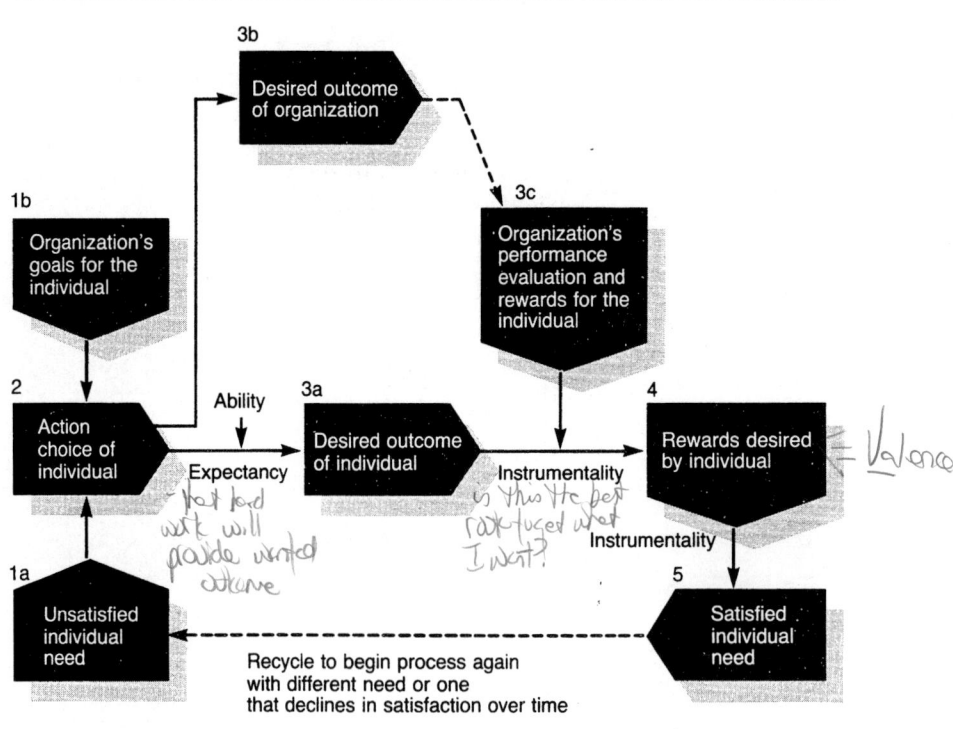

Source: Adapted from Vroom's Expectancy Theory, in V. H. Vroom, *Work and Motivation*, copyright © 1964 John Wiley & Sons, Inc.

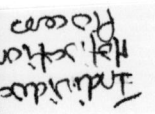

and that the outcome of her job is primarily determined by effort alone, her expectancy will be high. But if she doubts her capabilities and knows that her performance is heavily determined by others, her expectancy may be quite low. The fit between a person and a job is a critical aspect of this analysis. What type of job does a person hold, and how capable is he or she in the job? The next factor is the **instrumentality** that the desired outcome (arrow 3a) will actually lead to a reward (arrow 4). **Instrumentality is the link between desired outcome and desired rewards. Instrumentality is very important in the model because it links the motivation of an individual to actions of the organization.** If Betty believes that high productivity in her organization almost always leads to a promotion, her instrumentality for high productivity will be quite significant. But if she believes that such factors as luck and who a person knows sometimes determine promotions, her instrumentality for high productivity may be lower.

Valence is the actual value or importance a person places on a reward (arrow 4). If Betty's promotion is very important to her, her valence will be quite high. If it is only moderately important, the valence will be lower. In actual practice, the valence is really based on another instrumentality link—rewards desired to satisfy needs (arrows 4 and 5). In other words, if Betty feels that a promotion is very important in satisfying her need for recognition, the valence of the promotion will be high. If she is not as sure about this link, the valence of the promotion will be lower. **The need to be satisfied carries its own valence that affects the valence of the rewards desired.**

For a person to be highly motivated to work harder in a job, the expectancy between action and desired outcome (arrows 2 and 3a) must be high; the instrumentality between desired outcome and desired rewards (arrows 3a and 4) must be high; and the valence of the reward must be high. And as mentioned, this means that the instrumentality between reward and satisfied need (arrows 4 and 5) must be high. Furthermore, the need which is to be satisfied must be very important to a person. **If the expectancy or instrumentality connections are weak, or if the valence of the reward and the satisfied need are low, your motivation will be low.** The reason is that the process is multiplicative in nature. It is like a chain whose strength is determined by its weakest link. In our example, if Betty is unsure whether high productivity will lead to a promotion (low instrumentality between arrows 3a and 4), her motivation to work hard will tend to be lower, regardless of the valence and expectancy.

Thus far in our analysis, it should be clear how both Expectancy Theory and content theories relate to the integrative model. Expectancy Theory is the basis for the model, and the content theories elaborate on the types of needs that people act to satisfy. Herzberg's Two-Factor Theory helps managers understand the link between rewards and satisfied need (arrows 4 and 5). The reason for this is that all of the hygiene and motivating factors relate to actions and aspects of work—that is, the rewards desired by a person (arrow 4). The other content theories relate directly to the needs in arrows 1a and 5. Furthermore, we have acknowledged how Job-Design Theory ties into the instrumentality and expectancy aspects of the model. Meaningfulness, responsibility, and feedback, as spelled out in the job-design theory, are rewards that people may desire in addition to or in place of financial rewards. Both skill variety and autonomy also relate to the action options by expanding the range of options and the control a person has over the options.

The dynamic nature of the model

The explanation of the model, however, is still not complete. We have not yet dealt with the dynamic nature of the process. Let us explore this aspect of the model by returning to our example and tracing what happens as Betty begins to work harder and tries to satisfy her need for recognition. Whether her hard work pays off in increased productivity depends heavily on her ability. **Performance is a function of both motivation and ability, plus opportunity to perform.** Thus, Betty may work very hard (high motivation) but still not be very effective if she lacks the abilities needed for certain aspects of her job. If Betty's organization or her boss inhibits her chance to use her skills and motivation, she may also perform below par. However, if Betty does fail to achieve higher productivity, she may learn something about herself and her organization that will affect her motivation in the future. For example, she could decide that she will never get a promotion in her company and become motivated to look for another job.

At this point, we must also consider Betty's actions as they relate to Goal-Setting Theory, that is, to the desired outcomes of the organization (arrows 1b and 3b). Obviously, Betty's superiors and coworkers will be evaluating her hard work. And her superiors will evaluate her performance in light of organizational goals. The ideal situation occurs when actions achieve both personal desired outcomes (arrow 3a) as well as desired outcomes of the organization (arrow 3b). **In fact, it would be ideal to work in an organization where an employee's every action enhanced both his or her goals and the organization's goals simultaneously; and this matching might be viewed as a task for managers in organizations.** Questions such as, Does an employee know what the organization expects of him or her? and Does the organization tie rewards to its goals? are important as managers consider the interaction of arrows 1b, 2, 3a, and 3b in the integrative model. In our example, perhaps Betty can work hard and increase productivity, but because of a lack of clear organizational goals, she may increase productivity in the wrong areas. Perhaps in her hard work she ignores certain organizational norms that are considered just as important as performance goals. Or perhaps the organization actually throws obstacles in front of her such as changing goals or devising procedures that tie up her efforts. These events all come together in the instrumentality between the high productivity and the desired reward (promotion) that the company controls (arrows 3a, 3c, and 4). This also marks the point at which goal setting combines with reinforcement theory in the model. Providing desired rewards for behavior an organization desires should increase the likelihood that those behaviors will be repeated. And if the reward does not come, motivation to continue the behavior desired by the organization will decrease.

Let us assume that Betty's hard work has led to better performance, but she does not get the desired promotion. Instead, she receives a nice pay increase. What went wrong? Did she misread the desired outcomes of the organization? Did the organization misread her goals? Another piece of information helps complete the puzzle. Assume that Betty finds out that the promotion she wanted went to someone else who just happens to be connected to the boss's family and who plays golf with the boss on weekends. Betty thinks she has misread the real criteria for promotion and feels cheated. Suppose, however, that another coworker receives the promotion, but the boss explains to Betty why she was passed over this time. The pay raise is meant to tell her that she is doing a good job. If she keeps up the good work, the next promotion will be hers. Obviously, Betty's future motivation will be influenced quite differently in these two situations. Equity Theory and Social Facilitation Theory help managers understand this aspect of the model. The rewards employees value and the actions they believe will lead to those rewards are clearly influenced by what happens to them in comparison to others in the organization.

Now, let us assume instead that Betty receives the promotion she wanted. Everything has worked out for her as she desired. Is Betty's need for recognition satisfied? What is the actual link between promotion and need satisfaction (arrows 4 and 5)? Perhaps Betty finds that the feeling of recognition is not as great as she thought it would be. Thus, her need is still unsatisfied; Betty's cycle must begin again. Or perhaps Betty's need for recognition is satisfied, but she finds the new job too constraining. She is less free than she was in the old job. Thus, Betty's need for achievement or greater challenge may rise and become the focus of her motivational energies.

From this description, it should be clear why motivation is a complex process. It involves many pieces, much like a huge puzzle, and clearly that process is dynamic. The motivation process involves sequential steps that occur in a cyclical process over time. Many of the model's pieces require a look at the past in order to make a current assessment of those pieces—for example, instrumentality, expectancy, and needs all grow out of a time context. They do not just appear at a given moment. Change and evolution can enter the process at almost any point. As we consider another example for applying the model, think about these dynamic properties; we will return to them later.

Insight 6–1 presents the situation faced in the 1980s by graduates of MBA programs. As the article suggests, the situation was rather bleak and resulted in a reconsideration of the appropriate actions. Since the action to obtain an MBA (arrow 2 in the model) and the achievement of the desired outcome of the MBA degree (arrow 3a) often did not result in the desired reward of a good job (arrow 4), the instrumentality between ovals 3a and 4 was reduced. Therefore, people like Rachel Russo were led to question past decisions, as suggested in the quote from Tom Keffer. In Rachel's case, she decided to look for a job as a secretary. That is, she changed her desired reward (arrow 4). But how motivated would she be in that secretarial position? A related situation is presented by Bill Schwochow's choice to slack off on schoolwork in order to work harder to find a job. In Bill's case, he decided that the appropriate action (arrow 2) for getting a job (arrow 3a) was not more schoolwork, but rather more job searching. Of course, this decision certainly affected his motivation in the classroom; hence, Bill's decision may not have satisfied the organizational goals as represented by the teacher (arrows 1b and 3b). These examples demonstrate how the choice process of the motivational model works and how the process is affected by outcomes and rewards further on in the process. These examples point out the potential for changes in action choices, as well as changes in the other components of the model. Let us now turn to a more systematic discussion of the dynamic and development aspects of the motivational model. Then we will apply our integrative model to the Home Computers case.

CHANGES IN MOTIVATION OVER TIME

As suggested in discussing the model of motivation in Exhibit 6–1, many factors can change over time and affect the motivation of employees. The primary factor in the developmental nature of motivation is change that occurs in employees over time. However, changes in an organization and a job can also interact with employees to create changes in motivation.

Changes in people

Chapters 3 and 4 made the point that people are unique as a result of their background. Therefore, **managers must deal with a multitude of motivational issues if they manage a number of people.** In addition, the fact that these employees may represent different life, family, and

---

I N S I G H T 6–1

New MBAs Are Scrambling for Jobs as Recession Brings Drop in Hiring

Rachel Russo graduated last June from Northwestern University's J. L. Kellogg Graduate School of Management, one of the best business schools in the country. Today, she can't find a job.

She spends 10 to 20 hours a week writing letters, telephoning and interviewing at companies—so far without success. "In terms of getting a job," she says, "graduate school was a waste of time."

If she doesn't soon find a job in her field—personnel management—Mrs. Russo may try to be a secretary. But that, too, poses problems. "How many people want a secretary who has more education than they have?" she asks.

"There's no question there are fewer opportunities," says Karen K. Stauffacher, director of placement at the University of Wisconsin's Business School in Madison. She advises students to take advantage of personal connections at companies and to be flexible in considering salary, locations and jobs. The school's alumni placement file has grown to 250 names from 75 in the past year; the list of job openings has shrunk to two pages from 10.

"A lot of people gave up good jobs to get an MBA here," says Tom Keffer, editor of the Wharton Journal. "A lot feel they've wasted their time."

Letting schoolwork slide

The tight job market means many students will have to work harder wooing employers. "I'll be honest with you: I'm letting my work slide to prepare for these interviews," says Bill Schwochow, a 23-year-old University of Wisconsin student who has been searching since December. Before interviews, he spends one to two hours reading annual reports and business publications to bone up on companies. So far he hasn't had any success. "I try to avoid taking (rejection letters) personally," he says.

Over the long term, the MBA markets should improve as the post World War II baby boom population thins. After reaching a peak of about 59,000 business graduates in the 1984–1985 academic year, the number should decline to less than 55,000 by 1989, according to the National Center for Education Statistics.

Comments Albert P. Hegyi, president of the Association of MBA Executives Inc., a professional group: "You're going to see some excellent opportunities at the end of the decade."

---

career stages means their motivational needs will differ. On top of this variation, the motivational needs of people will change over time. Maslow saw his hierarchy of needs operating over a person's lifetime.[2] He saw the various needs that motivate people being different for a young person than for an older person. More recently, research by Sheehy, based upon Levinson's work, has outlined life phases and key events that occur during each life phase (see Exhibit 6–2).[3] A look at these will demonstrate how motivation might vary across life phases.

EXHIBIT 6–2

Adult Life Phases as Adapted from Sheehy and Levinson

Age	Key Events	Basic Issues
Late teens/ early twenties	Striking out on your own; college, job, military service. Early thoughts on a career and family life. Possibly marriage.	Achieving independence from your family. Search for identity. Determining what one should do in life.
Late twenties/ thirties	Change in occupation. Return to school. Marriage or possibly divorce. Family activities and children are important. Important job promotion.	What is life really about? What do I want in life? Achieving a sense of stability. Self doubts and awareness of getting older.
Forties	Realization that life goals may not be achieved. Change of career. Death of parents.	Real awareness of aging of your body. Stagnation in life, career, family. Who am I, really?
Fifties	Reaching your highest career level. Substituting new goals for your life.	Feeling of satisfaction with life versus self doubt. Development of a sense of wisdom.
Sixties and beyond	Retirement. Health problems. Aging.	What to do? Death of others and self. Need to belong. Importance of family and friends.

Source: G. Sheehy, *Passages* (New York: E. P. Dutton, 1976), and D. Levinson, *The Seasons of a Man's Life* (New York: Alfred A. Knopf, 1978).

The following paragraphs are general statements about people. And the stages discussed can vary a great deal from person to person. In fact, the key events may even occur at different life points for different people. The point of presenting these life stages and the motivation implications is to provide a general framework that must be modified based on each individual's background. As the Home Computers Company case in Chapter 4 illustrated, Steve probably needed more in terms of belongingness than did Louise. Thus, the best way to motivate these two people would vary, even though they were in the same life stage.

Sheehy points out that the late teens and early 20s are a time of trying to locate oneself in a peer group apart from the home and family. It is also the time of trying out an occupation. The questions being asked are: Who am I? What do I want to do? What is really occurring at this time is the combination of the exploration stage of a person's career (as discussed in Chapter 2) and the adolescence personality stage (as discussed in Chapter 4). The person at this stage is searching for both a career and an identity. Sheehy describes two primary alternative scenarios. In one, the teen/20s person looks for a ready-made form to fit into.

In the other, the individual jumps from one personal encounter and one job to another. Managers must know that basic needs motivate these people. **The teen/20s person typically seeks a sense of belonging; friendships and coworker relationships are important.** Thus, to be effective, managers try to provide this opportunity and also provide feedback directed toward the person's search for identity. This feedback also tells the person how he or she is doing on the job.

The next life stage occurs during the late 20s and 30s. In this period, a settling process takes place for most people. There may be a job change. A person may go back to school. Marriages usually occur in this period, and children may enter the picture. Essentially, this stage is an interaction of the young adult personality stage and the career stage of establishment (as discussed in Chapters 4 and 2, respectively). It is a time of asking: What do I want out of life? Will I be able to achieve my life goals? For many people, this is a time of growing stress as they pass into true adulthood. The birth of children begins a process that draws a person away from work, while conflicting forces attract the person to see what he or she can accomplish professionally. **The result for the 20s/30s employee is likely to be an unusual combination of needs for security and income with needs to succeed and progress in an occupation.** For the blue-collar worker, the need for progression may be replaced by a need to be recognized for accomplishments and abilities. In either event, effective managers should probably define opportunities that will use the talents of a 20s/30s employee, while recognizing the family demands the employee may be experiencing at this time. This recognition can come simply through an interest in the employee's personal life, though managers should never interfere where they are not wanted. Again, however, analysis of an individual employee will determine which behaviors of the manager will motivate him or her.

During the next life phase, the 40s, people begin to realize whether or not their life ambitions will be achieved. And because of the process of aging and physical decline, people experience what is known as the midlife crisis. Basically, people realize that they are getting older and that time for achieving their ambitions is limited. These same issues continue into the next life phase, the 50s, and set the stage for the critical issues of the adulthood personality stage (as discussed in Chapter 4). People must come to grips with whether they are basically satisfied with their life or whether they sense failure. This life stage interacts with the career stage of maturity (discussed in Chapter 2).

If the 40s/50s person senses possible failure or a plateau of ambitions, security needs will be predominant, along with needs to belong. Insight 6–2 shows that this time of life is often one of conflict between the dreams of a person's 20s and the realities of a person's 40s. Managers may then want to provide support for these people—and perhaps some

Dream vs. Reality
Harvard MBAs Find Investment Banking Is a Mixed Bag at Best

Many in Class of '69 Consider Personal Sacrifice Too Big, But Class of '87 Plunges In

Bull Market Remains a Lure

*H*arvard Business School graduates venturing into investment banking this summer are a charmed group, and they know it. What other recruits, after all, have immediate access to the inner circles of corporate power along with eye-popping starting salaries?

But earlier inductees into the elite club—Harvard M.B.A.s who preceded them into the field 18 years ago—have found that the glittering prizes are by no means guaranteed and often come only at a huge personal price.

Interviews with members of the classes of 1987 and 1969 present a classic contrast of youth's boundless optimism with the sobering experience of maturity. And because both groups embarked on their careers during a booming stock market and torrid investment-banking growth, the past may hold some sobering lessons for the freshly minted M.B.A.s.

To graduates of this year's class, investment banking offers a chance to deal as peers with client senior managers while earning as much as $100,000 the first year.

They are prepared to work 80-hour weeks, but insist that personal relationships needn't be sacrificed. They enter a field soiled by scandal but are confident ethical conflicts can be avoided. Success, they are convinced, is theirs for the grabbing.

The potential rewards

Members of the Class of 1969 were afire with the same ambition and assurance when they started out, and many haven't been disappointed. The work is exciting, and compensation can top $1 million a year. But some were forced from jobs in the intervening years by a slumping stock market that dried up the mergers, acquisitions and corporate financings that are the lifeblood of their business. Some found they didn't like the work. Others paid for career success with failed marriages.

Navigating the pressures and temptations and emerging a winner "isn't that simple," observes Richard S. Pechter, the 42-year-old chairman of the Financial Services Group of Donaldson, Lufkin & Jenrette Securities Corp. "I'm glad they have the self-confidence," he says of the Harvard M.B.A.s moving into investment banking, as he did in 1969. But, he says, success "requires a lot of things to come together, a lot beyond their control."

counseling as to how to handle this plateau or decline. The 40s/50s employee can be expected to be very loyal to the company, but his or her performance will depend heavily on the support managers and coworkers provide. **On the other hand, if the 40s/50s person feels successful in life, he or she will want to remain involved and productive in the company.** Thus, managers should probably try to utilize the expertise and wisdom of the older employee. And if the person is capable, the manager should provide a number of ways to involve this person in the company.

As people move into the life stage of the 60s, they begin to experience a sense that they are at the end of their working life. There is a tendency to review past accomplishments and to view their job in perspective with other important aspects of life, such as family and friends. Obviously, the career stage of decline (Chapter 2) and the later-life personality stage interact to yield either a sense of integrity or a sense of disappointment for these older workers. To get the most out of these employees, managers must endeavor to make them feel important so they gain a sense of integrity. **Self-esteem and belonging needs tend to be predominant in older employees, and managers must provide ways for these needs to be met if these workers are to be motivated.**

In addition to changes that occur over a lifetime at different ages, there are historical changes that also occur. People who come from different generations tend to view the world quite differently—consider, for example, a child and his parents. People who are currently in senior management positions in companies were children of the depression of the 1930s. They tend to view the world with more pessimism and caution than do their more junior managers who are children of the 1950s and 1960s. These younger managers are more impatient. They want authority now; they are smart; and they are willing to take risks. Further, they tend to be more optimistic, having never faced depression, and they seem to be less loyal to any one company. A 1986 *Business Week* article summarized the differences, as shown in Exhibit 6–3.[4] It is important that managers consider these differences in trying to motivate people from different generations. Their needs are not the same, and they desire different kinds of rewards and opportunities. Furthermore, they may desire different types of jobs.

Indeed, an exploration of these differences in generations and changes in people should illustrate that jobs must change for people to remain motivated over a career and from generation to generation. As people become better educated and more experienced, they demand more from their jobs. Can jobs keep up with the rate of change in people? Can people adjust to the changes in jobs? Do the changes in jobs affect the motivation of the people in the jobs? Let us look for answers to these questions as we look at the changes that occur in jobs.

EXHIBIT 6–3

Tomorrow's Executives: How They May Be Different

Generalizations are difficult to make. But according to management experts interviewed by *Business Week*, some broad differences do exist between today's executives and tomorrow's.

The Old Generation	The New Generation
Cautious	Eager to take risks
Insecure	Optimistic
Resistant to change	Flexible
Loyal to company	Willing to job-hop
Value job security	Want to make impact
Male	Male or female
White	Ethnically diverse
A good day's work	Workaholic
Comfortable in bureaucracies	Crave autonomy, power
Conservative Republican	Independent
People-oriented	Numbers-oriented
Slide rules, legal pads	Computers, data networks
College degree	Advanced degrees
25-year career plan	Instant gratification

Source: Reprinted from November 10, 1986 issue of *Business Week* by special permission, copyright © 1986 by McGraw-Hill, Inc.

Changes in the job

Changes that occur in a job will affect the motivation of people in the job. Almost any popular business magazine reports about technological advances that are vastly changing jobs. Machinists' jobs that in the past involved manual expertise now require an ability to interact with a computer. Secretaries now use word-processing equipment rather than electric typewriters. Robots perform many of the jobs that workers previously performed in the manufacturing of automobiles. The list could go on and on, but the point is that these changes affect the motivation of employees. Sometimes, automation takes away the meaningfulness, challenge, and responsibility of a job. For some people this makes the job much less interesting. In addition, technological advances may make the skills of a worker obsolete. This can result in frustration and eventual lack of motivation for the employee. The need to deal with changes in technology is a growing problem. And managers are right in the middle of this revolution. **The key point to remember is that technological advances must be viewed in terms of their impact upon the employee and the job.** If management invests heavily in new technology, it must also invest in showing employees how to get the most out of the technology. Otherwise, managers can wind up with some difficult motivational problems. Indeed, management must change its approach as changes are made in the technology, if employees are to stay motivated.

At the heart of this problem is the rapid technological advances that occur today. Job skills become obsolete at an increasingly faster rate. As a 1987 *U.S. News & World Report* article reported, this creates a growing mismatch between the skills employees have and the skills they need to do a job.[5] Three fourths of all new jobs require some college education and skills, while only half of all new employees complete high school. What this situation will do is create opportunities for women and minorities who have the technical skills needed in jobs. The down side for managers is that the imbalance will create fewer skilled workers to select from in the labor pool. This gap may leave managers with workers who have potential but who lack certain skills. As the excerpt in Insight 6–3 suggests, the answer to this problem will involve greater levels of training for employees than have been typical in the past.

Changes in the organization

At the macro level of an organization, managers can anticipate changes that will affect the motivation of employees. As mentioned earlier, growing organizations provide many opportunities for people to take on responsibilities and challenges. In fact, the changes due to company growth may come so fast that they are almost overwhelming. Often, this can result in poor communications, unclear directions, and managers expecting more than subordinates can deliver. Also, it can allow people to move into positions for which they are not yet qualified. This can create problems for both the individual and the organization. Of course, some people thrive in this rapid-growth environment; it gives them a chance to use their talents. Other people may be left behind. In the Home Computers case, for example, Louise would probably thrive in this rapid growth situation, but Steve might have some problems.

Of course, all organizations do not grow rapidly; some may even decline. And with decline, there are usually shrinking opportunities for employee growth and development. In fact, some employees may be confronted with the loss of their jobs. Others will operate out of fear of losing their jobs. The effect of company decline on people and their motivation can be severe. As Insight 6–4 shows, some people are motivated to start their own businesses, and some to go to work for small businesses. Whatever the case, most find the experience quite discomforting.

Another source of organizational change lies in company direction. Perhaps top management decides to bring out a different product line, go into different markets, switch from a production to a marketing orientation, or make other strategic changes. Each of these changes

Helping Workers to Work Smarter

*B*efore the line began to roll last winter at General Motors' new truck plant in Fort Wayne, Indiana, each assembly line worker received 400 to 500 hours of paid training. Electricians and other skilled maintenance workers got 1,000 hours apiece—the equivalent of almost six months—with full pay and benefits. All told, training for the Fort Wayne work force came to more than a million hours. The cost: an estimated $23 million in wages and benefits alone, and millions more for instructors and facilities. The factory itself cost $500 million.

Though the amount of training the Fort Wayne workers got is extraordinary by the standards of most industries, it represents a powerful new trend. As service companies have done for years, manufacturers making everything from tires to semiconductors are now spending heavily to teach workers new skills and upgrade their old ones. In a study last year for the Department of Labor, the Rand Corp. found that nearly 40% of U.S. workers have taken part in training programs while on their current jobs. Rand also concluded that the training increased earnings more than any other type of education and sharply reduced the likelihood of unemployment as well.

Many companies are coming to regard training expenses as no less a part of their capital costs than plant and equipment. Anthony Patrick Carnevale, chief economist for the Washington-based American Society for Training and Development, a professional group, estimates that corporate expenditures on formal training and education, away from the office or shop floor, now total roughly $30 billion a year, or almost a third of what the U.S. spends on all college-level education. That's a conservative estimate, Carnevale says. When you add wage and benefit costs, the total may well match the $238-billion annual bill for all public education.

Companies are starting to see clear payoffs from such efforts. Two years ago Motorola decided to raise its training outlays by $20 million. Says Motorola training head Bill Wiggenhorn, who came over in 1980 from Xerox, a pioneer in training: "Just as when you buy a piece of capital equipment, you put aside money to maintain that equipment, we required that 1.5% of payroll be put aside to maintain the competency level of the employees." With the pace of technological change accelerating in semiconductors and electronic communications, Motorola's key markets, that figure is now running about 2.6%, or close to 1% of sales. Much of the training has been tied to plant and office automation, as well as to bringing in production process control techniques aimed at reducing defects virtually to zero—the permissible rejection rate at each manufacturing step is 3.4 parts per million. In any given year almost a third of the company's 90,000 employees get a total of two million to three million hours of training; taking into account training expenses, wages, and benefits, the cost amounts to around $90 million.

The results have been dramatic. Says Wiggenhorn: "We've documented the savings from the statistical process control methods and problem-solving methods we've trained our people in. We're running a rate of return of about 30 times the dollars invested—which is why we've gotten pretty good support from senior management."

By Michael Brody, *Fortune*, June 8, 1987, © 1987 Time Inc. All rights reserved.

Laid-Off Managers of Big Firms Increasingly Move to Small Ones . . .

When Du Pont Co. offered early retirement to employees back in 1982, Keh Lin jumped at the chance. Du Pont wanted to trim its work force; Mr. Lin, then a 42-year-old chemical engineer with a 14-year career at Du Pont, wanted to turn his part time real estate pursuits into a full-time job. Today, as founder and president of Leisure International Enterprises Inc., he markets vacation homes with the slogan "We sell dreams."

His own, at least, seem to have come true. Last year, three years after he left Du Pont, his company's revenue was $24 million. He has 32 part- and full-time employees. One of his recent hires is Kenneth Mayhew, a 51-year-old former Du Pont project engineer who also took early retirement.

During the cutbacks of recent years, throngs of middle managers have opted to leave or been squeezed out of large corporations. A number of them have taken similar jobs at other big companies or simply retired. Most, however, have been forced to adapt to a job market increasingly oriented toward smaller businesses. For the first time in several decades, more than half of the country's workers are on the payroll of businesses with fewer than 100 employees.

Wrenching shift

But the shift in the job market can be wrenching. Some managers, for instance, look for jobs in small businesses—but they don't necessarily like it. "It's not likely a big corporation will find a need for a person like me," says 56-year-old Peter Koval, a human relations manager. "(Big companies) grow their own." After 30 years with Uniroyal Inc., Mr. Koval lost his job almost a year ago in corporate cutbacks. He's now sending resumes to smaller companies.

Older job seekers especially can feel daunted, despite decades of corporate experience, by the prospect of looking for work at a small company. They aren't used to looking for jobs at any corporation, big and small. And they often have a hard time pitching themselves to a small company; while they know what skills a large corporation appreciates, they are at a loss when trying to please a small one.

"They have to claw the positions out of rock with their bare hands," says Arnold Menn of Arnold Menn & Associates, an outplacement firm in Austin, Texas. "They may have to contact 600 to 900 potential employers."

The solution for many managers, therefore, is to start their own businesses. That's risky; of all small companies started, only about half survive past the fifth year, according to the Small Business Administration.

By Amanda Bennett, *The Wall Street Journal*, July 25, 1986. Reprinted by permission of *The Wall Street Journal*, © Dow Jones & Company, Inc. 1986. All rights reserved.

could create a significantly different situation for the employees. Such redirection could, for example, raise or lower the status of a particular department. For instance, in the switch from production to marketing orientation, the status of marketing may increase; the status of production may decline. Certainly, this might affect the motivation of people in the two departments. In addition, such changes might mean relocation of some employees both geographically and from one work group to another. This change will have an effect on the affiliation needs of the employees, and this cannot be ignored.

The 1984 breakup of the old AT&T Company is a good example of this situation. Brought on by the courts, the breakup resulted in eight new directions for the company—one for each regional phone company and one for the parent company. Employees in all of the companies were confused about their new roles, their security, and their work relationships. Motivation was clearly affected—in many cases, for several years.

The key point to remember is that change at the organizational level can result in changes in the need satisfaction and rewards of employees, as well as in the action options afforded them. Now that we have explored the dynamic aspects of the motivational model and thus gained a more complete understanding of the model, let us explore the concept of congruence and then use it to help us apply the model to the Home Computers case from Chapter 5.

THE CONCEPT OF CONGRUENCE

Exhibit 6–1, as previously discussed, provides a useful model for understanding the motivation of people in a work setting. The model makes clear several key elements in the motivational process: individual needs, feedback of information, desired rewards, impact of supervisors and peers, and organizational goals. And as noted, the job itself is also important. To make the best use of these elements in analyzing actual work settings, it is helpful to think of them as constituting a puzzle. **For motivation to be maximized, each of these elements must fit together with all of the other elements into a congruent whole, as suggested by Exhibit 6–4.**

In order for an individual to be truly motivated and effective, there must be a high degree of congruence (or fit) between the person and the work itself; between the person and other people at work; between the person and the reward system; and between the person and the information system. Likewise, there must be a high degree of fit between the other people at work and the work itself; between the other people and the information system; between the other people and the reward system—and so forth for the other three elements in Exhibit 6–4. **In essence, managers can determine the degree of fit that exists between**

EXHIBIT 6-4

Motivation as a Process of Fit

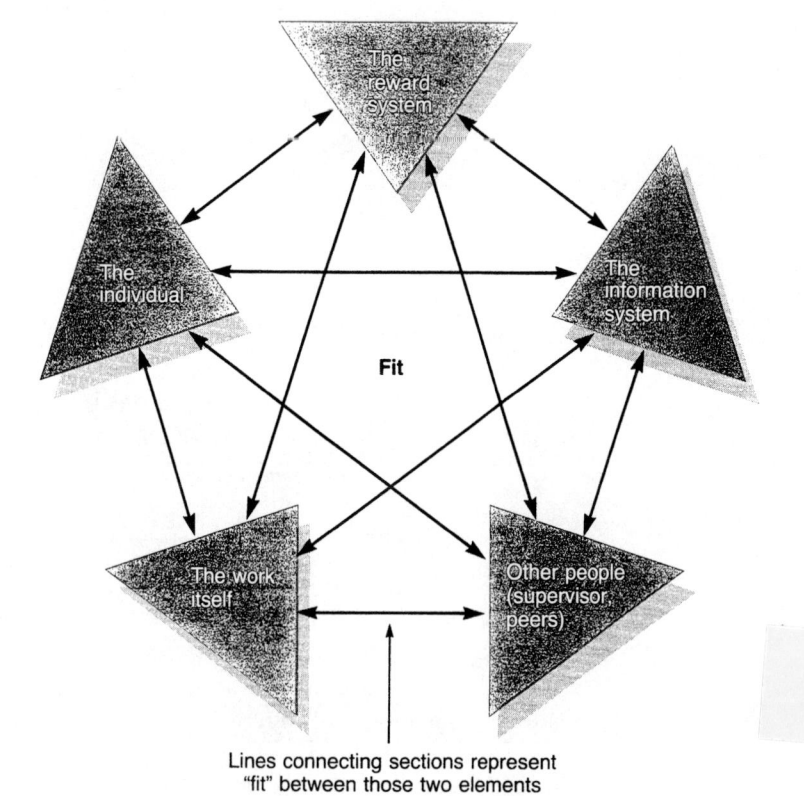

Lines connecting sections represent
"fit" between those two elements

these various elements by asking a series of questions. To illustrate this point, let us proceed through the series of questions, as applied to the Home Computers Company case from Chapter 5. (You may first want to reread the case.)

Application to Home Computers Company

Obviously, there are some motivational problems at HCC. Absenteeism and turnover (including managerial turnover) are high, and productivity is down. Let us try to understand why by looking at the changes that have developed in the company over the years.

What has happened to the work itself? The involving, challenging, and responsible craft work of the late 1970s—where each employee assembled an entire computer—has been replaced by assembly-line work

"Your background in creative decision making is interesting, but we're looking for someone with a strong background in creative order following."

that is not exciting, challenging, or responsible. Each person does only a part of the assembly job, and quality is checked by someone else. In addition, having shift operations means that employees are affected by the work performed by other people they seldom see. There is probably a sense of a loss of control in the job. As discussed in Chapter 5, job-design theory suggests several ways in which the jobs might be altered to better meet the needs of employees.

What has happened to the information system? Home Computers Company has become more bureaucratic, with five hierarchical levels replacing the original team approach. Obviously, this is necessary when a plant grows from 16 to 490 employees. However, with this more complex organization, feedback becomes much more difficult. People can begin to feel left out. The informal information system of the early company has been replaced by a more structured system that invariably results in distorted information and a lack of information for some people. On the survey, both employees and managers reported they felt left out on key information. This was especially apparent on the feedback questions. Perhaps a return to self-assessment of quality would be sufficient to improve the information system. The managers also seem to want a clearer picture of the HCC's overall goals and strategies. They need to know how the company plans to compete against other companies in the marketplace. Then, too, managers' own unit goals are sometimes not well defined. Perhaps Harvey should lay out some plans and goals for the future. Once these are shared with the middle managers, a dialogue could allow for sharing reactions and receiving additional details. This clarification exercise should enable the managers to guide employee actions to achieve both organizational and individual goals (arrows 1b, 3a, 3b, and 5 in Exhibit 6–1).

What has happened to the reward system? The only information given on this element is that the bonus system has been dropped. The impact of this change would be to decrease the typical employee's sense of involvement and responsibility. And this is consistent with the changes in the jobs, which are also demotivating. The previous section supplies a suggestion for this question, as well. With better-defined goals, it should be possible for managers and employees alike to assess performance. A financial reward could be tied to goals achieved, much like the old bonus system. Or the reward might need to be a promotion or something else the managers determine would be appropriate. Clearer goals for a particular job and unit, plus the suggested job changes should make it possible to establish a reward system that can motivate desired performance.

What has happened to supervisors and peers in the organization? First, there is a sizable degree of managerial turnover—probably a result of some of the factors mentioned previously (such as decreased responsibility). This means that employees must constantly adjust to new supervisors who may lack supervision experience. Indeed, in a company that grows rapidly (like HCC), it is not unusual for people to be promoted too quickly into positions for which they are not prepared. For example, a good computer technician may not make a good manager. The problem at HCC seems to be that the workers are rarely praised, but often reprimanded for mistakes by their new, inexperienced supervisors. The data from the survey suggest that some of the managers feel overwhelmed by the job, especially with increased competition in the marketplace. Perhaps more management training could help alleviate this problem. Clear goals could also help provide a sense of direction and control. Second, the company's rapid growth has probably meant hiring people with more widely divergent values and needs. Some of the workers seem bored with their jobs. Others like the lack of responsibility. Since these people must interact on the job, there is the possibility of motivation being reduced even further for the high-potential people. Quite likely, clearer goals, better information, and more task interaction will improve these interrelationship problems.

What has happened to the employees at HCC? Here, managers encounter the difficulty of knowing exactly what is going on inside people's heads; however, they do have some clues. In the earlier days, the company probably attracted people who wanted to be involved, challenged, and responsible. Why else would someone go to work for a brand-new company that might not be around tomorrow? Hence, these people probably liked the opportunity to make a complete computer, earn bonuses, receive informal and timely information, and work with others who also wanted challenge and responsibility. As the situation changed, some of these people moved on. Others moved up in the growing organizational structure. Some of those who moved up encountered a situation they could not handle, and some of them moved on. Others who moved up found increasing constraints as HCC attempted to get a grasp on its rapid growth.

At the worker level, some employees who have been around for several years have grown to want more responsibility, but less is being given. Some of the newer employees do not want much responsibility. This more heterogeneous mixture creates obstacles to finding satisfaction of people's needs. Things that please some people upset others—and the job of management is made more difficult.

Hence, it should be clear that analyzing motivation in an organization is a very complex task. Many elements and interactions are involved, and all aspects are subject to change. Our analysis has made clear the need for using a developmental perspective in understanding motivation in organizations. The past history of Home Computers Company and each of the elements in Exhibits 6–1 and 6–4, plus the 10 theories from Chapter 5 have been extremely important in this analysis. The integrative model and idea of fit have been helpful in our analysis of the motivational problems at HCC. Certainly, they have allowed us to generate a substantial list of suggested changes for the company. The final section of this chapter will review some motivation problems with new solutions that are being tried in industry today.

MOTIVATION APPROACHES COMPANIES ARE TRYING

Over the last 25 or so years, a number of approaches based on various theories of motivation have been tried in industry. This section briefly summarizes several of the more promising applications. As we discuss them, think about how they relate to the integrative model of motivation.

Job-oriented approaches

One approach—which this text has already discussed to some extent—is the redesign of work itself. Beginning with the suggestion of Herzberg, job enrichment has become a popular way to increase a job's ability to satisfy higher-level needs of employees.[6] Two industrial applications have gained widespread attention; they have also introduced other names for the approach, such as **industrial democracy, job redesign,** and **sociotechnical job design.**

The Gaines Pet Food company built a plant in Topeka, Kansas, in 1968 that would aid in developing meaningful and challenging jobs.[7] The plant was designed around self-governing work teams. The teams determined their own hiring and firing policies, scheduled their own workers, and made other major decisions which affected their work. All employees in the plant were classified under a single job classification, and the work teams were provided information formerly available only to management. The results have been outstanding. Costs are down; quality is up; absenteeism and turnover are down; and employee attitudes are good. A number of problems have had to be addressed, however, due primarily to concerns expressed by two groups: former middle managers, many of whose jobs were eliminated, and some workers who did not like making peer evaluations, pay decisions, and other typical managerial decisions. Still, the company hails the experiment as a success and is using the idea in other settings.[8]

The other widely noted experiment in job redesign took place at the Volvo plant in Sweden.[9] This particular effort was truly sociotechnical in nature. Both the people aspects of the jobs and the technical way of making cars were changed. A new carrier was designed to transport an entire car around the plant to various work teams responsible for major parts of the assembly. There is no assembly line. Each work team has control over its work pace, inspections of work, and scheduling of its workers. The team members must meet to resolve any problems they encounter. The results of this experiment have been dramatic. Turnover has been reduced, and worker attitudes are greatly improved. Quality of the cars did seem to suffer at first, but many of those problems now appear to be solved. And even General Motors has adopted this idea for some of its plants.[10] Furthermore, some Alcoa plants and some NCR plants now use autonomous work teams, suggesting that the concept is finding a receptive audience in a variety of manufacturing settings.

A related development has been a reduction in the number of supervisors and managers used in some organizations. Downsizing and decline of organizations, as discussed in Chapter 2, plus the need for greater efficiency in a more competitive world have contributed to this reduction. And employees have shown they can be productive without supervisors. One such example occurred in the old Bell system at Mountain Bell.[11] From 1983 to 1985, 100 telephone operators worked under a single second-level manager to run a $2.4 million facility that operated 24 hours a day, 7 days a week. This operation experienced lower absenteeism, fewer grievances, and fewer customer complaints than traditionally run, similar offices. It seems that such delegation can increase commitment and hence tap into employees' potential in a significant way. It is also clear that such delegation requires detailed plans and goals, increased training ahead of time, and more time spent in meetings. The salaries of the first-line supervisors are not saved; they are shifted into these activities. However, if the results are better, as they have been at Mountain Bell, there can be an increase in productivity measures.

The other major change occurring in jobs is **automation.** More and more, simple and boring jobs are being eliminated through automation. The Japanese, for example, have revolutionized automobile manufacturing by designing robots to make the many thousands of spot welds needed to make a car. Their machinists now must be computer operators, as well as technicians. The result seems to be more exciting jobs for the workers who are retrained. But whether automation results in a net loss or a net gain in jobs remains a point of controversy. Certainly, automation can mean relocation and retraining of many workers. The results could be quite positive for employees, since companies would have to take a greater interest in their development over their entire career. And such employer commitment is likely to result in greater commitment on the part of employees.

It is clear that these changes in jobs affect the **work itself** component of the motivation model. And they directly address the employee needs related to achievement, responsibility, and satisfaction with work.

Context-oriented approaches

A number of motivation approaches have related to the context in which employees work. Their design is consistent with the organizational aspects of the model of motivation. In particular, these approaches affect goals and rewards of employees.

One approach, **management by objectives (MBO),** involves a more concerted effort to define and clarify employee goals.[12] Really an application of Goal-Setting Theory, MBO has been widely used since the mid-1960s. Sometimes objectives are set jointly by the employee and the manager; sometimes the manager merely lays out the objectives. The basic idea is that if employees know clearly what their goals are, they will work to achieve them. Furthermore, specific and difficult goals inspire the greatest effort from individuals.[13] Coupled with the goal setting is the promise of rewards for accomplishing the goals. This is consistent with the connection in the motivation model between desired organization outcomes and rewards desired by the person (see Figure 6–1, arrows 3a and 4). Goal setting depends heavily on the individual's self-control and need to have responsibility. Often the goal is specified, but the means to accomplish it must be determined by the employee.

Another application that alters an employee's motivation is called **behavior modification.**[14] In many ways, behavior modification is similar to goal setting, but there are some significant differences. The primary difference is that behavior modification focuses specifically on behaviors of the employee and consequences that follow these behaviors. If the employee performs the desired behavior, a reward is given. If the employee does not perform the desired behavior, the reward is withheld, or in some cases, a punishment is administered. (Chapter 5 discussed Reinforcement Theory as a theory of motivation and Chapter 3 as a theory of learning.) Behavior modification is merely an application of Reinforcement Theory. As with goal setting, the choice of reward is critical to the success of the program. Rewards must satisfy needs of the employees if the program is to succeed. The case of Emery Air Freight discussed in Chapter 3 is a good example of the application of this approach. The company (through behavior-modification principles) motivated and helped workers to learn to use bulk cargo containers instead of small containers for shipping packages. The result was a tremendous savings for the company and satisfaction of some of the workers' important needs.

Another approach to motivation involves **ownership of the business by the workers.** The basic idea is to appeal to the entrepreneurial spirit of the workers. Ownership gives the workers responsibility, advancement, and opportunity for achievement—not to mention the chance to make more money if the company succeeds. Naturally, the risk is also higher. But having so many people committed to making the company work is certainly a secure feeling.

A related approach that has received renewed attention lately is *gain sharing,* sometimes referred to as profit sharing.[15] Basically, gain sharing allows employees to share in the benefits of increased productivity, cost reductions, and improved quality through regular cash bonuses. If the employees help the organization make more money, they share as a group in the gain. With recent declines in U.S. productivity growth, as well as the decline in the United State's position in world markets, many senior managers have begun to use gain sharing as part of an overall strategy of human resource management. This approach is even growing in popularity with large firms as competition in the marketplace increases. For example, Insight 6–5 talks about how telephone workers are getting in on the act.

Individually oriented approaches

Some of the other approaches to motivation have been designed to directly satisfy the needs of employees, without changing the basic structure of either the job or the organization. One of the most straightforward approaches is modifying the work week. Basically, two forms seem promising. One is called the **4/40 work week:** employees work ten hours a day for four days each week and have a three-day

Phone Workers on Verge of Profit-Sharing

New Era Seen in Labor-Management Relations

*T*he nation's telephone workers, soon to vote on new labor contracts, are on the verge of relinquishing bigger guaranteed wage increases for an opportunity to share in the telephone companies' growing profits.

In theory, linking part of phone workers' pay to the companies' financial performance—in essence, profit-sharing—will spark workers to strive continually to help improve profits, or so the industry's management is betting. "Team spirit" is thus engendered.

But the proposed change in compensation packages poses risks all around, union leaders and telephone managers alike acknowledge. For the companies, the idea of bonuses based on total company performance might be too fuzzy to inspire individual workers. For the rank and file, if growth projections prove illusory, there won't be more pay. Nonetheless, the telecommunications industry's management and union leaders say the risks are worth taking.

They and securities analysts label the proposed performance-based pay as a notable provision resulting from the first labor bargaining between the seven regional Bell concerns and the Communications Workers of America union since the Bell system breakup in 1984. But more important, the analysts and company and union officials point to the provision as the primary example of important changes that recognize the companies' increasingly competitive environment in the wake of industry deregulation. The new contracts thus herald a new era in telecommunications management-labor relations.

Emerging relationship fits a trend

The emerging relationship in telecommunications fits a trend in other industries, notes Robert Morris III, an analyst with Prudential-Bache Securities Inc. "More and more companies are trying to create a spirit within the corporation of participation at all levels, so everyone feels it is in their interest to have a healthy company," he says.

At Pacific Telesis, the performance bonus, or "team award," is a major building block for improved relations. Mr. Dial says the formula for determining workers' bonuses is the same as that used for calculating those of executives. "This is the first tangible linkage that says if the company does well, employees will do well," he adds. "It puts employees in a business partnership with the company."

By Johnnie L. Roberts, *The Wall Street Journal*, August 13, 1986. Reprinted by permission of *The Wall Street Journal*, © Dow Jones & Company, Inc. 1986. All rights reserved.

weekend. The other is **flexitime**.[16] It designates a core time each day when everyone must be present at work—say, 9:30 A.M. to 4 P.M. Starting time is anytime from 7:30 A.M. to 9:30 A.M.; quitting time can range from 4 P.M. to 6 P.M. Everyone is expected to work the normal eight hours a day. Obviously, a good record-keeping procedure is necessary, though experience with flexitime has shown little abuse of the system.

Another individually oriented approach is **job sharing,** where two people split a 40-hour-a-week job between them. Each works half the time, but the complete job gets done. Typically, the two employees do not receive full fringe benefits (unless they contribute a larger portion of their salaries), but they do have more free time to pursue other interests. On the other side of the coin, companies often get more than 40 hours a week from the two people, but coordination of effort can create some inefficiencies.

Another approach that seems to be gaining renewed emphasis is the **quality-of-work-life (QWL) approach** of giving workers a voice in plant decisions.[17] In some applications, this approach has resulted in far-reaching changes in the management of plants (for example, the Mountain Bell plant discussed earlier where workers operated totally without supervisors). But in many applications, the workers' decisions are limited in scope. One example is **quality circles,** where workers meet regularly to discuss production problems and recommend solutions. On technical grounds, this approach makes sense because of the workers' intimate involvement with production processes. The employees work with the production problems every day; thus, it makes sense that they would have ideas that management might overlook. It also makes sense in terms of the satisfaction of the workers' higher-level needs. Their needs for power, esteem, and growth can be tapped through the QWL approach to worker motivation. Employees can begin to feel more a part of the organization and can have more pride in solutions that they themselves help develop. One example of quality circles has been at the General Motors plant in Van Nuys, California.[18] Team leaders are chosen on the basis of leadership skills, not seniority, and the teams meet daily. Quality has increased such that the Van Nuys plant, long at the bottom of General Motors quality audits, has risen to number three. All is not perfect, but the quality teams appear to be providing a sense of purpose that has long been missing in auto plants.

Related to the general quality-of-work-life issue is the more specific focus of child care for employees' children. By 1990, roughly 65 percent of the people entering the labor market will be women, and about 60 percent of married men who work will have spouses who also work.[19] Companies are finding that they must become involved in the child care issue if they hope to attract and keep employees who are motivated. Studies are already finding that companies that help employees with child care issues have lower absenteeism and turnover rates.[20] As the number of dual-income families increases, managers and the companies they work for will have to become better at dealing with this issue if they want to keep motivated employees.

Then, too, the increase in dual-income families, as well as a recognition of a more heterogeneous work population, is causing an increase in *cafeteria benefit plans.* Such plans offer a menu of options for employees so they can tailor the benefits to their individual needs. Employees can spread a set amount of benefits among such options as life insurance, dental insurance, disability, retirement, or even vacation. As Insight 6–6 indicates, these plans are becoming popular at small as well as large companies. And where they have been tried, cafeteria plans, though more complex to administer, seem to be paying off in employee satisfaction.

Finally, a number of companies are experimenting with **health enrichment programs.** The idea has grown out of the increased interest in health by people in general. More and more people are jogging and joining health spas (probably to address their self-esteem and self-actualization needs). Some companies are providing these opportunities at work in hopes of gaining commitment and attracting and keeping better-quality employees. It is difficult to determine the bottom-line impact of such programs, but they are clearly gaining in popularity.

Persistent problems

In spite of the many theories of motivation, the years of study, and the numerous approaches just discussed, problems persist in motivating workers and managers. Probably the most serious is the inability to deal effectively with individual differences of the employees. Any solution applied to a group of employees is bound to satisfy some workers but not others. As stated many times in this text, each employee is unique. A second problem relates to the systems nature of the motivational process. As we discussed in these last two chapters, many elements affect motivation (the work, the person, rewards, information, other people—see Exhibit 6–4), and their effects are interactive. A solution such as goal setting must consider the work and the person as well as the reward if it is to be successful. For example, if the work requires a great deal of dependence on other people, the goals may have to be geared toward the group rather than the individual.

In addition to these two primary problems, there are several other persistent ones. First, technological constraints may negate control by the workers. Second, the cost-versus-benefits ratio of the motivational approaches is often difficult to measure. This is especially disconcerting when the costs are high. Third, management often wants quick solutions and is not willing to properly diagnose a given situation. As illustrated by the Home Computers Case, motivational problems can be quite involved. They can result from a series of developments over time and any solution may take time to yield results; things may get worse before they get better. Finally, managers, workers, and unions may resist change, fearing that things will actually get worse. For example, unions have often viewed QWL experiments as management attempts to get more work for the same pay.

```
I N S I G H T   6-6
```

To Each According to His Needs: Flexible Benefits Plans Gain Favor

Gary Encinas, a lawyer for Pacific Gas & Electric Co., is 37 years old, single and in "very good physical shape."

So when his San Francisco-based employer offered a choice of medical plans, he opted for one that provided less coverage than he had before. That choice, along with similar selections on fringes like dental care and life insurance, "saved" Mr. Encinas $565 in benefits pay—money he put into a 401(k) account, a tax-deferred savings plan sponsored by the company.

"The bottom line is that 'flex' is making people better consumers of health care," he says.

Flexible benefits plans—in which workers can trade off among various kinds of insurance, vacation time and cash—have been around for about 10 years. But compensation specialists say the popularity of flexible plans is poised to spread rapidly as more companies look for ways to control health-insurance costs. Moreover, despite the prospect of paying a greater share of premium costs or accepting reduced coverage, employees seem to like the ability to tailor benefits packages to their needs.

Towers, Perrin, Forster & Crosby, a New York consulting firm, predicts that, among companies of more than 1,000 employees, the number with flexible plans will more than double in the next two years. For the most part, participants are non-union white-collar workers.

Companies and employees are also finding traditional benefits plans increasingly unfair and unnecessarily costly for a work force no longer dominated by males with nonworking wives and children. Jeanne Kardos, director of employee benefits for New Haven, Conn.-based Southern New England Telephone Co., says fewer than 20% of the company's workers fall into that category. Many, she says, are part of two-income families—resulting in duplicate coverage—or single people who don't need a more expensive family plan.

By Larry Reibstein, *The Wall Street Journal,* September 16, 1986. Reprinted by permission of *The Wall Street Journal,* © Dow Jones & Company, Inc. 1986. All rights reserved.

In short, many problems remain for managers to grapple with. The theories and the analytical model provided in the last two chapters will be useful tools in this endeavor. As Tom Peters argues in his 1987 book *Thriving on Chaos,* the job is not going to get easier, and organizations are going to need employees who are motivated and trained to achieve organizational goals if they are to compete in the coming years.[21]

CHAPTER HIGHLIGHTS

This chapter completes our study of individual behavior. In it, we built upon the 10 motivation theories from Chapter 5 to provide an integrative model of motivation. This model is based primarily on Vroom's expectancy theory, but draws from the other motivation theories as well.

The model is an attempt to tie together content and process theories along with social-facilitation and job-design theories. The goal here has been to provide a model that will help managers better use the many theories of motivation found in the literature. **The model focuses on individual needs and action choices, as well as outcomes and rewards desired by an individual. In addition, it focuses on outcomes desired by the organization, as well as the organization's evaluation of an individual's performance and the forthcoming rewards.**

The amount of motivation for various actions an individual may choose depends on several factors according to the model. Most basic is the importance of an unsatisfied need to a person. Other factors include the organization's goals, the probability that the rewards given by the organization will help satisfy a need, and the probability that the desired outcome will lead to the desired reward. There is also a probability associated with whether a chosen action will lead to a desired outcome. Finally, the links in the model are like links in a chain. If one link is weak, the resulting motivation will be low. **So managers must be concerned with all of the links in the motivation model as they relate to employees.**

In completing the description of the motivation model, we stressed its dynamic nature. Depending on what happens as a person progresses through the model, his or her need is either satisfied, not satisfied, or partially satisfied. This result will influence future action choices because it may alter the instrumentalities of expectancy factors in the model, or it may even alter the valence of the need. In discussing this aspect of the model, we explored several scenarios to illustrate this important point.

The next section of the chapter explored the three major factors in the motivation puzzle (people, jobs, and organizations) in terms of how changes in these elements influence the motivation of employees. First, we looked at changes in people. Managers must manage people at different life, family, and career stages; therefore each person presents a particular challenge. Employees in their teens and early 20s will have different needs than those in their late 20s and 30s. Likewise, employees in their 40s and 50s will have different needs than their younger colleagues. The same is true for employees in their 60s. And employees born in different times in history will be different from each other. **As discussed, managers must recognize the unique needs of different people (where age is only one influential factor) and try to provide rewards and actions that help satisfy those needs.** This means that continuing analysis of employees will be necessary in order to stay current with their needs.

Second, we explored how changes in a job can create changes in the motivation of employees. **Changes in jobs thus must be viewed in terms of their impact on motivation** if the maximum benefits from the changes are to be achieved. And it seems that technological change is occurring at a growing rate of speed.

Third, we considered how changes in an organization can create changes in employees' motivation. **Whether organizations grow, decline, or change strategies, employee motivation is affected.** Rewards may be altered, as may action choices and needs to be satisfied.

The next section discussed a framework for analyzing motivation in work settings. Basically, the text suggested that for motivation to be greatest, there must be a high degree of fit between the individual, the work, the reward system, the information system, and other people in the work setting. A series of questions was applied to the Home Computers Company case to help us analyze the motivational problems that exist there.

The final section of the chapter briefly discussed several approaches to motivation that have been tried in industry. These approaches relate to the model of motivation. First, we discussed three job-oriented changes: redesign of work, reduction of the number of managers and supervisors, and automation of menial jobs. Second, we discussed four context-oriented approaches: management by objectives, behavior modification, employee ownership, and gain sharing. Last, we covered several individually oriented approaches: modified work week, flexitime, job sharing, quality-of-work-life plans, quality circles, child care centers, cafeteria benefit plans, and health enrichment programs.

Finally, we discussed several persistent motivation problems in organizations: dealing with individual differences, the systems nature of the problem, technological constraints, costs of programs versus benefits, quick-solution attempts, and resistance to change by employees, managers, and unions. In spite of the persistent problems, the model provided in this chapter plus the theories in Chapter 5 can equip managers to better deal with motivation in organizations.

REVIEW QUESTIONS

1. Explain the integrative model of motivation that is presented in this chapter. What are its important elements? How is the amount of motivation determined? How is the model dynamic?

2. Explain why motivation is developmental in nature. What changes in people lead to developmental influences on motivation? What changes in the job or the organization create developmental influences?

3. Explain the concept of *fit* as we have applied it to the analysis of motivation in work settings. What are the elements in this framework for analysis?

4. Describe the approaches to motivation which industry has been trying and that were mentioned in this chapter. What are the basic categories within which the approaches fall?

5. What motivation problems persist that managers have to face?

RESOURCE READINGS

Levinson, D. *The Seasons of a Man's Life.* New York: Alfred A. Knopf, 1978.

Peters, T. *Thriving on Chaos.* New York: Alfred Knopf, 1987.

Pinder, C.C. *Work Motivation: Theory, Issues, and Applications.* Glenview, Ill.: Scott, Foresman, 1984.

Ronen, S. *Alternative Work Schedules: Selecting, Implementing and Evaluating.* Homewood, Ill.: Richard D. Irwin, 1984.

Sheehy, G. *Passages: Predictable Crises of Adult Life.* New York: E. P. Dutton, 1976.

Steers, R. M., and L. W. Porter, eds. *Motivation and Work Behavior.* 4th ed. New York: McGraw-Hill, 1987.

Tichy, N. M. "Problem Cycles in Organizations and the Management of Change." In *The Organizational Life Cycle,* ed. J. R. Kimberly and R. H. Miles. San Francisco: Jossey-Bass, 1980.

Walton, R. E. "Establishing and Maintaining High Commitment Work Systems." In *The Organizational Life Cycle,* ed. J. R. Kimberly and R. H. Miles. San Francisco: Jossey-Bass, 1980.

NOTES

1. V. H. Vroom, *Work and Motivation* (New York: John Wiley & Sons, 1964).

2. A. H. Maslow, *Motivation and Personality* (New York: Harper & Row, 1954).

3. G. Sheehy, *Passages: Predictable Crises of Adult Life* (New York: E. P. Dutton, 1976); D. Levinson, *The Seasons of a Man's Life* (New York: Alfred A. Knopf, 1978).

4. T. Carson and J. A. Byrne, "Fast-Track Kids," *Business Week,* November 10, 1986, pp. 90–92.

5. R. J. Shapiro with M. Walsh, "The Great Jobs Mismatch," *U.S. News & World Report,* September 7, 1987, pp. 42–43.

6. F. Herzberg, B. Mausner, and B. Snyderman, *The Motivation to Work* (New York: John Wiley & Sons, 1959).

7. E. M. Glaser, *Productivity Gains through Worklife Improvements* (New York: Harcourt Brace Jovanovich, 1976).

8. R. E. Walton, "The Topeka Work System: Optimistic Visions, Pessimistic Hypotheses, and Reality," in *The Innovative Organization,* ed. R. Zager and M. P. Rosow (Elmsford, N.Y.: Pergamon Press, 1982), ch. 11.

9. P. G. Gyllenhammar, *People at Work* (Reading, Mass.: Addison-Wesley Publishing, 1977).

10. R. H. Guest, "Tarrytown: Quality of Worklife at a General Motors Plant," and D. L. Landon and H. C. Carlson, "Strategies for Diffusing, Evolving, and Institutionalizing Quality of Worklife at General Motors," in *The Innovative Organization*, ed. Zager and Rosow, chs. 5 and 12.

11. T. O. Taylor, D. J. Friedman, and D. Couture, "Operating Without Supervisors: An Experiment," *Organizational Dynamics* (Winter, 1987), pp. 26–38.

12. G. S. Odiorne, *Management by Objectives* (New York: Pitman, 1965).

13. E. A. Locke, "Toward a Theory of Task Motivation and Incentives," *Organizational Behavior and Human Performance* 3 (1968), pp. 157–89.

14. W. C. Hamner and E. P. Hamner, "Behavior Modification and the Bottom Line," *Organizational Dynamics* (Fall 1976), pp. 2–21.

15. M. Schuster, "Gain Sharing: Do It Right the First Time," *Sloan Management Review* (1987), pp. 17–25; and R. E. Majerus, "Workers Have a Right to a Share of Profits," *Harvard Business Review*, September-October, 1984, pp. 42–50.

16. P. Dickson, *The Future of the Workplace* (New York: Wybright and Talley, 1975).

17. L. E. Davis and A. B. Cherns, eds., *The Quality of Working Life* 2 (New York: Free Press, 1975).

18. A. Gabor with J. A. Seamonds, "GM's Bootstrap Battle: The Factory-Floor View," *U.S. News and World Report*, September 21, 1987, pp. 52–53.

19. D. E. Friedman, "Child Care for Employees' Kids," *Harvard Business Review*, March-April, 1986, pp. 23–34.

20. Ibid.

21. T. Peters, *Thriving on Chaos* (New York: A. A. Knopf, 1987).

CASE: John the discouraged

John has worked for a large shipping company for nine years. While in college, John worked part-time, unloading trucks at night. John formed close associations with his coworkers, most of whom were young college men. The spirit of the night shift was teamwork. Everyone worked together to accomplish the company's goal of fast, efficient package handling. The company sponsored team competitions with recognition factors for winning teams such as steak dinners, team photographs in the company magazine, and company paraphernalia. John, putting forth 100 percent effort for his team, worked hard and enjoyed his work.

John developed a strong commitment to the company. Realizing this was a solid company with a good future, John decided to build a career with the company. The company had a strong policy of promoting hard-working em-

Source: Adapted from a course assignment prepared by Terry Wise for Dr. Alan Randolph, 1987.

ployees. John's job dedication was rewarded by promotions through the career ladder of night operations.

Upon reaching the top of the career ladder, John was promoted to full-time truck driver. John differed from the other truck drivers in age, family associations, and personal goals. Although he knew most of the drivers on a first name basis, John had little interaction with them. While the company's goal remained the same, emphasis of goal achievement shifted from teamwork to individual performance. Because the company expected 100 percent effort by each individual, feedback was not praise for a good job but reprimand for poor performance. The company offered no rewards, such as public recognition, for hard work in his driving job. The yearly pay raise was not based on performance evaluations but was controlled by the Teamsters Union. After two years of driving, John experienced job dissatisfaction.

The company decided to build a regional office at John's facility. Seeing opportunities for advancement and new challenges, John applied for a job in management. John was assigned as the air operations staff member to the Industrial Engineering department. Because the company had only recently begun offering next day delivery, air operations was a new division in the company. This meant many aspects of John's job were undefined. A few of John's assignments were to write job descriptions for union workers, to complete work measurements, to do monthly audits at air centers in the region, and to project package volume. There were few guidelines, policies, or goals for John to follow. Also, John had two supervisors—one was the district air operations manager and the other was the district industrial engineer manager.

John was to be trained by a man who had worked in an air industrial engineering department at another facility. The trainer was busy designing and organizing the operations at the new facility; he did not spend time adequately training John. After six weeks, the trainer was promoted to another facility. John was left not knowing how to do many aspects of his job.

John had a difficult time organizing his work. He received conflicting directions from his supervisors. John began reports for air operations only to be told by the industrial engineer manager to stop and work on reports for the Industrial Engineering department. John developed a weekly schedule but never managed to follow his schedule because of unforeseen reports.

At first, John's work was a few days behind schedule, and reports contained some errors. Now John's work is consistently late and of poor quality. One work measurement was five months late. Monthly audits have not been completed for the last two months. John feels he is so far behind in his work that he will never get caught up. John feels discouraged that his new job is so difficult.

Questions

1. Why is John so discouraged? What aspects of the job, the situation, and John himself might be contributing?
2. Is this a motivational problem or an ability problem, or is it both?
3. What could be done to correct the problem?

EXERCISE: Motivation congruence

Objectives

The purpose of this exercise is to give students practice in dealing with the congruence aspects of motivation.

Instructions

Before coming to class, each student should choose a job that they have previously held or about which they have intimate knowledge. Those who are employed full-time may want to use their present job. They should then write up a short description of the major duties and responsibilities involved. In addition, each person should describe the information and reward systems, as well as the supervisor and peers.

Divide up into groups of four to six. Each group then chooses one job to be analyzed. Pick a job with which each member of the group is reasonably familiar. The group will consider the following questions:

1. What is the nature of the job in terms of core job dimensions?
2. What kind of information does the job holder receive?
3. What is the manner in which rewards are given to the job holder?
4. What norms and expectations come from peers and the supervisor?
5. What are the characteristics of the job holder?

The group will then discuss what changes could be made to create a more motivational situation. Once the group has decided on its recommendations they will be presented to the entire class. Everyone is responsible for analyzing the recommendations. The class should carefully consider whether or not the job changes are reasonable and workable. In addition, they should look closely at the recommended changes to determine what elements of motivation theories are being applied.

Source: Alan Randolph, 1988.

C H A P T E R 7

Individual Outcomes

C hapters 3 through 6 discussed many of the variables and theories that can help managers understand themselves and other individuals in organizational settings. People are the basic building blocks for organizations, and it is vital that managers be able to manage themselves and others toward desirable outcomes. This chapter explores many of the possible outcomes that managers may observe with individuals in organizations. Some of these outcomes are desirable to the organization, while others are not. The text also explores some of the interrelationships among these outcomes. The connection between these outcomes and the issues of interpersonal, group, and organizational relationships will form the basis for the remainder of the book.

What outcomes do managers like to see from people in organizations? Perhaps managers want high performance, commitment and loyalty to them and the organization, and high job satisfaction. What outcomes do managers not like to see from people? Perhaps managers wish to avoid absenteeism, tardiness, extensive turnover, and stress that hurts the employees and their performance. To introduce these issues, let us drop in for a visit at Home Computers Company. As we do, we will refer to the consultant's survey discussed in the Home Computers case in Chapter 5.

Home Computers Case

Individual Outcomes at Home Computers Company

Harvey sat across the table from Louise, scratching his head as he tried to explain the results of the consultant's survey. Louise responded by saying she was puzzled, too. For herself, job satisfaction and commitment to HCC were very high, and she felt her performance was very good. She could also think of many employees who were satisfied with their jobs and exhibited high commitment to the company. Some people even had to be sent home on the weekends and literally forced to take a vacation; they seemed to love their work! But, admittedly, others in the company were not satisfied and were frequently absent or late for work. How could there be such diversity among employees in the same company?

Harvey pointed out, "Louise, you and most of the other managers around here are more satisfied and committed because you feel more in control of what happens in your job. You understand the big picture better. And, of course, you make a much higher salary." The consultant had told Harvey that people higher up in the organization usually feel more job satisfaction, are more committed, and are not absent or late as often as people lower in the organization. Harvey further explained to Louise that the survey results had shown that many of the employees liked their pay and the working conditions, but were unhappy with their supervision, coworkers, and level of responsibility.

Louise said, "I guess this is helpful information, but it certainly makes it difficult to know what to do. How do we deal with the fact that some people are satisfied and committed, while others doing the same jobs are not."

Harvey responded, "I know what you mean. People are so hard to predict. And what's more, I'm concerned that we're losing some of our best people."

As they continued to discuss the situation, Louise and Harvey agreed that commitment to the organization and its goals depended not only on what was happening in the organization, but also on what was happening in other companies. During the early years of HCC, growth had been so rapid that the only reason people left was because they could not stand the pace. Now, the opportunities for promotion had slowed down, and for many people, the grass looked greener in other organizations. Indeed, some of HCC's best people were leaving to start their own companies. It seemed to Harvey and Louise that people of the younger generation wanted to do their own thing, and more and more of them were deciding that the only way to do this was to start their own business.

Harvey and Louise also agreed that be that as it may, they still had to do their best to keep good people who were committed to HCC and who performed well for the company. They had to figure out ways to handle absenteeism, tardiness, and turnover, so that they could keep overall company performance up. Louise pointed out how the company tended to put more and more work on their best people, thus creating tremendous stress for them.

Harvey responded, "Stress—tell me about it! What with the demands of my job and my wife talking about divorce, my blood pressure is up. Sometimes I wonder how I will cope with it." With that, Harvey shook his head, and they both headed down the hall to deal with the realities of the day.

POSITIVE INDIVIDUAL OUTCOMES

As we begin to explore the positive and negative individual outcomes in organizations, keep this situation at Home Computers Company in mind. Think about how the issues we discuss might help the managers at HCC. Let's begin our analysis on a positive note by looking at desirable outcomes. In particular, let's begin by looking at one of the most studied outcomes—that is, job satisfaction.

Job satisfaction

As discussed in Chapter 4, job satisfaction is an attitude. It is defined as **the extent to which an employee expresses a positive affective (or feeling) orientation toward a job.**[1] In other words, job satisfaction has to do with whether a person likes a job. Do most people like or dislike their jobs? Perhaps surprisingly, large-scale surveys conducted over many years and across many occupations regularly report that between 81 and 92 percent of employees are relatively happy with their jobs.[2] A recent survey conducted for *USA Today* revealed somewhat lower but still quite high statistics in reporting that nearly two thirds of employees like their work "a great deal," while 80 percent usually or always enjoy going to work.[3] What the *USA Today* survey also points out is that how a person views a job has a great deal to do with his or her level of satisfaction. If people view their work as part of a career, 79 percent say they like their job "a great deal." But if people view their work as just a job, only 37 percent say they like their job "a great deal." For more information from the survey, see Insight 7–1. Other more rigorous studies report similar findings in that managers, technical people, and professional employees—all of whom tend to view their work as part of a career—report higher levels of satisfaction than blue-collar personnel who tend to view their work as just a job.[4]

Research studies have also found different levels of job satisfaction for different groups of employees.[5] Older employees tend to report higher levels of satisfaction than younger employees. One obvious reason is that older employees see fewer opportunities for other jobs; thus, they may rationalize that they like the job they have, or perhaps they have just become comfortable with what they have in their present job. Minorities and women also tend to report lower levels of satisfaction (though the gap is decreasing), especially with regard to pay and promotion opportunities.

Such research studies use satisfaction surveys to assess employees' current feelings about their jobs. One of the most popular job satisfaction surveys is called the Job Descriptive Index (JDI for short).[6] It presents a series of adjectives and asks respondents to rate their job on five different aspects: the work itself, pay, promotional opportunities, supervision, and coworkers. Turn to the end of this chapter and take a few minutes to complete and score the abbreviated JDI as it relates to your current job or a job you had in the past. What is (or was) your level of satisfaction?

As we can see, and as Harvey and Louise at Home Computers realized, the plot with regard to job satisfaction thickens even more as we look at different aspects of a job. **Besides satisfaction with pay and promotion opportunities, managers must work for employee satisfaction with the work itself, satisfaction with supervisors, satisfaction**

We Enjoy Work 'A Great Deal'

Nearly two-thirds of all workers like their work "a great deal," according to a recent USA TODAY poll. And four out of five of us say we usually or always enjoy going to work.

The poll conducted by Gordon S. Black Corp. questioned 802 adult workers across the USA between April 4 and 6.

In another major finding, job satisfaction was cited as the most important thing about a job, beating out security, money and future opportunities.

What's so thrilling about the daily grind?

"Think about the last time you went to the dentist," says psychologist Arthur Brief, a New York University professor who specializes in workers' attitudes. "Chances are the experience wasn't as bad as you'd expected, right?

"Work is like that for many people. Work isn't as bad as we thought it was going to be, and so we're relieved and satisfied. That's my guess."

Call your work a career and you're more likely to find the dentist visit a breeze: Nearly four-fifths of those who consider their work a "career" liked it a great deal, compared with about a third who said their work was just "a job."

Windsor Thompson, 24, of North Augusta, S.C., for example, works at a *job* as a clerk in a shipping company, while training for a *career* as a nurse in a hospital intensive care unit.

The difference: Clerking is "boring stuff, the same thing every night," while health care is "difficult, challenging, with a constant turnover of people."

From *USA Today*, June 15, 1987.

with coworkers, and satisfaction with working conditions. These factors were discussed in Chapter 6 as they related to motivation. If managers want people to be motivated, they must help them achieve a fit between these various factors; if they want them to have high job satisfaction, they must not only achieve fit but also the desired levels for each factor.

Working conditions

When people feel that reward systems, promotion practices, and company policies are fair to them and others, they will feel a higher level of job satisfaction. Likewise, when they feel they are informed about what is going on around them, they will be more satisfied. There is the saying that "bosses do not like surprises." Well, neither do subordinates. Employees feel more job satisfaction if the general working environment is safe and comfortable.

The work itself

As stated in Herzberg's motivation theory (Chapter 5), the work itself is an important factor in employees' job satisfaction. People tend to feel higher satisfaction when their work is interesting and challenging, but not too challenging for their own desires.[7] A related aspect of the work itself is clarity about the goals that the employees are to achieve. When people know what is expected of them, they tend to feel more satisfied on the job, so long as the expectations are realistic.[8]

Others in the workplace

Another key variable in the satisfaction equation is the people with whom employees work on the job. Managers play a critical role here. When employees see their manager or supervisor as competent, honest, fair, and influential in the organization, their satisfaction tends to be higher. Employees also like to feel that their supervisors respect them as competent people. And employees are more satisfied if they feel their coworkers are cooperative and if they feel a sense of kinship with their coworkers.[9]

The changing individual

One final and important element in the job satisfaction equation deserves attention. Job satisfaction is clearly influenced by the person in the job. Quite often two people hold the same job, but one is satisfied and one is not. In this case, all of the above factors (working conditions, coworkers, etc.) appear to be equal, but the levels of job satisfaction for the two people are not. Personality, as discussed in Chapter 4, plays an important role in determining a person's job satisfaction. Recall the discussion of internals and externals in Chapter 4. Research has shown that internals, who feel in control of their lives, often report higher levels of satisfaction than externals, who feel a lack of control.[10] It is also true that people's career plans and where they are in these career plans can impact job satisfaction. The basic question is whether there is a fit between people's career plan and their current job.[11] Based on the discussion in Chapter 2, it is clear that things will change over the path of a career. A job that fits a career plan today may not fit tomorrow, as things change. And if the fit is not good and stays that way for a period of time, a person may find himself or herself looking for another job. But if the fit is good and remains good over a period of time, a person may find that his or her level of job satisfaction will stay high and commitment to the organization will also increase.

Commitment

Commitment has been defined as having a strong belief in an organization's values and goals, such that a person desires to remain a part of the organization and is willing to expend considerable effort for the organization.[12] In short, commitment is something like loyalty. And when people are loyal to something, they want it to succeed and will work to help it succeed. As an example, think about some people's loyalty to their undergraduate college or university's football team. Most people want very much for their team to win, and they remain loyal to their team long after graduation. In addition, they may even have gone to games in the rain and cold and yelled their lungs out to help their team win. Obviously, such commitment from the employees in an organization would be ideal. Let us now look at some of the determinants of commitment and at its potential relationship to other desirable outcomes.

When we talk about commitment, we have to focus on the question: "Commitment to what?" In an organizational setting, the most obvious focus of an employee's commitment is the manager and the goals of the organization. In fact, as a recent book by Warren Bennis and Burt Nanus points out, in the minds of employees, goals and the manager are highly interrelated.[13] Managers must formulate and articulate the organization's goals for their employees. Hence, if people are committed to a manager, they will probably be committed to the organization's goals, as well. And if they are committed to the goals a manager articulates, they will probably be committed to the manager as their leader. The bottom line of all of this is that if managers want commitment from their people, they will have to spell out the goals to which people must be committed. Certainly, that sounds simple, but it is amazing how few managers really spend the time and continued energy to think through and then share the goals of their organization. Indeed, Harvey and Louise at Home Computers Company may need to step back from the pressures of their jobs to spell out company goals more clearly.

Exhibit 7–1 provides a model of how commitment to goals develops.[14] Obviously, goal commitment is a result of external factors (such as authority of the leader, peer group influence, and rewards); interactive factors (such as participation); and internal factors (such as expectancy and internal rewards). All of these factors work together through a cognitive process to yield an employee's level of goal commitment. It is easy to see that the same factors that relate to goal commitment also relate to job satisfaction, discussed earlier in this chapter. This suggests that commitment is probably an extended form of job satisfaction.

External factors

When an employee feels that a manager has the legitimate authority to establish goals, the employee will be more committed to the goals than if he or she perceives the manager to lack authority. Part of this sense of authority is gained by a manager's ability and willingness to handle rewards and incentives in a way that employees feel is equitable and fair and that is connected to goal accomplishment. Another way of stating this is to say that management has to keep its promise to be committed to employees if management expects employees to be committed to the

EXHIBIT 7–1

Goal Commitment Model

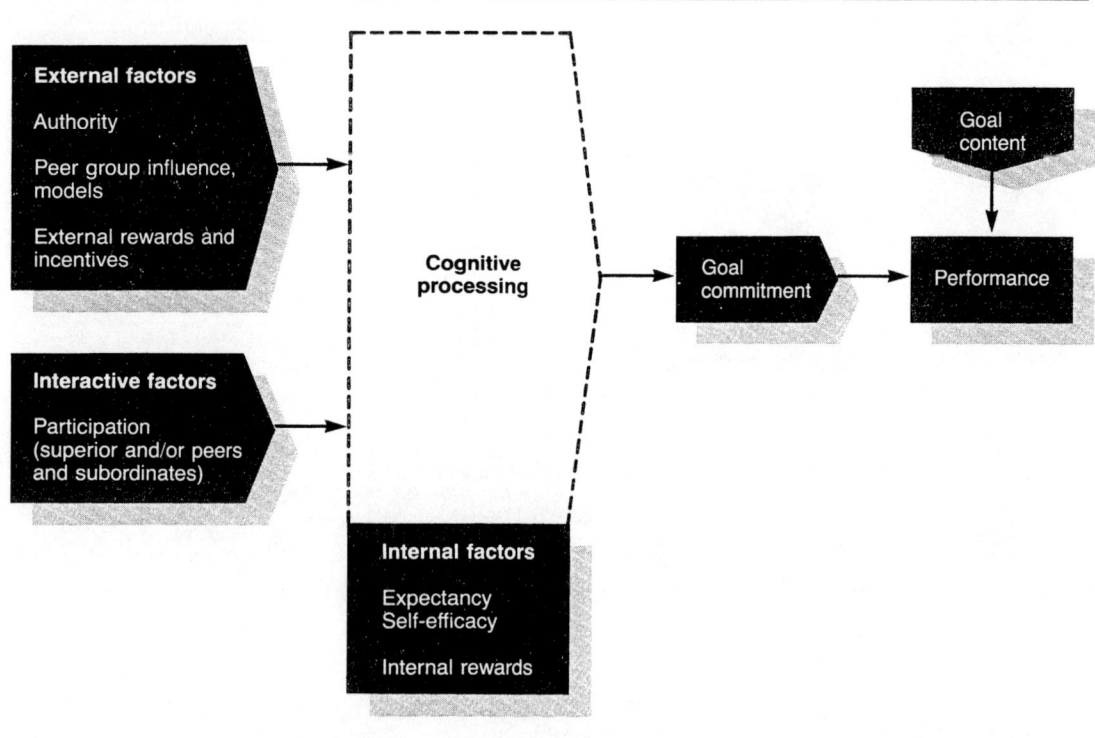

Source: E. A. Locke, G. P. Latham, and M. Erez, "The Determinants of Goal Commitment," *Academy of Management Review* 13 (1988), pp. 23–39.

organization. And if an employee's peers believe in the goals and provide encouragement, the employee will be more committed to the goal. Clearly, this is the essence of teamwork that helps groups achieve remarkable results in spite of numerous obstacles. If coworkers are not committed, it can clearly impact on an employee's level of commitment. (See Insight 7–2.)

Interactive factors

The primary interactive factor the author of this article presents is the level of an employee's participation in setting goals. Basically, the author suggests that if goals are set in a participative fashion between manager and employee, the worker's commitment to the goal will be higher than if the goal is simply assigned to the employee by the manager. The research results have not all been clear-cut in this regard. Perhaps em-

---

INSIGHT 7-2

Managing

What About Workers Who Are Left Behind?

Much research has been devoted to why people quit jobs, but academics are now starting to explore the effect turnover has on the workers who remain.

In a recent study, Joel Brockner, a Columbia University Business School professor, found that workers' job satisfaction and commitment to their companies declined when they felt a colleague left for a better job. Lateral or "downwardly mobile" job switches made remaining workers feel better or the same about their jobs. "It's where you are vs. where you see them going," says Prof. Brockner.

A variety of factors affect those reactions. For instance, low self-esteem employees, who typically are more easily influenced by others, were unhappier than more secure workers when a colleague left for a better job.

Is there anything a manager can do to buoy up remaining workers? One strategy, Prof. Brockner suggests, is to deflate the stature of the new job, but without bad-mouthing the departing employee. Or, he says, the manager might send the message that if the employee does well, there are plenty of places to advance within the company.

By Larry Reibstein, *The Wall Street Journal*, January 15, 1988. Reprinted by permission of *The Wall Street Journal*, © Dow Jones & Company, Inc. 1988. All rights reserved.

---

ployees are so used to having no clear goals at all that even assigned goals are better than nothing. Hence, employees become committed to goals that are both participatively and autocratically set. A recent book on planning and managing projects presents this exact point in saying that **commitment comes primarily from clear goals, but can be further enhanced when people feel they can contribute their ideas through participation.**[15]

Internal factors

Lastly, commitment to goals depends on several factors internal to the employee. As discussed in regard to motivation (Chapters 5 and 6), the employee's expectancy and self-efficacy (that is, self-confidence) that he or she can deal with situations presented on the job in an effective manner influences the level of goal commitment. If employees feel they can be effective with the goal, their level of commitment to it will be higher. If they feel they cannot be effective, why should they commit to it and risk failing? By not committing to the goal, they can always say they failed because they did not try. By the same token, if employees administer internal rewards, such as, "I feel I did a good job," that, too, can help build commitment to the goal.

The last element to point out in the model in Exhibit 7–1 is the relationship between commitment to the goal and performance. In other words, what are the possible consequences of varying levels of commitment?

Consequences of levels of commitment

Sometimes, it seems that the commitment of employees is declining. Employees of today expect more from life and from their places of work, and if they do not feel a commitment from the organization to address those expectations, they tend to lower their own levels of commitment to the organization.[16] They quit jobs, transfer their loyalty to nonwork activities, miss a lot of work, or just come in late too often. Hence, it is easy to jump to the conclusion that managers should strive to obtain the highest level of commitment they can from employees. But **there is some evidence that high levels of commitment, just like low levels, can have negative consequences. And it is possible that low commitment can have some positive consequences.** A table of these possibilities is shown in Exhibit 7–2.[17] Notice that the table defines positive and negative consequences for both the individual and the organization at three levels of commitment. Besides organizational goals, the table also brings in many of the outcomes discussed in this chapter. Indeed, commitment is a concept that impacts numerous aspects of an organization.

Low commitment consequences

First of all, let us look at the consequences of low commitment. For the individual, the negative consequences are slow career advancement, personal costs as a result of not supporting the organization in cases of wrongdoing, and possible exclusion from the organization. For the organization, the negative consequences are higher turnover and absenteeism and lower quality of work, among others. But notice that a positive consequence of low commitment for the organization is also turnover. Maybe the people that leave are the ones that should leave, thus making room for newer and better employees. For the individual, such turnover may allow the employee to find a job with another organization where higher levels of commitment are possible, thus making more effective utilization of human resources.

High commitment consequences

At the other end of the spectrum are the consequences of high commitment. The consequences of high commitment for the individual are career advancement opportunities, rewards from the organization, and a passionate pursuit that yields a real sense of accomplishment. But notice the possible negative consequences for the individual. Individu-

EXHIBIT 7–2

Possible Consequences of Levels of Commitment

Level of Commitment		Individual		Organizational	
		Positive	Negative	Positive	Negative
Low		*Individual* creativity, innovation and originality *More* effective human resource utilization	*Slower* career advancement and promotion *Personal* costs as a result of whistle-blowing *Possible* expulsion, exit, or effort to defeat organizational goals	*Turnover* of disruptive/poor performing employees limiting damage, increasing morale, bringing in replacements *Whistle*-blowing with beneficial consequences for the organization	*Greater* turnover, tardiness, absenteeism, lack of intention to stay, low quantity of work, disloyalty to the firm, illegal activity against the firm, limited extra-role behavior, damaging role modeling, whistle-blowing with damaging consequences, limited organizational control over employees
Moderate		*Enhanced* feelings of belongingness, security, efficacy, loyalty, and duty *Creative* individualism *Maintenance* of identity distinct from the organization	*Career* advancement and promotion opportunities may be limited *Uneasy* compromise between segmental commitments	*Increased* employee tenure, limited intention to quit, limited turnover, and greater job satisfaction	*Employees* may limit extra-role behavior and citizenship behaviors *Employees* may balance organization demands with nonwork demands *Possible* decrease in organizational effectiveness
High		*Individual* career advancement and compensation enhanced *Behavior* is rewarded by the organization *Individual* provided with a passionate pursuit	*Individual* growth, creativity, innovation, and opportunities for mobility are stifled *Bureaupathic* resistance to change *Stress* and tension in social and family relationships *Lack* of peer solidarity *Limited* time and energy for nonwork organizations	*Secure* and stable work force *Employees* accept the organization's demands for greater production *High* levels of task competition and performance *Organizational* goals can be met	*Ineffective* utilization of human resources *Lack* of organizational flexibility, innovation, and adaptability *Inviolate* trust in past policies and procedures *Irritation* and antagonism from overzealous workers *Illegal*/unethical acts committed on behalf of the organization

Source: D. Randall, "Commitment and the Organization: The Organization Man Revisited," *Academy of Management Review* 12 (1987), pp. 460–71.

als who commit everything to one organization's goals may limit their growth potential, be resistant to change, experience stress and tension in other parts of their lives, and find limited time for nonwork activities. In later life, this person may look back on his or her commitment and the rewards from the organization as well as the costs extracted and ask, "Is that all there is?" From the organization's point of view, highly committed employees tend to stay longer, accept the organization's demands on their time, work very hard, and achieve the organization's goals. On the negative side for the organization, the employees that stay may not be as good as others the company could hire if there were room. Such highly committed employees may be inflexible to change, resist the efforts of new employees who have good ideas, and engage in illegal or unethical acts on behalf of the organization.

Moderate commitment consequences

Is the answer, then, moderate levels of commitment? Would organizations and individuals then have the best of both worlds? As shown in Exhibit 7–2, there are both positive and negative consequences for the individual and the organization even for moderate levels of commitment. On the positive side, the individual may have enhanced feelings of belonging to an organization while still feeling some creative individualism and an identity separate from the workplace. For example, the person is more than just a manager for IBM. For the organization, the positive consequences of moderate commitment are increased stability in the work force, lower turnover, and increased job satisfaction. On the negative side of things for the organization, employees may be less willing to do extra things for the organization, may seek a balance between their job and their personal life, and may not achieve as high levels of performance. For the individual, moderate commitment may lead to limited career advancement because there will be others who are willing to forsake all for the company. The individual may also feel an uneasy compromise in trying to balance work and nonwork parts of life. Questions like, "Should I go to my child's school play tonight, or should I go to dinner with my client?" become uneasy battlegrounds when a person tries to balance commitment to work and family.

A manager's work with employee commitment is quite complicated. Do managers want their employees to be highly committed all the time or just some of the time? Sometimes this question will be essential, such as when managers need that "above the call of duty" extra effort. Should employees sometimes have moderate or low commitment? In general, moderate commitment may be best, but if an employee is a poor performer, managers may hope for low commitment and thus high turnover.

And for managers themselves, what should their level of commitment to the organization and its goals be? Clearly, all of this talk about commitment and job satisfaction has something to do with performance on the job. Let us now turn our attention to performance as an outcome from individuals.

Individual performance

Do managers get paid to get high job satisfaction and high commitment from employees, or do they get paid to achieve high performance from employees? Obviously, the answer is to get high performance—to get the job done and to get the product out the door. But managers may also be thinking, "Aren't job satisfaction and commitment related to performance?" The answer is yes, but unfortunately the link is quite complex. Let us look at individual performance as an outcome, first in terms of a definition and then in terms of its relationship with other outcome variables.

Here, when we talk about performance, we are talking about the performance of individuals. Later on in the book, we will look at the performance of groups and the performance of organizations, which in some way are the sum of individual performances. For now, we want to look at how well an individual employee achieves his or her goals. Does John get his budget report done on time, and is it accurate? Does Susan get her assembly work on the computer moving down the assembly line done in a timely fashion and in a way that meets quality standards? In a way, we are talking about measures of productivity—a ratio of outputs to inputs. We are talking about the extent to which certain organizational goals are accomplished. If the goal is to reduce the percentage of rejects coming off the computer assembly line to 1.0 percent, achieving a 1.5 percent reject rate is poor performance, while achieving a 1.0 percent rate is good, and achieving a rate of .5 percent is excellent. Finally, we are talking about utilizing the potential abilities of an individual.

On many of these outcomes, the United States has not been doing too well during the 1980s. Productivity rates have risen slowly (though the picture is getting brighter), and quality of products has long been a problem in the United States.[18] Managers complain constantly about employees not doing their jobs. A survey conducted by the Public Agenda Forum in the early 1980s found that less than 25 percent of employees feel they are working at full potential, 50 percent do only enough to keep their job, and 75 percent feel they could be significantly more effective.[19] Clearly, managers need to understand individual performance as an outcome measure. Managers shouldn't be afraid to let people perform and share in the rewards of their high performance. (See Insight 7–3)

As noted in Chapter 6 on motivation, individual performance depends on both the ability and the motivation of an individual. When leadership is discussed in Chapters 8 and 9, these same elements will be used to help managers determine the appropriate leadership style to use with an individual to achieve high performance. **The key point here is that performance depends on both ability and motivation.** If a stu-

---

I N S I G H T   7-3

Notable & Quotable

*C*hrysler Chairman Lee A. Iacocca, asked about his 1985 compensation package—$1,617,455 in salary and bonus, and more in stock options—at a press conference April 22:

Well, I'm not a socialist, you know. I believe in our system. I probably should answer you by saying in salary and bonus, I'm probably overpaid. My board pays me and they think I'm worth that kind of money. . . . But when you talk about stock options, I'm very candid about this. When we were dying, they brought me into the company—I didn't know how bad off we were. I wouldn't have come—but I had to bring the people you see in this front row plus a couple hundred others into the company and I had nothing to offer them. They said we'll never have a bonus again—it looked like we would never do it—and our salaries were about two-thirds of the going rate of other auto company salaries. So I would issue paper. I would give 'em stock options . . . $6 and most of 'em looked at me and said "I've talked to my wife about leaving a good, cushy job and coming with you and all you gave me was a lot of paper that she says that I will paper my room with some day." Now, they lived through this for five, six years and the stock went, on the pre-split basis, to $65. What the hell is wrong with that? Isn't that the American system? They grew with the company. We shouldn't feel ashamed about that part of it.

The Wall Street Journal, May 23, 1986. Reprinted by permission of *The Wall Street Journal,* © Dow Jones & Company, Inc. 1986. All rights reserved.

---

dent tries to write a research paper for a class, it does not matter how hard he tries if he lacks the basic ability to write clearly. The finished product will not be that good. And of course, if the student has the ability to do a good job but is not motivated to do his best, the finished product will also suffer. It takes both the ability to write the paper and the motivation to work hard in order to produce an excellent paper.

Performance and other outcomes

Many people have tried to convince managers that increased job satisfaction leads to better performance of an individual. In 1982, the popular book titled *The One Minute Manager* included the quote, "People who feel good about themselves produce good results."[20] Three years later in 1985, a sequel titled *Putting the One Minute Manager to Work* included the quote, "People who produce good results feel good about themselves."[21] Putting the two quotes together probably reflects the picture most accurately. **Job satisfaction does impact future performance, but higher performance also makes people feel more satisfied, if they are properly rewarded for that performance. It is a cycle of events**

that is clearly in keeping with the developmental perspective. It is also clear that just having satisfied employees does not guarantee high performance.

There are many factors in organizations which affect performance, besides job satisfaction.[22] One of those factors is past experience in similar jobs. If people have performed well in similar jobs in the past, they are likely to have been rewarded for that performance and are likely to do well on their current job. **But managers often make the mistake of promoting people into a job which is quite different from the job in which they were performing so well.** Good salespeople often are promoted to sales managers; good engineers are promoted to engineering managers; and good professors are promoted to deans. But the differences in these job pairs is so great that organizations wind up, for example, losing a good salesperson and gaining a poor sales manager. As discussed in the chapters on motivation, it is critical for high motivation and also for high performance to strive for a fit between the person and the job. If the person's abilities and motivation fit the job, then high performance is much more likely, so long as the person can work well with his or her supervisor and colleagues.

What all of this suggests is that many of the same factors that affect job satisfaction and commitment also affect performance on the job. It is all tied together in a complex package of individual behavior, where the theories and issues discussed in Chapters 3 through 6 are an integral part of the picture. What organizations like Home Computers Company do to try to orchestrate this complex picture is have personnel departments and informed managers. We will not get into all of these issues in detail, since the managerial issues will be our focus in Chapters 8 through 14, and since courses on personnel management deal with the functions of a personnel department.

Briefly, personnel departments focus on the ability variable in the equation in trying to help in the selection and hiring of people with the abilities needed to do a job. Of course, this means that they must conduct job analyses to better understand job demands. Then, personnel, in conjunction with line managers, interview, give tests, and use assessment centers in order to choose the best people from the prospective candidates—both internal and external—for the job. Clearly, issues in validation are critical if managers hope to get the right person for the job. Once the person is on the job, personnel gets involved in developing and providing training for both the employee and the manager so that abilities improve. On the motivation side of the performance equation, personnel is involved in developing performance appraisal and feedback instruments and training managers how to conduct meaningful appraisals. Personnel is also involved in the distribution of financial rewards to reinforce good performance and in outplacement counseling when things do not work out.

NEGATIVE INDIVIDUAL OUTCOMES

Now that we have discussed the positive individual outcomes, let us turn our attention to the negative individual outcomes, since as we know, we do not always get what we want. First, we will discuss several forms of employee withdrawal, namely tardiness, absenteeism, and turnover. Finally, we will discuss stress and its possible effects on employee performance.

Tardiness and absenteeism

In many ways, employees who come to work late or who do not come at all create more problems for managers than employees who quit. When employees are tardy or absent, managers often will not be able to replace them. Hence, managers have to get the job done when they are shorthanded. Imagine the manager of a nine-person work team that works on an assembly-line operation. The employees are highly interdependent in a serial fashion as the product moves down the line. What happens if one of the team members comes in 30 minutes late? The other eight employees cannot do their jobs unless they figure out some way to cover the missing employee's work station. The same problem arises if the employee calls in to say he will be absent. In this case, managers probably have to locate a floater to fill in, have the other eight cover for the missing employee all day, or fill in themselves—all of which will reduce the effectiveness of the group that day. In the United States, these events occur all too often. Some estimates are that in the United States, over 400 million workdays (roughly 5.1 days per employee) are lost each year to absenteeism.[23] Imagine how high the figure might go if we added in the hours and minutes lost to tardiness in the mornings, around breaks, and around lunch, and to leaving early in the afternoon. Such figures are enough to make managers old before their time.

Let us look at some of the factors which research has shown relate to higher levels of absenteeism and tardiness. One rather obvious factor is the degree of the employee's job satisfaction. If people are dissatisfied with their job, their supervisor, and/or their coworkers, they are more likely to be absent or tardy.[24] But managers have probably also known very dissatisfied employees who came to work regularly, and managers wished they would stay home because they were so disruptive. Obviously, there are other factors which affect the rate of an employee's absenteeism and tardiness.

One such factor is the perception that an employee has about his or her ability to get another job. If employees feel they could easily get another job, there may be a tendency for them to be absent more often, but they will call in with an excuse.[25] However, if workers desire to stay with their present employer and feel a sense of involvement in their job, their rate of absenteeism will be low.[26] Some researchers have found that once people start to be absent or tardy, they easily get into this habit.[27]

Many factors outside the workplace could affect employees' tardiness and absenteeism. Problems with a car, a sick child or spouse, family problems, and so forth can all have an impact on an employee's attendance record. The set of factors affecting absenteeism and tardiness are quite complex, as Harvey and Louise of Home Computers Company realize. Still, there are a few things managers can do to positively impact attendance. First of all, managers should make sure the goals of work are clear for employees and that the level of challenge is appropriate for them. Second, managers must strive for a productive operation where employees are recognized more for their contributions than for their mistakes. Third, managers should work to develop a team spirit, a productive leadership relationship, and working conditions that are satisfying to employees. In addition, organizations today are trying many ways to help employees avoid tardiness and absenteeism. (See Insight 7–4) But no matter what managers and organizations do, some tardiness and absenteeism is to be expected. If it becomes a serious problem with an employee, there will usually be company policies and procedures that managers can utilize. But managers must deal with the problem clearly and directly. One person's problem should not affect other people.

Turnover

The ultimate form of withdrawal is when an employee quits an organization. Sometimes managers might be glad to see the person go because he or she has been a poor performer and a management obstacle. Other times, managers may lament the fact that they are losing one of their best employees. Regardless of who leaves, the process of finding, hiring, training, and socializing a replacement is costly. It is not easy to actually measure the dollar cost of turnover, but some estimates suggest that for a clerical employee, the cost of turnover exceeds $2,500 for each incident; for Navy fighter pilots, the figure is $100,000.[28] Clearly, the range is wide, and these figures do not take into account the strain created for managers when they must still get their job done while finding and bringing on board the replacement person.

As one might expect, the process of an employee voluntarily leaving an organization is quite complex. Numerous models of the process and the factors in the process have been developed by researchers over the years. Probably none has received more support for its accuracy than the model shown in Exhibit 7–3.[29] Actually, the model is simpler than it first appears.

Child-Care Center at Virginia Firm Boosts Worker Morale and Loyalty

*T*he polls showed employees at Dominion Bankshares Corp. in Roanoke, VA, were having enormous problems balancing their families with work. More than half of those with children under six said they would probably use an on-site center. Parents were having difficulty arranging quality child care—and as a result there was more absenteeism in the workplace, more turnover and more stress.

Indeed, more than a quarter of Dominion's working mothers had considered quitting because of child-care problems. Barbara Martinet, age 37, a vice president, had lost three child-care providers, for various reasons, in two years. "The third time, I just sat in my office and cried," she recalls. She began to wonder "whether the stress was worth the satisfaction of work." She considers Dominion's center "manna from heaven."

Company officials considered the risks and benefits from every angle. Among their concerns were potential costs, the acceptability of the idea to Dominion's directors, and possible feelings of inequitable treatment among childless employees or those working in other areas at offices without on-site centers. Still, Dominion received only four comments from employees raising questions about fairness.

The path nevertheless took some rocky turns. The project was almost shelved when Dominion went through some less profitable times. Directors worried about the center's effect on profits, though they subsequently supported the project. And skeptics sent Mr. Dalhouse, Dominion's President, newspaper clippings about child abuse and other problems at day-care centers. In the end, Mr. Dalhouse says, the project "got done because I wanted it done."

"There are no altruistic motivations," Mr. Dalhouse says. "We do everything we do with the objective of profit." And enhancing earnings is precisely what the bank holding company believes the day-care center will do—by lowering turnover and absenteeism, improving productivity and morale, and attracting the best workers.

The Dominion program is a pioneer of sorts as corporations cope with the changing demographics of a workplace increasingly dominated by working mothers, single parents and dual-career couples. Nationally, about 3,000 employers provide some form of child-care support, including referrals or help with financing. But Dominion is one of only about 150 that have day-care centers at or near their offices.

The three basic types of factors in the model are the organization, the individual, and the economic labor market, as shown across the top of Exhibit 7–3. The combination of organization and individual factors influences job-related perceptions (like commitment), expectations about the job, and the level of job satisfaction. All of these have been shown to be related to turnover.[30] The combination of economic labor market

EXHIBIT 7–3

A Model of the Employee Turnover Process

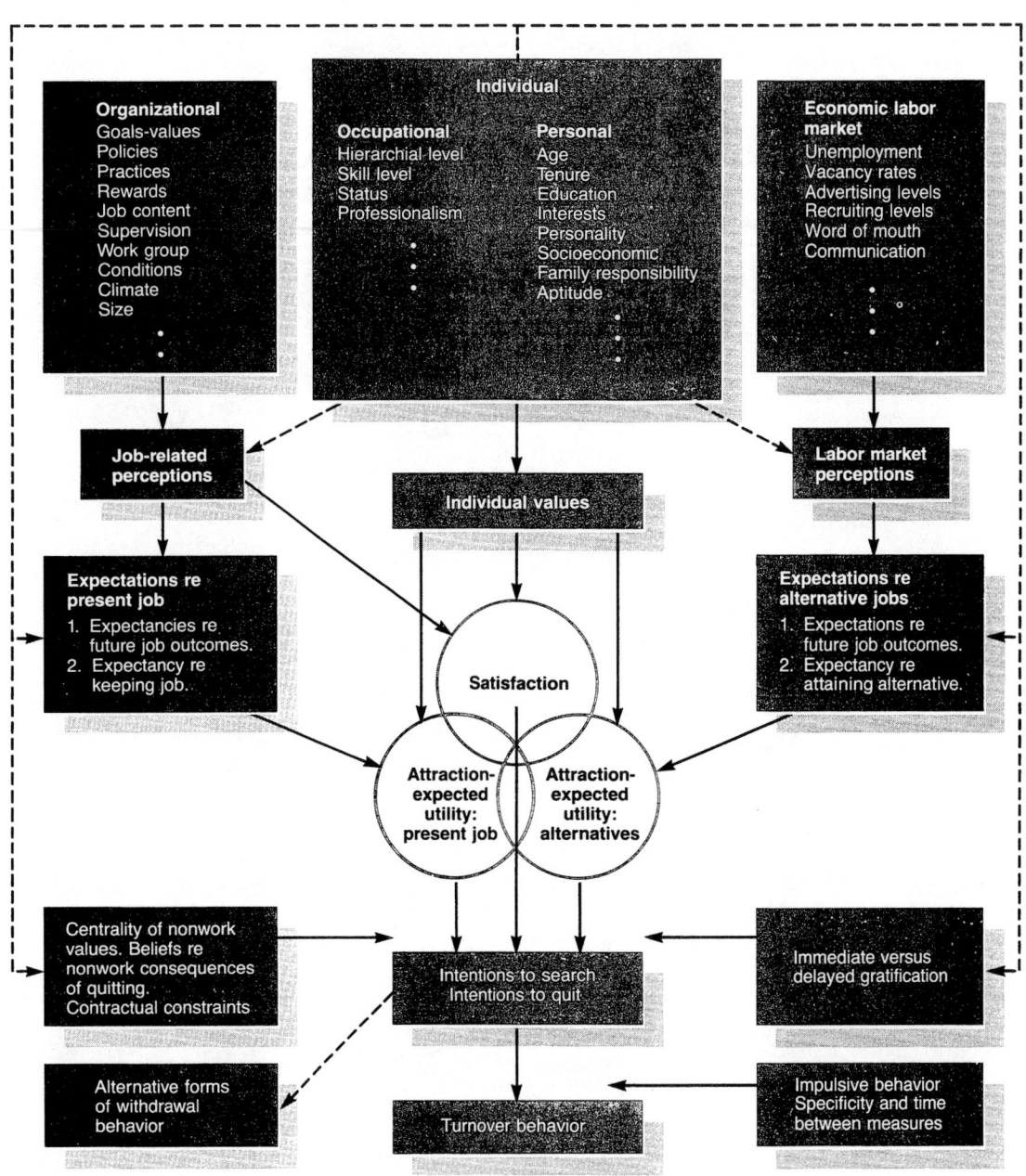

Source: W. Mobley, R. Griffeth, H. Hand, and B. Meglino (1979). A review and conceptual analysis of the employee turnover process. *Psychological Bulletin* 86:517. Copyrighted 1979, American Psychological Association. Reprinted by permission of the publisher and author.

and individual factors influences the attractiveness of other job options. Especially for the better performers who will always have other opportunities, the conditions in the marketplace play an important role in whether or not management can retain these high performers. If the opportunities are better in other organizations, managers can expect to lose some of their best people.[31] The process by which turnover develops is a comparative one. **If satisfaction with the current job plus its attractiveness outweigh the attractiveness of other jobs and the dissatisfaction with the current job, an employee is not likely to begin a search for another job.** Nor is the employee to be that tempted by other job offers. If the scale tips in the other direction, an employee will begin a search for a better job and may ultimately leave. What does seem clear, also, is that this process is not a gradual one that leads smoothly to the employee leaving one day. Over several months or even years, the tension between leaving and staying builds to a point where the person decides, "I'm leaving!" Once they cross this threshold emotionally and mentally, their behavior can change dramatically, as the focus shifts from staying to leaving.[32]

Turnover creates problems for managers, but sometimes an employee's staying does, too. While focus here has been on the employee's decision to leave, this topic must not be closed without at least making mention about turnover initiated by the manager. Managers will say that the most difficult thing to do is to fire someone. Yet, effective managers are not dissuaded from firing someone just because it is uncomfortable. Sometimes, it may be more uncomfortable for the manager, the other employees, and even the problem employee to keep him or her around. If handled properly, fired employees will often say (after they get over the shock), "Being fired from that organization was the best thing that ever happened to me. I probably never would have left on my own, but I am much better off in my new job." But remember, it is the manager's responsibility to set up conditions so a person has the best chance of succeeding. A manager must set clear goals, give people clear feedback on performance, and coach them toward success. But if an employee is not working out after every attempt to help him succeed, the manager must not be bashful about helping him with a career change.

By the same token, letting people go can often appear to be the best solution when it is not. Whenever people are fired from a job, there can be numerous negative consequences. Termination can affect a person's psychological and physiological well-being, as well as family relations.[33] Indeed, losing a job is one of life's most stressful events, as discussed next in this chapter. Also, when managers let people go, it can negatively affect those who are left behind (see Insight 7–2). On the other hand, if managers can keep employees when turnover seems inevitable, it can sometimes pay big dividends, as shown in Insight 7–5.

INSIGHT 7-5

Effective Turnarounds Do Not Require Employee Turnover

*T*he current wave of downsizing, restructuring and reorganizing—often euphemisms for firing people—has an alternative, as was refreshingly demonstrated a few years ago by Hugo Mann, managing director of Deutscher Supermarkt HandelsGmbH, a West German food retailer. When Deutscher acquired a marginally profitable food chain, Mr. Mann returned the chain to an acceptable return on investment without reducing personnel. At the outset he promised that no one would be fired if the employees helped him achieve a 5% sales increase by year end.

This is the story Mr. Mann told at a European seminar conducted last fall. He had learned that the food chain might be for sale. Quietly, he visited all 90 of its stores, noting their strengths and weaknesses. His staff provided demographic data and competitive analysis. He hypothesized that the fundamentals were in place that would return the firm to profitability if he could achieve a modest sales increase. When financial data were provided, his hypothesis was confirmed: A 5% sales increase, augmented by other operating efficiencies, would restore profits with no reduction in personnel or pay. Granted, Mr. Mann operates in Germany, where custom, regulations and union constraints make it more difficult to lay off or fire

people than in the U.S. In this instance, however, he had the option of firing people—he just chose not to do so.

Mr. Mann's reasoning was a model of clarity: "I can achieve the sales increase in the following ways: I can sell more per shopping trip to present customers through better in-store merchandising. I can improve my service so my customers will forsake the competition and shop with me more often. I can attract new customers. Or, I can achieve a combination of all three—and I can achieve it easier with an experienced, motivated, enthusiastic work force."

Immediately following the acquisition, Mr. Mann met with employees to present his proposition: "No layoffs if you will help me achieve a 5% increase in sales." The employees accepted the challenge enthusiastically. That was 1982. Today, the acquired chain is still profitable and growing steadily.

True, Mr. Mann's experience may be the exception, not the rule. Many troubled companies can be returned to long-term profitability only after the removal of unproductive managers and employees along with ill-advised or out-moded ventures. But most terminations and divestitures are irreversible and should be decided only after careful thought and painstaking analysis.

Stress

For most people living in the 20th century, stress is an everyday occurrence. People feel time pressure, pressure from their boss, demands from their families, and the list could go on and on. To cope, people reach for an Anacin, go for a run, yell at someone, or go to a therapist.

Again, the list could go on as people try to deal with both their psychological and physiological reactions to these stressful situations.

To understand stress, we need to distinguish between **stressors—those environmental factors that have the potential to create stress—and stress reactions, which are the physiological and psychological reactions of a person to those environmental factors.**[34] In everyday language, people tend to use stress to describe both the reactions to a situation and the situation itself. "She was under a great deal of stress," meaning that there were numerous stressors in her situation (for example, conflicting demands on her time). The distinction made here is an important one. Two people can be put into situations with the exact same stressors. One person will experience several stress reactions, such as headaches and feelings of anger, while the other person will handle the situation with no real problems. To understand the process of stress in people, let us explore in more detail three aspects of stress: its causes, our reactions to it, and our ways of managing it. The model in Exhibit 7–4 summarizes these aspects and helps us see the overall picture.

Sources of stress from the workplace

Many of the sources of stress in our lives can be traced to the workplace. The **demands of the job** can certainly contribute to stress. And some jobs just have more stressors than others. A national survey of over 130 occupations found that physician, office manager, foreman, and waitress/waiter were among the highest stress jobs, while maid, craft worker, and farm laborer were among some of the lowest.[35] But what is it about the demands of a job that make it stress producing? **Research has shown that when jobs require decisions, the constant monitoring of situations, repeated exchange of information, and/or threatening physical conditions, they create a situation where the employee is likely to feel stress.**[36]

Delving deeper into the workplace, the **dynamics of the employee's role** also contribute to feelings of stress. A person's role can produce stressors in a number of ways. First of all, there can be a basic conflict between the person and the job. For example, someone may be asked to take charge in a situation that demands an autocratic leader, but he or she believes very strongly in participative decision making. Second, if a person works on projects in an organization, he or she will often have two bosses—the department head and the project manager. Such situations are typified by conflicting demands from the two bosses, placing the person in the stressful situation of trying to satisfy both bosses, which is almost impossible, or of choosing which boss to satisfy. Third, there can be conflicting aspects of a work role which produce stress. For example, a university professor is supposed to help a student learn a

EXHIBIT 7-4

A Model of Stress

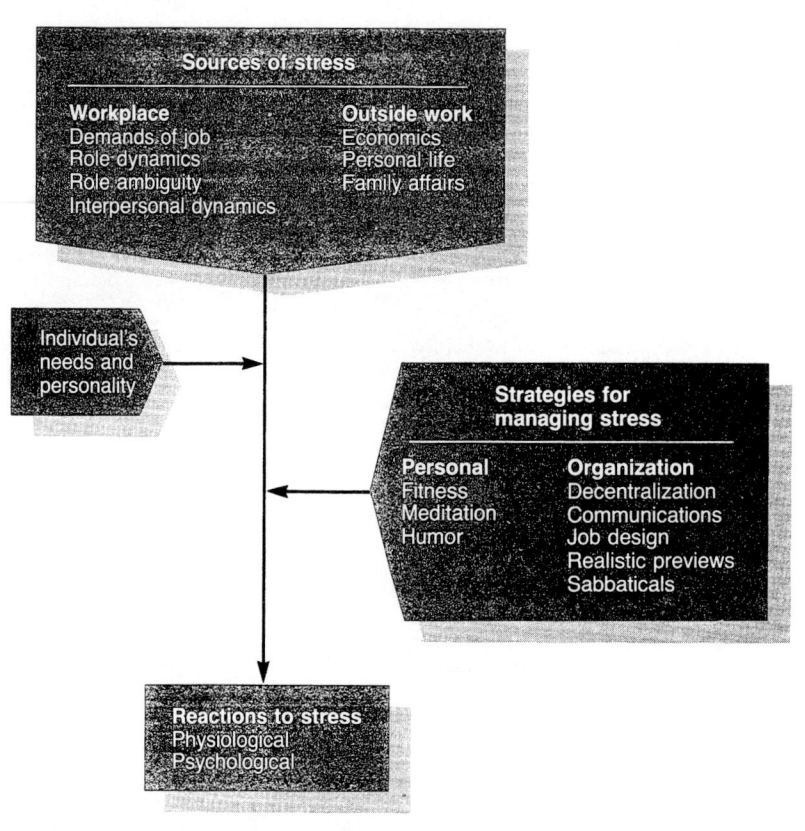

subject, but the professor must also play the role of judge in giving grades. Finally, a work role can be stressful because a person has too much to do in the time he or she has available. The worker just does not know where to start, and sometimes the stress can cause the person to do nothing. For example, a student may have three exams next Monday; which one does the student study for first and for how long? But it is interesting that having too little to do can also create stress in the form of boredom. Children often feel this form of stress during the summer months away from school. After about three weeks, they may constantly ask, "What can I do now?"

The other aspect of role-related stress at work is created by **uncertainty about what to do.** When employees are unclear about their responsibilities, the limits on their authority, the specific criteria used in evaluating their work, and/or the timetable for their work, they are in a stressful situation referred to as **role ambiguity.** As we will discuss in the chapters on leadership (8 and 9), even if people are highly skilled and motivated, they cannot perform well if their role is ambiguous. And in addition to lower performance, they will also experience stress reactions, which may have other negative consequences. Research has shown that as many as 60 percent of employees experience role ambiguity to some extent.[37] Of course, the interpersonal relationships people experience at work can also contribute to stress. Such simple things as noisy coworkers, telephone calls at the wrong time, people walking into the person's office, and so forth have been shown to be great sources of stress, largely because they take away the person's feeling of control.[38] Insight 7–6 gives a sense of this situation in describing an ad used by the Afscme union to try to attract state government employees. Then, too, the interpersonal relationship which places managers in a position of responsibility for others places them in a stressful situation. If managers must get work done through others, motivate them, reward and punish them, and evaluate their performance, managers will likely experience greater levels of stress. When people are having problems related to work, it is the manager who must listen to them and try to provide some help. Managers must listen to their complaints and sometimes settle disputes, and these activities create stress. Likewise, when people do not perform well or create problems for other employees, it is the manager who must bite the bullet and discipline the problem employee.

The flip side of this responsibility can also be a stressor. People who have been through a performance appraisal can understand this. When a superior's evaluation of an employee's performance has implications for the employee's career, it is almost always a stressful situation at the performance appraisal meeting.

Obviously, there are many factors in the workplace which can be stressors. As a way of gaining a better understanding of these factors, turn to the Stress Diagnostic Survey at the end of this chapter and take a few minutes to complete it about your current job, or if you are not working, about a job you have had in the past. See just how stressful your job is, or was.

Sources of stress from outside the workplace

In addition to the stressors from within the workplace, there are many stressors from outside the workplace. Certainly, **economic** conditions can create stress. If a person invests heavily in the stock market and it falls dramatically, as it is prone to do every so often, he or she could lose a great deal of money. This event might threaten plans for a new house or new car or any number of other financial decisions. On the other

New-Collar Jobs
Unions Court People in Service-Type Work to Stem Fall in Ranks

Columbus, Ohio—In a television commercial here, Bernice, a state government worker, endures 30 seconds of contemporary workplace hell.

People rush through her office barking orders and dropping off work. Her phone rings and a supervisor brays in the staccato style of Federal Express ads: "Keep Wednesday open and by the way we're cutting your sick days." A colleague asks, "Honey, can you answer our phone, too? Our girl's been laid off." The mail boy confides, "They're canceling our summer vacations."

In the final frame, Bernice clutches the telephone in her office late at night. "Hello, Afscme?" she says. A closing line declares simply: "We Win Respect."

The television ad, shown last year as part of the campaign of the American Federation of State, County and Municipal Employees to organize Ohio state employees, symbolizes organized labor's attempt to market itself to a changing work force that isn't much interested in its traditional appeals.

Baby Boomer Jobs

What Afscme and other unions are after—in Ohio and the rest of the nation—is the big demographic bulge of workers who make up the new service economy. They are the roughly 20 million members of the Baby Boom generation who mostly work in service jobs that are neither traditional blue-collar nor professional white-collar.

Ralph Whitehead, a University of Massachusetts professor, calls them the "new-collar" workers, the backbone of "the post-industrial working class."

Their ranks include clerical workers, insurance agents, keypunchers, nurses, teachers, mental health aides, computer technicians, loan officers, auditors and salespeople.

One convert is Sandra Winkle, a 26-year-old daughter of the middle-class who concedes she "never knew anyone who was in a union." Her vote for Afscme reflected a need for an ally against stressful working conditions.

Her work—keying information from tax forms into computers—is monitored to see if she meets a daily goal. After receiving several warnings about not meeting goals, she was suspended for a day. "I don't think there should be pressure like that on any job," she says. "I need somebody to help me get the point across."

Still, the union still has far to go in worker acceptance. Even some of its new members say they think it remains an old-style bureaucracy emphasizing matters like seniority rights over professional concerns. Unions, says William R. Cody, a state landscape architect, "probably work best for guys out driving snowplows."

hand, sometimes a person's economic situation can be so successful that it creates stress. Most people probably think, "Bring on this problem; it's one I'd like to have." But when people make a lot of money quickly, they feel the stress of how to keep it. What investments should they make? How will they maintain that high level of income? Where can they spend it? These are just some of the questions people face when they get into a situation where they are making money quickly.

An individual's **personal life** can also be a source of stress. For example, moving to a new city is very disruptive to people's lives. They have to locate a new dry cleaner, find a new place to have their car serviced, and determine the best route to work. They have to make new friends and meet their neighbors. Of course, a serious injury, such as a person might suffer in a car accident, can put life on hold and be a source of stress. Should a person decide to marry or to get a divorce, he or she will experience personal stress. The individual dealing with the death of a spouse is experiencing one of the most stressful events imaginable. Researchers have found that events in personal lives do create varying degrees of stress and can even have consequences on a person's health. Exhibit 7–5 summarizes these findings.[39] The larger the point value for an event, the more stressful it is. And if during the course of a year, a person experiences a combination of events where the point total exceeds 300, research has shown that that person has a 70 percent chance of becoming seriously ill due to the stress created in his or her life.[40]

What this list also suggests is that **family affairs** are potential nonwork stressors. For instance, married people with young children tend to get less sleep; and the demands of a small child can be quite physically tiring. As children get older, they learn to talk back to their parents, to make their own demands, and to have their own set of activities. And living in a household with teenage children can be a most stressful situation. Two-career families have enough stressors to give anyone an ulcer! Schedules conflict, time together as a family is reduced, each spouse has to be concerned with his or her own career, and there are endless conflicts which create stress. As discussed in Chapter 4, the combination of family stages with career stages and life stages can make for a delicate balancing act at times. The pressures of family life create their own strain and demand time, but pressures at work also create strain and demand time. The combination of the two can make for a very stressful situation to which an individual must respond.[41]

Reactions to these stressors

As suggested earlier in this chapter, the stressors in the situation are only part of the picture. **The characteristics of the person in the stressful situation have a great deal to do with the actual stress which will be experienced.** If a person's needs are such that he or she is ambitious,

EXHIBIT 7–5

The Social Readjustment Rating Scale

Life Event	Mean Value
1. Death of spouse.	
2. Divorce.	
3. Marital separation.	
4. Jail term.	
5. Death of close family member.	
6. Personal injury or illness.	
7. Marriage.	
8. Fired at work.	
9. Marital reconciliation.	
10. Retirement.	
11. Change in health of family member.	
12. Pregnancy.	
13. Sex difficulties.	
14. Gain of new family member.	
15. Business readjustment.	
16. Change in financial state.	
17. Death of close friend.	
18. Change to different line of work.	
19. Change in number of arguments wit	
20. Mortgage over $10,000.	
21. Foreclosure of mortgage or loan.	30
22. Change in responsibilities at work.	29
23. Son or daughter leaving home.	29
24. Trouble with in-laws.	29
25. Outstanding personal achievement.	28
26. Spouse begins or stops work.	26
27. Begin or end school.	26
28. Change in living conditions.	25
29. Revision of personal habits.	24
30. Trouble with boss.	23
31. Change in work hours or conditions.	20
32. Change in residence.	20
33. Change in schools.	20
34. Change in recreation.	19
35. Change in church activities.	19
36. Change in social activities.	18
37. Mortgage or loan less than $10,000.	17
38. Change in sleeping habits.	16
39. Change in number of family get-togethers.	15
40. Change in eating habits.	15
41. Vacation.	13
42. Christmas.	12
43. Minor violations of the law.	11

Source: Reprinted by permission of the publisher from Holmes, T. H. and Rahe, R. H. The Social Readjustment Rating Scale, *Journal of Psychosomatic Research, 11,* 213–18. Copyright © 1967 by The American Psychosomatic Society, Inc.

strives for perfection, and wants it all now, the person is likely to experience greater levels of stress than someone who is less hard-driving. Chapter 4 talked about Type A and Type B personalities. The Type A is this hard-driving person, and research has shown that Type A personalities feel stress more than Type B personalities.[42]

When we are in stressful situations, we respond both psychologically and physiologically. On the psychological side, we experience feelings of frustration, tension, and even anxiety. In the extreme, these reactions can result in negative shifts in moods and emotion—even feelings of depression. Stress can also cause low self-esteem and personality changes. An example can help illustrate this point. Imagine a situation where an employee must prepare an important report for his boss—a stressful situation. If the person's tension and anxiety result in a poor report, his self-confidence can be decreased. This event could lead to a shift from extroversion toward introversion. A very common reaction to stress is a reduction in job satisfaction, which (as discussed earlier in this chapter) is a very important individual outcome.

On the physiological side of things, stress has been associated with a variety of common ailments and illnesses, including headaches, stomachaches, ulcers, high blood pressure, and heart disease.[43] People in stressful situations who react to the stressors will tend to experience some or all of these and other ailments and illnesses. In addition, an employee under high levels of stress may not be a good performer on the job. Indeed, employees under high stress may turn to drugs or alcohol as a means of coping. Such measures usually make matters worse for the individual and often lead to accidents which hurt other people. Employees under prolonged levels of high stress will often suffer **burnout, defined as emotional, physical, and mental exhaustion.** Good employees are often lost due to such situations. Performance declines, they start being tardy or absent, and they may quit or eventually suffer a breakdown. **Managers must know how to manage stress in a positive way, both for their employees as well as for themselves.** Let us now look at some of those ways of managing stress.

Managing stress

There are essentially two ways to manage the stress that people experience in their lives. First, there are **personal strategies,** and second, there are **organizational strategies.** Individuals can be sure to stay physically fit. Exercise on a regular basis not only makes people stronger and better able to withstand the physiological reactions to stress, but it also helps to relieve the psychological tension leading to negative stress reactions (see Insight 7–7). Besides, fitness has been shown to relate closely to lower absenteeism and higher productivity.[44] Good nutrition and the ability to relax while in the midst of stressful situations are also important ways to manage stress. Simple meditation exercises can be used by anyone to deal with stress in a positive way. Also, humor can often be used to relieve the pressures of stress; there is nothing quite like a good laugh to help reduce stress.

Managers must also think about what an organization can do to help people deal with stress. Sometimes organizations can be reorganized in a way that reduces the stress on employees. Decentralization, which is explored in Chapters 17 and 18, can sometimes be used to get people more involved and allow them to feel more control, thus reducing their level of stress in the job. Also, improved organizational communications, which is discussed in Chapter 11, can help people feel in control of what is happening around them. Sometimes, the kinds of changes discussed in Chapter 6 regarding job design can be utilized to create jobs which are more compatible with the people in them. An organization can also prepare new employees to deal with stress by providing them with **realistic previews** of what their jobs will really be like, thus helping people to begin preparing for the jobs before they even start.[45]

Finally, an organization can help employees deal with stress by providing training in relaxation techniques and fitness, as discussed above, as well as by developing a policy to provide employees with time away from the organization, that is **sabbaticals.**

CHAPTER HIGHLIGHTS

With this chapter, we conclude the section on individual behavior and ready ourselves to begin looking at interpersonal behavior. **This chapter reviewed a number of important individual outcomes, for which managers are at least partially responsible.** In addition, employees are partially responsible for their own levels of these individual outcomes. We looked at three positive individual outcomes—job satisfaction, commitment, and individual performance—and three negative individual outcomes—tardiness/absenteeism, turnover, and stress. Let us review them now.

Overall, most employees report reasonably high levels of satisfaction with their jobs. But job satisfaction does vary from person to person, depending on such things as the person's gender and age and the type of job held. This should come as no surprise given all of the individual differences discussed in Chapters 3 through 6. In addition, job satisfaction can vary depending on different aspects of the job. For example, an employee may like his or her job very much, but not be happy with the supervisor, coworkers, or working conditions. **So while job satisfaction is an important outcome variable, it is also a complex variable which managers need to grasp.**

Next, we explored the commitment a person has to an organization and its goals. **Commitment is critical for employees if they stay with an organization and work hard toward its goals.** In order to have committed employees, managers will have to clearly explain organizational goals and expectations to them. Because without something to commit to, most people are not going to be committed—it's that simple. But it is also more complicated than just setting clear goals. As seen in Exhibit 7–1, **such factors as peer group influence, external and internal rewards, participation, and individual expectancies play an important role in the commitment of an individual.**

It is also important for managers to remember that regardless of whether people exhibit low, moderate, or high levels of commitment, there will be both positive and negative consequences for both the individual and the organization. Everyone knows the negative consequences of low commitment—slower career advancement, personal costs, and even loss of job. But most people do not think about the positive consequences of low commitment, such as individual creativity and better utilization of people by getting them into the right jobs and getting rid of the more disruptive employees. Likewise, everyone knows the positive consequences of high commitment—career advancement, rewards, a stable work force, and higher performance. But people fail to recognize the negative consequences of high commitment, such as stifling of individual creativity, resistance to change, stress in nonwork relationships, lack of organizational innovation, and even illegal acts committed on behalf of the organization. Managers must manage the outcomes of commitment to the organization and its goals, trying to achieve positive outcomes but being on the lookout for negative outcomes.

Next, we explored the bottom-line outcome of job performance—the variable for which managers are ultimately responsible. We looked at how performance can be measured in terms of goal accomplishment and productivity. In exploring performance, it became quite clear that performance is tied to the other positive outcomes, as well as the negative outcomes in a complex picture. **It is a manager's job to understand the relationships between performance and things like job satisfaction, commitment, absenteeism, turnover, and stress so that he or she can work with the organization and the employees to achieve long-term high-performance levels.**

By looking at performance as an outcome, it also became clear that certain negative individual outcomes must be managed. As discussed, tardiness and absenteeism create many headaches for managers. In trying to keep control over these outcomes, managers have to try to keep job satisfaction and commitment up. But employees' perception of the ease of getting another job, external events in their lives, and everyday things such as car problems and sickness which are out of a person's control are all going to have an impact on tardiness and absenteeism.

In addition, managers must be concerned about turnover as an outcome. Whenever managers lose an employee, they must not only find a replacement, but they must train and socialize the replacement. There are some significant costs incurred. We discussed how **organizational, individual, and economic labor market factors combine to create the level of turnover managers must deal with in their organization.** But it is important to remember that turnover can be positive for both the organization and the individual when there is a lack of fit between the two.

The final topic for this chapter was stress. **There are numerous stressors in the workplace, such as the demands of the job, role conflict and ambiguity, and responsibility for others. There are also numerous stressors from outside the workplace, such as in your personal and family life.** These stressors interact to create stressful situations to which people respond, with varying degrees of felt stress, in both psychological and physiological ways. Since stress is a fact of life in the 20th century, it is important for us to learn to deal with it. We discussed such personal coping strategies as exercise and relaxation techniques. Managers also need to understand organizational strategies which can help both them and their people. We discussed such things as decentralization of responsibilities, realistic job previews, and sabbaticals.

Throughout this chapter, it has been implied that the various individual outcomes, both positive and negative, are partially a product of the individual. The factors of perception, learning, values, attitudes, personality, and motivation which were discussed in Chapters 3 through 6 all play a part in these individual outcomes. Clearly, these outcomes are also influenced by many interpersonal factors like leadership, power and politics, and communications as discussed in Chapters 8 through 11. They are also influenced by many group and intergroup issues as discussed in Chapters 12 through 14. They are also impacted by many aspects of the overall organization in which the person works. These are explored in Chapters 15 through 19. Finally, the developmental overlay which forms the frame for this entire book and which was explained in Chapters 1 and 2 must not be forgotten. **Individual outcomes, positive and negative, must continually be managed. Just because they are bad today does not mean they will remain that way; and likewise, just because they are good today does not mean they will remain that way either.**

REVIEW QUESTIONS

1. What is job satisfaction, and why is it so important for managers to understand the factors that influence it?
2. Explain how working conditions, the job itself, others in the workplace, and the changing individual impact job satisfaction.
3. What do we mean when we talk about commitment of an employee? What do people commit to in organizations?
4. Explain how commitment develops in an employee. What are the key factors affecting employee commitment?
5. What are the positive and negative individual and organizational consequences of low, moderate, and high commitment?
6. What do we mean by individual performance, and how is it related to the other individual outcomes?
7. Why might we say that tardiness and absenteeism are more nagging problems than actual turnover of employees? What factors affect tardiness and absenteeism?
8. Explain how organizational, individual, and market factors influence whether an individual leaves or stays with an organization. Why is the decision to stay or to leave a comparative process?

9. What is the difference between stressors and stress? Explain the causes of stress from both within the workplace and from outside the workplace.

10. What are some typical psychological and physiological reactions to stress? Why do people respond differently to stressful situations?

11. What are some of the best personal and organizational ways for you and others to cope with and manage stress?

RESOURCE READINGS

Brief, A. P.; R. S. Schuler; and M. VanSell. *Managing Job Stress.* Boston, Mass.: Little, Brown, 1981.

Locke, E. A. "The Nature and Causes of Job Satisfaction." In *Handbook of Industrial and Organizational Psychology,* ed. M. D. Dunnette. Skokie, Ill.: Rand McNally, 1976.

Locke, E. A.; G. P. Latham; and M. Erez. "The Determinants of Goal Commitment." *Academy of Management Review* 13 (1988), pp. 23–39.

McGrath, J. E. "Stress and Behavior in Organizations." In *Handbook of Industrial and Organizational Psychology,* ed. M. D. Dunnette. Skokie, Ill.: Rand McNally, 1976.

Mobley, W. H. *Employee Turnover: Causes, Consequences, and Control.* Reading, Mass.: Addison-Wesley Publishing, 1982.

NOTES

1. P. C. Smith, L. M. Kendall, and C. L. Hulin, *The Measurement of Satisfaction in Work and Retirement* (Skokie, Ill.: Rand McNally, 1969).

2. R. P. Quinn and G. L. Staines, *The 1977 Quality of Employment Survey* (Ann Arbor, Mich.: Institute for Social Research, 1979).

3. *USA Today,* "Pulse of the USA," June 15, 1987, p. 1.

4. C. N. Weaver, "Job Satisfaction in the United States in the 1970's," *Journal of Applied Psychology* 65 (1980), pp. 364–67.

5. R. A. Barron, *Behavior in Organizations: Understanding and Managing the Human Side of Work,* 2nd ed. (Boston: Allyn and Bacon, 1986), p. 157.

6. Smith et al., *The Measurement of Satisfaction in Work and Retirement.*

7. J. R. Hackman, G. Oldham, R. Janson, and K. Purdy, "A New Strategy for Job Enrichment," *California Management Review* 27 (1975), pp. 57–71.

8. E. A. Locke, "The Nature and Causes of Job Satisfaction," in *Handbook of Industrial and Organizational Psychology,* ed. M. D. Dunnette (Skokie, Ill.: Rand McNally, 1976).

9. E. A. Locke, D. M. Schweiger, and G. P. Latham, "Participation in Decision Making: When Should It Be Used," *Organizational Dynamics* 14 (Winter 1986), pp. 65–79.

10. Barron, *Behavior in Organizations.*

11. C. S. Granrose and J. D. Portwood, "Matching Individual Career Management," *Academy of Management Journal* 30 (1987), pp. 699–720.

12. L. W. Porter, R. M. Steers, R. T. Mowday, and P. V. Boulian, "Organizational Commitment, Job Satisfaction, and Turnover Among Psychiatric Technicians," *Journal of Applied Psychology* 5 (1974), pp. 603–9.

13. W. Bennis and B. Nanus, *Leaders: The Strategies for Taking Charge* (New York: Harper & Row, 1985).

14. E. A. Locke, G. P. Latham, and M. Enez, "The Determinants of Goal Commitment," *Academy of Management Review* 13 (1988), pp. 23–39.

15. W. A. Randolph and B. Z. Posner, *Effective Project Planning and Management: Getting the Job Done* (Englewood Cliffs, NJ: Prentice–Hall, 1988).

16. M. R. Driver, "Career Concepts—A New Approach to Career Research," in *Career Issues in Human Resource Management,* ed. Ian R. Katz (Englewood Cliffs, NJ: Prentice–Hall, 1982), pp. 23–32.

17. D. Randall, "Commitment and the Organization: The Organization Man Revisited," *Academy of Management Review* 12 (1987), pp. 460–71.

18. J. Rutledge and D. Allen, "We Should Love the Trade Deficit," *Fortune* (February 29, 1988), pp. 125–26.

19. D. Yankelovich and Associates, *Work and Human Values* (New York: Public Agenda Foundation, 1983), pp. 6–7.

20. K. Blanchard and S. Johnson, *The One Minute Manager* (New York: William Morrow & Co., 1982), p. 19.

21. K. Blanchard and R. Loember, *Putting the One Minute Manager to Work* (New York: William Morrow & Co., 1985), p. 18.

22. K. I. Miller and P. R. Monge, "Participation, Satisfaction, and Productivity: A Meta-Analytic Review," *Academy of Management Journal* 29 (1986), pp. 727–53.

23. R. M. Steers and S. R. Rhodes, "A New Look at Absenteeism," *Personnel,* November-December 1980, pp. 60–65.

24. K. D. Scott and G. S. Taylor, "An Examination of Conflicting Findings—the Relationship Between Job Satisfaction and Absenteeism: A Meta-Analysis," *Academy of Management Journal* 28 (1985), pp. 599–612.

25. E. W. Larson and C. V. Fukami, "Employee Absenteeism: The Role of Ease of Movement," *Academy of Management Journal* 28 (1985), pp. 464–71.

26. G. J. Blau, "Job Involvement and Organizational Commitment as Interactive Predictors of Tardiness and Absenteeism," *Journal of Management* 12 (1986), pp. 577–84.

27. J. M. Ivancevich, "Predicting Absenteeism from Prior Absence and Work Attitudes," *Academy of Management Journal* 28 (1985), pp. 219–78.

28. W. H. Mobley, *Employee Turnover: Causes, Consequences and Control* (Reading, Mass.: Addison–Wesley Publishing, 1982).

29. Ibid.

30. J. P. Curry, D. S. Wakefield, J. L. Price, and C. W. Mueller, "On the Causal Ordering of Job Satisfaction and Organizational Commitment," *Academy of Management Journal* 29 (1986), pp. 847–58; R. P. Vecchio, "Predicting Employee Turnover from Leader-Member Exchange: A Failure to Replicate," *Academy of Management Journal* 28 (1985), pp. 478–85; J. L. Cotton and J. M. Tuttle, "Employee Turnover: A Meta-Analysis and Review with Implications for Research," *Academy of Management Review* 11 (1986), pp. 55–70.

31. G. M. McEvoy and W. F. Cascio, "Do Good or Poor Performers Leave? A Meta-Analysis of the Relationship Between Performance and Turnover," *Academy of Management Journal* 30 (1987), pp. 744–62.

32. J. E. Sheridan, "A Catastrophe Model of Employee Withdrawal Leading to Low Job Performance, High Absenteeism, and Job Turnover During the First Year of Employment," *Academy of Management Journal* 28 (1985), pp. 88–109.

33. C. R. Leana and J. M. Ivancevich, "Involuntary Job Loss: Institutional Interventions and a Research Agenda," *Academy of Management Review* 12 (1987), pp. 301–12.

34. J. E. McGrath, "Stress and Behavior in Organizations," in *Handbook of Industrial and Organizational Psychology*, ed. M. D. Dunnette (Skokie, Ill.: Rand McNally, 1976), pp. 1351–95.

35. National Institute for Occupational Safety and Health, Department of Health, Education, and Welfare. (Washington, DC: Government Printing Office, 1978).

36. J. B. Shaw and J. H. Riskind, "Predicting Job Stress Using Data from the Position Analysis Questionnaire," *Journal of Applied Psychology* 68 (1983), pp. 253–61.

37. J. E. McGrath, "Stress and Behavior in Organizations."

38. R. I. Sutton and A. Rafaeli, "Characteristics of Work Stations As Potential Occupational Stressors," *Academy of Management Journal* 30 (1978), pp. 260–76.

39. T. H. Holmes and R. H. Rahe, "Social Readjustment Rating Scale," *Journal of Psychosomatic Research* 11 (1967), pp. 213–18.

40. Ibid.

41. J. H. Greenhaus and N. J. Beutell, "Sources of Conflict Between Work and Family Roles," *Academy of Management Review* 10 (1985), pp. 76–88.

42. M. S. Pittner, B. K. Houston, and G. Spiridigliozzi, "Control Over Stress, Type A Behavior Pattern, and Response to Stress," *Journal of Personality and Social Psychology* 44 (1983), pp. 627–36.

43. M. Frese, "Stress at Work and Psychosomatic Complaints: A Causal Interpretation," *Journal of Applied Psychology* 70 (1985), pp. 314–28; A. A. McLean, *Work Stress* (Reading, Mass.: Addison–Wesley Publishing, 1980).

44. L. E. Falkenberg, "Employee Fitness Programs: Their Impact on the Employee and the Organization," *Academy of Management Review* 12 (1987), pp. 511–22.

45. J. P. Wanous, *Organizational Entry: Recruitment, Selection, and Socialization of Newcomers* (Reading, Mass.: Addison–Wesley Publishing, 1980).

CASE: Is anyone irreplaceable?

Background

Marilyn Owens has been employed by Enertrol Manufacturing Company for 32 years. Thirty of those years have been spent in the company's claims department as a secretary. Marilyn is one of two secretaries who work for the claims investigators. Because of her length of service, Marilyn is senior over the other secretary, but does not have any substantial formal authority. Marilyn is known as a perfectionist. Mr. Mills, the claims agent and department head, often relies on Marilyn to carry out the department's secretarial duties with expertise because Marilyn's quality of work output and her loyalty to the department are outstanding.

Janice Martin, a recent graduate of Adams Business College, was hired two months ago as the number two secretary for the claims department. From her transcripts it could be seen that Janice excelled in shorthand, typing, business English, and had many other necessary secretarial traits. In her short time with the claims department Janice had shown her ability to communicate well with the public and had a friendly and cooperative attitude with the investigators in the office. Mills feels that she added to the professional and efficient atmosphere of the department.

In the past two years, there have been seven female employees in the number two secretarial position. Most have had "personality conflicts" with Marilyn and departed within a short time.

Incident

During the early stages of Janice's employment it seemed that she and Marilyn worked well together. Mills felt that the two women were a great asset to the department. One afternoon, however, Mills found Janice terribly upset. He asked her to step into his office. Through the conversation that followed, he learned that the secretaries were not as compatible as he had thought. It seems that Marilyn found some minute flaw with *all* of Janice's work and condescendingly pointed them out. Janice said she was losing her self-confidence and was finding it harder and harder to work under such pressure. Mills assured Janice that she had been doing a fine job and that he would speak with Marilyn.

Mills called Marilyn into his office. He related the incident that had just occurred with Janice and asked for Marilyn's views. She quickly became

Source: J. E. Dittrich and R. A. Zawicki, *People and Organizations* (Plano, TX: Business Publications, 1981), pp. 119–20.

defensive and said, "I'm always the heavy around here." She went on to state that all the young girls hired as number two secretary "seem like they know it all when actually they know very little." She exclaimed, "It takes years of experience, not school courses, to become proficient in the secretarial field."

Mills told Marilyn he would have to think the matter over, but while doing so, she should display patience with Janice.

Decision

Mills reflected over the past events. This was not the first time that Marilyn had unjustly turned against the woman in the number two secretarial spot. He felt that Marilyn was insecure about young competition; but he was torn in his decision—he needed Marilyn to run the clerical end of his department. She had always done an excellent job in the past and she continued to do so now. But he was also tired of the turnover that kept occurring in the number two spot.

Questions

1. What positive outcomes is Marilyn impacting?
2. What negative outcomes is she impacting?
3. What should Mills do? Should Mills consider firing Marilyn?

CASE: Labor relations: Reconnecting the lines

For years, it had been considered one of the most innovative labor-management relationships around. Every few months, top American Telephone & Telegraph Co. managers met with leaders of the company's two unions in so-called common interest forums. The two sides pored over financial figures normally given only to the board of directors, a key step in building mutual trust. More than that, they discussed how to improve products and services. Management sought advice, and the unions gave it.

In 1985, however, the process all but collapsed. With costs running out of control, AT&T was anxious to show Wall Street a solution could be found. Robert E. Allen, then AT&T's president, broke a decades-old tradition of job security. He started to eliminate 75,000 jobs, both union and nonunion, or 20% of the work force, over three years. The company's once-enviable labor relations deteriorated. The low point came during a 1986 strike that lasted 17 days.

The damage to morale has turned out to be one of AT&T's most serious post-divestiture problems. But now, slowly, relations are starting to improve. "Everything's still not hunky-dory at AT&T," says Morton Bahr, president of the Communications Workers of America (CWA), which represents 148,000 AT&T employees. "But I think we've seen the worst of it."

Crisis busters. The most progress has come in dealing with layoffs. Even to many white-collar employees, AT&T handled its initial job reductions

Source: Aaron Bernstein, *Business Week*, January 18, 1988, p. 59.

clumsily. But the company learned from its mistakes. In the fall of 1986, AT&T's Information Systems (IS) Div. decided that it had approximately 1,400 surplus technicians and clerical workers. Instead of just firing them, it set up a joint crisis team with the CWA to find jobs. The team offered early retirement to technicians in a different division, AT&T Communications, even though that unit wasn't overstaffed. This opened up employment for 747 IS technicians. Some 60 others took temporary two-year jobs with AT&T Communications in California, while some clerks got jobs in the operator services division.

In the end, all 1,047 IS employees who remained after 353 had taken early retirement were offered jobs, although 287 workers quit rather than relocate. Says Tom Hickman, an assistant to the president of the International Brotherhood of Electrical Workers(IBEW). "It took the cooperation of the company, which went beyond the contract."

AT&T also worked with the unions last year to revamp its retail phone store operations. Increased competition had made many of the outlets unprofitable. But instead of closing them, management ran an experiment with the unions, who agreed to let some sales clerks be paid on commission instead of at the union wage. It worked, keeping nine endangered phone stores open.

Such successes have led to the return of common interest forums between local union officials and division managers. Both the unions and Ray Williams, the AT&T vice-president spearheading the rebuilding of labor relations, think that senior management and top union officials should get involved again, too. "We'll be making some suggestions to the unions about this," he says.

Happy endings?   First, the two sides must settle one problem. In the 1986 contract dispute, the IBEW accepted a last-minute company offer that the CWA rejected before it walked out. The division helped AT&T to force the CWA to settle on its terms. To avoid this in the future, Bahr has proposed that a single team of representatives from both unions negotiate with AT&T next time—a process called coordinated bargaining. It's not an unprecedented idea, but Williams is leery of the notion. Nonetheless, union and company officials say that they're likely to reach an agreement on the plan.

It may be that AT&T could have avoided some of its current morale problems had it maintained cooperative relations instead of ending them so abruptly. Still, the story has an upbeat ending: AT&T has tried confrontation and cooperation, and it's found that cooperation is better.

Questions

1.   What do you think about the way AT&T handled this situation?
2.   What could they have done differently that would have been better?

QUESTIONNAIRE: Sample items from the Job Descriptive Index (JDI)

Think of your present work. What is it like most of the time? In the blank beside each word given below, write

__Y__ for "Yes" if it describes your work

__N__ for "No" if it does NOT describe it

__?__ if you cannot decide

Work on Present Job

_____ Fascinating

_____ Frustrating (R)

_____ Boring (R)

_____ Respected

Total
Score _____

Think of the kind of supervision that you get on your job. How well does each of the following words describe this supervision? In the blank beside each word below, put

__Y__ if it describes the supervision you get
          on your job

__N__ if it does NOT describe it

__?__ if you cannot decide

Supervision on Present Job

_____ Asks my advice

_____ Impolite (R)

_____ Praises good work

_____ Doesn't supervise
          enough (R)

Total
Score _____

Think of the majority of the people that you work with now or the people you meet in connection with your work. How well does each of the following words describe these people? In the blank beside each word below, put

__Y__ if it describes the people you work
          with

__N__ if it does not describe them

__?__ if you cannot decide

People on Your Present Job

_____ Stimulating
_____ Lazy (R)
_____ Stupid (R)
_____ Responsible
Total
Score _____

Think of the pay on your present job. How well does each of the following words describe your pay? In the blank beside each word given below, write

__Y__ for "Yes" if it describes your pay

__N__ for "No" if it does NOT describe it

__?__ if you cannot decide

Present Pay

_____ Income adequate for normal expenses
_____ Barely live on income (R)
_____ Income provides luxuries
_____ Insecure (R)
Total
Score _____

Think of the opportunities for promotion in your job. How well does each of the following words describe the opportunities? In the blank beside each word below, put

__Y__ if it describes the promotion opportunities you have on your job

__N__ if it does NOT describe it

__?__ if you cannot decide

Opportunities for Promotion

_____ Good opportunity for promotion
_____ Opportunity somewhat limited (R)
_____ Promotion based on ability
_____ Dead-end job (R)
Total
Score _____

In the five categories above, for each item *with* (R) after it, give yourself 0 points for "yes," 1 point for "?," and 3 points for "no"; for each item *without* (R) after it, give yourself 3 points for "yes," 1 point for "?," and 0 points for "no." Total your score in each column separately. A higher score indicates greater job satisfaction.

Source: Patricia C. Smith, © 1985, Bowling Green State University, Bowling Green, OH 43403.

QUESTIONNAIRE: Stress Diagnostic Survey©

The following questionnaire is designed to provide you with an indication of the extent to which various individual level stressors are sources of stress to you. For each item you should indicate the frequency with which the condition described is a source of stress. Next to each item write the appropriate number (1–7) which best describes how frequently the condition is a source of stress.

Write *1* if the condition described is *never* a source of stress
Write *2* if it is *rarely* a source of stress
Write *3* if it is *occasionally* a source of stress
Write *4* if it is *sometimes* a source of stress
Write *5* if it is *often* a source of stress
Write *6* if it is *usually* a source of stress
Write *7* if it is *always* a source of stress

		Answer
1.	My job duties and work objectives are unclear to me.	_____
2.	I work on unnecessary tasks or projects.	_____
3.	I have to take work home in the evenings or on weekends to stay caught up.	_____
4.	The demands for work quality made upon me are unreasonable.	_____
5.	I lack the proper opportunities to advance in this organization.	_____
6.	I am held accountable for the development of other employees.	_____
7.	I am unclear about whom I report to and/or who reports to me.	_____
8.	I get caught in the middle between my supervisors and my subordinates.	_____
9.	I spend too much time in unimportant meetings that take me away from my work.	_____

10. My assigned tasks are sometimes too difficult and/or complex. _____

11. If I want to get promoted I have to look for a job with another organization. _____

12. I am responsible for counseling with my subordinates and/or helping them solve their problems. _____

13. I lack the authority to carry out my job responsibilities. _____

14. The formal chain of command is not adhered to. _____

15. I am responsible for an almost unmanageable number of projects or assignments at the same time. _____

16. Tasks seem to be getting more and more complex. _____

17. I am hurting my career progress by staying with this organization. _____

18. I take action or make decisions that affect the safety or well-being of others. _____

19. I do not fully understand what is expected of me. _____

20. I do things on the job that are accepted by one person and not by others. _____

21. I simply have more work to do than can be done in an ordinary day. _____

22. The organization expects more of me than my skills and/or abilities provide. _____

23. I have few opportunities to grow and learn new knowledge and skills in my job. _____

24. My responsibilities in this organization are more for *people* than for *things*. _____

25. I do not understand the part my job plays in meeting overall organizational objectives. _____

26. I receive conflicting requests from two or more people. _____

27. I feel that I just don't have time to take an occasional break. _____

28. I have insufficient training and/or experience to discharge my duties properly. _____

29. I feel that I am at a standstill in my career. _____

30. I have responsibility for the future (careers) of others. _____

Scoring Each item is associated with a specific individual level stressor. The item numbers and the appropriate categories are listed below. Add your responses for each item within each category to arrive at a total category score.

Your Score

Role Ambiguity:
1, 7, 13, 19,25   ___ + ___ + ___ + ___ + ___ = ___

Role Conflict:
2, 8, 14, 20, 26   ___ + ___ + ___ + ___ + ___ = ___

Role Overload—Quantitative:
3, 9, 15, 21, 27   ___ + ___ + ___ + ___ + ___ = ___

Role Overload—Qualitative:
4, 10, 16, 22, 28   ___ + ___ + ___ + ___ + ___ = ___

Career Development:
5, 11, 17, 23, 29   ___ + ___ + ___ + ___ + ___ = ___

Responsibility for People:
6, 12, 18, 24, 30   ___ + ___ + ___ + ___ + ___ = ___

The significance of the total score in each of the stressor categories will, of course, vary from individual to individual. In general, however, the following guidelines may be used to provide a perspective for each score:

Total scores of less than 10 are indicators of low stress levels.

Total scores between 10 and 24 are indicative of moderate stress levels.

Total scores of 25 and greater are indicative of high stress levels.

Source: J. M. Ivancevich, M. T. Matteson, *Stress and Work: A Managerial Perspective* (Glenview, Ill.: Scott–Foresman, 1980), pp. 118–20. Reprinted by permission.

Mutt and Jeff

Mutt and Jeff, both engineering graduates of Midwest University, had been hired into the management training program of the Crocko Company's Columbus (Indiana) plant. Although similar in many respects, they were also diametric opposites in others.

Mutt, a mechanical engineer, had lived all his life in the Columbus area with the exception of the time spent at Midwest. His large family lived in a small town just south of Columbus, where his father was presently employed as a used car salesman. Over the last twenty years, there was very little work in or around Columbus that his father had not tried but he always returned to selling. Presently, Mutt's father was nearing retirement age, but had not spent sufficient time with any one company to accumulate pension benefits. Mutt, being single, had decided to live at home while working at Crocko because of the congenial family atmosphere and the knowledge that his income could help the family when his father reached the compulsory retirement age.

Throughout school, Mutt had been an excellent student and had graduated with honors. He was affectionately known to his friends as the "worm" because of the long hours he spent in the library and studying in his room. Extracurricular activities didn't interest him and, throughout his four years of college, he never joined any clubs or organizations. After joining Crocko, a company that expressed an interest in community involvement by employees, he neither joined any of the local service clubs nor participated in any company activities.

Jeff, on the other hand, was an industrial engineer who had lived many places around the country. His father, an analytical chemist, had

Source: Reprinted with permission of Macmillan Publishing Company from *Organizational Behavior: Readings and Cases*, 2nd ed. Copyright © 1981 by Theodore T. Herbert.

routinely switched jobs and companies in his travels up the corporate ladder. The year after Jeff entered college, he had pooled his resources with large loans to purchase a small chemical plant in Georgia which was faltering. The plant, which had specialized in agricultural products, had run into problems with governmental agencies over the use of some of its insecticides. Through the use of prudent management and his technical expertise, Jeff's father had alleviated the problems and was ready to expand the business by the time Jeff graduated from college. He also wanted Jeff to work for him after graduation, but Jeff had felt it was better to obtain experience elsewhere; he also wished to avoid the stigma of being the "boss's son." Jeff had refused offers of assistance throughout college and had financed his own way with the help of a merit scholarship and numerous summer jobs.

While in school, Jeff was active in many activities, ranging from the golf team to the school newspaper; he was coeditor during his senior year. He was also president of his fraternity and was well known as a "ladies' man" on campus. During his senior year Jeff married. Upon going to work for Crocko, he became active in Jaycees and Kiwanis.

Somehow, although he was always busy, Jeff had also managed to keep his grades high enough to graduate with honors. During his sophomore year he had been having academic difficulties, soon corrected when he changed majors from chemical to industrial engineering. According to Jeff, "Chemical engineering is too restrictive. I don't want to spend my life designing processes. I'd rather be involved in the production itself." All of Jeff's electives were taken from the school of industrial management.

The Crocko Company employed a total of 4,400 employees in five widely scattered plants. Corporate offices were located in Paramus, New Jersey; each plant was treated as an independent profit center, with headquarters providing technical assistance to requesting plants. The Paramus staff functions included finance, marketing, sales, and personnel; personnel was a small group, whose primary concern was benefit coordination and compliance with federal guidelines and regulations. The chief administrator at each plant was the plant manager, who normally had total autonomy in plant operations, personnel hiring and firing, and union negotiations.

For many years the Columbus plant had been the backbone of the Crocko organization. It had the highest capital investment and had always been responsible for a large percentage of the corporate profits. The product of the Columbus plant was mobile homes. Two other plants also produced mobile homes, but Columbus was responsible for the top of the line models. These units were generally 50 to 60 feet in length and sold at $15,000 and up. Although only seven basic models were produced in Columbus, the immense number of options made each unit almost unique. The company was proud of its ability to deliver a custom-built unit to a customer within a week by manufacturing subassemblies and adding all the options after the order had been received.

The Columbus plant employed slightly over 700 union workers and 180 salaried workers. Over 60 percent of the salaried workers were either clerical or first-line supervisors. The plant manager at Columbus felt the main asset of the plant was its salaried employees; in fifteen years on the job he had never discharged anyone. When a person was found to be incompetent in his job, another position was found (or created) for him, and someone else would be promoted from within to the vacated position. The plant manager felt that this was only fair to the employees and that this security helped keep the better employees from leaving.

Although the plant manager did not own any stock in Crocko, he had often expressed the belief that Columbus Works was *his* plant. He enjoyed the freedom granted by headquarters to run the plant as he saw fit; along with this freedom, he recognized, went an awesome responsibility to his employees. To keep abreast of operations and in touch with all levels, he insisted on being consulted on or informed of even seemingly routine matters around the plant. Department managers knew that if they were going to institute even a change that would affect only their own departments, the change proposal should be discussed with the plant manager. Changes were often overruled.

Profits of the Crocko Company were decreasing because of slackening demand for the plusher mobile homes. Sales of competitors' comparable models were steady or increasing. The Paramus office, feeling that part of the reason for the slump might be a lack of innovation or stagnation of ideas in the key Columbus plant, decided to hire two young engineers and train them for management positions in Columbus. Tom Gilman, vice-president of personnel, visited the Midwest campus to recruit graduating seniors.

During this interview trip, Gilman interviewed over twenty prospective graduates, but was particularly impressed by Jeff and Mutt. Mutt had not been undergoing intensive interviewing; he had only stopped in to interview Crocko because he knew of their plant in Columbus. Jeff had been averaging three interviews per day and was concentrating on those companies that had openings in management training programs.

Tom Gilman told both Mutt and Jeff of the sales slump being experienced and the Paramus view of the reasons for it. An apparent lack of promotable personnel was of significant interest to Jeff; he left the interview with the feeling he would have much opportunity to advance with this company. He was also intrigued by the flexibility of the training program, which would give him broad exposure to many different aspects of the company's operations over a short period of time. Mutt was impressed by the salary range mentioned and the guarantee that the job would be in Columbus; he had also been told of the policy of relative autonomy for each plant, so he felt there was no chance he would be transferred. In turn, Gilman was impressed by the scholastic achievements of both Mutt and Jeff.

Mutt and Jeff accepted the job offers of Crocko and began working the day after graduation. Unknown to them at this time was Mutt's starting at a slightly higher salary level; Crocko used published data on nationwide averages for different academic degrees to determine starting salaries. Both Mutt and Jeff began in the Time Study and Methods Department for basic orientation to the company policies, methods, and personnel. During his one-month stay in this department Jeff devised a method of using available statistical programs to standardize and report much of the data generated by the department. The department head liked the idea and convinced the plant manager to give it a try. Mutt was then assigned the task of adapting or writing new computer programs that were necessary to implement the system.

When Mutt had completed two months of relatively routine programming, he was (unwillingly) transferred to the Cost Department to learn the accounting and cost system for his future use. Although he did not distinguish himself in any way, the supervisor felt he was intelligent and eager to learn. The one hesitation he had about Mutt was that he really didn't feel that Mutt fit in his closely knit, highly gregarious group.

Following the three months in the Cost Department, Mutt moved successively to Maintenance, Design Engineering, and finally Manufacturing Engineering—which was to be his first permanent assignment after the training program. In this position it was anticipated that Mutt would begin with the basics by learning the manufacturing specifications and by doing some elementary drafting. After this he was to advance to detail drafting and then quickly to machine design. Mutt quickly learned the specifications and did an excellent job of elementary drafting. The detail drafting consisted of taking rough sketches made by a senior engineer and turning them into fully descriptive engineering drawings. Mutt's work in this area was excellent, although at times his work was overly detailed; in general, he spent more time on each drawing than was really necessary. As a result of his excellence in detail drafting and his apparent slowness, Mutt never advanced to machine design as was originally planned.

Jeff moved to the Personnel Department following his stay in Time Study and Methods. While in Personnel, Jeff handled all employment screening and interviewing; in addition he proposed a manpower requirements forecasting plan for both exempt and nonexempt employees. He filled in for the personnel manager during one week of his vacation, and also began pursuing an M.B.A. degree at Indiana University at night.

Following nine months in Personnel, Jeff was transferred to Quality Control, an area in which he had shown an interest. The Quality Control Department was comprised of a manager and four technicians. Jeff was assigned to special projects in which he could use his quality control and engineering background. After three months on the job, Jeff was offered the opportunity to move to Industrial Engineering but declined, stating that he wished to drop out of the training program and remain in Quality Control. The plant manager accepted this because he felt that this was one important area in which the plant could use assistance.

Two months later the manager of Quality Control suffered a serious heart attack. Since it was anticipated that he would return, no acting manager or replacement was named. The department ran smoothly without the manager for the first few days, but after a week the manager's paperwork had backed up; Jeff took it upon himself to clear it up. A crisis also developed from a backlog of finished mobile homes awaiting Quality Control approval before shipment to the customer. Jeff inspected the homes and assumed the responsibility of releasing them for shipment.

Prior to the manager's illness, Jeff had been working on a new system of total quality control for the plant. His systems would guarantee that defective materials would never get into the product and that a defective subassembly would never be put into a final assembly. It also called for increased reporting of the cause of losses and computerized manipulation of data. Although the manager's formal authorization was unavailable, Jeff implemented the system in the plant. The four technicians complained of the increased work load but accepted it.

When the manager returned after two months, he put Jeff back on special projects. He also criticized Jeff for implementing the total quality control program without prior approval, and canceled the program until he could study how it would affect his existing systems. Jeff attempted to discuss it with the plant manager but was told to work it out with his supervisor. Jeff became noticeably less involved in both his work and community activities, and increased his class load at school.

The Crocko corporate personnel office was planning to hire a pair of engineers for a similar program in their Easton, Pennsylvania, plant. To determine the effectiveness of the flexible training program, Tom Gilman came to the Columbus plant to talk to Mutt and Jeff. After talking to their supervisors in the morning and taking both young engineers to lunch, Gilman took them aside individually and asked them to evaluate the program and the experience they had received, along with their general opinions of the company.

MUTT: The program has been extremely beneficial to me. The wide background in many departments has made me see many aspects of this company which some of the other engineers can't understand. If, for some reason, I were no longer needed in Manufacturing Engineering, I think I could fill in quite well in any of the areas that I've worked in. I mean, I'm happy where I am. The work is real interesting and I enjoy doing a good job, but I could be just as happy in the other departments.

The only part of the program I disliked was the changing of jobs so often, because as soon as I really got to the point that I knew the people and what I was doing, it was time to move. Looking back at it, however, the experience was well worth the frustration it caused.

The salary, benefits, and pension plan also seem very good to me.

JEFF: You asked me to be frank with you, so I will. I hope you won't take any of this the wrong way.

I believe that you unintentionally didn't tell me the whole truth when we talked on campus. Maybe you didn't realize the situation in this plant, but I can't see any opportunity for advancement because no one ever leaves or is fired here and even the plant manager is only fifty-one years old.

This place is also too archaic for me. No one even wants to listen to a proposal for change. You hired us to generate new ideas but when we do, no one will listen. My quality control plan and manpower forecasting plan were both turned down without even being seriously considered.

Only two of the jobs I've held have had any challenge at all. The first was filling in for the personnel manager that week and the other was filling in for the quality control manager. I was doing a better job than him but no one even said "thanks."

I just got chewed out for trying to improve the system and save some money.

No, I haven't been very happy and if you're planning on instituting a similar program somewhere else, you should be honest with the graduates and be sure that someone else doesn't have plans which vary from yours.

Gilman was totally confused by the two opposite reactions to the same program.

QUESTIONS

1. Describe Mutt's and Jeff's personalities. How do you think they developed?
2. Explain Mutt's and Jeff's different perceptions of the training program at Crocko Company.
3. What did Mutt and Jeff learn during their experiences in the training program?
4. Explain the different positive and negative outcomes of Mutt and Jeff in the training program.
5. Use the expectancy model of motivation to explain Mutt's and Jeff's opposite reactions to the same program.

A Developmental Framework for Studying Organizations

DYNAMIC ENVIRONMENTAL INFLUENCES

Past	Present	Future
Change	**Organizations** Environments Goals/Effectiveness Structure Design Development	Change
Develop	**Work Groups** Structure Processes Cohesion Groupthink Intergroup Behavior	Develop
Evolve	**Interpersonal Relationships** Leadership Power Politics Communications	Evolve
Grow	**Individuals** Perception Learning Attitudes Values Personality Motivation Outcomes	Grow

PART THREE

Interpersonal Relations in Organizations

CHAPTER

Leadership in Organizations

Now that we have completed our analysis of individuals, we will begin to explore interpersonal relations in organizations. We will look at the interaction patterns of people and how these interactions can be managed. To be effective, managers must understand the critical aspects of interpersonal interactions. **The very essence of managerial work is to do things through other people.** If managers cannot effectively interact with others, they will never be truly effective. A manager's interactions with subordinates help determine their motivation to do a job, helps provide them with the knowledge to do a good job, and helps resolve problems that may arise. In addition, a manager's interactions with other managers on the same level helps determine the effectiveness of the work unit, helps resolve conflicts between work units, and helps ensure a smoothly running organization. Also, a manager's interactions with superiors influences the manager's future career with the company, helps provide critical information up the organizational hierarchy, and helps resolve problems that may affect both the manager's work unit and the organization as a whole. To be effective over time, managers must know how to apply the theories that relate to leadership, power, politics, and communications in organizations.

Chapters 8 and 9 deal with leadership processes and their developmental and contingency aspects in organizations. By understanding the factors that are critical for effective leadership, managers will learn more about themselves as leaders and how to enhance their leadership abilities.

Chapter 10 explores power and politics in organizations as vehicles for exerting leadership. Managers must learn how to determine their own and others' sources of power. And managers must learn how to use this power to help them lead more effectively. The final chapter in this section (Chapter 11) looks into communications in organizations. Some managers have referred to communications as the lifeblood of an organization. And managers must learn how communications play a vital role in leadership, politics, and motivation.

Throughout these chapters, keep in mind the material covered in Part 2 of this book—Individuals in Organizations. Also, recall from Chapter 1 the model of organizations that is guiding this analysis of organizational behavior. Remember that people are the basic building blocks of any organization. This section of the book focuses on the next level in the building block process—the interactions of individuals. ■▶

J ust as each person is unique, the interactions between any two people or between any leader and a group of people are also unique. And, each interaction has a beginning, continues into the future, and may have an end. As discussed in Chapter 1, change is the nature of relationships in organizations. As we move into a discussion of leadership, think about your past and present relationships in work situations, and in the school situation where you are now. This chapter will help you better understand the leadership interactions you have with others in these settings.

THE IMPORTANCE OF LEADERSHIP TO A MANAGER

Leadership is the process of influencing the behavior of other people or groups of people toward the achievement of organizational goals.[1] There are two important aspects of this definition. First, leadership involves two or more people, but the designation of an appointed leader is not mentioned in the definition. Indeed, there is a distinction between being the **leader** and exerting **leadership.** While an appointed leader can and should exert leadership, he or she may or may not be the only leader of a group of people. Any member of the group can influence the behavior of the members of the group and thus provide leadership. The appointed leader draws upon the formal management hierarchy, which includes different sources of power from a leader who emerges from informal networks that cut across hierarchical lines.[2] Chapter 10 discusses these different power sources in detail. For now, we can all think of situations where people followed someone other than the appointed leader. The point is that **leadership is more than being the appointed manager; it has to do with who other people are following.** A second aspect of leadership is important in organizational settings: Managers exert leadership within a context. There are the followers; there are the peers; there are people higher in the organization than the manager; and there are the organizational goals and constraints on behavior. Leaders receive their authority to lead from each of these sources. In turn, each of these factors acts to determine the appropriate behavior of the leader if he or she is to have others follow effectively. But as some researchers have suggested, leadership's importance in the scheme of things can be overplayed.[3] If we feel we can use leadership behavior to explain performance, we tend to attribute stronger reactions to both positive and negative outcomes. What we often do, then, is to downplay such factors as the people involved in the situation, the task to be performed, the technology for the task, the organizational constraints on behavior, and the environment in which all of the factors coexist. In short, we romanticize the impact of leadership. Certainly leadership does serve a symbolic role, though. Leaders do manipulate symbols and manage meaning of work for their people. When a person is in a leadership position, be it first-line supervisor, manager, or CEO, he or she will be expected to influence others. Hence, leaders need to recognize both the limits of leadership and the potential difference it can make in a manager's effectiveness.

Why study leadership?

As the definition and comments above imply, there are several reasons why managers should study leadership.

First, managers must be able to influence the behavior of their subordinates. Once a person crosses the line from worker to supervisor or manager, he or she becomes dependent on other people to get work done. Managers acquire certain legitimate forms of influence to get the work done (for example, pay increases, promotions, and disciplinary actions). To be a truly effective manager, a person's leadership must be willingly accepted by his or her subordinates.[4] This means that managers have to rely upon other, more personal, sources of influence (for example, their expertise, charisma, and ability to relate to people).

The second reason managers study leadership is that it is so closely connected to the motivation of subordinates and other people managers try to influence. And as discussed in Chapters 5 to 7, the growing need for more complete use of human resources means managers have to depend more and more on their ability to tap the motivation of people. In turn, managers' abilities to motivate will depend upon their abilities to exert appropriate leadership.

Third, managers study leadership because it seems to be such a scarce resource in the world of organizations today. This statement should not be misunderstood, though. There are plenty of managers around. Business schools in the United States graduate 60,000 to 70,000 new MBAs every year. Unfortunately, as Warren Bennis and Burt Nanus found in their studies, most managers "do things right," while organizations need leaders who "do the right thing."[5] And as discussed in Chapter 5, changes in technology and the environment are creating an increasing need for people who can provide leadership. The first question is: What is the right thing to do? The second is: How does a manager do it right? For example, Insight 8–1 shows how GE has been training its managers to be leaders.

A recent book by Tom Peters titled *Thriving on Chaos* devotes nearly 100 pages to the topic of leadership.[6] And two other recent books—*The Leadership Challenge* by Jim Kouzes and Barry Posner and *A Passion for Excellence* by Tom Peters and Nancy Austin—also tell of the importance of leadership.[7] The books maintain that leadership can occur at all levels of organizations. Regardless of where managers find themselves, they can become leaders.

I N S I G H T   8–1

GE'S Training Camp: An 'Outward Bound' for Managers

Jack Welch is a tough, pragmatic, intuitive manager. And what does the chairman of General Electric think of management theory and academics? "Not much," reports Noel M. Tichy, a University of Michigan business professor who has worked at GE.

So it may seem surprising that Welch is putting more money into GE's Management Development Institute in Croton-on-Hudson, N.Y. But Crotonville, as it's called, is no ordinary corporate training center. Yes, there are lecture halls and blackboards—but there are also river-rafting races and mandates to tackle real GE problems. And, yes, there are some courses in finance—but far more that encourage team-building and networking. Instead of using Crotonville to teach traditional business subjects, Welch wants it to be a "change agent."

Crotonville's mission: to make GE managers more action-oriented, more risk-oriented, more people-oriented. It's supposed to develop leaders, not just managers. Says Welch, "Yesterday's idea of the boss, who became the boss because he or she knew one more fact than the person working for them, is yesterday's manager. Tomorrow's person leads through a vision, a shared set of values, a shared objective."

Lessons in change. Instilling those skills is no easy task, and GE had to invent much of its course work. New managers, for example, come to Crotonville about six months after their promotions—time enough for them to have made mistakes. They come with critiques of their performance from subordinates and supervisors. They learn what they've been doing wrong and promise to change. They discuss issues in teams, partly

so they know they're not alone in their experiences.

Since last year, Crotonville has offered what Tichy—who headed Crotonville for two years until September—calls "a business Outward Bound experience." It's a four-week course that lets employees crack a real GE business problem. First, participants do preparatory case studies, bone up on the business problem, and learn to work in teams. That's where the rafting comes in: The teams build rafts, then race each other up the Hudson River. Or they spend a few days performing other physical tasks to build trust among team members. Later, they visit the business and meet with customers—or anyone else they wish. Then they make recommendations and present them, in competition with another team, to the appropriate vice-president. Besides teamwork and analytical skills, the course teaches people that they can handle bigger problems than they thought.

Participants seem to relish the course. Bonnie L. Ayres, a radar programs manager in GE's aerospace business, was part of a team devising ways to expand a service business in GE's power systems group. "It's an 'up' experience," she says. "You feel tremendously stimulated and excited about what's happening at the company." Ayres took some lessons home, too: Feedback from teammates prompted Ayres, who manages 400 people, to delegate more.

Global issues. In words that would warm Welch's heart, Ayres adds "there was a large reinforcement of the company's desire to look outward—at markets—instead of inward, and to think competitively." That's deliberate. Many of the business problems focus on global issues. And Welch harps on competitiveness when he visits Crotonville, a dozen times a year, to meet with students. "Yesterday, he was up there [at the board] sketching global organizational forms—strategic alliances, and what they might look like," Tichy says.

As competition increases, many experts believe, old-fashioned bureaucratic management is simply not going to cut it anymore. "The evidence that leadership is so much more important today is overwhelming," says

Harvard business school professor John Kotter. "Yet the average corporation is not doing anything." Once again, he adds, GE is ahead of the pack.

By Judith Dobrzynski. Reprinted from the December 14, 1987 issue of *Business Week* by special permission, copyright © 1987 by McGraw-Hill, Inc.

This last sentence is precisely the fourth reason managers must study leadership—because it is a process that they can learn to use in organizations. It is probably true that some people are just born leaders—or at least their early development results in traits and abilities that make them natural leaders. But it is also true that most people can improve as leaders if they study the process of leadership and work to apply the principles that have been determined through research. Leadership is, however, a complex process to master. It involves the **abilities and traits of a manager,** the **abilities and motivation of his or her subordinates,** and the **relationships between the manager and the subordinates.** Furthermore, leadership involves the **nature of the task,** especially as it relates to the abilities and experience of the manager and his or her subordinates. Leadership also involves the kind of **situation** in which managers must lead: Is there time pressure? Is there ambiguity? Are there enough resources? Finally, leadership involves the **context** in which managers must lead. Even managers are still a subordinate to someone in the organizational hierarchy, and a peer to other managers on their level. This context both constrains leadership and provides opportunities to exert it sideways, upward, and downward in the organization. Insight 8–2 provides an interesting example of these context factors at work as they relate to women and minority managers. In addition to there being many factors that determine a manager's situation, the factors are themselves constantly changing. Thus, managers must lead in a complex and **dynamic** situation.[8]

Leadership as a dynamic process

As with other topics covered in the first seven chapters of this book, leadership also has developmental aspects. **This means that effective managers cannot use the same style of leadership with all people, in all situations, and without change over time.** Indeed, each person managers wish to lead must be viewed as a unique leader–member relationship for a given set of tasks.[9] For example, managing a 49-year-old experienced machine operator would call for a different leadership approach than managing a 23-year-old inexperienced machine operator.

I N S I G H T 8-2

Women and Minority Workers in Business Find a Mentor Can Be a Rare Commodity

J ames I. Nixon remembers the first time an older executive tried to take him under his wing. It was in the mid-1950s, when Mr. Nixon was a young engineer at General Electric Co.'s flight-propulsion center in Cincinnati. The manager, who had taken an interest in Mr. Nixon's career, suggested a friendly game of squash at the local YMCA.

They never played the game. Because Mr. Nixon is black, he wasn't allowed on the court, he says. "That was the end of that mentoring relationship," recalls Mr. Nixon, now the 54-year-old managing director of North American Venture Development Group in New York.

Today, "the problems are not as overt," says Mr. Nixon's 32-year-old son, James Nixon III, an architect with Nadler-Philopena Associates in Mt. Kisco, N.Y. Yet in corporate suites still dominated by white males, mentoring remains a rite of passage into the old-boy network. Minority and women employees often continue to be shut out of this network for at least part of their working lives, unable to find older executives willing to coach them, protect them and push their careers.

'Missed a lot'

Suzanne Burton Armour, the only black female among a dozen pharmaceutical production managers at Upjohn Co. in Kalamazoo, Mich., says two white males counseled her for a time earlier in her career, but after one died and the other was promoted out of reach, she was on her own. "I missed a lot," she says. "What a white male talks to me about is different from a black female or a black male."

On lacking a mentor, she says, "I feel intuitively it has limited my career." Jobs she wanted went to "friends of friends" of those in power, she says. "My ambitions and goals—nobody knew about them."

Some firms try to overcome barriers of race and sex by assigning mentors to promising young executives. At BankAmerica Corp., a senior manager may be asked to counsel three or four juniors for a year at a time, says Robert N. Beck, executive vice president of human resources.

Many mentoring specialists caution that such company intervention often proves fruitless. But Gail Lantrip, a 35-year-old Bank of America branch manager in Sacramento, Calif., says just being picked for the program has boosted her self-esteem, a central goal of any mentoring effort.

But even more important, a manager would have to alter his or her leadership style as the 23-year-old grew in experience and skill over the various life stages discussed in Chapter 6.

Also, people have developed into the kind of leaders they are now as a result of their past experiences. And people change and develop different abilities, perceptions, and motivations as time passes. These changes may also result in changes in their leadership. Furthermore, a manager's superiors and peers may develop different expectations that will influence the leadership approach a manager uses. For example, as managers move through the career stages discussed in Chapter 2, they may be given added responsibilities. This may mean that managers must delegate some of their past responsibilities to others if they are to continue to be successful.

Changes in the tasks and technology for a manager's unit in the organization can also create the need for changing an approach to leadership. Suppose that a person manages a clerical department that has depended heavily on calculators, typewriters, and outside computer services for certain aspects of the work. Now top management decides that employees will all have computer terminals at their work stations. The terminals will allow direct access to the main computer and to the files stored there. It will also allow word processing functions to be performed and will eliminate the need for typewriters. Under these new conditions, the manager may have to provide more directive leadership than he or she has in the past—at least during the transition period. Some of the workers may be resistant to the changes while others welcome the new challenges. A manager's leadership may have to vary from person to person.

This point suggests another factor that is developmental in leadership: The group of people a person manages will change over time. If they stay together over a long period, they will develop as a group (a topic discussed in Chapters 12 and 13). But more likely, some people will be leaving and some people will be joining the work group. Such changes can influence the group's ability and motivation—which again exerts a force for change on a manager's leadership.

Another developmental aspect of leadership concerns the fact that managers will probably move up the corporate ladder. And as discussed in Chapter 2, management at different levels requires different skills. As managers move up, the need for technical skills declines; the need for conceptual skills increases; and the need for human relations skills remains about the same. As managers move up the hierarchy, their jobs tend to become broader and more ambiguous. Furthermore, subordinates tend to be both more capable and more motivated. A manager's leadership must adjust to these conditions if he or she is to continue to be successful.

Finally, changes in the organization and its environment can create the need for changes in a manager's leadership approach. In a tight economy or a declining organization, the reins of leadership may need to be held tighter. Managers may have to deal with people who are fearful of losing their jobs. In a rapidly growing industry or organization, managers may be constantly challenged by subordinates who want to move up the ladder. Their responsibilities may increase faster than they can handle, and this may dictate the need to train subordinates to handle increasingly greater delegated responsibilities.

AN INTRODUCTION TO THEORIES OF LEADERSHIP

Now that we have discussed what leadership is and why we need to study it, let us explore the leadership theories that have been developed over the years. Unfortunately, there is no definitive single theory. Rather, the evolution of leadership research has resulted in the development of many theories—and each one can claim at least some empirical support. Thus, we should view these theories not as competitors, but rather as pieces of the leadership puzzle.[10]

The evolution of leadership theories

Serious study of leadership dates back about 80 years. It began with efforts to identify a set of traits common to all good leaders. Traits that were studied fell primarily into six categories: (1) physical characteristics, (2) social background, (3) intelligence and ability, (4) personality characteristics, (5) task-related characteristics, and (6) social characteristics.[11] While a definitive answer might make life simpler, research has not been able to distinguish a meaningful relationship between these traits and leader effectiveness. But the point here is not that traits are totally irrelevant in predicting leadership abilities. Rather, it is that **traits alone cannot predict leadership ability and performance.** In fact, some current researchers have reintroduced traits into the study of leadership.

The growing dissatisfaction with trait theories in the 1940s was positive for the study of leadership. It resulted in the emergence of the behavioral theories of the 1950s. These theories focused on what a leader does and began the search for a best style of leadership. Early attempts to categorize leader behavior identified two extremes on a continuum: (1) authoritarian leadership, and (2) democratic leadership.[12]

Another approach to behavioral leadership theory, developed at The Ohio State University, identified two basic dimensions of leadership that remain with us to this day: (1) initiating structure, and (2) consideration.[13] A great deal of effort went into the study of these two dimensions. Some researchers proposed that a leader must exhibit behavior high in both dimensions to be effective.

In fact, a training program based on this research but developed elsewhere was designed to teach people this high initiating structure/ high consideration style of leadership.[14] The program was known as the Managerial Grid, and this style was called the Team Leader. Tens of thousands of managers have completed the program since it was started in the 1960s.

As more and more studies were conducted, effective managers were found with the other combinations of initiating structure and consideration.[15] Researchers began to realize that **the best leadership style is contingent on the situation and needs to vary over time.** Since the 1960s, several contingency theories of leadership have been developed. These contingency theories try to define **situational** characteristics which determine how favorable the situation is for the leader. Then, depending on the situation, the leader can select the most effective style of leadership.

The remainder of this chapter will review all six of these leadership theories in more detail. Chapter 9 will tie them together in an integrative model of leadership. Before proceeding, however, let us define what we mean by effective leadership for a manager. **Effective leadership results in the accomplishment of the task assigned to the work group and in the development of the capabilities of the people in the work unit so that long-run performance is also good.** Effectiveness is more than just getting the job done. It also includes the idea that people do the job because they want to do it.[16] People may do it out of a sense of loyalty, obligation, or duty, but they do it because they want to.

TRAIT THEORIES OF LEADERSHIP

While researchers have noted many problems with trait theories of leadership, managers cannot totally dismiss them. Recent books by Kotter (*The General Managers*), Bennis and Nanus (*Leaders*), and Garfield (*Peak Performers*) support the idea that traits, along with behaviors, do help us understand a manager's leadership abilities.[17] Many motivational, interpersonal, temperamental, and cognitive factors are important in distinguishing effective and ineffective managers. In fact, one researcher has suggested a number of traits for successful senior managers. (See Insight 8–3.) **Traits are primarily useful in determining whether a leader is able to exhibit the appropriate style of leadership.** Traits can help or hinder the fit between the manager and the leadership style appropriate for a given situation. For example, if a situation calls for a leader to delegate

Why Are Some Managers Top Performers? A Researcher Picks Out Characteristics

Senior managers require a number of defined characteristics to work at the top of their form. "The corporate culture is much more complex and requires more skills than sports, arts or science cultures," says Mr. Garfield. [Charles Garfield is a consultant who has studied peak performers in many organizations.]

Good business managers at any level have the same six characteristics that mark top performers in other fields, he notes. These people transcend previous performance, avoid getting too comfortable in their jobs, enjoy the art of their work, vividly rehearse coming events in their minds, don't hold trials to place blame for mistakes, and examine the worst consequences of an action before taking the risk.

At the level of general manager of, say, sales, research or advertising, four more traits and skills come into play. Top performers at this level always have time for planning and didn't merely swing from crisis to crisis like monkeys caught in a forest fire. "Lower-performing managers would tend to get wrapped up in anything that looked like a crisis," says Mr. Garfield. "High performers were able to sift through and sort out the real crises."

They also were adept at selling their ideas, and sought responsibility instead of artfully dodging it, like bureaucrats. They bore rejection and loss well. Finally, they were inclined to champion new ideas and projects rather than letting them die untried.

The ability to act

In the upper reaches of management, the additional characteristic most apparent was an ability to reject perfectionism and act. "Many others were paralyzed by perfectionism," says Mr. Garfield. "They felt that if they tried it out and it didn't work, they'd be in trouble."

The best senior managers usually didn't have nicknames like Genghis Khan or Bloody Mary, either. They created a balance between autonomy and direction, setting goals for subordinates but not dictating how those goals were to be met. They were good team-builders, too, limiting the number of staffers involved in projects to avoid "bureaucratic neutralization."

The most effective senior managers sought quality rather than just quantity in their work, and saw clearly that the training and development of other managers and employees was a vital function. "To them, it's more than just a nice thing to do to give people management training," adds Mr. Garfield.

The Wall Street Journal, January 21, 1983. Reprinted by permission of *The Wall Street Journal,* © Dow Jones & Company, Inc. 1983. All rights reserved.

responsibility, a highly motivated, temperamental, power-seeking leader may have difficulty.

As Kotter points out, we must take a long-term view of a manager if we are to understand his or her personal characteristics. **The traits and personalities that people exhibit are developed over an entire lifetime.** Childhood, family, and early career experiences all interact to determine who a person is (discussed in Chapters 3 and 4). So, to understand ourselves and others as managers, we need to know something about who we and the others are. By knowing something about a manager's traits, we may gain a clue about what behavior to expect in a given situation. As we have stressed, traits do not tell us enough about effective leadership. We must look further at behavioral and contingency theories to gain a more complete understanding of the process.

BEHAVIORAL THEORIES OF LEADERSHIP

The behavioral theories of leadership of the 1950s provide useful, descriptive categories of leadership styles. Indeed, they are the basic styles used in the integrative model in Chapter 9. Let us consider the two most popular behavioral theories.

Autocratic-democratic continuum

One behavioral theory of leadership developed in the 1950s labeled behavior along a continuum from autocratic to democratic.[18] Exhibit 8–1 shows the continuum and identifies the sources of authority. **The autocratic leader makes decisions and announces them to his or her subordinates.** The autocratic leader relies heavily on power inherent in the manager's position to get people to carry out his or her decisions and can utilize punishment for those who do not carry out these decisions. On the other hand, **the democratic leader permits subordinates to function within limits defined by the manager; the leader shares the decision-making responsibility.** The democratic leader relies less on power inherent in the position of manager and more on powers of persuasion. As the continuum in Exhibit 8–1 indicates, there are many types of leadership between these two extremes. The use of authority by the manager and the amount of freedom allowed the subordinates vary along the continuum to create different leadership styles.

For example, suppose Louise of Home Computers Company decided that she should receive a progress report each Monday morning from her project teams. She could choose to be autocratic and announce her decision to begin the reports next week. She also could specify the frequency and format of the reports. Programmers who complied would receive praise and a good rating on their performance review. Those

EXHIBIT 8–1

The Autocratic–Democratic Continuum

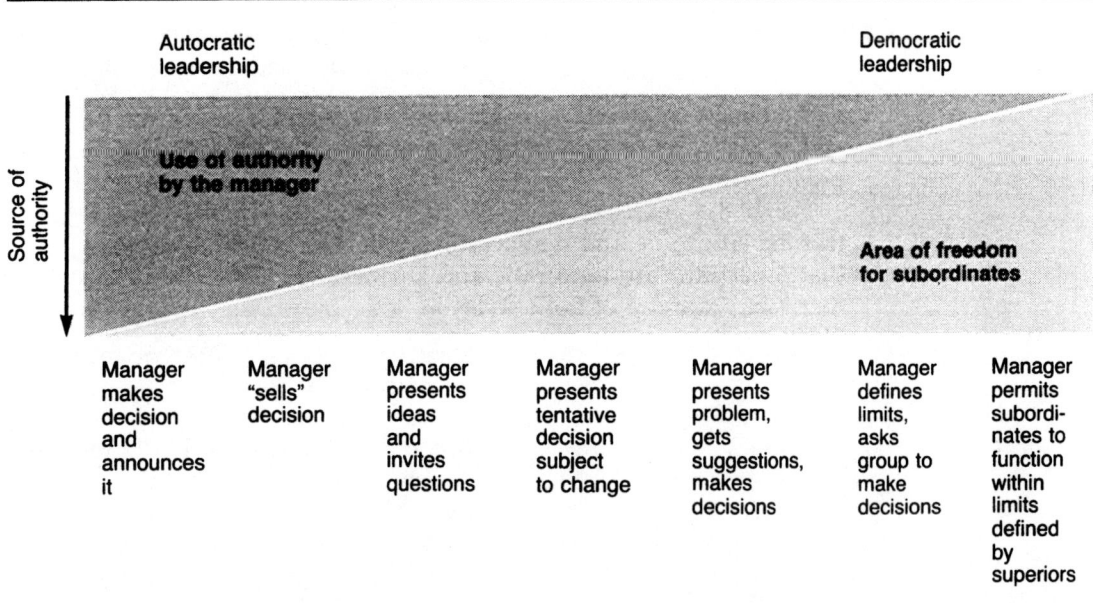

Autocratic leadership

Democratic leadership

Source of authority

Use of authority by the manager

Area of freedom for subordinates

| Manager makes decision and announces it | Manager "sells" decision | Manager presents ideas and invites questions | Manager presents tentative decision subject to change | Manager presents problem, gets suggestions, makes decisions | Manager defines limits, asks group to make decisions | Manager permits subordinates to function within limits defined by superiors |

who failed to comply would be reprimanded and perhaps rated lower on their review. In other words, as an autocratic leader, Louise would use the power of her position to get compliance from the programmers. If, on the other hand, Louise chose to be democratic, she would share the decision-making responsibility with the programmers: she would allow them to operate more freely, within certain limits. Louise would depend less on the power of her management position and more on her power of expertise, experience, and persuasion. She might sit down with the programmers and explain the need for update reports and then lead a discussion on ways to provide them on a timely basis. The reports are needed; that parameter has been set. But the programmers can have a say in their format and frequency. Louise is still responsible for the decision that is made, and the programmers who must implement it have input into the decision.

Under the autocratic approach, Louise will probably get the reports as she wants them, but what will be the long-run effectiveness of this approach? Performance may remain good while long-run resentment is building. This resentment could eventually lead to less productive programmers or even the loss of good programmers. This point emphasizes the developmental aspect of leadership. Under the democratic approach, Louise will probably still get the reports—though the format and frequency may not be as she prefers. And if the programmers do not have the information, expertise, and desire to make a responsible decision, Louise will be asking for trouble. Still, the programmers will probably appreciate the chance to have had a say in the decision, and it may improve working relationships between Louise and the programmers.

Insight 8–4 describes two powerful leaders who demonstrate the contrasting autocratic and democratic styles. The article does not suggest that Americans are autocratic and Japanese are democratic. Certainly, there are examples of both styles in both countries. These are but two illustrative examples.

The problem with the autocratic–democratic continuum theory is that leadership is viewed as a one-dimensional concept. Subsequent research has discovered at least two dimensions: initiating structure and consideration. Furthermore, this model does not really guide a manager in choosing a leadership style along the continuum; it just describes the behavior. Tannenbaum and Schmidt do indicate that managers should analyze: (1) forces in themselves, (2) forces in subordinates, and (3) forces in the situation. For example, what are a manager's values? How secure does he feel? How much confidence does he have in his subordinates? Are his subordinates self-motivated? What are the norms of his organization? How much time pressure does he face? Unfortunately, Tannenbaum and Schmidt do not provide much guidance on how to use the answers to these questions to choose along the continuum. Still, their ideas were a forerunner to the contingency theories of the 1960s.

The Ohio State model

The other popular behavioral leadership theory from the 1950s was developed at The Ohio State University.[19] It defined two dimensions for describing leadership behavior. **Initiating structure** was defined as the degree to which the leader organized and defined the task for subordinates. **Consideration** was defined as the degree to which the leader developed a trusting and supportive relationship with the subordinates. By combining these two dimensions, there are four possible combinations of initiating structure and consideration that define four styles of leadership, as shown in Exhibit 8–2 on page 316. Since the 1950s, these four leadership styles have been those most frequently used by both researchers and practicing managers. You may be interested in learning which of the four is most descriptive of your leadership. A copy of the Leader Behavior Description Questionnaire (LBDQ) and scoring instructions are included at the end of this chapter for your use. Take a

---

I N S I G H T 8–4

Autocratic

A Management Styles Passes With Death of Henry Ford II

*T*ime was when Mellons, Carnegies and Rockefellers stalked the executive suites of America's great corporations, absolute rulers over family-founded empires. But in these waning years of the 20th century, the men of such privilege and power gradually have disappeared.

Except at Ford Motor Co., where Henry Ford II for 35 years held sway as captain of his grandfather's company. He was the last descendant of one of America's founding corporate families who truly ran the place—who came to power because of who he was and kept power because of how he was.

He was more than an automobile magnate. In his prime, his wealth, celebrity and stature assured continued recognition inside and outside Ford Motor. He was probably America's most famous businessman.

Being called to his office "was like being summoned to see God," said Lee A. Iacocca, now Chrysler Corp. chairman and perhaps the most famous of a line of former Ford presidents first beknighted and later beheaded by Mr. Ford. With one disparaging sentence, Mr. Ford could throw a wrench into months of work by company car planners. Or he could bring a car to market simply by pointing and saying, as he did while viewing various early design proposals for the Lincoln Mark III, "I'd like to drive *that* home."

—Leonard M. Apcar

Democratic

Man Likely to Become Japan's Next Leader Lives to Compromise

*M*atsue, Japan—As far back as boarding school, Noboru Takeshita, the man widely expected to be Japan's next prime minister, showed a natural talent for cooling conflict.

He was assigned to a dormitory room where the older high-school boys were taking special delight in tormenting one young student, sometimes searing his arms with red-hot metal. Other schoolboys were amazed when the unimposing, jug-eared Mr. Takeshita stopped the bullies, not by fighting but by talking with them. "He did it so he wouldn't get bullied himself," recalls Uemon Takeuchi, a high-school and college buddy of his who is now the mayor of a small town. "He was always an adjuster."

Today, the 63-year-old Mr. Takeshita is known primarily as that, an adjuster who is clever, cautious and quiet. His supporters say those are his great strengths, for he is able to forge compromise and get opposing sides headed in the same direction. Detractors say he lacks the independence, international stature and vision to guide the world's No. 2 economic power in a period of rising tensions with the U.S. and Europe.

—Damon Darlin

EXHIBIT 8–2

The Ohio State Leadership Dimensions

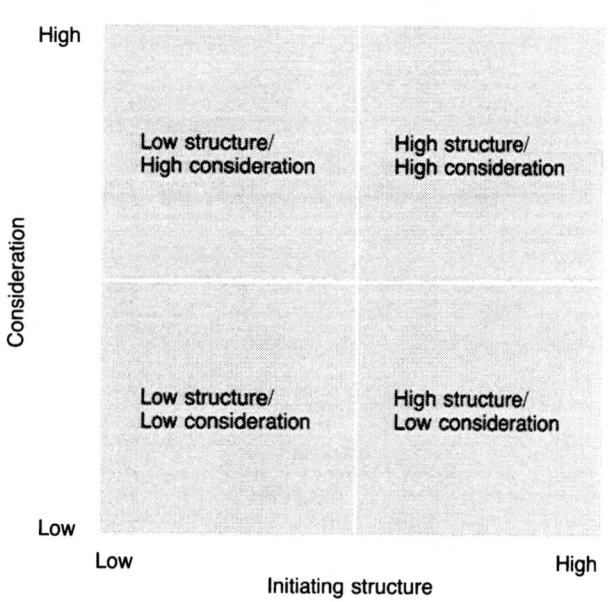

Source: J. K. Hemphill, *Leader Behavior Description* (Columbus, Ohio: Ohio State University Press, 1950).

few minutes now to complete and score the questionnaire. Then plot your scores on the grid provided. If you do not have much leadership experience, try to imagine how you would respond to each statement in the questionnaire.

Regardless of how your score comes out, it should be viewed as your perception of yourself. And since **we know that leadership is situational in nature, your general style may not always describe what you would do in a given situation.** Nevertheless, if you score high in structure and low in consideration, you tend to be directive in your leadership. High scores in both dimensions means you tend to be both directive and people-oriented. A high score in consideration and a low score in structure means you tend to be more people-oriented than directive. And finally, if you score low in both dimensions, you tend to delegate to people and stay out of the way.

Unfortunately, we do not know from the LBDQ if you are an effective leader. As we said before, early research on the model suggested that effective managers exhibit both high initiating structure and high consideration; and the best leadership style is contingent on the situation.

Thus, what we can say is that your style would be effective in some managerial situations but not all. The following contingency theories of the 1960s and 1970s can lend some insight into which situations these might be.

CONTINGENCY THEORIES OF LEADERSHIP

Fiedler's theory

One of the most widely researched contingency theories of leadership was developed by Fred Fiedler.[20] The central idea of this model is that the effectiveness of a work group in accomplishing its immediate task depends on the favorableness of the situation in combination with a leadership characteristic Fiedler calls the least preferred coworker score. First, let us briefly define the three situational characteristics Fiedler specifies. **Leader–member relations** relates to the degree of confidence, trust, and respect that subordinates feel for a manager. **Task structure** is the degree to which a group's task is clearly specified. This includes the clarity of goals, the ways to accomplish goals, and the ease of evaluating goal accomplishment. For example, an assembly-line worker's job would be more structured than that of a researcher in a laboratory. The final situational factor, **position power,** is the amount of power inherent in a leader's position in the organization. To what extent does the leader have the power to influence the behavior of subordinates?

These three factors, according to Fiedler, determine the overall favorableness of the situation and suggest the appropriate style of leadership. However, Fiedler's definition of different leadership approaches is really based on an aspect of the leader's need structure—the least preferred coworker (LPC) score. The LPC instrument asks people to assess the coworker with whom they would least like to work. A copy of the LPC is included at the end of the chapter. Take a minute now to fill out and score your LPC.

A **low LPC score** means that you are basically ready to reject those coworkers with whom you would least like to work. This is basically an **attitude** that you have; but we can infer that your behavior would tend to be task-oriented, much like the people who score high in initiating structure. On the other hand, a **high LPC score** means that you perceive even your worst coworker in a relatively positive light. The behavioral approximation of this attitude is one of working toward successful interpersonal relationships, much like the people who score high in consideration. Compare your scores on the LPC with the LBDQ which you completed earlier; there will probably be a consistency between the scores. However, if there is not, do not be alarmed. It is probably the different approaches of the instruments. Remember, the LBDQ was designed to describe behavior, while the LPC was designed to assess attitude.

Combining the three situational factors and the LPC score, Exhibit 8–3 indicates in which situations low LPC leaders and high LPC leaders will be most effective, according to Fiedler. Situation categories 1 through 3 define a favorable situation, and according to Fiedler, the low LPC (high initiating structure) leader will be the most effective. The same low LPC leader will be most effective in situation category 8, which is a very unfavorable situation. For the middle categories 4 through 7, the situation is moderately favorable, and according to Fiedler, the best leader will be the high LPC (high consideration) leader.

Fiedler's leadership theory is quite useful to managers in understanding the contingency aspects of leadership. The theory provides three important situational factors, and the relationship between LPC score and a work group's productivity has been supported repeatedly with research. Still, there are several concerns about the theory.[21] Fiedler contends that it is easier to alter a situation than to change a leader's LPC score, since it is a fundamental aspect of the person. It may be more

EXHIBIT 8–3

Fiedler's Contingency Model of Leadership

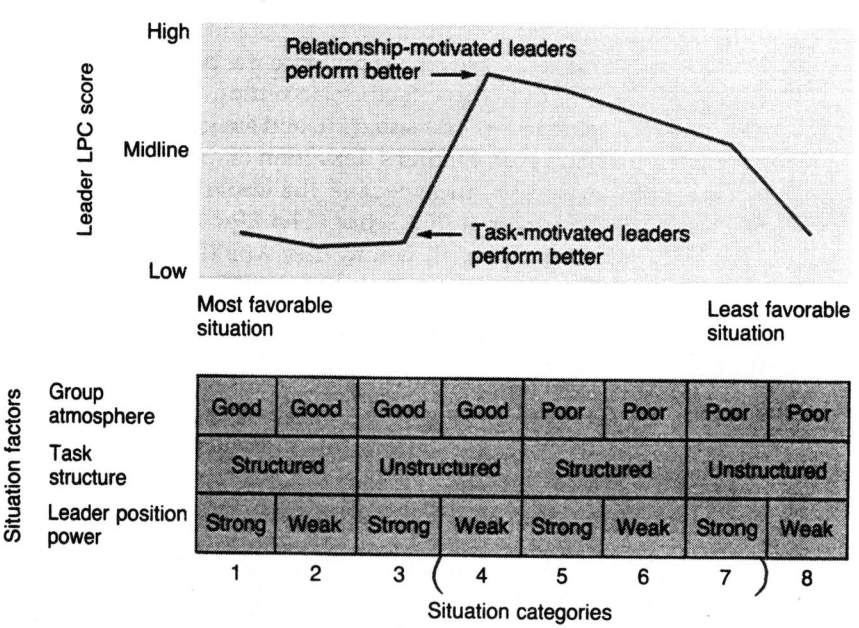

Source: Adapted from F. Fiedler, *A Theory of Leadership Effectiveness* (New York: McGraw-Hill, 1967).

accurate to say that both are somewhat difficult to change. Second, the theory assumes that a leader who exhibits initiating structure cannot at the same time exhibit consideration. But the Ohio State studies have clearly shown this to be an oversimplification. Third, the definition of effectiveness used in the theory is restricted to "getting the group's task done in an efficient manner." The definition ignores future implications about the development of subordinates' abilities and the potential for developing resentment among them. Fourth, the subordinate's impact on the situation is minimized. Task structure, for example, is a relative term. A highly trained programmer might view as relatively structured a task that an inexperienced programmer would see as very unstructured. Furthermore, as the inexperienced programmer gains experience, the same task might seem more and more structured over time. Finally, a leader can interact with situational variables to change them over time—and the model does not seem to account for this possibility. For example, a friendly leader is likely to improve leader–subordinate relations, while an aloof leader is likely to make them worse. Still, the theory has much to offer a manager's understanding of contingency-based leadership.

The Hersey-Blanchard situational leadership theory

Unlike Fiedler's theory, the Hersey-Blanchard theory has not been widely researched, but it has been widely used in industry for manager training since it was originally published in 1969.[22] Only recently has there been some research on this model.[23] The Hersey-Blanchard theory is based on the four leadership styles from the widely researched Ohio State model. The theory explicitly focuses on the fit between situation and subordinates by defining the situation in terms of the **readiness** of the subordinates. Readiness is defined in a unique way as: (1) the capacity of subordinates to set high but attainable goals (need for achievement); (2) the willingness and ability of subordinates to take responsibility for their work; and (3) the task-relevant education and experience of the subordinates. **Basically, readiness is the subordinates' ability and willingness to do the job.**

By determining the subordinates' readiness level, a manager can choose the appropriate leadership style, using Exhibit 8–4. In this model, the readiness continuum (which reads from right to left for increasing readiness) and a developmental curve are simply added to the four leadership styles from the Ohio State model. The situational leadership model is used in the following manner. If analysis shows the subordinates' readiness to be low (R1), managers can draw a vertical line up from the point on the readiness continuum to where it intersects the developmental curve to determine the appropriate leadership style. Hence, the developmental curve indicates the leadership style needed

EXHIBIT 8–4

The Hersey-Blanchard Situational Leadership Model

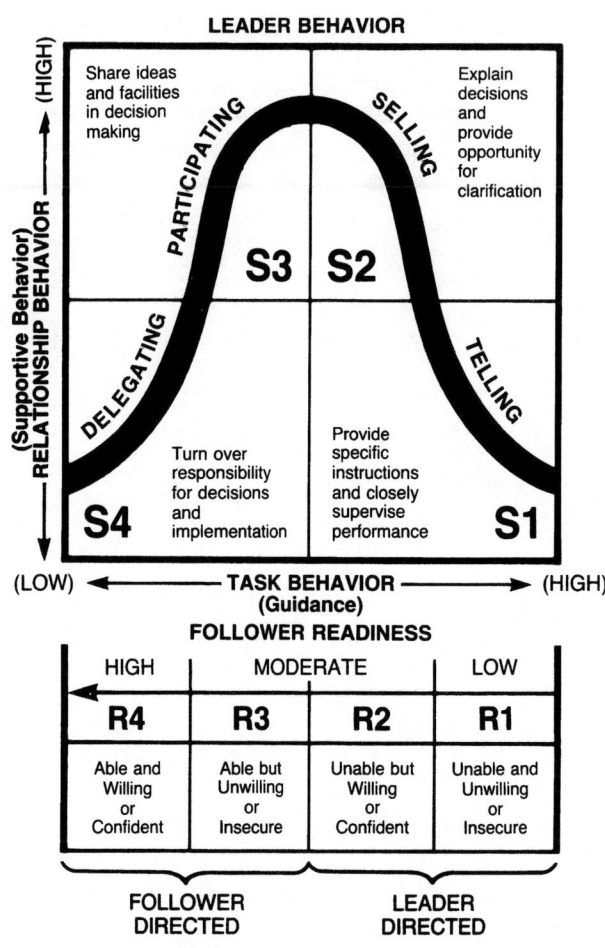

Source: P. Hersey and K. H. Blanchard, *Management of Organizational Behavior: Utilizing Human Resources*, 5th ed. (Englewood Cliffs, N.J.: Prentice-Hall, 1988), p. 171. The original model published in the first edition in 1969 used the label *maturity* instead of *readiness*.

for high performance, given a particular level of subordinates' readiness. For example, low subordinate readiness (R1), which is defined as unwilling and unable to do the job, calls for high-task/low-relationship leadership.

Now, managers may question this analysis. If the subordinate is low in readiness, would it not be good to provide high-relationship behavior? Indeed, some people might argue that participative leadership is desirable with all employees today. But research has shown that participative management can sometimes be harmful. In a recent *Organizational Dynamics* article, Ed Locke and his colleagues cited several studies that support the contention that nonparticipative leadership is best where employees have little job expertise.[24] In fact, to ask a subordinate who has little expertise to participate in deciding what to do and how to do it is setting the employee up for productivity failure and low job satisfaction.

As subordinates grow in their knowledge of the job, they can begin to contribute. Thus, when managers consider followers with increasing readiness, they must first reduce their task orientation and increase their relationship orientation. Managers must move along the developmental curve from right to left as the followers' readiness increases. For an R2 follower, defined as willing but unable to do the job, a high-task/high-relationship style is suggested. However, past the midpoint of the readiness continuum, both task and relationship orientations need to decrease. For example, moderately high readiness followers (R3), defined as unwilling but able to do the job, need low-task/high-relationship leadership. But even this much involvement from the leader may be too much for a highly skilled and motivated employee (R4). As Locke and his colleagues suggested, and as the Hersey-Blanchard theory prescribes, low-task/low-relationship leadership (that is, delegation) is best for such high readiness employees.[25]

As mentioned earlier, some research by academics has focused on the Hersey-Blanchard model. One study found that leaders whose behavior matched the prescriptions from the theory were viewed by experienced managers no more favorably than leaders who did not behave according to the theory.[26] This study suggested that if managers want the respect of employees, they should be high in relationship behaviors. But what about real effectiveness? A more robust test of this model found partial support for the theory.[27] This study found support for the model for low-readiness followers, but the results were mixed for moderate-readiness followers and were nonsupportive for high-readiness followers.

Blanchard's modified situational leadership theory

Perhaps because of such concerns and because of feedback from the thousands of managers using the Hersey-Blanchard situational leadership model, Blanchard has undertaken a significant revision of the model.[28] Let us review those changes.

First of all, Exhibit 8–5 shows the revised situational leadership model. The first thing to notice is the change in some of the terms. Task behavior is now called *directive behavior*, and relationship behavior is called *supportive behavior*. Directive behavior still refers to setting goals, telling people how to do things, monitoring performance, and close

EXHIBIT 8–5

Blanchard's Revised Situational Leadership Model

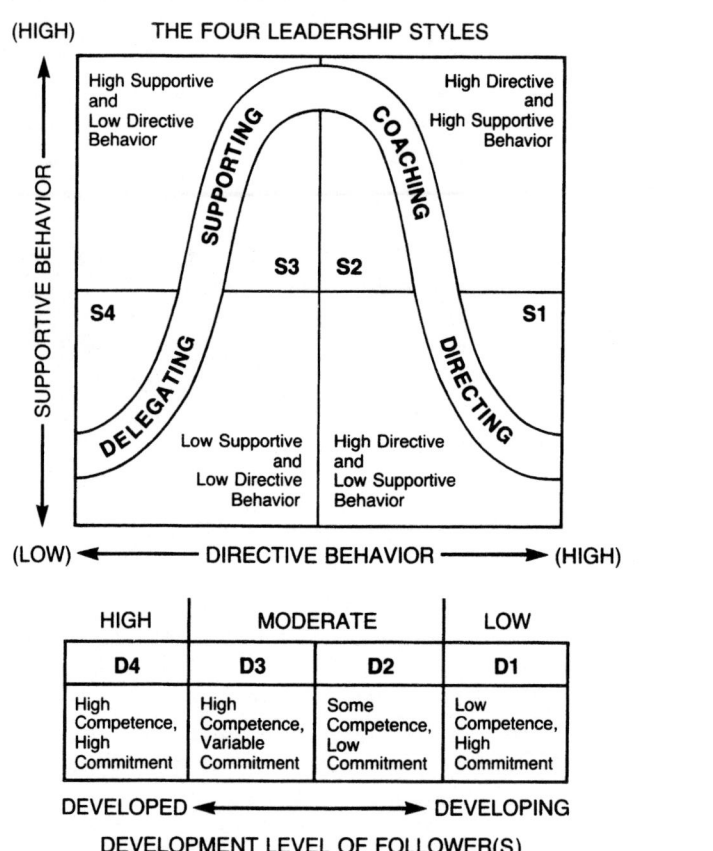

Source: Adapted from K. H. Blanchard, P. Zigami, and D. Zigami, *Leadership and the One Minute Manager* (New York: William Morrow and Co., 1985), pp. 50 and 68.

supervision. And supportive behavior still refers to praising work, listening to followers, and facilitating problem solving among followers. Only the labels are different. Likewise, the four styles (S1, S2, S3, and S4) are still defined in the same way, but the labels are less evaluative. The high-directive/low-supportive style is now called *directing,* instead of *telling.* The high-directive/high-supportive style is called *coaching,* instead of *selling.* The low-directive/high-supportive style is called *supporting,* instead of *participating.* And the low-directive/low-supportive style is still called *delegating.*

The revised model still calls for matching between the follower and the task as the key indicator of the appropriate leadership style for a given situation. But instead of referring to the *readiness* of the followers, the revised model calls it *development level* of the followers. And development level is defined in terms of the follower's current competence and commitment to do the job. Competence is the follower's *current* knowledge, training, experience, and skills to do the task at hand. Competence is not to be confused with the follower's *potential* to learn to do the job well. Commitment focuses on the follower's *current* motivation and confidence to do the task at hand. Two points are critical in determining the follower's development level. First, *development level* is not a global concept that applies to a person. Rather, it applies to the person in relation to a specific task. Second, development level is not a static variable. Both competence and commitment can change over time; hence, the follower's development level can change.

In applying this revised model of situational leadership, a manager must first determine the task to be performed by a given follower. Then, by assessing the follower's competence and commitment, the manager can determine the follower's development level to be D1, D2, D3, or D4, as shown in Exhibit 8–5. The question that then guides the manager's choice of leadership style is: What does the follower need from the leader in terms of directive and supportive behaviors for this task at this time? For example, the D1 follower is defined by the model to be low in competence and high in commitment. What type of leadership does this follower need? Clearly he or she needs high-directive behavior, but supportive behavior can be low because of the follower's own internal high commitment. Hence, the directing style in Exhibit 8–5 is suggested. The D2 follower is defined as having some competence but low commitment. Hence, what this follower needs is high-directive and high-supportive behaviors, the coaching style in Exhibit 8–5.

These definitions are one of the big theoretical differences between the revised situational leadership model and the original Hersey-Blanchard model. In the original model, low readiness (R1) was defined as being both unable and unwilling, rather than as the revised model suggests unable (low competence) and willing (high commitment) (D1). In the original model, R2 readiness was defined as unable but willing, where as the revised model defines D2 as unable (some competence) and unwilling (low commitment). Basically, D1 and D2 are reversed from R1 and R2.

Three reasons have prompted this change by Blanchard and his associates. First, managers have said they would not hire a D1 person for a job if the person was both unwilling and unable. They do expect the person to be low on competence initially, but they expect to see high commitment. Then, as a person gains experience on the job, his or her competence increases while the initial high commitment drops, due primarily to differences between reality and initial expectations about the job. Second, research on the development of groups and individuals suggests that the revised model better reflects the stages through which people and groups develop.[29] And third, the revised model is more consistent in applying a leadership style that logically fits the needs of the follower.

Thus, to complete the description of the revised model, consider the definitions of the D3 and D4 development levels. D3 is defined as the follower being high in competence and variable in commitment for a given task at the present time. Hence, the leader need not provide much direction, but rather should provide high support, which is the supporting style in Exhibit 8–5. And finally, the D4 follower is high in both competence and commitment, thus calling for the delegating style of leadership.

As a way of further understanding this theory, take a look at several questions from a questionnaire based on the Hersey-Blanchard model, as modified by Blanchard, and called the Leader Behavior Analysis.[30] First, four questions are listed so you can decide which of the four alternative actions (*a, b, c, d*) you would choose for the given situation. This procedure should generate some interesting discussion among your colleagues in class. We will discuss the scoring and rationale for each question when you finish.

1. The interdepartment task force that you manage has been working hard to complete its divisionwide report. You have been assigned a new task force member. He must complete some cost figures for his department by next week but knows nothing about the task force's requirements for the format of the report. He is excited and enthused about learning more concerning his role on the task force. You would:

    a. Tell him exactly what is needed in this report and closely monitor his progress.

    b. Ask if there is anything you can do to help him, and support his excitement about being a new task force member.

    c. Specify the report format and information requirements, but incorporate any ideas or suggestions he may have.

    d. Welcome him to the team, and put him in touch with other members of the task force who could help him get ready to present the cost figures.

2. Recently, you have begun to have trouble with one of the people you supervise. He has become lackadaisical, and only your constant prodding has brought about task completion. Because of past experience with him, you suspect he may not have all the expertise

needed to complete the high-priority task you have given him. You would:

    a. Continue to direct and follow up on his efforts to complete this task.

    b. Continue to supervise his work, and try to draw out his attitudes and feelings concerning this task assignment.

    c. Involve him in problem solving with this task, offer support, and use his ideas in the task completion.

    d. Let him know that this is an important task, and ask him to contact you if he has any questions or problems.

3. Because of budget restrictions imposed on your department, it is necessary to consolidate. You have asked a highly experienced member of your department to take charge of the consolidation. This person has worked in all areas of your department. In the past, she has usually been eager to help. While you feel she has the ability to perform this assignment, she seems indifferent to the importance of the task. You would:

    a. Take charge of the consolidation, but make sure you hear her suggestions.

    b. Assign the project to her, and let her determine how to accomplish it.

    c. Discuss the situation with her. Encourage her to accept the assignment in light of her skills and experience.

    d. Take charge of the consolidation, and indicate to her precisely what to do. Supervise her work closely.

4. Your staff has asked you to consider a change in their work schedule. In the past, you have encouraged and supported their suggestions. In this case, your staff is well aware of the need for change and is ready to suggest and try an alternate schedule. Members are very competent and work well together as a group. You would:

    a. Allow staff involvement in developing the new schedule, and support the suggestions of group members.

    b. Design and implement the new schedule yourself, but incorporate staff recommendations.

    c. Allow the staff to formulate and implement the new schedule on its own.

    d. Design the new schedule yourself, and closely direct its implementation.

The following table indicates, using the revised situational leadership model in Exhibit 8–5, how each of the four choices would be labeled in terms of leadership style, and also which styles would be the most and least effective for the particular situation.

Question	Directing	Coaching	Supporting	Delegating
1	a^b	c	b	d^w
2	a	b^b	c	d^w
3	d^w	a	c^b	b
4	d^w	b	a	c^b

Note: *w* indicates worst choice.
     b indicates best choice.

Let us explore the rationale for the best and worst choices above. For question 1, the individual is clearly motivated to do the work, but lacks the ability to do it alone. Thus, the person has a low development level (D1) situation, and Exhibit 8–5 indicates a directing style would be the best choice. Delegating would obviously be the worst.

For question 2, the employee is declining in performance and motivation. It appears that motivation is low, at least in part because he does not know how to do the task. It would seem that he is in the low-competence/low-commitment or D2 development level, and Exhibit 8–5 suggests a coaching style is most effective. On the other hand, to leave the person alone (delegating) would clearly be the worst style of leadership.

In question 3, you have assigned a task to someone who clearly has the ability to perform the task, but seems to lack the motivation. Hence, it appears the employee had a moderately high development level (D3), and Exhibit 8–5 suggests a supporting style of leadership is most effective. On the other hand, directing would apply too much task orientation and be the worst style—it would undercut the person's confidence.

Finally, in question 4, you are dealing with a very competent and motivated group that is aware of the need for change—a high development level (D4). Exhibit 8–5 suggests the best leadership style is delegating, while directing would be the worst. It undercuts the group's ability and is not a good use of the manager's time.

The four questions thus allow us the chance to practice identifying the four different leadership styles, as applied to real situations. They also allow us to see how the theory can be used to help us analyze real world situations.

The primary strengths of the Situational Leadership Theory revolve around its explicit inclusion of subordinates, its developmental focus, and its expanded definition of effectiveness. By focusing on the subordinate and the fit with the task, we are forced to recognize that managers must simultaneously lead more than one subordinate. Thus, for a given task, managers may have to lead both high-development-level and low-development-level subordinates and will need to vary their leadership style from person to person. Likewise, people may be at a high level of development for one task and at a low level of development for another task. Thus, managers may have to <u>vary their style from task to task for the same person</u>.

This model also recognizes that situations may change (develop) over time. **In fact, it is quite probable that a group of subordinates will move toward the D4 development level over time as they gain experience with the task.** For one thing, time on the job will increase task-relevant experience, if nothing else (unless there is a great deal of turnover of personnel). Thus, the leader's style must change over time to maintain effectiveness. If an individual or a group that a person manages reaches a high stage of development for a task, the manager should delegate to them (low-directive/low-supportive leadership).

But wait a minute. What do managers do with their time when they get to the point of delegating? It is all too easy to forget that **leadership in organizations involves more than just managing the tasks of the work group. It <u>also involves managing the relationships with other work groups and with higher-level managers in the organization</u>. Furthermore, <u>leadership should involve developing subordinates' abilities and motivation</u>.** The situational leadership theory takes this broader definition of effectiveness. This is <u>one of the major differences from Fiedler's model, which focuses only on getting the job done</u>.

In fact, this difference in definition leads to a very different choice of effective leadership style in the favorable (or high development level—D4) situation. Fiedler's results orientation leads to selecting the high directive leader (see Exhibit 8–3). In the favorable situation, the theory's focus on developing subordinates and getting results leads to selecting delegation (low directive/low supportive). (See Exhibit 8–5.) However, <u>there are some similarities between the</u> models. In the unfavorable (low-development level—D1) situation, both theories suggest a high directive/low-supportive leadership style as best. In the moderately favorable (moderate levels of development—D2 and D3) situations, both models suggest high-supportive styles of leadership. Both models use task structure as one aspect of the situation. The strengths of both theories will be used in developing the integrative model of leadership in Chapter 9. The revised situational leadership theory will be central to it.

The biggest concerns about the situational leadership model revolve around the limited research that has specifically addressed it. But as pointed out earlier, researchers have begun to rigorously test the model and have found some support for it. Still, additional research is needed on the model. Furthermore, the model assumes that a manager can learn to adapt his or her style to each situation in rapid succession. Such changes may not be that easy. Much research on people suggests that it is not easy to change something as fundamental as leadership style from moment to moment.[31] But then, many situations change in evolutionary rather than dramatic ways—and this developmental change may be more in line with what situational leadership is about. Plus, thousands of managers have learned to use this model of leadership and have found it helpful. It has stood the test of use by managers in real settings and has been found reasonably accurate in their eyes.

House's path-goal theory

House's path-goal leadership theory is closely related to the expectancy model of motivation discussed in Chapter 5. The basic idea of the model is that a manager's job is to increase the motivation of workers by "increasing personal payoffs to subordinates for work–goal attainment, and making the path to these payoffs easier to travel by clarifying it, reducing roadblocks and pitfalls, and increasing the opportunities for personal satisfaction en route."[32] This model thus ties together leadership and motivation aspects of management: **what a manager does in terms of leadership affects a subordinate's motivation.** And increased worker motivation should lead to both increased performance and satisfaction.

Path-goal theory explains how managers can choose from among four leadership styles the best style for a given situation by analyzing characteristics about both the subordinates and the task. The basics of this model are presented in Exhibit 8–6.

The four leadership styles can be defined as follows:

Directive leadership is the clarifying of paths to the goals for subordinates. It is similar to the high-initiating structure/low-consideration style of leadership.

Supportive leadership is the giving of support and consideration to subordinates. It is similar to the low-structure/high-consideration leadership style.

EXHIBIT 8–6

House's Path-Goal Theory of Leadership

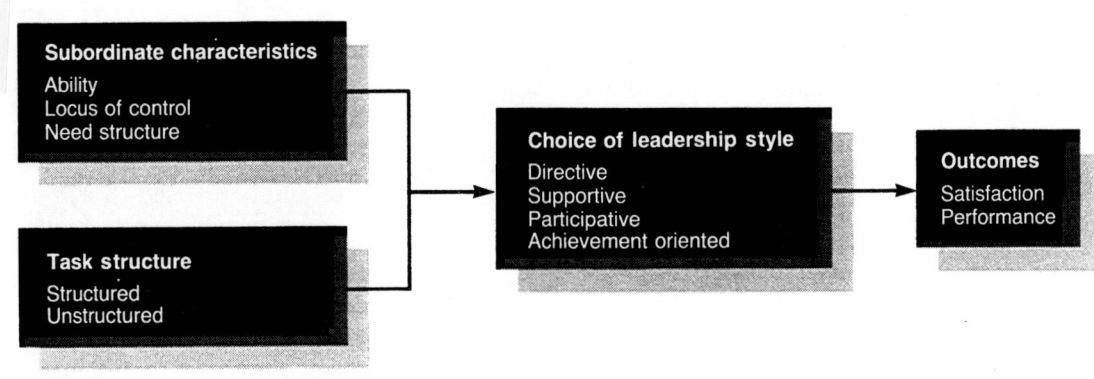

Participative leadership is characterized by sharing information and consulting with subordinates in making group decisions. It is similar to the high-structure/high-consideration style of leadership.

Achievement-oriented leadership is characterized by setting high goals for subordinates, seeking improved performance, and showing confidence that subordinates will perform well. It is most similar to the low-structure/low-consideration (delegation) style of leadership.

As to the **subordinates**, the model defines three employee characteristics that help define the situation and relate to the most effective leadership style: (1) ability, (2) locus of control, and (3) need structure. **The greater an employee's ability to perform the task, the less he or she will want directive leadership.** As in the situational leadership model, the high-ability employee will prefer achievement-oriented leadership (delegation). Locus of control, as discussed in Chapter 4, focuses on the follower's sense of internal and external control. It is similar to the "willingness to take responsibility" idea of Hersey-Blanchard, and the prediction from path-goal theory is consistent with their ideas. **The more an employee desires control in a situation, the less he or she will be satisfied with directive leadership.** Rather, this worker will desire participative or achievement-oriented leadership. Finally, need structure refers to Maslow's hierarchy of needs. The question is: Does the employee desire high- or low-level needs? **The more an employee desires high-level needs, the less he or she will want directive leadership.** More specifically, people who desire safety and security needs will respond positively to directive leadership. Those who desire belongingness will respond positively to supportive leadership. And those desiring self-esteem and self-actualization will respond positively to participative and achievement-oriented leadership.

Finally, as to the **task**, House refers to the degree of task structure in a manner similar to both Fiedler and Hersey-Blanchard. Like the other theories, path-goal theory suggests that **employees working on an unstructured task will want directive leadership.** In these unstructured task situations, the manager's job must be to initiate structure, clarify goals, and define expectancies for the subordinates. When managers can do this, they reduce worker uncertainty, and this leads to increased motivation and performance. **If the task is structured, supportive and participative leadership styles will be more effective.** This prediction is consistent with the situational leadership model.

To date, the biggest drawback with path-goal theory is that it has not been researched as a total theory. Rather, relationships between particular subordinate or task characteristics and particular leadership styles have been explored independently. This creates a problem for managers who must operate where all three subordinate characteristics and task structure are simultaneously present. For example, if an employee's ability is high, locus of control is medium, need structure is low, and task structure is medium, path-goal theory is not too helpful. High ability suggests using achievement-oriented leadership; but concern for lower-level needs suggests using directive leadership. Rather than being a complete theory of leadership, path-goal theory seems to be a set of independent propositions. However, one recent review of 48 studies of the path-goal theory does appear to offer additional overall support for the model.[33] Still, path-goal theory, unlike Fiedler's theory, does not specify leadership styles for all possible combinations of the situational characteristics.

A second problem with path-goal theory is that the outcome variable in the model is employee satisfaction/motivation, rather than performance. It is not difficult to imagine situations where employees are satisfied, but where productivity is low. Furthermore, path-goal theory implicitly assumes that employee satisfaction leads to higher performance, but research has indicated that it may be that high performance leads to satisfaction.[34] In the long run, it may be that both variables influence each other in a developmental manner. For example, high performance leads to satisfaction which leads to motivation to yield high performance.

Despite these criticisms of path-goal theory, it is still useful because it helps integrate leadership and motivation. The theory is also consistent with the other two contingency theories in several important areas. Most importantly, when subordinates must deal with an unstructured task, they appreciate and respond well to directive leadership. But as their ability develops, they respond better to participative leadership and finally to delegation.

By understanding these traits, behavioral, and contingency theories of leadership, managers have a great deal of information they can apply to leadership in organizations. Unfortunately, no single theory seems adequate in a practical and analytical sense. Managers need a way to integrate the six leadership theories from this chapter, so they can capitalize on the strengths of each one. But this chapter has gone on long enough now. Rather, let us save the integrative model and an application to the Home Computers Company case for Chapter 9.

CHAPTER HIGHLIGHTS

This chapter began with a discussion of the importance of leadership to managers. **Leadership was defined as the process of influencing the behavior of other people or groups of people toward the achievement of organizational goals.** Leadership thus takes into account both the interpersonal nature and the situational aspects of the process. While leadership does not encompass all of the variables in interpersonal influence processes, managers must understand leadership to be effective.

Next, the text mentioned six reasons why it is important for managers to understand the leadership process. First, managers must be able to influence the behavior of other people. Second, leadership is closely connected to the motivation of subordinates. Third, leadership appears to be a scarce resource in today's world. Fourth, managers can learn to use the process of leadership to make them more effective. Fifth, leadership is a complex process and requires study if managers are to understand it. Lastly, managers need to learn how the context in which they operate influences and constrains their leadership style choice.

The text then explained the developmental aspects of leadership. **As people (managers included) and situations change over time, managers must change their leadership style to remain effective.** Managers and their subordinates develop as discussed in Chapters 3 through 7; and their tasks and technology can also change over time. Managers may also have people leave or join a group of subordinates, and this can necessitate changes in their leadership. And managers must be able to alter their leadership style as they move up the organizational hierarchy. Finally, changes in the overall organization to which managers belong and its environment may create the need for managers to alter their leadership style.

The next section of this chapter introduced a number of leadership theories by reviewing how they have evolved over the past 75 years. We then began to delve into the theories in more detail.

First, we looked at trait theories, which tell us something about a leader's abilities. More important, **traits are useful in determining whether managers can exhibit the style of leadership called for by the situation.** Traits are also developed over an entire lifetime; they therefore help emphasize the importance of viewing leadership developmentally. Unfortunately, traits alone do not tell us enough about leadership.

So we next turned to a discussion of the behavioral theories of leadership that were developed in the 1950s. These theories provide descriptive categories for leadership behavior. We first explored the autocratic–democratic continuum. **Autocratic leadership is the style in which the leader makes all the decisions and announces them to the subordinates.** On the other hand, **democratic leadership is the style in which the leader allows the subordinates to become involved in the decision-making process.**

We then explored another popular behavioral theory developed at Ohio State University. This model identifies two dimensions of leadership behavior that have been important for over 30 years: initiating structure and consideration. Next, we turned to the contingency theories developed since the 1960s to learn more about the situational aspects of leadership.

The first contingency theory discussed was the most extensively researched, namely Fiedler's model. We explored how **leader–member relations, task structure, and position power of a leader help determine
how favorable the situation is for the leader.** In turn, the favorableness
of the situation determines whether a high or low LPC leader will be
effective. And **Fiedler defined LPC as the attitude a person has toward
the "least preferred co-worker."**

In reflecting on this theory, we mentioned several concerns. For example, the theory assumes leaders cannot change their LPC score very
easily. It assumes that initiating structure and consideration cannot be
exhibited simultaneously. It defines effectiveness only in terms of "getting the job done in an efficient manner." It minimizes the impact of
subordinates in a given situation. And it does not allow for developmental changes in the situational variables. Still, Fiedler's theory will be
useful in developing the integrative model in Chapter 9.

Next, we discussed the contingency theory developed by Hersey and
Blanchard. This theory adds a subordinate readiness dimension to the
Ohio State grid to define how favorable a situation is for a leader. The
text pointed out that **readiness is basically the ability and desire of
subordinates to do the job.** The higher the subordinates' need for
achievement, willingness to take responsibility, and task-relevant education and experience, the higher their maturity and the more favorable
the situation for the leader.

We also discussed the revised Situational Leadership Model developed by Blanchard and his associates. We talked about development
level instead of maturity and the task-specific nature of development
level. We reviewed the new labels applied to the four leadership styles,
and we discussed the different assessments for the lower end of the
developmental continuum for subordinates.

The primary strengths of the situational leadership model are its
explicit inclusion of subordinates as they relate to the task at hand, its
developmental focus, and its expanded definition of effectiveness. Concerns about the Hersey-Blanchard theory and the revised model revolve
around a lack of rigorous research on the model and the assumption
that leaders can easily change their style from moment to moment.
However, the text pointed out that some rigorous research is beginning
to appear, and literally thousands of managers use the revised model on
a daily basis.

The final contingency theory discussed was House's path-goal theory.
This theory is useful for linking leadership and motivation. **What a
manager does in terms of leadership affects the subordinates' motivation.** Path-goal theory is based on three employee characteristics: ability,
desire for control, and the level of needs desired, plus the degree of task
structure. Limited research has supported relationships between these
situational factors and the four leadership styles defined for the theory:

directive, supportive, participative, and achievement-oriented. The linkage of leadership and motivation this theory provides makes it useful to managers.

The chapter closed by suggesting the need for a way to integrate these six leadership theories to help managers better use them in organizational settings. The development of such an integrative framework will be the focus of Chapter 9.

REVIEW QUESTIONS

1. What is leadership? How is exerting leadership different from being the appointed leader?

2. Why is it important for managers to know about leadership and be able to apply it to managerial situations?

3. What factors suggest that a manager's leadership will have to vary from situation to situation and from time to time?

4. Why is it important to define effectiveness as more than just getting the job done as efficiently as possible?

5. Why is it important to include trait theories as a basis for understanding leadership?

6. What are the trade-offs a manager makes between autocratic and democratic leadership styles?

7. What is the biggest weakness of the Ohio State model of leadership? Why do you think this theory has been so popular for over 30 years?

8. Define the three situational factors in Fiedler's model of leadership, and explain how they determine the best leader (based on LPC score) for a given situation. What are the biggest weaknesses of Fiedler's model of leadership?

9. Explain how Hersey-Blanchard define readiness of subordinates and how maturity determines the best leadership style for a given situation. What are the primary strengths and weaknesses of the Hersey-Blanchard model of leadership?

10. What are the differences between the Hersey-Blanchard model of leadership and the revised situational leadership model by Blanchard and his associates?

11. What are the fundamental differences between Fiedler's theory and Situational Leadership Theory? How are they similar?

12. Explain the relationships between the three employee characteristics and task structure and the four leadership styles defined in House's Path-Goal Theory? How does Path-Goal Theory link leadership to motivation? What are the biggest weaknesses of this theory?

RESOURCE READINGS

Bass, B. *Stogdill's Handbook of Leadership.* New York: Free Press, 1981.

Blanchard, K. H.; P. Zigarmi; and D. Zigarmi. *Leadership and the One Minute Manager.* New York: William Morrow and Company, 1985.

Fiedler, F. *A Theory of Leadership Effectiveness.* New York: McGraw-Hill, 1967.

Garfield, C. *Peak Performers.* New York: William Morrow and Company, 1986.

Hemphill, J. K. *Leader Behavior Description.* Columbus, Ohio: Ohio State University Press, 1950.

Hersey, P., and K. H. Blanchard. *Management of Organizational Behavior: Utilizing Human Resources.* 5th ed. Englewood Cliffs, NJ: Prentice–Hall, 1988.

House, R. "A Path-Goal Theory of Leadership. *Administrative Science Quarterly* 16 (1971), pp. 321–38.

Kotter, J. P. *The General Managers.* New York: Free Press, 1982.

Tannenbaum, R., and W. H. Schmidt. "How to Choose a Leadership Pattern." *Harvard Business Review* 36 (March-April 1958), pp. 95–102.

NOTES

1. B. Bass, *Stogdill's Handbook of Leadership* (New York: Free Press, 1981).

2. L. B. Barnes and M. P. Kriger, "The Hidden Side of Organizational Leadership," *Sloan Management Review* 28 (Fall 1986), pp. 15–26.

3. J. R. Meindle and S. B. Ehrlich, "The Romance of Leadership and the Evaluation of Organizational Performance," *Academy of Management Journal* 30 (1987), pp. 91–109.

4. C. Barnard, *The Functions of the Executive* (Cambridge, Mass.: Harvard University Press, 1938); and more recently reemphasized by T. Kochan, S. Schmidt, and T. DeCotiis, "Superior-Subordinate Relations: Leadership and Headship," *Human Relations* 28 (1975), pp. 279–94.

5. W. Bennis and B. Nanus, *Leaders: The Strategies for Taking Charge* (New York: Harper and Row, 1985).

6. T. Peters, *Thriving on Chaos: Handbook for a Management Revolution* (New York: Alfred A. Knopf, 1987).

7. J. M. Kouzes and B. Z. Posner, *The Leadership Challenge: How to Get Extraordinary Things Done in Organizations* (San Francisco: Jossey-Bass, 1987); T. Peters and N. Austin, *A Passion for Excellence: The Leadership Difference* (New York: Random House, 1985).

8. K. Weick, "Middle Range Theories of Social Systems," *Behavioral Science* 19 (1974), pp. 357–67.

9. R. M. Diensch and R. C. Liden, "Leader-Member Exchange Model of Leadership: A Critique and Further Development," *Academy of Management Review* 11 (1986), pp. 618–34.

10. A. G. Jago, "Leadership: Perspectives in Theory and Research," *Management Science* 28 (March 1982), pp. 315–36.

11. Bass, *Stogdill's Handbook*.

12. R. Tannenbaum and W. H. Schmidt, "How to Choose a Leadership Pattern," *Harvard Business Review* 36 (1958), pp. 95–102.

13. J. K. Hemphill, *Leader Behavior Description* (Columbus, Ohio: Ohio State University Press, 1950).

14. R. R. Blake and J. Mouton, *The Managerial Grid* (Houston: Gulf Publishing, 1964), and *The New Managerial Grid* (Houston: Gulf Publishing, 1978).

15. A. Korman, "Consideration, Initiating Structure, and Organizational Criteria: A Review," *Personnel Psychology* 19 (1966), pp. 345–62; and S. Kerr and C. Schriescheim, "Consideration, Initiating Structure and Organizational Criteria: An Update of Korman's 1966 Review," *Personnel Psychology* 27 (1974), pp. 555–68.

16. B. Bass, *Leadership, Psychology and Organizational Behavior* (New York: Harper & Row, 1960).

17. J. P. Kotter, *The General Managers* (New York: Free Press, 1982); Bennis and Nanus, *Leaders;* C. Garfield, *Peak Performers* (New York: W. Morrow & Co., 1986).

18. Tannenbaum and Schmidt, "How to Choose a Leadership Pattern."

19. Hemphill, *Leader Behavior Description*.

20. F. Fiedler, *A Theory of Leadership Effectiveness* (New York: McGraw-Hill, 1967).

21. C. Schriescheim and S. Kerr, "Theories and Measurement of Leadership: A Critical Appraisal of Current and Future Directions," in *Leadership: The Cutting Edge,* eds. J. Hunt and L. Larson (Carbondale, Ill.: Southern Illinois University Press, 1977), pp. 22–27.

22. P. Hersey and K. H. Blanchard, *Management of Organizational Behavior: Utilizing Human Resources,* 1st ed. (Englewood Cliffs, NJ: Prentice–Hall, 1969). Also, see 5th ed., 1988, for concept of *readiness*.

23. H. A. Hornstein, M. E. Heilman, E. Moore, and R. Tartell, "Responding to Contingent Leadership Behavior," *Organizational Dynamics* 15 (1987), pp. 56–65; C. L. Graeff, "The Situational Leadership Theory: A Critical View," *Academy of Management Review* 8 (1983), pp. 285–91; R. P. Vecchio, "Situational Leadership: An Examination of a Prescriptive Theory," *Journal of Applied Psychology* 72 (1987), pp. 444–51.

24. E. A. Locke, D. M. Schweiger, and G. P. Latham, "Participation in Decision Making: When Should It Be Used," *Organizational Dynamics* (Winter 1986), pp. 65–79.

25. Locke, et al., "Participation in Decision Making."

26. Hornstein, et al., "Responding to Contingent Leadership Behavior."

27. Vecchio, "Situational Leadership: An Examination of a Prescriptive Theory."

28. K. H. Blanchard, P. Zigarmi, and D. Zigarmi, *Leadership and the One Minute Manager* (New York: William Morrow and Company, 1985).

29. R. B. Lacoursiere, *The Life Cycle of Groups: Group Developmental Stage Theory* (New York: Human Service Press, 1980).

30. The complete Leader Behavior Analysis questionnaire (20 questions) and scoring instructions are available from Blanchard Training and Development, Inc., 125 State Place, Escondido, CA 92025. Also available from Blanchard Training and Development are videotapes and a board game which can be used to teach the theory to people.

31. F. Fiedler, "Engineer the Job to Fit the Manager," *Harvard Business Review* 51 (1965), pp. 115–22.

32. R. House, "A Path-Goal Theory of Leadership," *Administrative Science Quarterly* 16 (1971), p. 322.

33. J. Indrik, "Path-Goal Theory of Leadership: A Meta-Analysis," *Academy of Management Proceedings* (1986), pp. 189–192.

34. D. P. Schwab and L. L. Cummings, "Theories of Performance and Satisfaction," *Industrial Relations* 9 (1970), pp. 408–30.

CASE: One of the boys

Barry Lawton joined the Fairchild Manufacturing Company as a production worker immediately upon graduation from high school. The company manufactured a wide variety of electric switching equipment that was used in industrial settings.

Barry got along well with his coworkers, but not with his foreman. Barry and his coworkers were united against the foreman because they felt he was too autocratic and rule-oriented and treated them like children. Because of this, there were many conflicts between the foreman and the workers. The whole climate of the work group suffered, and worker morale was low (although productivity remained at a satisfactory level). As time passed, it became clear that Barry had a knack for smoothing over the work-related conflicts that were caused by the foreman's attitudes. Barry prided himself on this ability, and he worked at refining it further. He felt that it was important for management to treat workers with more respect and dignity, and he said this to anyone who would listen. His coworkers enthusiastically agreed with his idea that if management treated workers well, they would be happier and more productive.

Two years after Barry joined Fairchild, the much-despised supervisor was transferred. The plant superintendent approached Barry and offered him the job. Barry immediately accepted, and set out to implement his ideas about managing people. For the first few weeks, things went well. The workers were very happy to be rid of the old autocratic boss, and they told Barry that it was nice to have "one of the boys" as their new foreman. For his part, Barry consciously treated his new subordinates in precisely the way he had always said subordinates should be treated.

As time passed, Barry began to be concerned about his section because it was obvious that productivity had not increased under his leadership. In fact, a trend was developing in the opposite direction. Barry knew how this would be viewed by the plant superintendent, so he started to gently apply pressure

Source: J. L. Gray and F. A. Starke, *Organizational Behavior: Concepts and Applications*, 3d. ed. (Columbus, Ohio: Charles E. Merril Company, 1984), pp. 252–53.

for more output. The workers didn't take this pressure too seriously, and joked that Barry shouldn't worry so much. This pattern continued for several months, and output continued to decline. By now Barry was deeply concerned and was plagued by doubts about the validity of his leadership ideas. One day as he was passing the ceramic switch line, he saw four workers looking down at the floor and laughing. As he came closer, he saw several switch boxes (each worth $700) lying broken on the floor. He asked what had happened and was told in a lighthearted fashion that the production line had been left unattended for a few minutes and the boxes had simply fallen off. Barry was furious and loudly chewed out the workers who were at fault. He then stormed back into his office. Thirty seconds later Joe Mankiewicz, one of the four workers, charged into Barry's office.

Joe: What do you think you're doing, Barry?!! You can't talk to me like that in front of our friends.

Barry: You mean your friends! You guys are not friends of mine anymore. Ever since I took over as foreman, you've been taking advantage of me and loafing on the job.

Joe: Aw, come on, Barry. Don't get upset. It was only three switch boxes that broke. The company can afford it. We've got to stick together.

Barry: Don't give me that "we've got to stick together" nonsense! If you guys don't increase your productivity, you won't have a job to come to.

Joe: That sounds like a threat. What happened to all your big talk about treating workers with dignity and respect? Since you got into management, you're a changed person.

Barry: Go back to your station, Joe. I don't want to discuss this any more.

Barry sat in his office and wondered how things had gotten so fouled up.

Questions

1. What is the problem here? What mistakes has Barry made?
2. What do the leadership theories presented in this chapter suggest should be done in this situation?
3. Discuss the impact of using different leadership styles in this situation.
4. What should Barry Lawton do now?

CASE: Ed the loan officer

The Jobs-Economic Development Authority was created by an act of the state legislature in 1983. Its mission was to create employment opportunities by encouraging the start-up and expansion of small private businesses. The tool for achieving this objective was a revolving loan pool.

The agency's loan pool was capitalized with funds obtained from a federal community development grant program, and its operating budget was ini-

Source: Adapted from a course assignment prepared by Robert Drake for Dr. Alan Randolph, 1987.

tially funded with federal administrative grants and annual appropriations from the state legislature.

The agency staff consists of twelve individuals: an executive director, an operating officer, two loan officers, a loan administrator/program compliance officer, a financial analyst, an accountant, three administrative assistants, a graduate student intern, and a receptionist/typist. The loan staff which handles lending functions consists of the executive director, operating officer, two loan officers, loan administrator, and financial analyst. This group ranges in age from 27 to 60 years. While each person on the loan staff has attended college, five of the group have degrees and three of the degrees are MBAs. The annual salaries range from $25,000 to $55,000.

The executive director is concerned because the performance of one of the loan officers is below his expectations. His concern is based upon his personal observations and reports from other members of the loan staff.

He has observed that the loan officer experiences difficulty:

- Completing routine tasks on time;
- Presenting credit requests to the loan committee; and
- Communicating with clients.

Members of the loan staff have complained to the executive director about the lack of initiative on the part of this loan officer. Among other things, the complaints allege that he exercises no independent judgment and relies on others to solve problems with his loan accounts. An example of this is the loan closing which generally requires only one staff person. When this officer is responsible for the closing, two people are required to represent the agency. Meetings with clients often involve two or three staff people in addition to this officer.

The executive director fears that this situation will deteriorate further. He has concluded that the job performance of the loan officer is not improving, and resentment of other employees is growing.

A profile of this individual, who we will refer to as Ed, indicates that he has been employed with the agency for one year. Ed is married and is approximately 60 years old. Although he has no previous experience as a loan officer, he has over 30 years experience in small retail businesses. Based on his comments to several colleagues, it is known that Ed did not wish to retire when he closed his private business and that he made several applications for employment before being hired by the agency.

One interesting point which may explain what motivates Ed is the importance he places on the employee insurance benefits provided by the state. He has confided to several colleagues that these benefits are much more important to him than salary or opportunities for advancement.

Evaluation of Ed's performance indicates that he has difficulty with many aspects of his job. He is unable to complete his work on time which results in delays in the consideration of credit requests. His credit analyses contain numerous errors which make their reading and understanding difficult. His understanding of technical terms used in credit analysis is limited; therefore, he often experiences difficulty in communicating his thoughts to others.

In managing his loan accounts, he relies heavily on the judgment of others and avoids making even simple decisions. He is quick to call a problem to someone's attention but slow to suggest a solution. His over-reliance on others has become a major problem within the agency. His colleagues complain about his lack of judgment and often attempt to ignore his requests for assistance.

Questions

1. Analyze this case using the contingency leadership theories.
2. What leadership style would you use to correct the problems with Ed?

QUESTIONNAIRE: Ohio State Questionnaire on Leader Behavior (LBDQ)

Put a check in the column that describes you.	always	often	occasionally	seldom	never			always	often	occasionally	seldom	never
1. I make my attitudes clear to the group	✓						2. I do personal favors for subordinates				✓	
3. I try out my new ideas with my group			✓				4. I do little things to make it pleasant to be a member of the group				✓	
5. I rule with an iron hand				✓			6. I am easy to understand				✓	
7. I speak in a manner not to be questioned			✓				8. I find time to listen to subordinates		✓			
9. I criticize poor work		✓					10. I mix with subordinates rather than keeping to myself		✓			
11. I assign subordinates to particular tasks			✓				12. I look out for the personal welfare of individuals in my group	✓				
13. I schedule the work				✓			14. I explain my actions to subordinates		✓			
15. I maintain definite standards of performance	✓						16. I consult subordinates before action		✓			
17. I emphasize the meeting of deadlines			✓				18. I back up subordinates in their action				✓	
19. I encourage the use of uniform procedures				✓			20. I treat all subordinates as equals	✓				

Put a check in the column that describes you.	always	often	occasionally	seldom	never			always	often	occasionally	seldom	never
21. I make sure that my part in the organization is understood	✓						22. I am willing to make changes				✓		
23. I ask that subordinates follow standard rules and regulations			✓				24. I am friendly and approachable	✓					
25. I let subordinates know what is expected of them			✓				26. I make subordinates feel at ease when talking with them	✓					
27. I see to it that subordinates are working up to capacity		✓					28. I put suggestions made by my group into action		✓				
29. I see to it that the work of subordinates is coordinated	✓						30. I get group approval in important matters before acting		✓				
Total	4	2	5	4	0		**Total**	4	7	4	0	0

Directions for Scoring LBDQ

Total the checks in each column of the previous page and enter in the square below each column. The columns on the left hand represent the Initiating Structure values. The right hand columns represent Consideration values. Record the column totals in the Initiating Structure and Consideration boxes below. Multiply each of these totals by the weighting factors indicated. Add these for a grand total representing the Initiating Structure value and Consideration value.

Initiating structure

Always	4 × 4 = 16
Often	2 × 3 = 6
Occasionally	5 × 2 = 10
Seldom	4 × 1 = 4
Never	× 0 = 0

Total 36

Consideration

Always	4 × 4 = 16
Often	7 × 3 = 21
Occasionally	4 × 2 = 8
Seldom	× 1 = 0
Never	× 0 = 0

Total 45

Locating Yourself on the Ohio Model

Directions: In order to locate yourself in one of the four quadrants of the Ohio State Model below examine your score for *Initiating Structure*. If this score is 40 or above you would be considered high on that dimension; if it is below 40 you would be considered low on that dimension. For *Consideration*. If this score is 40 or above you would be considered high on that dimension; if it is below 40 you would be considered low on that dimension. In which quadrant does your score place you?

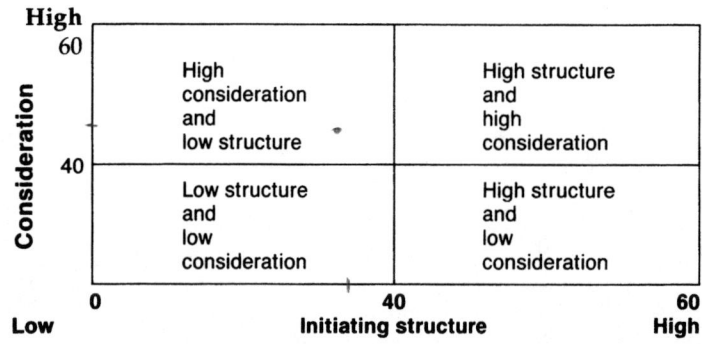

Source: J. K. Hemphill and A. E. Coons, "Development of the Leader Behavior Description Questionnaire." In R. M. Stogdill and A. E. Coons, eds., *Leader Behavior: Its Description and Measurement* (Columbus, OH: Ohio State University, 1957).

QUESTIONNAIRE: Fiedler's Least Preferred Co-Worker Scale (LPC)

Think of a person *with whom you have had difficulty working*. It does not have to be a person you really dislike, just someone you *must* work with and with whom working is difficult. Describe the person on each of the scales below by checking the number between each pair of adjectives that best describes that person. Then transfer the numbers to the spaces at the right and total them.

Pleasant	:__:__:__:__:__:__:__: Unpleasant	8 7 6 5 4 3 2 1	5
Friendly	:__:__:__:__:__:__:__: Unfriendly	8 7 6 5 4 3 2 1	8
Rejecting	:__:__:__:__:__:__:__: Accepting	1 2 3 4 5 6 7 8	4
Tense	:__:__:__:__:__:__:__: Relaxed	1 2 3 4 5 6 7 8	1

Distant	:__:__:__:__:__:__:__:	Close	2
	1 2 3 4 5 6 7 8		
Cold	:__:__:__:__:__:__:__:	Warm	2
	1 2 3 4 5 6 7 8		
Supportive	:__:__:__:__:__:__:__:	Hostile	3
	8 7 6 5 4 3 2 1		
Boring	:__:__:__:__:__:__:__:	Interesting	3
	1 2 3 4 5 6 7 8		
Quarrelsome	:__:__:__:__:__:__:__:	Harmonious	4
	1 2 3 4 5 6 7 8		
Gloomy	:__:__:__:__:__:__:__:	Cheerful	8
	1 2 3 4 5 6 7 8		
Open	:__:__:__:__:__:__:__:	Guarded	6
	8 7 6 5 4 3 2 1		
Backbiting	:__:__:__:__:__:__:__:	Loyal	5
	1 2 3 4 5 6 7 8		
Untrustworthy	:__:__:__:__:__:__:__:	Trustworthy	4
	1 2 3 4 5 6 7 8		
Considerate	:__:__:__:__:__:__:__:	Inconsiderate	6
	8 7 6 5 4 3 2 1		
Nasty	:__:__:__:__:__:__:__:	Nice	4
	1 2 3 4 5 6 7 8		
Agreeable	:__:__:__:__:__:__:__:	Disagreeable	4
	8 7 6 5 4 3 2 1		
Insincere	:__:__:__:__:__:__:__:	Sincere	4
	1 2 3 4 5 6 7 8		
Kind	:__:__:__:__:__:__:__:	Unkind	4
	8 7 6 5 4 3 2 1		

Total   77

There are two different leadership styles which are measured by the Least Preferred Co-worker scale.

1. *Relationship-motivated* (High LPC—score of 64 and above). These leaders seem to be most concerned with maintaining good interpersonal relations and accomplishing the task through these personal relationships. Sometimes the high LPC leader becomes so concerned with relating to group members that it interferes with completion of the assignment or mission. In relaxed and well-controlled situations, this type of leader tends to impress the boss.

2. *Task-motivated* (Low LPC—score of 57 or below). These leaders place primary emphasis on task performance. Low LPC leaders work best from guidelines and specific directions and if these are lacking, the low LPC will make the organization and creation of these guidelines the first priority. However, under relaxed and well-controlled

situations when the organization is running smoothly, the task-motivated leader takes time to attend to the morale of group members.

Source: F. Fiedler, *A Theory of Leadership Effectiveness* (New York: McGraw-Hill, 1967).

An Integrative Approach to Leadership

I n Chapter 8, we reviewed six different theories of leadership, plus a revision of one theory. Each helps managers better understand leadership in organizations. However, to be most effective, managers really need to draw on all of these theories. The integrative framework of leadership presented in this chapter is designed to make that possible. It also places leadership in a larger perspective.

This integrative model will be useful in analyzing situations to determine which of four leadership styles to use, and whether that style can be used by a particular manager in a given context. A basic premise of the model is that managers must continually work to develop the skills of the people they supervise.[1] Thus, the model emphasizes the need to view leadership as a developmental process, where the goals are both to get results through people and to develop employees to the point where delegation is possible. After developing the model, we will apply it to the Home Computers case for illustration. The chapter closes by considering several implications of the model.

AN INTEGRATIVE MODEL OF LEADERSHIP

All six theories discussed in Chapter 8 contribute to the analytical model developed here. The theories suggest that we must analyze the leader, subordinates, task, and general context if we are to determine the leadership style that will be most appropriate in a given situation. The integrative model will be developed in two steps: (1) picking the leadership style most appropriate for the task/subordinate fit, and (2) adjusting that choice based on leader and context characteristics. It will become clear very quickly that Blanchard's revised Situational Leadership Theory forms the basis of this model. We add to it from the other theories to make it more complete. The situational leadership model is chosen as the basis primarily because of its developmental orientation and because it is easy to grasp. Also, it is capable of incorporating points from the other theories. The basics of our integrative model (related to step 1 above) are shown in Exhibit 9–1.

The basic style choices are shown in the two-dimensional diagram, where initiating structure and consideration are the two dimensions. As noted earlier, these two dimensions became popular in the 1950s and have remained so. Indeed, they seem to capture the two most critical elements of a manager's job: the task to be done and the people who must do it. The integrative model includes the four basic leadership styles:

1. High structure/low consideration (cell 1, called *directing*).
2. High structure/high consideration (cell 2, called *coaching*).

EXHIBIT 9–1

A Framework for Analyzing Leadership Situations

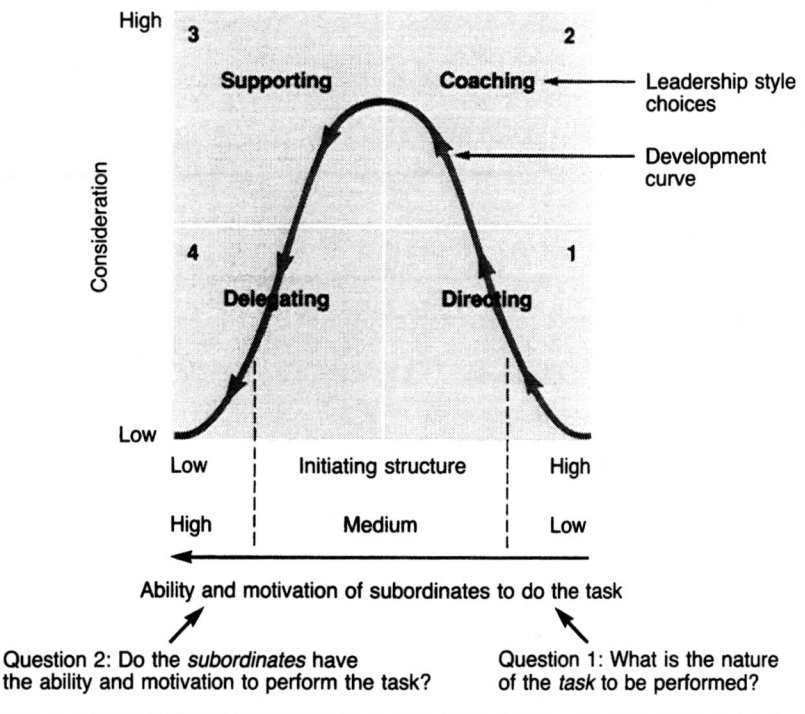

3. Low structure/high consideration (cell 3, called *supporting*).

4. Low structure/low consideration (cell 4, called *delegating*).

Now the question is: How do managers know when to use which leadership style, and do they move along the developmental curve in Exhibit 9–1 as the situation changes over time?

To determine the appropriate leadership style for a given situation, we draw heavily on the contingency theories developed in the 1960s. The developmental curve in the integrative model and the ability and motivation continuum are an adaptation of Blanchard's leadership model. If managers can determine where an individual or a group of subordinates lies on the ability and motivation scales for a particular task, they can then choose the right style of leadership. In so doing, managers must recognize the potential need to vary their leadership style from person to person, as well as from task to task. An initial analysis consists of addressing task characteristics and subordinate characteristics. Once these are assessed, the leader can ask what the follower needs in terms of structure and consideration to get the job done. This then helps determine the right leadership style to use. A walkthrough of the model—beginning with task characteristics—follows.

Task characteristics

The first question is: What is the nature of the task to be performed? (See the lower right-hand corner of Exhibit 9–1.)[2] Thinking back to Chapters 5 and 6 on motivation, goals were said to be important determinants of the motivation of people. Clearly, managers want to tap the motivation of people to do a task, and research has often shown the impact that clear goals can have on performance.[3] Thus, the starting point for diagnosing a leadership situation is to clarify the task that has to be performed. Hard as it may be to believe, many managers do not do a very effective job of setting goals and defining tasks for their employees. It is certainly logical that having clear goals and tasks to pursue enhances the probability of success. Managers, therefore, must clarify what has to be done, by when, and according to what standards. They must be sure to specify what a good job looks like by spelling out the standards for measuring performance on the task.

All of the contingency theories (Fiedler, Hersey-Blanchard, Blanchard, and House) consider the degree of task structure as an important situational variable. Fiedler and House explicitly state that managers need to know the degree to which subordinates' jobs are clearly defined. Hersey-Blanchard and then Blanchard alone look at the fit between task structure and employee capability. Hence, to answer the first question, managers need to analyze the task characteristics of structure, variability, and intrinsic motivation. Is the task clearly specified in terms of goals, the means to the goals, and the manner of evaluating goal accomplishment? Is the task highly variable in what must be done from day to day, and is it difficult to predict these variations? Also, is the task intrinsically motivating—that is, challenging and meaningful? Recall the job design model in Chapter 6. By looking at these task characteristics, managers can get a feel for how complex or how routine a job is. And if managers consider the past and present of these characteristics, they can tell whether a job is becoming more or less difficult.

Subordinate characteristics

Coupled with this analysis of the task, managers must analyze the subordinates' characteristics. Clearly, employees' levels of skill, motivation, and need can all act to influence the appropriate leadership style for a given task.[4] Thus, **the second question is: Do the subordinates have the ability and motivation to perform the task?** (See the lower left-hand corner of Exhibit 9–1.)[5] The Hersey-Blanchard, Blanchard, and

House theories all suggest that managers must determine if subordinates are motivated toward higher-level needs (such as achievement). The more they are, the more leaders need to emphasize consideration instead of initiating structure. House's path-goal theory also suggests the need to assess the employee's desire for control, while Hersey-Blanchard and Blanchard suggest managers assess the employees' ability (experience and education).

Several subquestions can be asked to get a handle on the subordinates' characteristics as related to the job. Do the employees have the ability to take responsibility for the task? Are they willing to take responsibility for it? Do they have the education and experience that is relevant to the task? Do they have a high need for achievement (as defined in Chapter 6)? Are the employees interested in higher-order needs (such as self-actualization and self-esteem) or in lower-order needs (such as safety and physiological needs)? Finally, do the employees want control over their daily job activities? Each of these questions must be answered in terms of the task to be performed. **It is the current match between employees and tasks that really dictates whether the ability and motivation of the subordinates to perform a task is high, medium, or low.** A manager must not fall into the trap of considering employee potential to do the job. Hopefully, all employees have the potential to develop high levels of ability and motivation, but a manager's current leadership style must reflect current levels of ability and motivation if employee potential is to be fully developed. And if the manager considers the past and present of employee motivation and ability for the task at hand, the analysis will reveal trends about this match. Is it becoming better or worse?

A manager's analysis thus far will reveal where the subordinates are along the ability and motivation scale in Exhibit 9–1. If the employees are unable but motivated to do a job, they will be at the low end of the scale (to the right). As they become more able, they will move through a period of lower motivation where the coaching style is most appropriate. As ability to do the job continues to increase, thus moving the follower to the left on the ability/motivation continuum, motivation should increase. If the potential is there and the manager guides its development, the followers may attain high levels of both ability and motivation for the task, thus allowing the manager to delegate. At each point in time, the manager needs to locate the employees' position on the scale and then draw a vertical line from that point on the continuum up to the developmental curve in the diagram. This will determine what style of leadership is appropriate for the given task/employee combination. This process helps the manager answer the question: What do the subordinates need from the leader in terms of initiating structure and consideration to accomplish the task? For example, if a person's ability/ motivation is low, the dashed line in Exhibit 9–1 indicates that high structure and low consideration, or directing, leadership is the best choice. On the other hand, if a person's ability and motivation are high, the dashed line in the figure indicates that low structure and low consideration, that is, delegating, leadership is the best choice.

Up to this point, the integrative model is similar to Blanchard's revised situational leadership theory. The integrative model uses House's and Fiedler's theories to make the considerations of the task more explicit and has formulated two questions to ask. The model has also drawn upon House's path-goal theory to help managers more fully understand how to assess subordinates' ability and motivation to do a task.

After managers think through the two questions about task and subordinates as they apply to a situation, they should be able to determine the best leadership style to help a particular set of subordinates perform a given task effectively. As pointed out earlier, managers are likely to have to alter their leadership style for each leader–member relationship, since different people may be at different points along the ability/motivation continuum, even for the same task. Managers may also have to vary their leadership style from task to task for the same person. As the example in Insight 9–1 suggests, it really is critical to fit leadership style to the situation. If managers do not, regardless of how hard they try to guide and motivate employees, they are likely to fail.

Insight 9–1 also raises an important question that leads us into Phase 2 of the integrative leadership model. Can a leader actually deliver the appropriate style of leadership for the situation? In addition, it is difficult to tell what kind of influence the surrounding environment will have on a manager's ability to use the desired leadership style. Exhibit 9–2 depicts the second phase of the integrative model by adding these two considerations at the top of the figure as questions 3 and 4. The answers to these two questions may necessitate an adjustment to the leadership style chosen as a result of the answers to the first two questions.

Leader characteristics

The third question to ask is: What characteristics of a leader might influence his or her ability to use the chosen leadership style? (See the upper left-hand corner of Exhibit 9–2 on page 351.)[6] Fiedler suggests that poor leader–member relations will generally call for a leadership style high in consideration. The trait theories suggest that a leader's experience and knowledge, power needs, and personal bases of power may be important in determining his or her effectiveness. Some recent research has also supported the idea that the level of achievement and affiliation power needs can impact a person's ability to lead.[7] Thus, managers must analyze their relations with their employees. Are they good, fair, or

---

I N S I G H T 9–1

Steel Target:
Critics Fault Trautlein for Failure
to Revive an Ailing Bethlehem

*B*ethlehem, Pa.—Donald H. Trautlein envisioned it as an inspirational meeting to rally his Bethlehem Steel Corp. troops. Instead, last year's retreat of top managers quickly turned bitter.

Mr. Trautlein angrily rebuked his subordinates when they complained that repeated white-collar pay cuts had undercut staff morale. "He shouted it was our problem," recalls one manager who quit a month later. "We all left that meeting feeling lost."

Such disillusionment typifies the atmosphere of Bethlehem during Mr. Trautlein's six-year reign. Once deemed the company's savior, the stocky accountant is singled out by critics today as the executive whose mistakes hastened its turbulent decline. The 59-year-old Mr. Trautlein is bowing out this month—under pressure, some say, from the board he helped recruit. A new chairman hasn't yet been named.

Bethlehem is reeling from $1.94 billion in losses since the start of 1982. It is so strapped for cash that it is auctioning its few earning assets and even such longtime symbols of corporate prowess as a private jet fleet. With the company fighting for crucial labor concessions, top executives concede that a bankruptcy filing is "not impossible."

Bethlehem's slide reflects more than the onslaught of imports and the shrinking demand that have bludgeoned all U.S. steelmakers. It is also a story of strategic errors and paralyzing indecision—flaws that can undo any company, but especially one in a declining industry.

"The tougher the environment, the more crucial it is to have good leadership," says Michael E. Porter of Harvard Business School, discussing management strategies for troubled companies. "Just because you're in a declining industry doesn't mean you can't make money. You need a management that's decisive and willing to bet on a strategy early on."

---

poor? Does the manager have the bases of power and influence needed to exercise the desired leadership style? Does the manager have the experience and knowledge? And what are the manager's power needs?

If managers have a high need for power, they may tend to exert structure when it is not needed. If managers have a high need for affiliation, they may tend to show consideration when it is not desirable. Insight 9–2 on page 352 illustrates how strongly personality can influence style of leadership. Personality and needs influence perception of a situation (as discussed in Chapter 3). In turn, perception influences analysis of a situation and thus the choice of one leadership style over

EXHIBIT 9–2

An Expanded Framework for Analyzing Leadership Situations

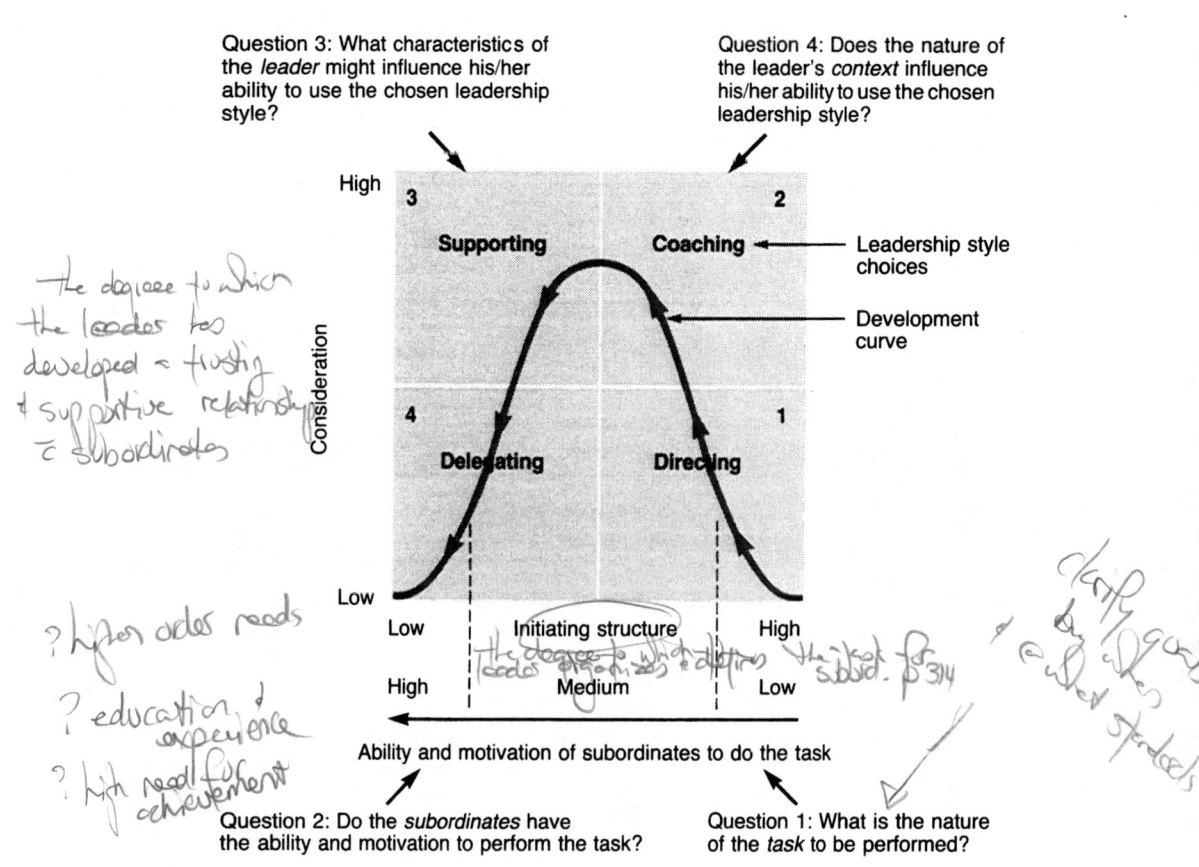

Question 3: What characteristics of the *leader* might influence his/her ability to use the chosen leadership style?

Question 4: Does the nature of the leader's *context* influence his/her ability to use the chosen leadership style?

Question 2: Do the *subordinates* have the ability and motivation to perform the task?

Question 1: What is the nature of the *task* to be performed?

another. Then too, a manager's experience and knowledge may allow him or her to be more directive (that is, high in structure). But if a manager lacks experience, it may be difficult to be directive, even if the situation calls for it.

As for relations with subordinates and bases of power (topics discussed at length in Chapter 10), high charismatic or expertise power and good relations with subordinates may enable managers to be directive when it is needed. If, however, a manager's relations with employees are not very good, high relationship behavior may actually lead to improved relations. On the other hand, poor relations may necessitate directive leadership for short-run effectiveness. Finally, if a manager's

---

I N S I G H T 9–2

**Numbers Man Hasn't Found
the Key at GM**

Just what skills and methods does GM need at the top right now? This isn't meant to be the gratuitous "Roger-bashing" that has become popular around Detroit lately—even among people who were hailing Mr. Roger Smith, CEO of General Motors, as an industrial visionary just a year ago. But like any man, the 61-year-old Mr. Smith has his strengths and weaknesses.

Mr. H. Ross Perot, GM Board Member, addressed those last May in an interview about GM's situation and Mr. Smith's leadership. "What you've got here is a numbers guy, and what we've got is a people problem," he said. "But let me defend him for a minute. This is the way he's been brought up."

Mr. Smith's biggest strength is brains. His mind works so fast that, in interviews, he often doesn't complete his sentences, because his mind moves on to his next thought faster than his mouth completes the thought he's finishing.

What's more, Mr. Smith can be appealingly unassuming for the head of the largest company on earth. In an interview last April he was looking for a document he wanted to use to make a point, but he couldn't immediately find it. Instead of summoning one of his secretaries, Mr. Smith walked over to a cabinet, got down on his hands and knees, and started rummaging until he found what he wanted.

---

expert power is low, he or she may not be able to be directive even though it would be appropriate.[8] Rather, the manager may have to depend more on relationship-oriented leadership than the model in Exhibit 9–1 would indicate.

Finally, the 1970s and 80s have marked the emergence of women into managerial jobs. Numerous studies have tried to determine if being a male or female leader will impact the leadership style a manager uses. It is encouraging to note that a recent review of those studies found no real differences between male and female use of the various leadership styles nor in their ratings of effectiveness.[9]

Still, some leader differences can impact the integrative model. The key point in adding leader characteristics to the model is that the best style of leadership, as defined by the task/subordinate fit, may have to be altered due to characteristics of the leader. For example, if being relationship oriented is not a manager's best style, it may be better for her to start with high structure and try to adapt her leadership style over time. Or perhaps the employees can adapt to the manager's style and still yield good results. Managers need to be aware of who they are in leadership situations if they are to lead effectively.[10]

Context characteristics

In addition to the leader characteristics, social and organizational context characteristics can also alter our analysis from Exhibit 9–1. **The fourth question is: Does the nature of a leader's context influence his or her ability to use the chosen leadership style?** (See the upper right-hand corner of Exhibit 9–2.)[11] Fiedler's theory points out the need to consider the power a leader derives from a position (a topic discussed at length in Chapter 10). The autocratic–democratic continuum indicates that leaders must have position power in order to exercise initiating structure styles of leadership. Thus, how much power do managers have because they are managers (that is, position power)? Can they fire someone? Can they give someone a pay raise? If managers' position power is low, they may have to depend more on personal power bases, such as the admiration of their employees or their own expertise. This is likely to result in more relationship-oriented leader behavior than the model in Exhibit 9–1 might suggest. Of course, a great deal of position power would allow managers to exercise directive leadership when it is suggested by the model.

The other context variables relate to the climate of a person's position as manager. What was the leadership style of the previous manager in the position? What is the leadership style of people around the manager in the organization (that is, peers and superiors)? And what are the norms of the organization? If previous leaders in a position and other leaders in the organization are directive leaders, a manager may be better off to move gradually toward coaching leadership rather than adopt it at once—even if the subordinate/task fit suggests the coaching style. This idea is consistent with the Hersey-Blanchard and Blanchard models, since they indicate it is not appropriate to radically change the leadership style used with a group of employees.

And there are many pressures in an organization to conform to certain expectations and adhere to norms of behavior. Managers who ignore these pressures usually encounter difficulty in their careers. Insight 9–3 illustrates how expectations of people around a leader can exert constraining forces on his or her behavior. Of course, most managers' situations may not be as extreme as the one described by Mr. Henderson. Still, norms and tradition will be important factors influencing a manager's choice of an effective leadership style. These context variables clearly stress the importance of viewing leadership as a developmental process. **The situation into which a leader walks will always have a past and a future. Managers must read the developmental process of the context if they are to be effective leaders.**

Now that we have fully discussed the integrative model of leadership, let us consider the following situation involving Louise of Home Computers Company, since we already know quite a lot about her from earlier chapters. We will then apply the model to the case.

INSIGHT 9–3

Firm Teaches Third World Managers

*M*anagement skills taught by U.S. business schools often don't apply in the developing world. Robert Youker, who teaches at Economic Development Institute, a training center run by the World Bank in Washington, says sophisticated techniques often are "totally unrealistic."

Verne E. Henderson, a management psychologist and protestant minister who teaches MEI's course in ethics, cites the case of an African student who worked for a bank. The student had been assigned to help open the first bank office in his home village. The first loan applicant was the village elder, whose tribal authority was un-questioned but whose credit rating wasn't. The elder couldn't meet the bank's lending guidelines; the student turned him down.

When the student went home that evening, Mr. Henderson says, his family was "up in arms." The student agonized over the issue of violating either his bank's guidelines or his tribe's traditions. Mr. Henderson says he advises students to resolve such questions by stating goals and consequences of actions. In this case, he says, granting the loan would have been both ethical and pragmatic, because without the elder's support, the branch would fail.

The Wall Street Journal, February 3, 1983. Reprinted by permission of *The Wall Street Journal,* © Dow Jones & Company, Inc. 1983. All rights reserved.

Home Computers Case

Leadership and Louise of Home Computers

When Louise took over the project manager's job in Phoenix, she realized that she had stepped across a significant boundary. She was now management, where before she had just been a systems analyst. In her old position, she had relied heavily on establishing good relationships with other programmers whose services she needed on her projects. Now as a manager, she had other legitimate sources of power to use. As she contemplated this new position, she recalled her first boss Sam Stewart and how he had given very clear direction—but a great deal of discretion—in how she did her work. She had liked that approach, and she wondered if it would work for her in Phoenix.

Many of the programmers in Louise's office were very new in their jobs. Some of them seemed quite capable; others appeared to need a great deal of guidance. The Phoenix office was growing quite rapidly, and many of the customers were engineering companies with extremely technical problems to be solved. Louise found the Phoenix office in a state of real disunity. The new programmers, while they had good credentials, did not know what to do. The more experienced programmers jumped from one project to another to try to put out fires as they arose. It appeared that the rapid growth of the office had led to the signing of many contracts without determining how the work could be done.

While Louise was not the systems manager for the entire office, she had several projects under her responsibility, and she decided to try to get those projects in good shape. She also decided to work with the systems manager, John Wood, to see if she could help correct the overall office problems. But she knew she would first have to develop some credibility with John, so she focused her energies on the projects directly under her.

Louise analyzed the situation in the following manner. The job facing her and her programmers was somewhat ambiguous in that the technical problems of the customers were difficult. Furthermore, the quantity of work was great. Fortunately, the work was very challenging—in fact, too challenging for her new, inexperienced programmers. They wanted to perform well because they saw this job as a great opportunity. But they were in over their head. The history of the company suggested that Louise was expected to produce, no matter what it took. Indeed, Louise was in a tough situation, and her boss John was so inundated that he could not help her very much.

Fortunately, Louise had a great deal of self-confidence. In addition, she was alert and outspoken and enjoyed solving problems by applying logic. Her experience suggested that her group would have to cut back on the number of new projects and focus on the ones they had, or they would be in danger of putting out a bad product. Louise knew that in the long run taking on new projects would cause more problems than cutting back production. John was not too sure about this solution, but when he saw Louise was so adamant, he consented to her wishes.

Louise proceeded to establish priorities among the existing projects and to refuse new projects for the time being. She then organized the programmers by mixing experienced and inexperienced programmers on each project. Each project was given specific instructions on how to proceed and strict deadlines to meet. Once these parameters were established, she appointed a project leader to carry out the plans. Then, each week she would meet with all project teams to discuss problems and progress toward the deadlines. The previous project manager had constantly been on the backs of the programmers and was always showing them how he would do the job; the programmers resented him.

The programmers responded well to Louise's leadership. They became very involved in turning out a good product in a reasonable time. In fact, after about 18 months, it became apparent that Louise's group was not only turning out excellent products, but they were beginning to turn them out faster. Many new clients wanted Louise to handle their projects, and many programmers in the office wanted to work in her group.

Louise began to have a great deal of influence with the other project managers in the office, as well as with John Wood, her boss. Her ability to handle the rapid-growth situation and get the most out of her subordinates made other managers want to listen to her. In fact, many of her peers began to come to her for advice instead of John. Fortunately, her unit had clear direction, and her staff had developed to the point that she did not have to devote all of her time to the unit. She saw this as her opportunity to begin directly influencing John and the entire Phoenix office, but she wondered if the same approach that had been so successful with her programmers would also work for the entire office.

By analyzing the situation much as she had done when she first came to Phoenix, Louise determined that she would have to focus more on her relationship with John than on the pure task of reorganizing the office. For one thing, she did not have the authority to tell John what to do. Furthermore, John was a very capable manager. Then, too, company protocol suggested that employees should respect the chain of command at all times. Louise adjusted to the new situation; and soon everyone knew that she was the one responsible for making the Phoenix office one of the best in the company. In 1975, when John was promoted to a larger, more established office on the West Coast, Louise was rewarded with the systems manager's job at Phoenix.

APPLYING THE INTEGRATIVE MODEL TO LOUISE'S SITUATION

Let us now apply the integrative model in Exhibit 9–2 to the Home Computers Company case by asking the four questions in the figure. First, what is the nature of the task to be performed? As a project manager, Louise faced a situation that was not well structured and was constantly changing. The projects were ambiguous, overwhelming, yet very challenging and meaningful. The programmers had a rather difficult task, thus pointing toward a need for an initiating structure leadership style. But what about their abilities and motivation?

The second question in the model addresses this issue: Do the subordinates have the ability and motivation to perform the task? The programmers appear to be motivated; the experienced programmers jumped from project to project to do the best they could to keep things on track. They were willing to take responsibility and had a high need for achievement. They also had a high desire for control over their work. These clues also suggest that they were capable within reasonable limits. In other words, they appeared to have the potential to be excellent programmers, but the situation was so unstructured they could not apply them effectively. As for the new programmers, they had good credentials and (by inference) reasonable abilities, but they were unclear about what to do.

So, what was the level of ability and motivation of the programmers to handle the task? The programmers did not appear to lack ability and motivation; rather, their jobs were so unstructured that they did not know what to do. They were willing but not able due to the lack of clear direction; thus, the ability/motivation appears to be low. The lack of task structure was overriding the capabilities of the employees. They wanted to perform well, but the unstructured task made them unable to do so. From the model in Exhibit 9–2, it appears that the appropriate leadership style was high on structure and low on consideration (that is, directing leadership style). This is what Louise did: she restricted the number of projects to be handled and set priorities for each project. She also gave specific guidelines for each project. She mixed the experienced and new programmers and met with each project team weekly to discuss progress. Otherwise, Louise left things up to the project leaders. As the case reports, Louise and her programmers performed very well, indeed.

The case also illustrates another aspect of the model. By providing the overall structure to the task, Louise created a better fit between the task and the programmers. This quickly moved their ability from low toward medium-low, by providing the needed structure. This movement, the bad relationship with the previous leader, and the fact that Louise was new then created the need for her to move into cell 2 of the model and increase her consideration (that is, coaching). As things progressed, she was able to move to cell 3 (supporting) because the ability/ motivation of the employees moved to medium-high. And as the case mentions, she actually moved into cell 4 (delegating) within 18 months, as the programmers moved into high ability/motivation. This developmental process is consistent with the model that indicates that such development is both natural and a goal of an effective leader.

Thus far, the model in Exhibit 9–2 suggests that initially the best leadership style for Louise was high in structure and low in consideration. Leader and context characteristics also need to be factored in. The third question in the model is: Which characteristics of the leader might influence his or her ability to use the chosen leadership style? Louise has a great deal of self-confidence, and she is also alert and outspoken. Information on Louise from Chapter 4 indicates she has a lot of knowledge and expert personal power. These factors suggest that Louise will be comfortable with an initiating structure leadership style. If Louise had not had experience and self-confidence, she might have found it difficult to stand up to John Wood and to initiate the structure of reducing the number of projects. On the other hand, since Louise is new in the position, she has no working relationship with the employees in Phoenix; thus, the leader–member relations rather quickly exert a force toward a consideration leadership style. In short, Louise is well suited to the style of leadership suggested by the model—she would appear to have the ability and personal characteristics to exercise both the directing and the coaching style of leadership. But it is not difficult to imagine a person who might lack the knowledge and self-confidence to get the job done. It also appears that Louise can be flexible, since she gradually moved to a supporting style and then to a delegating style.

The final question from Exhibit 9–2 is: Does the nature of the leader's context influence his or her ability to use the chosen leadership style? It would appear that the necessary position power is present for Louise to set priorities and control the situation faced by her programmers. Thus, she can follow through with the initiating structure needed in Phoenix. And what we know about her boss John Wood suggests that Louise has flexibility in her position. John is not so demanding about the situation as to dictate a style of leadership to Louise.

Finally, the case notes that the previous project manager was constantly on the programmers' backs and forever showing them how to do their jobs. Thus, Louise stepped into a situation where her predecessor had been almost all structure and very little consideration. But he structured the details of the jobs rather than the larger picture which Louise attacked. The previous leader's style probably made it easy for Louise to change the situation, since the programmers did not like his style. By structuring the overall situation, allowing the programmers their freedom, and showing consideration for the programmers, Louise was moving in a direction the potentially able and motivated programmers desired. But the company's past history suggests that it was wise to move initially no further along the developmental curve than the coaching style of leadership.

Thus, in this case, the two leader and context questions do not contradict the basic model; rather, they provide added support for the choice from the basic model. More importantly, it is easy to imagine how the leader and context characteristics could, in some cases, alter the choice of leadership style. **By analyzing not only the subordinates and the task, but also the leader and the context, we are able to gain a realistic perspective on the leadership style which will work in a given situation.**

IMPLICATIONS OF THE MODEL

With the integrative model now fully described and applied to Louise, we can look at several important implications of the model. First, the developmental curve in the model highlights the changing nature of both task and subordinate characteristics. **By analyzing the past history of the task and the subordinates' ability and motivation, managers gain an idea of how to handle the present situation. And the analysis must continue into the future, since both task and subordinates may**

undergo change. It has been argued that one of the manager's jobs is to move the subordinates along the ability and motivation continuum by moving leadership along the developmental curve from right to left.[12] Indeed, normal forces usually create a right-to-left evolution along the curve. Over time, the ability of subordinates to do the task will tend to increase through experience.

The second implication follows from the first. Past performance of subordinates will influence the appropriate leadership style choice for managers. And future performance of subordinates will influence adjustments in leadership style. Yes, **subordinate behavior affects leadership style just as leadership style affects subordinate behavior, as should be clear if managers take a developmental view of the situation.**[13] Louise chose a style that got positive results. She then shifted her style along the developmental curve. But suppose the chosen style had failed to work. She would then have had to shift to another style.

The new style Louise would have chosen leads to the third implication from the model. Would she attribute the continued poor performance to problems with the task? Or to problems with the subordinates' ability? Or to problems with their motivation? Obviously, Louise's attribution would affect her choice of appropriate leadership style.[14] And we can imagine that different leaders might interpret the same phenomena differently—just as Louise might interpret them differently at different times in her career. Indeed, the development of the leader is an important aspect of the integrative model.

It also is important to remember that the followers and other observers in a given situation will formulate their own attributions.[15] Hence, the fourth implication of the model is to recognize that the behaviors of the leader only partially determine performance, in spite of the fact that people will tend to attribute significant causality to the leader's behavior. To state it another way, the leader may not be as important in a given situation as we give him or her credit for.[16] One series of research studies documented how we tend to assign great credit to a leader's actions when performance is good, and to assign great blame to the leader when performance is bad.[17] But many other factors also affect performance of the people a person manages. For example, the factors that go to make up the personalities, motivation, and so forth of a manager's people can have a great impact on performance. Yet, these factors can be only partially influenced by a manager's behavior. In addition, more macro factors such as overall company performance, industry growth or decline, technology and structure of the company, and group and intergroup dynamics play a role and are only partially affected by a manager's leadership behaviors. These factors will be discussed in later chapters of the book. For now, it is important simply to know that managers will be held accountable for performance, even though they are only part of the equation affecting performance. By the same token, they are an important part of the equation. Managers need to understand how to make the most out of their leadership efforts.

A fifth implication from the model is actually the recognition of a limitation to the analytical aspects of leadership. Often managers will have to make numerous rapid-fire decisions in using the leadership model—the task, the person, the fit. And sometimes what managers know they should do may be different from what they will do. In these cases, managers will need to draw not only upon all of their analytical skills, but also upon intuition.[18] As a manager's stockpile of experiences builds and he or she organizes that information into meaningful chunks, the manager will learn to draw upon intuition, especially in these complicated and rapid-fire situations. The point is that managers must recognize that being a leader is not only analysis and acting by design; it is also acting as appropriate on intuition and feeling.

The sixth implication is that a manager must lead a number of people in performing a number of tasks. **Since each subordinate and each task may differ slightly, the manager will need to vary his or her leadership style from task to task and from person to person.**[19] Indeed, Louise might well have varied her leadership style between the experienced and new programmers. The implication here is important: it suggests the need to analyze not only the group of subordinates but also each subordinate individually.

The seventh implication is apparent from the Home Computers case. When Louise created structure for the programmers by limiting the number of projects and setting priorities among them, she reduced the need for daily structuring of programmer activities. These rules and procedures, plus the mixing of new with experienced programmers, actually serve as substitutes for leadership.[20] The task-relevant experience and education already in the integrative model are other substitutes for leadership. Remember, managers must provide the direction and support that people do not get from other sources, such as the job itself, company rules and procedures, and colleagues. If people get direction and support from these other sources, they will not need it from managers.[21] But if they do not receive support from other sources, managers must fill this void. The key point is that **if employee motivation and ability are high, and if the task is structured, leader behavior can be minimized.** In the model, this situation would put managers in cell 4 where delegating is the appropriate leadership style.

THE CHALLENGE OF LEADERSHIP

One final issue to deal with is the overall challenge facing managers who try to be leaders. As noted earlier, "managers do things right; leaders do the right things."[22] Additionally, leaders develop their people in hopes of one day being able to delegate tasks to them. Two of Tom Peters recent books, *A Passion for Excellence* and *Thriving on Chaos,* argue vehemently that there is a desperate need in today's organizations for leadership and the tapping of the real potential of people.[23] And in the forward to a book titled *The Leadership Challenge,* Tom Peters says, "The manager–to–leader revolution is not optional if you are interested in your children's well-being."[24] And we might add, "if you are interested in your own career." The point is one made at the beginning of Chapter 8: leaders are a scarce resource in organizations today. The material that follows sums up what leaders do that sets them apart from managers, as reported in two books titled *Leaders,* and *The Leadership Challenge,* and a recent *Organizational Dynamics* article.[25]

First leaders establish and share a vision of what they want for the future of their organization, their department, even their shift. And they work to share that vision with all of the people that they work with and for. A vision is not very helpful unless it is bought into by all of the people whose efforts must make it happen. As Insight 9–4 shows, the late Ray Kroc of McDonald's created a very clear vision for all of the McDonald's employees.

Second, leaders work very hard to enable others to be successful, to model the way to be successful, and to develop a plan of action that builds in accountability, reliability, predictability, and persistence. Along the way to the vision, leaders show people how to do things when they need help. They set up opportunities to win, and they encourage the heart of the employees, both as individuals and as a team, at every opportunity. Leaders also recognize those situations when they can enable others to act on their own, that is, they delegate. One way of looking at this is to say that leaders work for their people. They do everything in their power to make it possible for their employees to perform up to their potential. But leaders will not tolerate people who do not perform up to their potential.

The third point to recognize about leaders is that they constantly work to develop their people to the point where they can delegate to them. Most managers are afraid to really delegate because delegation means giving up control while still being accountable to the organization for the results of their people. Sometimes when leaders delegate, they will watch people mess up a job they could do so much better; sometimes leaders will watch employees do it not worse, just different from the way they would do it. And leaders may also watch while employees get better at a job than the leaders have been.[26] But, as pointed out in the integrative model of leadership, and as research has shown, the effects of delegation on a subordinate's job performance is dependent on the subordinate's job competence and on the match between subordinate and leader goals, which would definitely affect the subordinate's motivation.[27] In other words, leaders must create the vi-

---

Fast-Food Leader:
McDonald's Combines a Dead Man's Advice with Lively Strategy

Oak Brook, Ill.—In a room suitably dimmed for a seance, new employees of McDonald's Corp. gather to contact Ray A. Kroc, the fast-food company's founder.

Their voices hushed, half a dozen workers tap into rows of desktop computers offering 1½ hours of videotaped messages from the late Mr. Kroc. Wearing a sport coat and looking in the pink, the short, balding executive appears on their screens, barking pronouncements from telephones at each terminal.

On cleanliness: "If you've got time to lean, you've got time to clean." On the competition: "If they were drowning to death, I would put a hose in their mouth." On expansion: "When you're green, you grow; when you're ripe, you rot."

Ten years after Mr. Kroc stepped away from day-to-day operations at the world's largest fast-food chain, his ghost lives on. His office at McDonald's headquarters here is preserved as a museum, his reading glasses untouched in their leather case on the desk.

Mr. Kroc wasn't averse to new ideas. In fact, he encouraged them—and had his own, some of them awful. But McDonald's main strategy can be summed up in his three-decades-old philosophy of assembly-line cooking and preparation, fast service, a wholesome image and a near-religious devotion to the hamburger. Today a new generation of McDonald's executives cheers his axioms.

Impact Grows

Few departed corporate chiefs have left such an imprint. Today's executives at McDonald's cite Mr. Kroc so often that he still seems to be in charge. His photo smiles down on every desk. "When Ray died, people worried that his vision couldn't be kept alive," says Sharon Vuinovich, assistant vice president for accounting. "But we're doing that."

---

sion, develop employees' skills, and tap employees' motivation before they can delegate. But that is exactly what a person should be working to do with every employee on every task—that is, if the person wants to be a leader and not just a manager. It is not easy to delegate, but as Insight 9–5 shows, Byron Denenberg found it was essential if he wanted his small business to grow.

The final point is that leaders are self-confident in their abilities and their sense of what needs to be done. Leaders challenge the status quo, and they learn from their mistakes. They transform and change things to make them better.[28] They develop charisma by essentially doing the things in points one through three, by being trustworthy, by being

INSIGHT 9-5

Strength in Numbers

For Many Entrepreneurs, the Hardest Task Is Sharing Power with a Management Team

*T*hese days, more and more entrepreneurs are learning the same lesson: One of the keys to making a small business grow is putting together a management team. Despite the popular myth of "hero entrepreneurs"—founders who single-handedly take care of marketing, operations, finance and planning—most companies can't grow unless the founder hires a management team and delegates authority, experts say.

"The ones that don't do it well fall by the wayside," says Stuart L. Meyer, a management professor at Northwestern University.

But management teams in small business still aren't all that common, partly because the smallest businesses can't afford to hire marketing experts or financial whizzes. The experts generally say that a company needs a management structure when it reaches annual sales of several million dollars. But even as small companies grow and it becomes clear that more managers are needed, many entrepreneurs create the wrong kind of organization. They hire assistants who do as they are told or they hire clones who, like the founder, do a little bit of everything depending on the crisis of the day.

Thanks to good instincts, good advice and lots of trial and error, Mr. Byron Denenberg and MDA Scientific, Inc., created the right kind of structure.

He created a development team, and forced himself to be more patient. "It's not my way, but it's the way for the people who are doing the project," he says. "I try to tighten the screw, and what I get back are squeals that tell me we may save some time on the front end but lose it at the back."

Getting that far wasn't easy. Mr. Denenberg says hiring managers was a natural move, but Richard P. Posner, a former Chicago commercial financier who has been MDA's consultant for seven years, says it took months during late 1981 and early 1982 to convince Mr. Denenberg to change. "He kept resisting and telling me that he didn't have the ability to delegate," Mr. Posner says. "We had a lot of heavy discussions. He used to say to me, 'Richard, that's not my style. I've got to have my hands in the operation.'"

Even after accepting the idea of a team, Mr. Denenberg says he was still worried about finding the right people and then getting them to do the right things. Mr. Posner helped with the interviews, trying to decide if the applicants would work well with Mr. Denenberg. Over three years, they created a five-person team that includes Mr. Denenberg and managers in charge of operations, finance, marketing and technical affairs.

"He was finally convinced that you have to take the same entrepreneurial risk with people that you take with businesses," Mr. Posner says.

By Mike Connelly, *The Wall Street Journal,* May 19, 1986. Reprinted by permission of *The Wall Street Journal,* © Dow Jones & Company, Inc. 1986. All rights reserved.

skilled in what needs to be done, and by building power bases that get things done with their people.[29]

The challenge of leadership is definitely not easy, but clearly leaders are needed in today's world. You should now have a better understanding of leadership and how the six theories from Chapter 8 tie together to provide a useful framework. If managers work with the integrative model, they will be able to better analyze leadership situations. And through experience, managers will also learn to implement the leadership style appropriate for given situations. And in so doing, people actually become leaders, rather than just managers.

CHAPTER HIGHLIGHTS

This chapter has developed an integrative model of leadership which will be useful to managers in analyzing situations to determine the appropriate leadership style. The six leadership theories from Chapter 8 were used to develop the integrative model of leadership. The model includes four styles of leadership: directing, coaching, supporting, and delegating. By drawing from Blanchard's revised situational leadership model, plus the Fiedler and House models, **managers ask two questions about task and subordinate characteristics to determine the ability and motivation of subordinates to handle the task at the present time.** To apply the model, managers would first analyze the task structure and variability and its intrinsic motivation. To determine the fit between task and employees, managers would then analyze the subordinates' ability and willingness to take responsibility, their task-relevant education/experience, their need for achievement, their present need structure, and their desire for control. From this analysis, managers could determine where on the ability and motivation continuum in Exhibit 9–2 to place their employees. By drawing a vertical line up to intersect the developmental curve, managers could select the appropriate style of leadership for the situation.

Next, the model calls for an analysis of leader and context characteristics (using two more questions) to see if the chosen style can be implemented. **The leader characteristics of relations with subordinates, experience/knowledge, power needs, and personal power bases will influence a leader's analysis of the situation.** In addition, **the context characteristics of the position power of the leader, the style of previous people in the leader's position, the style of other leaders around the manager, and organizational norms of operation will act to constrain the leadership choices available to the manager.** These additional aspects can influence the choice of appropriate leadership style for a given situation.

The integrative model was then applied to the Home Computers case, after which we discussed several of its implications. First, the model emphasizes the developmental aspects of the leadership process. Second, it allows for the fact that subordinate behavior can affect leader behavior, as well as the reverse. Third, the leader's attributions regarding performance influence the analysis and adjustments that he or she makes. But the fourth implication was that the followers also make their attributions about performance, thus reminding us that leaders only partially determine performance in a given situation. Fifth, we recognized the limits to analytical aspects of leadership by pointing out the importance of intuition and feeling. Sixth, managers must vary their leadership style from subordinate to subordinate and from task to task. Last, a leader's behavior influences the context in which he or she must operate.

In the final section of this chapter we explored the true challenge facing managers in becoming leaders, rather than just being managers. We talked about the need for creating and sharing a vision of where leaders want their people to go. The text then discussed the need to enable and develop people so leaders can tap their true potential. Important in this regard is the recognition that leaders must always be working toward delegation, even though it is very difficult to give up control. Finally, the text talked about how leaders are self-confident and how they challenge the system.

The goal of this chapter has been to draw on a number of leadership theories in developing an integrative model of the leadership process that will be useful to managers in analyzing situations to determine the appropriate leadership style to use. What remains is for managers to become proficient in its use and experienced in putting into practice the leadership styles appropriate for the situations they encounter. What remains is for people to become not just managers, but to become leaders.

REVIEW QUESTIONS

1. What are the four basic leadership styles in the integrative model? What are the basic factors which determine the appropriate leadership style for a given situation?
2. Explain how the basic integrative model presented in this chapter can be used to analyze a given situation and determine the best leadership style for that situation.
3. How might leader characteristics and context characteristics cause managers to alter the leadership style chosen in the basic integra-

tive model (Exhibit 9–1)? Is it appropriate to consider altering the basic choice based on leader and context variables?

4. Explain the expanded model of leadership in Exhibit 9–2 as it relates to the leadership theories from Chapter 8. Speculate on the next generation of leadership theories that will help managers better understand the process of leadership.

5. Explain the issues inherent in the challenge of becoming a leader instead of a manager.

6. What are the important implications of the integrative model of leadership?

RESOURCE READINGS

Bennis, W., and B. Nanus. *Leaders: The Strategies for Taking Charge.* New York: Harper & Row, 1985.

Graen, G. "Role-Making Processes in Organizations." In *Handbook of Industrial and Organizational Psychology* ed. M. D. Dunnette. Skokie, Ill.: Rand-McNally, 1976.

Kerr, S., and J. M. Jermier. "Substitutes for Leadership: Their Meaning and Measurement." *Organizational Behavior and Human Performance* 19 (1978), pp. 370–87.

Kouzes, J. M., and B. Z. Posner. *The Leadership Challenge: How to Get Extraordinary Things Done in Organizations.* San Francisco: Jossey-Bass, 1987.

Peters, T. *Thriving on Chaos: Handbook for a Management Revolution.* New York: A. A. Knopf, 1987.

Pfeffer, J. "The Ambiguity of Leadership." *Academy of Management Review* 2 (1977), pp. 104–12.

Vroom, V. H. "Can Leaders Learn to Lead?" *Organizational Dynamics* 4 (1976), pp. 17–28.

NOTES

1. C. D. Orth, H. E. Wilkinson, and R. C. Benfari, "The Manager's Role as Coach and Mentor," *Organizational Dynamics* 15 (Spring 1987), pp. 66–74.

2. The task characteristics and the resulting questions are based on Fiedler, *A Theory of Leadership Effectiveness* (New York: McGraw-Hill, 1967); House, "A Path-Goal Theory of Leadership," *Administrative Science Quarterly* 16 (1971), pp. 321–38; and J. R. Hackman, G. Oldham, R. Janson, and K. Purdy, "A New Strategy for Job Enrichment," *California Management Review* 27 (1975), pp. 57–71.

3. G. P. Latham and T. P. Steele, "The Motivational Effects of Participation Versus Goal Setting on Performance," *Academy of Management Journal* 26 (1983), pp. 406–17.

4. J. P. Howell, P. W. Dorman, and S. Kerr, "Moderator Variables in Leadership Research," *Academy of Management Review* 11 (1986), pp. 88–102.

5. The subordinate characteristics and the resulting questions are based on Hersey and Blanchard, *Management of Organizational Behavior: Utilizing Human Resources,* 5th ed. (Englewood Cliffs, N.J.: Prentice-Hall, 1988); and House, "A Path-Goal Theory."

6. This section draws on the work of several researchers: B. M. Bass, *Leadership and Performance Beyond Expectations* (New York: Free Press, 1985); F. E. Fiedler, *A Theory of Leadership;* D. C. McClelland, "Power Is the Great Motivator," *Harvard Business Review* 54 (1976), pp. 100–10; V. H. Vroom, "Can Leaders Learn to Lead?," *Organizational Dynamics* 4 (1976), pp. 17–28.

7. R. M. Sorrentino and N. Field, "Emergent Leadership Over Time: The Functional Value of Positive Motivation," *Journal of Personality and Social Psychology* 50 (1985), pp. 1091–99.

8. F. E. Fiedler, "When to Lead, When to Stand Back," *Psychology Today* (September 1987), pp. 26–27.

9. G. H. Dobbins and S. J. Platz, "Sex Differences in Leadership: How Real Are They?" *Academy of Management Review* 11 (1986), pp. 118–27.

10. W. Bennis and B. Nanus, *Leaders: The Strategies for Taking Charge* (New York: Harper and Row, 1985).

11. This section draws on several researchers: Fiedler, *A Theory of Leadership;* B. J. Calder, "An Attribution Theory of Leadership," in *New Directions in Organizational Behavior,* ed. B. M. Staw and G. R. Salancik (Chicago: St. Clair Press, 1977), pp. 179–204; J. Pfeffer, "The Ambiguity of Leadership," *Academy of Management Review* 2 (1977), pp. 104–12.

12. Hersey and Blanchard, *Management of Organizational Behavior.*

13. G. F. Farris, "Organizational Factors and Individual Performance: A Longitudinal Study," *Journal of Applied Psychology* 53 (1969), pp. 87–92; C. N. Greene, "A Longitudinal Investigation of Modifications to a Situation Model of Leadership Effectiveness," *Academy of Management Proceedings* (1979), pp. 54–58.

14. W. A. Knowlton and T. Mitchell, "Effects of Causal Attributions on a Supervisor's Evaluation of Subordinate Performance," *Journal of Applied Psychology* 65 (1980), pp. 459–66.

15. G. H. Dobbins and J. M. Russell, "Self-Serving Biases in Leadership: A Laboratory Experiment," *Journal of Management* 12 (1986), pp. 475–83.

16. J. Pfeffer, "The Ambiguity of Leadership," in *Leadership: Where Else Can We Go,* eds. M. W. McCall and M. M. Lombardo (Durham, N.C.: Duke University Press, 1978), pp. 13–34.

17. J. R. Meindl, S. B. Ehrlich, and J. M. Dukerich, "The Romance of Leadership," *Administrative Science Quarterly* 30 (1985), pp. 78–102.

18. H. A. Simon, "Making Management Decisions: The Role of Intuition and Emotion," *Academy of Management Executive* 1 (1987), pp. 57–64.

19. G. Graen, "Role-Making Processes in Organizations," in *Handbook of Industrial and Organizational Psychology,* ed. M. D. Dunnette (Skokie, Ill.: Rand-McNally, 1976).

20. S. Kerr and J. M. Jermier, "Substitutes for Leadership: Their Meaning and Measurement," *Organizational Behavior and Human Performance* 19 (1978), pp. 370–87.

21. Howell, et al., "Moderator Variables in Leadership Research."

22. Bennis and Nanus, *Leaders.*

23. T. Peters and N. Austin, *A Passion for Excellence* (New York: Random House, 1985); T. Peters, *Thriving on Chaos* (New York: A. A. Knoff, 1987).

24. J. M. Kouzes and B. Z. Posner, *The Leadership Challenge* (San Francisco: Jossey-Bass, 1987), p. xiii.

25. Bennis and Nanus, *Leaders;* Kouzes and Posner, *The Leadership Challenge;* and R. E. Byrd, "Corporate Leadership Skills: A New Synthesis," *Organizational Dynamics* (Summer 1987), pp. 34–43.

26. T. W. Firnstahl, "Letting Go," *Harvard Business Review,* September-October 1986, pp. 14–17.

27. C. R. Leana, "Predictors and Consequences of Delegation," *Academy of Management Journal* 29 (1986), pp. 754–74.

28. K. W. Kuhnert and P. Lewis, "Transactional and Transformational Leadership: A Constructive/Developmental Analysis," *Academy of Management Review* 12 (1987), pp. 648–57.

29. J. A. Corger and R. N. Kanungo, "Toward a Behavioral Theory of Charismatic Leadership in Organizational Settings," *Academy of Management Review* 12 (1987), pp. 637–47.

CASE: The world according to John Sculley

Apple's chairman is going public—and into print—with his dreams for the company's future.

John Sculley is everywhere these days. In *Esquire,* the Apple Computer Inc. chairman shows off his favorite room, the study in his Woodside, (Calif.) home. In *Playboy,* he is the subject of a nine-page interview. Next month, he'll be in *Inc.* He'll soon be seen on talk shows, promoting his new book.

Why is the shy and reserved Sculley, who spent his childhood battling a speech impediment, unabashedly seeking the limelight? For starters, the timing is right. Points out former Apple Marketing Director Michael R. Murray: "Apple is red-hot once again, and John is maximizing his personal situation." Indeed, after two years of Sculley's leadership, the company has come a long way. The organizational chaos and inadequate products that put Apple in jeopardy in 1985 have been replaced by professional management and new Macintoshes that are grabbing a chunk of the business computer market.

Sculley insists that his new visibility isn't "just another CEO ego trip," however. He's going public to show the world what John Sculley, and his Apple, are all about—a mixture of hard-headed management and lofty vision. The combination is solid enough for big business to depend on, he says, yet an imaginative foil to a conservative International Business Machines Corp.

Source: Katherine M. Hafer, *Business Week,* September 28, 1987, pp. 71–72.

New era

Apple's new public persona is a clear departure from its offbeat past, when two kids cobbled a computer together in a Silicon Valley garage. And although his book includes a steamy blow-by-blow of his power struggle with co-founder Steven P. Jobs, Sculley hopes that what will stick with readers are his views of American business, society, and computers—especially Apple's. "This is John's way of saying Apple still has a visionary leader with ideas, that it's not a boring company now," says one Apple insider.

In that respect, Sculley is simply taking up a decade-old tradition of using the personality of Apple's leaders to identify the company in the minds of computer buyers. The marketing of John Sculley is, in large measure, the marketing of Apple. His book, *Odyssey*, coauthored by BUSINESS WEEK Management Editor John A. Byrne, has become part of a corporate-image campaign. "We've realized the book will be very good for Apple," says Jane Anderson, the Regis McKenna Inc. publicist who handles Apple. Last fall, Sculley began paying Anderson to work on the book with money from his $250,000 advance. Now Apple is picking up the tab.

Marketing himself and his ideas is nothing new to Sculley. Before being wooed to Apple by the charismatic Jobs and a $2 million first-year compensation package in 1983, the former Pepsi-Cola Co. president had earned a reputation as a consummate marketer during the Pepsi-Coke "cola wars." But instead of focusing on marketing at Apple, he immersed himself in learning the computer industry and nurturing his friendship with Jobs. After he forced Jobs out, Sculley concentrated on putting his imprint on Apple internally. He staffed the executive suite with serious-minded managers whom he either hired or picked out for promotion. Apple's chief financial officer, Deborah A. Coleman, and chief operating officer, Delbert W. Yocam, both were hired by Jobs but shepherded up the ranks by Sculley.

Over the past six months, however, the 48-year-old Wharton MBA has begun using the skills he knows best. He started by reorganizing Apple's marketing group. He wants to double sales to $5 billion in the early 1990s. To get the business customers he needs to reach that goal, he's hired top salespeople from companies such as Data General Corp. and IBM.

Polished ads

Sculley has also left his mark on Apple's advertising efforts. He dropped Chiat/Day Inc., the Los Angeles agency that created a slightly irreverent image for the young Apple. The replacement is BBDO International Inc., the Madison Avenue agency that dreamed up the "Pepsi Generation" commercials for Sculley in the 1970s. Under Phil Dusenberry, BBDO's chief creative officer and Sculley's longtime friend, the agency has produced a series of slick vignettes that dramatize the Macintosh's usefulness in business.

With his public appearances, Sculley also is working hard to show that within Apple, at least, it is possible to combine old-fashioned business discipline with creativity and innovation. "Apple is a company driven by a vision to change the world," he says. "That never wavered even during its most difficult moments." His speech is peppered with talk of visions, dreams, and journeys—terms patented by Jobs. But in place of Job's simple credo—to put computers in the hands of the masses—Sculley articulates a more convoluted vision of Apple's mission. Influenced by Apple Fellow Alan Kay, Sculley speaks of computers that will change "paradigms" for the way people work, think, learn, and communicate. The goal: for "the Information Age to create value . . . [for our] affluent, middle-class society." Concedes one insider: "It does get a bit hard to follow."

Taking risks

Chairman Sculley also is putting his stamp on the Macintosh itself, the computer that represents Jobs's most tangible legacy. Sculley has personally championed Hypercard, a database package that uses a Rolodex format. After the program had been given short shrift by Apple marketing managers, its developer, William D. Atkinson, went to Sculley, who made it his pet project. By backing Hypercard, Sculley took personal risks. He insisted on including it with each new Macintosh, despite objections by his staff and protests by some of Apple's largest independent software developers, who consider Hypercard a threat to their products.

Sculley says that Hypercard will make possible a panorama of new computer applications. Chief among them, he hopes, will be a Sculley-inspired "10th-generation Macintosh" called the Knowledge Navigator, which he describes in the final chapter of his book. Little more than a gleam in Sculley's eye at the moment, Knowledge Navigator would vastly extend the powers of a personal computer. "Everything else had already been done, or at least started, before I got to Apple," he says. "The Knowledge Navigator is something I could put my fingerprints on."

The emergence of Sculley as public personality and author might finally dispel the ghost of Jobs. For two years, Sculley has spoken of his rift with Jobs only in generalities. By finally telling his version of the story, people close to Sculley speculate, he hopes to put it to rest for good. There's a question whether the legend of the boy entrepreneur will ever die at Apple. "The religion is still Steve's, but its voice is John's," observes Esther Dyson, publisher of *Release 1.0,* an industry newsletter. "Steve is still the Messiah, but John's the Pope." Agrees Sculley: "You can't change history." But you sure can try to set its future course.

Questions

1. What do you think about John Sculley's vision for Apple?
2. What will he have to do as a leader to make his vision a reality?

CASE: The director of finance position

The government claims agency recently divided the state into four service delivery regions with a central office to oversee operations, provide technical assistance, and manage the overall fiscal affairs. The agency has placed a regional center into each of the four areas to provide the actual delivery of

Source: Adapted from a course assignment prepared by James Ward for Dr. Alan Randolph, 1987.

services to clients and lend technical assistance to community-based service providers. Each regional center has within its organizational structure a division of finance which is responsible for budgeting, accounts payable, receipt of client income, and client trust fund accounting. The operations of this department are supervised by a director of finance. The regional center organization also includes a reimbursement office which oversees the client, third party, and insurance billing activities, the generation of client unearned income, and trust account bank reconciliation procedures. Operations of this office are directed by a claims and collections officer. Within each region, the overall operation of the divisions of finance and reimbursement is under the general supervision of the same program administrator. This person also has several other service support areas for which he is responsible.

The divisions have traditionally been separate service entities within the regional organizational structure. In 1983, several changes were made that altered the structure within one region. The director of finance left to assume a new position within the center. The regional center management decided, with concurrence from central office, to combine the leadership responsibilities of the division of finance and the reimbursement officer into one position. The leadership role was assumed by the existing claims and collections officer, and his title was changed to director of finance. The decision to combine these positions was based on several considerations. A duplication of effort was evident in several of the day-to-day activities of the divisions. Management, therefore, expected to realize a better utilization of limited resources. The previous director of finance and the claims and collections officer spent a great deal of time "comparing notes" and coordinating many of their activities. Management also expected to reduce the duplication of data since both offices maintained separate financial records on each client. Regional and central office managment also expected to save money by reducing the number of high-cost positions.

Very little direction was given to the new director other than to keep the office running smoothly and get the work done. Functionally, the transition was a smooth one, and results were better than expected. Clerical and accounting staff performance increased over that experienced before the change. Work in the finance area that had been several months behind was caught up, and all work was current within five months. Some staff members were able to expand their experience base and delve into areas of the fiscal operation of the agency that had previously been closed to them.

Within one and one-half years, the director of finance was promoted to the central office division of finance. Due to the previous success, the regional center wanted to continue the concept of the combined positions and again received concurrence from the central office. The search began for a person with an unusual combination of skills, including accounting training and experience, knowledge of government reimbursement programs and strategies, budgeting skills, and microcomputer experience.

Within six months, a person with an adequate combination of existing skills and the ability to learn quickly was hired. While acquainting himself with reimbursement procedures and agency operations, he was able to further streamline the divisional activities. This regional finance office also served as the test site for a new electronic client trust fund accounting system which was placed into operation during the first three months of the new director's tenure. Even with all of these pressures, the regional office maintained its high level of production.

The conclusion reached by regional and central office management was that the combination of the two areas of functional responsibility within this area of the organization could be accomplished with good to excellent results. Expansion of the concept to other regions within the agency should prove beneficial.

A similar situation developed several months later in one of the other three regions when the director of finance decided to retire. The regional program administrator, aware of the success experienced by the first region in merging the finance and reimbursement areas, wanted to attempt such a consolidation within his program area.

The claims and collections officer in this region was a very capable individual. Jill had served in the military for several years early in her career, and she completed a government-sponsored MBA program. Prior to beginning work in the fiscal area of the region, she served as a regional personnel specialist. Immediately before starting the job as claims and collections officer, she served the region as a reimbursement officer.

Jill is recognized as being knowledgeable in the reimbursement area and has attained a reasonable level of proficiency with microcomputers. Having been a part of the agency for several years in various capacities, she understands the overall organization and its operation. It should be noted that this employee has tried unsuccessfully to move into various available positions in the regional and central offices during the past several years. Several managers have indicated that her inability to secure these positions is directly tied to problems she has in getting along well with others.

At the time the merger of the division of finance and the reimbursement office was proposed to Jill, she expressed a great deal of concern regarding the staff resources that would be available to complete the work. She was also concerned about adequate compensation for the increased responsibility and workload. However, staff members were made available to the same extent as in the region discussed earlier and, while delayed somewhat in implementation, her position was upgraded and her salary was increased.

Unfortunately, performance over the past several months has fallen short of expectations. Jill is consistently late with periodic bank reconciliations to the extent that these reconciliations are now over a year delinquent. This has resulted in audit exceptions and yields management information that is not justifiable. She is often abrasive and demanding with subordinates as well as with other staff members within the organization. The budget and accounts payable areas tend to be in a state of turmoil much of the time. Jill makes frequent demands of the central office staff to move funds among accounts in an effort to cover shortfalls in various areas. This indicates poor fiscal planning and management.

Jill also seems to have a difficult time delegating authority and assigning work to subordinates. Superiors have noted on several occasions that even after they suggest that Jill delegate a specific job, she prefers to perform the task herself rather than spend a few moments instructing a subordinate.

As noted earlier, Jill is quite proficient in certain technical aspects of the job. She has spent a great deal of time learning about the microcomputers acquired by the agency over the past two years. This has led to her becoming the regional computer "guru." In this informal capacity, she has spent many hours installing printers, diagnosing hardware and software problems, answering technical questions from less experienced users, and providing the general technical support normally supplied by the central office data processing staff or lower ranking regional support staff. Obviously, these activities severely limit the amount of time she is able to devote to managing the operation of the division of finance.

Questions

1. What is the nature of the situation faced by Jill? What leadership style should she be using?
2. Do Jill's characteristics and the organizational context inhibit her from using the desired leadership style?
3. What leadership style does Jill need from her superior?

Power and Politics in Organizational Behavior

I n the last two chapters we explored a number of leadership theories and developed an analytical, integrative model of leadership. In so doing, managers were given a tool to use in determining which of the four leadership styles is the most appropriate for a given situation. But leadership is more than simply knowing which style to use; it is being able to use that appropriate style. And it is even more than using the appropriate style. **Influencing the behavior of others—the definition of leadership—involves using power that is available to managers and understanding and using organizational politics for the good of the organization.**

THE NEED FOR POWER AND POLITICS IN ORGANIZATIONS

Some managers may not like the idea of using power and politics to influence the behavior of others. Still, power and politics are facts of life in organizations, and both power and politics can be used for good purposes as well as bad. Chapter 5 stated that to be a leader, managers must have a base of power. Chapter 9 explored how power bases can affect the choice of leadership style in a situation. Yes, **power is essential to a leader.** But this does not mean that managers have to carry a big club. There are other power sources, which we will explore in this chapter. As Kotter found in his research, successful general managers want power and are not afraid of it.[1] They use it to achieve the goals desired by the organization.

In addition to power, political behaviors are a natural part of every organization. Take, for example, a young marketing analyst just out of college. Upon landing his first job, Hank discovered that favoritism, little white lies, going outside the chain of command, and other political behaviors were rampant in the large oil company for which he worked. Being naive about organizations, Hank was shocked at these behaviors. Engineering training had taught him that rational and logical decision making was the norm in successful organizations and for effective managers. Thus, Hank left business to find a less political world—one he thought existed in universities. But again Hank was shocked to find that political behaviors were the norm in both graduate school and the universities for which he has worked since graduation. From Hank's experiences, it is evident that politics is a part of every organization. As the cartoon shown below suggests, more than logic is needed to succeed as a manager. Indeed, politics is a part of human existence—in families, churches, clubs, and wherever people operate collectively. **Politics is not always bad. It is simply a tool which people can use for the good of an organization or for personal gain.** In this chapter we will explore both the positive and negative aspects of politics in organizations.

Reprinted with special permission of King Features Syndicate, Inc.

Thus, our starting point is that power and politics in organizations are as natural and necessary as leadership. Indeed, power and politics complement leadership behaviors. **Managers cannot lead without developing bases of power to call upon.** While leadership is usually viewed as behavior that is expected in achieving organizational goals, organizations do not always work according to plan. **Political behaviors can be used to complement leadership, to deal with flaws in an organization, and to help ensure the achievement of organizational goals.** In this chapter, we will learn where power comes from in organizations and how to develop and use these bases of power. We will also learn what political behaviors are designed to achieve and why people engage in organizational politics. In so doing, we will learn how to become effective in organizations that are powerful and political, as well as rational.

POWER AND ITS SOURCES

Mention the word **power** and almost everyone has some image of what it means.[2] Many of us will think of someone negative—Muammar Gaddafi, Adolph Hitler, Al Capone, a boss who belittled us, or a teacher who embarrassed us in front of the class. But we could also think of Pope John Paul, Gandhi, President John F. Kennedy, a boss we really respected, or a teacher who was challenging and stimulating. **Power is neither good nor evil. It is simply the capacity to influence other people's behaviors.**[3] As Kanter elaborates, power is the ability "to mobilize resources, to get and use whatever is needed for the goals a person is attempting to meet."[4] Also, it is possible to use managerial power to give power to subordinates—that is, to make employees feel influential

---

INSIGHT 10–1

Chrysler Typifies the Hard Times of the Industrial Giants

*T*o understand the fall of American industrial might, you need look no further than Chrysler Corp.

Chrysler in 1979 was nearly driven to insolvency by mismanagement, stiff competition, inefficient plants, high labor costs and a relentlessly volatile economic climate. Even today, the brink remains uncomfortably close.

Their experiences dramatize, among other things, the importance of swift and decisive management action in troubled times.

Iacocca's High Marks

Bankers and suppliers give Chrysler management, particularly Lee Iacocca, high marks for aggressive and consistent leadership. He was visible and forceful, whether testifying in Congress or jabbing a finger at the American public in his television commercials. "There was a conscious strategy to put Iacocca out front, to say to the world,

"Everything's all right, Jack, come to the dealership," says a source familiar with Chrysler.

Chrysler had resorted to some desperate measures. At a press conference, it threatened to close a plant in Belvidere, Ill., if a bank near there didn't agree to the rescue plan. Company officials said that bankruptcy was just days away unless the bank fell in line. When a horde of angry workers thereupon lined up to close their accounts, the bank caved in.

Chrysler lobbied hard for the federal loan guarantees, shuttling dealers into Washington to talk to their congressmen. Before the government intervened by guaranteeing up to $1.5 billion in loans, current and former Chrysler officials insist, bankers were prepared to pull the plug. "The bankers were dragged into it by the government, kicking and screaming," a former company official says.

By Hal Lancaster and Sue Shellenbarger, *The Wall Street Journal*, January 28, 1983. Reprinted by permission of *The Wall Street Journal*, © Dow Jones & Company, Inc. 1983. All rights reserved.

---

in the organization. Indeed, powerlessness may be more harmful to productivity, morale, and feelings of managerial effectiveness than having power.[5]

The now famous situation at Chrysler described in Insight 10–1 points out the importance of "swift and decisive management action in troubled times." Could Mr. Iacocca have taken such action without a base of power? No! Indeed, this article also illustrates the political aspects of using power to influence behavior, as Chrysler did with the banks. Chapter 8 defined leadership as the process of influencing the behavior of other people or groups of people toward the achievement of organizational goals. Since power is the capacity to influence other people's behavior, it is thus necessary to the process of leadership. **Power essentially provides the resource which is the basis for leadership.** Where does a person get this resource called power? In other words, what sources are available for gaining power in organizations? As this chapter discusses, there are personal sources of power in organizations, position sources, and some organizational sources.[6]

Personal sources of power

The two most commonly recognized personal sources of power are **referent** and **expert**.[7]

Referent power comes from the admiration, respect, and identification that one person feels for another. Managers might have a reputation, personal attractiveness, or charisma that makes subordinates want to be like them. Thus, as these subordinates try to copy managers' behavior, they can give managers a great deal of power to influence their behavior. But what can managers do to develop this kind of power? Unfortunately, while referent power is based to some extent on accomplishments in the job, it is also a matter of style that may be difficult to pinpoint. For example, John Kennedy as president in the early 1960s was not responsible for passing nearly as many pieces of legislation as his successor Lyndon Johnson. But Kennedy was more revered and admired because he had that "something" which other people wanted to imitate. He exuded a great deal of confidence that many people admired and respected.

Expert power comes from a person's abilities, skills, and talents. Managers will have expert power if they can exhibit competence in performing certain aspects of the job. Perhaps a manager is especially good at analyzing and evaluating situations. As this becomes known to fellow workers, the manager will gain power to influence employees' behavior in this particular area. **Expert power is normally very limited in range in contrast to referent power which is wide in scope.** For example, a master machinist may have a great deal of expert power in the use of certain equipment in a plant. New workers and even inexperienced supervisors may yield to the advice of this expert craftsperson. However, if the company switches to computer-guided machinery that does not require the machinist's expertise, the expert power he or she once held is now greatly reduced.

Both referent and expert power are developed over time, and they can also decline over time. Before a manager's subordinates recognize their leader's expert power, the manager must show that he or she has more expertise than others that they work with—and it must be expertise in an area that employees value. For example, for a machinist to be an expert in English literature would probably not be important to workers at the plant. With referent power, the same developmental process takes place. People learn to admire managers because of what they do on their current job. Or, a manager's reputation may precede him or her on a new job. A good example of expert power is shown in Insight 10–2 on page 380. Mr. Johnson clearly impacts companies by analyzing situations and correctly moving to reorganize and/or divest for the long-term good of the company. However, when managers use expert power, they need to be right more often than not. Otherwise their expert power can quickly erode.

On the other hand, once it is established, referent power is more difficult to reduce than expert power. The two most likely ways for managers to lose referent power are for managers to do something to tarnish their attractiveness or reputation, and for someone more attractive and with more charisma to come along. On the other hand, expert power can easily be lost if managers teach others about their area of expertise. For example, if a manager tells a subordinate all she knows about a particular client, her expert power is reduced. Perhaps this is one reason why managers usually do not tell all to their subordinates. Of course, this same action could increase the manager's referent power; employees might admire a manager who uses this more participative style of leadership.

Position sources of power

French and Raven also identified three sources of power that are more attributable to the manager's position than to the person.[8]

Reward power is based on a person's ability to reward other people for desired behavior. If managers have some control over pay, promotions, time off, praise, and so forth, their subordinates will be inclined to do what managers want in order to receive these rewards. However, **the reward must be valued by the subordinate if it is to influence behavior.**

Chapter 3 made this point in discussing reinforcement theory as applied to learning. Chapters 5 and 6 also discussed using rewards as a way to motivate people. Since rewards are useful in changing people's behavior (that is, helping people learn), reward power may be most useful with new employees or with employees who are asked to learn something new in their work. The best-selling book *The One Minute Manager* emphasizes the use of praise rather than reprimand in helping employees become more effective performers, especially when they need to learn things they do not already know.[9] In other words, if employees' abilities need to be improved, managers must motivate employees to learn new behaviors. Reward power can be used very effectively in these cases.

The counterpart to reward power is **coercive power.** Coercive power is based on a person's ability to punish others for not doing what the person wants. To stop undesired behavior, managers can use punishment in the form of reprimands, reduced pay, demotion, undesirable

New Ballgame:
RJR Nabisco Is Jolted by a Boss Who Arrived through a Takeover

Johnson, 3 Weeks in Office, Is Selling the Liquor Unit and Moving Headquarters

Nowadays, in Winston-Salem, North Carolina, and at RJ Reynolds, there is little doubt about who Mr. Ross Johnson is. In the eyes of many people in this old tobacco city, he is a crafty stowaway in a Trojan horse—a man whose company, Nabisco, got acquired by RJR but who emerged to become the acquirer's chief executive.

Mr. Johnson received that title Jan. 1, a year and a half after the merger, which created a $20 billion consumer-products giant. In the past two months he has roared through RJR like a conqueror, laying waste its venerable white-collar staff and sweeping his own management team into power.

On Thursday, his 15th day as CEO, he fired an even bigger salvo: a plan to move RJR headquarters to Atlanta.

And the next day, he announced the $1.2 billion sale of RJR's Heublein Inc. wine and liquor business.

More changes seem sure to come. There could be a big acquisition before the year is out, many believe. And there is much speculation—denied by Mr. Johnson—that eventually the tobacco business will be sold or spun off.

Ross Johnson typifies a corporate phenomenon of the 1980s, what might be called the non-company man. He has little loyalty to even a venerable organization's businesses and traditions. In the name of shareholders, he has drained or sold off mother brands, moved into new lines, laid off lifelong employees.

Twice he has given up control of a company—when he merged his Standard Brands Inc. into Nabisco in 1981 and when he sold Nabisco to RJR in 1985. But in each case, the surrender of control was temporary. In all, the 55-year-old executive has three times slashed through somewhat stodgy companies, shaking up or ousting their managements. At all three companies, Mr. Johnson has won directors' support, even for moves as sudden and publicly unpopular as RJR's departure from Winston-Salem.

Quick Study

Thomas A. Gray, a descendant of one of RJR's leading families, is horrified by some of Mr. Johnson's early actions. And he fears for the effects on his native Winston-Salem. But as a shareholder, he says the new regime "is probably in the end going to be a good thing for the company."

Executives who have worked with Mr. Johnson describe him as decisive and a wizard with numbers. "He is the only person I've ever met who can, in five or 10 minutes in a budget presentation, understand my budget better than I did after studying it for two weeks," says John Gora, the president of Chuckles Co., a former Nabisco unit sold to management last year.

But much of his success, friends and co-workers think, comes by dint of personality. "He is a charmer, a raconteur, a real knee-slapping kind of guy," says Philip L. Thomas, once a public-relations consultant to Mr. Johnson. "He can walk among land mines, and they never go off."

work assignments, termination, and so forth. **But the punishment must be viewed negatively by the subordinate if it is to have the desired effect.** For example, a manager might reprimand an employee only to find the employee thankful for receiving attention that was lacking in the past. Thus, the undesired behavior may continue.

Chapter 3 discussed punishment as it relates to learning and to motivation. As pointed out, punishment has the disadvantage of working only to eliminate undesirable behavior. Employees still have to learn to do what is desired. Of course, if employees already know what to do, the threat of coercive power may make them perform as desired. As *The One Minute Manager* suggests, a reprimand is appropriate when dealing with a better employee who has let a manager down. **The key is to use the reprimand on the employee's behavior and couple it with praise of the employee as a valuable asset to the organization.**

The final source of power proposed by French and Raven was **legitimate power.** Legitimate power is based on the perception that a person has the right to influence behavior because of his or her position in the organizational hierarchy. This power base also includes the perception that subordinates are obligated to obey managers. Clearly, legitimate power is based on the position of the manager in relation to the position of the subordinate. For example, it is generally recognized that an Army drill sergeant has the right to tell trainees what to do and that the trainees have an obligation to obey the drill sergeant.

Since legitimate power is based on a manager's position in an organization relative to others around him or her, it has a developmental aspect. As people move up the ranks of the organization, they will gain in legitimate power. A general has more legitimate power than a major, who has more legitimate power than a lieutenant. Conversely, a person's legitimate power can be reduced if he or she is assigned to a position that is perceived to have less influence and status within the organization. For example, if a person moves from the engineering department in a highly technical organization to the personnel department, his or her legitimate power may be reduced.

Another aspect of legitimate power is the area of responsibility within which managers have the right to make decisions. As long as they remain within the perceived zone of their legitimate power, they can use this source of power to influence the behavior of employees. If managers move outside this zone, however, their power drops off rapidly. For example, managers may have the legitimate power to get employees to work overtime, but they may not have the power to make employees use a company's product in their personal lives. For example, some people who work for Chrysler drive Fords.

Much as been written about how managers' range of influence over their employees has declined over the last several decades. In the early 1900s, before the days of union influence, the limits to managerial legitimate power were very few. As unions gained in strength, however, they reduced this power by giving employees a strong voice to counter unreasonable managerial requests. And during the 1960s, a cultural revolution brought into question many of the rights that managers had previously assumed.[10] Today, employees feel that they have certain rights, and these rights limit the legitimate power of managers. A number of changes in the workplace have reduced the legitimate power of lower-level managers and supervisors. Computers have taken away part of their job. A **worth ethic** has developed to replace the old work ethic.[11] Employees feel they have worth beyond their jobs and thus feel obligated to follow only those orders that relate directly to their jobs and that demonstrate respect for them as individuals. However, the recession of the 1980s tended to increase the perceived legitimate power of managers because employees were more concerned about job security than they had been during the 1960s and 1970s. These events should make it clear that legitimate power is susceptible to change, both increasing and decreasing. Legitimate power is also influenced by societal events and by movement through the hierarchy.

In a moment, we will take a look at Home Computers Company to see power in operation. But first, take a few minutes to complete the PBS—Self questionnaire at the end of this chapter to find out which sources of power appeal most to you. There is no one best answer, so be honest with yourself. By answering and scoring this questionnaire, you will gain insight into yourself in terms of these five power sources, plus relations power, discussed later in this chapter. You will determine which ones you may like to rely on and which ones you may be ignoring.

Home Computers Case

The Home Computers Case—Rob and Tom

Both Rob and Tom have worked as production engineers for HCC since joining the company in 1979 in the Dayton, Ohio, plant. They both graduated from Ohio State University with degrees in engineering in 1979 and immediately joined HCC. Until 1984, Rob's and Tom's careers were remarkably similar. Starting out as first-line supervisors on the production line for the EZ2 computer, both Rob and Tom demonstrated an ability to get the job done. Furthermore, they both learned a great deal about the internal workings of the computer and about the history of Home Computers Company.

But there are some differences in the way they each have operated and how they are perceived. Rob always praises his employees for their good work. Furthermore, he uses every opportunity to get raises for his employees. His people seem to have a great deal of respect and admiration for Rob. They also put out a good effort and typically beat their quota in both quantity and quality. On the other hand, Tom comes down hard on his employees when they make a mistake and is seldom seen giving them a pat on the back for a job well done. Tom expects a good job and does not reward his people for doing only what is expected. Tom believes that he should reward employees only for doing something above and beyond the call of duty. Tom's people do what he says partly out of fear and partly because they respect the company. The result is a good product, but sometimes Tom has problems in terms of quality—especially when he has to be away from the floor for some reason.

In 1984, Rob was promoted based on his outstanding record as a supervisor, to the job of section head. As section head Rob was responsible for the work of several first-line supervisors, including Tom. Rob and Tom had been good friends, but their relationship was now altered by their status difference within the company. As section head, Rob continued to operate much as he had as a supervisor, relying on his technical expertise, the respect he had gained in the company, and his praising of employees. As often happens, Rob found that his promotion gave him more control over rewards and punishments in the organization. Furthermore, it seemed that his employees showed even greater respect for him than they had previously.

Tom, however, was disappointed about not receiving the promotion himself. He decided to show the company that he was really better suited for the job than Rob was. He knew that as a section head Rob would be dependent on the first-line supervisors for information important for the decisions he would have to make. Tom also knew that Rob's connections with the other supervisors might be weakened due to the normal distance between supervisors and section heads. Tom thus began to withhold certain information from Rob and to make comments to the other supervisors about how Rob was not representing their best interests. Indeed, this was true, since Rob did not have all of the information he needed to make the best decisions. In fact, Tom would sometimes introduce the missing information at important supervisors' meetings. As he introduced this information, Tom was always sure to talk about how he wanted to help the company achieve its goals. Rob was often caught off guard.

After awhile, Rob began to feel as though he were out to sea in a boat without a paddle. Many activities in his section occurred without his involvement, and his weakened position with the supervisors also weakened his position with superiors. It was clear to Rob's superiors that he had talent and was generally liked by his people, but he was not getting the job done. Both the quality and quantity of computers produced by his people were declining. It was not long before the decision was made to move Rob into the personnel department and to promote Tom into the section head position. Tom quickly held a supervisors' meeting to ensure them he wanted their ideas and suggestions—he would be a different leader from Rob.

After a year in these positions, Rob again demonstrated his ability to get a job done. Tom was also doing a good job, though he did not appear to be popular with his employees.

THE POWER SOURCES IN ACTION

It is not enough to merely have a strong power base; power must be used if it is to influence the behavior of others. If we stop to analyze the Home Computers case, we can identify the sources of power used by Rob and Tom. Both Rob and Tom appear to have expert power in the job of first-line supervisor. They know what to do, and they get it done. They understand both the product and the company. Since they both had the same position to start, they had the same amount of legitimate, reward, and coercive power; these depend on the position more than the person. However, the extent to which Rob and Tom relied on these three sources of power does vary. Tom relied more on coercive power, whereas Rob relied more on reward power. In using these different power bases, Rob and Tom were using the legitimate power they had to act in a supervisory role. Rob appears to have had more referent power than Tom, and this may be because of greater reliance on reward power, as opposed to coercive power. Indeed, the interactions among these five sources of power must also be considered.

Interactions among the power sources

As managers use their power bases, they usually find that the way they use one power base influences the other power sources. For example, Rob's use of reward power seemed to enhance his referent power, while Tom's use of coercive power seemed to reduce his referent power. However, if Rob had rewarded desired behavior and punished undesired behavior, his expert power would have increased. He would have demonstrated his ability to specify desired behaviors and to distinguish between desired and undesired behaviors.

Also, Rob's promotion, which increased his legitimate power, initially increased his referent power. Increases in legitimate power can also result in an increased expert power if people assume that promotions are based upon good performance on the job. For example, the best salesperson in a territory gets promoted to sales manager, thus increasing the perception that this person has expertise as a sales manager. Finally, referent power can cause an increase in all other sources of power. If managers are admired and respected, coworkers are more likely to assume they are an expert and that they effectively use both rewards and punishments. There are also some other important aspects of power that can be learned from the Home Computers case.

Organizational sources of power

In addition to legitimate, reward, coercive, expert, and referent power, the case illustrates several other important sources of power. First, Tom used **information power** to create problems for Rob and gain his own goal of a promotion. Information power is based on a person's access to information or knowledge that is of value to others.[12] In any managerial job, information is important for coping with the uncertainty that exists. Those people who through their knowledge and information can help ensure a smooth flow of work in an organization are perceived as more powerful because of the uncertainty they control. It is clear that once he was promoted, Rob's lack of information diminished his ability to manage the production of high-quality computers. Rob could not cope with the uncertainty in the job, and his power was thus reduced.

Tom also used **connection power,** which is based on a person's links with important and influential people in the organization.[13] His connections with the other supervisors allowed him to discredit some of the legitimate and referent power Rob had. Connection power can also be used to gain influence over another person because of that person's desire to gain favor from someone with whom a manager is connected. In his book *The General Managers,* Kotter talks about network building, which is very similar to developing connection power.[14] Managers need to build a network of people to help carry out agendas and plans.

Another source of power closely related to connection power is one discovered through research on the five French and Raven bases of power. It is called **relations power,** and it has to do with the nature of the relationship between two people. If managers are good listeners, show they care about people's nonwork life, and act essentially as a friend, they gain a certain power with employees. For example, is a person more likely to do a favor for a close friend or an acquaintance? The answer is pretty clear, and the reason is relations power. You may want to look again at the power questionnaire at the end of this chapter to reflect on your relations power score.

One final source of power is **resource power,** which is best defined as "the person who controls the gold makes the rules." To the extent that managers control employees, money, equipment, supplies, raw materials, customers, and so forth, they will have influence over the behavior of others.[15] In the Home Computers case, for example, if Rob as section head had been the key contact with a particular supplier of a critical part for the computers, Rob's centrality in the access to this resource would have greatly increased his power. If, on the other hand, he held no such critical position (as was apparently the case), he would not have any great degree of resource power. Another aspect of resource power is the degree to which it is easy to replace the resource provided by a manager. If it is easy to substitute for the resource or to get it from other managers, then a manager's resource power will be diminished. In fact, some managers go to great lengths to ensure that there is something unique about their contribution to the organization just so they have greater resource power. For example, it is not hard to imagine that Tom tried to develop information that was both critical and unique to him in order to strengthen his position relative to Rob's position.

Some other important aspects of power

Another aspect of power evident from the Home Computers case is that power is dynamic. When Rob was promoted, his legitimate power increased, but his expertise as a manager was not as great as his expertise as a supervisor. Recall from Chapter 2 that as people move up the organizational hierarchy, there is a decreasing need for technical skill and an increasing need for conceptual and administrative skill. Thus, after his promotion, Rob's expert power was based on a different area—managerial expertise. His managerial expertise was apparently lower than his technical expertise, and this created problems for Rob.

Managers have to be aware of the development and erosion of power bases over time. A popular book from some years back titled *Power: How to Get It, How to Use It*, details the two sides of this coin of developing and keeping power.[16] Some ways of doing this follow.

1. Try to put yourself in a position to deal with critical issues affecting the organization.

2. Try to gain control over resources that are valued by others.

3. Demonstrate your ability to deal effectively with organizational problems.

4. Try to gain a position in the organization which is central to the work flow.

5. Make sure you develop some unique aspects to your contribution to the organization.

6. Demonstrate behaviors that will be admired and respected by others.

7. Be sure that you are as successful as possible when you use your power bases.[17]

SUCCESSFUL USE OF POWER

As we have said, it is not enough merely to have power. Managers must use it and use it well. To use power successfully, managers will have to recognize a number of things.[18]

First, managers must recognize the power sources that are available and develop them for their use. In so doing, managers will need to use the power they have to help develop other power bases. For example, a manager may be able to use his or her expert power in a position to gain a promotion which will yield greater legitimate and referent power.

Second, managers must recognize whether they have a tendency to shy away from using power. Some research in particular has suggested that women have a slight tendency to use power less frequently than men even when the power available to both is equal.[19] What managers

"Sorry you can't come any closer, but that's the way my power consultant wants it."

© Sidney Harris

have to realize is that power is essential to being a leader. They should not be afraid to use the power they have and to develop other sources of power, as well. Remember, if managers have power and do not use it, they lose it.

A third point is that if a situation is uncertain and marked by scarce resources, managers can expect that resource power will be used. These situations will be appropriate times to use the power managers have—unless they perceive others to have greater power. In that case, managers may decide to save their power for another situation where they have a greater chance of influence.

Fourth, managers must recognize that there are costs to using power. Managers may lose the issue at hand; they may lose some of their power; or they may create long-term negative effects if they use power inappropriately. If managers are going to use power—especially if it is political—they need to win. And if managers lose, they should lose with finesse. But remember, too, that managers have a responsibility to use power in an ethical way and in ways that benefit an organization and society as a whole. All bases of power can be abused. It is up to each manager to decide whether he or she will abuse them or not.

Fifth, successful managers constantly work to develop additional power sources and to shore up the ones they have. Over a range of situations, managers will probably have occasion to use many sources of power. Therefore, **managers need as many sources of power as possible, and they must know when to use each one.** For example, former Secretary of State Shultz used expert and referent power, while staying within the limits of his legitimate power (see Insight 10–3). Also, Mr. Shultz used his power effectively throughout his tenure as secretary of state. A recent counter example where referent power was misused is the Jim and Tammy Bakker scandal at the PTL Club. The admiration and respect afforded the Bakkers by PTL followers were exploited to great personal advantage by the Bakkers.

Fortunately, a specific connection between power bases and leadership styles has been made by Hersey and Blanchard.[20] They suggest that if leaders manage people who are low in ability and motivation, leaders need to rely more on coercive power in order to achieve compliance (see Exhibit 10–1 on page 390). This coercive power will help managers establish a high-task/low-relationship style of leadership. As shown in Exhibit 10–1, for subordinates who are at a medium-low level of ability and motivation, first connection power and then reward power become important means of influence. A manager's connection with powerful people in an organization is important to these subordinates as they become interested in better performance. And managers' use of rewards can encourage them to continue to improve their performance.

As Exhibit 10–1 shows, legitimate power is important in this middle range of subordinate ability and motivation. Unless employees believe

I N S I G H T 10–3

The State of State:
Shultz's Logical Style Wins Him High Marks at Home and Overseas

As debate in the meeting developed, Mr. Shultz quietly pulled out a piece of paper and began jotting down a list of specific agricultural trade issues each side mentioned. Finally, he spoke up and proposed a solution: Rather than debate trade philosophy, both sides should examine the list of detailed complaints to see whether they could find practical solutions. His suggestion evolved into an agreement to undertake an intensive joint study of agricultural exports. The two sides emerged and announced that they had averted a full-blown trade war.

That incident typifies the Shultz style: cool, methodical, logical. Some would call it uninspiring. But the style is making Mr. Shultz a success, in the eyes of most U.S.

and foreign officials, after five months in office. It has enabled him not only to ease serious squabbles with the European allies but also to pilot through administration councils big foreign-policy initiatives like the Middle East peace plan. And his mastery at piecing together a consensus and mediating disputes has prompted the White House to pull him into domestic budget deliberations.

Reporters accompanying the secretary on his European trip suggest that he appears more animated and sure-footed when discussing domestic economic matters than when talking about foreign policy. Still, Mr. Shultz's restrained style makes it unlikely he will throw his weight around on domestic issues. Aides predict he will avoid the risk of antagonizing people who could hurt him on his own foreign-policy turf.

managers have the right to be the decision makers, it is unlikely they will respect managers' desires as managers move from the position types of power to the personal types. Indeed, at the medium-high level of ability and motivation, Hersey and Blanchard suggest that referent power is the appropriate source to draw on, assuming managers have developed referent power. In using a high-relationship/low-task style of leadership, managers are, to some extent, giving up the use of their position as a means of influence. Therefore, people must respect a manager if he or she is to have influence as a supporting leader.

Finally, for employees of high ability and motivation, a manager's power base must be one of information and expertise. Without these, subordinates will be doubtful of the goals and problems a manager delegates to them. By using the appropriate power base, managers can have more confidence in achieving desired results. Of course, if managers do not possess some of the power bases, this can limit their ability to effectively use the appropriate leadership style.

Other research on the five power bases from French and Raven, plus relations power, has suggested that the proposed relationships in Ex-

EXHIBIT 10–1

Power Bases and Leadership Styles

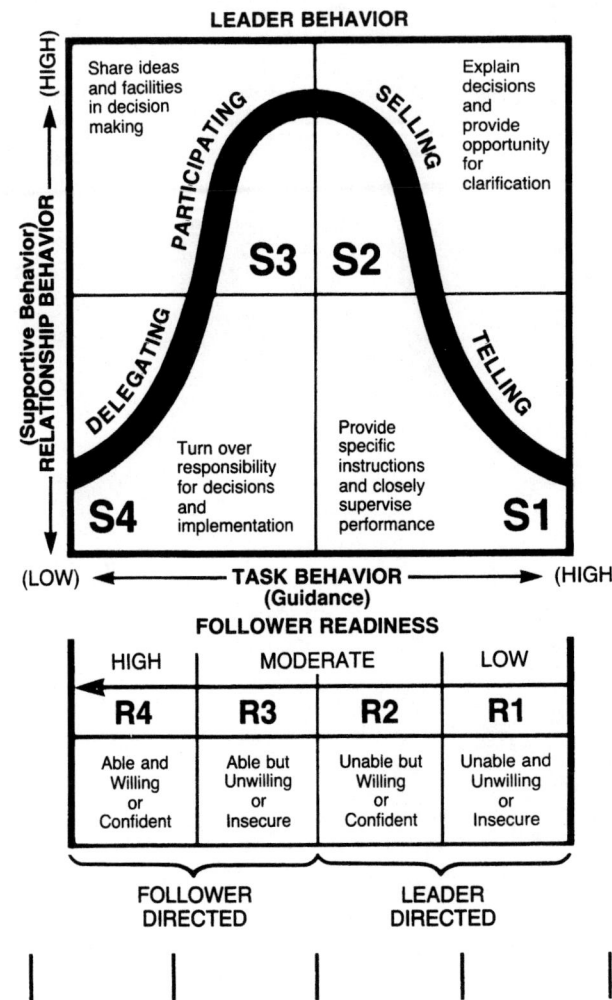

Source: Adapted from P. Hersey and K. Blanchard *Management of Organizational Behavior* 5th ed. (Englewood Cliffs, N.J.: Prentice-Hall, 1988) pp. 171, 218.

hibit 10–1 may not be entirely accurate.[21] Exhibit 10–2 shows the results of this research, which was drawn only from practicing managers. The model suggests that reward power is the most important with all four leadership styles. For Style 1 (directing), it appears that legitimate and expert power are more important than coercive power. However, this does make sense given that with the directing style of leadership a leader wants the follower to be receptive to the directions being given. For Styles 2 and 3 (coaching and supporting) after reward power, the same three power bases come into play, though the order is somewhat different. For Style 2, the order is referent, expert, and relations. For Style 3, expert power is ahead of referent power. This makes sense given that in the coaching style, the leader wants the follower to be participative, and referent power would be important to get the follower to open

EXHIBIT 10–2

Power Bases and Situational Leadership

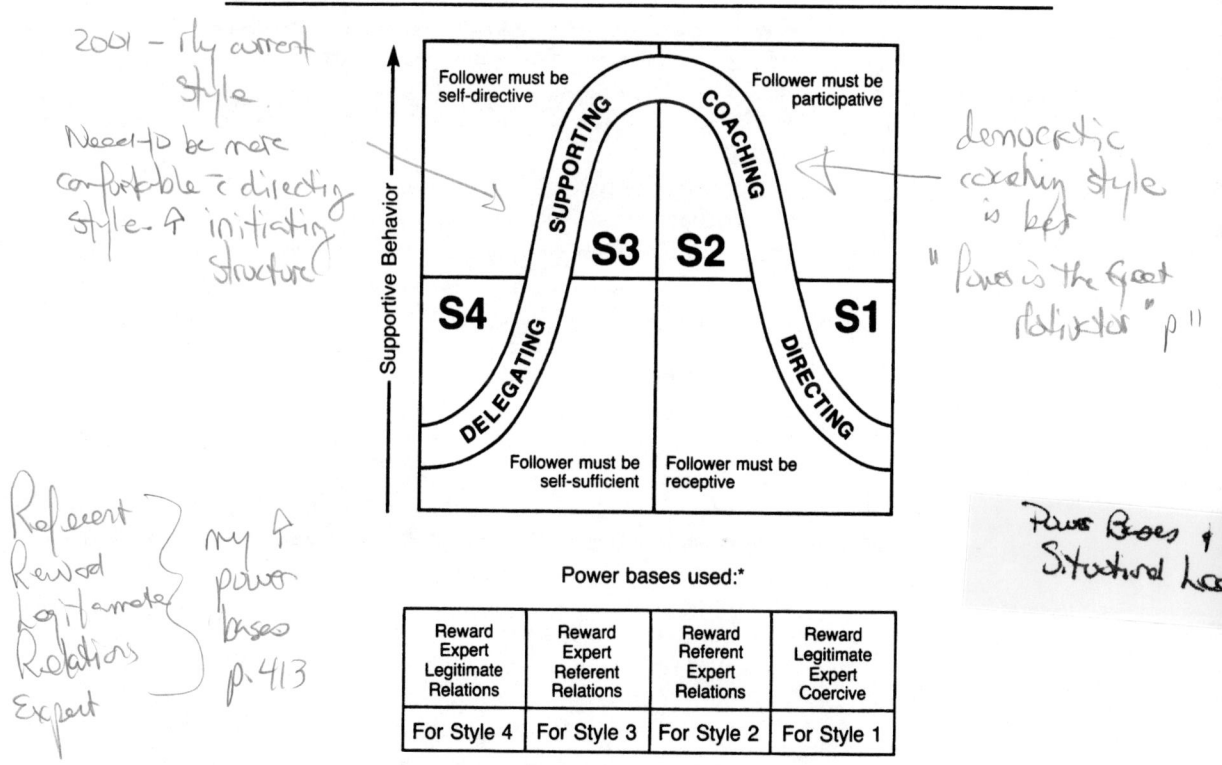

Power bases used:*

Reward Expert Legitimate Relations	Reward Expert Referent Relations	Reward Referent Expert Relations	Reward Legitimate Expert Coercive
For Style 4	For Style 3	For Style 2	For Style 1

*The power bases are listed in order of decreasing importance.

Source: Unpublished research by W. Alan Randolph.

up. For the supporting style of leadership, the leader wants the follower to be self-directive, and expert power will be important for knowing when to let the follower be self-directed and to inspire the follower's confidence to forge ahead.

Finally, for Style 4 (delegating), expert power again follows reward in importance. Interestingly, legitimate power then pops up, followed by relations power. At first this may seem strange, but for the follower to be self-sufficient, the leader must give him or her the authority to operate. And to grant authority, managers must have it—as in legitimate power.

However, Exhibit 10–2 is not the final answer. It merely provides additional data for consideration. Further research will help managers resolve this important issue. For now, reflection and discussion with others will help us grapple with the issue of which power bases are needed to effectively use the four leadership styles.

Possible reactions to power

Before we end this section on power, let us briefly consider the potential outcomes of using power. There are basically four responses managers can expect from people when they use power to influence employees' behavior: compliance, identification, internalization, and alienation.[22] Which one managers get will depend upon whether they have used the power base appropriate to the situation. A discussion of the four reactions follows.

Compliance (or **calculative behavior** as Etzioni calls it) is based on a subordinate's response to a manager's use of rewards and punishments. The employee tries to engage in behavior that will maximize the receipt of rewards and minimize the receipt of punishments. For example, if a manager asks his employees to work overtime to finish a project, they may do it because they expect extra pay or recognition or because they fear the consequences if they say no. The employees are complying with the manager's request because of the sanctions he or she controls, not necessarily because they agree with what the manager wants them to do.

A second response to a manager's use of power is **identification**. Subordinates may follow a request because they admire or respect their manager. Employees may hope that carrying out a manager's request will result in further improvement in their relationship. Employees may also feel that their manager would work late to finish a project. They are therefore willing to do the same because of a desire to be like the manager. Referent power is strongly at work in this case.

Internalization is the third response to a manager's assertion of power, and it is based on a congruence between a manager's request and the subordinates' values and priorities. Thus, Etzioni calls this response *moral*. When a manager asks someone to work late, the subordinate sees that this is needed and feels a responsibility to get the project done right and on time. The employee does not think about receiving a reward or about the manager–employee relationship. The allegiance here is to the project. Even if the manager had not made the request, the employee might have stayed late if he or she knew the deadline might be missed. Most likely, this response would be coupled with a manager's use of expert and information power, and it is also consistent with a delegating type of leadership.

The final response is one that managers hope to avoid in using power: **alienation** of the employee. Especially with the use of coercive power, managers must be careful to avoid alienating their subordinates. If a manager frequently demands that people work late and threatens them if they do not, the manager will likely destroy relationships and build up alienation. In the long run, managers will have to pay the price for such alienation by losing good people, failing to get good work, or other undesirable outcomes.

Exhibit 10–3 summarizes the discussion up to this point. Nine sources of power are shown along with four possible reactions to the use of power. It should be clear that managers would want to avoid the alienation response. Instead, managers would like to see the internalization response so they can do more delegating and thus be freed for other activities. But compliance and identification can also be useful responses as managers move people along the develop-

EXHIBIT 10–3

Power, Its Sources and Possible Reactions

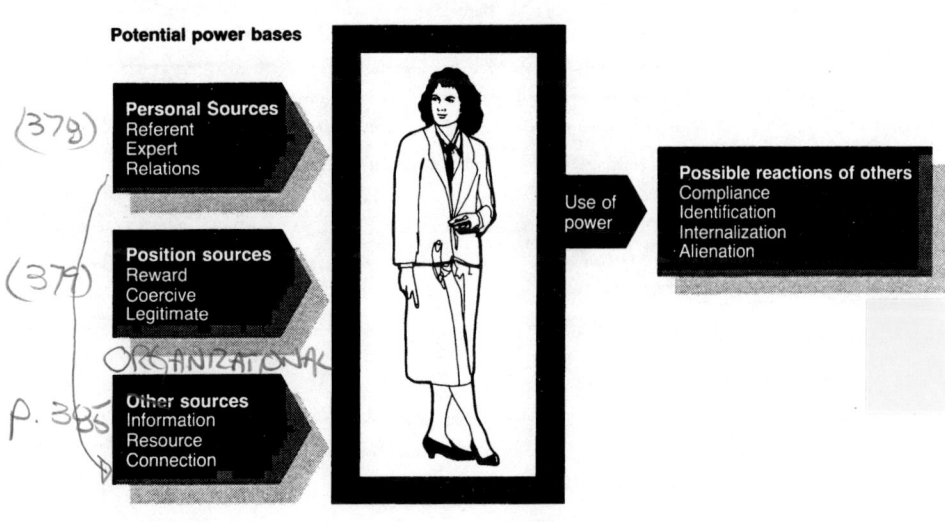

mental curve in the leadership model discussed in Chapter 9. The key is to have all of the power sources available and to use each one at the appropriate time.

POLITICAL BEHAVIORS

In addition to power and its use in organizations, we also need to think about political behaviors.[23] Politics in organizations is an important element in a manager's use of power sources. Indeed, understanding and using politics is essential for anyone who hopes to have a successful career as a manager.[24] Like power, politics can also be used to help accomplish organizational goals or to achieve personal goals at the expense of the organization. **Political behaviors are as common in organizations as are leadership behaviors.**

Everyone probably has his or her own definition of organizational politics. Some people define politics as "ways to get ahead in an organization."[25] Others define it more broadly as a "dynamic process of influence that produces organizationally relevant outcomes beyond the simple performance of job tasks."[26] In this text, organizational politics is **the management of influence to obtain ends not sanctioned by the organization or to obtain sanctioned ends through nonsanctioned influence means.**[27] As with leadership, political behaviors involve using the power bases a person has. The following sections explore these political behaviors in more detail.

Defining political behaviors

The broad definition of organizational politics used here points out the possibility that politics can be used for or against the organization and its members. Furthermore, this definition emphasizes that we need to consider both **ends** and **means** (that is, goals and behaviors) as critical factors in organizational politics. A good example of the distinction between means and ends is shown in Insight 10–4. The means (tactics) of the Soviets appear to be approved by the international community, but the ends remain in question. Such consideration of both ends and means helps managers determine when politics are positive or negative. Exhibit 10–4, on page 396, depicts the four cells that follow from combining the two dimensions of ends and means.

In Exhibit 10–4, both cells 1 and 3 lead to functional behavior as far as the organization is concerned. Cell 1 describes the behavior that is expected in an organization. The ends and the means are both sanctioned by the organization. This type of influence characterizes the leadership behaviors discussed in the last two chapters. The influence is nonpolitical.

I N S I G H T 10–4

Moscow's Mood:
Soviet Summit Tactics Reflect
Gorbachev Bid to Firm Grip on Party

Recent Steps on Arms Talks Are Viewed
as PR Moves Rather Than Policy Shifts

General Secretary's Iron Teeth

*B*onn—Soviet diplomats, journalists and scientists have been knocking on doors here in West Germany over the past few weeks, making the rounds like traveling salesmen testing a new product.

What is your reaction to our moratorium on underground testing? Was the American response of inviting us to watch their test adequate? What did you think of General Secretary Gorbachev's interview with the American magazine *Time*? What are your country's reservations about President Reagan's Star Wars program?

Unusual Activity

"The Soviets have entered their most active foreign-policy period for years," Mr. Voigt, Social Democratic Party spokesman, says. "Their people are measuring response to their policies and preparing new initiatives. They are doing their homework well, and their tactics at the moment are more flexible than those of the United States."

The question in everyone's mind, however, is whether the Soviet moves are merely propaganda. Although details of the Soviet's latest arms-reduction proposal at Geneva are still vague, U.S. negotiators are dissecting them to judge how much of the offer

might involve genuine concessions. The optimists believe that the economics-minded Mr. Gorbachev might finally be willing to concede points at the table in order to free resources to solve domestic problems, but even they warn that the Soviets will try to win a maximum of propaganda points with a minimum of concessions.

The Internal Motives

West European experts say Soviet foreign policy rarely if ever changes; only the tactics change. The aim of advancing the world-wide cause of communism remains Moscow's moving force, but the measures now are more sophisticated and nicely packaged. However, West Europeans with intimate knowledge of the Soviet Union say that the only way to properly understand Moscow's current approach is to recognize that Mr. Gorbachev's highest priority isn't the November summit but a meeting far more crucial to his future: the Communist Party Congress in February.

Before he can fully put his personal stamp on foreign and economic policy, he must extend his control over the Soviet apparatus by consolidating his hold of the party's lower-level leadership. He will be less interested in genuine concessions that would lead to superpower agreements in Geneva than in building an international image that will help free his hand internally.

EXHIBIT 10–4

Dimensions of Organizational Politics

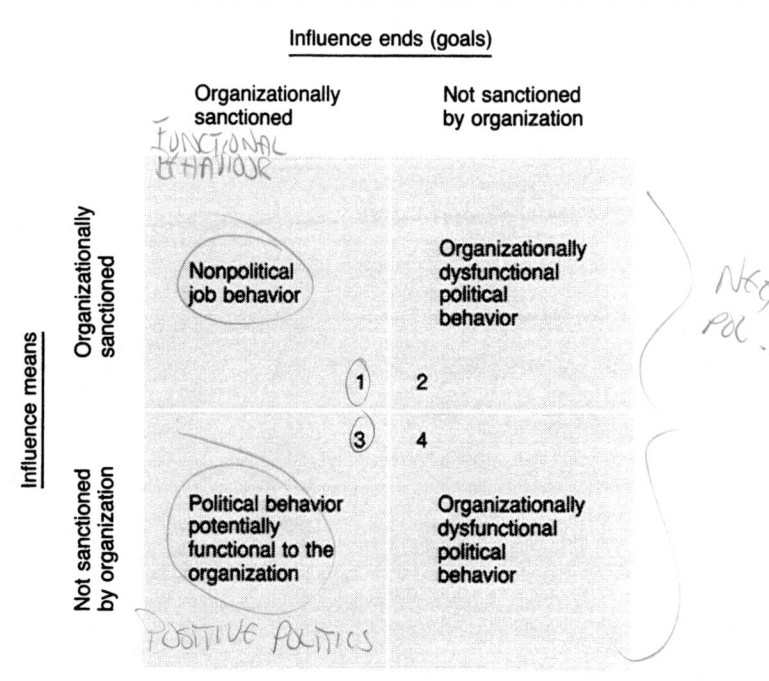

Source: B. T. Mayes and R. W. Allen, "Toward a Definition of Organizational Politics," *Academy of Management Review*, Volume 2 (1977) p. 675.

Cell 3 describes means (behaviors) that are not sanctioned (that is, approved and expected) by the organization, but they are geared toward ends sanctioned by the organization. For example, perhaps a manager needs some critical information from one of the salespeople in the field. The sanctioned means are to go through channels up to the manager's boss, then across to the sales manager, and then down to the salesperson from whom the manager needs information. The information would then reverse this path back to the manager. The manager knows this will take several days at best, and she needs the information by tomorrow for an analysis she is completing. So what does the manager do? She picks up the telephone and calls the salesperson directly. In so doing, the manager intrudes on the salesperson's time without approval from his or her boss. So while the manager's goal is proper, her behavior might be questioned by some. The manager's behavior is clearly political, but this kind of behavior is often called *positive politics*.

Cells 2 and 4 in Exhibit 10–4 both depict behaviors that are geared toward goals which are not sanctioned by the organization (that is, negative politics). Perhaps in this case the manager is more concerned about how he will appear in the situation than about accomplishing the organization's goals. At Home Computers Company, Tom's behavior could be classified as political, falling into one of these two cells. His goal was to achieve the position that Rob got—even if it meant discrediting Rob and hurting the organization in the process. But did Tom's actions fall in cell 2 or cell 4?

Cell 2 portrays behavior that is sanctioned by the organization, even though the goals are not. Hence, the political behavior is more covert. On the other hand, cell 4 portrays both behavior and goals which are dysfunctional to the organization, that is, more overt political behavior. It would appear, then, that Tom's behavior fell in cell 4. He withheld important information from Rob and tried to discredit him with the other supervisors. As a result, the organization suffered in terms of both quality and quantity, even though Tom got his promotion. And certainly all managers meet such people in their career, as well—people who put their self-interests above the organization or anyone else.

A recent article in *Organizational Dynamics* relates to this issue from the point of view of ethics.[28] Whenever managers engage in political behaviors, they must remain ethical; otherwise, they become destructive to the organization. The long-term welfare of the organization is threatened; battle lines are drawn; and organizations begin to come apart at the seams. Leaders have the responsibility to constantly make explicit the discussion of values and behaviors that do not lead to the abuse of power and politics. And it is important for managers to understand political behaviors so they can counteract the efforts of individuals who become destructive to the organization.

Notice that one strong point of this four-cell definition of political behaviors is that it is not culture-bound. By addressing the question of what means and ends are sanctioned by an organization, managers can take into account different cultural bases. For example, in the United States, pursuing a goal sanctioned by an organization by using kickbacks to customers (a nonsanctioned means) would place the action in cell 3 (functional political behavior for the organization though some people might say it was illegal). In Italy, on the other hand, such kickbacks are considered normal, legal ways of doing business (hence sanctioned means), which places the action in cell 1 (nonpolitical behavior).

Let us now use the definition of organizational politics to look at some typical political behaviors, as well as why people engage in politics and what types of people are most likely to be political in organizations. But first, turn to the end of this chapter and complete and score the Political Behavior Inventory. As with the power questionnaire, there are no right or wrong answers, so just be honest with yourself, and see how political you might be.

Typical political behaviors

What are the most typical behaviors used by managers? In a study conducted in 1979, managers at several levels were asked about typical political behaviors in their organizations.[29] The ones mentioned most often were:

1. Attacking or blaming others.
2. Selective use of information.
3. Image building.
4. Developing a base of support.
5. Praising others.
6. Coalitions with strong allies.
7. Creating obligations for others.

The first political behavior, **attacking or blaming others,** should be fairly obvious. This is one way that coercive and information power can be used. Blaming another person for a problem puts the person on the defensive from the start. Often this tactic is used with a third party, when the person being blamed is not present. Thus, the opportunity for the accused to present a defense is greatly hampered. The third party, who is probably influential in the organization, has formed an opinion before even speaking to the person who was blamed.

The **selective use of information** means that a person controls what information is in the hands of others and when it reaches them. Clearly, this behavior uses information power, and others become dependent upon the person who uses information in this manner. By timing the release of information and weighing the choice of information, a person can obviously distort the perception that others will form from the information. For example, some of the information Tom withheld from Rob in the Home Computers case might have been brought up at a meeting between Rob and the production managers just as Rob was about to make a decision that could have been altered by this information. By introducing the information at this time, Tom made Rob look unprepared, while he appeared to have helped the department avoid a serious mistake. Tom thus earned respect from his peers at the expense of Rob—a form of negative politics.

Image building is the process of appearing to always do the right thing at the right time. It relies on referent power while also enhancing referent power. For example, a person may be out for personal gain (even at the expense of the organization), but he constantly cites organizational goals as the reason for his behavior. This person may also be very careful to understand and adhere to the norms of the organization and to the preferences of the boss. Thus, the person appears to be doing things for the good of the organization, while he is really upgrading his own image.

Establishing a base of support is the process of gathering people and resources to back a person up in times of critical decisions. By doing favors for others, feeding superiors critical information and building relationships with key people, some people develop a network of supporters. As Kotter noted in his book, network building is a primary means for implementing the goals people wish to accomplish.[30] A person who builds a reputation in the eyes of others, makes them feel obligated to him, makes them feel dependent on him, and encourages them to identify with him by praising them, can develop a network that will support his efforts. Indeed, this base of support builds a person's connection and resource bases of power.

Praising others is one means of building a relationship with them. By complimenting them, they are more likely to repeat those behaviors (as discussed in both Chapters 3 and 5). Furthermore, managers develop the kind of referent power that is desired by political actors. People do the things a manager wants because they like and admire the manager. Praising others can be negative politics when managers do it to benefit themselves and simply build up their referent power. But praising others can be positive politics if managers use it to complement limited financial rewards and thus help accomplish organizational goals.

Forming coalitions with powerful people in an organization is primarily a means for increasing a manager's connection and legitimate power. By doing things for powerful people in the organization, a manager can become a part of the coalition whose members do things to help each other. This association with those in power will make others perceive the manager as more powerful. It will appear that what the manager wants to do is what the coalition wants to do, and she is less likely to encounter resistance in achieving her goals and agendas. This, too, is part of the network process described by Kotter.[31] Of course, a manager can form coalitions to help achieve organizational goals (positive politics) or simply to advance his or her career (negative politics).

The final tactic to discuss is **creating obligations from others.** By doing a favor for someone, a manager builds up a credit or an IOU that can be called in at a later date. Thus, the manager may get someone to support an idea by supporting one of his or hers. Obviously, the manager will have to keep tabs on the balance of credits and debits in the political account to avoid using credits foolishly. The manager must weigh each situation to determine if it warrants the calling in of an IOU. This behavior is a way managers build connection and coercive power.

There is, however, another set of more subtle political actions which Pfeffer has identified and which are discussed briefly here.[32] These actions include the political use of language, ceremonies, symbols, and settings. In legitimizing and justifying decisions and various organizational behaviors, people can use **language** that draws on the sanctioned goals and means of the organization—even when pursuing more personal goals and when using means that are not sanctioned by the organization. For example, at HCC, when Tom planted ideas about Rob in the heads of his peers, he used the language of the organization and talked up the good of the organization while trying to get himself promoted. Furthermore, upon being promoted he used the promotional **ceremony** to mobilize support and quiet any opposition that might have developed. Indeed, Tom assured the supervisors that he would be soliciting their ideas to avoid the misinformed decisions that Rob had made. In other words, Tom used the ceremony to try to completely alter the situation which he had created before his promotion.

As one way to achieve this change, Tom set up a symbolic meeting for the purpose of letting his people give him ideas and information. Besides serving the real meaning of information sharing, this meeting was a **symbol** that Tom intended to do things differently from his predecessor. Certainly, symbols are an important aspect of legitimate power that goes with various positions in an organization. People can use their titles, their reserved parking spots, the size of their budgets, and other such symbols to achieve their desired goals. Finally, closely related to symbols are the **settings** in which people operate. The size, location, and arrangement of a physical setting are all important aspects of the political behaviors that occur in organizations. For example, where does a manager meet with subordinates—in his or her office or theirs? By meeting in the manager's office, he has the advantage of home turf, which can be used to help him get what he wants. Likewise, if at a meeting a manager sits at the head of a table or near the head person, she can gain a political advantage. Indeed, these subtle issues are quite important to successful political actors in organizations. Managers would do well to learn as much as they can about these issues if they want to be successful.

Certainly, these few political behaviors are not the only ones managers will see in organizations. They are intended only to illustrate some of the more common ones. For example, look at Insight 10–5 to see what political behaviors and power bases corporate raider Carl Icahn used to bring about a long-sought settlement in the lawsuit between Texaco and Pennzoil. Notice his development of a base of support, his relating with others, and his use of the perceived threat of a takeover.

Why people engage in politics

With this understanding of typical political behaviors, we can discuss why people engage in these actions.[33] Study indicates that it is not simply because of personal ambition. The primary reason people engage in organizational politics is that there are always at least two sets of goals for employees to pursue: individual goals and organizational goals.[34] As

INSIGHT 10-5

How Icahn Got Texaco and Pennzoil to Brink of Elusive Settlement

*I*t was Friday, Dec. 4, and Carl Icahn was acting more like Henry Kissinger the shuttle diplomat than Carl Icahn the corporate raider. Arriving at Texaco Inc.'s Harrison, N.Y., headquarters, Mr. Icahn was eager to resolve the largest legal judgment ever against an American corporation. "So you get yourself down to the Waldorf and cut a deal," he told James W. Kinnear, Texaco's chief executive.

Mr. Kinnear's response: No.

Next stop, Pennzoil Co., and its wildcatting chairman, J. Hugh Liedtke. "Hugh, you can trust me, you can work with me. I've never shafted anybody," Mr. Icahn said. "This deal has got to be done for the good of everyone. Kinnear may go all the way through to the Supreme Court, and you could lose everything."

To get the Texaco-Pennzoil settlement, Mr. Icahn moved fast, but his first step was a mistake and cost him precious time. Even though the judge had given creditors the right to submit a joint settlement plan without Texaco's concurrence, Mr. Icahn focused his efforts at shuttle diplomacy on Texaco executives. Two days after the judge's ruling, he arrived in Mr. Kinnear's office to say that Mr. Liedtke would take a single-lump settlement of $4 billion. He also held at least two other meetings with Mr. Kinnear in five days.

But Mr. Kinnear wasn't interested, and Mr. Icahn soon decided to focus his attention on Mr. Liedtke. Seeking a way to influence the Pennzoil chairman, he struck up a telephone friendship with Mr. Liedtke's colorful lawyer and hunting buddy, Joseph Jamail, whose Texas humor makes the Brooklyn-born Mr. Icahn laugh. "I found [Mr. Icahn] to be reasonable. We talked at length," says Mr. Jamail, who met with Mr. Icahn two weeks

ago in New York over drinks and lunch.

The key may have been Mr. Icahn's recent purchase of 2% of Pennzoil's stock—an acquisition he didn't need to remind Mr. Liedtke or Mr. Jamail about. An alternative to a settlement, he told the Pennzoil chairman, could be five years of waiting for a court resolution and payment—with Mr. Icahn as one of Pennzoil's largest shareholders. "Things could get very messy," Mr. Icahn said. A takeover threat was only implied, but Mr. Liedkte "got the message," says an individual familiar with the conversations.

By Dec. 5, Mr. Icahn was back in Harrison with an offer from Mr. Liedtke of $3.5 billion, and the next day he phoned again to say Mr. Liedtke would take $3 billion. Texaco turned all the offers down, adopting the strategy that "he lowered his number by $1 billion in three days; he'll go lower," the same source says.

Convinced by last Monday that he was wasting his time with Texaco, Mr. Icahn set about fashioning an agreement between Mr. Liedtke and the equity, or shareholders, committee. Meanwhile, on Tuesday morning, shareholders' representatives gathered at the Roosevelt Hotel to decide what they would offer Mr. Liedtke if Judge Schwartzberg gave them a role in formulating a reorganization and settlement. Since Mr. Liedtke had told the equity committee's chairman, Robert Norris, the night before that he wouldn't take a penny less than $3 billion, the shareholders decided to offer $3.01 billion. A few hours later, the judge included the shareholders in the settlement group.

By Tuesday night, Mr. Icahn was dining at New York's Maurice Hotel with shareholder representatives, including Mr. Norris, a Colorado rancher who once played the archetypal cowboy in Marlboro cigarette commercials. Table talk focused on the settlement that the committee had agreed to support. After dinner, Mr. Norris and two co-people pursue their own goals, they also pursue their perceptions of the organizational goals which affect them on their job. And since political actions involve both goals and behaviors, people who agree on the same goals may still want to use different means to achieve them. In the Home Computers case, even before Rob's promotion, he and Tom went about achieving the same goals using very different means and power bases.

At another level, individual goals relate to a person's career. People typically work not only to do well in their present job, but they also do things which will lead to the achievement of their career goals. In fact, this career influence was apparently at the heart of Tom's political behaviors at HCC to get himself appointed as a section head. Of course, such behaviors may not always be as obvious as Tom's. People often push for a goal which will benefit the organization, but there is a clear slant to favor their own career goals.

A third reason people engage in politics is their affiliations with different segments of the organization.[35] When an organization is divided into departments and divisions, each unit develops its own goals, norms, priorities, and time frameworks. As people in the departments interact, they operate with these different backgrounds. Often the politics of these interactions become quite obvious when it is time to allocate money or other scarce resources to the various departments. Each department's goals become its primary focus, while organizational goals fall behind. For example, as a department head, a manager might have a need to hire an additional employee. But other department heads have the same need, and there will not be enough new-hires to go around. As the manager starts to make his case for the new employee, he downplays other departments' needs, exaggerates his own needs, and engages in other political behaviors to get a new person. The manager's departmental goal is his primary focus, whether or not he really needs another person as badly as other departments may.

The final reason people engage in politics is simply that there are limits to the amount of information, number of criteria, and points of view that people can handle. It is impossible for decisions and behaviors to be totally rational, and this leaves the door open for nonrational and political behaviors. For instance, most managers have their hands and minds full just running their own departments and dealing with other departments with which they must routinely interact. Understanding all individual departments in an organization plus the overall picture in detail may be next to impossible. Hence, political behavior may be managers' only choice if they are to achieve the organizationally sanctioned goals for their department. Managers cannot always know the best course of action for an entire organization; since each views a situation from the perspective of their own areas of responsibility. **Managers must accept that political behaviors are inevitable and work to ensure that they have positive rather than negative results for the organization and themselves.**

There are two conditions that actually determine how prevalent politics will be in an organization. First, how important are the issues over which there is conflict? If an issue is not important to a manager, he or she might be better off to save political resources for the more important issues. Second, what is the distribution of power? If a manager has very little power relative to the other parties involved in a situation, the manager may be foolish to try to use political behaviors to win. It is probably safer to use political behaviors when the manager has equal or greater power, although political tactics may be useful for balancing power when a manager has only slightly less power. But when managers use political behaviors, they must recognize the ethical responsibility that goes with them. While organizational goals are usually the desired end, along with satisfaction of personal goals, managers must have respect for justice (fair play) and for the rights of others. Otherwise, they can easily fall into political behaviors that have long-term negative effects on both the organization and themselves.

Personal characteristics and politics

Some people are more willing to engage in organizational politics than others (recall your own Political Behavior Inventory score). And research has identified several characteristics which seem to be related to using politics. **Political activities are used more often by people who are: (1) high in the need for power, (2) high in Machiavellianism, (3) internal in their locus of control, and (4) willing to take risks.** Let us explore each one in turn.

First, people who are high in need for power are more likely to use political behaviors than people low in need for power. As noted in Chapter 5, a high need for power seems to be related to success in organizations, at least in terms of progression up the hierarchy.[36] And political behaviors are more prevalent at higher levels of organizations.[37] Thus, a high need for power seems compatible with the situation where politics are most common—high up in the organization.

A second personal characteristic of political actors is Machiavellianism which, as discussed in Chapter 4, is the tendency to use deceit in interpersonal relations.[38] People with Machiavellian views of the world see guile and deceit as natural ways of influencing other people. They tend to be manipulators of others, and they are very good at using power in interpersonal relations. In addition, Machiavellian individuals seldom trust others to a great degree. In short, it is easy to imagine a Machiavellian person pursuing goals that are not sanctioned by an organization and using means that also are not sanctioned.

A third characteristic of political actors is that they believe that things that happen to them are largely under their control. That is, these people have a high internal locus of control.[39] People with an external locus of control believe that powerful others, chance, or luck determine what happens to them; thus, they tend to be passive people in organizations. But since **internals** assume that they can make a difference, they are likely to also recognize that political actions are necessary in some situations.

A fourth characteristic associated with political behaviors is a person's willingness to take risks. Since political behaviors almost always have some risk associated with them, people who are **risk seekers** are more likely to engage in politics than are **risk avoiders**.[40] When people pursue goals that are not sanctioned by the organization or use means that are not approved by the organization, they are obviously taking a risk, even if they successfully achieve their goal.

By understanding these personal characteristics, managers are in a better position to recognize political behaviors when they occur. Such recognition may allow them to counter negative politics and to appreciate the need for positive politics. Understanding these factors may also help managers appreciate their tendencies toward political behaviors.

In summary, political behaviors in organizations are inevitable, and they are not always bad. Managers need to recognize the situations where the use of politics is possible (as described earlier) and be able to determine whether political behavior would be desirable for them and their organization at that time. **As with leadership style, it is important to understand that politics must be adjusted to fit the situation.** Managers should not take the risk of using politics if the situation is not favorable. But if the situation is favorable, managers should be willing to use political behaviors to help both the organization and themselves achieve desired goals. And remember the ethical responsibility that goes with the use of political behaviors. Most likely, political behavior will be judged ethical if it is best for the organization, as well as for the manager, and if it creates a fair distribution of benefits and burdens.[41] Indeed, the questions of legality, fairness, and feelings discussed in Chapter 4 should be a constant part of a manager's analysis of political behaviors. Political actions need to be both ethical and beneficial to the organization. Otherwise, managers hurt the organization and ultimately hurt themselves.

CHAPTER HIGHLIGHTS

This chapter has complemented the material on leadership by focusing on the use of power and politics in organizations. While some people may not like the idea of using these means to influence the behavior of others, **both power and politics are facts of life in organizations. Furthermore, they can be used for good as well as bad purposes.** Managers cannot lead without power. In addition, politics are necessary for dealing with the flaws in organizations and to help managers achieve organizational and personal goals.

This chapter defined power as the capacity to influence other people's behavior. Two personal sources of power are available to managers. **Referent power** is based on respect. **Expert power** is based on ability. Both referent and expert power are developed over time and can decline over time. People must learn to admire managers and to know abilities before these sources of power become meaningful. Likewise, if managers do something that people do not respect, they can lose their referent power. If managers teach others about their area of expertise, they can lose their expert power.

Three sources of position power were then discussed. **Reward power** is based on giving desired rewards. **Coercive power** is based on giving punishment. **Legitimate power** is based on a person's rights as a manager. Since these sources of power vary by position in the organization, they, too, have a developmental aspect. As managers move up the hierarchy, they will usually gain in legitimate, reward, and coercive power. However, societal influences have tended to decrease position sources of power over the past few decades.

Next, we looked into the situation at Home Computers Company involving two production engineers, Rob and Tom. We saw how the five sources of power interacted with one another. We also saw that merely having a source of power does not mean much unless the power is used. The case also suggested that there are other sources of power: **information, resource, relations, and connection.**

To successfully use power, managers must recognize their power sources, recognize situations where power can be used, understand the costs of using power, and continuously work both to develop new sources of power and to maintain existing ones. In closing, this section discussed how the various sources of power can be related to the leadership model developed in the previous two chapters. The text also mentioned four possible reactions that other people may have to a manager's use of power: **compliance, identification, internalization, and alienation.**

With this discussion of power, the chapter then focused on political behaviors that put power to work. **Political behaviors were defined as** unsanctioned means that achieve organizational goals or sanctioned means that achieve personal goals at the expense of the organization. This led to definitions of two dimensions of politics (ends and means) and a four-cell grid. Behaviors involving organizationally sanctioned ends and means are defined as *nonpolitical job behavior.* If the ends are sanctioned by the organization, but the means are not, this results in political behavior that is potentially functional to the organization. If the ends are not sanctioned but the means are, this results in covert organizationally dysfunctional political behavior. Finally, if both ends and means are not sanctioned, this results in overt organizationally dysfunctional political behavior.

Several common political behaviors follow.

1. Attacking or blaming others.
2. Selective use of information.
3. Image building.
4. Developing a base of support.
5. Praising others.
6. Developing coalitions with strong allies.
7. Creating obligation for others, that is, IOUs.

In addition, the text briefly discussed a subtle set of political behaviors involving language, ceremonies, symbols, and settings.

The text moved on to discuss why people engage in politics in organizations. The primary reason is that **people are always pursuing two sets of goals: individual goals and organizational goals, and these two sets may not always be compatible.** Closely related is the fact that people work not only to succeed at their present jobs, but also to succeed in a career. A third reason for engaging in politics is that people represent different parts of an organization, each with its own goals, norms, priorities, and time frameworks. Fourth, people engage in political behaviors because there are limits to the amount of information, number of criteria, and points of view they can handle—decisions cannot be totally rational.

The final section of this chapter mentioned four characteristics that are associated with a tendency for people to be political. **People tend to be more political the higher their need for power, the more Machiavellian they are, the more their locus of control is internal, and the more they are willing to take risks.**

The chapter concludes by saying that **the use of power and politics in organizations is essential for managers to be successful.** By understanding and developing sources of power, managers will be in a better position to influence others toward the goals of the organization and to satisfy their own personal goals.

REVIEW QUESTIONS

1. Why is it so necessary for managers to understand the use of power and politics in organizations?
2. What is power, and why is it neither good nor bad?
3. Define the two sources of personal power, and explain why they are personal—as opposed to positional—in nature.
4. Define *reward, coercive,* and *legitimate power,* and explain the importance of the value of the reward or punishment to the person managers wish to influence. Also, why are these sources of power positional, rather than personal?
5. Explain the importance of information, resources, and connections as sources of power.
6. Why is power developmental in nature? Be specific with regard to the various sources of power.
7. How do the various power bases relate to the leadership models discussed in Chapters 8 and 9?
8. Of the four reactions to the use of power, what determines the reaction a person will get in a given situation? In other words, how can managers be successful in using power in an organization?
9. Using the four categories of political behaviors defined in this chapter, explain why organizational politics are present in all organizations.
10. When are people most likely to engage in political behaviors in an organization?
11. Explain how people in organizations use the most common political behaviors, as described in this chapter, to achieve the goals that they desire.
12. Give a profile of a person who is most likely to engage in political behaviors.

RESOURCE READINGS

Block, P. *The Empowered Manager: Positive Political Skills at Work.* San Francisco: Jossey-Bass, 1987.

Josefowitz, N. *Paths to Power: A Woman's Guide from First Job to Top Executive.* Reading, Mass.: Addison-Wesley, 1980.

Kelly, C. M. "The Interrelationships of Ethics and Power in Today's Organizations." *Organizational Dynamics* 16 (Summer, 1987), pp. 5–18.

Kotter, J. P. *The General Managers.* New York: Free Press, 1982.

Kouzes, J. M., and B. Z. Posner. *The Leadership Challenge: How to Get Extraordinary Things Done in Organizations*, San Francisco: Jossey-Bass, 1987.

Mintzberg, H. *Power In and Around Organizations.* Englewood Cliffs, N.J.: Prentice-Hall, 1983.

Pfeffer, J. *Power in Organizations.* Marshfield, Mass.: Pitman Publishing, Inc., 1981.

NOTES

1. J. P. Kotter, *The General Managers* (New York: Free Press, 1982).

2. A. T. Cobb, "An Episode Model of Power: Toward an Integration of Theory and Research," *Academy of Management Review* 9 (1984), pp. 482–93.

3. G. R. Salancik and J. Pfeffer, "Who Gets Power—And How They Hold on to It: A Strategic-Contingency Model of Power," *Organizational Dynamics* 3 (1977), pp. 3–21.

4. R. M. Kanter, *Men and Women of the Corporation* (New York: Basic Books, 1977), p. 166.

5. L. A. Mainiero, "Coping with Powerlessness: The Relationship of Gender and Job Dependency to Empowerment-Strategy Usage," *Administrative Science Quarterly* 31 (1986), pp. 633–53.

6. W. G. Antley, and P. S. Sachdera, "Structural Sources of Intraorganizational Power: A Theoretical Systems," *Academy of Management Review* 9 (1984), pp. 104–13.

7. J. R. P. French and B. Raven, "The Bases of Social Power," in *Studies in Social Power*, ed. D. Cartwright (Ann Arbor: University of Michigan Institute for Social Research, 1959), pp. 150–67.

8. Ibid.

9. K. Blanchard and S. Johnson, *The One Minute Manager* (New York: Wm. A. Morrow Co., Inc., Publishers, 1982).

10. C. A. Reich, *The Greening of America* (New York: Random House, 1970).

11. B. Z. Posner, W. A. Randolph, and M. Wortman, "A New Ethic for Work? The Worth Ethic," *Human Resource Management* 14 (1975), pp. 15–20.

12. B. H. Raven and W. Kruglanski, "Conflict and Power," in *The Structure of Conflict*, ed. P. G. Swingle (New York: Academic Press, 1975), pp. 177–219.

13. P. Hersey and M. Goldsmith, as noted in P. Hersey and K. Blanchard, *The Management of Organizational Behavior*, 5th ed. (Englewood Cliffs, N.J.: Prentice-Hall, 1988), pp. 171, 218.

14. J. Kotter, *The General Managers.*

15. J. D. Hackman, "Power and Centrality in the Allocation of Resources in Colleges and Universities," *Administrative Science Quarterly* 30 (1985), pp. 61–77.

16. M. Korda, *Power: How to Get It, How to Use It* (New York: Random House, 1975).

17. M. W. McCall, Jr., "Power, Authority, and Influence," in *Organizational Behavior*, ed. S. Kerr (Columbus, Ohio: Grid, 1979), pp. 185–206.

18. R. C. Benfari, H. E. Wilkinson, and C. D. Orth, "The Effective Use of Power," *Business Horizons*, May-June 1986, pp. 12–20.

19. D. Instone, B. Major, and B. B. Bunker, "Gender, Self Confidence, and Social Influence Strategies: An Organizational Simulation," *Journal of Personality and Social Psychology* 44 (1983), pp. 322–33.

20. Hersey and Blanchard, *Management of Organizational Behavior*.

21. M. Mulder, R. D. de Jong, L. Koppelaar, and J. Verhage, "Power, Situation, and Leader's Effectiveness: An Organizational Field Study," *Journal of Applied Psychology* 71 (1986), pp. 566–70; and unpublished research by W. Alan Randolph.

22. These four responses are drawn from H. C. Kelman, "Compliance, Identification, and Internalization: Three Processes of Attitude Change," *Journal of Conflict Resolution* 2 (1958), pp. 51–60, and A. Etzioni, *A Comparative Analysis of Complex Organizations* (New York: Free Press, 1961).

23. A. T. Cobb, "Political Diagnosis: Applications in Organizational Development," *Academy of Management Review* 11 (1986), pp. 482–96.

24. S. Young, "Politicking: The Unsung Managerial Skill," *Personnel* (June 1987), pp. 62–68.

25. M. Wallace and A. Szilagyi, *Managing Behavior in Organizations* (Glenview, Ill.: Scott, Foresman, 1982), p. 181.

26. B. T. Mayes and R. W. Allen, "Toward a Definition of Organizational Politics," *Academy of Management Review* 2 (1977), pp. 672–78.

27. Ibid, p. 675.

28. C. M. Kelly, "The Interrelationships of Ethics and Power in Today's Organizations," *Organizational Dynamics* 16 (Summer, 1987), pp. 5–18.

29. R. W. Allen, D. L. Madison, L. W. Porter, P. A. Renwick, and B. T. Mayes, "Organizational Politics: Tactics and Characteristics of Its Actors," *California Management Review* 22 (1979), pp. 77–83.

30. J. P. Kotter, *The General Managers*, pp. 67–75.

31. Ibid.

32. J. Pfeffer, *Power in Organizations* (Marshfield, Mass.: Pitman Publishing, 1981), pp. 211–29.

33. This section is based primarily on R. H. Miles, *Macro Organizational Behavior* (Glenview, Ill.: Scott, Foresman, 1980), pp. 154–61; and Pfeffer, *Power in Organizations*, ch. 3.

34. D. A. Ralston, "Employee Ingratiation: The Role of Management," *Academy of Management Review* 10 (1985), pp. 477–87.

35. M. A. Welsh and E. A. Shusher, "Organizational Design as a Context for Political Activity," *Administrative Science Quarterly* 31 (1986), pp. 389–402.

36. D. C. McClelland and D. H. Burnham, "Power Is the Great Motivator," *Harvard Business Review* 54 (1976), pp. 100–10.

37. J. Gandz and V. V. Murray, "The Experience of Work Place Politics," *Academy of Management Journal* 23 (1980), pp. 237–51.

38. G. R. Gemmill and W. J. Heisler, "Machiavellianism as a Factor in Managerial Job Strain, Job Satisfaction, and Upward Mobility," *Academy of Management Journal* 15 (1972), pp. 48–58.

39. L. W. Porter, R. W. Allen, and L. L. Angle, "The Politics of Upward Influence in Organizations," *Research in Organizational Behavior* 3 (1981), pp. 109–49.

40. Ibid.

41. M. Velasquez, D. J. Moberg, and G. F. Cavanagh, "Organizational Statesmanship and Dirty Politics: Ethical Guidelines for the Organizational Politician," *Organizational Dynamics* 12 (Autumn, 1983), pp. 65–80.

CASE: To air condition or not to air condition

Bruce was the new general manager for an Italian company that was planning to build a new plant in the southern United States. Bruce had recently been hired to oversee building the new plant, hire the new employees, and then operate the new plant for manufacturing fiber optic cable. An immediate problem arose over whether the plant should be air-conditioned.

Bruce felt that the plant had to be air-conditioned if he hoped to get his employees to work in the summer. After all, it was 1984, and all new plants in the deep South were air-conditioned. But the Italians had never built an air-conditioned plant and saw no need to start now. Besides, air-conditioning the plant would cost $2 million, according to Georgio, the engineering vice president in Italy. And Georgio was "always right." He had to win all of his arguments, and he did not trust Americans. And to top things off, he was the brother of the president of the worldwide company.

Bruce, on the other hand, was the new kid on the block. He was American, and he felt the plant must be air-conditioned. Bruce had also been told by his technical people that the plant could be air-conditioned for $550,000, and he had checked, double-checked, and triple-checked this figure. He knew he was right. But could he win if he argued on the cost figures and the lack of motivation that would occur if the plant was not air-conditioned? What would you do in this situation, especially given the fact that you do not like Georgio?

Bruce decided that this was the issue he would use to expose the incompetence of Georgio. To do this, he escalated the issue by going up the hierarchy to his boss, the vice president of United States operations. Bruce told the VP that the air-conditioning would cost only $550,000, not $2 million. Of course, the VP said, "Are your sure?" Bruce said, "Yes." The VP relayed this information to the president of United States operations, who, after asking the same set of questions, then passed the information on to the president of worldwide operations in Italy. The stakes were rising, but Bruce had confidently assured everyone that he was right.

Six months later, the air conditioning was installed for $550,000, and Georgio, who has assured the president, his brother, that it could not be done,

Source: Related by a manager at the company to Dr. Alan Randolph, 1987.

had egg on his face. The president was embarrassed, since he had originally sided with his brother. Bruce came out smelling like a rose and had exposed Georgio, at least temporarily, as interfering with the best interests of the company. What the future of this relationship will be, we can only speculate.

Questions

1. Was Bruce right to handle this issue in this way?
2. What would you have done?

EXERCISE: Diagnosis of the sources of power

Step 1: Think of the three people who had the most influence over you in the last year. Choose one experience where each person influenced you. Describe each of these experiences in one paragraph.

Step 2: In pairs, identify the sources of power used in each experience. Reach consensus with your partner.

Step 3: With the class as a whole, the instructor will tally the frequency of each source of power used. Then the instructor will ask you to describe the outcomes or consequences (behaviors and attitudes) of each influence experience.

Step 4: Discussion. In small groups or with the entire class, answer the following questions:

Description

1. Which sources of power were used most frequently? Least frequently?

Diagnosis

2. Under what circumstances was each type of power used? Does a pattern emerge?
3. Which types were most effective? Least effective?

Prescription

4. How could these people tap into additional sources of power?

*Source: J. Gordon, *A Diagnostic Approach to Organizational Behavior* 2nd ed. Boston: Allyn and Bacon, 1987, p. 497.

QUESTIONNAIRE: PBS—Self and scoring

Self

Please indicate the degree to which each of the statements below describes you. Do this by writing the appropriate number (based on the scale below) in the blank to the far left of each statement. Please make your assessment as objectively and factually-based as you can, without considering what you think the best answer is. If your work experience is limited, please indicate what you think you *would* do in a job.

The scale to use is as follows:

Very little extent	Little extent		Some extent		Great extent		Very great extent
1	2	3	4	5	6	7

To what extent do you or would you:

6 1. Know a great deal about how to do your and other's jobs?

7 2. Warrant people's trust and respect?

6 3. Expect others to do what you suggest because you're the boss?

5 4. Make yourself available to talk about non-job related matters?

7 5. Behave in ways others would like to behave?

7 6. Influence how much of a pay increase others receive?

7 7. Serve as a source of information and advice on job related issues?

7 8. Pull "rank" in asking others to do a task?

7 9. Demonstrate behavior that others really respect?

7 10. Have an impact on promotions in your organization?

7 11. Express interest in talking with others about things not related to the job?

2 12. Make people feel uncomfortable when they have made an error or broken a rule?

5 13. Have knowledge that is important to others in performing their jobs?

2 14. Criticize others and their work?

6 15. Assume that subordinates have a duty to follow your requests?

2 16. Reprimand people for making mistakes?

6 17. Provide answers to others about how to do a job better?

_7_ 18. Have a say about the size of a pay increase or a promotion that others might receive?

_7_ 19. Act in a manner that others admire and aspire to be like?

_7_ 20. Make yourself available to listen to others' concerns?

_7_ 21. Use your position (or authority) to get people to do their tasks?

_5_ 22. Give out penalties or write reports for someone's pesonnel file for doing a poor job?

_6_ 23. Recognize good performance in a way that is meaningful to people?

_6_ 24. Rely on friendship to get work done?

_2_ 25. Publicly criticize people when they have made a mistake?

_ _ 26. Demonstrate characteristics and behavior that others admire?

_7_ 27. Let people have a day off or similar benefit for doing a good job?

_7_ 28. Teach people how to do their jobs more effectively?

_7_ 29. Believe you have the right to make decisions that affect others on the job?

_7_ 30. Depend on good interpersonal relations between yourself and others?

Scoring

In the numbered spaces below corresponding to the numbered statements from the PBS, please record your answers (scale of 1 to 7). Then add the total in each column to determine the extent to which each power base is used. A higher score means the power base is used more. The numbers below are the mean scores for each power base from a national sample of managers. They can be used for comparison, _but do not necessarily represent a best score._

	Referent	Expert	Relations	Legitimate	Reward	Coercive
	2. 7	1. 6	4. 5	3. 6	6. 7	12. 2
	5. 7	7. 7	11. 7	8. 7	10. 7	14. 2
	9. 7	13. 5	20. 7	15. 6	18. 7	16. 2
	19. 7	17. 6	24. 6	21. 7	23. 6	22. 5
	26. 7	28. 7	30. 7	29. 7	27. 7	25. 2
Total	35	31	32	33	34	13
National survey mean	(23.75)	(24.50)	(24.05)	(18.70)	(29.60)	(13.40)

QUESTIONNAIRE: The political behavior inventory

To determine your political appreciation and tendencies, answer these questions. Select the answer that best represents your behavior or belief, even if that particular behavior or belief is not present all the time.

1. You should make others feel important through an open appreciation of their ideas and work.
   ____✓__ (True) _____ False

2. Because people tend to judge you when they first meet you, always try to make a good first impression.
   ____✓__ (True) _____ False

3. Try to let others do most of the talking, be sympathetic to their problems and resist telling people that they are totally wrong.
   _____ (True) _____ False

4. Praise the good traits of the people you meet and always give people an opportunity to save face if they are wrong or make a mistake.
   ____✓__ (True) _____ False

5. Spreading false rumors, planting misleading information and backstabbing are necessary, if somewhat unpleasant, methods to deal with your enemies.
   _____ True ___✓__ (False)

6. Sometimes it is necessary to make promises that you know you will not or cannot keep.
   _____ True ___✓__ False

7. It is important to get along with everybody, even with those who are generally recognized as windbags, abrasive, or constant complainers.
   _____ True ___✓__ (False)

8. It is vital to do favors for others so that you can call in these IOU's at times when they will do you the most good.
   _____ True ___✓__ (False)

9. Be willing to compromise, particularly on issues that are minor to you, but important to others.
   ____✓__ (True) _____ False

10. On controversial issues, it is important to delay or avoid your involvement if possible.
    _____ True ___✓__ (False)   5/10

The more questions answered "true," the greater your political behavior
Source: J. F. Byrnes, "Connecting Organizational Politics and Conflict Resolution," *Personnel Administrator* (June 1986), p. 49, Figure 2.

C H A P T E R 11

Communications in Organizations

I n closing this section on interpersonal behavior, it is fitting that we focus on communications in organizations. Every organization has communications problems. And researchers have well documented the fact that managers spend a great deal of their time communicating.[1] But why are communications so important to organizations and to managers? And why are communications so problematic?

The answer to the first question lies in the fact that communications are the lifeblood of an organization. Just try to imagine an organization without communications. It is impossible. Without communications, there would be no way to create the coordination of effort that must be present in any organization. There would be no way for managers to lead and influence their subordinates. There would be no way to move information around in an organization. And there would be no way to achieve the wide range of goals that are present in every organization. Without communications, there would be no way to resolve differences and move toward the combined effort of people that is so necessary in organizations. And there would be great difficulty in justifying past actions, without communication.[2] Furthermore, a great deal of research has shown that communications have important effects on the performance and satisfaction of employees and on the cohesiveness of groups.[3] Hence, it is typical to find managers spending up to 75 percent of their time in meetings, face-to-face communications, telephone conversations, and reading and preparing written documents.[4]

The second question—why communications are a problem in organizations—is a little more complicated to answer. In fact, unless people have experienced working interdependently with others, it may be difficult to imagine that communications could be a problem. **Communication mistakes abound in organizations because the communications process itself is quite involved, with many factors that can inhibit the process.** In this chapter, we explore how the process of communications works, and discuss some new technologies that are impacting it. The chapter also discusses possible outcomes to the process, as well as factors that may inhibit it. Finally, the text explores a number of techniques that managers can use to improve communication.[5]

THE PROCESS OF COMMUNICATIONS

In order to understand why communications are so problematic in organizations, managers must understand how the process of communications works. In its simplest form, communication occurs when information is passed from one person to another. The initiator of the communication is called the **sender**. He or she transmits a message through a **channel** to the other person, who is called the **receiver**. As

EXHIBIT 11–1

The Process of Communications

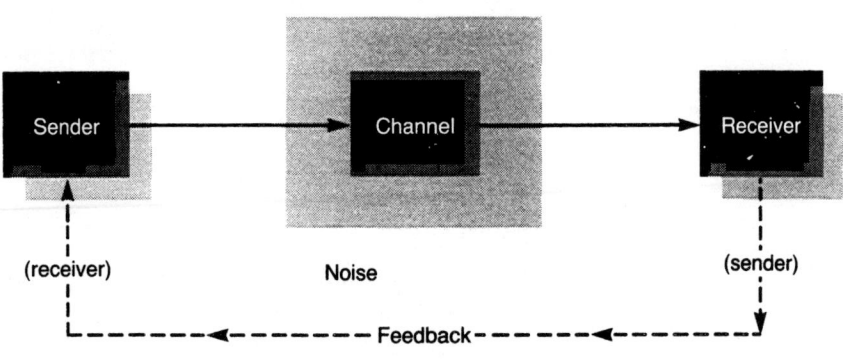

Source: Shannon and Weaver, *The Mathematical Theory of Communication* (Urbana, Ill.: University of Illinois Press, 1948).

shown in Exhibit 11–1, there are also two other important parts to the process of communications—**feedback** and **noise.**[6] Let us explore each of these elements in turn.

First, the initiator of a communication episode, the **sender,** determines the need for information to be transmitted to or from another person. It may be that the sender needs to tell the other person to do something, to ask a question of the other person, or to communicate for a variety of other purposes (which we will discuss later). The sender must first decide what message is to be transmitted to the receiver. The sender must then decide how the message is to be translated into a set of words, gestures, signals, or nonverbal symbols. This step in the communications process, called **encoding,** involves the sender's choice of media to use in transmitting the message to the receiver. The sender may choose a written message, verbal contact, telephone contact (even from the sender's car), computer network, video-conference, or other high- and low-tech media.

Once the sender transmits the message, it enters the **channel** that connects the sender to the receiver. Basically, this channel is the medium by which the message is carried from sender to receiver. The channel may be the air waves between two people as they communicate face-to-face. The channel may be the telephone lines connecting the two people, perhaps even in pictures via video-conferencing. The channel may be interoffice mail or Federal Express. The channel may also involve other people: for example, the manager gives the supervisors a message, and they in turn tell the workers, who were the manager's intended receivers.

The next step in the process is that the message reaches the **receiver.** Ideally, the receiver is aware that the message has arrived and interprets the message in the manner intended by the sender. This interpretation part of the process is known as **decoding** the message, and **communication has not occurred until the message intended by the sender is received and understood by the receiver.** Up until that point, there is merely transmission. For example, imagine a person making a telephone call when the line is slightly out of order. He or she can hear the person on the other end of the line repeating "Hello" louder and louder. It becomes obvious that the other person cannot hear the caller. Thus, the caller is only **transmitting** a message; the message is not being received. Hence, there is no real communication taking place. A humorous example of this aspect of communications is shown in the cartoon below.

The last step in the process of communications is **feedback.** The sender receives back from the receiver an indication of whether or not the message was received and understood as intended. Feedback may be a behavior that the receiver exhibits; it may be something said; or it may be a written message. The point is that feedback reverses the communications process. That is, the original receiver becomes the sender,

"It's not really all that important that we understand each other . . . just that you understand me."

From *The Wall Street Journal,* with permission of Cartoon Features Syndicate.

and the original sender becomes the receiver. And in this sense, the process may go through a number of cycles of sending and receiving, as happens when people carry on a conversation.

This cyclical aspect of the process illustrates the developmental nature of communications. As the process goes through repeated cycles, sometimes over extended periods of time, additional information is made available for each successive cycle. In Chapter 1 we saw how relationships develop over time; and certainly communications play an important role in this process. For instance, a new employee has an initial conversation with a coworker, and a relationship begins to develop. Over the next days, weeks, and months, their communication develops so that they each know the other better and better. Communications develop from the superficial level to deeper and deeper levels, so long as both parties feel comfortable with this growing knowledge of one another. Chapter 4 discussed how such feedback and sharing help to enlarge the open area in the Johari Window of understanding.

The last element in the communications process is **noise.** In Exhibit 11–1, the arrows show that noise can enter the communications process at any point along the way. **Noise** is anything that inhibits the flow of information from sender to receiver. Noise can be physical like that encountered on the floor of a factory. Or time pressure can cause a sender to abbreviate a message, making it more difficult for the receiver to understand. Noise can also be psychological. For example, the sender may have something else on his or her mind that leads to poor preparation of the transmitted message. Likewise, the receiver may have something else on his or her mind that decreases receptivity to the message being sent. For example, perhaps the receiver was just chewed out by the boss and is not ready to talk with a coworker about how to repair a machine that is down.

This chapter discusses several dimensions of this communications process—purpose, media, and direction—as well as context variables that influence organizational communications. The chapter also discusses potential outcomes to communications, barriers to effective communications, and ways of improving organizational communications. First, however, let us return to Rob of Home Computers Company (who we met in Chapter 10) and delve into the communications aspects of his job as a section head—before Tom's political games led to Rob's transfer to personnel.

Home Computers Case

The Home Computers Case—More on Rob

Rob, the newly promoted section head, arrived for work around 7:30 A.M. He grabbed a cup of coffee and thought about what lay ahead for him that day: supervisors' meeting at 9:00, personnel problems with one of his people, briefing meeting with his boss, and then just the regular matters of meeting production deadlines.

Shortly thereafter, he saw Jim Adams, one of the supervisors, walk by his door. Rob stepped to the door and called Jim over to discuss the production schedule for the day. They stood in the hall to go over a few minor problems and to try to ensure some better coordination between Jim's area and Tom's area. They ended the conversation with Rob asking Jim about the cabin he was building on a nearby lake.

Rob then walked to Tom's office to discuss the coordination issue with him. He was not there, so Rob left a note on Tom's desk, asking Tom to drop by his office.

Back in his office, Rob quickly went over the morning mail. He had received a couple of brochures about training programs, a quality-control report, and two memos from his boss. One of the brochures was on assertiveness training. Rob wondered if it might help him to be a better communicator, but he did not have time to think about it then. Through his electronic mail system, Rob received a memo from his boss dealing with a coordination problem between work shifts under Rob. The memo suggested Rob discuss remedies with some of the other section heads.

Rob picked up the telephone to call Hal Walker, one of the other section heads. Hal was out in the plant, so the receptionist paged him, and he called Rob back. They discussed the coordination among shifts, with Rob asking a lot of questions. Hal offered some useful ideas and said he would be willing to meet with Rob to go over some forms he had developed to help out with the coordination among shifts. But Rob wondered how Hal really felt about his inquiry. Rob was not sure, but he thought he sensed in Hal's tone of voice a belief that Rob should have been able to solve such a simple problem on his own.

By now it was 8:30, and Rob began to think about the regularly scheduled supervisors' meeting at 9:00. He called up some information from his computer file, and printed out what he wanted to share with meeting participants. Rob then headed down the hall for the meeting.

Rob opened the meeting by complimenting the supervisors on their efforts the past week. Next, he told them about a new version of the EZ2, which would soon be reaching the production stage. This new version was intended for use in schools and libraries, and it would be slightly different from the standard home and business versions of the EZ2. Rob then told the supervisors that he was not happy with the increasing number of personnel problems in his group. Absenteeism was too high, work quality was beginning to suffer, and employees seemed generally dissatisfied. Rob then opened the floor for questions and brief reports from each supervisor. Surprisingly, there were no questions about the new product, and there were no ideas about the personnel problems.

As he left the meeting, Rob saw several of the supervisors talking in the hall. He could not hear what they were discussing, and they dispersed as he approached. He did catch one comment made by Tom about Rob not knowing why the personnel problems were occurring. Rob wondered what Tom's ideas were and decided to ask him later when he responded to Rob's note.

As Rob walked through the plant, he thought about the memo from his boss regarding the coordination among shifts. Rob decided that the technology of production seemed to cut down on the frequency of communication not only between shifts, but also up and down the hierarchy. Everything was routine and highly structured. People on each shift and in each department felt a great deal of ownership for their work. They were always too busy trying to do a good job to have time to work out difficulties with other shifts and departments. Just last month Rob had an argument with one of the design engineers about the best production method for the new version of the EZ2. Rob had felt like he was talking to a brick wall, unable to get through to this engineer.

Rob returned to his office and decided to let his boss know about his concerns regarding the coordination problems in the plant. He was pretty clear on *what* was going wrong, but he was not altogether sure of *why*. And he did not want to come across to his boss as not knowing how to solve the problem. He contemplated whether to write a letter to his boss, to call him on the phone, to set up an appointment to talk with him, or just to let it ride for awhile.

Rob decided to let it ride for awhile. After a few days, he realized that Tom had never responded to his note, so he tried to call him about it. Tom was not in. Rob went around to see him several times but never found him in. He finally decided to drop it since it really was not that important. Over the next several months, it seemed that more and more of Rob's communications were not received or reacted to in the fashion he desired. His supervisors started avoiding him in the halls, and the weekly supervisors' meeting was becoming less and less productive. Hardly anyone talked but Rob, and he could make no eye contact with anyone except Jim Adams. Occasionally Tom would interject some information that would catch Rob totally off guard, but otherwise, the meetings were pretty quiet.

Rob decided to ask Jim to come to his office for a chat. He asked Jim what was going on in the plant, and after some pushing on Rob's part, Jim reluctantly said that Rob was not respected by the supervisors. Jim knew that Rob cared about his people and worked in their behalf, but the grapevine had it that Rob only did these things to get ahead. Rob was seen as not being well informed on matters that really counted to his people, and it was thought that Rob did not really respect their opinions. Rob was shocked, but he thanked Jim for his honesty. Jim said he liked Rob and wanted to see things get better. They shook hands as Jim walked out. Rob sat back down and gazed around his office at the diplomas and certificates hanging on the walls. He wondered what had gone wrong.

What has gone wrong for Rob? Several things are obvious. First, Rob does not listen very well to the nonverbal messages people send him, like when his staff dispersed as he walked up after the meeting. Also, he is not always able to ensure that his message has gotten through as intended, as with the design engineer. Rob is not in touch with the grapevine, and he is reluctant to talk to his boss. He also does not communicate well with people in other departments, as with section head Hal Walker. Finally, Rob is often unsure of the best medium to use to send his messages. For example, his note, phone calls, and visits to Tom were ineffective. Perhaps he should have used the more formal approach of sending a memo for a scheduled meeting. The case also demonstrates the developmental aspects of the communications process, as communications degenerate and result in many undesirable outcomes. Let us now discuss the dimensions of the communications process and how they can help us better understand Rob's problems.

DIMENSIONS OF COMMUNICATIONS

The following sections discuss several dimensions of communications: the purposes of communications; the media used; and the direction of communications in an organization (vertical, horizontal, and diagonal).

Purposes

There are many purposes for which people communicate in organizations.[7] Even single messages can serve more than one function. **The primary purposes of communications include: control, instruction, motivation, problem solving, feedback and evaluation, information exchange, social needs, and political goals.** Let us look at each one individually.

Control communications are designed to integrate and coordinate the activities of people in an organization. Formal communication channels that follow the organization chart often are for the purpose of control. Another example would be the standard operating procedures that organizations use to keep records and to locate necessary facts. Such communications serve the purpose of creating order in an organization, so that multiple goals and tasks can be pursued.

Instruction communications are used to let people know what they must do in their jobs. When routine problems arise, instructions can help solve the problems. And when an employee moves to a new job or is asked to perform a new task or to do a job a different way, there is a need for instruction.

The third purpose, **motivation,** serves the function of influencing the behavior of people in an organization. This purpose is the basis for earlier chapters on motivation and leadership. Motivation communications are used by managers to encourage and stimulate employees to work toward the accomplishment of organizational goals. Such communications may include issuing orders, making job assignments, and rewarding behavior and performance. As discussed in Chapters 5 and 6 on motivation and also in Chapters 8 and 9 on leadership, a key function of a manager is to formulate and communicate goals to which people can become committed. Indeed, some writers have suggested that this may be the most important role for a manager.[8]

Problem-solving communications usually involve the asking of many questions and are used on problems that do not have an easy solution. Managers and subordinates engage in a give-and-take discussion to determine what to do in these situations. For example, the telephone conversation Rob of Home Computers Company had with Hal Walker was a problem-solving communication.

Feedback and evaluation communications let people know how they are doing on the job. Often feedback and evaluation are linked together in a developmental fashion with instruction and motivation communications. For example, a manager explains a new procedure to an employee in the department. The manager then checks to see if the employee does the procedure correctly. If the person does it approximately right, the manager may praise the progress. And the manager may also evaluate performance and explain what needs to be done to improve. This example illustrates the use of instruction, motivation, evaluation, and, again, instruction communications in a developmental sequence.

The sixth purpose, **information exchange,** is the most basic of all communication purposes. In fact, all of the other purposes are special cases of this one. Communications always have an information purpose of some description. This category is intended for communications that are purely informational in nature—like Rob's telling HCC supervisors about the new EZ2 for schools and libraries.

Social needs communications relate to the emotional and nontask-oriented interactions that occur in every organization. Employees need to talk about baseball games, the weather, politics, and so forth. And while such communications do not directly affect the performance of the organization's tasks, they serve the need for employees to feel a connection with others at work. And it is not uncommon for these communications to include discussions of pay, treatment on the job, the boss's personality, and so forth. Obviously, these issues are more closely related to the job than is the baseball game, though, again, they are not directly a part of the job. Still, how employees feel about their work conditions can influence their performance on the job.[9]

The final category of communications purposes, **political goals,** is a little different from the others. Political communications are outside the expected range of communications. They can be positive if directed toward accomplishing organizational goals but involving nontraditional channels or media (that is, positive politics as discussed in Chapter 10). Or political communications can be negative if directed toward accomplishing personal goals at the expense of organizational goals. As people strive for personal gain, they may distort information, give poor feedback, and fail to use the positive side of the communications purposes discussed above.

Media

Just as there are many purposes for which people communicate in organizations, there are also many media people can use to convey their message—and the list has been growing with technology advances.[10] There are four basic media categories: written, verbal, nonverbal, and high tech. And within each of these broad categories, are several different types of media. As we explore these media, we will discuss some of the advantages and disadvantages of each one.

Written communications can, for example, take the form of a procedures manual, report, memo, letter, handwritten note, or file. **The basic advantage to written communications is that they can be thought out and carefully prepared to serve the sender's purpose.** Furthermore, the sender need not be present when the receiver reads the message. But herein lies **the major disadvantage of written communications—they are basically one-way in nature.** Feedback is often limited, so how can the sender know if the receiver interprets the message as intended?

In transmitting any written message, the sender must decide which written form to use in a given situation, as Rob did in the Home Computers case. A letter is more formal than a memo, and a typed message is more formal than a handwritten one. The signature on a letter also is an important indicator: first name only is less formal; full name is more formal. Addressing a letter "Dear Mr. Smith" is more formal than is "Dear Jim." Who is copied on a letter can be important. For example, copying the receiver's boss is a subtle way of putting pressure for response or action on the receiver. Sending a letter Federal Express or Faxmail indicates its urgency. And with the advent of electronic mail, messages may be sent almost instantly. Although the list of subtleties of written communications could go on and on, the purpose here is just to raise the issues; managers must be aware of them if they are to effectively communicate in organizations.

Verbal media can also take many forms. For example, there are formal and informal one-on-one conversations, formal and informal meetings, telephones, and even cellular phones for automobiles. Several of these were applied in the Home Computers case. **The biggest advantage to verbal communications is that they permit immediate feedback as to whether the message had been received as intended.** They allow for a two-way form of communications where the people involved are both sender and receiver. Verbal communications are particularly useful in dealing with complex and ambiguous problems.[11] **One disadvantage to verbal communications is that they may be less well planned than written communications, and there is no record of the exchange of information.**

Managers should consider several factors in deciding which type of verbal media to use in a given situation. A formal group meeting can be very similar to written communications in terms of preparation, but the meeting can more easily involve several people simultaneously. A formal one-on-one meeting, such as a performance review session, can be a good way to document issues of concern and make plans for future action. Of course, formal meetings can consume a great deal of time and can actually hinder productivity if they are not properly conducted.[12] Informal meetings and impromptu one-on-one conversations can be used effectively to transfer information, solve problems, and stimulate action. In fact, research suggests that such impromptu meetings are the most common form of interaction for high-level managers.[13]

Finally, there is the telephone, and many managers do make good use of this verbal medium.[14] The telephone can make it very easy to reach someone quickly, even though the sender and receiver are not in the same building, or even in the same city, state, or country. And telephone answering machines, beepers, voice mail, and portable cellular telephones have made it easier to reach a person in a relatively short time period. As Insights 11–1 and 11–2 show, portable phones and voice mail systems are changing people's lives. For example, teleconferencing makes meetings possible among people who are in different cities. But in using the telephone, managers give up another very important medium of communications—nonverbal communications—unless they use the new video-conferencing technology that produces both voice and picture. This option is discussed later under high-tech media.

Nonverbal communications are all communications that do not involve the use of words. Some researchers estimate that over two thirds of people's communications are through nonverbal media.[15] As discussed in Chapter 10, ceremonies, symbols, and settings are important nonverbal means of communicating.[16] In addition, nonverbal media include head, face, and eye behavior (for example, eye contact and facial expressions); posture and body language; distance between sender and receiver; gestures; tone of voice; volume; silence; color (for example, blushing); touch; smell; time; signals; objects; office layout; and clothing.[17] Managers need to develop their skills for reading these signals in other people, so they can get beyond the words people say. It is apparent

Portable Phones Are Prompting Change in Business and Life Styles

William Joy, a vice president at Sun Microsystems Inc., used to get impatient cooling his heels in office lobbies. No more. "Now I can step outside, whip out my portable phone and make calls," he says. "For people who are truly workaholics, it's a benefit."

Hand-held cellular telephones like Mr. Joy's are the latest techno-toys starting to spread through the business world. Although they are still rare, the growing number of dedicated users say they make a more profound change in life styles than even car-based mobile phones.

"I think they're the greatest thing to come along since wheels," says O'Donald Carroll, general manager of CBA Security Services Inc., a Las Vegas company that has given portable cellular phones to all its executives and supervisors. Handling security for prize fights and events like the Jerry Lewis Telethon, "you have celebrities that have to be coordinated," he says. "You can't stop and walk 20 yards to a pay phone to get in touch."

Fans say that the increasingly common cellular car phones are just a technological way station en route to personal pocket phones. "Car phones are simply a resting point for this technology," says Daniel R. Croft, general marketing and sales manager for Centel Cellular Co., a Chicago unit of Centel Corp. "We're headed for people phones—not car phones or house phones."

Expensive Communications

That doesn't mean it's time to junk the wall unit in the kitchen. (Portable cellular phones aren't related to home portables, which work from a base unit.) Even enthusiasts concede that portables have some drawbacks that will prevent them from capturing a substantial portion of the phone market for several years.

The first is price. Even the cheapest models cost about $1,500. (By contrast, car phones cost as little as $500.) And operating charges average about $150 a month.

While portable phones don't work as well in cars as do car phones, they do work. Financier Bernard Cornfeld says that he replaced his old mobile phone with a portable because "I found I was using the car with the phone all the time, even though I have several cars. Now, one phone is applicable to all of my cars."

They also work, to some degree, on trains and in planes and taxis. Michael Kolowich, a Lotus Development Corp. vice president, says he carries his when he goes to New York on business. When traffic makes him late, he can call his appointments. "The worst thing about being late is the anxiety about the people you're visiting. This eliminates it," he says.

Dial 'O' for Options: Computers Enhance Phone-Answering Gear

Computerized answering machines may do for switchboard operators what automated teller machines have done for bank tellers.

A new generation of sophisticated telephone-answering devices is helping businesses and institutions to handle calls more efficiently and accurately. The simplest "voice-mail" machines let callers leave a recorded message, just like a standard tape answering machine. But many of the systems—the so-called automated attendants—do a lot more, directing callers to select from among various options using the buttons on a touch-tone phone. Such devices now enable some 40,000 students at Texas A & M University to register for classes by phone, and in the coming weeks a computer will tell callers to the Butterball turkey hotline how to thaw their holiday birds.

Although reaction to the devices has been cool in some quarters, a growing number of businesses are resorting to them to protect costly employees from time-consuming, and sometimes annoying, outside callers. Falling prices have made them even more attractive.

"Five years from now, when calling the overwhelming majority of companies, people will reach automated attendants," predicts Blair Pleasant, a researcher with Yankee Group, a Boston-based consulting firm.

'Thank You for Calling'

That's already the case for those who call American Airlines to check on flight delays. A slightly disembodied feminine voice says:

"Thank you for calling American Airlines' automated information system. For flight arrival information, press one. For fare and schedule information, press two. For assistance anytime, press asterisk and zero."

If the caller presses one on a touch-tone phone and then taps out the flight number, the voice reports on its status. (As with most similar systems, an operator assists those calling from rotary-dial phones.)

Is this progress? Some people don't think so. Carlton Vogt, an editor with Design News magazine in Newton, Mass., says sometimes the computers make him go through so many steps that "I just hang up." And the Internal Revenue Service concedes that more than one-third of the callers to its three-year-old TeleTax service, which tells taxpayers when they can expect to receive refunds, hang up without getting their information.

But most callers, who have become used to answering machines of one form or another, put up with communicating with computers. Some even like it.

Consider the system at Citizens & Southern National Bank in Atlanta. Every day—24 hours a day, seven days a week—the bank receives some 16,000 calls from customers who can tap in a password and an account number to find out about account balances, credit-card payments or whether certain checks have been cashed. Mary Farrell of Perception Technology, the Canton, Mass., firm that developed the system, says it handles about 80% of the bank's phone inquiries.

EXHIBIT 11–2

What Are These Facial Expressions Saying?

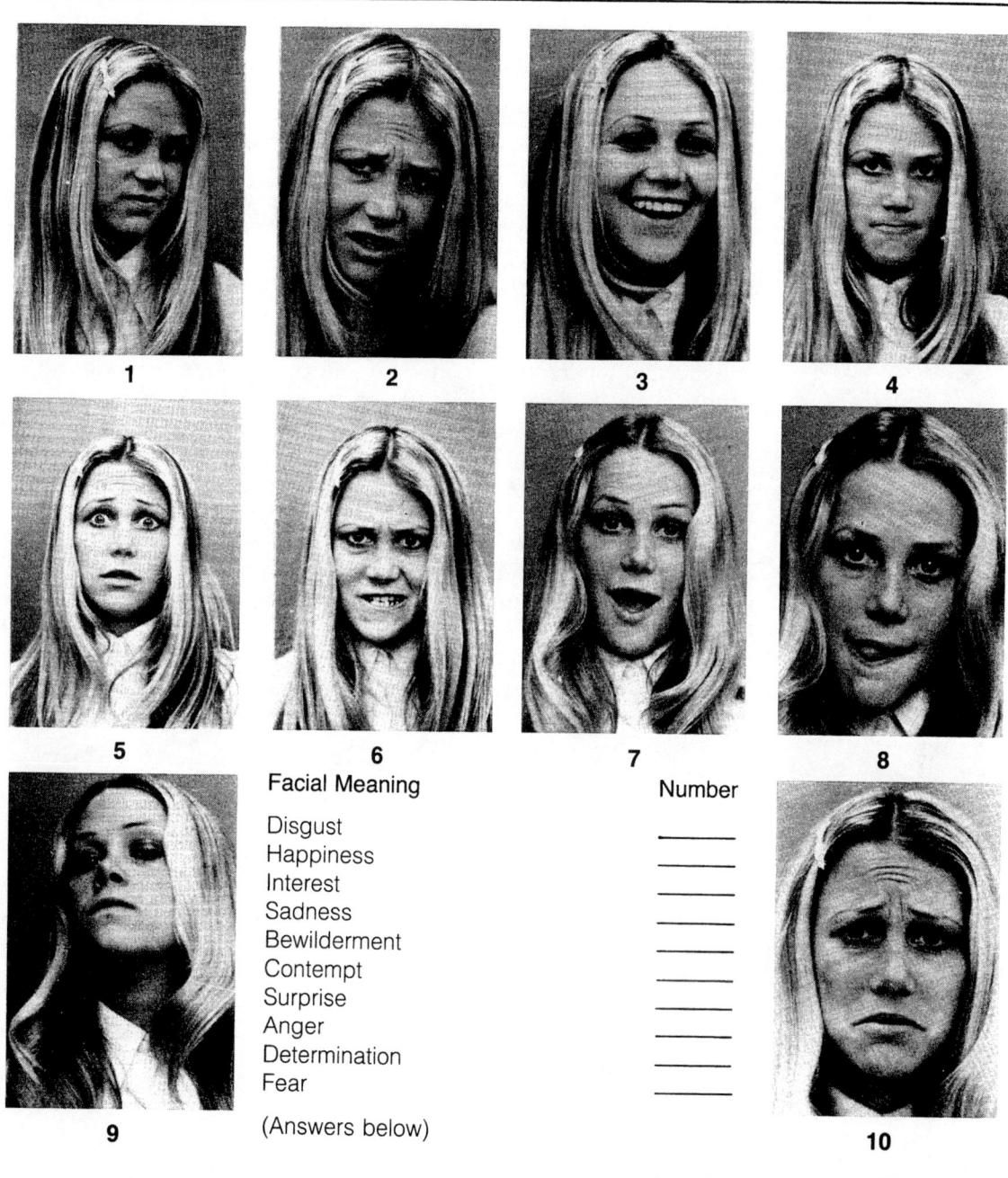

Facial Meaning	Number
Disgust	_____
Happiness	_____
Interest	_____
Sadness	_____
Bewilderment	_____
Contempt	_____
Surprise	_____
Anger	_____
Determination	_____
Fear	_____

(Answers below)

(Correct answers: Disgust = 1, Happiness = 3, Interest = 8, Sadness = 10, Bewilderment = 2, Contempt = 9, Surprise = 7, Anger = 6, Determination = 4, and Fear = 5.)

Source: Dale G. Leathers, *Nonverbal Communication Systems* (Boston: Allyn and Bacon, 1976), pp. 26–28. Printed with permission of Dale G. Leathers.

in the Home Computers case that Rob does not do a good job reading nonverbal cues. And that is unfortunate since most of these cues are straightforward. Still, several nonverbal cues do deserve some comment. Facial expressions are the primary means by which people transmit emotions, such as happiness, anger, disgust, and surprise.[18] Take a look at Exhibit 11–2 on page 430 to see how well you can identify the emotions that go with the 10 facial expressions shown. **Body language** refers to signals given by such actions as standing versus sitting, open versus crossed legs and arms, facial expressions, and eye contact or lack thereof. **Silence** is just that. By not answering someone's question, a person conveys a message. For example, if an employee asks for a raise and the boss says nothing, the employee has received his answer. The **color** of a person's office carpet and walls could convey harshness if they were red, whereas a pale blue would convey more warmth. **Smell** includes body odor, bad breath, and nice cologne, each of which conveys a message the sender may or may not intend. And **clothing** conveys things about a person, as well. For example, a man or woman wearing a conservative business suit is seen as more powerful than a man wearing a plaid sport coat or a woman in a brightly colored, high-fashion dress.[19]

Time can indicate a person's degree of interest in something. For example, if a manager answers a request for information the next day as opposed to three weeks later, the time difference may suggest how the manager feels about the original sender or the request. **Signals** include such things as fire alarms, horns indicating lunch break or shift change in a plant, a watch that beeps as a reminder of a meeting, or the beep on a word processor to indicate a mistake. Finally, **objects** are the focus of work, and they can convey a message. For example, a dishwasher in a restaurant who sees the busser bring a load of dishes to the kitchen window, needs no words exchanged to know to begin washing the dishes.

Finally, in the last 10 years, **high-tech** media have burst onto the scene in an array of forms.[20] For example, personal computers networked together create easy means to store and communicate vast amounts of information. Unfortunately, some managers have become enamored with how much information can be generated with computers. Thus, managers may simply flood people with information that often has no meaning to the receivers. Managers may forget that the purpose of communications is not information, but rather the transfer of meaning. If meaning is transmitted, communications time is reduced, thus generating higher productivity. For example, in a recent Business Week article, IBM reported reducing new-product development time by 15 to 20 percent by using computer networking to help people share design proposals.[21]

A more extreme example of high-tech communications is **artificial intelligence** or **expert systems.** Essentially these computer programs store the knowledge and thinking of experts so that others can access it, much like talking to the experts themselves. For example, Boeing has used expert systems to tell skilled workers how to assemble the 5,000 multiple electrical connectors on an airplane, based on nearly 20,000 pages of cross-referenced specifications. Use of the system has reduced the search time for specifications from 42 minutes to only 5 minutes per connector.[22]

On another level of high-tech media, satellites, telecommunications, video cameras, and fiber-optic cables have created other options. Video-conferencing can allow companies to simultaneously transmit messages to thousands of people in a variety of locations. It can also allow groups to communicate live with each other via cameras and cable transmission of the picture and sound, even though the groups are hundreds or even thousands of miles apart (see Insight 11–3). One researcher observed such a session involving engineers in the United States having a video-conference meeting with engineers in Germany. Of course, the equipment for such communications systems can be quite expensive, costing anywhere from $75,000 to $150,000, plus transmission costs of about $1,000 per hour. And it is interesting to note that people still seem to prefer face-to-face meetings. Indeed, studies have shown that people still prefer conventional media like the telephone, mail, and personal meetings over the high-tech options like electronic mail, videoconferencing and computer networks.[23] But changes are occurring, and no doubt everyone will be using high-tech media more and more frequently in the future. Technology has come a long way in just the last 15 years or so in the use of personal computers and videocassettes. Other high-tech changes will also occur.

Directions

The last dimension of communications, **direction,** takes into account the *people* who are engaged in communication. More specifically, **directions of communications help people focus on the organizational roles of the sender and the receiver.** Basically, communications can be vertical, horizontal, and diagonal, as determined by their relationship to the organizational chart.[24]

Vertical communications flow in two directions: upward through the hierarchy, and downward through the hierarchy. Usually **downward communications** are used for control, instruction, motivation, and evaluation purposes. For example, managers in organizations are expected to set priorities and tasks for subordinates, to tell them what their jobs are, and to motivate them. Rob of the Home Computers Company case was using downward communications when he told his supervisors about the personnel problems in the section. And Rob learned the hard way that if subordinates' perceptions of a manager's communications are poor, their performance also tends to be lower.[25]

INSIGHT 11-3

Face to Face

*T*here are times when a picture may be worth considerably more than a thousand words. Say you have a designer in Chicago who needs to show a drawing to an engineer in Atlanta. Or maybe it's time to inspire a far-spread salesforce with a personal message from the chairman. What if there's just been an unexpected upheaval in your business—something akin to the stock-market crash last October—and you must get up-to-the-minute instructions out to branch offices all across the country? If your company is an innovator, you're probably already mastering these situations with something called videoconferencing. If not, you may be using it soon.

Videoconferencing is an umbrella term—it refers not to one, but two, technologies that use live video to unite widely dispersed company operations. The more popular type of videoconference is business television. Relying on the same basic technology that brings Alf and Bill Cosby into our homes, business-television networks enable companies to deliver powerful messages to thousands of employees simultaneously. For more intimate meetings, there is point-to-point digital videoconferencing—think of it as two small groups in faraway places meeting via live television pictures.

Televised instruction covers a spectrum as wide as a manager's imagination, including technical sessions for service reps, new product overview for sales staffs, management courses for executives, even general enrichment classes. It's like having an auditorium full of employees who can watch demonstrations, listen to the experts, and even raise their hands to ask questions—business TV networks permit call-in responses from viewers. But of course, a private network can reach many more people than can be crammed into an auditorium.

The savings derived from business TV account for much of its popularity. When Hewlett-Packard first used a telecast conference to announce a new product in 1981, it cut product introduction costs in half.

But business TV is only part of the videoconferencing picture—albeit the larger, more widely utilized and, yes, more glamorous part. The other important technology is point-to-point digital videoconferencing. Think of it as a private meeting, with a few people in one conference facility conversing via a television with a few people in another, distant conference room.

"It enables you to hold an interactive meeting," says Kathleen J. Hansell, president of KJH Communications, a market research firm based in Atlanta.

By Jeffrey Zygmont, *Sky Magazine*, February, 1988. This article has been reprinted through the courtesy of Halsey Publishing Co., publishers of Delta Airlines' *Sky* magazine.

Upward vertical communications are typically used for information exchange, problem solving, and as a response to downward communications.[26] In a great many organizations, upward communications are not used nearly so frequently as downward communications. The primary reason for this is that lower-level organization members are expected to initiate these communications when there may be no incentive, channel, or precedent for doing so. If upper-level managers would solicit and encourage an upward flow of information, this direction could become a more important vehicle for improved communications in organizations. The Home Computers case illustrates this well, both with Rob's decision to delay contacting his boss about the coordination problems in the plant and with the lack of communications flowing up to Rob from his supervisors.

Horizontal communications can also be broken down into two categories. First, there are communications with peers in the same department and/or shift. Typically, these communications are for information exchange, minor problem solving, and social needs purposes. Peers sometimes are also involved in rating each other's performance. Research has suggested, however, that negative peer ratings can significantly reduce group cohesiveness and satisfaction in later situations.[27] Second, horizontal communications may cut across department and/or shift boundaries to people at the same level in an organization. For example, Rob's contact with Hal Walker, another section head, was interdepartmental horizontal communication. Typically, interdepartmental horizontal communications are for control, information exchange, problem solving, and social needs purposes.

Diagonal communications are like the interdepartmental horizontal communications except that they link people at higher or lower levels in an organizational hierarchy. For example, a supervisor may need to get a particular new procedure initiated in another department of the plant. In order to do this, it might be necessary for the supervisor to talk directly with that department head, who is two levels up in the hierarchy. The supervisor could go up the chain of command to the department head level and let his or her department head discuss the issue with the other department head. But it will take longer; and it may be that the supervisor has been requested to handle this matter personally. Such situations occur frequently in organizations, and they point out the importance of personal power sources and politics, as discussed in Chapter 10. Furthermore, these situations highlight the fact that communications paths often do not trace the lines connecting people on an organizational chart.

The **informal communications system** (or **grapevine** as it is sometimes called) is another direction of communications. The grapevine does not adhere to an organizational chart, yet it impacts almost everyone in an organization. There are people in every organization who always seem to have the latest news or gossip. Others gravitate to these people instead of to their bosses to find out what is going on. And since a great deal of important information is transmitted via this informal communications system, it is probably safe to say that organizations would be less effective without it.

STRUCTURAL, TECHNOLOGICAL, PHYSICAL LAYOUT, AND HISTORICAL INFLUENCES

In addition to the purpose, media, and direction dimensions of communications, managers must be aware that organizational communications occur within a **context,** consisting of organizational structure, technology, physical layout, and past history.[28] Exhibit 11–3 illustrates this point and summarizes our discussion up to now. Let us briefly explore each of these four context variables.

First, the **structure** of an organization directly influences its intended communications. People are grouped into one department because they perform similar work and because they need to communicate more closely with each other than with people in other departments. However, as the discussion of the grapevine suggests and as research has

EXHIBIT 11–3

Organizational Communications: Process, Purposes, Media, Directions, and Context

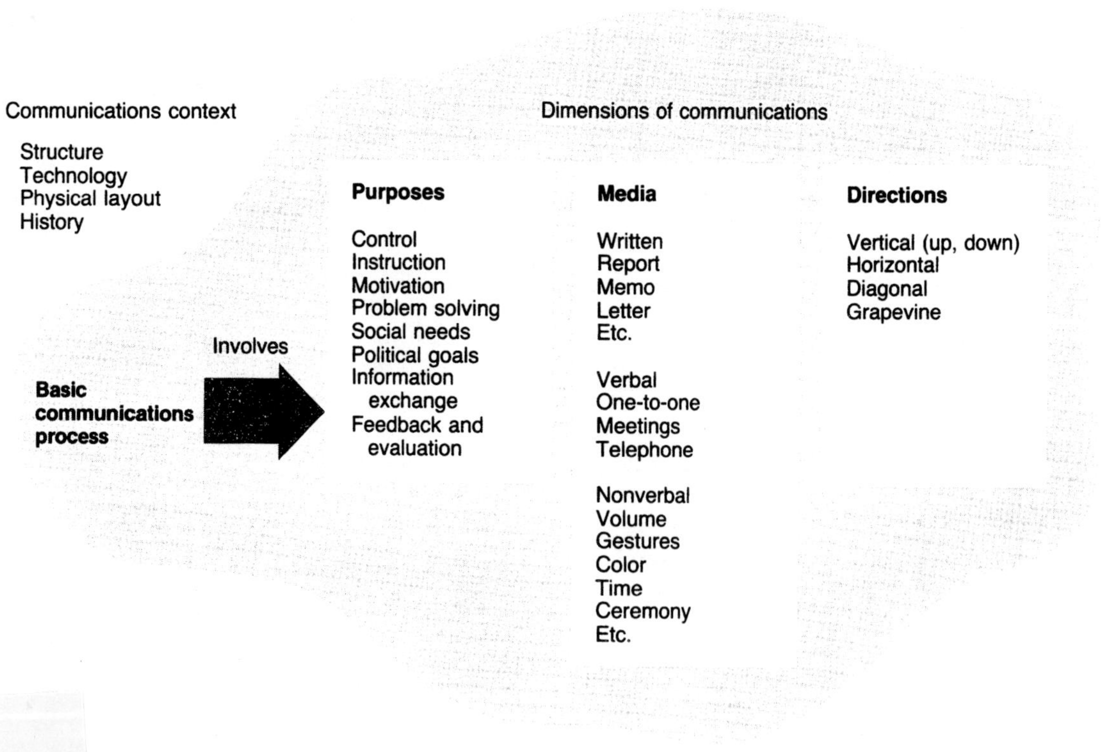

Communications context

Structure
Technology
Physical layout
History

Involves →

Basic communications process

Dimensions of communications

Purposes	**Media**	**Directions**
Control	Written	Vertical (up, down)
Instruction	Report	Horizontal
Motivation	Memo	Diagonal
Problem solving	Letter	Grapevine
Social needs	Etc.	
Political goals		
Information exchange	Verbal	
Feedback and evaluation	One-to-one	
	Meetings	
	Telephone	
	Nonverbal	
	Volume	
	Gestures	
	Color	
	Time	
	Ceremony	
	Etc.	

demonstrated, the organizational structure may not coincide very well with the actual communications networks that emerge.[29] In fact, the formal structure can sometimes inhibit the flow of necessary information. The structure certainly inhibited the flow of communications at HCC between Rob (the superior) and Tom (the subordinate) and between Rob and all of his supervisors.

In addition to structure, the **technologies** in organizations influence the communications that emerge.[30] As the technology becomes more routine, the frequency of communications tends to decrease. For example, the assembly-line section at HCC that Rob supervises would probably have fewer communications than the research and development department. Communications also tend to be more horizontal and less vertical with more routine technologies. Furthermore, increases in technological routine tend to result in more instruction and motivation communications and fewer problem-solving communications.

Physical layout can also have an impact on communications. For example, one study found that clerical employees in an open office with fewer walls between work stations communicate more freely than those in more traditional, walled-off offices. But managerial and professional people, who must think about things in more depth, tend to communicate less freely in an open-office setup.[31] The key point here is that the layout of offices has an impact on communications. **Managers should not physically relocate people without considering the effect it may have on communications.** If managers break up existing communication flows with the change in layout, productivity will probably drop.

Finally, communications in organizations take place within a **historical context.** People in organizations have had an opportunity to interact over time. They have seen the power and status differences and have learned about the norms and incentives in the organization. For example, employees may learn over time that a person should never disagree with the boss in public. Or they may learn that notes to people get a better response than do telephone calls. Past communication experiences in an organization are thus part of the historical context. **The pattern of communications in any organization develops over a period of time, and it will continue to evolve into the future.** As technologies, structures, and people change, so will the communications in an organization.

OUTCOMES ASSOCIATED WITH COMMUNICATIONS

There can be many outcomes of communications in an organization— some positive and some negative. As discussed earlier, **communications are the primary vehicle by which leadership is activated, people are motivated, and relationships are developed.** At its most basic level, communication is how managers influence people in an organization. Communication by a manager can result in: (1) compliance of others, (2) a calculated response designed to get something in return, or (3) total lack of compliance.[32] These outcomes concern managers on an almost daily basis. But there are also some long-term outcomes that are of concern to managers.

A new member of an organization or one who makes a departmental move learns through communications how to become effective in the new position. That is, the person becomes **socialized,** as discussed in Chapter 4. The job is learned, as are the norms of the organization and the expectations of peers, subordinates, and superiors. If communications are open in an organization, it is possible that good relationships can develop with the other employees. A feeling of support and honesty can develop that will make working together both a pleasure and a real success in terms of organizational goals. If, however, communications are guarded, the person will not become properly socialized to the organization and will be less effective in the job.

Second, through communications, it is possible to develop **liking** and **respect** for others. Most managers want their subordinates both to like and respect them. If managers develop communications that convey a sense of warmth, trust, and closeness with their employees, liking will tend to develop. If managers convey a sense of aloofness and distance, liking probably will not develop.[33]

Managers must also have the respect of their people. Indeed, respect may be more important than liking for getting a task done. If communications convey a sense of a manager's competence and a respect for the employees' abilities, that respect will tend to be returned. If, on the other hand, a manager conveys a sense of superiority and disrespect for the subordinates' abilities, the subordinates probably will not respect the manager much, either.[34]

Closely associated with the outcomes of respect and liking is the **trust** that can develop via communications. If liking and respect are present, trust probably is, too. In relationships, trust is something that develops slowly over time. Usually it requires that one or both people involved take risks with each other, and the manager plays a key role in creating a climate that promotes trust. Supportive exchanges are essential in building trust.[35] For example, letting a subordinate be responsible for a task without looking over her shoulder while she does the job helps build trust. A certain level of trust is necessary for any organization to run properly.[36]

As discussed in Chapter 3, communications can also be important in aligning perceptions held by different people. If messages are clearly sent and received, perceptual errors are more likely to be discovered and corrected. And when perceptions are aligned, working to achieve the organization's goals will be more unified. For example, when the players on a college basketball team clearly agree on the perceptions of each other's abilities and strengths, they know what to count on from each other and hence tend to perform well as a team. Indeed, research has shown that accuracy of communications and the related perceptions are associated with improved performance.[37] And research has shown also that communications can increase participative decision making, cohesiveness, and morale in a group. But if communications are not handled well in a group, they can lead to increases in conflict and distrust, as discussed in Chapters 12 and 13.[38]

Each of the outcomes discussed above has both a positive and a negative side, and this is determined by the way the communications process and its dimensions are used by the people in an organization. Many factors can inhibit effective communications and lead to negative outcomes. We turn now to these factors and then to some ways of improving communications in an organization.

FACTORS THAT INHIBIT COMMUNICATIONS

In discussing the factors that can inhibit the flow of communications in an organization, it is helpful to tie any comments to the basic model of the communications process in Exhibit 11–1 and the basic dimensions of communications in Exhibit 11–3.[39] Let us look first at the problems from the point of view of the sender.

Problems related to the sender

As the originator of a communication, the sender has the responsibility of ensuring that the message is transmitted so that the receiver has the greatest chance of receiving and understanding it. A primary problem can occur in the encoding of a message: the sender may select the wrong set of words and symbols for the receiver. For example, at Home Computers Company, Rob felt he was communicating with a brick wall when talking to one of the design engineers about production methods for the new EZ2. Rob was probably using different terminology than the design engineer typically used. This problem can also exist between different levels of an organization, as illustrated in Insight 11–4 on page 439.

Another problem is that managers sometimes abbreviate a message, thus making it unclear. For example, a manager may explain steps one, three, and five of a six-step process, assuming that an employee will be able to fill in steps two, four, and six to complete the required task. The manager assumes that the employee has as complete an understanding of the process as does the manager, but this may not be true. What happens is that both sender and receiver must interpret communica-

"What do you mean. I don't communicate? Didn't you read the memo
I left you at breakfast?"

From *The Wall Street Journal*, with permission of Cartoon Features Syndicate.

tions based on his or her own set of experiences—which, as discussed
in Chapter 3 on perception, may be quite different and lead to different
interpretations.[40]

Another reason for sending an incomplete message is that the sender
is not sure of the response the receiver will send back. For example, an
employee may be reluctant to disclose the details of a costly mistake he
made for fear of what the boss's response may be. Thus, the employee
tells only part of the story and tries to correct the problem before the
boss finds out any more. Recall in the HCC case how Rob decided not
to communicate with his boss about the coordination problems in the
plant.

This problem can often lead to the more general problem of a poor
relationship between the sender and the receiver. If the relationship is
not good or if the status differences are too great, communications may
be altered as they are transmitted from the sender. The personalities of
the sender and the receiver (as discussed in Chapter 4) play an important role in the developmental aspects of communications. And they can
create real barriers to the flow of information between sender and receiver. For example, we can speculate that Rob is a feeling type (see
Chapter 4), and this could be part of his communication problem with
Tom, who may be a thinking type. Rob's high-relationship style of lead-

ership may come across as weak with Tom because their past experiences have created such different personality types.

A related issue is the degree of trust that the sender has in the receiver. If past experience has shown that the receiver seldom understands and acts on the sender's messages, a lack of trust may develop and make the sender uncertain about how to ensure that communications are complete.

Finally, the sender can fail to recognize the time implications associated with a communication. For example, in the Home Computers case, Rob may ask a supervisor to do something that will take more time than Rob has allowed in his request. The supervisor may then hear only the part of the message he or she feels can be accomplished in the allotted time. On the other side of the coin, Rob might be telling employees about the new EZ2 version too far in advance to hold their interest. If he announces it six months in advance, they may not give it as much attention as if he announced it two months in advance. The point is that the sender must be aware of the appropriate timing of the message in order to increase its probability of reception.

Problems related to the receiver

The primary problems associated with the receiver are lack of awareness of the message, misinterpretation of the message, and lack of acceptance of the message. People are bombarded with many messages and other stimuli, and they simply must ignore some messages. For example, suppose a manager comes back from lunch to find six phone messages taped to his office door, three reports and three memos in his in-basket, and someone waiting to see him. While the manager is talking to the visitor, his phone rings twice, his secretary buzzes him, and he tries to sneak a glance at the reports. Is it any wonder that the manager may miss some of the messages intended for him?

As John Naisbitt, author of *Megatrends,* suggests, this problem of information overload will drastically increase in the information society of the coming years.[41] Naisbitt comments that **information float,** the time it takes for messages to be transmitted from sender to receiver, will be greatly reduced. For example, instead of taking three or four days to send a letter across the country and three or four days for it to return, that week's float will be reduced to a matter of seconds with the advent of electronic mail. Just imagine what reduced float time will do to the amount of correspondence managers will have to deal with each day at work!

One way that receivers respond to this flood of communications is to use programmed responses and decision rules to determine which messages they pay attention to. As receivers use such devices, they run the risk of missing important information or an important request. And as people's working world becomes more international, the chance of misinterpreting a message can go up dramatically.[42]

The second receiver problem revolves around decoding the message that is received. If the sender uses language unfamiliar to the receiver, the message may be misinterpreted. The receiver may also read between the lines and assume messages that were not intended. For example, at Home Computers Company, when Rob wondered about Hal's tone of voice and interpreted it in a defensive manner, he may have been receiving a message that Hal did not intend. Insight 11–5 shows how such problems can easily occur, especially in a world that is becoming increasingly international.

The final receiver problem is that the receiver may not accept the message, even if it is heard and understood. For example, suppose a subordinate tells a manager of a problem with one of the manager's decisions. The manager may ignore the comment because she does not want to hear criticism, even if it is accurate. Here, the credibility of the sender is important. As discussed in Chapter 10, the sender's expert power may make the difference in the receiver's acceptance of the mes-

I N S I G H T 11–5

How to Read Your Japanese Partners' Hai Signs

*T*he ritual first step in any encounter with a Japanese business person is the exchange of business cards (*meishi*). This exchange formalizes the introduction process and establishes the status of the two parties relative to each other and within their respective organizations. When a Westerner accepts a card from a Japanese, it is essential he read the entire card (to himself) and then make a statement acknowledging it. Never take a Japanese person's business card and put it directly into your pocket. That implies you think your counterpart is unimportant, an unintended offense from which your meeting might never recover.

Once the introductory formalities have been completed, do not assume it is time to get down to business. The rituals have just begun, and for the Westerner, sensing the proper time to raise business topics will require a large amount of perception and patience. Don't rush the business discussion. The Japanese know why you are there, and you should not force a conversation or decision to go any faster than your guests deem appropriate.

Because form is substance for the Japanese, their conversations are layered. Westerners value being direct, and the English language stresses precision. The Japanese value the process of communication, and their language is deliberately vague. In what is said and what is not said, the Japanese are distinguishing between *tatemae* and *honne*. Tatemae is the official stance, the public truth, while honne is the true intention, the real truth. Not understanding the difference has led to many a missed opportunity.

For example, because the Japanese will, as a courtesy, attempt to tell the Westerner what he wants to hear—and because of the Japanese aversion to saying "no"—the Westerner may think he is being deceived while the Japanese person thinks he is being polite. For astute executives, conversations with the Japanese can consist almost entirely of trying to perceive the often unspoken honne behind the tatemae. Both are there, but it is the tatemae to which most Westerners usually react.

Japanese conversations are also interactive. In English, one party speaks while the other politely listens; to interrupt in English is considered rude. In Japanese, the listener gives signals to indicate he understands. Sometimes the listener will even finish the speaker's sentence for him. The alert Westerner observes these signals and unobtrusively responds in kind when the Japanese speak. Slight nods and soft comments (such as yes, uh huh, I understand, I see) are perfectly appropriate.

When Westerners speak, Japanese will often say "*hai*" (yes). This hai means "Yes, I understand you," *not* "Yes, I agree with you." It is always safe to assume that, instead of giving you his personal opinion or making a decision, a Japanese person is only acknowledging that he has understood what you have said.

sage. Likewise, a lack of trust in the sender can be a barrier to communications.

Thus, the ego of the receiver can be an important barrier to the flow of information. If the message sent seems to create the need for the receiver to make a change or admit a mistake, the receiver's ego may make it difficult to really hear, understand, and accept the message.

Problems in the channel

Problems in the communications channel arise when the sender chooses a medium that is inappropriate for the receiver or for the message. For example, at HCC, Rob chose to leave a note for Tom, to call him, and to drop by his office when maybe he should have used a more formal channel, such as a memo. Sometimes the structure of an organization dictates the choice of media. If two people are located in offices 2,000 miles apart, the only logical media may be the telephone for quick contact—at least until electronic mail becomes common.

Another problem with the channel is that it may involve several conflicting media. For example, suppose a husband shouts that he is not mad at his wife, while standing over her with crossed arms and a red face. The nonverbal cues clearly contradict the words—and the wife would probably listen more to the nonverbals, even though her husband might be calming down and really mean what he says.[43]

Finally, the channel may involve more than one person in linking the originating sender to the ultimate receiver. The problem is that a message tends to get distorted as it passes through several people, all with their own biases, priorities, and communications abilities. Research has indicated that up to 80 percent of a message can be lost in communications cycles completed by five successive people.[44]

Problems related to the context

In addition to the barriers to communications that deal with purpose, media, direction, and process, we must consider the **context** in which communications occur. Because the **structure** of an organization creates status differences, authority and responsibility differences, and incentives for action, it can also create a barrier to communications. People cannot communicate simply as people; they must communicate as role occupants in the organizational structure. For example, the roles that Rob and the design engineer fill at HCC create barriers to communications that might not exist if the two of them were playing golf together. And the status difference between Rob and his boss may be the factor inhibiting Rob from communicating about the coordination problems across shifts.

Furthermore, people communicate to some extent through stereotypes. As more women have entered the ranks of management, the old stereotypes of differences between the sexes have created barriers to communication.[45] For example, touch, while generally having a friendship connotation, can suggest other things when it occurs between a man and a woman on the job. Fortunately, such stereotypes are changing, as men and women work together on a more equal basis in the workplace.

Another factor inhibiting the communications between Rob and the design engineer at HCC is that they work in different departments. The more that organizations form highly specialized departments that function in a very formalized manner, the more communications between departments will be inhibited. As the departments become more separated in their activities, they will develop their own priorities, norms of behavior, and time frames. Thus, what may be of critical and immediate importance to Rob may be much less important to the design engineer. And this difference will make the engineer less receptive to what Rob wants.

As for **technological** barriers, if the technology of an organization is complex and nonroutine, there will be a great chance for miscommunication, even though communications will be very frequent. On the other hand, if the technology is routine, the frequency of communications will be reduced, and the accuracy should be increased. However, over time the routine technology can lead to bored workers who get careless with their communications, thus leading to reduced accuracy.

The **history** of communications can also become a barrier to current communications. A past history of miscommunications between managers and subordinates can lead to severe conflict. It appears that this is what happened to Rob. As he chose not to deal directly with the symptoms of poor communications in his section, they became worse and worse. A sense of distrust developed among his people, and finally Rob was reassigned to another department.

WAYS TO IMPROVE COMMUNICATIONS IN ORGANIZATIONS

Considering all these problems of communications, the complexity of the communications process, the many dimensions of the process, and the context variables, it is no wonder it is difficult to have good communications in an organization. We will now explore several ways to improve communications. To provide order to this discussion, we will use Exhibit 11–4 as an outline of some steps for improving communications in organizations.

EXHIBIT 11–4

Steps to Improve Communications
in an Organization

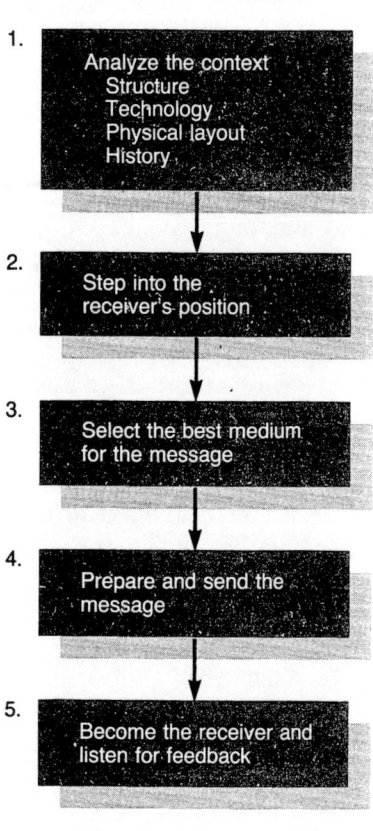

Step 1: Analyze the context

The first step in improving communications in organizations is to understand the context in which the communications must occur. Managers need to assess the technological, structural, physical layout, and
historical context in which the communications occur. Changes in this
context can be used to improve communications. For example, use of
computer-based information systems can improve communications. As
Naisbitt suggested, managers have computer terminals right on their
desks, and they must know something about basic programming to
effectively use the computer.[46] Managers without computer skills will
be lost in a sea of rapidly changing information.

An example of a structural change is when companies employ communications specialists and special work units.[47] When a situation is

very complex or rapidly changing, the hierarchical order of communications may need to be altered. The use of task forces, special ad hoc committees, and special project groups can be especially helpful in linking departments in an organization, when strong differences make it difficult for the departments to communicate.

It may also be possible to link machinery to computers to reduce the need for communications among the people in an organization. The emergence of robots in the workplace illustrates the potential of this device for improving communications.[48]

But managers may not always be able to use technology and structure to their advantage. Instead, technology and structure may actually constrain a manager's behavior, as noted earlier. Managers need to understand these constraints in order to maintain effective communications. Managers' communications in a very routine and highly structured situation will be much more controlled than in an unstructured and nonroutine situation.

Another aspect to consider is the political context of communications as discussed in Chapter 10. Often decisions and other important communications are heavily influenced by the politics of the situation; and it will not always be best to engage in open communications.[49] The cultural network determines what type of communications will be most effective. It may be formal communications, or it may be informal, spontaneous communications.[50] The point is that **managers must understand the situation if they are to communicate effectively in it.**

Step 2: Step into the receiver's position

The sender needs to understand the receiver in order to communicate effectively. For example, a supervisor dealing with a relatively uneducated worker on the shop floor must choose his words differently than when communicating with his boss. Likewise, if a receiver is very angry, the sender must communicate differently than when the receiver is calm. Perhaps when a person is angry, the sender should wait until the person calms down. Remember, **if the sender does not transmit in an appropriate language and manner, and at a time when the receiver can hear the message, the chances of effective communication are greatly reduced.** Communication is basically a marketing concept. As Insight 11–6 shows, people do not necessarily have to change their product (or their idea), just the way they push it.

A recent book describes a related process called **active listening** as a vehicle for getting inside another person's viewpoint.[51] The concept suggests that the receiver listen for total meaning; that is, the receiver should try to get not only the content of messages, but also the sender's feelings. To do so, the receiver must listen to all the cues being sent, especially the nonverbal ones. In addition, the listener should give feedback, paraphrasing the speaker's words so that they reflect the feelings

---

INSIGHT 11-6

Wooing Aging Baby-Boomers

*T*he house of Seagram has a new quality-of-life spiel for aging baby-boomers. Says Peter Dimsey, executive vice president of marketing: "When they were younger, they wanted to do everything differently from their parents, and they did not acquire a taste for drinks like whiskey." But cocktails and hard liquor are making a comeback with baby-boomers, who are changing their drinking patterns. "They have become more affluent and are intrigued with the reemergence of elegance," explains Dimsey. "Cocktails and martini glasses are all vehicles for formal entertainment."

Seagram's ads used to equate quality with the high cost of such brands as Crown Royal and Chivas Regal. More expensive is better was the message. The company's new print campaign (distillers do not advertise on TV) is still fairly snooty, but the emphasis has shifted from it-costs-a-fortune to a social situation that aging boomers can identify with. The setting for one Crown Royal ad is a room decorated with an exquisite modern chair and a minimalist painting. "I don't know the guy throwing this party, but he's got lousy taste in art," goes the written text of a witty conversation be-

tween two people who are not visible in the ad. When he realizes he's talking to his host, the speaker quickly adds: "And great taste in cocktails."

Some advertisers have not formally identified the older half of the baby boom, but their ads are evidence that someone at the company or ad agency is tuned in to the aging trend. Diet Rite's straight-shooting commercials are intended for ages 18 through 34. Yet they feature Tony Danza, 36, the popular star of the TV sitcom *Who's the Boss?*, and $6 million man Lee Majors, 47. Beads of sweat roll down the bionic man's brow after a strenuous workout at the gym, while a jingle plays: "It doesn't matter who you are, it's gonna be a tough fight . . . Everybody's gotta Diet Rite."

Saatchi & Saatchi created the Diet Rite ads. Says Penelope Queen, executive vice president and research director: "Most diet soda commercials show a young, shapely girl walking along the beach." But that approach implies that a slim figure is the effortless result of drinking the product. Queen went for reality instead. "We wanted to show the vulnerability and the struggle." Older consumers can certainly relate to that!

Fortune, February 1, 1988.

---

of the speaker. This helps draw out the speaker and helps the listener really understand what is being communicated. And people who use active listening are much more likely to be able to communicate their messages effectively.

Step 3: Select the best medium for the message

Once the message's context and the receiver's position have been analyzed, the sender must think about the best vehicle for transmitting the message. As we have discussed, written communications have the advantage of thoughtful presentation, and the receiver can reflect on the message in privacy. On the other hand, if the message is complex, research has shown that the two-way process of verbal communications is most effective.[52] Of course, several media can be used together (for example, a phone call to make a request, followed by a memo repeating the request). New high-tech media coming on the scene offer even more options.

Further, managers should not forget that nonverbal media are an integral part of any communication. For example, the timing and location of a communication are both part of the media decision. Usually, the more immediate the communication, the better, though at times it may be smarter to let some time pass (for example, when someone is angry).

Step 4: Prepare and send the message

With all of the information in hand from Steps 1 through 3, it is now time to actually formulate and send the message. At this point, it helps the sender rethink the message to be sure he or she still wants to send it. **If the sender is open to the feedback received in analyzing the situation and the receiver, he or she may decide to change the message originally planned.** For example, a manager may have intended to reprimand an employee for poor performance. But after analyzing the situation, the manager felt that the context actually created the poor performance and that the receiver was doing his best in the situation. Hence, the manager may change the message to a problem-solving session with the employee. Above all else, the sender must be sure to send a message that shows respect for the receiver. The sender knows what he or she wants understood; it is the receiver who must now understand it.

Development of a message over time is possible if people are open to the information available to them in an organization. And if people also listen and observe while sending their messages, they can make adjustments in their communications as the process unfolds. For example, in some assertiveness training programs, people are taught to combine understanding with their assertiveness. The understanding allows people to actively pay attention to the receiver. It also allows for three distinct levels of assertiveness.

1. **Understanding–assertive,** where the focus is primarily on understanding the receiver, though not to the point of being submissive.
2. **Equally assertive–understanding,** where there is a balance between listening to the receiver and getting across the sender's ideas.
3. **Assertive–understanding,** where the focus is primarily on getting across the sender's ideas, though not to the point of being aggressive and running over the receiver.

"How do you want this proposal – technical, credible or entertaining?"

During an exchange, it is possible to shift gears through all three levels, depending on how a situation unfolds. And it is important to recognize that a situation may unfold over a few minutes in an exchange or over several months in a series of exchanges.[53] Of course, a person can also communicate in an aggressive or submissive fashion as well. Aggressive communications seek to get the speaker's point across, regardless of the ideas or feelings of the receiver. Submissive communications let the receiver run over the speaker. To find out just how assertive, submissive, or aggressive you are, take a few minutes now to complete the Assertiveness Inventory at the end of this chapter.

Step 5: Become the receiver and listen for feedback

When a message has been sent, the sender needs to switch roles and become the receiver of feedback. **The sender must listen to be sure the message got through and was understood as intended.** Part of the sender's responsibility is to ensure that the feedback loop is completed. Such feedback may be verbal or written, as in a request for information. Or it may be behavioral. That is, when the sender asks the receiver to do something, the sender can watch what the receiver does. For example, at HCC, it was feedback to Rob when Tom did not respond to his note to come by the office. When the feedback indicates that the message was not received, the sender has to go back to Step 1 and begin a follow-up cycle to try to complete the intended communication.

Following these five steps and incorporating an understanding of the process, dimensions, context, outcomes, and inhibitors of communications can make managers better communicators, if they work at it. Remember, **as the sender, a manager is responsible for transmitting a message that the receiver can understand and for ensuring that the manager receives feedback. As the receiver, a manager is responsible for understanding a message that is sent to him or her and for ensuring that feedback is received by the sender.**

CRITICISM AND FEEDBACK

In closing this chapter, we will focus even more specifically on effective communications in two key areas for managers: (1) giving and receiving criticism, and (2) giving and receiving positive feedback.[54] **Giving criticism** that works to correct behavior is vital to any manager. The main rule in being effective with criticism is to focus on the *behavior* and not on the person. Managers should get to the point with the bad news first by specifically describing the problem. And managers must be sure to know the problem before criticizing. It is also good to share feelings of anger, frustration, and disappointment. But in the end, managers must be sure to reinforce the fact that the person criticized is OK. Managers must let the person know how valuable he or she is to the organization and that they know the employee can correct the problem. Remember, **managers must never criticize someone for something when they did not know what to do or how to do it.**

In **receiving criticism,** the key thing to do is absorb the criticism without becoming defensive. If the criticism is correct, admit it; if the criticism is close to correct, acknowledge the possibility; and if the criticism seems wrong, get more information by asking questions. But never attack back. The receiver's goal is to understand the criticism.

On the more positive side, managers need to learn to **give praise** effectively. As with giving criticism, managers need to get to the point and describe the positive situation. The goal is to be as specific as possible in giving the feedback to ensure understanding by the receiver. Again, managers should share feelings of pride, happiness, and satisfaction with the receiver. The objective is for the employee to feel really good when the praising is finished. And remember, **unless managers share their praise verbally or in writing, it will do little good.** Just thinking good thoughts is not enough. These thoughts must be expressed.

Finally, **receiving praise** may make one feel uneasy if he or she is not used to it. But one should just let it soak in; enjoy it; and then say thank you. With practice, it will feel better and better.

CHAPTER HIGHLIGHTS

This final chapter of the section on interpersonal behavior in organizations focuses on communications as a vital organizational process. **Communications are the lifeblood of any organization.** Organizations simply cannot operate without them. And communications in organizations are typically very problematic.

First, we explored the process of communications. The **sender** decides what message to send, encodes the message, and transmits it via the media channel. The message then reaches the intended **receiver,** who decodes it for its intent. Until the receiver gets the message and interprets it as intended by the sender, communication has not occurred. In fact, this means that the last step in the communications process is actually **feedback.** And **it is this cyclical aspect of the communications process that makes communications developmental in nature.** Finally, the last aspect of the process, **noise,** inhibits the flow of communications.

We then looked in on Rob at Home Computers Company. Following that, we discussed three basic dimensions of communications: **purpose, media,** and **direction.** We defined eight basic purposes for which people communicate in organizations: control, instruction, motivation, problem solving, feedback and evaluation, information exchange, social needs, and political goals.

We then discussed four basic types of media that can be used to send messages to other people: **written, verbal, nonverbal,** and **high-tech.** The written category includes procedures manuals, reports, memos, letters, handwritten notes, and files. The basic advantage to written communications is that they can be thought out to ensure better clarity. The biggest disadvantage is that written communications are essentially one-way.

Verbal communications include formal and informal one-on-one conversations, formal and informal meetings, voice mail, and telephone (both stationary and portable). The primary advantage to verbal communications is that they are essentially two-way. The disadvantage is that they may be less well planned, and there is no record of the communication.

Nonverbal communications include head, face, and eye behavior; posture and body language; distance between sender and receiver; gestures; tone of voice; volume; silence; color; touch; smell; time; signals; objects; office layout; clothes; ceremony; symbols; and settings. Some researchers estimate that over two thirds of people's communications are sent via nonverbal media.

High-tech media include such things as networked personal computers, expert systems, videoconferencing, and a growing array of options. At present, many people resist these powerful (and expensive) options, but time will bring down both the price and the resistance.

The last dimension of communications that we discussed was direction: **vertical, horizontal, diagonal,** and the **grapevine.** Vertical communications can be upward and downward. Horizontal communications can be within a department or between departments at the same level. Diagonal communications are also interdepartmental, but they are links to people at higher or lower levels in other departments. Finally, grapevine communications do not follow an organizational chart. **Each direction serves particular purposes, and effective managers are skilled at using each direction.**

The next section discussed the context in which communications occur. The context is influenced by an organization's **structure, technology, physical layout,** and **history.** Furthermore, each of these contextual factors changes over time and creates forces for change in the communications of an organization. Thus, the communications of an organization develop over a period of time.

We then discussed several outcomes associated with communications in organizations—some positive and some negative. In the short run, managers may get compliance, a calculated response, or lack of compliance. In the longer run, through communications, people become socialized to an organization; develop liking and respect for coworkers; develop trust or distrust; and develop, more or less, closely aligned perceptions. The quality of communications determines whether the outcomes are positive or negative.

We then explored a number of factors that can inhibit communications and yield negative outcomes. First, there can be problems related to the sender. The sender can encode the message improperly or send an incomplete message. A poor relationship between sender and receiver can inhibit communications. The sender can also fail to recognize the time aspects of communications.

There can also be problems related to the receiver. The receiver may not be aware of the message, may misinterpret it, or may not accept the message as sent. And an increase in international operations is sure to make this problem worse. There can also be problems in the communications channel: the sender can choose the wrong medium; the sender may send conflicting messages through different media; and the message may have to travel through several people.

Finally, there can be problems in the context of the communications. The organizational structure creates different statuses, authorities, responsibilities, and incentives, and it can inhibit communications for people who are performing their organizational roles. Stereotypes about people can also inhibit communications. The organizational structure places people in different departments, and this can also inhibit communications. And the technology and history of an organization can also create barriers in the communications process.

The final section of the chapter explained five steps to improve communications in organizations. First, analyze the context. Second, step into the receiver's position. Third, select the best medium for the message. Fourth, prepare and send the message. And fifth, become the receiver and listen for feedback. By using these five steps and applying the understanding of process, dimensions, context, and inhibiting factors set forth in this chapter, managers will be in better shape to deal with the problematic nature of communications in organizations. And managers will be better able to give and receive both the criticism and positive feedback that are so vital to being effective.

REVIEW QUESTIONS

1. Why are communications so important in organizations?

2. What are the main reasons why communications in organizations are so problematic?

3. Explain why communication has not occurred until the message is received and understood by the receiver.

4. Why are communications developmental in nature?

5. Explain the basic purposes for which people communicate. Why are some purposes more positive than others in terms of organizational goals?

6. Explain the advantages and disadvantages of each of the four basic types of communications media.

7. What purposes are typically associated with the basic directions of communications?

8. How do the context factors of communications suggest that communications are developmental in nature?

9. What communications outcomes develop over a period of time, again supporting the understanding that communications are developmental in nature?

10. What are the factors that tend to inhibit communications as related to the sender, the receiver, the channel, and the context?

11. Explain the steps managers can use to improve communications in an organization. Explain the cyclical aspect to these steps.

12. Explain how to give and receive both criticism and feedback.

RESOURCE READINGS

Fisher, D. *Communication in Organization.* St. Paul, Minn.: West Publishing, 1981.

Goldhaber, G. *Organizational Communication.* 3d ed. Dubuque, Iowa: Brown, 1983.

Haney, W. V. *Communicational and Interpersonal Relations.* Homewood, Ill.: Richard D. Irwin, 1979.

Harper, R. G.; A. N. Weins; and J. D. Matarzzo. *Nonverbal Communication: The State of the Art.* New York: John Wiley & Sons, 1978.

Kaplan, R. E. *Trade Routes: The Manager's Network of Relationships.* New York: American Management Association, 1984.

Putnam, L., and M. Pacanowsky. *Communication and Organizations: An Interpretive Approach.* Beverly Hills, Calif.: Sage Publications, 1983.

Rice, R. E. *The New Media: Communication, Research, and Technology.* Beverly Hills, Calif.: Sage Publications, 1984.

NOTES

1. H. Mintzberg, *The Nature of Managerial Work* (New York: Harper & Row, 1973); J. P. Kotter, *The General Managers* (New York: Free Press, 1982); F. Luthans and J. K. Larsen, "How Managers Really Communicate," *Human Relations* 39 (1986), pp. 161–78.

2. A. Donnellon, B. Gray, and M. G. Bougon, "Communication, Meaning, and Organized Action," *Administrative Science Quarterly* 31 (1986), pp. 43–55; J. F. Rand and R. E. Wolfe, "Stage Negotiation: The Best Route to Agreement," *Personnel,* January 1985, pp 57–63.

3. C. A. O'Reilly and L. R. Pondy, "Organizational Communication," in *Organizational Behavior,* ed. S. Kerr (Columbus, Ohio: Grid, 1979), pp. 119–50.

4. Mintzberg, *The Nature of Managerial Work*; Kotter, *The General Managers*; C. R. MacDonald, *Performance Based Supervisory Development: Adapted from a Major AT&T Study* (Amherst, Mass.: Human Resource Development Press, 1982, pp. 113–33).

5. C. M. Kelly, "Effective Communications—Beyond the Glitter and Flash," *Sloan Management Review* (Spring 1985), pp. 69–79.

6. C. Shannon and W. Weaver, *The Mathematical Theory of Communication* (Urbana, Ill.: University of Illinois Press, 1948); S. R. Axley, "Managerial and Organizational Communications in Terms of the Conduit Metaphor," *Academy of Management Review* 9 (1984), pp. 428–37.

7. This section draws primarily from W. G. Scott and T. R. Mitchell, *Organization Theory: A Structural and Behavioral Analysis* (Homewood, Ill.: Richard D. Irwin, 1976), ch. 9; and L. Thayer, *Communications and Com-*

munications Systems (Homewood, Ill.: Richard D. Irwin, 1968), pp. 187–301.

8. I. S. Shapiro, *America's Third Revolution* (New York: Harper & Row, 1984).

9. Scott and Mitchell, *Organization Theory*.

10. W. V. Haney, *Communicational and Interpersonal Relations* (Homewood, Ill.: Richard D. Irwin, 1979).

11. W. Whitley, "An Exploratory Study of Managers' Reactions to Properties of Verbal Communication," *Personnel Psychology* 37 (1984), pp. 41–59.

12. G. W. Soden, "Avoid Meetings or Make Them Work," *Business Horizons*, March-April 1984, pp. 47–55.

13. Mintzberg, *The Nature of Managerial Work*, and Kotter, *The General Managers*.

14. Mintzberg, *The Nature of Managerial Work*.

15. R. G. Harper, A. N. Wiens, and J. D. Matarzzo, *Nonverbal Communication: The State of the Art* (New York: John Wiley & Sons, 1978).

16. J. Pfeffer, *Power in Organizations* (Marshfield, Mass.: Pitman Publishing, Inc., 1981).

17. D. Fisher, *Communication in Organizations* (St. Paul, Minn.: West Publishing, 1981); A. J. DuBrin, *Contemporary Applied Management* (Plano, Tex.: Business Publications, 1982).

18. H. L. Wagner, C. J. MacDonald, and A. S. R. Manstead, "Communication of Individual Emotions by Spontaneous Facial Expressions," *Journal of Personality and Social Psychology* 50 (1986), pp. 737–43.

19. DuBrin, *Contemporary Applied Management*, 1982.

20. R. E. Rice, *The New Media: Communication, Research and Technology* (Beverly Hills, Calif.: Sage Publications, 1984).

21. C. L. Harris, J. B. Levine, J. B. Treece, F. Seghers, J. Brott and R. Mitchell, "Office Automation: Making It Pay Off," *Business Week*, October 12, 1987, pp. 134–46.

22. A. Kupfer, "Now, Live Experts on A Floppy Disk," *Fortune*, October 12, 1987, pp. 69–82.

23. C. H. Sullivan, Jr., and J. R. Smart, "Planning for Information Networks," *Sloan Management Review* (Winter 1987), pp. 39–44.

24. This section draws primarily from R. E. Kaplan, *Trade Routes: The Manager's Network of Relationships* (New York: American Management Association, 1984); and D. Katz and R. L. Kahn, *The Social Psychology of Organizations* (New York: John Wiley & Sons, 1966), ch. 9.

25. R. A. Snyder and J. H. Morris, "Organizational Communication and Performance," *Journal of Applied Psychology* 69 (1984), pp. 461–65.

26. M. J. Glauser, "Upward Information Flow in Organizations: Review and Conceptual Analysis," *Human Relations* 37 (1984), pp. 613–43.

27. A. S. DeNisi, W. A. Randolph, and A. G. Blencoe, "Potential Problems with Peer Ratings," *Academy of Management Journal* 26 (1983), pp. 457–64; R. C. Liden and T. R. Mitchell, "Reactions to Feedback: The Role of Attributions," *Academy of Management Journal* 28 (1985), pp. 291–308.

28. O'Reilly and Pondy, "Organizational Communication."

29. T. Allen and S. Cohen, "Information Flow in R&D Laboratories," *Administrative Science Quarterly* 14 (1969), pp. 12–20.

30. W. A. Randolph and F. E. Finch, "The Relationship Between Organization Technology and the Direction and Frequency Dimensions of Task Communications," *Human Relations* 30 (1977), pp. 1131–145; and W. A. Randolph, "Organization Technology and the Media and Purpose Dimensions of Organization Communications," *Journal of Business Research* 6 (1978), pp. 237–59.

31. M. D. Zalesny and R. D. Farace, "Traditional Versus Open Offices: A Comparison of Sociotechnical, Social Relations, and Symbolic Meaning Perspectives," *Academy of Management Journal* 30 (1987), pp. 240–59.

32. B. H. Drake and D. J. Moberg, "Communicating Influence Attempts in Dyads: Linguistic Sedatives and Palliatives," *Academy of Management Review* 11 (1986), pp. 567–84.

33. S. L. Kirmeyer and T. R. Lin, "Social Support: Its Relationship to Observed Communication with Peers and Superiors," *Academy of Management Journal* 30 (1987), pp. 138–51; W. Bennis, D. Berlew, E. Schein, and F. I. Steele, *Interpersonal Dynamics*, 3d ed. (Homewood, Ill.: Richard D. Irwin, 1973).

34. Bennis et al., *Interpersonal Dynamics*, 1973.

35. C. E. Beck and E. A. Beck, "The Manager's Open Door and the Communication Climate," *Business Horizons* January-February (1986), pp. 15–23.

36. W. Ouchi, *Theory Z: How American Business Can Meet the Japanese Challenge* (Reading, Mass.: Addison-Wesley Publishing, 1981); and T. J. Peters and R. H. Waterman, Jr., *In Search of Excellence* (New York: Harper & Row, 1982).

37. For example, see C. A. O'Reilly and K. H. Roberts, "Task Group Structure, Communication and Effectiveness in Three Organizations," *Journal of Applied Psychology* 62 (1977), pp. 674–81.

38. O'Reilly and Pondy, "Organizational Communication" and T. M. Harrison, "Communication and Participative Decision Making," *Personnel Psychology* 38 (1985), pp. 93–102.

39. This section draws primarily from H. Guetzkow, "Communications in Organizations," in *Handbook of Organizations*, ed. J. G. March (Skokie, Ill.: Rand McNally, 1965), pp. 534–73; L. W. Porter and K. H. Roberts, "Communication in Organizations," in *Handbook of Industrial and Organizational Psychology*, ed. M. D. Dunnette (Skokie, Ill.: Rand McNally, 1976), pp. 1553–89; and O'Reilly and Pondy, "Organizational Communication."

40. J. D. Hatfield and R. C. Huseman, "Perceptual Congruence about Communication as Related to Satisfaction: Moderating Effects of Individual Characteristics," *Academy of Management Journal* 25 (1982), pp. 349–58.

41. J. Naisbitt, *Megatrends* (New York: Warner Books, 1982).

42. C. L. McKenzie and C. J. Qazi, "Communication Barriers in the Workplace," *Business Horizons* March-April (1983), pp. 70–76.

43. A. Mehrabian, *Silent Messages* (Belmont, Calif.: Wadsworth, 1971).

44. I. J. Lee and L. L. Lee, *Handling Barriers in Communication* (New York: Harper & Row, 1968), p. 69.

45. P. Dubono, "Attidues Toward Women Executives: A Longitudinal Approach," *Academy of Management Journal* 28 (1985), pp. 235–39; L. R. Cohen, Nonverbal (Mis)Communication Between Managerial Men and Women," *Business Horizons* January-February (1983), pp. 13–17; N. A. Steckler and R. Rosenthal, "Sex Differences in Nonverbal and Verbal Communication with Bosses, Peers, and Subordinates," *Journal of Applied Psychology* 70 (1985), pp. 157–63.

46. Naisbitt, *Megatrends*, p. 35.

47. J. Hage, *Communications and Organizational Control* (New York: John Wiley & Sons, 1974).

48. Naisbitt, *Megatrends*, p. 29.

49. E. M. Eisenberg and M. G. Witten, "Reconsidering Openness in Organizational Communication," *Academy of Management Review* 12 (1987), pp. 418–26.

50. T. E. Deal and A. A. Kennedy, *Corporate Cultures* (Reading, Mass.: Addison-Wesley Publishing, 1982), ch. 5.

51. J. Brownell, *Building Active Listening Skills* (Englewood Cliffs, N.J.: Prentice-Hall, 1986).

52. For example, see J. Short, "Effects of Medium of Communication on Experimental Negotiation," *Human Relations* 27 (1974), pp. 225–34.

53. W. A. Randolph and R. A. Randolph, "Asserting Your Way to Better Planning," *Supervision Training Update*, Spring 1985, pp. 4–5.

54. This material is drawn from K. H. Blanchard and S. Johnson, *The One Minute Manager* (New York: Morrow, 1982) and H. Weisinger and N. M. Lobsenz, *Nobody's Perfect: How to Give Criticism and Get Results* (New York: Warner Books, 1981).

CASE: The sales department at BSC

Budget Systems Corporation (BSC) began in 1972 as the data processing department for a large southeastern insurance company. The responsibility of this department was to develop and maintain the computer resources for processing the company's insurance policies, invoices, and reports.

BSC was quite successful with its efforts and, in 1978, expanded to become a formal subsidiary of the large insurance company. As a subsidiary, BSC became a money-making entity by providing its software products and services to other insurance companies nationwide. BSC continued to expand its product lines and developed a worldwide customer base. In 1984, the subsidiary issued its own stock and became a fully incorporated entity.

Source: Adapted from a course assignment prepared by Hunter Griffin for Dr. Alan Randolph, 1987.

While BSC continues to expand, most of the company's recent growth has been attributed to acquisitions of other insurance service companies. Growth in domestic sales has suffered as a result of heavy losses in the insurance industry and market saturation with the BSC products. The sales division has come under increasing pressure to generate new sales.

The sales department is staffed with approximately 30 salespeople who are on the road dealing with prospective customers four days each week. To assist the sales department in its sales efforts, the marketing support department has the responsibility for information-gathering, product presentations and demonstrations, and sales proposal development. The support department is staffed with six support representatives and one department manager. The employees in this department are highly motivated individuals who have transferred from the various production divisions to gain marketing experience for a potential career in sales.

Each representative in the marketing support team is specifically trained and responsible for at least two BSC products and has a general knowledge of all products. The department manager assigns an account representative to a sales project when a salesperson makes a request for support services. Ideally, a support representative would be solely dedicated to a project from beginning to end; however, with more than 30 salespeople, the 6 support representatives are involved with several projects at any time.

The salespeople are out of the office most of the time; as a result, most of the support requirements are discussed with the representative over the telephone. Quite often, the end result of a support representative's effort does not meet the expectations of the salesperson and more importantly, the sales prospect. Salespeople almost always need information immediately; however, the projects usually involve expertise in several products. In such cases, the support representative must jump through many hoops to seek assistance from fellow representatives or from employees in the product development areas.

The support representatives put in much overtime and weekend time to meet the demanding deadlines imposed by the salespeople. In the earlier years at BSC, a representative's effort was often rewarded with a bonus recommended by the salesperson. However, these awards are contingent upon product sales, and sales have recently been declining. Additionally, the intense schedules require so much of the support representative's time, that he or she does not have the time to participate in actual sales training. The general attitude is that the marketing support department is no longer the launching pad to a career in sales.

The pressure to generate new sales is pervasive throughout the corporation, and it has become more and more essential for effective support of the sales department. But the frustrations and dissatisfaction in the support department have led to a decline in the quality of sales support.

Questions:

1. What is the context (technology, structure, physical layout, and history) of communications between the salespeople and sales support staff? How do these factors inhibit effective communications?

2. Which communications media might be used to improve communications in the sales department?

3. What role can listening and nonverbal media play in improving communications?

EXERCISE: Getting your point across

Purpose:

To examine common means of disrupting communication through poor listening.

Group Size:

Any number of groups of four to five members.

Time Required:

30–45 minutes.

Preparation Required:

None.

Materials:

None.

Room Arrangement Requirements:

So it is possible for four to five members to sit facing one another.

Related Topics:

Interpersonal Relationships

Exercise Schedule:

1. (2 min.) Divide into groups of four to five members each. Any class members left over and not in a group can act as group observers.

2. (2–3 min.) One volunteer in each group will talk for two to three minutes on any topic. Suggested topics include current events and topics covered earlier in this course. The task for the other three members in each group is to make *irrelevant* comments every time there is a break in the "speech." For example, if the speaker is describing a trip he or she took recently, the other group members intervene with statements like "I had a hamburger for supper last

night," or "Gee, you're nice." Members can also key their nonverbal behavior to this mode of response. One person can act as observer.

3. (3 min.) Each group should discuss the experience within the group. In particular, the speaker should indicate how this kind of response made him or her feel. How many times have you had this kind of response happen to you, have observed it, or done it to others? What impact does it have on the speaker?

4. (3 min.—optional) The instructor will lead a general class discussion to see whether different groups had different experiences. The observers can relate their observations at this time.

5. (15–27 min.) Steps 2, 3, and 4 will be repeated three more times. Another volunteer will speak each time, and the other group members will respond in the ways noted below.

   a. *Tangential responses:* The second time, the task of the group members, whenever they can, is to make tangential responses—i.e., to move the focus of attention from the speaker to the person making the response. For example, if the speaker is talking about a recent trip, the responder might break in and start describing a trip of his own, picking up something in the talk which enables him to "butt in" and take over the conversation. This is a widely used technique which you all recognize. You will find that you can be very creative in moving the conversation back and forth between people. In your discussion, you should note its impact on how people feel and on the organization of the interaction.

   b. *Interrogative responses:* As with tangential responses, you will proceed through steps 2, 3, and 4 above. Another volunteer will be given a topic, and the task of the other three members is to make interrogative responses. With interrogative responses, you question the speaker. It may seem that you are interested in the speaker, but questioning limits the speaker and takes the conversation in directions dictated by the questioners. Interrogative responses are very useful in keeping the focus of the conversation on the speaker—sometimes in ways he or she does not intend. The responder in this mode is really in control of the conversation. This response can be useful in clarifying misunderstandings, but it can also be used to manipulate the conversation.

   c. *Reflective responses:* Again, a volunteer (some may volunteer twice—it is not necessary for all to be a speaker) will speak on any topic. The task for the other three members is to make reflective responses. These should reflect both content and the feelings behind the content. Try to match your nonverbal behavior to this mode of responding, You will probably feel uncomfortable using this mode. (Afterwards, check to see which responses you were most comfortable in using.) Proceed through steps 3 and 4.

General Discussion

6. (5–10 min.) The instructor will lead a general discussion of the exercise.

Source: F. E. Finch, H. R. Jones, and J. A. Litterer, *Managing for Organizational Effectiveness: An Experiential Approach* (New York: McGraw-Hill, 1976), pp. 163–64. Used with permission.

QUESTIONNAIRE: Assertiveness inventory

Below are listed 20 situations in which you might find yourself. Please fill out the description in your own mind to make the situation realistic for you.

Then, using the five choices below, please indicate in the space to the left of each situation how you would feel in that situation. Be as honest with yourself as you can; the results from the inventory are for you. In each of the 20 situations, would you feel:

1 = Not very comfortable at all
2 = Not comfortable
3 = Somewhat comfortable
4 = Fairly comfortable
5 = Very comfortable

For now, ignore the blanks to the right of each situation.

Degree of Comfort			Likelihood of Behavior
_____	1.	When you are in a hurry and someone cuts in front of you in a line, ask him/her to go to the rear of the line.	_____
_____	2.	Tell your boss you cannot agree to his/her request because it seems unreasonable.	_____
_____	3.	Tell a close friend you are angry because of something he/she did.	_____
_____	4.	Ask a big favor of a friend.	_____
_____	5.	Apologize to your spouse or a close friend for saying something that offended him/her.	_____
_____	6.	Raise an objection to a position that is being pushed by your boss.	_____

_____ 7. At a social gathering, walk up to a public figure you _____ admire and introduce yourself.

_____ 8. Speak up during a discussion at a public gathering, _____ such as a city council or school board meeting.

_____ 9. Clearly express your opinions during a meeting involving your boss and several of your coworkers. _____

_____ 10. Ask your boss, who interrupts you in the middle of _____ a point you are making, to let you finish.

_____ 11. Discuss openly with a coworker his/her criticism of _____ your behavior.

_____ 12. Request a meeting with your boss to discuss a problem in his/her department. _____

_____ 13. Ask someone who will not take no for an answer to _____ stop bothering you.

_____ 14. Admit to your boss that you are confused about _____ what to do next on a project.

_____ 15. Ask someone who is making too much noise beside _____ you in an important meeting to stop or move away from you.

_____ 16. Thank your boss when he/she compliments you for _____ something you have done.

_____ 17. Tell a waiter you are not satisfied with a steak that _____ has been overcooked.

_____ 18. Tell a friend how much you appreciate a favor he/ _____ she did for you.

_____ 19. At a party, introduce yourself to an attractive person _____ of the opposite sex.

_____ 20. Insist that a painter who has worked on your house _____ come back to repaint something with which you are not satisfied.

Now, put your hand over your responses in the degree of comfort column and go back over the 20 situations. This time use the five choices below to indicate in the space to the right the likelihood that you would engage in the behavior described in each situation. Again, be as honest with yourself as you can; the results are for you. In each situation, would you:

1 = Almost never do it
2 = Rarely do it
3 = Do it about half the time
4 = Usually do it
5 = Do it without hesitation

Finally, total your responses in each column to get your <u>Degree of Comfort</u> score and your <u>Likelihood of Behavior</u> score. Record these below.

☐	Total of left column equals Degree of Comfort score.	Total of right column equals Likelihood of Behavior score. ☐

Source: © W. A. Randolph and R. A. Randolph, 1985. Used with permission.

Hammond General Hospital

Dave Smith came to Hammond General Hospital in October 1985 to become director of food service. Mr. Smith was employed by Master Host Company, a large, national food service corporation that had just been awarded the management contract for the department. The previous food service director had been employed by the hospital in the same capacity for the last 28 years and had also been a registered dietitian. The hospital had always operated its own food service.

Dave recalls his reception at Hammond. "Prior to assuming official control of the department, I spent a week there just getting to know the people and learning the current system. I immediately met resistance from the acting director, Ms. Pat Stone, R.D. Ms. Stone felt she should have been promoted and that an outside food service was not needed. She had been acting director for six months and prior to that had been the assistant director for ten years. Further resistance was quickly made obvious by the entire dietitian staff, who all felt that the director should be a registered dietitian (R.D.). There was also concern among the nursing staff at the hospital that a man had taken a position that had traditionally been held by a woman." (Detailed impressions gathered by Dave in his interviews are related in the section on the food service department.)

"After encountering nothing but resistance wherever I went, I made an appointment to see the assistant administrator to whom I reported at the hospital. His name was John Block, and he had only been at Hammond General for one month himself. In fact, his first assignment was to hire an outside company and then approve me as the director."

Source: This case was prepared by Cyril C. Ling and David Skeehan and is intended as a basis for class discussion. Presented and accepted by the refereed Midwest Case Writers Association Workshop, 1986. All rights reserved to the authors and to the Midwest Case Writers Association.

"Upon hearing my problems, John smiled and said, 'That's nothing. I understand the entire city is upset that a big company has taken over the department; the hospital's board of directors is having second thoughts; and the president of the hospital, Dan Schultz, is not comfortable with my selection of you as director.'"

"The very next day John was admitted to Hammond as a patient for emergency surgery and would be out for two months. I was now virtually alone to succeed or fail," Dave said.

The industry

Approximately 15 percent of all hospital food service departments are contracted. This is still a very young and growing industry. "My company has approximately 50 such contracts, making them about fourth in the industry as far as size is concerned," Dave related.

The general procedure is for the contractor to supply a director and an assistant director and provide the support systems such as recipes, production systems, and accounting procedures. The company charges the hospital for the salaries and benefits for the management team and a fee for service. The director would report to a hospital administrator as well as to the company's district manager.

The hospital

Hammond General Hospital is a 334-bed general hospital located in a small midwest town of approximately 45,000 people and serves a county-wide population of approximately 140,000. The area is heavily dependent on manufacturing supporting various vehicle industries. Consequently, in 1985, there was still unemployment, and jobs were not as plentiful as people would have liked.

The hospital is one of the largest employers in the city. The administrative team is young and aggressive, but feels a genuine obligation to provide a safe, pleasant, and positive work environment.

The food service department

The food service department has 58 full-time equivalents (F.T.E.s). This consists of 40 full-time employees and 25 part-time employees. (See Exhibit A for an organization chart.) Dave Smith and Doris Horn were the only two staff members employed by Master Host. All others were hospital employees. (See Exhibit B for personnel profiles.)

Clinical staff. Headed by the chief dietitian, Cynthia Thomas, R.D., the staff consisted of three clinical dietitians and four diet clerks.

Operations. Headed by one of Master Host's new assistant managers, Doris Horn, R.D. Her responsibilities included food production, all san-

EXHIBIT A

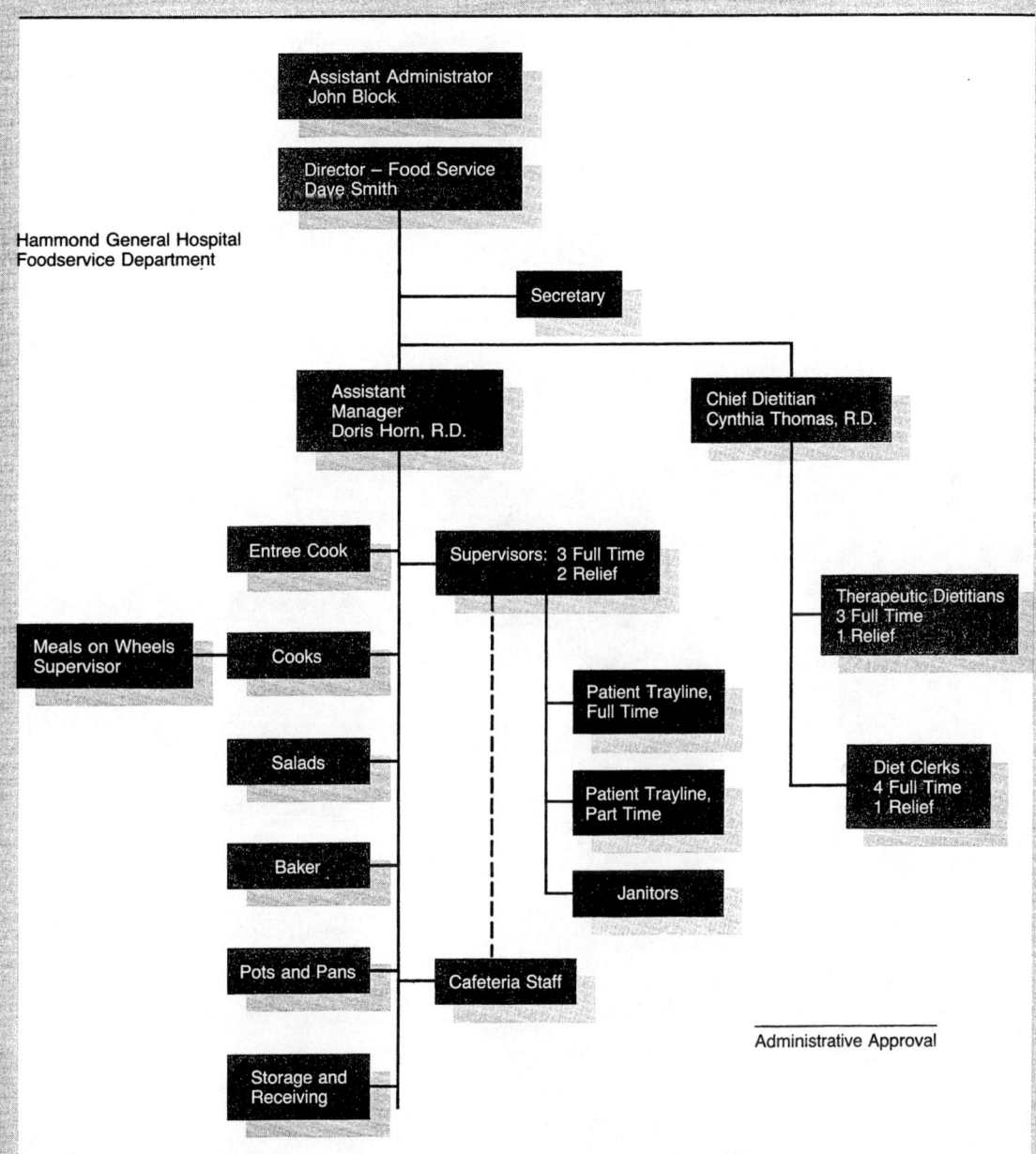

Hammond General Hospital
Foodservice Department

Assistant Administrator
John Block

Director – Food Service
Dave Smith

Secretary

Assistant Manager
Doris Horn, R.D.

Chief Dietitian
Cynthia Thomas, R.D.

Entree Cook

Supervisors: 3 Full Time
2 Relief

Meals on Wheels
Supervisor

Cooks

Therapeutic Dietitians
3 Full Time
1 Relief

Patient Trayline,
Full Time

Salads

Patient Trayline,
Part Time

Diet Clerks
4 Full Time
1 Relief

Baker

Janitors

Pots and Pans

Cafeteria Staff

Administrative Approval

Storage and
Receiving

EXHIBIT B

Personnel Profiles (1978)

Dave Smith—32 years old. Held a bachelor's degree from a good state university in the East, in Business Administration. Had been with the company for almost seven years, five as a director of food service.	Doris Horn, R.D.—25 years old. Held a bachelor's degree from a state university in Illinois in Nutrition. Had only been with the company for one month, but had been an administrative dietitian in another hospital for two years.	Cynthia Thomas, R.D.—26 years old. Held a bachelor's degree from a state university in Michigan. Had been a clinical dietitian at Hammond for three years before becoming chief dietitian.	Pat Stone, R.D.—50 years old. Held a bachelor's degree from a fine private institution in the East. Had been assistant director of food service at Hammond General for ten years. Prior to that, had been an administrative dietitian in the military.

itation, patient trayline, and the employee cafeteria. There were three supervisors who reported to her—one each for mornings and afternoons and a relief supervisor.

Catering and special projects. Ms. Pat Stone, R.D., was put in charge of all catering events and was responsible for coordinating many of the new changes that would come with the management change.

The management of the department

John Block explained that the reasons for contracting with the Master Host firm to run the department were:

1. The department was considered to be overstaffed by ten F.T.E.s.
2. The food and supply costs were excessive in comparison with industry standards.
3. Department morale was at an all-time low. The department had supported a recent unsuccessful attempt by the Teamsters to unionize all hourly employees in the hospital.
4. The medical staff was unhappy with the quality of patient food.
5. The hospital employees were unhappy with the quality of the cafeteria food.
6. Overtime pay in the department was the highest in the entire hospital.

7. Performance evaluation had not been taken seriously for several years.

8. Ordering of food lacked systematic procedures and was not well related to dietary planning or cost estimates.

Block summed it all by saying, "The department was run last year the same way it was 28 years ago. There have been no new systems, improvements, or changes in management philosophy for more than a quarter of a century."

Supervisors

Ms. Sally Manley, A.M. supervisor, said, "We are supervisors in name only. We make no decisions, take no disciplinary actions, are not involved in performance appraisals, and are not involved in interviewing new hires. If we do discipline someone, it is usually overturned."

Ms. Jane Harper, P.M. supervisor, said, "The morning shift does everything wrong. There is no procedure that we do the same as them. People that cross shifts don't know what to do. When we ask management for a decision as to what to do, they say, 'Do whatever will work for you.' Also, we have no authority to discipline, so no one pays any attention to us."

Ms. Sheila Rafferty, relief supervisor, said, "This place is a zoo. No one knows what in the hell they're supposed to do. There is no direction and no management whatsoever. The employees do what they damn well please, and nobody does anything about it."

Food service employees

Millie Park, head cook, said, "Hell, I have been here for 20 years, and this place gets worse each year. No one in there (the office) ever comes out here. I'll bet they don't even know what's on the menu today. They order food and don't even take inventory; they do it sitting on their butts. I'll bet there is $30,000 in outdated food in the basement. Also, no one else can cook. They pay dishwashers as much as cooks, so we have two cooks who can't even read a recipe if we had some—which we don't."

Pat Baker, cook, said, "We never have enough food to cook what is on the menu. We are always running out, and we get blamed. We can't cook what we don't have. Also, everyone else in the other departments thinks everyone in the kitchen is a stupid jerk, when they (management) are the only stupid ones."

Lora Lee Butram, cafeteria cashier, said, "We run out of food halfway through lunch. No one in the kitchen knows what is going on. Everyone in the hospital thinks everyone in this department is an idiot."

James Wilson, janitor, said, "They want us to clean the kitchen. I don't even have a good broom or a mop. Half the time, I don't even have soap to use on the floor. How the hell can I clean the kitchen?"

Jean Allen, diet clerk, said, "They want us to have a high school diploma plus a year of additional schooling, yet we don't make any more money even though we do as much as dietitians."

Hospital employees

Ed Norton, maintenance, said, "They should close food service and have McDonald's deliver. No one in that whole department can do anything right."

Mrs. Allie Crow, head nurse, said, "The patients don't get what they ordered. The trays are late, incomplete, and the food is cold. If a patient has a problem, we can't get a dietitian to come visit them."

Noreen Watson, housekeeping, said, "We are supposed to clean the cafeteria at night. Food service is supposed to clean it during the day. They don't. It is a mess, and no one can do anything about it."

Ralph Mason, director of personnel, said, "I think there are a lot of good people in food service. I think they care, but they need help and a lot of it."

The first management meeting

On the first official day of the management contract, Mr. Smith met with his assistant manager, Doris Horn, R.D. Her comments were, "Let's bomb this place and go home. It's hopeless! Look what we face:

1. "No one wants us here.
2. Our budget is unrealistic. It is based on having people that can, at least, walk and chew gum at the same time.
3. The assistant director thinks she should be the director, and she hates you for taking her job.
4. The chief dietitian is 100 pounds overweight (great example, eh,), and she is afraid of her 'old school' dietitians who don't want to leave their desks.
5. There are no systems of any kind.
6. The place is filthy.
7. The whole hospital hates the department.
8. The supervisors can't manage people and don't.
9. Administration thinks we will have the best food service department in one year because our salesperson said we would.
10. Why the hell did I take this stupid job?"

Dave's reply was, "We will fix the department the same way you would eat an elephant—one bite at a time. Let's get 'em all (managers, dietitians, and supervisors) in here and start right now.

QUESTIONS

1. Analyze the situation at Hammond General Hospital using the models and theories from Chapters 8–11. What is the nature of the situation Dave faces?

2. What type of leadership should Dave exercise?

3. What specific steps should he take? How should his actions be communicated?

4. What power bases does Dave have that will help him succeed? Which ones does he lack that might inhibit him?

5. How might Dave's leadership need to evolve if his first steps are successful?

A Developmental Framework for Studying Organizations

DYNAMIC ENVIRONMENTAL INFLUENCES

Past	Present	Future
Change	**Organizations** Environments Goals/Effectiveness Structure Design Development	Change
Develop	**Work Groups** Structure Processes Cohesion Groupthink Intergroup Behavior	Develop
Evolve	**Interpersonal Relationships** Leadership Power Politics Communications	Evolve
Grow	**Individuals** Perception Learning Attitudes Values Personality Motivation Outcomes	Grow

PART FOUR

Work Teams in Organizations

*H*aving now completed our analyses of both individuals and interpersonal relations in organizations, we will explore the behavior of groups of people in organizations. Chapter 12 will look at why groups are so important to managers in an organization. We will examine a number of individual and situational inputs to the behavior of groups. Overlaying this discussion will be an explanation of the developmental aspects of groups.

Chapter 13 will explore the emergent structural and process elements of groups in organizations. Managers should understand how norms, status and power relationships, cohesiveness, communications, leadership, decision-making methods, and roles of group members help define the behavioral patterns, daily operation, and effectiveness of groups. It will become clear that these emergent elements are essential factors for managers to manage if they are to lead or belong to an effective work group. In essence, the input variables discussed in Chapter 12 form the context in which the structural and process elements in Chapter 13 must be managed.

The final chapter in this section (Chapter 14) will deal with the interactions among different groups that make up an organization. It is not enough that leaders manage only the group of people who report to them. Managers must also be concerned with other groups to which they belong and those with which their group must interact to accomplish its work. Chapter 14 will deal with managing the inevitable conflicts and problems of coordination that develop among groups in organizations.

Throughout these three chapters, it will be important to remember the material covered in Parts Two and Three of this book, "Individuals in Organizations" and "Interpersonal Relations in Organizations." Also, it will be necessary to recall the model of organizations presented in Chapter 1 as the guiding framework for our analysis. It is repeated on the following page for your reference, with the focal points of this section highlighted. People are the basic building blocks of any organization, and along with interpersonal relations, they form the basis for this section on group behavior. ◼

Groups of People at Work

J ust as people and their interpersonal relations are always unique and developing, so too are groups. **Each group in an organization will have a unique character, and this character will have developed over time and will develop positively or negatively into the future.** As we discuss group behavior, think about various work groups, study groups, committees, church groups, and so forth to which you have belonged. By applying what we discuss to your own experiences, you will benefit more from the material presented in this chapter.

THE IMPORTANCE TO A MANAGER OF UNDERSTANDING GROUPS

Effective managers must be able to work with and in groups of people. This statement is an extension of the one made in Chapter 8; that is, **the very essence of managerial work is to do things with or through other people**. The difference is that by focusing on groups, we realize that "doing things with or through other people" takes place in a collective atmosphere. In an organization, managers often cannot work with people in a one-on-one fashion. Instead, they must work with groups of people who interact with each other, as well as with managers. Indeed, one way of viewing an organization is as a collection of groups, rather than as a collection of individual persons.

Few jobs in an organization can be done alone. People must assist each other with the work to ensure that the total job gets done. Hence, **groups are a fact of life in organizations**. Unlike a school atmosphere, where students depend primarily on themselves and where grades are individually determined, performance in a work organization is highly dependent on other people. Organizations simply could not exist without groups that divide the labor and coordinate individual effort. And groups are becoming even more important with the advent of quality circles, worker participation in management decisions, and entrepreneurial ventures in large companies. For example, Insight 12–1 illustrates how a team strategy has been used at Procter & Gamble to focus on being a more competitive company. The teams at P&G have been credited with turning around several products that were about to go under.

As another example, the early Hawthorne studies clearly established the importance of groups in affecting individual behavior.[1] As researchers increased lighting levels, rest periods, and incentives, performance improved. But performance continued to improve even as the lighting levels, rest periods, and incentives were decreased. This study showed that the group impact on individual performance was more important than external factors. Throughout history, there have been many instances where workers have held back on production because of group

**Team Strategy: P&G Makes Changes
in the Way It Develops and
Sells Its Products**

*P*rocter & Gamble CEO John Smale has
been leading the company's metamorphosis.
"We're moving to a greater use of what we
call business teams," he told the Harvard
Business Review in an interview. "A business team is . . . a concept that says, 'When
you're going to address a problem, get the
people who have something to contribute in
the way of creativity, if not direct responsibility. Get them together.' "

An early, experimental team formed in
1980 was assigned the task of turning
around unpopular Pringle's—or killing the
chip. Its mission also was to overcome what
P&G's advertising vice president called the
"dog-sled approach," in which only the lead
dog, or brand manager, saw the landscape.
The Pringle's team developed new flavors,
introduced a new oil-application method,
and designed new ads that promoted taste
rather than package design. Sales of Pringle's increased sharply.

More recent teams are credited with in-
venting a popular drip-proof cap for Liquid
Tide, rushing Ultra Pampers to market in
nine months—half the usual time—and now,
two years later, introducing an improved Ultra Pampers Plus. "Working on a team with
12 or 20 others, it takes longer to reach decisions, but once that's done you've got everyone you need in place to move a product to
market faster," says David Browne, a former
brand manager of P&G's Tenderleaf tea.

Teams also can help prevent costly
mistakes. Mr. Browne recalls one brand-
management group that rushed a promotional package to market only to find it didn't
fit most supermarket shelves. "A team perspective probably would have prevented the
mistake," he says.

Anxious to limit the dominance of marketing managers, some teams elect their leaders. And one, now developing a new citrus
product, deliberately held its early meetings
on neutral ground away from company
offices.

Still, team spirit is proving difficult to instill
at a company used to clear lines of authority.
To the layers of midlevel marketing managers at P&G and its competitors, brand
management "is the Holy Grail and they're
reluctant to tinker with it," says Mr. McHenry
of McKinsey & Co. Adds a P&G advertising
manager: "Sharing authority is always
painful."

Friction also erupts occasionally on
teams between brand managers, who are
used to calling the shots, and manufacturers
and research managers, who now have a
much more equal say. While brand managers feel pressured to make a mark quickly,
their counterparts in slower-moving career
paths—in manufacturing and research, for
example—"don't have that sense of urgency," says Mr. Baynham, the former Fol-
gers-decaffeinated manager.

Conflicts occur, too, between brand managers and colleagues in jobs that didn't exist
five years ago. For instance, the category
manager for P&G's Joy, Ivory, Dawn, and
other dishwashing liquids cut manufacturing
and packaging costs by giving all the products similarly shaped bottles and making the
soap formulas more alike. Meanwhile, however, brand managers still are expected to
find ways to set their products apart.

pressure, even though it cost them money to do so. For example, the FAA Air Controllers' slowdown of several years ago was a vivid example of the strength of groups against an organization—in this case the federal government. On the other hand, group pressure can also cause people to perform at peak levels of performance if the group accepts the organizational goals. A good example of this is an athletic team with less talent beating a stronger team, as when Kansas beat Oklahoma for the NCAA national basketball title in 1988. **Managers must realize that the work group they supervise is a potential competitor with their leadership in influencing the behavior of group members; however, the group can also be a manager's ally in influencing group members.** Managers need to understand groups so they can achieve the significant positive outcomes of which groups are capable.

Another reason groups are important to managers is that managers simultaneously belong to several groups within an organization. They supervise one group of people. They belong to a group consisting of peer managers and their boss. They may belong to a special committee, project group, or task force with people from various levels and departments of the organization. Managers might also belong to groups based on common interests (like bowling or photography) or on friendships that cut across both departmental and hierarchical lines in the organization. Furthermore, managers no doubt belong to groups outside the organization, such as a family, club, or church. Our focus here, however, is on groups within an organization. As members of multiple groups in an organization (as summarized in Exhibit 12–1), managers encounter many forces that affect their behavior. They must know how to deal with these often conflicting forces if they are to be successful, both as managers and as group members.

Finally, groups are important to understand because they are complex entities. Many factors influence whether or not a group will be effective. The remainder of this chapter and the next chapter will be devoted to these factors, but we will briefly preview them here. Groups both influence and are influenced by the behavior of individuals. Further, the context in which the group operates influences its development and effectiveness. Over time, groups develop particular norms, role relationships, power relationships, and internal status differences, and they use various communications, leadership, and decision-making processes. And since all of these elements are constantly changing and interacting, it is difficult to be a group member or to manage a group well.

In this and the next chapter, we will discuss a model that should be helpful in understanding and analyzing groups. We also will discuss some ideas on how to effectively manage groups and work as a member of groups in organizations. Let us begin by exploring the definition of *groups*.

EXHIBIT 12–1

The Multiple Groups of an Organization

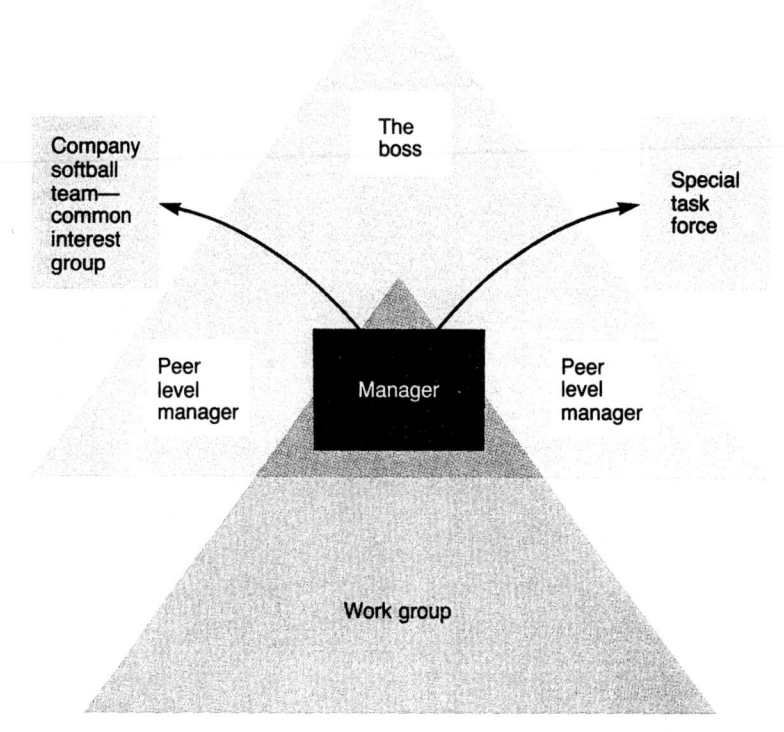

THE DEFINITION OF A GROUP

The literature on groups has been fairly consistent in defining the term: **A group in an organization is a collection of two or more people who, over a period of time, develop shared norms of behavior, are interdependent, and interact with each other for the purpose of achieving some common goal or set of goals.**[2]

Group **norms** provide a sense of identity. The **interactions** of group members reinforce the group as an entity and can help the group achieve its purposes. The **interdependence** of group members in achieving group goals helps define different roles for the various group members. For example, a task force assigned to solve a quality-control problem at Home Computers Company may divide this task into various parts for different group members: research the technical design, look into the production process, interview customers, prepare a written report. Finally, while the **time dimension** of groups has not often been made explicit in the various definitions, it is important from a developmental perspective. And the importance of the time dimension will become even clearer as we proceed in our discussion of groups.

Unfortunately, the definition of a group does not really help us understand *why* groups are formed in the first place. Basically, **groups are formed because they have the potential to accomplish more than would the same number of people working alone.** Groups allow for specialization of function by their members. They also permit a synergistic effect, where the whole is greater than the sum of its parts. However, the reverse can also occur: groups can result in the whole being *less* than the sum of its parts. For example, as mentioned earlier, some athletic teams with excellent talent at every defensive and offensive position lose to a less talented team that plays together well. The point is that **groups are an essential part of every organization, but it is very difficult to make them work effectively over time.** As Insight 12–2 suggests, there are always competing interests between individuals and the group, and this may be most evident in the university setting. Still, as this article points out, businesses feel teamwork is important.

Types of groups

To further understand the definition of groups, we need to look at the two basic types of groups: formal and informal. **Formal groups are those prescribed by the organization.** Within the departments of any organization, groups of people (often called *sections* or *units*) are assigned particular tasks to perform. Management might also assign an employee to a project group, committee, task force, quality circle, or autonomous work group. Project groups are typically formed to accomplish a particular short-range task—for example, to design the modifications on HCC's EZ2 for the school and library markets. Committees and task forces are usually formed to manage either ongoing or problem-solving issues within an organization. Quality circles are problem-solving groups of workers within the production sector of society.[3] Typically, these groups meet once a week for an hour or so to try to solve production problems. Effective use of such groups has led to the implementation of many successful solutions. Finally, autonomous work groups operate on a day-to-day basis by supervising themselves. They distribute work, determine the pace of work, and organize their own breaks. Research has shown that members of such groups experience high levels of satisfaction; but they also feel greater stress, since they must manage all of their work and interactive processes alone.[4]

Informal groups are not prescribed by an organization, but develop because of proximity, common interest, and individual need satisfac-

INSIGHT 12-2

Teamwork, M.B.A.-Style: Some Students See Cooperation as a One-Day Adventure

Chapel Hill, N.C.—In a forest near here, 30 people are standing in a circle with their hands around each other's shoulders. They all turn sideways and plop down on each other's laps. Then each gives the stranger sitting in his or her lap a back massage.

Sound like the warmup for an orgy, or at least a seminar with Dr. Ruth? This gathering in the woods is actually part of the MBA program at the University of North Carolina at Chapel Hill. "MBA Adventure" day brings new students into the woods to teach them to work together.

A growing number of business schools have begun emphasizing teamwork in their programs over the past 10 years, says John Van Maanen, a professor of sociology at MIT's Sloan School of Management who has studied such programs. Mr. Van Maanen says, however, that the teamwork approach only veils competition. "The group method is very smiling on the surface and savage underneath," he says. Mr. Van Maanen says his studies show that students organized in teams vie to take charge in their group and strenuously compete for jobs after graduation.

Such subtle competition is certainly evident during Chapel Hill's "MBA Adventure"— one of the few business school teamwork programs run outside the classroom.

For "Adventure," conducted by Executive Adventure Inc. of Atlanta, 160 of the 199 first-year MBA students turn out, arriving at Camp New Hope in worn T-shirts and gym shoes. Groups of 15—three study groups, spend the day in exercises that J. R. Ewing

wouldn't be caught dead doing; they arrange themselves in numerical order, for instance, a tough task because only they know their number and they are blindfolded and mute. (Clue for the baffled: this eventually involves running around repeatedly hitting others to signify one's number.)

First-year student Joe Bryson, a former mechanical engineer, calls Adventure day at Chapel Hill a "look with rose-colored glasses." He contends that team spirit groomed in the forest won't last on campus. When the class begins and "we don't have time, then it all breaks down and gets into individual concerns," he predicts of the year ahead.

Will the team approach make these MBAs more attractive to prospective employers when they graduate in 1989? It's impossible to predict, but several corporations randomly surveyed applaud the approach: "We foster the teamwork concept in our own company, patterning ourselves after the Japanese," says Joseph McInnes, vice president of human resources at Blount Inc., a Montgomery, Ala.-based construction concern. "If students were exposed to teamwork I think it would have some attractiveness to us."

Maybe so, but some "graduates" of Adventure day think their experience will mostly provide comic relief for the short term, as their study teams focus on cramming. "When we're studying at 2 a.m., we'll remember when we fell and caught each other," says student Jerry McGee. He expects to say to his teammates at that time, "I won't do that again."

tion. For example, a car pool group may develop among several people who live in the same neighborhood. And they may not even work for the same organization, just ones in close proximity. Company baseball teams or bridge groups form because of a common interest in those activities. Groups may also form at break and lunch times as people come together to complain about things in the company—for example, pay and working conditions.

Even more significant informal groups have been referred to as **networks.** Indeed some networks are referred to as the dominant coalition of an organization, and some authors have suggested that networking is one of the key tasks of an effective manager.[5] Research has suggested that a person's promotions, influence in an organization, and general effectiveness depend to some extent upon his or her success in networks.[6] Recall from Chapter 10 on politics how networking and politics are so critical to managers. Not everything gets done through the formal, rational organization. And good managers know how to use the informal, sometimes nonrational, parts of the organization to compensate for this shortcoming.

Each type of group serves particular needs, and each develops its own personality. To be an effective member of these groups, people need to understand how groups operate. Furthermore, since people belong to more than one group at the same time, it is important to recognize the conflicting demands the different groups may make. An informal group sometimes opposes the goals of an organization and has a negative impact on people in the group. But informal groups can also help an organization if they accept the primary organizational goals. **As with formal groups, informal groups can either help or hinder an organization; which result occurs depends in part on what group members and managers do.**

Group development stages

To truly understand and manage groups, though, managers must learn to recognize the developmental stages groups go through. Since the late 1940s, a number of group development models have been proposed by various authors. Indeed, the very number of models (roughly 20) suggests the strong support for the conclusion that groups do move through stages of growth in a developmental process. Chapter 1 discussed the model proposed by Schutz with the three stages of inclusion, control, and affection.[7] A more complete model for our purposes here was proposed by Tuckman.[8] The two models are very similar in the basic stages defined, but Tuckman's model (shown in Exhibit 12–2) defines stages in terms of both interpersonal relations and task functions that are essential concerns of any group. A group must manage both task and interpersonal relations to be effective over the long run.

EXHIBIT 12–2

The Process of Group Development

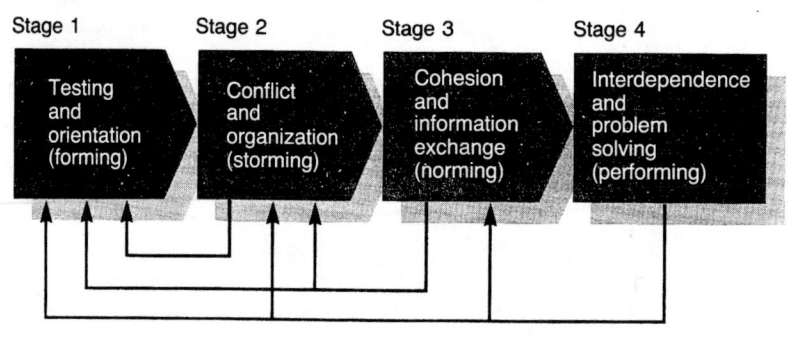

Source: B. W. Tuckman, "Developmental Sequence in Small Groups," *Psychological Bulletin* 63 (1965): 384–99. Copyright 1965 by the American Psychological Association. Adapted by permission of the author.

The length of time spent in each of Tuckman's group development stages can vary greatly. Group development is typically a process that occurs over weeks and months. And it may be more like a start–stop, jerky movement, rather than a smooth progression.[9] **Each stage lasts until its paramount issues are essentially resolved; the group then moves on. And the stages are not so clearly marked that there is no overlap between them.** As always, models of behavior are much neater than the actual behavior. Groups really operate to varying degrees in all of the stages, all of the time. The issues of one stage will, however, usually be primary at any one time as the group evolves. Groups also sometimes regress to earlier stages of development. The addition of new members, a change in the group's task, and other factors can cause this backtracking. In other words, the process of group development is on-going and complex. With this background, let us now review each of the four stages of Tuckman's model, especially as applied to work groups.

Stage 1: Testing and orientation (forming)

In Stage 1, group members try to determine what behaviors will be acceptable to the group, what skills and resources each member brings to the group, what goals and motivations each member has, and who will psychologically commit to the group. In this stage, people are becoming acquainted with one another and want to know what is expected of them. Group members depend on the leader to set the rules, establish an agenda, and make sure things happen. Likewise, group members depend on the leader to define the task, establish group goals, and basically be responsible for task accomplishment. This stage is consistent with the leadership situation where the subordinates are not yet competent enough as a group to be productive, though motivation and expectations are often high. Thus, a leader (either formal or informal) must provide a great deal of structure.

Stage 2: Conflict and organization (storming)

As a group moves into Stage 2 of development, conflicts tend to emerge. Often, group members begin to doubt the people who have exercised leadership, as they experience a gap between reality and their initial expectations about the group. Other members besides the leader begin to exert influence on the group, and a fight for control of the group can follow. A group in this stage may have difficulty making decisions and communicating effectively.

Coupled with these interpersonal conflicts are the task functions of becoming organized. A leader must have followers, and the group must determine who will be responsible for what. Norms of expected behavior, standards, and work rules start to develop during this phase. And as the conflicts are resolved, some uncommitted group members may leave the group, either physically or psychologically. If a group gets through Stage 2 successfully, it is well on its way to becoming an effective group. However, it is often difficult to fully resolve the leadership and organizational conflicts of this stage—especially if there is much turnover in the group or many changes in its task and situation. In this stage, the leader must continue to provide structure while shoring up the group that is suffering through low motivation and confidence.

Stage 3: Cohesion and information exchange (norming)

During Stage 3, a real sense of cohesion and teamwork begins to emerge. Group members feel good about each other and really identify with the group. They share feelings, give and receive feedback, and begin to share a sense of success. During this stage, however, a group runs the greatest risk of falling into groupthink.[10] **Groupthink occurs when the feelings of cohesion override the realistic appraisal of alternative courses of action.** Groupthink makes a group think of itself as invulnerable; and group members tend to withhold expressing any thoughts that are not consistent with the group consensus. Groupthink can lead to carelessness, which results in mistakes and lower productivity.

But groupthink does not have to occur. The other option for Stage 3 groups is to develop the potential for exchanging all kinds of information relevant to a task. With the group oriented and organized, it is primed for the exchange of information that will help the group accom-

"Rose colored glasses in place?"

From *The Wall Street Journal*, with permission of Cartoon Features Syndicate.

plish the task effectively. If group members focus on information that is necessary rather than just on what people want to hear (as with groupthink), Stage 3 can be marked by conflict over ideas, rather than conflict between egos and personalities. By arguing over ideas while supporting each other as people, group members can avoid groupthink, maintain cohesiveness, and be very productive.[11] Stage 3 is a junction point. If the issues of the first two stages have not been settled, the group will tend either to erupt into serious conflict or to fall prey to groupthink. If the group has resolved those issues, the conflict level will rise slightly as ideas are exchanged and groupthink is avoided. At this stage, the leader can back off on providing structure—the group knows what to do now. But the leader must be a listener and encourage idea disagreement to help avoid groupthink and make the group productive.

Stage 4: Interdependence and problem solving (performing)

Stage 4 of development is difficult to achieve for most groups. The interpersonal relations in this stage are marked by a sophisticated level of interdependence. Group members can now work well with everyone in the group. Everyone can and does communicate with everyone else. Decisions are made with full agreement by everyone and after a comprehensive discussion of all alternatives. Group members understand the roles they need to perform if the group is to be highly effective. The group is very much oriented to maintaining good relationships among its members and to getting its task accomplished.

INSIGHT 12–3

Quality Circles: Rounding Up Quality at USAA

"It's 9 o'clock, time for our meeting," announces one of the advertising specialists in the USAA Marketing Department. At that signal, several other employees leave their desks and head for the conference room. They start right to work on the problem they have been spending an hour a week on for the last two months. Then, regardless of how much or how little they accomplish, the meeting is adjourned exactly one hour later.

Hardly typical of a business meeting, this is a quality circle in operation. One of the first insurance companies in the country to implement quality circles as a management technique for improving quality and productivity, USAA now has 44 active circles with more planned.

Japanese companies have successfully used quality circles to promote worker in-volvement and improve efficiency for the past 20 years. But there are those who say that the concept is just another fad with American companies. However, USAA's success is proving that quality circles work and will become even more important in the future.

Bob Gaylor coordinates and directs USAA's quality circle program. "The logic behind Quality Circles is that the people who do the work know the most about it, and are the best qualified to improve it," says Gaylor. "USAA's program has been successful largely because of the support of management. With that support and the enthusiasm of our employees, there's no limit to what we can accomplish."

Source: Excerpted from "Quality Circles: Rounding up Quality at USAA," *AIDE Magazine* (Fall 1983), p. 24. Used by permission.

Indeed, the task function side of the ledger suggests that the group has matured into a real team. It can solve complex problems and implement the solutions. There is commitment to the task and to experimentation in problem solving. This stage is really an extension of Stage 3. Cohesion has progressed to the point of collaboration of effort, and information exchange has advanced to real problem solving. People in the group really care about each other, but they are also not afraid to speak their minds. Confidence reaches a high level for the few groups who achieve this stage. Many companies are finding that such highly developed teams can be vital in today's more competitive and rapidly changing world. Insight 12–3 illustrates how American companies have begun to use quality circles to solve problems. And the trend continues even today.

Unfortunately, even if a group reaches Stage 4, it still faces the difficult job of staying there. Many factors can force the group back to earlier stages and thus reduce productivity.[12] For example, even some very well-respected and successful groups of organizational behavior researchers revert to Stage 1 when one member of the team moves to another university. Such breakups can create real havoc for a group and lead to poor performance. Then, too, addition of a new member also raises many of the issues of Stage 1 again.[13] And if a group gets a new leader, it must deal again with many of the issues of Stage 2 (conflict and organization). Plus, any major change in the technology or task of a group raises issues on task development that are typical of Stages 1 and 2. For example, as offices become automated, work groups are being forced to relearn their jobs and the nature of their interrelationships. Indeed, as the arrows in Exhibit 12–2 indicate, **the group developmental process is a never-ending process**. Groups never reach a position where they can simply sit back and continue to be effective. Thus, managers must constantly work to move their groups toward Stage 4 in a never-ending process of team development.[14]

The remainder of this chapter and Chapter 13 will develop a model of group behavior. But first, we will look at several quality circle groups at Home Computers Company. As you read the case, think about the developmental stages and how leaders could analyze and work with these groups to achieve effectiveness.

Home Computers Case

Quality Circle Groups at Home Computers Company

Harvey, the president of Home Computers Company, has been exploring a number of personnel and production problems with the help of a consultant. Their focus has been primarily on the Dayton plant, which was the original HCC plant in 1977. Over the years, this plant has become very routine in its operation: assembly lines are the primary form of production; workers are paid by the hour; and most decisions are made by the plant manager. Somehow, this highly structured approach is not working well. The workers say they do not feel like they belong; they have no sense of achievement in their jobs. A number of the original HCC people have left the company, and many of those remaining are very unhappy with their jobs. Production at the plant is starting to suffer in terms of quality and quantity. Harvey knows something must be done. Demand for HCC's computers is growing again, and Harvey is considering opening a third plant.

The consultant suggested that they start up some quality circles, including people from different shifts and different departments. His suggestion was to get the workers and lower-level supervisors involved in solving the morale and production problems plaguing the Dayton plant. Harvey had some doubts, but decided to give it a try. The consultant suggested that they use the Denver plant as a comparison to determine if the changes in Dayton have a positive effect.

Shortly after this discussion, three quality circles were begun in Dayton, one for each of the three computer product lines—home use, schools and libraries, and small businesses. Each quality circle was assigned three people from production, three from sales, and two from personnel. Two different levels of the hierarchy and all shifts were represented. Since there were many indicators of friction between sales and production, a personnel person was appointed to head up each circle. Each quality circle was given a meeting room and an appointed time to meet each week. An hour and a half was allocated for each meeting. In addition, the members were encouraged to meet informally during the week on their breaks or at mealtime to keep ideas and energy flowing on the task.

Harvey was present at the first meeting of each group to explain the purpose of the quality circle. He asked them to come up with recommendations that would help solve the production and personnel problems of the plant. He assured them that their ideas would be implemented if at all possible, and that they would get a response to every suggestion. Harvey told the groups that this was their plant to make successful or unsuccessful. He also said that if he did not have confidence in them, he would not even try this quality circle approach. The consultant then worked with each circle to help the members become acquainted with each other and to help them determine how their strengths and resources could help the circle. The consultant also worked with the circle leaders on how to set an agenda and run an effective meeting. This process went on over several months until each circle and leader felt comfortable in their roles.

In two cases, it became clear that the circle leader had a great deal of expertise about the HCC operation. Furthermore, the status of these two leaders was enhanced by their being from the neutral personnel area rather than either production or sales. Both of these groups developed norms of hard work and commitment to the goals laid out by Harvey. There were some conflicts between production and sales about whose fault the problems were; but the circles overcame these and became well organized within about three months. Cohesion and a sense of teamwork were strong in both groups. They moved quickly into providing problem definitions and solutions that were useful to plant management.

In the other group, however, the appointed leader from personnel was not so experienced, and several group members were particularly antagonistic to one another. Problems developed soon after the consultant pulled out. Some of the team members were higher in the hierarchy than the leader, and several members constantly vied with him for the leadership of the group. They tried to coordinate and summarize the actions of the circle, and they often disagreed with the leader on important decisions. Instead of moving into a sense of teamwork and cohesion, this circle became mired in conflict and disorganization. The meetings were difficult and unproductive. Some members even began to avoid the circle members. Finally, the team leader went to the consultant to ask for additional help.

What would you suggest if you were the consultant? What has gone wrong with this group? Could something still go wrong with the other two groups? After a brief introduction of a model of group behavior, we will answer these questions as we explore the model in detail in this and the next chapter.

A MODEL OF GROUP BEHAVIOR

As we analyze what is happening with the quality circles at HCC, it would help to understand some basic principles of groups. For example, how do groups operate? What factors influence their behavior? We will explore such questions as we discuss the model presented in Exhibit 12–3, which summarizes the aspects of group functioning. This model draws on a number of theories related to groups. The remainder of this chapter will deal with the two sets of input variables—individual and situational—and their impact on group structures, processes, and outcomes such as performance, satisfaction, and turnover. Chapter 13 will explore the structure and process elements shown in Exhibit 12–3. The end result will be a complete model for understanding how to be an effective manager and group member. We begin with a quick overview of the model presented in Exhibit 12–3.

The individual and situational input variables form a context within which managers must work with a group of people. Section II of this book dealt extensively with understanding individuals as the basic building blocks of an organization. Because groups are made up of individuals, **individual variables** (such as those discussed in Chapters 3 through 7) are inputs to a group because they are brought in by each member of the group. How people learn; their attitudes, perceptions, abilities, values, and personalities; what motivates them; and past individual outcomes all impact on a group and its ability to function effectively.

Likewise, **situational variables** form part of this context for a group. The size of the group, as well as its composition of people (for example, a homogeneous group of engineers or a heterogeneous group of engineers, accountants, marketers, and production people) affect the way a group operates and how effective it is. In addition, the type of task that

EXHIBIT 12–3

A Model of Group Behavior

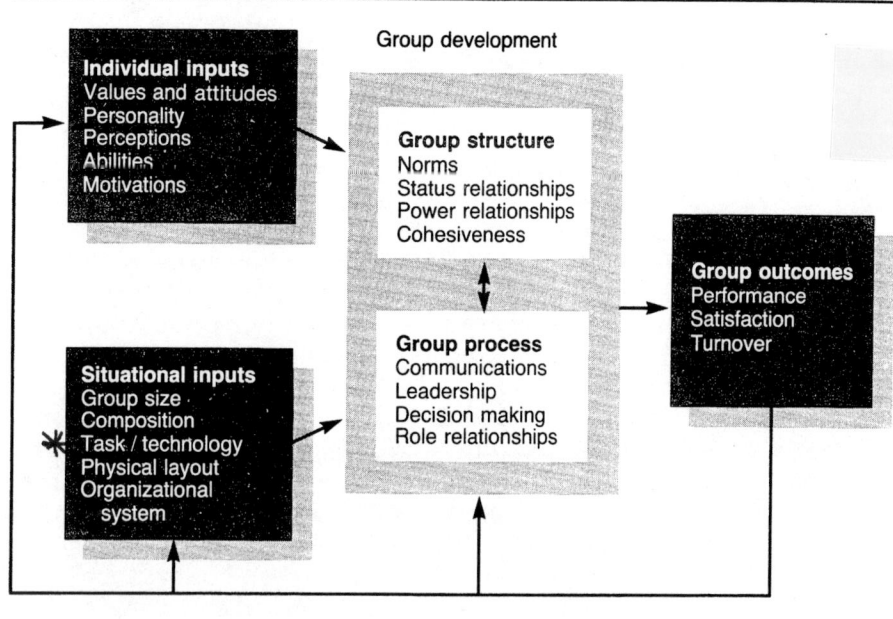

a group must accomplish and the physical layout of the group also affects its functioning. For example, an assembly-line operation where the work is routine and people are spread out over a long, noisy distance will be different from a problem-solving committee where people sit around a table to discuss a complicated situation. Finally, other groups in a department—and even in the entire organization—form a part of the context that will affect a group's functioning.

Once these individual and situational inputs come into play, a group begins the developmental process discussed earlier. Through the operating processes and structure that emerge over time, the group develops a character of its own that ultimately affects the outcome variables. By **group structure**, we mean the norms, status and power relationships, and cohesiveness that develop as a group operates. And by **group process**, we mean the communications, leadership, decision making, and role relationships that are a part of a group's activities.

All of these factors converge to yield the outcomes of a group, as shown in Exhibit 12–3. Is the group effective in accomplishing its task? Are the group members satisfied with being a part of the group? Is there a great deal of absenteeism and turnover in the group? These outcomes serve as feedback to both the group development and inputs parts of the model, as a group moves forward in its developmental process. A successful group will receive reinforcement for its structure and processes. An ineffective group may feel pressure to make changes, even in the input variables.

With this introduction, let us now explore in detail the two sets of input variables. We will save the structure and process variables for Chapter 13.

Individual inputs

Part 2 of this book dealt with understanding individuals. Thus, we will only briefly look at these inputs here. **Remember that each person brings to a group a unique set of characteristics, and each person can potentially be in a different stage of personal development.** As these unique people come together to form a group, the interaction among these characteristics can influence both positively and negatively the group's processes, structure, and performance.

The quality circles at HCC are probably made up of people who have different attitudes and values, as well as several of the 16 personality types described in Chapter 4. The impact of this can be seen in the way the group functions.[15] For example, extroverts and feeling types could be expected to talk more than introverts and thinking types. Thinking types (along with sensing types), however, may be able to analyze situations in greater detail than either feeling or intuitive types. If the appointed leader happens to be an introvert, it may be difficult for him or her to effectively lead extroverts. The variety of personality types allows group members to enhance each other's strengths by compensating for the weaknesses. In other words, the combination of different personality types can result in either positive or negative group outcomes, but their major impact will be on the group processes and interaction.[16]

In addition, the backgrounds of the group members, as reflected in their perceptions, abilities, and past experiences, can be unique. Indeed, such differences are one of the strong points of groups. One person may perceive a situation incorrectly or may not have the ability to perform a task that is necessary. Through interaction and group development, a group of people can learn to use their differences to achieve a high level of effectiveness. For example, in a student group working on a case analysis, only one person may really know how to use the computer to analyze data. Another person may know how to write well and type. Either person working alone would have a hard time completing the task, but together they can complete an excellent report. At HCC, the successful quality circles may be successful partly because they use the differences in the individual members, while the unsuccessful quality circle lets these differences destroy it.

Finally, each group member may be motivated by something different. Chapters 5 and 6 discussed many things that can motivate people. Some of the group members may be motivated by the feeling of belonging that they get from the group interactions. In an unsuccessful group, people may be motivated by power and the desire to influence. Still others may be motivated by the challenge of the task. These different motivations can create problems for a group if they lead to conflict rather than cohesion as the group develops. But different motivations can also lead to a real synergy of effort if directed toward the goals of a group. Indeed, different motivations, perceptions, and abilities can help a group avoid groupthink if they are directed toward the goals of the group.

Overall, the point is that individuals make up a group, and individuals are all different. **An effective member or manager of a group needs to appreciate the potential effects of individual inputs**. A person must learn to work with the differences in a group to capitalize on the mix of people in the group. Otherwise, the person could wind up in the position of the unsuccessful quality circle leader at HCC. The situation probably contributed to the difficulties encountered by this leader, but the leader is still held accountable for the problems of the group and must find ways to cope with the problems.

Situational inputs

The model of group behavior also includes several situational factors that influence both group development and performance: size, composition, task/technology, physical layout, and the organizational system. A group's task/technology may be the most critical input variable in terms of impact on the group—but let us explore each variable in turn.

Group size

Size is simply the number of people in a group. The effects of size on several other group variables have been widely researched.[17] Small groups (two to four people) tend to be characterized by greater tension and greater seeking of harmony and agreement than larger groups.[18] The logical reason for this is that people in a small group must work more intimately with each other. In larger groups (five or more), more interactions will be directed toward releasing tension and toward getting information out on the table for discussion. Also, some people will be reluctant to speak out in a larger group. Thus, larger groups may take longer to move through the developmental stages.

Size has also been found to affect the satisfaction, level of absenteeism, and turnover of group members. Given the greater degree of involvement in smaller groups, it is not surprising that people in small groups tend to be more satisfied and have less absenteeism and turnover. As the discussion of motivation in Chapters 5 and 6 suggests, there would appear to be more motivating factors present in small groups than in larger groups. For example, people in a small group more easily identify with the whole task and feel a sense of belonging. On the other hand, there appears to be no direct relationship between group size and **performance.** As we will explore shortly, the nature of the group task tends to dictate the group size. Certain complex tasks simply require more people to be involved. Still, a number of successful, large U.S. companies are working hard to keep work units small and to make workers feel involved, as described in the Minnesota Mining & Manufacturing Company example in Insight 12–4.

Finally, group size is a variable that can change over time. Changes in a group task that necessitate changes in group personnel, as well as people leaving or joining a group, can easily cause changes in group size. And these changes then affect the other variables we have just discussed.

Group composition

Group composition focuses attention on the combined effects of the individuals in a group.[19] **Each person brings a unique character to the group. But once the group has formed, the particular combination of people in the group begins to have an impact.** In particular, are the group members alike in many ways—a **homogeneous** group? Or are they different in many ways—a **heterogeneous** group?

In a homogeneous group, communications should be enhanced and conflict reduced. For example, one study found that all-male groups, when compared to mixed-sex groups, reported less difficulty working together, lower levels of competition and stress, and higher levels of working efficiency and cooperation.[20] A homogeneous group should move rather quickly through the first three stages of group development. And if the group's task is routine—for example, on the assembly line for a simple product—homogeneity of the group can lead to increased performance and satisfaction. However, too much homogeneity can cause a group to overlook good alternatives and miss out on vital pieces of information when problem solving.

At Home Computers Company, the quality circles were heterogeneous, and the differences in the people probably caused the development of the groups to proceed slowly. With people from several different departments, the potential for conflict was increased. Communications were made more difficult by the various backgrounds of the people. (Recall from Chapter 11 how communications can be inhibited between people from different levels and departments of an organization.) The advantages of heterogeneity are that it broadens the perspective of the

INSIGHT 12-4

Some Firms Fight Ills of Bigness by Keeping Employee Units Small

St. Paul, Minn.—For a company with 87,000 employes and annual sales in excess of $6 billion, Minnesota Mining & Manufacturing Co. spends a lot of time "thinking small."

"We are keenly aware of the disadvantages of large size," says Gordon W. Engdahl, the company's vice president for human resources and its top personnel officer. "We make a conscious effort to keep our units as small as possible because we think it helps keep them flexible and vital," he says. "When one gets too large, we break it apart. We like to say that our success in recent years amounts to multiplication by division."

Mr. Engdahl's comment is no conceit. 3M's average U.S. manufacturing plant employs just 270 people, and management groups as small as five guide the fortunes of the company's numerous household, industrial and scientific products. In the 1970s, its sales and earnings grew almost fourfold, while its U.S. work force increased by 40%.

In light of the attention given in recent years to "alienated" workers in big companies, firms have been seeking ways to ameliorate the effects of bigness. Some have adopted programs to make work groups smaller, to improve communications between workers and supervisors, and to give rank-and-filers more say over the way they do their work.

Worker involvement

3M uses a broad array of worker-participation devices, including regular work-crew and management-group meetings and voluntary "quality circles" that assess work procedures.

3M's exhortations to its workers are relentlessly upbeat. At a multipurpose company plant in Menominee, Wis., cartoon figures mouth safety slogans from the walls, and posters proclaim "Safety Day" records instead of injury counts.

Many of the plant's employees have small radios on their workbenches, quietly playing the music of their choice. The radios replaced a plant-wide system of piped-in music that workers complained was too bland. Informality is the rule; not only does everyone go by his first name, but nicknames such as Bob, Jerry and Joe adorn managers' doorplates.

Marge Froeschle has worked at the plant for six years. She is a "group leader," a sort of assistant foreman in work crews that range in size from two or three to a dozen employes. This is her first factory job, and she likes it. "I get to do different things around the plant, and I can put in my two cents' worth whenever I want," she says. "It's not at all what I thought working for a big company would be like."

group and should lead to better solutions when dealing with complex tasks.[21] Indeed, that was Harvey's hope in forming the three quality circles at HCC.

Task/technology

The **task and technology** of a group are important factors in determining the effects of other situational variables.[22] Indeed, along with the individuals in the group, task and technology may be the most important input variables. Different task types have different effects on groups.[23] **Simple tasks** require simple and routine technologies. They can be highly structured, with very few exceptions to the work and only simple problems to solve. In addition, simple tasks require only low-level technical and interpersonal skills. On the other hand, **complex tasks** require nonroutine and complex technologies. There are many alternatives, many exceptions to the work, and very difficult problems to solve. In addition, complex tasks require high levels of both technical and interpersonal skills. Information needed to complete the task tends to be spread among many people. The issue of task/technology is usually more complicated than this analysis, but this level of detail serves the purpose here.

When a group deals with simple tasks, group structure and process can develop in straightforward ways. Group satisfaction and performance can be expected to be high and turnover low if the group members do not desire challenging work (as discussed in Chapters 5 and 6 on motivation). With simple tasks, smaller groups can be expected to be more successful than larger groups, and homogeneous groups will tend to outperform heterogeneous ones.[24] In other words, there must be a match between the people and the task/technology if effectiveness is to result.

When a group must deal with complex tasks, such as the one facing the quality circles at HCC, the development of group structure and process will be more problematic. For one thing, the group will tend to be larger and more heterogeneous (eight people from three departments in the HCC quality circles). Increased size and diversity in a group means more difficult communications, more conflict, and a probable slowdown in the developmental process. There also is a greater likelihood that status differences and power differentials will be larger, thus slowing down the development of norms and cohesiveness. Still, because of the complex task, larger, more heterogeneous groups should be more effective in terms of performance. And if group members desire challenging work, then satisfaction should also be high and turnover low. As discussed in Chapter 13, a critical factor in achieving these results with a complex group task is the type of group process that develops. And the members of the group are the keys to how group process develops.

Physical layout

Another situational input, **physical layout,** is closely associated with the task/technology input. If the physical layout of a group places people close together, interactions tend to increase, unless noise or other factors inhibit them. And **increased interaction among group members should lead to quicker development of the group.**[25] It should also lead to faster development of group norms and cohesivenss. If a group is spread out along an assembly line, the individuals are less likely to become a cohesive group as quickly as a group of office workers working at adjacent desks with no partitions between them. At HCC, the physical layout is constantly changing. The quality circle members work in their own departments with some members seeing each other more frequently than others. Then once a week they sit down around a table for a meeting. It is quite likely that such an arrangement might slow down the group development and make it more difficult for the groups to perform effectively.

But physical space can change over time, with continuing effects on a group. With the advent of automated offices, floor designs are changing. Some companies are going from a large open space with nothing separating the desks to partitions separating the employees. A feeling of teamwork is definitely inhibited by such changes. Indeed, at one large computer manufacturer, the constant moving of portable cubicle walls has created some serious group development problems that have affected employee morale. Likewise, automated office equipment is moving the task/technology of work groups toward the complex end of the continuum. The primary point to remember is that task/technology and physical layout are important influences on a group, and both are highly subject to change. Managers need to be aware of the effects of such changes. They need to manage these changes if their groups are to be effective.

The organizational system

The final situational input is the **organizational system** surrounding a particular group. Other groups with which a group must work are an important influence, as discussed in Chapter 14. The culture and norms of the organization also influence a group.[26] It is difficult for a group to have norms and power relationships that run counter to the overall organization. For example, the takeover of Conoco by DuPont created many cultural adjustments for the groups of employees at Conoco (see Insight 12–5). And this era of deregulation and customer focus has brought on the need for numerous such cultural adjustments for groups in many organizations. For example, one of the authors of this text has worked with a large utility making the cultural shift to be more competitive via decentralization and customer focus. The shift has created nu-

Honeymoon's End

Du Pont, Once a Hero, Has Become a Bother, Many at Conoco Feel

*L*ess than a year ago, Du Pont Co. was a hero to most of Conoco Inc.'s employees. The chemicals giant rescued the coveted oil company from two unwanted suitors—Mobil Corp. and Seagram Co.—and promised there would be no bloodbath, no major shake-up.

But after eight months of living with Du Pont, some Conoco people believe that the $6.8 billion takeover—the biggest ever—has turned out to be a mixed blessing. They tell of anxiety over what Du Pont has in mind for its new subsidiary, of squabbling over who moves into whose office and of more serious conflicts involving corporate style and strategy.

Constructive relationships

Du Pont says it hasn't been callous in its treatment of Conoco. Rather, it says, it has purposely been making changes slowly to ease the adjustment pains. "All things considered, I'm pleased with the response from the Conoco side of the house," says Du Pont Chairman Edward Jefferson, who has been mingling with Conoco employees in their plants and offices, at Christmas parties and on golf-course fairways. "For every difference of opinion," he says, "I think there is an example of a constructive relationship."

The major culture shock for some Conoco people is Du Pont's financial conservatism. Used to the fast-paced, wheeling-dealing nature of the oil business, they are a bit confounded to find that some Du Pont executives value restoring the company's triple-A credit rating more than making a big oil discovery. "Conoco wasn't nearly as conservative about debt. Their attitude was you borrow like hell to search for oil," says Harold May, a Du Pont man who was appointed vice president of corporate studies this year to help map strategies.

Not as much fun

Some chemical workers say they are having fits adjusting to Du Pont's bureaucratic management and its emphasis on paper work. "It was really fun at Conoco Chemicals," an employee says. "You could make mistakes—not the same one twice—and it felt like you really made a difference. But the merger has knocked a lot of that out." He says he recently was called to task for taking the initiative of writing a letter expressing his views on some environmental legislation. Du Pont executives didn't disagree with him. They were just miffed, he says, because he hadn't cleared the letter with them.

By Ronald Alsop, *The Wall Street Journal*, June 16, 1982. Reprinted by permission of *The Wall Street Journal*, © Dow Jones & Company, Inc. 1982. All rights reserved.

merous problems for staff and line groups throughout the company, and the change has taken several years.

A number of factors define the culture of an organization—for example, rules, roles of people, provisions for training, and reward systems. And certainly one of the most important of these factors is the reward system. In many organizations, the reward system encourages individual behavior from people who must work in groups. For example, project teams at one medical products manufacturer are not rewarded as teams, but rather as individuals. Their rewards are determined by their respective department heads. Is it any wonder that such groups have difficulty becoming cohesive teams? When conflicts between department needs and project needs arise, the employees invariably focus on department needs, thus inhibiting project team effectiveness. In other organizations, the reward system is based on group behavior, and highly effective work teams often result.[27] An effective group member or manager must work with these situational inputs by adjusting to them and to their impact on the groups. Then, too, a member or manager may sometimes be able to alter the situational inputs to yield a more favorable effect on the groups.

Overall, then, situational and individual factors are important for managers to understand. They do appear to have an impact on the **performance** of a group. But perhaps even more important, these factors have an impact on the development of a group's **structure** and **process** (elements discussed in Chapter 13). And in turn, group structure and process directly influence the performance of the group and satisfaction of its members.

Furthermore, the performance of a group serves as feedback to affect the input variables. If a group is successful, new people may desire to join it, thus altering the group slightly (for example, size increases and composition changes). And if a group is not successful, some members may leave the group while others join, again affecting the group's composition and perhaps size. Certainly, too, poor performance may lead to changes in physical layout, technology, rewards, and so forth. A manager or group member needs to know how to improve group effectiveness by managing the input variables. So we will next look into ways to design more effective groups.

IMPROVING GROUP EFFECTIVENESS BY MANAGING THE INPUT VARIABLES

Perhaps the **first step in understanding how to more effectively manage and belong to groups in organizations is to accept the fact that groups are a way of life in organizations.** Managers must get work done both through formal and informal groups of people. Synergy of effort is the desired goal, in addition to effort directed toward accomplishment of organizational goals. Both informal and formal groups can improve communications and enhance interpersonal relations that are beneficial to an organization, so long as they accept the goals of the organization. Beyond this first step, it is important to recognize that group effectiveness involves many factors. Up to this point, we have focused only on the input variables that can be used to design a work group. In Chapter 13, we will focus on the emergent structure and process variables that characterize the daily operation of a group.

For now, we need to place the input (design) variables in a framework which will make managing them more understandable. As explained in Chapter 1, managing a group is similar to putting together the pieces of a puzzle—except for three points.

1. There is no guarantee that all the pieces will be present.
2. There is no guarantee that the pieces will fit together.
3. There is no guarantee that the pieces will not continue to change through growth and development.

Still, understanding the variables that must fit together in the puzzle helps a person become both a better manager and a better group member. The framework shown in Exhibit 12–4 is based on the same concept of congruence as defined in Chapter 6 when talking about the fit of variables that determine the motivation of an employee. A good fit or match between the variables shown in Exhibit 12–4 should lead to higher group effectiveness. And a continuing fit over time, as these inputs develop, should lead to both long-term and short-term effectiveness.

To use the framework in Exhibit 12–4, start with an analysis of the **task/technology** variable. As noted earlier, the nature of the task/technology influences the effects that other input variables have upon group performance. And the task/technology variable determines the type of people who would best fit in a group. The more complex the task/technology, the more highly skilled people are needed. Although managers often cannot alter the technology, sometimes they can make important changes in the tasks. For instance, a manager can alter tasks to make them more intrinsically motivating (as discussed in Chapter 5). Some of these same variables (skill variety, task significance, task identity, autonomy, and feedback) can make a job more or less complex to better fit the people in the group.

Thus, the second critical variable from Exhibit 12–4 is the **individuals** who make up the group. Managers need to work toward understanding the personalities, perceptions, abilities, and motivations of group members. In fact, this information will be useful whether a manager is the leader of the group or simply a group member. Perhaps through selection or training a manager can find people who are best suited for the type of task the group must do. Or by understanding the people, perhaps managers can alter the task or other variables to fit the people they have. It really does not matter. **The key point is to achieve as good a fit as possible between the people and the task.**

The next fit variable to consider is the **group size and composition.** Usually smaller groups perform better than larger ones. One reason for

EXHIBIT 12–4

The Fit of Group Input Variables

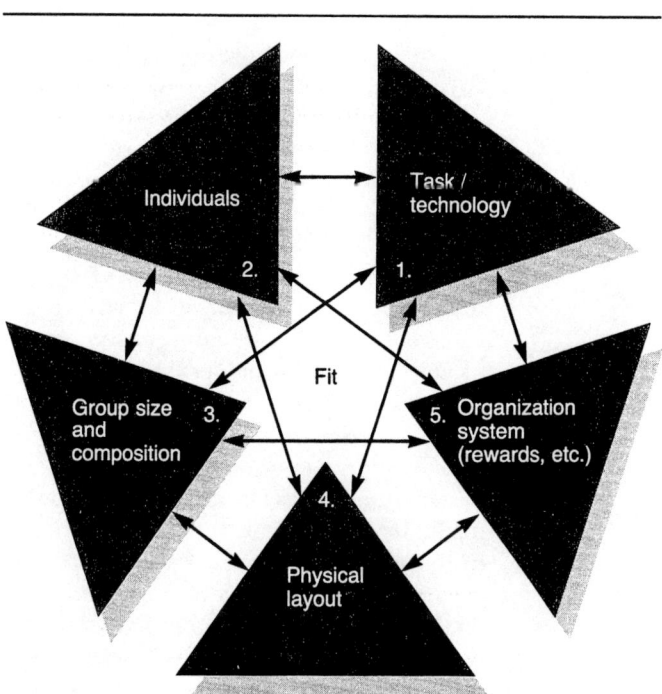

this tendency is that the number of interpersonal connections grows rapidly as size increases. And this makes it harder to work out all of the conflicts and communications problems that inhibit group cohesion. For the same reason, homogeneous groups are easier to manage than heterogeneous groups. Of course, if the group task is complex, group size may need to increase, and the composition will probably need to be more heterogeneous to cope with the task. Indeed, when the task is complex, larger heterogeneous groups tend to outperform smaller homogeneous groups, providing their interactions are well managed. Again, **the fit between size/composition and the task and people is the critical issue to manage.**

In considering the **physical layout** as an input variable, managers are in some respects returning to the task/technology variable. Although a group's physical layout will be largely determined by the task/technology, there is usually some room for adjustment. Usually people in a group should be located close to one another so they can easily interact, since interaction will help move them through the stages of group development. And interaction also leads to greater cohesion and hence, greater effectiveness. But again, a group's physical layout must be consistent with the other input variables. If people must perform different parts of a task, and technology dictates that they must be performed in different ways, the physical layout of the group may separate members. The key then becomes the use of certain group members as links between the different subgroups that will form in each physical space.

Finally, to the greatest extent possible, managers should use the **organizational system** (such as rules, procedures, rewards, and goals) to emphasize group effort. Managers should establish individual jobs that are clearly linked to group goals, which have been spelled out to group members. Managers should then reward behaviors that are consistent with these goals and group effectiveness.[28] An example of this is found in a grocery store chain in North Carolina. Departments in each store receive a bonus each month based on the sales of their department, and group cooperation is very high. Without such group-oriented reward systems, a group can easily destroy itself as individuals strive to receive individual rewards.

The actions of a manager, plus the organizational system, will determine whether a heterogeneous group that is physically spread out working on unique aspects of the group task will pull together or pull apart.[29] In the Home Computers case, the organizational systems input will be very important in moving the quality circles through the group stages and making them effective in both the short and long term. When a group is homogeneous, small, close together, and working on a simple task, managerial emphasis on these organizational issues can probably be reduced. However, these issues are always important for a manager and a group, given society's cultural orientation toward individual performance.

The final point to be made in using Exhibit 12–4 is to manage the developmental aspects of each of the fit variables. Each fit variable can and will change over time.[30] To the degree that a manager keeps the fit variables matched, a group will move through the stages of development more quickly. In starting up a new group, if the input variables are properly matched, the group will move rapidly through the early stages of group development. And to the extent that the manager keeps the inputs in congruence, the group will continue to be effective and move toward the final, desirable stage of development.

For example, task/technology variables tend to move from the complex toward the simple over time. At the same time, individuals tend to develop from lower to higher levels of skill. Thus, at the early stages of group development, the technology may be more complex than the people can effectively handle. This means that the manager will have to provide skill training, structure, procedures, and rewards to compensate for this mismatch. Over time, the group's skills may surpass the demands of the technology. When this happens, the manager will need to loosen up on the structure and encourage greater innovation on the part of the group. Again, the point is continuous management of the group input variables.

Once a group is set up with the input variables and starts to operate, the emergent structure and process variables in Exhibit 12–4 come into play. In Chapter 13, we will deal with those issues in detail as we focus on the behavioral aspects of making work groups effective.

CHAPTER HIGHLIGHTS

This chapter has marked a shift from the interpersonal level of organizational behavior to the group level. In introducing this part of the book, the opening text stressed the importance of building upon the interpersonal and individual behavior material discussed in the previous two parts of the book. Furthermore, the text pointed out that just like individuals and interpersonal relations, groups move through developmental stages.

The chapter opened by relating the importance to managers of understanding groups. The main reason for this is that **the essence of management is doing work through groups of people.** Indeed, groups are an essential fact of organizational behavior. And managers and their people will belong to several groups within an organization. **Groups are very complex entities;** and the goal of this chapter has been to begin the process of understanding them.

Early on, the chapter **defined a group as a collection of two or more people who exist over some period of time, develop shared norms of behavior, are interdependent, and interact over time for the purpose of achieving some shared set of goals.** To further elaborate the definition, we discussed several types of groups and their developmental stages. We mentioned formal and informal groups (including networks), both of which can be a help or a hindrance to an organization. A manager's job is to ensure the positive outcomes.

In discussing group development, the text presented Tuckman's four-stage model, which focuses on both interpersonal and task elements of development. The first stage of development is called **test and orientation, or forming.** It is the stage where group members become acquainted with one another and also learn what is expected of them on a task.

The second stage is called **conflict and organization, or storming.** Here, group members begin to have conflicts over who is the real leader of the group. It is also the time when norms, standards, and work rules emerge to give a group a sense of organization. Stage 3 is called **cohesion and information exchange, or norming.** In this stage, group members begin to feel really comfortable with each other. It is at this time that groups are most vulnerable to **groupthink**, where cohesiveness overrides analytical processes. But in this stage, a group can also become good at exchanging information relevant to a task.

The final stage of group development, which many groups never reach, is called **interdependence and problem solving, or performing**. At this stage, a group works like a team, both in terms of interpersonal and task issues. **This group developmental process is never ending. Many factors, such as new members, a new leader, or a task or technology change, can cause groups to slide back into previous stages of development**.

After discussing these stages, we checked in on Home Computers Company for a look at its quality circles. We then examined a model of group behavior, consisting of individual and situational inputs, structure, process, and outcomes (shown in Exhibit 12–3).

In terms of individual inputs, the personalities of different group members might influence (either positively or negatively) group interactions and performance. Perceptions, abilities, and motivations of group members are also important inputs. **An effective manager of a group needs to manage the potential effects of individual inputs**.

We then discussed the various situational inputs in Exhibit 12–3. **Group size** was mentioned as an important situational input that affects the interactions of a group. A larger group moves more slowly through the stages of group development.

Group composition (the particular combination of people in a group) was categorized as either homogeneous or heterogeneous. Homogeneous groups communicate more easily and have fewer conflicts. They work best on simple tasks. But with complex tasks, heterogeneous groups tend to do better.

The task/technology input variable tends to moderate the relationships between the other input variables and group outcomes. When dealing with a simple task/technology, smaller homogeneous groups tend to perform better and move more rapidly through the stages of group development. With complex task/technologies, more effective groups tend to be larger and more heterogeneous, though they will be more difficult to manage.

Physical layout was treated briefly as a variable closely connected to the task/technology. **People who work in close proximity interact more frequently and should be expected to develop as a group more rapidly**.

The final situational input variable discussed was the **organizational system**. Other groups, as well as rules, procedures, and reward systems, are important factors that can affect a group.

Exhibit 12–4 presented a framework for managing group behavior based on a proper fit among all of the individual and situational inputs. In essence, we talked about the process of designing groups for high performance. But because of the developmental aspect of groups, there needs to be a continuing process of assessment and adjustment among the inputs for a group to have continued high performance.

In using the framework in Exhibit 12–4, managers should start with an analysis of the task/technology of a group, since it seems to influence the relationship between the other inputs and performance. The next fit variable to consider is the people. By understanding their employees, managers work toward a good fit between task/technology and the members of the group.

Next, managers should consider the size and composition of the group to be sure they design a fit between size/composition and task and people. To the extent that physical layout can be altered, it, too, should be congruent with the other input variables. Finally, managers need to be sure that the group's design is consistent with the organizational system in terms of norms, rules, procedures, and rewards.

With this basic understanding of groups and group development, and how to manage group input variables, we are ready to discuss the action phase of managing group structure and process. And it is to that task we turn in Chapter 13.

REVIEW QUESTIONS

1. Why is it important to keep in mind the material discussed in Parts 2 and 3 of this book (individual and interpersonal behavior) when exploring group behavior in organizations?

2. Why is it important for managers to understand groups in organizations?

3. Why is the developmental aspect of groups so important in the definition of a group?

4. Why is it important that managers understand the individual and situational inputs to group behavior shown in Exhibit 12–3, even though they may be difficult to influence?

5. Explain the four stages of group development presented in this chapter. Does this developmental process make sense when applied to groups to which you have belonged?

6. Why is the group development process never ending?

7. Which aspects of individuals would be most important to consider as inputs for understanding group behavior?

8. What are the impacts of group size and composition on the interactions and performance of a group? Why are these two situational inputs perhaps less important than the task/technology input variable?

9. Explain what is meant by the task/technology input variable and how it impacts on the size, composition, and physical layout input variables.

10. Which aspects of a surrounding organization have influence on group behavior and performance?

11. Explain how Exhibit 12–4 can be used to help in the design process for input variables to group behavior and performance.

RESOURCE READINGS

Lawler, E. E. III. *High Involvement Management*. San Francisco: Jossey-Bass, 1986.

Shaw, M. E. *Group Dynamics: The Psychology of Small Group Behavior*. 3rd ed. New York: McGraw-Hill, 1981.

Tuckman, B. W., and M. A. C. Jensen. "Stages of Small Group Development Revisited." *Group & Organization Studies* 2 (1977), pp. 419–27.

Walton, R. E. "Reestablishing and Maintaining High Commitment Work Systems." In *The Organizational Life Cycle*, ed. J. R. Kimberly and R. H. Miles. San Francisco: Jossey-Bass, 1980, pp. 208–90.

NOTES

1. E. Mayo, *The Social Problems of an Industrial Civilization* (Boston, Mass.: Harvard University Graduate School of Business, 1945).

2. For example, see M. E. Shaw, *Group Dynamics: The Psychology of Small Group Behavior*, 2d ed. (New York: McGraw-Hill, 1976).

3. E. E. Lawler III and S. A. Mohrman, "Quality Circles: After the Honeymoon," *Organizational Dynamics* 15 (Spring 1987), pp. 42–55.

4. T. D. Wall, N. J. Kemp, P. R. Jackson, and C. W. Clegg, "Outcomes of Autonomous Workgroups: A Long-Term Field Experiment," *Academy of Management Journal* 29 (1986), pp. 280–304.

5. J. P. Kotter, *The General Managers* (New York: Free Press, 1982).

6. D. J. Brass, "Men's and Women's Networks: A Study of Interaction Patterns and Influence in an Organization," *Academy of Management Journal* 28 (1985), pp. 327–43.

7. W. C. Schutz, "Interpersonal Underworld," *Harvard Business Review*, July–August 1958, pp. 38–56.

8. B. W. Tuckman, "Developmental Sequence in Small Groups," *Psychological Bulletin* 63 (1965), pp. 384–99; B. W. Tuckman and M. A. C. Jensen, "Stages of Small Group Development Revisited," *Group & Organization Studies* 2 (1977), pp. 419–27.

9. C. J. G. Gersick, "Time and Transition in Work Teams: Toward a New Model of Group Development," *Academy of Management Journal* 31 (1988), pp. 9–41.

10. I. L. Janis, *Groupthink*, 2d ed. (Boston: Houghton Mifflin, 1982).

11. C. R. Leana, "A Partial Test of Janis' Groupthink Model: Effects of Group Cohesiveness and Leader Behavior on Defective Decision Making," *Journal of Management* 11 (1985), pp. 5–17.

12. R. Katz, "The Effects of Group Longevity on Project Communication and Performance," *Administrative Science Quarterly* 27 (1982), pp. 81–104.

13. R. Moreland, "Social Categorization and the Assimilation of 'New' Group Members," *Journal of Personality and Social Psychology* 48 (1985), pp. 1173–90.

14. S. J. Lieborvitz and K. DeMeuse, "The Application of Team Building," *Human Relations* 35 (1982), pp. 1–18.

15. R. W. Napier and M. K. Gershenfeld, *Groups: Theory and Experience*, 2d ed. (Boston: Houghton Mifflin, 1981), pp. 214–15.

16. Shaw, *Group Dynamics*.

17. This section draws primarily from L. L. Cummings and C. J. Berger, "Organization Structure: How Does It Influence Attitudes and Performance?," *Organizational Dynamics* 5 (1976), pp. 34–49, and R. M. Steers, *Introduction to Organizational Behavior*, 3d ed. (Glenview, Ill.: Scott, Foresman, 1988).

18. R. F. Bales and E. F. Borgatta, "Size of Group as a Factor in the Interaction Profile," in *Small Groups*, ed. A. P. Hare, E. F. Borgatta, and R. F. Bales (New York: Alfred. A. Knopf, 1956); M. E. Shaw, *Group Dynamics: The Psychology of Small Group Behavior*, 3d ed. (New York: McGraw Hill, 1981).

19. This section draws primarily from A. P. Hare, *Handbook of Small Group Research* (New York: Free Press, 1962).

20. S. W. Alagna and D. M. Reddy, "Self and Peer Ratings and Evaluations of Group Processes in Mixed-Sex and Male Medical Training Groups," *Journal of Applied Social Psychology* 15 (1985), pp. 31–45.

21. M. R. Callaway, R. G. Marriott, and J. K. Esser, "Effects of Dominance on Group Decision Making: Toward a Stress-Reduction Explanation of Groupthink," *Journal of Personality and Social Psychology* 49 (1985), pp. 949–52.

22. J. Kelly and J. McGrath, "Effects of Time Limits and Task Types on Task Performance and Interaction of Four Person Groups," *Journal of Personality and Social Psychology* 49 (1985), pp. 395–407.

23. This section draws primarily from D. M. Herold, "The Effectiveness of Work Groups," in *Organizational Behavior*, ed. S. Kerr (Columbus, Ohio: Grid, 1979), and W. A. Randolph, "Matching Technology and the Design of Organization Units," *California Management Review* 23 (1981), pp. 39–48.

24. Hare, *Handbook of Small Group Research*, p. 201.

25. D. Cartwright, "The Nature of Group Cohesiveness," in *Group Dynamics*, 3d ed., ed. D. Cartwright and A. Zander (New York: Harper & Row, 1968), pp. 91–109.

26. T. E. Deal and A. A. Kennedy, *Corporate Cultures* (Reading, Mass.: Addison-Wesley Publishing, 1982).

27. R. E. Walton, "Establishing and Maintaining High Commitment Work Systems," in *The Organizational Life Cycle*, ed. J. R. Kimberly and R. H. Miles (San Francisco: Jossey-Bass, 1980), pp. 208–90.

28. G. C. Elliott and B. F. Meeker, "Achieving Fairness in the Face of Competing Concerns: The Different Effects of Individual and Group Characteristics," *Journal of Personality and Social Psychology* 50 (1986), pp. 754–60.

29. R. Hackman and R. E. Walton, *The Leadership of Groups in Organizations* (New Haven, Conn.: Yale University Press, 1985).

30. Walton, "Establishing and Maintaining High Commitment Work Systems."

CASE: John Berkely

John Berkely was a production worker at Universal Manufacturers, Inc., which made components and accessories for the automotive industry. He had worked at Universal for almost six years as a welder, along with twelve other men in the crew. All had received training in welding, both on the job and through external courses. The members of the work group got along very well with one another. There was a lot of kidding around, the usual baseball and football pools, and the group always ate together in the company cafeteria. Most of the fellows had been there for some length of time, except for two men who had been hired in the last two months.

Berkely was generally considered to be the informal leader of the group, so it was no surprise that when the foreman of their crew was transferred and his job was posted, Berkely applied for the job and got it. There were only three other applicants for the job, one from another department and two from the outside. When the appointment was announced on Friday afternoon, everyone in the group congratulated Berkely, took him out to a bar, and bought him several beers to celebrate.

On Monday morning, Berkely came to work a foreman. It was company practice for all the foremen to wear blue work coats, a white shirt, and tie. Each man's coat had his name badge sewn onto the left-hand pocket. The company had supplied Berkely with his coat which he proudly wore to work on Monday.

Upon entering the work area, all the men crowded round "admiring" his new blue coat. There was a lot of kidding such as, "Hey, John, yer ole' lady go out and buy you a new wardrobe?" or "Good grief! Mama's little boy got all dressed up to come to work!" One of the guys went back to his locker and returned with a can of shoe polish and acted as though he were polishing Berkely's shoes. After about five minutes of horseplay, all of the men went back to work and Berkely went to his office to get more familiar with his new job.

Source: J. L. Gray and F. A. Starke, *Organizational Behavior: Concepts and Applications*, 3d ed. (Columbus, Ohio: Merrill Publishing Co., 1984), p. 466. Reprinted by permission of the publisher.

At noon, all the men broke for lunch and went to the cafeteria to eat and talk as usual. Berkely was busy when they left but followed after them a few minutes later. As he came though the food line and paid the cashier, he turned to face the open cafeteria. Back to the far right-hand corner of the room was his old work group; on the left-hand side of the cafeteria sat all the other foremen in the plant, all dressed in their blue coats.

A hush fell over the cafeteria as both groups looked at Berkely, waiting to see which group he would eat with.

Questions

1. Whom do you think Berkely will eat with? Why?
2. If you were one of the other foremen, what could you do to make Berkely's transition easier?
3. What would you have done if you were in Berkely's shoes? Why?
4. What stage of group development are the foremen in with regard to Berkely? What about the worker group?

CASE: Ted Lofton's problem

Ted Lofton was aghast. He had just completed his first inspection of the plant and had seen so many problems he didn't know where to begin. This was Ted's first major management position and he knew that his future with the company depended on how he handled this job. The East Hampton plant had a reputation in the company as a real trouble spot. He knew that if he could get things straightened out, he would be on his way.

And suddenly, Ted knew just where to begin. As he toured the plant, the most shocking scene had been in Section C. There were five older women down there who had turned the place into a living room. Whereas everyone else had worked at tables arranged in neat rows, these five had their tables arranged in a circle. They had put down a carpet and even hung some pictures on the wall. They had stashed a small refrigerator off to one side and kept a radio playing music. Ted didn't understand why they needed the radio, though. They talked incessantly and couldn't possibly have heard anything. And, Ted was sure, the talking and other distractions were surely hurting productivity. Yes, Ted thought, that's where I'll start.

Late that evening, after everyone else had gone, Ted sent a maintenance crew down to Section C. He had them unplug the radio and refrigerator and set them in a corner. The carpet was rolled up, the pictures taken off the wall, and the work tables arranged in a neat straight line.

The next morning, Ted fully expected the women to come storming into his office, and he was prepared to deal with them. He was surprised, however, when they simply sat down and went to work. He was equally surprised

Source: Ricky Griffin, *Management*, second edition. Copyright © 1987 by Houghton Mifflin Company. Used with permission.

to find three days later that output from Section C was down 75 percent. He immediately raced to the floor to find out how the women were cutting back, but he couldn't find any evidence that they were working at anything but maximum efficiency.

Ted next went back to his office and did something he realized he should have done much earlier. He looked at the performance records of the five women. Three pieces of information were especially enlightening. The women had worked together in the same section for over fifteen years, and they consistently produced at a rate of 70 to 80 percent above the standard established for their jobs. Finally, their supervisor had noted several times in their files that they were all very dedicated and committed employees.

Questions

1. Can you characterize the work group in Section C both before and after the changes Ted made?
2. At what stage of development was the work group in Section C?
3. What group input variables help in understanding what has happened?
4. What should Ted do now?

Option

Role play Ted's next step with the group of five women.

C H A P T E R 13

Group Structure and Process

I

n the preceding chapter we began our exploration of groups in organizations. Besides discussing the importance of groups, we examined the developmental stages that groups pass through. We also focused on understanding and managing the input variables that create the context for the development of group structure and process. With that background, we are now ready to delve inside the operation of a group to study the emerging structure and process and to learn how to manage these key group variables. For convenience, the model of group behavior from Chapter 12 is repeated here with the parts of the model that will be our focus in this chapter highlighted (see Exhibit 13–1).

Once a group has been designed by determining the individual and situational input variables, the group begins to function, and the structure and process variables determine just how successful the group will be. Indeed, **getting the most out of a group depends heavily upon the group structure and process that emerge during the developmental stages.** A group manager or member will have more direct influence over these variables than over the input variables. In many ways, the input variables are givens that a manager works with; they are constraints on the manager's and the group's actions (especially with a preexisting group). Thus, the structure and process variables become the key variables to understand and manage. That is the challenge of this chapter.

THE GROUP STRUCTURE VARIABLES

As the model in Exhibit 13–1 reflects, once a group begins to operate and develop over time, group structure and process begin to emerge. Also, the group outcomes serve as feedback to the emergence of structure and process. This section will explore group structure and how it develops over time. **Group structure is the pattern of relationships that develops among group members and influences the group's outcomes.** As shown in Exhibit 13–1, group structure consists of norms, status relationships, power relationships, and cohesiveness. Each of these four elements, which are discussed below, is influenced by the individual and situational inputs and the group outcomes. And each element emerges in a developmental fashion.[1]

Norms

Norms are the rules of behavior that are developed by group members and provide guidance to group activities.[2] They are present in every group; in fact, without norms, it would be difficult for a group to exist. Norms direct the behaviors of individual members toward the group's

EXHIBIT 13–1

A Model of Group Behavior

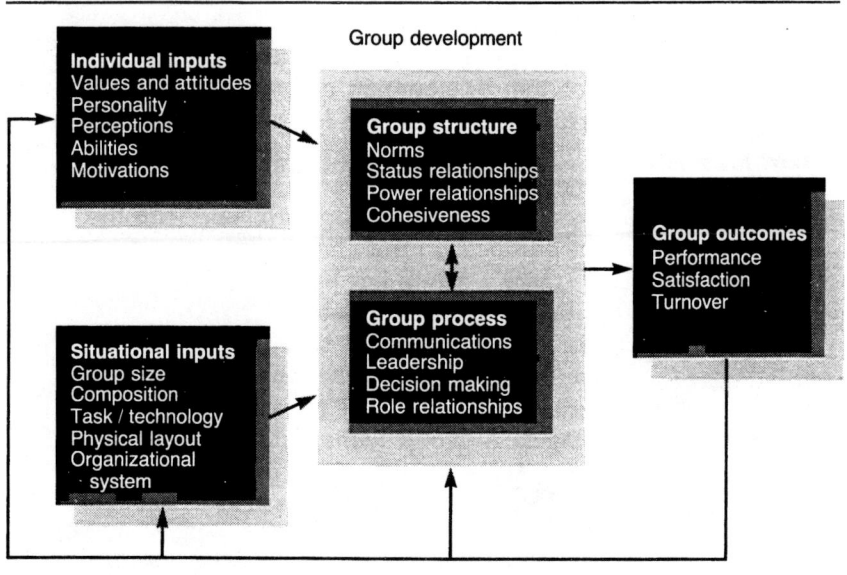

goals. A manager must be concerned that group norms are congruent with the goals of the organization, since norms are a powerful influence on group member behavior. If, for example, a group develops a norm of restricting performance to the minimum requirement, it can be very difficult for the manager to achieve a higher level of performance. Hence, it will be best for a group leader to work to develop desirable group norms.[3]

Norms usually develop and change gradually in a group. As members learn what behaviors are truly important for the accomplishment of group goals, they develop expected standards for those behaviors. It is possible, however, for groups to set norms quickly by verbally agreeing to a particular guiding behavior. For example, a group might decide that everyone on a committee is expected to come to the meetings on time and prepared.

And there are consequences associated with violation of group norms. Group members are expected to adhere to the norms that are developed. But what happens to someone who deviates from the group norms? At first, other group members usually communicate more frequently to try to bring the deviate back into the group.[4] But if the deviate continues to ignore the group norms, a time will come when the group rejects this person. Group members may stop talking to and psychologically withdraw from the deviate. In the movie and the book *Lords of Discipline,* the drumming of a cadet out of a military school is a vivid reminder of what can happen to someone who deviates from accepted norms.[5] Because the cadet stole gas from a fellow cadet, he was forced to walk out of the school down a path lined, on either side, by his peers. As he passed, each one turned his back on the cadet, vowing never to speak his name again. Honesty was a strong norm which this cadet violated. It is true that such stringent measures are rare in the business world. In fact, having someone in a group who deviates from the norm may enable a group to more clearly identify group norms for new members.[6] When the deviant person is disciplined by the group, the contrast between his or her behavior and that of other group members makes the norms much clearer.

However, all norms do not apply equally to all people in a group. High-status members can sometimes ignore group norms more easily than lower-status members. However, even the high-status person must be careful of the side effects of ignoring group norms. A manager might, for example, ignore a norm of being on time for meetings with the work group. In return, the group might not work as hard for the manager. Or group members might be less punctual in coming to work each day than . they would if the manager respected the group norm.

The development of group norms

Different types of group norms are associated with the four stages of group development.[7] During the **testing and orientation (forming) stage,** norms develop around who is and who is not a member of the group, attendance, and commitment. Once these issues are basically settled, the group develops norms about leadership, status, ways of doing work, and organization as it moves into the **conflict and organization (storming) stage.** If a group succeeds at this stage and moves into the **cohesion and information exchange stage,** norms about relationships among group members, ways of showing caring in the group, and the balance between task and interpersonal relationships will develop. During the final stage, **interdependence and problem solving (performing),** a group can be expected to develop norms that relate to how much experimentation will be allowed, how much adaptation is desired, and ways of maintaining a highly cohesive group.

As with the group development stages, the focus on norms may not proceed in a highly orderly fashion. Many factors influence the development of group norms.[8] Let us briefly concentrate on how the input variables in Exhibit 13–1 impact norms. First of all, different individuals respond differently to norms. The more intelligent group members are, the less likely they are to develop and conform to norms. The same is true for people who are authoritarian in nature.

The size and composition of a group can also influence the development of norms. Larger groups tend to have a stronger sense of norms—perhaps they have to in order to create cohesion among the larger number of people. Homogeneous groups tend to develop norms more rapidly than heterogeneous groups.

As for the task/technology input, the more routine and well defined the task, the quicker norms will develop. But once norms are developed, new ambiguous tasks may cause groups to fall back on established norms as a form of security. For example, the departmental groups at one large utility company, when faced with the new challenge of being customer focused, invariably relied on the old norm: "Don't do anything unless someone tells you to do it." Instead of taking initiative as current conditions demanded, group members waited for specific guidance from company management. Indeed, this may be one reason groups tend to resist change so strongly. The physical layout of a group can affect norm development because groups that are in close proximity tend to interact more frequently. And groups that interact more frequently develop stronger norms.

The norms of the organization in which a group is located will also influence the development of group norms. Most group norms will be consistent with the organization's norms. If, however, the organization's norms are highly unfavorable to the group, the group can develop strong norms that run counter to the organization. A good example of this is the union action that occurs in some organizations. The union establishes norms with its members about speed and quantity of work. No matter how hard management tries, it may not be able to get union members to work faster.

The group process variables of communications, decision making, leadership, and member roles that emerge also have an impact on group norms (see Exhibit 13–1). Likewise, the performance, satisfaction, and turnover of group members will influence group norms. A successful group tends to maintain existing norms and to develop new norms that are consistent with existing ones. On the other hand, an unsuccessful group may feel the need to alter the status quo and develop new norms it hopes will lead to better outcomes.

Status and power relationships

Status and power relationships are treated together in this section because of their similarity. **Status is the importance ranking associated with each group member.** Not all members will have the same status, and hence, a set of status relationships will develop in a group. These differences in status may be based on individual characteristics, job title, level of authority and responsibility, among other things.

For example, in considering group composition as an input, a department head of data processing might be in a group along with the plant manager and two section heads from accounting, working on an accounting project for the plant. The plant manager would have a higher status than the data processing manager, who would have a higher status than the accounting section heads because she is a department head. It is easy to imagine how communications and decision making might be influenced by this configuration of status relationships.

In addition to these status differences, there will be power differences, as well. In Chapter 10 we discussed numerous bases of power: referent, expert, reward, coercive, legitimate, relations, information, connection, and resource. In the example above, the accounting section heads may have more expert power than the data processing manager or the plant manager, since the task is to solve an accounting problem. But the data processing manager has the resources that they need— namely, the computer system and analysts. Hence, there are both power and status differences in this group.

With these differences, inconsistencies that will create conflicts in the group can emerge easily.[9] No one group member has all the status and power variables in his or her favor. Indeed, these differences are sometimes a primary reason for forming a project group that must deal with a complex problem.[10] But these inconsistencies can create problems. During the conflict and organization (storming) stage of development, for example, conflicts may be more heated when there are inconsistencies in status and power, and the group might develop more slowly. However, these differences may also help clarify the roles for group members and ultimately lead to a very effective group.

What, then, affects the status and power relationships in a group? Individuals bring various status and power bases with them as inputs to a group. Thus, an initial set of status/power relationships already exists when a group is formed. The larger and more heterogeneous the group, the greater the chance of status inconsistencies. The same is true for a complex task/technology and a physical layout that spreads people out: these cases invite status/power differences. But such differences do not always have negative effects on a group. If properly managed, they can be helpful. Take a look at Insight 13–1. What impact does the status/ power differences between J. R. Houghton (as chairperson) and the other managers at Corning Glass Works have on the management team? Who dictates at top-management meetings?

As a group begins to develop, the process variables will influence the emergent status/power relationships. While some differences and inconsistencies in status and power may not be apparent during the design of a group, they will become obvious as the group begins to operate. And the performance and satisfaction of group members will feed back into the development of these relationships. A successful group will move forward with the status and power relationships that were prescribed

---

With New Chairman, Corning Tries to Get Tough and Revive Earnings

Corning, N.Y.—Corning Glass Works' management-training program, so the joke on Wall Street goes, consists of three weeks of polo, three weeks of squash and nine weeks of platform tennis.

Corning clearly has a reputation for a laid-back management style—a reputation that observers inside and outside the company say is deserved. They blame the company's 41% drop in net income since 1979 partly on management's unwillingness to make difficult, but necessary, decisions on cost cutting, acquisitions and divestitures.

Last week, Corning decided to try to change course. Amory Houghton Jr., Corning chairman and chief executive for almost two decades, stepped down at age 56, and was replaced by his 47-year-old brother, James R. Houghton. The new boss, who had been vice chairman, has a reputation for toughness and is the chief architect of strategy, including management reorganization

and extensive writeoffs, that Corning hopes will revive its sagging fortunes.

"I'm viewed around here as a little bit of a hard-ass," says the new chairman, who confesses to having just reread Machiavelli's "The Prince." "I have a reputation for asking hard questions and sometimes not being very nice in meetings. I guess I don't put up with too much explanation for lots of problems."

Changing a culture

Still, most people believe he won't have it easy. It is hard to change a corporate culture, and the one at Corning has been around a long time.

Moreover, that culture of paternalism and an easy-going, risk-averse style has been provided by the Houghton family, which started Corning 130 years ago here in upstate New York.

By Ann Hughey, *The Wall Street Journal*, April 22, 1983. Reprinted by permission of *The Wall Street Journal*, © Dow Jones & Company, Inc. 1983. All rights reserved.

---

in designing the group and that emerge during group development. An unsuccessful group will encounter much greater conflict in determining the relationships that will develop.

Cohesiveness

Group cohesiveness is one of the most researched of the group variables. In some ways, it is an outcome variable, but most researchers agree that cohesiveness is a property of a group that affects both performance and satisfaction. Hence, cohesiveness is usually referred to as a group structure variable. **Cohesiveness is the degree to which members of a group are attracted to one another and motivated to work together.**[11] In simpler terms, it is the degree to which a group feels like a team. As discussed in Chapter 12, the development of cohesiveness marks one of the four stages of group development. Indeed, without cohesiveness, a collection of people cannot really be referred to as a group.

Since group cohesiveness develops over time, it is influenced by the group process variables we will shortly be discussing. In fact, frequency of communications, a process variable, is a key factor influencing the development of cohesiveness. More frequent interactions lead to greater cohesiveness.[12] Frequency of interactions will be influenced by the status/power relationships that develop in a group, by a group's size, and by the task/technology. Status/power relationships must be resolved during the conflict and organization stage of development for cohesiveness to develop in a group. Internal conflicts can cause problems in developing a sense of cohesiveness for a group.

As group size increases, interactions per person will be more limited because of the finite amount of time for communications. And with the decrease in interactions, cohesiveness will develop more slowly. Increased size also makes it more difficult to agree on common goals and activities. Finally, increases in group size bring about the need for subgroups to form to get the work done. This division of labor is another obstacle to the development of cohesiveness.[13]

With regard to task/technology, the more complex it is, the more group interaction is necessary; and this should lead to increased cohesiveness.[14] However, the complexity of the task could also make it more difficult for a group to achieve cohesiveness, unless group members can agree on some common goals and activities. This usually means that the group needs an overall goal that everyone in the group wants to achieve.[15]

Agreement on group goals is at least partially dependent on the people in a group. Compatible personalities, perceptions, motivations, and abilities can make the development of cohesiveness easier. Thus, the composition of a group is really the key variable affecting the interpersonal attraction among its members and the cohesiveness that develops. Research has consistently shown that people who are attracted to one another tend to be become a cohesive group more quickly than people who are not.[16] But as discussed in Chapter 12, too much cohesiveness can lead to groupthink. Thus, managers need to consider the personalities, motivations, and attitudes of people making up a group. Managers must try to form a group in which the members are compatible and can develop cohesiveness. But managers must also recognize that some heterogeneity can help avoid excessive cohesiveness, which may lead to groupthink.[17]

Another important factor in the development of cohesiveness is the performance and satisfaction that a group achieves. This feedback loop reinforces the developmental aspect of the group structure variables. A group that is successful in achieving its goals will develop cohesiveness more quickly than a group that is unsuccessful.[18] Success makes group members feel good about each other and their efforts to date. It may also make them feel good compared to less successful groups—a sense of superiority that leads to better feelings about each other. On the other hand, failure can lead group members to throw the blame at each other as they search for a scapegoat. It is not hard to see how such conflict could lead to decreased cohesiveness, and perhaps dissolution of the group.

The final factor that can affect cohesiveness is the organizational system input variable. If a group is in an organization that encourages group performance through its reward structure, cohesiveness will tend to increase. Cohesiveness may not increase if the reward system encourages individual performance. Likewise, the fewer the resources of the organization, the more chance cohesiveness has to develop.[19] When resources are lacking, groups tend to pull together in hopes of winning against other groups. Hence, a shortage of personal computers available in an organization may cause departments to fight over who gets one, and this process may make a department group more internally cohesive—at least until the resources increase.

Effects of cohesiveness

It is logical that a cohesive group can accomplish more than one that is not cohesive.[20] The question is, what goals are these groups working toward? A very cohesive group that sets performance goals consistent with the organization's goals can be very productive. But a group that decides to go counter to the organization can be a very powerful negative force. **Managers must work to ensure compatibility between group and organization goals so that cohesiveness can work for them.** Otherwise, managers could encounter problems like those between union and management described in Insight 13–2. Cohesive groups that do not accept the goals of an organization can be very problematic, indeed.

Cohesiveness provides greater satisfaction for group members, and membership in the group becomes very valuable. Group members want to participate in the group, and they exhibit great loyalty to it. Cohesiveness also leads to greater communications among group members and stricter adherence to group norms.

In fact, herein lies the groupthink pitfall. Cohesiveness is an illusive quality for a group, and once it is achieved, groups do not want to give it up, even at the risk of making mistakes and performing poorly. Deviance may not be tolerated in a group that is too cohesive, for fear of rocking the boat. Conformity becomes more valuable than high performance. The goal of the manager and group members is to help move the group into the fourth stage of development (interdependence and problem solving) where cohesiveness is high, but internal conflict is a positive norm that will help the group continue to be successful.

I N S I G H T   13-2

Work Rules Shape Up as Major Battleground in U.S. Labor Disputes

Industry Seeks to Slash Costs and the Unions Dig In Fearing Decline in Ranks

A Key Issue in AT&T Strike

Work rules are turning into the next big battleground between management and labor.

Since company profits have risen from the depths of this decade's recession, further wage cuts have become less of an issue. So industry, still eager to cut costs, has turned instead to work rules—everything from the frequency of restroom breaks to who operates which machine. Unions, determined to preserve every remaining job, are digging in.

At American Telephone & Telegraph Co., 155,000 workers went on strike Sunday, largely because they oppose job reclassifications that they say could reduce pay for some technicians. At Trans World Airlines, flight attendants offered to take a 15% wage cut but went on strike in March rather than accept crew and scheduling changes that would lengthen their workday; they have since softened their stand, but the company has replaced almost all the striking attendants.

Caterpillar and GM

At Caterpillar Inc., workers have said they will strike rather than accept certain work-rule changes. And at a General Motors Corp. plant in Indianapolis, workers have refused to combine job categories, even though their refusal will mean a one-third reduction in the plant's work force over the next few years.

The stakes are particularly high this year, which is a big one for labor talks. Negotiations in the telecommunications, steel and heavy-equipment industries and at some railroads are all focusing largely on work rules. That has led to at least one costly showdown—at AT&T—and the results there and elsewhere could set the pattern for other industries for years to come.

By Alex Kotlowitz, *The Wall Street Journal*, June 4, 1986. Reprinted by permission of *The Wall Street Journal*, © Dow Jones & Company, Inc. 1986. All rights reserved.

GROUP PROCESS

Now we are ready to explore group process variables, which in many ways are much easier to observe in groups. **Process variables are the daily interactions that occur as a group works together to accomplish its tasks; they relate to how the group works together.** As such, process variables can be influenced by managers and group members on a regular basis. And process variables relate very closely to some of the leadership material discussed in Chapters 8 and 9.

To explore this point a little further, researchers of groups make a distinction between group **process** and group **content. Content is the**

task that group members work on. Are they solving a budgeting problem? Are they trying to decide how to introduce a new product? Are they trying to complete a difficult task in a short period of time? Often, academic training focuses on the content aspects of group work. Students learn in courses and seminars what analytical techniques best apply to a given problem. And they learn to make rational decisions. But they often do not receive enough training in **group process, which is how a group works together in trying to achieve a quality solution that can be implemented.** As is pointed out in the best-seller *In Search of Excellence,* analytical techniques are necessary, but not sufficient for solving the often irrational problems managers encounter.[21] Furthermore, they do not help that much in ensuring that good decisions are implemented. And what good is an excellent decision that is never properly implemented? The process aspects of group work deal with these issues explicitly. The following pages explore these aspects.

Member participation

One of the first things a manager or a group member can observe is the participation level of group members. Usually, some people speak up more than others, and some have very little at all to say. And there may be shifts in these involvement patterns. Some people may have a great deal to say when information is being shared and less to say as decision time approaches. For others, the pattern may be just the reverse. What is important for group development is that members participate in a manner appropriate to their ability to contribute.

Over time, group member involvement tends to even out so that no one member dominates the group; but there will still be differences in involvement level. As discussed in Chapter 4, some people are just more extroverted than others and are likely to be more outspoken. And there are some people who will try to get by on less, especially if the group is large. They essentially hope to be carried along by the group.[22] Indeed, some researchers have coined the phrase *social loafing* to describe this phenomenon.[23] When group members feel that the responsibility for a task is shared, some people will tend to loaf, hoping others will carry them through. In a developmental way, if certain group members feel that others in the group are putting in less effort than they are, there is a tendency to cut back on their own effort in order to achieve some level of equity.[24] But if the task is highly visible, such as a major project for the company, social loafing is not so high, and people may also work hard to make up for those who do loaf.[25]

Managers must be concerned with such participation issues. They want to maximize participation of people aimed at getting the job done. **But a key concern for a manager is to avoid too much participation by people who really have little to contribute at a particular time and to**

avoid too little participation by people who are holding back valuable information. People who are not participating need to be drawn into the group; and people who tend to dominate need to be toned down. As we will discuss later, there is ample opportunity for all group members to become involved. True group cohesiveness, as well as high performance, are both dependent on active involvement by all group members.

Group communications

Communication in a group is also one of the easiest of the process variables to observe. Yet, communication is extremely important, for it underlies all of the other process variables. As explained in Chapter 11, communication is the means we have for moving information from one person to another, and it is an extremely complex process to understand fully. However, in a group, observers can see who communicates with whom. People seldom communicate with the entire group. They tend to make eye contact with people they respect or like, even if their words may be spoken for all to hear. But people may also selectively communicate with only some members of the group. By noting the communications pattern that emerges, an observer can better understand the dynamics that are unfolding.

If we were to observe a group of people communicating over a period of time, we might witness a variety of communications patterns. A number of these patterns have been analyzed in terms of their impact

"Our communications are excellent, but we're communicating the wrong things."

upon various group outcome variables. Five of these patterns are shown in Exhibit 13–2.[26]

The first pattern, called the **wheel** or **star,** looks very much like an organizational chart. In Exhibit 13–2, the wheel clearly shows that person X is the leader of the group. Unfortunately, the lack of opportunity for communication for the other group members leads to low levels of member satisfaction. Only the leader is really satisfied in this pattern. And even the leader's satisfaction may be short-lived if the group is working on a complex task, since the wheel pattern is associated with low performance on such tasks. The pattern can, however, be very effective on simple tasks if group members accept the leader's authority. The Y pattern is very similar to the wheel. In fact, the only real difference is that the person at the bottom of the Y (person Z) is one person further removed from the leader (person X).

The **chain** pattern of communications results when group members communicate only with certain people in the group, but everyone is somehow connected with someone else in the group. In this pattern, it is not clear who the leader is. A variation of this pattern that may be more common in organizations is the formation of cliques within a group. For example, persons 1 and 2 in the chain talk to each other, but not to the other three people. And persons 3, 4, and 5 communicate with each other, but not with the other two people. It is as though the

EXHIBIT 13–2

Five Possible Group Communications Patterns

Communication pattern	Wheel or star	"Y"	Chain	Circle	All channel
Group characteristics					
Clarity of leadership	High	High	Moderate	Low	Low
Group member satisfaction	Low	Low	Moderate	Moderate	High
Quality of work					
Complex	Low	Low	Moderate	Moderate	High
Simple	High	High	Moderate	Moderate	Moderate

chain is broken between persons 2 and 3. In such situations, it is also unclear who is leading the group. In fact, with cliques, there may be two or more leaders. Member satisfaction tends to be better than in the wheel pattern, but not as high as in some of the other patterns. In terms of performance, chain patterns tend to work moderately well for both simple and complex problems. The biggest drawback facing groups with chain patterns is a lack of coordinated effort. The groups do not function like a team, and leadership is also weak.

The **circle** pattern is quite similar to the chain pattern; the only difference is that the two end people are now connected. And as shown in Exhibit 13–2, the results associated with the circle are very similar to the results with the chain, including the lack of clear leadership.

The final pattern shown is the **all-channel** pattern. At first glance, this network looks like chaos, with everyone talking at once. And indeed, if no one is listening to other group members, it would be chaos. But to depict chaos, the lines would be drawn from each group member but not connecting to other group members. In other words, ideas would die on the table. With the all-channel pattern, everyone in the group can talk to everyone else, and over time they do. The result is that leadership is unclear because it is shared by all members. As we will discuss later, this is possible because of the many functions that must be performed in a group that exhibits sustained high performance. With the all-channel pattern, group satisfaction tends to be quite high, as does performance on complex tasks. One might even argue that this type of interaction is essential for dealing with complex tasks. On the other hand, if the task is simple, the performance of a group using the all-channel pattern will be only moderate, primarily because it will take longer than it takes using the wheel pattern. And since time is such a valuable resource, it might be better to use the wheel pattern for solving simple tasks, unless the intent is to develop people for long-term effectiveness—as discussed in Chapters 7 and 8 on leadership.

It is clear from Exhibit 13–2 that each communications pattern has strengths and weaknesses. A manager or group member must weigh these trade-offs, remembering both **solution quality** and **implementation** as critical criteria. Later we will discuss how to make a decision about the appropriate network. For now, it is enough to recognize the effects of the patterns and to think about how they might be altered as necessary. For example, a manager of a group with a wheel pattern may feel that this pattern is not working. Therefore, the manager might consider exciting the group about a goal and then leaving the room so that a more all-channel pattern can emerge. President John Kennedy used just such a maneuver to arrive at a decision about how to handle the Cuban missile crisis, when missile sites were being built in Cuba by the Soviet Union.[27] This tactic helped avoid groupthink and a confrontation with Russia. With the advent of computer networking and greater use of telephone and videoconferencing, it will be possible to have group meetings that are not really face to face. How people will accept these approaches remains to be seen. It is not clear how the approaches will impact quality of work decisions and the acceptance of those decisions. One study did compare computer-based communications in group decision making to face-to-face interaction. The study found that the computer-based communications resulted in greater group member participation, more uninhibited behavior of group members, and more shifting from members' initial positions.[28] Such results, if typical, may mean that computer-based group communications may actually result in higher-quality decisions, since they seem to suggest greater involvement and more open discussion of issues. Only more experience and research will yield the answer.

Group decision making

Often groups are confronted with problems to solve or decisions to make. How should they deal with a new vacation plan? How should they solve a production problem that is resulting in too high a defects rate? **Decisions that are high in quality (that is, their implementation will resolve the problem) and to which everyone in the group can commit must be made.** A good decision that is not implemented is worthless. But how do groups make decisions? There are several ways, each with its own set of strengths and weaknesses. These decision methods are summarized in Exhibit 13–3 and explained in the following paragraphs.[29] As you read through this section, think about which of these decision-making approaches best describes the Frito-Lay situation in Insight 13–3.

The first method of making a decision is "decision by default" or **lack of response.** In essence, this means that a group member's idea is de-

EXHIBIT 13–3

Ways Groups Make Decisions

	Decision Characteristics			
	Quality		Group	Group Time
Decision Method	**Complex**	**Simple**	**Acceptance**	**Needed**
1. Lack of response	?	?	?	None
2. Authority rule	Bad	Good	?	Very little
3. Minority rule	Bad	Good	Poor	Little
4. Majority rule	OK	Good	Fair	Moderate
5. Consensus	Good	Good	Good	Great deal
6. Unanimous	Good	Good	Good	Very great deal

Source: Adapted from Edgar Schein, *Process Consultation*, © 1969, Addison-Wesley Publishing Co., Inc., Reading, Massachusetts. Pages 53-57. Reprinted with permission.

I N S I G H T 13–3

The Public Doesn't Get a Better Potato Chip without a Bit of Pain

*D*allas—Twenty managers at Frito-Lay Inc. sit at a conference table, nibbling thick, white tortilla chips. The chips taste good, but the managers aren't here for idle munching.

Small tortilla-chip makers in the West have been winning customers who like corn chips to eat with meals, rather than just as a snack. Their paler, blander chips are hurting sales of two Frito stars, Doritos and Tostitos. The chips the Frito managers are sampling, a proposed new offering called Sabritas, are supposed to put a stop to that.

But there are problems. The marketing people want Sabritas to be made only of white corn so they will be pale, but Frito-Lay plants now use yellow corn or a yellow-white mix. Will a new grain bin have to be built for the white corn?

Another thing: The competing chips have a twist tie around the top of the bag. Twist ties are expensive and are a bother to put on. But shoppers might not think of Sabritas the way they do the others if Sabritas' bag doesn't look the same.

Wayne Calloway, the company's president, gives the objectors a meaningful look. "Jerry, Jim, we need to get with this one," he says. "We're already late." A committee is formed to solve the problems so that test marketing can begin. The product manager for Sabritas has scored a small victory.

In the chips

This may seem like a rather elaborate approach to a commodity most people just crunch absent-mindedly. But Frito-Lay didn't get to where it is by taking tortillas for granted. The PepsiCo Inc. subsidiary takes in $2 billion on snack food a year, easily topping big rivals like Nabisco and Borden, not to mention the regional makers. Frito-Lay's earnings from operations have been growing an average of 23% a year, though the pace slowed a bit in recent months. The $311 million Frito earned last year made it the biggest contributor to PepsiCo's profits.

Coming up with new products is essential to keeping this lead, and Frito-Lay is good at it. Company managers consider hundreds of suggestions each year, but their screening process is so tough that only five or six get much past the idea stage. To go from being a gleam in the eye to a bag on the shelf, a new chip has to make it through the test kitchen, consumer taste testing, naming, package design, and planning, manufacturing and test-marketing. A poor grade on one of the tests—or a poor decision about the name or ad theme—can kill a new product.

A successful one, though, can be worth $100 million or more a year in added revenue. So, although Frito-Lay develops certain products to meet specific competitive threats, its researchers are constantly trying to dream up new ideas simply in hopes of selling more snacks.

cided upon because no one speaks either for or against it. It is simply ignored. In such cases, it is difficult to determine either the quality or acceptance of the decision. It may be a good idea that gets ignored, or maybe it was ignored because it was a bad idea. Who can say? In some cases, one such idea is plopped on the table, only to be followed by another lack of response decision, and another. If group members are simply not communicating with each other, nothing can happen. The group is stuck.

The second decision form, and one that requires a little more time, is **authority rule.** Here, the leader makes the decision for the group. Referring back to the leadership material, the leader is using a directive style. Such decisions can be either good or bad, depending on whether or not the leader has all of the information and skill necessary to make the best decision. For a simple task, such as having people in a group complete a time-log of activities, the leader may have all of the information to make a good decision. The main question may be whether the leader can get the group to accept the decision and properly implement it. Will the group start completing the reports as requested? A lot will depend on the leader's position power, relationship with the group, and presentation of the idea. If, on the other hand, the leader must decide on a complex matter, such as cutting down on waste in the production process of the group, it may be difficult to have all of the information necessary to make a good decision. Hence, an authority rule approach may result in a manager not considering the best alternative solution.[30] And the acceptance of an authority rule decision in this situation may be more difficult because there will be many different opinions about how to solve the problem.

The third decision method, **minority rule** (commonly called railroading), involves a little more time and yields about the same results as authority rule. Essentially, a few people in a group make the decision for the group as a whole. If these people have all of the relevant information and a good relationship with the other group members, this method can work very well. But often this is not the case, especially with complex problems. Some group members wind up feeling coerced and are reluctant to accept the "group" decision. Often this results in problems in implementing the decision.[31] For example, a minority of group members may decide that the solution to the waste problem mentioned above is a rotation of jobs so that employees can check up on each other and not become bored with a particular task. But some group members who were left out of the communications clique that made this decision feel that the "solution" will just make the situation worse because employees will constantly be adjusting to a new task. Hence, these group members may work half-heartedly through the task changes, making many mistakes and demonstrating how bad the decision really was.

The same potential for disgruntlement exists with the next decision method, **majority rule.** This method involves taking a group vote on the best method for solving the waste problem. What could be wrong with this method? Is this not how all important issues are decided in America's democratic society? The possible solutions are presented and discussed until group members are ready to vote. Then, after the vote, everyone accepts and works with the majority decision. This process does result in better quality decisions and greater acceptance than any of the methods discussed so far. Think for a moment about the voting process, however. Suppose two solutions are being considered. When the vote is taken, five people in the group are for solution 1, and three people are for solution 2. Thus, the decision is for solution 1. But what about the commitment of those three people who lost the vote? They lost, and they may not at all like the solution that was chosen. The question is, will they be able to psychologically commit to implementing a solution they so clearly opposed? Thus, acceptance may only be fair (see Exhibit 13–3).

On the quality issue, majority rule has the potential for reasonably good decisions in complex situations. The biggest problem lies with the question of whether all truly useful solutions are adequately discussed and presented. The politics of the situation (as discussed in Chapter 10) can enter into and affect the rational process of majority rule. For example, a person may be tempted not to bring up a solution because of who might be against it. And furthermore, since people are associated both with the solutions they suggest and with the solutions for which they vote, they will be cautious if there are potential political repercussions. Group members may feel they cannot vote against another group member who is more powerful than they are. Or they may vote for the solution of one group member in order to get something from that member later on. One final point with regard to majority rule: it does take a moderate amount of time, and with the potential problems just mentioned, it may not be a good idea to place so much faith in this method. But what else is left?

Consensus decisions, which we will come back to in a minute, and unanimous decisions still remain to be discussed. In a **unanimous decision,** everyone in the group feels a particular solution is the best one. This means that acceptance will be high, and implementation will be much easier. Clearly, this decision process would be very desirable. The problem is that in order to get a unanimous decision, a great deal of discussion must take place, even for relatively simple problems. Everyone has been involved in meetings where a "simple" matter seemed to take up a great deal of time. For a complex problem, the discussion to reach a unanimous decision may take far too much time to be practical. And if there are external pressures or threats related to the decision, information sharing may be reduced, and reaching the decision may be emphasized. A manager or group member needs to monitor one problem which can easily arise in such situations. Sometimes groups make a unanimous decision rather quickly because they fall into the groupthink trap. What appears to be a unanimous decision is actually a disguised disagreement. People appear to agree when, in fact, they have reservations. And these reservations come out during implementation or when the group later discovers that a bad decision has been made. Have you ever been in a meeting where everyone seemed to agree, but afterward in the hall began to raise all sorts of questions about the decision and how it would work? If so, you may have been through groupthink.

To avoid groupthink, the last decision method, **consensus,** can be utilized. In essence, consensus decisions are a cross between majority rule and unanimous decisions. They are like majority rule in that if people were asked to vote, they might still have their preferences for how to solve a problem. But at this point, they are also willing to commit to a particular solution and do their best to make it work, which is like a unanimous decision. The psychological commitment is there, even though the analytical process still leaves some questions. In complex situations, the consensus method may be the best managers can hope for, since unanimous decisions take too long or may never be achieved. In fact, with complex issues, consensus decisions also take up a great deal of time because of the process of encouraging and considering a wide array of options. But consensus decisions tend to be worth it in terms of good decision quality and acceptance by group members.[32] Furthermore, the time spent to ensure acceptance may result in better relationships both among group members and with the group leader, so that down the road, an authority rule decision may have a greater chance of acceptance. This developmental aspect of consensus decisions makes them especially useful for developing a group into a high-performing team.

Some structured decision-making approaches

Thus far, we have discussed group decision making as though it all occurs in a face-to-face discussion format. But there are several other more structured methods, some of which are not even face-to-face: nominal group technique, delphi technique, dialectical inquiry, and devil's advocacy. Let us briefly explore each of these methods.

The **nominal group technique** is designed to stimulate creative group decision making, where members cannot agree and where individual members have incomplete knowledge about the problem.[33] Individual members' inputs are essential, but disruptive conflict is likely. The technique consists of five steps:

1. Group members write down their ideas and solutions to the problem.
2. These ideas are read aloud with no criticism or discussion allowed.
3. The ideas are recorded for all to see while they are read aloud.
4. All of the ideas are then openly discussed for clarification only. Evaluative comments are not allowed.
5. A written voting procedure allows members to individually prioritize these ideas. The votes are then tabulated to yield an overall priority list. Sometimes another vote is held after discussion of these initial priorities. This vote yields the group's decision and a sense of closure.

Research has shown that the nominal group technique is quite effective for solving complex tasks that have many parts. It is less useful for simpler tasks.[34]

The **delphi technique** was developed by the Rand Corporation to allow groups to make decisions without face-to-face meetings.[35] In fact, the members can be scattered all over the world and still use the delphi technique. The technique can be summarized in four steps:

1. A questionnaire stating the problem and asking for alternative solutions is sent to all group members.
2. These solutions are summarized by a coordinator.
3. The written summary is returned to all group members, asking for additional input.
4. These results are summarized by the coordinator and sent out with the solutions for another round. The process continues by repeating steps 3 and 4 until a consensus is reached on the best solution.

Clearly, this technique is tedious and depends solely on written communications, which we know from Chapter 11 have their limitations. Perhaps with computer networking the delphi technique can be used more efficiently.

The last two techniques (dialectical inquiry and devil's advocacy) were developed to deal with complex, strategic decisions.[36] Both techniques encourage intense, heated debate among group members. The **dialectical inquiry** operates as follows:

1. Divide the group in half.
2. One subgroup prepares in writing a recommended solution, with assumptions and key data.
3. The other subgroup develops plausible assumptions to negate the other group's ideas. This subgroup also prepares a set of recommendations.

4. Both subgroups present their arguments to each other, orally and in writing. The groups debate the two positions.

5. Agreement is then reached on which assumptions survived, and recommendations are developed, based on these assumptions.

6. Final recommendations are recorded in writing.

It is easy to see that this technique can often yield very heated discussion and debate.

The **devil's advocacy technique** is similar in process, but has some distinct differences. The steps are as follows:

1. Divide the group in half.

2. One subgroup prepares a set of recommendations for solving the problem and builds an argument for them.

3. This subgroup presents its recommendations to the second subgroup.

4. The second subgroup critiques the recommendations, trying to uncover everything wrong with them.

5. The critique is presented to the first subgroup, which then revises its recommendations to try to satisfy the criticisms.

6. Steps 3 through 5 are repeated until both groups are satisfied with the recommendations.

7. Final recommendations are recorded in writing.

Again, the devil's advocacy technique can provoke some very heated discussions, but it can also yield excellent solutions to problems. Indeed, one research study found that both the devil's advocacy technique and the dialectical inquiry technique led to higher-quality recommended solutions than the consensus method discussed earlier. But the consensus method led to higher group member satisfaction and a greater desire to continue to work together.[37] And as we have discussed, a solution to a problem is only good if it can be implemented successfully. Clearly, group members' desires to work together can affect implementation.

Let us now explore one framework which may prove useful to managers in determining the best way to lead a group decision-making effort—best in terms of both quality and acceptance of group members. This framework draws upon the leadership theories discussed in Chapters 8 and 9 and also leads to the process topic of leadership in groups.

The Vroom and Yetton model

Victor Vroom and Philip Yetton developed a model to guide group leaders in determining how best to make group decisions.[38] Their model is built on choosing among five basic decision-making options to maximize the decision's quality and acceptance to the group. The model is also designed to help groups make decisions as efficiently as possible, in terms of time.

The five decision-making options for the leader range from authority-rule decision making to consensus decision making as follows:

A_1 The leader solves the problem or makes the decision alone, using information he or she has at the time.

A_2 The leader obtains the necessary information from team members individually, then decides on the solution to the problem. The leader may not even tell members what the problem is when he or she is getting the information. The role group members play in making the decision is merely to provide the necessary information to the leader. They do not get involved in generating or evaluating alternative solutions.

C_1 The leader shares the problem with relevant team members individually, getting their ideas and suggestions without bringing them together as a group. Then the leader makes the decision, which may or may not reflect their influence.

C_2 The leader shares the problem with team members as a group. They collectively share their ideas and suggestions. Then the leader makes the decision, which may or may not reflect their influence.

G_1 The leader shares the problem with team members as a group. Together they generate and evaluate alternatives. An attempt is made to reach consensus on a solution. The leader's role is much like that of chairperson. The leader does not try to influence the group to adopt his or her solution and is willing to accept and implement any solution that has the support of the entire group.

Based on a series of questions that address both quality and acceptance issues, the Vroom and Yetton model guides managers to the proper choice of decision-making style. The basic rules underlying the choices are built on logic, as follows. With regard to the quality of decisions, if the leader does not have sufficient information to make the decision, then the authority-rule decision cannot be used. On the other hand, if group members do not share an organization's goals, using a consensus decision process will not be best. With regard to group acceptance of a decision, if acceptance is critical to implementation and is not likely to result from an authority-rule decision, managers must use the more participative decision processes.

The series of questions in the model is summarized in Exhibit 13–4. The first three questions address the quality issue. The last four help address the acceptance issue. To use the model, a manager simply asks each question in order from left to right, and follows the response (yes or no) to the next question. Eventually, the manager will come to the decision style that research has shown is most effective in a particular situation.[39]

EXHIBIT 13—4   Decision Process Flow Chart

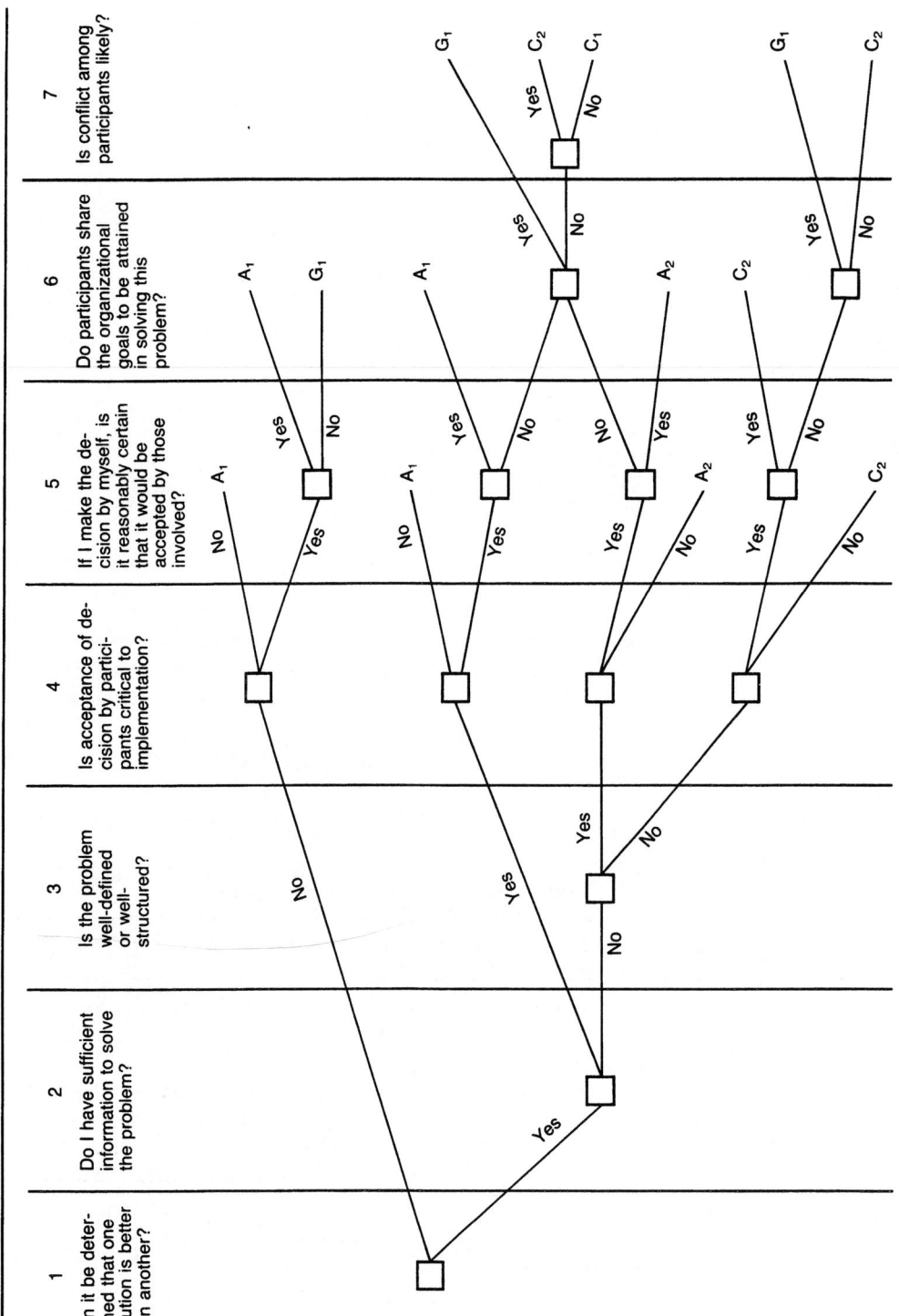

1	2	3	4	5	6	7
Can it be determined that one solution is better than another?	Do I have sufficient information to solve the problem?	Is the problem well-defined or well-structured?	Is acceptance of decision by participants critical to implementation?	If I make the decision by myself, is it reasonably certain that it would be accepted by those involved?	Do participants share the organizational goals to be attained in solving this problem?	Is conflict among participants likely?

Source: Adapted and reprinted from *Leadership and Decision-Making* by Victor H. Vroom and Philip W. Yetton by permission of the University of Pittsburgh Press. © 1973 by University of Pittsburgh Press.

An example provided by Vroom and Yetton may prove helpful for understanding how to use the model. Imagine the following scenario:

> The general foreman in charge of a large crew laying an oil pipeline needs to estimate his expected rate of progress in order to schedule material deliveries to the next field site. The foreman knows the nature of the terrain he will be traveling. He has the historical data needed to compute the mean and variance in the rate over that type of terrain. Given these two variables, it is a simple matter to calculate the earliest and latest times at which materials and support facilities will be needed at the next site. It is important that the general foreman's estimate be reasonably accurate. Underestimates result in idle foremen and workers. Overestimates result in tying up materials for a period of time before they are to be used. Progress has been good to date. The general foreman's five foremen and other members of the crew stand to receive substantial bonuses if the project is completed ahead of schedule.

Starting with question 1 in Exhibit 13–4, the answer is yes—one solution is better than another. This leads to question 2, where again the answer is yes—the general foreman has sufficient information. This leads to question 4, where the answer is yes—acceptance is critical. Next comes question 5 where the answer is yes—the crew will accept the decision. This leads to the A_1 style, which advocates the foreman's making the decision himself.

Leadership in a group

Let's be brief here, since we have already spent two chapters on leadership and will return to this variable when we later discuss group member roles. In observing a group to which a person belongs, he or she should be aware of who is leading the group. Is it one person, two people, or several group members? As we discussed in Chapter 12, a central issue in the conflict and organization stage of group development is: who are the leaders? Especially important is whether there is conflict between the appointed group leader and another member of the group who wants to be the leader.

One of the key aspects of group involvement is that it is possible for there to be more than one leader in a group; in fact, everyone in the group can be a leader. There are many aspects that contribute to the effective functioning of a group. Thus, different group members can exert influence in different areas, making everyone a leader. One might even argue that a group that operates like a team will exhibit such leadership by almost all group members. This leadership will, however, be well coordinated so that conflicts are not dysfunctional. We will return to this point in more detail when we discuss the roles that people can play in a group.

A final point on leadership is to observe the methods of influence that group members use in exerting leadership (as discussed in Chapters 8, 9, and 10). Do they use coercive power, expert power, position power—or another base of power? Is their style of leadership directing, coaching, supporting, or delegating? Do the group members' methods vary from time to time as the group moves through its developmental stages and deals with different problems? Answering such questions will help managers better understand what is happening in the groups to which they belong.

Exhibit 13–5 integrates some of the group process variables discussed thus far. It shows what leadership style and decision-making method most likely correspond with each of the five communications patterns from Exhibit 13–2. As the exhibit shows, the wheel pattern is most likely to be associated with authority rule decisions and directive leadership. The leader is clearly in command in this case. In moving across to the right, the commuications patterns open things up for group members and allow first minority rule and coaching leadership and then majority rule and supporting leadership. And consensus decisions that need supporting leadership to facilitate the exchange of information are most likely associated with the all-channel communications pattern.[40] With these associations, which of the three process variables (communications, decision making, or leadership) would be easiest to observe in a group setting? Probably communications. Thus, a group leader or member who pays attention to communications in the group can learn a great deal about how decisions are being made and about the leadership that will be exercised. As mentioned in Chapter 11, communications are the lifeblood of an organization. This statement applies equally well to a group. We now turn to the final group process variable, group member roles.

Group member roles

In observing a group over time, it is possible to see many types of behaviors exhibited by group members. Three categories of behavior called **roles** are particularly important as they relate to group effectiveness: self-oriented roles, task roles, and maintenance roles. Examples of these types of roles are shown in Exhibit 13–6. In almost any group, it is possible to see people performing all three types of roles. **Self-oriented roles are self-serving behaviors that actually hinder the performance of a group.** A **blocker** is someone who always seems to get in the way of group progress toward completion of its task. A **recognition seeker** tries to gain personal distinction, even at the expense of a group. Such people are not team players. A **dominator** tries to run everything, whether it is best for a group or not. And an **avoider** just does not contribute to a group and cannot be counted on. As we might expect, research has shown the presence of these roles in a group to be associated with poor performance.[41]

EXHIBIT 13–5

Integrating Communications Patterns with Decision-Making Methods and Leadership Style

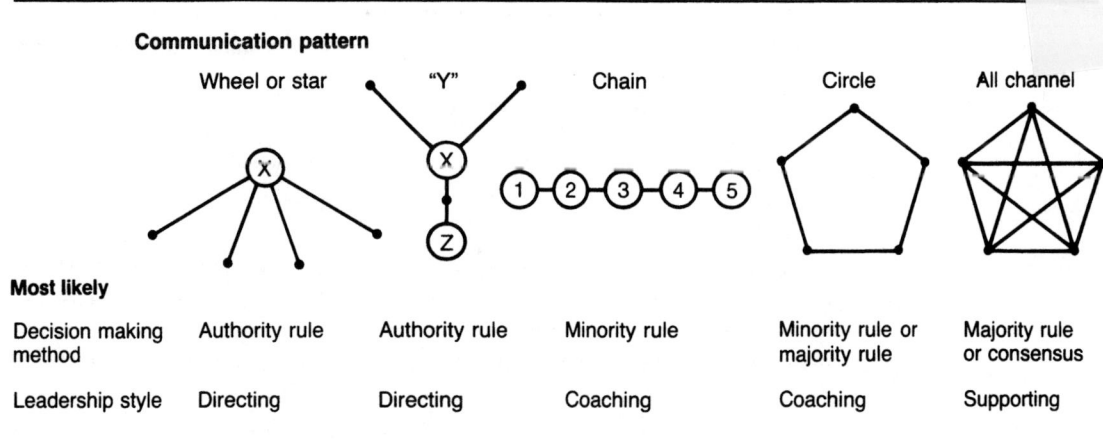

	Wheel or star	"Y"	Chain	Circle	All channel
Most likely					
Decision making method	Authority rule	Authority rule	Minority rule	Minority rule or majority rule	Majority rule or consensus
Leadership style	Directing	Directing	Coaching	Coaching	Supporting

We now turn to the more positive side of the group-roles picture as we look at **task** and **maintenance** roles. These types of activities in a group should sound familiar: they are essentially the same as the two key dimensions of leadership we focused on in Chapters 8 and 9. **Every group must not only get the task done, but also maintain itself over**

EXHIBIT 13–6

Three Categories of Group Member Roles

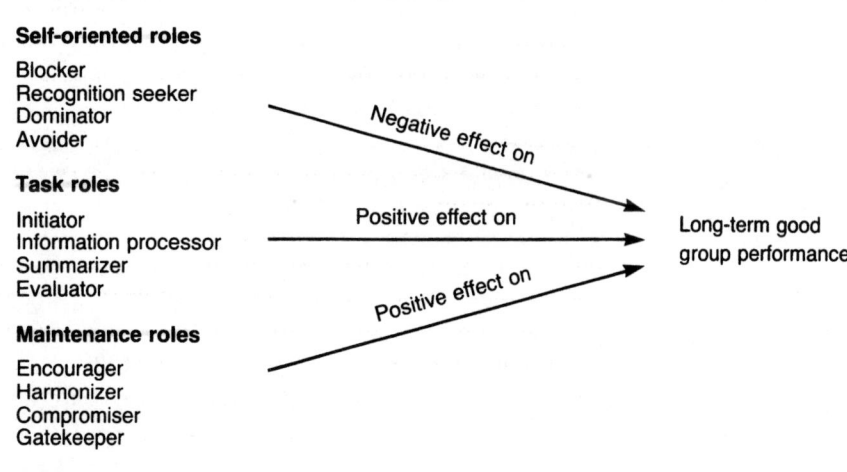

Self-oriented roles

Blocker
Recognition seeker
Dominator
Avoider

Negative effect on

Task roles

Initiator
Information processor
Summarizer
Evaluator

Positive effect on

Maintenance roles

Encourager
Harmonizer
Compromiser
Gatekeeper

Positive effect on

Long-term good group performance

time as a group.[42] The task and maintenance roles shown in Exhibit 13–6 are instrumental in accomplishing these two ends. Research has found support for a positive relationship between the performance of task and maintenance roles and group effectiveness.[43]

What are the task roles? An **initiator** is someone who offers many ideas and suggestions to a group. The **information processor** both seeks and gives information that will be useful to a group in performing its task. The **summarizer** restates, clarifies, and organizes the information and ideas that are offered and helps a group remain clear about its goals. The **evaluator** helps a group test its ideas and problem solutions against logical and rational benchmarks. The evaluator also helps select the best alternative decision from among several choices.

As for the maintenance roles, the **encourager** praises the ideas and contributions of others and supports the efforts of other group members. The **harmonizer** acts to resolve differences of opinion and reduce tension that may develop in a group. Similarly, the **compromiser** tries to help group members locate an acceptable middle ground which everyone can support. This function is invaluable in helping a group achieve consensus in a complex situation. Finally, the **gatekeeper** ensures that everyone gets a chance to speak openly by drawing out people who sit back or by toning down the dominators in a group.

These task and maintenance roles are important for a group to perform in order to be effective. Which roles are most vital will vary as the group works through a problem, and even from one group development stage to another. For example, during the testing and orientation stage, the gatekeeper and initiator roles would prove helpful in providing a group with the guidance and involvement that is needed to get off to a good start. During the conflict and organization stage, the summarizer, information processor, harmonizer, and compromiser roles can help a group resolve the inevitable conflicts and move into the productive stage of cohesion and information exchange. During this and the final stage of interdependence and problem solving, almost all of the roles are important if a group is to maintain a record of high performance. In the ebb and flow of daily activities, the emphasis on particular roles may be high or low; but over time, an effective group will take care of both task and maintenance needs, while avoiding the self-oriented roles.

Exhibit 13–7 summarizes this point. As with the leadership material, the performance of task roles goes on the horizontal axis, and the performance of maintenance roles goes on the vertical axis. Then, by observing which roles are present and which are absent, the group can be categorized into one of the four cells in Exhibit 13–7. For example, a group that has many of the task roles present but few of the maintenance roles could be called a **task-oriented group.** In the short run, this might be appropriate to meet a deadline or for a temporary committee, but over the long haul, such a group will tend to die from the inside

EXHIBIT 13–7

Types of Groups Based on Performance of Task and
Maintenance Roles

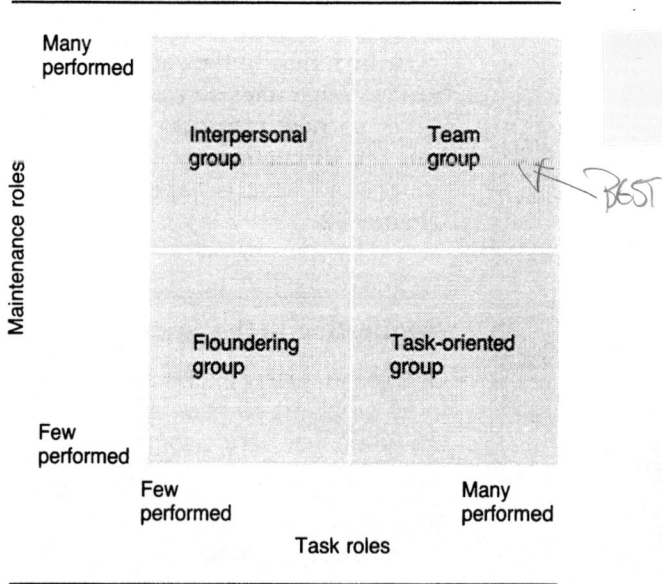

out. A leader or member of such a group could be of most help by
performing some of the maintenance roles to help move the group into
the team category.

The **team group** is one with both task and maintenance roles performed. **The team group should be the best performing group over the
long run.** The leader of such a group can delegate much of the work to
the group and thus be free to work more with peers and superiors. If,
however, the group is high on the maintenance roles, but low on the
task roles, it is called an **interpersonal group.** Here, the manager needs
to provide the task roles so the group will not love itself to death and
ignore the task that must be performed.

Finally, the **floundering group** has neither task nor maintenance
roles. The group is probably not very effective and needs both task and
maintenance roles performed. But can a manager do both simultaneously? Probably not. Hence, drawing upon the leadership material
from Chapters 8 and 9, a directing style focusing on the task roles
should be applied first. Then, as the group experiences some success,
the manager can back off the task roles and focus more on the maintenance roles. Or perhaps someone in the group will start to take up this
slack. **The key point here is that leadership style and group roles are
quite interconnected.** To positively influence a group, managers must

determine which roles are missing that would be present in a team group. Managers can then try to perform those roles to help the group move toward being a team. And in this case, a person can use Exhibit 13–7 to help exercise this kind of influence in a group, even if he or she is not the appointed leader. To further focus your attention on these roles, turn now to the end of the chapter and complete the Group Roles Survey. What roles do you feel you usually perform in a group?

Let us now return to the Home Computers Company case to see how our discussion of group structure and process can help us better understand what is happening in the problematic quality circle from Chapter 12.

Home Computers Case

Application to the Home Computers Company Case

One of the quality circles started by the consultant Sally Barnes encountered problems as soon as the consultant left. Many conflicts surfaced, the group was very disorganized, meetings were difficult and unproductive, and people began to avoid the meetings of the circle. A norm seemed to develop rather quickly that the meetings were not important and members should go only if they had nothing else to do. Jim Andrews, the team leader, was outranked in the organizational hierarchy and in terms of experience, and could not seem to get the team members to follow his lead. The group just was not very cohesive and looked like it would soon self-destruct. Wisely, Jim went to Sally for help.

Jim's first questions dealt with why he had been placed in such a difficult situation. Jim felt he did not have either the status or the power to influence the group in the desired direction. The consultant's answer was that Jim was the only person for the job. This quality circle was in the relatively new product area for schools and libraries. Most of the people in the quality circle were excellent technically, but lacked the managerial expertise needed. On the other hand, while Jim was young and relatively new in the company (two years), he did have a master's degree in business administration, as well as an engineering degree. Unfortunately, the group was developing in the wrong manner. Sally told Jim she would work with him to teach him how to better manage the group by understanding the communications, decision-making, and leadership aspects of the group. Then they would work with the entire group on the same task. Jim agreed, though he had his doubts.

Sally began to explain the process side of group development to Jim. She also explained the stages of group development. Together, Sally and Jim determined that the quality circle group was stuck in the conflict and organization stage of development. After explaining the process variables of communications, leadership, decision making, and roles, Sally helped Jim analyze the quality circle in terms of these variables.

First they looked at the communications in the group. Sally asked Jim who did most of the talking. Jim said he did. Sally asked if people in the circle listened to him. Jim's response was, "I'm not sure." Sally decided to attend the next meeting of the quality circle to observe the group in action and to explain how she wanted to help them become a real team. When Sally attended, she discovered Jim was right; he did most of the talking, but few people really listened. At times, the group would override Jim and make its own decisions. Things were really out of hand.

After the meeting, Sally and Jim discussed what had happened. She told Jim that he was running the group in a very directive manner. The communications mostly came from Jim, and sometimes the others did not listen to him. She noticed that a particular clique of engineers railroaded a number of decisions.

Sally then explained how consensus decisions can be used to achieve high-quality decisions to which everyone is committed. She suggested that Jim did not have all of the information needed to make a high-quality decision. And he did not have the power or status to get the group to accept his decision. Yet, their acceptance of a high-quality decision was critical for implementation that would solve their problems. Sally suggested that Jim needed to use a more participative style of leadership to provide structure and also get everyone involved.

"But how can I do that?" asked Jim. "The group does not seem to respect me. How will I be able to get them involved?" Sally showed Jim a diagram similar to Exhibit 13–7. She explained about the task and maintenance roles, and they identified the group as being interpersonal—high on maintenance roles and low on task roles. The group needed someone to perform some task roles to help push them toward being a team group. "Of course," said Sally, "you will have to carefully select the roles to play to avoid coming across as too directive." Jim suggested that perhaps he could be more of an information seeker and summarizer of the ideas of others. By using this approach, maybe he could get others to initiate ideas and could draw out Sam and Mary, who were excellent at evaluating solutions to problems. Jim and Sally also decided that while the group was high on some maintenance roles, it lacked a harmonizer and compromiser. People encouraged each other in their cliques and communicated freely in the cliques, but the conflicts between cliques and between the group and Jim were ignored. Thus, Jim decided to speak to Harold in private to encourage him to serve these roles. Harold seemed to have the respect of most of the circle members.

Jim immediately put his plan into action. Sally continued to observe and to help Jim and the others play their roles effectively. Gradually, the group became more cohesive and productive. Members attended meetings more regularly, as a new norm of interest in the group developed. The circle gained a new respect for Jim and his ability to bring the group together. Finally, the group began to come up with some good solutions to the problems confronting them. Within six months, this quality circle was operating as an effective team.

What can managers learn from this episode at Home Computers Company? First, there is a need in such situations, for a manager to be a problem solver. This means that the manager must collect facts on group process (communications, decision making, and leadership), determine what the group's problems are, and determine solutions to solve the problems. A recognition of the power/status differences, norms, and cohesiveness (group structure variables) will certainly be helpful in this process. By observing the communications in the group, the consultant was able to determine a great deal about both Jim's style of leadership and the decision-making approach of the group. This analysis helped Jim determine the leadership/decision-making approach that seemed best for this quality circle.

The second point to be emphasized is that Jim still needed some guidance in how to be the kind of leader the group required. By analyzing the roles being performed in the group, Jim and Sally determined some specific actions which Jim could take to implement the chosen leadership/decision-making approach. In other words, role analysis helped make Jim's job much more explicit. Also, by taking the perspective of analyzing the roles performed in the group, Jim had something he could monitor as the group progressed.

And the group did progress. As the case ends, the quality circle has become both cohesive and productive. An observer of this group would probably find a good balance between the task and maintenance roles. Furthermore, this should free Jim from having to shoulder the entire burden of the group. He can delegate responsibility to group members and work with them to achieve positive ends. And as long as group members can keep focused on the goals of the organization, they should be very productive as a quality circle.

We must give several warnings here, however. First, if there is much turnover of personnel in the circle, some of the cohesiveness could be decreased, and the group could slide back into previous stages of development (such as conflict and organization). Second, if new procedures, techniques, or tasks are introduced for the group to deal with, this, too, could bring about the need for reanalysis and adjustment to the new situation. Third, other groups in the organization with which this group must interact could create forces for change in the quality circle. For example, the production department could make changes that would affect the engineering department. Chapter 14 discusses these issues of intergroup conflict and coordination. But first let us summarize what we have learned about groups in these last two chapters.

WHAT A MANAGER SHOULD KNOW ABOUT GROUPS

Whether taking over the management of a group at work or joining a group as a member, the first thing a person should do is to analyze both the people who make up the group and the situational aspects of the group. For instance, what kind of task does the group have to perform? What is the size and composition of the group? What are the members' personalities, abilities, and motivations? By drawing on the material from Chapter 12, a person can then determine whether there is a fit between the people and the situation. Are the conditions ripe for a successful group? If not, maybe something can be altered in the people or the situation to achieve a better fit. And of course, if a person is starting up or joining a new group, there is the opportunity to more immediately influence these factors.

The second thing a person should do is determine the stage of group development. What problems are facing the group currently? By analyzing the existing group structure and the nature of group processes, the person can determine the stage of group development. And knowing this, a person can better predict where the group is headed. The process variables, especially, can be helpful in analyzing where a group is and where it is headed. They are relatively easy to observe, and they clearly affect the emerging structure variables. And if problems are developing with norms, cohesiveness, and status and power relationships, the process variables serve as early warning signals.

Conversely, the structure variables for an existing group may help a person understand why the process variables are problematic. A group that has status and power problems, for example, will probably exhibit communications and decision-making difficulties. And a group with strong cohesiveness and norms that conflict with the organization may be using its process variables to work against the organization. Analysis of these variables can prove most useful in determining what can be done to help get the group on the right track. But what is the right track?

A group that is functioning well will exhibit several key properties, aside from good performance. Problems in these areas may foretell problems in the group's performance down the road. First, **group members should be willing to argue with one another about ideas and opinions without the argument becoming too personalized.** Members should avoid arguing just to win an argument. The goal should be the best for the group. Second, group members should take responsibility for **both hearing what others say and for getting their own ideas across.** Closely tied in here is the fact that group members must be willing to change their mind. They should want what's best for the group, not just to get their own ideas across. Third, **all members of a productive group perform roles which are important for the group (that is, task and** maintenance roles) and avoid performing self-oriented roles. In other words, members all serve as leaders of different functions the group must perform. Remember, the reason for having a group in the first place is to achieve a whole which is greater than the sum of its parts— that is, synergy. **Groups are difficult to run effectively over time, and if synergy is not achieved, the group may not be worth the trouble.** To assess a group, one can use the Team Building Checklist at the end of this chapter. Take a look at it, and respond to the 14 statements based upon the last group experience you had. If you make the effort to use the material covered in these last two chapters, your group can score high on the Team Building Checklist, and you can be both a good group leader and a good group member.

CHAPTER HIGHLIGHTS

This chapter has completed the analysis of what happens inside groups in organizations. Having looked at the design aspects of groups in the last chapter, we focused on the emergent properties of groups in this chapter. We first looked at group structure variables and then at process variables.

Group structure is the pattern of relationships which develop in a group over time and influence outcomes. Group structure consists of norms, status relationships, power relationships, and cohesiveness. **Norms** are the rules of behavior that provide guidance to group activities. They develop over time and provide a basis for determining what is expected of people in a group. **Each group will develop its own unique set of norms in its own unique way.**

We then examined **status and power relationships** together because of their similarity. **Status** is the importance ranking associated with each group member. **Power** relates to the sources of influence that each group member has to draw on. Both variables relate to the different group members' abilities to influence the behavior of other group members. Status/power differences also help managers understand some of the conflicts that can arise in a group. People bring to a group varying positions in an organization and varying bases of power, but the emergence of relationships is influenced by the group processes that transpire over time.

Next, we dealt with one of the most heavily researched group variables—cohesiveness. **Cohesiveness is the degree to which group members are attracted to one another and motivated to work together.** Cohesiveness develops over time and is influenced by input variables, group process, **and group performance.** To the extent that group members perform well together, they tend to become more cohesive. The text mentioned two important negative effects of cohesiveness for managers to keep in mind. First, a cohesive group that does not accept the organization's goals can be a serious problem. And second, a cohesive group can fall prey to groupthink, resulting in serious mistakes affecting the group's performance.

Next, we looked at **group process variables, which are some of the most important variables to understand in working with and in groups.** This is because group process variables occur everyday and can be changed more quickly than the other group variables we have discussed. The text made a distinction between group content and group process. **Content is what the group is doing, while process is how the group is doing it.** Process includes member participation, communications, decision making, leadership, and group member roles.

Member participation was defined as a way to focus on whether all of a group's resources are being utilized. The text introduced the theory of social loafing, where some members of a group may try to ride on the efforts of others. Next, we discussed one of the key process variables, communications, because of its relationship to all of the others. **Communication** is an easy variable to observe. We discussed five patterns of communications: wheel, Y, chain, circle, and all-channel. The wheel pattern seems to be most effective with simple tasks and problems, though it tends to result in low group member satisfaction. At the other extreme, all-channel communication seems to work best with complex problems and also tends to result in high member satisfaction.

Then we turned to group **decision making** and discussed the fact that group decisions must not only be of high quality, but also acceptable to those who must implement them. We discussed six approaches to interactive decision making: lack of response, authority rule, minority rule, majority rule, consensus, and unanimous. Each of these approaches was described and related to time needed, quality of decision, and acceptance. We also discussed four rather structured approaches to decision making: the nominal group technique, the delphi technique, the dialectical inquiry technique, and the devil's advocacy technique.

This discussion led us to explore the Vroom and Yetton model for deciding what decision-making style to use in a given situation. The model focuses on both quality and acceptance of a decision, and a choice among five different decision-making styles. The model, shown in Exhibit 13–4, guides managers via a series of questions to the best decision-making style for the situation.

We then discussed leadership in a group. The key point here was that **it is possible to have more than one leader in a group; indeed, everyone in an effective group can be a leader if this leadership is handled properly.** We also examined how communications, decision making, and leadership are interrelated. The wheel pattern of communications is often seen with authority rule and autocratic leadership. On the other hand, the all-channel pattern is often associated with consensus decisions and participatory leadership.

The final process variable discussed was group member roles. There are three types of roles: self-oriented roles, which are dysfunctional for a group, and task and maintenance roles, both of which serve useful purposes for the group. After defining a number of these roles, we defined four types of groups depending on the presence of these roles: task-oriented group, interpersonal group, team group, and floundering group. And we talked specifically about how to use this grid (Exhibit 13–7) to be a better group member or manager.

We then went back to the Home Computers Company quality circle experiencing some problems and explored the group using some of our new tools.

In closing, the chapter summarized what a manager should know about groups. First, managers should determine if there is a fit between the people and the situation. Second, managers should determine the stage of group development. And third, managers must study the group's structure and process to determine what actions can be taken to improve its performance. The chapter's final paragraph summarized what a well-functioning group should look like to achieve the synergy that justifies the effort it takes to make a group work, and introduced readers to the Team Building Checklist at the end of the chapter.

REVIEW QUESTIONS

1. What is *group structure,* and how does it develop over time?
2. What kinds of norms might be associated with each of the four stages of group development?
3. Why do status and power differences develop in a group? What effects can these differences have?
4. How can cohesive groups create problems for managers?
5. Why is it important to understand group process variables, in addition to analytical aspects of content?
6. Why are different communications patterns effective when dealing with complex tasks as opposed to simple tasks?
7. In deciding which of the six interacting decision-making approaches to use, what factors should managers keep in mind?
8. Explain how the nominal group technique, the delphi technique, the dialectical inquiry technique, and the devil's advocacy technique structure the decision-making process.

9. Explain how the Vroom and Yetton model in Exhibit 13–4 helps managers make high-quality decisions that are acceptable to the group members who must implement them.

10. How do leadership, communications, and decision making interrelate in the functioning of a group?

11. How can a person use group member roles to help him or her determine the leadership needs of a group?

12. What are the characteristics of a group that is functioning well?

RESOURCE READINGS

Dyer, W. G. *Team Building: Issues and Alternatives.* 2nd ed. Reading, Mass.: Addison-Wesley Publishing, 1987.

Eddy, W. B. *The Manager and the Working Group.* New York: Praeger Publishers, 1985.

Hackman, R., and R. E. Walton. *The Leadership of Groups in Organizations.* New Haven, Conn.: Yale University Press, 1985.

Janis, I. L. *Groupthink.* 2nd ed. Boston: Houghton Mifflin, 1982.

Napier, R. W., and M. K. Gershenfeld. *Groups: Theory and Experience.* 2nd ed. Boston: Houghton Mifflin, 1981.

Schein, E. *Process Consultation.* Reading, Mass.: Addison-Wesley Publishing, 1969.

NOTES

1. S. L. Obert, "Developmental Patterns of Organizational Task Groups: A Preliminary Study," *Human Relations* 36 (1986), pp. 37–52.

2. R. W. Napier and M. K. Gershenfeld, *Groups: Theory and Experience,* 2nd ed. (Boston: Houghton Mifflin, 1981), p. 122.

3. R. Spick and K. Keleman, "Explicit Norm Structuring Process: A Strategy for Increasing Task-Group Effectiveness," *Group & Organization Studies* 10 (1985), pp. 37–59.

4. L. Berkowitz and R. C. Howard, "Reactions to Opinion Deviates as Affected by Affiliation Need and Group Member Interdependence," *Sociometry* 22 (1959), pp. 81–91.

5. P. Conroy, *Lords of Discipline* (Boston: Houghton Mifflin, 1980).

6. R. A. Dentler and K. T. Erikson, "The Functions of Deviance in Groups," *Social Problems* 7 (1959), pp. 98–107.

7. D. A. Nadler, J. R. Hackman, and E. E. Lawler, *Managing Organizational Behavior* (Boston: Little, Brown, 1979), pp. 124–26.

8. This section draws primarily from H. T. Reitan and M. E. Shaw, "Group Membership, Sex Composition of the Group, and Conformity Behavior," *Journal of Social Psychology* 99 (1969), pp. 45–51.

9. W. A. Randolph and B. Z. Posner, *Effective Project Planning and Management: Getting the Job Done* (Englewood Cliffs, N.J.: Prentice-Hall, 1988).

10. J. B. Gustafsen, "Cooperative and Clashing Interests in Small Groups, Part I," *Human Relations* 34 (1981), pp. 315–39.

11. M. E. Shaw, *Group Dynamics: The Psychology of Small Group Behavior* (New York: McGraw–Hill, 1976).

12. G. C. Homans, *Social Behavior: Its Elementary Forms* (New York: Harcourt Brace Jovanovich, 1961).

13. E. J. Thomas and C. F. Fink, "Effects of Group Size," *Psychological Bulletin* 60 (1963), pp. 371–84; A. P. Hare, "Group Size," *American Behavioral Scientist* 24 (1981), pp. 695–708.

14. W. A. Randolph and F. E. Finch, "The Relationship Between Organization Technology and the Direction and Frequency Dimensions of Task Communications," *Human Relations* 30 (1977), pp. 1131–145.

15. M. Sherif, *Group Conflict and Cooperation: Their Social Psychology* (Boston: Routledge & Kegan Paul, 1967).

16. A. J. Lott and B. E. Lott, "Group Cohesiveness as Interpersonal Attraction: A Review of Relationships with Antecedent and Consequent Variables," *Psychological Bulletin* 64 (1965), pp. 259–309.

17. N. R. F. Maier, "Assets and Liabilities in Group Problem Solving: The Need for an Integrating Function," *Psychological Review* 47 (1967), pp. 239–49.

18. M. Sherif and C. Sherif, *Groups in Harmony and Tension* (New York: Harper & Row, 1953).

19. N. E. Friedkin and M. J. Simpson, "Effects of Competition on Members' Identification with Their Subunits," *Administrative Science Quarterly* 30 (1985), pp. 377–94.

20. R. T. Keller, "Predictors of the Performance of Project Groups in R & D Organizations," *Academy of Management Journal* 29 (1986), pp. 715–26.

21. T. J. Peters and R. H. Waterman, Jr., *In Search of Excellence* (New York: Harper & Row, 1982).

22. R. Albenese and D. D. Van Fleet, "Rational Behavior in Groups: The Free Rider Tendency," *Academy of Management Review* 10 (1985), pp. 244–55.

23. N. Kerr, "Motivation Losses in Small Groups: A Social Dilemma Analysis," *Journal of Personality and Social Psychology* 45 (1983), pp. 819–28.

24. J. Jackson and S. Harkins, "Equity in Effort: An Explanation of the Social Loafing Effect," *Journal of Personality and Social Psychology* 49 (1985), pp. 1199–206.

25. G. Jones, "Task Visibility, Free Riding and Shirking: Explaining the Effect of Structure and Technology on Employee Behavior," *Academy of Management Review* 9 (1984), pp. 684–95.

26. This section draws from H. J. Leavitt, "Some Effects of Certain Communication Patterns on Group Performance," *Journal of Abnormal and Social Psychology* 46 (1951), pp. 38–50; H. Guetzkow and H. Simon, "The

Impact of Certain Communication Nets upon Organization and Performance in Task-Oriented Groups," *Management Science* 1 (1955), pp. 233–50; and A. Bavelas, "Communication Patterns in Task-Oriented Groups," in *The Policy Sciences*, ed. D. Lerner and H. D. Lasswell (Palo Alto, Calif.: Stanford University Press, 1951).

27. I. L. Janis, *Groupthink*, 2nd ed. (Boston: Houghton Mifflin, 1982).

28. J. Siegel, V. Dubrovsky, S. Kiesler, and T. W. McGuire, "Group Processes in Computer-Mediated Communication," *Organizational Behavior and Human Decision Processes* 37 (1986), pp. 157–87.

29. E. Schein, *Process Consultation* (Reading, Mass.: Addison-Wesley Publishing, 1969), pp. 53–57.

30. C. R. Leana, "Partial Test of Janis' Groupthink Model: Effects of Group Cohesiveness and Leader Behavior on Defective Decision Making," *Journal of Management* 11 (1985), pp. 5–17.

31. D. L. Gladstein and N. P. Reilly, "Group Decision Making Under Threat: The Tycoon Game," *Academy of Management Journal* 28 (1985), pp. 613–27.

32. J. P. Wanous and M. A. Youtz, "Solution Diversity and the Quality of Group Decisions," *Academy of Management Journal* 29 (1986), pp. 149–59.

33. A. L. Delbecq, A. H. Van de Ven, and D. H. Gustafson, *Group Techniques for Program Planning: A Guide to Nominal and Delphi Processes* (Glenview, Ill.: Scott-Foresman, 1975).

34. D. M. Hegedus and R. V. Rasmussen, "Task Effectiveness and Interaction Process of a Modified Nominal Group Technique in Solving an Evaluation Problem," *Journal of Management* 12 (1986), pp. 545–60.

35. A. L. Delbecq et al., *Group Techniques for Program Planning*.

36. R. A. Cosier, "Methods for Improving the Strategic Decision: Dialectic Versus the Devil's Advocate," *Strategic Management Journal* 3 (1982), pp. 373–74.

37. D. M. Schweiger, W. R. Sandberg, and J. W. Ragan, "Group Approaches for Improving Strategic Decision Making: Analysis of Dialectical Inquiry, Devil's Advocacy, and Consensus," *Academy of Management Journal* 29 (1986), pp. 51–71.

38. V. H. Vroom and P. Yetton, *Leadership and Decision Making* (Pittsburgh: University of Pittsburgh Press, 1973).

39. G. A. Field, "Test of the Vroom-Yetton Normative Model of Leadership," *Journal of Applied Psychology* 67 (1982), pp. 523–32.

40. A. Vinokur, E. Burnstein, L. Sechrest, and P. Wortman, "Group Decision Making by Experts: Field Panels Evaluating Medical Technologies," *Journal of Personality and Social Psychology* 49 (1985), pp. 70–84.

41. W. A. Randolph and S. A. Youngblood, "An Analysis of Group Processes: The Relationship between Performance of Group Roles and Task Effectiveness of Interacting, Problem-Solving Groups" (Paper presented at the National Academy of Management meeting, Atlanta, 1978).

42. J. Misumi and M. K. Peterson, "The Performance-Maintenance (PM) Theory of Leadership: Review of a Japanese Research Program," *Administrative Science Quarterly* 30 (1985), pp. 198–223.

43. W. A. Randolph and S. A. Youngblood, "An Analysis of Group Processes."

CASE: The problem with problem solving

Part I

In mid-October, twenty-nine-year-old Bill Meister, president of Artisan Industries, had to meet with his management group to consider increasing prices. A year before, he had taken over the failing $9-million-a-year wooden gift manufacturing company from his father. It had been a hectic year, but he had arrested the slide to bankruptcy. However, much work was still needed in almost every area of the company.

People in his office for the 11:00 meeting are described in the following paragraphs.

Bob was the thirty-year-old VP of finance. He had three years with the company, coming from the staff of a Big Eight accounting firm. He headed accounting and the office staff.

Cal was thirty-five years old and had been with the company eight years. Although he had a bachelor's degree in accounting, he had held many jobs in the company. Now he was installing a small computer system and reported to Bob.

Edith was Bill's forty-year-old sister and manager of the routine sales activity as it interfaced with the home office. The sales force was made up of independent sales reps. Only clerical people reported to Edith. She had no college training.

Bill called the meeting to order in the presence of a management consultant who happened to be visiting to discuss other plans for improvement.

Bill: OK. We've been discussing the need for a price increase for some time now. Bob recommends increasing prices 16 percent right away. I'd like to get all of your thoughts on this. Bob?

Bob: My analysis of profit statements to date indicates that a 16 percent increase is necessary right now if we are to have any profit this year. My best estimate is that we're losing money on every order we take. We haven't raised prices in over a year and have no choice but to do so now.

Cal: I agree. What's the sense in taking orders on which we lose money?

Bob: Exactly. If we raise prices across the board immediately, we can have a profit of about $300,000 at year end.

Cal: It would've been better to have increased prices with our price list last May or June rather than doing it on each order here in the middle of our sales season, but we really have no choice now.

Bob: There's just no way we can put it off.

Bill *(pausing, looking around the room):* So, you all recommend a price increase at this time?

Cal and Bob: Yes.

Bob: We can't wait to increase prices as new orders are written in the field or through a new price list. Right now we already have enough of a backlog of orders accepted at the old prices and orders awaiting our acknowledgment to fill the plant until the season ends in six to eight weeks. We must only accept orders at the new prices.

Cal: If we acknowledge all the orders we have now, like that thirty page one Edith has for $221,000, then the price change won't even be felt this year.

Bob: No, we should not acknowledge any orders at the old prices. I would hold the orders and send each customer a printed letter telling them of the price increase and asking them to reconfirm their orders with an enclosed mailer if they still want them.

Cal: Orders already acknowledged would keep the plant busy until they responded.

Bill: So, is this the best thing to do?

Bob: We're in business to make money; we'd be crazy not to raise prices!

Bill: Edith, you look unhappy. What do you think?

Edith *(shrugging):* I don't know.

Bob *(visibly impatient):* We're losing money on every order.

Edith: I'm just worried about trying to raise prices right in the middle of the season.

Cal: Well, if we wait, we might as well forget it.

Bob: Just what would you suggest we do, Edith?

Edith: I don't know. *(Pause).* This order *(picking up the thirty-page order)* took the salesman a month to work up with the customer. There are over 175 items on it, and the items must be redistributed to the customer's nine retail outlets in time for Christmas. I'm worried about it.

Bob: It's worthless to us as it is.

Cal: Look, in our letter we can mention the inflation and that this is our first increase in a long while. Most customers will understand this. We've got to try. It's worth the risk, isn't it Edith?
(Edith shrugs.)

Bill: What do you suggest, Edith?

Edith: I don't know. We need the increase, but it bothers me.

Bob: Business is made of tough decisions; managers are paid to make 'em.
(All become quiet, look around the room, and finally look at Bill.)

Questions for Part I

1. Explain what happened at this meeting: What was each person's role? What was each person doing and trying to do? Diagram the interactions. Was it a good meeting? Why?

2. What is the decision going to be? Give all the specifics of the decision.
3. What do you think of the decision? Can you think of ways to improve upon it?
4. What would you do if you were there?

Part II

Consultant *(calmly):* I think Edith has raised a good point. We *are* considering making a big move right in the middle of our busy season. It will cause problems. If we can't avoid the increase, then what can we do to avoid or minimize the problems?

Bob *(hostile and obviously disgusted):* It would be ridiculous to put off the price increase.

Consultant *(calmly):* That may be true, but is it being done in the best way? There are always alternatives to consider. I don't think we are doing a good job of problem solving here. *(Pause.)* Even with the basic idea of an increase, it can be done poorly or done well. There is room for more thought. How can it be done with the least penalty? *(All quiet, as consultant looks around the group, waiting for anyone to add comments. Hearing none.)* For example, by the time we mail them a letter and they think about it and mail it back, two or three weeks may pass. The price increase wouldn't take effect until the season is almost over. How can we get the increase making us money right away? And though we are bound to lose some orders, what can we do to minimize these? *(Pausing to allow comments.)*

Edith: Yes, that's what I meant.

Consultant: On this order, for example *(picking up the $221,000 order)*, we could call them right now and explain the situation and possibly be shipping at the higher prices *this afternoon.*

Bob *(with no hostility, and with apparent positive attitude):* OK. I will call them as soon as we leave here.

Cal: We have a pile of orders awaiting acknowledgment . . .

Bob: Right, we can get some help and pick out the bigger orders and start calling them this afternoon.

Consultant: How about involving the sales force?

Edith: Yes, the salespeople know the customers best. We should call them to contact the customer. They got the order and know the customer's needs. But we will have to convince the salespeople of the necessity of the increase. I can start getting in touch with them by phone right away.

Bob: OK, we can handle the bigger orders personally by phone and use the letter on the small ones.

Consultant: What do you think about making them act *to keep* the order? Why not make it so *no action* keeps the order. Tell them that we are saving their place in our shipping schedule and will go ahead and ship if they don't contact us in five to seven days. Is it best to put the control in their hands?

Edith: That bothered me. Increasing the price is serious, and we need to handle it carefully if it's to work. I think most people will go ahead and accept the merchandise.

Bob: Edith and I can get together this afternoon on the letter. *(All become silent again.)*

Bill: OK, can you all get started after lunch? Let's meet in the morning to see how it's going.

Questions for Part II

1. What do you think of the decision now? Is it improved? Why might you call the first decision "suboptimal"?
2. Would the group have made the new decision without help? Why?
3. It can be said that initially the group was not involved in problem solving. Why?
4. What did the consultant see that had to be done with the group? How could she do it? Did the consultant want to make the decisions herself? Could Bill have taken this role?

EXERCISE: Lost at sea

Step 1

Instructions: You are adrift on a private yacht in the South Pacific. As a consequence of a fire of unknown origin, much of the yacht and its contents have been destroyed. The yacht is now slowly sinking. Your location is unclear because of the destruction of critical navigational equipment and because you and the crew were distracted trying to bring the fire under control. Your best estimate is that you are approximately one thousand miles south-southwest of the nearest land.

Below is a list of fifteen items that are intact and undamaged after the fire. In addition to these articles, you have a serviceable, rubber life raft with oars large enough to carry yourself, the crew, and all the items listed below. The total contents of all survivors' pockets are a package of cigarettes, several books of matches, and five one-dollar bills.

Your task is to rank the fifteen items below in terms of their importance to your survival. Place the number 1 by the most important item, the number 2 by the second most important, and so on through number 15, the least important.

Step 2

Instructions: This is an exercise in group decision-making in ranking the fifteen items below. Your group is to employ the group consensus method in reaching its decision. This means that the prediction of each of the fifteen survival items must be agreed upon by each group member before it becomes a part of the group decision. Consensus is difficult

Things Available to You on the Yacht	Step 1 Individual Ranking	Step 2 Team's Ranking	Step 3 Survey Ranking	Step 4 Difference between Steps 1 and 3	Step 5 Difference between Steps 2 and 3
Sextant					
Shaving mirror					
Five-gallon can of water					
Mosquito netting					
One case of U.S. Army C rations					
Maps of the Pacific Ocean					
Seat cushion (flotation device approved by the Coast Guard)					
Two-gallon can of oil-gas mixture					
Small transistor radio					
Shark repellent					
Twenty square feet of opaque plastic					
One quart of 160-proof Puerto Rican rum					
Fifteen feet of nylon rope					
Two boxes of chocolate bars					
Fishing kit					
Totals					

Team Number

	1	2	3	4	5	6	7	8
Step 6: Average individual score								
Step 7: Team score								
Step 8: Gain score								
Step 9: Lowest individual score								
Step 10: Number of individual scores lower than team score								

to reach. Therefore, not every ranking will meet with everyone's complete approval. As a group, try to make each ranking one with which all group members can at least partially agree. Here are some guides to use in reaching consensus.

1. Avoid arguing for your own individual judgments. Approach the task on the basis of logic.

2. Avoid changing your mind if it is only to reach agreement and avoid conflict. Support only solutions with which you are able to agree at least somewhat.

3. Avoid "conflict-reducing" techniques such as majority vote, averaging, or trading in reaching your decision.

4. View differences of opinion as a help rather than a hindrance in decision-making.

Source: Reprinted from J. William Pfeiffer and John E. Jones (eds.), *The 1975 Annual Handbook for Group Facilitators.* San Diego, CA: University Associates, 1975, pp. 28–34. Used with permission.

QUESTIONNAIRE: Group roles survey

Think about past times when you have participated in group work. Perhaps it was a task group or committee at work or a student project group. Did you:

	Never	Seldom	Often	Frequently
Task behaviors				
1. Initiate ideas or actions	1	2	3	4
2. Facilitate introduction of facts and information	1	2	3	4
3. Clarify issues	1	2	3	4
4. Evaluate issues	1	2	3	4
5. Summarize and pull together various ideas	1	2	3	4
6. Keep group working on task	1	2	3	4
7. Ask to see if group is near decision (take consensus)	1	2	3	4
8. Request further information	1	2	3	4
Maintenance behaviors				
1. Support and encourage others	1	2	3	4
2. Reduce tension	1	2	3	4
3. Harmonize (keep peace)	1	2	3	4
4. Compromise (find common ground)	1	2	3	4
5. Encourage participation	1	2	3	4
Self-oriented behaviors				
1. Express hostility	1	2	3	4
2. Seek recognition	1	2	3	4
3. Avoid involvement	1	2	3	4
4. Dominate group	1	2	3	4
5. Nitpick	1	2	3	4

Now look at which roles you feel you frequently perform. Are they mostly task, maintenance, or self-oriented roles? Which of the four group types discussed in the chapter (task-oriented, team, interpersonal, or floundering) do you encourage with your actions?

Source: Adapted by permission from *Organizational Behavior*, 4th Edition, by Hellriegel, Slocum and Woodman; copyright © 1976, 1979, 1983, 1986 by West Publishing Company. All rights reserved. Page 243.

QUESTIONNAIRE: Team-building checklist

To what extent is there evidence of the following problems in your group?

		Low Evidence		Some Evidence		High Evidence
1.	Loss of production or work-unit output.	1	2	3	4	5
2.	Grievances or complaints within the work unit.	1	2	3	4	5
3.	Conflicts or hostility between unit members.	1	2	3	4	5
4.	Confusion about assignments or unclear relationships between people.	1	2	3	4	5
5.	Lack of clear goals, or low commitment to goals.	1	2	3	4	5
6.	Apathy or general lack of interest or involvement of unit members.	1	2	3	4	5
7.	Lack of innovation, risk taking, imagination, or taking initiative.	1	2	3	4	5
8.	Ineffective staff meetings.	1	2	3	4	5
9.	Problems in working with the boss.	1	2	3	4	5
10.	Poor communications: people afraid to speak up, not listening to each other, or not talking together.	1	2	3	4	5
11.	Lack of trust between boss and member or between members.	1	2	3	4	5
12.	Decisions made that people do not understand or agree with.	1	2	3	4	5
13.	People feel that good work is not recognized or rewarded.	1	2	3	4	5
14.	People are not encouraged to work together in better team effort.	1	2	3	4	5

Scoring: Add up the score for the fourteen items. If your score is between 14–28, there is little evidence your unit needs team building. If your score is between 29–42, there is some evidence, but no immediate pressure, unless two or three items are very high. If your score is between 43–56, you should seriously think about planning a team-building program. If your score is over 56, team-building should be a top priority item for your work unit.

Source: Wm. G. Dyer, *Team Building*, © 1987, Addison-Wesley Publishing Co., Inc., Reading, Massachusetts. Pages 42–43. Reprinted with permission.

Managing Intergroup Conflict and Coordination

T his chapter focuses on the interactions that occur between groups in an organization—that is, intergroup behavior. As organizations grow, management must break down tasks for multiple groups of people to perform. But these group tasks are usually interrelated, at least to some extent, since they all relate to overall organizational goals. Thus, there will need to be interactions among these groups, just as there are interactions among people in an organization. It is important that managers learn to manage these intergroup interactions. They must learn to manage the conflicts that arise and achieve a coordinated effort.

THE IMPORTANCE OF UNDERSTANDING INTERGROUP BEHAVIOR

As we turn our attention to intergroup behavior, we are actually beginning to look at the organization as a whole. This chapter is a bridge between the behavior of people in organizations and the behavior of organizations. As we proceed, we are building on all the material on individuals, interpersonal behavior, and group behavior that we have discussed in the first 13 chapters. Effective management of intergroup behavior is contingent on using this knowledge as a basis. **And managers must learn to deal with the dynamics of intergroup behavior if they aspire to upper-management levels.** A look at any organization chart makes it clear that as people move up the hierarchy, they move from managing people to managing groups of people. For example, Exhibit 14–1 depicts career situations for managers over time. A young production manager might be responsible for eight workers—that is, for one group of people. But later in his or her career, as product manager, he or she might be responsible for four groups under two subassembly managers.

Even at relatively low levels of an organization, managers and their groups are affected by the actions of other groups in the organization. For example, in Exhibit 14–1, production manager A may manage the first-shift operation, while manager B manages the same work on second shift. If B's people leave the machines in disrepair, that will create problems for A. But if B warns A about a problem they had on second shift, A may be able to avoid a downtime loss. Such intergroup interactions can make the difference between a manager's success and failure.

In many ways, managing intergroup interactions is really a balancing act: Will the interactions result in conflict or in coordinated effort? When groups of people are placed in a situation where each group develops a unique culture because of the different tasks it must perform; where groups must compete for scarce resources; and where interaction must take place, it is not surprising that there is potential for conflict. Yet these same factors can help create needed specialization within a well-

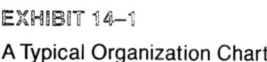

EXHIBIT 14–1

A Typical Organization Chart

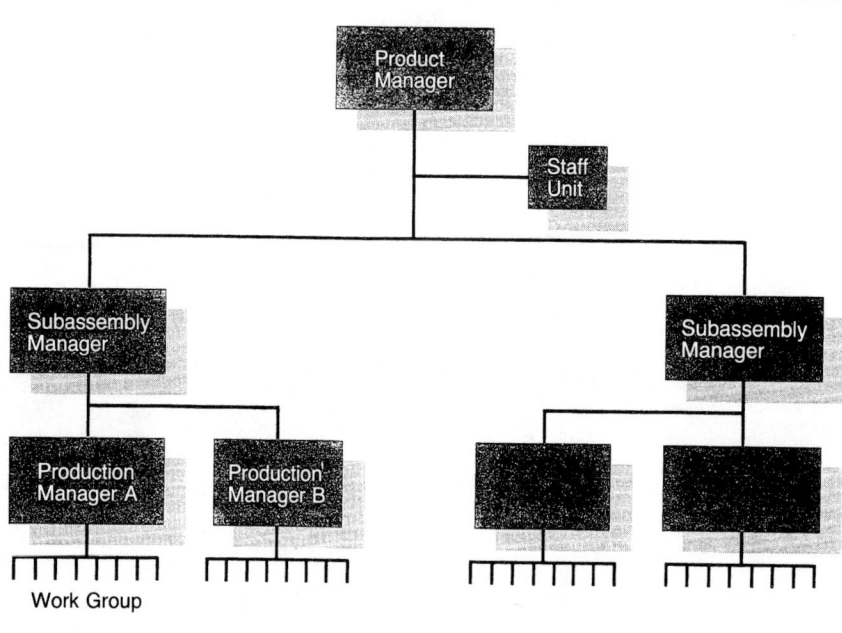

Work Group

coordinated, whole organization. Unfortunately, the rational behavior choices intended by top management are not always possible between groups. Sometimes the ambiguity of a situation or the desires of one individual or group may make political actions (such as those discussed in Chapter 10) necessary. For these reasons, the task of managing and living with intergroup behavior is difficult.

But why are organizations made up of interacting groups with different goals and different perspectives? The answer has to do with the growth of an organization. As we saw with Home Computers Company in Chapter 1, the start-up organization consisted of only two people. But as HCC grew and more and more people were added, it was not possible to run the company as one big group. Some people had to sell the product while others produced it and still others designed it. Such specialization is necessary for organizations to deal with the uncertainty that always exists in running a business. By breaking the organizational task into parts, each part of the overall task can be better managed. The problem is that this division of labor creates problems in coordinating the efforts of different organizational subunits. Division of labor also creates the potential for intergroup conflict which develops over time as an organization grows and adjusts to technological and product changes.

The focus in this chapter is on achieving the coordinated effort among groups in an organization that is necessary if success is to be achieved. To do this, managers should explore why there is always potential for conflict among groups. Managers also must explore both positive and negative aspects of intergroup conflict. Finally, managers must explore both ineffective and effective ways to manage conflict in an organization and thus create coordinated intergroup effort. Companies sometimes go to great lengths to teach managers how to deal with conflict.[1] As a first step, let us visit HCC to gain a more realistic perspective on intergroup interaction.

Home Computers Case

Intergroup Behavior at Home Computers Company

As HCC grew from a fledgling company operating out of a garage, it developed specialization along several functional lines. Production is handled primarily out of two plants (one in Denver and one in Dayton). Assigned to each plant are salespeople, accountants, and design engineers. As the largest and oldest plant for HCC, the Dayton plant is looked upon as the guiding light for the company, especially since the corporate offices are located there.

Over the years, the Dayton plant moved into assembly-line production and became very bureaucratic. Some of the original employees left during this transition, feeling that the company had become too rigid. But production had to become more highly structured, since the plant was using three shifts. Furthermore, production errors were very costly, and not every computer that went out the door could be completely tested for defects. Production quantity fell off, and product quality became an issue as customers complained to the salespeople.

Further, the salespeople were constantly complaining about the plant's slowness and the poor quality of computers coming out of the plant. The personal computer industry was rapidly expanding, and customers expected machines that worked right all the time and for a long time too. The salespeople had to focus on short-term goals and problems, and they knew that their pay depended directly on the volume of sales they could generate.

To deal with the frustration of the production problems, the salespeople often distorted information sent to production on their sales orders. Primarily, they indicated a deadline earlier than was actually needed. They complained to management that production would not cooperate with their needs. And they also restricted their contact with the production people as much as they could. They drew together as salespeople and worked hard to outsmart the production people. One sales rep was even heard to say, "We have to do everything we can to protect ourselves and our customers from the problems in production."

On the other hand, the people in production felt the salespeople were unorganized and made impossible demands. As a result, production would also distort information about meeting the sales deadlines. Even when it was possible to meet the deadlines, they gave reasons why they could not get the job done as requested. In fact, some production people would do things to put production behind schedule just to hurt the sales-people. If confronted with these problems, the production people would refer the problem up the hierarchy, saying that if they had better lead time and planning from sales, they could do their job right. But if they were rushed, quality problems were likely to occur.

When Harvey met with consultant Sally Barnes to discuss the problems between sales and production, he was hoping she would have some ideas about what to do. How could he keep his very successful organization from going down the tubes because of the conflict and lack of coordination between sales and production?

INTERGROUP CONFLICT AS A DEVELOPMENTAL PROCESS

Imagine yourself as the consultant to HCC. What would you tell Harvey? How would you analyze the situation to determine the causes of the problems facing the company? It is clear that there is conflict between sales and production when there needs to be cooperation. But why does this happen? What is causing the groups to be in conflict? How could they avoid conflict and achieve coordination? The issues of conflict and coordination in intergroup behavior are crucial for managers to learn to handle. Therefore, let us explore answers to these questions.

Before answering the questions above, we must define intergroup conflict. **Intergroup conflict exists when one group attempts to achieve its goals at the expense of the goal attainment of another group in the organization.** Thus, conflict is the opposite of the desired cooperation and coordination between groups in an organization. Unfortunately, it is all too common. To complete the definition of conflict, managers need to recognize that **intergroup conflict is a cyclical process involving four repeated steps: frustration, conceptualization, behavior, and outcome.** Exhibit 14–2 illustrates the process of conflict and its cyclical nature.[2]

The first step in the conflict process is the **frustration** that develops when a group feels blocked from achieving a goal. Examples might include blockage from a performance goal, from the completion of a

EXHIBIT 14–2

The Process of Intergroup Conflict

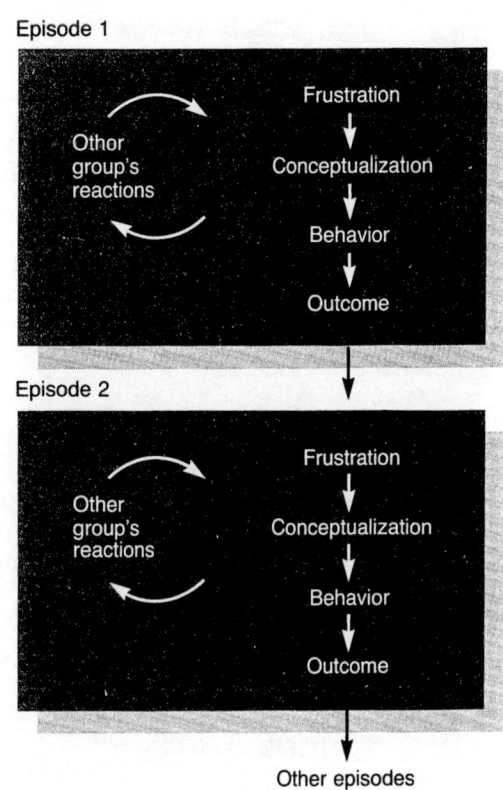

Source: K. Thomas, "Conflict and Conflict Management." In *Handbook of Industrial and Organizational Psychology*, ed. M. D. Dunnete. Copyright © 1976 John Wiley & Sons. Reprinted by permission of John Wiley & Sons, Inc.

task, from information that is needed, or from financial or personnel resources. Such frustration can create negative attitudes toward another group when it is seen as the cause of the blockage.

The second step in the process is **conceptualization** of the conflict. This means that group members attempt to understand why they are frustrated and who is responsible. In addition, they begin to plan a reaction to the frustration and may even anticipate the subsequent reaction from the group responsible for the frustration. Conceptualization is the problem-solving and strategy stage in the process that precedes actual behavior in response to the conflict situation. Sometimes it is a subconscious step that is influenced by the past history and attitudes of the groups involved.

Behavior is the third step in the conflict process. There are many possible behaviors that a group can use in reacting to a conflict situation. It can give in to the other group; it can fight with the other group; it can hope the conflict will go away; or it can try to work out a compromise or joint solution to the problem.

As a result of a group's choice of behavior and the reaction of the other group to the behavior, the **outcome** of the conflict is determined. **Outcome** takes in the satisfaction, attitudes, goal attainment, and intergroup relations of the two groups involved. Unless both groups are really satisfied with the resolution, the seeds for future conflicts are sown. Hence, the second conflict is often an outgrowth of an unresolved conflict in the first episode.

Thus, the definition and process of conflict make it clear that intergroup conflict and lack of coordination do develop over time. Past episodes in the relationship between two groups—just as with two people in interpersonal relations—are a big factor in determining what will happen next. This developmental aspect of intergroup behavior also suggests that problems cannot be solved overnight. It takes time for problems to build up, and it takes time for them to be resolved. The Home Computers case and Insight 14–1 about Microsoft and Ascii provide excellent examples of how conflicts develop over time. They also suggest that it will take time to work through these conflicts. With these examples and the definitions in hand, let us now turn to the task of developing a model of intergroup conflict, including causes and outcomes.

A MODEL OF INTERGROUP CONFLICT

As we develop a model of intergroup conflict, we will first explore some of the causes of conflict. We will then look at both negative and positive potential outcomes and explore both ineffective and effective strategies for dealing with conflict. As we proceed, think about how the model can be applied to the Home Computers case and what suggestions the consultant should make to Harvey.

Causes of intergroup conflict

The first step in developing the model is to explore the causes of intergroup conflict. We often hear the comment, "It was a personality clash that created the conflict." Certainly, some conflicts are truly the result of a personality clash. But **most conflicts between people in an organization are really conflicts between the jobs and departments that the people represent.** Some form of conflict would be likely no matter which two people were in the positions, though the intensity of conflict will

High-Tech Saga:

How 2 Computer Nuts Transformed Industry before Messy Breakup

*T*hey were unlikely candidates to be industry titans.

William Gates was one of America's first computer nerds, a compulsive hacker with big glasses and messy hair. Kazuhiko Nishi was a tubby, hyperactive engineering student from Kobe, Japan. When they became partners in 1978, they were both 22-year-old dropouts obsessed by an esoteric new technology: the personal computer.

But over the next seven years, through a combination of foresight and theatrics, Mr. Gates and Mr. Nishi helped transform personal computers from a novelty into a giant, explosive industry. Mr. Gates and a high-school friend founded Microsoft Corp., and Mr. Nishi set up a company in Japan that worked with Microsoft. With Mr. Nishi's guidance, Microsoft played a crucial role in designing Japan's first personal computer. Then, thanks to an impromptu airborne sales job by Mr. Nishi, Microsoft developed one of the first portable personal computers. And Mr. Nishi's impetuous counsel in a late-night debate spurred Mr. Gates to make a lucrative alliance with International Business Machines Corp.

But as Microsoft grew bigger, relations between Mr. Gates and Mr. Nishi started to wear thin. By 1983, Microsoft was doing business with some three dozen companies in Japan, most of which snapped up MS-DOS for their machines. Mr. Gates worried that Mr. Nishi was spending too much time chasing new technology schemes and not enough attending to these customers.

In the U.S., Mr. Gates was putting more complex organizational structures in place at Microsoft and hiring a corps of older, sea-soned managers to run them. Some of them began to bristle at the unorthodox way that Mr. Nishi and his company, Ascii Corp., were running Microsoft's Asian operations.

So did some of Mr. Nishi's own colleagues in Japan. "In the cowboy age, Billy the Kid can be a star," says Susumu Furukawa, who left Ascii this year to run Microsoft's Japanese subsidiary. "But Microsoft became an army, and Kay was still playing like Billy the Kid. Kay's not a general who can manage an army."

Then came the dinosaur episode. Mr. Nishi set out to produce a television show that would make computers enticing to schoolchildren and promote his company's products. He conceived an elaborate story featuring a young boy who uses Microsoft software to re-create a brontosaurus.

The tensions finally came to a head in March, the day after Microsoft completed a very successful public offering. Mr. Gates had gone to Australia to visit Microsoft's Sydney office and take a celebratory cruise on the Great Barrier Reef. Mr. Nishi met him there, and the two boarded a plane together for Tokyo.

In a wrenching 30-hour session, they haggled about restructuring their partnership. "We'd talk about our vision, and then we'd get mad at each other, and then we'd apologize," recalls Mr. Gates. "You can get kind of mad when you're gone from the guy, but then I'm reminded what a great guy he is."

There was no resolution, though. "Kay would rather see it all go down in flames than feel like he's compromised in some way," says Mr. Gates. The two finally decided to dissolve the partnership.

A messy split

The separation was messy. Microsoft opened its own Japanese subsidiary and infuriated Mr. Nishi by quickly hiring away 18

Ascii employees. In public statements, Microsoft officials declared that they bore Mr. Nishi no ill will and hoped to keep working with him. But Mr. Nishi doesn't believe it. "Give me a break," he says, spitting out the words. "They are all liars."

Mr. Gates says he sympathizes with his former partner's anger and frustration. "The guy's life is a mess," he says sadly. "He's worth negative half a million and I'm worth X million—that's certainly seeds for bitterness."

be influenced by the particular people involved. This was certainly the case between Bill Gates and Kazuhiko Nishi in Insight 14–1. Two points are important for managers to understand here. First, intergroup conflict involves conflict between **people.** In groups and organizations, people are the actors who create the dynamics everyone experiences. Second, however, even though intergroup conflicts involve people, the people are only actors in **roles** that are in conflict with one another.

In the next few pages we will explore eight different causes of intergroup conflict:

1. Task interdependence.
2. Different goals, norms, and time frames.
3. Ambiguity of roles.
4. Limited common resources.
5. Reward systems.
6. Communications obstacles.
7. Status and power differences.
8. Personnel skills and traits.

These causes are summarized in Exhibit 14–3, which indicates their effect on the conflict process. These causes set up the conditions for conflict, and the intensity of conflict is then determined as the conflict process unfolds. We will explore each of the eight causes in turn.

Task interdependence

A primary cause of intergroup conflict is that one or both of the groups in question cannot do their work unless the other group also does its work. For example, at Home Computers Company, the salespeople cannot sell the computers on any reliable basis unless production gets the product out in a timely manner. Likewise, production needs to produce computers only if sales can effectively sell them. In an organization, all groups are at lest minimally interdependent or they would not be part of the same organization. The question is, how interdependent are they?

EXHIBIT 14–3

A Partial Model of Intergroup Conflict: Causes and Process

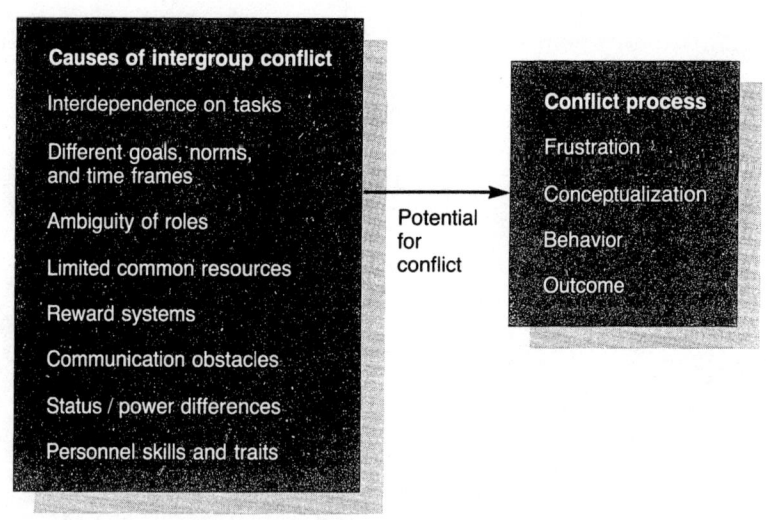

Three basic types of interdependence have been identified by researchers: pooled, sequential, and reciprocal.[3] They are depicted in Exhibit 14–4 and described below.

Pooled interdependence between two groups in an organization means that they can perform their tasks at the same time with very little need for interaction. For example, the accounting group in the HCC plant in Dayton is essentially independent from the production group there. The only interdependence comes from the fact that they are both part of HCC.

Sequential interdependence means that the outputs from one group are the inputs to another group. In other words, there is a one-way type of interdependence. In Exhibit 14–4, group B is dependent on group A finishing its work so that group B has some work to do. On the other hand, group A is not dependent on group B, unless group B is so slow in its work that inventory backs up and blocks group A's output. At HCC, the salespeople are sequentially interdependent with the production people. They cannot sell the computers until they are produced. Production is dependent upon sales in a more limited and long-term fashion.

The most highly interdependent situation is **reciprocal interdependence. Outputs from each group can serve as inputs to the other group.** In other words, there is a two-way type of interdependence. If either

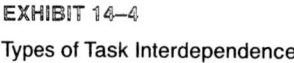

EXHIBIT 14-4

Types of Task Interdependence

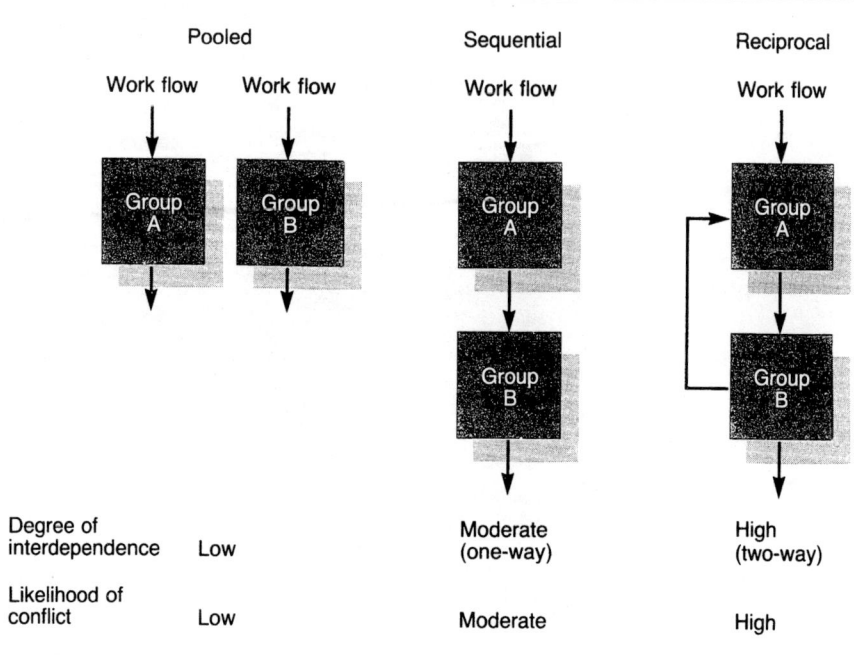

	Pooled	Sequential	Reciprocal
Degree of interdependence	Low	Moderate (one-way)	High (two-way)
Likelihood of conflict	Low	Moderate	High

group has problems, they will be felt by the other group. For example, at HCC, research and development (R&D) and market research must work hand in hand to come up with a computer that is technically sound and will sell. Otherwise, both groups and the company as a whole will suffer.

The type of interdependence that exists between two groups does not guarantee more or less conflict. It simply sets up a situation where conflict is easy, and coordination of effort is difficult. Pooled interdependence creates the least potential for conflict, except perhaps at budget time. Sequential interdependence creates more potential for conflict, and reciprocal interdependence creates the most potential for conflict.

Differentiation

Another extremely important cause of coordination problems among groups is the **differentiation** that occurs in the design of the groups. As discussed earlier, organizational growth results in the need to create different functional work units. And the logical way to divide up the work in an organization is to create work groups with different responsibilities and specialties.[4] At Home Computers Company, it makes sense for one group to be concerned with selling the computers—the salespeople—and another group to be concerned with manufacturing them—the production people. The results of this specialization are twofold. First, specialization allows people to become experts and to develop a sense of identity with their tasks and goals. But over time, these groups learn to do things differently and focus only on their unique goals. This focus can create coordination problems for the organization.[5]

Differentiation in groups can be summarized along four major dimensions:

1. Goal orientation.
2. Time orientation.
3. Formality of structure.
4. Nature of interpersonal relationships.

With different groups there will obviously be different **goal orientations.** Production groups focus on goals related to cost control and utilization of manufacturing technology. Sales groups focus on goals related to consumer response to the product and generation of sales revenue. Research and development groups focus on contributions to science and applications of science to new products. Such different goal orientations can lead to conflicts in the priorities of certain activities. For example, a marketing analyst's need for information to complete an analysis may be his number 1 priority. But the salesperson from whom he had to get this information may consider this task a number 10 priority. Obviously, the potential for conflict exists. Insight 14–2 further explores how employees become focused on their own department's goals to the exclusion of organizational goals.

Closely associated with the goal orientation that results from differentiated work groups is a difference in **time orientation.** Because of the particular goals assigned, some groups may develop long-term orientations while others develop short-term perspectives. For example, at HCC, the salespeople have probably developed a short-term orientation, since they must respond to a rapidly changing and demanding marketplace. On the other hand, production people probably have developed a somewhat longer-term perspective. They must be concerned with the costs of changing setups from manufacturing one product to another—and long runs of the same product are cheaper than short runs and frequent changes. In the R&D department at HCC, employees might have an even longer-term orientation, since their endeavors are scientific in nature. These differences in time orientation can create tension between sales (which wants the new product on the market as soon as possible) and research (which wants to develop a product that will

---

I N S I G H T 14-2

Silencing the Refrain, 'It's Not My Job, Man'

It's a familiar story: The restaurant patron asks a passing waiter, "Can you tell me the time?" and the answer comes back, "Sorry, sir, this ain't my table."

Or the airline passenger who asks a flight attendant, "Where's seat 12A?" and is told, "I'm not on duty." The executive who recounted this episode insisted that "So long as she's wearing the airline uniform she's on duty! She's still a company representative."

These situations arise from the notion that "it's not my responsibility." The weak links in an organization are usually at the point where departments are supposed to meet. It's at these joints that institutional arthritis attacks. When departments are separated like national frontiers, fully equipped with barbed-wire fences, bristling watchtowers and buried mine fields, serious losses occur.

Theoretically, efficiency is served by departmentalization, specialization and division of labor. The goal, however, can be achieved only if management strives for coherence by constantly reminding people that they are not isolates working in their own cubbyholes but parts of a larger whole. Here is what executives, conscious of the problem, recommend:

- From the very beginning of a relationship with employees, even in the hiring interview, it is important to stress that the individual will be working for the company—not just for a division, department, unit or particular supervisor.

- By presenting prospects for advancement, the company can demonstrate that looking beyond the narrow confines of the immediate assignment will open windows of personal opportunity.

- In the course of periodic employee appraisals, cooperation with others and the display of initiative in discovering and filling gaps should be treated as major performance criteria. Managers should seek every opportunity to reward subordinates for their contributions that benefit the whole organization.

By Mortimer R. Feinberg and Aaron Levenstein, *The Wall Street Journal*, November 12, 1985. Reprinted by permission of *The Wall Street Journal*, © Dow Jones & Company, Inc. 1985. All rights reserved.

---

perform well over a long period of time) and production (which must produce a reliable product while keeping costs down).

The third effect of differentiation is a difference in the **formality of the structure** that develops in different groups. Some groups may develop a great many rules and paperwork procedures to guide their work, such as might be seen in the production group at HCC. But others may do things more informally by word of mouth and with very few rules, such as in sales at HCC. In addition, the clarity with which roles within groups are defined may vary substantially. Closely associated with the formality of structure is the **nature of interpersonal relationships.** Some units develop norms of behavior that are very task oriented; other groups tend to be more <u>relationship oriented</u>. As just noted, these differences tend to make it more difficult to coordinate activities that cut across group lines.[6] For a summary of how differentiation can impact different types of work units, see Exhibit 14–5.

 Ambiguity of roles

The effects of differentiation and task interdependence are both influenced by the degree of ambiguity and task uncertainty that exists in a group. When the tasks assigned to different groups are not clearly defined, ambiguity about responsibility can result. This ambiguity can result from top management not doing their homework in setting up the groups, but it can also result from a technology that is uncertain and nonroutine. If the company works in a rapidly changing and complex industry like the personal computer industry, defining clear tasks can be difficult.[7] And if the technologies used in the company are characterized by many exceptions to the work plan and difficult problems in the sequencing of work, it will be difficult to clearly define group tasks.[8] Regardless of the reason, task uncertainty for groups and ambiguity about group roles open the door for conflict.[9] And they also open the door for responses that are politically determined and dysfunctional for the organization.

Resources and rewards

Two additional causes of intergroup conflict and politically oriented responses are **limited common resources** and **reward systems.** When two groups are both dependent upon the same set of resources—be it people, machinery, or dollars—and when these resources are limited,

EXHIBIT 14–5

Differentiation among Various Types of Work Units

Dimensions of Differentiation	Types of Work Unit			
	Basic Research	Applied Research	Production	Sales
Primary goal orientation	Development of new knowledge	Cost reduction and quality control	Cost reduction and process efficiency	Consumer problems and competition
Time orientation	Very long-term	Intermediate-term	Short-term	Short-term
Interpersonal orientation	Intermediate	Intermediate	Performance emphasis	People emphasis
Formality of structure	Very low formality	Low formality	Very high formality	High formality

Source: Adapted from Paul R. Lawrence and Jay W. Lorsch, *Organization and Environment: Managing Differentiation and Integration* (Boston: Graduate School of Business Administration, Harvard University, 1967), pp. 36–38.

there is potential for conflict over their distribution. The typical reaction is competition for scarce resources. The same potential exists where rewards are limited and associated with comparative performance. For example, if two shifts at HCC are rewarded according to how many nondefective computers they turn out compared to the number turned out by the other shift, destructive competition may result. Each shift may do things at the end of the shift to make it difficult for the following shift to get started quickly. Insight 14–3 relates other examples of how reward systems have encouraged destructive competition. A relevant question here is, "What good is it to be the best group in a company that is out of business?" **So long as resources and rewards are allocated based on individual group criteria, as opposed to criteria based on contribution to intergroup success, conflict will almost be inevitable.**

Communications obstacles

Another factor that relates to intergroup conflict is **communications obstacles.** There may be: (1) physical barriers, such as geographical separation; (2) time barriers, such as shift work; (3) information barriers, such as when one group knows something the other group doesn't; and (4) semantic barriers, such as engineering jargon versus sales jargon versus accounting jargon.[10] In general, when different groups lack information about the work, goals, and priorities facing other groups, communications will be difficult.

Status and power differences

Another factor that can create intergroup problems is the **difference in the status and power of groups.** For example, if HCC is a market-oriented company, the salespeople may be viewed by top management as more important than the production people. The salespeople may be responsible for **absorbing the uncertainty** from Home Computers Company's markets. In other words, the salespeople use their abilities to satisfy customer demands while allowing production and R&D the time they need to create a viable new product. Of course, production and R&D may see things somewhat differently; but to the extent that sales can handle this uncertainty for the company, they are in a more powerful position than the other two groups. Closely associated with this basis of status difference is the **substitutability** of each group. If the salespeople at HCC are viewed as indispensable, while production is viewed as something that could be subcontracted out, sales is going to have greater status and power in the organization.

Such status and power differences between groups create the potential for intergroup conflict. Furthermore, the weaker group often feels it must give in to the more powerful group, and this can lead to decreased

I N S I G H T 14–3

Pitting Workers against Each Other Often Backfires, Firms Are Finding

*T*o prod branch managers to perform better, a European bank encouraged them to compete against each other to produce the most improved results.

The winner was promised a bonus. But the outcome was disappointing. The bank discovered that a greedy officer had steered a customer to a rival bank rather than help another branch manager win the bonus.

Companies often pit manager against manager in the hopes that the race will bring out the best in both. When monitored properly, internal competition can boost employees' egos and help them feel they control their own destiny. "It's healthy," says organizational psychologist Raf Haddock. "There's a human drive to compete and to strive." But the competition can get out of hand when the stakes are too high or supervisors get careless.

Sales contests

Chase Manhattan Bank hoped to create healthy competition between divisions by linking employees' bonuses to the fees their divisions generated. But the bonus plan encouraged employees to aim for high-volume customers rather than good credit risks. One group built a huge portfolio with a tiny new company called Drysdale Government Securities Inc. In May, Drysdale defaulted on interest payments on securities it had borrowed through Chase. Chase forecasts it will take an after-tax write-off of $117 million in the second quarter as a result.

What works?

Just posting performance rankings hurt the efficiency of a Los Angeles-based workman's compensation insurance company. It ranked offices according to how frequently they distributed disability payments on time. But a former employee recalls that when one office got a claim that was meant for another, workers frequently used the mail rather than the telephone to reroute the information in an attempt to lower the rankings of the competitors.

By Heywood Klein, *The Wall Street Journal*, July 19, 1982. Reprinted by permission of *The Wall Street Journal*, © Dow Jones & Company, Inc. 1982. All rights reserved.

satisfaction and lower overall performance.[11] To achieve the greatest degree of coordination in an organization, groups should be essentially equal in status and power.

⑧ Personnel skills and traits

The final cause of intergroup conflict discussed here is the **skills and traits of personnel** in the groups. As mentioned earlier, even though intergroup conflict involves the groups, the **people** in the groups are the actors in the situations. Hence, the extent to which the people are dom-

"It's not surprising. The production department is in Spain, the warehouse is in Korea, the accounting division is in Bolivia, the board of directors is in Canada . . ."

ineering, aggressive, and tolerant of ambiguity determines the potential for intergroup conflict.[12] Different personality types, as discussed in Chapter 4, deal with conflict in different ways.[13] For example, **thinking** types tend to be more conflict oriented than **feeling** types, since they like things handled in a logical fashion and can get along without harmony. And **judging** types tend to be more conflict-oriented than **perceptive** types, since they like to get things settled and finished. In addition, communications and problem-solving skills of group members might be important predictors of the potential for intergroup conflict. And as we might anticipate, one study found that perceptions of the people in a group can significantly influence reactions to this group. Specifically, if an employee feels that a person representing another group is sincere in his or her disagreement, the employee will tend to respond more favorably than if he or she feels that the person is insincere.[14]

Summarizing the causes of intergroup conflict

In looking over the eight causes of intergroup conflict in Exhibit 14–3, note that all but the last of them are situational in nature. That is, the *people* in the situation are not a factor in these causes. **People come into play as the conflict process unfolds. The causes of conflict merely create conditions that are ripe for conflict.** True, the causes create some base level of conflict. The question is: How severe will the conflict be? Will conflict win out in a destructive manner, or will coordinated intergroup effort win out? Here is where people come into play. **The actions of people determine whether negative or positive outcomes will result as the conflict process unfolds.**

Outcomes from intergroup conflict

We now turn our attention to the possible outcomes of the conflict process. Exhibit 14–6 extends Exhibit 14–3 to include the negative and positive outcomes to conflict. We will first explore the negative outcomes, since they are probably the most familiar. Then we will explore the often surprising positive outcomes to intergroup conflict.

Negative outcomes

Think back to situations where conflict existed between two groups. One good example, and one where conflict is supposed to occur, is in a soccer game between two college fraternity or sorority teams. In this situation, it is easy to recall some of the negative outcomes shown in Exhibit 14–5.[15] Information is concealed—each team keeps its plays secret from the other team. Players obviously feel concern only for their own team, and they may be only mildly concerned when one of the other team's players goes down hurt. Players feel distance between their team and the other team; they do not interact with the other team until the game is over. A climate of distrust and a *we-they* attitude develops. In short, the soccer game is a conflict situation full of negative outcomes, as competitive sports are supposed to be.

But imagine how these negative outcomes might develop in Home Computers Company between sales and production; and further, imagine the effects on the company as a whole. What will happen now that sales and production have begun concealing information from one another? Will that help sales and production do their jobs in the long run? No. And as they operate this way over time, the distance between the groups will increase. Sales and production may each become more concerned with only their own goals and objectives. Pressures will develop within each group to do things for itself and against the other group.

EXHIBIT 14–6

A Partial Model of Intergroup Conflict: Causes, Process, and Outcomes

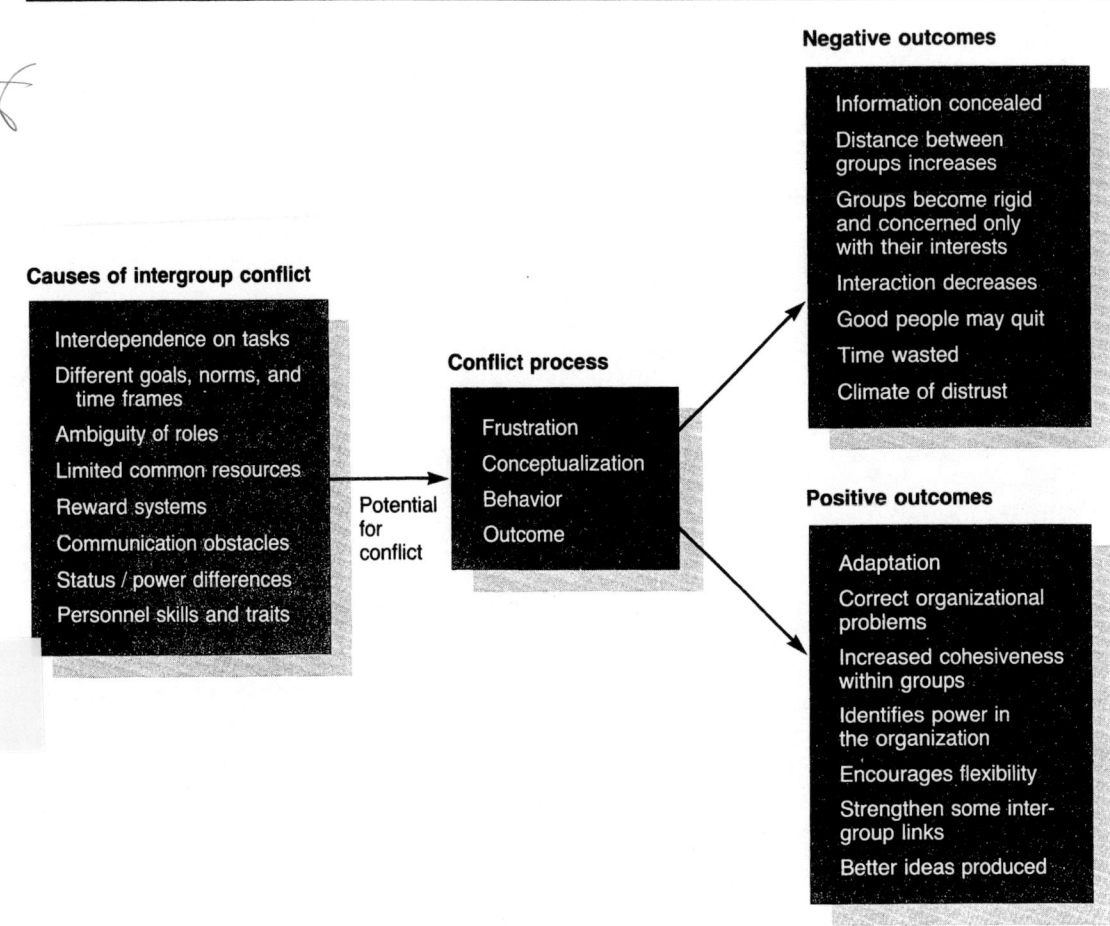

As these pressures mount and result in decreased interaction between sales and production, distrust will run rampant. Sales will imagine that production is doing even more than they really are to hinder the work of the salespeople; and production will exaggerate in the same way about sales. A great deal of energy in each group will be directed toward the conflict instead of toward cooperative work which is productive for the organization. In time, the productivity of both groups will suffer. Good people may quit to get out of this destructive situation. The negative outcomes that are expected and accepted on the soccer field are not helpful at HCC or at any other organization. What good will it do for sales or production to win the conflict if HCC goes out of business in the meantime? Insight 14–4 on page 576 shows an example of how such intergroup conflict nearly destroyed Apple Computer Company several years ago.

Positive outcomes

Believe it or not, positive outcomes can occur as a result of intergroup conflict. Indeed, some degree of conflict in an organization is inevitable and desirable. This statement may be hard to believe; and, in fact, not long ago management literature encouraged the elimination of all conflict in organizations.[16] But since the 1940s, the literature has shown more acceptance of the fact that intergroup conflict is inevitable given the divisionalized design of organizations. More recently, researchers have recognized that elimination of all conflict may be as bad for an organization as having too much conflict. As noted earlier, groupthink and lack of conflict can cause a group to make serious mistakes. The same rationale applies to intergroup behavior. As discussed below and as shown in Exhibit 14–6, **intergroup conflict can serve as a signal that problems exist and as a motivator to correct these problems.** In other words, conflict can be viewed as a way of questioning the status quo and motivating improvements. Let us explore this point further as we look at several positive outcomes of intergroup conflict.[17]

Intergroup conflict can have very positive effects **within the groups** that are involved. Internal cohesiveness typically increases for groups in conflict, and interpersonal conflicts within groups tend to be overlooked in light of the larger intergroup conflict. A good example of this would be the New York Yankees baseball team of the early 1980s. While the Yankees were winning the World Series, they were able to put aside their personal differences and play as a team to win. But after the intergroup conflict (the World Series) was over, the interpersonal conflicts among the players and their manager and owner boiled over. This example also points out the tendency for intergroup conflict to make the groups attend more carefully to the tasks they are assigned. It makes the groups adapt more readily internally to do a better job. Of course, as stated before, extreme amounts of intergroup conflict can absorb so much energy that group tasks and adaptability can be hindered.

At the **organizational level,** intergroup conflict can make people aware of the problems that exist in terms of the variables that cause conflict. For example, a reward system that encourages competition rather than collaboration among groups may be an obvious cause of conflict. Or power differences that are dysfunctional for the organization may come into view as a cause of intergroup conflict.

As a result of highlighting problems and making people uncomfortable, intergroup conflict can also **motivate people to find solutions to**

INSIGHT 14-4

Intergroup Conflict at Apple Computer

As a result of a general softening in the personal computer market and also some internal difficulties, Apple experienced a major drop in its business and in the value of its stock as well. This appears to have brought into the open intergroup conflicts that had been present for some time. Initially, the major conflict was between the company's two major product divisions, the Apple II products division and the Macintosh division.

The Apple II division handled the basic computer line that had originally made the company so successful. These computers continued to sell well, and the division accounted for a large share of the company's earnings. The division was headed by Delbert Yocam, who had come up through manufacturing; it contained a group of effective managers in their forties, including William Campbell, brought in from Eastman Kodak to push field sales to dealers.

The Macintosh division originally had the task of getting its new, highly sophisticated personal computer to the market as quickly as possible. It did this, but was unable to meet projected sales figures. The division was headed by Steven Jobs, the company's board chairman (but not chief executive officer), co-founder, and largest stockholder. His group included: Michael Murray, director of marketing; Robert Belleville, director of engineering; Deborah Coleman, manufacturing director; and Susan Barnes, controller. The division maintained the image of a young elite, and indeed many, including Jobs, were in their early thirties.

Conflicts between the two groups swirled around the perception that the Apple II people were making the profits and the Macintosh people were getting all the publicity and perks. Trivial matters like free fruit juice and a masseur on call for the Macintosh team became major issues. Jobs was very protective of his people and frequently attacked members of the Apple II team, which he described as the "dull and boring product division." As the conflict escalated, turnover in the management ranks became a real problem. Steve Wozniak, co-founder of the company and the designer of the original Apple computer, left with some very angry words.

As the Macintosh computer continued to encounter difficulties, including delays in getting out new components of the system, a third group joined the fray. This consisted of John Sculley, president and chief executive of the company, and a majority of the company's board of directors—including Arthur Rock, an outside director and venture capitalist, who played an important role. The fight became increasingly one between Job's people and Sculley's people—between advocates of technological innovation and advocates of financial soundness. Jobs and Sculley, in turn, tried to get each other fired from their respective positions. Jobs failed, Sculley, with the support of his friends on the board, succeeded. Jobs was removed from all operating responsibilities, and several members of his group, including Belleville, resigned.

Although the company is still financially sound, many fear Apple has lost the spirit and vision that made it into a business phenomenon.

Source: Adapted from Bro Uttal, "Behind the Fall of Steve Jobs," *Fortune*, August 5, 1985, pp. 20–24. © 1985 Time, Inc. All rights reserved.

problems causing the conflict. It can strengthen linkages between certain groups by forcing their interaction to resolve the problem. In a manner of speaking, the conflict is a force for growth within groups. As such, intergroup conflict can increase flexibility in the way groups interact, result in the generation of better ideas for their interaction, and lead to structural and power changes that reduce the negative impacts of conflict. For example, at Home Computers Company, sales has greater status and power than production. The conflict that this produces could be reduced if Harvey were to start emphasizing quality and cost as much as he emphasizes meeting customer delivery demands. Or perhaps less conflict would result if some of the production work were subcontracted. The point is that intergroup conflict can motivate action to resolve the difficulties between sales and production. Some organizations thrive on conflict that helps them solve problems more effectively. Recall the New York Yankees example.

Strategies for managing intergroup conflict

The causes of conflict shown earlier in Exhibit 14–6 have a great deal to do with creating the conditions for conflict. Indeed, they may determine the first episode in the process of conflict. But whether conflict escalates to the dysfunctional level and results in negative outcomes or is maintained at a healthy level and results in positive outcomes depends on the **behaviors** in the first and subsequent conflict episodes. There are both ineffective and effective strategies for managing intergroup conflict.[18] **The ineffective strategies try to suppress the conflict; the effective strategies accept it and try to keep it under control or alter its causes.** The effective strategies do not always work well, and the ineffective ones sometimes work out all right, but managers can better handle intergroup conflict if they understand the differences between the two sets of strategies. Before discussing some of the specific strategies for managing conflict, it will help to distinguish among some basic dimensions of the conflict management process.

Actions designed to deal with intergroup conflict fall into one of three categories: win/lose, lose/lose, and win/win.[19] In **win/lose,** one group gains a goal at the expense of the other group. In **lose/lose,** the conflict results in both groups being denied their goals. And in **win/win,** both groups manage to achieve their goals. These categories can also be discussed along the two dimensions of **cooperativeness** and **assertiveness.** These two dimensions define five ways of dealing with conflict, as shown in Exhibit 14–7.[20]

In the upper left-hand corner of Exhibit 14–7, **competing** is a win/lose strategy. A competing group asserts its position and tends to ignore the position of the other group. In some cases, this may be the right ap-

EXHIBIT 14–7

Categories of Conflict Management

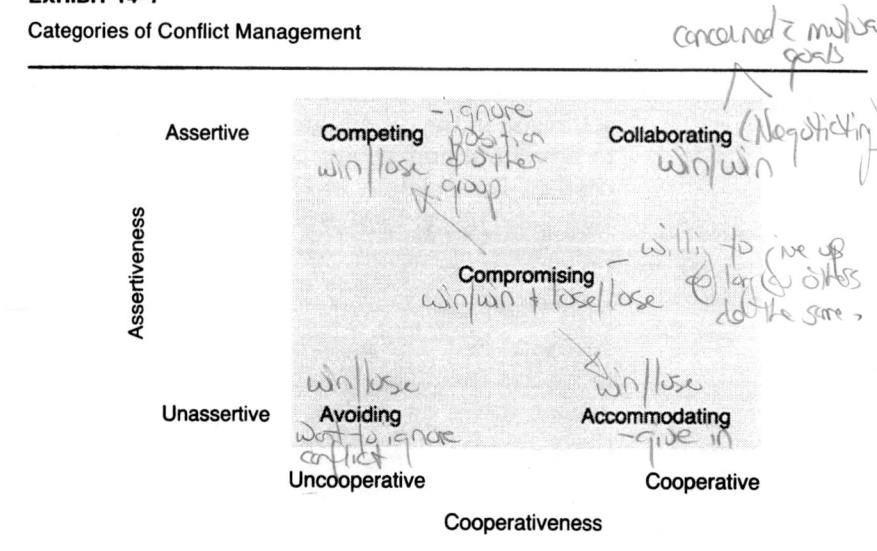

Source: K. Thomas, "Conflict and Conflict Management." In *Handbook of Industrial and Organizational Psychology.* Ed. M. D. Dunnette. Copyright © 1976 John Wiley & Sons. Reprinted by permission of John Wiley & Sons, Inc.

proach if a group feels strongly about its position. But in such situations, we might expect to see some of the political behaviors we discussed in Chapter 10, such as blaming others, image building, and developing a base of support. In the long run, this approach might well result in an undercurrent of distrust. Also, if both groups employ this win/lose strategy, it can turn into a lose/lose situation when two equally strong combatants tangle.

In the lower right-hand corner of the exhibit, **accommodating** is also a win/lose strategy. This time, however, the accommodating group gives in to the other group, probably because of a large power difference or because the issue at stake is not too important to the group. In such cases, accommodating might be the best strategy to follow. But accommodation in the short run may be a political strategy to win in the long run—sort of a lose-the-battle-to-win-the-war strategy. Such behaviors can result in long-term problems for the organization; so again we must question the wisdom of this strategy in most cases. And if both parties employ an accommodating strategy, the result may be a lose/lose situation. The parties are so cooperative that they fall prey to an intergroup type of groupthink.

In the lower left-hand corner of Exhibit 14–7, **avoiding** is a strategy where a group takes no action and hopes the conflict will go away over time. If this group encounters a competing group, the result will probably be win/lose, with the avoiding group losing. Or the avoiding group could wind up winning if it is dealing with an accommodating group. Sometimes, avoiding may be the best strategy, especially if the issue is unimportant to a group; but avoiding usually just delays the negative outcomes associated with intergroup conflict. From this discussion we can see that **the behavior of one group is important only in relation to what the other group does.** The outcomes of a conflict depend on the behaviors of both groups.

In the upper right-hand corner of the exhibit, **collaborating,** sometimes called negotiating, is a win/win strategy. The collaborating group is concerned with the goals of both groups and those of the larger organization. Thus, even if this group encounters a competing, accommodating, or avoiding group, the potential is still there for a win/win resolution, so long as they maintain their collaborating behavior. A book titled *The Win-Win Negotiator* spells out four steps for collaborating/negotiating.[21] First, managers should establish win-win plans. (What's the big picture?) Second, managers should develop win-win relationships. (It's hard to collaborate if you dislike the other person.) Third, managers should form win-win agreements and write them down. And fourth, managers should perform win-win maintenance. (Work hard to keep the agreements working.)

The **compromising** behavior in the center of Exhibit 14–7 is a middle ground; each group may give up something in order to gain something else. This might be referred to as a half win/win and half lose/lose situation because each group asserts itself on some points and cooperates on others. Often, people view compromise as the best alternative for resolving conflicts. In highly critical situations, however, it may not be desirable for each group to give up something. In such cases, win/win collaboration may be the only alternative, even though it can be quite time consuming.

These general conflict management strategies provide a framework for understanding some specific ineffective and effective strategies for dealing with intergroup conflict.

Ineffective management strategies

Exhibit 14–8 shows seven ineffective strategies for managing conflict. **These strategies are ineffective because they attempt to ignore the conflict in hopes it will go away or because they are too much oriented toward group goals rather than organizational goals.**

Avoiding strategies. The first three strategies fall into the category of avoiding, which was identified in Exhibit 14–7. **Nonaction/avoidance** is rather straightforward in meaning, but administrative orbiting and due-process nonaction deserve further comment.[22] **Administrative orbiting**

EXHIBIT 14–8

A Model of Intergroup Conflict: Causes, Process, Management Strategies, and Outcomes

geared toward win/lose → result l-ti conflict.

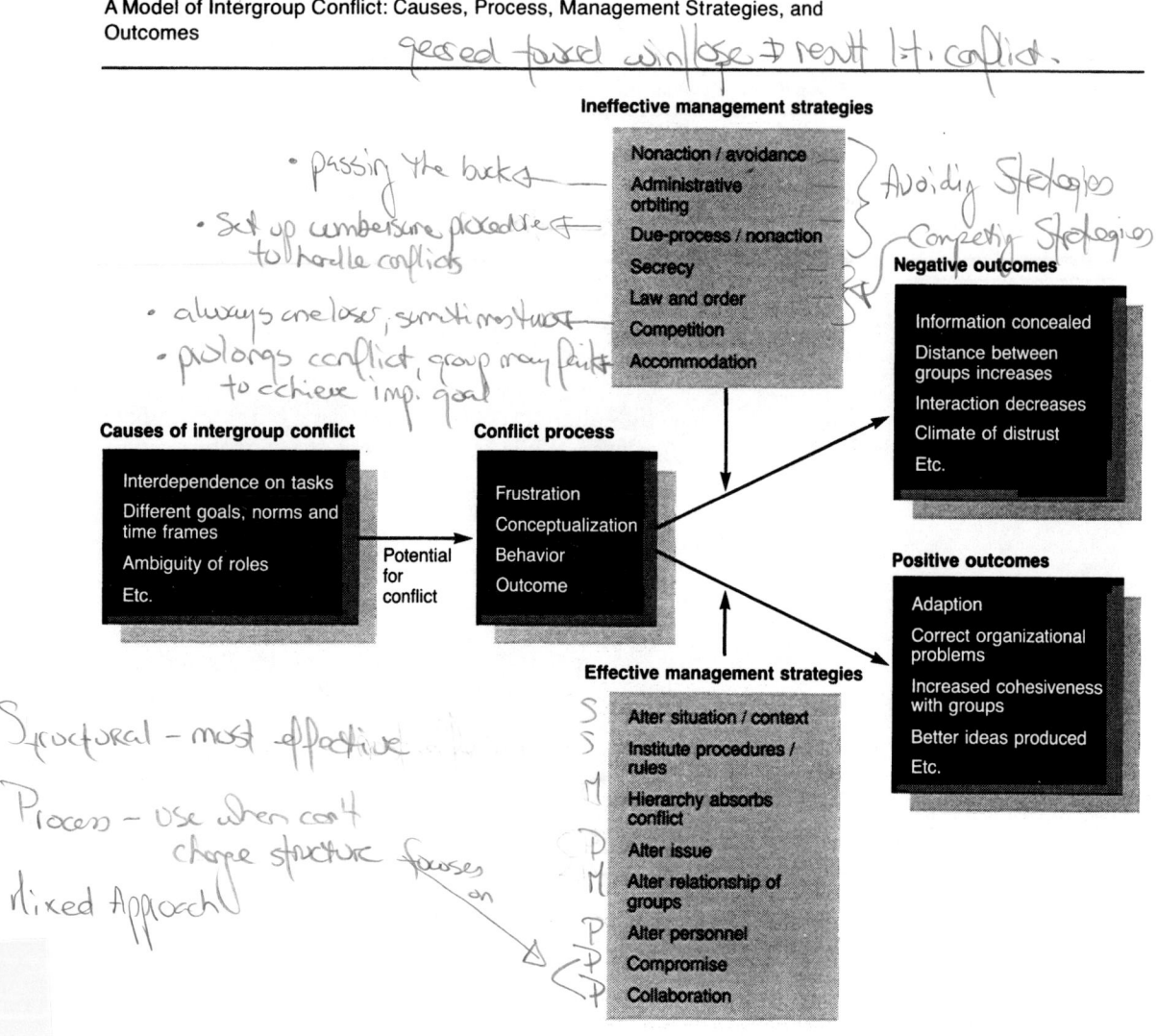

· passing the buck

· Set up cumbersome procedures to handle conflicts

· always one loser, sometimes two

· prolongs conflict, group may fails to achieve imp. goal

Avoiding Strategies

Competing Strategies

Ineffective management strategies

- Nonaction / avoidance
- Administrative orbiting
- Due-process / nonaction
- Secrecy
- Law and order
- Competition
- Accommodation

Negative outcomes

- Information concealed
- Distance between groups increases
- Interaction decreases
- Climate of distrust
- Etc.

Causes of intergroup conflict

- Interdependence on tasks
- Different goals, norms and time frames
- Ambiguity of roles
- Etc.

Potential for conflict

Conflict process

- Frustration
- Conceptualization
- Behavior
- Outcome

Positive outcomes

- Adaption
- Correct organizational problems
- Increased cohesiveness with groups
- Better ideas produced
- Etc.

Effective management strategies

- S — Alter situation / context
- S — Institute procedures / rules
- M — Hierarchy absorbs conflict
- P — Alter issue
- M — Alter relationship of groups
- P — Alter personnel
- P — Compromise
- P — Collaboration

Structural – most effective

Process – use when can't change structure focuses on

Mixed Approach

is more commonly called *buck-passing.* Rather than making a decision, for example, a manager will refer the issue to a higher manager or form a committee to study the situation. As the process continues, the conflict simply goes on unresolved and gradually worsens. **Due-process nonaction** is an extension of administrative orbiting. It involves setting up a procedure for handling conflicts that is so cumbersome or risky that groups are reluctant to use it. Or if groups do use it, they become mired in the details of the process.

Competing strategies. Secrecy and law and order strategies could most easily be classified as competing strategies. They are actions that try to ensure that one group's goals are achieved, even at the expense of another group's goals. Indeed, **secrecy** involves the concealing of information, which was identified as a negative outcome of intergroup conflict. When groups that must work together withhold information from each other, the outcome will at best be win/lose. Over time, the outcome is most likely to be lose/lose and dysfunctional for the organization as a whole. Likewise, the **law and order** strategy is an implementation of the golden rule: "He or she who holds the gold makes the rules." The group with the greatest power will attempt to discredit or stigmatize the other group in the name of organizational security or the status quo. It is also possible on some occasions for a low-power group to use this same strategy to gain the upper hand with a more powerful group, but usually the organization will suffer from this process.

Open competition between two conflicting groups is usually an ineffective strategy because in competition there is at least one loser, and sometimes two. The hostilities that can result from competition often lead to attitudes that create long-lasting problems between groups in an organization.[23] Such negative attitudes and behaviors can become a natural part of the groups involved, lasting far beyond the tenure of the present members of the group. Indeed, the socialization processes for groups can grow to include the establishing of a we-they attitude for new members of each group.

In many ways, the **accommodating** strategy can be almost as bad. This strategy ensures some problems for the group using it and perhaps for the organization as a whole. The accommodating group may fail to achieve a goal that is really just as important to the organization as the goal of another group. And such behavior may be a smoke screen for long-term competitive behavior. Thus, the accommodating strategy only prolongs the conflict and allows it to smolder, only to burst into a raging fire at a later date.

In summary, the ineffective strategies tend to ignore conflicts in hopes they will disappear, or to create win/lose situations. Sometimes these strategies do result in positive outcomes, but usually they only delay the surfacing of conflict and allow it to grow worse without being resolved. Fortunately, there are better alternatives, which are discussed in the following sections.

Effective management strategies

Exhibit 14–8 shows eight effective strategies for managing conflict. **These strategies are effective because they focus on altering the causes of intergroup conflict or on collaboration.**[24] The eight effective strategies in Exhibit 14–8 fall into one of three basic categories: structural, process, and mixed approaches.[25] As we explore the strategies in each category, we must recognize that no strategy works every time.

Structural approaches.   These approaches focus on altering some of the causes of intergroup conflict. The first effective strategy—**alter the situation/context**—is clearly a structural approach. Perhaps goals of the organization and the various groups can be made clearer. Perhaps rewards can be devised to promote intergroup cooperation. Perhaps assigned tasks can be altered so that interdependence is reduced toward the pooled end of the continuum. But probably the simplest way to alter the situation is to help the groups focus on goals they have in common rather than on those where they have conflict. If a common goal can be identified and the goal will last over time, this strategy can go a long way toward bringing intergroup conflict under control. But as Insight 14–5 shows, companies often struggle to maintain the proper balance between coordination and freedom to act. For example, if the sales and production people at Home Computers Company can be made aware of the threats from other computer firms, especially larger more established companies, the goal of beating these competitors could help sales and production work together more effectively.

Another structural strategy is to **institute particular rules and procedures** for handling conflicts that are bound to arise. A good example of such a strategy is a procedure to handle employee grievances. When an employee has a complaint that is not satisfactorily handled by his or her supervisor, the employee and the supervisor know the procedure to follow. Rules serve the same type of function by specifying behaviors that must be carried out by each of the groups involved in a conflict situation. For example, at HCC, rules could be established for setting the lead time sales must give production to fill an order. This should eliminate the fighting over the timing of an order. In the situation of a personal computer manufacturing company, one disadvantage of rules and procedures is that they reduce flexibility and are not easily changed to fit rapidly changing situations. Groups must be careful to use rules and procedures to help manage conflict, rather than let rules become due-process nonaction tools.

Two other structural approaches can be mentioned, but they are clearly less effective and may not be possible in a given situation. First, it may be possible to **separate the groups** so that they need not have much contact. Second, it may be possible to **relocate particular individuals** who are intensifying the intergroup conflict. Transfers, job rotation between groups, and promotions are all possibilities. But as we have discussed, many personality conflicts are much more than that. And by moving people around, managers may only temporarily cover up the **role** conflict.

INSIGHT 14-5

IBM's Plan to Decentralize May Set a Trend—but Imitation Has a Price

Since International Business Machines Corp.'s announcement that it would decentralize its management structure, management consultants have been predicting that other companies will follow.

For many companies, it could be an expensive imitation.

In recent years an increasing number of companies have learned that pushing decision-making down the ranks is a management luxury they can't always afford, especially in a competitive environment. The benefits can be undermined by staff duplication, marketing confusion and out-of-control local units. That's been especially true as companies shed units and return to a single, core business.

Companies have found that small, decentralized sales forces can be inefficient when dealing with large customers.

3M used to sell products like stethoscopes, elastic bandages, scrub brushes and plastic hospital drapes out of two different medical-products divisions. That worked well when individual doctors made buying decisions, because 3M's slew of sales agents could contact each one and tout the products' features.

But when buying decisions began to be made by hospital groups, 3M's decentralized sales strategy became inefficient. Hospitals were more interested in price and bulk purchases, and they preferred buying from one sales representative rather than dealing with sales agents from two divisions.

So the company merged the two divisions in 1984. "We can now offer bundles of products to large hospital groups and have fewer people in the field," says Jerry E. Robertson, executive vice president, life sciences sector.

Another problem with decentralization has arisen when companies find that their units are competing with each other. While that may spur innovation and aggressiveness at some companies, sometimes it leads to confused customers.

Hewlett-Packard, for instance, had at least three autonomous divisions making different—and incompatible—computers aimed at the professional and office markets. "The fact is, those products were being sold competitively against one another by the various divisions," a spokesman says. "Customers were telling us we didn't have a coherent strategy."

Process approaches. Process approaches involve changing the behaviors and attitudes of the members in conflicting groups. These approaches focus on collaboration and compromise. The primary means for accomplishing these changes fall under the approach called **altering the relationship of groups** in Exhibit 14–8. Through confrontation among the groups involved, compromise and/or collaboration can be accomplished. One strategy involves holding direct negotiations between the groups: let them sit down and talk about the problems facing them. Often, such negotiations will also involve a third party who acts as a mediator. And a strategy commonly used by such third parties is called *image exhange*.[26] For example, sales and production at Home Computers Company can get together in a neutral place to work out their differences. Each group member is asked to write down perceptions of his or her own group and of the other group, focusing on both pros and cons. These lists are then shared in an open meeting. Next, the sales and production people return to their separate groups to discuss what they have learned and how they can use this information to improve the relationship between the two departments. The groups then get back together to share and discuss their ideas on how to work together more effectively. The focus in this process is on *beginning* the development of a feeling of collaboration. One half-day or all-day meeting of this sort will not immediately erase the years of conflict behavior between sales and production.

This strategy can lead to another process strategy, which is to **require regular and extended interaction between groups** in order to resolve the conflicts that exist between them. Frequent and regular meetings between sales and production can lead to changes in attitude and behavior that will benefit the company as a whole.

Another process strategy closely related to the two above is to **alter the issue in dispute**.[27] Often when groups are brought together for image exchange, they begin to see the issue of conflict in a different way. The issue of conflict can be broken down into parts and dealt with one part at a time. The hope is to reduce the issue to manageable size. Alternatively, sometimes the issue can be dealt with more effectively if it is expanded. By expanding the conflict issue, it may be possible to find areas of common concern that can serve as the basis for beginning coordination between the groups. For example, sales and production at HCC might define their ordering conflict as a conflict between customer needs and HCC's capabilities. This new definition may make it possible for the groups to agree on a plan to better meet customer needs, without arguing over the timing of orders in relation to production. The objective in expanding or breaking down a conflict is to search for common concerns and manageable conflict issues. Other aspects of altering the issue include removing issues that are a matter of principle and limiting the scope of precedents set in resolving conflicts. In matters of principle and precedent, groups are more likely to hold strongly to their position, since the stakes seem so high. If the stakes in the conflict can be reduced, it is more likely that the desired reduction in conflict will be achieved.

The final process-oriented strategy falls under the **alter-the-people** category. To change attitudes and behaviors, training can equip people to deal more effectively with intergroup conflicts. People can be taught better communication, assertiveness, and negotiating skills. They can also be cross-trained for jobs in both groups. Finally, the groups themselves can also be trained in intergroup team building. Such alteration of the people can be expensive—but then, so is conflict and lack of coordination between groups in an organization.

The key point of process strategies for dealing with intergroup conflict is to accept that the basic causes of conflict cannot be substantially changed and to deal with the reactions of the people involved. Where possible, structural strategies for conflict management are probably the most effective because they deal directly with the causes of conflict. But in some cases, structural changes are not practical, and process changes offer a viable alternative. For example, Harvey might consider reducing the interdependence between sales and production at HCC, or he might expand the size of the common resource pool. But these changes would not be likely, given the nature of the product and the competitiveness of the industry.

Mixed approaches.   Mixed strategies for intergroup conflict management are just that—a mixture of structural and process elements. When the **hierarchy absorbs the conflict** by a manager's decision, the structural aspect of the manager's power and authority to make such a decision comes into play. The manager would have responsibility over both of the conflicting units. But a manager's style in handling the conflict would also enter the process. Such a strategy can be effective in the short run, but to use managers on a long-term basis for this purpose can be dysfunctional to an organization. The use of rules and procedures or some of the other mixed approaches discussed below would be preferable for the long run.

Several mixed approaches fall under the category of **altering the relationship of the groups.** First, the groups can appoint liaison or boundary-spanning people. Such people would provide lateral communications as needed to improve the interactions of the two conflicting groups. Liaison people at HCC could interact daily between sales and production to make sure that both units can respond to customer demands in a timely manner and still maintain cost and quality goals. If the liaison people are versed in both sales and production responsibilities, they effectively keep the channels for coordination open between the two groups.

Second, if the problems between sales and production are more complex, it might be necessary to use a **temporary task force**—that is, a group of people working on the problem to find solutions. Task forces are especially useful when more than three groups are involved in the conflict. For example, if the research and development department was also involved in the conflict between sales and production at HCC, it might be useful to form a task force of people from each group to work on the problem. When the problem is resolved to the point that a liaison or other strategy can handle the coordination, the task force members return to their respective jobs full time. **A task force, then, is a temporary group that deals with the process of solving a coordination problem in an organization.**

Third, if the coordination is extremely difficult, it may be desirable to form a permanent **integrating department.** The integrating department may consist of only one person, or of several people. It would function much like the temporary task force, but it would be viewed as more permanent. The department's sole responsibility would be to enhance the coordination between groups that are by nature in conflict. Integrating departments usually have real authority and responsibility for the groups they work to coordinate. They may report to a manager who is above both of the groups, or they may have an impact on the budgets of the two groups. Either way will give integrating departments some clout, but they must also depend on some intangible factors as well. They must be viewed by the conflicting groups as neutral but also skilled in the specialties of the groups.[28] Further, they must be viewed as having skills which can help the groups achieve the desired goal of coordination. Thus, here is a mixture of the structural aspects of formal assignment and authority and the process elements of skill and impartiality.

In summary then, we have discussed a number of effective strategies for dealing with intergroup conflict. In most cases, the structural approaches will probably be the most effective because they deal directly with the causes of the conflict.[29] Still, the process and mixed approaches can be very effective when they are used properly. But for any of these strategies to be successful, managers will have to analyze the causes of intergroup conflict.[30] Also, they will have to deal with the actors in the conflict. Thus, both behaviors and attitudes must often change in order to manage intergroup conflict and achieve the desired coordination of effort.

CHAPTER HIGHLIGHTS

In this chapter, we have begun to cross over from organizational behavior into what researchers call organization theory. As stated early in the chapter, **understanding intergroup behavior is vital for managers if they are to manage effectively in an organizational context.** The goal of intergroup behavior is to achieve coordination of group efforts so that organizational goals are achieved. The problem is that group goals can become so important to groups that conflict arises between the groups and begins to hurt the organization. The objective here has been to explore why this happens and how to deal effectively with intergroup conflict.

After looking in on Home Computers Company to illustrate intergroup conflict, we discussed **intergroup conflict as the situation where one group attempts to achieve its goals at the expense of another group in the organization.** Furthermore, intergroup conflict is a process consisting of a series of episodes, each made up of four steps: (1) frustration, (2) conceptualization, (3) behavior, and (4) outcome. The outcome of one episode can lead to the frustration that begins the next conflict episode. **Intergroup conflict is a developmental process that builds over time; it also takes time to bring conflict under control.**

To better understand intergroup conflict and how to manage it, we then began exploring a model. First, we looked at eight causes of conflict (shown in Exhibit 14–3), which set up the conditions where conflict is likely. **The primary cause of conflict among groups appears to be the interdependence that is necessary for the groups in doing their tasks.** We discussed three types of task interdependence: pooled, sequential, and reciprocal.

Probably **the second most important cause of conflict is the differentiation that occurs as a result of the specialization among task groups.** The different goal and time orientations, formalities of operation, and interpersonal relationships in various groups create problems in coordinating their efforts without conflict.

Further complicating the matter can be several other causes of conflict—**ambiguity of roles, common limited resources, and reward systems.** If groups are unclear about their responsibilities in relation to those of other groups, coordination efforts become difficult. If people, equipment, and financial resources are also limited, groups can easily feel the need to compete. And often, **reward systems encourage competition by rewarding each group based upon how they perform compared to other groups.**

Finally, we discussed three other causes of conflict. To the extent that there are **communications obstacles** and **differences in status and power** between groups, coordination will be more difficult. And if **group members lack conflict management skills,** the groups will have greater difficulty in their interactions.

Having discussed the causes of conflict, we turned our attention to the potential outcomes of intergroup conflict, as shown in Exhibit 14–6. We talked about **negative outcomes,** such as concealing information, increasing distance between groups, increasing groups' self-interest, decreasing interaction among groups, wasting energy, loss of good people, and the development of a climate of distrust.

Most people are quite familiar with these negative outcomes, but probably less familiar with the **positive outcomes.**

Intergroup conflict can signal that problems exist in the organization and serve as a motivator to correct these problems. Furthermore, intergroup conflict leads to increased cohesiveness within the conflicted groups and can strengthen certain intergroup linkages. It can also encourage adaptation and flexibility in solving problems, and thus lead to better ideas produced by the groups. And intergroup conflict can lead to the identification of power differences among groups in an organization.

What really determines, over time, whether negative or positive outcomes of conflict result, are the strategies people use to manage intergroup relationship. Thus, we next discussed various strategies for managing conflict. We identified three general categories of behavior: win/lose, lose/lose, and win/win. And we further defined five basic strategies based on the degree of cooperativeness and the degree of assertiveness of a group: competing, accommodating, avoiding, collaborating, and compromising.

We then moved to a more specific discussion of both ineffective and effective strategies for managing intergroup conflict, as shown in Exhibit 14–8. The first three ineffective strategies (nonaction/avoidance, administrative orbiting, and due-process nonaction) are basic **avoiding** strategies, which are used in hopes the conflict will go away. The next four (secrecy, law and order, competition, and accommodating) are all basically **competing** strategies. They are geared toward win/lose and usually result in long-run increases in conflict.

As Exhibit 14–8 shows, there are also a number of effective conflict management strategies. **Structural approaches are geared toward altering the causes of conflict.** Managers can alter the situation or context that groups must manage, or they can institute rules and procedures. Managers can also separate groups or transfer particular people to reduce the conflict. The **process approaches are geared toward changing the behaviors and attitudes of the people without changing the situation.** For example, managers can alter the relationships among people through negotiation or confrontation, can alter the issue in dispute, or can train people to handle conflict situations. The third category is a **mixture of structural and process approaches.** For example, the hierarchy can absorb the conflict, liaison or boundary spanner personnel can be appointed, task forces can be formed on a temporary basis, and integrating departments can be put into place.

Structural strategies are probably the most effective, but they may not always be possible. In such cases, the process and mixed approaches can be very effective, if both the behaviors and attitudes of group members are altered. Managers' long-term effectiveness, especially as they move up the corporate ladder, will be enhanced if they become skilled in using strategies that lead to positive outcomes from intergroup conflict.

REVIEW QUESTIONS

1. Why is it important for managers to understand how to manage intergroup conflict and coordination?

2. What is *intergroup conflict,* and why is it a developmental process?

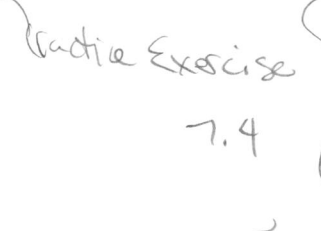

3. How might task interdependence and differentiation together create a great deal of potential for intergroup conflict?

4. How do resources and rewards, as well as status differences, ambiguity of roles and communications obstacles, help to create the potential for intergroup conflict?

5. How are people skills and traits important in the level of conflict that develops between two groups in an organization?·

6. Discuss both negative and positive outcomes to intergroup conflict.

7. How is the ultimate level of intergroup conflict determined? Distinguish among the five categories of conflict behavior that are determined by the levels of cooperativeness and assertiveness that groups exhibit.

8. What are the common factors among the various ineffective conflict management strategies discussed in this chapter?

9. What are the structural approaches to conflict management, and how do they differ from the process approaches? Which ones tend to be more powerful?

10. Why are some approaches to conflict management called *mixed approaches?* What are some of these approaches, and how effective are they?

RESOURCE READINGS

Lawrence, P. R. , and J. W. Lorsch. *Organization and Environment: Managing Differentiation and Integration.* Homewood, Ill.: Richard D. Irwin, 1967.

Likert, R., and J. Likert. *New Ways of Managing Conflict.* New York: McGraw-Hill, 1976.

Miles, R. H. *Macro Organizational Behavior.* Glenview, Ill.: Scott, Foresman, 1980, chap. 5.

Robbins, S. P. *Managing Organizational Conflict: A Nontraditional Approach.* Englewood Cliffs, N.J.: Prentice-Hall, 1974.

Thomas, K. W. "Conflict and Conflict Management." In *Handbook of Industrial and Organizational Psychology,* ed. M. D. Dunnette. Skokie, Ill.: Rand McNally, 1976, pp. 889-935.

Walton, R. E. *Managing Conflict: Interpersonal Dialogue and Third Party Roles.* Reading, Mass.: Addison-Wesley Publishing, 1987.

NOTES

1. P. S. Shockley-Zalabak, "Current Conflict Management Training: An Examination of Practices in Ten Large American Organizations," *Group & Organization Studies* 9 (1984), pp. 491–507.

2. K. W. Thomas, "Conflict and Conflict Management." In *Handbook of Industrial and Organizational Psychology,* ed M. D. Dunnette (Skokie, Ill.: Rand McNally, 1976), pp. 889–935.

3. J. D. Thompson, *Organizations in Action* (New York: McGraw-Hill, 1967).

4. D. Katz and R. L. Kahn, *The Social Psychology of Organizations,* 1st ed. (New York: John Wiley & Sons, 1966).

5. P. R. Lawrence and J. W. Lorsch, *Organization and Environment: Managing Differentiation and Integration* (Homewood, Ill.: Richard D. Irwin, 1967).

6. This paragraph draws primarily from Lawrence and Lorsch, *Organization and Environment.*

7. W. R. Dill, "Environment as an Influence on Managerial Autonomy," *Administrative Science Quarterly* 2 (1958), pp. 409–43.

8. C. Perrow, *Organizational Analysis: A Sociological View* (Belmont, Calif.: Wadsworth, 1970).

9. M. E. Schnake and D. S. Cochran, "Effect of Two Goal-Setting Dimensions on Perceived Intraorganizational Conflict," *Group & Organizational Studies* 10 (1985), pp. 168–83.

10. R. H. Miles, *Macro Organizational Behavior* (Glenview, Ill.: Scott, Foresman, 1980), chap. 5.

11. R. E. Walton, *Managing Conflict: Interpersonal Dialogue and Third Party Roles,* 2d ed. (Reading, Mass.: Addison-Wesley Publishing, 1987).

12. Miles, *Macro Organizational Behavior.*

13. R. E. Jones and C. S. White, "Relationships Among Personality, Conflict Resolution Styles, and Task Effectiveness," *Group & Organization Studies* 10 (1985), pp. 152–67; R. J. Sternberg and L. J. Soriano, "Styles of Conflict Resolution," *Journal of Personality and Social Psychology* 47 (1984), pp. 115–26.

14. R. A. Baron, "Reducing Organizational Conflict: The Role of Attributions," *Journal of Organizational Pyschology* 70 (1985), pp. 434–41.

15. This section draws primarily from R. E. Walton and J. M. Dutton, "The Management of Interdepartmental Conflict: A Model and Review," *Administrative Science Quarterly* 14 (1969), pp. 73–84.

16. S. P. Robbins, *Managing Organizational Conflict: A Nontraditional Approach* (Englewood Cliffs, N.J.: Prentice-Hall, 1974).

17. The following section draws primarily from Miles, *Macro Organizational Behavior,* chap. 5.

18. L. Greenhalgh, "Managing Conflict," *Sloan Management Review,* Summer 1986, pp. 45–52; M. A. Rahim, "A Strategy for Managing Conflict in Complex Organizations," *Human Relations* 38 (1985), pp. 81–89; B. J. Hill,

"An Analysis of Conflict Resolution Techniques: From Problem-Solving Workshops to Theory," *Journal of Conflict Resolution* 26 (1982), pp. 109–38.

19. A. Filley, *Interpersonal Conflict* (Glenview, Ill.: Scott, Foresman, 1975).

20. K. Thomas, "Conflict and Conflict Management"; W. A. Randolph and B. Z. Posner, *Effective Project Planning and Management: Getting the Job Done* (Englewood Cliffs, N.J.: Prentice-Hall, 1988), chap. 8.

21. R. R. Reck and B. G. Long, *The Win-Win Negotiator* (Escondido, Calif.: Blanchard Training and Development, 1985).

22. Miles, *Macro Organizational Behavior.*

23. G. A. Youngs, Jr., "Patterns of Threat and Punishment Reciprocity in a Conflict Setting," *Journal of Personality and Social Psychology* 51 (1986), 541–46.

24. This section draws largely from Miles, *Macro Organizational Behavior*, and R. Likert and J. G. Likert, *New Ways of Managing Conflict* (New York: McGraw-Hill, 1976).

25. D. A. Nadler, J. R. Hackman, and E. E. Lawler III, *Managing Organizational Behavior* (Boston: Little, Brown, 1979).

26. E. H. Schein, *Organizational Psychology,* 2d ed. (Englewood Cliffs, N.J.: Prentice-Hall, 1970).

27. Miles, *Macro Organizational Behavior.*

28. P. R. Lawrence and J. W. Lorsch, "New Management Job: The Integrator," *Harvard Business Review* 45 (1967), pp. 142–51.

29. Nadler, Hackman, and Lawler, *Managing Organizational Behavior.*

30. H. Prein, "A Contingency Approach for Conflict Intervention," *Group & Organization Studies* 9 (1984), pp. 81–102.

CASE: Winthrop Hospital

Winthrop Hospital is located in a medium-sized suburban community. A general hospital, it serves a large portion of the surrounding area and is usually operating at, near, or sometimes beyond its capacity. Each floor of the hospital has its own particular structure with regard to the nurses who staff it. This formalized hierarchy runs from the supervisor (who must be a registered nurse) to registered nurses (RNs) to licensed practical nurses (LPNs) to students and nurses' aides. Professionally, there are some duties that are supposed to be performed only by the RNs; these are spelled out in the hospital manual. In practice, however, the LPNs do much of the work that is supposed to be done by the RNs. The RNs are glad for the help because they are very busy with other duties. Through time the work done by the RNs and the LPNs has meshed so thoroughly that one just does the work without thinking of whose job it is supposed to be. The hospital is normally so

Source: T. Kolakowski in S. J. Carroll, *The Management Process,* 2d ed. (New York: MacMillan Publishing Co., Inc., 1977), pp. 429–31.

crowded that, even with everyone performing all types of work, there never seems to be enough time or enough help.

The procedural manual used at Winthrop Hospital was first used in 1947 and has not been revised. Everyone connected with the hospital realizes that it is extremely outdated, and actual practice varies so greatly as to have no similarity to what is prescribed in the manual. Even the courses that the student nurses take teach things entirely differently from what is prescribed in Winthrop's manual.

The vacation privileges for nurses at the hospital show extreme differences for the different types of nurse. RNs receive two weeks' vacation after nine months on the job, whereas LPNs must be on the staff for ten years before receiving their second week of vacation. The LPNs believe this to be extremely unfair and have been trying to have the privileges somewhat more equalized. Their efforts have met with little cooperation and no success. The hospital superiors have simply told them that the terms for vacation are those stated in the hospital manual and that they saw no need to change them.

Some of the individual nurses at Winthrop then began to take matters into their own hands. The LPNs on the fourth floor of the hospital decided that if they couldn't have the extra vacation because of what was written in the manual then they would follow the manual in all phases and go strictly according to the book. Difficulties surfaced as soon as the LPNs began to behave in this manner. The RNs now seemed to have more work than they could handle adequately and the LPNs were just as busy doing solely their ".prescribed" duties. The same amount of effort put forth previously was being exerted, but less was being accomplished because of the need to jump around from place to place and job to job in order to work strictly according to the book. An example of this wasted effort occurred in the taking of doctors' orders. Doctors phone in the type of treatment that a patient is to receive—medicines, times for dispensing such, diet, and so forth. These doctors' orders are supposed to be taken by an RN, but in practice whoever was nearest the phone had taken the order. If an LPN took the order she had it signed by the supervisor (stationed at the desk) as a safeguard. This procedure saved the time and effort involved in getting an RN to the phone for every order. Now, however, the LPNs refused to take the doctors' orders and called for an RN. The RN had to leave the work she was doing, go to the phone, take the order, then go back to her unfinished work. This procedure wasted the time of the doctors, the RN, and the LPN who had to locate the RN. The LPNs' practice of going by the book brought about hostile feelings among both groups of nurses and among the doctors who had to work on the floor. The conflicts led to a lessening in the high degree of care that the patients had been receiving.

The conflict initiated by the difference in vacation privileges brought about more complaints from both parties. In the manual the categories for vacation privileges listed: "supervisors," "RNs," "lab technicians," and "others." The LPNs resented being placed in the "others" category. They felt that they deserved a separate listing, especially because they had the same amount of training as other groups, such as the lab technicians. Adding further fuel to the fire was the fact that the lab technicians got a second week of vacation after only one year on the job. Another item of controversy was the fact that RNs were allowed to sign themselves in on the job when they reported, whereas the LPNs were required to punch in. The LPNs felt that the RNs thus could hide any incidents of lateness, whereas the LPNs had strict account kept of their time and were docked in salary for any time missed.

The RNs now complained to the hospital superiors more vehemently than ever about being understaffed. They felt that they simply needed more RNs on every floor on every shift to meet what was required of them; this was a demand they had been voicing even before the conflict began. The shortage was especially acute at nights, when unfamiliarity with individual patients often led to mix-ups in the treatments.

The ill feelings led to arguments among the nurses. The LPNs felt that they were always doing more work than the RNs, that they spent more time with the patients because the RNs had more to do at the desk, and that they knew more about treatments because they more often accompanied doctors on their rounds. They now voiced these opinions. The RNs argued superiority on the basis of a longer period of formal training.

All these factors combined to bring about a tremendous drop in morale and a marked decrease in efficiency, and the conflict was in danger of spreading to the other floors in the hospital.

Questions

1. Why is there such conflict between these groups?
2. What are the consequences of this conflict?
3. What might be done to alleviate the problem?

EXERCISE: Win as much as you can

Directions: Your class will be divided into organizations consisting of four groups each. Groups should range from four to six people. For 12 successive rounds, you and your group will choose and record in the "choice" column either an "X" or a "Y". The instructor will ask you to announce your group's choice after each round. You are to confer with your group on each round and make a joint decision. Before rounds 5, 8, and 10, you confer with the other groups in your organization, then with your group for the final choice. The "pay-off" for each round is dependent upon the pattern of choices made by the four groups in your organization. You are not to talk to people in other groups unless given specific permission to do so. The objective of the exercise is to win as much as you can.

Payoff Matrix for the Four Groups in Each Organization

| 4 Xs: Lose $1 each |
| 3 Xs: Win $1 each
1 Y : Lose $3 each |
| 2 Xs: Win $2 each
2 Ys: Lose $2 each |
| 1 X : Win $3 each
3 Ys: Lose $1 each |
| 4 Ys: Win $1 each |

Round	Strategy Time Allowed	Confer with	Choice	$ Won	$ Lost	$ Balance	
1	2 mins.	group					
2	1 min.	group					
3	1 min.	group					
4	1 min.	group					
5	3 mins. + 1 min.	organization group					Bonus round: pay-off is multiplied by 3
6	1 min.	group					
7	1 min.	group					
8	3 mins. + 1 min.	organization group					Bonus round: pay-off is multiplied by 5
9	1 min.	group					
10	3 mins. + 1 min.	organization group					Bonus round: pay-off is multiplied by 10
11	1 min.	group					
12	3 mins. + 1 min.	organization group					Bonus round: pay-off is multiplied by 20

Source: Adapted from W. Gellermann in J. W. Pfeiffer and J. E. Jones, *A Handbook of Structured Experiences for Human Relations Training—Vol. II.* La Jolla, Calif.: University Associates, 1974, pp. 62–67.

Joe Johnson: Production Foreman

Joe Johnson started work at the plant right after leaving school. The town was small and did not offer much opportunity for employment to a young man 17 years of age seeking his first job. Furthermore, the economic picture in the country was poor, and it was no time to do anything but grasp whatever kind of work came along and hold on tight. What came along for Joe was a chance to join one of the loading crews at the factory. He quit school before graduation in order to be sure the opportunity did not slip through his fingers. His father, who had worked in the maintenance department at the plant practically since it started up, felt it would be best for Joe to take the job. Also, several of Joe's friends who were already employed on the same crew urged him to join them.

Although the loading-crew jobs were usually considered starting positions from which people moved into production as openings occurred, this particular crew remained almost intact for a number of years. Characteristically, when a promotion was offered to a young man in the crew, he would turn it down, indicating that he preferred to stay with his present group. Joe was no exception. He declined three offers of better-paying jobs before finally moving to a production unit, and even then he accepted the transfer only because his crew was being broken up. Unfortunately, he had hardly started his new work when orders arrived for him to report for military service.

Four years passed before Joe returned to his home town to stay. He turned up at the plant personnel office several days later. A few questions brought out the facts that he wanted to return to his old job, that he had married a local woman while home on leave, and that he was very glad to be home. Military service had been all right, but he preferred the friends he had grown up with to the hodgepodge of people

Source: J. B. Miner, *Organizational Behavior: Performance and Productivity* (New York: Random House, 1988), pp. 285–88.

from everywhere that he had been exposed to in the Army. His service record was satisfactory, although he had never risen above the rank of corporal. There was little question about his being given a job. Legal requirements regarding the reemployment of returning veterans were of course important, but in addition his previous employment record carried the notation, "A willing employee, completing all work promptly with a minimum of errors; has done a commendable job." Everyone was glad to have him back.

The years that followed were relatively uneventful. Several of the boys from the old loading crew went away to college on the GI bill. Some took higher-paying jobs in the city, although many of them eventually drifted back to the plant. Joe held on tight to what he had and stayed with the people who understood him. He was well thought of and well liked, and it was obvious that he enjoyed his friends at work and his family. There were occasional opportunities to work elsewhere—both outside the plant and with other groups within—but none were sufficiently attractive to Joe.

As time went by, Joe accumulated more and more seniority. With his service years added in, he began to develop a real stake in his job. He talked about this a lot: the fact that he was an old-timer, that he remembered how things used to be, and that he had stayed with the gang through thick and thin. Gradually, opportunities to take increased responsibility arose. The foreman was often away because of conferences, illness, or vacations. It was traditional that the senior person take over in his absence. Joe was that person. He was never formally selected, and in fact, the superintendent was not even consulted. It had just always been done that way.

However, when the foreman rather suddenly took a disability retirement, a more formal decision had to be made with regard to a replacement. Several candidates were considered, but Joe Johnson obviously had the inside track. It would be hard to turn him down. He knew the work, had had supervisory experience as an alternate to the foreman, and, perhaps most important, was popular throughout the plant. The combination of seniority, experience, and popularity was hard to argue against. If Joe was not selected, a number of people—especially the old-timers—might be rather unhappy. There was little point in running the risk of stirring them up. After all, Joe probably was the best person for the job. The appointment went through without a hitch.

The work continued much as before. The new foreman seemed to be doing all right; at least, there was no trouble from his group. Grievances and disciplinary actions were in fact at an all-time low. The unit was overstaffed according to company standards for the type of work done, but so were a number of other groups in the plant. Also, breakdowns seemed to be rather frequent. However, that could not be considered Joe's fault. The equipment was old and the maintenance department overworked. Nobody could break any production records with that kind of a situation. Yet it was because of the maintenance problem that the trouble started.

Late one afternoon a maintenance foreman, who had a reputation as a good "management man" and also as one of Joe Johnson's least ardent admirers, reported a strange situation to his boss. He and his crew had been working on the equipment again and finished up in Joe's area about mid-afternoon. But the operators were nowhere in sight. A check of the time cards indicated that the three men were in the plant, although nobody seemed to know where at the moment. Joe said he would take care of it and tell the men what the maintenance crew had done when they were located. When the maintenance foreman went through the area an hour later to get some parts, the three men were still not there, although they were still punched in.

An informal check was made just before five o'clock and the three men were clearly not in evidence. Yet their time cards were punched out as of quitting time. Joe was called on the carpet the next morning. He had very little to say. The men must have been around the plant somewhere. Things had been pretty hectic the preceding afternoon, and he had not had time to look for them. No, they had not checked with him before leaving the area, but he had had to be off the floor several times early in the afternoon. No, he had not seen them check out at five.

One of the three workers, however, was less reticent. When the breakdown occurred and the maintenance people were called, he said, he and the other two workers had washed up, gone out the gate, and stopped at a bar down the street for a beer. They just had not made it back by quitting time. With this start the rest of the story could be pieced together rather easily. Apparently the foreman had not seen his three men leave, but when their absence became evident he had done nothing to find them. Presumably he knew from past experience where they were. He had asked the others to work a little harder so that the absences would not show up in the production figures. This had been done. At first it was not completely clear who had punched the men out at quitting time. However, by a process of elimination the field was narrowed down to two men, one of whom was Joe. A second period of questioning brought a confession. Yes, he had been the one.

Further investigation unearthed a number of similar instances. One man who had frequently arrived at work under the influence of alcohol on Monday mornings only to be sent home had never lost any pay because of these episodes, a fact which he himself found hard to understand. Apparently his time card had always been turned in to indicate a full day's work. Another man whose absenteeism was so excessive as to make continued employment questionable suddenly started working very steadily—at least, on the record. However, questioning indicated little change in his actual behavior. The company was obviously paying for a good deal of work that was not being performed. A decision was tentatively reached to discharge Joe Johnson for inability to fulfill the requirements of his job.

When this conclusion was told to Joe, he launched into a long and impassioned plea for "just one more chance." He was in debt, his youngest child was sick, and his father, who had retired from the company just over a year before, had been ill for several months. The effect of his discharge on the father's condition might be drastic. But there was more to be taken into account that just his personal problems. For one thing, he had not intended to do anything wrong, but only to protect the gang so they would not get in trouble. The gang was likely to be rather unhappy if he tried to take action in cases like this. It seemed best not to stir them up. In the end it was easier to punch the time cards for them and forget the whole thing. There was less trouble that way, and anyhow it was a good thing for a foreman to remain popular with his people. By the time he had finished, Joe had created the impression that he had not only exhibited admirable loyalty to his group but also had done the company a good turn by keeping the workers happy and morale at a high level. Even the superintendent felt a little sorry for him.

Questions

1. How do you feel about Joe Johnson and his behavior? Was what he did right? Was it in the company's interest? Was it the way a supervisor should behave?

2. What exactly are the group factors that produced Joe's performance problems? Do you think these are common sources of difficulty for managers?

3. Is there any evidence that the company might have been in part responsible for the situation that developed? If so, how?

4. What factors other than the direct group influences can you identify as contributing to Joe's difficulties? Were any individual factors operating, for instance?

5. If you were faced with making the decision in Joe's case, what would you do? Why?

6. It is clear that the superintendent felt sorry for Joe. Would you tend to feel the same way? If so, do you think this feeling might have influenced the decision you indicated in your response to question 5?

A Developmental Framework for Studying Organizations

DYNAMIC ENVIRONMENTAL INFLUENCES

Past	Present	Future
Change	**Organizations** Environments Goals/Effectiveness Structure Design Development	Change
Develop	**Work Groups** Structure Processes Cohesion Groupthink Intergroup Behavior	Develop
Evolve	**Interpersonal Relationships** Leadership Power Politics Communications	Evolve
Grow	**Individuals** Perception Learning Attitudes Values Personality Motivation Outcomes	Grow

PART FIVE

Organizations and Their Environments

*T*hus far, we have examined organizational behavior from a number of different perspectives. We started our discussion with the individual, since organizational behavior is about the attitudes and behaviors of people in organizations. We moved on to consider people interacting with others and the nature of the relationships that develop between people in organizations. One set of relatively permanent relationships are those that develop around work groups. That was the topic of the third part of this book. Then we considered the processes and relationships that arise as work groups interact in an organization.

We have one last perspective on organizations to discuss. This perspective has been given a number of labels: macro organizational behavior and organization theory, to name two. This final perspective looks at an organization as a whole. That is, we assume that people and work groups are givens, and now we are interested in looking at the bigger picture of the whole organization in relationship to other organizations and to the organization's environment.

To do this effectively, we need to understand the *context* in which organizations operate. In Chapter 15, we explore the ways in which elements of the *external* and the *internal environments* affect a firm. In Chapter 16, we examine the role of goals in organizations and investigate a number of different kinds of goals. We also consider some ways to determine how well an organization is doing.

Organizations structure and adapt themselves in response to a variety of factors that change, evolve, and develop over time, including environments and goals. Chapters 17 and 18 discuss how organizations are structured. This part of the text concludes with discussion of organizational change and development in Chapter 19. We examine the change process and methods for making these changes.

Organizational Environments: External and Internal

T his chapter looks at an organization's environments, both external *and* internal. **The external environment refers to factors outside the boundaries of an organization, while the internal environment refers to factors within organizational boundaries.**

The external environment comprises **sectors** or areas of potential interest for an organization. And each sector changes at different rates for different organizations. Two dimensions describe the external environment more succinctly: **complexity** and **stability.** The nature of each dimension determines the uncertainty of an organization's environment. This chapter examines different levels of environmental uncertainty and discusses how organizations can respond to it.

Of equal importance to an organization is top management's ability to anticipate what might happen in the environment in the future. With environments changing so rapidly, organizations can no longer be content to simply react to changes. Survival and success require the effective management of the environment. Thus, this chapter considers a number of strategies available for **proacting with** rather than **reacting to** the environment.

Finally, we examine the internal environment: the **corporate culture.** We consider what corporate culture is, how it develops, and how it can be maintained or changed. Let's start by checking in with Harvey Brown of Home Computers Company on his way into the office.

Home Computers Case

Home Computers Company and Its Environments

Harvey Brown, President of HCC, was making good time on his drive to the office. This was a good sign. He usually spent an hour a day tied up in expressway traffic. To pass the time, Harvey would listen to a local radio station or to some classical music on the cassette player. Unlike some people, Harvey found commuting a good time to think—particularly about what was happening at HCC. His days were busy, and he rarely had time at the office to think about long-range or strategic problems.

But now, tail lights flashed in front of him, and he slowly pumped his brakes. Harvey knew that he would have more time for thinking today. Unlike some of the drivers who were leaning on their horns and shouting at no one in particular, Harvey refused to let traffic jams get him upset and frustrated. In the bigger scheme of things, honking, swearing at other drivers, and beating on the steering wheel made no difference. The radio station was playing a set of songs from the 70s. And the music brought back a rush of memories.

When Harvey and his cousin Bill Adams founded HCC back in the mid-70s, they did so on a wing and a prayer. Were it not for the financial assistance of Mr. Hearn, HCC would probably have gone the way of many other small computer companies that had started up in those heady days set off by Apple Computer Company.

But survive they did, and Harvey thought of how the company had grown from a garage production facility to a multimillion dollar corporation with three divisions, two plants, a national salesforce, and some 800 employees. Getting there had not been easy. Both Harvey and Bill had paid a price, personally and professionally. Bill was no longer with the firm; and the major decisions now belonged to Harvey.

The personal computer industry had been through some rough times. Foreign competition, inflated market projections, nonexistent cost controls, and, in some cases, just plain bad management had forced many companies out of business. But the industry seemed to be on the rebound, and Harvey would soon have to make some substantial decisions—decisions about adding a new production facility, restructuring the organization for quicker responses to change, and entering the growing market of network systems.

With red tail lights flashing ahead, Harvey tuned the car radio to the all-news station. In the 20 minutes it took to reach his exit, Harvey heard at least a half a dozen news stories that directly or indirectly could have an impact on HCC. One of his major competitors just announced a new line of PCs built around a more powerful chip. There was a story about a possible computer chip shortage. In Switzerland, a team of scientists had developed yet another new superconducting alloy. If it could be manufactured commercially, it would eventually place the power of a mainframe computer on the desk of every employee. Congress was considering legislation aimed at increasing levels of mandatory employee benefits. (In fact, Harvey had just spent time the day before with his vice president of personnel, discussing with her the implications of a parental leave program.) And the ongoing tragedies of drugs, alcoholism, and AIDS reported in the news touched firms like HCC in a number of ways: employee selection, drug testing, employee-assistance programs, and insurance rate hikes. The list of events that could affect HCC seemed endless.

This laundry list of possible problems stood in stark contrast to the earlier, simpler years. Bill and Harvey's only concerns then were finding enough solder and one or two buyers for their first machines. How the environment had changed—and so quickly! Harvey found himself wondering how well HCC had responded to those changes. Did the firm spend too much time *reacting* to changes and not enough time *anticipating* them? What should HCC be doing to take advantage of opportunities in the environment while not letting unanticipated problems overwhelm the company?

And what of the internal environment at HCC? Harvey pulled into a parking space at corporate headquarters. For all HCC employees, parking was on a first-come, first-served basis, regardless of position or rank. This was one of the elements of corporate culture—or at least that's what the reporter on the radio had said. The reporter had been talking to a consultant about corporate culture, and how it might have a bottom-line impact for companies. Harvey used to think that corporate culture was one of those management fads that spring up every so often. But culture seemed to have some substance, and Harvey made a mental note to give the corporate culture at HCC some added thought.

For now, it was time to take a deep breath and plunge into the day's activities.

ORGANIZATIONS AS SYSTEMS

Harvey's firm has come a long way since he and Bill put together the first EZ1. In those days, they were like the crafters of colonial times. Years ago, products and services were supplied primarily by individual artisans who were not particularly concerned about the environment. The resources they needed were usually available—for example, in the nearby forests for the cabinetmaker. There was little to fear in the way of government interference. The technology used to produce the products was relatively straightforward, and there was little need for major financial expenditures. A collection of guilds maintained the appropriate number of artisans, minimizing competition. And since the market was limited to the local area, an extensive distribution system was not necessary.

However, as consumer demand outstripped the artisans' capabilities, larger organizations appeared. Using elaborate and expensive technologies, these firms increased output to meet the increased demand. Scientific management techniques and assembly lines increased the supply of goods to customers in an ever-expanding market. Initially, researchers interested in how organizations operated tended to view firms as larger versions of the individual artisan. These organizations were seen as **closed systems, operating so that their environments had little impact on their activities.** This perspective viewed organizations as comprising three major subsystems: an input subsystem, a throughput subsystem, and an output subsystem.[1] This closed system was assumed to exist in a relative vacuum, so that few, if any, outside forces could disrupt operations.

As organizations grew larger and their environments more complex, it became unrealistic to describe them as closed systems. A different perspective was needed to understand what went on in expanded organizations. This perspective viewed the organization as an **open sys-**

EXHIBIT 15–1

Closed and Open System Perspectives

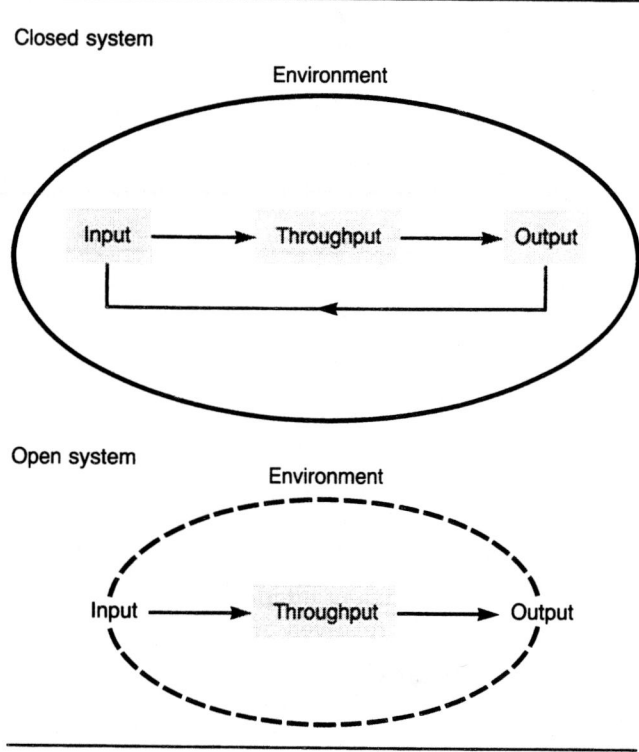

Closed system

Open system

tem. **The open-systems approach suggested that managers could no longer ignore their environments.** The environment affected all the major subsystems in their organizations.[2] Exhibit 15–1 suggests the differences between the closed and open systems views of organizations.

Aspects of the environment become relatively more or less important as organizations evolve over time. New organizations are more concerned about acquiring financial resources than are older, more established firms, for instance. Older firms with substantial investments in existing technologies are more sensitive to changing technologies in their industries. Large firms pay added attention to actions by legislative bodies or to the rulings of regulatory agencies because their large size makes these firms more visible to these governmental entities.

Viewing organizations as open systems means managers must be more aware of their environment. The next section examines the nature of the external environment.

THE EXTERNAL ENVIRONMENT

A firm's **external environment includes factors that exist outside the formal boundaries of an organization with the potential to impact the organization.**[3] As a manager once defined it in an executive development course, "The environment is what's out there."

Why should managers be concerned about the external environment? What do these environments do to or for an organization? In general, organizations interact with their external environments in three ways:[4]

1. The external environment **makes demands** on organizations to supply the goods and services that customers or clients wish to purchase.

2. The external environment **imposes constraints** on the way organizations can meet these demands through legislation, judicial decisions, and social norms.

3. The external environment **provides opportunities** for organizations that have positioned themselves advantageously.

To help us understand the external environment, we can divide it into the primary environment and the secondary environment.[5] The **primary environment includes areas that influence an organization most directly,** including human, financial, and material resources; and technology, industry, and customer sectors. The **secondary environment includes areas that are more likely to influence an organization indirectly:** the government/political, economic, and cultural/demographic sectors. A note of caution: While making distinctions between primary and secondary environments will help to clarify our discussion, at times the different sectors may seem part of both environments. Exhibit 15–2 illustrates how these different sectors impact the various organizational subsystems.

Sectors in the primary environment

The **primary environment includes three resource sectors (human, financial, and material); the technology sector; the industry sector; and the customer sector.** These sectors have a more direct effect on the input, throughput, and output subsystems of an organization than sectors in the secondary environment. Let's examine each of these sectors in more detail.

Human resources sector

Many corporate CEOs argue that the key to the success of any organization is the people. If a company can't attract, hire, and retain qualified people, it will have difficulty supplying sufficient products and services

EXHIBIT 15–2

Environmental Sectors and Their Impact on Organizational Systems

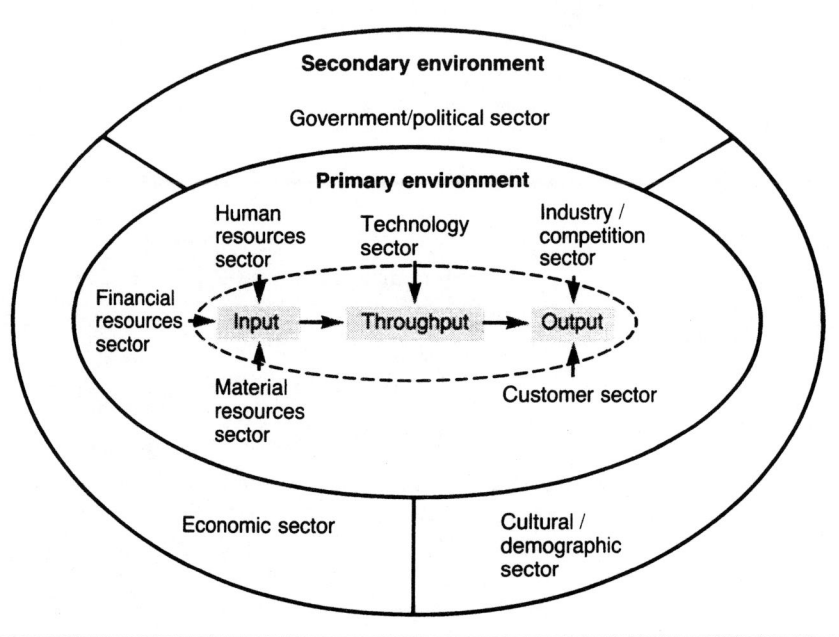

at profitable levels. The nature of the human resources sector will also influence a firm's recruitment, selection, and training programs. It will affect the level of compensation needed to attract, motivate, and maintain quality employees. As the excerpt in Insight 15–1 illustrates, the market collapse of October 19, 1987, made business students wary of working on Wall Street and more available to other types of firms.

Financial resources sector

Another primary external sector revolves around the financial resources available to a firm. Availability of credit at relatively attractive interest rates can fuel an organization's growth. Lack of such resources can retard development, forcing it to redirect its strategic planning, or even driving it into bankruptcy.

At Home Computers Company, the major cash infusion from Mr. Hearn allowed the fledgling company to survive the early years. Larger, well-established organizations can usually raise funds in the stock or bond markets or through lines of credit at financial institutions. Smaller,

I N S I G H T 15-1

For Many Business Students Wall Street Loses a Lot of Its Magic

On a recent trip to the University of Pennsylvania's Wharton School, First Boston Corp. recruiters could fill only a third of a 300-seat amphitheater they had packed just a few months earlier.

The next day 175 prospective M.B.A.s crammed into a 100-seat room to hear accountant Touche Ross & Co. make a pitch for its consulting division.

The Class of '88 has met the Crash of '87—and the result is that many of the nation's premier business students are turning their backs on Wall Street.

Of course, Wall Street is also turning its back on the students, as Black Monday and the ensuing layoffs have cut sharply into the number of jobs available to new M.B.A.s. But there's more to it than that. Many business students look at the turmoil on Wall Street and see an insecure future they prefer to avoid. Moreover, the October debacle has brought to the surface issues students dismissed when times were good; now, they frequently voice concerns about the prospect of 18-hour days and the idea that they could be nothing more than asset shufflers.

Banner year

As a result, students are increasingly turning to big consulting firms, commercial banks, service companies and even once-moribund manufacturers. "The Fords and Exxons and Eli Lillys are looking for 1988 to be the banner year in which they once again get their share of the best and the brightest," says James Beirne, Wharton's placement director.

Until last October students didn't have to concern themselves with worries about job

security or reduced pay packages. Now they do. Sajan K. Thomas, a 26-year-old Wharton student, recently took a job with an investment division of Prudential Insurance Co., working on leveraged buy-outs and private placements. "Prudential is a rock in more ways than one," he says. "I feel very confident that if there were a major recession, I wouldn't have to worry about my job."

Similarly, at Stanford University, students are worried that "something else like Oct. 19 could happen," says Elizabeth Meyer, director of the school's career management center. Four of five Stanford business school students offered Wall Street jobs so far have rejected them. And some students, put off by forecasts of further layoffs on the Street, are simply skipping their investment firm interviews.

Meanwhile, other students aren't even signing up for them. These future M.B.A.s share the opinion, long voiced on "Main Street," that Wall Street is obsessed with money for money's sake, and that deal making has become an end in itself—and not a desirable end, either.

Many students are shunning Wall Street for opportunities that will teach them to run a company, not just finance it.

Harvey Packer of Wharton, for instance, entered graduate school seriously interested in investment banking. Now the 28-year-old is bent on operations management or consulting for a manufacturer. "There's something about making a tangible product, something that you can get your arms around," says Mr. Packer, who's interviewing with 16 consulting firms and eight manufacturers.

In another instance, Maria Bettino, a 25-year-old Columbia M.B.A. candidate, grew disillusioned with investment banking after working last summer for Merrill Lynch. "You become a technician," she says. "I like the idea of being able to run a company and

newer companies are often forced to seek financing from venture capitalists who invest in infant organizations in hopes of gaining major returns once the companies become successful.

Material resources sector

This primary external sector includes all the sources that a firm counts on for the raw materials and component parts it uses to produce its products or services. For some organizations, like social service agencies or hospitals, people are the raw materials for the services provided. For most firms, however, materials or parts come from a variety of sources. Also, as these inputs change in relative importance to the organization, so will the relative importance of the source. At HCC, Harvey and Bill looked to Texas Instruments as the key supplier of the computer chips that went into the earliest versions of the EZ1. As chip technology changed, HCC changed suppliers, getting most of their new chips from Intel or Motorola.

In 1988, a booming personal computer (PC) market, trade restrictions, and an earthquake that damaged a major Japanese dynamic random access memory (DRAM) computer chip maker forced Sun Microsystems and Daisy Systems Corporation to reduce production levels on products using these chips. But bad news for some in the environment can be good news for others in the same environment. Micron Technology, one of the two U.S. makers of the needed chips, was inundated with orders and planned to expand its manufacturing capacity.[6]

Technology sector

The technology sector includes the methods, techniques, and knowledge needed to produce an organization's products and services. Ford Motor Company uses an assembly-line technology to produce automobiles, for instance. Volvo and Saab use a work group-oriented technology to produce their automobiles.[7] Having a proprietary right to certain knowledge can also mean tremendous rewards to the lucky firm. Insight 15–2 (p. 614) describes the benefits that Johnson & Johnson will likely reap from their Retin-A anti-wrinkling skin cream.

The nature of an organization's technology (or technologies, since many firms use more than one) will influence and be influenced by the human, financial, and material sectors. Education levels of employees must match the sophistication of the technology. Changes in technology often require sizable financial resources to buy new machinery. General Motors, for instance, has spent $2 billion to develop new approaches to producing cars at its Selma, Tennessee, facility.[8]

Organizations must constantly scan this sector for potential changes in technologies. Failure to keep abreast of major technological changes can have dramatic consequences for a firm. The decline of the American steel industry in the late 70s was due, in part, to the industry's unwillingness to invest in new steel producing technologies.[9] Misuse of technologies or adoption of new technologies without thoughtful analyses can also prove costly. Many large corporations believed the use of robots would be a way to save many millions of dollars in labor costs. These corporations invested heavily in these mechanical employees who didn't take coffee breaks. Unfortunately, the software needed to make the robots effective in the workplace had not yet caught up with the hardware. Companies were left with noncoffee-drinking robots, able to perform only the simplest of tasks.[10]

Industry sector

The basic element in this sector is the nature of a firm's competition. Characteristics of the industry can influence the design of a firm's distribution system, for instance. The fast-food industry chains establish many outlets so that customers will not have to travel too far for "good food for fast times." And these chains constantly monitor their competition to determine if new menu items should be added. Like the fast-food industry, the computer industry is extremely competitive, with a few large participants and a number of smaller ones. Smaller firms in both industries have been quite successful in providing products to customers that the larger organizations have chosen to ignore.

For instance, as MacDonald's, Burger King, and Wendy's expanded their menus and raised the prices of their products, firms like PD Quix attracted customers by doing now what the Big Three used to do: providing basic hamburgers in a spartan facility at prices lower than the competition. Despite its size, HCC became successful by offering personal computers that could be expanded with many options, and that could communicate with nearly every other PC on the market. Apple Computer's early machines were not nearly so flexible, and this strategy cost them a major share of the PC market. Succeeding generations of machines have been far more open.[11]

Anti-Wrinkle Cream Gives Maker's Sales a Rosy Complexion

J ohnson & Johnson's Fountain of Youth—its Retin-A anti-wrinkle cream—appears to be overflowing.

First-quarter sales already have exceeded expectations for all of 1988, industry analysts say. Larry Feinberg of Drexel Burnham Lambert Inc. said sales of Retin-A will be $50 million to $60 million in the first quarter—his original estimate for the full year. As a result, he raised his 1988 sales projections to between $180 million and $200 million.

Last year, sales were just $38 million for Retin-A, a Vitamin A compound approved for treating acne, yet effective as an anti-wrinkle agent.

"Clearly this is a much bigger product than we expected," said Mr. Feinberg. "This could be an initial surge that will level out. Still, I'm raising my 1989 projections from $100 million to $250 million" for Retin-A.

The analyst also will boost his estimate of the New Brunswick, N.J.-based health-care-products maker's 1988 per-share earnings to $5.70 from $5.55. He adds that Retin-A could contribute 40 cents to 50 cents a share to 1988 earnings.

In New York Stock Exchange composite trading yesterday, Johnson & Johnson shares rose $1.625 to close at $85.125.

Though Johnson & Johnson wouldn't release first-quarter results for the drug, a spokesman called the $50 million estimate "reasonable." He added, however, "We can't speculate on how long the increased demand will continue. And we aren't endorsing any long-range estimates."

On Jan. 22, the Journal of the American Medical Association suggested that Johnson & Johnson's potent prescription cream, on the market 17 years as an acne treatment, could help smooth sun-aged skin.

A few days later, the company was so inundated with orders that it devised an allocation system, boosting all clients' original orders 15%. And it stepped up production, adding a third shift to its facilities, the spokesman stated, saying that it hopes to alleviate the situation by May.

Pharmacists and dermatologists in the New York area said they are deluged with requests for the latest solution to the problem of aging skin. Ronald Sherman, a Manhattan dermatologist, said the number of requests for Retin-A last month was 10 times what it had been a year ago.

At C.O. Bigelow Chemists Inc. in New York's Greenwich Village, orders in the first two months this year are at least six times the level for the like period last year, said Joel Eichel, a pharmacist there. "And just think, the press coverage didn't even begin until late January," he added.

He now stocks about two dozen of most strengths and sizes of the product, rather than three or four of each, as he did last year. Mr. Eichel and others said they don't intend to boost the price. For the most common prescription of Retin-A, Bigelow charges about $18.

Neil Sweig, analyst at Prudential-Bache Securities Inc., said Retin-A is "in a sold-out position." But he said Retin-A sales would have to reach at least $300 million a year to significantly affect Johnson & Johnson's sales and earnings. In 1987, he said, the product contributed "less than one-half of one percent of the sales at what is an $8 billion company."

In evaluating this sector, an organization must know who the competition is—and what it is planning to do. Nonprofit organizations that assume their competition to be other nonprofit organizations are often surprised. Museums and art galleries, for instance, find that competition for the public's leisure-time dollars includes sporting events, TV, movies, and VCR rentals. Failure to recognize the true nature of the industry sector can prove fatal to an organization.

Customer sector

This sector of the primary external environment includes the customers or clients for the products or services a firm offers. Without customers or clients, organizations do not survive. The size of an overall market and a firm's current and potential market share can influence a number of key decisions. Should the firm grow or retrench? Should it spend resources on new equipment or repair existing equipment? Should it continue advertising to existing markets or focus on new ones? These questions can only be answered with knowledge about what is happening or what is about to happen in the customer sector of the environment. An example of changes in this sector is the targeting of new markets, as illustrated in Insight 15–3.

Each of these six sectors can have a direct impact on the success of most organizations. The company that fails to acquire needed resources, to provide products and services with a competitive technology, or to sell its outputs to an appropriate share of the market will not survive long.

Sectors in the secondary environment

Other sectors in the external environment indirectly affect the input, throughput, and output subsystems of a firm. These sectors are in the firm's secondary external environment. The following paragraphs consider three of them: the governmental/political, economic, and cultural/demographic sectors.

Government/political sector

Businesses confront constraints (and opportunities) as a result of the regulatory, legal, and political climate within which they operate. Any one or all of these elements can impact the input, throughput, and output subsystems of a company. For instance, consider the various points at which Home Computers Company might be affected by this sector of the environment. Personnel policies, health and safety regulations, and trade legislation means that Harvey's staff must keep attuned to changes in this sector if HCC is to compete successfully.

Consider the effects of two Federal Drug Administration (FDA) decisions on Genentech, the gene-splicing company. In May 1987, an FDA

More Firms Court Hispanic Consumers—But Find Them a Tough Market to Target

*L*ast year when Campbell Soup Co. launched a major assault on the Hispanic market, it used three different ad campaigns on Spanish-language television: one aimed at Hispanics of Caribbean origin, another for Mexican-Americans, and a third that mixed elements from the other two.

Hispanics, clearly, are not an easy group to target. Yet an increasing number of major companies are courting the Hispanic consumer. To these companies, Hispanics—the second fastest-growing population group in the U.S.—is a market that can't be ignored.

Last fall, the Census Bureau reported that since 1980, the country's Hispanic population had increased by 30%, to 18.8 million from 14.5 million—five times the growth rate of non-Hispanics. And although the Hispanic advertising market is still small at $491 million, it grew 23% last year, according to *Hispanic Business* magazine.

"Anybody who looks at the size of the Hispanic consumer segment would have to be nuts not to do business there," says Charles E. Morrison, a vice president of Coca-Cola USA, a unit of Coca-Cola Co.

Other companies agree. In the past year such major marketers as Pillsbury Co.'s Burger King Corp., Southland Corp.'s 7-Eleven Stores, and Domino's Pizza Inc. began comprehensive Spanish-language advertising campaigns for the first time.

Coca-Cola has used such Hispanic celebrities as Los Angeles Dodger pitching star Fernando Valenzuela, while Pepsi Cola has featured the Miami Sound Machine. In Miami, the wealthiest Latin enclave in the U.S., American Express Co. plans to feature prominent Hispanics in a Spanish-language version of its Portraits campaign.

"It's a population whose importance can't be denied any longer," says Liz Castells, product manager for Campbell Soup's Hispanic food unit. "That's the bottom line."

Still, it's an embryonic market and some agencies remain unconvinced of its importance. It also isn't an easy market to understand—or crack.

The Hispanic population, for instance, is highly concentrated, which might seem to make a wide-reaching national ad campaign fairly easy to execute. Fifty-four percent live in just two states—Texas and California. According to Strategy Research Inc., a Miami market research firm, 32.8% live in seven other states.

But the concentration is a bit deceiving. Mexican-Americans make up about 63% of U.S. Hispanics and dominate the market in California and the Southwest. Cubans are a far smaller group, but their higher income and heavy concentration in South Florida make Miami the country's most important Hispanic media market, after Los Angeles. New York, the nation's third-richest Hispanic market, has significant Dominican and Puerto Rican populations.

"We are just a bunch of segmented markets within a large market," says Carlos Rossi, the Puerto Rican president of New York-based Conill Advertising Inc., who helped to design the Campbell ads.

Some companies use one ad for the entire Hispanic community. But others, like Campbell Soup, opt for a varied ad campaign in an effort to reach specific audiences. What plays to Caribbean Hispanics, they find, doesn't necessarily work with Mexican-Americans.

The Campbell ads, for instance, all feature a woman cooking but differ in such details as the age of the character, the setting and the music. The version for Caribbean Hispanics has a grandmother cooking in a plant-filled kitchen to the sounds of salsa and merengue. The Mexican-American ad shows a young wife, preparing food in a brightly colored "southwestern-style"

kitchen, with pop music playing in the background, according to Mr. Rossi.

advisory panel recommended to the agency that Genentech's blood-clot dissolving drug TPA not be approved for public sale. This action drove Genentech's stock price down, along with that of nearly every other biotechnology company. Six months later, in November 1987, the FDA reversed this decision and approved the commercial sale of TPA. Genentech's stock rebounded immediately in the face of what could eventually be a billion-dollar market.[12]

Economic sector

Earlier, we discussed how a customer's willingness to purchase a firm's products or services is an important primary environmental influence. From a broader perspective, general levels of national and international economic activity represent important aspects of the secondary external environment. Factors such as levels of consumer spending, unemployment and interest rates, inflation, the value of the dollar versus foreign currencies, and changes in tax policies can influence hiring practices, wages, and capital availability. A firm's ability to anticipate and adapt quickly to economic changes could spell the difference between its ultimate success and failure.

Cultural/demographic sector

This secondary external environment sector includes the broader set of cultural norms and values held by society at large. The culture of the society in which an organization operates influences what behavior is or is not acceptable. For example, Japanese management styles are far different than American management styles. This is due, in large part, to the major cultural differences between the two countries. Even within the same country, acceptable behavior can differ by region. What might be considered acceptable in southern California might not be acceptable in the more conservative Midwest or South.

Norms or values can change over time. Corporate actions resulting in pollution, price gouging, or employee injury were tolerated 50 years ago. They are illegal today. Failure to act as a responsible corporate citizen can prompt the wrath of many different groups (as the accompanying cartoon implies) and finish an organization. People may choose not to work for or purchase the output of firms that violate society's trust. For instance, one local barbecue restaurant went under following a boycott of it. Citizens were angered that the restaurant had cut down a large stand of mature trees, ostensibly to improve visibility for its sign. Even replacing the cut trees with new ones did little to stem the outrage of some individuals. Within three months of the tree-cutting incident, the restaurant was up for sale.

"Looks as if the clean-air crowd turned out in force."

Changing norms with respect to alcohol consumption were at least partially responsible for the furor that arose around the Spuds Mac-Kenzie (the Original Party Animal) campaign that the Anheuser-Busch Companies used to promote Bud Light beer. The brewer feels such a campaign was appropriate and within legal guidelines. But the one-time director of New York State's Alcoholism & Alcohol Abuse Division asked the federal Bureau of Alcohol, Tobacco & Firearms to investigate the campaign. He claimed that the sale of Spuds MacKenzie toys and apparel was aimed at those under the legal drinking age for consuming alcoholic beverages. Anheuser-Busch argued that stores were selling "bootleg" products to underage kids in defiance of corporate policy. The brewer took legal action against stores selling these products.[13]

The other major element of this sector addresses the demographic characteristics of the population. The term *demographics* includes a population's location, distribution of income, composition (sex, race, age, etc.), educational levels, and so on. On the input side, improved education levels in the work force has improved the quality of new employees and the complexity of the jobs they can handle. On the other hand, a reduction in the birth rate may reduce the availability of qualified employees in the next 20 years. On the output side, the aging of the population makes the production of goods and services for the elderly increasingly attractive. Similarly, as more women enter the labor force, convenience items and services become more attractive to consumers. Firms must adjust their mix of outputs to meet these changes.

The nine sectors we have just discussed represent the major external environmental elements that should be systematically evaluated by an organization. For some companies, certain sectors are more important and relevant than others. Successful managers can determine the relative importance of each sector for the survival of their firm and allocate more resources to sectors of major significance.[14] Obviously the external environment can have dramatic effects on an organization. So what can firms do to survive in an increasingly complex and turbulent world? Fortunately, managers and researchers have learned a great deal about ways for organizations to adapt to the uncertainty created by external environments. Let's discuss this uncertainty and examine how organizations can respond to it.

UNCERTAINTY IN THE ENVIRONMENT

Harvey is trying to decide whether or not HCC should build a new production facility. This is an extremely difficult decision because he does not have all the information he needs. He's not sure what the PC market will be like in two years—the time when the new plant would come on line. In an ideal world, Harvey would have enough information about the external environment to know exactly what actions to take now and in the future. Unfortunately, we don't live in an ideal world. It is impossible for anyone to know all there is to know about what is or what will be happening in the environment. To the extent that such information is not available, the environment is said to be *uncertain.*[15] But how much environmental uncertainty does an organization face, and what can be done to reduce this uncertainty to a level where top management can act without endangering a firm?

To clarify the discussion, let's consider levels of uncertainty as best explained as a function of two dimensions: the **complexity** and the **stability** of the environment.

Complexity and stability

Complexity represents the number of environmental sectors that can have important implications for the organization.[16] In complex environments, many or all of the environmental sectors can interact in important ways with the organization. Biotechnology firms exist in complex environments, since a large number of sectors influence their success or failure.

A **simple environment,** on the other hand, **contains few sectors that interact with the organization.** Compared to biotechnology firms, cardboard box manufacturers exist in a fairly simple environment. Only a few of the sectors we discussed earlier are likely to have major influences on box makers.

At one time, the differences between simple and complex environments were more distinct. But today, given changes in the economy and the widespread impact of many legislative and judicial actions, few (if any) firms could describe their environments as simple. We might be better off conceding that all environments are complex. Some are just more complex than others.

Stability refers to the extent to which the relevant sectors change over some period of time.[17] In stable environments, sectors tend to change little for lengthy periods of time. For example, until the advent of nuclear power generation and citizen oversight boards, local utilities operated in relatively stable environments. Demand and costs (both operating and construction) could be predicted with some accuracy. The technology of nonnuclear electricity production was well understood; and in most markets, there was no competition.

With the advent of nuclear power, increased concern about utility safety and costs, and new opportunities for cogeneration programs, the environments of public utilities have become far more **dynamic.** The discoveries of new superconducting materials suggest that additional technological changes may be on the horizon for utilities. They must make plans now to deal with this wide array of environmental changes.

Combining the two dimensions

The dimensions of complexity and stability are placed along the axes in the diagram in Exhibit 15–3. By combining these dimensions, we can summarize the varying types of environmental uncertainty confronting today's organizations.[18]

The diagram suggests three levels of environmental uncertainty. Uncertainty is lowest in simple–stable environments. Moderate uncertainty exists in simple–dynamic or in complex–stable environments. The highest level of uncertainty is found in complex–dynamic environments.

Before ending this discussion of environmental uncertainty, we must consider a few additional issues. First, there are more than just three levels of uncertainty. The environmental uncertainty diagram is presented for ease of understanding. In reality, there are infinite levels of uncertainty—or at least as many levels as there are managers. Individual perceptions determine uncertainty levels to which managers then respond.

EXHIBIT 15–3

Four Types of Environmental Uncertainty

	Simple	**Complex**

Stable	**Low uncertainty**
	Few important external sectors
	Sectors remain the same or change slowly over time
	Examples:
	  Container firms
	  Bottlers
	  Car makers
		Moderate uncertainty
		Many important external sectors
		Sectors remain the same or change slowly over time
		Examples:
		  Colleges
		  Universities
		  Hospitals

Dynamic	**Moderate uncertainty**
	Few important external sectors
	Sectors change rapidly and unexpectedly
	Examples:
	  Fashion industry
	  Music industry
	  Toy industry
		High uncertainty
		Many important external sectors
		Sectors change rapidly and unexpectedly
		Examples:
		  Airlines
		  Electronic firms
		  Aerospace firms

Environmental Stability (vertical axis)

Environmental Complexity (horizontal axis)

Source: Reprinted from "Characteristics of Organizational Environments and Perceived Environmental Uncertainty" by Robert B. Duncan, published in *Administrative Science Quarterly* 17, no. 3, 1972, pp. 313-27, by permission of *Administrative Science Quarterly*.

Second, managers from the *same firm* may perceive supposedly identical environments as having *different levels* of uncertainty. In Chapter 3, we discussed the perceptual process and the factors that can distort a common reality. Lack of agreement among managers about uncertainty levels can hinder collective actions needed to deal with the environment.

Third, organizations within the *same industry* likely confront different levels of uncertainty within the industry environment. For instance, small, well-established firms tend to face less uncertainty than larger organizations. But small, entrepreneurial firms likely face more uncertainty than firms that have been around awhile.

Fourth, environmental uncertainty levels are not static; they change over time. Thus, an organization's location in Exhibit 15–3 may also change over time. As organizations grow, they usually move from confronting less uncertainty to confronting more. However, it is also possible for the environment to become less, rather than more, uncertain. For example, legislation designed to reduce the likelihood of hostile takeovers would remove at least one element of uncertainty from the environments of many companies. Uncertainty increased for the Suzuki Motor Company after a complaint was filed with the National Highway Transportation and Safety Administration by the Center for Automotive Safety. The complaint alleged that the Suzuki Samurai all-terrain vehicle (ATV) was unsafe. In an attempt to reduce this uncertainty, Suzuki made what was characterized as an unusually combative response, vehemently denying the allegation. The company promised to investigate the source of the charges and do what it could to halt the allegations, "including appropriate legal action."[19]

When faced with unacceptable levels of uncertainty, a firm acts to reduce the uncertainty to the point where the company can operate successfully. To do this, the organization can respond in two general ways. It can design **internal mechanisms** to deal with changes in the environment. Or it can increase control of its **external environment** so that the need for internal responses is minimized. The following sections look at each of these general responses.

INTERNAL RESPONSES TO UNCERTAINTY

An organization's actions in a simple–stable environment will differ from its actions in a dynamic environment. When faced with little uncertainty, a firm responds to few changes. These responses can be accomplished in a deliberate fashion, since change is not rapid. In a complex-dynamic environment, however, there are many changes; and they occur rapidly. Organizational responses must also be frequent and rapid.

Organizations most frequently need to adapt and develop responses as their environments move from lesser to greater uncertainty. What options are available for managers to cope with this increasing uncertainty? We examine some of these next.

Boundary-spanning roles and units

In new organizations, the owner/manager is often responsible for all aspects of the firm's operations. To respond to the environment, this manager plays a number of **boundary-spanning roles—positions that link the firm to other firms in the external environment.**[20] For example, in HCC's early years, Bill and Harvey acted as salespersons, purchasing agents, and distributors—as boundary spanners. As a firm grows, however, one or two people cannot adequately respond to all the essential sectors in the environment. **Boundary-spanning units are then formed to accomplish two basic tasks: the collection, interpretation, and communication of environmental information to top managers; and the representation of the organization to important environmental sectors.**[21]

Increased environmental complexity requires increased organizational complexity in the form of additional boundary-spanning units. The units are formed to protect the basic throughput technology of the organization—the heart of the organization. This throughput technology, called the **technical core,** is directly responsible for providing the products and services.[22] Other organizational units exist primarily to serve the core; to buffer the technical core from the uncertainty in the environment; and to absorb as much uncertainty shock as possible. This way, the core can carry on its important activities with minimal disruption.

What might some of these buffering units look like, and what roles do they play? *Advertising and marketing* units interact with customers to ensure that output can be sold. This prevents excess inventory from clogging up the production process. *Quality control and customer service* units ensure that what gets to the consumer is in acceptable condition— or is repaired or replaced if it is not. This keeps irate customers from dashing into the core facilities and berating the first employee they see with complaints about products or services purchased. *Purchasing, inventory control, and production scheduling* units ensure a smooth flow of resources and production. As demand for products or services increases, these units buffer the core by maintaining a constant and cost-effective production flow.

Even in service organizations like hospitals, consulting firms, and colleges and universities, buffering units work to enable the technical core to function as effectively and efficiently as possible. Hospitals have separate units to handle admissions, billing, and pharmaceutical serv-

ices. Colleges and universities have admissions, business, and placement offices. Individual faculty members are not required to evaluate
applicants, to determine tuition levels, or to find jobs for graduates.

The type of boundary-spanning units formed will be related to those
environmental sectors a firm thinks are most important. Thus, while a
defense contractor devotes organizational resources to monitoring the
technological and political sectors, a museum will monitor the demographic and economic sectors more intensely.

Differentiation and integration

As boundary-spanning units continue to buffer the technical core, they
become increasingly specialized or **differentiated** in their activities.[23]
And as certain sectors of the environment become more important than
others, the boundary units devoted to those sectors also become more
powerful.

Too much differentiation can result in work units that are unable to
communicate effectively with each other because they do not understand each other's specialized languages. Extreme differentiation can be
dangerous to an organization's health, particularly in rapidly changing
environments. When rapid, coordinated responses to environmental
change are needed, some type of **integration** mechanism is needed to
help the diverse units communicate with each other.[24] Chapter 18 discusses a variety of mechanisms, including liaison personnel, task forces,
and task teams, to name a few. For our purposes here, it is enough to
say that whatever it takes, communications and coordination must be
maintained in uncertain environments. The more turbulent the environment, the better the quality of integration required for organizational
success.[25]

Planning and control

Organizations must also develop **planning and control processes** that
fit the environmental demands they confront. Consider the impact that
varying uncertainty levels have on planning activities. In a simple–
stable environment, two kinds of planning are appropriate: short-term
operational planning and long-term strategic planning. When a firm
knows its environment well (uncertainty is low), short-term plans can
be made with relative confidence. Long-term plans will be relatively
stable, and reflect responses to only a few possible planning scenarios.

As environmental uncertainty increases, operational planning remains important; but long-range planning becomes both more important and more difficult. Assumptions about environmental changes will
be more tenuous in complex–dynamic environments. Managers must
consider a far greater number of possible planning scenarios. As sectors
change, organizations may be forced to reevaluate the assumptions on

which their long-range plans were built. And as the planning horizon lengthens, planning uncertainty increases and confidence in a plan decreases. Examples of volatile planning assumptions abound—from predicting the moves of the stock market to estimating the price of imported oil.

Organizational control processes must also change to match external environment changes. In a complex–dynamic environment, the successful organization responds quickly and effectively to unanticipated environmental changes. In more stable environments, less flexibility is needed.

Two British researchers, Burns and Stalker, provided some early insights to this question.[26] They examined the control processes used in 20 British industrial firms operating in different kinds of environments. The researchers' findings provided solid evidence about the relationships between control systems and the environment. Burns and Stalker characterized their 20 firms as either **mechanistic** or **organic** systems. They found that the mechanistic style worked best in the stable environment and the organic style worked best in the complex environment.

Mechanistic systems

These systems were characterized by elaborate collections of written rules and procedures imposed in a top-down fashion through a clear organizational hierarchy. Jobs were broken down into specialized tasks. Decisions about how tasks were to be done were centralized at the top of the organization. Official communications came from the top down. Because simple–stable environments do not change quickly, they do not demand quick responses. The mechanistic systems served organizations in this setting quite well.

Organic systems

At the other end of Burns and Stalker's control range was the organic organization. These systems were marked by less formal interactions between employees and work units. To ensure quick responses in a changing environment, these firms had fewer written rules and procedures to follow. Formal hierarchies were often ignored as employees adjusted or redefined their roles to get the job done. Since environmental changes occurred frequently, there was little time for decision requests to be sent up the hierarchical chain of command. Decision-making expertise and authority were located where needed. To ensure coordination, communications were predominantly horizontal across the organization, rather than up and down. Top management still provided overall objectives and goals; but they left lower-level managers and employees alone to accomplish their tasks as quickly as possible.

EXHIBIT 15–4

Organizational Reactions to Environmental Uncertainty

<table>
<tr><td rowspan="2" style="writing-mode:vertical">Stable

Environmental Stability

Dynamic</td><td>

Low uncertainty

Mechanistic structure—
  formal, centralized

Few departments

No need for integration
  between units

Planning for operations

</td><td>

Moderate uncertainty

Mechanistic structure—
  formal, centralized

Many departments to span
  boundaries with key
  sectors

Little integration between
  units

Some planning

</td></tr>
<tr><td>

Moderate uncertainty

Organic structure—informal,
  decentralized

Few departments to span
  boundaries with key
  sectors

Little integration between
  units

Some planning

</td><td>

High uncertainty

Organic structure—informal,
  decentralized

Many departments to span
  boundaries with key
  sectors

Much integration between
  units

Extensive planning and
  forecasting

</td></tr>
</table>

Simple   **Complex**

Environmental Complexity

Source: Adapted from R. Daft, *Organization Theory and Design*, 2nd ed. (St. Paul, Minn.: West
Publishing Co., 1986), p. 67.

Exhibit 15–4 summarizes the appropriate organizational responses to
environmental uncertainty. Note that these are not independent responses; choosing one response does not preclude a manager from
choosing another. In fact, many companies use a variety of internal
responses to cope with a rapidly changing environment.

As noted, changing the internal mechanisms of an organization is
one general approach for dealing with an increasingly complex environment. Using this approach exclusively, however, assumes that organizations can only *react* to their environments. Managers can only hope to
reduce reaction time by monitoring the environment and reacting as
quickly as the organization's control systems permit.

EXTERNAL RESPONSES TO UNCERTAINTY

A second approach to surviving in a changing external environment
assumes that a firm can actually manage the environment—much like
it manages other important resources. These strategies are externally

oriented and call for a **proactive** rather than a reactive stance toward the environment. Two sets of suggested tactics are presented below. One set deals with linkages to other organizations, such as mergers, joint ventures, contracts, and the like. The second set contains tactics directed at influencing the nature of the environment in which an organization must operate.

Links with other organizations

One way to reduce uncertainty is to purchase controlling interest in or to **merge** with companies in sectors crucial to the success of the buying organization.[27] For instance, IBM felt some uncertainty in both the material resources and the technology sectors of its environment. IBM reduced its uncertainty in these areas by investing in Intel (chip manufacturing) and Rolm (telecommunications).[28] This ensured favorable responses to IBM's requests for input and throughput needs. Ownership in another organization can range from purchase of a small portion of the firm, through a controlling interest to a complete takeover or merger of two companies. Many mergers result in benefits for both firms. However, the rationale behind some mergers is less clear, as the cartoon suggests.

A less dramatic way to reduce uncertainty in key environmental sectors is through joint ventures or contracts between firms. In a **joint venture,** two or more organizations pool their resources to take advantage of an opportunity that may be too risky or expensive for one organization to undertake alone. For example, American and foreign automakers have joined forces to produce new lines of automobiles in this country. This gives the foreign companies access to U.S. markets, and gives the American automakers access to Japanese manufacturing technology and cost-control systems. In this case, foreign companies reduce market uncertainty, and domestic companies reduce technological uncertainty.

To reduce uncertainty in a major international market, Johnson & Johnson entered a joint venture to make Band-Aid adhesive bandages in China. Band-Aids are produced by Shanghai Johnson & Johnson Ltd., a joint venture in which the U.S. manufacturer owns 60 percent of the new company, and Shanghai Hygienic Supply Works owns the remaining 40 percent.[29]

Similarly, **long-term contracts** between an organization and key suppliers or customers provide a measure of security for both parties. But both firms must realize that if either party goes out of business, uncertainty for the remaining firm increases greatly. For that reason few companies choose to put all of their resource eggs in one basket.

Companies frequently forge links with key sectors of their environments by including **representatives from those sectors on their boards**

Source: Drawing by Ed Fisher. © 1988 *Harvard Business Review.* Reprinted by permission of Ed Fisher.

of directors. For instance, current members of the Home Computers Company board include a banker, a broker, a lawyer, and an officer from a key supplier. By including these individuals on the board, Harvey gains insights into future trends in their particular sectors. They also act as a sounding board, providing predictions of sector reactions to strategic changes planned at HCC. More recently, some firms have placed union representatives on their boards. In 1980, Douglas Frazier, the now-retired president of the United Auto Workers, became the first union board member when he joined the Chrysler Corporation board during Chrysler's attempts to avert bankruptcy. Union representation has expanded since then, with union members currently serving on the boards of Wheeling-Pittsburgh Steel, Pan Am, Kaiser Aluminum, and Weirton Steel.[30]

Recruiting executives from organizations in key environmental sectors is another way to manage the environment by attempting to learn more about it. For instance, members of presidential administrations and key personnel from government agencies are often hired by organizations in the belief that their contacts within the government can provide assistance in securing new contracts or advanced information about moves that government agencies might make in the future. The practice of hiring executives from other companies can also reduce uncertainty. As some professionals change companies, they frequently bring customers or clients with them to their new firms. This may reduce uncertainty in the customer sector, but it increases it in the legal sector if the former company sues for these actions. For example, Microsoft Corporation, a major software publisher, sued Borland International to prevent a senior marketing executive from accepting a job with Borland.[31]

On a more general level, environmental control or influence is also possible through **advertising and public relations activities.** Advertising provides closer links between an organization and its current or potential customers. Public relations efforts attempt to improve a firm's reputation in the eyes of key environmental sectors. Insight 15–4 gives an example of an attempt to recast a once-hostile corporate image as somewhat more understanding. This approach combines advertising and public relations to strengthen ties with the governmental and customer sectors.

Managing the environment

Organizations can also try to *change* their external environment. Consider the following tactics for accomplishing such changes.

Top management makes a conscious decision about the **domain** (environment) in which it will operate. A firm can alter its domain by leaving the existing domain, by diversifying into other domains, or by divesting units that operate in overly complex domains. If a firm's current domain is simply too competitive, for instance, the firm may choose to leave it and to look for a friendlier domain in which to operate. In its early years, Home Computers Company had few substantial competitors, except for Apple. It took time to convince customers that personal computers were something that everyone needed; but once that obstacle was overcome, HCC became a great success. Unfortunately, the eventual entry of IBM into the market forced both HCC and Apple to alter their approaches to business. Apple modified its original domain to concentrate on school systems, so that it would not have to compete head on with IBM. Apple also chose to produce hardware that would not run IBM software. HCC also switched domains, but by closely monitoring IBM's entry into the PC market, HCC chose to continue making machines that were IBM-compatible. Insight 15–5 (p. 632) presents an example of a smaller firm that was forced by the environment to adopt a diversification strategy.

Companies attempt to protect favorable environments by undertaking **lobbying activities.** These activities are directed at influencing governmental actions limiting the ability of new organizations to enter the

Dow Chemical Tries to Shed Tough Image and Court the Public

Midland, Mich.—Employees at Dow Chemical Co. know that beaten-down feeling all too well. First they went through the public outcry over napalm during the Vietnam War. Then came the discovery of dioxin contamination right in Dow's corporate back yard. Then Agent Orange, raging battles with environmental authorities and humiliating attempts to defend the company's integrity on national television.

Top management only made matters worse; it seemed to relish a good public fight. A string of combative chief executive officers angrily shouldered through controversy—and drew lines in the sand, daring regulators and environmentalists to step across. By 1983, one manager recalls sadly, morale had sunk so low that long-time chemists and researchers removed their company pins before boarding business flights.

Today, corporate confrontation is out, or so Dow says, and a new age of sensitivity is in. In fact, the company is seeking nothing less than public redemption through an extraordinary image-makeover campaign.

The ingredients: a schmaltzy $60 million advertising effort; a performance-review system that takes into account a manager's public-relations skills; the sharing of more information with regulators; support for legislation that is pleasing even to environmentalists; and, not surprisingly, extra effort to cozy up to the media.

Dow's bout with self-analysis was long overdue. "We had made a lot of enemies who could influence our future," says Richard Long, then Dow's Washington public-affairs manager who headed a company task force to deal with its image problem. "We recognized we had to clean up our act."

They also recognized a new fact of corporate life: Dow, once mainly a commodities chemical maker, has thrust itself into pharmaceuticals and consumer products, a move that may have made it even more sensitive to public opinion. Dow's campaign also reflects broader efforts by the chemical industry to buff up its image. Skeptics scoff at Dow's campaign as glitz with no substance. Ralph Nader, just one of the consumer advocates watching the company, believes that Dow has got off easy during the conservative Reagan years; others say the truth about Dow's apparent enlightenment won't be known until the next crisis hits the company.

Indeed, old personas do die hard. In 1985, not long after Dow's image-switching campaign started, a manager was caught circulating results from a confidential blood test that incorrectly said a Greenpeace activist arrested on Dow property had a venereal disease.

Dow has opened its plant sites around the country to hundreds of tours. It has invited, for example, a Texas state senate subcommittee to its Gulf Coast operations and has shown Rep. James J. Florio, a New Jersey Democrat and big backer of the Superfund, around its Louisiana facility. Its scientific "road shows" and its advice to line managers to join more community groups are raising its profile.

What's more, the company has sent out thousands of copies of its Public Interest Report, which lists Dow's philanthropic activities. It has made organ-donor education its public cause, and bowing to "growing public concern," it begrudgingly pulled out of South Africa earlier this year. It set up a special 800 inquiry line for reporters, supported a science-journalism project and launched a "Dow Lets You Do Great Things" ad campaign. A Dow-commissioned survey says the campaign has raised positive reaction to the company six percentage points, to 29%, within a few months.

It also is trumpeting its expertise in hazardous-waste reduction, even joining last month with environmentalists at a news conference endorsing related new legislation. "This is the first time the Sierra Club was on

the same side of an issue as Dow," says Anne Woiwode, a member of Sierra's Michigan chapter.

market, or to change the rules under which the industry operates to favor existing companies over new ones. On the international level, lobbying for trade restrictions on foreign imports is an example of using political actions to control or change an organization's environment to make it less uncertain.

Firms that consider the political sector important, but are not large enough to undertake their own political activities, often link up with similar firms in **professional or trade associations.** Their collective resources and professional expertise are put to use by the association staff on behalf of member firms. Associations also try to preempt governmental bodies from establishing industry regulations by offering their own less-burdensome policy suggestions.

Our earlier discussion of Suzuki's response to charges against its Samuri ATV indicates a strategy somewhat at odds with other ATV manufacturers. Early complaints about accidents with these vehicles prompted makers to attach safety-warning labels to each machine. But proposed industry standards also would have allowed eight-year-olds to ride the smallest models. Attempting to preempt more restrictive legislation, the industry argued that accidents were almost entirely due to operator error. Honda claimed that in its ads, drivers always wore helmets and obeyed all safety rules. Honda officials believed states should enact tougher licensing and training requirements for ATV drivers as a means to reduce accidents.[32]

Finally, although this book does not condone or encourage illegal activities by individuals or organizations, a discussion of controlling the environment would be incomplete and naive without considering the illegal activities some firms frequently use to reduce environmental uncertainty. Anyone who reads the newspaper or the business press knows that payoffs for contracts, bribes, illegal political contributions, and insider information have been used to increase some organizations' control over elements in the environment. These activities have been around since organizations became an acceptable form of operation. The robber barons of the late 1800s practiced questionable activities to such excess that major legislation was passed to limit the ways businesses could operate. Illegal and unethical activities in the stock market have

---

INSIGHT 15–5

**Small Cigar Maker Finds
It Is Forced to Diversify**

Geneva—Zino Davidoff, who likes a fine cigar more than money, doesn't want to play the luxury-goods industry's expansion game. But he has to.

The maker of the Davidoff Anniversario 80, at 42 Swiss francs ($32) perhaps the world's most expensive smoke, accuses other luxury-goods companies of "becoming big bazaars and financial businesses. They're turning into empires, and empires can fall. All it takes is a management change."

To avoid that, the 82-year-old Mr. Davidoff took in a partner some years ago by selling a controlling stake to Ernst Schneider, a kindred spirit who also owns a big tobacco distributor. "As long as I'm around," Mr. Schneider vows, "we won't go on the stock market." And Mr. Schneider also wants to prevent the Davidoff line of cigars from becoming mass consumer items. "If everyone has a Cartier jewel, is it still a luxury product?" he asks.

However, Davidoff, like other luxury companies, is diversifying; it also makes neckties, an after-shave lotion, watches and a cognac to go with the cigars. But Messrs. Davidoff and Schneider say they diversified only because the company's name was showing up, without its approval, on T-shirts, wine, watches and other products. Each time, Davidoff sued the counterfeiters and won, but under the court rulings it had to launch similar products to maintain control over its brand name.

Mr. Schneider often gets proposals to put the Davidoff name on clothes, jewelry, eyeglasses and even underwear, but he turns most of them down. "I could make a small fortune just by putting our name on a product, but the brand would be killed," he says. And Mr. Davidoff laments, "I'm not interested in any product outside of tobacco. I like being small. . . . But you can't go against the commercial storm."

The Wall Street Journal, November 23, 1987. Reprinted by permission of *The Wall Street Journal,* © Dow Jones & Company, Inc. 1987. All rights reserved.

---

sparked calls for more restrictive stock trading regulations. Illegal activities may seem beneficial to an individual and an organization in the short run. But history has shown that the disastrous long-run consequences make the use of such tactics highly ill-advised.

Our discussion of the external environment has shown that it comprises different sectors, some more important to an organization than others. These sectors and the rate of change within them produce various levels of environmental uncertainty, requiring managerial attention. Exhibit 15–5 summarizes much of the preceding discussion about managing the environment; it also offers some additional suggestions for dealing with specific environmental sectors.

The external environment represents only half of the environmental context, however. Understanding the other half requires an investigation of a firm's internal environment.

EXHIBIT 15–5

Managing Sectors in the Environment

Source	Examples of Strategic Actions
Government	Lobby for favorable treatment Recruit former government officials Relocate to a different governmental jurisdiction
Competition	Advertise to build brand loyalty Select a less competitive domain Merge with competition to gain larger market share Negotiate a cooperative agreement with competition
Unions	Negotiate a long-term collective-bargaining agreement Build facilities in countries with a large, low-cost labor supply Appoint prestigious union official to board of directors
Suppliers	Use multiple suppliers Inventory critical supplies Negotiate long-term contracts Vertically integrate through merger
Financial institutions	Appoint financial executives to board Establish a line of credit to draw upon when needed Diversify by acquiring a financial institution Use multiple financial resources
Customers	Advertise Use a differentiated price structure Ration demand Change domain to where there are more customers
Public pressure groups	Appoint critics to board Recruit critics as employees Engage in visible activities that are socially conscious Use trade association to counter criticism

Source: Adapted from Stephen P. Robbins, *Organization Theory: Structure, Design, and Applications*, 2/e, © 1987, p. 300. Reprinted by permission of Prentice-Hall, Inc., Englewood Cliffs, New Jersey.

THE INTERNAL ENVIRONMENT: CORPORATE CULTURE

Advertisements for two car dealers recently appeared on a local TV station. In one, a fast-talking actor *demanded* that the viewer get down to the local dealership, "NOW!" In the other ad, a soft-spoken, sincere voice promised no pressure and no hype from the sales staff. The viewer was *invited* to stop by; but if the invitation was not accepted, that was fine.

Visits to both dealerships revealed that the personalities of the two firms were as different as their advertising campaigns. The first firm *was* hard-charging and high-pressured. A customer barely set foot in the showroom door before a pack of salespeople descended. The second firm *was* more sedate and laid-back. Customers were free to just look around; and if assistance was needed, a salesperson was available. There was no pressure and no hype. Surprisingly, research indicated that both dealerships were equally profitable and equally respected in the community.

These two different philosophies toward doing business contribute to another important organizational environment—the one found *within* an organization. This **internal environment** is influenced by factors in the external environment; but it has recently emerged as a topic of interest in its own right under the label **corporate culture.**

Corporate culture is defined as **"the set of key values, beliefs, and understandings that are shared by members of an organization."**[33] Culture could also be described as the personality of an organization. While people cannot actually *see* a corporation's culture, they can *infer* a lot about it by observing the following:

1. The basic philosophy of the organization.
2. The values that underlie organizational norms.
3. The norms that guide behaviors.
4. The status accorded to certain individuals.
5. The formal and informal rules that have developed for getting a task done.
6. The type of language used in the organization.[34]

Developing a corporate culture

The development of a corporate culture is profoundly affected by the values and philosophies of a firm's founder or a particularly strong leader somewhere in its history. Stories (true or exaggerated) of the activities of this person surviving in a hostile environment become the basis for the beliefs and norms that guide subsequent generations of managers and employees. These beliefs become part of the corporate culture. The impact of such notable founders as Ray Kroc at McDonald's, James Cash Penney at J. C. Penney, and Thomas Watson at IBM is well known.

Consider for a moment Burton A. Burton, the founder of Casablanca Fan Company. As founder, Burton positioned Casablanca at the premium end of the home fan market. Where import fans were selling for under $100, Casablanca fans sold for $500. His secret was marketing; and his efforts became part of company legend. He spent over a million dollars to refurbish two old railroad cars, and toured the country in them to promote his product. Burton entered floats in the Rose Bowl parades. He handed out T-shirts that read "Blow Your Wad, Cool Your Bod with Casablanca Fans." Did he have an impact on the firm? When he sold the company in 1981, Casablanca had sales of nearly $50 million and an aftertax profit of 21 percent. Four years later, the company was facing a $2.5 million dollar loss and an employment drop of 20 percent. The new owners rehired Burton A. Burton. After one year back on the job, Burton had raised the company's earnings to more than $2 million.[35]

Maintaining the corporate culture

Organizations maintain their cultures with a variety of mechanisms. In particular, five approaches have been suggested to maintain a culture within a company.[36] Each of these is discussed briefly below, and the set is summarized in Exhibit 15–6.

Reactions to crises

IBM has a long-established, though unofficial, policy of lifetime employment. In the mid-1980s, IBM experienced its worse financial performance in 60 years. The company chose a variety of tactics to improve its situation. For many firms, personnel layoffs would have been an obvious

EXHIBIT 15–6

Developing and Maintaining a Corporate Culture

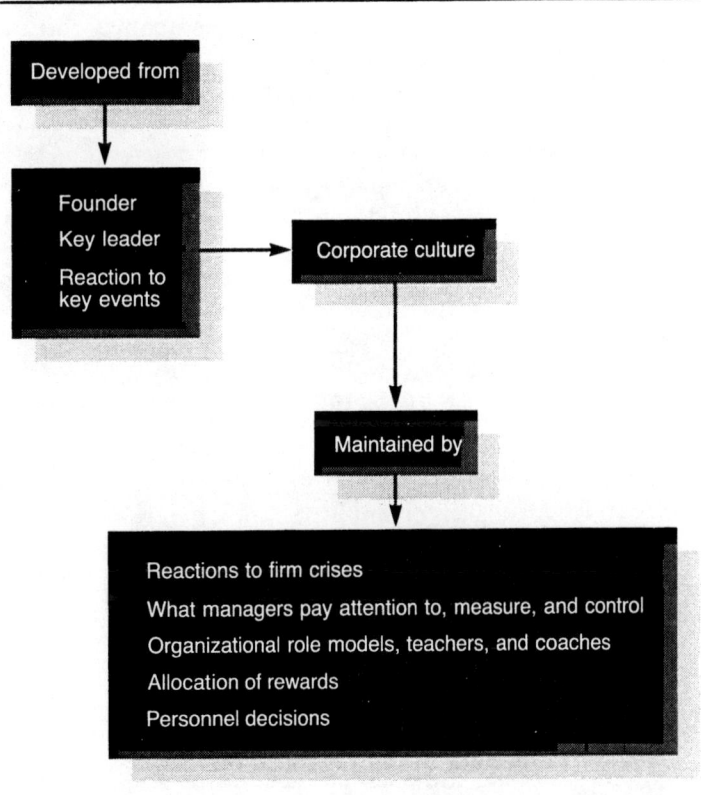

response to this crisis. True to its culture, IBM did not lay off a single employee. This action reinforced the corporate culture in the minds of its employees. How a company handles an organizational crisis offers employees a vivid reminder of the core values of the corporate culture. In fact, some might argue that the way an organization reacts in a crisis reflects its corporate culture more clearly than the way it conducts its routine activities.

What managers pay attention to, measure, and control

In an earlier chapter we discussed how reinforcement influences employees to behave in certain ways. It is an old, but true, saying, that "what gets measured is what gets done." Managers can reinforce certain aspects of an organization's culture simply by paying attention to them. For example, HCC's culture stresses creativity and innovation. Harvey and his managers pay attention to and support creative behavior, even though that behavior occasionally leads to some creative failures. In Harvey's mind, too few failures means that his team is not taking enough risks.

Paying attention to a company's culture occurs not only by direct reinforcement, but also by indirect or symbolic actions taken by managers. The equality in parking spaces and a common dining room for executives and employees at HCC are two examples of symbolic, ongoing measures that define and maintain the HCC culture.

As Boeing Corporation worked to reduce costs, Boeing managers emphasized the importance of cost control. In one case, the manager of a department that produces airplane interiors dumped three large truckloads of scrapped parts and paperwork in the middle of the factory floor. He stood next to the scrap pile while talking to the employees about pride on the job.[37]

Role models, teachers, and coaches

How managers behave on a day-to-day basis provides information to employees about the nature of the corporate culture. Managers can explicitly or implicitly incorporate elements of the corporate culture in their training programs and in their informal ongoing feedback to employees. Is the firm authoritarian, democratic, or paternalistic? Managers' interactions with subordinates, peers, and customers can tell a great deal about the values and norms underlying the corporate culture.

Allocation of rewards

Similar to the measuring tactic discussed earlier, this tactic reveals in real and often tangible terms which actions and attitudes are most important to the organization. Rewards can include the usual monetary ones; but they can also include some of the nonmonetary rewards considered in Chapter 6, such as promotion, time off, and more challenging work assignments. Not only is it true that what gets measured is what gets done, but what gets *rewarded* also gets done.

Personnel decisions

Recruiting or selecting people who fit is another way to maintain a culture. Criteria used in making personnel decisions like promotion and termination send signals about the corporate culture. Regardless of how an organization *actually* arrives at these decisions, the criteria *perceived* by employees for taking such actions help maintain or inhibit the corporate culture.

Impact of corporate culture on the organization

The recent interest in corporate culture was sparked by Peters and Waterman's book *In Search of Excellence* and from the study of Japanese management styles, following Japan's remarkable economic performance of the 70s and 80s.[38] Regardless of the rationale, many managers have taken the concept of corporate culture to heart. They believe that having a culture (and in some cases they believe *any* culture) is good for a firm. At a minimum, culture has an impact on the language used in firms. For instance, at Walt Disney Company, employees describe a positive event as "good Mickey," a negative event as "bad Mickey," and lunch at the company's expense as "on the mouse."[39]

What do we know about the impact of culture on some important areas of a company? Knowing what an organization's culture is and how it came to be provides employees important information about their firm's history and suggests the nature of activities anticipated in the future. **Thus, corporate culture and its values and norms can work to control employee behaviors.** A strong culture is particularly useful for controlling behaviors in areas where no formal rules or regulations exist, such as a willingness to protect the organization from harm or to refrain from speaking negatively about the organization in public. Finally, as employees learn and accept the corporate culture, they usually become more committed to the corporate philosophy, values, and objectives.[40] This increased organizational commitment helps to reinforce activities directed at accomplishing key organization goals. We can conclude, therefore, that strong cultures have more influence on organizational members than do weak ones.[41]

But do certain cultures lead to higher levels of performance than other cultures? Most research on this issue has provided mixed evidence on the relationship between culture and performance.[42] The differential impact of culture on organizational performance is well illustrated in Insight 15–6. In one case, two computer companies with contrasting cultures have *nearly identical levels of performance*. In the second case, two

INSIGHT 15–6

The Impact of Culture on Performance

SUN MICROSYSTEMS INC.

West Coast—
Mountain View, California

Standardized machines, cheaper to produce, easier to sell to varied market

"Ebullient and, at times, down right loony. The Company throws beer bashes, and on Halloween employees report to work in gorilla suits. Attitude of sheer, unrestrained invincibility. Style is the open-collar, open-door, protocol-free ambiance of California.

"On April Fool's Day, engineers torment their bosses. One year they placed an executive's Ferrari on a platform in the middle of the company's decorative pond.

"They're a Fortune 500 company, but the president has trouble finding a parking space at 5:30 P.M.

APPOLLO COMPUTER INC.

East Coast—
Chelmsford, Massachusetts

Machines incompatible with other machines, higher in price, superior product

"Buttoned-down, traditional company. Trying to build an image of solid, long-term reliability. Atmosphere is decidedly corporate with closed doors, scheduled meetings, and a library hush in the executive suite.

"It's a more buttoned-jacket style. From 9:15 to 9:20, you discuss an issue, and at 9:20 you approve it. We have people doing fun stuff. That doesn't mean . . . you don't wear suits.

"The parking lots are almost empty in the evening and on weekends. Executives urge the staff to work harder."

THE RESULTS

23% of work-station market
Revenues—$141 million
Earnings—$10.2 million

26% of work-station market
Revenues—$123 million
Earnings—$6.4 million

PILGRIM PLANT

Location—Plymouth, Massachusetts
Owner—Boston Edison, Co.

Views nuclear power as similar to existing technology. "It was just another way to generate steam and make electricity.

"We have to make a profit. We do what we have to do. We don't do more than we have to do."

Has had three plant supervisors in one year.

Staff reported to one supervisor when plant operated; another one when plant was closed.

Operators rarely saw the supervisor in the control room.

MILLSTONE PLANT—1

Location—Waterford, Connecticut
Owner—Northeast Utilities

Views nuclear power generation as completely different from fossil fuel power generation.

Motto on the wall of a training facility: "Excellence in operations is the sum of many small details done right."

Has had two plant supervisors in five years.

Staff reports to one supervisor.

Supervisor visits the control room nearly every day.

Not one of the plant supervisors has been promoted into the Edison corporate hierarchy.	VP-Nuclear Operations, Senior VP-Nuclear Operations, Executive VP-Engineering and Operations, and ex-President were all plant supervisors.

THE RESULTS

In the past 15 months, Pilgrim has generated NO electric power.	Millstone 1 has generated enough power to supply a city of 540,000
NRC fines—$660,000	NRC fines—$0
Radiation Exposure: 1949 rem/emp	Radiation Exposure: 645 rem/emp

Adapted from W. Bulkeley, "Two Computer Firms with Clashing Styles Fight for Market Niche," *The Wall Street Journal,* July 6, 1987; and D. Wessel, "Pilgrim and Millstone, Two Nuclear Plants, Have Disparate Fates," *The Wall Street Journal,* July 28, 1987. Reprinted by permission of *The Wall Street Journal,* © Dow Jones & Company, Inc. 1987. All rights reserved.

utility firms with contrasting cultures have *widely different levels of performance.*

Some research *has* found that different corporate cultures lead to different levels of performance. **The effect of culture on performance is contingent on a number of different organizational elements,** including the external environment, the organization's technology, etc.[43] In one context, a very paternalistic culture is appropriate for higher levels of performance. Another organization in a different setting finds that an autocratic culture is most effective. An innovative, risk-taking culture (like HCC's) is warranted in a dynamic environment, but would be inappropriate in a stable environment.

Changing the corporate culture

Our social culture and accepted actions in that culture have developed over many years. And that culture influences everything that happens in society. Given this situation, imagine trying to change a culture. It would seem to be a nearly impossible task. And what about attempts to change corporate cultures? Even though these cultures exist within the boundaries of an organization, and they have not been developing as long as social cultures, changing corporate cultures remains a difficult task.

For instance, the breakup of AT&T presented the Baby Bells with tremendous changes in their environment. They went from operating in the stable environment of a protected monopoly to competing in a rapidly changing environment. A new marketing-oriented culture was needed to replace the former service-oriented culture. Banks and other financial institutions have been forced to confront the same types of environmental changes in the wake of banking deregulation.

These examples of situations in which it becomes necessary to change a corporate culture prompt an interesting question. Under what conditions might successful corporate culture change be most likely? Let's consider the impact of a number of factors.[44]

A major crisis

Researchers suggest that before a change in culture can occur, some sufficiently dramatic event must happen. This event shocks management and employees into realizing that the old way of doing things is no longer useful, and that new approaches may be needed to deal with the crisis. Examples of such crises might include the collapse of the stock market, the loss of a major legal battle, or a hostile takeover. The court-ordered breakup of AT&T remains a perfect example of such a crisis.

Changes in leadership

The replacement or retirement of an organization's founder or other key executives provides another opportunity for attempting a cultural change. Since leadership positions transmit the values underlying a culture, changes in these positions may assist a change in culture. Leaders brought in from outside the firm may be viewed by employees as bringing new cultural values. John Sculley had this impact at Apple Computer, as did Lee Iacocca at Chrysler, and Jack Welch at GE.

Age or stage of the firm

Which companies have stronger cultures— young or old? Not surprisingly, the strength of a corporate culture is strongly related to the age of the firm. Younger firms have less-entrenched cultures, making the existing culture easier to change. In older firms, corporate cultures are usually the result of many years of development and reinforcement. All else equal, cultures in these older companies are much more difficult to change.

Closely related to age is the stage of a firm's development. And related to development is the ease of cultural change. As organizations experience the problems associated with rapid growth, major shifts in culture and operations may be needed. For example, perhaps the entrepreneur/founder no longer knows each employee's name, and the family atmosphere is lost as more formalized operating procedures are instituted. Changes in culture may occur as a result of this depersonalization of processes and a growth in organizational size. Similarly, as existing corporations diversify or merge, the need for cultural change may also exist. Such is the situation at General Electric. GE has placed a high premium on the value of training as a way of acculturating recent organizational additions to the GE family. A further discussion of this process appears in Insight 15–7.

I N S I G H T   15–7

Culture Class: GE's Management School Aims to Foster Unified Corporate Goals

As a boss, do you have this problem?

"Your budget has been cut, but the work load increases. You've been told to reduce staff while maintaining the current level of productivity, but receive no advice on how people are to keep up."

If you were a new manager at General Electric Co., you would find answers to these and 80 other problems in the "Trouble-Shooting Guide" of your New Manager Starter Kit. The kit as well as mandatory attendance at a one-week course at GE's Crotonville Management Development Institute in Ossining, N.Y., are among the tools GE is using these days to develop its future leaders—and help assimilate the diverse operations it recently has acquired.

As GE has increased its pace of acquisitions and divestitures to focus on services and technology under Chairman John F. Welch Jr., it has stepped up the importance of the 31-year-old Crotonville program. The campuslike facility, spread over 50 rolling acres near the Hudson River, has become much more than an in-house school for accounting, finance and marketing. It also spreads Chairman Welch's vision of the company and molds a common GE culture.

Other companies have management-development programs, but Crotonville is one of the most intense and systematic. As a result, it is closely studied by other companies establishing their own schools.

Although Crotonville is given much credit for helping instill GE's often-praised management style, some say such programs can be too insular.

GE is aware of that risk, says James Baughman, manager of corporate organization, management development and executive compensation. But because of the acquisition of RCA Corp., Kidder, Peabody & Co., and other concerns in recent years, as well as major changes within the parent company, he says, GE needs a program such as Crotonville to rally managers around common goals.

That program ranges from 2½-day mandatory sessions for the 2,500 new college graduates GE hires each year, to monthlong programs for mid-level and upper-level managers. Lecturers include GE executives, a retired officer from the U.S. Military Academy at West Point, and visiting professors from top business schools including Harvard, Emory and Yale.

A regular guest at Crotonville is Mr. Welch, who rarely misses his monthly visits to speak to classes and answer questions. In July, two days before GE announced the sale of its consumer-electronics business, he flew to New York from Washington so that he could address a mid-management group at Crotonville. He then left for Indianapolis to discuss the impending sale with GE officials.

And what does GE recommend in the case cited at the top of this story? The "Trouble-Shooting Guide" advises, hold brainstorming sessions with staff, don't discourage negative comments, look for more efficient methods, and focus on top priority tasks.

As organizations grow larger and more sophisticated, cultural change becomes more difficult. Not only will a general culture become more firmly entrenched, but separate cultures may develop as functional areas are identified in the organizational structure.

Finally, cultural change in mature organizations is nearly impossible without the threat of crisis or changes in executive leadership. A downturn in organizational performance may require personnel cutbacks, divestments, or other dramatic signs of retrenchment. These activities can suggest a crisis to the remaining employees and signal a need to carefully reevaluate the existing way of doing things.

One or more of these situational factors could enhance a firm's ability to change the corporate culture. An actual change in culture is best implemented by using one or more of the tactics discussed earlier for maintaining a culture. Thus, an organization's culture can be altered by changing:

- The way the firm responds to crises.
- Its managers.
- The way existing managers behave.
- What gets measured or controlled.
- The criteria for allocating rewards.
- The bases for personnel decisions.

If a crisis forces a company to move from an individualistic culture to one of teamwork and cooperation, managers would have to evaluate and reward team performance as opposed to individual performance. IBM's decision to move people from staff positions into more productive sales positions is a reaction to changing market conditions, changing leadership, and a return to the original motto of its founder, Thomas Watson: "Service to the Customer and Respect for the Individual."[45]

We have seen that the internal environment, the corporate culture, can play an important role in the functioning of an organization. To a large extent, the nature of the corporate culture acts as an invisible glue that can hold the organization together in times of crisis. Like societal cultures, however, corporate cultures develop over relatively long periods of time. They have a strong influence on the attitudes and behaviors of employees, and they are extremely difficult to change.

CHAPTER HIGHLIGHTS

Organizations are most usefully viewed as **open systems**. This means that they are influenced by their environments. This chapter examined two environments—the external environment and the internal environment, also called the **corporate culture.**

A firm's **external environment includes factors that exist outside of the organization's boundaries.** The environment makes demands, imposes constraints, and provides opportunities.

An organization's external environment comprises a number of sectors that can be grouped into primary and secondary environments. **The primary environment contains sectors that most directly influence a firm,** including human resources, financial resources, material resources, technology, industry, and customers. **The secondary environment contains sectors that have an indirect impact on a firm.** Included in this environment are the government/political, economic, and cultural/demographic sectors. For some companies, certain sectors will be more important than others; and these should be monitored more intensively.

The number of important sectors **(complexity)** and the rate of change in those sectors **(stability)** contribute to managerial perceptions of environmental uncertainty. **Uncertainty can vary from low in a simple–stable environment to high in a complex–dynamic environment.**

Organizational responses to the environment can be directed at changes in the internal organization processes or attempts to manage the external environment. Internal changes include the formation of **boundary-spanning positions and units, increased differentiation and integration, and the imposition of differing planning and control processes.** We distinguished between the formalized and centralized control processes of the **mechanistic** organization and the informal, decentralized processes of the **organic** organization.

Attempts to better control or manage the environment can be undertaken by establishing links with important environmental sectors, or changing the domain in which the organization operates. Tactics for establishing linkages include joint ventures or mergers, contracts, board memberships, and advertising. **Domain management tactics** include political activities and trade association memberships. Organizational responses to environmental uncertainty are not independent; and **choosing one approach does not preclude choosing others.** Organizations typically undertake a variety of activities to reduce environmental uncertainty to more acceptable levels.

While a firm's external environment is important, managers cannot forget the significance of their internal environment or corporate culture. **Corporate culture is defined as shared values, beliefs and understandings.** Corporate culture arises from the values and personality of the founder or other dominant leader. **To maintain the culture, managers can use a variety of tactics, including measurement and control emphasis, crisis reactions, role modeling, reward allocation, and personnel decisions.** The strength of a culture is related to a number of important organizational outcomes like commitment and control. **But the relationship between culture and performance is not strong.** Culture's relationship to performance is probably dependent on a number of other factors.

Finally, we discussed ways to change an organization's culture. **There is a set of situational factors (crisis, leader change, company age, and stage of development) whose presence could make cultural changes easier.** It was also suggested that changes in any of the tactics designed to maintain a current culture could be used to change that culture. **Successful cultural change frequently requires a major upheaval that completely shatters the existing culture.** Obviously, this is neither a painless nor a cost-free process.

An organization's external and internal environments provide a context within which the other elements of the organization must operate. As a starting point, an understanding of the external environment gives managers information about appropriate strategic goals and objectives for their organization. The next chapter examines the issues of organization goals and objectives, as well as ways in which the effectiveness of organizations can be determined.

REVIEW QUESTIONS

1. What is meant by the term *external environment?* Why does the open system perspective make environments more important for managers?

2. In what three ways can the environment influence a firm?

3. Explain the difference between primary and secondary external environments. What sectors are usually found in each environment?

4. Which environmental sectors are currently important for each of the following organizations?
   a. Your college or university
   b. General Motors or Ford
   c. A local hospital
   d. Chase Manhattan Bank
   e. Al & Alice's Bowling Emporium

5. What is *environmental uncertainty?* How do stability and complexity contribute to uncertainty?

6. What boundary-spanning units exist at your college or university? What core technology are they designed to buffer? Why might some boundary units be more powerful than others?

7. What are the basic differences between mechanistic and organic approaches to organizational control? In what environment is each approach likely to be effective?

8. "The environment is simply too big to manage." How would you respond to this statement?

9. Describe how links between organizations help to reduce uncertainty.

10. If the environment is so important for organizational survival, why do so many managers fail to keep in touch with their environment?

11. Since managers cannot actually see a corporate culture, what aspects of the organization might allow them to make some guesses about the nature of the culture?

12. How does a corporate culture usually develop?

13. What are some of the ways to maintain a corporate culture?

14. What are the major differences between cultures in:
    a. A high school and a college or university.
    b. Different college or university classes.
    c. Different campus organizations.

15. What situational factors would probably work to support a successful change in a corporate culture? Why are these important?

16. What are the relationships between corporate culture and important organizational outcomes?

RESOURCE READINGS

Aldrich, H. *Organizations and Environments.* Englewood Cliffs, N.J.: 1979.

Deal, T., and A. Kennedy. *Corporate Culture: The Rites and Rituals of Corporate Life.* Reading, Mass.: Addison-Wesley Publishing, 1982.

Meyer, M., and associates. *Environments and Organizations.* San Francisco: Jossey-Bass, 1978.

Sathe, V. *Culture and Related Corporate Realities.* Homewood, Ill.: Richard D. Irwin, 1985.

Schein, E. *Organizational Culture and Leadership.* San Francisco: Jossey-Bass, 1986.

Wilkins, A., and N. Bristow. "For Successful Organizational Culture, Honor Your Past." *Academy of Management Executive,* August 1988, pp. 221–29.

NOTES

1. J. Thompson, *Organizations in Action* (New York: McGraw-Hill, 1967), pp. 4–13.

2. Ibid.

3. R. Daft, *Organization Theory and Design,* 2d ed. (St. Paul, Minn.: West Publishing, 1986), p. 49.

4. Thompson, *Organizations in Action*.

5. W. Dill, "Environments as an Influence on Managerial Autonomy," *Administrative Science Quarterly*, June 1958, pp. 409–43.

6. B. Schlender and J. Miller, "Shortage of Memory Chips Forces Some Computer Firms to Curtail Output," *Wall Street Journal*, February 26, 1988.

7. W. Dowling, "Job redesign on the assembly line: Farewell to the blue collar blues," *Organizational Dynamics*, Autumn 1973, pp. 51–67.

8. T. Moore, "Make-or-Break Time for General Motors," *Fortune*, February 15, 1988, pp. 33–40.

9. P. Lawrence and D. Dyer, *Renewing American Industry* (New York: Free Press, 1983), pp. 55–85.

10. H. Brody, "U.S. Robot Makers Try to Bounce Back," *High Technology Business*, October 1987, pp. 18–24.

11. J. Sculley, "Sculley's Lessons From Inside Apple," *Fortune*, September 14, 1987, pp. 108–18.

12. J. Hamilton, "Birth of a Blockbuster: How Genentech Delivered the Goods," *Business Week*, November 30, 1987, pp. 138–42.

13. E. Ehrlich, "Are Wine Coolers Leading Kids to Drink," *Business Week*, October 26, 1987, p. 38.

14. D. Hickson, C. Hinings, C. Lee, R. Schneck, and J. Pennings, "A Strategic Contingencies Theory of Intraorganizational Power," *Administrative Science Quarterly*, June 1971, pp. 216–29.

15. R. Duncan, "Characteristics of Organizational Environments and Perceived Environmental Uncertainty," *Administrative Science Quarterly*, September 1972, pp. 313–27.

16. Ibid.

17. Ibid.

18. Adapted from R. Duncan, "What is the Right Organization Structure," *Organizational Dynamics*, Winter 1979, p. 63.

19. J. White, "Suzuki Threatens Legal Actions to Halt Complaints About Samurai Sport Vehicle," *Wall Street Journal*, March 1, 1988.

20. J. Thompson, *Organizations in Action*.

21. R. Leifer and A. Delbecq, "Organizational/Environmental Interchange: A Model of Boundary Spanning Activity," *Academy of Management Review*, January 1978, pp. 40–41.

22. J. Thompson, *Organizations in Action*.

23. P. Lawrence and J. Lorsch, *Organization and Environment* (Homewood, Ill.: Richard D. Irwin, 1969).

24. Ibid.

25. Ibid.

26. T. Burns and G. Stalker, *The Management of Innovation* (London: Tavistock, 1961).

27. J. Kotter, "Managing External Dependence," *Academy of Management Review,* January 1979, pp. 87–92.

28. G. Lewis, "Big Changes at Big Blue," *Business Week*, February 15, 1988, pp. 92–98.

29. "Johnson & Johnson Joins Chinese Venture," *Wall Street Journal*, December 3, 1987.

30. J. Hoerr, "Blue Collars in the Boardroom: Putting Business First," *Business Week*, December 14, 1987, pp. 126–28.

31. K. Wells, "Microsoft Sues to Stop Former Employee from Working for Borland, a Rival Firm," *Wall Street Journal*, December 10, 1987.

32. D. Moskowitz, "Why ATVs Could Land In a Heap of Trouble," *Business Week*, November 30, 1987, p. 38.

33. E. Schein, *Organizational Culture and Leadership* (San Francisco: Jossey-Bass, 1986), p. 6.

34. Ibid.

35. J. Hyatt, "The Indispensable Man," *INC.*, September 1987, pp. 78–86.

36. E. Schein, *Organizational Culture and Leadership.*

37. K. Labich, "Boeing Battles to Stay on Top," *Fortune*, September 28, 1987, pp. 64–72.

38. T. Peters and R. Waterman, *In Search of Excellence: Lessons From America's Best-Run Companies* (New York: Harper & Row, 1982); R. Pascale and A. Athos, *The Art of Japanese Management* (New York: Warner Books, 1981); and W. Ouchi, *Theory Z: How American Business Can Meet the Japanese Challenge* (Reading, Mass.: Addison-Wesley Publishing, 1981).

39. M. Miller, "At Many Firms, Employees Speak A Language That's All Their Own," *Wall Street Journal*, December 29, 1987.

40. Schein, *Organizational Culture and Leadership.*

41. Peters and Waterman, *In Search of Excellence.*

42. See, for example, R. Kilman and associates, *Gaining Control of the Corporate Culture* (San Francisco: Jossey-Bass, 1985).

43. Ibid.

44. Adapted from E. Schein, *Organization Culture and Leadership,* and T. Deal and A. Kennedy, *Corporate Culture: The Rites and Rituals of Corporate Life* (Reading, Mass.: Addison-Wesley Publishing, 1982).

45. D. Kneale, "Cutting Output, IBM Tells Workers: Move, Retire, or Quit," *Wall Street Journal*, April 8, 1987.

CASE: Dillard department stores

Headquartered in Little Rock, Arkansas, Dillard Department Stores Inc. is considered something of a plain jane in the retailing industry, particularly in

Adapted from M. Totty, "Expansion-Minded Dillard Is Catching Some Attention," *The Wall Street Journal,* March 16, 1988. Reprinted by permission by *The Wall Street Journal,* © Dow Jones & Company, Inc. 1988. All rights reserved.

comparison to glitzier rivals like Bloomingdale's and Saks Fifth Avenue. But Dillard has some ambitious expansion plans. It decided to open eight new stores in 1988, including its first in Iowa and Nebraska, and through a joint-venture is advancing north by acquiring Higbee Co. of Cleveland. It plans to use Higbee's 14 stores as a springboard to learn about Yankee shoppers' buying patterns.

Dillard was founded in 1938 by William Dillard, a drop-out from a Sears, Roebuck management training program. His vision was to offer name-brand merchandise that wouldn't be found in Sears' or Penney's stores. The company has long been tightly held by the Dillard family. Four of the five top executives are Dillard men—a situation that some critics say forces too many decisions to be made in Little Rock, hampering innovation. Some managers chafe at the lack of independence. Dillard buyers are required to submit each new vendor to Little Rock for approval, a process that some complain limits diversity and slows Dillard's ability to react quickly to fashion trends.

The move out of the Southwest will be challenging. The small cities where Dillard has flourished aren't much of a training ground for the markets it wants to enter. Up north the competition will be different. So what makes a no-nonsense, Arkansas-reared retailer think it can make it in the fast-changing world of fashion?

For starters, Dillard is hardly a ragtag Confederate retailer. In the past four years it has successfully consolidated a total of 73 stores accumulated in three major acquisitions. It reported a 22.5 percent jump in profit in 1987 to $91 million. Dillard keeps its buying, accounting, data processing, and advertising staffs in its four-story downtown Little Rock headquarters, giving it a comparatively lean regional staff. It also has an elaborate, much-envied management information and control system that provides hourly updates on sales and inventory in each store's department.

To be successful, Dillard recognizes that some changes are needed. It may have to revamp its highly centralized inventory control system and dress up the lackluster—some say "dull"—atmosphere in its stores. It will have to do a better job of "selling the sizzle."

Questions

1. What is the nature of the environment that Dillard is confronting as it moves to expand its operations? What environmental sectors should have the biggest impact on the success or failure of Dillard's moves?

2. How would you describe the level of uncertainty in Dillard's environment? How stable is the environment? How complex?

3. Given your assessment of the environmental uncertainty, what recommendations would you make to Dillard's management with regard to the kinds of control systems that would be most appropriate for its operations?

EXERCISE: Diagnosing corporate culture

We can assess an organization's corporate culture in a number of different ways. For instance, we could go into a firm and observe what happens in that firm over a long period of time, much like an anthropologist studies people in cities, towns, or villages. But this would be time consuming, and our judgments would be limited by the quantity and quality of our observations.

We could amass all of the published information about a firm and try to determine the nature of its corporate culture from our interpretation of this material. Again, we would be limited in our interpretation by our ability to find this information.

Finally, we could undertake a broader investigation by using an interview or survey approach. In this procedure, a number of employees would be selected to take part in an interview or to complete a survey designed to measure the corporation's culture. One example of such an interview/survey form is presented below.

Instructions: Working alone or in groups, select several individuals who work in the same organization. This could be a campus organization, a local establishment that serves your campus, or a larger manufacturing, service, or nonprofit organization. Provide each employee the following set of questions.

Diagnosing Corporate Culture

Directions: Please answer the following six questions related to your organization. Each of these items contains descriptions of four organizations. Please distribute 100 points among the four descriptions, depending on how similar the description is to your own organization. None of the descriptions is any better than the others; they are just different. For each question, please use the full 100 points.

In question 1, for example, if Organization A seems very similar to your organization, B seems somewhat similar, and C and D do not seem similar at all, you might give 70 points to A and the remaining 30 points to B. C and D would not receive any points.

1. Dominant Characteristics (Divide 100 points.)

   a. _____ Organization A is a very personal place. It is like an extended family. People seem to share a lot of themselves.

   b. _____ Organization B is a very dynamic and entrepreneurial place. People are willing to stick their necks out and take risks.

    c. _____ Organization C is a very formalized and structured place. Bureaucratic procedures generally govern what people do.

    d. _____ Organization D is very competitive in orientation. A major concern is with getting the job done. People are very production and achievement oriented.

2. Organizational Leader (Divide 100 points.)

    a. _____ The head of organization A is generally considered to be a mentor, a facilitator, or a parent figure.

    b. _____ The head of organization B is generally considered to be an entrepreneur, an innovator, or a risk taker.

    c. _____ The head of organization C is generally considered to be a coordinator, an organizer, or an efficiency expert.

    d. _____ The head of organization D is generally considered to be a hard driver, a producer, or a competitor.

3. Organizational Glue (Divide 100 points.)

    a. _____ The glue that holds organization A together is loyalty and commitment. Cohesion and teamwork are characteristic of this organization.

    b. _____ The glue that holds organization B together is a focus on innovation and development. The emphasis is on being at the cutting edge.

    c. _____ The glue that holds organization C together is formal procedures, rules, or policies. Maintaining a smooth-running organization is important.

    d. _____ The glue that holds organization D together is an emphasis on production and goal accomplishment. Marketplace aggressiveness is a common theme.

4. Organizational Climate (Divide 100 points.)

    a. _____ The climate inside organization A is participative and comfortable. High trust and openness exist.

    b. _____ The climate inside organization B emphasizes dynamism and readiness to meet new challenges. Trying new things and trial-and-error learning are common.

    c. _____ The climate inside organization C emphasizes permanence and stability. Expectations regarding procedures are clear and enforced.

    d. _____ The climate inside organization D is competitive and confrontational. Emphasis is placed on beating the competition.

5. Criteria of Success (Divide 100 points.)

    a. _____ Organization A defines success on the basis of its development of human resources, teamwork, and concern for people.

    b. _____ Organization B defines success on the basis of its having unique or the newest products. It is a product leader and innovator.

    c. _____ Organization C defines success on the basis of efficiency. Dependable delivery, smooth scheduling, and low-cost production are critical.

    d. _____ Organization D defines success on the basis of market penetration and market share. Being number one relative to the competition is a key objective.

6. Management Style (Divide 100 points.)

    a. _____ The management style in organization A is characterized by teamwork, consensus, and participation.

    b. _____ The management style in organization B is characterized by individual initiative, innovation, freedom, and uniqueness.

    c. _____ The management style in organization C is characterized by security of employment, longevity in position, and predictability.

    d. _____ The management style in organization D is characterized by hard-driving competitiveness, production, and achievement.

In the spaces below, sum the number of points given to Organization A (alternative *a*) for all six items. Then divide by 6 to obtain an average number of points for Organization A. Do the same for the points you assigned to the other three organizations.

Total Points Assigned   **Average Points for**

Organization A items	divided by 6	Organization A
Organization B items	divided by 6	Organization B
Organization C items	divided by 6	Organization C
Organization D items	divided by 6	Organization D

    If you have found more than one employee for the organization you are investigating, do the same calculations for each one. Then sum their average results for each organization, and divide by the number of people you talked to. This will give you the overall description of the company's culture.

Interpreting Your Results

You can interpret the results of your research efforts by plotting the values of the individual or group responses for each corporate culture dimension on the profile sheet in Exhibit 1. The responses for alternative *a* should be plotted in the upper-left-hand quadrant of each chart; alternative *b* should be plotted in the upper-right-hand quadrant; alternative *c* should be plotted in the lower-left-hand quadrant; and alternative *d* should be plotted in the lower-right-hand quadrant. Each hash mark counts 10 points. In some cases, the plots may need to be extended beyond the end of the line, if, say, 60 or 70 points were given to an alternative. After plotting each point, connect the points with straight lines. Summing and averaging the *a* alternatives, the *b* alternatives, and so on for all six questions produces an overall cultural profile. It should be plotted on the overall profile sheet (Exhibit 2). Your instructor will provide additional information regarding an interpretation of your results.

Source: Adapted from K. S. Cameron, "Conceptual Foundations of Organizational Culture," in J. R. Smart (ed.) *Higher Education: Handbook of Theory and Research*, Vol. 4 (New York: Agathon, 1988). Reproduced in R. E. Quinn, *Beyond Rational Management* (San Francisco: Jossey-Bass, 1988) pp. 142–47.

EXHIBIT 1:

Organizational Culture Plots

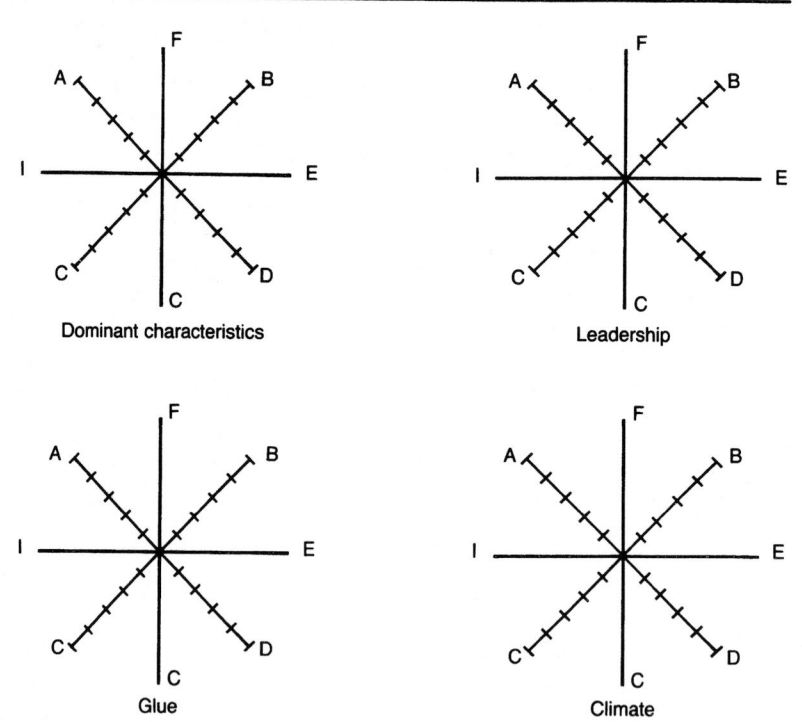

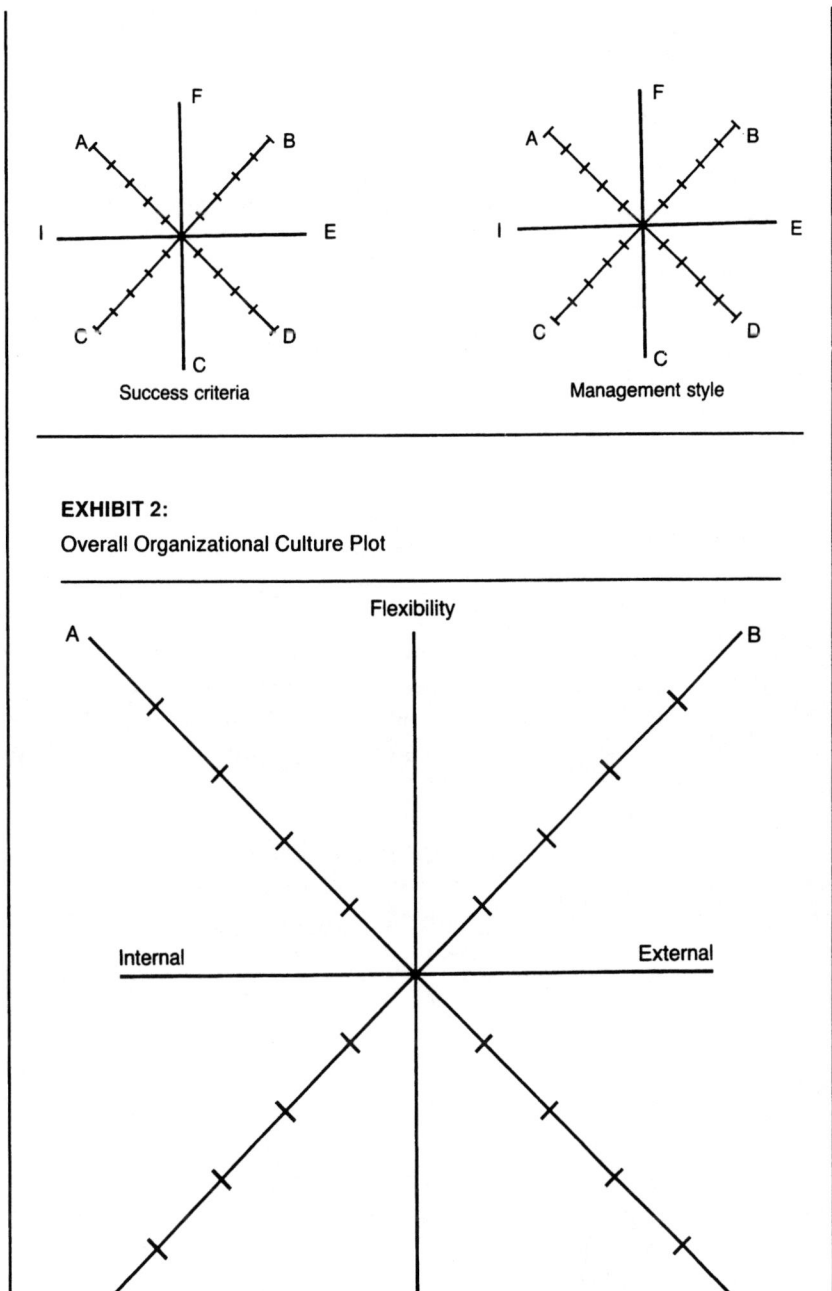

Success criteria

Management style

EXHIBIT 2:

Overall Organizational Culture Plot

Flexibility

Internal

External

Control

Organizational Goals and Effectiveness

I n the last chapter we examined two important elements of an organization's context: its external and internal environments. An equally important element of this context are the **goals and objectives** of an organization. The question of which comes first, the establishment of goals or an appreciation of the environment, might provoke an interesting debate. On the one hand, the environment allows firms to pursue only certain kinds of goals. On the other hand, goals can be established that allow an organization to operate in more-or-less tolerant environments.

Regardless of which comes first, a discussion of organizational goals is useful. We discussed the importance and significance of *individual* goals in an earlier chapter; but our discussion here examines goals and objectives from an *organizational* perspective. In particular, we will consider why goals are important for organizations, as well as the types of goals that organizations establish. We also will discuss a set of guidelines for selecting and implementing goals throughout an organization.

Goals provide a set of outcomes that managers and others can use to evaluate how well a firm is performing. This evaluation is one way to determine **organizational effectiveness**—the topic of the last half of this chapter. Since effectiveness should mean more than impressive numbers on a balance sheet, we will discuss four options for measuring a firm's effectiveness. Each is designed to assess a different aspect of a firm's operations.

Finally, the chapter offers some guidelines for choosing which option (or options) to use when evaluating an organization's effectiveness. Before we get into these issues, however, let's visit the annual board meeting at Home Computers Company.

Home Computers Case	**Home Computers Company—The Annual Board Meeting** At 4:30 P.M., Harvey Brown brought the gavel down sharply on the oak block and declared the annual HCC board meeting adjourned. Since incorporating the firm seven years ago, the annual board meeting was the highlight of the year for Harvey and his management team. This year was no exception. Harvey was able to report increases in profitability, revenues, and market share. He felt he had reason to be proud of his accomplishments. Once again, however, the board meeting was marked by the usual haggling over where HCC should be going in the future. And despite Harvey's feelings of accomplishment, there had also been some discussion of how effectively Harvey and the management team had conducted the affairs of the corporation for the past year.

As usual, the discussion of corporate goals and strategies consumed a large amount of the board's time and energy. Board members seemed torn between the twin goals of profit maximization and market share increase. While the two goals were not incompatible, Louise, vice president of sales, pointed out that increasing market share usually required reducing prices and increasing advertising and promotion expenditures. She reminded the board that unless other costs could be contained or reduced, this strategy might erode profit margins substantially.

Two new board members representing several nonbusiness constituencies reminded Harvey (and the board) of HCC's continuing responsibility to be a good corporate citizen. In addition to establishing financial and market goals for the next fiscal year, this meant continued efforts in behalf of various charitable organizations. It also meant renewed assurances that HCC's manufacturing processes would not pollute the environment or expose employees to hazardous working conditions.

As the meeting continued, Harvey caught himself wondering how other chief executive officers balanced these multiple and occasionally conflicting goals. He also realized that goals established at the board level often bore little resemblance to relevant goals set elsewhere in the firm. Now, that was a management problem!

ORGANIZATIONAL GOALS

Organizational goals are not only **"a desired state of affairs that an organization attempts to realize;"**[1] they are more than this. For instance, HCC has a variety of goals it wants to achieve; and it appears that some of them can only be achieved at the expense of other goals. And HCC's goals have been changing. They are not static or chiseled in stone. Rather, they are dynamic; they change as a result of top management decisions made in the face of a constantly changing environment. Goals, like other organizational inputs, can be viewed as resources; and resources must be managed. Thus, we begin our discussion of goals by considering why they are important for a firm.

Why are goals important?

To paraphrase the title of a book on individual goal setting, if an organization does not know where it is going, it will probably end up somewhere else.[2] Goals give a firm the direction it needs, so it will end up where it wants to be. Properly managed and communicated, goals play many important roles for organizations and their employees. HCC—like most firms—developed its goals for three basic reasons: to give legitimacy to the firm; to provide direction, motivation, and commitment; and to establish performance standards.[3] These reasons are discussed more fully below.

To give legitimacy to the firm

Organizations succeed when they convince key sectors in the external environment that they can provide a product or service at an appropriate price within the constraints imposed by that environment. Primary and secondary environment sectors need to know what an organization intends to do and how it intends to do it. The establishment and communication of goals to employees and to these external environments accomplishes this purpose.

For instance, in its corporate mission statement, HCC claims that its organizational goals include the following:

■ To conduct business with integrity.
■ To maintain an atmosphere of respect for employees.
■ To maintain financial strength to meet all obligations.
■ To provide for customers' future requirements.
■ To earn reasonable returns for investors.
■ To be a responsible corporate citizen.

If important sectors of the environment accept these goals as legitimate, then HCC will be allowed to continue. If one or more of these goals are viewed as illegitimate (unwanted, unneeded, illegal, harmful to society, or immoral), then HCC would not be allowed to continue—or would fail because no one would buy its products.

To provide direction, motivation, and commitment

While goals serve an external purpose of securing legitimacy, they also serve several internal purposes. In the face of constantly changing environments, goals provide a broad set of guidelines to direct employee behaviors at all levels in an organization. Goal or mission statements inform employees about the major purposes of a company. For instance, the three major TV networks have each established different goals for what viewers might see as the same environment. NBC is interested in broad diversification. ABC, already diversified, seeks to upgrade prime-time programming. And CBS is willing to maintain the status quo, although some argue that Laurence Tisch, CBS's chief executive, is directionless.[4] Only time will tell which of these goals is most appropriate for the industry's environment.

If employees believe in a firm's mission, they are more likely to be committed and motivated to work toward these outcomes. For instance,

Chairperson James Olson needed his executives to commit to new goals for AT&T after the breakup of the company's monopoly on telephone service. In 1986, Olson had been unable to implement a modest change in goals for the firm because he "hadn't gotten [his] managers to buy into it." At a planning session in 1988, Olson and 27 key executives met to develop a new set of goals for AT&T. At the end of the session, Olson invited each executive present to stand. "Are you with me?" he asked. Not surprisingly, each executive publicly bought into the new set of goals.[5]

Goals also direct specific employee behaviors, particularly when these behaviors are not or cannot be covered by policies or procedures. Exciting and acceptable goals may also attract new employees.

To establish performance standards

Finally, goals establish at least one set of possible performance criteria for an organization. This set can be as specific or as general as top management wishes. For example, the HCC board's evaluation of Harvey's performance was based on such typical organizational goals as profits, revenues, return on assets, and return on investments. But the board also evaluated nonfinancial outcomes, such as market share, turnover rates, production volumes, and customer complaints. The extent to which a company achieves its goals and meets its standards becomes one indicator of organizational effectiveness.

Insight 16–1 illustrates how new executives at Westinghouse use organizational goals to serve these three important functions.

The family of goals

Some people might think that a goal by any other name is still a goal. But when we talk about goals in an organizational context, we distinguish three different types: official or strategic goals; operative or tactical goals; and operational goals. As we'll discuss shortly, operational goals are developed from operative goals. These, in turn, are derived from official goals. Thus, there exists a hierarchy within this family of goals. We begin our discussion with the most general and highest-level goals—the official goals of a firm.

Official goals

Insight 16–2 (p. 660) presents Procter & Gamble's statement of purpose. This is an example of a set of official or strategic goals. **Official goals refer to outcomes that the organization publicly and formally identifies as worthy of pursuit.**[6] Usually found in organizational charters, annual reports, and corporate mission statements, an official goal "provides the foundation for priorities, strategies, plans, and work assignments. It is

---

I N S I G H T 16-1

Westinghouse's New Top Executives Set Goal of 10% Per-Share Profit Rise in '88

*P*ittsburgh—Westinghouse Electric Corp.'s new top executives said they expect per-share earnings growth of at least 10% in 1988 on a sales gain of about 8.5%.

John C. Marous, chairman and chief executive officer, and Paul E. Lego, president and chief operating officer, also said they intend to move Westinghouse from a "good" corporation to a "great" one by enhancing shareholder value and becoming "quality obsessed."

In a news conference on their first day in office, the executives said they plan "to stick closely" to the strategic direction of Mr. Marous's predecessor, Douglas D. Danforth, who retired. Mr. Lego's positions are new. But they indicated they want to communicate better "exactly what Westinghouse is and what it does."

Financial analysts have complained that the company hasn't defined itself well or disclosed where it's going.

Westinghouse has interests in electronics, defense electronics, broadcasting, finan-

cial services, industrial and energy systems, among other things. But many consumers still think the company makes light bulbs and appliances, two fields it left years ago. And, although only 20% of its business comes from the electric utility market, Westinghouse usually is categorized as an electric company along with General Electric Corp. and Emerson Electric Corp.

Mr. Lego, 57, said Westinghouse anticipates that about 35% of its revenue growth this year will come from acquisitions and growth of new internal businesses. The company has focused attention on developing such new businesses as waste-to-energy systems, hazardous-waste and toxic-waste management, and providing sophisticated security systems. He said the company will continue to pare costs.

One analyst who follows the company applauded the attention to defining Westinghouse. "Right now no one thinks it exists. They must continually address that goal to try and earn credibility," said the analyst, requesting anonymity.

---

the starting point for the design of managerial jobs and structures. It specifies the fundamental reason why an organization exists."[7]

While official goals are designed to give direction and in some way define acceptable organizational performance, their basic function is to provide acceptance by the external environment. These goals give the organization legitimacy. Official goals tell important sectors of the environment what an organization intends to accomplish. Thus, these goals must be communicated to the public—to become the basis by which potential employees and investors choose to place their efforts or their money, for instance. While no goal is ever permanent, official goals change little over time.

I N S I G H T   16–2

Procter & Gamble's Statement of Purpose

We will provide products of superior quality and value that best fill the needs of the world's consumers.

We will achieve that purpose through an organization and a working environment which attracts the finest people; fully develops and challenges our individual talents; encourages our free and spirited collaboration to drive the business ahead; and maintains the Company's historic principles of integrity, and doing the right thing.

Through the successful pursuit of our commitment, we expect our brands to achieve leadership share and profit positions and that, as a result, our business, our people, our shareholders, and the communities in which we live and work, will prosper.

These are the principles that guide our actions as a Company and our attitudes about our employees:

- We will employ, throughout the Company, the best people we can find without regard to race or gender or any other differences unrelated to performance. We will promote on the same basis.

- We recognize the vital importance of continuing employment because of its ultimate tie with the strength and success of our business.

- We will build our organization from within. Those persons with ability and performance records will be given the opportunity to move ahead in the Company.

- We will pay our employees fairly, with careful attention to the compensation of each individual. Our benefit programs will be designed to provide our employees with adequate protection in time of need.

- We will encourage and reward individual innovation, personal initiative and leadership, and willingness to manage risk.

- We will encourage teamwork across disciplines, divisions and geography to get the most effective integration of the ideas and efforts of our people.

- We will maximize the development of individuals through training and coaching on what they are doing well and how they can do better. We will evaluate Procter & Gamble managers on their record in developing their subordinates.

- We will maintain and build our corporate tradition which is rooted in the principles of personal integrity; doing what's right for the long-term; respect for the individual; and being the best in what we do.

Reproduced with permission from The Procter & Gamble Company.

Official goals are important for both large and small firms. For instance, the mission statement at 3M encourages "the promotion of entrepreneurship" and "the preservation of individual identity." At a small shoe-repair shop in Cambridge, Massachusetts, the official goal is mounted on the wall for all to see: "We are dedicated to the saving of soles, heeling, and administering to the dyeing."[8]

"Don't you ever worry about your lack of long-range goals?"

Source: © 1988 James Stevenson

Operative goals

Official goals are too general to be of great help in actually determining how an organization will operate. If official goals specify generally *what* an organization is trying to accomplish, then operative goals specify *how.* **Operative goals represent the primary means or tactics by which an organization plans to achieve its official goals.**[9] One of HCC's official goals is "to be a responsible corporate citizen." In Harvey's mind, this includes protecting the environment from harm. A related operative goal for HCC reads, "To minimize pollution levels in gaseous, liquid, and solid waste discharged by our manufacturing facilities." The time horizon for achieving operative goals is typically two to five years.

Operational goals

At lower levels in an organization, **operational goals, derived from the firm's operative goals, identify specific performance objectives for each work unit and, in some cases, for each employee.**[10] Since operational goals function at a specific level, they can also act as standards against which work unit or individual performance can be evaluated. Following from HCC's operative pollution goal, an operational goal for the manufacturing plants might read, "To maintain levels of sulfide emissions at no more than 15 parts per billion." Time horizons for these goals are typically set in terms of months, but may be as short as weekly or even daily. Exhibit 16–1 illustrates relationships between and examples of the different types of goals.

Achieving these goals

Associated with each type of goal are the relevant processes by which these goals can be achieved. **Organizational strategies** are designed to give top management general directions on how to achieve official goals. **Organizational policies/tactics** facilitate the achievement of operative goals. Finally, **rules, regulations, and standard operating procedures** direct the accomplishment of operational goals.[11]

EXHIBIT 16–1

Relationships among the Organizational Goals

Hierarchy of Goals		Hierarchy of the Firm
Official goals	established by	Board of directors and top management
Operative goals	established by and to be used by	Top- and middle-level management
Operational goals	established by and to be used by	Middle- and lower-level management and other employees

Examples of the Different Types of Goals

Official goals	Operative goals	Operational goals
Fair return on investment	Provide 12% rate of return	Net profits of $150 million
Respect for employees	Improve morale 10%	Reduce turnover; 3% firmwide gain on attitude survey
Be a good corporate citizen	Increase community activities	Managers will join local service groups

Source: Adapted from R. Webber, M. Morgan, and P. Browne, *Management,* 3d ed. (Homewood, Ill.: Richard D. Irwin, 1985), pp. 229–301.

Goal selection and implementation

Simply deciding on a goal and announcing it does not guarantee that the goal will be pursued successfully. In selecting and implementing official, operative, and operational goals, top management must consider several important factors.[12]

1. All organization goals must *contribute* in some way to the desired outcomes of the organization. Goals and strategies for their achievement should minimize possible goal conflicts; and the rationale for the goals and strategies should be known to all managers. No manager or supervisor should ever say, "I don't know why we do it that way. It's just our policy."

2. From this perspective, then, organizational goals, strategies, policies, procedures, and rules should be *congruent*—both horizontally and vertically. **Horizontal congruence requires minimizing possible conflicts between goals at the same level regarding different organizational outcomes.** For example, in the HCC board meeting, Louise was concerned about possible conflicts between profit goals and market share goals. She was not sure these two goals could be congruent.

The Timberland Company, a U.S. shoe and boot maker, has established a strong image as a maker of premium boots and hand-sewn shoes. But declining sales in early 1987 forced the firm to establish new goals. Major conflicts arose in developing the goals needed to turn the company around. Marketing wanted to move into even more expensive shoes. Sales wanted to design a special line of lower-priced footwear and move toward the middle of the shoe market. Since these goals could not be achieved simultaneously, there was little horizontal goal congruence at Timberland.[13]

Vertical congruence requires minimizing possible conflicts between goals at different levels regarding *the same* organizational outcome. At HCC, the pollution abatement goals were congruent at all three levels. On the other hand, consider the company's official goal: "To maintain an atmosphere of respect for all employees." If HCC decided to reduce costs (an operative goal) by imposing mandatory overtime requirements (an operational goal) instead of hiring new employees, this lower-level goal would not be congruent with the official goal of maintaining a respectful climate.

The congruence guidelines ensure that the pursuit of different goals at the same level or the same goal at different levels will not create unwanted or unexpected outcomes.

3. Goals should be viewed as both *feasible* and *realistic* by those responsible for their implementation and achievement. This point, made earlier about individual goals, also holds for organizational goals. Organizational goals at every level must be developed after a realistic as-

sessment of what the market wants or needs or can be made to want; what the environmental opportunities and constraints are; and what organizational resources are available to achieve the goals.[14] Unrealistic or impossible goals will not be accepted by the external environment—and Chapter 5 indicated the same resistance could be anticipated from managers and employees.

4. Goals should be sufficiently *flexible* for an organization to meet unanticipated opportunities or challenges from the environment. It was suggested earlier that official or strategic goals tend to be of longer duration than operative or operational goals. But a balance must be struck: goals are not cast in bronze; neither should they be changed on mere whim.

5. At every level, goals should be *written, publicized, communicated, and taught.* This is an important implementation step for two reasons. First, if a firm is unwilling or unable to put its goals in writing, then these goals are probably too unclear or ambiguous to be of use to the organization. Second, if top management fails to publicize, communicate, and teach its goals, then management may fear for the legitimacy of some goals and the company's ultimate survival. Insight 16–3 contains an excerpt from a manager who believes passionately in the importance of writing and communicating goals.

6. Finally, like all organizational resources, goals should be *managed.* They should be reexamined on a regular basis and revised or maintained as needed. At each level, flexible goals should allow response to changes in the internal or external environment. For instance, the breakup of AT&T required a major reexamination of organizational goals. Executives in that firm had to answer such questions as: What businesses should AT&T now be in? Should it continue to rely on Bell Labs to design new products, or should it buy some from the outside? Fortunately, after three years of struggling to answer these questions (and three years of lack-luster performance), the company identified acceptable goals and righted itself.[15] If goals become obsolete in a rapidly changing environment and are not replaced, then the organization will likely fail.

The factors influencing effective goal selection and implementation are summarized in Exhibit 16–2 (p. 666).

Goals: A developmental perspective

Like individuals, organizations go through a series of developmental stages. To a large extent, the duration of each stage is a function of the relative success of the organization. Successful companies may grow larger and mature faster than unsuccessful ones. Still, at each stage in its development, the organization confronts differing and usually more complex environments. As an organization grows larger, its goals, man-

---

I N S I G H T 16–3

Robert Townsend on "Objectives"

One of the important functions of a leader is to make the organization concentrate on its objectives. In the case of Avis, it took us six months to define one objective—which turned out to be: "We want to become the fastest-growing company with the highest profit margin in the business of renting and leasing vehicles without drivers."

That objective was simple enough so that we didn't have to write it down. We could put it in every speech and talk about it wherever we went. And it had some social significance, because up to that time Hertz had a crushingly large share of the market and was thinking and acting like General Motors.

It also included a definition of our business: "renting and leasing vehicles without drivers." This let us put the blinders on ourselves and stop considering the acquisition of related businesses like motels, hotels, airlines, and travel agencies. It also showed us that we had to get rid of some limousine and sightseeing companies that we already owned.

Once these objectives are agreed on, the leader must be merciless on himself and on his people. If an idea that pops into his head or out of their mouths is outside the objective of the company, he kills it without a trial.

Peter Drucker was never more right than when he wrote in his 1964 book *Managing for Results*:

Concentration is the key to economic results . . . no other principle of effectiveness is violated as constantly today as the basic principle of concentration . . . Our motto seems to be: 'Let's do a little bit of everything.'*

It isn't easy to concentrate. I used to keep a sign opposite my desk where I couldn't miss it if I was on the telephone (about to make an appointment) or in a meeting in my office: "Is what I'm doing or about to do getting us closer to our objective?" That sign saved me from a lot of useless trips, lunch dates, conferences, junkets, and meetings.

*Managing for Results, New York: Harper & Row, 1964.

Adapted from "Objectives," in R. Townsend, *Further Up the Organization* (New York: Alfred A. Knopf, 1984), pp. 155–56.

---

agement styles, and structure will change. The focus here is on the nature of organizational goals in each of four stages: entrepreneurial, early maturity, midlife, and maturity.[16]

In the **entrepreneurial stage, survival is the major goal of the new organization.** At the official level, legitimacy is sought from government agencies, suppliers, and customers. At the operative and operational levels, meeting cash flow requirements tends to be the dominant goal.

As the firm solidifies its position and moves into the **early maturity stage, goals change from a concern for survival to a concern for growth.** Growth goals may be stated in terms of market share or profits, for example. Official goals may now include concerns for employee development and corporate social responsibilities.

EXHIBIT 16–2

Factors Influencing Effective Goal Selection and Implementation

---

Goals should contribute.

Goals should be congruent—horizontally and vertically.

Goals should be feasible and realistic.

Goals should be flexible.

Goals should be written, publicized, communicated, and taught.

Goals should be managed.

Source: Adapted from F. Paine and W. Naumes, *Strategy and Policy Formation: An Integrative Approach* (Philadelphia: W. B. Saunders, 1974).

The larger the organization becomes, the more difficult it is for a single entrepreneur or small management team to control activities throughout the firm. In its **midlife stage**, professional managers are hired, and operative and operational goals become more important for giving direction to subordinate employees and for measuring performance of these managers. **Goals may shift from an emphasis on growth to increased concerns for stability of organization systems, successful interactions with the environment, and maintenance of market share.**

In the **mature stage, top management becomes more concerned with potential problems of stagnation.** Excellence of reputation remains an important organizational goal; but managers now direct their attention to developing the unique competencies of the firm that will allow it to remain competitive. In addition, more effort must be directed at ways to revitalize old products or services and/or develop new outputs. Operative and operational goals change accordingly at this stage.

For many years, this model offered a satisfactory description of development in many companies. Developmental models have traditionally assumed continued growth in a firm. In the mature stage, it was assumed that organizational needs for resources, technology, and market share would continue to be met. Within the past few years, however, international competition and global economic upheavals have added another, less inviting stage to the development process of many firms. This fifth stage is called **decline or resurgence.** Many companies have had to confront the realities of **shrinking resource bases, loss of technological superiority, and eroding market share from aggressive international competitors.**

In this decline/resurgence stage, many organizations have been forced to revert to the goals of the early entrepreneurial stage. They find themselves driven by the **survival** goal. Other firms, not so hard pressed, have shifted their goals to an emphasis on cost controls, including major personnel cutbacks. These new goals are an attempt at resurgence. Goals in this stage often require dramatic new strategies, including the sale of major assets or the redevelopment of those assets through a major restructuring. Other organizations have decided that even survival is unlikely, and their only goal becomes the liquidation of the organization at the most economically advantageous price.

Our discussion of goals would be lacking without a final comment with regard to the establishment of goals in organizations. The goal-setting process is not as straightforward or as rational as it might seem from the discussion here. Many groups inside and outside a firm have ideas about the appropriateness of certain goals. The process by which goals are chosen is often political, dominated by groups with relatively more power and influence. And organizational performance relative to chosen goals becomes an important determinant of a firm's effectiveness in the eyes of many different constituencies.

To begin a fuller discussion of organizational effectiveness, let's return to the Home Computers Company board meeting, as the board begins its evaluation of how well the company is doing.

Home Computers Case

Home Computers Company: The Annual Board Meeting (continued)

The second half of the board meeting was devoted to an examination of how well the management team had performed during the past year. Harvey was proud of his achievements. Market share, sales, and profits were up. Quality problems with one of the production lines had been resolved. And employee morale seemed to be on the mend. Still, two board members made inquiries about whether the organization was being run as efficiently as possible. They made the point of distinguishing between HCC's *effectiveness* at getting the job done, and the firm's *efficiency*—getting the job done with the minimum amount of resources. The question was also raised about whether or not financial performance measures, like return on investment, return on assets, and debt-to-equity ratios, were the only (and the best) measures of how well HCC performed last year.

Harvey assured the board members that his evaluation of HCC's effectiveness did not stop with financial indicators. He proudly pointed out the role the firm had played in a recent fund-raising campaign for the local symphony orchestra; and he reminded the board of the company's ongoing financial commitment to the Special Olympics.

The board agreed that Harvey and HCC had done a good job in the past year. The profit sharing formula for rewarding all HCC employees was approved. The board accepted the proposed operating budget, as well as Harvey's plan to add a third manufacturing facility. Finally, the board endorsed a new set of performance criteria against which Harvey and the HCC management team would be judged during the next fiscal year.

As Harvey walked back to his office, he was still pondering the broader implications of the board's discussion of organizational goals and effectiveness. Things had changed dramatically as HCC expanded over the past 15 years. When the management team was just Harvey and Bill Adams, determining the goals of the company was an easy task. In those first years, the only goal was survival—ensuring sufficient cash flow to pay the bills. Measures of organizational effectiveness were equally easy to determine. Could HCC open its doors tomorrow and pay the employees and the bills? If the answer was yes, then Home Computers Company was effective.

But as HCC grew, the number of organizational goals had grown, and decisions about which goals to pursue had become more complex. The same thing could be said for determining how effective the organization was. Now that HCC had gone public, there were new external constituencies with different perspectives for assessing how well the firm was doing. The assessment of the firm's effectiveness now entailed far more than simple survival and the ability to pay the bills.

ORGANIZATIONAL EFFECTIVENESS

Harvey's report to his board of directors was not nearly as emotional or depressing as the report Mr. Dithers is giving in the accompanying cartoon. But Harvey's discussion does highlight concerns that surface when attempting to evaluate how well a company is doing. Earlier we

Source: Reprinted with special permission of King Features Syndicate, Inc.

discussed individual performance and the difficulties encountered in trying to assess how well an individual is performing. Unfortunately, the evaluation process is equally difficult at the organizational level. However, to some people it might seem that this is not really the case. For instance, some might argue that all a person needs to do to determine HCC's effectiveness is to examine its stock price, profit levels, or market share. From one perspective, this approach might be useful: these figures do give a basis for comparing HCC's financial statistics with those of other organizations. However, many factors other than top management and employee activities can influence these financial measures of organizational performance.

For instance, poor financial indicators might lead people to believe that HCC was an ineffective organization, if they did not know that fires, floods, shipping wars, or other circumstances beyond the managers' control resulted in low financial indicators. In reality, management may have been extremely effective by keeping the financial performance from being even worse!

Also, measures of economic or financial well-being don't indicate *how* an organization achieved its numbers. Did management defer necessary but costly maintenance to next year, for instance? Or did they burn out their employees so the firm looked more productive in the short run, only to find that half of the work force quit the following year? In this case, new employees must be hired at substantially higher wages.

When we talk about organizational effectiveness, we need to take a much broader perspective on the issue. And we need to make a distinction between organizational effectiveness and organizational efficiency at the start. **Getting the job done or accomplishing some particular objective is synonymous with organizational effectiveness. Getting the job done using the least resources suggests organizational efficiency.**[17] If HCC can meet its target of, for example, 300,000 EZ2 computers produced for the fiscal year, we call the firm *effective*. If it can accomplish that task under budget or with minimal resources, we call it *efficient*. Most organizations (like HCC) can get the job done and get the products or services out the door. But the survivors in a particular industry are the organizations that can accomplish their tasks at costs lower than their revenues and less than or equal to their competitors.

Failure to achieve either of these cost conditions will, in time, lead to the failure of an organization—unless the organization is so large and of such strategic value that it can convince key environment sectors to keep it alive. Chrysler did this in 1979 when it obtained a $1.5 billion federal loan guarantee. The company used this loan to forestall bankruptcy and turn itself around. Chrysler repaid the loan ahead of schedule and is now a healthy organization.[18] Most failing organizations are not as fortunate as Chrysler, however.

Approaches to organizational effectiveness

What criteria should a firm choose to determine its level of effectiveness or efficiency? What options are available? Many answers have been provided to these questions. For example, consider the 30 effectiveness criteria that have been suggested in Exhibit 16–3. They reflect the diversity of the organizations being evaluated, as well as the position of the individuals or groups doing the evaluating. By themselves, the criteria are not overly helpful in an attempt to evaluate organizational effectiveness, since, in some cases, the criteria are contradictory: for example, stability and growth or efficiency (the absence of slack resources) and flexibility (requiring the presence of slack).[19]

For a more useful response to the quest for options and criteria to assess effectiveness, recall our discussion of an organization's environment. An organization was described as an open system, and it was said that sectors of the environment had different influences on the three organizational subsystems: input, throughput, and output. The systems approach also is useful when managers consider how to evaluate an organization's performance. It suggests that each subsystem can and should be evaluated individually. Exhibit 16–4 suggests how each major subsystem and an organization as a whole can be evaluated by one of four approaches: the systems resource approach, the internal

EXHIBIT 16–3

Thirty Criteria of Organizational Effectiveness

1.	Overall effectiveness	16.	Planning and goal setting
2.	Productivity	17.	Goal consensus
3.	Efficiency	18.	Internalization of goals
4.	Profit	19.	Role/norm congruence
5.	Quality	20.	Managerial interpersonal skills
6.	Accidents	21.	Managerial task skills
7.	Growth	22.	Information management
8.	Absenteeism	23.	Readiness
9.	Turnover	24.	Utilization of environment
10.	Job satisfaction	25.	Evaluations by external sectors
11.	Motivation	26.	Stability
12.	Morale	27.	Value of human resources
13.	Control	28.	Participative decision making
14.	Conflict/cohesion	29.	Training/development emphasis
15.	Flexibility/adaptation	30.	Achievement emphasis

Source: Adapted from J. Campbell, "On the Nature of Organizational Effectiveness," in P. Goodman and J. Pennings, eds., *New Perspectives on Organizational Effectiveness* (San Francisco: Jossey-Bass, 1977), pp. 36–41.

EXHIBIT 16–4

Relationships among Effectiveness Approaches and Organizational Subsystems

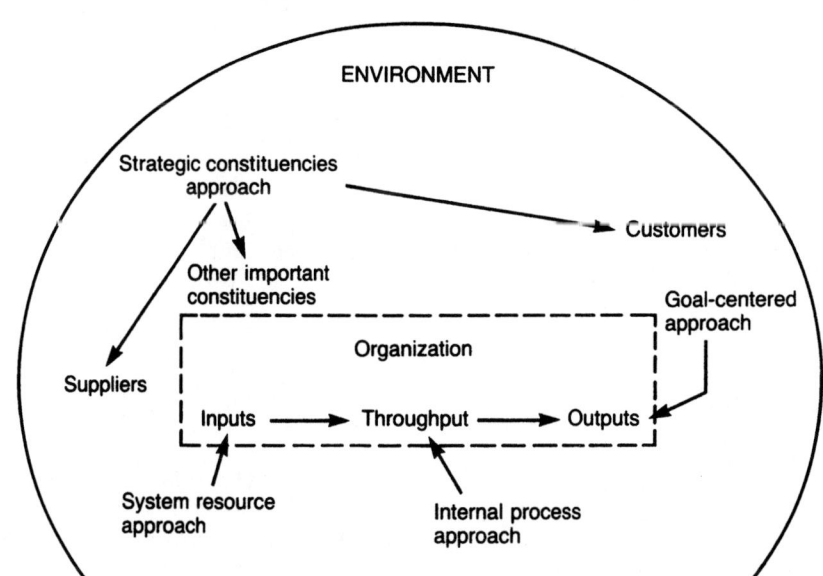

Source: Adapted from *Organizations: A Micro/Macro Approach* by Richard Daft and Richard Steers. Copyright © 1987 by Scott, Foresman and Company. Reprinted by permission.

process approach, the goal-centered approach, and the strategic constituencies approach.[20] The following sections describe each of these and then suggest several models to guide the selection of the appropriate approach.

Systems resource approach

Emphasizing the input subsystem, the system resource approach to effectiveness evaluates a firm's ability to obtain necessary resources from the environment. The organization that can obtain needed inputs is effective. The organization that is able to obtain these resources at lower cost than competitors is both effective and efficient. This approach, while not widely used, is useful when managers want to compare firms with different goals. For example, the missions of social service agencies vary widely. A systems resource approach could measure inputs, such as acquisition of funds, personnel, equipment, and office space. After allowing for the influence of agency size on these inputs, useful comparisons could be made about relative agency effectiveness. This approach would also be appropriate where competitors' facilities and technologies are nearly identical within an industry. Once again, the organization that is better able to acquire resources will be the more effective (and successful) firm.

On the other hand, where input resources are readily available and acquiring such resources does not provide a competitive advantage to an organization, emphasis for assessing effectiveness should shift to examining a firm's ability to internally process these inputs into outputs.

Internal process approach

This approach focuses on how well the throughput subsystem operates. It assesses such process factors as machine downtime, maintenance costs, absenteeism rates, employee satisfaction levels, etc. This perspective is also concerned with the morale of employees and the functioning of internal systems that facilitate employee productivity, like compensation, communications, decision making, and conflict management. The effective and efficient organization from this perspective could be called a healthy organization.

William Evan proposed a more quantitative approach for evaluating internal effectiveness.[21] He suggested that as a first step, managers determine the financial costs of the firm's input (I), throughput (T), and output (O) subsystems. These costs can then be used to develop a number of different ratios of organizational performance. Evan's most popular ratio compares outputs to inputs (O/I). In a business firm, return on investment or return on assets would be two examples of such a ratio. A T/O ratio for a college or university could be instructional costs per graduate.

The internal process approach is appealing; but using it exclusively can give an incomplete picture of how well or poorly a company is doing. There are many situations in which inputs to a firm are excellent, but the outcomes far less so. Politics and sports are two examples where this can occur. For instance, President John Kennedy surrounded himself with "the best and the brightest." Yet these individuals were responsible for the Bay of Pigs fiasco and the initial commitment of troops to Vietnam. Similarly, before his fellow owners put pressure on him, George Steinbrenner, owner of the New York Yankees, spent lavishly to acquire many talented baseball players. His results have not been impressive. The Yankees have not won the pennant since 1981.

How well inputs are used and how healthy a company is internally is a useful way to determine another aspect of effectiveness. However, this perspective says little about the quality of the outputs or their desirability to the environment. If this is an important consideration, a firm might be better off examining its ability to achieve its goals.

Goal-centered approach

The approach most widely used to determine effectiveness evaluates an organization's ability to meet its various goals. This suggests a focus on the output systems (although at lower levels in an organization, goals might be set for many other organization systems). The better able an organization is to achieve its goals, the more effective it is. For most business organizations, output goals are typically quantitative in nature: market share, profits, and return on investments, for example. For a college athletic team, one goal may be the number of wins in a season; another goal may be the player graduation rate.

This approach to effectiveness is useful only if an organization's goals can be identified, and if top management can actually influence these goals. The approach also requires that managers be in general agreement on the goals to be pursued, and that progress toward or achievement of the goals is measurable or can be determined. When it is difficult to measure goals, or when there are multiple goals with differing priorities, developing a single measure of organizational effectiveness can be difficult with this approach.

Finally, assessing only goal achievement ignores the processes used to achieve those goals. For instance, the check-kiting scam uncovered at E. F. Hutton was tolerated by upper-level management as a means to achieve organizational profit goals. Many illegal and unethical actions have been defended by managers who find them necessary to accomplish unrealistic goals set by upper management. This is highlighted in Insight 16–4.

Strategic constituencies approach

This fourth approach takes the broadest perspective on organizational effectiveness. With this approach, management assesses a firm's effectiveness by gathering relevant performance information from strategically important environmental sectors. **A strategic constituency is any group of individuals with a stake or interest in an organization and its operations.**[22] These constituencies could include customers, suppliers, employees, regulators, bankers, and countless others. While all firms have a variety of constituencies or stakeholders, it has been only recently that the importance of these groups has been publicly acknowledged. For instance, NCR Corporation launched a major public relations effort to assure constituencies that their concerns were important to the

I N S I G H T 16–4

Some Middle Managers Cut Corners to Achieve High Corporate Goals

*T*o hear some middle managers there tell it, the "pressure-cooker" atmosphere at Pittsburgh's H. J. Heinz Co. wasn't confined to the concern's steamy food-processing plants.

"When we didn't meet our growth targets, the top brass really came down on us," recalls a former marketing official at the company's huge Heinz U.S.A. division. "And everybody knew that if you missed the targets enough, you were out on your ear."

In this environment, some harried managers apparently resorted to deceptive bookkeeping when they couldn't otherwise meet profit goals set by the company's top executives. Invoices were misdated and payments to suppliers were made in advance—sometimes to be returned later in cash—all with the aim, insiders say, of showing the sort of smooth profit growth that would please top management and impress securities analysts.

Annual meeting delayed

Today, Heinz officials won't comment on the profit-juggling practices or on what led to them until an investigation is completed by the board of directors' audit committee. However, what began as an attempt to satisfy demanding superiors undoubtedly has tarnished the image of one of the country's corporate stalwarts: The Heinz annual meeting has been delayed and the outside auditors' opinion of the company's fiscal-1979 report has been withheld until the juggling schemes' precise effect—currently estimated at a cumulative $8.5 million—on previously reported Heinz earnings is determined.

Whether at Heinz or at any of the thousands of other U.S. companies, pressure to achieve goals is, of course, an everyday fact of life. Properly applied—through threat of punishment or promise of reward—such pressure can motivate employees to turn in their maximum performance. Sometimes, though, corporate goals are set too high or are simply unreasonable. Then, an employee often confronts a hard choice—to risk being branded incompetent by telling superiors that they ask too much, or to begin taking unethical or illegal shortcuts.

corporation. This effort was accompanied by an advertising campaign and student essay contest on the topic, "Creating Value for all Stakeholders in Corporations and/or Not-For-Profit Organizations." The standards against which NCR wanted to be judged by six different sets of stakeholders are presented in Insight 16–5.

Each constituency will likely be interested in different effectiveness criteria. Exhibit 16–5 (p. 676) presents some typical organizational effectiveness criteria for selected constituencies in Home Computer Company's environment.

I N S I G H T 16–5

NCR's Stakeholder Advertising Campaign—Standards for Stakeholders

Stakeholders: We believe in building a mutually beneficial and enduring relationship with all of our stakeholders, based on conducting business activities with integrity and respect.

Employees: We respect the individuality of each employee and foster an environment in which employees' creativity and productivity are encouraged, recognized, valued, and rewarded.

Supplier: We think of our suppliers as partners who share our goal of achieving the highest quality standards and the most consistent level of service.

Customers: We take customer satisfaction personally: we are committed to providing superior value in our products and services on a continuing basis.

Shareholders: We are dedicated to creating value for our shareholders and financial communities by performing in a manner that will enhance returns on investments.

Communities: We are committed to being caring and supportive corporate citizens within the worldwide communities in which we operate.

From *Fortune*, November 23, 1987, pp. 221, 223, and 225.

From this perspective, an organization is effective if it provides outcomes of value to each of these constituencies. This, of course, requires a delicate balancing act by top management. As has been noted elsewhere, "managers who ignore their organization's impact on constituencies may find themselves fighting legal battles and losing customers so that profit performance, resources, and internal efficiency will all suffer."[23]

Such an approach is particularly useful if a firm's survival depends on favorable evaluations by important sectors of its environment. Schools, political organizations, social service units, and other public institutions that exist at the pleasure of different strategic constituencies (Congress, parents, funding agencies, etc.) might find this approach valuable.

Not surprisingly, an evaluation that requires careful scrutiny of key environmental sectors is not problem free. First, the organization must determine the criteria that define some constituencies as strategically important and some as not. Second, as the environment changes, so might the relative importance of strategic constituencies. For instance, when government administrations change, organizations associated with the in-group will seek additional public support. Organizations associated with the out-group may have to refocus their requests for support to privately funded groups. Third, different strategic constituencies will likely have different determinants of an organization's effectiveness. In a service organization, for instance, funding agencies will be concerned with the efficient use of resources. Recipients of the services will be more concerned with the quantity or quality of services provided. These two criteria of effectiveness are not unrelated.

Finally, if all of these concerns have been dealt with successfully, the organization must develop procedures for measuring constituency satisfaction, and then find a way to combine these ratings into some useful index of its effectiveness. Using such an approach appears to be more trouble than it might be worth. Most organizations that adopt this option often take an effectiveness-by-exception approach to its implementation. That is, key executives assume that the organization is meeting constituency expectations, unless they hear otherwise. If this occurs, organizational resources are redirected to satisfy the offended constituency.

If Congress complains about spending in the Defense Department, that agency may reduce its budget request the next year. If clients complain about service levels, services are increased. Not surprisingly, any one action may offend a number of constituencies. Fortunately, most of these organizations' strategic constituencies are sufficiently unorganized or sufficiently bureaucratic to afford plenty of time to successfully redirect organizational resources.

EXHIBIT 16–5
Effectiveness Criteria of Important HCC Constituencies

Constituency	Criteria
Shareholders	Dividends, earnings, return on investment
Employees	Levels of pay, fringe benefits, satisfaction with various aspects of the firm
Customers	Price, quality, variety, service, cutting-edge technology
Investment community	Financial health, cash flow, indebtedness
Suppliers	Timeliness of payments, levels of sales
Local communities	Respect of local environment, contribution to community organizations, participation in community groups
Governmental agencies	Adherence to laws

Which approach is best when?

The preceding paragraphs have described four options managers can use to evaluate their organizations. Each approach addresses a different system component—one of the three major subsystems or the external environment. Any one of the four options can be useful for understanding how well an organization is performing. But is there a best approach for assessing organizational effectiveness? The answer to this question is, not surprisingly, "It depends." To this answer, the text will add some insights. The following sections look at three models that will assist managers in determining the approach(es) most appropriate for different organizations: the combined model, the domain-emphasis model, and the diagnostic model.

Combined model

This is the simplest model to use. Advocates of the model suggest that managers need a balanced analysis of how their organization is doing.[24] Undue emphasis on input, throughput, output, or the environment can miss problems in less-emphasized areas. To give top management a more complete view of a firm's performance, the combined model advocates evaluating activities from all four perspectives simultaneously. Rather than a single index of organizational effectiveness, this model suggests a profile of indicators as the best way to evaluate firm performance. Top management must decide the relative weight given to each element in the effectiveness profile. For example, while all four approaches are used, the internal process results may account for 40 percent of the profile in one organization, with the remaining 60 percent distributed evenly among the other three approaches. A different organization may decide that 25 percent of their profile will be determined by each of the four evaluation options.

Domain-emphasis model

This model suggests that an organization's domain—defined here by where the firm places itself along two important dimensions—should guide the evaluation process.[25] Exhibit 16–6 indicates one approach to this model. In this exhibit, the vertical dimension is labeled **agreement on goals.** This refers to whether or not top managers can agree on the important goals for an organization and on ways to measure these goals. The horizontal dimension, **understanding of cause–effect,** indicates how well managers understand an organization's throughput process. For example, an automobile assembly line provides a well-understood relationship between input and output. The treatment of patients in a mental hospital reflects a less clear relationship between cause and effect, however. A treatment that works for one patient may not work for another.

The diagram that results from combining these two dimension suggests that—depending on the extent of agreement on goals and the understanding of cause–effect relationships—a particular effectiveness option is appropriate.

Cell 1—The system resource approach.   When managers are in agreement about their goals and have a good understanding of how the throughput system works, the systems resource approach is recommended for evaluating effectiveness. In this case, effective and efficient resource acquisition should be of primary concern for managers. They know where they are going and how they are going to get there: they only need to minimize the costs associated with the journey.

EXHIBIT 16–6

A Domain-Model for Choosing Organizational Effectiveness Evaluation Options

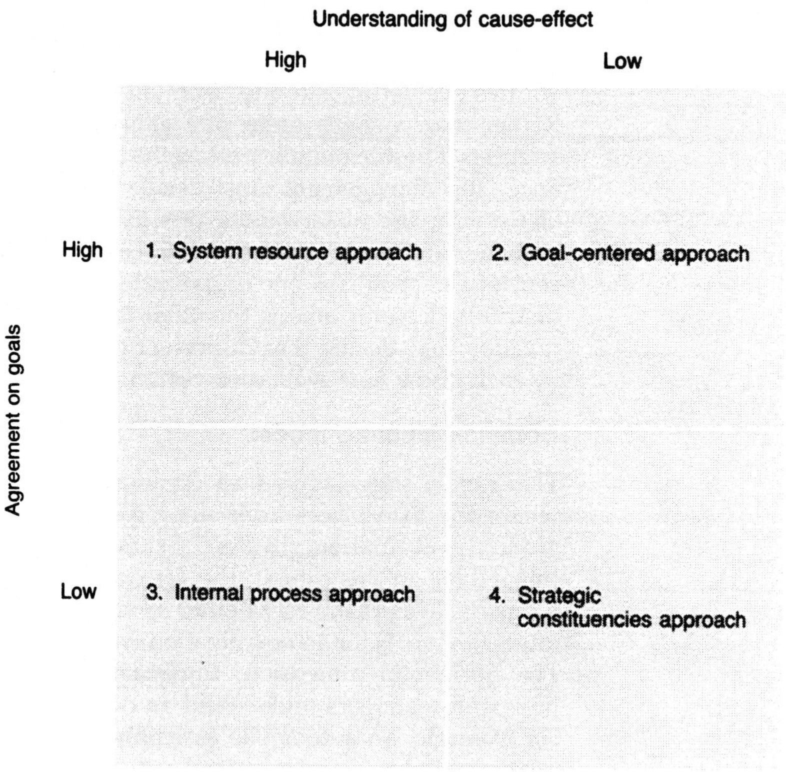

	Understanding of cause-effect	
	High	Low
High	1. System resource approach	2. Goal-centered approach
Low	3. Internal process approach	4. Strategic constituencies approach

Agreement on goals (vertical axis label)

Source: Adapted from J. Thompson, *Organizations in Action* (New York: McGraw-Hill, 1967), p. 85; R. Daft and R. Steers, *Organizations: A Micro/Macro Approach* (Glenview, Ill.: Scott, Foresman, 1986), p. 347.

Cell 2—The goal-centered approach. In this cell, managers agree on the nature of the goals they wish to pursue, but disagree on the process necessary to achieve them. Many nonprofit organizations find themselves in this situation. University officials agree that turning out educated students is a desirable goal, for instance. Problems arise in attempting to gain consensus on the best approach for accomplishing that goal. Since educators cannot agree on the nature of the process, emphasis is placed on ensuring acceptable outcomes and meeting outcome goals. Less attention is paid to how efficiently the process producing those outcomes is operating. Effectiveness is measured by the organization's ability to achieve its output goals. Professional sports teams would be another example found in this cell.

Cell 3—The internal process approach. In the opposite situation, top managers agree on the processes required to move their firm in some general directions, but are unable to identify or agree on specific goals. In this situation, managers may believe that if appropriate support services are provided, and employees can work in a satisfactory internal environment, then generally acceptable outcomes should be produced. Since these organizations lack identifiable or agreed-upon goals, a goal-centered approach for assessing effectiveness is illogical. At best, the organization can hope the internal processes are working well.

A research institute may have a complex, but relatively well-understood process for developing new ideas into useful products. Top managers of the institute may not know what those new ideas will or should be, or they may not agree as to whether outputs should be commercially feasible. The struggle between basic and applied research outcomes can be severe in these organizations. In this case, effectiveness would be assessed by the extent to which the internal processes facilitate any outcomes. If things are working well in an organization and employees are satisfied with their situations, then the organization would be effective. In this domain, management assumes that sufficiently useful outcomes will eventually emerge; but the presence or absence of such outcomes cannot be used as the basis for assessing organizational effectiveness.

Cell 4—The strategic constituencies approach. In the fourth quadrant, top managers agree neither about the nature of the goals to pursue nor about the relationships between inputs and outputs in a firm. Many governmental organizations are in this domain. Since the goals they develop must satisfy a variety of constituencies, goal agreement may be difficult. At the same time, these organizations are not certain what outcomes their policy decisions will produce. With lack of clarity in both goals and processes, the best indicator of effectiveness will be the extent to which the various constituencies are satisfied. If the strategic constituencies remain satisfied, the organization is effective.

Diagnostic model. Recently, a more sophisticated model to evaluate approaches to organizational effectiveness has been proposed.[26] From this perspective, neither the combined approach nor the domain-emphasis approach is viewed as sufficiently specific to assist in making the choice of which effectiveness option(s) to use. Meaningful effectiveness assessments can be made only when certain decisions are made in advance of the actual evaluation process. These decisions are framed as six diagnostic questions, each of which is discussed below.[27] The diagnostic questions are summarized in Exhibit 16–7.

1. Which major organization activity will be the focus of the evaluation? Since organizations operate in a number of areas (production, R&D, sales, etc.), a summary effectiveness measure is not particularly meaningful, regardless of the perspective chosen. Managers must be clear as to which activity or set of activities will be evaluated at any one time. This ensures a focus in the evaluation efforts.

EXHIBIT 16–7

The Diagnostic Model for Selecting an Organizational Effectiveness Approach

QUESTION 1:	Which major organization activity should be the focus of the evaluation?
QUESTION 2:	What perspective should be taken? Internal External
QUESTION 3:	At what level should effectiveness be assessed? Individual Group Organization
QUESTION 4:	What time frame should be used? Short-term Long-term
QUESTION 5:	What kind of information about organizational effectiveness should be used in the evaluation? Subjective Objective
QUESTION 6:	What standards should be used to determine the level of organizational effectiveness? Comparisons with other firms Norms or "ideals" Organizational goals Improvements over time Organizational traits

Source: Adapted from K. Cameron, "Critical Questions in Assessing Organizational Effectiveness." Reprinted, by permission of the publisher, from *Organizational Dynamics*, Autumn 1980, pp. 66-80. © 1980 American Management Association, New York. All rights reserved.

2. What perspective should be taken—internal or external? Managers must determine what perspective to take in the evaluation of their organization. Employees (or unions), the financial staff, and the board of directors may be interested internal parties in an assessment of the relative effectiveness of their organization. Externally, managers find many environment sectors, including suppliers, customers, and governmental bodies. It is likely that evaluations of effectiveness in one activity from one perspective would be different when viewed from another perspective.

This issue is becoming particularly thorny with the increased takeover activity seen in corporate America. Managers attempt to protect themselves from these efforts by developing a variety of anti-takeover defenses. If implemented, many of these defenses end up costing the individual shareholder money, while top managers or stock speculators make money.

Consider the problem from the perspective of Hicks B. Waldron, chairperson of Avon Products. Waldron is concerned about having to manage his company to pacify holders of large blocks of the corporation's stock—to assure that quarterly profit and dividend figures are sufficient to discourage attempts to replace his management team with another. "We have 40,000 employees and 1.3 million representatives around the world. We have a number of suppliers, institutions, customers, communities. None of them has the democratic freedom shareholders do to buy or sell their shares. They have much deeper and much more important stakes in our company than our shareholders."[28]

Since firms like Avon find it difficult to satisfy all constituencies simultaneously or at the same level, they must consider the following options.[29] First, managers can identify the most important sector and satisfy it to the greatest extent possible. Second, if a dominant constituency cannot be identified, managers can try to satisfy all constituencies at some minimally acceptable level. To paraphrase George Orwell, "All constituencies are equal, but some are more equal than others." Most likely, greater efforts will be made to satisfy the more equal constituencies than the less equal ones.

3. At what level should effectiveness be assessed—individual, group, or organization? As we have seen, effectiveness at one level in an organization may not reflect effectiveness at another level. Similarly, the outcomes to be evaluated and the procedures used are determined by the level of the evaluation. Measuring individual performance requires different criteria and techniques than measuring group performance, for instance. And the last few pages have discussed the difficulties and options for assessing organizational performance.

4. What time frame should be used? Managers must determine the time frame to be used as the basis for the assessment of organizational effectiveness. An earlier chapter suggested that reinforced behaviors tend to be repeated by individuals. If an organization assesses and rewards short-term organizational gains, then its managers will act to accomplish (and be rewarded for) short-term gains. Evaluation of annual earnings per share or quarterly profits are two well-known examples of short-term effectiveness criteria. Some have argued that American management's predisposition for short-run criteria has contributed to the country's decline in international competitiveness. Top management has been unwilling to invest for the long run because their effectiveness is assessed in the short run.

This is not to say that short-term accomplishments are not needed. In fact, when organizational survival is threatened, a short-term mentality is a must. There is not time for long-term thinking: in the long run, the organization may no longer exist. But many organizations pursue short-term effectiveness criteria long after the question of organizational survival has been successfully answered. Longer-term thinking is necessary and should become the basis for some effectiveness evaluations once the challenges to organizational survival have been overcome.

5. What kind of information about organizational effectiveness should be used in the evaluation? There are two basic types of effectiveness information. First, subjective information can be gathered by asking key managers or constituency representatives for their perceptions of how well the organization is doing. Second, more "objective" information can be gathered from company records and reports or from data available outside the organization. The word *objective* is in quotes to indicate that figures taken from published reports or other records may simply *seem* less biased than personal reports. However, those figures were first generated and then reported and recorded by individuals whose original perceptions or calculations may have been flawed.

Both types of information have their advantages and disadvantages in terms of their relative accuracy, costs to gather and to process, etc. In the long run, the most accurate information about organizational performance requires a combination of data-gathering techniques.

6. What standards should be used to determine the relative level of organizational effectiveness? When people say that their organization is effective, they should be asked, "Effective relative to what?" Without knowing the standards against which performance has been compared, an assertion of effectiveness is meaningless. To reduce this problem, consider the following five bases for making effectiveness judgments.

a. Comparisons—Performance results for one organization can be compared to similar results for another firm in the same business. This is an appropriate standard if the two businesses operate in similar environments, if evaluation and reporting procedures are similar, and if comparable effectiveness information is available. If these similarities are not present, then comparative judgments are inappropriate.

For example, the Royal Dutch/Shell Group and Exxon Corporation have waged an intense but low-key battle over which firm will be the largest oil company in the world. As one analyst summarized Shell's strategy, "The only corporate strategy Shell has got is to exceed Exxon on earnings and be the largest oil company in all respects."[30] Shell's effectiveness at achieving this goal will be determined by comparing its earnings to those of Exxon.

b. Norms—Rather than comparing the performance of two organizations, results could be compared to some "ideal" level of performance established by top management. This approach reduces the need to gather information about other organizations; but it raises problems if top management's ideal state is unrealistic. The definition of the ideal state may·be either over- or under-inflated.

c. Goals—Goals are one basis for determining an organization's effectiveness. Using this approach, the extent to which a firm's goals (official, operative, and operational) are accomplished provides the means of assessing its effectiveness.

d. Improvement—This implies some change in performance over time. Thus, the effectiveness of an organization can be judged in comparison to its performance at some earlier time. This perspective makes some assumptions about the relative importance of organizational functions over time so that meaningful comparisons can be made. It also assumes that measurement procedures are comparable at the different points in time.

e. Traits—Some managers assume that if their organization possesses certain traits, it will be effective by definition. For instance, an organization that is innovative, creative, frugal, or flexible could be defined as effective. This view assumes that an organization with such traits will also be a high performer. The trait perspective requires top managers to identify and then measure organizational standing on some set of traits. It also requires evidence that such traits do lead to higher levels of performance. Such a relationship may or may not exist, depending on other factors in the organization's environment.

The use of this diagnostic process allows top managers to choose an evaluation approach best suited to their needs. The model chosen from this process will most likely depend on the major activity areas of the firm, the extent to which internal or external constituencies are important, and the ease with which information can be gathered, processed, and reported.

ORGANIZATIONAL EFFECTIVENESS: A DEVELOPMENTAL PERSPECTIVE

As an organization matures, different effectiveness approaches should become more or less appropriate. From the combined perspective, more weight might be placed on the system resource and goal-centered approaches when the organization is relatively young. As the organization matures, the efficiency emphasis of the internal process approach may become more important. If the organization remains successful and becomes larger, more complex, more visible, and more influential, the strategic constituencies approach may be added to the evaluation process.

The domain-emphasis perspective requires an assumption that goal clarity and cause–effect clarity change over time. New organizations should agree strongly on goals, especially survival goals. Depending on the nature of its technology, the firm may or may not have a grasp of cause–effect links. This would suggest that either the system resource or the goal-centered approaches would be emphasized. Organizational evolution and increasing complexity in mature organizations might lead to a reduction in goal clarity, suggesting that the internal process or the strategic constituencies approach be selected.

Finally, from the diagnostic perspective, where an organization is in its evolution will likely influence the nature of the responses to the six diagnostic questions. Choices of focus, points of view, levels of analysis, time frames, data type, and standards can change as an organization becomes more complex and more mature.

The judgment of organizational effectiveness probably lies in the eye of the beholder. Using any one of the models above, one manager may consider an organization effective while another manager using an alternative model might see it as ineffective. The key point to remember, however, is that like individual performance, **organizational performance is multidimensional and multifaceted.** To use only financial or market indicators of how well an organization is doing is to lose an appreciation for the many different aspects of organizational effectiveness. Professional photographers take hundreds of shots of their subjects, using a variety of films and lenses. This is the only way that they can get a good picture. Managers, too, must take multiple snapshots of their organization's performance if they hope to get a realistic assessment of its effectiveness.

CHAPTER HIGHLIGHTS

The first chapter of this text described organizations as goal-seeking entities. This chapter examined these goals in greater detail. **Goals specify the outcomes a firm hopes to attain. They can give legitimacy to the** firm, provide direction for employees, and serve as standards for assessing organizational effectiveness.

Organizations exist at the pleasure of society. To maintain that legitimacy, firms publish official goals in their corporate mission statements. **Official goals provide general information to important environment sectors about what a firm intends to accomplish.** But official goals are too general to provide specific guidance to employees. **Operative goals reflect the primary tasks required to accomplish the official goals. Operational goals are derived from operative goals and represent the performance expectations for work units or individuals.**

Establishing goals is only half the battle. In choosing and pursuing various levels of goals, managers must ensure that at each level, **goals contribute to desired outcomes and are congruent, both horizontally and vertically.** The goals selected must be both **feasible** and **realistic.** And since environments change, goals must be **flexible.** To be useful, goals must be **communicated, both orally and in writing.** These requirements suggest that at all levels, goals must be **managed.** Goals are an organizational resource and must be treated as such.

The second half of the chapter examined the topic of organizational effectiveness. **Effectiveness means getting the job done. Efficiency means getting the job done with minimal resources.**

Most companies use financial or market indicators as the primary determinants of how they have performed. This chapter argued that this was a limited perspective and might mask problems elsewhere in the firm. Four approaches for assessing effectiveness were discussed. **The system resource approach defines effectiveness as a firm's ability to acquire the resources needed to produce its outputs.** These resources can be financial, material or human. **Examining the quality of the process by which a firm transforms inputs into outputs is the basis for the internal process approach to effectiveness.** The health of a company is determined by examining a variety of processes or ratios. **The traditional goal-centered approach defines effectiveness as the ability of a company to achieve certain desired outcomes.** Each of these three models concentrates on one of the major organizational subsystems. The fourth approach, **the strategic constituencies approach, centers on how well key sectors in the environment think an organization is doing.** Rather than focusing on individual subsystems, this option examines the performance of the complete organizational system from an environmental perspective.

Choosing which approach or approaches to use is not an easy task. So three models were presented that make the job a little easier. **The combined model suggests that all four approaches be used to provide the most comprehensive picture of the firm.** Top management still must decide on the relative importance of each effectiveness indicator and develop a meaningful profile to summarize the results.

A second model proposes that the evaluation option selected be determined by the extent to which managers agree on corporate goals and know the relationship between inputs and outputs. **Goal clarity and clear cause–effect relationships suggest the system resource approach is appropriate. The internal process approach is best when agreement on goals is not strong, but cause–effect relationships remain clear. When these relationships become muddied but goal agreement is strong, the goal-centered approach is best. If goal agreement is weak and cause–effect relationships remain unclear, the strategic constituencies approach is the best way to assess how well a firm is doing.**

Finally, a diagnostic model was presented to assist managers in choosing an evaluation procedure. **By answering six questions regarding focus of evaluation, point of view, level of analysis, time frame, type of data, and standards, an appropriate evaluation strategy can be selected.** This model requires that managers think carefully about a number of important aspects of the effectiveness evaluation process.

Establishment of goals sets the stage for organizational actions. Assessment of organizational effectiveness allows managers or members of key constituencies to determine how successfully these actions have been carried out. The next two chapters examine the structures and processes required to turn goals into actions and actions into effective outcomes.

REVIEW QUESTIONS

1. What are the three reasons that organizations develop goals?
2. What is the difference between and among official, operative, and operational goals? Who establishes each level of goals?
3. Give an example of each type of goal for each of the following organizations.
   a. Your college or university
   b. General Motors or Ford
   c. A local hospital
   d. Chase Manhattan Bank
   e. Al & Alice's Bowling Emporium
4. What factors influence the selection and implementation of goals? Which of these factors do you believe is the most important? Why?
5. What organizational goals might conflict with each other? If goals conflict, how can they also be congruent?
6. What is the difference between effectiveness and efficiency?
7. What effectiveness approach would be most appropriate to use in each of the organizations listed in Question 3?

8. How can managers use the strategic constituencies approach to evaluate an organization?

9. The domain-emphasis model provides one way to determine which evaluation approach to use. What two factors determine each domain, and which approach is appropriate in each domain?

10. Suppose you were asked to evaluate the effectiveness of your organizational behavior class. What questions would you want to ask before deciding on the approach to take?

RESOURCE READINGS

Cameron, K. "Critical Questions in Assessing Organizational Effectiveness." *Organizational Dynamics,* Autumn 1980, pp. 66–80.

Cameron, K., and D. Whetten, eds. *Organizational Effectiveness: A Comparison of Multiple Models.* New York: Academic Press, 1983.

Goodman, P., and J. Pennings, eds. *New Perspectives on Organizational Effectiveness.* San Francisco: Jossey-Bass, 1977.

Perrow, C. "The Analysis of Goals in Complex Organizations." *American Sociological Review,* December 1961, pp. 854–66.

Quinn, R. *Beyond Rational Management.* San Francisco: Jossey-Bass, 1988.

Quinn, R., and J. Rohrbaugh. "A Spatial Model of Effectiveness Criteria: Toward a Competing Values Approach to Organizational Analysis." *Management Science,* 1983, pp. 363–77.

Richards, M. *Setting Strategic Goals and Objectives, 2nd ed.* St. Paul, Minn.: West Publishing, 1986.

NOTES

1. A. Etzioni, *Modern Organizations* (Englewood Cliffs, N.J.: Prentice-Hall, 1964), p. 6.

2. D. Campbell, *If You Don't Know Where You're Going, You'll Probably End Up Somewhere Else* (Niles, Ill.: Argus Communications, 1974).

3. H. Simon, "On the Concept of Organizational Goal," *Administrative Science Quarterly,* March 1964, pp. 1–22.

4. P. Sellers, "Lessons from TV's New Bosses," *Fortune,* March 14, 1988, pp. 115–30.

5. J. Keller et al., "AT&T: The Making of a Comeback," *Business Week,* January 18, 1988, pp. 56–62.

6. C. Perrow, "The Analysis of Goals in Complex Organizations," *American Sociological Review,* 1961, pp. 854–66; C. Perrow, *Complex Organizations,* 3d ed. (New York: Random House, 1986), pp. 10–11.

7. J. Pearce, II and F. David, "Corporate Mission Statements: The Bottom Line," *Academy of Management Executive,* May 1987, pp. 109–16.

8. L. Nash, "Mission Statements: Mirrors and Windows," *Harvard Business Review,* March-April 1988, pp. 155–56.

9. C. Perrow, "The Analysis of Goals in Complex Organizations."

10. R. Daft and R. Steers, *Organizations: A Micro/Macro Approach* (Glenview, Ill.: Scott, Foresman, 1986), p. 324.

11. R. Webber, M. Morgan, and P. Browne, *Management,* 3d ed. (Homewood, Ill.: Richard D. Irwin, 1985), pp. 264–82.

12. F. Paine and W. Naumes, *Strategy and Policy Formation: An Integrative Approach* (Philadelphia: W. B. Saunders, 1974).

13. S. Flax, "Boot Camp," *INC.,* September 1987, pp. 99–104.

14. R. Webber et al., *Management.*

15. J. Keller et al., "AT&T: The Making of a Comeback."

16. R. Quinn and K. Cameron, "Organizational Life Cycles and Some Shifting Criteria of Effectiveness: Some Preliminary Evidence," *Management Science,* 1983, pp. 33–51.

17. A. Etzioni, *Modern Organizations,* p. 8.

18. L. Iacocca with W. Novak, *Iacocca: An Autobiography* (New York: Phantom Books, 1984).

19. S. Robbins, *Organization Theory,* 2d ed. (Englewood Cliffs, N.J.: Prentice-Hall, 1987), p. 27.

20. R. Kanter and D. Brinkerhoff, "Organizational Performance: Recent Developments in Measurement," *Annual Review of Sociology,* 1981, pp. 321–49; K. Cameron, "Critical Questions in Assessing Organizational Effectiveness," *Organizational Dynamics,* Autumn 1980, pp. 66–80.

21. W. Evan, "Organization Theory and Organizational Effectiveness: An Exploratory Analysis," in *Organizational Effectiveness: Theory, Research, Utilization,* ed. L. Spray (Kent, Ohio: Kent State University Press, 1976), pp. 15–28.

22. T. Connolly, E. Conlon, and S. Deutsch, "Organizational Effectiveness: A Multiple-Constituency Approach," *Academy of Management Review,* April 1980, pp. 211–17.

23. R. Daft and R. Steers, *Organizations,* p. 343.

24. Ibid.

25. Ibid., p. 345.

26. K. Cameron, "Critical Questions in Assessing Organizational Effectiveness."

27. Ibid.

28. B. Nussbaum and J. Dobrzynski, "The Battle for Corporate Control," *Business Week,* May 18, 1987, pp. 102–9.

29. K. Cameron, "Critical Questions in Assessing Organizational Effectiveness."

30. J. Tanner and A. Sullivan, "Two Giant Oil Firms Battle for Supremacy with Differing Tactics," *Wall Street Journal,* July 8, 1987.

CASE: If you can't fire the team, fire the coach!

It happens all the time in pro sports. The team does poorly or doesn't make the playoffs, and the coach is fired. The same thing happens in the college ranks, though not so frequently. The team does poorly, doesn't finish in the top 20, doesn't play in a bowl game or in the NCAA basketball tournament, and the coach is released. But lately, something different has occurred in the college coaching ranks. Educational institutions are now firing or releasing seemingly successful coaches. For instance, Dick Crum's record at the University of North Carolina–Chapel Hill was 72–41–3. He had taken his teams to 6 bowl games and won 4 of them in his 10 years at the school. But his teams were called "dull," "unexciting," "unemotional," and had trouble beating teams in the top 20. The Rams Club, alumni supporters of the school's athletic programs, bought out the remainder of Crum's contract for $800,000.

Earle Bruce's record at Ohio State was 81–26–1—the best overall record of current coaches in the Big Ten Conference. In 1987, his football team was rated number one in many preseason polls. Problems during the season gave the Buckeyes a record of 6–3–1 going into the last game of the season against archrival Michigan. Complaints about Bruce's coaching style were similar to those voiced about Crum's. His play calling and offensive game plans were compared to the conservative attire he wore on the sidelines: typically a suit and hat. The University released Bruce the week before the Michigan game, paying him $471,000 to buy out the final year of his contract. His team then went out and beat Michigan.

Finally, Walt Hazzard was fired as the basketball coach at UCLA in the spring of 1988. His career record after four years at UCLA was 77–47. Like Ohio State fans, UCLA fans were expecting big things of Hazzard's 1987–88 Bruins. They had tied for the PAC 10 basketball title in 1987 and were picked to finish high in the standings in 1988. But defections from the team and substandard play by veteran players left his team with a 16–14 record, a defeat in the PAC 10 post-season tournament, and no invitation to post-season NCAA tournament play. At a school remembered for its 10 NCAA basketball championships in 12 years, Hazzard's performance was not up to expectations. He joined the line behind four other UCLA coaches who had left the school since the retirement of the legendary John Wooden, the coach who had made UCLA synonymous with championship basketball. Hazzard was the first coach at the school since Wooden to leave involuntarily.

In each case, the fired coach had a winning record, overall. But apparently winning wasn't enough. And because it wasn't enough, something had to give. You can't fire the team, you can only fire the coach!

Source: Adapted from "Former Buckeye Coach Bruce Waits . . . and Waits for Job," *Durham Morning Herald*, April 9, 1988; A. Wolff, "Call Him Irreplaceable," *Sports Illustrated*, April 11, 1988; Conversation with the Sports Information Office, Department of Athletics, University of North Carolina at Chapel Hill.

Questions:

1. In most sports, winning is the primary goal. At these institutions, winning apparently wasn't the only goal. What do you think are (or should be) the most important goals in college athletics?

2. Identify three official goals for a college or university athletic team or program. How might those official goals be translated into operative and then into operational goals?

3. Given our discussion of organizational effectiveness, how would you assess the effectiveness of a college or university athletic team or program?

4. Given your answers to these questions, why do you think each of the coaches discussed in the case was released from his coaching duties?

Organizational Structure

$\mathbf{T}$he first chapter of this text defined an **organization** as **an invention of people that is a goal-directed vehicle for coordinating a set of activities for individuals and groups.** The text also noted that at least five elements interact to determine an organization's effectiveness: people, tasks, environment, technology, and structure.[1]

Succeeding chapters considered a number of these topics: people, tasks, and environment, in particular. The next two chapters will shed some light on such topics as organizational structure, organizational design, and the factors that make up and influence these two important concepts.

As a framework for our discussion, think about the way people put a jigsaw puzzle together. How do they go about doing it? Some people sort the pieces by general color. Some find the pieces that make up the puzzle's border. Whatever people's strategy, their rationale is to learn more about the pieces that will eventually contribute to the picture. We can take the same approach here.

Before we can talk about structure or design, we need to know more about the individual pieces that make up these concepts. For instance, to be able to talk about the structure of United Parcel Service as centralized, or that of the federal government as bureaucratic, we need to know what those terms mean. Examining this kind of information (like sorting the puzzle pieces into piles) makes it easier to understand how the pieces fit together to make a coherent picture. Thus, our discussion builds from the specific to the general.

In this chapter we look at the pieces of structure that combine to determine the bigger picture: organizational structure. Then, in Chapter 18, we put additional pieces together and consider what managers can do to develop a better fit between and among some of these macro level elements. To give us a context within which to place this chapter, let's visit Home Computers Company again. Harvey is about to meet with the members of HCC's top management team following the recent board meeting.

Home Computers Case

Home Computers Company: The Weekly Executive Committee Meeting

To keep in touch with operations at HCC, Harvey schedules regular, Monday morning staff meetings with his key managers. At these 8:30 A.M. sessions, managers report what has happened in the past week, and what is planned for the upcoming one. This meeting also allows managers to voice concerns they have about events in their divisions or work units, and it allows Harvey to identify opportunities and problems he has noticed at HCC.

One Monday morning, the managers settled themselves around the table in the large conference room, checking their notes for the meeting. Most of those present had helped themselves to the fruit juice, coffee, and hot danish. The meetings were normally not long-winded affairs, but the presence of a visitor at this meeting suggested that the session might run longer than normal. Harvey sat with Sally Barnes at the head of the conference table. Sally was the consultant Harvey had been working with to help him examine the way HCC was run.

As the two of them waited for the managers to get their coffee and find their seats, Harvey went over in his mind the state of the corporation, the reactions of the board of directors to his report, and the agenda for the meeting. HCC had weathered the recession and the shake-out in the PC industry—but not without some difficulties. Now that the competitive picture had cleared, major decisions had to be made about adding a third manufacturing plant to those in Denver and Dayton. And regardless of that decision, there were increasingly bothersome problems of what seemed to Harvey to be a lack of coordination between some of the major operating functions within HCC.

The problems at the Dayton plant were typical. Harvey continually got reports from the plant manager of situations in which production was unable to meet the delivery dates promised by the marketing function. And sales made commitments to deliver customized machines that it knew full well production could not realistically meet within its operating budget.

At the individual employee level, the recent unsuccessful union certification vote indicated that all was not well at the Dayton plant. Harvey had heard complaints that the company was too bureaucratic. He felt the increasing pressure of his personal involvement in far too many decisions. It seemed that all decisions, both large and small, ended up on his desk, either for review or for action.

Harvey and Sally had discussed these problem areas prior to the meeting. They hoped input from the managers would further pinpoint the causes of the problems and provide assistance in overcoming these concerns. Sally had suggested that the key question the committee needed to answer was whether these issues represented people problems or structural problems.

Harvey asked her to clarify this difference. Sally responded that one way of making this distinction was for Harvey and his managers to consider replacing or removing certain individuals or work units. If that happened, would the problems persist? If the answer to that question was yes, then HCC had serious structural problems.

Harvey was convinced that too much bureaucracy, overcentralized decision making, and poor coordination were structural problems. Even if the players changed, the problems would remain. In Harvey's mind, the issues boiled down to what could be done about HCC's organizational structure to remedy these situations. Harvey wondered, given the coordination and cooperation problems, if HCC had the right structure for its environment, goals, and technology. And what, if anything, could or should be done to reduce or eliminate these problems.

Harvey hoped that with Sally's expertise, his manager's input, and his own commitment to and support for eliminating (or at least greatly reducing) these problems, they could develop some useful solutions to the issues. In any case, he knew that this would not be a typical staff meeting.

Harvey's concerns are probably not much different than those of most managers. To develop answers to his questions, Harvey needs to gather some basic information about organizational structure. In particular, it would help if he knew more about this notion of **bureaucracy.** Most people probably use the term to describe experiences (usually bad) with some large organization. But what does it mean to be too bureaucratic? Might bureaucratic organizations actually be beneficial in some situations? And what—if any—suggestions can be drawn from this way of running an organization?

Harvey also needs to answer some questions about **centralization.** What does it mean? And is it the only way of describing the processes that go on within an organization's structure? Finally, Harvey needs to examine the nature of coordination problems that can occur in many firms. What are the ways to coordinate activities effectively? And when are some ways more appropriate than others?

DEFINITIONS AND DESCRIPTIONS OF STRUCTURE

It is useful to begin the discussion with a definition of structure. Many definitions have been suggested, such as:

- **Structure is the allocation of responsibilities.**
- **Structure is the designation of formal reporting channels.**
- **Structure is the systems and mechanisms that underlie the effective coordination of effort.**[2]

These are all formal, classroom definitions of structure, however. The most useful definition of organizational structure might be the one that Harvey would give you if you stopped him in the hall at HCC. He would probably say that **structure is the way a company is put together.**

To make these definitions useful, we need to put some meat on their bones. Rather than talking about definitions of structure, let's talk about some different **descriptions of structure.**

Harvey was hearing complaints that as HCC grew larger, it was becoming more impersonal, more bureaucratic. He was extremely concerned at the thought of his organization being too bureaucratic. And anyone who has confronted the red tape usually associated with bureaucracies at one time or another would probably be quick to agree with Harvey. But as we'll see shortly, bureaucracies were not originally designed to be difficult to deal with, nor are they the only way to put a company together.

Organizational structures can be described in four different ways. The **classical approach** examines bureaucratic characteristics in more detail. Following directly from this is the **configurational or organizational chart approach.** A person can describe a firm's structure with a snapshot or picture of how various elements in the organization are related. This picture is referred to as the organization chart and represents the formal configuration of the company. Third, managers can take the **process approach.** In a structural context, managers consider the policies, procedures, and systems that determine employee and work-unit activities within an organization. If the configuration approach explores the skeleton of an organization, the process approach examines its neuromuscular or circulatory system. Finally, managers can combine these perspectives to view structure from a **holistic approach** and describe five generic types of organizational structures.

Since organizational structure is a complex topic, our discussion is also complex. The following pages investigate each approach individually in hopes that examination from multiple viewpoints will increase your understanding.

THE CLASSICAL APPROACH

Bureaucracy

We have talked often about the variety of developmental processes that occur in organizations. But we have yet to answer the question: Where did modern organizations come from originally? Most large private and public organizations are a relatively recent phenomenon. Except for the church, national governments, and the military, earlier generations satisfied their own needs or purchased necessary products or services from craftspeople. But needs grew more sophisticated, and demand for products outpaced the supply available in a craft economy. The Industrial Revolution brought explosive growth in the rail, oil, and steel industries. These large organizations required managers and—perhaps more important—structures able to oversee and control increasingly large undertakings.

Not surprisingly, many different types of administrative and organizational structures arose in response to this need. Some were more effective than others; and organizations that adopted these structures tended to survive. Firms that adopted less appropriate approaches frequently disappeared. One of the earliest investigators of these organizing approaches was Max Weber, a German sociologist. Weber was interested in organizing techniques available to governments. From his study of a variety of governmental organizations, he distilled a set of characteristics representing an ideal way to structure an organization. He called this particular structure a **bureaucracy**.[3] The salient characteristics of a bureaucracy, as well as the ideal and real outcomes usually associated with the structure, are highlighted in Exhibit 17–1 (p. 698) and discussed below.[4]

Clear division of labor

Job responsibilities and levels of authority are clearly defined for each employee. Authority is commensurate with the level of job responsibility, and there is no overlap of responsibility between jobs.

Employment decisions based on merit

Selection into and promotion within an organization are based solely on qualifications, ability, and performance. Employment decisions are not based on family relationships, friendships, or political persuasion.

Formal hierarchy of authority

Each position in an organization is controlled by and reports to a single position one level up in the hierarchy. This ensures that the overall goals of the organization take precedence over individual employee goals.

Job and job-holder remain separate

Employees must not use the rights and privileges of their jobs to enrich themselves. They are paid a sufficient wage or salary to eliminate the need or temptation to accept bribes or graft.

Impersonal approaches to all interpersonal activities

To eliminate favoritism in dealings with employees, customers, or clients, employees must treat each other on an equal basis—impersonally and fairly.

Rules and regulations

To ensure impersonality in organizational transactions, written rules and regulations exist for each position. This also allows organizational activities to be performed in a predictable and routine manner.

Maintenance of written records, communications, and rules

A written record of organizational activities keeps rules and regulations visible to all participants. It also allows the evaluation of past decisions and activities and adds to the organizational memory. This gives an organization continuity over time.

Weber's characteristics represent an ideal that he believed should be the goal of every organization. To anyone reading through his recommended characteristics, it should be apparent that in this ideal state, organizations would be good places to work and should provide efficient service to customers or clients. We frequently hear complaints about the ineffectiveness of bureaucratic organizations. Yet adherence to Weber's principles by the federal government or the military services enables both institutions to provide a vast array of services to large numbers of people all over the world (and in outer space).

EXHIBIT 17–1

Bureaucratic Organizations: Characteristics and Outcomes

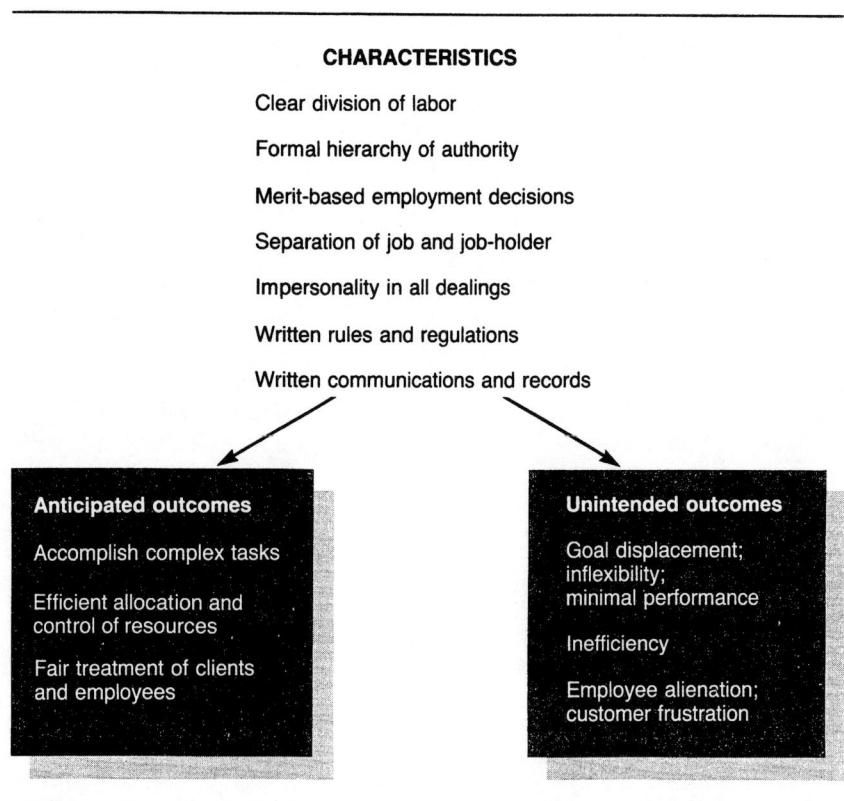

It is also possible that organizations that fail to follow Weber's recommendations could be less efficient or effective—or even fail. Recall the organizational excesses that were exposed after the fall of the Marcos government in the Phillipines. Mrs. Marcos was said to have had 3,000 pairs of shoes. Mr. Marcos allegedly had purchased real estate in the United States that was worth over a billion dollars. All of this was accomplished on an annual salary of $27,000. Either the Marcos family spent its money carefully and invested it wisely, or this is an excellent example of what can happen when family ties, political favoritism, bribery, and graft infect a national government. Compared to the corruption exposed in the Phillipines, the plusses of bureaucratic organizations easily outweigh the possible minuses. This was exactly why Weber made his recommendations.

More recently, the demise of E. F. Hutton as an independent firm has been attributed to its failure to adhere to some of Weber's most basic principles. Included among these violations were employment decisions based on the whims of the CEO; a "me first" attitude among employees and board members; a lack of information, communication, and rules; and no clear lines of authority.[5] As a writer in *Fortune* magazine commented, "At Hutton, selfishness was a business. The company lived—and died—by it."[6]

Problems with bureaucracies

If a bureaucracy is such an effective and efficient way to organize, why do we cringe when we hear the word *bureaucracy?* Why is Harvey concerned that Home Computers Company has become too bureaucratic? What are some of the problems that can arise when organizations adhere too closely to Weber's principles? Consider, for example, the potential pitfalls of the overly bureaucratic organizations illustrated in Insight 17–1.

But more substantive drawbacks of the bureaucratic form also exist. A major concern with the bureaucratic organization is **goal displacement—work unit or personal goals displacing organizational goals in day-to-day activities.**[7] The specialization and division of labor called for by Weber (and present in many companies today) creates many different subunits, each with different goals. Although the discussion in Chapter 16 suggested that lower-level goals must be congruent with the overall goals of an organization, this is not always the case. Some of HCC's problems with relationships between sales and production may be the result of unit goals displacing the organization's goals. Thus, sales makes promises to customers that the production unit can meet only by ignoring its own schedules and one of its important goals—predictable production.

INSIGHT 17–1

Would You Believe? Examples of Bureaucracies at Work

*T*he following stories have appeared in newspapers across the country!

■ Received at Disneyland—a letter from the Selective Service System addressed to "Mickey M. Mouse" and opening with these words: "Dear Registrant: Our records indicate you have not responded to our initial request for necessary date-of-birth information. . . ."

■ The FBI is opening dossiers on citizens who write to the FBI to ask whether it is keeping dossiers on them.

■ The New York Department of Mental Hygiene produced and distributed a three-page illustrated memorandum on how to split an English muffin.

■ The U.S. Fish and Wildlife Service agreed to let the Air Force use almost 75 percent of the Desert National Wildlife Range in Nevada for bombing exercises. "We feel we will still have control over the area," said Bob Yoder of the Wildlife Service. "We feel the animals are in safe hands."

■ After seventeen years of careful deliberation, the British government announced official standards for the stiffness of toothbrushes.

■ Every employee whose last name consists of three or fewer letters was dropped from the Department of Agriculture phone book.

By E. Knoll, *No Comment* (New York: Vintage Books, 1984).

Although the bureaucratic characteristics can produce a high degree of organizational reliability and predictability, **overly detailed procedures, rules, and regulations can reduce adaptability and flexibility.**[8] Slavish adherence to rules and regulations can become the driving force in a firm, even though such behavior reduces the likelihood of accomplishing organizational goals. Probably everyone has been a victim of this problem at one time or another—in situations where it seemed that organizational employees were more concerned about following the rules than they were about actually helping to solve a problem. Take the example that drives many people (and at least one cartoonist) crazy: even though the express lane (eight items or less) is open at the grocery store, customers still must wait in line at the regular checkout lane if they have one too many items. The organization's goal was to serve the customer as quickly and as courteously as possible—but the rules became more important than that goal.

For most organizations, rules and regulations establish not only what is acceptable and unacceptable in terms of behavior, but in many cases, these **rules establish minimum levels of acceptable performance.**[9] Un-

ON SALE TODAY   By Carol Sherman

"She tried to pay by check in the express lane."

Reprinted by permission: Tribune Media Services.

less other incentives are provided to the employee, there is little reason for the bureaucratic employee to perform above these minimal levels.

Another shortcoming of the bureaucratic organization is the **incorrect usage of rules and regulations.**[10] Well-known procedures and regulations give employees a sense of security. As long as they apply the rules as they know them, they cannot be blamed if something goes wrong. ("I was only following the rules.") Suppose a slightly different situation arises—one that calls for an alternative approach or a little-known rule or procedure. In this situation, the employee may incorrectly apply the standard, well-known procedure, unaware of the situation's uniqueness or unwilling to consider alternative, less familiar procedures. Or the employee may refuse to deal with the situation at all, claiming that he or she is not responsible for the activity. In either case, correcting this oversight at some later date costs the organization and the customer or client.

Finally, what happens to those who work in or deal with bureaucracies? Bureaucratic impersonality, designed to prevent favoritism and provide impartial treatment of customers and clients, can also have negative effects on employees and customers.

Internally, we find higher levels of employee alienation in bureaucratic firms.[11] The impersonality designed into the system can reduce employees' commitment to the firm and add to the belief that the firm cares little for employees as individuals. Specialization and routine activities can result in many of the problems presented earlier in our discussion of job design. Employees feel they are being used or the organization doesn't appreciate their contributions. This may be part of the reason behind the complaints of HCC's employees. As HCC grew, there was more specialization and less interaction between employees and the organization. This feeling can be heightened when others in the organization make it difficult for employees to do their jobs by enforcing bureaucratic rules and procedures for even the simplest request. Filling out five forms and waiting two weeks to get a dozen new pencils is a perfect example.

Externally, the frustrations that afflict employees can also afflict those who deal with the bureaucracy. Customers or clients may confront the same extreme adherence to rules and unwillingness to make exceptions. This bothersome problem can be temporary if competing organizations offer the same service. Customers and clients simply take their business to a less bureaucratic organization—one willing to respond quickly to the customers' particular needs. Many start-up organizations succeed because they are willing to handle exceptional situations without bureaucratic red tape.

Unfortunately, many of this country's largest bureaucracies are governmental institutions or regulated monopolies (utility companies, for example). Dissatisfaction with their service cannot be voiced by going to a competitor. Even though these organizations exist to serve the customer, client, or taxpayer, more often it seems as though their actions are designed to frustrate those they serve.

Despite these problems, the bureaucratic model is with us and will likely stay with us for some time to come. When implemented with care, with appreciation of employee needs, and with sufficient flexibility to handle changing customer or client demands, it can be an extremely effective and efficient administrative structure.

THE CONFIGURAL/ORGANIZATIONAL CHART APPROACH

The classical or bureaucratic approach to organizations and the publication of a variety of management principles prompted the development of administrative structures that allowed increased control of large or-

ganizations. Implementation of these structures produced the traditional **pyramid-shaped organization.** One representation of this
structure is in the organization chart. This graphic portrayal of relationships between key elements in an organization offers a second perspective on organizational structure.

To better understand the organization chart and the configural description of structure, we must think developmentally for a moment. At
HCC, when Harvey and Bill started building personal computers, they
handled everything—from buying parts and components, to assembling
machines, to selling them, to taking cash to the bank. If someone had
asked either founder to draw a chart of their organization, they might
have looked at that person strangely. There was no organization chart
as such. Harvey and Bill were responsible for everything.

But their product was good, customers paid a competitive price
for it, and demand soon outpaced their ability to supply the needed output. At this point, they had two options. They could hire more employees, with each new employee making more of the product. Or
they could divide up the manufacturing job and let each new employee perform only a few of the manufacturing tasks, assembly-line
fashion.

Harvey chose this second option as the only way for HCC to meet
customer demands for each of its products. Dividing up the labor this
way has its advantages and disadvantages, which the discussion of job
design in Chapter 5 highlighted.

Differentiating jobs also called for additional efforts by upper-level
management at HCC. More managers were needed to make sure the
work proceeded smoothly. This differentiation also required that HCC
develop systems and procedures to integrate the parts—so that at the
end of the production process, the firm would have a quality product.
Suggestions for such procedures were many, but Harvey and Bill's
eventual structure developed out of trial and error. A partial organizational chart of HCC (Exhibit 17–2) reflects the influence of Weber's
bureaucratic ideal and the management principles proposed by the early
practitioners.

As earlier firms gained experience with new approaches to organizing the workplace, management principles appeared, offering guidance
on how best to integrate differentiated jobs. While these guidelines have
attained the status of managerial commandments for some managers,
they are more accurately viewed as suggestions or recommendations.
They may need to be violated or ignored in the name of organizational
survival. These principles were offered in the belief that they represented the *one* best way to build effective organizations. As we will see
later in this chapter and in the next, there are, in fact, a *variety* of ways
to build organizations—the best structure being a function of both internal and external factors. Still, these principles do provide a founda-

EXHIBIT 17–2

Partial Organization Chart—Home Computers Company

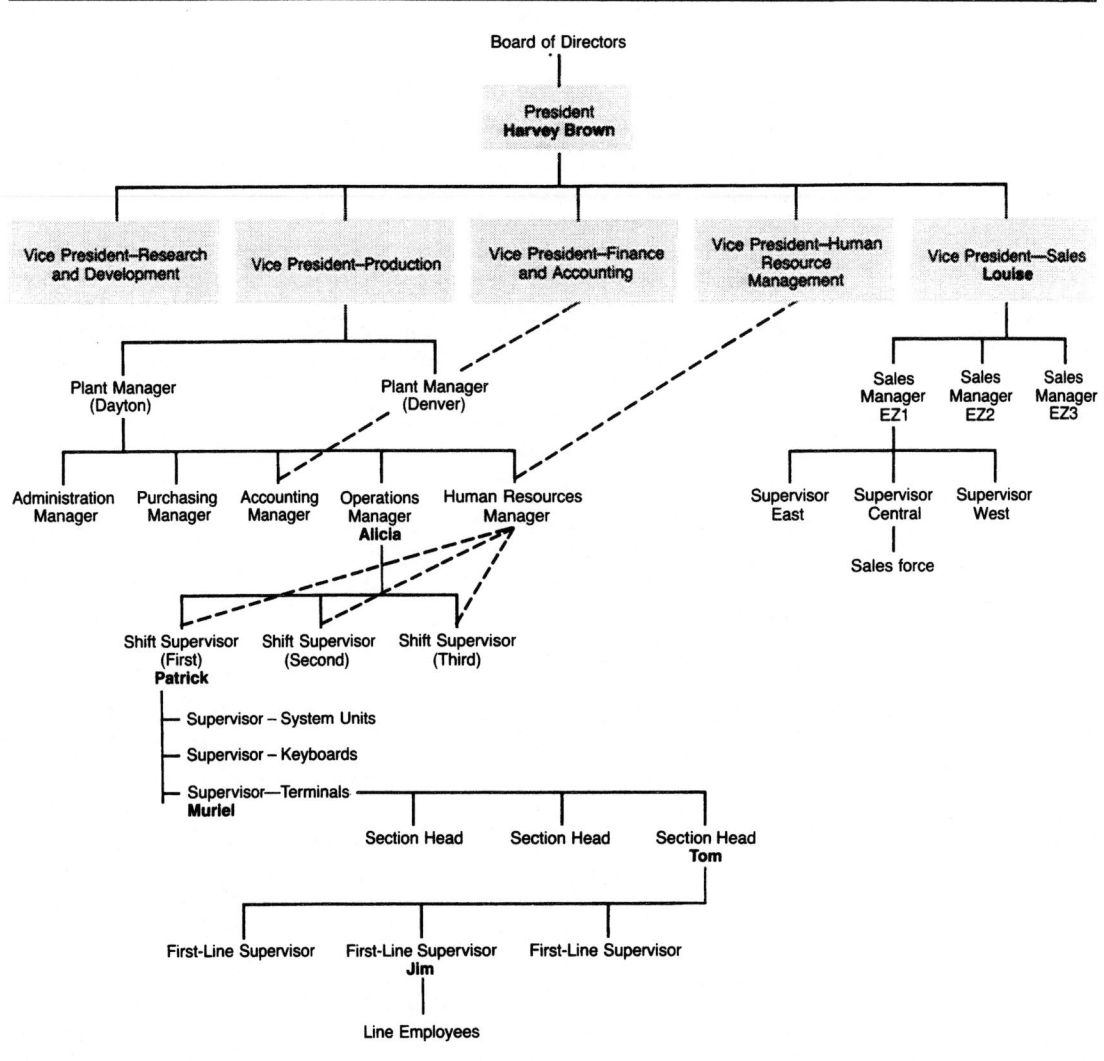

tion on which to build a discussion of structure from a configural approach.

Refer again to Exhibit 17–2. This chart is a visible representation of the invisible reporting relationships that exist at Home Computers Company. Note that in this chart, Patrick reports to Alicia, while Tom is responsible for the three first-line supervisors. The chart is a snapshot or map of HCC at the time it was drawn. As we will see shortly, in many cases, any similarities between what a chart shows and what really goes on in a firm is, as they say in the movies, purely coincidental.

Note that the chart contains boxes connected by horizontal, vertical, and diagonal lines, some dotted, most solid. Each box represents a position held by one or more employees. The lines represent authority and information-exchange relationships between positions. Boxes (positions) at the same level in the chart should have the same legitimate authority and responsibility. Vertical lines connecting the boxes indicate power and authority differences by virtue of job level in the hierarchy. Dotted lines represent advisory relationships. Job-holders in these boxes exchange information, and formal authority relationships vary. The number of different boxes in the chart indicates the division of labor within HCC. This division or differentiation occurs along two dimensions: horizontal and vertical.[12]

Differentiation

Horizontal differentiation refers to the way work is divided at the same level in an organization. By *same level,* we mean jobs that have the same formal levels of authority and responsibility. At HCC, the vice presidents of R&D, production, finance and accounting, human resource management, and sales are differentiated horizontally. And, on paper at least, they have the same levels of power. **As organizations confront increasingly complex environments, they typically become more differentiated—developing specific boundary-spanning units to deal with key sectors in the external environment.** (The next chapter considers a number of ways organizations differentiate themselves horizontally.) As firms become more differentiated and develop new units or restructure old ones, communications and coordination across the units become more difficult. Communication and coordination mechanisms are needed for the company to function effectively. These mechanisms are discussed later in this chapter.

Vertical differentiation refers to the number of authority or hierarchical levels between the lowest and highest levels in a firm. At HCC, there are seven levels between Harvey and his line employees. One can also describe the extent of vertical differentiation: tall firms have many levels; flat firms have few levels. Tall firms have more opportunities for advancement and offer increased numbers of checks on lower-level decisions. On the downside, tall firms can create communications problems and slow responses to opportunities or crises, as information must be filtered through many levels before action is taken. HCC is a relatively tall firm for the number of employees it has. This might be one explanation for employee complaints about poor communications and overly bureaucratic management.

But tall from one individual's perspective may not be tall from another's vantage point. For instance, organizational changes at Lotus Development Corporation, the publisher of the popular 1-2-3® spreadsheet computer software, prompted some programmers to complain that the firm had become stuffy and bureaucratic, with five levels of management between them and senior management.[13] Conversely, Tom Peters, management consultant and author of *Thriving on Chaos*, suggests that successful firms of the future will be flatter, with no more than five layers of management, no matter how large the organization.[14]

The discussions of power and political processes in Chapter 10 caution that the actual exercise of power by managers can vary from what is reflected in the organization chart. Sources of managerial power (other than legitimate power) can increase or decrease a manager's ability to influence activities. HCC's organization chart also allows us to discuss four other principles of organization and management: chain of command, unity of command, span of control, and parity of authority and responsibility.[15]

Chain of command

Each position in an organization chart has a superior position to which it is accountable. This results in the chain of command. This chain of command allows communications and information to flow up and down the hierarchy. If appropriately used, the chain of command ensures that all employees contribute to the overall efforts of a firm. This principle requires communications to flow upward through the chain of command. In Exhibit 17–2, if Muriel needs to talk with Alicia, she must go through her immediate supervisor Patrick—through the chain of command. Even Harvey is accountable to the board of directors.

The principle seems valid, since violating the chain in either direction might cause confusion. Employees could receive conflicting instructions from persons other than their own supervisors, or could provide information upward, bypassing their superiors. In most cases, adherence to the chain of command is appropriate.

However, there are situations when strict observance of the chain of command would not be wise. In situations where the problem *is* the immediate supervisor, skipping a hierarchical level to report this is appropriate. And in emergency situations, subordinates need to be able to communicate with those at upper levels if the immediate superior is not available. Finally, discussions with others in the chain of command about routine issues should be allowed without passing these communications through the chain of command.

An alternative view of the chain of command is offered in Insight 17–2. Is this the preferred way to structure a chain of command? Our answer no doubt depends on whether we are at the top or the bottom!

INSIGHT 17–2

An Alternative View of the Chain of Command

Source: W. E. Scott, Jr., and L. L. Cummings, *Readings in Organizational Behavior and Performance,* rev. ed., 1973, p. 236.

Unity of command

To reduce the likelihood of receiving multiple or conflicting instructions from others in the hierarchy, **the unity of command principle requires that each individual in the chain have only one direct superior.** A look at Exhibit 17–2 indicates that this principle is operating at HCC. However, even though the chart suggests that unity of command has been maintained, there are circumstances when others in the organization may attempt to influence the actions of subordinates.

To understand how this problem arises, we need to distinguish between staff and line units. **Line units contribute directly to the production of a firm's products or services.** Thus, manufacturing, production, and operations divisions contain most of the line units. **Staff units provide support services to the line units.** General counsel, public affairs, human resource management, and finance and accounting are examples of staff units.

For example, the purchasing, accounting, personnel, and operations managers are directly responsible to the plant manager. But these individuals may also have to respond to requests from R&D, instructions on hiring, promoting, or firing from personnel, and financial or cost reporting requirements from finance and accounting.

In Exhibit 17–2, the dotted lines represent these advisory reporting relationships. How is this apparent violation of the unity principle handled? There are a variety of ways in which staff activities can be managed to minimize conflicting directions. The most effective procedure requires that all staff recommendations be made *through* the plant manager. As this manager reviews and approves such changes, only then are they communicated downward to subordinate managers. Note that this problem can arise between corporate headquarters and the plants, as well as within the plants themselves.

Many firms have begun to realize that they have become inefficient because they have too many staff members, given the number of line employees in the company. For instance, General Foods dismantled its corporate staff hierarchy and eliminated most of its 2,000 headquarters jobs. Nucor Steel Company manages a work force of 3,700, with a headquarters staff of 17. Kenneth Iverson, Nucor CEO, noted that the 17 figure was up 6 percent from the previous year because the company added one staff person.[16]

Span of control

The principles of chain of command and unity of command combine to suggest a third management principle: Managers should supervise the appropriate number of subordinates. **Span of control refers to the number of subordinates reporting directly to the same supervisor.** Exhibit 17–3 shows three examples of differing spans of control—from small to

EXHIBIT 17–3

Comparing Spans of Control

Employees in each level

Assumed span of control at each level

Level in the firm	4	8	16
1 Highest	1	1	1
2	4	8	16
3	16	64	256
4	64	512	4096
5	256	4096	
6	1024		
7 Lowest	4096		

Total Number:

	4	8	16
of Non-managers	4096	4096	4096
of **Managers**	**1365 (Levels 1-6)**	**585 (Levels 1-4)**	**273 (Levels 1-3)**
of Employees	5461	4681	4369

Factors influencing span of control

Job Factors	**Employee factors**	**Organizational factors**
Job significance	Job Knowledge	Appraisal system
Job similarity	Maturity levels	Supervisory demands
Interdependence	Experience	Managerial salaries
Job dispersion	Training	Perception of upward mobility
Job routineness		Culture (trust versus mistrust)

large—for the same size firm. Note that the tallest firm has the most levels and the most managers. The flattest firm is able to supervise the same number of employees with only 273 managers.

Originally, the appropriate span of control was thought to be about seven. It is not clear where this number came from, but it may reflect employee skill levels or technologies used in early industrial organizations. Smaller spans of control suggest that managers can observe employee actions more closely. But within two organizations of similar size, an organization with a smaller span of control would likely pay out more in managerial salaries. On the plus side, a small span of control should allow subordinates easier access to—as well as more attention from—their managers, if needed.

Larger spans of control might prevent managers from maintaining close supervision of their employees, but should reduce salary expenses. Subordinates might have more difficulty getting to see their supervisor and receive less attention on the job if spans are too large.

In determining an appropriate span of control, there are a number of factors that might influence its size. Consider the following characteristics and their impact on span of control, as identified in Exhibit 17–3. Span of control should vary as a function of the predictability of the job, the maturity level and job knowledge of subordinates, the significance of the job to organizational survival, the extent to which job performance can be measured, and the levels of interdependence between employees in the work unit or between this unit and other units.

When jobs are simple, repetitive, relatively unimportant, easily measured, and performed by well-trained and motivated employees, the supervisory span of control can be quite large, even up to 40 or 50 subordinates. For example, although the head coach of a professional football team has a number of assistant coaches, the head coach has a span of control of 45 football players. The players' jobs may or may not be simple and unimportant, but the jobs are repetitive, easily measured, and usually performed by well-trained, motivated players. At the other extreme, jobs that are complex, unique, important to a firm's survival, not easily evaluated, or performed by poorly trained, inexperienced, or poorly motivated employees may require a much smaller span of control; say, one supervisor to every two or three employees.

Parity of authority and responsibility

The final principle deals with the relationship that should exist between the responsibility to perform a task and the authority given to accomplish it. The term **parity means that the authority given to an individual or position should be equal to the responsibilities required of that position.** Suppose a manager gave an employee the responsibility to increase sales levels among subordinates, but did not give that person the authority to hire or fire salespeople or to change job assignments or compensation plans. In this case, parity does not exist, and the employee will have a difficult time accomplishing his or her task. Note that in the cartoon, the absence of parity is apt to cause a devilish time on the job.

The configural or organizational chart approach and our discussion of management principles give us a second approach on structure. We will see more examples of organization charts in Chapter 18. Unfortunately, while useful, the configural approach is a static approach. It's like looking at a snapshot and not a motion picture. Or more graphically, it is like looking at a skeleton and trying to describe the living person. We need to examine structure from a more dynamic approach. We need

From now on, you will be in charge of a department
for which you have total responsibility and zero authority. Good luck.

to determine what gives an organization its life. The next section examines some of the *processes* that exist in an organization as a third way of understanding organizational structure.

THE PROCESS APPROACH

The lines joining the boxes in an organization chart provide little information about what decisions are made where. The boxes themselves offer little insight into the nature of the jobs within each work unit. And nowhere in the chart is there any suggestion about the nature of the rules, regulations, policies, or procedures that guide the day-to-day activities of employees and work groups. In other words, the organization chart doesn't indicate much about *how* or *why* an organization works the way it does. In fact, when Harvey looks at his organization chart, he gets no hints at all as to why he is making so many apparently trivial decisions. The **process** perspective offers some assistance to Harvey on this problem.

One of our earlier definitions of structure included such terms as *systems, procedures, processes,* etc. Individuals interested in structure from the process perspective believe that a better understanding of what actually happens within an organization can be gained by examining key organizational processes. These processes represent the glue that holds the organization together. We are not talking about the particular processes discussed earlier, like reward, promotion, or disciplinary processes. Rather, we are thinking in a broader sense about more general or pervasive processes that underlie these more specific systems.

While a number of different labels have been proposed for these broader processes, disagreement remains on the best way to describe them. We will examine four of the major process dimensions: complexity, formalization, centralization, and coordination.

Complexity

Complexity is the process dimension most evident on an organization chart. **Complexity refers to the degree of differentiation of jobs and work units within an organization.**[17] It is the process dimension most directly related to the specialization and division of labor principles discussed earlier. Like differentiation, complexity has both vertical and horizontal components and can influence a firm in a number of ways.

From a developmental perspective, as organizations grow larger, they also grow more complex. Such is the case with Home Computers Company. There are more and different jobs now at HCC than there were when the firm was founded in 1974. As organizations become more complex, communications, coordination, conflict, and control problems can also increase. Dividing up the labor and the authority for getting a job done requires systems, procedures, and processes to ensure that the different parts are integrated properly. It also requires additional levels in the hierarchy. Specifically, increased complexity requires that managers pay more attention to problems with coordinating the various parts of the work.

As Richard Hall points out, increasing complexity can increase organizational effectiveness and efficiency as units are formed to deal with key areas in the external environment.[18] But it also requires an increase in the number of managerial positions and systems to coordinate and control this increased number of tasks. The successful organization is the one best able to ensure that the efficiencies of the division of labor are not lost in the integrating processes and positions needed to coordinate employee efforts.

Formalization

One way to coordinate and control the various jobs and work units in a company is through the use of written rules, regulations, or procedures. **Formalization represents the extent to which written rules guide or direct employee or work unit activities.**[19] This dimension is closely related to Weber's requirement for rules, regulations, and written records. Formalization usually increases as jobs become specialized and an organization becomes more complex. The need for coordination and control is now greater. Specifying in writing what can and cannot be done on the job reduces a manager's need to constantly observe subordinates.

For example, at United Parcel Service, each activity is carefully controlled according to productivity standards. Employees know exactly what is required of them. Package sorters at a UPS hub near Chicago are expected to load between 500 and 650 packages per hour into the UPS trucks. Each stop of a driver's route is timed with a stopwatch. Superiors usually know within six minutes how long a driver's pick-ups and deliveries should take.[20]

When HCC changed from a craft approach to an assembly-line approach, employees' jobs became more specialized. Job descriptions, work rules, and procedures appeared in policy manuals and management handbooks. Little discretion remained for lower-level employees on how to do their jobs. Higher levels of formalization may be one reason that some employees feel that HCC has become more impersonal and bureaucratic.

A number of issues must be considered in this discussion of formalization. First, the establishment and publication of policies and procedures does not guarantee that they will affect employee behavior. Chapter 3 indicated that to influence behavior, consequences must be associated with that behavior. If formal rules and regulations exist but are not enforced, they will soon mean little to employees.

A second issue concerns whether only written rules and regulations influence employees. Earlier discussions of employee socialization and corporate culture suggested that employee activities can be influenced as much by unwritten norms and cultures as by written rules and regulations. Our working definition of formalization refers to rules presented in written documents. In truth, behavior can also be controlled by unwritten constraints. We have already considered the impact of values and attitudes on employee behavior in Chapter 4. This realization is important because written rules and regulations that unintentionally contradict employee socialization or corporate culture can cause employee frustration and lead to unpredictable actions. It is more than likely that their attitudes and values will take precedence over formal rules and regulations.

Conversely, if employees are upset with the firm for some reason, one way to make this displeasure known is to follow formalized rules exactly. If employees chose to work to the rules and follow written policies and procedures to the letter, many organizations would grind to a halt. Unions frequently dramatize their demands by working to the rules. The air traffic controllers' work actions in 1981 were an example of this tactic. Scrupulous adherence to FAA requirements for intervals between landings and takeoffs, and the number of aircraft handled by any one controller, enabled the union to cause lengthy delays at individual airports and near chaos in the air transport system.[21]

Third, it is important to recall that levels of formalization vary throughout an organization. Formalization is usually higher for lower-level positions, where it is easier to describe the exact requirements and procedures covering a particular position. As an employee moves up in the organizational hierarchy, or into more ambiguous jobs (like a research and development position), the level of formalization decreases.

Finally, unlike the organizational rules listed in Insight 17–3, rules and regulations in contemporary firms usually constrain job-related behaviors only. While some firms do address the nature of punishments associated with illegal or immoral activities outside the workplace that put the company in a bad light, typical organizational policies do not affect most off-the-job behaviors.

Our discussion thus far suggests that excessive formalization is widely viewed as an obstacle to creative and innovative behavior on the job. This may be true in some firms. But before we indict formalization as unacceptable, we must also remember that formalization is the reason that Burger King, McDonald's, and other franchised eateries can ensure that food and service will be identical at every outlet. Even if people do not like the food, they can trust the quality, regardless of where they get it.

Centralization

As jobs become more fragmented, resolution of coordination, conflict, communications, and control problems becomes more difficult. Top management must determine where or at what level decisions about resolving these problems should be made. **Centralization refers to the location or dispersion of decision-making authority within a company.**[22] Weber's call for a formal organizational hierarchy and parity between authority and responsibility influence where important decisions are made.

A firm that makes most significant decisions at the top is described as *centralized*. Firms that push decision-making authority and responsibility down the organizational hierarchy are said to be *decentralized*.

One of the problems facing Harvey at HCC is the highly centralized decision structure that has developed. Nearly all company problems, major and minor, end up on Harvey's desk. He would like to decentralize this process to give his subordinates more responsibility for some of the firm's decisions. But the outcomes of centralizing or decentralizing operations can be more or less desirable depending on the firm. Wang Laboratories has pushed decision making down to managers in the

INSIGHT 17-3

Organizational Work Rules

*T*hese rules were printed in the *Boston Globe* some years ago and were reported to be the rules posted by the owner of a New England carriage works in 1872, as a guide to his office workers.

ANNOUNCEMENT

1. Office employees will daily sweep the floors, dust the furniture, shelves, and showcases.
2. Each day fill lamps, clean chimneys, and trim wicks. Wash the windows once a week.
3. Each clerk will bring in a bucket of water and scuttle of coal for the day's business.
4. Make your pens carefully. You may whittle nibs to your individual taste.
5. This office will open at 7 A.M. and close at 8 P.M. except on the Sabbath, on which day we will remain closed. Each employee is expected to spend the Sabbath by attending church and contributing liberally to the cause of the Lord.

6. Men employees will be given off one evening each week for courting purposes, or two evenings a week if they go regularly to church.
7. After an employee has spent his 13 hours of labor in the office, he should spend the remaining time reading the Bible and other good books.
8. Every employee should lay aside from each pay a goodly sum of his earnings for his benefit during his declining years, so that he will not become a burden on society or his betters.
9. Any employee who smokes Spanish cigars, uses liquor in any form, or frequents pool and public halls, or gets shaved in a barber shop, will give me good reason to suspect his worth, intentions, integrity and honesty.
10. The employee who has performed his labors faithfully and without a fault for five years, will be given an increase of five cents per day in his pay, providing profits from the business permit it.

By Paul Dickson, *The Official Rules* (New York: Dell Publishing Co., 1979), pp. 191–92.

field.[23] On the other hand, Hewlett-Packard Company has cut costs by centralizing research, marketing, and manufacturing decisions. These had previously been scattered among diverse and autonomous divisions.[24]

The centralization dimension seems relatively straightforward; but transferring the concept from the textbook to the company is neither easy nor direct. For instance, centralization is not an either–or dimension. That is, we should not describe companies as either centralized or decentralized. It is possible, indeed probable, that employees at the same hierarchical levels in a firm have different levels of decision-making authority. Since some decisions are more important than others, top management may decentralize routine decisions and retain control of the most important ones. In this situation, we could describe the firm as both centralized and decentralized.

A second issue that clouds the clarity of the centralization dimension is the level of formalization in a firm. For example, assume a line manager believes he has decision authority in an apparently decentralized operation. But the amount of this decision authority may be limited by policies and procedures. The manager can decide on expenditures up to $500, for instance; but decisions about larger expenditures must be made at higher levels. In this case, the decentralized decision authority of the manager is limited by formalized regulations.

Similarly, the advent of sophisticated on-line computer systems can encourage a false sense of decision decentralization among middle managers. For example, at Mrs. Field's Cookies, the control systems used by top management to monitor lower-level decisions can also be used to override decisions that management may feel are incorrect.[25] This reduces the apparent decentralized decision-making authority of subordinate managers. It does appear that—like beauty—centralization may be in the eye of the beholder.

However apportioned, decision-making authority is a key management tool. Managerial decision making is a time-consuming process, regardless of a person's level in the company. Appropriate decentralization can minimize the number of less important decisions that clutter top management agendas and ensure timely decisions within an organization. It can be a complex dimension to fully understand; but its wise use can be crucial to organizational effectiveness. Consider the major decentralization effort undertaken by IBM in an attempt to develop new products more quickly, as outlined in Insight 17–4.

Relationships among the three dimensions

Having examined each dimension individually, we will now examine possible relationships that might exist between dimensions. For instance, do the dimensions tend to be found together in organizations, such as high complexity, formalization, and centralization in one firm versus low complexity, formalization, and centralization in another firm? Researchers have also been interested in this question for a number of years; but their answers are not as clear-cut as we might like.

The clearest of the three relationships is between **centralization and complexity.** Most investigations find that as organizations become more complex and the number of different jobs increases, the organizations' ability to maintain centralized control over decision making is reduced.[26] As firms become more complex, they become less centralized. To what extent this relationship will change as computerized management information systems become more widespread, allowing information to move quickly up an organization, is unknown at this time.

I N S I G H T 17–4

IBM Unveils a Sweeping Restructuring In Bid to Decentralize Decision Making

New York—International Business Machines Corp., frustrated by three years of disappointing results, unveiled a sweeping effort to decentralize decision-making at the world's largest computer company.

IBM Chairman John Akers described the changes as the company's biggest restructuring in at least six years and possibly its biggest in three decades. They shift broad responsibility from Mr. Akers's beleaguered management committee to IBM's six main product and marketing groups.

IBM, based in Armonk, N.Y., also took steps to resolve some deep in-house marketing clashes that had pitted rival products in competition for the same customers. It moved its personal computer division into the same group as its older typewriter division, a sign that those two markets are converging. It also moved a slow-selling line of midrange computers into the same group as IBM's core business: the large mainframe computers that run most big companies' and governments' finances.

Company insiders said the restructuring was entirely Mr. Akers's plan, and wasn't forced on him by the IBM board. A director said the board learned of the plan at its meeting last Tuesday. "John found everything was coming onto his desk, and he had more than he could cope with," another director said. "He wanted an organization which resolved more problems before they got to him."

In part, Mr. Akers's restructuring of IBM is simply an effort to reinvigorate his troops and shine up the company's tarnished image. He rechristened every one of IBM's blandly named product groups, giving them some uncharacteristic new glitz. For example, the old Information Systems & Storage Group will become IBM Enterprise Systems.

"These kinds of changes are part of IBM's culture," said Bob Djurdjevic, an industry consultant and former IBM employee. "This recharges the top executives' batteries. It kicks the year off on a high note and starts them running in a new direction."

Mr. Akers emphasized that one of his most urgent objectives is to make IBM faster at bringing out new products. "Our development and manufacturing teams will frankly spend less time at corporate headquarters," he said. In addition, he said that over the next couple of years, "many thousands" of corporate staff members will be moved into posts that bring them into closer contact with customers."

The relationships between **complexity and formalization** are less clear-cut.[27] In some cases, more complex firms have low levels of formalization. In other cases, complex organizations have high levels of formalization. On their face, these results appear contradictory. A closer look at the jobs being done in these different situations offers an explanation for the differences. In the first situation, highly trained professionals were the subject of the research. Their training precluded control by a great many written rules and regulations. In fact, in many cases, it would have been nearly impossible to write such formal job requirements. In this situation, increased complexity of a professional nature was associated with reduced levels of formalization.

In the other situation, researchers were looking at routine, assembly-line jobs. These jobs were easily described in formal job descriptions and were controlled by a large number of written policies and procedures. Increased complexity of a routine nature was associated with increased levels of formalization.

Finally, what about the association between **formalization and centralization?** To make sense of this relationship, we need to take two other factors into consideration: employee skill levels and types of decisions. High levels of formalization and centralization are frequently used in dealing with relatively unskilled employees. Both of these process dimensions act as controls in this situation.

Highly skilled, professional employees require less control in terms of formal rules or procedures. Similarly, these employees prefer retaining the authority to make decisions on issues directly affecting their work. Thus, for job-related decisions, there is a positive relationship between formalization and centralization—low formalization and low centralization. These professionals are usually content to allow upper levels in the organization to make nontask-related decisions. For these decisions, the relationship between formalization and centralization is negative: low formalization is associated with high centralization.[28]

These relationships are summarized in Exhibit 17–4.

Coordination

Formalization and centralization are two ways to maintain control in complex organizations. But control is only a partial answer to the integration of specialized and complex jobs. Of equal importance is the coordination of the interdependencies among jobs. **Coordination refers to the strategies, processes, or procedures that ensure that various jobs are accomplished in the proper order.** Mintzberg argues that organizations use one or more of five coordinating mechanisms to integrate the various jobs. These mechanisms include mutual adjustment, direct supervision, and standardization of work processes, outputs, and skills. Each of these is examined below.[29]

Mutual adjustment

The least formal approach to coordination is mutual adjustment. **Mutual adjustment refers to the person-to-person communications needed to accomplish tasks involving more than one person.** At HCC, Harvey

EXHIBIT 17–4

Relationships among Three Process Dimensions

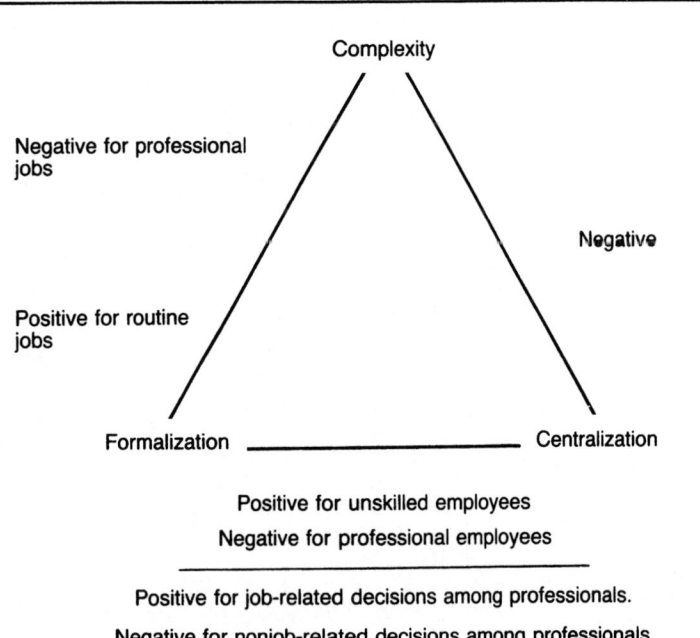

Positive for unskilled employees

Negative for professional employees

Positive for job-related decisions among professionals.

Negative for nonjob-related decisions among professionals.

communicates daily with each of his plant managers to ensure that they have the resources to accomplish their jobs. The sales staff and sales managers frequently interact on a person-to-person basis to resolve marketing issues. For instance, at Pizza Hut, employees taking orders communicate directly with the employees making pizza. Coordination efforts that bypass the formal chain of command are usually of this type.

Direct supervision

Harvey and most of his managers also coordinate by means of direct supervision. **Direct supervision requires that managers inform certain subordinates about when and how to act in relationships with other subordinates.** The nature of a manager's direct supervision is a function of the extent to which an organization is centralized or decentralized, the level of power available to the manager, and the manager's span of control.

Standardization

Home Computers Company also coordinates activities between individuals and work units by standardizing some of these activities. **Standardization refers to the extent to which jobs and related activities are done in a uniform fashion.** Highly standardized jobs are all performed in exactly the same manner. Assembly-line jobs are usually highly standardized. High-level executive positions are much less standardized. Each is done in a unique fashion. This method of coordination can be accomplished in three different ways, each of which is discussed below.

Standardization of work processes. This coordination approach is similar in effect to formalization. **When the work process is standardized, specific procedures are provided for accomplishing a particular task.** At HCC, the accounts payable clerks have specific procedures for paying bills to ensure accurate control of expenditures. Computer assemblers also have explicit instructions on how to do their jobs. This allows any one assembler to step in for another with only a short training period. These specifications reduce the amount of mutual adjustment or direct supervision needed to complete a task and allow managers to have a larger span of control.

Standardization of outputs. At other levels in HCC, coordination among different jobs or work units is achieved by **specifying the nature of the results or outputs desired in a particular job or work unit.** At the plant level, the HCC plant managers at Denver and Dayton receive production and budgetary goals from corporate headquarters. Within each plant, the plant manager is free to use whatever processes thought appropriate for accomplishing these desired outcomes. At Harris Corporation, an electronics conglomerate, salary increases for division executives are tied to improvements in earnings.

This particular coordination mechanism is particularly useful if it is difficult to specify the most effective means to achieve a particular outcome. For instance, the programming unit at HCC headquarters coordinates its efforts with other HCC units by promising to produce one new software package every six months. Knowing that this output has been specified allows other units to better coordinate their activities on the assumption that new software products are coming twice a year.

Standardization of skills. Finally, in some areas, HCC coordinates activities as **a function of the standardized skills that certain employees are assumed to bring to their jobs by virtue of their education, socialization, or previous job training.** For instance, in HCC's research and development division, coordinating individual scientists by specifying work processes or outputs is not feasible. Few scientists are willing to operate under such constraints. Rather, Harvey and his vice president of research and development assume that coordination among the R&D staff will occur through the relatively similar education and training that each scientist brings to the job. This socialization allows R&D staff members to coordinate their activities, knowing what their colleagues have done or will be doing in the future.

Merck & Company is one of the premier drug companies in the world. In 1986, it was named as the most admired U.S. corporation in a poll by *Fortune* magazine. The head of the firm's research and development noted that Merck allows its scientists to control their own destiny. "If you have bright, highly motivated people who feel responsible for their work, they will discover great things."[30]

The four process dimensions of structure—complexity, formalization, centralization, and coordination—evolved from the earlier classical and configural perspectives. They were developed to provide additional insights into the way in which organizations are put together. Individually and in combination, the process dimensions offer a more complete explanation of organizational structure. They allow us to explain more fully the nature of the relationships only hinted at in the organization chart. As you think about the structures of the organizations to which you belong, consider how you would describe each of them in terms of their complexity, formalization, centralization, and coordination.

We have now examined three approaches on the way organizations are put together. The classical approach looked at structure in terms of Weber's bureaucratic characteristics. The configural approach and its underlying managerial principles allowed only a static view of structure—like looking at a picture of an organization. To get a more dynamic view, we examined four process dimensions of structure that influenced how work, information, and decisions are aligned within a company. That is, we tried to see how the boxes and lines in the organization chart truly interacted. But we are still talking about the bits and pieces of structure.

Now we need to consider what kinds of structures emerge when we put some of the pieces together. We need to find out what structures actually exist in organizations, and we need to examine how organization structures can be classified. For this purpose, we turn to a classification scheme suggested by Henry Mintzberg.

THE HOLISTIC APPROACH

A word of caution is warranted before we begin our discussion. Any classification scheme of organizational structures will, of necessity, be overly simplistic. In reality, there are probably as many different kinds of specific structures as there are organizations. On the other hand, the differences may be relatively minor—particular twists that make a general structure work a little better for a given firm. But if we look at general structures across many firms, some approaches seem to occur more frequently than others.

One of the most popular classification schemes has been proposed by Mintzberg.[31] He believes there are five basic structural configurations. Each is the result of the interplay of five organizational components and coordinating mechanisms that allow the components to function effectively. His approach allows us to take a more holistic look at organizational structures.

Although Mintzberg might take us to task for oversimplifying his categories, for our purposes, we can say that his classifications of structure are based on two concepts. One was just considered—his description of coordination mechanisms available to an organization. The second concept is derived from his assertion that there are five basic parts to any company. These parts, illustrated in Mintzberg's own unique representation in Exhibit 17–5 and discussed below, include the strategic apex, operating core, middle line, technostructure, and support staff.

According to Mintzberg, key executives and top managers reside in what he calls the strategic apex. In the **strategic apex are individuals who ensure that an organization serves its mission effectively**—and that it serves the needs of those who control or otherwise have power over the organization. Harvey, his vice presidents, and probably his plant managers are the strategic apex at Home Computers Company.

At the other end of the organizational hierarchy is the operating core. In the **operating core are employees who perform the basic work related directly to the production of products and services.** From a systems perspective, these are the individuals responsible for securing the necessary inputs, transforming inputs into outputs, and distributing outputs. In addition, the operating core includes those organizational activities that provide direct support to these key subsystems, such as maintenance and inventory control. From this perspective, the operating core contains much more than simply operations and manufacturing units. It also contains units like purchasing, receiving, selling, and transportation.

Joining the strategic apex and the operating core is a group of employees called the middle line. This **middle-line connection between apex and core is made by the chain of middle managers with formal authority.** Actually, middle-line members range from first-level supervisors to senior managers, one level removed from the strategic apex. Managers in the middle line are responsible for implementing the goals and objectives of the strategic apex by managing efforts of employees in the operating core.

EXHIBIT 17–5

Basic Structural Elements

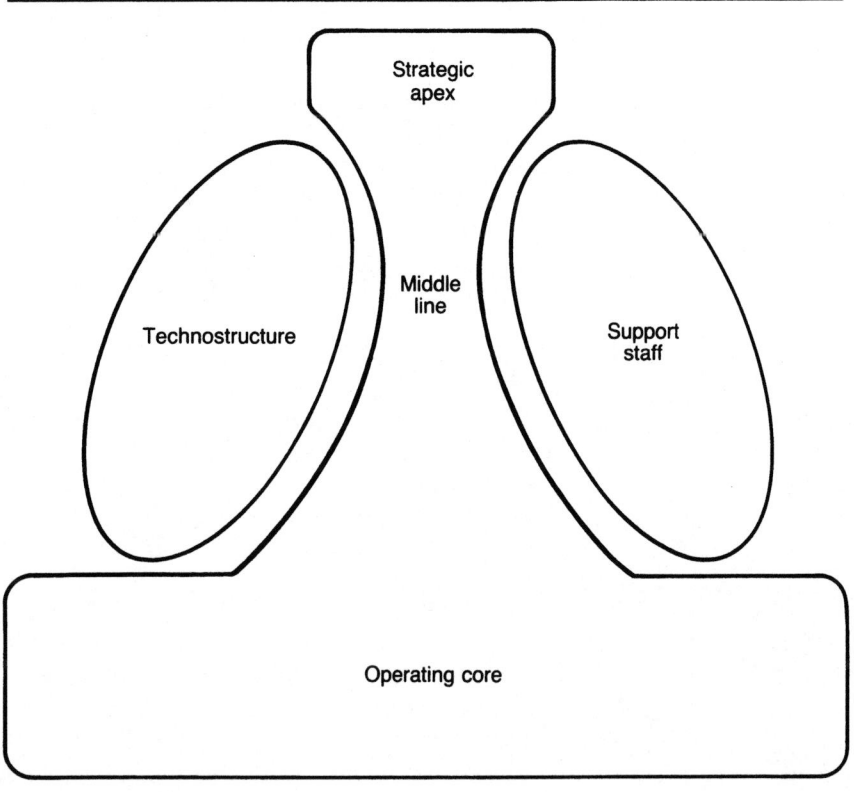

Source: Henry Mintzberg, *The Structuring of Organizations*, © 1979, p. 20. Reprinted by permission of Prentice–Hall, Inc., Englewood Cliffs, New Jersey.

Two organizational elements provide assistance to the key operational units of an organization: the technostructure and the support staff. The **technostructure consists of employees and work units that do not operate in the work flow.** Rather, they design, plan, or change the work flow. Or they train the people who do it; but they do not operate in the work flow themselves. The technostructure provides procedures for standardizing operations and activities in the firm. For instance, the industrial engineering department works to standardize work processes at a variety of levels. Planners, financial analysts, and cost accountants standardize many work outputs by establishing organizational objectives or budgets. The human resource management department, by establishing selection, training, evaluation, and promotion procedures, standardizes employee skill levels.

The last of Mintzberg's five structural elements is the support staff. The **support staff provides support to the organization outside of the operating work flow.** Unlike the technostructure units that were concerned with standardizing activities in support of the operating core, the support staff provides *indirect* support to basic organizational missions. Examples of support units at HCC might include corporate legal counsel, public relations, research and development, the mailroom, the company cafeteria, and the grounds crew. The direction of emphasis for the technostructure is inward toward the firm. The thrust of support staff concerns is both internal and external. Legal counsel and public relations staffs interact more frequently with external environmental sectors than do the units in the technostructure, for instance.

Together, the technostructure and the support staff are commonly referred to under the single title of *staff* as opposed to *line,* which refers to units contributing directly to the basic mission of a firm. Given our discussion here, there are significant differences between units found in these two elements. Their impact on the various design options becomes apparent in the following section.

Structural options

Mintzberg found that as one or more of these five organizational elements dominates in a firm in conjunction with certain coordination processes, five generic organizational structures emerge. These generic structures are simple structure, machine bureaucracy, professional bureaucracy, divisionalized form, and adhocracy. Each of these is described below and illustrated in Exhibit 17–6.

Simple structure

When Harvey and Bill started HCC, their organization's structure would have been described by Mintzberg as a *simple structure.* In a **simple structure,** the strategic apex is the dominant element, with centralized control exercised over an operational core marked by low levels of complexity and formalization. The coordination exercised by Harvey and Bill in those early years was basically mutual adjustment and direct supervision. When they needed to understand or integrate activities, HCC was small enough to do this on a person-to-person basis.

Machine bureaucracy

As HCC grew in size, and as demand for its products increased, jobs became more specialized, and the organization became more complex. Horizontal and vertical differentiation increased, requiring increases in formalization. While the strategic apex remained important, the impact

EXHIBIT 17–6

Mintzberg's Five Organizational Configurations

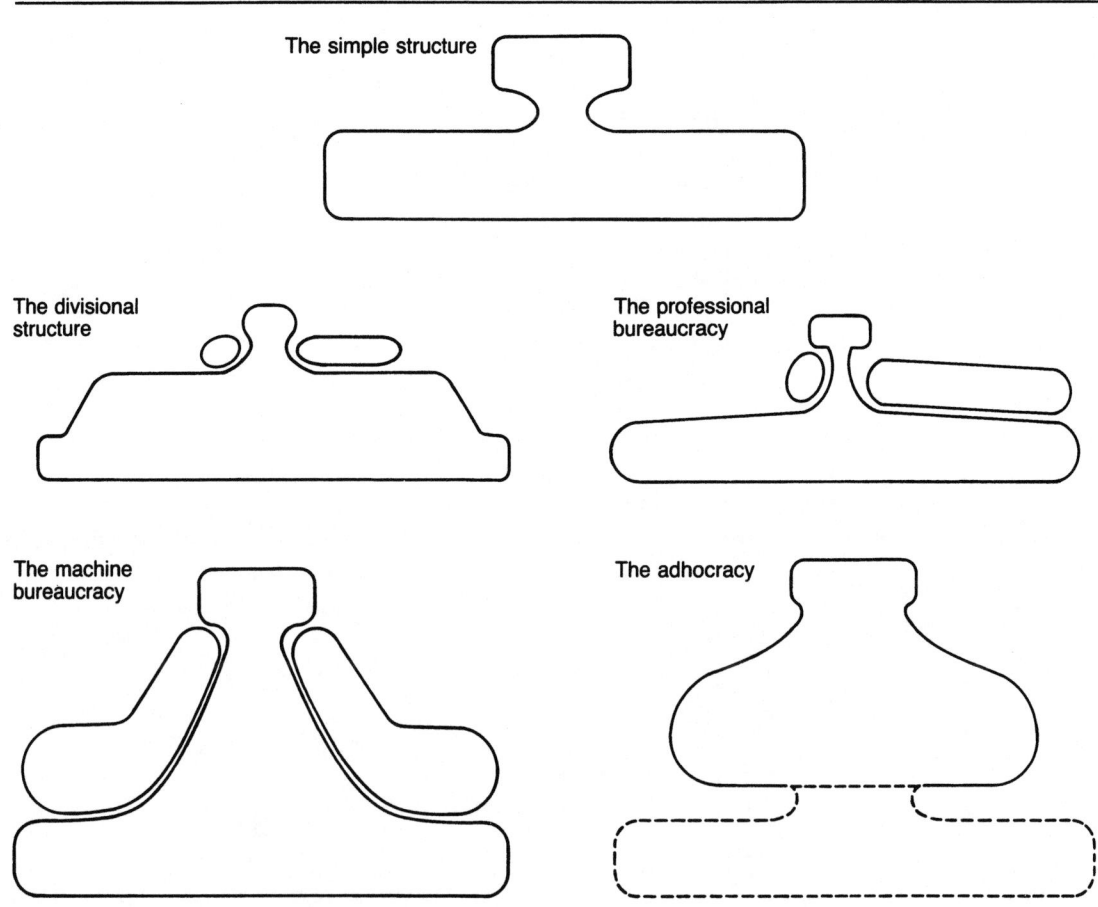

The simple structure

The divisional structure

The professional bureaucracy

The machine bureaucracy

The adhocracy

Source: Henry Mintzberg, *The Structuring of Organizations*, © 1979, pp. 307, 325, 355, 393, 443. Reprinted by permission of Prentice–Hall, Inc., Englewood Cliffs, New Jersey.

of the analysts in the technostructure increased. Efficient production of the early computers became an important contribution to the survival of the firm. The diagram of the resulting **machine bureaucracy** reflects this dual emphasis. Coordination and control in these structures is usually through direct supervision and standardization of work processes. HCC's evolution into a large-scale manufacturer of computers and accessories made this structure appropriate. Mintzberg found this structure in such diverse organizations as the post office, a security agency, a steel company, a custodial prison, and an automobile manufacturer.

Professional bureaucracy

Machine bureaucracies are well suited to large organizations. The **professional bureaucracy** can come in many different sizes, however. As illustrated in Exhibit 17–6, the basic difference between the two structures is the highly trained, professional operating core found in the professional bureaucracy. This core is composed of specialists with high degrees of specialized training and skills. Operating core activities are controlled through the standardization of these skills. This encourages substantial autonomy and decentralization in the specialized tasks in the operating core.

Exhibit 17–6 also indicates that a large support staff is necessary to provide adequate service to the core professionals. The support staff in areas outside the professional core are often highly formalized and centralized. Universities, consulting firms, and medical clinics are typical examples of professional bureaucracies. HCC, a manufacturing firm, is not a candidate for such a structure. Still, certain functions within the company, notably the R&D areas, could be structured in this way. Similarly, many of the software firms that write programs for HCC machines are probably structured as professional bureaucracies.

Divisional structure

The **divisional structure** incorporates a number of relatively independent units within a broader hierarchy, controlled at corporate headquarters. In this structure, the middle-line is emphasized. It is the link between the divisional units of the operating core and the strategic apex at headquarters. Within each division, there are smaller machine bureaucracy structures characterized by high levels of complexity, formalization, and centralization. Control in these organizations is through the standardization of outputs, with each independent unit treated as a separate profit center. Managerial performance and organizational effectiveness is evaluated relative to these profit targets. These structures are frequently found in older and larger firms, particularly firms with multiple product lines.

For instance, IBM's reorganization, discussed earlier in the chapter, will result in six main product and marketing groups.[32] Gulf & Western has three core businesses: Paramount Pictures, Simon & Schuster Publishing, and the Associates, a commercial and consumer loan company.[33] Borden Inc. has grouped some 40 separate companies into six areas: dairy, pasta, snacks, specialty industrial chemicals, consumer do-it-yourself items, and "niche" grocery products (like ReaLemon juice and Eagle sweetened condensed milk).[34]

Adhocracy

The label attached to this last structure comes from the Latin phrase *ad hoc*, meaning *for a specific purpose.* The **adhocracy** structure allows specialists to be drawn from different disciplines into ad hoc project teams as the environment demands. The adhocracy structure illustrated in Exhibit 17–6 suggests the relative importance of the five organizational elements in this structure.

Many companies use a version of an adhocracy when forming task forces to deal with problems that require expertise from many different functional areas. The structure is characterized by individuals or groups working on different aspects of a project or different projects. Team members are usually professionals, who may or may not be full-time employees of the organization. Given the high levels of professional expertise, there are usually low levels of formalization and centralization and high levels of complexity in organizations that adopt this structure. Coordination usually occurs through mutual adjustment and the standardization of skills.

There is little need for technostructure in an adhocracy, since the nature of the technology used by any group differs over time. The strategic apex works closely with the operating core (composed of a variety of work groups). Of the five structural elements, the support staff plays the most important role here, supplying and coordinating staff services to a constantly changing labor force.

Although Harvey does not preside over a true adhocracy at HCC, he has formed various task groups to address critical organizational issues, like plant locations and new product introductions. The efficiencies demanded of his organization by the marketplace reduce the usefulness of this structure.

Adhocracies are appropriate structures for organizations facing complex and dynamic environments. In HCC's early years, before Harvey and Bill successfully produced the EZ1, the two of them were likely operating some sort of occasional adhocracy. They might have been unaware that such a label could be applied to those chaotic first few years; but the structure did allow them to respond quickly to the needs of their environment.

Mintzberg's classification scheme offers a more in-depth perspective on structure, but provides few insights into how or why a company moves from one structure to another (or back again, if necessary). The next chapter addresses this issue by examining factors or contingencies that influence organizational designs and the designs that work best for a given set of contingencies. The next chapter will make reference to the discussion here of process dimensions, coordination mechanisms, and structural configurations.

EXHIBIT 17–7

Relationships among the Structural Characteristics and Mintzberg's Configurations

Characteristic	Simple Structure	Machine Bureaucracy	Professional Bureaucracy	Divisional Structure	Adhocracy
Coordinating mechanism	Direct super-vision	Standardization of work	Standardization of skills	Standardization of output	Mutual adjustment
Key part	Strategic apex	Techno-structure	Operating core	Middle-line	Support staff
Complexity	Low	Much horizontal and vertical	Much horizontal	Some horizontal and vertical	Much horizontal
Formalization	Low	High	Low	High within divisions	Low
Centralization	High	High	Low	Limited	Low
Control profile	Organic	Mechanistic	Mechanistic	Mechanistic	Organic
Appropriate environment	Simple and dynamic	Simple and stable	Complex and stable	Simple and stable	Complex and dynamic

Source: Henry Mintzberg, *The Structuring of Organizations*, © 1979, pp. 466–467. Adapted by permission of Prentice–Hall, Inc., Englewood Cliffs, New Jersey.

As a way of summarizing much of what has been discussed in this chapter, Exhibit 17–7 describes each of Mintzberg's five configurations in terms of some of the other descriptions of structure presented in the chapter.

CHAPTER HIGHLIGHTS

In our two-chapter module on organizational structure and design, this first chapter presented a discussion of the pieces that contribute to an increased understanding of structure. This chapter defined structure in a variety of ways, allowing that structure can mean many things to many different people. We examined four different approaches to structure, including the classical, configural, process, and holistic approaches.

The classic approach of Weber's ideal bureaucratic organization was discussed in the context of the historical development of complex and large organizations. **Weber's ideal organization was designed to ensure impartiality, rationality, efficiency, and effectiveness.** Dismayed at the quality of governmental organizations he had observed, Weber proposed an organizational structure, calling for a **division of labor, employment decisions based on merit, hierarchy of authority, separation of job and job-holder, impersonality, written rules and regulations, and written records and communications.**

729

If these characteristics were implemented successfully, and if both the letter and the spirit of the suggestions were observed, the resulting bureaucratic organization would be both effective and efficient. Unfortunately, in many settings, implementation is unsuccessful; and a variety of problems soon beset most bureaucracies. **We identified some of the key disadvantages of bureaucracies: goal displacement, rules as minimal levels of acceptable performance, incorrect use of rules, and red tape leading to employee alienation and customer or client frustration.**

Early investigations into the way organizations were structured prompted a great deal of speculation among practicing managers. Efforts to codify what they viewed as the best ways to structure a firm led to the publication of a series of management principles. From these principles and the work of Weber, the traditional pyramid-shaped organization arose. To examine this organization structure, we considered the configural approach. **The management principles underlying the configural approach are differentiation, chain of command, unity of command, span of control, and parity of authority and responsibility.**

The classical and configural approaches provided some useful information about the way firms put themselves together; but the picture they provided was too static. The organization chart told little about the relationships between the boxes and along the lines. For a more dynamic approach, we considered four different process dimensions of structure: **complexity, formalization, centralization, and coordination.** Each of these has its roots in Weber's bureaucratic characteristics. Individually and jointly, they impact an organization in fairly predictable ways. We discussed the relationships among the first three process dimensions and concluded that **an understanding of these relationships requires knowledge about the nature of jobs, employee skill levels, and types of decisions being made.**

Our discussion of coordination mechanisms identified five ways activities in a firm can be appropriately controlled and integrated. **Mutual adjustment refers to person-to-person interactions. Direct supervision represents the typical superior–subordinate relationship. The three forms of standardization (of work process, outputs, and skills) suggest that uniformity in actions can also assist in coordinating diverse activities.**

Finally, we put the pieces together by exploring five general structural options that Henry Mintzberg argues allow people to describe most of the structural forms in modern organizations. **His five options arise as a function of which basic structural element is dominant, and which coordinating mechanism is used to integrate the elements. The strategic apex includes key executives and is responsible for overall guidance of a firm. The operating core contains those employees and work units that provide a firm's products and services. These two ele-**

ments are linked by the middle-line, comprising lower- and middle-level managers. Staff assistance to the operating core is provided by the technostructure and to the remainder of the firm by the support staff.

By combining these five elements with the earlier coordinating mechanisms, Mintzberg identified five structural options: **simple structure, machine bureaucracy, professional bureaucracy, divisional form, and adhocracy.** As we will see in the next chapter, each of these is an appropriate structure for dealing with progressively more complex external environments.

REVIEW QUESTIONS

1. What is meant by the term *organizational structure?*
2. Identify the major characteristics of Weber's bureaucratic organization.
3. Weber believed that his bureaucracy would be an effective and efficient organization. What problems can arise in a bureaucracy? Why do you think these problems occur?
4. What are the advantages and disadvantages of using an organization chart to understand an organization's structure?
5. What is the difference between the concepts of *chain of command* and *unity of command*?
6. In what types of organizations would managers have relatively small spans of control?
7. A time-honored statement in the military asserts, "A commander can delegate authority, but never responsibility." How does this statement compare with the requirement of parity between authority and responsibility in organizations?
8. What is the relationship between the division of labor in a firm and the complexity of that firm?
9. How does formalization act to control or coordinate the interaction between organizational jobs or work units?
10. "This organization is too centralized." Why might the validity of this statement be questioned in a large organization?
11. What are the advantages and disadvantages of centralization?
12. What factors tend to influence the relationships that are found between complexity, formalization, and centralization?
13. Coordination by standardization can occur in three different ways. Describe each method, and indicate the setting in which each would be appropriate.

14. What are the five structural elements common to all organizations?

15. Describe each of the five structural options. When is each the appropriate option and why?

RESOURCE READINGS

Daft, R. *Organizational Theory*, 2nd ed. St. Paul, Minn.: West Publishing, 1986

Hall, R. *Organizations: Structure and Process*. Englewood Cliffs, N.J.: Prentice-Hall, 1977.

Mintzberg, H. *Structure in Fives: Designing Effective Organizations*. Englewood Cliffs, N.J.: Prentice-Hall, 1983.

Van Fleet, D. "Span of Management: Research and Issues." *Academy of Management Review*, 1983, pp. 546–52.

Weber, Max. *The Theory of Social and Economic Organizations*, translated by A. Henderson and T. Parsons. New York: The Free Press, 1947.

NOTES

1. R. Katz, "Skills of the Effective Administrator," *Harvard Business Review*, January-February 1955, pp. 33–42.

2. J. Child, *Organizations* (New York: Harper & Row, 1977), p. 10.

3. Max Weber, *The Theory of Social and Economic Organization*, translated by A. Henderson and T. Parson (New York: Free Press, 1947), pp. 328–40.

4. Ibid.

5. J. Steingold, "How They Tore Hutton to Pieces." *The New York Times-Business*, January 17, 1988.

6. B. Fromson, "The Slow Death of E. F. Hutton." *Fortune*, February 29, 1988, pp. 82–88.

7. R. K. Merton, "Bureaucratic Structure and Personality," *Social Forces*, May 1948, pp. 560–68.

8. Ibid.

9. A. W. Gouldner, *Patterns of Industrial Bureaucracy* (New York: Free Press, 1954).

10. Merton, "Bureaucratic Structure and Personality."

11. G. A. Miller, "Professionals in Bureaucracies: Alienation Among Industrial Scientists and Engineers," *American Sociological Review*, October 1967, pp. 755–68.

12. P. Lawrence and J. Lorsch, *Organizations and Environment* (Boston: Harvard University Graduate School of Business, Division of Research, 1967).

13. "The Drill Instructor Who Made Lotus Snap to Attention," *Business Week,* November 16, 1987, pp. 190–92.

14. P. Pasarella, "Tom Peters Invites Chaos for Survival," *Industry Week,* October 19, 1987, pp. 48–53.

15. L. Urwick, *The Golden Book of Management: A Historical Record of the Life and Work of Seventy Pioneers* (London: N. Neames, 1966).

16. T. Moore, "Goodbye Corporate Staff," *Fortune,* December 21, 1987, pp. 65–76.

17. S. Robbins, *Organization Theory,* 2d ed. (Englewood Cliffs, N.J.: Prentice-Hall, 1987), p. 56.

18. R. Hall, *Organizations: Structure and Process* (Englewood Cliffs, N.J.: Prentice-Hall, 1982), p. 90.

19. D. Pugh, D. Hickson, C. Hinings, and C. Turner, "Dimensions of Organizational Structure," *Administrative Science Quarterly,* June 1968, p. 75.

20. K. Labich, "Big Changes at Big Brown," *Fortune,* January 18, 1988, pp. 56–64.

21. D. Rosenbloom and J. Shafritz, *Essentials of Labor Relations* (Reston, Va.: Reston Publishers, 1985), pp. 154–56.

22. Robbins, *Organization Theory,* p. 73.

23. "How the Doctor's Son Is Getting Wang Back on Its Feet," *Business Week,* January 25, 1988, pp. 84–85.

24. J. Levirce, "Mild Mannered Hewlett-Packard is Making Like Superman," *Business Week,* March 7, 1988, pp. 110–14.

25. T. Richman, "Mrs. Fields' Secret Ingredient," *INC.,* October 1987, pp. 65–72.

26. J. Child, "Organizational Structure and Strategies of Control: A Replication of the Aston Study," *Administrative Science Quarterly,* March 1972, pp. 163–77.

27. Pugh et al., "Dimensions of Organizational Structure," pp. 65–105.

28. See, for example, Pugh et al., "Dimensions of Organizational Structure"; L. Donaldson, J. Child, and H. Aldrich, "The Aston Findings on Centralization: A Further Discussion," *Administrative Science Quarterly,* September 1975, pp. 453–60; and P. Grinyer and M. Yasai-Ardekani, "Dimensions of Organizational Structure: A Critical Replication," *Academy of Management Journal,* September 1980, pp. 405–21.

29. H. Mintzberg, *The Structuring of Organizations* (Englewood Cliffs, N.J.: Prentice-Hall, 1979), p. 3.

30. "The Miracle Company," *Business Week,* October 19, 1987, pp. 84–90.

31. Mintzberg, *The Structuring of Organizations,* pp. 305–467.

32. M. Miller and P. Carroll, "IBM Unveils a Sweeping Restructuring in Bid to Decentralize Decision-Making," *Wall Street Journal,* January 29, 1988.

33. M. Williams, "Can a Tough Boss Mellow," *Fortune,* December 21, 1987, pp. 105–12.

34. B. Saporito, "How Borden Milks Packaged Goods," *Fortune,* December 21, 1988, pp. 139–44.

CASE: The Medtek Corporation (A)

"We have a basic problem of performance here in the technical division." John Torrence, Senior Vice-President of the Medtek Corporation and Director of the company's technical division (R&D) was talking with several members of a consulting team he had brought in to help with problems in the division. "We have a bad case of technical constipation; this division has not brought out a successful new product in two years. If we don't do something about this problem soon, the whole company is going to be in big trouble."

Company background

The Medtek Corporation is an international company that designs, manufactures, and markets automated instruments for the analysis of blood and serum as well as for similar industrial applications. The company was founded in 1949 by Paul Torres; the father of the present chairman and chief executive officer, Arthur Torrence; and the grandfather of the present senior vice-president for research and development, John Torrence. Torres died in 1978.

Medtek was formed in 1949 as a small operation in a Bronx loft. They handcrafted a new device called the Automed, a product still manufactured by the company. This product automated the preparation of human tissue for microscopic examination by pathologists.

In the early 1960s the firm employed approximately twenty-five people. The R&D section was composed of two engineers and two draftsmen. The organization was very informal. New employees and consultants were brought in as needed to work on specific tasks.

During this period, Ben Kless, one of Medtek's salesmen, met an inventor named Dennis Rettew. Rettew was employed in a Cleveland hospital. After observing both the kidney dialysis and laboratory procedures in the hospital, he applied the mechanical techniques used in dialysis to the development of a rudimentary device that could automate one laboratory procedure.

Rettew and his invention were brought to Medtek. Technical development of this device resulted in the single channel Autoxam—an innovation which today is still one of the company's major products.

The single channel Autoxam works by plucking up a small blood sample and pumping it through a continuous system in which the sample is properly diluted; reagents added and mixed; the solution heated and/or cooled, filtered, pigmented, and spectrographically analyzed; and the results recorded and compared to a norm. Successive samples can be introduced continuously to the Autoxam. The innovation of separating the samples with a small air bubble both permitted the continuous flow of samples and scrubbed the pathway clean of the previous sample. Prior to the Autoxam, each sample was handled manually by a lab technician. Obviously the new device allowed a saving in lab technicians' time and in the amount of reagents used. Further

Source: Adapted from David A. Nadler, Michael L. Tushman, and Nina G. Hatvany, *Managing Organizations: Readings and Cases*, pp. 551–57. Copyright © 1982 by David A Nadler, Michael L. Tushman, and Nina G. Hatvany. By permission of Scott, Foresman and Company.

savings were realized by the Autoxam's ability to examine a larger number of samples per day than a technician.

In 1967 the Autoxam was introduced to the market. It was a great success and ushered the firm into an era of rapid and continuous growth. By the early 1970s the firm had grown to about 125 employees. The bulk of the research and development work was centered around the blood analyzer. Development work during this period focused on a multichannel version of the Autoxam that could automate additional laboratory tests and could also automate some industrial tests such as the measurement of trace metals in water used in powering steam turbines for generating electricity. New applications and new clinical procedures compatible with Autoxam technology were developed both internally and by users and researchers external to and independent of the company. Much new information came to Medtek through professional journal reports of research inspired by the introduction of the Autoxam.

The years 1977 and 1978 brought a crisis to Medtek. This crisis was precipitated by the development of the 60/12, a second generation analyzer that produced a patient profile of 12 lab tests from one sample at the rate of 60 tests per hour. First, an internal fight arose over whether to finance an expansion of the company to tap the possible profits of the 60/12 or whether to restrain the firm's growth. Second, the rapid growth resulted in errors and slippage for which no one was accountable. A consulting firm proposed a vast change in the formal organization in order to better handle these accountability problems. Vice presidents, senior vice-presidents and a divisional structure were introduced. Some believed that the switch to this formal structure was too quick and that the company did not have enough properly trained personnel to staff the new organization. Third, the company went public through a sale of common stock, the implications of which still seem to be sensitive.

The choice was made to expand, and the period of 1979 to 1982 was a time of extremely rapid growth. The technical division grew to 150 employees. Its 1981 budget was some five times greater than its 1977 budget. Lou Bidder, who was brought on in the early 1960s to work on the Autoxam hydraulics, became the first technical division vice-president.

The 60/12 was a huge success. The company moved to suburban Washington, D.C. Task groups were introduced in the technical division. This innovation changed the long-standing structure of the three departments: mechanical, electrical, and clinical chemistry. Development focused on HORSE (High Operation Repeated Sequential Examiner), a third generation computer-controlled blood analyzer with a capacity of 20 tests per profile and 150 tests per hour.

The years 1982 to the present have not been easy ones for the company. The National Institute of Health retrenched, and federal funds to buy Medtek's products were no longer as readily available to hospitals. HORSE developed numerous technical problems. Underwriters' requirements for insuring installed HORSEs varied from city to city and in the international market necessitating modifications to fit local conditions. The company experienced problems with its formal organization structure.

In addition to the analyzers the firm also offers a white cell testing and diagnosis device, reagents for the analyzers, an infrared analyzer, and a hospital-oriented management information system. The analyzers, however, continue to account for the vast majority of hardware sales. Organization charts for the company as well as financial highlights are included as Exhibits 1, 2, and 3.

The technical division

As the R&D arm of Medtek, the technical division is responsible for basic research in areas relevant to the products of the firm. Its major goal, however, is the development of new product ideas that can be developed successfully into new commercial products for the firm. In addition, the division is responsible for development and refinement of existing products as well as investigating and responding to problems with products already in the field.

John Torrence, age 30, was given the assignment of heading up the technical division about a year ago after having rotated through a number of different positions within the company at large. He has been charged with revitalizing the division and increasing its performance.

In initial discussions with this new consulting team, Torrence provided some perspective on the problems the technical division faces:

> Our biggest problem, of course, is the failure to come up with new products. The future of the company depends upon us developing new technologies that will be commercially successful. Many of the prob-

EXHIBIT 1

Organization Chart of Medtek

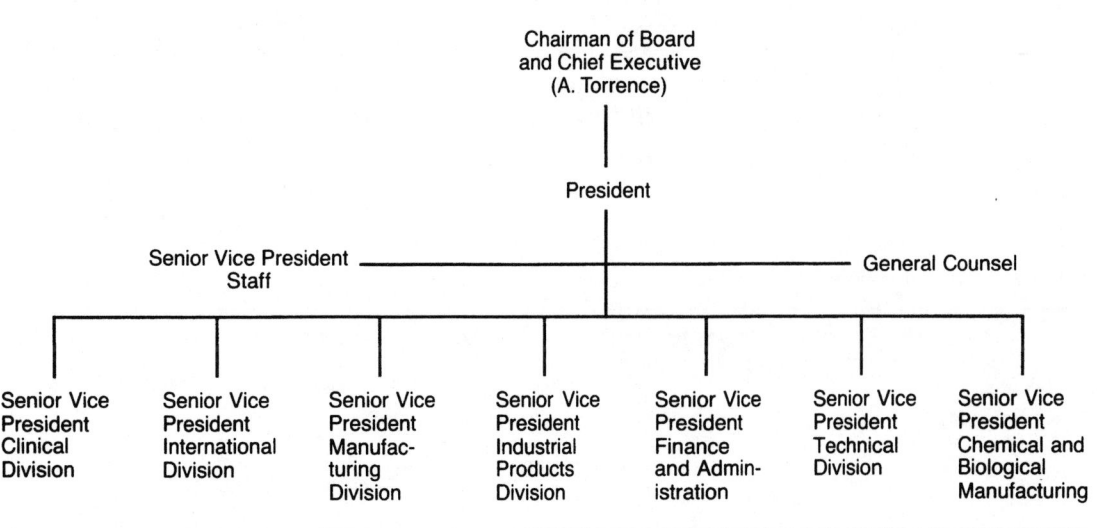

EXHIBIT 2

Organization Chart of the Technical Division

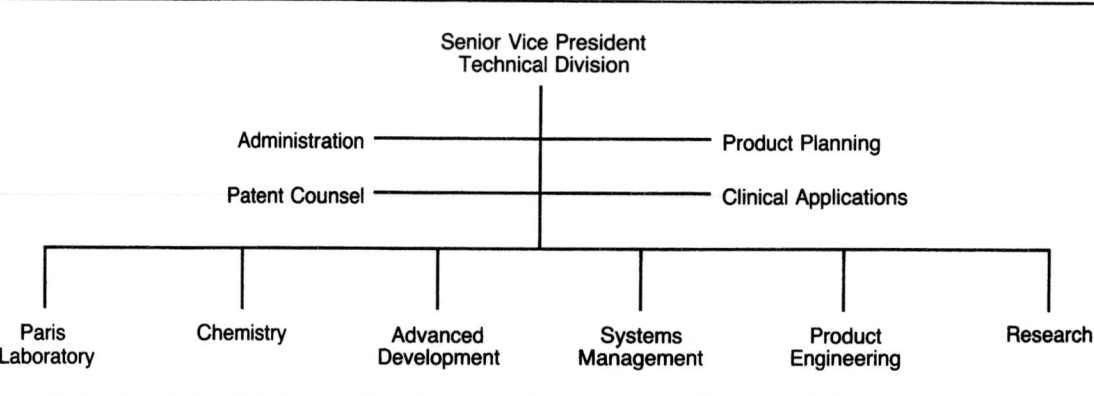

lems, I think, stem from the way that we manage ourselves. With a few exceptions, we have high quality people here in the division. We do have the necessary scientific and technical talent. The problem is that they are not coming up with new ideas; and when they do come up with ideas, they don't seem to be able to get through the process of moving an idea to the product stage. Part of our problem, I think, is the way we are organized within the division. I have too many people reporting to me, and I am thinking about changing the structure. Beyond that, however, there are problems in the attitudes of people. When I talk to people in the division, they just don't seem to have much drive or ambition. They don't seem fired up. This attitude is reflected in the large number of projects that are either behind schedule, over budget,

EXHIBIT 3

Selected Financial Data (years 1975–1985)

	1975	1976	1977	1978	1979	1980	1981	1982	1983	1984	1985
Sales (millions)	23	32	44	54	79	102	100	109	131	166	202
R&D expenditures (millions)	.9	1.3	2.0	2.9	4.9	9.8	10.6	10.1	10	10.5	
R&D expenditures as percentage of sales	4	4	4.5	5.4	6.2	9.6	10.6	9.3	7.6	6.3	
Number of employees		50		150						250	
Introduction of major products			60/12						HORSE		

or both. Finally, we don't seem to have a good feel of where we are going as a division, where we ought to be putting our resources, and how we determine priorities.

Questions:

1. To what extent, if any, might the bureaucracy at Medtek be responsible for some of the problems in the technical division?

2. John Torrence complains, "I have too many people reporting to me, and I am thinking about changing the structure." Given our earlier discussion of the appropriate size for a manager's span of control, why might John feel the way he does? What do you think he can do to reduce his span of control?

3. John is also concerned that there is a shortage of new product ideas, and that when new ideas do surface they rarely make it to the product stage. How might levels of centralization and formalization be hampering new product development in the technical division?

4. What would be the most appropriate coordination mechanism(s) in the technical division? How might these affect or be affected by levels of centralization and formalization?

5. According to Mintzberg's classification scheme, what type of organization structure does Medtek currently have? If John decides to reorganize the technical division, which of Mintzberg's structural options might be appropriate? Why do you believe this to be the case?

EXERCISE: Measuring the process dimensions

To learn more about the process dimensions of structure, identify someone who is currently working in an organization. This could be a relative or a friend. Use their responses to the following questions to determine the relative levels of complexity, centralization, and formalization. Compare your results with those of your classmates.

Complexity: Check which of the following activities in the firm are dealt with **exclusively** by at least one **full-time** person who:

a. Is responsible for PR, advertising, or promotion. _____

b. Disposes of, distributes, or services the output. _____

c. Carries outputs, resources, and other material from one place to another. _____

d. Acquires and allocates human resources. _____

e. Develops and trains personnel. _____

f. Takes care of employee welfare, security, or social services. _____

g. Obtains and controls materials and equipment (purchasing and stock control). _____

h. Maintains and erects buildings and equipment . ____
i. Records and controls financial resources (accounting). ____
j. Controls workflow (planning, scheduling). ____
k. Takes care of quality control (inspection). ____
l. Assesses and devises ways of producing output (work-study methods, operations study, etc.). ____
m. Devises new outputs, equipment, and processes (design and development). ____
n. Develops and carries out administrative procedures (statistics, information systems, filing, etc.). ____
o. Deals with legal and insurance requirements. ____
p. Acquires information on the market (market research). ____

Count the number of check marks you have made. The greater the number of check marks, the more complex is the organization.

Centralization: Which level in your firm has the authority to make the following decisions? (Circle a score of 5 if the level is above the chief executive—like the board of directors or the owner; a 4 if the level is that of the chief executive; a 3 if it is a divisional or functional manager, such as production or sales manager; a 2 if it is a subdepartment head; a 1 if it is a first-level supervisor; or a 0 if the decision is made by employees at the operating level.)

Decisions concerning:

a. The number of employees required 0 1 2 3 4 5
b. Whether to employ a worker 0 1 2 3 4 5
c. Internal labor disputes 0 1 2 3 4 5
d. Overtime at the shop level 0 1 2 3 4 5
e. Delivery dates/order priorities 0 1 2 3 4 5
f. Production plans 0 1 2 3 4 5
g. Dismissal of an employee 0 1 2 3 4 5
h. Methods of personnel selection 0 1 2 3 4 5
i. Equipment to be used 0 1 2 3 4 5
j. Method of work to be used 0 1 2 3 4 5
k. Allocation of work among employees 0 1 2 3 4 5

Total up the number of points circled. The higher the number, the more centralized the organization you are investigating.

Formalization: Check which of the following applies to the documents used in the firm.

a. Written contract of employment? ____ NO ____ YES

b. Information booklets treating, for example, security, working conditions, employment rules and regulations, etc. are given to:

No one	_____ 0
Only a few employees	_____ 1
Many employees	_____ 2
All employees	_____ 3

c. An organization chart is given to:

Chief executive only	_____ 1
Few top executives only	_____ 2
Chief executive and most managers	_____ 3
All managers and supervisors	_____ 4

d. Written job descriptions are available for:

| Direct production workers | _____ NO |
| | _____ YES |

| Clerical workers | _____ NO |
| | _____ YES |

| Supervisors | _____ NO |
| | _____ YES |

| Specialists | _____ NO |
| | _____ YES |

| Chief executive | _____ NO |
| | _____ YES |

e. In this organization, is there:

| A written business policy? | _____ NO |
| | _____ YES |

| A written manual of procedures/rules? | _____ NO |
| | _____ YES |

| Written operating instructions for employees? | _____ NO |
| | _____ YES |

Add up all the YES answers in a, d, and e and the values in b and c. The higher the number, the more formalized is your organization.

Follow-up questions:

1. How easy was it for your interviewee to provide this information?
2. Did the information apply to the entire organization or only to your interviewee's work unit?
3. Do the results of this survey match your impressions of the firm?
4. Are the three process dimensions related in the ways talked about in the chapter?

Source: Adapted from D. Miller and C. Droge, "Psychological and Traditional Determinants of Structure," *Administrative Science Quarterly,* December 1986, pp. 539–60.

Organizational Design

Home Computers Company: 15th anniversary party
Differentiation
By function
By product
By customers
By location
Hybrid departmentation
Functional organizations
Advantages of the functional organization
Disadvantages of the functional organization
Environmental changes and linking mechanisms
Memos and reports
Person-to-person exchanges
Full-time liaison positions
Task forces
Product/program managers
Task teams
Divisional organizations
Advantages of the divisional organization
Disadvantages of the divisional organization
Matrix organizations
Responsibilities in a matrix organization
Advantages of the matrix organization
Disadvantages of the matrix organization
Power flows in a matrix organization
Contingency factors and organizational design
Environmental uncertainty
Goals and strategic choices
Technology
Size
An integrative approach
Chapter highlights
Case: Aquarius Advertising Agency

In Chapter 17, we discussed ways to describe a firm's structure; however, we did not offer much insight into *why* firms adopt some structures and not others. Discussions in earlier chapters did hint that just one "best way" to structure an organization does not exist. For example, Chapter 15 described two different organizational control profiles (mechanistic and organic) that were appropriate in different environments. And in Chapter 17, we considered Mintzberg's description of five organizational configurations.

This suggests that not all organizational structures are the same; and no one structure is ideal for all organizations. One of top management's major tasks is to identify the right structure for the firm. This process—the decisions and actions that result in an organization's structure[1]—is the process of **organizational design.** The raw materials for these design activities are the various structural, control, and configural characteristics discussed in the last chapter. The factors that influence design choices are called **contingency factors.** That is, design decisions are contingent on—or depend on—these factors. This chapter examines the organizational structures that result from various design decisions. We also consider how these structures evolve as a function of four contingency factors.

In particular, we will look at several outcomes of the organizational design process. One outcome, the functional structure, is appropriate when a firm must efficiently produce products or services in a stable, simple environment. As information processing demands increase, however, some firms redesign their structures to add linking mechanisms. These linkages ensure rapid and coordinated responses to changing environments. As flexibility and adaptability become more critical, firms may need to redesign their underlying structures again into self-contained or divisionalized units. Continuing demands for both efficiency and adaptability may yield a final design outcome, the matrix structure.

Our discussion here will also examine four contingency factors that can influence the appropriate design: an organization's environment (and environmental uncertainty), goals, technology, and size. Finally, the chapter presents a framework that helps us better understand the relationships between contingencies, design decisions, structures, and organizational effectiveness.

We begin our investigation of design and contingency factors by joining Harvey and his employees at the 15th anniversary party for Home Computers Company.

Home Computers Company: 15th Anniversary Party

On the occasion of HCC's 15th anniversary, Harvey rented a plush private dining room in one of the city's poshest hotels. He hosted his headquarters staff and their spouses and friends to a sumptuous feast—shrimp cocktail, standing rib roast, and a dessert cake decorated to look like the original EZ1 computer.

After cocktails, dinner, and dessert, discussions turned both nostalgic and forward-looking. Conversations were punctuated with phrases like "Remember when . . ." and "Those were the days." Each "good old days" remark was balanced by an excited comment about what the future might hold for the firm.

Harvey and his management team had been thinking long and hard about precisely that issue—particularly since the present was filled with concerns about new technical developments, competitors' activities, and problems within HCC. Harvey and his executives often spent time analyzing where they have been, where they are now, and where they want to be in the future.

One major concern that surfaced was the current structure of the firm. HCC began as a functional organization, with all employees doing the same task, housed within the same work unit. Then it shifted to a structure organized along product lines, with many different kinds of employees bringing their particular skills to a particular product. Now a variety of problems had arisen at HCC; and the management team wondered whether the current organizational structure contributed to some of these problems.

Harvey frequently asked himself, "What happened to the spirit, to the entrepreneurial excitement we had when we were smaller? Is this the price we pay for being successful? What can I do to recapture that old feeling?"

Harvey often read about IBM's independent business units and the "skunkworks" in other organizations, where new product ideas were farmed out to "intrapreneurs" who operated free of the red tape of the larger organization. Did HCC's current structure prevent such creative and innovative outcomes?

Harvey gazed around at the partygoers. He wondered if the staff had the same concerns about HCC's setup. Originally, it was just Harvey and Bill, building machines in an old garage. Since then, HCC had grown considerably. Its environment had changed, and its goals were different. As HCC grew, the way the organization operated also changed. The technology changed from having two or three employees build each machine to an assembly-line approach. Now employees needed different skills as robots were used to help build the machines.

As the organization grew, many things happened to the original HCC structure. New divisions were added, along with several layers of management hierarchy, including managers, line supervisors, and shift supervisors. To what extent—if any—had these changes stifled creativity and innovation?

As the last of the partygoers headed for the door, Harvey loosened his tie and poured himself a last glass of champagne. A long list of difficult questions dampened the excitement of the evening. What could he do to recover the entrepreneurial spirit at HCC? What factors had interfered with the successful change from a functional to a divisional structure? Could the current structure have contributed to the symptoms that Harvey identified? What factors needed to be considered before HCC made another change in the way it was put together?

Harvey's questions and concerns are probably no different than those confronting many CEOs. For our purposes, Harvey's questions can be combined under the general management issue of **organizational design—top management's decisions and actions that result in the development of specific organizational structures.**[2]

DIFFERENTIATION

One set of design decisions revolves around the processes of **differentiation** and **integration**.[3] Namely, how should complex tasks be broken up, and how should they be regrouped (integrated) into appropriate work units? We discussed the topics of differentiation and integration in Chapter 17, but their impact on design and the developmental or evolutionary nature of design is considered in this chapter in more detail.

To accomplish organizational goals, tasks can be divided up and integrated in a variety of ways. In 1974, Harvey and Bill did all of the work required by their new firm. There was little differentiation. But success and the accompanying demands for growth required that some activities or functions be delegated to others. Harvey and Bill could no longer do everything. Purchasing, sales, accounting, manufacturing, and other tasks had to be delegated to employees and work units if the firm was to succeed. There are numerous bases for this differentiation of tasks. Let's examine a few of them.

By function

One of the most popular ways to differentiate an organization is shown in Exhibit 18–1A. This is an example of departmentation by function. **In a functional organization, individuals and work groups with similar functions or common tasks are grouped together.**[4] In the exhibit, the

EXHIBIT 18–1

Types of Organizational Departmentation

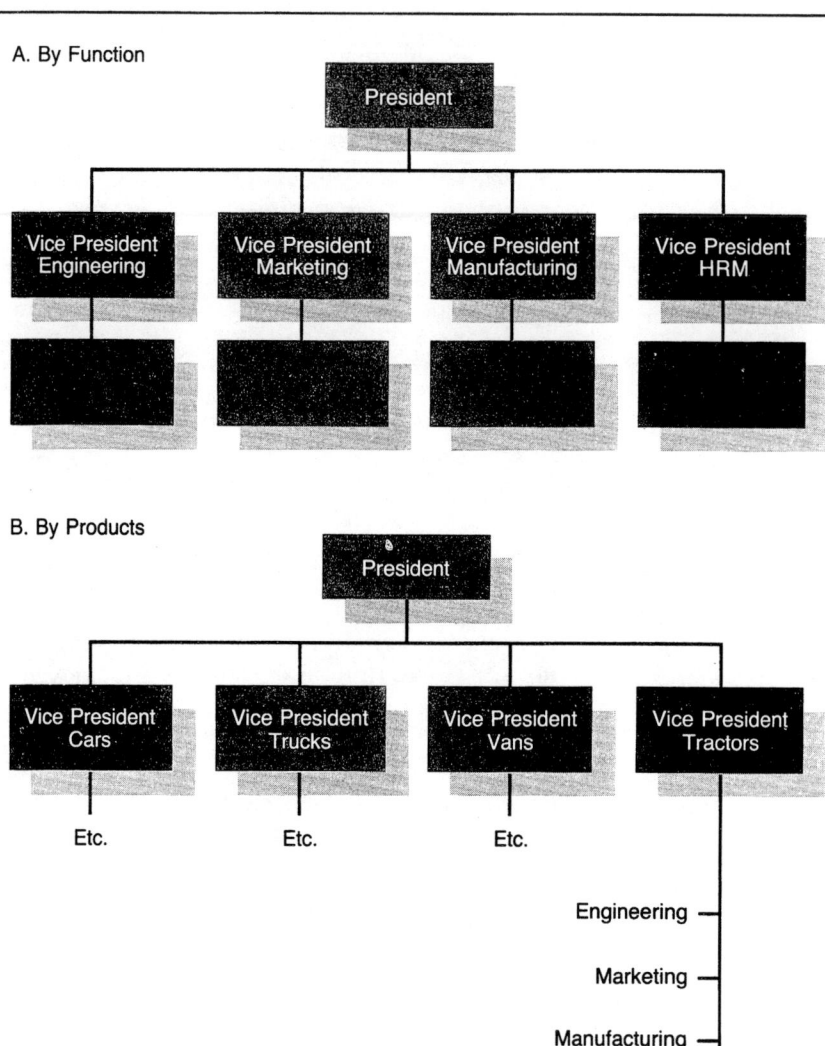

A. By Function

President

Vice President Engineering

Vice President Marketing

Vice President Manufacturing

Vice President HRM

B. By Products

President

Vice President Cars

Vice President Trucks

Vice President Vans

Vice President Tractors

Etc.

Etc.

Etc.

Engineering

Marketing

Manufacturing

Human Resource Management

C. By Customers

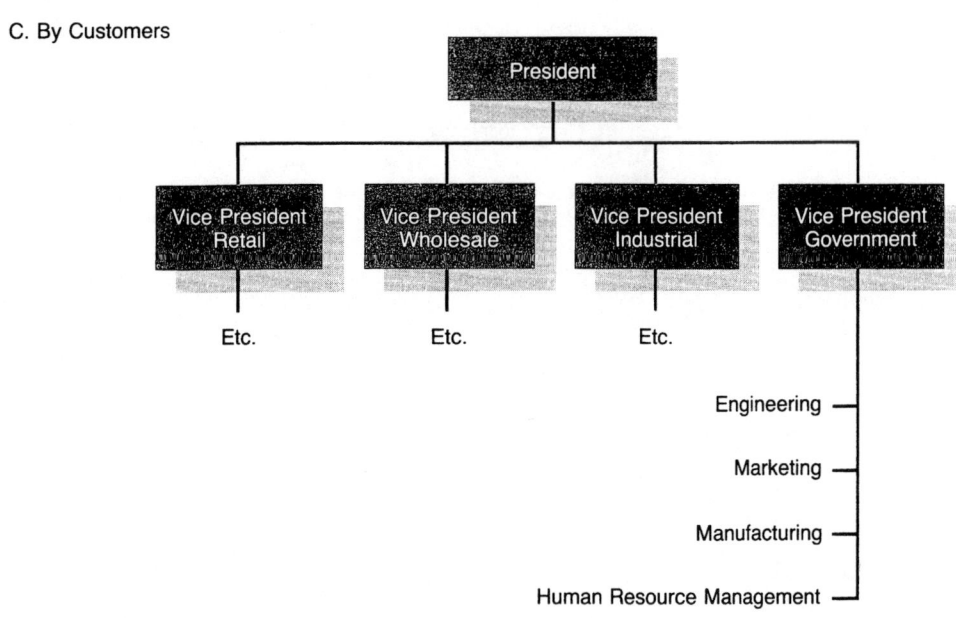

D. By Location

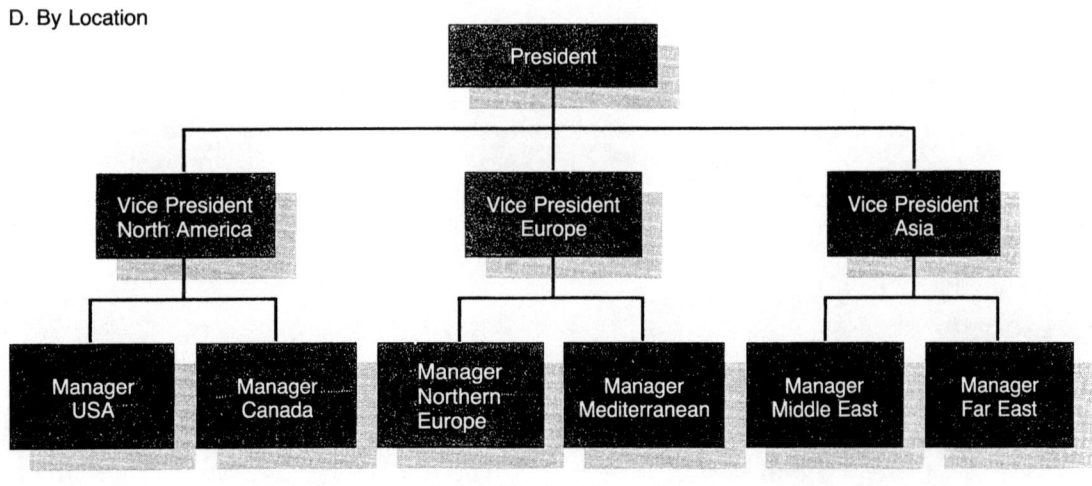

organization has engineering, marketing, manufacturing, and human resources functions, among others. Within each of these functional areas, employees are responsible for engineering, marketing, manufacturing, and human resource issues, respectively.

A second departmentalization scheme is what Mintzberg classified as the **divisional form**.[5] This design has also been called a **goal-oriented** or **self-contained unit structure**.[6] The divisional design forms groups of employees from the basic organizational functions to produce a given product, provide a particular service, or serve a particular set of customers or geographic areas.

By product

Exhibit 18–1B shows an organization chart for a firm structured on the basis of the products it provides. One of the best-known product-based structures is General Motors. Prior to a reorganization a few years ago, GM divided itself at the very top of the organization into five car divisions: Chevrolet, Buick, Pontiac, Oldsmobile, and Cadillac. Within each of these self-contained divisions were most functions necessary to produce a particular line of vehicles. In 1984, GM reorganized into a two-division, product-oriented firm, with a division for large vehicles (Buick, Oldsmobile, and Cadillac) and one for small vehicles (Chevrolet and Pontiac).[7]

By customers

Exhibit 18–1C illustrates an organization that is structured around its major customers. This firm has executive vice presidents responsible for the needs of a different set of customers: retail, wholesale, industrial, and governmental. Once again, all of the needed organizational functions are located within each self-contained division.

By location

Exhibit 18–1D shows the chart for a firm organized around the major geographical areas that it serves. This chart is for a large, multinational firm, and there are divisions for major areas of the globe. Similarly, within each of these major divisions, further differentiation occurs by specific groupings of countries.

Hybrid departmentation

Some organizations, especially large ones, frequently combine bases for departmentation in what could best be described as a **hybrid** design. For example, Exhibit 18–2 provides an example of a hybrid organization.

EXHIBIT 18–2

Hybrid Departmentation

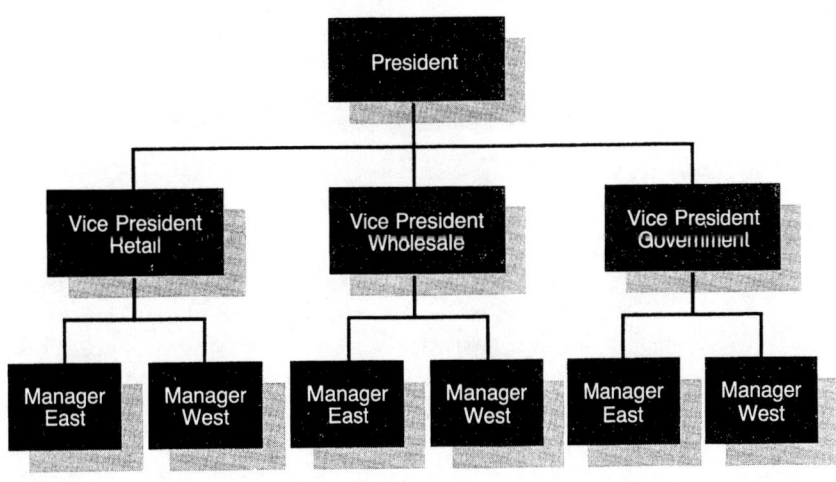

Note that at upper levels in the firm, differentiation is by customer, while within the divisions, differentiation is by location.

These different types of departmentation have a variety of advantages and disadvantages. As we will see shortly, the approach(es) chosen will be the result of many factors. Before discussing these factors, let's examine some of the distinguishing characteristics of the basic functional and divisional designs. We'll also consider how these designs develop over time, depending on the nature of an organization's environment.

FUNCTIONAL ORGANIZATIONS

In functional structures, all of the people or equipment doing the same thing are located in the same department.[8] In Exhibit 18–1A, all of the engineers are in the engineering department, all of the salespeople are in the sales department, etc. Functional structures are most appropriate when the environment is stable, and when an organization's goals emphasize efficient production. Stable environments allow managers to determine customer needs well in advance and to plan for long, efficient production runs. Top management usually treats functional areas as cost centers, with performance evaluation based on ability to minimize the costs associated with each function.

Advantages of the functional organization

There are a number of advantages of the functional structure, and these are discussed below.[9]

First, **resources are used more efficiently.** Since employees with specific skills and the necessary equipment are located in the same functional division, expertise and equipment can be used by the entire firm. Rather than hiring four electrical engineers and assigning one to each division, where only half of his or her time might be used, a firm can hire two engineers and schedule their time over the demands of the entire organization. Duplication of human resources and equipment is minimized in the firm. Honeywell Bull, a multinational joint venture of France's Group Bull, Japan's NEC Corporation, and Honeywell, Inc. reorganized along functional lines—strategic planning, development, manufacturing and marketing—in an effort to save $40 million in manufacturing costs.[10]

In a stable environment, top management has time to make strategic decisions relative to the major functional areas of the firm. **Decisions and directions are centralized at the top levels** to maintain the efficient operation of all units. When John Sculley took over as the head of Apple Computer, he reorganized along functional lines. He did this because he learned at Pepsi that it was at least one good way of giving [him] immediate control over a very serious situation.[11]

Employees within functions share many characteristics—socialization, training, and job experience, for instance. They identify closely with their function, and they can communicate easily with others in the same function because they speak the same technical language. This promotes **better coordination of activities within the function.** For instance, Compaq Computer Corporation reorganized along functional lines. By centralizing marketing operations for all of its products in one function, the company could prevent a new model from cannibalizing the market for the company's current products.[12]

From an individual developmental perspective, working within a functional area provides **opportunities for supervision and training by specialists.** Entry-level salespeople, for instance, are frequently paired with experienced sales managers for their first few months on the job; and junior engineers work alongside senior engineers. Professional development within a function ensures that employees keep current with the latest technical developments.

Similarly, as an individual's skills and abilities within a function increase, promotions and other **career development activities occur within the professional specialty.** Promotion is based on an employee's performance in the functional area. Junior engineers become senior engineers and then managing engineers, for instance.

Disadvantages of the functional organization

The advantages of a functional structure can quickly turn to disadvantages if a stable environment becomes too dynamic. Consider the following problems that can arise in functional firms.[13]

Although coordination within functions is good, **coordination across functions can be difficult.** In each function, socialization, training, and experience may prompt employees to identify more closely with the function than with the firm. Functional unit goals become more important than organizational goals—and coordination suffers. At HCC, for instance, the sales and marketing unit makes promises that the production function cannot possibly fulfill. Finally, each function may develop its own technical language. Inability to understand the jargon and technical language of another function hampers communications and coordination between functions.

Centralization can overburden top management. Conflict and coordination problems involving more than one function frequently require senior management resolution. If these conflicts become too numerous, managers are soon overwhelmed. Excessive demands on management time can lead to slower decisions. If decisions are rushed, decision quality may be lower.

Difficulties in communications, coordination, and decision making can combine to slow organizational adaptions to changes in the environment. If key sectors of the environment change, and a different response is required, **response times can be slow, and innovative reactions are difficult.** This is particularly true if many different functional areas must coordinate response efforts.

Since outcomes in a functional firm require the interdependent actions of many units, **responsibility for unit success or failure is difficult to determine.** Managers could reward or punish some functions incorrectly.

From an individual career perspective, promotions within a particular functional area provide **little training for general management positions.** Specialized development within a function reduces the ability of functional managers to develop important general management skills. This problem can be minimized by planning career paths to ensure that potential general managers experience a variety of different functional assignments.

ENVIRONMENTAL CHANGES AND LINKING MECHANISMS

We have seen that the functional firm can be effective and efficient in stable and simple environments. The mechanistic processes discussed in Chapter 15 work well when firms can plan major activities in advance and when timely responses to changes in key environmental sectors are unnecessary. What happens to these firms as their environments become more dynamic and complex? What options are available to enable the functional firm to respond more quickly to important environmental changes? To answer these questions, consider the role of **horizontal linkage mechanisms—methods to improve coordination across functional units.**[14]

Memos and reports

Most functional organizations maintain at least minimal coordination, communications, and information exchange across functions with memos and reports. Intended to keep functions informed of what is happening (or needs to happen) in other functions, this approach is cumbersome if much information must be exchanged. It limits opportunities for different functional areas to develop joint actions in response to environmental changes. And if language barriers do exist between functions, memos and reports may be filed and not read—or read but not understood.

Person-to-person exchanges

Person-to-person discussions provide an alternative to exchanging memos and reports about common problems or environmental opportunities or threats. While direct contact can be expedient, it, too, poses problems. It can be time consuming if the manager must discuss situations with many other employees. If lower-level managers engage in such exchanges without notifying their superiors, coordination difficulties arise. Meaningful exchange on a face-to-face basis can also be difficult if technical language barriers exist between individuals.

Full-time liaison positions

If coordination and communications between functions become a full-time requirement, it may be necessary to establish a formal, full-time liaison position between functions. The liaison employee acts as a translator or interpreter of problems across functional boundaries. An R&D specialist who, by virtue of training or experience, has spent time working with marketing specialists might facilitate coordination between these two functional areas. United Technologies Corporation, concerned that scientists and engineers had only casual knowledge of what their counterparts in other divisions were doing, created the post of chief technical officer to facilitate the sharing of technological information.[15] Tom Peters, author of the management best-seller *Thriving on Chaos* argues that in the future, middle managers will be called on more frequently to play this liaison role.[16] He expands on this idea in Insight 18–1.

I N S I G H T 18–1

Tom Peters on Horizontal Management

We will have to "recognize the middle-management job as one of facilitator and functional boundary-basher, instead of expert and guardian of functional units," Mr. Peters insists. Self-managing teams make no sense unless we make this change, he tells *Industry Week.*

In this new role, the middle manager "must become 1) expeditor/barrier destroyer/facilitator, 2) on-call expert, and 3) diffuser of good news. In short, the middle manager must practice fast-paced 'horizontal management,' not traditional, delaying 'vertical management.'"

Again and again, in both the interview and the new book, Mr. Peters refers to "horizontal management." The concept is central to his *Chaos* book, since the barriers between groups and departments get in the way of responding to the customer and making continual improvements in productivity and quality.

Mr. Peters distinguishes between this "proactive skid greasing" in order to get things done and conventional "coordination," which generally "emphasizes the horrid role of protecting one's function."

Adapted from P. Pascarella, "Tom Peters Invites Chaos for Survival," *Industry Week,* October 19, 1987, p. 53.

Memos, direct contacts, and liaison positions are effective if coordination and communications concerns are limited to exchanges between few functions. If environmental pressures require coordination among many functional areas, these linking mechanisms will not suffice. Mechanisms are needed that allow the simultaneous interaction of many functions. Three approaches to this requirement—task forces, product/program managers, and task teams—are discussed below.

Task forces

A **task force is a group of employees drawn from across hierarchical levels and functional areas to deal with a particular event, problem, or opportunity that affects many functions.** For example, Johnson & Johnson responded to the tampering with their Tylenol bottles by mobilizing a task force. The crisis required a quick and knowledgeable response to the problems with inputs from experts in many functional areas. The company's reaction to this disaster is held up as a model of a good organizational response to a crisis situation.[17] Insight 18–2 suggests that other firms are following this example.

The second distinguishing feature of a task force is that it is **temporary.** As soon as the event that generated the need for the task force has passed, the task force is disbanded, and employees return to their functional areas.

Preparing for the Worst: Firms Set Up Plans to Help Deal with Corporate Crises

One day early this year, a Boston area supermarket received a call from a man who said he had poisoned several cans of Campbell tomato juice with strychnine.

As soon as word of the call reached Campbell Soup Co.'s headquarters in Camden, N.J., the company's new crisis-planning and management team assembled and secured approval for a regional recall of the product. Within six hours, Campbell employees had removed two truckloads of tomato-juice stock from all 84 stores in the New England supermarket chain.

Companies like Campbell are organizing crisis teams, developing responses for selected emergencies and even staging mock disasters—complete with clamoring reporters—to see how their personnel perform. "We have to be prepared in case the unimaginable ever happens," says Robert A. Smith, director of corporate safety and services for Dow Chemical Co.

Mock disasters are played out by Niagara Mohawk Power Corp., a Syracuse, N.Y.-based utility and nuclear power plant operator. The company formed a crisis-management task force last year because of mounting concern about possible emergencies in its industry and an incident in which a temporary meter reader was murdered on the job.

The fact that a company has established a crisis-management program, consultants say, doesn't guarantee that problems will be resolved quickly and painlessly. Many programs, experts say, emphasize short-term solutions—particularly damage control in the media and in the courts—at the expense of long-term preventative measures, such as stress-management training or simulated crises. Other plans are overly complicated, denying a company the flexibility it may need in a crisis.

SmithKline Beckman Corp., a Philadelphia-based pharmaceuticals company, came face to face with that problem in March 1986 when it recalled its Contac cold medicine capsules. Government investigators had discovered traces of rat poison in several capsules.

Following the incident, some company executives suggested that SmithKline put together a thick manual with step-by-step instructions on how to deal with various crises. Instead, the company decided on a one-page memo identifying potential threats and listing key employees who should be contacted in each case.

"You want to quickly analyze the situation, approach the right people and get organized to make the decisions that are necessary," says Thomas M. Collins, vice president for corporate affairs at SmithKline. "The clarity of thinking and the responsiveness are what you're looking for."

It used to take Honeywell four years to design and build a new thermostat. A customer, dissatisfied with this delay, threatened to take its business to a competitor. In response, Honeywell established a special "tiger team" to reduce design time. The team was composed of employees from marketing, design, and engineering, and the company gave the team the freedom to pursue the problem in any feasible manner. Honeywell Vice President and General Manager John Bailey commented, "We told them to break all the rules, but to get the job done in 12 months." The team did.[18]

Product/program managers

If the need for coordination across functional areas is longer term, but the organization wants to maintain the basic resource efficiency of the functional design, it may establish the position of **product/program manager**. This is a **full-time position, responsible for coordinating activities across a number of functional units**. Unlike the liaison position that was housed in a particular function, product/program managers are independent of functions. For example, Exhibit 18–3 shows an organization chart with four functional areas and three full-time product/program managers.

Procter & Gamble's traditional use of brand managers is an example of this design option. In the past, brand managers were responsible for devising marketing and advertising strategy, planning sales promotions, and coordinating package design. They had little contact with manufacturing or purchasing. They also had little formal authority; nearly every decision had to be approved by upper levels of management. Still, these employees were responsible for the successful production of their particular products.[19]

P&G redefined the role of brand manager and created additional management positions to integrate brand managers under broader supervision.[20] Insight 18–3 explains further the new roles of brand managers at P&G.

Task teams

As Insight 18–3 illustrates, P&G is moving to a greater use of teams in its operations. **Task teams** are the most complex integrative mechanisms for use across functional areas. Similar in composition to the task force, task teams are **formed in response to on-going problems or opportunities**. Task forces are designed to respond quickly and effectively to situations and then disband. They are temporary additions to a firm's structure. Task teams on the other hand are **permanent additions**.

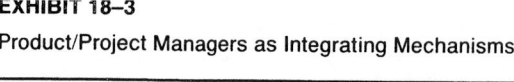

EXHIBIT 18–3

Product/Project Managers as Integrating Mechanisms

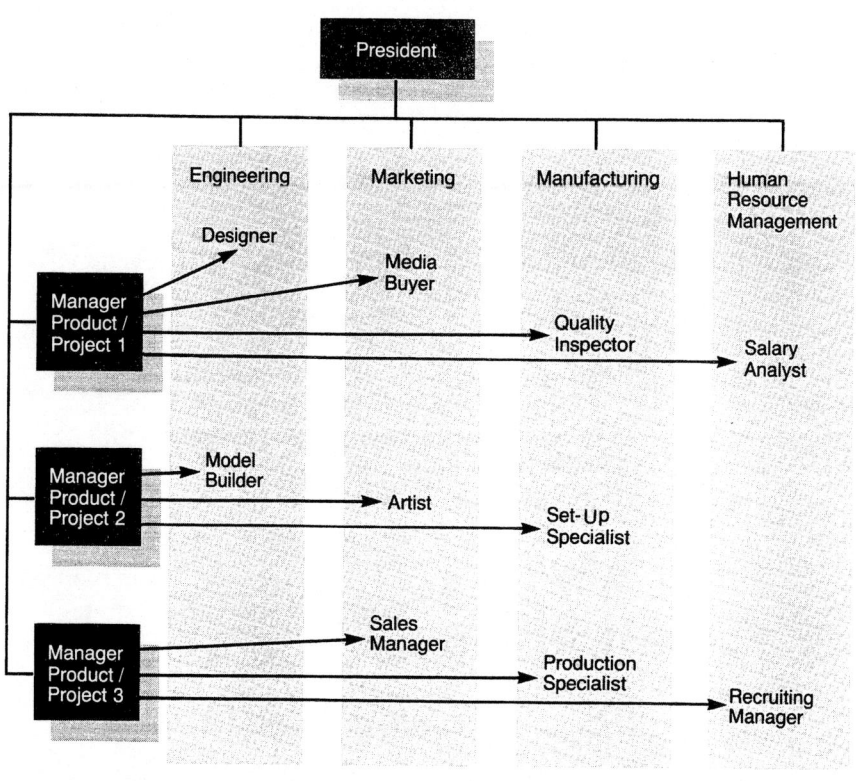

Task teams can be of two types. Exhibit 18–4A (p. 757) shows an organization chart where the task team (indicated by the dotted line) is composed of employees who maintain their position in the function. The teams meet on a regular basis for coordination and communications purposes, but employees remain assigned to specific functional areas for training, compensation, evaluation, and promotion. Time is split between team and functional area activities. These teams are called **integrated** teams.

A second type of task team removes the employee from the functional area entirely to become a member of a separate, permanent structural entity. All administrative concerns are handled within the task team or through staff services. This approach is illustrated in Exhibit 18–4B (p. 757), with task teams indicated by solid lines. These teams are called **free-standing** teams.

An example of this type of task team was used by Ford in the design and production of its Taurus automobile. Traditionally, American cars

P&G Makes Changes in the Way It Develops and Sells Its Products

Cincinnati—For four years, Bruce Miller spent most waking moments thinking about Crisco. "My whole life was grease," he says.

From his small office at Procter & Gamble Co., he mulled over everything about the cooking fat—from its can size and label to the cents-off coupons offered at the nation's supermarkets. And he avidly watched competitors, especially his colleague down the hall handling P&G's Puritan brand.

That was the life of a brand manager, tapped to champion a single product and promised a fast-track rise at P&G if successful. P&G created the system, which set standards in classrooms at Harvard Business School and served as a model for most other consumer-products companies.

But classic brand management isn't working any longer, and P&G and its competitors are scrambling to overhaul the way they develop and sell products. The result: a revolution as they alter what one consultant calls "the most sacred of sacred cows."

"Brand management isn't dead—it just isn't enough today," asserts Scott McHenry of McKinsey & Co., the consulting company, which is completing a study of changing management systems at 19 top packaged-goods companies. "And there isn't any one answer. The smartest companies must tailor the organization of each of their business units to support their individual strategies."

The new chart

A close look at this change at P&G, the nation's largest and most influential household-products marketer, illuminates the upheaval occurring in modern merchandising. P&G officials are reluctant to discuss the changes, but the changes are more and more apparent.

Consider the company's shifting organization chart. Grafted onto the system of brand managers—who still play an important role—are such executives as category brand managers, who in some cases oversee an entire group of related products and emphasize cooperation, not competition, among brands; "future" brand managers, who plan long-term marketing strategies; and a few regional marketing managers, who work directly with sales executives.

Most striking, P&G's brand managers no longer operate like mini-czars but are assigned to teams with manufacturing, sales and research managers, people they once outranked. P&G currently has scores of teams for its vast array of products.

In the past, although every decision a brand manager made required approval from layers of superiors, often right up to the chief executive, his office was nevertheless the critical starting point for marketing and advertising strategy, planning sales promotions and coordinating package design. "We thought of ourselves as the hub of the wheel," says Mr. Miller, the former Crisco brand manager. "We didn't have much contact with manufacturing or purchasing. We'd go to research and ask for something and they'd say, 'That's impossible.' We'd say, 'Do it anyway.'"

The total emphasis on marketing proved too limiting at times to deal with the complexities of developing and introducing new products.

Another disadvantage of the old system: With marketing executives dominating the company, P&G's large research staff often couldn't get an audience for even major technological breakthroughs. Olestra—the cholesterol and calorie-free fat substitute for which P&G is currently seeking government approval—languished in labs for more than two decades because of the company's "rigid organizational structure," charges Hercules Segalas, an analyst at Drexel Burnham Lambert Inc. and a former P&G engineer.

The team approach appears advantageous for P&G, but it has prompted some brand managers to re-evaluate their own careers. For instance, the former Tenderleaf tea manager left P&G last year for a job as

chief operating officer at Optica, a high-fashion eye-wear chain.

"With teams, it's difficult to make your own mark and see how good you really are," he says. "I wanted the opportunity to dig my own grave or build my own pedestal."

have been developed sequentially. They are designed in one unit, and that design is translated into a prototype vehicle by an engineering unit. Manufacturing attempts to build the car from engineering's specifications, and sales and marketing then figure out how to sell the final product. This approach has been slow and has led to some major cost and quality problems in the automotive industry.

To overcome these problems, Ford used a task team approach to produce the Taurus. Initially, Team Taurus consisted of automotive designers, engineers, and manufacturing specialists. Eventually, the team drew on the expertise of assembly-line employees, customers, and even the competition. Ford's use of teams to produce the Taurus flew in the face of automotive tradition, but resulted in the development of one of the best-selling cars in Ford's history.[21]

The need for the various linking mechanisms arose because the functional structure could not respond quickly enough to changing environmental demands. Taking coordination to the extreme, an organization could redesign its structure so that all functional units are disbanded and functional employees become members of task teams—each team attempting to respond to some part of the changing environment. The resulting reorganization has been labeled a **self-contained unit structure,** a **goal-oriented structure,** or what Mintzberg called the **divisional structure.** The following sections discuss divisional structures.

DIVISIONAL ORGANIZATIONS

Unlike the functional design, in which each function contains large numbers of employees doing the same type of job, the **divisional structure contains elements of all the needed functions to complete a product or provide a service.**[22] Exhibits 18–1B through 18–1D (pp. 744–745) illustrate different divisional structures. Comparing this design with Exhibit 18–1A (p. 744), it is apparent that elements of each function now reside within each division.

EXHIBIT 18–4
Task Teams as Integrating Mechanisms

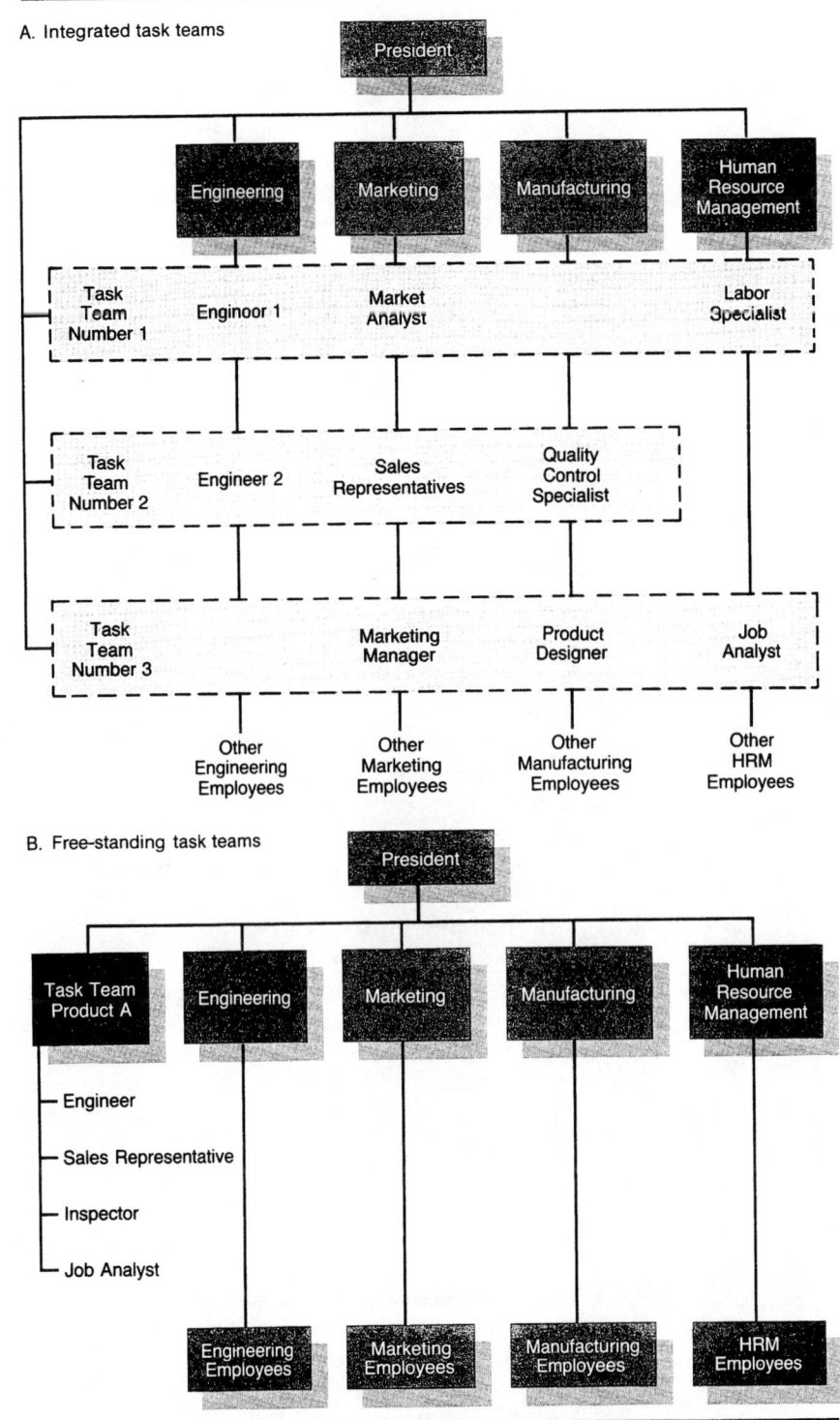

A. Integrated task teams

B. Free-standing task teams

The divisional structure is usually found in large firms that produce a number of specific products or serve a number of geographic areas, for instance. It is the appropriate structure when environmental uncertainty is relatively high, and an organization chooses to compete (and survive) on its ability to respond to changes in the environment. Whereas functional units are frequently viewed as cost centers by top management, **self-contained divisional units are usually viewed as profit centers.** Authority is decentralized, and division managers have considerable autonomy to run their operations as they see fit. Their basic standard of performance is the level of profit they return to the company. At Harris Corporation, an electronics conglomerate, CEO John Hartley reorganized and tied raises for division executives to earnings improvements. He hoped to replace a sense of complacency with a sense of urgency by making managers more accountable for division performance.[23]

Advantages of the divisional organization

It should not be surprising that many of the disadvantages associated with the functional design become advantages in the divisional design.[24]

Functional structures are frequently plagued by coordination problems. In the divisional structure, however, all of the necessary functional activities are located within the division. Employees find it easier to communicate, resulting in **better coordination within the unit.** This coordination **reduces the time needed to deal with environmental changes.** Divisions are frequently smaller than functional units, providing more opportunity for face-to-face interactions to meet environmental demands.

Depending on the basis for forming divisions (products, customers, or regions), greater emphasis can be placed on these elements. **Employees identify more readily with the division's goals and focus their efforts on these outcomes.** Hartley of Harris Corporation has streamlined his formerly sluggish bureaucracy with units designed to slash development time and to ensure that products are better suited to customer needs. A similar reorganization was undertaken by a Swedish firm, SKF, the world's largest manufacturer of rolling bearings. The company now has three different business areas "to react more effectively to customer requirements and respond more efficiently in satisfying their needs."[25]

Finally, from a career perspective, **coordination requirements within divisions expose managers to a broad range of interactions with various functions.** Managers learn the language of these functions and acquire the skills needed to integrate the activities of the many functional specialists. These managers develop a grasp for the big picture—unconstrained by functional loyalties. These experiences provide a better training ground for general management positions than do experiences in functional firms.

Disadvantages of the divisional organization

As with the functional structure, the divisional structure also has its disadvantages.[26] Perhaps the major problem with the divisional structure is its **potential for inefficient use of resources.** Look again at Exhibit 18–1A (p. 744). A functional firm may have three compensation specialists handling wage and salary issues for the entire firm. A divisional firm may require a compensation specialist in each of its many units—an inefficient use of human resources. Some divisional firms solve this problem by establishing corporate staff units to supply specialized services to each division.

Again, in the functional firm, manufacturing equipment can be scheduled to run 24 hours a day, producing products for the entire firm. But that machinery may stand idle at times in a divisional company, since each division needs its own equipment to make its own products. President John Young of Hewlett-Packard was able to reduce operating costs substantially by restructuring some functions in his firm and by centralizing research, marketing, and manufacturing operations, which had been dispersed among autonomous divisions.[27]

Emphasis on product, customer, or other divisional-level goals can come at the expense and appreciation of overall corporate goals. **Division goals may displace organizational goals in importance;** and little thought may be given to the impact of divisional decisions on corporate results. This focus on divisional goals can, if not properly managed, result in the same coordination difficulties across divisions that we found across functions in the functional structure. For example, John Hoffman, a consultant with Cresap, the consulting arm of Towers Perrin Company, tells of a chemical division seeking higher immediate profits. It sold its product to an outside customer at a higher price than it could have gotten from a sister division. But the corporation was the ultimate loser because the sister division would have made even higher profits by adding greater value to that product.[28]

Coordination problems are frequently made more serious by the decentralized nature of the divisional design. With divisions acting as profit centers, top managers relinquish a great deal of control to their division counterparts. Without a strong chief executive, division managers might run their divisions like personal kingdoms.

From a career perspective, employees in a divisional firm find **less specialized professional interaction in each division.** They are less likely to be trained, supervised, and evaluated by a specialist in their own area of expertise. In a division firm, for instance, an engineer may be the only one with a specific set of engineering skills. This isolation from the profession can prevent technically skilled employees from maintaining state-of-the-art knowledge about their specialties. Professional employees might be concerned that this could hamper their career development. Insight 18–4 summarizes the nature of these divisional disadvantages, as viewed from IBM's decision to decentralize some of its decisions to six divisional executives.

We have seen that, in a general sense, functional structures are appropriate in stable environments where efficiency is an important basis for survival. Divisional designs are useful as the environment becomes more complex, and adaptability or flexibility becomes more important. What happens when the environment makes dual demands on a firm— for efficiency *and* for adaptability or flexibility? One solution would be to design a firm with the advantages of both the functional and the divisional structures. Such a structure does exist. It is found in a **matrix organization.**

MATRIX ORGANIZATIONS

Two design principles provide the foundation for the matrix structure shown in Exhibit 18–5.[29] First, note that there are **dual hierarchies.** A functional hierarchy has been laid over a product hierarchy. Functional and product managers in *both* hierarchies report to the chief executive. The dual hierarchy means that some employees will have two bosses— a functional manager and a product manager.

The second principle requires that a **balance of power** exist between the two hierarchies. This balance must be carefully maintained so that one hierarchy does not come to dominate the other. In large firms, it is often difficult to manage the dual hierarchies and the necessary balance of power. Face-to-face interactions are easier in smaller firms and provide the communications and coordination needed to manage the twin organizing principles. But the administrative overhead associated with the matrix precludes its use by very small firms. Thus, the matrix structure is most appropriate in medium-sized firms that produce or supervise a modest number of products or programs. However, large organizations like Boeing and NASA have also used this design outcome. The relative flexibility of the matrix structure makes it suited to environments that are highly uncertain and change frequently. This was clearly the case with these two firms.

Responsibilities in a matrix organization

To understand how to manage this balance of power between function and division, we need to understand what life is like in a matrix organization. Many employees are simultaneously members of both a functional unit and a product unit. As product needs expand or contract due

I N S I G H T 18-4

IBM's Plan to Decentralize May Set a Trend—but Imitation Has a Price

Since International Business Machines Corp.'s announcement that it would decentralize its management structure, management consultants have been predicting that other companies will follow.

For many companies, it could be an expensive imitation.

In recent years an increasing number of companies have learned that pushing decision-making down the ranks is a management luxury they can't always afford, especially in a competitive environment. The benefits can be undermined by staff duplication, marketing confusion and out-of-control local units. That's been especially true as companies shed units and return to a single, core business.

As a result, many companies, including Hewlett-Packard Co. and Minnesota Mining & Manufacturing Co., are in fact moving slightly in the other direction—either consolidating functions or reining in their divisional managers.

What IBM did

IBM, hoping to become more responsive to customers and spur innovation, shifted broad responsibility from corporate headquarters to six product and marketing groups that will have wide latitude in decision-making. In addition, the company says that over the next couple of years "many thousands" of corporate staff members will be moved into positions that put them closer to customers.

Students of corporate history have plenty to look at in gauging the effectiveness of such a move. For the past 50 years, decentralization has come and gone several times as a management trend. And so its pitfalls are well known.

The first is that it can lead to costly duplication. Hewlett-Packard, for instance, has since 1959 allowed its units to operate as minicompanies, each with its own manufacturing, marketing, finance and personnel staffs. But about three years ago, the company decided that sometimes such duplication was too expensive.

For example, each of Hewlett-Packard's units manufactured circuit boards for its particular product—even though the boards are often interchangeable. This setup allowed unit managers flexibility and control over volume and quality. But the company says that system was "redundant" and a cost it no longer could afford in the face of strong competition. To eliminate the overlap, the company has consolidated the circuit-board manufacturing at fewer sites, says Lewis E. Platt, executive vice president of Hewlett-Packard's technical-systems sector.

Stiffer global competition has forced companies like Johnson & Johnson, cited by management experts as a model of a well-run decentralized company, to make adjustments to trim duplication. Last year, it consolidated about 75% of the manufacturing of sanitary-protection products in Europe into a single plant in Germany.

The products had been made at plants run by previously autonomous units. But as more and different types of sanitary-protection products were developed, a spokesman says, the company could no longer afford installing in each plant the necessary sophisticated machinery.

"To compete with the products consumers want, we can't afford to manufacture locally," a company spokesman says.

Another problem with decentralization has arisen when companies find that their units are competing with each other. While that may spur innovation and aggressiveness at some companies, sometimes it leads to confused customers.

Hewlett-Packard, for instance, had at least three autonomous divisions making different—and incompatible—computers aimed at the professional and office markets. "The fact is, those products were being sold competitively against one another by the various divisions," a spokesman says. "Customers were telling us we didn't have a coherent strategy."

So last year the company stripped the divisions of their autonomy, placing them under one group, reporting to one manager.

Among the first changes: Products were made technologically compatible.

Despite all the problems, however, nobody thinks decentralization will go away—if only because of the image it presents.

"Nobody wants to admit to being centralized," says Jay Lorsch, a Harvard Business School professor. "The American feeling is it's good to let people make decisions and be autonomous."

Adapted from L. Reibstein, "IBM's Plan to Decentralize May Set a Trend—Imitation Has a Price," *Wall Street Journal* February 19, 1988.

EXHIBIT 18–5

The Matrix Organization

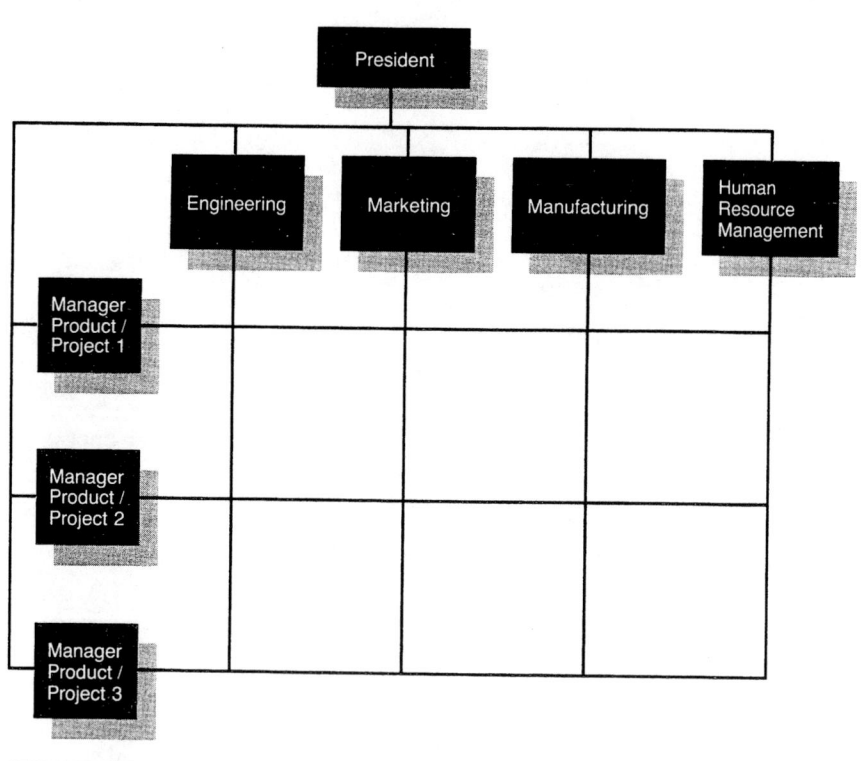

to changing environmental demands, functional specialists are drawn from or returned to human resource pools maintained by functional managers. In the pool, employees are available for reassignment to new or existing products, as needed. Exhibit 18–6 summarizes the different responsibilities of functional and program/product managers in a matrix organization.[30]

Advantages of the matrix organization

Given these responsibilities, certain advantages accrue with the matrix structure.[31] They reflect many of the advantages present in the functional and divisional designs.

First, since resources can be shifted between products or projects as needed, there is **relatively efficient use of limited resources.** The matrix is not as efficient as a purely functional structure, since there are costs associated with moving resources among products. But the matrix is more efficient than the divisional structure because the need for multiple sets of identical employee skills and equipment is reduced.

The matrix organization **can respond relatively quickly to changing environmental demands.** Its adaptation and innovation levels are superior to the functional design because resources can be moved about as needed, and coordination within products is easier. On the other hand, the requirement to move functional resources between products means that adaptability levels may not be as high as in the divisional firm.

From a career perspective, individuals who move through a matrix organization gain **experience from both a functional and a general management perspective.** Employees retain a functional "home," enabling them to keep their professional contacts and specialist knowledge base. Successful product management requires them to devleop a variety of interpersonal, conflict management, negotiation, and bargaining skills.

EXHIBIT 18–6

Responsibilities in a Matrix Organization

Functional Managers	Product Managers
1. Recruit and hire functional specialists.	1. Recruit functional specialists for each product.
2. Ensure that products meet technical specifications.	2. Ensure that product is completed on time and within budget.
3. Maintain technical expertise of functional specialists.	3. Ensure that functional specialists comply with product goals.
4. Provide training and technical evaluations of functional employees.	4. Direct and evaluate progress toward product completion.

Source: Adapted from S. Davis and P. Lawrence, *Matrix,* © 1977, Addison-Wesley Publishing Co., Inc., Reading, Mass. Reprinted with permission.

Disadvantages of the matrix organization

Reporting to two superiors and the ongoing need to negotiate trade-offs between product completion and balanced functional staffing can lead to a number of problems with the matrix design.[32]

The **dual lines of authority in the matrix can lead to numerous conflicts.** Functional and product managers may disagree about resource availability and product completion deadline priorities. Managers with two bosses may have to satisfy the conflicting demands of both, simultaneously. Some managers thrive in this atmosphere and view conflict as a challenge. For others, the constant attempts to reconcile conflicts can be draining.

Conflicts can result in high levels of frustration, anxiety, and stress. These frustrations occur most frequently among the two-boss managers and upper-level managers responsible for resolving conflicts. The need to resolve conflicts and coordinate ongoing staffing demands for projects of varying importance and length means that **a great deal of management time is spent in meetings.** Time in meetings means time away from the management of functional or product activities.

Matrix managers need a particular set of management skills unlike those required of their counterparts in traditional firms. Consequently, more firm resources must be devoted to managerial development. Training must also be provided to other employees to inform them about the peculiarities of this nontraditional design and their relationships in the dual hierarchies.

Finally, to maintain a true matrix organization, upper management must **ensure the balance of power between the two hierarchies.** This is not an easy task. Success depends on functional and product manager personalities, organizational reward systems, top-management skills, and continual monitoring of changing environmental demands. This last issue deserves a more complete discussion.

Power flows in a matrix organization

How does a matrix organization respond to changes in its environment? Consider what happens to the successfully balanced matrix firm when major environmental demands shift—perhaps to an emphasis an effectiveness and efficiency over flexibility and adaptability. Say, for instance, that a low-cost competitor unexpectedly enters the market, or the economy undergoes a recession. Which way would the power flow in the matrix? Since minimizing costs now becomes a pressing concern, power would likely shift toward the functional hierarchy and away from product managers. If these efficiency demands persist, the product side of the matrix might disappear completely, with the firm evolving into a strictly functional design to retain the efficiency advantages.

Conversely, if environmental demands shift so that flexibility and adaptability become crucial, the product hierarchy would likely become more powerful, relative to its functional counterpart. If need for flexibility persists, the matrix structure might evolve into a strictly divisional structure designed to maintain the flexibility advantages.

Both of these design changes occurred at a well-known business school. The school was originally designed as a matrix organization. School administration consisted of academic program directors who managed admissions, curriculum planning, and placement activities for undergraduate, MBA, and doctoral programs. Department chairs in finance, accounting, marketing, and organizational behavior managed the selection and professional development of department faculty members. Program directors and department chairs negotiated the assignment of faculty to teach in the various programs and the time allocated for faculty to pursue their own research agendas.

In the late 1970s and early 1980s, market demand increased for topflight business school graduates at all levels. Reflecting the environmental change, the program directors increased their power, relative to department chairs. Graduates were now of greater importance than faculty research. Curriculum changes were made to reflect market desires; and teaching assignments, once negotiated, were now mandated by the more powerful program directors.

As frequently happens in many organizations, market forces abated. A glut of business school graduates and negative publicity surrounding the number-crunching mentality of many MBAs resulted in a renewed emphasis on the quality of program graduates, rather than just the quantity. Graduate quality was viewed as a function of quality faculty. In academic circles, faculty quality is typically measured by intellectual development and research productivity. These activities were in the purview of the department chairs, and the power in the matrix shifted back to these individuals. Teaching assignments were now made by the department chair in the interests of faculty development. Program demands were of secondary concern. The ultimate resolution of these design shifts has yet to be determined. Most likely, the cyclical nature of the environment will prompt additional power swings in the future.

Our discussion thus far has identified three general organizational designs and the advantages and disadvantages associated with each. The pros and cons of each design are summarized in Exhibit 18–7. We also considered how these particular designs might evolve as a function of the changing nature of an organization's environment. But the environment is not the only factor that influences how firms are put together. The following section discusses some of these other factors.

EXHIBIT 18–7

Pros and Cons of Functional, Divisional, and Matrix Designs

Functional Designs	
Advantages	**Disadvantages**
1. Efficient use of resources	1. Poor cross-function coordination
2. Centralized decision making	2. Over-burdened management
3. Good within function coordination	3. Slower response times
4. Supervision by specialists	4. Difficult to assign responsibility
5. Career advancement within profession	5. Poor training for general management positions

Divisional Designs	
Advantages	**Disadvantages**
1. Better within unit coordination	1. Inefficient use of resources
2. Quicker response time	2. Goal displacement
3. Identification with division goals	3. Coordination problems between divisions
4. Good training for general positions	4. Less professional interaction

Matrix Designs	
Advantages	**Disadvantages**
1. Relatively efficient use of limited resources	1. Frequent conflicts
2. Relatively quick response times	2. High levels of frustration, anxiety, and stress
3. Experience from both a functional and general management perspective	3. Much time spent in meetings
	4. Increased training demands
	5. Difficult to ensure balance of power

Source: Adapted from R. Duncan, "What is the Right Organizational Structure?" *Organizational Dynamics*, Winter 1979.

CONTINGENCY FACTORS AND ORGANIZATIONAL DESIGN

So far, we have considered a number of organizational design outcomes. We have only indirectly considered what influences the types of outcomes that occur, however. We now know that there are many ways to design organizations. One explanation for the many structures found in today's organizations is offered by **contingency theory.** Contingency theory proposes that the structure or design of an organization is contingent on—or depends on—a number of factors. Two assumptions provide the foundation for this perspective:

Assumption 1.   There is no one best way to organize.

Assumption 2.   Some ways of organizing are more effective than others.[33]

The first assumption presumes that the early management principles are not applicable to all firms at all times. The second assumption counters the assertion that it is useless to look for underlying principles of successful designs. Together, these assumptions fuel the search to find out how and why some ways of organizing are better than others. The assumptions lead to the proposition that **effective designs depend on certain contingency factors.**

The remainder of this chapter looks at four of these factors: organizational environments, goals, technology, and size. Because the first two factors were considered important enough to warrant separate chapters in this text, discussion of these factors here will be brief. The following sections pay more attention to the impact of technology and size on the way firms are structured.

Environmental uncertainty

Part of the discussion in Chapter 15 dealt with environmental uncertainty. It was argued that organizations attempt to structure themselves to reduce uncertainty to manageable levels. Greater uncertainty means greater amounts of information to be processed to achieve acceptable levels of performance.[34] Chapter 15 also presented suggestions about structures that could best respond to varying levels of uncertainty and information.

As environmental uncertainty increases, firms would likely become more decentralized, less formalized, and more complex. These characteristics allow firms to respond quickly to environmental changes and to process information more rapidly. The chapter also discussed the usefulness of boundary-spanning units to assist in gathering and processing information. Finally, the text suggested that the nature of organizational control systems—mechanistic or organic—are also related to environmental uncertainty. Organic systems are appropriate in highly uncertain settings, while mechanistic systems are appropriate in situations of greater certainty.

The first half of the current chapter highlighted the role of the environment (and an organization's ability to process information) in the development of various organizational designs. As environments become more complex and uncertain, designs evolve from purely functional structures, through functional structures with increasingly intensive linking mechanisms, to divisional structures. If dual sources of environmental uncertainty confront a firm, then a matrix design is appropriate. Clearly, the nature of the environment can have a significant impact on organizational design and structure.

Goals and strategic choice

In Chapter 16, we discussed organizational goals—particularly different types of goals and the roles they play in organizations. But how do goals influence organizational design decisions? Senior managers make choices about the goals pursued by their firms. The selection of these goals is referred to as **strategic choice.**[35]

The basic goal of most organizations, public or private, profit or nonprofit, is survival.[36] All other goals become secondary if survival is threatened. The most important strategic choice concerns a firm's basis for survival. Most firms choose to compete and, ultimately, to survive in one of three ways: efficient production, custom production, or customer responsiveness.[37] We will look at each of these below.

The first approach is to compete with others on the basis of the **most efficient use of resources.** The pursuit of such a goal requires that several suppliers of a similar product or service compete in a market; that customers perceive product quality to be nearly equal; and that customers purchase the least expensive product or service. The successful firm is the one that can supply its products at the lowest cost. Examples of firms that might choose this approach include a cardboard box manufacturing company, a steel producer, a bedding company, and, for the present, Home Computers Company. United Parcel Service prides itself on the fact that it makes the most efficient use of its resources by running "the tightest ship in the shipping business."[38]

Efficiency-based organizations work best in simple, stable environments, where demand for products or services is predictable and allows for long, efficient production runs. We have already determined that in such an environment, mechanistic control processes and functional designs are appropriate.

A second strategic approach rests on a firm's ability to **produce one-of-a-kind or custom-designed products or services for customers or clients.** Building a nuclear power station, a dam, or a space station would be examples of such outcomes. While some concern with efficiency is present, customers willingly pay premium prices to gain the particular (and in some cases unique) expertise of the firm to ensure timely project completion. Bechtel Corporation, the nation's largest construction and engineering company, is an example of an organization whose survival depends on its unique abilities to complete massive projects all over the world.[39]

A third group of firms compete or survive on the basis of their ability **to adapt quickly to the changing needs of clients or customers.** The usefulness and timeliness of the product or service, rather than the cost, are the primary concerns to customers and clients. By design, these organizations are not overly efficient. Extra personnel and equipment must be kept on hand to ensure quick responses to changing customer demands and requirements. Fashion design houses, advertising agencies, and specialized computer software firms are examples of these organizations.

Organizations competing on the basis of custom design or customer adaptability thrive in environments that are more dynamic and complex. The competitive edge here is to provide customers or clients with special services that are needed on an ad hoc and unplanned basis. To respond quickly to these needs, organic control processes encourage informal communications and decentralized decision making. Divisional firms or functional firms with extensive linking mechanisms are appropriate in this setting.

Don't be misled by these examples, however. Companies in the same industry can choose to operate on different bases for their survival. For instance, General Motors, Ford, and Chrysler try to operate on an efficiency basis. Rolls Royce, Lamborghini, and Maseratti operate in the custom-design automotive market. In fact, the success of many small, start-up companies can be attributed to their ability to provide the personalized service to customers unavailable from efficiency-based organizations.

Remember that the structural options discussed here represent the extremes of a design continuum. As mentioned earlier, few organizations can ignore the need to operate within certain efficiency constraints. Additionally, many organizations have adopted hybrid designs in which some units emphasize efficiency, while other units emphasize adaptability.

Technology

Some investigators have suggested that a third contingency factor—a firm's technology—has an impact on structure and design. We used the term technology earlier, without definition, on the assumption that most people have an idea of what it means. This discussion calls for a more explicit understanding of the concept. **Technology represents the activities, equipment, and knowledge necessary to turn organizational inputs into desired outputs.**[40] It is not hard to visualize a number of different kinds of technologies. For instance, at Chrysler, the basic technology that probably comes to mind is the assembly line. The same can be said for Home Computers Company. But at North Shore Community

Hospital, a different type of technology is used to help sick people. It is also important to realize that firms can change their technologies in response to competition. An example of this is illustrated in Insight 18–5.

Before investigating the impact of technology on design, let's distinguish between organizational technology and work unit technology. **Organizational technology represents the dominant technology used by a firm.**[41] In many manufacturing companies, the assembly line represents the dominant technology. But this is not the only technology at work in these firms. Other work units may use different technologies. R&D efforts, for instance, do not lend themselves well to an assembly-line approach. Sales and marketing groups have their own technologies. **Work unit technologies refer to the particular activities, equipment, and knowledge needed to turn work unit inputs into desired outputs.**[42] Given this distinction, we need a way to describe technologies in a more simplified fashion. Just as we could describe structures and environments using a limited number of dimensions, we can do the same for technologies.

Work unit technologies

Work unit technologies can be described along two different dimensions: *task variety* and *problem analyzability.*[43] **Task variety refers to the amount of variation or number of exceptions that can occur in a particular job or work unit.**[44] Some jobs have little variety; they are routine and change little from day to day. Making pizzas, collecting tolls, and putting front bumpers on Fords might be examples of jobs with low levels of task variety. Other jobs change constantly; little in the job remains the same from day to day. The work contains many different requirements. Consultants, physicians, and college professors usually have jobs with a great deal of variety.

Problem analyzability describes the extent to which job activities and procedures are well defined.[45] In highly analyzable jobs, employees know exactly what to do at all times. Due to education, experience, training, or the availability of standard operating procedures, these employees know or can quickly determine how to meet each task requirement. Many engineers, airline mechanics, and even accountants likely find themselves in jobs that are highly analyzable. On the other hand, some jobs have few available solutions for problems that occur. Solutions to these problems may only be discovered through trial and error. Artists, research scientists, and textbook authors likely have jobs low in analyzability.

The chart in Exhibit 18–8 (p. 772) combines the dimensions of task variety and problem analyzability.[46] Each cell in the exhibit contains a description of the work unit technology, a sample of the kinds of work

U.S. Shoe Revamps

*F*ive years ago, U.S. Shoe Corporation began tapping to a new beat. Survival was at stake, and managers wore out some leather studying the ways of successful U.S. and Japanese firms.

Result: a complete turnaround in the way U.S. Shoe makes shoes, views its employees, and develops goals, says Robert Stix, senior vice president for manufacturing.

Armed with higher production quality, a new flexibility, and market responsiveness, U.S. Shoe six months ago became the first U.S. shoemaker in recent times to export women's fashion footwear to Europe. So far, it has shipped 80,000 pairs to West Germany, Britain, Switzerland, and Sweden. Next target: shoe king Italy.

"The company is probably one of the most efficient for footwear manufacturing," says analyst Jeffrey Stein, who follows Cincinnati-based U.S. Shoe for McDonald & Company. U.S. Shoe replaced traditional assembly lines with manufacturing modules in its 11 Ohio and Kentucky factories. Each module houses a team of nine cross-trained employees who swap tasks, make their own decisions about how to meet quality and productivity goals, and get bonuses for meeting or exceeding them.

That and a similar revamping of management methods gives U.S. Shoe a telling edge: It once took the company 20 days to begin turning out a new design. Now, it takes 24 hours.

By J. Odato, "U.S. Shoe Revamps," *USA Today,* March 24, 1988. Copyright 1988, *USA Today.* Reprinted with permission.

units meeting these descriptions, and the structural characteristics usually associated with each technology.

Variability and analyzability are positively related in most work units. That is, a person is likely to find more work units in the routine and nonroutine cells in Exhibit 18–8 than in the craft and engineering cells. Also note the arrow that points from Cell 1 to Cell 3. This suggests that most work units have technologies that range along a continuum from routine to nonroutine.

Given previous contingency discussions, you can probably predict the general relationships between routineness of work unit technology and work unit structural characteristics. Investigations into these relationships provide support for the structural properties listed in Exhibit 18–8. Routine technologies (Cell 1) are best managed with highly structured designs. As work unit technology becomes less routine, greater flexibility is required in the work unit structure for nonroutine work units (Cell 3).

Engineering technologies (Cell 2) maintain flexibility with reduced formalization, but ensure that the standardized knowledge is available

EXHIBIT 18–8

Work Unit Technologies

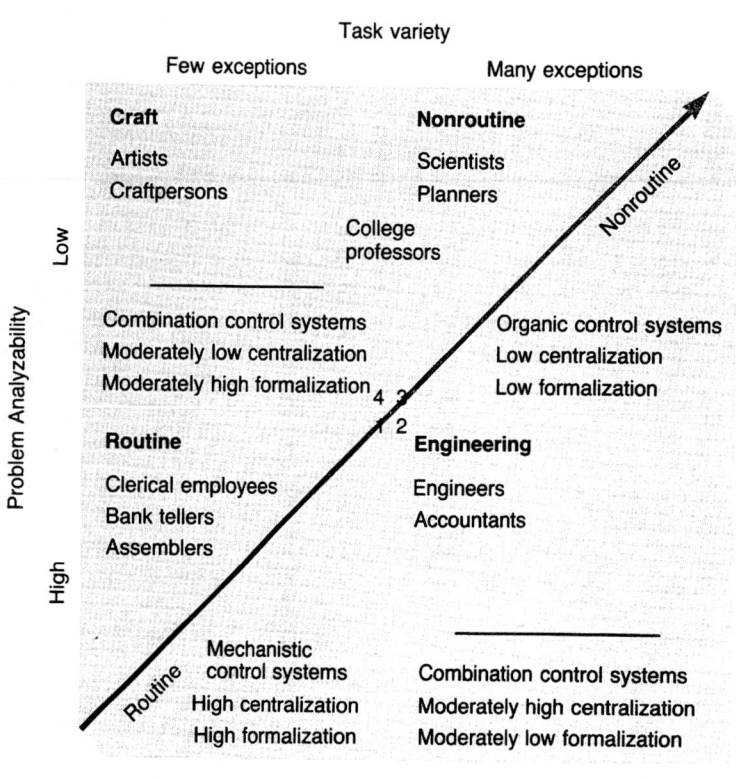

Source: Adapted from C. Perrow, "A Framework for the Comparative Analysis of Organizations," *American Sociological Review*, 1967, pp. 194–208.

with higher levels of centralization. The reduced variety of problems confronting work units using a craft technology (Cell 4) means that increased levels of formalization can be used to maintain control over operations. Finding solutions to problems that do arise requires that problem resolution remain close to the craftsperson. This is accomplished with increasing decentralization.

Given this discussion, describing an entire firm as centralized, formalized, or complex, for instance, is nonsensical. The impact of technology on work unit structure and the large number of work units in most organizations explains why a firm could have many levels of formalization, centralization, and complexity.

Organizational technologies

An important study that helps managers understand the impact of organizational technology on structure was undertaken in Great Britain.[47] In examining the nature of a number of English firms, researchers discovered an interesting relationship between technology and structure and a firm's performance.

In this research, organizational technologies were classified into three groups: unit or small batch, mass production, and continuous flow. Each group represented technologies of increasing technical complexity. Firms employing a small-batch technology produced custom-made (frequently one-of-a-kind) products, requiring specialized skills and equipment. Such firms might include makers of antique furniture reproductions, custom-designed jewelry, or ocean-going yachts. Mass production firms used an assembly-line technology to manufacture large quantities of the same product, like automobiles or air conditioners. Continuous-flow technologies were used by equipment-intensive firms processing bulk inputs, as in oil refineries, chemical companies, and breweries.

Different structures emerged around each type of organizational technology.[48] Exhibit 18–9 profiles these structural differences. In general, the mass-production technologies operated with a more mechanistic profile. These firms were highly differentiated (more complex) and exercised control through higher levels of formalization and centralization. The small-batch and continuous firms presented the opposite picture. Their technologies resulted in an organic profile. High levels of formalization and centralization were inappropriate with the small batch's customized production requirements and were not needed in the equipment-intensive, highly automated, continuous-process firms. Similarly, there was far less complexity in firms with these two technologies than in the mass-production firms.

This research also discovered that the relationship between structure and technology had an impact on organizational success in the companies examined.[49] Success was determined by looking at firm profitability, market share, and stock price. These results indicated that the closer a firm in a particular category was to the average profile in Exhibit 18–9, the more successful that firm tended to be. Firms with structures that departed from this profile tended to be less successful.

As with much organizational research, this study has been criticized because it looked at a sample of manufacturing firms.[50] This limited the ability to apply its results to other nonmanufacturing organizations. Additionally, the organizations studied were relatively small, and technology may play a more significant role in smaller companies. The critics argue that larger firms are able to develop units that buffer the main

EXHIBIT 18–9

Summary of Relationships among Different Organizational Technologies

Structural Characteristics	Technology		
	Unit Production	Mass Production	Continuous Production
Number of levels	3	4	6
Average span of control	24	48	14
Complexity	Low	High	Low
Formalization	Low	High	Low
Centralization	Low	High	Low

Source: Adapted from J. Woodward, *Industrial Organization: Theory and Practice* (London: Oxford University Press, 1965).

technology of the firm.[51] The larger the firm, the less likely it is that operating technologies will have a major impact on structure. These critics suggest that rather than technology influencing structure, organizational size may be the most important contingency factor. Let's briefly examine this argument.

Size

Our discussion of the contingency factors and their influence on structure often seems like the old chicken and egg question—which comes first, contingency factor or structure? This question can certainly be asked about the relationship between size and structure. Do organizations change their structures as they grow larger to better manage more complex and diverse activities? Or do certain structures (or technologies, or goals, for that matter) allow organizations to grow larger? A developmental perspective would suggest that both processes probably occur in the life of a firm. A manager's complaint, "We've got to get organized," might indicate the need to restructure operations to gain better control of an organization grown too large. That certainly seems to be the concern of the poor fellow in the cartoon.

Simultaneously, however, this restructuring could enable or even encourage additional growth until further restructuring is needed. At this point, we simply cannot say whether size causes structure or structure causes size. We do know, however, that associations have been found between size and some of the dimensions of structure considered earlier. These relationships are discussed below.

Almost by definition, as firms grow larger, they expand horizontally, vertically, or in both directions. New job titles and work units are formed, and additional levels of hierarchy are required to manage these new units. This increased complexity may allow for even further increases in size. **There is a positive relationship between size and com-**

"And so you just threw everything together?
... Mathews, a posse is something
you have to *organize*."

plexity.[52] Humorous evidence of this result comes in the form of a quote from David Jackson, founder and chief executive officer of Altos Computer Systems. Jackson noted, "In my experience, the real turning point in a company is when you go from one to two people. Then, at last, there's someone to answer the phone while you eat your lunch."[53]

As firms expand, control and coordination become more difficult. To maintain control, organizations increase the number of rules, policies, and procedures governing employee behavior. As formalization increases, so might spans of control as supervision becomes easier. This suggests that additional employees can be adequately supervised despite the increase in size. **There is also a positive relationship between size and formalization.**[54]

Combining increased complexity with the increased control afforded by formalization results in the increased decentralization frequently seen as an additional means for managing larger firms. This effect is most obvious as an organization moves from a functional to a divisional structure, decentralizing many responsibilities to divisional managers. Moving the decision-making authority to lower levels in a firm allows management to exercise corporate control over a larger number of divisions. This ability enables the firm to grow even larger, if it chooses. **There is a negative relationship between size and centralization.**[55]

AN INTEGRATIVE APPROACH

Exhibit 18–10 presents a summary of appropriate design outcomes based on our discussion of the four contingency factors.

At this point, you may be wondering which contingency factor has the biggest effect on the way firms are put together. Organizational researchers have sought the answer to this question since the turn of the century. Some have proposed a technological imperative: a match between technology and structure is imperative if a firm is to be successful. Others have offered similar arguments for size, goals, and environmental uncertainty. Not surprisingly, no one contingency factor has consistently reached a lofty position in helping managers understand organizations and effectiveness. What is offered here is an integrative framework that brings together the possible influences of the four contingency variables on design decisions and the resulting structural characteristics. Exhibit 18–11 illustrates this framework.

Environmental sectors and niches influence what organizations *want* to do, but also constrain what organizations are *permitted* to do. Thus, the environment influences strategic choices and organizational goals. By choosing goals carefully, however, senior management can determine which environmental sectors will be allowed to have the greatest impact on the firm.

EXHIBIT 18–10

Summary of Contingency and Design Relationships

	Contingency Factors			
Design Outcomes	**Environment**	**Goals**	**Technology**	**Size**
Functional design	Simple, stable	Efficiency	Routine	Small-medium
Divisional design	Complex, dynamic	Adaptability	Interdependencies	Large
Matrix design	Complex, dynamic	Efficiency, adaptability	Nonroutine	Medium

Source: Adapted, by permission of the publisher, "What Is the Right Organization Structure?" by R. Duncan, *Organizational Dynamics*, Winter 1979 © 1979 American Management Association, New York. All rights reserved.

EXHIBIT 18–11

An Integrative Framework

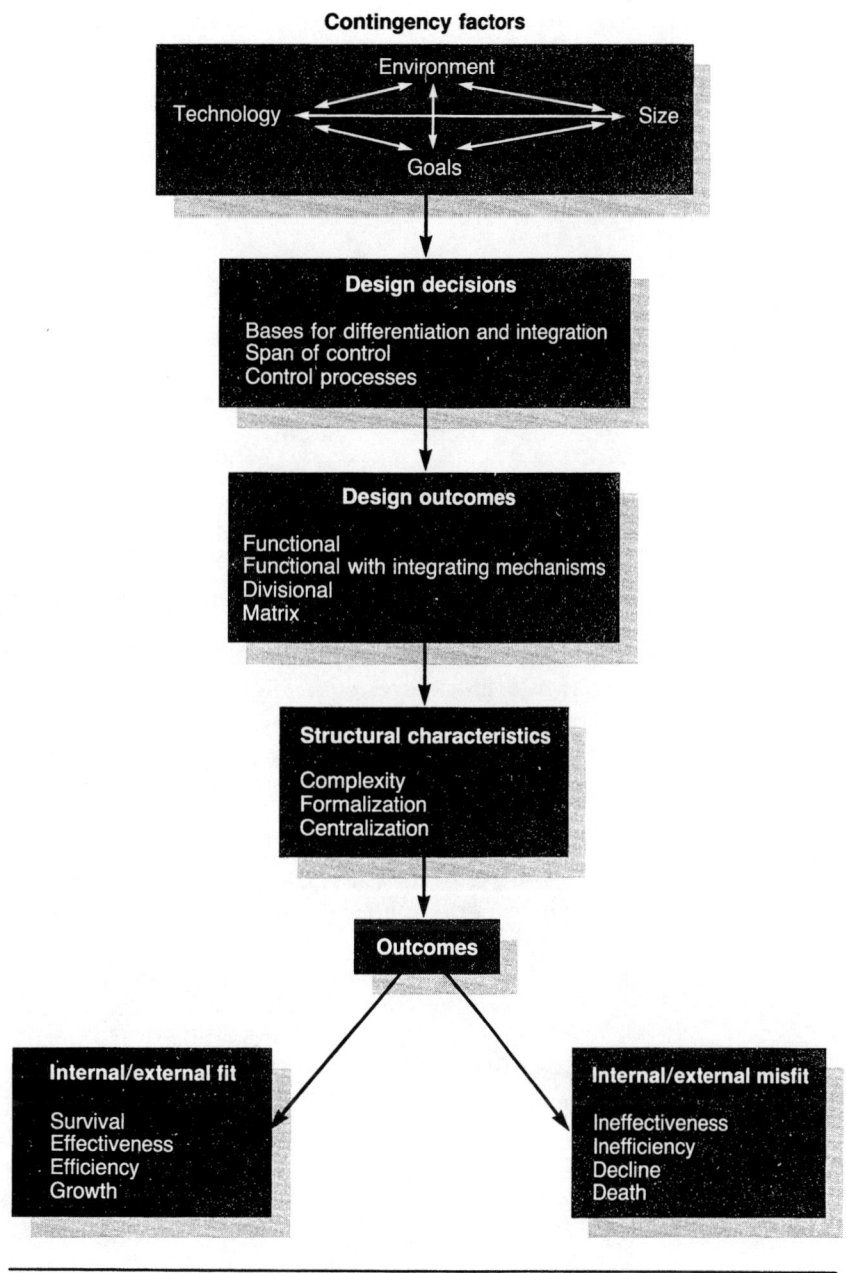

Top management can also choose to operate at a certain size. This choice influences which sectors pay attention to the firm. Bigger firms naturally attract more attention than smaller ones. The environment will allow firms to grow only so big and powerful, as antitrust suits aimed at blocking mergers and acquisitions would indicate.

Similarly, the environment limits which technologies are available and which make sense, given the nature of the competition. Organizational size constrains the technologies a firm can afford. The selection of certain technologies may require the development of buffering units to ensure that the technology remains effective and efficient. Larger organizations are better able to add these units. Smaller companies may not be able to make these structural changes.

In some combinations, these contingency factors impact on the design outcomes available to an organization. These outcomes include the bases for departmentation and integration, spans of control, and types of control systems to be used. Decisions about these characteristics determine the structure of a firm: functional, functional with linking mechanisms, divisional, or matrix.

Each of these design outcomes can be established with varying levels of the three process dimensions. A factor in choosing the levels is the internal fit between the way a firm is configured and the way processes are expected to operate. Functional organizations tend to be mechanistic in nature with higher levels of complexity, formalization, and centralization. Organic processes are better suited for divisional and matrix firms. To overlay organic processes on a functional structure or mechanistic processes on a divisional or matrix structure may defeat the advantages inherent in the configurations and control processes.

The extent to which these aspects of design and structure are internally congruent and fit with the particular combination of contingency factors influences important organizational outcomes. All else equal, a good fit (internally and externally) should lead to organizational survival. But more than that, this fit should produce an effective, efficient, growing organization. Conversely, all else equal, a mis-fit (internally or externally) will likely lead to much less desirable outcomes, including the possible death of a firm.

It is senior management's responsibility to ensure that the latter outcomes do not occur. Improving or maintaining effectiveness and efficiency should be an important goal for any organization. If symptoms of ineffectiveness do surface, it is time to consider changing certain elements of the organization. To this end, a key managerial skill is the ability to diagnose, organize, and successfully implement organizational change. This is the topic of the next chapter.

CHAPTER HIGHLIGHTS

There is a close relationship between organizational structure and design. Structures are the outcomes of the design process. As a basis for design, **firms can be differentiated or departmentalized by function, product, customer, location, or by combining two or more of these organizing perspectives in a hybrid firm.**

With employees in the same function, performing the same types of jobs, the functional design offers a number of **advantages, including efficient use of resources, centralized decision making, good coordination within units, enhancement of technical skills, and career development within a profession.** Unfortunately, the following **disadvantages** can arise with this design: **poor cross-function coordination, slow response to environmental changes, difficulty in placing responsibility for performance, and poor training for general managers.**

The functional design is appropriate in simple and stable environments. As the environment becomes more complex and dynamic, however, linking mechanisms are needed to increase communications and coordination between functional units. **Memos, person-to-person contact, and liaison positions are useful linkages if only a few units must interact.** Complex coordination among many units requires more complex linking mechanisms. **Task forces are temporary groupings** of specific employees from functional units affected by a particular issue. When the issue prompting the formation of the task force has been resolved, task force members return to their functional units.

Product/program managers coordinate activities across a number of functional areas. These managers negotiate with functional managers for human and technical resources to produce a product or complete a program.

Task teams represent the most intensive coordinating device. Similar to task forces in terms of functional composition, task teams are a **permanent addition** to a firm. They deal with on-going problems or opportunities.

Divisional structures build work units around the other bases of departmentation noted earlier. Employees in each division represent the functions necessary to produce a product or run a program. There are a variety of **advantages** to this structure, including **greater within-unit coordination, quicker responses to environmental changes, greater focus on basis for departmentation, and improved training for general managers.** On the **downside**, in the divisional firm, there is **coordination difficulty across divisions, goal displacement, inefficient use of resources, and professional isolation. The divisional structure is an**

appropriate design in more complex environments where reactions to changing environments can be managed more quickly within divisions than across functions.

When environments make dual demands for both efficiency and adaptability, a matrix structure is useful. In a matrix firm, functional and product managers negotiate among themselves for the efficient distribution of functional resources among a changing array of product units. The flexibility of the design provides a variety of advantages, including the relatively efficient use of resources, relatively quick responses to environmental demands, and a variety of career experiences. On the other hand, the dual reporting requirements of some managers and the efforts required to maintain the balance of power between the two sides of the matrix can lead to the following disadvantages: frequent conflicts, excessive frustration, need for specialized management skills, and difficulty in maintaining the balance of power.

Selecting the design that is correct for a given firm is not easy, and will likely be contingent on the organization's environment, goals, technology, and size.

In relatively certain environments, functional configurations and mechanistic control systems allow for the efficient use of resources. As environmental uncertainty increases, the need for integrating mechanisms increases. Sufficient environmental complexity may require a shift of structure to the divisional or matrix form.

Goals and strategic choices also influence structure and design. Top management can choose to compete (and ultimately survive) on the basis of efficient production, custom production, or customer responsiveness. Efficient production calls for a functional design. Custom production and customer responsiveness call for a divisional, a functional with linking mechanism, or a matrix structure.

Technology can also influence structure at both the work unit and the organizational level. Work unit technologies can be divided into routine, craft, engineering, and nonroutine categories, based on the extent to which the problems confronted are numerous (or not), and whether task problems are easily analyzable (or not). As work units move along the routine–nonroutine dimension, the appropriate control structure shifts from mechanistic to organic.

At the organization level, mass-production firms tend to be more centralized, formalized, and complex. Small batch and continuous-process firms have the opposite structural profile: low centralization, formalization, and complexity. Firms with technologies closer to the average profile within a category are more successful than those whose technologies diverge from this average.

The causal relationship between size and structure is still a matter of debate. There are, however, associations between size and structural dimensions. In particular, **larger firms tend to be more complex, more formalized, and less centralized than smaller firms.**

The chapter closed with an integrative model relating the contingency factors to issues of structure, design, and effectiveness. **While no single factor has a universal and unique influence on firms, the environment comes close.** Most likely, contingency factors work in various combinations. Successful managers identify the nature of their contingencies, match configurations, and control processes accordingly to ensure organizational survival.

REVIEW QUESTIONS

1. What are the major methods of departmentalizing an organization? What determines which method(s) is (are) selected by a firm?

2. Why are functional firms most effective in simple and stable environments? What are the disadvantages associated with the functional design?

3. Rank the horizontal linking mechanisms from least intensive to most intensive.

4. Discuss the similarities and differences between task forces and task teams. Give an example of each.

5. When are divisional firms most appropriate? What are the relative advantages and disadvantages of this design?

6. A matrix organization is developed around two basic principles. What are they? In what sort of environment is this the preferred design?

7. Identify the advantages and disadvantages of the matrix design.

8. In their best-seller *In Search of Excellence*, Peters and Waterman argued that firms were becoming disillusioned with the matrix. Given that their book was written during an economic recession, why might some firms have felt this way about the matrix?

9. What are the underlying assumptions of the contingency theory of structure and design?

10. What two dimensions are used to describe work unit technology? When these dimensions are combined, how would you describe the resulting categories? What are some organizational examples of each technology?

11. What are the structural implications for work units at various points along the routine–nonroutine technology dimension?

12. How did we classify organizational technologies? What were the "average" structures found within each category?

13. What is the relationship between the structure–technology fit and firm performance?

14. Which of the contingency factors is the most important in determining an appropriate structure or design? Why?

RESOURCE READINGS

Davis, S., and P. Lawrence. *Matrix.* Reading, Mass.: Addison-Wesley Publishing, 1977.

Duncan, R. "What is the Right Organization Structure?" *Organizational Dynamics,* Winter 1979, pp. 59–80.

Fredrickson, J. W. "The Strategic Decision Process and Organizational Structure." *Academy of Management Review,* April 1986, pp. 280–97.

Galbraith, J. *Organization Design.* Reading, Mass.: Addison-Wesley Publishing, 1977.

Hulin, C., and M. Roznowski. "Organizational Technologies: Effects on Organizations' Characteristics and Individuals' Responses." In *Research in Organizational Behavior,* ed. L. L. Cummings and B. Staw. Greenwich, Conn.: JAI Press, 1985, pp. 39–85.

Rousseau, D., and R. Cooke. "Technology and Structure: The Concrete, Abstract, and Activity Systems in Organizations." *Journal of Management,* Fall-Winter 1984, pp. 345–61.

Yasai-Ardekani, M. "Structural Adaptations to Environments." *Academy of Management Review,* April 1986, pp. 9–21.

NOTES

1. H. C. Wilmott, "The Structuring of Organizational Structure," *Administrative Science Quarterly,* September 1981, pp. 470–74.

2. Ibid.

3. P. Lawrence and J. Lorsch, *Organization and Environment* (Homewood, Ill.: Richard D. Irwin, 1969).

4. A. Filley, *The Compleat Manager* (Champaign, Ill.: Research Press Company, 1978).

5. H. Mintzberg, *The Structuring of Organizations* (Englewood Cliffs, N.J.: Prentice-Hall, 1979).

6. A. Filley, *The Compleat Manager.*

7. W. Hampton and J. Norman, "General Motors: What Went Wrong," *Business Week,* March 16, 1987, pp. 102–110.

8. A. Filley, *The Compleat Manager.*

9. This discussion follows from R. Duncan, "What is the Right Oganiza-tion Structure?: Decision Tree Analysis Provides the Answer," *Organizational Dynamics*, Winter 1979, pp. 59–80.

10. P. Houston, "Why Honeywell Bull is on a Turnaround Track," *Business Week*, February 22, 1988, pp. 152–54.

11. "Corporate Antihero: John Sculley," *INC.*, October 1987, pp. 49–60.

12. G. Lewis, "Who's Afraid of IBM," *Business Week*, June 29, 1987, pp. 68–74.

13. This discussion follows from R. Duncan, "What is the Right Organization Structure?: Decision Tree Analysis Provides the Answer."

14. J. Galbraith, *Designing Complex Organizations* (Reading, Mass.: Addison-Wesley Publishing, 1973).

15. R. Mitchell, "After Harry Gray: Reshaping United Technologies," *Business Week*, January 18, 1988, pp. 46–48.

16. P. Pascarella, "Tom Peters Invites Choas for Survival," *Industry Week*, October 19, 1987, pp. 48–53.

17. N. Jeffrey, "Preparing for the Worst: Firms Set Up Plans to Help Deal With Corporate Crises," *Wall Street Journal*, December 4, 1987.

18. J. Bussey and D. Sease, "Manufacturers Strive to Slice Time Needed to Develop Products," *Wall Street Journal*, February 23, 1988.

19. J. Solomon and C. Hymowitz, "P&G Makes Changes in the Way It Develops And Sells Its Products," *Wall Street Journal*, August 11, 1987.

20. Ibid.

21. J. Treece et al., "Can Ford Stay on Top?" *Business Week*, September 28, 1987, pp. 78–86.

22. A. Filley, *The Compleat Manager.*

23. G. DeGeorge, "Why Harris Has to Make It Outside the Pentagon," *Business Week*, November 2, 1987, pp. 138–40.

24. This discussion follows from R. Duncan, "What is the Right Organization Structure?: Decision Tree Analysis Provides the Answer."

25. G. DeGeorge, "Why Harris Has to Make It Outside the Pentagon"; and information in an advertisement, "SKF Restructures for Closer Customer Contact," *The Wall Street Journal*, October 1987.

26. This discussion follows from R. Duncan, "What is the Right Organization Structure?: Decision Tree Analysis Provides the Answer."

27. J. Levine, "Mild-Mannered Hewlett-Packard is Making Like Superman," *Business Week*, March 7, 1988, pp. 110–14.

28. L. Reibstein, "IBM's Plan to Decentralize May Set A Trend—but Imitation Has a Price," *Wall Street Journal*, February 19, 1988.

29. S. Davis and P. Lawrence, *Matrix* (Reading, Mass.: Addison-Wesley Publishing, 1977).

30. Ibid.

31. This discussion follows from R. Duncan, "What Is the Right Organization Structure?: Decision Tree Analysis Provides the Answer."

32. Ibid.

33. These assumptions have been paraphrased and adapted from J. Galbraith, *Designing Complex Organizations.*

34. Ibid.

35. J. Child, "Predicting and Understanding Organization Structure," *Administrative Science Quarterly,* March 1973, pp. 168–85; and D. Hambrick, "Environment, Strategy, and Power within Top Management Teams," *Administrative Science Quarterly,* June 1981, pp. 253–76.

36. A. Filley, *The Compleat Manager.*

37. Ibid.

38. K. Labich, "Big Changes at Big Brown," *Fortune,* January 18, 1988, pp. 56–64.

39. "Bechtel Reports Fourth Year of Revenue Decline," *The Chapel Hill Newspaper,* March 27, 1988.

40. C. Perrow, "A Framework for the Comparative Analysis of Organizations," *American Sociological Review,* 1967, pp. 194–208.

41. Adapted from R. Daft and R. Steers, *Organizations: A Micro/Macro Approach* (Glenview, Ill.: Scott, Foresman, 1986).

42. R. Hall, "Intraorganizational Structural Variation: Application of the Bureaucratic Model," *Administrative Science Quarterly,* June 1962, pp. 295–308.

43. C. Perrow, "A Framework for the Comparative Analysis of Organizations."

44. Ibid.

45. Ibid.

46. Ibid.

47. J. Woodward, *Industrial Organization: Theory and Practice* (London: Oxford University Press, 1965).

48. Ibid.

49. Ibid.

50. L. Donaldson, "Woodward Technology, Organizational Structure and Performance: A Critique of the Universal Generalization," *The Journal of Management Studies,* October 1976, pp. 255–73.

51. J. Gibson, J. Ivancevich, and J. Donnelly, Jr., *Organizations* (Plano, Tex.: Business Publications, 1988), pp. 493–94.

52. N. Hummon, P. Doriean, and K. Teuter, "A Structural Control Model of Organizational Change," *American Sociological Review,* December 1975, pp. 813–24.

53. Quoted in "Quote of the Month," *INC.,* May 1987, p. 138.

54. W. Rushing, "Organizational Size, Rules, and Surveillance." In *Organizations: Structure and Behavior,* 3d ed., ed. J. Litterer (New York: John Wiley & Sons, 1980), pp. 396–405.

55. P. Khandwalla, "Mass Output Orientation of Operations Technology and Organization Structure," *Administrative Science Quarterly,* March 1974, pp. 74–97.

CASE: Aquarius Advertising Agency

The Aquarius Advertising Agency is a mid-sized firm, offering two basic professional services to its clients—customized plans for the content of an advertising campaign (e.g., slogans, layouts, etc.) and complete plans for media, such as radio, TV, newspapers, billboards, and magazines. Additional services include aid in marketing and distribution of products and marketing research to test advertising effectiveness.

The company's activities are organized in a traditional manner. (The formal organization chart is presented in Exhibit 1.) Each of the functions includes similar activities, and on top of that, each client account is coordinated by an account executive who acts as a liaison between the client and the various specialists on the professional staffs of the operations and marketing divisions. The amount of direct communications and contacts between and among various Aquarius personnel and clients is indicated in Exhibit 2. This information was gathered by a consultant who conducted a study of the patterns of communications within the firm. Each cell in Exhibit 2 indicates the relative frequency of communications between clients and agency personnel.

Although an account executive was designated to be the liaison between the client and various agency specialists, communications frequently occurred directly among parties without involving the account executive. These direct contacts involved a wide range of interactions, such as meetings, telephone calls, and letters. A large number of communications occurred between agency specialists and their counterparts in the client organization. For example, an agency art specialist working on a client's account might be contacted directly by the client's in-house art specialist. Some of these unstructured contacts led to more formal meetings with clients in which agency personnel made presentations, interpreted and defended agency policy, and committed the agency to certain courses of action.

Both a hierarchical and professional system operated within the departments of the operations and marketing divisions. Each department was organized hierarchically, with a director, an assistant director, and several levels of authority. Professional communications were widespread and mainly concerned with sharing knowledge and techniques, technical evaluation of work, and development of professional interests. Control in each professional department was exercised mainly through control of promotions and supervision of work done by subordinates. Many account executives felt the need for more control. One commented:

> Creativity and art. That's all I hear around here. It is hard as hell to effectively manage six or seven hotshots who claim that they have to do their own thing. Each of them tries to sell his or her idea to the client, and most of the time, I don't know what has happened until a week later. If I were a despot, I would make all of them check with me first to get approval. Things would sure change around here.

Source: Adapted from J. Yanouzas, "Aquarius Advertising Agency." In *The Dynamics of Organization Theory*, 2d. ed., ed. Veiga and Yanouzas (St. Paul, Minn.: West Publishing, 1984), pp. 212–17.

EXHIBIT 1
Aquarius Advertising Agency Organization Chart

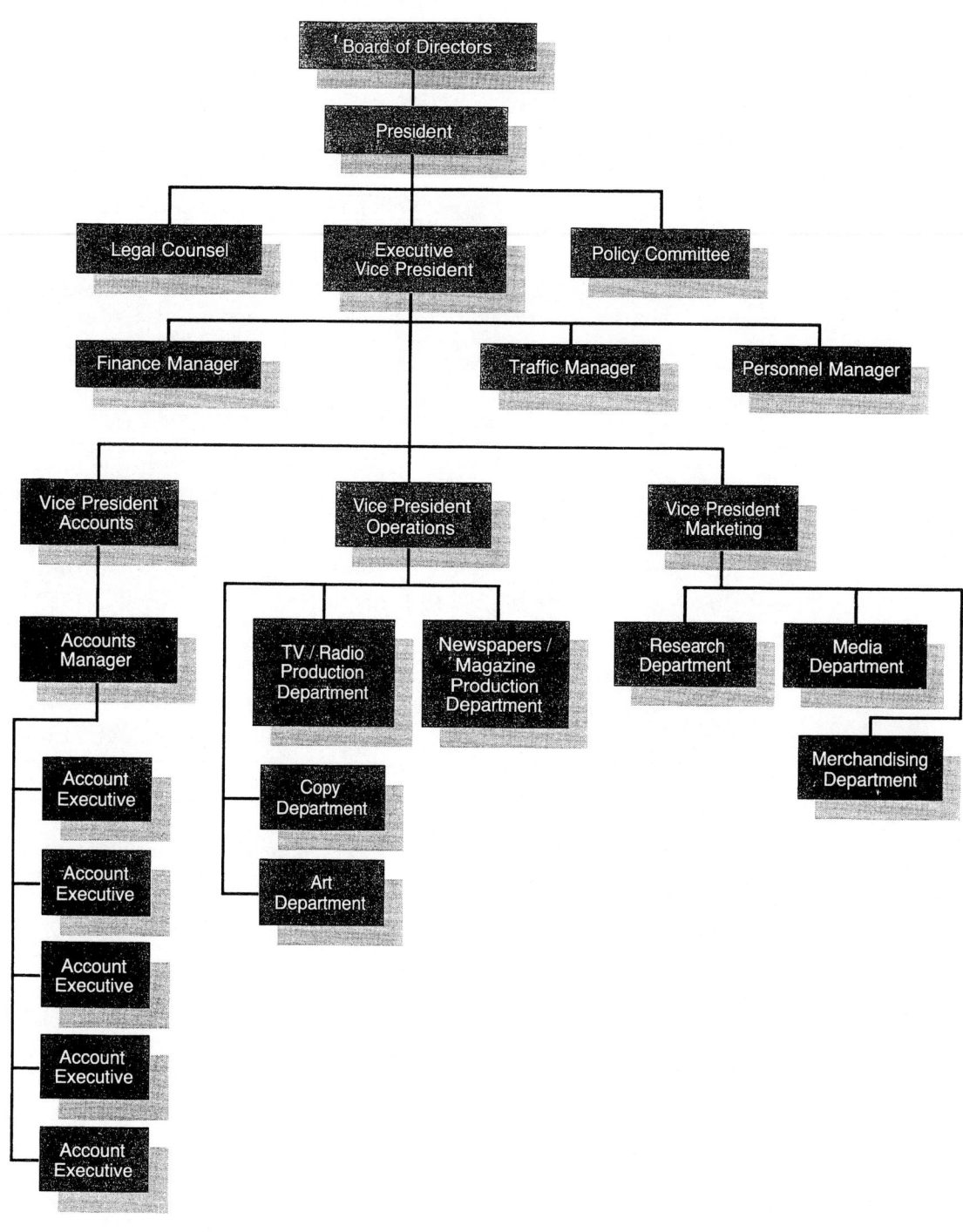

EXHIBIT 2

Direct Communications and Contacts between Aquarius Employees and Clients

	Account manager	Account executives	TV / radio specialists	Newspaper / magazine specialists	Copy specialists	Art specialists	Merchandising specialists	Media specialists	Research specialists	Traffic
Clients	D	D	N	N	O	O	O	O	O	N
Account manager		D	N	N	N	N	N	N	N	N
Account executives			D	D	D	D	D	D	D	D
TV / radio specialists				N	O	O	N	N	O	N
Newspaper / magazine specialists					O	O	N	O	O	N
Copy specialists						N	O	O	O	N
Art specialists							O	O	O	N
Merchandising specialists								D	D	N
Media specialists									D	N
Research specialists										N

D = Daily O = Occasionally, once or twice per project N = Never

The need for reorganization was made even more acute by the changes in the environment. Within a short period of time, there was a rapid turnover in the major accounts handled by the agency. It was not atypical for advertising agencies to gain or lose clients quickly, often with no advance warning, as consumer behavior and lifestyle changes emerged and product innovations occurred.

An agency reorganization was one of the solutions proposed by top management to increase flexibility in this unpredictable environment. The reorganization was aimed at reducing the agency's response time to environmental changes and at increasing cooperation and communications among specialists of different types.

Questions:

1. Given our discussion in this chapter, what kind of organization structure does Aquarius have right now? Given the nature of its environment, is it the appropriate structure? Why or why not?

2. What are the organizational goals at Aquarius? What is the nature of its technology? Given your examination of these contextual variables, do you think a reorganization is appropriate at this time? Why or why not?

3. Having analyzed the context and the nature of the communications between and among the agency's specialists and the clients, how would you respond if the president recommended reorganizing the agency around client accounts? What if the president recommended a matrix structure?

Organizational Change and Development

I n this chapter we will discuss some important aspects of change and the change process. We will consider what *change* means—distinguishing between change and innovation—and cover where changes are likely to occur in a company. The most important section of the chapter looks at change as a process of unfreezing the old, making the desired changes, and then refreezing the new. We will examine what forces in a firm are likely to support or interfere with the unfreezing process. We also will look at how changes can best be implemented and then successfully refrozen. (Of course, things are changing so rapidly that we may change our minds!)

Louise of Home Computers is also confronting the need to make changes. Let's visit her at an executive development program she is currently attending.

Home Computers Case

Louise of Home Computers

Louise had been with Home Computers Company for nearly 10 years. She was now the national sales vice president for HCC. In that position, she had direct access to Harvey, CEO of HCC. As part of Harvey's plan to eventually retire from HCC, he identified Louise and two other key HCC executives as possible successors. To prepare for the eventual change at the top, and to ensure that the new leader of HCC had every opportunity to succeed, Harvey arranged for the three candidates to attend the Senior Management Executive Development Program at a major university.

The program was directed at upper-level executives who had been identified as possible CEO material. It lasted eight weeks and consisted of intensive day and evening classes taught by university professors and CEOs from a number of different companies. Louise was one of 50 class members who had come from all over the world to take advantage of the unique training opportunity.

It was the last week of class, and graduation exercises were planned for the weekend. Harvey had promised to attend, and Louise's husband Steve was bringing their daughter to the ceremony. Steve was also pleased that the course was finally coming to an end. Except for a three-day weekend in the middle of the course, he had not seen Louise for two months. Their daughter was beginning to wonder if she still had a mother. Louise had been sensitive to this, but she felt it might be the price that both sexes paid for making dual careers work.

The last morning's class was entitled "Taking It Home and Making It Work." The topic for discussion was how to take what students had learned in the past two months back to their companies and use it successfully.

Louise knew that she was one of the candidates to succeed Harvey when he stepped down as the president of HCC. With that in mind, she had approached the program hoping that she could make immediate use of what she had learned. Louise had not been disappointed. She already knew some of the changes she wanted to make in the sales division. And she was beginning to think strategically about future directions for HCC.

As the instructor entered the classroom, Louise was pleased to see the third female faculty member of the program. This was a refreshing change. The predominantly male faculty she had seen so far had convinced her that the educational institution was perhaps unable to make the kinds of changes the faculty kept advocating to its executive students. The professor began the class by asking what they thought about change.

One classmate from a small company raised his hand and answered, "I try not to think about change. In my company, I have all I can do just managing the day-to-day operations and keeping my head above water." There were chuckles around and murmurs of agreement. Another student raised her hand. "I can appreciate Rob's problem, but in my company, we believe that change is inevitable. If we are not prepared for the changes that we know will be coming down the pike, we won't survive for very long in our industry."

The professor asked for a show of hands as to which position the class members supported. Somewhat sheepishly, someone asked, "Can we vote twice?" When the professor allowed two votes, the class was nearly unanimous in supporting both positions. It was clear that among these managers, surviving the daily hassles and managing change simultaneously required significant managerial skills.

Given the results of the vote, the professor asked, "If change is inevitable, then why does everyone seem to resist most changes so strongly?" There was a moment of silence as the class pondered this question. Then, from the back of the class, a lone voice reminded them, "Not everyone resists change." As heads turned to identify the speaker, he continued, "One person who loves change is a wet baby." And with the accompanying boos and hisses, the class was off into another stimulating discussion of an important management topic.

WHAT IS CHANGE?

Louise was being asked to consider the topic of change. And she will do so from both a personal and professional perspective. Her own life will undergo significant change if Harvey asks her to become the new president of HCC. And she is certain that HCC must change if it is to survive in the increasingly competitive personal computer market.

That change is inevitable in almost any setting is an incontrovertible fact. As one unknown pundit put it, "The only thing certain in this world is change." Bill McGowan, founder of MCI Communication Corporation, puts it a slightly different way. He argues, "The only (management) practice that's now constant is the practice of constantly accommodating to change—and if you're not changing constantly, you're probably not going to be accommodating to the reality of your world."[1] These two comments suggest that the more managers know about and understand change, the more successful they should be dealing with it.

To put some boundaries around what can be a complex topic, the following pages make two important distinctions about change. First, the text distinguishes between planned and unplanned changes. **Planned change is the planned and purposeful shift from one state of existence to another.**[2] This definition applies to changes that occur within a person or within an organization. **All other change is unplanned change.** Obviously, unplanned changes occur frequently, forcing personal or professional changes based on minimal planning. But the changes talked about here are those over which managers have some control. Louise's change to a product-oriented structure in the sales division at HCC was a planned change. If she took the wrong turn on her way home from the airport, this would be an unplanned change, and one that does not interest us here.

A second distinction is between change and innovation. **Organizational change refers to the adoption of an idea, procedure, process, or behavior that is new to an organization.**[3] **Organizational innovation refers to the adoption of an idea, procedure, process, or behavior that is new to a broad spectrum of organizations in an industry, market, or general environment.**[4] If HCC adopted a technology currently used by a competitor, this would be an organizational change. If HCC was the first company in the personal computer industry to implement a technology based on superconducting compounds, this would be an organizational innovation.

LEVELS OF CHANGE

Historical change

Our discussion of change can take place at many levels. At one extreme, there is change of an epic nature. Exhibit 19–1 summarizes some changes that have taken place in a number of work-related areas and activities through three different ages. The developers of this table believe that individuals and organizations are now entering the Information Age. Changes within a firm must, in some way, reflect the importance of information and ideas and their flow through the firm.

EXHIBIT 19–1

Changes through the Ages

Elements	Agriculture Age	Industrial Age	Informational Age
Basic technology	Craftspeople	Clockwork	Software
Key resources	Seeds, soil, and water	Money	Ideas
Products	Food	Mass-produced items	Information
Organizing principles	Seasons	Product design	Information flow
Communication	Conversation (transfer ideas locally)	Conferences (transfer ideas by transferring people)	Teleconference (transfer ideas by transmitting images)

Source: Adapted from "Changes through the Ages," *The Futurist*, July-August 1987, p. 19.

An evolutionary model of organizational change

At a somewhat less cosmic level, there are changes that most organizations confront as they develop. Louise of HCC read one article for her class on change that described changes in organizations as both **evolutionary** and **revolutionary.** Chapter 1 referred briefly to this same article as a useful way to describe how organizations grow and develop. We will discuss it here in greater detail.

Greiner studied the nature of changes in organizations over time.[5] He concluded that most organizations grow through **five** phases. **Movement between phases is usually the result of a particular organizational crisis in the previous phase.** Change within each phase is usually controlled and **evolutionary.** Change during periods of crisis is frequently chaotic and **revolutionary.** Greiner's model of phases and crises is shown in Exhibit 19–2. Note that Greiner's approach indicates that this progression of evolution and revolution is related to a firm's age and size.

Phase 1: Creativity

Growth in this first phase occurs as a result of the entrepreneurial talents of a firm's founder(s). Creative ideas are directed at producing products and finding markets for them. The simple structure described in Chapter 17 is most likely used in this phase. If a firm is successful here, it may confront a **crisis of leadership.** The founder may lack the

EXHIBIT 19–2

Greiner's Five Phases of Organizational Growth

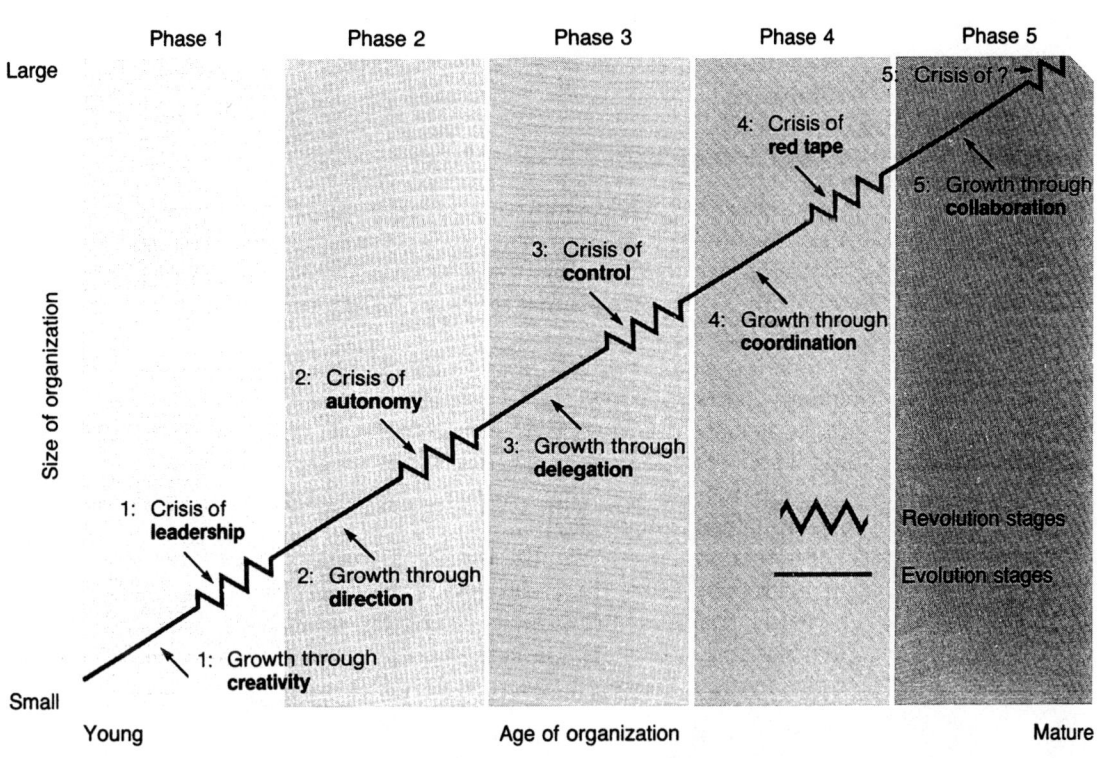

required management skills to lead a larger and more sophisticated company. The informal communications and centralized decision making of an entrepreneurial firm cannot cope with the increasing complexity in the environment. Founders are often unwilling to spend time on management tasks, preferring instead to tinker with the technology that launched the firm.

The decline and fall of Adam Osborne and the Osborne Computer Company in September 1983 is a classic example of this problem. In the fall of 1982, "raging chaos had begun to overtake Osborne Computer. . . ." Only eight salespeople were handling millions of dollars in business. Running a department was like playing poker, a former manager commented. "Somebody would say, 'I'm going to get 150 pack-

ages of software out,' and someone else would say, 'Let's make it 200.' "
Osborne told one of his vice presidents, "In six months, you will be
in over your head, and I may be as well." In October 1982, Osborne
knew the company had major problems. He and the board of directors
agreed to find a new president. But it was already too late for Osborne Computers. A new management team was unable to save the
company.[6]

Phase 2: Direction

Assuming that leadership talent can be found, professional managers
formalize relationships within an organization. To meet demand in a
cost-effective manner, firms in this phase frequently adopt a functional
structure with a traditional managerial hierarchy to control communications and decisions.

But increased centralization, formalization, and specialization frequently frustrate lower-level managers. They prefer the freedom to
make decisions related to their functions. Conflicts arise as functional
managers pursue their own goals. Top management is hesitant to reduce
its influence on the organization. These competing perspectives can
prompt a **crisis of autonomy.**

Such a crisis apparently hit Intel Corporation, the world leader
in microprocessors. In early 1987, Intel was described as the fastest-
growing major semiconductor company. However, Intel had grown
too big and found its markets changing too rapidly to be as tightly
controlled as Andrew Grove, Intel's CEO, would prefer. But it proved
difficult to decentralize operations as rapidly as some managers
would have liked. A former Intel manager commented, "People are so
used to checking with Andy that they don't know how to operate on
their own."[7]

Phase 3: Delegation

The autonomy crisis can be resolved if top management appreciates
the need for individual unit managers to be able to respond quickly
to changes in the environment. Autonomy is given to unit managers,
often by restructuring a firm along divisional lines. Top management
is then free to devote its time and energy to long-range planning and
the development of control systems to monitor the newly autonomous
managers.

Once these control systems are in place, top management often interprets the data generated as indicating that each division is headed off in
its own direction. Such may not actually be the case; but sufficient
concern can result in the partial reimposition of centralized top-level

decision making to ensure common direction of efforts. This reduction in autonomy can lead to a **crisis of control.**

Phase 4: Coordination

To resolve the control crisis, a firm decentralizes decision making. However, to ensure that line-unit activities remain coordinated with company goals, staff units are formed. These groups are responsible for reviewing, controlling, and coordinating the line units. If authority relationships between line and staff units are clear, then control and coordination occur without hampering the decision-making responsibilities of line managers. If these relationships are not clear, then conflict between line and staff members becomes a burden. Line managers are confronted by new, seemingly unnecessary rules, policies, procedures, and reports. This **crisis of red tape** can become so severe that line managers devote a greater percentage of their time to the bureaucratic requirements of the staff than to the important task of producing products and services.

In 1970, Weyerhaeuser, the forest products, paper, and real estate company, was organized in a highly integrated fashion to maximize the highest possible return from each tree on each acre. That required large corporate and business unit staffs, which greatly increased the cost of doing business. But George Weyerhaeuser, president and CEO, cut staff. Today, quality and productivity are up, costs are down, and morale is high.[8]

Phase 5: Collaboration

Greiner found firms that successfully overcome the red-tape crisis by increasing opportunities for interpersonal collaboration among employees. He found that a strong corporate culture could supplant the need for increasing staff controls. Many of the integrating mechanisms discussed in Chapter 18, like liaison personnel, task forces, and task teams, serve this function. At an extreme, the matrix structure may be adopted. Since the firm now faces a more complex environment, the need for increased collaboration is clear.

At AT&T's Components and Electronic System Works in Reading, Pennsylvania, highly skilled employees were dissatisfied with the firmly structured corporate hierarchy. They felt it denied them a voice in decisions affecting their jobs. Now the firm has developed teams of employees from all levels to make decisions about how to operate the business. They have established 45 project teams to address issues ranging from the appraisal process to pension plans.[9]

Greiner is unsure of what, if any, crisis marks the end of the collaborative phase. That crisis might well depend on the nature of an organization's environment. If sudden environmental changes force a firm to downsize, the company may return to some earlier phase in the model. Chapter 18 suggested that as environmental demands change, the relative power in a collaborative structure (like the matrix) shifts to favor either the product or the functional side. Thus, these organizations may return to Phase 2, 3, or 4.

If the environment remains healthy and provides opportunities for further growth, the resulting evolution may be back to Phase 1, as independent units are spun off from the larger firm. Recent experiences of many older and larger firms offer some evidence that this might indeed be the case. Intrapreneuring and the use of independent business units free of organizational red tape give managers with new product ideas and an entrepreneurial flair a chance to develop a new product from the ground up. Consider the case of Art Fry of 3M Corporation who is profiled in Insight 19–1.

Greiner's approach provides interesting information about changes that confront organizations through their lives. But, it also raises some interesting questions. Do all organizations grow through the same phases that Greiner has identified at the same rate? Do all firms grow through each of the five phases? The likely answer to both questions is no. Some companies decide early in their existence that they will remain small and entrepreneurial. And some have succeeded in this. Others may spend a great deal of time in a purely functional structure (Phase 2), with few autonomy problems to cause a crisis. Similarly, some companies may skip one or more of Greiner's phases or crises as a function of rapid environmental changes or careful managerial planning. Thus, small entrepreneurial firms that hit it big may have a founder who is completely aware of his or her lack of management skills and can avoid the crisis of leadership. While it took a major slump in sales to awaken Steven Jobs of Apple Computer to the need for a seasoned executive, he appreciated that need and brought in John Sculley of PepsiCo to run the business.[10]

One or more of the phases or crises between creativity and collaboration may be skipped if the environment is sufficiently volatile or if top management is sufficiently insightful.

Despite the questions that Greiner's model fails to answer, it does highlight major organizational changes, as well as when such changes may occur. Whatever the crisis that follows collaboration, it is clear from Greiner's work that organizations usually must change substantially over time if they are to survive. And each adjustment they make can generate its own collection of perils.

This broad description of historical and general organizational change provides the context within which we discuss change as it can occur within a particular organization.

INSIGHT 19–1

Art Fry: Persisting with a Good Idea

Art Fry of 3M is the inventor and intrapreneur of Post-It Notes, those ubiquitous little yellow note pads with peelable stickum along the top of the back side. Art's brand of intrapreneuring is important. He made use not only of corporate funds, but of proprietary corporate technology and pilot plants, manufacturing facilities, and marketing channels. Equally important was strong loyal sponsorship from his immediate supervisor and the technical director in his division.

Art began working on Post-It Notes in 1974 while singing in the church choir. He would mark hymns in his hymnal with slips of paper. By the second service, however, some of the markers would fall out. He needed a page marker that would adhere to the page but not damage it when it was pulled off. Taking advantage of a 3M policy that gives technical people 15 percent of their time to work on their own ideas, Art began work on a prototype peelable hymnal marker.

One of the great virtues of 3M is the relative ease with which intrapreneurs like Art can get to use the equipment in other divisions to try out their ideas. "It takes patience to locate all the different kinds of paper coaters and handlers available at 3M and then find out when they have open time,"

says Art. "It can't be done through formal channels."

If the equipment was available only at night, Art worked at night. His dedication is, in fact, legendary. When he got official permission to use a pilot plant, he worked five consecutive eight-hour shifts, without stopping.

Strictly speaking, the way 3M is organized, designing the production process for the Post-It notes was not Art's job. He was supposed to design the product while process engineering people worked on how to make it. The problem was that manufacturing told him it was impossible. But Art wouldn't accept that. He invented a machine that looked like it might just do the job. Unfortunately, the manufacturing engineering function said the machine he designed would take six months to build and cost a small fortune. The anguish of that barrier proved too much for Art's somewhat limited political instincts. The next morning when people came to work they found Art's new process up and running. He had built a crude version of the machine overnight in his basement, brought it to work, and installed it. It was working.

Post-It notes are now a multimillion dollar product for 3M.

Adapted from "Profile—Art Fry: Persisting with a Good Idea," in Gifford Pinchot, III's *Intrapreneuring* (New York: Harper & Row, 1985), pp. 137–42.

TARGETS FOR CHANGE

Exhibit 19–3 indicates that there are a variety of elements in an organization that can be changed. Which elements are chosen is partly determined by a manager's ability to accurately diagnose a firm's problems or opportunities. The following sections briefly examine each of these areas of possible change. These targets exist at the individual, interpersonal (group), organizational, and environmental levels.

Individual targets

At the individual level, organizations can target a number of change areas. These changes fall under the general category of human resource changes. They include decisions to increase or decrease the number of employees. Employee changes may also be made by retraining and repositioning employees. In addition to changing the number and skills of the human resources component, management can also consider programs aimed at changing levels of employee motivation and performance. Change in these areas usually occurs as the result of new staffing strategies or through employee training or development programs. IBM's approach to this problem is described in Insight 19–2.

Interpersonal and group targets

In this area, managers might consider changing the nature of relationships between managers and subordinates or relationships within work groups. As discussed in Chapters 8 through 14, targets here might

EXHIBIT 19–3

Targets for Change

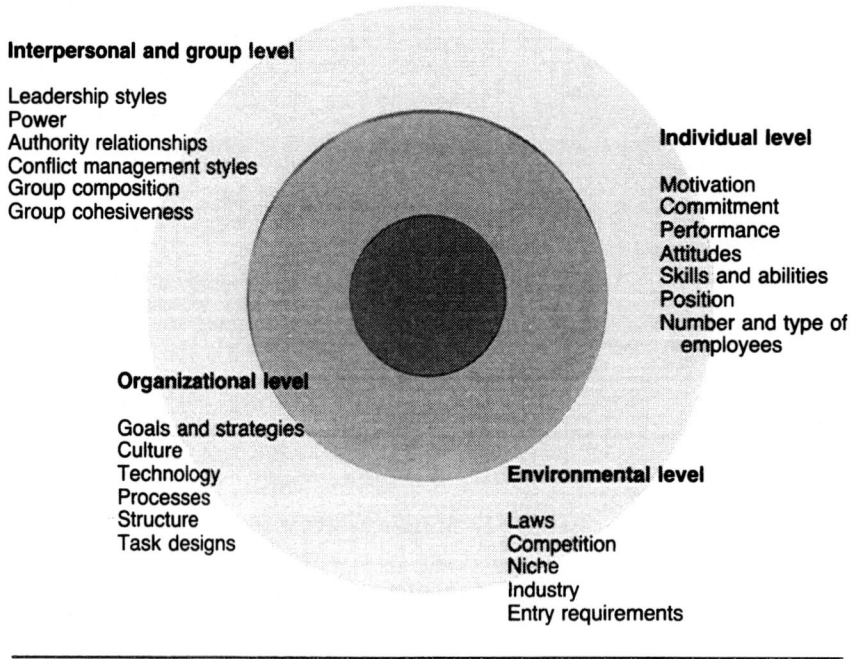

Interpersonal and group level

Leadership styles
Power
Authority relationships
Conflict management styles
Group composition
Group cohesiveness

Individual level

Motivation
Commitment
Performance
Attitudes
Skills and abilities
Position
Number and type of
    employees

Organizational level

Goals and strategies
Culture
Technology
Processes
Structure
Task designs

Environmental level

Laws
Competition
Niche
Industry
Entry requirements

I N S I G H T   19–2

How and Why IBM Avoids Layoffs

*I*nternational Business Machines Corp. is having a rough time now. Tough enough so that many would urge the company to abandon its no-layoff, full-employment policy to sustain earnings performance. But its policy, like the company itself, is tough-minded optimism in action. It is based on respect for the individual, a tenet that is deeply embedded in the company's culture and central to all management decision-making. It is a gutsy posture.

The idea is that there isn't just one giant switch labeled LAYOFFS that a company must pull when in a slump. There are plenty of intermediary steps, which can be a challenge to administer but which help the company in the long run. On the lower end, outside services are pared back, travel expenses are reduced, and summer hiring is lowered. On the higher end, employees change locations, are retrained to new jobs, or switch from staff to line or vice versa.

"We've been there before," says *Think,* the company magazine, referring to previous computer-industry slumps in 1957–58, 1961–62, 1971–72, and 1974–75. There were no layoffs during those slumps, but IBM did plenty of "resource-balancing."

Ultimately, the issue is one of costs. It costs money to retrain and rebalance the work force when times are tough, just as it costs money for companies to clean up their waste—to stop polluting. But one way or another, society pays the cost—just as it does for pollution—if IBM starts laying off when trouble hits. IBM takes a longer, broader view of things instead of buckling under pressure to prove its "worth" by keeping quarterly earnings up.

Excerpted from R. Waterman, *The Renewal Factor: How the Best Get and Keep the Competitive Edge* (New York: Bantam Books, 1987).

---

include changes in or redirection of management leadership styles; changes in group composition, cohesiveness, or decision-making procedures; changes in conflict resolution approaches; or changes in the allocation of power and authority among individuals and work groups.

Organizational targets

As the target levels become more macro and larger in scope, the possible targets become more numerous. At the organizational level, managers can change the basic goals and strategies of the firm, its domain, and the products or services it provides. Changes might include a shift from functional to divisional structure, the addition or deletion of work units, or the de- or recentralization of decision-making authority. Organizational processes, such as reward, communications, or information processing systems, could be changed. And as suggested in Chapter 15, an organization's culture could also be a target for change.

Environmental targets

Finally, an organization can work to change portions of its external environment. Chapter 15 discussed a number of ways in which both primary and secondary sectors in the external environment can be influenced and changed.

Making changes in any one target area can be a complex task. Making changes in more than one area at a time is even more difficult. The target areas are highly interdependent, and changes affecting one target area will frequently require changes in others. In an interview with *Fortune* magazine, H. Ross Perot, founder of Electronic Data Systems and one-time General Motors board member, was asked how he would turn General Motors around. His answer consisted of 13 different suggestions, ranging from reduction of internal conflicts between the financial staff and the car builders, to developing new relationships with the United Auto Workers, to the replacement of all current outside board members.[11]

It is virtually impossible to make a change in one aspect of an organization and not have something change elsewhere in the firm. It is true in organizations, as it is in many other settings, that management cannot make just one decision. Changes in the products or services offered may require a new technology or distribution system. Technological change might require a change in the type of employee hired or a revamping of corporate training procedures. Managers must appreciate the possible ripple effects of changes they plan to make. Once again, the interconnection of systems and subsystems makes the job of management an extremely complex and challenging endeavor.

The difficulty in making an organizational change is illustrated in the following discussion between Louise and Harvey of HCC.

Home Computers Case

Home Computers Company: Harvey and Louise Plan a Change

Louise and Harvey were having a working lunch in Louise's office. Since her return from the executive development program a week ago, Louise had been constantly on the go. With eight weeks of sales activities to review and problems to iron out, most of her lunch hours were filled with work. This one was no exception. When Harvey dropped by to invite her to join him for lunch in the company cafeteria, Louise convinced him to order in; she was expecting an important call from one of HCC's best customers. His corned beef on rye and her ham and cheese on toast were still warm, and as Harvey opened a bag of chips, he shared a recent concern with Louise.

The new manufacturing plant in Dallas was coming on line in a few months. Ignoring for the moment all the headaches the project had already caused at HCC, Harvey reminded Louise that this increased capacity meant more EZ computers to sell. And because the profit margins on their PCs were smaller than margins on the mainframes sold by some of their larger competitors, HCC's ability to maintain or increase profits was going to be a function of increasing market share and sales volumes. Harvey suggested to Louise the possibility of developing a new sales compensation plan.

HCC's sales staff was on a salary-plus-commission plan: 70 percent of their take-home pay was salary, and 30 percent was based on sales commissions. To remain competitive, Harvey wanted to change this formula—to tie monetary rewards more directly to actual sales. In fact, to meet Harvey's estimated sales figures, he thought a 40-percent-salary, 60-percent-commission plan was needed. He also thought a tiered commission plan that would trigger higher commission rates when individual sales volumes reached certain levels would be desirable. Harvey was certain that this change would benefit the company and the sales staff: HCC sells more computers, and the sales staff takes home more pay.

Louise agreed that a revamping of the current system was needed. She had been working on just such a system since her return to the office. She had not yet formally presented it to Harvey, the management team, or the sales force because there were still some bugs to be worked out. But Harvey was less concerned about potential problems. He wanted to put the plan into effect as soon as possible.

Louise cautioned against an immediate implementation of the plan, however. Although both she and Harvey felt that the change would benefit the sales force, Louise was not certain that a unilateral shift in compensation plans would be accepted by the sales staff. She reminded Harvey that the current plan had been installed to protect the income levels of the sales force when the PC market nosedived in the mid-1980s. The PC market had since rebounded; but Louise was not sure the sales staff would accept the new plan. It might mean increased income in a growth market, but what happened if the PC market hit the skids again? Also, the revised plan might send an unintended message to the sales force that sales were all important and that customer development was no longer a concern. Louise wondered how the sales staff in smaller markets would respond to a change like this in their compensation system. On average, incomes might rise, but what would happen to individual salaries? And Louise was concerned that such a package might foster unhealthy competition among salespeople. This could lead to cannibalizing territories, promising unrealistic delivery dates to get added sales, or (at worst) an increasing number of complaints about unethical sales tactics.

Between bites of his sandwich, Harvey shook his head thoughtfully, glad that he had someone like Louise as vice president of sales—someone able to think about these problems before he jumped in with both feet. Harvey asked Louise what she thought should be their next step.

Calling on both her experience and recent executive training, Louise suggested that a program of educating key sales managers about the importance of the change for HCC would be a good first step. At the same time, these sessions could be structured to give these managers an opportunity to participate in the detailed development of the plan. Implementing the change unilaterally and throughout the company would be unwise. Louise wanted to start on a small scale in just a couple of territories where she knew the sales managers would support this approach.

Harvey agreed with her suggestions and promised his complete support. He offered his assistance to resolve any problems that could not be handled at her level.

As they cleared away the remains of the lunch and crunched the last of their dill pickles, they agreed that the compensation change was necessary. Louise also realized that in addition to talking with the sales managers, she needed to communicate with her counterparts in finance and human resources. The finance people would want to know how much more this new approach would cost, and whether the projected increase in revenues would cover the increased salary expenses. The vice president of human resources was responsible for compensation systems for the entire corporation. Any system changes would have to be cleared through her unit; and concerns about perceptions of salary equity with other HCC employees would have to be addressed. In addition, the vice president of human resources had to consider the increased complexity of the new tiered commission schedules. Louise quickly realized that this was not going to be an easy task.

A MODEL OF CHANGE

Louise's concerns about the successful implementation of her new sales compensation package reflect the challenge of making changes in any organizational setting. Her change is related to just one organizational system—the compensation plan. And there were many other systems within HCC that might also be changing as a result of opening the Dallas facility. Her instructors at the executive training program had been right: managing change is an incredibly complex task.

A framework or model that can simplify our discussion of change was proposed by Lewin a number of years ago.[12] Lewin realized that merely introducing a change did not guarantee that the change would be successful. Instead, he believed that change could best be understood as a three-step process.

Unfreezing

Unfreezing is the first step in the change process. The preferred state for most people and organizations is one of stability and the perpetuation of the status quo. In such a state, forces attempting to change a firm are equally offset by forces that would maintain the status quo. Lewin called these *driving forces* and *resisting forces,* respectively. **The unfreezing of this equilibrium situation requires that a firm or an individual somehow move or be made to move from this point of balance.** Lewin suggested that unfreezing or disequilibrium can occur in one of three ways: (1) the driving forces are increased; (2) the resisting forces are decreased; (3) a combination of these two actions is undertaken.

Changing

If the status quo can be unfrozen, then Lewin's model indicates that it is possible to introduce a change or set of changes. How this change is actually introduced in people or organizations has been much debated. We will examine later a set of change strategies and identify some of the change techniques that are available.

Refreezing

Change pushes an individual or firm into a temporary state of disequilibrium. Unless this new point is established as the new status quo, the change will not be successful, and the old equilibrium point will resurface. **Lewin labeled this process of solidifying the new practice refreezing.** To make sure the change sticks, the individual or organization must undertake some additional activities.

We have briefly examined Lewin's model, and a pictorial representation of the model appears in Exhibit 19–4. Now let's go back and look at each of the three steps in more detail.

UNFREEZING: A FORCE-FIELD ANALYSIS

To be successful, any change process must work to overcome the status quo—to unfreeze old behaviors, processes, or structures. This requires the identification of possible driving and resisting forces and a determination of their number and magnitude. To call on a physics metaphor, **unfreezing occurs only if the strength of resisting forces exceeds the strength of resisting forces.**

One useful tool for taking a more systematic look at the forces in play around a proposed change is called a **force-field analysis.**[13] This may sound like something out of a *Star Trek* movie; but it is really just a

EXHIBIT 19–4
Lewin's Model of Change

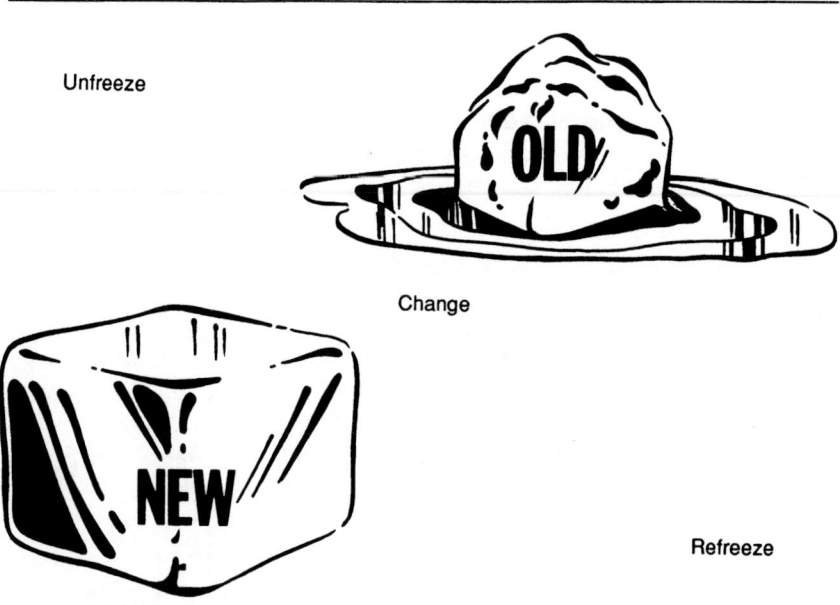

Unfreeze

Change

Refreeze

Source: Kurt Lewin, adapted from *Field Theory in Social Science* (New York: Harper & Row, 1951).

systematic process for examining the pressures that are likely to support or resist a proposed change. Exhibit 19–5 contains an example of a force-field analysis appropriate for the situation Louise faces at Home Computers Company.

Conducting a force-field analysis is not as difficult as the exhibit might suggest. The status quo represents the current situation that a manager wants to change. As we will discuss shortly, there are forces within individuals and organizations that work to support or to resist many changes. A force-field analysis requires those people who would make changes to think carefully about the source and strength of these supporting and resisting forces. In the exhibit, Louise has identified a number of forces that will support or resist the change she plans in the sales force compensation system. The length of the arrows in the force field represents the relative strength of each force in favor of, or opposed to, the planned change. Louise must now decide if the supporting forces are (or can be) sufficiently strong to overcome the resisting forces. If they are, she can continue with her change effort. If they are not, she needs to consider what she can do to further strengthen the supporting

EXHIBIT 19–5

Force-Field Analysis: Louise's Compensation System Change

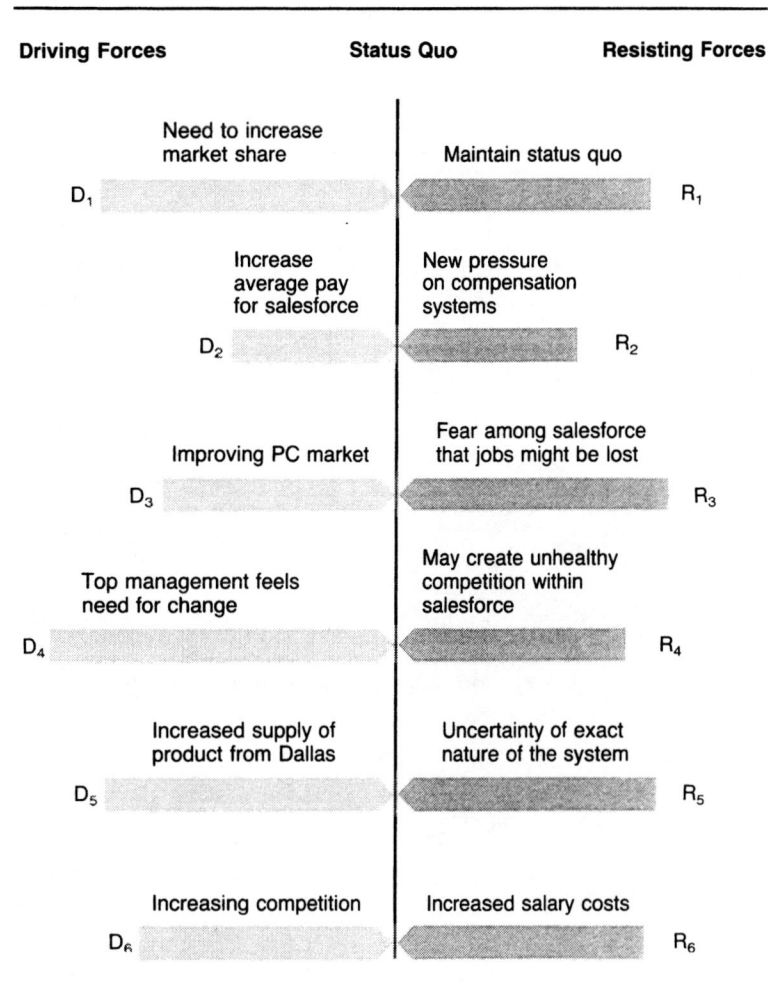

Driving Forces	Status Quo	Resisting Forces

forces and weaken the resisting forces. To develop a more detailed picture of the elements in the force field, let's examine some of typical forces supporting change.

Forces supporting change

Every change has a multitude of possible driving, sustaining, or supporting forces acting on it. **These are forces that work in favor of the change, either directly or indirectly.** Here, it is enough to list just a few of these forces. A manager planning a possible change will want to make a thorough inventory of these forces. Cultivating them will increase the likelihood that the change will be successful.

Threats to survival

The most pressing reason to make a change is in response to a threat to the survival of the individual, group, or organization. Major problems with organizational effectiveness or efficiency that call into question a firm's ability to continue suggest that drastic changes are needed, perhaps at a number of different levels.

For instance, to prevent the total collapse of ComputerLand Corporation, its founder and CEO Bill Millard was forced, in late 1985, to give up his title and his seat on the board of directors. This occurred after a court ordered the firm to pay a $141 million damage award and turn over 20 percent of its stock to a competitor.[14] This was a drastic change.

In many firms, the driving forces may not be as significant as a threat to the firm's existence. But many changes are made in response to serious internal or external events. Any one of these events could be a step or two away from threatening a firm's survival if it is not dealt with appropriately. For instance, Home Computers Company's inability to increase its sale of new computers would not immediately threaten the firm. But continued erosion of HCC's market share could raise the issue of survival. Harvey and Louise would probably deal with the more immediate concern before it became life-threatening for the company.

In 1986, the stock price of the Williams Companies, a natural resources conglomerate, was $17, half the book value of $34. Chairperson Joseph Williams started divesting parts of the corporation that winter. He comments, "With our stock going south and our earnings prospects poor, we said 'it's time to change our strategy, no matter how much we like it, no matter how long we've had it.' We had lived with these people for years. It wasn't fun to break that up." Williams's firm is now a pipeline and digital communications company; its stock price had doubled before the October 1987 crash.[15] The organization's survival was not directly threatened, but problems were serious enough to warrant a major change in corporate strategy.

The most frequently encountered driving or supporting forces can be classified as external or internal. The following paragraphs examine each of these sets of forces individually.

External forces

Changes in one or more of the key environmental sectors discussed in Chapter 15 might provide the impetus for change in an organization. For instance, new, low-cost manufacturing technologies could make the replacement of existing equipment mandatory. Introduction of new products or services by competitors requires a response in order to maintain market share and visibility. A strike at a major supplier or an embargo of raw materials may force a change in resource management techniques. The nature of these supporting forces that come from the external environment are as limitless as the environment itself. As Donald Kelly, chief executive of E-II Holdings, commented recently, "We are not in total control of our destinies. There is no protection in size. Some CEOs are pretending it can't happen to them. They're the most naive of all. They are living in an era that doesn't exist anymore. You can't relax."[16] And Time, Inc. CEO Richard Munro notes, "When you become a takeover candidate, you get your house in order. Where [earlier] you would tolerate marginal things, now you can't. You have to face up to decisions a lot quicker. The intensity increases geometrically."[17]

Internal forces

Change may also be initiated or supported in response to forces from within a firm. At top-management levels, changes in goals, strategies, and plans call for changes elsewhere in the organization. The availability of excess resources (also called **slack**) may allow an organization to make proactive changes, rather than reactive ones in the face of unexpected shortages. As suggested in the previous chapters, evaluation of an organization's structure or effectiveness could produce results suggesting that the structure is not working as desired and/or the firm is not as effective as required. This result suggests that changes be made if the firm is to remain competitive.

In some organizations, change is an accepted way of doing business. Thus, the corporate culture is a significant, internal, driving force for change. Corporate cultures in these organizations are innovative, creative, and encouraging of chance and risk. These firms reward risk taking, creativity, innovation, and change. They encourage these activities and clearly support change for change's sake. Similarly, this type of culture also encourages the development of **idea or product champions**—the individuals who find a new product or new idea, take the ball, and run with it. Product champions are confident in their abilities to get things done, and are sufficiently committed to the new idea or product that they personally act as a major supporting force for change—change to ensure that their idea or product sees the light of day.

Merck & Company gives its scientists extraordinary freedom to design an approach to developing a new drug and then seeing it through. The company lets the best people find the best way. Each potential new drug has a leader—a champion, Merck calls them—whose job is to keep the laboratories fueled with ideas and excited about the possibilities.[18]

At Home Computers Company, Louise's proposed change in the compensation package for her sales force was the result of forces both external and internal. Increased competition, maintenance of market share, and industry practices worked as external forces for the change. Internally, the need to ensure sales of the newly available products was a major driving force.

Felt need for change

Regardless of the pressures of these driving forces for change, most researchers who look at the change process conclude that the most important driving force (after survival, that is) is the presence of a **felt need for change** among those most affected by the proposed change.[19] **This term refers to the perception of a gap between a desired state of affairs and the current state.** In the absence of this felt need for change, change at any level will likely be unsuccessful. Individuals or work units will be unable to see why the change is necessary or unable to see the benefits to be derived.

Usually events occur that prompt this felt need for change—threats to a firm's survival being a primary one. In the absence of survival issues, this felt need becomes the primary driving force in the unfreezing process. In fact, one of Louise's biggest problems in successfully implementing the new salary program will be to convince her sales staff (as well as the compensation and finance managers) of the need for change. Since the sales force is perfectly satisfied with the existing program, it may well respond with that time-honored phrase, "If it isn't broken, don't fix it!" Salespeople will need to be convinced that this change will benefit them and the firm. It may seem logical (even obvious) to the dispassionate observer that the proposed change is a good one. But unless it is deemed necessary by the individuals and work units directly affected by or responsible for its implementation, the change will have a difficult time succeeding. Without such perceptions, neither individuals nor managers will admit that the status quo needs to be changed. Thus, whatever can be done to strengthen that need will serve the unfreezing process well.

Forces resisting change

If the presence of a felt need for change is a key driving force for change, then the *absence* of a felt need for change is a critical force resisting change. But it is not the only possible resisting force attempting to maintain the status quo. As with driving forces, resisting forces to a planned change can be classified as internal or external. A few of the many resisting forces are examined below.

Internal forces

Both individuals and firms can suffer from a **fear of the unknown** as well as the **uncertainty** associated with change. By its very nature, change means a movement from the known to the unknown. And the unknown can cause a great deal of anxiety. Employees are unsure what a new situation means in terms of skills required to succeed, the impact of new reporting relationships, etc. If previous change attempts have resulted in severe employee disruptions, if good-faith agreements about changes have been broken in the past, or if employees are simply unaware of the proposed change, they will likely resist the change. This reflects human nature. MCI's McGowan comments that major changes in many organizations are hampered by individuals whose "number one loyalty is to [protecting] their own tush."[20]

Also, change may threaten vested interests in an organization. Managers or employees may feel threatened by a loss of power, responsibility, authority, and prestige. For example, a major obstacle to the successful introduction of personal computers in many organizations was the fear among middle managers that they would become expendable. Upper-level managers could now monitor and control lower-level operations directly with the PC.[21]

For both individuals and organizations, **traditions, habits, and inertia** frequently stand in the way of successful change attempts. Statements like "We always do it this way" or "We've never done it that way before" or "That simply will not work here" all speak to people's desire to maintain the status quo. Change may require that they reevaluate the traditions, customs, and habits that have guided their behaviors and attitudes for many years.

TRW Corporation's interest in change, innovation, and creativity sparked a series of TV commercials and print ads describing how traditions stand in the way of change. In one ad, the caption above a brightly lit lightbulb reads, "I have an idea . . ." In succeeding frames of the ad, the light bulb becomes progressively dimmer, with each frame headed by such phrases as, "A word of caution . . ." "A little too radical . . . ," "I like it myself but . . . ," and "Its just not us . . ." In the last frame, the lightbulb is completely dark, and the caption reads, "Oh, it was just an idea. . . ."

The lack of two other internal factors (considered potential supporters of change) can become major inhibitors of change. **Excess organizational resources** (slack) can enhance a firm's ability to experiment with change efforts. But a **lack of key resources**—time, money, people, equipment, facilities—may prevent such change activities. The nature of an **organization's corporate culture** can also resist change. As we have seen, corporate culture can have a major impact on the way an organization operates. This culture permeates the organization and acts as a control of employee actions. Changes that seem to violate the accepted culture will have difficulty being implemented successfully. Just as there are innovative organizations that develop entrepreneurs and encourage the work of idea champions, there are also historically conservative firms that avoid change of any sort at all costs. And when these firms attempt change, the changes are usually of an incremental sort, rather than major innovations. An example of how firms with a conservative tradition have difficulty in undertaking major change activities is illustrated in Insight 19–3.

External forces

There are countless external forces that can inhibit organizational change; but two factors stand out. The first is the nature of interorganizational agreements the firm has made with other organizations. Labor–management contracts, contracts with major suppliers or customers, and joint-venture agreements are some examples. Chapter 15 suggested that these agreements could reduce environmental uncertainty. But the other side of the coin is that they could also reduce a company's freedom to make unilateral changes in areas covered by the agreements.

The second external resisting force exists in the various laws, regulations, directives, and judicial decisions that make some changes extremely difficult. Affirmative action laws govern all personnel changes. The Environmental Protection Agency and the Occupational Safety and Health Administration influence changes that can be made legally in manufacturing processes. The list here is a long one.

As an example of how these driving and resisting forces can be evaluated to determine the potential success of change, consider Home Computer Company's plan to revamp the sales force salary package. Louise not only looked for the driving and resisting sources, she also estimated the possible impact of each source. For instance, as shown in Exhibit 19–5, Louise identified six forces supporting the change. But a single resisting force (say, insufficient financial resources) might be enough to completely overwhelm the driving forces, and the new plan would not be implemented. Exhibit 19–5 also shows the resisting forces Louise found. From the results of this analysis, it is clear that Louise should continue with the plan's implementation. At this point, the strength of driving forces exceeds the strength of resisting forces. Louise has a good chance of moving things from the status quo.

Strategies for unfreezing

Having completed a force-field analysis, a manager must decide whether and how to complete the unfreezing process. If the resisting forces cannot be sufficiently reduced or the sustaining forces cannot be suffi-

Wrong Number: AT&T Manager Finds His Effort to Galvanize Sales Meets Resistance

William F. Buehler looks back on the past year and speaks in elegiac tones about his "noble experiment."

Here he was, 43 years old, just named a vice president at American Telephone & Telegraph Co., given a work force of 3,000 and put in charge of marketing phone systems to small business all over the U.S. What's more, his bosses at AT&T gave him considerable freedom to break with the Bell way of doing things.

And that's exactly what he did. In place of Bell's rigmarole of endless memos, interminable meetings and strict chain of command, the boyish-looking Mr. Buehler discarded planning manuals, threw out employee tests, put salespeople on the highest commission-based compensation plan in AT&T history and fired those who couldn't meet his tough quotas.

It worked. Salespeople say they caught "Buehler fever," and sales figures soared off the charts. His boss and the chairman of AT&T Information Systems, Charles Marshall, concedes that the Buehler unit that sold the smaller business systems is outperforming the rival unit-selling larger ones.

But today, 12 months later, Mr. Buehler isn't bathing in accolades. Instead, he is being removed from his job and put in an obscure planning position, though he remains a vice president.

As a result, the new corporate culture that he created has been weakened, if not snuffed out, and many of his subordinates are apprehensive even though they often found him difficult to work for. "We're all upset and worried that we'll lose our new culture," says James R. Lewis, an AT&T account executive in Southfield, Mich. Moreover, many observers wonder whether AT&T isn't discouraging the kind of competitive zeal it is going to need as it tries to change from a regulated monopoly into a company that can take on the likes of International Business Machines Corp.

To many within the company Mr. Buehler was removed because he was too menacing to the old Ma Bell culture. Despite his bottom-line success, he was viewed more as a maverick than as a visionary, they say.

An AT&T mistake?

Mr. Buehler may not be the only loser. Many inside and outside observers say AT&T is making a mistake by stifling Mr. Buehler and the new corporate culture that he tried to create despite the huge bureaucracy.

But for now, this battle between corporate traditionalism and innovation has produced a victory for the old line at AT&T. Yet Bill Buehler makes it clear that his campaign to create a new corporate culture there hasn't ended.

"I'm already meeting with my new planning staff," he says, "and they've never had an operations type like me leading them. So we're having a difference of opinion on how we view the world, but I'm used to this kind of resistance. Hey, it's not stopped me before, and it won't now."

Adapted from M. Langley, *The Wall Street Journal*, December 16, 1983. Reprinted by permission of *The Wall Street Journal*, © Dow Jones & Company, Inc. 1983. All rights reserved.

ciently increased, then the change should not be attempted. The effort would likely fail. On the other hand, if these forces can be managed, then the next step is to design a strategy that will reduce resistance and/ or stimulate support. What strategies are available, and which is the best? Kotter and Schlesinger suggest six strategies for dealing with this unfreezing step.[22] They include education and communication; participation and involvement; facilitation and support; negotiation and agreement; manipulation and cooptation; explicit and implicit coercion. Their suggestions are summarized in Exhibit 19–6 and discussed briefly below.

Education and communication

A felt need for change is one of the powerful driving forces for change. A lack of such understanding provides a powerful resisting force. This suggests that a program of education and communication about the need for change would be effective. This program should highlight the shortcomings of the status quo and the expected benefits of the proposed change. For example, in an interview with *INC. Magazine*, John Sculley, president of Apple Computer, commented on his efforts to facilitate changes at Apple after founder Steven Jobs left the company. Portions of this conversation are reproduced in Insight 19–4 (p. 816).

This approach assumes that the top-management team or the individual charged with making the change is trusted by those to be educated. If the team or individual lacks credibility, however, these efforts will be fruitless. The education and communication process is difficult if many individuals must be educated, or if there are time pressures involved in making the changes. Education and communication are time consuming. In attempting to turn around the Springfield Remanufacturing Center Corporation (SRC), President John Stack set up what was described as an extraordinary education program. Every employee in the SRC plant took a series of courses covering the basic elements of business, from accounting to warehousing. Ninety-six hours of training were offered, involving more than 1,300 hours of student instruction and preparation. To provide additional information about the status of the firm, every employee (top management to production employees) has access to the company's monthly financial report. And discussions of the figures in the report are held with small groups on a regular basis.[23]

Participation and involvement

If lack of understanding and fear of the unknown are key resisting forces, then the participation or involvement of those affected by the change could reduce their concerns. Again, trust and credibility must exist so that employees view the process as true participation. Other-

EXHIBIT 19–6

Summary of Methods for Dealing with Resistance to Change

Approach	Commonly Used in Situations	Advantages	Drawbacks
Education + communication	Where there is a lack of information or inaccurate information and analysis.	Once persuaded, people will often help with the implementation of the change.	Can be very time-consuming if lots of people are involved.
Participation + involvement	Where the initiators do not have all the information they need to design the change, and where others have considerable power to resist.	People who participate will be committed to implementing change, and any relevant information they have will be integrated into the change plan.	Can be very time-consuming if participators design an inappropriate change.
Facilitation + support	Where people are resisting because of adjustment problems.	No other approach works as well with adjustment problems.	Can be time-consuming, expensive, and still fail.
Negotiation + agreement	Where someone or some group will clearly lose out in a change, and where that group has considerable power to resist.	Sometimes it is a relatively easy way to avoid major resistance.	Can be too expensive in many cases if it alerts others to negotiate for compliance.
Manipulation + cooptation	Where other tactics will not work, or are too expensive.	It can be a relatively quick and inexpensive solution to resistance problems.	Can lead to future problems if people feel manipulated.
Explicit + implicit coercion	Where speed is essential, and the change initiators possess considerable power.	It is speedy, and can overcome any kind of resistance.	Can be risky if it leaves people mad at the initiators.

wise, participation becomes merely a sign-off on decisions already made elsewhere in the firm's hierarchy. The participation and involvement approach is helpful if employees can bring expertise to the change setting, as when a change in technology is planned. At SRC, all employees play an active role in changes made in the organization. They are directly responsible for helping make the changes work.[24]

On the other hand, this approach can also lead to poor-quality information if employees are not knowledgeable in the change area. Participation can be difficult in organizations where the culture has not supported such activities in the past. In such settings, employees may feel that participation is not their responsibility; management may feel that participation leads to a loss of power and authority. Like the education strategy, this one can also be time consuming.

INSIGHT 19-4

Corporate Antihero: Interview with John Sculley, CEO of Apple Computer Company

INC: You're sitting atop a troubled company. You've just ushered the founder out the door. How do you communicate to large numbers of people that you are not, in fact, the bad guy?

SCULLEY: I wasn't really focused on popularity. What I had to do was convince people that we were in a crisis, and that we weren't going to get out of it unless we pulled together. There were some decisions that were going to have to be made quickly from the top—and those were the relatively easy ones from someone coming from a big corporation: cutting expenses, putting controls in place. The thing that was going to be more difficult was finding a new direction for the company that people at Apple would continue to feel excited about. How were we going to hold onto the roots of Apple? And there were no shortcuts to that. It couldn't come from a business plan. It had to come, really, from the soul of the company.

INC.: And how did you tap into that soul?

SCULLEY The only way I knew how, which was to get groups of managers together and sit down and talk it through with them. We went over the mistakes and the successes. And then we tried to figure out what things were really important to us. It meant sitting down with many, many people. And it was something that we had to do under the fire of competition, with the media writing about us and reporting on us as though we were living through a soap opera. It was a stressful time.

INC.: You seem to be suggesting a role for the CEO that is much more focused on internal communications. Is that a part of the job that you think most managers underestimate?

SCULLEY: Absolutely. In the traditional second-wave corporation—the world I came from—stability is a characteristic that people most admire, and so the way information and ideas move through the organization is highly structured. The CEO is essentially at the end of a process of elimination designed to create consensus. But in a third-wave company like Apple, in a fast-growth industry, stability is really a sign of vulnerability. Third-wave companies have to be built around flexibility, and dissent is something that has to be cultivated, not stifled. That means that there is nothing more important than good internal communications.

Source: Adapted from S. Pearlstein and L. Rhodes, "Corporate Antihero," *Inc.*, October 1987, pp. 49–60. Reprinted with permission, *Inc.* magazine, October 1987. Copyright © 1987 by *Inc.* Publishing Company, 38 Commercial Wharf, Boston, MA 02110.

Facilitation and support

Change implies movement into areas that may be unknown to those affected. Fear of the unknown can have devastating effects on employees. Managers can develop support programs to reduce these fears and their effects. These facilitative activities include training programs in skill areas that will be useful after the change, employee counseling, and any other activities that make the transition from known to un-known easier. Unfortunately, these strategies don't always have the desired effect. Consider this example from AT&T. In the fall of 1986, Richard Ponsell, a 22-year AT&T veteran, killed himself. During AT&T's reorganization, Ponsell had been transferred three times in two years and moved between five jobs, only to be told that he wold probably be laid off. Prior to Ponsell's suicide, James Olson, chief executive officer at AT&T, had toured seven cities to personally explain AT&T's situation to 40,000 employees. Olson was particularly concerned about employees' distress at the changes being forced on their organization.[25]

Despite the tragic occurrence at AT&T, support programs can be extremely beneficial to employees and to organizations. They can also be both time consuming and expensive. As the story in Insight 19–5 indicates, J. C. Penney used a range of supportive efforts to convince its employees that moving its corporate headquarters from New York City to Plano, Texas would not be so traumatic as many supposed.

Negotiation and agreement

One way to increase acceptance of a proposed change is to trade with or buy off possible resisting forces. Negotiation occurs frequently when changes in union–management agreements are proposed, for instance. Job security is promised to employees in exchange for management's right to make changes in work rules.

But negotiations and agreements can also arise in less explicit ways. For instance, Louise of Home Computers Company might be able to gain the support of the vice president of finance for her salary plan by promising to support a change proposed by finance sometime in the future. The old adage, "You scratch my back, and I'll scratch yours," applies in this change situation.

Negotiation can be used to avoid major resistance; but the cost of gaining an agreement can be high in terms of what is traded. And once it becomes known that there is a willingness to negotiate, other parties may make the same demands. Succeeding change attempts may be met by additional attempts at corporate blackmail.

Manipulation and cooptation

Two of the less-desirable strategies for influencing forces may provide short-term advantages at the cost of long-term problems. Distorting facts, starting rumors, and selectively withholding or providing information can all be used to **manipulate** employee or work-unit attitudes toward change. **Cooptation** is an underhanded form of participation and involvement, whereby key individuals or groups opposed to a change are given what appear to be important roles in the change process. Their input is ignored, however. What is desired is their appar-

---

Would Liza Minnelli Ever Belt Out a Song about Plano, Texas?

PLANO, Texas—Shivering in over-aircon-ditioned tour buses, almost 100 J.C. Penney Co. employees are getting a glimpse of their future—and some are dismayed by what they see. "We'll have to wait 20 years for trees to grow here," one groans.

"Here" is Plano, Texas, where Manhattan-based Penney is planning to move its corporate headquarters next spring. Penney thinks the move is a great idea: Relocating to this Dallas suburb should save the big retailer up to $70 million a year. Now all it has to do is convince 3,800 New York employees that Plano is a pleasant place—a task that in many cases is roughly equivalent to promoting an outpost on the moon.

When the Penneyites arrived in Dallas, Plano volunteers took over with, among other things, a champagne reception and a four-hour bus tour. But the latter sometimes backfired. "It's pretty darn stark," says one Penney employee recalling how the bus passed isolated home developments and grazing cows on its way to Penney's 429-acre headquarters site. "I could see driving home at night and thinking you were in the Twilight Zone."

Plano boosters have joined Penney bosses in a concerted—and somewhat frantic—effort to sell Texas to the taxi set. Penney, for example, recently tried to induce employees to spend a long weekend in Dallas by paying the air fare (employees paid for their own hotels and meals). More than 1,000 Penney employees and their families took up the company on its offer.

Meanwhile, back in New York, Penney has been pulling out all the stops in its Texas-touting campaign. A jukebox in the company cafeteria played country music for about a week (reportedly annoying some potential converts to the Texas cause). Penney also has thrown a party for single employees who are considering making the move and might be looking for roommates. And the company offers a wide range of free seminars, including one on managing stress and another on Texas plants, soil and weather.

But all that is only part of the effort. To fight the notion that, as one employee puts it, "everyone is toting a gun and a Bible" in Texas, hot lines have been set up in Dallas to answer questions about real estate, Plano's teen-age life style and Dallas's Jewish community. Penney also runs a "Texas Information Center" in New York, whose offerings include videotaped testimonials from Penney managers already in Texas. (One ringing endorsement: "I'm not used to people saying hello to me for no reason.")

Employees have been given plenty of time to process all this information. They don't have to decide whether to make the move—or to stay behind and collect up to a year's severance pay—until 60 days before their department's moving date.

But when it comes to the pluses and minuses of Greater Dallas and Greater New York, even real-estate agents and relocation cheerleaders in this area have a sense of perspective. Dolores Gilliam, vice president for relocation of a Dallas real-estate firm, recalls a recent three-day mission to Penney headquarters—especially the part where she sneaked off to Macy's and Trump Tower. "We have wonderful shopping in Dallas," she says, "but, you know, New York is New York."

ent agreement with what has been proposed. The tradeoff of an apparent position of influence for support for the change can be attractive. These strategies are relatively inexpensive and quick methods for reducing resistance or sustaining support. In the long run, however, they can create major problems if the nature of the manipulation or cooptation is discovered. Undermining recent changes and difficulties in undertaking new changes might be the least of these problems.

Explicit and implicit coercion

Finally, if a person has the power and authority, he or she can simply order resistance to cease by threatening job loss, transfer, and the like. In the short run, this approach is relatively quick. But in the long run, commitment to changes made under threat will be low. Repeated use of explicit or implicit coercion could lead to violent reactions by those subjected to such strategies.

Look again at this list of unfreezing strategies, beginning with education and communication. A number of additional points should be made. First, most managers will likely use more than one of the strategies for a given change. Depending on time and levels of commitment desired, a manager might start at the beginning of this list, and work down, as a function of success at each step. In the order presented here, the list goes from strategies that consume the most time to those that consume the least. The ordering also represents strategies that yield the highest levels of commitment to change to those that result in minimal commmitment. In other words, the strategies are arranged from most to least preferred. It is easy to make such value judgments in a textbook. However, real managers in real situations are confronted by a variety of pressures. They may have no alternative but to implement what is identified here as a less-desirable strategy.

MAKING THE CHANGE

Closely tied to strategies for dealing with resistance and support are the tactics available for actually implementing changes. Exhibit 19–7 presents a continuum of possible change tactics. At one end is what might be called the Attilla the Hun approach. Here, the change is imposed in a rapid, unilateral fashion. This approach hopes to crush and/or ignore any resistance. Bill McGowan of MCI seems to prefer this approach to change. He argues, "Most organizations, left to their own devices, are going to atrophy, to get so institutional, so bureaucratic, that they get to the point where their original reason for existence has been lost, and they stagnate. So you have to have change, and by that I mean dramatic change."[26]

At the other extreme, change is implemented in a slower, evolving fashion that attempts to involve all those concerned. This approach accepts the likelihood of resistance, but uses education, communication, participation, and involvement to minimize that resistance.

Exhibit 19–7 is drawn to suggest that these two approaches represent the extremes available to implement change. Most changes are undertaken from positions between the extremes. For complex changes with little resistance in some areas and strong resistance in others, a quick implementation strategy might be coupled with an evolutionary approach.

Choosing an approach

One of a manager's responsibilities is to choose the location on this spectrum where he or she wants to operate in making changes. The choice a manager makes will be influenced by a number of factors. A few of these are discussed below.[27]

Importance

Of major concern is the importance of the change. If a firm is concerned about its survival, then the quicker the implementation of a change designed to preserve the firm the better. Closely related to importance, then, must be the nature of any time constraints under which a manager is operating. A realistic assessment of these is a major determinant of the appropriate change strategy. Consider the example of David Roderick, CEO of USX Corporation. He cut 63,000 employees from his payroll in the early 1980s in response to international competition. In addition

EXHIBIT 19–7

A Continuum of Change Tactics

Quick	**Slow**
Unilateral	**Participative**
Planned	**Evolving**
Eliminate Resistance	**Pacify Resistance**

◄────────────────────►

Our Choice—A Function Of
Importance of the change
Distribution of power
Organizational culture
Managerial styles
Need for commitment
Sources of resistance
Strength of resistance

Source: Reprinted by permission of the *Harvard Business Review.* An exhibit from "Choosing Strategies for Change" by John P. Kotter and Leonard H. Schlesinger (March/April 1979), p. 112.

to that, he demanded steep wage concessions from the Steelworkers Union in 1986. After a six-month strike, he got those, too. Roderick argues, "Either you slash cost, or you go Chapter 11 [bankruptcy]."[28]

Distribution of power

The extent to which a manager can impose a change in short order on a group of employees or an entire organization is largely a function of that manager's power. As discussed in Chapter 10, power derives from many sources. In this case, a manager needs sufficient levels of legitimate power to operate at the left-hand end of the change spectrum. If change is desired in the absence of power, a more democratic approach will be required.

Organizational culture/managerial styles

The generalized norms and values held by employees can determine the acceptable approaches to making changes in a firm. A corporation that encourages employee participation and involvement would likely rebel against a change imposed in an authoritarian fashion. Similarly, attempts to involve employees in change efforts in an autocratic culture might be met with great skepticism. Thus, change tactics counter to a corporation's culture can be met with great resistance. On the other hand, a tactic that is congruent with the culture should increase the chances for successful change.

An example of cultural resistance to change is seen in the case of Vatex Corporation, a small Richmond, Virginia-based printer of T-shirts and sweatshirts founded by Jerry Gordé. Gordé is not your typical CEO. His long hair and blue jeans are a throwback to the 1960s, when he organized street demonstrations with Yippie leaders Abbie Hoffman and Jerry Rubin. Gordé's goal with Vatex was to succeed at the capitalist's games, but to refuse to play by their rules. He wanted Vatex to be a community, as well as a business. Five percent of the firm's annual profits went to charity. Employees owned a large portion of the business.

Gordé wanted employees who were physically fit. He believed that fitness was an essential part of personal and organizational transformation. His board voted to spend $15,000 on exercise equipment, but few people took advantage of this opportunity. Gordé was displeased. He wanted people to be committed to the organization, not to the individual; he wanted employees to align their values with the company's. Individuals had to want what the group wanted, not what was in their own short-term interest. If employees wouldn't do it voluntarily, Gordé "would do what leaders since Moses had done when their followers failed them. He would kick ass." And he did, making participation in the fitness program a required, not an optional, part of the job.

Unfortunately, demanding this type of change in this way violated the employees' perceptions of the corporate culture. As one employee commented, "*Ask* me to exercise. *Encourage* me to exercise. I'll do it. Just don't *tell* me to exercise."[29]

Need for commitment

The use of change tactics that run roughshod over resistance or fail to involve those employees affected in the change process may reduce the levels of commitment to the change. In emergency situations, employees understand the need for quick, unilateral changes. But when the corporate culture supports involvement, and commitment is important for the long-run success of the change, tactics on the left side of the spectrum will probably not provide this support.

Sources and strength of resistance

The savvy manager realizes that for any change, there may be sources of resistance that simply cannot be crushed or overcome by unilateral changes. History is filled with examples of attempted changes that have failed because leaders failed to appreciate the strength of resistance. On the international level, the willingness of the Soviet Union to consider the withdrawal of their troops from Afghanistan in 1988 to 1989 is an excellent example of the impact of strong resistance on a proposed change. In the United States, strikes and work stoppages are common employee reactions to unwanted management changes. Unless managers are quite sure of the nature and strength of the resistance to change, they would do well to take an evolutionary approach.

There are probably a number of other factors managers should investigate before choosing the tactic(s) for implementing a change. But this list provides a sample of the issues that must be considered. Louise's implementation tactics for her new compensation plan would likely be chosen from options to the right of the change spectrum. Home Computers Company is not currently confronted with issues of survival. Louise does not have all the necessary technical information she needs to implement the plan. She must consider the implications for other key managers, as well as possible reactions from the sales staff.

Tactics for change

Many changes that occur in an organization—new machinery, new policies, new products—are, in isolation, relatively easy to implement. The purchase and installation of new equipment is costly and may be difficult to bring on line, but technical problems can usually be resolved. However, major difficulties can arise when dealing with the human reactions to such organizational changes or in attempting to change human actions and relationships directly. These problems can be addressed through education and training at the individual level and through development programs at the organizational level.

Education and training

Change in the human component can occur at a number of different levels. Lawrence and Lorsch suggested that organizational change involving individuals directly or indirectly can require changes in roles, technical skills, human relations skills, or values and attitudes.[30] These changes can be described as ranging from *cognitive* to *emotional* in content. According to these researchers, employee role change requires cognitive change and is the simplest change to make. Changes in employee skills also represent cognitive changes; but skills are more difficult to change than roles.

These two changes are frequently made with formal educational programs, where new roles can be explained and new skills taught. Training programs are typically developed for lower-level employees; management development programs are aimed at upper-level managers. (Louise of HCC attended such a management development program.) These programs are offered by the firm itself if training demands and resources are available. For example, GE, Xerox, IBM, GM, and most major accounting and consulting firms have their own management development institutes. Smaller firms or firms with relatively specialized training needs may work jointly with an educational institution to develop customized training or development programs. These are staffed by university faculty and are designed to address issues of importance to the contracting firm.

A third training option is the generic management development program operated independently by schools or private consulting organizations. These are directed at providing general training or development programs or more specialized programs of a highly technical nature. Home Computers Company's size restricted Louise's management training options to this last approach. Such training programs can range in length from a half a day to many weeks and cost several thousand dollars for longer sessions.

Organizational development

The primary tool for human changes of an emotional nature is called **organizational development,** usually referred to as **OD. Organizational development is "a change process that is planned, organization-wide, (and) managed from the top, to increase organizational effectiveness and health through planned intervention in organizational processes using behavioral science knowledge."**[31] Unlike the formal educational training programs discussed above, OD typically requires that an external OD consultant be brought in to assist a firm in its OD change efforts.

This consultant usually brings along a set of values and assumptions that may initially be at odds with the values and assumptions of top management. Organizational development values and assumptions usually include the following:

■ Most employees desire self-actualization.

■ Most employees desire to increase their contribution to the achievement of an organization's goals.

■ The open expression of individual feelings is appropriate, even desirable.

■ Levels of trust and openness in most organizations should be increased.[32]

If top management accepts this set of values, the OD process will likely have a successful launch. Disagreement about values must be resolved if OD programs are to have any chance of success. Failure to come to some agreement prevents top management from being fully committed to an OD program, and the effort appears transparent to other employees.

The organizational development process is shown in Exhibit 19–8. The first step in the process does not concern the OD consultant at all. Before any type of OD effort can occur, managers in a firm need to be aware that something is not as it should be. Symptoms might include low morale, reduced productivity, and inability to respond quickly to competitor moves, among countless others. Once management realizes that there are shortcomings in an organization, they must select an OD consultant. Depending on the size of the firm, these individuals can come from inside or outside. Many Fortune 500 firms have their own in-house OD consultants. Smaller firms may need to find an external consultant.

Working with management, the consultant plans a program of information gathering to determine why or how these problems arose. Information is usually collected from managerial and employee interviews, standardized and customized surveys (of job satisfaction, corporate culture, leadership styles, group interactions, and the like), and company records or archives. The collected information is then analyzed and synthesized, and the consultant provides a preliminary diagnosis of the causes for the company's problems. This information is fed back to management. Working together, the consultant and management develop a joint diagnosis of key organizational problems. The consultant wants to get beyond mere symptoms (like high turnover, low quality, etc.) to identify the underlying *causes* that led to the identified concerns.

To be effective, this diagnostic process must be a joint management–consultant endeavor. And the diagnosis must be accepted by management if the OD change process is to succeed. Once agreement is reached

EXHIBIT 19–8

The Organizational Development Process

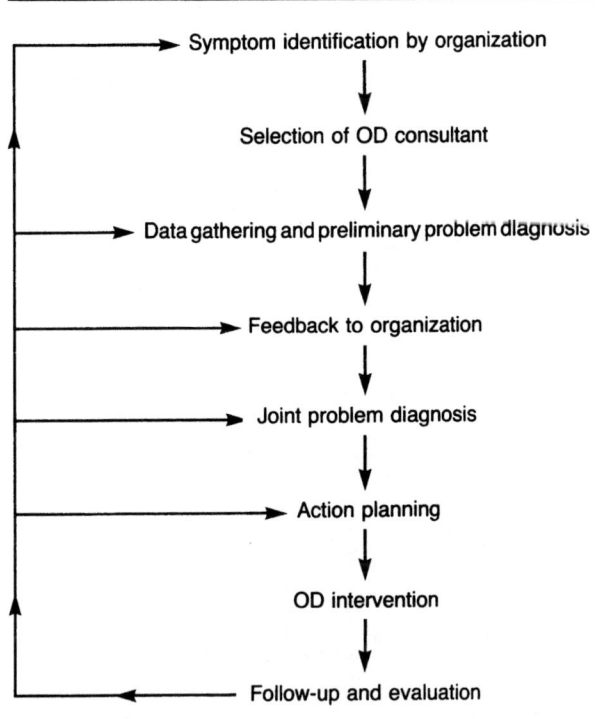

Source: © 1985 by the Regents of the University of California. Adapted from W. French, "Organization Development: Objectives, Assumptions and Strategies," *California Management Review*, vol. 12, no. 2, p. 26. By permission of The Regents.

on a diagnosis, plans are made as to the appropriate changes **(OD interventions)** needed and the level at which these changes will be made.

The proposed change or changes can include skill training, management development programs, and managerial retreats, among others. Whatever the nature of the intervention, management and the OD consultant continue to monitor events during and after the actual intervention to evaluate the relative success (or failure) of the intervention effort. The model in Exhibit 19–8 also contains a feedback loop, suggesting that the evaluation process could require further repetitions of the OD process.

A number of change techniques have become popular with OD consultants, including survey feedback, team development, and quality circles. The last of these techniques should sound familiar, as it was discussed in depth in Chapter 12. For that reason, we will discuss here only the first two approaches, survey feedback and team building.

Survey feedback

As the name implies, **survey feedback** requires the administration of standardized or customized survey questionnaires to appropriate managers and their employees. The intent is to gather accurate information anonymously about various aspects of an organization, work unit, and individual manager. Many large corporations, including Sears and IBM, survey their entire labor force over a period of three years. A brief sample of questions that might appear on a survey questionnaire follows.

		Agree		Neutral		Disagree
1.	My manager contributes to my level of performance.	1	2	3	4	5
2.	Compensation in this firm is fair and equitable.	1	2	3	4	5
3.	Top management cares little about lower-level employees.	1	2	3	4	5
4.	Working conditions around here are about as good as can be expected for our industry.	1	2	3	4	5

The key to successful survey feedback is in the feedback portion of the change attempt. Survey results are calculated for as many different organizational levels as needed. These results are presented to joint meetings of managers and their subordinates by the organizational development consultant. At the work unit level, the consultant provides feedback about what the results mean, how they compare to similar units in the company or to other companies, and why particular results might have occurred. This process is designed to encourage managers and subordinates to confront possible problem areas and to work with the consultant to develop actions plans to address them.

Successful survey feedback requires that managers (1) encourage open and free discussion of the findings, their probable causes, and possible implications for unit performance; (2) propose and encourage suggestions for ways to resolve problems; and (3) carry out agreed-upon changes as quickly as possible, usually with the assistance of the OD consultant. Frequently, follow-up surveys are completed after the change has had a chance to stick to see if it was successful.

Team building

One possible result of the survey feedback process is an awareness that a manager and his or her work group are not functioning as a team. **Team-building activities are designed to assist all employees to learn to act and function more effectively together.**[33] These activities require managers and work unit subordinates to participate in a series of workshops where exercises, case studies, and role playing require interaction, mutual assistance, and trust. The OD consultant works with team members to improve communications and conflict-resolution skills and group cohesiveness. More adventurous programs send employees on white-water rafting expeditions or rappeling down mountain sides as ways of increasing team interactions and appreciation for team members.

When does it work?

One final issue needs to be addressed before we conclude our discussion of organizational development. That issue is, "Does it work?" The success or failure of an OD change intervention is a function of a variety of factors: the commitment level of the OD consultant and of top management, the appropriateness of the OD intervention, and the reinforcement of the new values and attitudes resulting from the OD change.[34]

If OD consultants see organizations as simply a series of consulting jobs, or as opportunities to attempt their preferred intervention strategy regardless of the problem diagnosis, OD efforts will likely fail. Think about the child who gets a new hammer for his or her birthday. All of a sudden, everything the child sees needs to be hit. OD consultants with only one trick (say, survey feedback) in their bag of tricks frequently see all problems as calling for survey feedback as the appropriate response.

If top management views an OD intervention as useful because (1) everybody else is doing it; (2) it will shut the employees up for a while; or (3) it will keep the union out, then any intervention, even from the most capable and well-meaning consultant, will probably be doomed.

Lack of top-management support for the results of a well-conceived OD effort can also undermine its success. Sending a unit manager and subordinates for a week-long outward bound experience may work wonders for developing cohesiveness and teamwork. But if that cohesiveness is not reinforced once the work unit returns, the effects of the experience can fade quickly.

Similarly, extensive employee dissatisfaction with an OD approach can also spell disaster for some programs. At Pacific Bell, a subsidiary of Pacific Telesis, attempts were made to change the corporate culture using an OD consultant "who often veils his ideas in an impenetrable language, claims to make people rethink the way they think, and hence arrives at new ways of solving problems." Investigations of the process by the California Utilities Commission revealed hundreds of employee complaints about the process. "They hated the jargon and obscure language, the perceived threats that those who didn't adopt the new think would have no future at Pac Bell, the 'facilitators' who sat in as 'thought police' at meetings to make sure procedures were followed, and the implication that anyone who didn't get the new routine was stupid." Pac Bell suspended further training and began its own investigation. Eventually, the president took early retirement, and the executive vice president was demoted to the presidency of a smaller subsidiary.[35]

Successful OD change attempts require three elements: careful and informed selection of the OD consultant, top management willingness to participate in and support all steps of the process, and reinforcement of the changes after the formal intervention process has been completed. This final suggestion, the reinforcement of the OD intervention, leads to a discussion of the final step in the change model: refreezing the change.

REFREEZING THE CHANGE

Assuming that management has made the changes in organizational goals, products, processes, structures, or people, they still cannot sit back and simply expect the change to be maintained over time. Physics informs us that an object moved from equilibrium will tend to return to the original equilibrium point unless new forces are present to prevent this. Lewin reminds managers that new goals, structures, behaviors, and attitudes need to be refrozen.[36] The changes must become the new status quo. Consider the following approaches that should be useful in accomplishing this final step of the change process.

Gain top-management support

Formal or informal sponsorship for a change by top management is an important factor in giving the new outcome legitimacy. If employees elsewhere in an organization see that top managers support and accept the change, they will be more likely to do so themselves. Thus, if the change involves a redesign of the communications or information processing systems, top management must encourage the use of the new system by using it themselves.

Minimize surprises

As suggested earlier, if participants in a change are aware of the nature of that change, the implementation schedule, and expectations after the change is made, they should be more receptive to the change. One of the most stressful occasions for employees can be the unannounced surprises that happen in any firm. There are probably many of these over which management has only limited control. If management carefully plans a change, then the Holiday Inn approach to change is preferred: "The best surprise is no surprise."

Design for success

A change may be complex. It may have the potential to affect large segments of a company or to be somewhat controversial. In any of these situations managers should take every advantage they can in the initial implementation. For instance, managers and their work unit should not only believe in the change, but be willing to allow the change in their unit. Managers should do everything possible to make that change a success. They should publicize the success widely and spread the change to other units, as appropriate. Peer pressure and word-of-mouth advertising can smooth the change's entry into other units. Once others see the benefits of the change, they will be more willing to attempt it.

Expect the unexpected

In designing and implementing a change, it is always wise to assume that Murphy's Law will hold: "If something can go wrong, it will." To give change a chance to refreeze, managers must anticipate as many problems as possible and prepare contingency plans, should one or more of them arise. Nothing can doom a change faster than an unforeseen obstacle arising after the change has been in place. Like the pebble thrown in the pond, change will cause ripple effects throughout an organization, often in ways least anticipated. Managers must ask as many "what if" questions as possible and be prepared to provide the answers, if necessary.

Reinforce the new

Behaviors that are positively reinforced tend to be repeated. This book has made this point many times. In designing a change, attention must be paid to how the new approach will be reinforced. For example, one change made at SRC Corporation was the installation of a red electronic message board. The board flashes real-time reports of labor utilization in various manufacturing units. If goals are attained, work units become eligible for a bonus under an SRC plan known as STP-GUTR: "Stop the Praise, Give Us the Raise." Such systems seem to have worked at SRC. Sales grew 40 percent in 1986, and net operating income rose 11 percent. Absenteeism and turnover have nearly disappeared.[37] These outcomes suggest that reward systems should be carefully considered when planning changes, and redesigned, if necessary. If the rewards or reinforcements inherent in the change fall short of employee expectations, then the change will likely fail.

Evaluate the change

Finally, an important and often overlooked step in the refreezing stage of change is the evaluation step. Management needs to know if the change had its intended effects. Too many managers install changes, undertake training programs, and redesign structures with the mistaken belief that simply because the change was made, it will be successful. In many cases, this assumption proves incorrect. This is particularly true if the change was unilateral or was made without a felt need for change by those affected. Sabotage of managerial changes is not an unknown activity.

Evaluation is also beneficial because it forces the person making the change to establish the objectives or criteria by which the success of the change can be judged well before the change is made. This provides additional guidance when planning the tactics for making the change. It also forces this individual to give careful thought to how, or if, the results of the change will be measured at some time in the future.

CHAPTER HIGHLIGHTS

This chapter looked back and recalled the many different topics covered to this point. Any one or more of these topics provides the basis for change in someone's personal or organizational life. This chapter examined a number of different issues relating to the general topic of change.

The chapter began by making a distinction between planned and unplanned change. The interest here is with **change as the "planned and purposeful shift from one state to another."** The text also distinguished between **change—the adoption of ideas new to an organization, and innovation—the adoption of ideas new to an industry, market, or general environment.**

We examined the developmental nature of change at two broad levels. An epochal model of change provided a brief examination of changes across the ages. At a slightly less expansive level, an evolutionary model of organizational change proposed that most firms evolve through five separate phases: **creativity, direction, delegation, coordination, and collaboration.** Each of these phases was distinguished from the others by a series of crises concerning **leadership, autonomy, control, and red tape.**

Within this context of ongoing but slower-moving change, we discussed how change occurs **within** organizations. Starting with a consideration of targets for change at the individual, group, organizational, and environmental levels, the discussion centered on Lewin's three-step change model: **unfreezing, changing, refreezing.**

To determine the likelihood that the unfreezing step will be successful, managers need to identify **forces that support and forces that resist change.** Key supporting forces included **threats to organizational survival** as well as a **felt need for change** among those affected. A number of other supporting forces were classified as internal or external events. **Internal support likely comes from redirection of organizational goals, excess resources, ineffective structures or operations, corporate cultures that foster innovation, and idea or product champions. External support can be found within any number of key environmental sectors, including changes in technology, competitor moves, or legislative or judicial actions.**

Similarly, our discussion of possible resisting forces also categorized these forces as internal or external. **Internal resistance comes from fear of the unknown, uncertainty associated with change, threats to vested interests, traditions, habits, slack resources, and conservative corporate cultures. External resistance can come from interorganizational agreements with firms in key environmental sectors and from laws, regulations, or judicial decisions that inhibit certain changes.**

One way of determining the relative likelihood that a planned change will be successful is the **force-field analysis.** This process allows a manager to evaluate the number and strength of the various forces for and against change. **Only if the strength of driving forces exceeds the strength of resisting force can the change process begin.**

To increase support for or reduce resistance to a change, six different strategies were presented: **education, participation, facilitation, negotiation, manipulation, and coercion.** Each of these strategies could be appropriate under certain circumstances to expedite the change process; however, levels of long-term commitment to a change decrease as the strategies move toward manipulation and coercion.

Changes can be made in an infinite number of ways. **We considered the extremes: unilateral, imposed change and participative, evolving change.** The choice of change tactics to employ is a function of **the importance of the change, the distribution of power of those in the change process, corporate cultures, need for commitment, and the source and strength of resistance.**

To implement changes, especially at the individual level, requires a determination of the nature of the change—**cognitive or emotional.** Cognitive changes are best handled with formal employee training or management development programs. Emotional change may require an **organizational development intervention.** In this process, organizational development consultants work with top management to **develop an accurate diagnosis, collect accurate information related to the diagnosis, plan and implement appropriate change programs, and evaluate their success.** Organizational development practitioners use a variety of change tactics, including **survey feedback** and **team building.**

Finally, once a change is in place, steps must be taken to ensure that the new way is **refrozen.** We discussed a number of mechanisms to help in this refreezing process, including **gaining top management support, minimizing surprises, designing for success, expecting the unexpected, reinforcing the new, and evaluating the results.**

REVIEW QUESTIONS

1. What is *change?* How does it differ from *innovation?*
2. In Greiner's model of organizational evolution, what are the various phases and crises that organizations encounter?
3. The text offered some speculations about what the sixth phase of organizational evolution might be. What do you think the next phase will be? What crisis might prompt this next phase?
4. Using Greiner's model, describe the evolution of a firm that you know.
5. Describe how the various targets for change are related.
6. What are the three steps in Lewin's change model?
7. Think about a change you tried to make in your own life or in an organization that you belong to. What supporting forces did you encounter? What resisting forces?
8. Consider a change you want to make now. Complete a force-field analysis, and determine whether or not the change is possible.
9. Why is a felt need for change an important supporting force for change?
10. What strategies are available to managers for increasing support for or reducing resistance to change? Which of these is the quickest? Which will lead to the greatest commitment to change?
11. What factors will influence the tactics chosen to implement a change?
12. Define organizational development. What values do OD consultants usually bring to an OD intervention? What techniques do OD consultants use? What is needed to increase the likelihood of a successful OD project?
13. When refreezing a change, what can managers do to increase the chances that the change will be successful?
14. Why is top-management support important for a successful change?
15. What does the statement "You can't make just one decision" mean in the context of organizational change?

16. What specific recommendations would you make to Louise about how she should attempt to change HCC's sales force compensation system?

RESOURCE READINGS

Drucker, Peter. *Innovation and Entrepreneurship.* New York: Harper & Row, 1985.

French, W.; C. Bell; and R. Zawacki, *Organization Development: Theory, Practice, and Research,* rev. ed. Plano, Tex.: Business Publications 1983.

Goodman, Paul S., et al. *Change in Organizations.* San Francisco: Jossey-Bass, 1982.

Huse, E., and T. Cummings. *Organization Development and Change,* 3d ed. St. Paul, Minn.: West Publishing, 1985.

Kanter, R. M. *The Changemasters.* New York: Simon and Schuster, 1983.

Kotter, J., and L. Schlesinger. "Choosing Strategies for Change," *Harvard Business Review,* March-April 1979, pp. 106–14.

Peters, Tom. *Thriving on Chaos.* New York: Alfred A. Knopf, 1987.

Woodman, R., and W. Pasmore. *Research in Organizational Change and Development,* vol. 1. Greenwich, Conn.: JAI Press, 1987.

NOTES

1. "MCI Founder: Bill McGowan," *INC.*, August 1986, p. 38.

2. S. Robbins, *Organizational Theory* (Englewood Cliffs, N.J.: Prentice-Hall, 1987), p. 306.

3. J. Pierce and A. Delbecq, "Organizational Structure, Individual Attitudes, and Innovation," *Academy of Management Review,* April 1977, pp. 27–37.

4. Ibid.

5. L. Greiner, "Evolution and Revolution as Organizations Grow," *Harvard Business Review,* July-August 1972, pp. 37–46.

6. S. Coll, "The Man Who Would Be King," *California Magazine,* November 1983, pp. 89 and 92.

7. J. Wilson, "Can Andy Grove Practice What He Preaches?" *Business Week,* March 16, 1987, p. 68.

8. "Reorganizing at Weyerhaeuser," *Fortune,* Advertising Supplement, September 28, 1987.

9. "Participative Management at AT&T," *Fortune,* Advertising Supplement, September 28, 1987.

10. "Sculley's Lessons From Inside Apple," *Fortune,* September 14, 1987, pp. 108-19.

11. R. Perot, "How I Would Turn Around GM," *Fortune*, February 15, 1988, pp. 44–48.

12. Kurt Lewin, *Field Theory in Social Science* (New York: Harper & Row, 1951).

13. Ibid.

14. G. Critser, "The Est Factor," *INC.*, August 1986, pp. 69-76.

15. S. Lee and C. Brown, "The Protean Corporation," *Forbes*, August 24, 1987, pp. 76–79.

16. B. Nussbaum, "The Changing Role of the CEO," *Business Week*, October 23, 1987, pp. 13–28.

17. Ibid.

18. J. Byrne, "The Miracle Company," *Business Week*, October 19, 1987, pp. 84–90.

19. S. R. Michael, "Organizational Change Techniques," *Organizational Dynamics*, Summer 1982, pp. 67–79.

20. "MCI Founder: Bill McGowan," p. 36.

21. "How Computers Remake the Manager's Job," *Business Week*, April 25, 1983, pp. 51–61.

22. J. Kotter and L. Schlesinger, "Choosing Strategies for Change," *Harvard Business Review*, March-April 1979, pp. 106–14.

23. L. Rhodes and P. Amend, "The Turnaround," *INC.*, August 1986, pp. 42–48.

24. Ibid.

25. J. Keller et al., "AT&T: The Making of a Comeback," *Business Week*, January 18, 1988, pp. 56–62.

26. "MCI Founder: Bill McGowan," p. 38.

27. J. Kotter and L. Schlesinger, "Choosing Strategies for Change."

28. B. Nussbaum, "The Changing Role of the CEO," p. 17.

29. J. Case, "Chairman Jerry's Cultural Revolution," *INC.*, August 1987, pp. 58–65.

30. P. Lawrence and J. Lorsch, *Developing Organizations: Diagnosis and Actions* (Reading, Mass.: Addison-Wesley Publishing, 1969).

31. R. Beckhard, *Organizational Development: Strategies and Models* (Reading, Mass.: Addison-Wesley Publishing, 1969); W. Warner Burke, *Organizational Development: A Normative View* (Reading, Mass.: Addison-Wesley Publishing, 1987).

32. W. French and C. Bell, Jr., *Organizational Development* (Englewood Cliffs, N.J.: Prentice-Hall, 1973).

33. E. F. Huse and T. Cummings, *Organizational Development and Change*, 3d ed., (St. Paul, Minn.: West Publishing, 1985).

34. W. Dyer, *Team Building: Issues and Alternatives*, 2d ed., (Reading, Mass.: Addison-Wesley Publishing, 1987); R. Beckhard and R. Harin, *Organizational Transitions: Managing Complex Change*, 2d ed., (Reading, Mass.: Addison-Wesley Publishing, 1987).

35. J. Main, "Trying to Bend Managers' Minds," *Fortune,* October 23, 1987, pp. 95–108.

36. Kurt Lewin, *Field Theories in Social Science.*

37. L. Rhodes and P. Amend, "The Turnaround," p. 43.

CASE: Change in WP/DE

Helen Maxwell supervises the word processing/data entry (WP/DE) unit for the Department of Administration of State Government. She has held this job for about a year and is well liked by the employees in her unit. Helen took this job with the state as a step up from her former position as a data entry lead worker in an insurance company in the same city. Though Helen has a "task-oriented," professional approach to her work and high standards of quality, she also has good interpersonal skills and handles her employees well. Her supervisory style could be characterized as traditional—low in participativeness, but sensitive to employee needs and rights.

Alice Gifford is Helen's assistant. Alice has been a word processing employee since the new computerized equipment was installed four years ago. She was a secretary for many years before that. Her excellent work and leadership qualities were noticed, and she was promoted at the same time that Helen was hired. The two have gotten along well with each other. The WP/DE unit was created by Helen's predecessor in a difficult and stressful transition from individual units having their own secretary to the processing "pool" of employees with all computerized equipment. Data entry was added with the increased use of new information and decision support systems by various state agencies. At present, the work area consists of four circles of word processing equipment stations (16 employees) and a row of 10 data entry employees and their equipment. (See Exhibit 1)

Interestingly, the employees who handle word processing tasks are different in several ways from the data entry employees. Almost all of the WP employees had been secretaries prior to learning to use the computer equipment; this is not true of data entry employees. The WP employees typically wear formal business attire to work, while their counterparts in DE dress much more casually, including jeans and T-shirts. The immediate work spaces of the employees also differs, depending on their WP or DE work assignments. WP machines are covered with personal objects, like family pictures, radios, flowers, etc. The DE area has a noticeable lack of such decorations, with only an occasional cartoon taped to a machine. The DE employees are not as ownership oriented about their computers. Other, less visible differences in attitudes and behaviors also serve to create two distinct subgroups in Helen's unit.

Since the WP/DE unit was created, it continued to evolve and develop. Much of the work for the unit came in large batches due to project start-ups, committee report work with tight deadlines, and so on. When the legislature was in session, the DE employees sometimes received large batches of work

Source: Adapted from M. Gander and S. Willey, "Managing Change often Involves Managing Conflict," *Proceedings* of the 1986 Midwest Case Writers Association Meeting.

EXHIBIT 1

Physical Layout of the WP/DE Unit

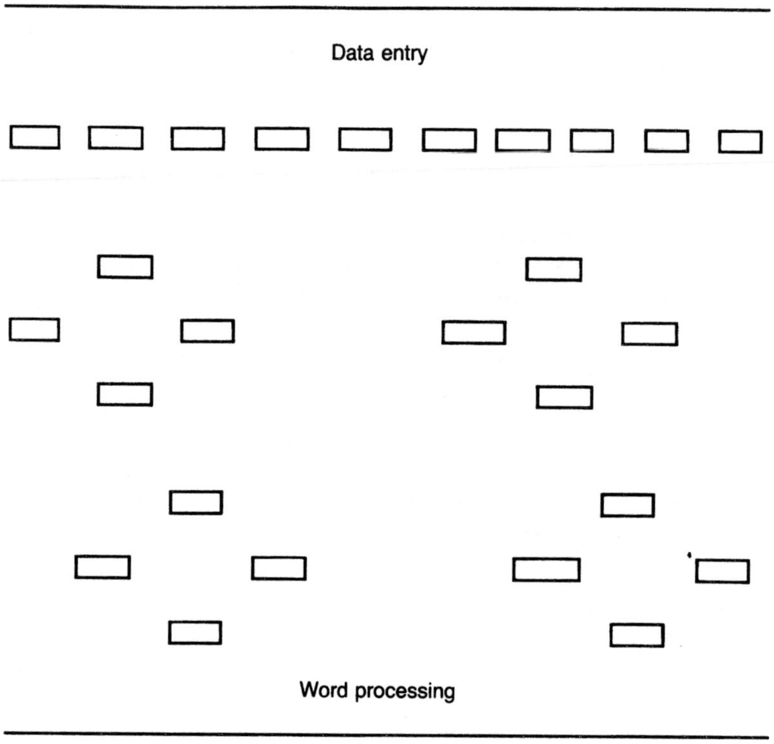

Data entry

Word processing

on very short notice. All too often, these employees are swamped with work while their WP counterparts barely have enough to keep them busy. The opposite situation also arises on occasion. And if a WP or DE employee calls in sick, that computer sits idle for the day. There is no provision to replace the absent employee, regardless of workload demands.

Recently, top administration decided that some new machines should be added to the WP/DE unit. In conjunction with those additions, Helen was to be responsible for having the DE employees learn how to use the WP equipment and vice versa. As Helen thought about the implementation of the cross-training requirement, she knew there might be resistance from some employees. She was careful to devise what she felt was a method to accomplish the cross-training over a period of three months—enough time to give her employees sufficient training support. She felt her plan was realistic and fair, and that the whole unit would be able to work more efficiently once that plan was accomplished. Her boss heartily endorsed the plan when she presented it to him.

Shortly after announcing the plan to her unit, Helen was confronted with major and unexpectedly hostile reactions from her employees. Many of them were upset about having to learn to operate the other machines. Others though it was a good idea and a good opportunity, but were uncertain about the three-month time table. Alice tended to agree that the plan was unfair and unreasonable. She expressed her concerns to Helen, but not to the other employees.

In an informal lunch meeting, 10 of the WP employees voted to resist the cross-training and later in the day, obtained support for their position from seven DE employees. They confronted Helen with their decision the next morning. Knowing that her boss was committed to the cross-training, Helen attempted to reason with her employees. But it seemed useless; they were adamant in their demands. Moreover, having heard about the resistance, the WP/DE employees who welcomed the cross-training opportunities united and indicated their support for the change. For the first time since Helen had been the supervisor of the unit, WP employee ranks were split on an issue, siding with DE employees who were of the same opinion. The situation in the unit was certainly a divisive and volatile one. Helen was under pressure to solve the problem as soon as possible.

Questions:

1. What are your reactions to the way Helen handled the proposed change?
2. Why do you think most of the employees are resisting the change? What factors contributed to this resistance?
3. What do you think will happen if Helen goes ahead with the cross-training, in spite of the resistance?
4. On the other hand, what will happen if she lets the employees who do not want the cross-training prevail?
5. What are some of the supporting forces for change in this situation?
6. What should Helen do now?

The Medtek Corporation (B)

John Torrence, senior vice-president of the Medtek Corporation and director of the company's technical division (R&D) was talking with several members of a consulting team that he had brought in to help him with problems in the division.

> We have a basic problem of performance here in the technical division. Related to this problem is the low morale in my division and increased pressures from other parts of the company.
>
> We have had a bad case of technical constipation; this division has not brought out a successful new product in two years. Given our competition, if we don't do something about this problem soon, the whole company is going to be in big trouble.

COMPANY BACKGROUND

The Medtek Corporation is an international company that designs, manufactures, and markets automated diagnostic instruments for clinical and industrial users. The company was formed in 1949 as a small operation in a Bronx loft by the late Paul Torres; the father of the present chairman and CEO, Arthur Torrence; and the grandfather of the present senior vice-president for research and development, John Torrence.

Mr. Torres started Medtek by hand-crafting a new device called the Automed, a product still manufactured by the company, which automated the preparation of human tissue for microscopic examination by pathologists. The firm continued to grow until, in the early 1960s, it employed approximately 25 people. The R&D section was composed of two engineers and two draftspersons. At this stage, Medtek was orga-

Source: D. Nadler, M. Tushman, and N. Hatvany, *Managing Organizations: Readings and Cases* (Boston: Little-Brown, 1982), pp. 551-557.

nized very informally. New employees and consultants were brought in as needed to work on specific tasks.

During this period, an inventor named Dennis Rettew was brought in. Rettew had been employed in a Cleveland hospital. After observing both the kidney dialysis and laboratory procedures in the hospital, Rettew applied the mechanical techniques used in dialysis to the development of a rudimentary device that could automate one laboratory procedure. Technical development of this device resulted in the single channel Autoxam, an innovation that is still the basic technology for Medtek's major products.

The single channel Autoxam works by plucking up a small blood sample and pumping it through a continuous flow system where the sample is properly diluted; reagents added and mixed; the solution heated and/or cooled, filtered, pigmented, and spectrographically analyzed; and the results recorded and compared to a norm. Successive samples can be introduced continuously to the Autoxam. The innovation of separating the samples with a small air bubble both permitted the continuous flow of samples and scrubbed the pathway clean of the previous sample. Prior to the Autoxam, each sample was handled manually by a lab technician. Obviously, the new device allowed a saving in lab technicians' time and in the amount of reagents used. Further savings were realized by the Autoxam's ability to examine a larger number of samples per day than a technician.

In 1967 the Autoxam was introduced to the market. It was a great success and ushered the firm into an era of rapid and continuous growth. By the early 1970s the firm had grown to about 125 employees. The bulk of the research and development work was centered around the blood analyzer. Development work during this period focused on a multichannel version of the Autoxam that could automate additional laboratory tests and could also automate some industrial tests such as the measurement of trace metals in water. New applications and new clinical procedures compatible with Autoxam technology were developed both internally and by users and researchers external to and independent of the company. Much new information came to Medtek through professional journal reports of research inspired by the introduction of the Autoxam.

The years 1977 and 1978 brought a crisis to Medtek. This crisis was precipitated by the development of the 60/12, a second generation analyzer that produced a patient profile of 12 lab tests from one sample at the rate of 60 tests per hour. First, an internal fight arose over whether to finance an expansion of the company to tap the possible profits of the 60/12 or whether to restrain the firm's growth. Second, the rapid growth and the associated organizational consequences resulted in substantial engineering errors as well as cost and timing slippages. A consulting firm proposed a basic change in the formal organization in order to better handle accountability and coordination problems. Vice-presidents, senior vice-presidents, and a divisional structure were introduced. Some believed that the switch to this formal structure was too quick and that the company did not have enough properly trained personnel to staff the new organization.

The choice was to expand, and the period of 1979 to 1982 was a time of extremely rapid growth. The technical division grew to 150 employees. Its budget was some five times greater than its 1977 budget. Lou Bidder, who was brought in the early 1960s to work on the Autoxam hydraulics, became the first technical division vice-president. During this period, Medtek moved to suburban Washington, D.C. and greatly expanded its facilities.

The 60/12 was an instant success. None of Medtek's competitors could match or duplicate the 60/12's technology, speed, or versatility. Given the success of 60/12, development was initiated on HORSE (High Operation Repeated Sequential Examiner), a third generation computer-controlled blood analyzer with a capacity of 20 tests per profile and 150 tests per hour.

In the early 1980s work began on Scan-Lon—a complex high-speed diagnostic instrument oriented to the pharmaceutical industry. Scan-Lon was designed to take advantage of Medtek's core technology. Medtek also produces a white cell testing and diagnosis device; in addition, Medtek has developed and patented a range of reagents for its analyzers.

Medtek also produces an infrared analyzer and a hospital oriented management information system. These two products, however, constitute only a small, but growing, part of Medtek's sales of clerical systems and associated reagents.

The years 1982 to the present have not been easy ones for the company. Besides having to cope with the organizational consequences of growth, Medtek faces a range of environmental pressures. First, federal cutbacks to hospitals have decreased their ability to buy Medtek's products. This problem is acute because most of Medtek's new (and expensive) products are oriented to large clinical settings. Second, underwriters' requirements for insuring diagnostic equipment changed during the early 1980s in a number of cities and in the international market. These changes required making numerous modifications to fit local conditions. Similarly, the government, mostly through the Food and Drug Administration began to require extensive testing and product documentation before it would permit the diagnostic machines to be sold. Finally, during the 1980s a number of major companies began to directly compete with Medtek's diagnostic product line.

The organization chart for the company, financial highlights, and a description of the different divisions are included as Exhibits 1, 2, and 3.

EXHIBIT 1
Organization Chart of Medtek

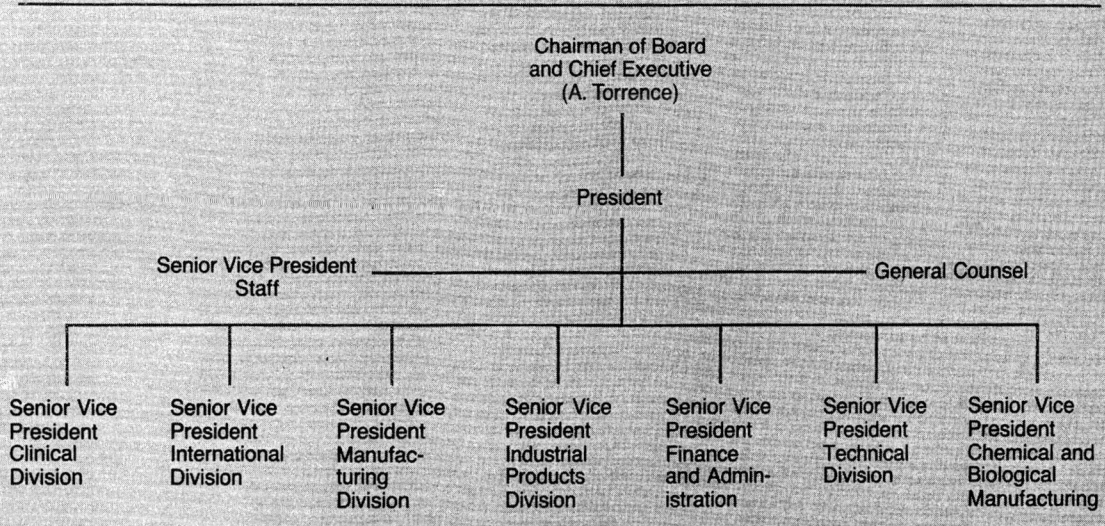

THE TECHNICAL DIVISION

As the R&D arm of Medtek, the technical division is responsible for basic and applied research in areas relevant not only to present but also to future products of the firm.

John Torrence, age 30, was given the assignment of heading up the technical division about a year ago after having rotated through a number of different positions throughout the company. He expressed his views on the strategy of the technical division to the consultants:

> As my father has articulated it, we are in the business of benefiting mankind by serving the health care community. The best way to do this is for Medtek to develop innovative technology and be first to the market with new and patentable products. We are a "me first," not a "me too" firm.
>
> The technical division is integral to this strategy and I believe that fully two-thirds of the division's time should be spent in generating new and creative ideas which can be developed into unique commercial products for the firm. The remainder of the division's time should be spent in developing and refining existing products.

The organization chart of the division can be found in Exhibit 2. Structurally, the division is organized into several departments. These

EXHIBIT 2

Organization Chart of the Technical Division

Senior Vice President
Technical Division

Administration   Product Planning

Patent Counsel   Clinical Applications

| Paris Laboratory | Chemistry | Advanced Development | Systems Management | Product Engineering | Research |

departments are briefly described in the order of their involvement in the work flow of a typical project.

Research

Research concentrates on areas that relate to Medtek's basic technology and processes. There are small projects (4–6 members) investigating phenomena such as wave scattering properties and electrochemical principles.

Advanced development

This department is chartered to do advanced development research (generating new knowledge or utilizing existing knowledge to solve a particular problem). The hydraulics, cell, and programming projects each conduct applied research on particular product problems in small

EXHIBIT 3

Selected Financial Data (years 1975–1985)

	1975	1976	1977	1978	1979	1980	1981	1982	1983	1984	1985
Sales (millions)	23	32	44	54	79	102	100	109	131	166	202
R&D expenditures (millions)	.9	1.3	2.0	2.9	4.9	9.8	10.6	10.1	10.0	10.5	
R&D expenditures as percentage of sales	4	4	4.5	5.4	6.2	9.6	10.6	9.3	7.6	6.3	
Number of employees		50		150						250	
Introduction of major products			60/12					HORSE			

teams. Each team's overall objective is to demonstrate the technical feasibility of a product idea.

Both these areas deal with state-of-the-art technology and are therefore particularly sensitive to new information from areas external to Medtek (universities, governmental agencies, professional societies). The technical personnel in these areas typically have advanced scientific or engineering degrees and are generally younger (with less organizational experience) than the rest of the staff in the division. Besides conducting research, these two departments are also responsible for assisting other divisional areas with technical problem solving.

Chemistry methods

This department is in charge of developing the clinical test methods to be used in each system. As such, the department is divided into areas covering new system methods, existing system improvements, and reagent development. Different from the research and advanced development departments, this area not only develops the feasibility of a particular analysis but also develops the processes and reagents used in the analyses. This department is staffed with a range of professionals including biochemists, physicians, hematologists, organic chemists and hydraulic engineers. These professionals must also keep track of information from areas outside Medtek. Furthermore, since their products are at an intermediate stage of the work flow, the chemistry methods staff requires information not only from other departments in the technical division but also from areas in the larger corporation, such as manufacturing and marketing.

Engineering services

This department provides support services to other departments in the division as well as to the larger corporation. The drafting design and model shop areas provide services to each product development program. The power supply area works on mechanical and electrical packaging questions as well as on power supply problems for each product line. A material assurance area monitors quality on all incoming technical components. The work in this department tends to be routine and requires less extradivisional communication than the other areas. The staff in this area tends to be older, more experienced within Medtek, and less educated than the rest of the division.

Systems management

This department has overall responsibility for taking a "feasible project" and developing a manufacturing prototype (that is, a working model, with detailed designs, to be handed over to manufacturing). The department is organized into product-line program areas (HORSE, 60/12,

Scan-Lon) as well as a systems support (computer) area. Each program has a product manager who has full responsibility for the project and a full-time technical project team. Since these teams do not have all the competence to carry a project to completion, the product manager must make arrangements with the different functional areas for assistance. Frequently a project will "buy" support teams from other areas for the full development phase of a project. Particularly important interfaces within the division are with chemistry methods and the service areas. Of vital importance to program development are effective links with manufacturing and marketing areas since the ultimate product must meet manufacturing constraints yet still meet market needs. The technical staff in this department are all engineers with varying amounts of experience at Medtek.

Product planning

This is a two-person department whose responsibility is keeping track of and evaluating existing programs as well as investigating the possibilities of new products and new acquisitions. Product planning is a new department whose members are not yet sure of their roles. Indeed, there is a general confusion in the division as to the legitimate role of this department.

The product-line programs carried out in the division are each *unique systems* focusing on some aspect of clinical information and data analysis. Each system is made up of a range of components to handle the various stages in the work flow from material preparation, material transfer, and multiple diagnostic tests to automatic analysis and interpretation. The various system components have to be integrated to produce an automated, high-speed, and precise system. In order to be commercially successful, each system has to be tailored to fit the particular market as well as the legal requirements in the different locations.

The Scan-Lon system provides an example of the complexity of a particular program. To meet a need in the pharmaceutical industry, Medtek initiated a program to develop a system that would allow high-speed assays of the most critical parameters facing the pharmaceutical producer. The system required the development of a new form of photometric analysis to be integrated with continuous flow core technology. Once the measurement concept was found feasible, the program team had to come up with specially designed test procedures, mechanics, power systems, and computer program. Each of the component systems had to be compatible with the overall design and within cost specifications. The system is now in production but not without some accuracy and maintenance problems.

SOME CURRENT ISSUES IN THE TECHNICAL DIVISION

In order to probe the reasons for the problems with both technical innovation and with morale, the consulting team conducted a number of
interviews in all parts of the laboratory.

The most frequently discussed problem was one termed "fragmentation." As one researcher suggested:

> The structure of the laboratory only encourages separate disciplines,
> each with a desire to do it their own way and with their own set of
> objectives. An example of this fragmentation problem was the initial
> photometric development by the advanced development department.
> Even though the research department had done substantial ground-
> work in the area, the advanced development group essentially started
> without the benefit of this in-house expertise.

Another researcher suggested:

> I think part of the fragmentation problem is that people in the various
> departments are so different. The guys in engineering services feel
> inadequate around us because, after all, their work really is not as im-
> portant in the overall scheme of things as ours is. However, when we
> do need them, they aren't very helpful.

A result of the fragmentation problem seemed to be inefficient transfer of work between departments. There was a tendency for each area to
overlook or fail to take into account other related areas. "Communication and coordination among areas can best be characterized as hit or
miss," said one division member.

The fragmentation problem was not unique to the technical division.
Important marketing or manufacturing information was often not available in the formative and problem-solving stages of a project. As one
researcher put it, "I am sick of receiving memos from marketing that
give me out-of-date information. What's the point of my doing feasibility
studies for a product without knowing about the regulation out there
which directly affects the product?"

Another major problem was the role of the product managers. Product managers were assigned between one and three projects; their role
was to marshal the needed resources and shepherd the project to completion. The power of these product managers varied greatly. As one
manager described it:

> We have full responsibility for projects, but we don't have the influ-
> ence—over budgets and staffing and so on—that we need to get the job
> done. The department heads have the authority here; except for one of
> us. We call him the Czar—he's a buddy of the chairman of the board.
> He gets all the resources and support he needs.

Day-to-day decision making seemed to present a basic problem for the product managers. In short, their real influence over divisional staff and other corporate personnel was minimal—coordination and joint problem solving suffered.

Another major problem faced by the division (and particularly by the product managers) was the absence of laboratory plans and project priorities and the attendant lack of systems to track and evaluate project progress. Ongoing projects were not subject to formal review procedures; there were no formalized cost, schedule, or timing systems. A product manager commented:

> Not only are reviews done on a "catch-as-catch can" basis, but it's also unclear whether I am supposed to be doing the evaluating or not. Sometimes, Torrence Senior suddenly takes over and sometimes it all gets so confusing that a department head does it. To make it all worse, Arthur Torrence has actually been known to walk into the lab and unilaterally start or stop a project. We don't have formal controls, so it leaves us open to unpredictable tampering by top management. One project was started and stopped three times over a two-year period. We call it the "yo-yo effect."

Contributing to the confusion of the staff was the problem of project definition and interproject coordination. Since projects changed direction so frequently and since the product managers did not always have current information, project members often did not know either what their own objectives were or how they should fit into the overall project objectives. This lack of general project direction reinforced the fragmentation problem and the feelings of "isolation in the midst of chaos" and further undermined the influence of the product managers. The lack of control and the general planning problem also adversely affected the coordination among projects: "Decision making about resource allocation—space, time, budgets, staff—among projects is often made arbitrarily and by the seat of management's pants; the point is that there are just no priorities to systematically guide project decision making."

A final problem that was frequently mentioned was the role of the research and advanced development departments. One researcher complained:

> We're supposed to be doing real applied research, but we hardly ever get a chance to actually do any. We spend all our time fire fighting on existing products. What research work we do is all but ignored by top management. I helped develop a process a few months ago, and then we heard that top management had gone outside to get exactly the same process. I still feel terrible about it.

Another example often given of management's lack of support for in-house expertise was the fact that the basic technology of Scan-Lon was not developed in-house, but was bought from an outside laboratory. The results of these management actions were very low morale in these departments and a lack of real research activity in a firm dependent on new technology and new clinical processes. As one interviewee put it, "The researchers have just stopped thinking; their creativity has been burned out by management's neglect."

While particularly an issue in the research areas, the problem of employee motivation and morale existed throughout the division. Many employees felt either that their work was not recognized by management or that they were simply not being used to their full potential. A survey indicated that a full 70 percent of the division's staff did not believe that they were effectively utilized. Further, more than two-thirds of the staff felt that the pay and career systems did not recognize or reward creative work.

These problem areas seemed to feed on each other. The lack of planning and control procedures and the resultant start-stop of the projects only accentuated the fragmentation problem as each functional area focused on its narrow task. Further, the lack of clear project objectives also contributed to the narrow focus of the departments. Defects in the planning and control system and weakness of the product managers worked to drive the departments away from each other. The lack of project stability, the poor structure of reward systems, and the nature of the stop-and-start work each reduced commitment and involvement of the staff. Similarly, the "yo-yo effect" undermined the role of the product managers and further reduced their ability to develop motivation within their project and to influence others in the larger organization.

These interrelated problems along with the lack of any real research activity contributed to low morale and low motivation in the division. Between departments, communication decreased as did the amount of effective collaboration and cooperation. The HORSE project developed a number of clinical and engineering problems, while the 60/12 system and the Scan/Lon system could not shake off persistent technical problems. The reputation of the division had fallen sharply in the eyes of the rest of the corporation, and the R&D personnel were openly complaining of the lack of leadership and direction in the division.

JOHN TORRENCE'S PERSPECTIVE

John Torrence was clearly frustrated. In discussions with the consulting team, Torrence provided some perspective on the problems faced by the technical division.

> Something is rotten here. Given our corporate objectives and our commitment to R&D, the laboratory should have the highest status individ-

uals in the company. Instead, our morale is low, and our reputation could not be lower within the firm as a whole. Our biggest problem, of course, is the failure to come up with new products. The future of the company depends upon our developing new technologies that will be commercially successful. Many of the problems, I think, stem from the way that we manage ourselves. With a few exceptions, we have high quality people here in the division. We do have the necessary scientific and technical talent. The problem is that they are not coming up with new ideas; also, they don't seem to be able to get through the process of moving an idea to the product stage. Part of our problem, I think, is the way we are organized within the division. I have too many people reporting to me, and I am thinking about changing the structure. Beyond that, however, there are problems in the attitudes of people. When I talk to people in the division, they just don't seem to have much drive or ambition. They don't seem fired up. This attitude is reflected in the large number of projects that are either behind schedule, over budget, or both. Finally, we don't seem to have a good feel of where we are going as a Division, where we ought to be putting our resources, and how we determine priorities.

Given their initial diagnosis, Mr. Torrence asked the consulting team for any interpretations as to what was going on. He also asked if they had any suggestions for new directions in the technical division.

QUESTIONS

Given the knowledge that you have gathered in the past five chapters, assume you are the head of the consulting team that has analyzed the technical division of Medtek. John Torrence, senior vice president of Medtek and head of the technical division, has asked you to prepare a report of your analysis and your recommendations for changes, if any, that you feel he should make. Your report would likely consider the following:

1. What is your evaluation of what is happening in the technical division?
2. What do you believe is causing the problems that you identified in your diagnosis?
3. How would you describe the nature of the environment in which Medtek operates?
4. What are the nature of Medtek's goals? What about the goals of the technical division?
5. Given these goals and the environment, are the current structures of the corporation and the technical division the appropriate ones? If so, why do you feel this way?
6. If they are not appropriate, what changes would you recommend?
7. How would you suggest that these changes be implemented? Remember to consider sources of support and resistance to these changes, the tactics for making the changes, and what can be done to ensure that the changes made will be successful.

A Developmental Framework for Studying Organizations

DYNAMIC ENVIRONMENTAL INFLUENCES

Past	Present	Future

Past: Change

Present: **Organizations**
Environments
Goals/Effectiveness
Structure
Design
Development

Future: Change

Past: Develop

Present: **Work Groups**
Structure
Processes
Cohesion
Groupthink
Intergroup Behavior

Future: Develop

Past: Evolve

Present: **Interpersonal Relationships**
Leadership
Power
Politics
Communications

Future: Evolve

Past: Grow

Present: **Individuals**
Perception
Learning
Attitudes
Values
Personality
Motivation
Outcomes

Future: Grow

PART SIX

Conclusion and Recap

Chapter **20**

Epilogue: A Note to
the Student

Epilogue: A Note to the Student

Analysis and action in organizations

The challenge

$\mathbf{A}$ s we close this book, it is helpful to think back to the first chapter which stated the purpose of this book. **Our purpose has been to help you gain an understanding of the dynamics of behavior in organizations and to help you learn to manage people in organizations effectively.** These were ambitious objectives, for, as stated in Chapter 1, it is difficult to live either with or without organizations. To be effective, managers must understand the many elements of an organization that operate in a dynamic and interactive manner.

We have focused on understanding and managing the people element in organizations. This means that people must be understood and managed as individuals, as interpersonal relationships, as groups, and as multiple, interacting groups. And they also must be understood and managed within the dynamic context of the tasks they perform, the technologies and structure of the organization, and the environment facing the organization. Throughout, we have referred to a developmental framework for analyzing and studying organizations. Managing all of the components of organizational behavior is indeed difficult, but using the information and models in this book should make your job as a manager easier.

Imagine that you are walking into Home Computers Company or some other company today to begin work as a new lower-level manager. What would you do? What questions would you ask? What elements of the organization would you explore? What would you find out about the organization's past? What about its expected future? How would you decide what actions to take to be an effective manager? Think about it for just a minute before proceeding. Then let us compare ideas.

ANALYSIS AND ACTION IN ORGANIZATIONS

In analyzing a situation like the one above and developing action plans, it is important to do two things. First, use a developmental analysis/action model to guide you in a general sense. Second, you should use the material from this book to provide detail to your analysis and help you decide on your action plan.

There are many issues that you must analyze as you begin the position of a new manager if you wish to be effective. Indeed, this entire text might be viewed as a developmental analysis/action model of organizational behavior. However, a general framework for analysis and action—such as the model shown in Exhibit 20–1—would be most helpful.

The first step is to diagnose and analyze the situation to understand the factors that are operating. In terms of this text, this analysis would include the individuals, their interpersonal relationships, groups, intergroup behavior, and the overall organization and its environment. The

EXHIBIT 20–1

A Developmental Analysis/Action Model of Organizational Behavior

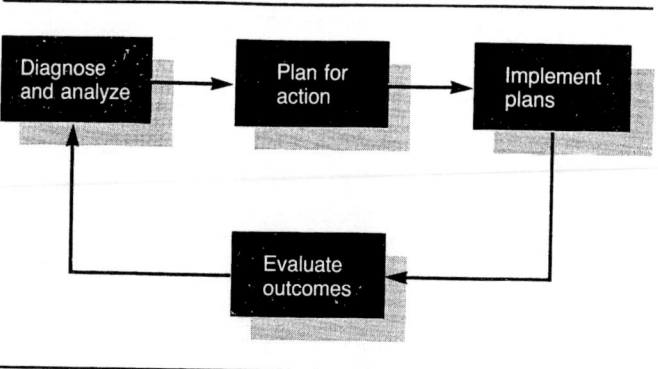

next step in the model is to develop a plan of action. What actions might help you become an effective manager and have a successful career? Then comes the time when you must implement your plan of action. This is a critical point. You must go beyond analysis if you are to be effective—**you must act upon your analysis.** And as you move into action, you move forward historically; your actions now become part of the situation. Hence, the important next step in the model is to evaluate the outcomes associated with your plan. In conducting this evaluation, you also begin the cycle in Exhibit 20–1 over again, since evaluation means the collection of data which must be diagnosed and analyzed. **This process should continue over and over again in a never-ending series of cycles as you work through your career.** By doing this, you are explicitly dealing with the developmental aspects of organizations. If your analysis misses a critical factor at one point in time, or if a critical factor changes, repeating the process helps you make valid analyses over time.

We must further emphasize the point about taking action. As this text has noted many times, managers are action-oriented people. Indeed, they must be. **Throughout your managerial career, you must be willing to take action, to try new things, and to take risks if you are to be really successful.** Superiors value managers who **learn** from their mistakes. You must be willing to try new things, to make mistakes, and to learn from your mistakes.

The comments recently made in a speech by a very successful manager highlight this point. The manager indicated that his success could be attributed to "making right decisions." When asked how he had learned to make right decisions, he replied, "Experience." And when some brave soul in the audience pressed him on how he had gained all this experience that now helped in making right decisions, his reply was, "Wrong decisions."

With the model in Exhibit 20–1 now in hand, you can begin to use the material from this book to help you analyze and take action in your new managerial job. If you think back over this book as a whole, we have explored individuals, interpersonal relationships, group behavior, and intergroup behavior, all in a dynamic, organizational context. Indeed, organizational task, technology, structure, and environment are critical contextual elements to understand if you want to be an effective manager.

THE CHALLENGE

Throughout this text, the challenge has been to help you understand the people element of organizations within the organizations' dynamic context. And it has also been this book's task to help you understand people as dynamic beings who exist in evolving relationships and groups. As you can now better appreciate, this is not a simple task. **In order to truly understand the elements of an organization, it is necessary to analyze their history, as well as their present status. This analysis then determines what you as a manger should do to be effective.**

Your job is not finished at this point, however. **You must then manage people as they and their context develop over time.** The job of an effective manager is one of analysis, action, evaluation, and action again in a never-ending cycle. This book can help you in this task. And we hope that you will accept the challenge to try the things suggested throughout the book, even if they are hard or do not work well the first time you try them. Becoming a successful manager—and staying one—is a challenge that must be tackled with great fervor and with the expectation that you will make mistakes. But remember to learn from your mistakes and to continue learning about management as you progress in your career. If you do this, and if you use the ideas from this book, you will become a more effective manager and turn "wrong decisions" into "right decisions." Good luck!

Glossary

accommodating A win/lose conflict-management strategy in which the accommodating group gives in to the other group in a conflict.

achievement-oriented leadership Leadership style characterized by setting high goals for subordinates, seeking improved performance, and showing confidence that subordinates will perform well.

adhocracy A structural option in which flexibility, adaptability, low formalization, and decentralization are present. As needed, ad hoc work teams are formed and disbanded to deal with changing organizational issues.

administrative orbiting (buck passing) A conflict-delaying tactic in which rather than making a decision, a manager refers the issue to a higher manager or forms a committee to study the situation.

advancement stage The career stage (ages 36-45) where a person works hard to develop a secure place in the chosen field of work.

alienation One outcome of power based on the use of coercive power.

attitudes Opinions held by individuals about things or people; that is, individual likes and dislikes.

authority rule A group decision-making rule where the leader makes the decision for the group.

autocratic leadership A leadership style in which the leader makes decisions and announces them to subordinates.

autonomy The degree to which a job provides freedom and independence for the employee to make important decisions related to the performance of the job.

avoiding role Someone who does not contribute to the group and cannot be counted on.

avoiding A conflict management strategy in which a group takes no action and hopes the conflict will go away over time.

behavior modification A motivational technique that focuses specifically on behaviors of the employee and consequences that follow behavior.

behavior stage The third step in the conflict process, during which a group may engage in many possible behaviors in reacting to a conflict situation.

856

beliefs Perceptions that relationships exist between two things.

blocking role Someone who always seems to get in the way of a group's progress toward completion of its task.

body language The signals given by standing versus sitting, open versus crossed legs and arms, facial expressions, and eye contact or lack thereof.

boundary-spanning units Units formed to accomplish two basic tasks: the collection, interpretation, and communication of external environmental information to top managers; and the representation of the organization to important external environmental sectors.

buffering units Units designed to protect (buffer) the core technology from changes in key environmental sectors.

bureaucracy A form of organization characterized by clear division of labor, employment decisions based on merit, a formal hierarchy of authority, job and job holder remaining separate, an impersonal approach to all interpersonal activities, rules and regulations, and maintenance of written records, communications, and rules.

burnout The emotional, physical, and mental exhaustion that can result from an excessively stressful job.

cafeteria benefit plans A benefits program that offers a menu of benefit options to employees so they can tailor the benefits to their individual needs.

career A sequence of work-related experiences and activities over a person's lifespan, including the person's sequence of attitudes and behaviors in these work-related experiences.

centralization The location or dispersion of decision-making authority within a company.

chain of command The management principle requiring each position in the organization to have a superior position to which it is accountable.

change agent An organizational development consultant responsible for facilitating organizational changes.

closed systems From an organizational perspective, operating in the belief that environments have little or no impact on organizational activities.

coercive power Power derived from a person's ability to punish other people for not doing what the person wants.

collaborating A win/win conflict management strategy in which the collaborating group is concerned with the goals of both groups and those of the larger organization.

commitment Having a strong belief in an organization's values and goals, such that an employee desires to remain a part of the organization and is willing to expend considerable effort for the organization.

communication channel The medium by which a message is carried from sender to receiver.

communication The process that occurs when a message intended by the sender is received and understood by the receiver.

competing A win/lose conflict-management strategy in which the competing group asserts its position and tends to ignore the position of the other group in a conflict.

complexity The degree of differentiation of jobs and work units within an organization.

compliance One outcome of power based on a subordinate's response to the use of rewards and punishments.

compromising role Someone who tries to help group members locate an acceptable middle ground which everyone can support.

compromising A win/lose conflict-management strategy in which each group may give up something in order to gain something else in a conflict.

conceptual skill The ability to see the organization as a system of interacting parts and as a system interacting with its environment.

conceptualization stage The second step in the conflict process, during which group members attempt to understand why they are frustrated and who is responsible.

connection power Power derived from a person's links with important and influential people in the organization.

consensus A group decision-making rule where everyone must eventually agree on the final group decision.

consideration The degree to which the leader develops a trusting and supportive relationship with subordinates.

content motivation theories Theories of motivation that deal with "what" motivates people (includes the need theories).

contingency theory An explanation for determining organizational designs that proposes the appropriate design of an organization is contingent on—or depends on—a number of different factors, such as goals, technology, size, and/or environmental uncertainty.

continuous process technology Organizational technology characterized by highly controlled, standardized, and nonstop production (oil refineries, for example).

cooptation An underhanded form of participation and involvement in a change whereby key individuals or groups opposed to the change are given what appear to be (but are not really) important roles in the change process.

coordination The strategies, processes, or procedures that ensure various jobs are accomplished in the proper order.

corporate culture The set of key values, beliefs, and understandings that are shared by members of an organization.

craft technology Work unit technology characterized by low task variety and low problem analyzability.

decentralization Low levels of centralization.

decoding The step in the communication process where the receiver interprets the message from the sender.

delphi technique A group decision-making technique that provides for written responses to group tasks, review and clarification of responses, additional written responses, sufficient iterations of this process to achieve consensus, and final group report.

democratic leadership A leadership style in which the leader permits subordinates to function within limits defined by the manager; the leader shares the decision-making responsibility.

devil's advocacy technique A group decision-making technique in which half of a group presents recommendations to the other half; the second group critiques these recommendations; the presenting group revises recommendations and presents again; cycle repeats until final recommendations are acceptable.

diagnostic model A sophisticated model to evaluate approaches to organizational effectiveness. The appropriate procedure to use is a function of the profile of answers given to seven diagnostic questions.

diagonal communications Communications between people at higher or lower levels in the organization hierarchy and in different functions.

dialectical inquiry technique A group decision-making technique that has one subgroup develop solutions to a group task; the other subgroup works to negate assumptions of first group; both groups present and debate their recommendations; agreement is reached on joint recommendations.

differentiation Specialization of operations and separation of those operations within specific work units in an organization.

direct supervision A coordination process in which managers inform certain subordinates about when and how to act in relationships with other subordinates.

directive leadership Leadership style characterized by the clarifying of paths to the goals for the subordinates.

divisional structure A structural option in which a number of relatively independent units within a broader hierarchy are controlled at corporate headquarters.

domain-emphasis model A model for determining the appropriate organizational effectiveness assessment procedure to use. The appropriate approach will be a function of the extent to which there is agreement on organizational goals and the extent to which cause-effect relationships are known.

dominating role Someone who tries to run everything, whether it is best for the group or not.

due-process nonaction A conflict-delaying tactic and an extension of administrative orbiting, involving setting up a procedure for handling conflicts that is so cumbersome or risky that groups are reluctant to use it.

encoding The process by which the sender chooses the media to use in transmitting a message to a receiver.

encouraging role Someone who praises the ideas and contributions of others and supports the efforts of other group members.

engineering technology Work unit technology characterized by high task variety and high problem analyzability.

environmental complexity The number of environmental sectors that can have important implications for the organization. Environments can range from simple (few sectors) to complex (many sectors).

environmental stability The extent to which relevant sectors in the external environment change over time. Environments can range from stable (few changes) to dynamic (many changes).

environmental uncertainty The extent to which information needed to operate effectively in a given environment is unavailable due to the number of and changes in environmental sectors.

equity theory A model of motivation which involves comparison of efforts and output with either some internal standard of performance or the performance of other employees.

establishment stage The career stage (ages 26 to 35) where a person has found an appropriate field of work and is trying to make a place in that field.

ethics Standards of conduct that assess whether actions are right or wrong in a moral sense.

evaluating role Someone who helps the group test its ideas and problem solutions against logical and rational benchmarks and also helps select the best alternative decision from among several choices.

evolutionary change Change that occurs over a period of time as the result of strategic decisions by top management.

expectancy theory A model of motivation that asserts effort is a function of the expectations that effort will lead to performance that will bring valued rewards.

expectancy An individual's assessment of the probability that a particular level of effort will lead to a desired level of performance.

expert power Power derived from a person's abilities, skills, and talents.

exploration stage The career stage (ages 15 to 25) where initial job choices are made and sampled in discussion, courses, and part-time work.

external environment Factors that exist outside of the formal boundaries of the organization with the potential to impact the organization.

extinction Failure to reinforce an undesirable behavior.

extroverts People who like action and interaction with people.

feedback (as job characteristic) The degree to which carrying out the work activities results in an employee receiving direct information about how well he/she is doing.

feedback (as a step in the communication process) When the sender receives back from the receiver an indication of whether or not a message was received and understood as intended.

felt need for change The perception of a gap between a desired state of affairs and the current state.

floundering group A group that has neither task nor maintenance roles.

force-field analysis A systematic process for examining the pressures that are likely to support or resist a proposed change.

formal groups Groups that are prescribed by the organization.

formalization The extent to which written rules guide or direct employee or work unit activities.

forming stage The first stage in the group development process during which group members try to determine what behaviors will be acceptable to the group, what skills and resources each member brings to the group, what goals and motivations each member has, and who will really psychologically commit to the group.

four/forty work week A work schedule under which employees work ten hours a day for four days each week and have a three-day weekend.

frustration stage The first step in the conflict process, which develops when a group feels blocked from achieving a goal.

functional organization design Design in which individuals and work groups with similar functions or common tasks are grouped together.

fundamental attribution error The tendency for individuals to underestimate the impact of external or situational causes on behavior and to overestimate the impact of internal or personal causes.

gain sharing A process that allows subordinates to share in the benefits of increased productivity, cost reductions, and improved quality through regular cash bonuses.

gatekeeping role Someone who ensures that everyone gets a chance to speak openly by drawing out people who sit back or by toning down the dominating individuals in a group.

goal displacement When work unit or personal goals are allowed to take priority over organizational goals in day-to-day activities.

goal-centered approach A procedure for evaluating an organization's effectiveness by assessing the organization's ability to meet its various goals.

goal-oriented organizational design Design in which employees from the basic organizational functions are grouped together to produce a given product, provide a particular service, or serve a particular set of customers or geographic areas. (Also known as a self-contained unit structure.)

goal-setting theory A model of motivation that asserts that we all have values and desires that determine the goals we set for ourselves.

group A collection of two or more people who, over a period of time, develop shared norms of behavior, interdependence, and interaction with each other for the purpose of achieving some common goal or set of goals.

group cohesiveness The degree to which members of a group are attracted to one another and motivated to work together.

group content The task that group members work on.

group norms The rules of behavior that are developed by group members to provide guidance for group activities.

group process The communications, leadership, decision-making, and role relationships that are a part of the group's activities.

group status The importance ranking that is associated with each of the group members.

group structure The norms, status and power relationships, and cohesiveness that develop as a group operates.

group substitutability The extent to which a group is perceived as indispensable by other groups in the organization. Lower substitutability results in greater status and power in the organization.

growth need strength The desire an employee has for development of skills and abilities and for performing interesting and challenging work.

halo (or horn) effect The process by which perceptions of observed traits influence perceptions of unobserved traits.

harmonizing role Someone who acts to resolve differences of opinion and to reduce tension that may develop in a group.

heterogeneous group Group composed of members that are different in many ways.

homogeneous group Group composed of members alike in many ways.

horizontal communications Communications that flow at the same level in the organizational hierarchy.

horizontal differentiation The way work is divided at the same level in an organization.

horizontal goal congruence Situation in which there is minimal conflict between goals at the *same* organizational level regarding *different* organizational outcomes.

human relations skill The ability to motivate, lead, and communicate with other people.

hybrid organizational design An organizational design in which different design options are used at different levels or in different units of the organization.

hygiene factors In Herzberg's two-factor theory, factors that relate to lower-level needs (physiological, safety, and some belonging).

idea or product champion An individual within an organization who finds a new product or new idea and pursues it until it is completed.

identification One outcome of power based on a subordinate's response to a request because of admiration or respect for a manager.

image building A political tactic in which the individual appears to always do the right thing at the right time.

implicit personality theories Development over time of a personal theory about people and their traits.

individualism The degree to which a person feels the key resource for work and problem solving is the individual versus the group.

informal groups Groups that are not prescribed by the organization, but develop because of proximity, common interest, and individual need satisfaction.

information power Power derived from a person's access to information or knowledge that is of value to others.

information processing role Someone who both seeks and gives information that will be useful to a group in performing its task.

initiating role Someone who offers many ideas and suggestions to a group.

initiating structure The degree to which a leader organizes and defines the task for subordinates.

instrumental values Means for achieving desired ends.

instrumentality An individual's assessment of the probability that the desired level of performance will lead to a desired reward.

integration Procedures undertaken in an organization to ensure coordination between differentiated work units.

intergroup conflict The state that exists when one group attempts to achieve its goals at the expense of the goal attainment of another group in the organization.

internal environment Factors within the organizational boundaries that influence the operations of the organization. (See **corporate culture**)

internal process approach A procedure for evaluating an organization's effectiveness by assessing how well the throughput subsystem operates.

internalization One outcome of power based on a congruence between a request and the subordinates' values and priorities.

interpersonal group A group that is high on maintenance roles, but low on task roles.

intrapreneuring Creating the spirit of entrepreneurship within an otherwise bureaucratic organization by rewarding risk-taking, creativity, and innovation.

introverts People who like to work alone and stay to themselves.

intuitive types People who work in bursts and are impatient with details.

job enlargement Combining jobs of equal difficulty into one bigger job.

job enrichment Increasing the levels of the five core job dimensions: task variety, skill identify, task significance, autonomy, and feedback.

job rotation Moving people from one job to another during the day.

job satisfaction An attitude reflecting the extent to which an employee expresses a positive affective (or feeling) orientation toward a job.

job sharing A situation where two people split a 40-hour-a-week job between them.

judging types People who like to follow a plan and make decisions, and who want only the essentials for their work.

lateral career movement Transferring horizontally to different functions, programs, or projects in the organization.

leader-member relations As an element of Fiedler's situational favorableness concept, this refers to the degree of confidence, trust, and respect that subordinates feel for the manager.

leadership The process of influencing the behavior of other people or groups of people toward the achievement of organizational goals.

learning The relatively permanent change in an attitude or behavior that occurs as a result of repeated experience.

least preferred co-worker (LPC) score Within Fiedler's contingency theory of leadership, LPC refers to the leader's disposition to emphasize tasks (low LPC) or relationships (high LPC) in dealing with subordinates.

legitimate power Power derived from the perception that a person has the right to influence behavior because of his or her position in the organizational hierarchy.

liaison An employee or work unit that acts as a translator or interpreter of problems across functional boundaries.

line units Organizational units that contribute directly to the production of the firm's products or services (manufacturing, production, and operations divisions, for example).

locus of control The extent to which a person feels in control of the events that affect his or her life (called *internals*) or feels that other factors, like fate, are in control (called *externals*).

lose/lose conflict management styles Conflict management techniques in which both groups are denied their goals.

machine bureaucracy A structural option in which most of the bureaucratic characteristics are present.

majority rule A group decision-making rule that involves voting on the best solution to a group problem.

management by objectives (MBO) A management tool involving a formalized effort to define and clarify employee goals.

masculinity (assertiveness) The degree to which a person feels managers should be assertive, independent, and insensitive to feelings.

mass technology Organizational technology characterized by mass production of similar items (automobile assembly lines, for example).

matrix organization An organizational design marked by dual hierarchies and a balance of power between functional and program/product managers. Functional employees are assigned to work on one or more projects or products.

maturity stage The career stage (ages 46-65) defined as the time to hold on to one's place in the chosen field of work.

mechanistic systems Control systems within organizations, characterized by high levels of complexity, formalization, and centralization.

middle-line Units or managers connecting the strategic apex and operating core in an organization.

minority rule (railroading) A group decision-making rule where a few people in the group make the decision for the group as a whole, frequently by dominating discussions.

motivation An internal force that energizes, directs, and sustains an individual to perform goal-directed actions.

motivators In Herzberg's two-factor theory, factors that relate to satisfaction of higher-level needs (self-actualization, self-esteem, and some belonging).

mutual adjustment Person-to-person communication needed to accomplish tasks involving more than one person.

need for achievement The desire to perform to high standards or to excel at a job.

need for affiliation The desire to develop close interpersonal relationships with others.

need for power The desire to influence and control others.

negative reinforcement Gaining the desired behavior from an individual by removing an undesirable consequence in the absence of that behavior.

noise Anything that inhibits the flow of information from sender to receiver.

nominal group technique A group decision-making technique that allows for silent generation of ideas, public listing of ideas, discussion for clarification, and rank-order voting for preferences.

nonroutine technology Work-unit technology characterized by high task variety and low problem analyzability.

nonverbal communications All communications that do not involve the use of words.

norming stage The third stage in the group development process, during which a real sense of group cohesion and teamwork begins to emerge.

official goals Outcomes that the organization publicly and formally identifies as worthy of pursuit.

open systems From an organizational perspective, operating in the belief that an organization interacts with and responds to changes in its environment.

operant conditioning (or reinforcement theory) A model for rewarding the kind of behavior desired from employees and not rewarding undesired behavior.

operating core Units of the organization with employees who perform the basic work related directly to the production of products and services.

operational goals Specific performance objectives for each work unit and, in some cases, for each employee.

operative goals The primary means or tactics by which the organization plans to achieve its official goals.

organic systems Control systems within organizations, characterized by flexibility in structure, informal communication, few rules and policies, and decentralized decision making.

organization An invention of people that is a goal-directed vehicle for coordinating a set of activities for individuals and groups.

organizational behavior The study of actions, feelings, and effectiveness of people in organizational settings.

organizational change The adoption of an idea, procedure, process, or behavior that is new to an organization.

organizational design Top management's decisions and actions that result in the development of specific organizational structures.

organizational development A change process that is planned, organizationwide, and managed from the top to increase organizational effectiveness and health through intervention in organizational processes using behavioral science knowledge.

organizational development interventions Techniques and procedures used by organizational development consultants to effect changes in individuals, groups, and organizations.

organizational domain That particular portion or niche of the marketplace in which an organization has chosen to sell its products or offer its services.

organizational effectiveness Getting the job done or accomplishing some particular goal or objective.

organizational efficiency Getting the job done or accomplishing some particular goal or objective using the least resources.

organizational goal A desired state of affairs that the organization attempts to realize.

organizational innovation The adoption of an idea, procedure, process, or behavior that is new to a broad spectrum of organizations in an industry, market, or general environment.

organizational policies/tactics Statements that facilitate the achievement of operative goals. They provide guidelines within which employee can operate.

organizational politics The management of influence to obtain ends not sanctioned by the organization or to obtain sanctioned ends through nonsanctioned influence means.

organizational strategies General directions established by top levels of management on how to achieve official goals.

organizational technology The dominant technology used by the firm.

outcome stage The last stage of the conflict process during which the outcome of the conflict is determined.

parity The management principle requiring that the authority given to an individual or position should be equal to the responsibilities required of that position.

participative leadership Leadership style characterized by sharing information and consulting with subordinates in making group decisions.

perception The process by which people select, organize, interpret, and assign meaning to external phenomena.

perceptive types People who adapt well to change, want to know all about a job, and may get overcommitted.

perceptual defense The process which takes selected phenomena and alters them to be consistent with existing perceptions.

performance A function of both motivation and ability plus opportunity to perform.

performing stage The fourth stage in the group development process, during which groups are able to accomplish tasks quickly and will not disband if conflicts arise.

personality An individual's total sense of self; an organizing force for the person's particular pattern of exhibited traits and behaviors.

planned change The planned and purposeful shift from one state of existence to another.

pooled interdependence Relationship between two groups in an organization such that they perform their tasks at the same time with very little need for interaction.

position power The amount of power inherent in the leader's position in the organization; a determinant of situational favorableness in Fiedler's contingency theory of leadership.

positive reinforcement The giving of a valued reward when an individual behaves in a desired manner.

power The capacity to influence other people's behaviors and not to be so influenced yourself.

power distance The degree to which a person feels there should be an unequal distribution of power in organizations.

primary environment Environmental sectors that influence the organization most directly, including human resources, financial resources, material resources, technology, industry, and customer sectors.

problem analyzability The extent to which job activities and procedures are well defined.

process motivation theories Theories of motivation that deal with "how" individuals are motivated (includes goal-setting, equity, expectancy, and reinforcement theories).

product/program manager A position responsible for coordinating activities across a number of functional units in the service of a particular product or program.

professional bureaucracy A structural option in which highly skilled professionals dominate the operating core, and the organization is marked by high levels of complexity, decentralization, and internalized professional standards.

projection The perceptual filter in which past or current knowledge and feelings sometimes cause the attribution to (or projection on) other people of traits or feelings that are really the perceiver's.

punishment Reducing an undesirable behavior by providing an undesirable consequence or by removing a desirable consequence when the undesirable behavior occurs.

quality circles An effort to increase employee participation in the workplace by having them meet regularly to discuss production problems and recommend solutions.

quality-of-work-life (QWL) A change approach which gives workers a voice in plant decisions.

radial career movement Moving toward greater or lesser amounts of influence in the organization.

receiver The intended recipient of a communication.

reciprocal interdependence Relationship between two work units in an organization such that outputs from either unit can serve as inputs to the other unit.

recognition seeking role Someone tries to gain personal distinction, even at the expense of the group.

referent power Power derived from the admiration, respect, and identification that one person feels for another.

refreezing The process of solidifying a change or a new practice.

relations power Power derived from the nature of the relationship between two people.

resisting forces Forces that work in opposition to a change, either directly or indirectly.

resource power Power derived from the control of vital employees, money, equipment, supplies, raw materials, customers, etc.

revolutionary change Change that occurs rapidly; most frequently as the result of crises within or external to the organization.

role ambiguity Lack of clarity about employee job responsibilities, the limits on job authority, the specific criteria used in evaluating a job, and/or the timetable for a job.

routine technology Work unit technology characterized by low task variety and high problem analyzability.

rules, regulations, and standard operating procedures Explicit directives that tell employees exactly what is or is not appropriate on the job. These are developed to direct the accomplishment of operational goals.

sabbaticals A policy to provide employees with time away from the organization.

secondary environment Environmental sectors that influence the organization indirectly, including the government/political, economic, and cultural/demographic sectors.

selective perception Having formed a perception of a person or a situation, the tendency to select into the perceptual process only external phenomena that support the original perception.

self-fulfilling prophecy The process by which the perception of another person actually alters the external phenomena to become consistent with our perception.

self-oriented group roles Self-serving behaviors that hinder the performance of a group.

sender The initiator of any communication.

sensing types People who like to approach a problem in a step-by-step organized way.

sequential interdependence Relationship between two work units in an organization such that the outputs from one unit are the inputs to the other unit.

simple structure A structural option in which the strategic apex exercises centralized control over an operational core and marked by low levels of complexity and formalization.

skill variety The extent to which a job involves doing different things and using different skills.

slack Excess resources that can either enhance the firm's ability to "play around" with change efforts, or make it "fat" and complacent and unwilling to experiment with new ideas.

social loafing The process that occurs when some group members, feeling that the responsibility for a task is shared, will tend to loaf, hoping others will carry them through.

socialization The process by which an individual is assimilated into and gains loyalty and commitment to an organization.

span of control The number of subordinates reporting directly to the same supervisor.

staff units Organizational units that provide support services to the line units (general counsel, public affairs, human resource management, and finance and accounting units, for example).

standardization The extent to which jobs and related activities are done in a uniform fashion.

standardization of outputs Standardizing work by specifying the nature of the results or outputs desired in a particular job or work unit.

standardization of skills Standardizing work by ensuring that certain employees bring similar levels of skills to their jobs by virtue of their education, socialization, or previous job training.

standardization of work processes Standardizing work by providing specific procedures for accomplishing a particular task.

stereotyping The process of assigning attributes to people on the basis of a category to which they belong.

storming stage The second stage in the group development process, during which conflicts tend to emerge and group members begin to doubt the people who have exercised leadership as they experience a gap between reality and their initial expectations about the group.

strategic apex The top levels of the organization where executives ensure that the organization serves its mission effectively, and that it serves the needs of those who control or otherwise have power over it.

strategic choice An organizational design contingency factor that allows a manager's ability to choose to influence the nature of the organizational design.

strategic constituencies approach A procedure for evaluating an organization's effectiveness by gathering relevant performance information from strategically important environmental sectors.

strategic constituency Any group of individuals or organizations with a stake or interest in a firm and its operations.

stress reactions The physiological and psychological reactions of a person to environmental stressors.

stressors Environmental factors that have the potential to create stress.

structure The allocation of responsibilities; the designation of formal reporting channels; and/or the systems and mechanisms that underlie the effective coordination of effort within an organization.

summarizing role Someone who restates, clarifies, and organizes the information and ideas that are offered and helps the group remain clear about its goals.

support staff Employees or work units that provide indirect support services to the organization outside of the operating work flow.

supporting forces Forces that work in favor of a change, either directly or indirectly.

supportive leadership Leadership style characterized by the giving of support and consideration for subordinates.

synergy The process by which the whole is greater than the sum of its parts.

survey feedback The administration of standardized or customized survey questionnaires to appropriate managers and their employees; the results of which are used to facilitate changes in organizations, as required.

systems resource approach A procedure for evaluating an organization's effectiveness by assessing the firm's ability to obtain necessary resources from the environment.

task force A group of employees from across hierarchical levels and functional areas temporarily brought together to deal with a particular event, problem, or opportunity that affects many functions.

task identity The extent to which a job involves performing a task from beginning to end (that is, a complete job).

task significance The importance of a job in the overall work of the plant or company.

task structure As an element of Fiedler's situational favorableness concept, the degree to which the group's task is clearly specified.

task teams Similar in purpose and composition to a task force, this group of employees is brought together on a permanent basis.

task variety The amount of variation or number of exceptions that can occur in a particular job or work unit.

task-oriented group A group that has many of the task roles present but few of the maintenance roles.

team group A group with both task and maintenance roles performed.

team-building A change technique designed to assist employees to learn to act and function more effectively as a team.

technical core The core operating technology of the organization.

technical skill The ability to perform the specific kinds of activities required in a job.

technology The activities, equipment, and knowledge necessary to turn organizational inputs into desired outputs.

technostructure Employees and work units that do not operate in the work flow, but design, plan, or change the work flow; or train the employees who work in the operating core.

terminal values Ends to be achieved.

unanimous decision A group decision-making rule where everyone in the group feels a particular solution to a problem is the best one.

uncertainty avoidance The degree to which a person feels that ambiguity and uncertainty should be avoided.

unfreezing Actions undertaken to move individuals, groups or organizations from an equilibrium situation to a situation that is more receptive to change.

unit or small-batch technology Organizational technology characterized by custom-made production or production in small, nonroutine lots (custom-made furniture or automobiles, for example).

unity of command The management principle requiring each individual in the chain of command to have only one direct superior.

valence The importance, attractiveness, or value placed on each possible reward.

values Basic and pervasive standards by which individuals evaluate end-states of existence and modes of conduct.

vertical career movement Career moves up or down the hierarchy of the organization.

vertical communications Communication that flows in two directions: upward through the organizational hierarchy, and downward through the hierarchy.

vertical differentiation The number of authority or hierarchical levels between the lowest and highest levels in a firm.

vertical goal congruence Situation in which there is minimal conflict between goals at *different* organizational levels regarding *the same* organizational outcomes.

win/lose conflict management styles Conflict management techniques in which one group gains a goal at the expense of the other group in a conflict.

win/win conflict management styles Conflict management techniques in which both groups manage to achieve their goals in a conflict.

withdrawal stage The career stage (age 66 and up) when abilities sometimes begin to decline and people reach retirement age.

work unit technology The particular activities, equipment, and knowledge needed to turn work unit inputs into desired outputs.

Index